Lecture Notes in Artificial Intelligence 11320

Subseries of Lecture Notes in Computer Science

LNAI Series Editors

Randy Goebel
University of Alberta, Edmonton, Canada
Yuzuru Tanaka
Hokkaido University, Sapporo, Japan
Wolfgang Wahlster
DFKI and Saarland University, Saarbrücken, Germany

LNAI Founding Series Editor

Joerg Siekmann
DFKI and Saarland University, Saarbrücken, Germany

More information about this series at http://www.springer.com/series/1244

Tanja Mitrovic · Bing Xue
Xiaodong Li (Eds.)

AI 2018: Advances in Artificial Intelligence

31st Australasian Joint Conference
Wellington, New Zealand, December 11–14, 2018
Proceedings

 Springer

Editors
Tanja Mitrovic
University of Canterbury
Christchurch, New Zealand

Xiaodong Li (ID)
RMIT University
Melbourne, VIC, Australia

Bing Xue (ID)
School of Engineering and Computer
 Science
Victoria University of Wellington
Wellington, New Zealand

ISSN 0302-9743   ISSN 1611-3349 (electronic)
Lecture Notes in Artificial Intelligence
ISBN 978-3-030-03990-5   ISBN 978-3-030-03991-2 (eBook)
https://doi.org/10.1007/978-3-030-03991-2

Library of Congress Control Number: 2018960680

LNCS Sublibrary: SL7 – Artificial Intelligence

This Springer imprint is published by the registered company Springer Nature Switzerland AG
The registered company address is: Gewerbestrasse 11, 6330 Cham, Switzerland

Tanja Mitrovic · Bing Xue
Xiaodong Li (Eds.)

AI 2018: Advances in Artificial Intelligence

31st Australasian Joint Conference
Wellington, New Zealand, December 11–14, 2018
Proceedings

 Springer

Editors
Tanja Mitrovic
University of Canterbury
Christchurch, New Zealand

Xiaodong Li ⓘ
RMIT University
Melbourne, VIC, Australia

Bing Xue ⓘ
School of Engineering and Computer
  Science
Victoria University of Wellington
Wellington, New Zealand

ISSN 0302-9743   ISSN 1611-3349 (electronic)
Lecture Notes in Artificial Intelligence
ISBN 978-3-030-03990-5   ISBN 978-3-030-03991-2 (eBook)
https://doi.org/10.1007/978-3-030-03991-2

Library of Congress Control Number: 2018960680

LNCS Sublibrary: SL7 – Artificial Intelligence

This Springer imprint is published by the registered company Springer Nature Switzerland AG
The registered company address is: Gewerbestrasse 11, 6330 Cham, Switzerland

Workshop Chairs

Jeremiah Deng	University of Otago, New Zealand
Lin Shang	Nanjing University, China

Publicity Chairs

Grant Dick	University of Otago, New Zealand
Zeng-Guang Hou	Chinese Academy of Sciences, China
Kourosh Neshatian	University of Canterbury, New Zealand
Su Nguyen	Latrobe University, Australia
Ke Tang	University of Science and Technology of China, China
Jing Liu	Xidian University, China
Xiaoying Sharon Gao	Victoria University of Wellington, New Zealand
Rohitash Chandra	University of Sydney, New Zealand

Panel Session Chairs

Peter Andreae	Victoria University of Wellington, New Zealand
Dongmo Zhang	University of Western Sydney, New Zealand

Webmasters

Harith Al-Sahaf	Victoria University of Wellington, New Zealand
Yiming Peng	Victoria University of Wellington, New Zealand
Qi Chen	Victoria University of Wellington, New Zealand

Senior Program Committee

Patricia Anthony	Lincoln University, New Zealand
Quan Bai	Auckland University of Technology, New Zealand
Stephen Cranefield	University of Otago, New Zealand
Eibe Frank	University of Waikato, New Zealand
Marcus Frean	Victoria University of Wellington, New Zealand
Reinhard Klette	Auckland University of Technology, New Zealand
Michael Kirley	University of Melbourne, Australia
Byeong Ho Kang	University of Tasmania, Australia
Yuefeng Li	Queensland University of Technology, Australia
Jie Lu	University of Technology Sydney, Australia
Tapabrata Ray	University of New South Wales, ADFA, Australia
Abdul Sattar	Griffith University, Australia
Michael Thielscher	University of New South Wales Australia
Brijesh Verma	Central Queensland University, Australia
Ruili Wang	Massey University, New Zealand
Stefan Williams	University of Sydney, Australia
Wai (Albert) Yeap	Auckland University of Technology, New Zealand

Preface

This volume contains the papers presented at the 31st Australasian Joint Conference on Artificial Intelligence 2018 (AI 2018), which was held during December 11–14 2018, in Wellington, New Zealand, hosted by the Victoria University of Wellington. This annual conference remains the premier event for artificial intelligence in Australasia, which provides a fórum for researchers and practitioners across all subfields of artificial intelligence to meet and discuss recent advances. This year the conference was held together with the IEEE/ACALCI Summer School on Artificial Life and Computational Intelligence.

AI 2018 received 125 submissions with authors from 26 countries. Each submission was reviewed by at least three Program Committee members or external reviewers. Subsequent to a thorough discussion and rigorous scrutiny by the reviewers and the dedicated members of the Senior Program Committee, 76 submissions were accepted for publication: 50 as full papers and 26 as short papers. The acceptance rate was 40% for full papers. In addition to the 76 paper presentations, we had four keynote talks by the following distinguished scientists:

- Jie Lu, University of Technology Sydney, Australia
- Zbigniew Michalewicz, Complexica, Australia
- Kay Chen Tan, City University of Hong Kong, Hong Kong
- Toby Walsh, University of New South Wales, Australia

AI 2018 also featured an exciting selection of workshops and tutorials, which were held on the first day of the conference and were free for all conference participants to attend. The workshop with its own proceedings is:

- The 5th Workshop on Machine Learning for Sensory Data Analytics.

The seven tutorials were on:

- Academia and Entrepreneurship: How to Start and Run a Technology Company, presented by Zbigniew Michalewicz
- Computational Intelligence for Brain Computer Interface (CIBCI), presented by Chin-Teng (CT) Lin
- Methods and Techniques for Combating False Information in Social Media, presented by Wei Gao
- Managing and Communicating Object Identities in Knowledge Representation and Information Systems, presented by David Toman and Grant Weddell
- Evolutionary Computation for Digital Art, presented by Frank Neumann and Aneta Neumann
- Machine Learning in Uncertain Environments, presented by Ke Tang
- Grammar-Guided Genetic Programming, presented by Grant Dick and Peter Whigham

AI 2018 would not have been successful without the support of authors, reviewers, and organizers. We thank the authors for submitting their research papers to the conference. We are grateful to authors whose papers are published in this volume for their cooperation during the preparation of the final camera-ready versions of the manuscripts. We thank the members of the Program Committee and the external referees for their expertise and timeliness in assessing the papers. We also thank the organizers of the workshops and tutorial speakers for their commitment and dedication. We are very grateful to the members of the Organizing Committee for their efforts in the preparation, promotion, and organization of the conference, especially the general chairs, Mengjie Zhang and Michael Blumenstein, for coordinating the whole event. We acknowledge the assistance provided by EasyChair for conference management. Last but not the least, we thank the Australian Computer Society (ACS) National Committee for Artificial Intelligence, Victoria University of Wellington, and Springer for their sponsorship, and the professional service provided by the Springer LNCS editorial and publishing teams.

September 2018

Tanja Mitrovic
Bing Xue
Xiaodong Li

Organization

General Chairs

Mengjie Zhang	Victoria University of Wellington, New Zealand
Michael Blumenstein	University of Technology Sydney, Australia

Program Committee Chairs

Tanja Mitrovic	University of Canterbury, New Zealand
Bing Xue	Victoria University of Wellington, New Zealand
Xiaodong Li	RMIT University, Australia

Advisory Board

Hussein Abbass	University of New South Wales, ADFA, Australia
Gill Dobbie	University of Auckland, New Zealand
Tom Gedeon	Australian National University, Australia
Geoff Holmes	University of Waikato, New Zealand
Nikola Kasabov	Auckland University of Technology, New Zealand
Zbigniew Michalewicz	Complexica, Australia
Xin Yao	South University of Science and Technology of China, China
Xinghuo Yu	RMIT University, Australia
Yanchun Zhang	Victoria University, Australia

Local Organizing Chairs

Will Browne	Victoria University of Wellington, New Zealand
Hui Ma	Victoria University of Wellington, New Zealand

Tutorial and ACALCI Summer School Chairs

Markus Wagner	University of Adelaide, Australia
Gang Chen	Victoria University of Wellington, New Zealand

Sponsorship Chairs

Andy Song	RMIT University, Australia
Yi Mei	Victoria University of Wellington, New Zealand

Program Committee

Mohamed Abdelrazek	Deakin University, Australia
Harith Al-Sahaf	Victoria University of Wellington, New Zealand
Brad Alexander	The University of Adelaide, Australia
Patricia Anthony	Lincoln University, New Zealand
Quan Bai	Auckland University of Technology, New Zealand
Partha Bhowmick	Indian Institute of Technology, Indian
Ying Bi	Victoria University of Wellington, New Zealand
Michelle Blom	The University of Melbourne, Australia
Michael Blumenstein	University of Technology, Australia
Mohammad Reza Bonyadi	The University of Adelaide, Australia
Will Browne	Victoria University of Wellington, New Zealand
Weidong Cai	The University of Sydney, Australia
Lawrence Cavedon	RMIT University, Australia
Gang Chen	Victoria University of Wellington, New Zealand
Qi Chen	Victoria University of Wellington, New Zealand
Stephen Chen	University of York, UK
Ran Cheng	Southern University of Science and Technology, China
Sung-Bae Cho	Yonsei University, South Korea
Stephen Cranefield	University of Otago, New Zealand
Michael Cree	University of Waikato, New Zealand
Hepu Deng	RMIT University, Australia
Atilla Elci	Aksaray University, Turkey
Daryl Essam	University of New South Wales, Australian Defence Force Academy, Australia
Eibe Frank	University of Waikato, New Zealand
Marcus Frean	Victoria University of Wellington, New Zealand
Tim French	The University of Western Australia, Australia
Wenlong Fu	SAP NZ Limited, New Zealand
Marcus Gallagher	The University of Queensland, Australia
Xiaoying Gao	Victoria University of Wellington, New Zealand
Tom Gedeon	Australian National University, Australia
Ning Gu	University of South Australia, Australia
Hans W. Guesgen	Massey University, New Zealand
Mingyu Guo	The University of Adelaide, Australia
Tim Hendtlass	Swinburne University, Australia
Byeong-Ho Kang	University of Tasmania, Australia
Reinhard Klette	Auckland University of Technology, New Zealand
Alistair Knott	University of Otago, New Zealand
Paul Kwan	University of New England, Australia
Ickjai Lee	James Cook University, Australia
Andrew Lensen	Victoria University of Wellington, New Zealand
Andrew Lewis	Griffith University, Australia
Xiaodong Li	RMIT University, Australia
Wan Quan Liu	Curtin University of Technology, Australia

Kevin Wong	Murdoch University, Australia
Brendon J. Woodford	University of Otago, New Zealand
Shuxiang Xu	University of Tasmania, Australia
Bing Xue	Victoria University of Wellington, New Zealand
Jianhua Yang	Western Sydney University, Australia
Wai Yeap	Auckland University of Technology, New Zealand
Fabio Zambetta	RMIT University, Australia
Fangfang Zhang	Victoria University of Wellington, New Zealand
Mengjie Zhang	Victoria University of Wellington, New Zealand
Xiuzhen Zhang	RMIT University, Australia

Additional Reviewers

Soumen Bag
Samantha Cook
Michael Dann
Xuelei Hu
Hung Nguyen
Shyamosree Pal
Lyn Pang
Sanjoy Pratihar
Nathaniel du Preez-Wilkinson
Alexandre Sawczuk Da Silva
Tom Smoker

Yang Song
Manou Rosenberg
Ye Tian
Ayad Turky
Chao Wang
Chen Wang
Yangxu Wang
Vithya Yogarajan
Yao Zhou
Jianlong Zhou

Sponsoring Institutions

- Australian Computer Society (ACS) National Committee for Artificial Intelligence
- Victoria University of Wellington
- Springer

Contents

Computer Vision

Knowledge Representation and Reasoning

Machine Learning and Data Mining

Planning and Scheduling

Text Mining and NLP

Agents, Games and Robotics

Compromise as a Way to Promote Convention Emergence and to Reduce Social Unfairness in Multi-Agent Systems

Shuyue Hu[(✉)] and Ho-fung Leung

Department of Computer Science and Engineering,
The Chinese University of Hong Kong, Sha Tin, Hong Kong
{syhu,lhf}@cse.cuhk.edu.hk

Abstract. Recently, the study of social conventions has attracted much attention. We notice that different agents may tend to establish different conventions, even though they share common interests in convention emergence. We model such scenarios to be competitive-coordination games. We hypothesize that agents may fail to establish a convention under these scenarios and introducing the option of compromise may help solve this problem. Experimental study confirms this hypothesis. In particular, it is shown that besides convention emergence is promoted, the undesirable social unfairness is also significantly reduced. In addition, we discuss how the reward of coordination via compromise affects convention emergence, social efficiency and unfairness.

Keywords: Convention emergence · Norm · Fairness · Compromise

1 Introduction

Social conventions (or conventions), such as driving on a particular side of roads and hand-shaking to greet, play an important role in human society. They are a type of social norms that specially focus on coordination problems and help maintain social order [1]. Recently, the concept of conventions have attracted much attention in multi-agent system research, in terms of how they promote coordination among agents. To introduce conventions into multi-agent systems, there are two branches of research [2], namely, *prescriptive* and *emergence* perspectives. The prescriptive perspective is usually concerned with central authorities [3], while the emergence one takes a bottom-up view and addresses the emergence of conventions from agents' local interactions [4,5]. In comparison, the emergence approach does not require any a priori central authority, and is usually more adaptive to an open and dynamic environment [6].

Early research work defines conventions in a game-theoretic framework and finds that conventions can naturally emerge from agents' repeatedly playing 2-action pure coordination games [7,8]. To improve social efficiency under such

© Springer Nature Switzerland AG 2018
T. Mitrovic et al. (Eds.): AI 2018, LNAI 11320, pp. 3–15, 2018.
https://doi.org/10.1007/978-3-030-03991-2_1

game setting, an amount of subsequent research attempts to promote convention emergence from multiple perspectives [9–11]. In particular, emergence phenomena from agents' playing games other than pure coordination games, e.g., anti-coordination and prisoner's dilemma games, have also been studied [12–14].

In this paper, we consider the scenario in which different agents may prefer different conventions, although establishing a global convention is in their common interest. In real life, Qualcomm and Huawei compete to set the 5G industry standards; open source programmers convince one another to adopt their own coding styles; and right-hand (or left-hand) vehicle owners try to enforce the rule of right-hand (or left-hand) traffic. Despite the commonness of these scenarios, they have rarely been investigated in the literature. To this end, following the conventional game-theoretic framework, we model the above scenario as 2-action *competitive-coordination* games, where there are two Nash equilibria in which players choose the same action, and each player prefers either of the equilibria to the other. We suspect that agents' divergence in preferences hinders convention emergence and may result in the undesirable discoordination among agents.

To tackle this problem, we introduce the option of *compromise* into multi-agent systems. The inspiration is derived from the fact that different parties usually give up parts of their own interests so as to achieve a win-win situation in human society. By compromise, agents with different preferences will receive the same acceptable payoffs. We hypothesize that this should facilitate convention emergence and reduce the undesirable social unfairness. However, it is still unclear a priori whether rational agents (which aim to maximize their own payoffs) are willing to compromise voluntarily.

To answer the above questions, we conduct an experimental study on systems of agents which repeatedly play competitive-coordination games with and without the option of compromise respectively. To measure the consequent social fairness and efficiency, we adopt two metrics, namely, Gini index and utilitarian social welfare. It is confirmed that in the absence of compromise, it is hard for social conventions to emerge, and agents generally receive highly unfair payoffs. More importantly, experimental results confirm that introducing the option of compromise helps promote convention emergence and lower social unfairness. Last but not least, from the engineering perspective, we discuss how the reward of compromise influences convention emergence, social unfairness and efficiency.

The remainder of the paper is organized as follows. Section 2 reviews the related work. Section 3 formalizes competitive coordination games with or without the option of compromise and defines the metrics of social efficiency and fairness. Section 4 presents our experimental study. Section 5 concludes the paper with some directions for the future work.

2 Related Work

Social conventions are solution to certain coordination problems, which, with time, turn normative [1]. Early research work [5–8,10] reveals the natural convention emergence from agents' repeatedly playing pure coordination games, where there are multiple equally good Nash equilibria in which players choose the same action. Pujol et al. [12] base their research on the coordination games in which a particular Nash equilibrium is Pareto-optimal. Hao and Leung [13] address convention emergence under stochastic coordination games in which the optimal Nash equilibrium is risk-dominated by the sub-optimal ones. Some more recent work [14–16] focus on language coordination games that are similar to pure coordination games in principle, but with an extremely large convention space. To evaluate convention emergence, Kittock [17] proposes that a convention is considered to emerge if at least 90% of agents converge to choose the same action. Following this *90% convergence* metric, most of the prior studies aim to increase social efficiency, in terms of the probability and speed of convention emergence [4,9,10]. Social fairness is rarely considered in these studies, since agents are indifferent to the particular convention that emerge in the above game settings.

Few research work on social norms also studies the emergent phenomenon but focuses on scenarios different than coordination problems. For example, under anti-coordination games the norms that emerge are discoordinations [18]. Some researchers [19,20] study norm emergence under prisoner's dilemma games in which the unique Nash equilibrium is not Pareto-optimal. In particular, Yu et al. [19] take social fairness as an appraisal signal to derive agents' emotions. Their main goal, however, is to engineer the emergence of the norm of cooperation, which maximizes social efficiency.

Therefore, in line with most of the prior studies, our main research goal in this paper is to facilitate convention emergence and to achieve coordination among agents. However, we focus on the scenario in which agents have different preferences, which has not been studied before. Social fairness, which is rarely considered in the prior studies, is one of the concerns in this paper.

3   Game Formalization and Quantitative Metrics

Consider a set $N = \{1, 2, \ldots, n\}$ of agents, each of which has a set $A = \{x, y\}$ of two available actions. By the 90% convergence metric [17], a social convention λ_a restricts at least 90% of agents of set N to choose a particular action $a \in A$. In this paper, we consider the situation in which agents tend to establish different conventions, although they share common interests in convention emergence.

3.1   Competitive-Coordination Game

We define agents' local interactions under the situation that we investigate to be competitive-coordination games. Agents prefer coordination via the same choice of action to discoorination. However, different agents may prefer different conventions. Let N_x and N_y be the sets of agents that prefer conventions λ_x and λ_y respectively, such that $N_x \cap N_y = \emptyset$ and $N_x \cup N_y = N$. Formally, we define the competitive-coordination game as follows.

Definition 1. *A competitive-coordination game G is a tuple $\langle P, A, (\tau_i), (r_i) \rangle$, where $P = \{1, 2\}$ is the set of players; $A = \{x, y\}$ is the set of actions available to each player; τ_i is the type of each player i, which reflects its preference over different conventions, such that $\tau_i = x$ if $i \in N_x$ and $\tau_i = y$ if $i \in N_y$; and r_i is the reward function of each player i such that $r_i(a_i, a_j)$ corresponds to player i's reward of the joint action (a_i, a_j), which is given by:*

$$r_i(a_i, a_j) = \begin{cases} \alpha & a_i = a_j = \tau_i \\ \beta & a_i = a_j, a_i \neq \tau_i \\ 0 & a_i \neq a_j \end{cases} \tag{1}$$

where $\alpha > \beta > 0$.

By Definition 1, an agent receives a reward α or β, when it coordinates to play the same action as its opponent's. However, it receives the highest reward α only when the coordination is achieved in its preferred way. Therefore, agents which prefer convention λ_x, i.e., $\tau_i = x$, are motivated to choose action x. On the contrary, agents which prefer convention λ_y, i.e., $\tau_i = y$, tend to choose action y. This suggests that agents with different preferences easily fail to coordinate on the same choice of actions. We present the example payoff matrices (with $\alpha = 10$ and $\beta = 2$) under different situations in Table 1. Under each situation, there are two Nash equilibria which denote two ways of coordination: (x, x) and (y, y). As shown in Tables 1a and b, when the two players have the same preference, their jointly preferred coordination results in the maximum payoff of 10 for both players. However, as shown in Tables 1c and d, when the two players have different preferences, either way of coordination dose not Pareto-dominate the other. Only one of the players can receive the payoff of 10, but at the sacrifice of the other player's receiving the payoff of 2.

Intuitively, once a convention emerges in systems where these games are played, some agents embrace their preferred convention, while the others have to sacrifice and put up with their non-preferred one. Consequently, as we shall show in Sect. 4.2, conventions may not emerge and agents may fail to achieve coordination. To tackle this problem, we shall introduce the option of compromise into these multi-agent systems in the next section.

Table 1. Payoff matrices of competitive-coordination game under different situations. The row player is i and the column player is j. α is set to 10 and β is set to 2.

	x	y
x	10,10	0,0
y	0,0	2,2

(a) $\tau_i = \tau_j = x$.

	x	y
x	2,2	0,0
y	0,0	10,10

(b) $\tau_i = \tau_j = y$.

	x	y
x	10,2	0,0
y	0,0	2,10

(c) $\tau_i = x, \tau_j = y$.

	x	y
x	2,10	0,0
y	0,0	10,2

(d) $\tau_i = y, \tau_j = x$.

3.2 Competitive-Coordination Game with the Option of Compromise

In real-life, compromise is a common way for different parties in conflict of interest to reach agreement. Each party gives up part of its own interests, so that a win-win situation is achieved. Inspired by this, we introduce an additional action, which is compromise c, into multi-agent systems. For individual agents, in addition to the original two ways of coordination via actions x and y, they can also achieve coordination via compromise c. Specifically, if agents coordinate to play compromise c, they will receive exactly the same acceptable reward γ. The reward γ is not as high as the reward α of preferred coordination, but is higher than the reward β of the non-preferred one as it serves as a fairer alternative. For simplicity, we here set the reward γ to be the average of the rewards α and β.[1] Formally, we define a competitive-coordination game with the option of compromise as follows.

Definition 2. *A competitive-coordination game G_c with the option of compromise is a tuple $\langle P, A, (\tau_i), (r_i) \rangle$, where $P = \{1, 2\}$ is the set of players; $A = \{x, y, c\}$ is the set of actions available to each player; τ_i is the type of each player i, which reflects its preference over different conventions, such that $\tau_i = x$ if $i \in N_x$ and $\tau_i = y$ if $i \in N_y$; and r_i is the reward function of each player i such that $r_i(a_i, a_j)$ corresponds to player i's reward of the joint action (a_i, a_j), which is given by:*

$$
r_i(a_i, a_j) = \begin{cases} \alpha & a_i = a_j = \tau_i \\ \beta & a_i = a_j, a_i \neq \tau_i, a_i \neq c \\ \gamma & a_i = a_j = c \\ 0 & a_i \neq a_j \end{cases} \tag{2}
$$

where $\alpha > \beta > 0$ and $\gamma = \frac{\alpha + \beta}{2}$.

We present the example payoff matrices (with $\alpha = 10$, $\beta = 2$ and $\gamma = 6$) under different situations in Table 2. Under each situation, there are three Nash equilibria which denote three ways of coordination: (x, x), (y, y) and (c, c). As shown in Tables 2a and 2b, when the two players have the same preference, their jointly preferred coordination still leads to the maximum payoff of 10 and thus they are not motivated to compromise. However, as shown in Tables 2c and 2d, when the two players have different preferences, coordination via compromise c is the unique Pareto-optimal outcome. As a result, both players receive the same acceptable reward, neither of which have to unfairly sacrifice.

We hypothesize that this may motivate a system of agents with different preferences to establish the convention of compromise, i.e., λ_c. Intuitively, if such a convention does emerge, all of the agents receive the same reward γ, which leads to both coordination and social fairness among agents. However, it is important to note that agents are autonomous and rational in the systems. Thus, they may not voluntarily compromise and the desirable compromise convention may not emerge.

3.3   Quantitative Metrics: Social Efficiency and Fairness

Obviously, frequent emergence of conventions is socially desirable, since agents achieve coordination among one another. From the view of utilitarianism, the

---

[1] The effect of the value of γ will be discussed in Sect. 4.4.

Table 2. Payoff matrices of competitive-coordination game with the option of compromise under different situations. The row player is i and the column player is j. α is set to 10, β is set to 2, and γ which is the average of α and β is set to 6.

	x	y	c
x	10,10	0,0	0,0
y	0,0	2,2	0,0
c	0,0	0,0	6,6

(a) $\tau_i = \tau_j = x$.

	x	y	c
x	2,2	0,0	0,0
y	0,0	10,10	0,0
c	0,0	0,0	6,6

(b) $\tau_i = \tau_j = y$.

	x	y	c
x	10,2	0,0	0,0
y	0,0	2,10	0,0
c	0,0	0,0	6,6

(c) $\tau_i = x, \tau_j = y$.

	x	y	c
x	2,10	0,0	0,0
y	0,0	10,2	0,0
c	0,0	0,0	6,6

(d) $\tau_i = y, \tau_j = x$.

convention which maximizes the total (or average) reward of the entire agent society should be established. However, this is indeed ethically unfair for agents which do not prefer the to-be-established convention.

We measure social efficiency by the utilitarian social welfare [21], which is the average (or sum) of individual agents' payoffs. Let $\hat{r}_i$ be the expected reward of any agent $i \in N$. The utilitarian social welfare is given as follows:

$$\mu = \sum_{i=1}^{n} \hat{r}_i. \tag{3}$$

By Eq. 3, when the social efficiency in terms of utilitarian social welfare is maximized, it is possible that most of the rewards concentrate on the hands of only few agents. To reveal such possible unfair situations, we adopt Gini index [22], a well-known index of wealth gap in economics, to measure social fairness. Formally, we define Gini index of a multi-agent system as follows:

$$g = \frac{\sum_{i=1}^{n} \sum_{j=1, j \neq i}^{n} |\hat{r}_i - \hat{r}_j|}{2n \sum_{i=1}^{n} \hat{r}_i}. \tag{4}$$

By Eq. 4, the value of Gini index is between 0 and 1. A higher value of Gini index indicates a larger degree of undesirable social unfairness. When all the agents receive exactly the same rewards, Gini index is 0. By contrast, when a particular agent receives all the rewards, Gini index is 1.

We can now ready to quantitatively measure social efficiency and fairness of a multi-agent system. An efficient and socially fair system should be of high utilitarian social welfare but of low Gini index.

4   Experimental Study

We consider a system of 500 agents, each of which is randomly connected to 20 other agents. Let ρ_x denote the ratio of agents that prefer convention λ_x to the total number of agents, i.e., $\rho_x = |N_x|/|N|$. We vary ρ_x from 0.1 and 0.9. When ρ_x is close to 0.9 (or 0.1), most agents prefer convention λ_x (or λ_y). As the ratio ρ_x becomes closer to 0.5, the numbers of agents preferring different conventions become more balanced.

4.1   Game-Theoretic Framework

We adopt the conventional *social learning* [4] as agents' interaction model. In this model, agents randomly choose their initial actions and then learn their strategies by playing games with their neighbours repeatedly. Specifically, at each time step, agents are first randomly paired with one of their neighbours. Each pair of agents then independently choose their actions and play games. Each agent receives a payoff from playing the game, based on which it reevaluates its choice on actions with reinforcement learning methods.

Following the convention [5, 9, 11], we equip agents with Q-learning [23] with ϵ-greedy exploration.In particular, we consider two type of Q-learners: individual action learner (IAL) and joint action learner (JAL) [24]. IALs update the Q-value for each individual action. By contrast, JALs update the Q-value for each joint action of themselves and their opponents. It is shown in the previous work [13] that JALs usually have better performance than IALs in terms of the probability of convention emergence.

4.2   Emergent Phenomena Without the Option of Compromise

We first let agents repeatedly play competitive-coordination games with one another. We set the reward α of the preferred coordination to 10 and focus on the following three values of the reward β of the non-preferred coordination: 8, 5 and 2. The decreasing trend in the value of β expresses that, to establish a convention, agents which do not prefer the to-be-established convention have to put up with the less (i.e., more unequal) rewards. For each of the above settings, we conduct 100 simulations each of which contains 5, 000 iterations.

Convention Emergence Conditioned on a Sufficiently Large β. We report the number of simulations that manage to establish each social convention in Fig. 1. Each column comprises the results of a type of learners and each row comprises the results of a certain value of β. From Fig. 1, it can be seen that with a sufficiently large reward of non-preferred coordination, i.e., β is 5 or 8 here, social conventions usually emerge. As the ratio ρ_x increases, there is a larger number of simulations that manage to establish convention λ_x. This can be expected, since there are more agents preferring convention λ_x, the choice of action x becomes more prevalent and thus there is a higher chance for convention λ_x to emerge.

Convention Non-emergence Conditioned on a Sufficiently Small β and a Balanced Ratio ρ_x. More importantly, we observe that with a small reward β of non-preferred coordination, it is hard for social conventions to emerge.When β is 2, as the ratio ρ_x gets closer to 0.5, conventions become less likely to emerge, especially in systems of JALs. When the ratio ρ_x is exactly 0.5, no simulation manages to establish a convention, no matter agents are IALs or JALs. In fact, we find that in these simulations, agents always attempt to achieve their preferred ways of coordination. Specifically, agents which prefer conventions λ_x and

λ_y persist in choosing actions x and y respectively, neither of which are willing to give in. Therefore, with a low value of β, agents with different preferences fail to achieve coordination with one another. JALs may even result in smaller chance of convention emergence, which contrasts with the prior finding [13].

Latent Low Social Efficiency and High Social Unfairness. We present utilitarian social welfare and Gini index under each of the settings in Fig. 2. The expected reward $\hat{r}_i$ of any agent $i \in N$, which is used in the calculation of these two metrics, is agent i's immediate payoffs averaged over the last 100 iterations. The results of the systems in which conventions generally do not emerge are marked with circles. From Fig. 2a, we observe that with respect to the ratio ρ_x changing from 0.1 to 0.9, the curve of utilitarian social welfare is generally 'V'-shaped. This result reveals that when agents with different preferences become more balanced, agents receive lower rewards on average. This is especially true in systems where conventions fail to emerge. On the other hand, it can be seen in Fig. 2b that the curve of Gini index is 'M'-shaped with a low value of β, but is 'Λ'-shaped with a sufficiently high value of β. Despite the difference in shapes of curves, in general, when ratio ρ_x is closer to 0.5, there is an increasing trend of Gini index. The exceptions are the results of systems where there is no convention emergence. That is to say, Gini index is low in systems where agents cannot establish a convention. However, it is high where conventions are able to emerge, especially if the ratio ρ_x is close to 0.5. Therefore, without the option of

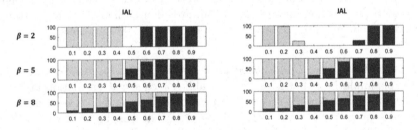

Fig. 1. The number of simulations that manage to establish each convention without the option of compromise. The x-axis is the ratio ρ_x and the y-axis is the number of simulations. The blue and yellow colors indicate conventions λ_x and λ_y respectively. (Color figure online)

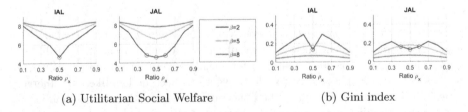

(a) Utilitarian Social Welfare   (b) Gini index

Fig. 2. Utilitarian social welfare and Gini index of systems without the option of compromise. The results are averaged over 100 simulations.

compromise, the social efficiency of certain systems is considerably hindered by the non-emergence of conventions and agents receive equally low payoffs. Even though agents manage to establish a convention, they may still suffer from the high degree of social unfairness.

4.3 Benefits of Introducing the Option of Compromise

To verify the benefits of introducing the option of compromise, we let agents play repeated competitive-coordination games with the option of compromise and adopt the same setting of rewards α and β as those in last section. That is, for every values of β which are 8, 5 and 2, we set the corresponding rewards γ of coordination via compromise to 9, 7.5 and 6 respectively. For each reward γ, we conduct 100 simulations in which agents randomly choose their initial actions.

Promotion of Convention Emergence. We report the number of simulations in which a convention emerges in Fig. 3. It can be seen that social conventions generally emerge under different systems. Besides conventions λ_x and λ_y, the compromise convention λ_c also manages to emerge. As the ratio ρ_x becomes closer to 0.5, a larger proportion of simulations establish the compromise convention λ_c. Specifically, when β is 2 and ρ_x is close to 0.5, the established conventions are mainly the compromise convention λ_c. We see in the last section that under the same setting of rewards α and β, it is hard for social conventions to emerge

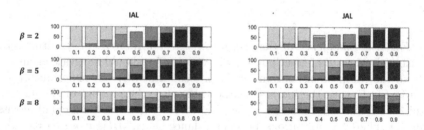

Fig. 3. The number of simulations that manage to establish each convention with the option of compromise. The x-axis is the ratio ρ_x, the y-axis is the number of simulations, and the blue, yellow and green colors indicate conventions λ_x, λ_y and λ_c respectively. (Color figure online)

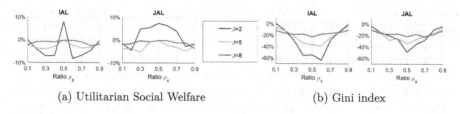

(a) Utilitarian Social Welfare   (b) Gini index

Fig. 4. Percentage change of utilitarian social welfare and Gini index with the option of compromise.

without the option of compromise. Therefore, introducing the option of compromise significantly promotes convention emergence by enabling the emergence of compromise convention.

Comparability of Social Efficiency and Significant Reduction of Social Unfairness. In Fig. 4, we present the percentage change of utilitarian social welfare and Gini index after introducing the option of compromise. It is shown that the utilitarian social welfare is at most 9% lowered. Occasionally, it is improved by 8%. On the other hand, Gini index mostly decreases by 20% or more. When β is 2, Gini index can drop by more than 60%. Therefore, utilitarian social welfare is generally comparable in systems with or without the option of compromise. Interestingly, Gini index is always significantly lowered with the option of compromise. That is to say, introducing the option of compromise maintains comparable social efficiency and significantly reduces undesirable social unfairness.

4.4 Effects of the Reward of Coordination via Compromise

We also investigate how the change of the reward γ of coordination via compromise affects convention emergence, social efficiency and fairness. Specifically, we vary the value of γ between the rewards α and β such that $\gamma \in (\alpha, \beta)$. This is to express that coordination via compromise is less desirable than an agent's preferred coordination but is still a better alternative than the non-preferred one.

More Frequent Emergence of Convention λ_c with the Increase of γ. Intuitively, increasing the reward of coordination via compromise should motivate agents to establish the compromise convention. This is confirmed by our experiments. As shown in Fig. 5, with the increase of the value of γ, the number of simulations in which convention λ_c emerges always increases. When the numbers of agents preferring different conventions become balanced, i.e., ρ_x is close to 0.5, the emergence of compromise convention is especially frequent. Due to the lack of space, we only present in this section the results for IALs. However, the results for JALs also show the same trend.

Lower Social Unfairness with the Increase in γ When $\gamma \geq \frac{\alpha+\beta}{2}$. When a comprise convention emerges, different individual agents receive almost the same payoff and thus Gini index is close to 0. Thus, with the emergence of compromise convention becoming more frequent, which is the result of the increase in γ, Gini index drops correspondingly. In Fig. 6, we present the percentage change of Gini index, when the option of compromise with different values of γ is introduced. The results confirm the decrease in Gini index as the value of γ rises. In addition, we find that if $\gamma \geq \frac{\alpha+\beta}{2}$, which means the reward of coordination via compromise is equal or greater than the average of the rewards of preferred and non-preferred coordination, there is almost always a significant reduction in the value of Gini index by introducing the option of compromise. However, we also find that given $\gamma < \frac{\alpha+\beta}{2}$, when β is small and the ratio ρ_x is close to 0.5, Gini index may be marginally increased. That is to say, to ensure a lower degree of social unfairness, the reward γ of coordination via compromise should be not smaller than the average of the rewards α and β.

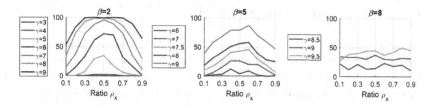

Fig. 5. The number of simulations that manage to establish convention compromise λ_c with different values of γ.

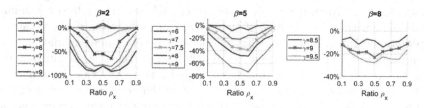

Fig. 6. Percentage change of Gini index, when the option of compromise with different values of γ is introduced. The results of $\gamma = \frac{\alpha+\beta}{2}$ are marked with crosses.

Higher Social Efficiency with the Increase in γ When $\gamma \geq \frac{\alpha+\beta}{2}$. We also investigate if the increase in social fairness is achieved at the cost of the decrease in social efficiency. We present the percentage change of utilitarian social welfare in Fig. 7, when the option of compromise with different values of γ is introduced. We observe that as the reward γ increases, in general, there is an increasing trend in utilitarian social welfare by introducing the option of compromise. However,

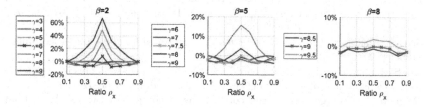

Fig. 7. Percentage change of utilitarian social welfare, when the option of compromise with different values of γ is introduced. The results of $\gamma = \frac{\alpha+\beta}{2}$ are marked with crosses.

we also find that when $\gamma < \frac{\alpha+\beta}{2}$, utilitarian social welfare is usually marginally reduced with the option of compromise. On then contrary, when $\gamma \geq \frac{\alpha+\beta}{2}$ and β is small, there is a significant increase in utilitarian social welfare by introducing the option of compromise. Therefore, to achieve a comparable or even higher social efficiency, the reward γ of coordination via compromise should not be smaller than the average of the rewards α and β.

5   Conclusions and Future Work

In this paper, we study the scenarios in which different agents may prefer the emergence of different conventions, although they share common interests in convention emergence. We formalize such scenarios to be competitive-coordination games. Our results confirm that when agents repeatedly play these games, they may fail to establish a convention or suffer from high degree of social unfairness. To solve this problem, we enable agents to compromise such that agents coordinate on compromise receive the same acceptable reward γ. Our main finding is that introducing the option of compromise, not only promotes convention emergence, maintains comparable social efficiency, but also significantly reduces social unfairness. To ensure the benefits, we identify that the value of γ should be not smaller than the average of the rewards of preferred and non-preferred coordination. Moreover, we find that the benefits become more significant with a higher value of γ. In our future work, we will consider the cases in which different agents prefer a convention to different degrees, there are a larger number of possible conventions, and agents may prefer more than one convention, to see if introducing the option of compromise still helps facilitate convention emergence and lower social unfairness.

References

1. Ullmann-Margalit, E.: The Emergence of Norms, vol. 11. Oxford University Press, Oxford (2015)
2. Savarimuthu, B.T.R., Cranefield, S.: Norm creation, spreading and emergence: a survey of simulation models of norms in multi-agent systems. Multiagent Grid Syst. **7**(1), 21–54 (2011)
3. Neumann, M.: A classification of normative architectures. In: Takadama, K., Cioffi-Revilla, C., Deffuant, G. (eds.) Simulating Interacting Agents and Social Phenomena. Agent-Based Social Systems, vol. 7, pp. 3–18. Springer, Tokyo (2010). https://doi.org/10.1007/978-4-431-99781-8_1
4. Sen, S., Airiau, S.: Emergence of norms through social learning. In: Proceedings of IJCAI (2007)
5. Hu, S., Leung, H.-F.: Achieving coordination in multi-agent systems by stable local conventions under community networks. In: Proceedings of IJCAI (2017)
6. Delgado, J.: Emergence of social conventions in complex networks. Artif. Intell. **141**, 171–185 (2002)
7. Young, H.P.: The Economics of Convention. J. Econ. Perspect. **10**(2), 105–122 (1996)

8. Shoham, Y., Tennenholtz, M.: On the emergence of social conventions: modeling, analysis, and simulations. Artif. Intell. **94**(1), 139–166 (1997)

9. Yu, C., Zhang, M., Ren, F., Luo, X.: Emergence of social norms through collective learning in networked agent societies. In: Proceedings of AAMAS (2013)

10. Villatoro, D., Sabater-Mir, J., Sen, S.: Social instruments for robust convention emergence. In: Proceedings of IJCAI (2011)

11. Marchant, J., Griffiths, N., Leeke, M.: Convention emergence and influence in dynamic topologies. In: Proceedings of AAMAS (2015)

12. Pujol, J.M., Delgado, J., Sangüesa, R., Flache, A.: The role of clustering on the emergence of efficient social conventions. In: Proceedings of IJCAI (2005)

13. Hao, J., Leung, H.-F.: The dynamics of reinforcement social learning in cooperative multiagent systems. In: Proceedings of IJCAI (2013)

14. Salazar, N., Rodriguez-Aguilar, J.A., Arcos, J.L.: Robust coordination in large convention spaces. AI Commun. **23**(4), 357–372 (2010)

15. Hasan, M.R., Raja, A., Bazzan, A.L.: Fast convention formation in dynamic networks using topological knowledge. In: Proceedings of AAAI (2015)

16. Wang, Y., Lu, W., Hao, J., Wei, J., Leung, H.-F.: Efficient convention emergence through decoupled reinforcement social learning with teacher-student mechanism. In: Proceedings of AAMAS (2018)

17. Kittock, J.E.: Emergent conventions and the structure of multi-agent systems. In: Proceedings of the 1993 Santa Fe Institute Complex Systems Summer School, vol. 6 (1993)

18. Sugawara, T.: Emergence and stability of social conventions in conflict situations. In: Proceedings of IJCAI (2011)

19. Yu, C., Zhang, M., Ren, F.: Emotional multiagent reinforcement learning in social Dilemmas. In: Boella, G., Elkind, E., Savarimuthu, B.T.R., Dignum, F., Purvis, M.K. (eds.) PRIMA 2013. LNCS (LNAI), vol. 8291, pp. 372–387. Springer, Heidelberg (2013). https://doi.org/10.1007/978-3-642-44927-7_25

20. Hu, S., Leung, H.-F.: Do social norms emerge? The evolution of agents' decisions with the awareness of social values under iterated prisoner's dilemma. In: Proceedings of SASO (2018)

21. Endriss, U., Maudet, N.: Welfare engineering in multiagent systems. In: Omicini, A., Petta, P., Pitt, J. (eds.) ESAW 2003. LNCS (LNAI), vol. 3071, pp. 93–106. Springer, Heidelberg (2004). https://doi.org/10.1007/978-3-540-25946-6_6

22. Gini, C.: Italian: Variabilità e mutabilità (variability and mutability). Cuppini, Bologna (1912)

23. Watkins, C.J., Dayan, P.: Q-learning. Mach. Learn. **8**(3–4), 279–292 (1992)

24. Claus, C., Boutilier, C.: The dynamics of reinforcement learning in cooperative multiagent systems. In: Proceedings of AAAI/IAAI (1998)

Hierarchical Population-Based Learning for Optimal Large-Scale Coalition Structure Generation in Smart Grids

Sean Hsin-Shyuan Lee$^{(\boxtimes)}$, Jeremiah D. Deng, Martin K. Purvis, and Maryam Purvis

Department of Information Science, University of Otago, Dunedin, New Zealand
sean.hslee@postgrad.otago.ac.nz,
{jeremiah.deng,martin.purvis,maryam.purvis}@otago.ac.nz
https://www.otago.ac.nz/info-science/index.html

Abstract. Large-scale Coalition Structure Generation poses a key challenge in the Cooperative Game Theory and Multi-Agent Systems in regards to its NP-hardness computation complexity. State-of-the-art algorithms, such as Optimal Dynamic Programming, could only solve the problem on a small scale, e.g. 20 agents, with an excessive running time. Our previous study, using population-based learning to deal with the same scale outperforms others and revels an immense potential of efficiency and accuracy. In this study we further advance the problem to large scales, e.g. 80 agents. Firstly, we show that our PBIL-MW algorithm could obtain an approximate optimal solution. Furthermore, we propose an approach of Hierarchical PBIL-MW with a termination scheme that achieves significant efficiency with only small losses in terms of accuracy. It provides an alternative solution, while time restriction is essential in some applications.

Keywords: Coalition Structure Generation · Optimisation
Dynamic Programming · Population-Based Incremental Learning
Smart Grids · Hierarchical Structure

1 Introduction

Coalition Structure Generation (CSG) [5], *aka* a "Coalitional Game in Partition Form" [13], is a concern in multi-agent systems technology when individual agents join together to form groups (coalitions) for achieving an optimal solution for the overall benefit of all the participating agents.

For example, because renewable energy sources, such as wind and solar power, have variable energy outputs across both space and time, it can be useful for them to form temporary coalitions in order to share their energy. That way communities having excess energy (i.e. they are producing energy in excess of their local consumption) can give their unneeded energy to other members in

© Springer Nature Switzerland AG 2018
T. Mitrovic et al. (Eds.): AI 2018, LNAI 11320, pp. 16–28, 2018.
https://doi.org/10.1007/978-3-030-03991-2_2

their coalition who are facing an energy deficit. For a large collection of communities producing renewable energy, it then becomes an optimisation problem as to what coalition arrangement (i.e. which energy-producing communities should join together to form the various coalitions) will result in the optimal distribution of available power. Because weather conditions can change rapidly, a solution for this CSG optimisation needs to be recalculated very often, say every hour.

However a straightforward algorithmic approach to reaching CSG optimization is NP-hard and so does not scale well with respect to increasing numbers of participating communities involved. Indeed, calculating CSG optimisation using this straightforward approach for just two dozen agents in this connection is infeasible. In this paper we explore more efficient ways to achieve near-optimal results that are more computationally tractable.

There are many investigations have been devoted to improving the efficiency of solving a CSG problem [10]. For instance, [14] propose a Dynamic Programming (DP) approach to find an exact solution without using an exhaustive search, [11] present a partial search algorithm which guarantees the solution to be within a bound from optimum; [6] use heuristic to select optimal values from sub-problems and choose the remained unassigned agents from other sub-problems; [9] combine DP with a tree-search algorithm to avoid the redundant process in DP and claim that the approach is the fastest exact algorithm for complete set partitioning. These DP variants, such as [9] and [4] run in $O(3^n)$ and $O(2^n)$ time respectively, which still restrict their application with limited numbers of agents. For example, all the DP variants will need to get all the possible subsets, i.e. coalitions, for n agents, which will be (2^n-1). While $n = 31$, the number of coalitions, $(2^{31}-1)$, will need to have $\approx 16\,\text{GB}$ RAM to store the fitness values in a float array, 64 *bites* each, which is the maximum size allowed on our experimental PC, and it makes the programs of DP variants difficult to manipulate. Clearly, using 80 agents as we do in our study is beyond the practical scope of DP. For large scale CSG, it remains impractical to search for a global optimum using the approaches. Alternatively, stochastic optimisation (SO) algorithms for CSG may provide a promising solution with great efficiency. For example, [12] use an Order-Based Genetic Algorithm as a stochastic search process to identify the optimal coalition structure. Though it does not guarantee finding an exact solution, it has suggested the potential for using SO algorithms to solve the CSG problems.

To our knowledge, there are few studies [10] employing SO algorithms to solve CSG problems. Specifically, based on the algorithm of Population-Based Incremental Learning (PBIL) [1], we have suggested an improved algorithm, Top-k Merit Weighting PBIL (PBIL-MW) [7], for solving CSG problems. The result has showed a promising ability both in accuracy and efficiency in comparison with other algorithms. Advancing upon the previous approach, we ave designed a new genotype encoding scheme [8], and the new results outperform a few SO counterparts, such as Genetic Algorithm and the original PBIL. Moreover, in comparison with DP, our approach has largely reduced the memory consumed in computation and shortened the running time significantly. In this study, we further proposed two approaches, a Hierarchical PBIL-MW algorithm and a termination scheme, and both have shown greater advantages for dealing with large scale CSG applications which the DP variants hardly achieve.

The rest of this paper is organised as follows: in Sect. 2 we first give the mathematical framework for forming a coalition structure of agents in smart grids, and we then propose our SO-based solutions, especially the hierarchical approach and the termination scheme, for investigating the optimal partition. Some results of experiment are shown in Sect. 4, with the algorithm's performance compared to the DP and our previous PBIL-MW method in terms of convergence speed and computational efficiency for larger scale optimization. Finally, we conclude the paper and point to some possible further directions.

2   Coalition Model for Large Scale Smart Grids

2.1   Coalition Structure

Within a cooperative game contains n agents, the set of all agents is denoted by S, such that $S = \{a_n\}$. The term "coalition", denoted by C_k, refers to k agents, $k \neq 0$, a subset of S. A coalition structure CS is a collection of coalitions, where CS $= \{C_k\}$, such that $\cup_k C_k = S$, $C_k \neq \emptyset$ and $C_k \cap C'_k = \emptyset$, if $k \neq k'$. The size of CS for S, denoted by $|CS_n|$, is known as a Bell number [3], $B(n)$, which is proven to satisfy [5]

$$(n/4)^{n/2} \leq |CS_n| = B(n) \leq n^n. \tag{1}$$

For example, in a set of three agents, there are five possible CS, i.e. $|CS_3| = B(3) = 5$, as listed below,

$\{a_1, a_2, a_3\}$, $\{\{a_1, a_2\}\{a_3\}\}$, $\{\{a_1, a_3\}, \{a_2\}\}$, $\{\{a_1\}, \{a_2, a_3\}\}$, and $\{\{a_1\}, \{a_2\}, \{a_3\}\}$.

To show its extraordinary growth rate, a few Bell numbers are listed below:

- $B(1) = 1$,
- $B(10) = 115,975$,
- $B(20) \approx 5.172 \times 10^{13}$,
- $B(40) \approx 1.575 \times 10^{35}$,
- $B(60) \approx 9.769 \times 10^{59}$,
- $B(80) \approx 9.913 \times 10^{86}$.

Furthermore, a coalition structure CS is said to be globally optimal for a characteristic function game G, if CS gives the maximal overall characteristic value [5]:

$$v(\text{CS}) = \sum_{C_k \in \text{CS}} v(C_k). \tag{2}$$

2.2   Coalition Model for Smart Grids

In comparison with other approaches for CSG in smart grids, we adopt our previous model [7,8] which requires that every agent in the coalition should have adequate renewable energy to support its own demand in general. However, according to the intermittence of renewable energy, the agent may frequently face shortage. Accordingly, keeping an agreement to share the surplus energy among others is a more profitable method in comparison with measures such as expanding the facility, installing larger backup capacity or dealing with power companies. Since the demand and supply are both dynamic, the model needs to engage a flexible mechanism to obtain the optimal CS endlessly. In the studies, we assume all agents exchange their power generation surplus and consumption needs regularly, e.g. on an hourly basis in this study. Thus, a faster algorithm, e.g. within 10 min, with acceptable accuracy will be an essential prerequisite for providing decision makers, such as agents or the coalition organizer, with sufficient time to allow agents to adjust their power demand and supply, and to reach a confirmed agreement among the agents.

Coalition Criterion. In every hourly period any agent a_i with extra power can share its surplus with shortage ones within the cooperative union. Our goal of the union is to maximise the total profit by forming coalitions. For the stability of power grids, the union joins every feasible coalition must have a power excess.

For instance, for a_1 and a_2, each has a 1.5 and 0.9 kWh excess accordingly, but a_3 has a shortage of 1.2 kWh . According to the requirement, a_1 and a_3 can team up as a feasible coalition $\{a_1, a_3\}$. On the other hand, a coalition such as $\{a_2, a_3\}$ is not acceptable. Consequently, a grand coalition cannot always be feasible and a game of CSG [13] should be constructed and needs to be resolved.

Distributed Agents in Regional Smart Grids. Based on our previous studies which focus on local coalition, to demonstrate the ability on a large regional scale, such as cities, we have extended the local model to four regional areas as shown in Fig. 1. The power transports among the inter-area need to be sent by a high voltage transmission network by way of transformers to exchange power between distribution and transmission lines. The power loss caused by the electrical lines is trivial in short distance; therefore, for a simplified coalition model, only the power losses of transformers, $\beta = 2\%$, per step up or down via a transformer, are calculated.

Coalition Evaluation. In our study, $v(C_k)$ is the fitness function of C_k given by

$$v(C_k) = \begin{cases} 0 & \text{if } |C_k| = 1, \\ Q_d \times P_r & \text{if } |C_k| > 1 \text{ and } Q(C_k) \geq 0, \\ -9999 & \text{otherwise,} \end{cases} \qquad (3)$$

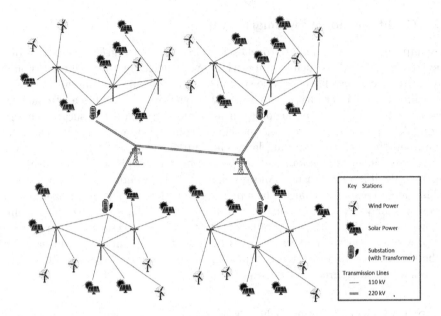

Fig. 1. Regional power connections structure

where $|C_k|$ denotes the size of the coalition C_k, P_r represents the price difference between getting power from the coalition and trading with power utilities, Q_d is the total power needed for deficit agents in the C_k, and $Q(C_k)$ is the net power of C_k. Furthermore, for giving penalty to an unfeasible coalition, we let $v(C_k) = -9999$. The goal is to arrive at the best CS and to maximize total profit. Certainly, an exhaustive search (ES) for the optimal CS could be a solution, but will be impracticable for a generous size of agents. Thus, as in [10], other options are essential for practically acquiring the optimum, or a near-optimal coalition structure.

3   Approaches of PBIL-MW for Solving a Large-Scale Coalition Structure Generation

3.1   PBIL-MW

As we know from the original PBIL algorithm [1,2,7], the probability vector $\mathbf{p}^{(t+1)}$ is updated depending on the top K elements $\mathbf{G}_i$ chosen from $\mathbf{G}$. In fact, K bests are utilized for updating $p_i^{(t)}$ by $p_j^{(t+1)}$ with equal weighting, i.e. $\frac{1}{K}$. However, it is reasonable that the fitness values $\{f_i\}$ may be used to tune the weighting when updating $\mathbf{p}^{(t+1)}$.

Our proposed adaptive algorithm, PBIL with merit weighting (PBIL-MW), incorporates this idea [7]. The first steps are the same as in PBIL until every fitness individual f_i has been evaluated in the first iteration. Then f_i is ranked and the weights are given by

$$w_i = \frac{f_i'}{\sum_{i=1}^{K} f_i'} \, , \qquad 2 \le K \le n, \qquad (4)$$

where $f_i' = f_i - \min_{i' \in i}(f_{i'}), \forall f_{i'} \ge 0$, and K is the number of chosen particles with the highest fitness values. Now that every w_i has been obtained, the probability vector $\mathbf{p}^{(t+1)}$ is given by

$$\mathbf{p}^{(t+1)} = (1 - \gamma)\, \mathbf{p}^{(t)} + \gamma \sum_{i=1}^{K} (w_i \mathbf{G}_i) \, . \qquad (5)$$

Note that every fitness f_i is considered and its weight w_i is given accordingly. The pseudocode of PBIL-MW is shown in Algorithm 1.

Algorithm 1. PBIL-MW

1: Initialise probability vector $\mathbf{P}^{(0)}$
2: **repeat**
3:   Generate a population $\mathbf{G}_n$ from $\mathbf{P}^{(t)}$
4:   Evaluate and rank the fitness f_i of each member $\mathbf{G}_i$
5:   Obtain w_i from Eq.(4)
6:   Update $\mathbf{P}^{(t+1)}$ according to Eq.(5)
7: **until** termination condition has been met

3.2   Set-ID Encoding Scheme

In our previous study [7], we proposed a novelty encoding scheme by using the coalition ID to allocate agents into separate groups in the process of searching for an optimal coalition structure.

For example, in an 8 agents scenario, the bit-length is 3 for one agent and $3 \times 8 = 24$ bits for a probability vector. The binary vector $[0, 0, 0]$ represents the number 0 set, and $[0, 0, 1]$ corresponds to number 1 etc. Hence, if the ID array for agents 1 to 8 is $[3, 2, 3, 7, 2, 2, 4, 0]$ then the coalitions will be
Coalition 0: $\{a_8\}$;
Coalition 2: $\{a_2, a_5, a_6\}$;
Coalition 3: $\{a_1, a_3\}$;
Coalition 4: $\{a_7\}$;
Coalition 7: $\{a_4\}$.
Therefore, the CS for this ID set is
$\{\{a_1, a_3\}, \{a_2, a_5, a_6\}, \{a_4\}, \{a_7\}, \{a_8\}\}$.

Consequently, agents with the same ID suggest that they are in the same coalition. For a set of n agents, the maximum coalition is n (all singletons) and the minimum coalition is 1 (the grand coalition). Therefore,

$$L = n \times \lceil \log_2 n \rceil (bits) \tag{6}$$

will be a sufficient length for the probability vector to represent all possible coalition structures.

3.3   Global PBIL-MW

To distinguish the organisational paradigms used in this study, we name "Global PBIL-MW" for the approach of searching the optimal CSG in a single PBIL-MW computation as previous studies [7,8].

Coalition Evaluation. Following Eq. (3), the net power $Q(C_k)$ of coalition C_k with respect to intra-area and inter-area are calculated separately. For example, a_1 and b_1 are surplus agents in different areas, a_2 is a deficit in same area as a_1. For Coalition $\{a_1, a_2\}$ the net power $Q(C_k) = Q(a_1) - Q(a_2)$, and for Coalition $\{b_1, a_2\}$ the net power $Q(C_k) = Q(b_1) \times (1 - 2\beta) - Q(a_2) = Q(b_1) \times (1 - 4\%) - Q(a_2)$.

Initial Probability Threshold. During our preliminary study, we found that different initial thresholds for numerous agents and their power statuses will lead the algorithms' iterations for finding a better solution in different speeds. Some results are shown in Fig. 2. Therefore, we have examined a series of initial probabilities from 0.5 to 0.01, the suggested initial thresholds for numerous agent size, in four hourly periods randomly chosen in data of year 2008, as shown in Table 1.

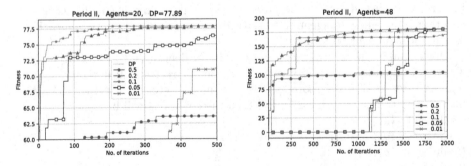

Fig. 2. Comparative results of different initial probabilities for period II

Table 1. Different initial probabilities used in Global PBIL-MW

Period	I	II	III	IV
Agent's size	Initial probability			
20	0.1	0.1	0.1	0.1
32	0.1	0.1	0.1	0.1
48	0.1	0.2	0.1	0.1
64	0.1	0.2	0.1	0.1
80	0.1	0.2	0.05	0.1

3.4 Hierarchical PBIL-MW

Once the number of agents becomes larger, the size CS_n will be very large. For instance, in the 80 agents experiment, $CS_{80} = B(80) \approx 9.913 \times 10^{86}$, any program written to implement DP variants might be unfeasible. Although the vector length $L = 80 \times \lceil \log_2 80 \rceil = 560$ bits will be moderate for PBIL-MW to search for the better CS, it will consume longer iterations to reach a global or local optimal solution, e.g. over 27 min and 1580 iterations on average will need in our experiment. Consequently, we propose a hierarchical structure of PBIL-MW to accelerate the process of exploring the CS.

Our hierarchical approach uses two steps of PBIL-MW iterations. First, it searches every local area separately to form a local optimal CS. Note that, since there is no transformer with the local area, the power losses are ignored. Secondly, we then employ all the local coalitions to explore the CS for the whole region. For instance, in the first step, a_1 to a_4 and b_1 to b_4 can form a local optimal CS such as $la_1 = \{a_1, a_2\}$, $la_2 = \{a_3, a_4\}$, $lb_1 = \{b_1, b_3\}$ and $lb_2 = \{b_2, b_4\}$. According to the local CS, the second PBIL-MW can look for the hierarchical optimal CS, such as $h_1 = \{la_1, lb_2\} = \{a_1, a_2, b_2, b_4\}$ and $h_2 = \{la_2, lb_1\} = \{a_3, a_4, b_1, b_3\}$.

From the framework we realize that after forming the local coalitions, then any agent in a local coalition would only be able to cooperate with other agents in a different local coalition by joining the two coalitions. Consequently, the best fitness will be less than or equal to the one by global PBIL-MW. However, by sacrificing the accuracy, this approach may shorten the time in return.

3.5 Termination Scheme

As seen in Fig. 4, we might find that some PBIL-MW can reach a maximum fitness with just a few iterations. For speeding up the running time, we have improved the algorithm by adding a threshold check to count the latest best repeating times during the iterations. Throughout the process, any latest global best fitness values and repeat times have been recorded. If a further new global best value is found, then the repeat time will return to one; otherwise, this duplicated time will be accumulated until its number meets the termination threshold, e.g. 10 times in our experiments. On that occasion the program will be terminated earlier.

4   Experiment

4.1   Data

To demonstrate the potentials for our approach to be utilized in real-world smart grids, we follow the same approach as in our previous works to construct a realistic dataset, which is composed of two diverse sources. The first part is power consumption of smart-meter readings in New Zealand. The second source is power generated by commercialized facilities of wind turbines and solar panels which are coupled with meteorological data of New Zealand from NIWA[1].

To assess the ability of sharing power in a regional area, the weather data of the four local cities, Dunedin, Balclutha, Middlemarch and Ranfurly, have been gathered from NIWA. The first two cities are located in a windy coastal zone, and the others are in sunny central Otago. The distance between cities is 40 to 80 km approximately. The power conditions of all agents are then given by subtracting demand from supply. The power(kWh) used is on an hourly basis, and the price $P_r = 20$ (¢/kWh).

However, we know that while the union has a net power surplus at some given hours, then the grand coalition will have trivial solutions. Thus, we consider only periods with overall power deficits. In our data, we have one year of hourly power demand and supply for 240 agents. Among those, four hourly periods with net power deficits are randomly chosen. Furthermore, in comparison with the efficiency of different approaches, we pick five sizes of union at random which are 20, 32, 48, 64 and 80 agents for the all four periods accordingly.

4.2   Setup

To our understanding, except Exhaustive Search, the algorithms of DB categories are the ones which can guarantee an exact optimal for CSG [10]. However, from Subsect. 2.1 we know that the running time of DP with respect to agent numbers grows rapidly. Figure 3 (left) shows the running time for four periods with each size from 4, 8, 12, 16 to 20 agents[2], and all the 20 agents' cases will spend more than 6 h to get an exact solution.

Since our further experiments have utilized 20, 32, 48, 64 and 80 agents for large scale CSG evaluation, and only the result of 20 agents obtained by DP could be available as the ground truth in comparison with other algorithms. Accordingly, instead of DP we will use max-fitness obtained from all approaches in each period to be the comparison index.

The algorithms used in experiments are Global PBIL-MW (G-PBIL-MW), Hierarchical PBIL-MW (Hi-PBIL-MW) and Hierarchical DP (Hi-DP). For two PBIL-MW algorithms we also use fixed iteration and termination scheme for comparison. Consequently, G-PBIL-MW-t and Hi-PBIL-MW-t will represent

---

[1] Meteorological data obtained from "CliFlo: NIWA's National Climate Database on the Web", https://cliflo.niwa.co.nz/.

[2] The code of the experiments is written and testing in Python 3.6 on Windows 10 PC with Intel core i5-4570 CPU and 16 GB RAM.

algorithms with a termination scheme. Note that DP and Hi-DP are run once, and all PBIL-MW experiments are repeated 20 times to obtain the average. Figure 3 (right) shows the running time for all PBIL approaches with each size from 20 to 80 agents accordingly.

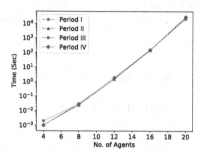 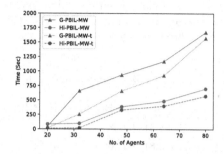

Fig. 3. Running time according to different number of agents. Left: DP with log-scale of time. Right: average running time for PBIL approaches.

4.3   Results

Case Study of 20 Agents. For the four periods, all the algorithms can reach the exact solution as DP's results. The optima of these periods are 111.047, 77.889, 98.845, 124.895 respectively. Table 2 shows the time required for each approach. It is clear from the table that excludes DP, all others are more than 200 times faster, and especially they could all reach the same optima as DP.

Table 2. Running time of different approaches for 20 agents

Period	DP	Hi-DP	G-PBIL-MW	Hi-PBIL-MW	G-PBIL-MW-t	Hi-PBIL-MW-t
I	21328.98	16.63	45.05	100.91	14.38	2.11
II	27565.86	14.50	43.94	76.94	36.54	39.91
III	29372.56	0.22	44.75	77.77	17.28	2.70
IV	28605.46	0.22	47.31	81.98	2.77	1.46
Mean	26718.21	**7.89**	45.26	84.40	17.74	11.54

Unit: sec

Case Study from 32 to 80 Agents. For the large-scale experiments, we select 32, 48, 64 and 80 agents to be the size for the whole four local areas. Hence, from Eq. 6 we know that the bits length of the probability vector are 160, 288, 384 and 560 accordingly. The population and number of iterations are consistently 500 and 4000. All PBIL-MW algorithms have run 20 times, and the results are summarised in Table 4. Since DP is unfeasible in these experiments, we follow the hierarchical structure of PBIL-MW to compute the fitness of CSG by hierarchical DP (Hi-DP), though it can be executing under 20 agents, while in some cases the local coalitions will exceed 20 which leads to Hi-DP becoming unfeasible again.

Furthermore, Table 3 shows the running time of different approaches for 32 agents. It is obvious from the table that Hi-DP is becoming slower than others. Thus we can know that Hi-DP will still be unfeasible while the agents' size becoming larger.

Table 3. Running time of different approaches for 32 agents

Period	Hi-DP	G-PBIL-MW	Hi-PBIL-MW	G-PBIL-MW-t	Hi-PBIL-MW-t
I	5608.41	622.88	111.58	171.01	43.68
II	423.81	624.66	101.97	752.01	25.34
III	0.16	676.16	89.33	20.28	2.03
IV	0.10	707.83	87.95	82.15	2.35
Mean	1508.12	657.88	97.71	256.36	**18.35**

Unit: sec

Table 4. Max-fitness of different approaches

Size	Period	Hi-DP	G-PBIL-MW	Hi-PBIL-MW	G-PBIL-MW-t	Hi-PBIL-MW-t
32	I	**147.75**	**147.75**	**147.75**	**147.75**	**147.75**
	II	164.04	**164.12**	163.70	**164.12**	163.58
	III	**119.29**	119.29	119.29	119.29	119.29
	IV	**199.43**	199.43	199.43	199.43	199.43
48	I	NA	**218.03**	218.03	218.03	218.03
	II	NA	**179.76**	179.35	**179.76**	179.38
	III	270.07	270.07	270.07	270.07	270.07
	IV	234.85	234.85	234.85	234.85	234.85
64	I	NA	**288.16**	288.16	288.16	288.16
	II	NA	**237.34**	235.65	**237.34**	235.65
	III	384.21	384.21	384.21	384.21	384.21
	IV	289.82	289.82	289.82	289.82	289.82
80	I	NA	**369.94**	369.94	369.94	369.94
	II	NA	**291.48**	291.39	**291.48**	291.29
	III	NA	**462.95**	462.94	**462.95**	462.94
	IV	372.40	372.40	372.40	372.40	372.40

unit: cent(¢)/hr

In general, we can find that G-PBIL-MW and G-PBIL-MW-t always have the max-fitness values, though in some cases the hierarchical approaches will have the same ones. Albeit, we have explained in Subsect. 3.4 that the best values of Hi-PBIL-MW will be less than the global approach sometimes. It is clear from Table 4 that even in the worst case, e.g. period II of 64 agents (as shown in Fig. 4), its best fitness is still close to the maximum.

Besides the accuracy, we have computed the average running time of all approaches as shown in Fig. 3. The faster converge speed of H-PBIL-t will be an appropriate alternative, while running time is an essential concern in some applications. Like the data of our study which are based on an hourly exchange, in the 80 agents' cases, the G-PBIL-MW or G-PBIL-MW-t will demand nearly half an hour to obtain the better result, and on the contrary, Hi-PBIL-MW and Hi-PBIL-MW-t take only 10 min less to gain a plausible solution. However, for the large case, e.g. 200 agents in an hourly-based case, the Hi-PBIL-MW and Hi-PBIL-ME-t could be the only two possible solutions to meet the time requirement.

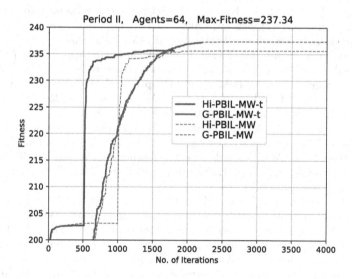

Fig. 4. Fitness VS. iteration for period II using different approaches

5 Conclusions

In this study, we demonstrate the superior speed and comparable accuracy of hierarchical PBIL-MW approaches for solving a large scale CSG. Though the stochastic optimization algorithms cannot guarantee finding the exact solution, since no other method could be used, then it could provide a viable alternative.

Renewable energy sharing in a large region is a critical component. Some areas have abundant wind power, while others have longer sunshine hours. Consequently, the cooperation among those areas may result in flourishing energy utilisation and reduce the demand for a backup system. Our study can provide a solution. While the subsidy of renewable energy is trivial, the prosumer could still be profitable by utilising the mechanism provided in this study.

For future work, we will bring more constraints and enlarge the region to form a multi-hierarchical CSG in smart grids.

References

1. Baluja, S.: Population-based incremental learning. a method for integrating genetic search based function optimization and competitive learning. Technical report No. CMU-CS-94-163, Carnegie-Mellon University Pittsburgh Pa Department Of Computer Science (1994)
2. Baluja, S., Caruana, R.: Removing the genetics from the standard genetic algorithm. In: Machine Learning: Proceedings of the Twelfth International Conference, pp. 38–46 (1995)
3. Bell, E.T.: Exponential numbers. Am. Math. Mon. **41**(7), 411–419 (1934). www.jstor.org/stable/2300300
4. Björklund, A., Husfeldt, T., Koivisto, M.: Set partitioning via inclusion-exclusion. SIAM J. Comput. **39**(2), 546–563 (2009)
5. Chalkiadakis, G., Elkind, E., Wooldridge, M.: Computational aspects of cooperative game theory. Synth. Lect. Artif. Intell. Mach. Learn. **5**(6), 1–168 (2011)
6. Changder, N., Dutta, A., Ghose, A.K.: Coalition structure formation using anytime dynamic programming. In: Baldoni, M., Chopra, A.K., Son, T.C., Hirayama, K., Torroni, P. (eds.) PRIMA 2016. LNCS (LNAI), vol. 9862, pp. 295–309. Springer, Cham (2016). https://doi.org/10.1007/978-3-319-44832-9_18
7. Lee, S.H.S., Deng, J.D., Peng, L., Purvis, M.K., Purvis, M.: Top-k merit weighting PBIL for optimal coalition structure generation of smart grids. In: Liu, D., Xie, S., Li, Y., Zhao, D., El-Alfy, E.S. (eds.) Neural Information Processing, ICONIP 2017. LNCS, vol. 10637, pp. 171–181. Springer, Heidelberg (2017). https://doi.org/10.1007/978-3-319-70093-9_18
8. Lee, S.H.S., Deng, J.D., Purvis, M.K., Purvis, M., Peng, L.: An improved PBIL algorithm for optimal coalition structure generation of smart grids. In: Workshop on Data Ming for Energy Modelling and Optimization (DaMEMO), The 22nd Pacific-Asia Conference on Knowledge Discovery and Data Mining. Springer (2018)
9. Michalak, T., Rahwan, T., Elkind, E., Wooldridge, M., Jennings, N.R.: A hybrid exact algorithm for complete set partitioning. Artif. Intell. **230**(C), 14–50 (2016). https://doi.org/10.1016/j.artint.2015.09.006
10. Rahwan, T., Michalak, T.P., Wooldridge, M., Jennings, N.R.: Coalition structure generation: a survey. Artif. Intell. **229**, 139–174 (2015)
11. Sandholm, T., Larson, K., Andersson, M., Shehory, O., Tohmé, F.: Coalition structure generation with worst case guarantees. Artif. Intell. **111**(1–2), 209–238 (1999)
12. Sen, S., Dutta, P.S.: Searching for optimal coalition structures. In: 2000 Proceedings Fourth International Conference on Multiagent Systems, pp. 287–292. IEEE (2000)
13. Shoham, Y., Leyton-Brown, K.: Multiagent Systems: Algorithmic, Game-theoretic, and Logical Foundations. Cambridge University Press, Cambridge (2008)
14. Yeh, D.Y.: A dynamic programming approach to the complete set partitioning problem. BIT Numer. Math. **26**(4), 467–474 (1986)

Empowerment-Driven Single Agent Exploration for Locating Multiple Wireless Transmitters

Daniel Barry$^{(\boxtimes)}$, Andreas Willig$^{(\boxtimes)}$, and Graeme Woodward$^{(\boxtimes)}$

University of Canterbury, Christchurch 8140, New Zealand
dan.barry@pg.canterbury.ac.nz,
{andreas.willig,graeme.woodward}@canterbury.ac.nz

Abstract. Unmanned Aerial Vehicles (UAVs) have attracted significant interest in recent years, as they have shown to be effective in supporting a wide range of applications in many different areas, including logistics, search and rescue (SAR) [3], public safety communications [8], infrastructure monitoring [9], precision agriculture [4], forestry [5], and telecommunications [2]. Specifically we focus on those of search and exploration in the context of search and rescue. In our presented work, success is measured in an agents ability to find all transmitters in as small a time as possible. Through the use of a challenging discretized simulation environment, we investigate the practicality of an empowerment-driven exploration behaviour (EEB) in order to locate an unknown number of wireless transmitters with minimal prior knowledge about the locations of obstacles, transmitters and their properties. With problem specific adaptations to the algorithm, including the ability to detect non-identifying signals from transmitters, when compared with a random walk agent and an idealistic Bayesian agent, the empowerment algorithm performs near to that of the Bayesian agent with unrealistic information about the environment. We show that our empowerment-driven algorithm has practical potential and lays a foundation for future work in this area.

Keywords: Empowerment · Search and rescue · Wireless transmitters

1 Introduction

We are interested in SAR operations and in particular on a scenario where several people carrying some kind of wireless transmitter (e.g. their cellphone, laptop, smart watch) are distributed over a fixed area and need to be located so that they can receive rescue assistance. We assume that their wireless transmitters frequently send out some signal, although the period is unknown. The overall aim is to minimize the (average) time required to detect and localize all wireless transmitters, assuming that an increased time (cost) taken to find these targets has negative consequences [1].

© Springer Nature Switzerland AG 2018
T. Mitrovic et al. (Eds.): AI 2018, LNAI 11320, pp. 29–37, 2018.
https://doi.org/10.1007/978-3-030-03991-2_3

We have chosen to investigate the viability of empowerment [7] to drive the behaviour of UAV agents for SAR. Bayesian search models have been proven effective in time-critical SAR operations, but there are still open questions about path planning [10]. Empowerment offers an intrinsic motivation for agents to search an environment, offering the ability to negotiate immediate loss of "reward" in favour of long-term opportunity to discover a transmitter. The empowerment-based algorithm developed in this paper comes with $O(|A|^N)$ time complexity, where $|A|$ is the number of possible actions and N is the look-ahead variable. We compare the performance of this algorithm against two baseline schemes and find that it offers detection times much shorter than a random search and competitive with the times achievable with an idealized Bayesian agent already knowing the environment.

2   Background

See Table 1.

Table 1. Nomenclature for equations in this paper.

A	Set of possible action states	L	Length of the environment in patches
B	Set of obstacles within the environment	n	Number of empowerment steps
C	Channel capacity	S	Set of possible sense states
ζ	Channel capacity with prediction decay	t	Discrete time step for the environment
$\mathfrak{E}$	Empowerment value	T	Set of transmitters
$f(\cdot)$	Function for calculating agent action	W	Set of possible world states
$g(\cdot)$	Function for internal agent update	λ	Information decay value

2.1   Perception Action Loop

We model our agent in a discrete-time perception action loop as shown in Fig. 1. At each time step (or tick), t, the real world is in state W_t. An agent (i.e. a UAV) is given sensor input S_t, updates its own internal world model to become the new internal model M_t, and then calculates an action to be carried out, A_t, which is taken from a finite set of actions available in the current internal state M_t. The action taken in turn has an impact on the real world state, which changes to become W_{t+1} at the start of the next round. An agent essentially wants to choose its action A_t so that it maximizes its chances of detecting or even localizing a transmitter. In picking its action A_t the agent can choose to consider the consequences of the actions into the future, for example over a time horizon of the next n steps (lookahead). The agent first updates its internal model using the behaviour g, i.e. $M_t = g(M_{t-1}, S_t)$, and then calculates its best action using behaviour f, i.e. $A_t = f(M_t, n)$. In this paper we look to define suitable representations for the sensor data S_t, the internal model M_t and the two behaviours $g(\cdot)$ and $f(\cdot)$.

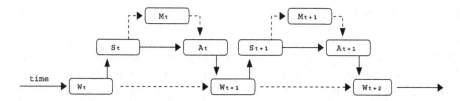

Fig. 1. Agent's perception action loop with memory.

2.2 Empowerment

Empowerment is an information-theoretic algorithm that describes the control an agent has over its environment (whether this is actual control or perceived control from an internal model) in the perception-action loop (see Sect. 2.1). Empowerment can also be interpreted as allowing an agent to estimate how much control it has and to choose its actions so as to maximize it's capability of maintaining many control options in the future [6]. In other words, an agent driven by empowerment aims to "keep its options" as open as possible. When applied to the SAR problem, we interpret the notion of "option" or "control" here by the opportunities to discover a transmitter.

With one-step empowerment we aim to choose our action A_t to maximize our information about the location of transmitters in the next step, i.e. to maximize our chances of getting the desired sensor inputs S_{t+1}:

$$\mathfrak{E}_1 := C(A_t \to S_{t+1}) \equiv \max_{p(a_t)} I(S_{t+1}; A_t) \tag{1}$$

With n-step empowerment we aim to choose A_t to maximize our information about the location of transmitters within the next n steps:

$$\mathfrak{E}_n := C(A_t \to S_{t+n}) \tag{2}$$

3   System Model and Evaluation Method

3.1   Environment

We assume that the search environment W (i.e. the pre-defined area within which to search for transmitters) is two-dimensional and has the shape of a square, with sides of length L. The obstacles are placed randomly, with a given probability $p(B)$ of finding an obstacle within a patch.

We have used an algorithm from maze design, particularly we are using a depth-first search (recursive-stack) backtracker to place obstacles. Obstacles are then randomly removed until the desired ratio of obstacles in the environment is obtained - whilst maintaining a fully explorable environment. Varying the number of obstacles in the environment changes the scenario difficulty.

3.2   Wireless Transmitters

The transmitters are randomly placed into the environment, particularly into patches without obstacles, such that no two transmitters are in the same patch. We choose a uniform distribution for placing transmitters into patches.

In this paper we use the simple *unit disc model* for transmitter detection. In this model there is given a radius around the transmitter. If the receiver is within this radius, a signal is received with 100% probability and if outside this radius, signal is 0% probability. A transmitter transmits signals periodically from a uniform distribution between 4 ticks and 10 ticks and do not contain any information allowing the UAV to uniquely identify the transmitter, the UAV can only tell whether a signal is detected or not. In our model signals do not overlap or interfere with one another.

3.3   State, Sensing and Action Spaces

The world state is given by a vector $(W_{x,y} : x, y \in \{1, \ldots, L\})$ with one state value $W_{x,y}$ for each patch (x, y). The patch occupancy is given by $W_{x,y} \in \{EMPTY, OBSTACLE, TRANSMITTER\}$.

With respect to sensing we make the following assumptions:

– The UAV agent has a GPS facility and can always tell with certainty in which patch (x, y) it currently is. The UAV is restricted to being in patches without obstacles.
– The UAV agent has a downward-facing camera, which allows to determine with certainty whether a transmitter is directly below the UAV agent or not. A transmitter in square (x, y) is detected with the downward camera only when the UAV position is (x, y), too.
– The UAV has further sensors allowing it to determine whether the eight neighboured patches contain obstacles (with obvious adaptations if the UAV is at the boundary of the environment). This is called the Moore neighbourhood.

All these quantities are being made available to the UAV as the sensing input S_t at the start of a tick. In addition there is the input from the radio receiver, which the agent receives while being in the current patch. The action space of the UAV agent reflects its options for movement, more precisely, when the agent is in patch (x, y) it gives the possible movements into any neighboured patch for the next tick, taken from the set $\mathcal{A} = \{NORTH, EAST, SOUTH, WEST\}$.

3.4   Performance Measure

We vary both the number of transmitters and the density of obstacles independently and record the average time to accurately detect all transmitters. The simulation keeps track of transmitters the agent has accurately located by visiting them (i.e. the agent being in the same patch and detecting the transmitter with the downward camera). The average is taken over a number of realizations of the maze.

4   Comparison Algorithms

The **random walk** algorithm is very simple and can be considered a lower bound. It does not keep any internal state (i.e. the state update function $g(\cdot)$ is empty) and it selects the next patch randomly with uniform distribution (it can tell which of the neighbouring patches is admissible based on sensor inputs, it does not need to keep track of the environment).

We also use a **Bayesian search** algorithm which we expect to perform quite well, by virtue of already having a-priori information about the environment, which EEB does not have. Particularly, the Bayesian search algorithm knows a-priori which patches contain obstacles and which ones don't. The location of transmitters is not known to the Bayesian search agent. Intuitively, the behaviour of the Bayesian search agent is always to go next to the nearest patch which it has not yet visited, this way exhausting all non-obstacled patches in a greedy fashion.

5   Empowered Exploration Behaviour (EEB)

5.1   Algorithm Overview

Building on empowerment, our agent employs a few key differences:

- A preference for information in the near future: suppose the agent considers two alternative paths of n steps each, and both with the same number of yet-unexplored patches, i.e. both allowing for the same information gain. According to the definition of empowerment both possible paths would be of the same value, but in our algorithm we give preference to the path which leads more quickly to expected information gain.
- The use of transmitter signals to prioritize search, i.e. when the agent receives transmitter signals in its current patch, it gives preference to close-by patches in order to quickly locate the transmitter(s) currently close to it. With this, the agent spends more time searching a given area with the expectation the signal may reveal a new transmitter.
- When there exists two or more actions of the same maximal empowerment value, we use a further heuristic to break the ties, where preference is given to the option that leads to a newly discovered transmitter with a higher probability. This is explained in more detail below.

5.2   Internal Memory

The EEB agent maintains an internal state M_t which is updated from the sensed information about the environment. More precisely, to each patch (x, y) the agent associates the following information:

- A belief value $W_{b(x,y)}$ which encodes the current knowledge of the agent about this patch, giving the probability of an undiscovered transmitter existing. As

$W_{b(x,y)} \to 0$, the probability of discovering a new transmitter is low and at 0 the agent has directly observed the patch and confirmed there is no transmitter. As $W_{b(x,y)} \to 1$, the probability of discovering a new transmitter is high. The agent operates under the assumption that there is always a new transmitter to be found, which cannot be confidently proved true or false until the entire environment is searched.

- Whether a patch can be explored (because of an obstacle) is stored in $W_{e(x,y)}$, where by default 1 indicates the state is explorable until an observation suggests otherwise, in which case $W_{e(x,y)} = 1$.
- The number $W_{s(x,y)}$ of radio signals heard while being on this patch: this is a counter incremented each time the agent is in this patch and hears a wireless signal.
- The location of transmitters found $W_{t(x,y)}$, 0 by default indicates no transmitter located, whereas 1 indicates a transmitter found.

Besides this information the agent knows its own position at any time, represented as the patch (x, y) it is currently in.

5.3   Update Function $g(\cdot)$

In each tick, we update our internal model M depending on the sensor input S as follows, assuming the agent is currently in patch (x, y):

1. *Increment signal reception counters*: When the agent has heard a signal while being in patch (x, y) the counter $W_{s(x,y)}$ is incremented according to the number of signals overheard.
2. *Record when no transmitter found:* When the downward sensor in the current location (x, y) indicates the absence of a transmitter we assign the belief value $W_{b(x,y)} = 0$.
3. *Record when transmitter found:* When the downward sensor in the current location (x, y) indicates the presence of a transmitter we assign the belief value $W_{t(x,y)} = 1$.
4. *Updating belief about neighboured patches:* The agent uses its further sensors to check neighbouring patches for the presence of obstacles. If, while the agent is in patch (x, y) these sensors indicate an obstacle in a neighboured patch (u, v), then we update the belief value $W_{e(u,v)} = 0$ and by extension, a transmitter may not exist and $W_{b(u,v)} = 0$.
5. *Keep track of update rates:* Whenever we update any part of our internal model during a tick, we increment the counter c by one. When calculating $1 - (c/ticks)$, we can calculate the average probability ρ under the assumption this invalidates our previous empowerment calculations of the world. As time passes, ρ will converge to 0, and we use ρ as a discount factor when weighing information gain on n steps.
6. *Identify areas with unaccountable signal(s):* We consider two scenarios: (i) the detected signal at $W_{s(u,v)}$ is within radio range of a transmitter $W_{t(i,j)} = 1$ and our current model is $W_z = W_b$, (ii) the detected signal cannot be

accounted for, in which case $W_{z(i,j)}$ is $W_{b(i,j)}$ times the sum of all local signals $W_{s(u,v)}$ divided by the total number of unexplored patches when the sum is not zero.

W_z is finally normalized. It is recalculated per tick and represents a heuristic, where larger values indicate a transmitter is more likely.

5.4 Action Function $f(\cdot)$

After the update function $g(\cdot)$, we compute an output A by performing a calculation on our internal model M.

As described by the empowerment Eq. 1, we probe actions A for our model W_z, and measure the resulting S to calculate the maximum expected information gain. To perform n-step as seen in Eq. 2, for each probed W_z, we perform this step again until n steps deep, choosing the action with the greatest expected information gain.

An exception to this process is that when calculating maximum mutual information for channel capacity, C, we decay this value for the current n-step value. The purpose of ζ is to apply a self inflicted cost function to favour near-future expected information gain. We consider the observed model update-rate as a approximation of model accuracy.

$$\zeta = \max_{p(a)} I(S;A) \cdot \rho^{n-1} \tag{3}$$

Finally, if our empowerment calculation yields no bias between two or more actions, we sum the probabilities represented by the competing actions and use the largest in order to attempt to split the tie: North: $\sum_{i=0}^{L} \sum_{j=0}^{y+1} W_{z=i,j}$, East: $\sum_{i=x}^{L} \sum_{j=0}^{L} W_{z=i,j}$, South: $\sum_{i=0}^{L} \sum_{j=y}^{L} W_{z=i,j}$, West: $\sum_{i=0}^{x+1} \sum_{j=0}^{L} W_{z=i,j}$. If still no clear action exists, one is randomly selected from the empowerment calculation stage.

6 Results

We have developed a simulator in Java for the purpose of a controlled comparison. For both the random and the Bayesian search algorithm we run 1,000 replications for each considered combination of parameters, where for each replication a new scenario is generated randomly. For EEB we have used >50 averaged replications per parameter combination, due to the computational complexity of this algorithm. The results for the first set of experiments are shown in Fig. 2a and b shows the results for the second set of experiments. We see that the EEB agent was easily able to outperform the random walk agent and generally performs close to the advantaged Bayesian search agent. Interestingly, in the second experiment the gap between EEB and Bayesian search widens somewhat as the number of transmitters is increased. We explain this by our heuristic to not look in the vicinity of already detected transmitters, which can have a tendency

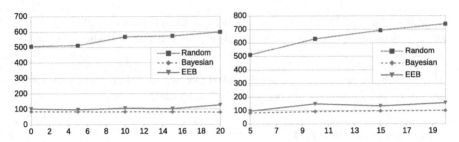

(a) % of obstacles $\{0, 5, 10, 15, 20, 25\}$ vs av-(b) % of transmitters $\{5, 10, 15, 20, 25\}$ vs
erage ticks (y axis), transmitters $= 5$.   average ticks (y axis), obstacles $= 5$.

Fig. 2. Comparison of algorithms where: (Length) $L = 10$, n-step $= 12$, transmitter radius of 4 with periods of 4 to 10 ticks.

to mask further transmitters close to already detected ones. With the exception of the random algorithm, the probability of obstacles had no measurable effect on the average performance, meaning that the EEB agent was able to successfully navigate around obstacles to find transmitters despite no prior knowledge of where obstacles were placed.

7 Conclusions

The EEB agent appears to be a practical algorithm which can find wireless transmitters efficiently while simultaneously mapping the environment. We see the EEB algorithm as a promising stepping stone towards the development of more refined and more realistic single-agent algorithms, but more importantly we also expect that it can be fruitfully carried over to the case where several agents are used in parallel and are allowed to collaborate with each other, e.g. by sharing belief and counter information. The EEB algorithm is an important step towards information-driven search and exploration agents with an unknown number of objectives. More work is required in order to reduce the computational overhead and allowing for real-time application.

References

1. Adams, A., et al.: Search is a time-critical event: when search and rescue missions may become futile. Wilderness Environ. Med. **18**(2), 95–101 (2007)
2. der Bergh, B.V., Chiumento, A., Pollin, S.: LTE in the sky: trading off propagation benefits with interference costs for aerial nodes. IEEE Commun. Mag. **54**(5), 44–50 (2016)
3. Erdos, D., Erdos, A., Watkins, S.E.: An experimental UAV system for search and rescue challenge. IEEE Aerosp. Electron. Syst. Mag. **28**(5), 32–37 (2013)
4. Gevaert, C.M., Suomalainen, J., Tang, J., Kooistra, L.: Generation of spectral-temporal response surfaces by combining multispectral satellite and hyperspectral UAV imagery for precision agriculture applications. IEEE J. Sel. Top. Appl. Earth Obs. Remote. Sens. **8**(6), 3140–3146 (2015)

5. Ghamry, K.A., Kamel, M.A., Zhang, Y.: Cooperative forest monitoring and fire detection using a team of UAVs-UGVs. In: Proceedings of 2016 International Conference on Unmanned Aircraft Systems (ICUAS), Arlington, USA, June 2016
6. Klyubin, A., Polani, D., Nehaniv, C.: Empowerment: a universal agent-centric measure of control. In: 2005 IEEE Congress on Evolutionary Computation, vol. 1, pp. 128–135. IEEE, Edinburgh Scotland (2005)
7. Klyubin, A., Polani, D., Nehaniv, C.: Keep your options open: an information-based driving principle for sensorimotor systems. PLoS One **3**, e4018 (2008). Sporns, O. (ed.)
8. Merwaday, A., Guvenc, I.: UAV assisted heterogeneous networks for public safety communications. In: Proceedings of Wireless Communications and Networking Conference Workshops (WCNCW), Istanbul, Turkey (2015)
9. Sa, I., Hrabar, S., Corke, P.: Inspection of pole-like structures using a vision-controlled VTOL UAV and shared autonomy. In: Proceedings of IEEE/RSJ International Conference on Intelligent Robots and Systems (IROS 2014), Chicago, Illinois, September 2014
10. Stone, L., Keller, C., Kratzke, T., Strumpfer, J.: Search for the wreckage of air france flight AF 447. Stat. Sci. **29**(1), 69–80 (2014)

A Logic for Reasoning About Game Descriptions

Dongmo Zhang[✉]

Western Sydney University, Penrith, NSW, Australia
d.zhang@westernsydney.edu.au

Abstract. General game playing aims to develop autonomous computer players capable of playing any formally described games. The biggest challenge for
such a player is to understand a game and acquire useful knowledge about the
game from its description. This paper aims to develop a logical approach for
reasoning about game rules. We introduce a modal logic with a sound and complete axiomatic system. The logic extends Zhang and Thielscher's framework
with two modalities to express game rules and reason about game outcomes. We
use a well-known strategy game, Hex, to demonstrate how to use the logic to
standardise game descriptions and verify properties of a game description.

1 Introduction

One of the ultimate goals of AI is to develop programs that can solve any complex problem without the need to be taught how. Along with many other efforts towards such general problem-solving systems, *General Game Playing* (GGP) aims to build AI systems
capable of playing any formally-described games without preset game-specific knowledge [1]. To describe a game to an autonomous computer player, a formal language,
game description language (GDL), was developed as the official language for the *AAAI
General Game Playing Competition* [2, 3]. GDL is highly expressive so that, in theory, it
can describe all finite-state, perfect-information games, including Checkers, Chess, Go
and many others. However, the way in which a game is described can dramatically affect
game players' efficiency [4]. This has been observed at the 2016 GGP Competition,
which featured several games that were described by two syntactically different sets of
rules—a computationally simple one used by the Game Manager and one that was much
harder to reason about for the players. It was observed that the "badly described" games,
mostly involving recursive definitions, resulted in many players becoming highly inefficient. Therefore a smart GGP player must be able to autonomously reformulate badly
written game rules in order to improve its efficiency [5,6]. The question is how this can
be systematically done.

Two approaches have been proposed in [1] for analysing a game from its GDL
description. The first approach is to create a *domain graph* from the formal game rules
to determine the dependencies of the variables therein. Such a graph can be useful
when we transform a GDL description into a more efficient data structure such as a
propnet [7]. The second approach is to create a *rule graph* from a game description
to analyse the structure of game rules [8]. A rule graph can be used to identify specific structural properties. Unfortunately neither of the approaches has been strictly for-
malised.

© Springer Nature Switzerland AG 2018
T. Mitrovic et al. (Eds.): AI 2018, LNAI 11320, pp. 38–50, 2018.
https://doi.org/10.1007/978-3-030-03991-2_4

Zhang and Thielscher introduced a formal logical system to transfer GDL into a propositional modal logic with a sound and complete axiomatisation [9, 10]. The language of their logic, denoted by $\mathcal{L}^{GDL^+}$, contains the basic components of GDL augmented by a modality of strategy and two prioritised connectives to represent and reason about game strategies. However, their logic was not specialised for representing and reasoning about game descriptions. Although a GDL-described game rule can be literally translated into a formula their language, the translated game rules must be treated as domain-dependent axioms and are combined with other domain-independent axioms for reasoning purpose. The generic game properties, such as playability, terminability and winnability, are not expressible in their logic. These properties must be discussed in a upper level language with their logical language as the metalanguage.

This paper aims to develop a logical language to describe game rules in the object-language level and reasoning facilities for formalising game properties and reasoning about game descriptions. We will extend Zhang and Thielscher's logical language with two modalities, one for representing game rules and the other for reasoning game outcomes (Sect. 2.1). We then show the semantics of the extended logic (Sect. 2.2) and discuss its properties (Sect. 2.3). By augmenting Zhang and Thielscher's axiomatic system with the axioms for the new introduced modalities (Sect. 2.4) we gain a sound and complete axiomatisation of the new logic. In Sect. 3 we demonstrate how to describe game rules in our logical language and how to formalise and verify game properties. We will use the well-known strategy game Hex as a running example to demonstrate how to use the logic to validate a game description and verify its properties. We conclude the paper in Sect. 4 with a brief discussion of related work and future work.

2 The Logic

In this paper we will focus on games with finite states played by finite number of players with complete information. To specify a game either syntactically or semantically, we assume that any game is associated with a *game frame* $\mathcal{F} = (N, \mathcal{A})$, where N is a non-empty, finite set of players and $\mathcal{A}$ is a non-empty, finite set of *actions* of players. We do not make an assumption about whether an action is actually a joint move, as in GDL, or a single player's move. We only assume that each state transition is caused by exactly one action. Therefore, in a simultaneous-move game, the actions are joint actions from all players while in a sequential game, each action is performed by a single player. In any case, all actions of a game must be fully specified by its description.

2.1 Syntax

Let us first introduce the syntax of our logic. To describe a game, we extend the propositional modal language $\mathcal{L}^{GDL^+}$ with the GDL variable *wins(.)* and two modal operators, □ and Υ.

Definition 1. Given a game frame $(N, \mathcal{A})$, let $\mathcal{L}^{GDL^{++}}$ be a propositional modal language which consists of a set, Φ, of propositional letters, the reserved GDL variables, *initial*, *terminal*, *does*(.), *legal*(.), *wins*(.), and modalities [.], $\lfloor . \rfloor$, $\square$ and Υ. The formulas of $\mathcal{L}^{GDL^{++}}$ are generated by the following BNF rule:

$$\varphi ::= p \mid \neg\varphi \mid \varphi \rightarrow \varphi \mid initial \mid terminal \mid wins(n) \mid does(a) \mid legal(a)$$

$$\mid \square\varphi \mid [a]\varphi \mid \lfloor a \rfloor\varphi \mid \Upsilon\varphi$$

where $p \in \Phi$, $a \in \mathcal{A}$ and $n \in N$. Other logical connectives ($\wedge$, $\vee$ and $\leftrightarrow$) and logical constants ($\top$ and $\bot$) will be introduced as usual with the standard order of precedence.

As in GDL, *initial* and *terminal* are used to represent the initial states and the terminal states of a game, respectively. *does*(a) means the action a is taken at the current state. *legal*(a) means that action a is legal to be taken at the current state. *wins*(n) means that the player n wins in the current state (*wins*(.) was not included in $\mathcal{L}^{GDL^{+}}$). The action modality $[a]\varphi$ means if action a is executed at the current state, φ will be true in the next state. With this modality, the next operators of temporal logic can be defined as:

$$\bigcirc \varphi =_{def} \bigvee_{a \in \mathcal{A}} (does(a) \wedge [a]\varphi) \tag{1}$$

Modality $\lfloor a \rfloor\varphi$ is inherited from $\mathcal{L}^{GDL^{+}}$ and means that if action a is chosen (but not yet executed), φ must be true in the current state.

The extended language does not include the strategy modality $\lfloor . \rfloor$ from $\mathcal{L}^{GDL^{+}}$ simply because strategic reasoning is not a major concern of this paper. Instead, $\mathcal{L}^{GDL^{++}}$ introduces the following two additional modalities:

- *Global modality* $\square\varphi$: φ holds in all states with all possible selection of actions.
- *Ultimate modality* $\Upsilon\varphi$: Ultimately φ will hold in the terminal state of every terminating path that starts from the current state.

The dual operators of both modalities can be defined as follows:

$$\Diamond\varphi =_{def} \neg\square\neg\varphi \qquad \langle\Upsilon\rangle\varphi =_{def} \neg\Upsilon\neg\varphi \tag{2}$$

$\Diamond\varphi$ means that there exists a state and a choice of action such that φ is true. $\langle\Upsilon\rangle\varphi$ means that there is a terminating path starting at the current state along which φ becomes true ultimately at the terminal state. The meanings of these new modalities will be clearer after the semantics is given in the next section.

2.2 Semantics

As a general practice for GGP, a GDL-described game is specified by a finite state transition system (or state machine). A state transition system can be defined as follows.

Definition 2. Given a game frame $(N, \mathcal{A})$, a *state transition model* M of $\mathcal{L}^{GDL^{++}}$ is a tuple (W, I, T, U, L, G, V), where

- W is a non-empty set of states;
- $I \subseteq W$ is the set of *initial* states;

- $T \subseteq W$ is the set of *terminal* states;
- $U : W \times \mathcal{A} \mapsto W \setminus I$ maps each pair of state and action to a non-initial state;
- $L \subseteq (W \setminus T) \times \mathcal{A}$ says which actions are legal in a state;
- $G : N \to 2^T$ specifies which player wins in which terminal states[1];
- $V : \Phi \to 2^W$ specifies which propositional letters are true in each state.

For simplicity, $U(w, a)$ is sometimes written as $u_a(w)$ sometimes. Let $w \in W$ and $a \in \mathcal{A}$, we call (w, a) a *move*. A sequence $\rho = w_0 \xrightarrow{a_0} w_1 \xrightarrow{a_1} \cdots \xrightarrow{a_{m-1}} w_m$ is called a *path* if

1. $w_j \in W$ for all $0 \le j \le m$ and $a_j \in \mathcal{A}$ for all $0 \le j < m$;
2. $(w_j, a_j) \in L$ for all $0 \le j < m$; and
3. $U(w_j, a_j) = w_{j+1}$ for all $0 \le j < m$.

We say that the path starts at state w_0, denoted by $\rho \uparrow w_0$, and ends at state w_m, denoted by $\hat{\rho} = w_m$. As an extreme case, a single state can be a path. A path is called a *terminating path* if it ends at a terminal state.

Similar to [9], we define the satisfiability relation as $M \models_{(w,a)} \varphi$ to mean that φ is satisfied when action a is taken at state w of M. We write $M \models_w \varphi$ as an abbreviation of "$M \models_{(w,a)} \varphi$ for all $a \in \mathcal{A}$".

Definition 3. Let M be a state transition model of $\mathcal{L}^{GDL^{++}}$. The *satisfiabilty relation* $M \models_{(w,a)} \varphi$ is defined as follows:

$M \models_{(w,a)} p$	iff $w \in V(p)$
$M \models_{(w,a)} \varphi_1 \to \varphi_2$	iff $M \models_{(w,a)} \varphi_1$ implies $M \models_{(w,a)} \varphi_2$
$M \models_{(w,a)} \neg\varphi$	iff $M \not\models_{(w,a)} \varphi$
$M \models_{(w,a)} does(b)$	iff $a = b$
$M \models_{(w,a)} legal(b)$	iff $(w, b) \in L$
$M \models_{(w,a)} initial$	iff $w \in I$
$M \models_{(w,a)} terminal$	iff $w \in T$
$M \models_{(w,a)} wins(n)$	iff $w \in G(n)$
$M \models_{(w,a)} [b]\varphi$	iff $M \models_{u_b(w)} \varphi$
$M \models_{(w,a)} \lfloor b \rfloor \varphi$	iff $M \models_{(w,b)} \varphi$
$M \models_{(w,a)} \Box\varphi$	iff $M \models_{(w',a')} \varphi$ for all $w' \in W$, $a' \in \mathcal{A}$
$M \models_{(w,a)} \Upsilon\varphi$	iff $M \models_{\hat{\rho}} \varphi$ for all terminating path $\rho \uparrow w$

where $p \in \Phi$; $a, b \in \mathcal{A}$; $n \in N$ and $\varphi \in \mathcal{L}^{GDL^{++}}$. Note again that $u_b(w)$ is an abbreviation of $U(w, b)$, meaning the next state after move (w, b) is taken.

As in any modal logic, φ is *valid* in M, written as $M \models \varphi$, if $M \models_{(w,a)} \varphi$ for all $w \in W$ and $a \in \mathcal{A}$. Similarly, by $\models \varphi$ we mean φ is valid in all state transition models.

---

[1] We allow tie situations in which more than one players can won or lose simultaneously.

2.3 Properties of the New Modalities

In this section, we show the basic properties of the new introduced modalities. First we consider the global modality $\Box$.

Proposition 1. *For any $a \in \mathcal{A}$ and any $\varphi \in \mathcal{L}^{GDL^{++}}$,*

1. $\models \Box\varphi \to \varphi$ *(Reflexivity)*
2. $\models \Box\varphi \to \Box\Box\varphi$ *(Transitivity)*
3. $\models \neg\varphi \to \Box\neg\Box\varphi$ *(Symmetry)*
4. $\models \Box\varphi \to [a]\varphi$ *(Inclusion - action execution)*
5. $\models \Box\varphi \to \lfloor a \rfloor\varphi$ *(Inclusion- action selection)*
6. $\models \lfloor a \rfloor\Box\varphi \leftrightarrow \Box\varphi$ *(Action selection reduction)*

With the diamond operator, these properties can be written in different forms. For instance, Symmetry can be simplified as:

$$\models \varphi \to \Box\Diamond\varphi$$

From the above proposition, it is easy to see that $\Box$ operator satisfies all the properties of the global modality [11] although it has to interact with other K modalities - action execution, action selection and ultimate modality.

Note that we do not have $\models \Box\lfloor a \rfloor\varphi \to \Box\varphi$. For instance, let $\Phi = \{p\}$ and $\mathcal{A} = \{a, b\}$. For any state transition system M with non-empty set W of states, $M \models_{(w,c)} \Box\lfloor a \rfloor does(a)$ but $M \not\models_{(w,c)} \Box does(a)$, where (w, c) can be any move in M.

Next we show the properties of Υ operator. Before that, let's define a new next operator $\oplus$:

$$\oplus\varphi =_{def} \bigwedge_{a \in \mathcal{A}} (legal(a) \to [a]\varphi) \tag{3}$$

Different from $\bigcirc$, $\oplus$ is hypothetical, which means that φ could be true after any legal action were taken no matter which action is actually chosen.

Proposition 2. *For any $a \in \mathcal{A}$ and any $\varphi \in \mathcal{L}^{GDL^{++}}$,*

1. $\models \lfloor a \rfloor\Upsilon\varphi \leftrightarrow \Upsilon\varphi$
2. $\models \Upsilon\varphi \leftrightarrow \Upsilon\lfloor a \rfloor\varphi$
3. $\models \Upsilon\ terminal$
4. $\models (\Upsilon\varphi \wedge terminal) \to \varphi$
5. $\models \Upsilon\varphi \to \oplus\Upsilon\varphi$
6. $\models ((terminal \to \varphi) \wedge (\neg terminal \to \oplus\Upsilon\varphi)) \to \Upsilon\varphi$

Properties (1) and (2) indicate that the ultimate operator only concerns about state status regardless selection of actions. Properties (3) and (4) show that the truth of ultimate operation is determined in the terminal states. This become more obvious if we put (4), (5) and (6) together:

$$\models ((terminal \to \varphi) \wedge (\neg terminal \to \oplus\Upsilon\varphi)) \leftrightarrow \Upsilon\varphi \tag{4}$$

This means that, to know if a property holds ultimately in all terminating states, we can check whether it is true whenever a terminal state is reached; or proceed to the next state and check. Such a recursive property can be seen in a number of modal logics, say temporal logic (future operator F) or dynamic logic (iteration operator $*$). Note that any terminating path must be finite because there is no legal action at a terminal state. This differentiates the ultimate operator from other temporal modalities in the traditional modal logics [11, 12][2].

2.4 Axiomatisation

In this section, we will develop an axiomatic system for the proposed logic. Since our logic is extended from [9]'s system, we will inherit most of their axioms but introduce the axioms for the new modalities and prove the soundness and completeness of the whole system. We call the logic with the following axiomatic system GDL^{++} while [9]'s system is referred to as GDL^{+}:

1. Basic axioms:
   - **(A1)** all axioms for propositional calculus
   - **(A2)** $\vdash \neg(does(a) \wedge does(b))$ if $a \neq b$
   - **(A3)** $\vdash \bigvee_{a \in \mathcal{A}} does(a)$
   - **(A4)** $\vdash \neg[a]initial$
   - **(A5)** $\vdash terminal \rightarrow \neg legal(a)$
   - **(A6)** $\vdash wins(n) \rightarrow terminal$

2. Axioms on the action execution modality:
   - **(B1)** $\vdash [a](\varphi \rightarrow \psi) \rightarrow ([a]\varphi \rightarrow [a]\psi)$
   - **(B2)** $\vdash \neg[a]\varphi \leftrightarrow [a] \bigvee_{b \in \mathcal{A}} \lfloor b \rfloor \neg\varphi$

3. Axioms on the action selection modality:
   - **(C1)** $\vdash \lfloor a \rfloor p \leftrightarrow p$ where $p \in \Phi \cup \{initial, terminal, legal(b), wins(n)\}$
   - **(C2)** $\vdash \lfloor a \rfloor does(a)$
   - **(C3)** $\vdash \neg \lfloor a \rfloor does(b)$, if $a \neq b$
   - **(C4)** $\vdash \lfloor a \rfloor \neg\varphi \leftrightarrow \neg \lfloor a \rfloor \varphi$
   - **(C5)** $\vdash \lfloor a \rfloor(\varphi \rightarrow \psi) \leftrightarrow (\lfloor a \rfloor \varphi \rightarrow \lfloor a \rfloor \psi)$
   - **(C6)** $\vdash \lfloor a \rfloor[b]\varphi \leftrightarrow [b]\varphi$
   - **(C7)** $\vdash \lfloor a \rfloor \lfloor b \rfloor \varphi \leftrightarrow \lfloor b \rfloor \varphi$
   - **(C8)** $\vdash \lfloor a \rfloor \Box\varphi \leftrightarrow \Box\varphi$
   - **(C9)** $\vdash \lfloor a \rfloor \Upsilon\varphi \leftrightarrow \Upsilon\varphi$

4. Axioms on the global modality:
   - **(E1)** $\vdash \Box(\varphi \rightarrow \psi) \rightarrow (\Box\varphi \rightarrow \Box\psi)$
   - **(E2)** $\vdash \Box\varphi \rightarrow \varphi$
   - **(E3)** $\vdash \neg\varphi \rightarrow \Box\neg\Box\varphi$
   - **(E4)** $\vdash \Box\varphi \rightarrow \Box\Box\varphi$
   - **(E5)** $\vdash \Box\varphi \rightarrow [a]\varphi$
   - **(E6)** $\vdash \Box\varphi \rightarrow \lfloor a \rfloor \varphi$

5. Axioms on the ultimate modality
   - **(F1)** $\vdash \Upsilon(\varphi \rightarrow \psi) \rightarrow (\Upsilon\varphi \rightarrow \Upsilon\psi)$
   - **(F2)** $\vdash \Upsilon\, terminal$
   - **(F3)** $\vdash \Upsilon \lfloor a \rfloor \varphi \leftrightarrow \Upsilon\varphi$
   - **(F4)** $\vdash (\Upsilon\varphi \wedge terminal) \rightarrow \varphi$
   - **(F5)** $\vdash \Upsilon\varphi \rightarrow \oplus\Upsilon\varphi$
   - **(F6)** $\vdash ((terminal \rightarrow \varphi) \wedge (\neg terminal \rightarrow \oplus\Upsilon\varphi)) \rightarrow \Upsilon\varphi$

6. Inference rules:
   - **(MP)** If $\vdash \varphi$ and $\vdash \varphi \rightarrow \psi$, then $\vdash \psi$.
   - **(GEN G)** If $\vdash \varphi$, then $\vdash \Box\varphi$.
   - **(GEN U)** If $\vdash \varphi$, then $\vdash \Upsilon\varphi$.

   where $a, b \in \mathcal{A}$, $n \in N$ and $\varphi, \psi, \alpha \in \mathcal{L}^{GDL^{++}}$.

Among the axioms and inference rules, (A6), (C8), (C9), (E1)–(E6), (F1)–(F6), (GEN G) and (GEN U) are new to GDL^{+}. We also removed inference rules (GEN A)

---

[2] For example, the ultimate operator looks similar to the future operator F in temporal logic. However, $[F]\varphi$ ($\langle F \rangle$) means that φ holds in all future time points (will hold in some future point). The ultimate operator checks only at the terminal states.

and (GEN C) from GDL^+ because they can be derived from (E5), (E6) and (GEN G). We excluded all the axioms in relation to the strategy modality because the strategy operator is not part of language $\mathcal{L}^{GDL^{++}}$.

As usual, a formula φ is derivable, denoted by $\vdash \varphi$, if it can be derived from the axioms and inference rules. For any set of formulas Σ and formula φ, $\Sigma \vdash \varphi$ means that there are $\varphi_1, \cdots, \varphi_m \in \Sigma$ such that $\vdash (\varphi_1 \wedge \cdots \wedge \varphi_m) \to \varphi$.

Theorem 1 (Soundness and completeness). *For any $\varphi \in \mathcal{L}^{GDL^{++}}$, $\models \varphi$ if and only if $\vdash \varphi$.*

The soundness for the additional axioms has been proved by Propositions 1 and 2. The proof of completeness is quite lengthy even for the extended components only. For better readability, we put the proof at the end of this paper as an appendix.

Although the common practice of implementing a GGP player is to compile a GDL described game into a state machine, search for game playing strategies over a state machine normally has exponential complexity. As mentioned earlier, the way to describe a game dramatically affects the efficiency of a GGP player. It is crucial for a GGP player to be able to reformulate a computationally unfriendly game description into more efficient ones before a game starts. Ideally, the process of rule reformulation can be done in syntactical level. The axiomatic system of the logic not only gives us hope for developing syntax-based approaches for game rule reformulation but also provide us two options for theoretical proofs - either in syntactical level or in semantical level (See Proposition 4).

3 Reason About Game Descriptions

The logic introduced in the previous section not only provides a formal language to describe game rules but also an inference mechanism for reasoning about a game.

3.1 Game Descriptions

Both $\mathcal{L}^{GDL^+}$ and $\mathcal{L}^{GDL^{++}}$ contain all the logical components of GDL. In order to reason about a GDL-described game, it seems that we only have to translate the GDL rules into a set of logical formulas in either $\mathcal{L}^{GDL^+}$ or $\mathcal{L}^{GDL^{++}}$. Unfortunately this is not true. A game description in GDL specifies an action theory, containing a set of initial state axioms, precondition axioms, effect axioms, frame axioms, terminal state axioms and wining conditions. This axioms must be treated as domain-dependent axioms when we use GDL^+ to reason. They are not expressible in the object level of GDL^+. However, with the global modality of $\mathcal{L}^{GDL^{++}}$, it is possible. To demonstrate how to describe a game in $\mathcal{L}^{GDL^{++}}$, we consider the following game, Hex, co-invented by Piet Hein and John Nash [13].

Example 1 *(Hex Game). Hex is a two-player game played on a rhombus-shaped board with $m \times m$ hexagonal cells ($m > 1$). The two players, Black (b) and White (w), alternate placing a stone of their colour in a previously unoccupied cell. The goal of each player is to form a connected path of their own stones linking opposing sides of the board (North and South for Black; West and East for White). The first player to complete his or her connection wins the game (see Fig. 1).*

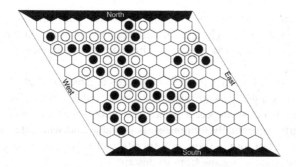

Fig. 1. An 11×11 hex game where the white player wins.

To specify the game in our language, let $p_{i,j}^n$ denote that cell (i, j) is occupied by player n's stone and $a_{i,j}^n$ the action of player n placing a stone in the cell (i, j), where $n \in \{b, w\}$ and $1 \le i, j \le m$. Furthermore, we recursively define a collection of propositional symbols $\gamma^n(i, j, i', j')$, for each $n \in \{b, w\}$ and $1 \le i, i', j, j' \le m$, as follows[3]:

- $\gamma^n(i, j, i, j) \leftrightarrow p_{i,j}^n$
- $\gamma^n(i, j, i', j') \leftrightarrow (p_{i,j}^n \land adjacent(i, j, i'', j'') \land \gamma^n(i'', j'', i', j'))$ where $adjacent(i, j, i', j') =_{def} (i' = i \land |j - j'| = 1) \lor (|i - i'| = 1 \land j' = j) \lor (i' = i + 1 \land j' = j - 1) \lor (i' = i - 1 \land j' = j + 1)$.

It is easy to see that $\gamma^n(i, j, i', j')$ represents the existence of a path for player n from (i, j) to (i', j'). With the variables defined above, the rules of Hex game on an $m \times m$ rhombus can be specified by the following formulas:

1. $\Box(initial \leftrightarrow turn(b) \land \neg turn(w) \land \bigwedge_{i,j=1}^{m} \neg(p_{i,j}^b \lor p_{i,j}^w))$

2. $\Box(wins(b) \leftrightarrow \bigvee_{j,j'=1}^{m} \gamma^b(1, j, m, j')) \land$
$\Box(wins(w) \leftrightarrow \bigvee_{i,i'=1}^{m} \gamma^w(i, 1, i', m))$

3. $\Box(teminal \leftrightarrow wins(b) \lor wins(w) \lor \bigwedge_{i,j=1}^{m} (p_{i,j}^b \lor p_{i,j}^w))$

4. $\Box(legal(a_{i,j}^n) \leftrightarrow \neg(p_{i,j}^b \lor p_{i,j}^w) \land turn(n) \land \neg terminal)$

5. $\Box(\bigcirc p_{i,j}^n \leftrightarrow p_{i,j}^n \lor does(a_{i,j}^n))$

6. $\Box(\bigcirc turn(w) \leftrightarrow turn(b)) \land \Box(\bigcirc turn(b) \leftrightarrow turn(w))$

where $n \in \{b, w\}$ and $1 \le i, j \le m$ whenever they occur as free variables. Let Σ_{hexp}^m denote the set of the above game rules. These are the rules, reformulated in our language, from the original GDL description for players from the 2016 GGP Competition[4].

---

[3] Since our language is propositional, each $\gamma^n(i, j, i', j')$ is treated as a propositional variable rather than a predicate. Different values for n, i, j, i', j' result in different variables.

[4] The original GDL description includes a $step(.)$ variable. Since it does not play a role in the rule compilation, we omitted it in our version.

The rules are quite intuitive. Rule (1) says that initially it is the black player's turn and all cells are empty. Rules (2) and (3) describe the winning and termination conditions, respectively. (4) and (5) specify legality and effects of each action. Rules (6) defines turn-taking.

In theory, any set of formulas in $\mathcal{L}^{GDL^{++}}$ specifies a game (or a set of games), therefore can be called as a *game description*, because they determines a set of state transition models. However, we expect a game description specifies a meaningful game, which can be started, eventually terminates, is playable and winnable. It is important to know whether a set of formula correctly specify such a game and, more importantly, how to derive properties of a game from its description.

3.2 Game Properties

Genesereth and Thielscher introduced a set of constraints to limit the scope of game descriptions so as to avoid problematic games [1]. These constraints were described informally as follows:

- *Termination*: A game description terminates if all infinite sequences of legal moves from the initial state of the game reach a terminal state after a finite number of steps.
- *Playability*: A game description is playable if and only if every role has at least one legal move in every non-terminal state reachable from the initial state.
- *Winnability*: A game description is *strongly* winnable if and only if, for some role, there is a sequence of individual actions of that role that leads to a terminal state of the game where that role's goal value is maximal, independent of the other players' moves. A game description is *weakly* winnable if and only if, for every role, there is a sequence of joint actions of all roles that leads to a terminal state where that role's goal value is maximal.
- *Well-formedness*: A game description is well-formed if it terminates and is both playable and weakly winnable.

With the help of our logic, we can formalise these concepts accurately. Let Σ be a set of formulas in $\mathcal{L}^{GDL^{++}}$. If we use Σ to describe a game, as a minimal requirement, we want the description to be logically consistent:

Consistency: $\Sigma \nvdash \bot$

In other words, at least one state transition model satisfies the game description.

Secondly, we require that the description of initial states and terminal states are valid:

Non-vacuity: $\Sigma \vdash \Diamond initial \land \Diamond terminal$

Semantically, either the set of initial states or the set of terminal states of any state transition model of the game description is non-empty.

Thirdly, we specify the condition of termination:

Termination: $\Sigma \vdash \Box(initial \rightarrow \langle \Upsilon \rangle terminal)$

The condition says that any initial state leads to a terminal state. In other words, a game must have a terminating path from each initial state. Since there is no legal action in the terminal states, all terminating paths are finite. Note that we do not require that any path from an initial state terminates in finitely many steps because in some games, such as Chess, states can be repeated forever unless there are special termination conditions enforced.

The following conditions express two variations of termination.

Weak Termination: $\Sigma \vdash \Diamond(initial \wedge \langle \Upsilon \rangle terminal)$

Strong Termination: $\Sigma \vdash \Box \langle \Upsilon \rangle terminal$

Weak termination means that there is at least one path that starts from an initial state and ends in a terminal state. Maze games satisfy weak termination, for example. Strong termination says that any state with any action can lead to a terminal state.

Next, we formalise the concept of playability.

Playability: $\Sigma \vdash \Box(\neg terminal \rightarrow \bigvee_{a \in \mathcal{A}} legal(a))$

The condition of playability requires that in every non-terminal state there must be at least one legal action to proceed. Thus for a turn-taking or simultaneous-move game, every player must have at least one legal move in every non-terminal state. Note that our concept of playability is slightly stronger and simpler than [1]'s because we do not require that non-terminal states are reachable.

Finally, we introduce concepts of winnability that also slightly differ from [1] due to the following two reasons. First, we do not assume all players make simultaneous moves. Weak winnability is then not generally applicable. Second, the original GDL contains a goal function which awards each player a natural number as its goal value when a game reaches a terminal state. However, including a function with values of natural numbers in a propositional modal logic would introduce significant complexity. Instead we simply use the propositional variables *wins(.)* with only two values, true and false, to represent a game outcome. Accordingly, our concepts of winnability are simpler but different.

Week Winnability: $\Sigma \vdash \bigwedge_{n \in N} \Diamond(initial \rightarrow \langle \Upsilon \rangle wins(n))$.

Strong Winnability: $\Sigma \vdash \bigwedge_{n \in N} \Box(initial \rightarrow \langle \Upsilon \rangle wins(n))$.

Weak winnability says that every player has a chance to win. Strong winnability says that every player has a chance to win no matter which initial state the game starts from. These concepts of winnability reflect a certain sense of fairness.

Finally we have the following definition:

Definition 4. A game description is *well-formed* if it is *consistent, non-vacuous, terminable, playable* and *weak winnable*.

3.3 Reason About Game Descriptions

We have demonstrated that the language of GDL^{++} is sufficient for formalisation of [1]'s informal constraints on game descriptions. However, expressing properties of game descriptions is not the main motivation of proposing this logic. The main motivation for the logic is to develop approaches for analysing game properties. In this section, we demonstrate how to use GDL^{++} for reasoning about game properties.

First we show the relationship between the game properties.

Proposition 3. *For any game description,*

1. Strong Termination implies Termination.

2. *Non-vacuity and Termination implies Weak Termination.*
3. *Strong Winnability implies Termination.*

Secondly, we show the game properties of Hex game.

Proposition 4. *For the game description Σ^m_{hexp} of $m \times m$-Hex,*

1. $\Sigma^m_{hexp} \models \Box(initial \rightarrow \langle \Upsilon \rangle terminal)$
2. $\Sigma^m_{hexp} \models \Box(initial \rightarrow \Upsilon \neg(wins(b) \wedge wins(w)))$
3. $\Sigma^m_{hexp} \models \Box(initial \rightarrow \Upsilon(wins(b) \vee wins(w)))$

Statement (1) says that Hex is terminable. Statement (2) says that the two players cannot win a game of Hex at the same time. Statement (3) is a well-known result which says any terminated Hex game must have a winner. It is worth noting that the proof of statement (3) requires to map Hex game models to planar graphs or to a fixed-point problem so that either the Four-Colour Theorem or Brouwer's Fixed-Point Theorem can be used to prove it [13].

We would like to remark that we did not provide syntactical proofs for these statements. The first two have simply syntactical proofs even quite lengthy. A syntactical proof for the third statement can be very challenging. Thanks to the soundness and completeness, which allows us a model-based proof using the well-known existing methods. However, it is interesting to know if an automated theorem prover can help.

Finally we show that Σ^m_{hexp} is a well-formed game description.

Theorem 2. *The game description Σ^m_{hexp} is well-formed.*

From the above examples we can see that although reasoning about game properties is possible but it cannot be easy, as [1] said, "*analysing a set of rules with the aim to acquire useful knowledge about a new game is arguably the biggest, and most interesting, challenge for general game-playing systems.*" A general practice in GGP player design is: syntactical approaches can be highly efficient but less guaranteed while model-based approaches can guarantee to use but less efficient. Normally syntactical approaches apply to large games and model-based approaches work only for simple games.

4   Discussion and Conclusion

We have introduced a modal logic system with formally defined syntax, semantics and sound complete axiomatic system. Although the logic was build up on Zhang and Thielscher's framework, the motivation and outcomes of these two pieces of work are significantly different. Zhang and Thielscher's work focuses on representation and reasoning about game strategies while this current work aimed at expressing game rules and analysing game properties. With the new modalities, we can describe game rules and game outcomes in the object language level. These operators interact with the existing operators nicely resulting in a highly expressive but simple, intuitive and elegant logical system.

There has been a number of logical frameworks that can be used for describing and reasoning about games, such as ATL, coalition logic and even dynamic logic or situation calculus [14–16]. Different frameworks have different focuses and different pros and cons with respect to either expressive power, inference facilities, or computational complexity. Among all the logics with similar expressive power, our logic looks the simplest with regarding to its semantics and axiomatic system. In addition, our logic is the only formal logical system fully expressing GDL without transformation. The proposed proof theory may be useful in the development of automated reasoning systems for GGP players.

There are a number of different directions for further extending the current work. The first direction is to extend the existing logic with epistemic operators or coalition operators in order to represent games with incomplete information and strategic ability and coalition of multi-agents [17]. The second direction is to extend the current logic with the strategy modality [9]. This can be extremely interesting because the strategy modality in [9] is reducible. However, with the ultimate modality, this operator is no longer reducible. This is very much like the announcement logic extending with common knowledge operator [18]. In addition, the combination of strategy modality and ultimate modality could allow us to express and even prove winning strategies for games. As a simple example, the following statement says that $\bigcirc(\neg p_{1,1}^b \wedge p_{1,2}^b)$ is a winning strategy for Black in the elementary 2×2-Hex game:

$$\Sigma_{hexp}^2 \models \langle\!\langle \bigcirc(\neg p_{1,1}^b \wedge p_{1,2}^b)\rangle\!\rangle \Upsilon wins(\mathsf{b})$$

However, with all modalities in one logic, the development of a sound and complete axiomatisation becomes a challenge.

Finally, as mentioned earlier, the way of describing a game can affect the efficiency of a GGP player significantly. It is ideal for a GGP player capable of autonomously reformulating a badly-written game description into an "equivalent" but more computationally-friendly description. Such equivalence is not necessarily logical equivalence but can be behaviourally equivalent. Implementation of algorithms for automated game equivalence verification and automated game description compilation and reformulation can be a common task for the GGP community in the future.

References

1. Genesereth, M., Thielscher, M.: General Game Playing. Morgan & Claypool Publishers, San Rafael (2014)
2. Love, N., Hinrichs, T., Genesereth, M.: General game playing: game description language specification. Technical report, Computer Science Department, Stanford University (2006)
3. Genesereth, M., Love, N., Pell, B.: General game playing: overview of the AAAI competition. AI Mag. **26**(2), 62–72 (2005)
4. Genesereth, M.M., Björnsson, Y.: The international general game playing competition. AI Mag. **34**(2), 107–111 (2013)
5. Swiechowski, M., Mandziuk, J.: Fast interpreter for logical reasoning in general game playing. J. Log. Comput. **24**(5), 1071–1110 (2014)
6. Romero, J., Saffidine, A., Thielscher, M.: Solving the inferential frame problem in the general game description language. In: AAAI-2014, pp. 515–521 (2014)

7. Schkufza, E., Love, N., Genesereth, M.: Propositional automata and cell automata: representational frameworks for discrete dynamic systems. In: Wobcke, W., Zhang, M. (eds.) AI 2008. LNCS (LNAI), vol. 5360, pp. 56–66. Springer, Heidelberg (2008). https://doi.org/10.1007/978-3-540-89378-3_6

8. Schiffel, S.: Symmetry detection in general game playing. In: AAAI-2010, pp. 980–985 (2010)

9. Zhang, D., Thielscher, M.: A logic for reasoning about game strategies. In: AAAI-2015, pp. 1671–1677 (2015)

10. Zhang, D., Thielscher, M.: Representing and reasoning about game strategies. J. Philos. Log. **44**(2), 203–236 (2015)

11. Blackburn, P., Rijke, M.d., Venema, Y.: Modal Logic. Cambridge Tracts in Theoretical Computer Science. Cambridge University Press (2001)

12. Goldblatt, R.: Logics of Time and Computation. CSLI, Stanford University, Stanford (1992)

13. Gale, D.: The game of hex and the Brouwer fixed-point theorem. Am. Math. Mon. **86**(10), 818–827 (1979)

14. Alur, R., Henzinger, T.A., Kupferman, O.: Alternating-time temporal logic. J. ACM **49**(5), 672–713 (2002)

15. Pauly, M.: A modal logic for coalitional power in games. J. Log. Comput. **12**(1), 149–166 (2002)

16. Ågotnes, T., van der Hoek, W., Wooldridge, M.: Reasoning about coalitional games. Artif. Intell. **173**(1), 45–79 (2009)

17. Jiang, G., Zhang, D., Perrussel, L., Zhang, H.: Epistemic GDL: a logic for representing and reasoning about imperfect information games. In: IJCAI-2016, pp. 1138–1144 (2016)

18. van Ditmarsch, H., van der Hoek, W., Kooi, B.: Dynamic Epistemic Logic. Springer, Dordrecht (2007). https://doi.org/10.1007/978-1-4020-5839-4

General Language Evolution in General Game Playing

Armin Chitizadeh$^{(\boxtimes)}$ and Michael Thielscher

UNSW Sydney, Sydney, NSW 2052, Australia
{a.chitizadeh,mit}@unsw.edu.au

Abstract. General Game Playing (GGP) is concerned with the development of programs capable of expertly playing a game by just receiving its rules and without human intervention. Its standard Game Description Language (GDL) has been extended so as to include incomplete information games. The extended version is named as GDL-II. Different algorithms were recommended to play games in GDL-II, however, none of them can solve coordination games properly. One reason for this shortcoming is their inability to generate the necessary coordination language. On the other side, most existing language evolution techniques focus on generating a common language without considering its generality or its use for problem solving. In this paper, we will extend GGP with language evolution to develop a general language generation technique. The new technique can be combined with GGP algorithms for incomplete-information games and assist players in automatically generating a common language to solve cooperation problems.

Keywords: General game playing with incomplete information
Language learning · Multi-agent coordination · Fictitious play
Evolutionary computing

1 Introduction

General Game Playing (GGP) is concerned with the development of a general Artificial Intelligence (AI) system that, in principle, can learn to play any game by only receiving its rules [8]. The rules are given in a formal language called Game Description Language (GDL) [12]. While the original language was restricted to games with full information, such as Chess and Go, a later extension of GDL, called Game Description Language with Incomplete Information (GDL-II) [23], can also model games with asymmetric information and chance, such as Poker. The current state of the art in GGP-II are three algorithms known as *Shodan Player* [3], *Norns algorithm* [7], and *HyperPlay-II* [15], respectively. However, none of these current algorithms is expressive enough to reach an agreement for a common plan or language in *cooperative* games.

In some cooperative games, agents need to share their knowledge about the world without this being explicitly described in the rules of the game.

© Springer Nature Switzerland AG 2018
T. Mitrovic et al. (Eds.): AI 2018, LNAI 11320, pp. 51–64, 2018.
https://doi.org/10.1007/978-3-030-03991-2_5

As an example, consider a simple game, taken from [15], with a random player ("Nature") and two agents, respectively called *cutter* and *viewer*. The game is named "cooperative spies game". It proceeds as follows: First, a bomb is armed by randomly choosing one of two wires. Only the *viewer* can see which wire the bomb is armed with. This player can then send one of two possible messages to the *cutter*. Finally, the *cutter* needs to cut the right wire for both agents to win. The crux in this game is the lack of any connection between the perception of the *viewer* (which wire has been used) and the message it can send to the *cutter*. This problem is mentioned as a limitation of all current methods for GGP-II [15]. We believe this limitation is due to the inability of agents to automatically generate a common language among themselves.

The study of common language generation in computer science can roughly be divided into two categories based on the environments that are considered: simulated or embodied. The embodied systems mainly focus on language games. There have been three main variants of the language game: object naming game, colour categorising and naming game, and lexicon spatial language game [1,16,18–21]. In simulated environments, agents do not need any interaction with the real world or image recognition, so they can focus on extending the communication to a population of agents [9]. This extension allows the simulation to test how a common language equilibrium will be affected when a new agent enters the environment [17].

Whether they use simulated or embodied environments, existing research methods are all limited to the design and evaluation of one specific problem. Recently, Reinforcement Learning (RL) has been suggested as a relatively general approach to generate a common language [6,13]. RL techniques consist of centralised learning and decentralised execution. They also assume there exists a communication channel for sending messages with no effect on the world. These assumptions limit the generality of the algorithms: Firstly, centralised learning means agents who will cooperate need to come together and train with each other. This reduces the applicability of these algorithms to games in which the cooperating agents will always be allies and enemies will always be opponents. Secondly, more complicated scenarios in which signalling might come at a cost for agents cannot be solved by these techniques. In these scenarios, agents need to weigh the benefit against the cost of signalling. Moreover, the RL techniques always need centralised learning even though some problems can be solved without requiring this. Later in this paper, we will present and discuss such a game.

In this paper, we will extend GGP with language evolution to develop a general language generation technique. Our main contributions are as follows: We extend GGP-II so that it can be applied to the field of language learning in AI with the aim to study general language learning algorithms that can be applied across a wide variety of problems. We also introduce a general language learning algorithm in this framework that allows agents to reach a common language for sharing information and correctly playing coordination games. Agents learning new common languages for problems solely by being given a formal problem description without a dedicated communication channel is new to both GGP as well as the field of language learning.

The rest of the paper is organised as follows: We first introduce the current framework of GGP-II, cooperative games, and our recent so-called Iterative Tree Search (ITS) algorithm for GGP-II [4]. We then introduce our new general language learning algorithm for GGP-II, followed by an analysis of the algorithm in a variety of different games. We also report on an experiment performed with the help of genetic algorithm and our algorithm. The paper ends with a summary and discussion of our results.

2   Background

This section provides a brief background on GGP-II, cooperative games, and Iterative Tree Search.

```
1     (role cutter)                          27    (<= (sees cutter a)
2     (role viewer)                          28       (does viwer tellA)
3     (role random)                          29    (<= (sees cutter b)
4     (init (round 0))                       30       (does viewer tellB)
5     (coulour red) (colour blue)            31    (<= (next (round 1))
6     (<= (legal random (arm ?c))            32       (true (round 0)))
7        (colour ?c) (true round 0))         33    ...
8     (<= (legal random noop)                34    (<= (next (armed ?c))
9        (not (true round 0)))               35       (does random (arm ?c)))
10    (<= (legal viewer noop)                36    (<= (next (armed ?c))
11       (true round 0))                     37       (true (armed ?c))
12    (<= (legal cutter noop)                38
13       (true round 0))                     39    (<= disarmed
14    (<= (legal viewer tellA)               40       (does cutter (cut c?))
15       (true round 1))                     41       (true (armed ?c)))
16    (<= (legal viewer tellB)               42    (<= exploded
17       (true round 1))                     43       (does cutter (cut c?))
18    (<= (legal cutter (cut blue))          44       (not (true (armed ?c))))
19       (true round 2))                     45    (<= terminal (true
20    (<= (legal cutter (cut red))           46       (round 3)))
21       (true round 2))                     47    (<= (goal ?role 100)
22    ...                                    48       (disarmed)
23    (<= (sees viewer red)                  49       (distinct ?role random))
24       (does random (arm red))             50    (<= (goal ?role 0)
25    (<= (sees viewer blue)                 51       (exploded)
26       (does random (arm blue))            52       (distinct ?role random))
                                             53    (<= (goal random 0)
```

Fig. 1. GDL-II description of the Cooperative Spies game.

2.1   General Game Playing with Incomplete Information

GGP systems can play any game whose rules are given in GDL format. Game states in GDL are defined as sets of state features that are currently true. The initial state and terminal states are distinguished. In GDL-II, "chance" is modelled by a so-called random player. The random player chooses its moves randomly with uniform probability, and it has the same reward value at all terminal states. Players' moves are hidden from each other. Logical rules are defined to describe the next states, legal actions, and perceptions. The only way of knowing past moves of other players is through perceptions. Rules of the game explicitly describe who perceives what after every action. If agents are given sufficient information then they can use logical inference and their perceptions to infer some past moves. When the game ends, players will be notified and given a reward value. In GGP the convention is that the minimum reward is 0 and the maximum reward is 100. The goal of players is to maximise their reward values.

As an example of how games are specified to players in the general game description language GDL-II, Fig. 1 formally describes the "Cooperative Spies Game" [15] from the introduction. Pre-defined GDL-II keywords are printed in bold. Keyword *role* in lines 1 to 3 is used to name the players in the game. Keyword *init* in line 4 is used to list the state features that compose the initial state of the game. Lines 6 to 21 use logical rules (that can be read like logic programming rules but use prefix syntax and "?" to denote variables [12]) to specify the legal moves that player have depending on the current position of the game. As an example, lines 6 and 7 are saying that the random player can perform action *arm(?c)* if the game is still at *round(0)* and ?c is a *colour*. Lines 23 to 30 describe the perceptions that players will get after a specific action. As an example, lines 23 and 24 say that after the random player arms the red wire, the viewer can see *red*. Lines 31 to 37 describe how the position of the game will change during the match. For example, lines 36 and 37 are saying that the armed wire will remain armed throughout the game. The *terminal* keyword at line 45 describes when the game comes to an end. Lines 47 to 53 specify the rewards of the players when the game terminates. For more details about syntax and semantics we refer to [12] and [8].

2.2 Cooperative Games

A cooperative game has a cooperative environment. Cooperative environment means agents will gain the most when they fully cooperate [14]. In this paper, we will consider cooperative games in which agents need to generate a common language in order to win. We also consider general games with a coordination problem. The latter means that there is more than one optimal joint policy [2]. "Battle of Sexes" is a famous example of a game with a coordination problem. Table 1 describes "Battle of Sexes" as a matrix game with rewards of either 1 or 0.

Table 1. Battle of Sexes with binary rewards

Man	Woman	
	Boxing	*Shopping*
Boxing	$(1, 0)$	$(0, 1)$
Shopping	$(0, 1)$	$(1, 0)$

Another example of a game with a coordination problem is called "pick a number". In this game, two agents are asked to choose a number simultaneously, e.g. between 0 and 100, and if they select the same, then both win. One technique to solve this type of games is to use a *focal point* [5]. According to the focal point technique, agents should choose the most distinct and unique object or path. In the example the median, 50, is the most unique and distinct number, so both agents should choose 50. This technique is easily understandable to humans and often applied in real life. However, as problems get more complicated, e.g. when a game becomes symmetric like the "Battle of Sexes" game with only 1 and 0 rewards, the focal point tewas chnique is not suitable to solve the problem. Language games, such as the Naming Game, all feature both a cooperative environment and a coordination problem.

The other common approaches for games with a coordination problem are policy learning and convention techniques. In policy learning, agents play a game several times and choose an optimal policy randomly each time. When they discover that they both chose the same optimal policy, then they will keep playing it. Social law or convention technique is one of the most basic approaches. With the help of a function that always chooses one unique element in a given set, this technique will assist agents to always choose the same joint strategy. Social convention technique has also been used to tackle the one-shot prisoner's dilemma problem [11,22]. The convention technique is relatively easy to implement with GDL. One convention function could be to return the maximal optimal joint strategies based on the alphabetic order of roles and their strategies. This, however, is not intuitive to other players or humans so that we will use the policy learning technique instead.

2.3 Iterative Tree Search Algorithm

Recently, we have developed Iterative Tree Search (ITS) as a new algorithm that can successfully play a wider variety of GGP-II games than previous techniques [4]. ITS searches on the incomplete information game tree to value information in games. It also iteratively plays against itself before the game starts in order to learn the optimal strategy against a rational opponent. However, it is incapable of playing coordination games such as the above-mentioned Cooperative Spies game. For a detailed description of the ITS algorithm we refer to [4]; in this paper, we will introduce a simplified version (called sITS). In this version, the algorithm searches the game tree only once and avoids further iterations. Iteration is required to model an opponent in a game and hence is not needed for the purpose of our work here since we are focusing on cooperative games. This dramatically reduces the time complexity of the algorithm. The simplified version is described in Algorithm 1.

3   General Language Algorithm

While traditionally the focus in GGP competitions has been on one-shot games [8], in order to solve a coordination problem we will use a policy learning technique for which we extend the GGP framework to go beyond one-shot games.

Algorithm 1. Simplified ITS algorithm

1: $firstState \leftarrow GenerateTheGameTree(GDL)$
2: $IS \leftarrow GenerateInformationSetHashMap$
3: $gameValue \leftarrow CalculateUtil(firstState)$
4: **return** $gameValue[thePlayer]$

5: **procedure** $CalculateUtil(state)$
6:     **if** $state \in terminals$ **then**
7:         **return** $state.reward$
8:     **else if** $state.playerToMove == random$ **then**
9:         **return** $CalculateRandomUtil(state)$
10:    **else**   ▷ If the player is an agent
11:        **return** $CalculatePlayerUtil(state)$

12: **procedure** $CalculateRandomUtil(state)$
13:    **return** $\sum_{m \in state.legalM} \frac{CalculateUtil(state.nextS(m))}{|state.legalMoves|}$

14: **procedure** $CalculatePlayerUtil(state)$
15:    **return**

$$\max_{m \in state.legalM} \left(\sum_{st \in IS(state)} \frac{Prob(st) \times CalculateUtil(state.nextS(m))}{|IS(state)|} \right)$$

This also requires that players keep information about their past matches. On this basis we can now introduce our General Language (GL) algorithm.

Only for the sake of clarity in our description of the algorithm, we will introduce a new syntactical element to GDL-II, a pre-defined keyword called *must()*. An instance (*must* (*does* ?*agent* ?*action1*)) forces an agent to choose the given specific action. Effectively, we are just removing all the legal actions except for one for a player in a state. We will refer to this rule as the *mustRule*.

Our General Language technique for GGP-II learning is as follows: A common language can be described as a set of *mustRules* added to the original GDL-II of the game. These rules connect perception tokens received by a player to the actions of that player. In other words, each *mustRule* forces an agent to play a particular move that triggers a specific percept if, and only if, the agent made a specific observation beforehand. A move that releases a percept must happen right after the triggering percept has been received by the player. This is a one to one relation. Formally, all the added *mustRules* have the following structure:

(⇐ (**must**(**does** ?agent1 ?action1)) (**sees** ?agent1 ?perception1))

where *action1* has the following consequence:

(⇐ (**sees** ?agent2 ?perception2) (**does** ?agent1 ?action1))

It is worth noting that *?perception1* is always received before *?perception2* in a game.

The first step of the GL technique is to generate a bag of different GDL games, each of which we refer to as *dialect*. The original GDL of the game is a *dialect*, and so are the original GDL with one or more *mustRules* added. We begin by adding *all* the possible *dialects*. Next, we run sITS on each *dialect* and set the returned value for each game as the value of the *dialect*. We then choose the *dialect* with the highest value and play the policy generated by running sITS on this *dialect*. If there is more than one *dialect* with maximum value, then we have a coordination problem. To solve this coordination problem, we will use the learning policy algorithm. Each agent chooses a *dialect* with maximum value randomly, then plays an optimal policy for it. If the coordination succeeds, they will stick with what the chosen *dialect* for all future rounds. If, however, it fails, then the agents repeat the process by randomly choosing a *dialect* with maximum value again. Algorithm 2 describes this GL algorithm more formally.

Algorithm 2. General Language Algorithm

1: $dialectList \leftarrow [\ ].add(theOriginalGDL)$
2: Populated $dialectList$
3: $maxReward \leftarrow -1$
4: **for all** $dialect \in dialectList$ **do**
5:     **if** $maxReward < sITS.Value(dialect)$ **then**
6:         $maxDialect.add(dialect)$
7:         $maxReward \leftarrow sITS.Value(dialect)$
8: $chosenDialect \leftarrow rand(maxDialect)$
9: **while** (time allows) **do**
10:     play according to $sITS(chosenDialect)$ policy
11:     **if** $matchReward < maxReward$ **then**
12:         $chosenDialect \leftarrow rand(maxDialect)$

Example: Cooperative Spies. To illustrate our technique, we will use the Cooperative Spies game by Schofield and Thielscher [15], who introduced this example to illustrate the limitation of their and all other existing approaches to general game playing with incomplete information. The crux is that in the description of the game (cf. Fig. 1) there is no logical dependency between the colour of the wire and the signal that the *viewer* can send. For this reason, none of the previous GGP-II approaches can solve this problem.

Recall from Fig. 1 the following *sees* rules for the *viewer*:

```
(⇐ (sees viewer redWire) (does random (arm red)))
(⇐ (sees viewer blueWire) (does random (arm blue)))
```

along with the following rules for the *cutter*:

```
(⇐ (sees cutter a) (does viewer tellA))
(⇐ (sees cutter b) (does viewer tellB))
```

For this game, there are four possible *mustRules* that can be added:

1. (⇐ (**must**(**does** viewer tellA)) (**sees** viewer redWire))
2. (⇐ (**must**(**does** viewer tellA)) (**sees** viewer blueWire))
3. (⇐ (**must**(**does** viewer tellB)) (**sees** viewer blueWire))
4. (⇐ (**must**(**does** viewer tellB)) (**sees** viewer redWire))

There are 16 combinations of the above *mustRules*[1]. However, any combination must keep the one-to-one rule and the received-perception-before-sent-perception rule. As a result, we will only have six legal combinations that can be added to the original GDL. We then run the sITS algorithm on all seven *dialects* and calculate their values. Consider, for example, the *dialect* with only *mustRule* 1. This *dialect* is similar to the original *GDL* but limits the viewer to only choose *tellA* after the random player chose to arm the red wire. In other words, the branch where *viewer* chooses *tellB* after the random player chose to arm with the red wire is removed from the game tree.

The value of the original GDL determined by sITS is 50. The value of *dialects* with only one *mustRule* is computed as 75. The value of the two *dialects* with two *mustRules* is 100. This shows that in this game, we have a coordination problem. Agents are required to choose between combinations of the first *mustRule* with the third *mustRule* or the second *mustRule* with the fourth *mustRule*. Let us assume that one agent chooses the first combination and the other choose the second one. They will fail and need to choose again. As soon as the agents make the same choice, they will stick to it for all future matches, thus having learned to cooperate through the development of a common language. Figure 2 illustrates the difference between the original game tree and the tree for an enhanced *dialect*. The utilities are calculated using the sITS algorithm. The left game tree belongs to a *dialect* with *mustRule* 1 and *mustRule* 2.

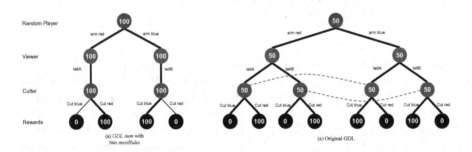

Fig. 2. Comparison of a dialect with two *mustRules* vs the original game in Cooperative Spies. (Color figure online)

---

[1] Later in this paper, we use a shorter version to represent a *mustRule* in figures. It is structured as <*action abbreviation*>-<*perception abbreviation*>. For example, (⇐ (**must**(**does** viewer tellA)) (**sees** viewer redWire)) will be shown as A-Red.

4   Analysis

In the following, we will describe different games and show how with the GL algorithm agents are always able to generate a common language and play the optimal move.

4.1   Naming Game

Naming Game is a game in which agents need to find a common language that connects an object to a name. In this game, any *dialect* with a number of *mustRules* equal to the number of objects is an optimal *dialect*. This class of games can be described in GDL-II as follows. The game has three players, one random player and two agents. The random player chooses an object at random. Both agents can see the chosen object. Then they should choose one among different actions. Each action sends a specific percept to the other agent. If both choose the same action they win and receive a score of 100, otherwise they lose and score 0. There are $\frac{n!}{obj!}$ optimal legal *dialects*, where obj is the number of objects and n the number of names. All of these optimal *dialects* contain exactly obj many *mustRules*. The value of each optimal *dialect* is 100 after running the sITS algorithm on them. Now agents can solve the coordination problem with the help of our policy learning. As can be seen, the GL algorithm can successfully play the Naming Game.

4.2   Air-Strike Alarm

Another simple game that we call "Air-Strike Alarm" is an example with only one optimal *dialect*. Games with one optimal strategy show the advantage of combining language learning with planning. In this category of games, agents do not need to use policy learning to reach a common optimal *dialect*. The Air-Strike Alarm game has three players: enemy, signalman and citizen. The enemy is played by the random player who attacks 10% of the time. Signalman sees aeroplanes coming toward the city. He can then sound the alarm or not. The citizen then needs to decide whether to take shelter or not. The game is similar to Cooperative Spies. The viewer is replaced by a signalman; the cutter is the citizen; perceptions 'a' and 'b' are replaced, respectively, by seeing or not seeing the aeroplanes; cutting wires are replaced by taking shelter or not taking shelter by the citizen; and the two messages the signalman can send are sounding the alarm or not. The main differences to the original game are, firstly, that raising the alarm causes auditory discomfort which comes at a cost of 10 points for everyone and, secondly, that the enemy will attack only 10% of the time.

Again, all the existing approaches to GGP-II would fail to optimally play this game, because the best strategy they find is always not to sound the alarm. People then know it is better to go about their normal life as only in 10% of the time an air-strike will occur. As a result, they get an average of 90 points. This mistake in choosing a non-optimal strategy occurs because there is no learning involved. On the other hand, RL techniques cannot solve games that involve a penalty for sending messages. Moreover, they always require prearranged centralised learning of agents.

Our GL algorithm finds seven *dialects*, similar to the Cooperative Spies game. sITS determines 90 as the value of the original GDL and 82 if the alarm is off during an air-strike and on during a safe situation. The optimal *dialect* is when the alarm is on during an air strike and off when it is safe. sITS returns 98 points for this *dialect*. If we assume that all the citizens are rational, then all of them will find the optimal *dialect* with the right language in it and play the optimal strategy to receive an average expected value of 99.

5   Experimental Analysis

In the following, we report on the experiments with *sITS* and its complete version, *ITS*. Our main focus is *sITS*, but we have also found that *ITS* can introduce some additional advantages over *sITS*.

Experiment with sITS. We have performed a language evolution experiment with *sITS* and Genetic Algorithm (GA) [10]. We let the population fluctuate to reach an equilibrium in which the majority has developed an optimal common language. This can also be used as a way to find an optimal *dialect*, provided the size of the optimal language is too large. A language, i.e. a set of *mustRules*, is hardcoded in each agent's DNA. Agents reproduce and die similarly to single-celled organisms. Agents whose language is less compatible with others in the society will be eliminated sooner. The more compatible agents survive longer and multiply more often. In other words, we use natural selection to show the evolution of a society without any language to an optimal society with an advanced common language.

For the purpose of the experiment, we have introduced a new matchmaker that is in charge of creating, penalising, death and organising games among the agents. The society starts with a group of agents with no *mustRule*. The matchmaker randomly chooses an agent from the society. Then if any agent with a similar language exists, the matchmaker randomly picks one. Otherwise, it randomly picks an agent with a different language. It lets them play a game. If they succeed, they both age by a *normal ageing* value. However, if they fail, both will be penalised by ageing faster (the *penalised ageing* value). All Agents have a *lifespan*. Any agent with an age equal or higher than the *lifespan* will die and be removed from the society. After playing some specific number of matches, a single agent gives birth to a new agent. This parameter is referred to as the *reproduction rate*. The new agent can have the same exact *dialect* (chromosome) of the mother or some mutation of it. A mutation is the addition or the removal of one *mustRule* (gene). The probability of a mutation is given by the *mutation rate*. To make it similar to a real society, we set a limit on reproduction. Reproduction in the society stops when the population reaches the *reproduction limit* value. The reproduction restarts when the population is reduced to the *restart reproduction* value.

All of these parameters can be varied but need to satisfy the following constraints. The *penalised ageing* value needs to be larger than the *normal ageing* value. Agents should be able to live long enough to reproduce. Some legal values might push the population to extinction with high probability. For example, high ageing values or low *restart reproduction* values. Some combinations of legal values for the parameters in the experiment can slow down reaching an equilibrium. As an example, having *penalised ageing* close to *normal ageing* or a low *mutation rate* will stop the population from changing quickly.

In a society with natural selection, the species which can successfully cooperate most of the times will remain in the society. Other species reduce dramatically in population or even become extinct. To show the effect of natural selection on language evolution, we have run a second experiment with identical parameters as in the first experiment except that *penalised ageing* was set equal to *normal ageing*.

Specifically, we ran experiments with an extended Cooperative Spies game where we doubled the number of wires. This extension has the effect that success by chance is unlikely and living without adaptation much more difficult. As we have discussed, in the Cooperative Spies game, an agent with the maximum number of *mustRules* is optimal. Optimal agents can fully cooperate with their own kind and partially cooperate with their primitive kind.[2] To make it similar to a real society, we set a limit on reproduction.

The values used for the parameters in our experiment were as follows: We set *lifespan* to 100 years, *penalised ageing* to 70 years reduction, *normal ageing* after each game to 1 year reduction, the *reproduction limit* to 60 agents, the value for *restart reproduction* to 58 agents, *reproduction rate* to 3 rounds for each agent and the mutation rate to 1%. As Fig. 3 indicates, the society started with some agents lacking any language. Then the common language slowly shifted towards a more complicated version with more *mustRules*. After 700 matches, an equilibrium was reached.

We were able to test the effect of natural selection by simply changing the *penalised ageing* value to just -1 in the second experiment. This way agents will face the same penalty if they succeed or fail. This simple change stops the society from evolving to a more cooperative society: As can be seen from Fig. 4, changes hardly happen in a society without natural selection. However, as in such societies all agents benefit equally, in an externally long run the society might turn into a scattered population of different kinds of agents. Our experiment without natural selection shows the society hardly changes even after 10,000 total games were played.

Experiment with Full Version of ITS. In the following, we describe another experiment with a similar four-wire Cooperative Spies game with ITS. The main difference between ITS and its simplified version is the addition of opponent modelling [4]. With the help of several self-plays, ITS can find Nash equilibria

---

[2] An agent is referred to as a primitive version of another agent if the language of the former is a subset of the language of the latter.

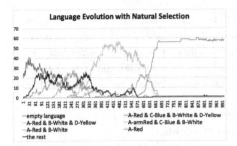

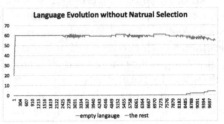

Fig. 3. Experiment on language evolution with natural selection

Fig. 4. No language evolution can be seen on a society without natural selection.

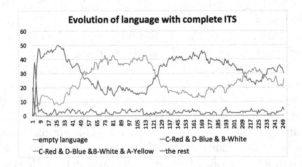

Fig. 5. Game tree for four cutting wire game with three *mustRules*.

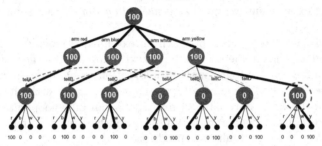

Fig. 6. The evolution of optimal language with ITS search algorithm.

in a variety of classes of games. The ITS algorithm helps the players with an incomplete language to fully cooperate. An incomplete language misses one or more *mustRule* compared to an optimal language. Our experiments show that smarter algorithms, such as ITS, can guess the missing *mustRule* in the games.

For our example game, only three *mustRule* suffice for a smart player to guess the missing *mustRule*. Figure 5 shows the game tree with three *mustRules*. State values are given after few iterations of the ITS algorithm on the tree. For the full details of the ITS algorithm we refer to [4]. Since ITS can guess the final *mustRule*, in the society the majority can have either four or three *mustRules*. As can be seen in Fig. 6, the majority oscillates between two languages: one of size three and another one of size four.

6   Discussion and Conclusion

We have introduced GGP-II, a well-known framework for general artificial intelligence, into the field of language learning. With just a few modifications to GGP-II, we were able to develop a general language learning method. The GL algorithm allows agents, at least in principle, in any game to generate a common language if there is a need for it. We have also shown that it can solve common problems in language learning such as the Naming Game. Moreover, with the help of planning in GL without repeating the match, agents can reach an optimal common language if there exists only one.

The general language evolution in GGP is general enough for it to be used as a framework for future research. One extension could be to involve a real natural language for the common language among the agents. This adds natural intuition to the language generation process. As an example, if a human needs to convey the information *red* but is only allowed to say "*blood*" or "*sky*", then the obvious choice would be the former. This reduces the need for policy learning.

Finally, the GL technique is not restricted to ITS as a solution; other algorithms can be used that might perform even better. For future work, we are interested in investigating ways in which AI agents might be able to acquire this background information with the help of machine learning and searching the web and/or online media. Also testing the GL with other current algorithms in GGP-II will be of interest.

References

1. Bleys, J., Loetzsch, M., Spranger, M., Steels, L.: The grounded colour naming game. Institute of Electrical and Electronics Engineers (2009)
2. Boutilier, C.: Sequential optimality and coordination in multiagent systems. In: IJCAI, vol. 99, pp. 478–485 (1999)
3. Černý, J.: Playing general imperfect-information games using game-theoretic algorithms. Bachelor's thesis, Czech Technical University in Prague, Czech Republic (2014)
4. Chitizadeh, A., Thielscher, M.: Iterative tree search in general game playing with incomplete information. In: Computer Games Workshop at IJCAI 2018. https://www.cse.unsw.edu.au/~mit/Papers/CGW18.pdf
5. Fenster, M., Kraus, S., Rosenschein, J.S.: Coordination without communication: experimental validation of focal point techniques. In: International Conference on Manufacturing Systems, pp. 102–108 (1995)
6. Foerster, J., Assael, I.A., de Freitas, N., Whiteson, S.: Learning to communicate with deep multi-agent reinforcement learning. In: Advances in Neural Information Processing Systems, pp. 2137–2145 (2016)

7. Geißer, F., Keller, T., Mattmüller, R.: Past, present, and future: an optimal online algorithm for single-player GDL-II games. In: ECAI, vol. 14, pp. 357–362 (2014)
8. Genesereth, M., Thielscher, M.: General Game Playing. Morgan & Claypool Publishers, San Rafael (2014)
9. Gonzalez, M., Watson, R., Bullock, S.: Minimally sufficient conditions for the evolution of social learning and the emergence of non-genetic evolutionary systems. Artif. Life **23**(4), 493–517 (2017)
10. Holland, J.H.: Adaptation in Natural and Artificial Systems: An Introductory Analysis with Applications to Biology, Control, and Artificial Intelligence. MIT Press, Cambridge (1992)
11. LaVictoire, P., Fallenstein, B., Yudkowsky, E., Barasz, M., Christiano, P., Herreshoff, M.: Program equilibrium in the prisoner's dilemma via Löb's theorem. In: AAAI Workshop on Multiagent Interaction without Prior Coordination (2014)
12. Love, N., Hinrichs, T., Haley, D., Schkufza, E., Genesereth, M.: General game playing: game description language specification (2008). http://logic.stanford.edu/reports/LG-2006-01.pdf
13. Lowe, R., Wu, Y., Tamar, A., Harb, J., Abbeel, O.P., Mordatch, I.: Multi-agent actor-critic for mixed cooperative-competitive environments. In: Advances in Neural Information Processing Systems, pp. 6382–6393 (2017)
14. Owen, G.: Game Theory. Emerald Group Publishing Limited, Bingley (2013)
15. Schofield, M.J., Thielscher, M.: Lifting model sampling for general game playing to incomplete-information models. In: AAAI, vol. 15, pp. 3585–3591 (2015)
16. Skubic, M., et al.: Spatial language for human-robot dialogs. IEEE Trans. Syst. Man Cybern. Part C (Appl. Rev.) **34**(2), 154–167 (2004)
17. Steels, L.: A self-organizing spatial vocabulary. Artif. Life **2**(3), 319–332 (1995)
18. Steels, L.: Language games for autonomous robots. IEEE Intell. Syst. **16**(5), 16–22 (2001)
19. Steels, L., Kaplan, F.: Aibo's first words: the social learning of language and meaning. Evol. Commun. **4**(1), 3–32 (2000)
20. Steels, L., Kaplan, F., McIntyre, A., Van Looveren, J.: Crucial factors in the origins of word-meaning. Trans. Lang. **2**(1), 2–4 (2002)
21. Steels, L., Spranger, M.: Can body language shape body image? In: Artificial Life, pp. 577–584 (2008)
22. Tennenholtz, M.: Program equilibrium. Games Econ. Behav. **49**(2), 363–373 (2004)
23. Thielscher, M.: A general game description language for incomplete information games. In: AAAI, vol. 10, pp. 994–999 (2010)

Intra-task Curriculum Learning
for Faster Reinforcement Learning
in Video Games

Nathaniel du Preez-Wilkinson[✉], Marcus Gallagher, and Xuelei Hu

School of Information Technology and Electrical Engineering,
The University of Queensland, Brisbane, QLD 4072, Australia
{uqndupre,marcusg,xuelei.hu}@uq.edu.au

Abstract. In this paper we present a new method for improving reinforcement learning training times under the following two assumptions: (1) we know the conditions under which the environment gives reward; and (2) we can control the initial state of the environment at the beginning of a training episode. Our method, called *intra-task curriculum learning*, presents the different episode starting states to an agent in order of increasing distance to immediate reward.

1 Introduction

Reinforcement learning [1] has surged in popularity in recent years due to the outstanding performance of deep reinforcement learning on Atari video games [2]. However, one draw back to reinforcement learning is the long training time it requires. Recently, there have been several impressive results for improving reinforcement learning training times [3–5] via general algorithms that make no assumptions about the environment. We are interested in using pre-existing knowledge to train an agent to solve a problem. A video game development team, for example, is more likely to be concerned with the upcoming deadline for a specific title than with how their approach will generalise.

2 Background

In reinforcement learning, an agent learns the best way to interact with an environment through trial and error [1]. The environment can take on one of a finite number of *states*, $s \in S$, and the agent interacts with the environment through *actions*, $a \in A$, that transition the environment from the current state, s_t, to a new state, s_{t+1}. After an agent's action changes the state of the environment, the agent receives feedback in the form of a *reward*, $r_t = r(s_t, a_t, s_{t+1})$, that indicates how desirable the choice of that action was while in that state. The goal of reinforcement learning is to develop an optimal *policy*, $\pi : S \rightarrow A$, a mapping from states to actions, for a given problem. An optimal policy maximises the

© Springer Nature Switzerland AG 2018
T. Mitrovic et al. (Eds.): AI 2018, LNAI 11320, pp. 65–70, 2018.
https://doi.org/10.1007/978-3-030-03991-2_6

total return, $R = \sum_{t=0}^{T} \gamma^t r_t$; where T is the total time the agent interacts with the environment; and γ is a discount factor applied to future rewards.

The type of reinforcement learning that we use in this paper is *Q-learning*. In Q-learning, each state-action pair is represented by a Q-value, $Q(s, a)$, that represents the expected total reward resulting from taking action a in state s, assuming greedy actions thereafter. After taking action a in state s, the Q-value, $Q(s, a)$, is modified according to the following update rule:

$$Q(s_t, a_t) \leftarrow (1 - \alpha)Q(s_t, a_t) + \alpha(r_t + \gamma \times max_a Q(s_{t+1}, a)) \qquad (1)$$

where α is a learning rate parameter.

3   Related Work

Eligibility traces [1] are numerical values that are stored for each state[1]. The eligibility trace for a state decays exponentially with each time step, but is increased whenever that state is visited. When a learning update occurs, the estimated value of each state is updated in proportion to its eligibility trace. Thus, states receive more credit for a reward if they have been visited recently.

Prioritised sweeping [1] is a model-based reinforcement learning algorithm that requires the model to be able to explicitly calculate, for a given state, what predecessor states may lead to it. When a reinforcement learning update occurs for a given state, the preceding states are checked to see if they should also be updated. If the change in estimated value for the predecessors is above a certain threshold then they are updated and *their* predecessors are also checked.

Rather than relying solely on an external reward function, agents can learn by using an internal reward function [4] that may be stimulated by, for example, curiosity [3] or the ability to correctly predict how an agent's actions will affect the environment [5]. The advantage of these internal reward functions is that they allow for learning updates to occur after processing every input sample.

4   Intra-task Curriculum Learning

Our approach makes two key assumptions: (1) we have knowledge of the conditions under which the environment gives reward; (2) we have the ability to control the initial state of the environment at the beginning of a training episode. Given these assumptions, we propose to present the states of a reinforcement learning problem to an agent *in order of increasing distance*[2] from immediate reward.

---

[1] Eligibility traces are recorded for each *value* in value function based reinforcement learning. We use the term "state" here, but in practice the values can also be stored for state-action pairs (e.g. in Q-learning).

[2] For the purpose of this paper, we define the distance form state s_a to state s_b as the *minimum* number of transitions required to get from s_a to s_b. This definition is sufficient because the environments we use have deterministic transitions, but a different definition would be required for stochastic environments.

For simple problems the distance to reward can be calculated explicitly for the entire state space. For more realistic problems the distance can be *approximated heuristically* on a sample of initial states that will be used in training. The actual distance to reward does not need to be calculated explicitly, as long as a relative ranking of the initial states can be determined.

States that are far from an immediate reward do not allow an agent the opportunity to update its internal state for a potentially very long time. This is especially true at the start of training, when an agent has no information about which actions are desirable, and is typically exploring randomly in the state space. Instead of letting the agent wander around randomly, we can *guide* the propagation of this information in order to speed up convergence to the optimal policy. We suggest that the "easier" (to learn) states in reinforcement learning are those that are *closer* to immediate reward, and that the "harder" states are those *further* from immediate reward.

In curriculum learning [6], training samples are provided to an agent in order of increasing difficulty. Thus, we propose that our method is a form of curriculum learning. We refer to our method as *intra-task curriculum learning* to indicate that we are ordering a collection of states within a task. Algorithm 1 (used in our experiments) introduces a form of intra-task curriculum learning where the training time is equally distributed across the difficulty levels in a task.

Algorithm 1. Intra-task curriculum learning training regime

Define T as the total training time
Define $|D|$ as the number of difficulty levels
Define S_d as the set of starting states of difficulty d
Define $|S_d|$ as the number of states in S_d
$t_d \leftarrow T/|D|$
for $d \leftarrow 1$ **to** $|D|$ **do**
  $t_s \leftarrow t_d/|S_d|$
  for all $s \in S_d$ **do**
    train using s as the start state until time t_s is reached
  end for
end for

---

5 Experimental Setup

The first problem we have designed is a 5×5 maze in which the agent starts in the bottom-left corner, and the goal lies in the top-right corner. The agent can move: up, down, left, and right. The agent receives a positive reward if it reaches the goal; and the goal state is terminal. For the curriculum we chose three different possible starting locations. The 2D maze is shown in Fig. 1a.

For this experiment we chose to store all of the Q-values in a look-up table. The Q-values were initialised to zero. A learning rate of 0.001 and a discount factor of 0.99 were used for the Q-learning update described in (1). For this experiment, the agent used a 100% uniform random exploration strategy.

The second problem we designed is a game played on a 9×9 grid where a piece of fruit (size 1×1) spawns at a random location at the top of the board and falls to the bottom. The agent controls a 3×1 paddle that starts in a random location at the bottom of the board. The paddle can: move left; move right; or remain in place. At each time step the agent is given the coordinates of the piece of fruit and the x-coordinate of the centre of the paddle. The terminal state for the game is when the fruit reaches the bottom of the board. The agent receives a reward of $+1$ if it catches the fruit, or a reward of -1 if it misses the fruit. The curriculum learning difficulty levels for this problem were mapped to the starting heights of the fruit. A visualisation of the game is shown in Fig. 1b.

In this experiment, we used a neural network as the agent model. The network had an input layer with 3 units to receive the fruit coordinates and paddle x-position. This was followed by a hidden layer with 64 fully connected units using the rectified linear activation function. The output layer contained 3 fully connected outputs with no activation function – representing the Q-values for the three possible agent actions, conditioned on the input state.

The agent in this experiment used the ϵ-greedy exploration strategy, with ϵ linearly annealed from 1 to 0.01 over the first 1000 training iterations. We also used double Q-learning [7], with a target network and memory replay buffer as described by [2]. We used the Adam optimisation algorithm with the mean squared error (MSE) loss function, and a learning rate of 0.00025.

6   Theoretical Analysis of 2D Maze

We can model the 2D maze as an absorbing Markov Chain. For our experiment the transition probabilities between states are known. The maze has 18 states[3]. Define $|T|$ as the number of transient (non-absorbing) states. From the transition matrix we can determine the fundamental matrix, N, of the absorbing Markov Chain. From this we can calculate the expected time before absorption for all transient states, $\mathbf{t} = N\mathbf{1}$; where $\mathbf{1}$ is a unit vector of length $|T|$; and $\mathbf{t}$ is a vector of length $|T|$ such that t_i is the expected time until absorption from state s_i. The expected time to complete the maze without curriculum learning is t_1.

$$\bar{t}_{NCL} = t_1 = 456 \tag{2}$$

The curriculum learning regime spreads training time evenly across all three designated start states[4]: s_1, s_{11}, and s_{13}. Therefore, the expected time to complete a game is the average of the expected time until absorption of these three states.

$$\bar{t}_{CL} = \frac{t_1 + t_{11} + t_{13}}{3} = 310.6\bar{6} \tag{3}$$

---

[3] We have a 5×5 grid with 7 walls; leaving 18 free spaces.
[4] We number the states in the 2D environment from left to right, bottom to top.

Using (2) and (3) we can find the relative difference between the two methods.

$$\frac{\bar{t}_{NCL} - \bar{t}_{CL}}{\bar{t}_{NCL}} = 1 - \frac{\bar{t}_{CL}}{\bar{t}_{NCL}} \approx 0.3187 \tag{4}$$

Thus, our analysis shows a 31.87% speed up from using curriculum learning on the 2D maze. This result is verified empirically in Fig. 2.

7   Results and Discussion

We compare the rewards obtained by different agents under testing conditions. The testing difficulty for each problem was the maximum difficulty. During testing the agents acted greedily according to their learned policies, and the policies were not updated.

For the 2D maze, the agents were given 100 testing iterations in which to finish the maze as many times as they could. Acting optimally, the maze takes 10 iterations to solve. With a reward of 10 upon reaching the goal, the maximum reward obtainable during testing is 100.

For the testing of the fruit catching game, the agents played the game ten times in a row. Under the optimal policy the fruit should be caught every time. With a reward of 1 per fruit caught, the maximum score achievable is 10.

Figure 3 shows the results of periodically sampling testing performance during training for the two agent training regimes in the two experiments. In both experiments, the testing reward for both regimes eventually converges to the maximum value, but the curriculum learning regime converges faster. The variance for both regimes increases initially but decreases as the testing score converges.

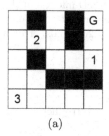
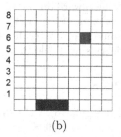

(a)   (b)

Fig. 1. A visual representation of the environments used in our experiments. (a) shows the 2D maze. "G" is the goal. Numbered spaces are different curriculum learning starting positions in order of difficulty. (b) shows the fruit game, with the paddle at the bottom and a piece of fruit falling. Numbers show different curriculum learning fruit spawning heights.

In conclusion, we have performed an investigation into reordering the states of a reinforcement learning problem. Our method, called "intra-task curriculum learning", reorders the states the agent sees according to distance from reward. Results indicate that starting an agent closer to reward, and moving them further away during training, improves the learning speed.

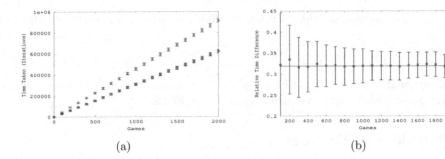

(a)   (b)

Fig. 2. Comparison of the time taken to complete a certain number of games between an agent trained with curriculum learning, and one trained without, for the 2D maze. (a) shows the absolute number of iterations taken for each method. Blue circles show curriculum learning results; red crosses show non-curriculum learning results. (b) shows the empirical (blue crosses) and theoretical (red line) results for the relative difference in training time between the two methods. Empirical results are the average of 200 trials; error bars show standard deviations. (Color figure online)

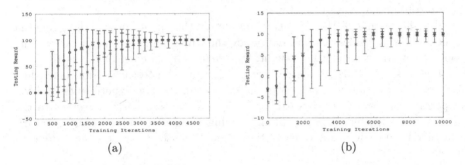

(a)   (b)

Fig. 3. Testing reward during training for agents in: (a) the 2D maze; and (b) the fruit game environment. Blue circles show curriculum learning results; red crosses show non-curriculum learning results. Results are the average of 200 trials; error bars show standard deviations. (Color figure online)

References

1. Sutton, R.S., Barto, A.G.: Reinforcement Learning: An Introduction, vol. 1. MIT Press, Cambridge (1998)
2. Mnih, V., et al.: Human-level control through deep reinforcement learning. Nature **518**, 529–533 (2015)
3. Pathak, D., et al.: Curiosity-driven exploration by self-supervised prediction. In: ICML (2017)
4. Chentanez, N., Barto, A.G., Singh, S.P.: Intrinsically motivated reinforcement learning. In: NIPS, pp. 1281–1288 (2005)
5. Dosovitskiy, A., Koltun, V.: Learning to act by predicting the future. In: ICLR (2017)
6. Bengio, Y., et al.: Curriculum learning. In: ICML, pp. 41–48 (2009)
7. van Hasselt, H., Guez, A., Silver, D.: Deep reinforcement learning with double q-learning. In: AAAI (2016)

An Approach for Task Execution in Dynamic Multirobot Environment

Amar Nath[✉], A. R. Arun, and Rajdeep Niyogi

Department of Computer Science and Engineering,
Indian Institute of Technology Roorkee, Roorkee 247667, India
anath@cs.iitr.ac.in, arunnadar1994@gmail.com, rajdpfec@iitr.ac.in

Abstract. In this paper we consider the problem of task execution in dynamic environments. We introduce a formal framework of a dynamic environment, and model the behavior of the robots using communicating automata. Based on the model we suggest a distributed approach for task execution that can handle multiple tasks that arrive at same instant of time. We have implemented the approach using ARGoS–a multirobot simulator.

Keywords: Dynamic environment · Robots · Task execution · ARGoS

1 Introduction

In automated environments (e.g., office, workshop), a team of mobile robots may be used to perform routine tasks like moving (carrying) a heavy box from one location to another, lifting a heavy object [1,2]. The environment is dynamic since the states of robots are changing, robots are moving from one location to another, robots may enter or leave the environment, and tasks may arrive at any instant of time at any location. Task execution requires all members of a team be present at the location where the task arrived.

If a robot is not engaged in any activity, finds a task at a location (which is in its range), it attends the task. When a robot r attends a task it can determine the size of the team needed for its execution. However, since r does not know the states and locations of other robots, it cannot determine the set of robots available for the task. This is because in a distributed system, no agent (robot) has a global view of the system. With such insufficient information, a team cannot be formed by r, and subsequently the task cannot be executed. Thus the necessary information has to be acquired by r by communicating with other robots. This necessitates the design of a distributed approach for task execution in such dynamic environments. Our proposed approach is described in Sect. 3.

Auction-based approaches for team formation (task allocation) are suggested in [3,4]. A bidder agent has some resources (e.g., data center, CPU) [4], who may bid for multiple auctioneers concurrently. In our work a non-initiator robot (bidder) will not express its willingness to multiple initiators (auctioneers) concurrently; when more than one request message arrives, the robot stores the requests

T. Mitrovic et al. (Eds.): AI 2018, LNAI 11320, pp. 71–76, 2018.
https://doi.org/10.1007/978-3-030-03991-2_7

in its local queue. Having one or more resources specified in the auction, is a sufficient condition for an agent to make a bid [4]. Having the required skills for a task is a necessary but not a sufficient condition for a robot to express its willingness to be part of a team, in our work. A robot's behavior, in our work (modeled using communicating automata), is determined by its current state, whereas in [3,4] states need not be taken into consideration. Our approach accommodates all these aspects and so it is substantially more complex than auction based protocols used in [3,4].

The rest of the paper is structured as follows. A formal framework of a dynamic environment is given in Sect. 2. The proposed approach is given in Sect. 3. The implementation is given in Sect. 4. Conclusions are made in Sect. 5.

2   Problem Formalization

Definition 1 *(Dynamic environment). A global view (snapshot) of an environment $\mathcal{E}$, with a set of locations L, taken at time t, is given by a 3-tuple $\mathcal{E}^t = \langle \mathcal{R}^t, \mathcal{T}^t, f \rangle$, where $\mathcal{R}^t$ is the set of robots present in the environment at time t, and $\mathcal{T}^t$ is the set of tasks that arrive in the environment at time t, $f : \mathcal{R}^t \times \mathbb{N} \mapsto L$, is a function that gives the location of a robot at a discrete instant of time represented by the set of natural numbers $\mathbb{N}$.*

Definition 2 *(Task). A task τ is specified by a 5-tuple $\tau = \langle \nu, l, t, k, \Psi \rangle$ where ν is the name of a task (e.g., move (carry) box B to location l', lift desk D), $l \in L$ is the location where the task arrived, t is the time at which the task arrived, $k > 1$ is the number of robots required to execute the task, and Ψ is the set of skills required to execute the task.*

Definition 3 *(Condition for multiple task execution). The tasks $\tau_1 = \langle \nu_1, l_1, t, k_1, \Psi_1 \rangle$ and $\tau_2 = \langle \nu_2, l_2, t, k_2, \Psi_2 \rangle$ can be executed if the following conditions hold:*

1. there exists a set $\mathcal{R}_1$ of k_1 available robots at some time $t'_1 > t$, such that $\psi_r \supseteq \Psi_1$ for all $r \in \mathcal{R}_1$, and at some time $t''_1 > t'_1$, $loc_r = l_1$ for all $r \in \mathcal{R}_1$.
2. there exists a set $\mathcal{R}_2$ of k_2 available robots at some time $t'_2 > t$, such that $\psi_r \supseteq \Psi_2$ for all $r \in \mathcal{R}_2$, and at some time $t''_2 > t'_2$, $loc_r = l_2$ for all $r \in \mathcal{R}_2$.
3. $\mathcal{R}_1 \cap \mathcal{R}_2 = \emptyset$.

Definition 4 *(Utility of a team for task execution). Let $\Gamma = \{x_1, \ldots, x_k\}$ be a team that can execute a task $\tau = \langle \nu, l, t, k, \Psi \rangle$ where each member of the team was located at loc_{x_i}. The utility of a team Γ for executing τ is $\mathcal{U}_{\langle \Gamma, \tau \rangle} = -cost_{\langle \Gamma, \tau \rangle}$, where $cost_{\langle \Gamma, \tau \rangle} = \sum_{x_i \in \Gamma} \mu_{\langle x_i, \tau \rangle}$ and $\mu_{\langle x_i, \tau \rangle} = \mathbf{p}(x_i, \tau) \times \frac{1}{\alpha_{x_i}} + \mathbf{d}(loc_{x_i}, l) \times \beta_{x_i}$ where $\alpha_{x_i}, \beta_{x_i} \in (0, 1]$ denote remaining battery coefficient and battery consumption rate respectively of (a robot) x_i, $\mathbf{p}(x_i, \tau)$ is the price of x_i for τ, $\mathbf{d}(l_1, l_2)$ is the distance covered when moving from l_1 to l_2.*

Problem Statement: Design a distributed approach to execute the tasks that arrive in a dynamic environment $\mathcal{E}$ at some time instant, where the team chosen for each task has maximum utility.

3   Proposed Approach for Task Execution

In a dynamic environment $\mathcal{E}$, let a robot i attend a task $\tau = \langle \nu, l, t, k, \Psi \rangle$ where $\psi_i \supseteq \tau.\Psi$; now $loc_i = l$. In order to form a team for the execution of task τ, r communicates with other robots. We refer to i as an initiator, and the other robots as non-initiators.

An initiator i broadcasts a *Request* message whose format is $\langle id_i, \tau.\nu, \tau.l, \tau.\Psi \rangle$, and waits for some time, say Δ. It is assumed that a broadcast message would be delivered only to the robots present in the environment at that time. A non-initiator j, who has the necessary skills, will send either a *Willing* message (whose format is $\langle id_j, \mathbf{p}(j, \tau), \alpha_j, \beta_j, loc_j \rangle$) or an *Engaged* message if its state is *Idle* or *Promise* respectively. Otherwise, it will ignore the *Request* message. The initiator increases its counter c when it receives a *Willing* message. After Δ time has elapsed, i checks if there are enough robots available to form a team ($c \geq k-1$). If yes, i selects the team with maximum utility as per Definition 4, and sends *Confirm* message to the other members of the team, *Not-Required* message to $(c-(k-1))$ non-initiators, if any. If no, i sends a *Not-Required* message to all c non-initiators who expressed their willingness to help. Depending on its queue status, i will change its state from *Ready* to *Idle* or *Promise*.

A non-initiator robot works as follows. The computations are done based on the current state that may be *Idle*, *Promise*, *Busy*, and *Ready*. Within a state, the type of message is checked and appropriate actions are taken. For example, when state is *Idle*, if a *Request* message is received, it becomes *Promise*, the identifier of the sender is enqueued, and *flag* is set to true; all these actions are done atomically (denoted by $\langle \ldots \rangle$). Now the robot sends a *Willing* message to the sender (initiator) and *flag* is set to false. A robot j maintains a local queue Q which keeps the identifiers of the senders, based on the incoming *Request* messages. The Q is used to avoid starvation since, more than one initiators may send *Request* messages at the same instant of time. The boolean variables *flag* and *flag'* are used to control the sending of *Willing* and *Engaged* messages respectively.

We use communicating automata (CA) [5] based model to capture the behavior of robots, shown in Figs. 1 and 2. A CA is like a finite automaton where the transitions may involve sending/receiving of messages. A label of a transition, in the CA that we use, has a more general form $\chi : \gamma$, where χ can either be an input a (send message $!m$, receive message $?m$), or a state condition g, or (a, g), and γ can either be a sequence of actions seq, or a sequence of actions that is to be performed atomically $\langle seq \rangle$, or empty. The semantics of the transitions are: $s \xrightarrow{a} s'$ means switch from s to s' on input a; $s \xrightarrow{g} s'$ means switch from s to s' if a condition g holds at s; $s \xrightarrow{(a,g):\langle seq \rangle} s'$ means switch from s to s' on input a if g holds at s, and the sequence of actions seq are performed atomically either just before or immediately after transiting to s'; $s \xrightarrow{(a,g):seq} s'$ means switch from s to s' on input a if g holds at s, and the sequence of actions seq are performed either just before or immediately after transiting to s'. Q^D in Figs. 1 and 2, denotes a queue Q after making one Dequeue operation.

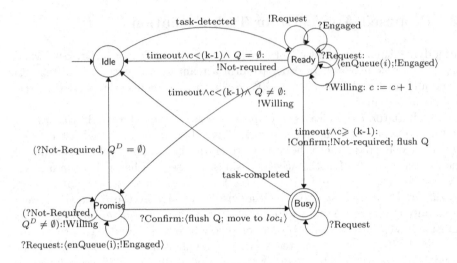

Fig. 1. Communicating automata model of initiator agent

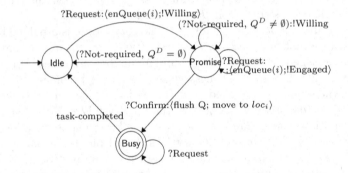

Fig. 2. Communicating automata model of non-initiator agent

4   Implementation

We consider an obstacle clearance scenario to illustrate the proposed approach (Sect. 3), where a corridor may be blocked by several obstacles. A team of robots should jointly move each obstacle to one side of the corridor. The proposed approach is implemented using ARGoS (Autonomous Robots Go Swarming) [6], a multirobot simulator. The code run in ARGoS can be directly deployed on a real robot system.

An example scenario is shown in Fig. 3, where the shaded portion in gray is the corridor (10 m × 5 m), obstacles are simulated by green movable cylinders of radius 0.2 m with a blue light on top. The robots are shown in blue. The overall process of removing an obstacle from the corridor is shown in Fig. 3. The robots in ARGoS use the inbuilt range and bearing sensor (rab) to communicate among themselves.

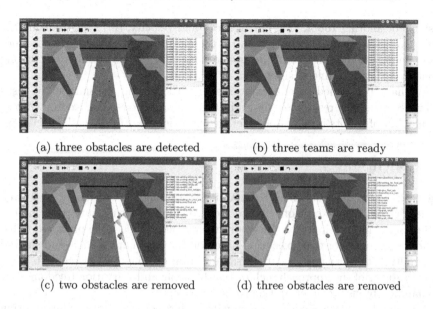

(a) three obstacles are detected   (b) three teams are ready

(c) two obstacles are removed   (d) three obstacles are removed

Fig. 3. Illustration of multiple task execution in ARGoS

In Fig. 3-a, the initial position of the robots and obstacles is shown. Three robots detect three obstacles and they start team formation. We assume that all the obstacles require two robots to move. In Fig. 3-b, initiator robots form their respective teams; the robots have reached the location of obstacles and they are ready to move the obstacles. Figure 3-c, shows that two obstacles have been shifted to one side of the corridor. Then the robots again visit the corridor and search for other obstacles, if any. Finally, in Fig. 3-d, the third obstacle is also detected and removed.

For the implementation we have written the required functions in Lua, a C-like language. These are (i) to control the movement of a robot to avoid obstacle or another robot based on proximity sensor data, where the sensor detects an

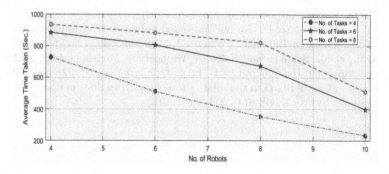

Fig. 4. Performance based on varying the number of robots and tasks

obstacle or another robot, (ii) control speed and velocity, (iii) synchronizing the robots for task execution, (iv) to control the movement of a robot when boundaries are detected using motor-ground sensors, and (v) communication among robots based on the line of sight.

We have performed several experiments with varying the number of tasks and robots, and the results are shown in Fig. 4. From the results, we find that as the number of robots is increased, average execution time of the tasks decreases.

5   Conclusion

The task execution problem in a dynamic environment is considered. A formal framework for task execution is introduced. Communicating automata models of the robots interacting with the environment are provided. We proposed a distributed approach for task execution based on the automata models and showed how multiple tasks that arrive at the same instant of time can be executed. Some salient aspects of the approach include non-blocking and starvation freedom, that are handled by using timer and queue respectively.

We introduced two new parameters with each robot that are used for selecting a team with maximum utility. The intuition behind these parameters is that a robot with more battery backup and lower battery consumption would last longer, and it would not fail due to battery failure during task execution. The approach has been implemented and simulated in ARGoS. We have performed several experiments and the results obtained are very encouraging. Our future work would be to address the problem of multi-task execution in a dynamic environment where the number of robots needed to execute a task is not known.

References

1. Farinelli, A., Iocchi, L., Nardi, D.: Distributed on-line dynamic task assignment for multi-robot patrolling. Auton. Robots **41**(6), 1321–1345 (2017)
2. Rosenfeld, A., Agmon, N., Maksimov, O., Kraus, S.: Intelligent agent supporting human-multi-robot team collaboration. Artif. Intell. **252**, 211–231 (2017)
3. Gerkey, B.P., Mataric, M.J.: Sold!: auction methods for multirobot coordination. IEEE Trans. Robot. Autom. **18**(5), 758–768 (2002)
4. Kong, Y., Zhang, M., Ye, D.: An auction-based approach for group task allocation in an open network environment. Comput. J. **59**(3), 403–422 (2015)
5. Bérard, B., et al.: Systems and Software Verification: Model-checking Techniques and Tools. Springer, Heidelberg (2001). https://doi.org/10.1007/978-3-662-04558-9
6. Pinciroli, C., et al.: ARGoS: a modular, parallel, multi-engine simulator for multi-robot systems. Swarm Intell. **6**(4), 271–295 (2012)

Monocular ORB-SLAM on a Humanoid Robot for Localization Purposes

Daniel Ginn$^{(\boxtimes)}$, Alexandre Mendes, Stephan Chalup, and Jake Fountain

School of Electrical Engineering and Computing, Faculty of Engineering and Built
Environment, University of Newcastle, Callaghan, NSW, Australia
{daniel.ginn,jake.fountain}@uon.edu.au
{alexandre.mendes,stephan.chalup}@newcastle.edu.au

Abstract. This work presents an application of ORB-SLAM in an iGus bipedal humanoid robotic platform. The method was adapted from its original implementation into the framework used by the NUbots robotic soccer team and used for localization purposes. The paper presents a description of the challenges to implement the adaptation, as well as several tests where the method's performance is analyzed to determine its suitability for further development and use on medium sized humanoid robots.

To conduct the tests, we determined the robot's real location using a high-accuracy, camera-based infrared tracking system. Two experiments were performed to estimate the robustness of the method to the vibration and constant camera wobbling inherent to a bipedal walk and its ability to deal with the kidnapped robot problem.

The tests indicate that ORB-SLAM is suitable for implementation into a medium sized humanoid robot in situations comparable to a robotic soccer environment, and requires relatively low computational resources, leaving enough CPU power for other tasks. Additionally, since ORB-SLAM is robust to the difficulties associated with humanoid motion, we conclude that it provides a good SLAM algorithm to enhance with features specific to the humanoid robotic platform.

Keywords: ORB-SLAM · Humanoid · Visual odometry
Visual SLAM

1 Introduction

One of the primary enabling capabilities of any autonomous mobile robotics platform is the ability to keep track of its location. Various methods have been utilized to achieve this, including odometry sensors, inertial measurement units (IMU) like accelerometers and gyroscopes, and SLAM (Simultaneous Localization and Mapping) techniques using cameras and Lidar. In the last decade, visual odometry and visual SLAM techniques have become increasingly capable of being run in real-time on mobile robotics platforms, with ORB-SLAM [6]

© Springer Nature Switzerland AG 2018
T. Mitrovic et al. (Eds.): AI 2018, LNAI 11320, pp. 77–82, 2018.
https://doi.org/10.1007/978-3-030-03991-2_8

widely considered state-of-the-art. The application of these SLAM techniques to various mobile robotics platforms has focused mainly on ground-based wheeled platforms, flying quadcopters and hand-held cameras. These platforms are relatively stable when in motion. However, considerably less work has been done on humanoid robots. Humanoid robots are bipedal which is a significantly more unstable method of locomotion, considerably reducing the accuracy of odometry measurements. This work focuses on the RoboCup soccer competition and thus the humanoid platform used supports only the strictly humanoid binocular cameras, which is one of the requirements of the humanoid league.

In this paper, we report on and discuss the suitability of using ORB-SLAM on a medium sized humanoid robot to provide visual odometry. This paper will only investigate monocular ORB-SLAM, due to the computational limitations of the robot, as all processing is done on-board. To the best of the authors knowledge, there has been no feasibility study on the use of the state-of-the-art monocular ORB-SLAM on humanoids.

Only one other 2018 RoboCup humanoid team (NimbRo[1]) mentioned using a visual odometry system. They report testing two state-of-the-art visual odometry (VO) techniques called SVO [3] and DSO [1]. They found that these techniques failed over longer periods of time and under rapid movement. We believe that a full visual SLAM system which provides loop closure, map building and relocalisation will be able to succeed in the same circumstances.

The remainder of this paper is organized as follows: Sect. 2 gives a brief overview of related work and concepts; Sect. 3 presents the humanoid robot and experiment design used in this paper; Sect. 4 presents the results of ORB-SLAM's performance on a humanoid robot; Sect. 5 provides a discussion on the advantages and disadvantages of ORB-SLAM; and Sect. 6 presents our conclusions.

2   Background

2.1   Related Work

The majority of works that implement SLAM onto humanoids use Lidar or RGB-D sensors. This choice is often made due to the superior accuracy of these sensors. Both however have their drawbacks, with Lidar sensors being quite expensive, and RGB-D sensors having a fairly limited range. Cameras in contrast are very cheap, and are usually already necessary for other vision processing tasks. Among the studies that implement passive visual SLAM onto a humanoid, Oriolo et al. [7] used odometry and foot pressure sensors to provide the state prediction for an EKF (Extended Kalman Filter), and PTAM and IMU data to provide the measurement update.

Scona et al. [8] used ElasticFusion [10] (an originally RGB-D camera SLAM method) on a 1.8 m tall humanoid robot, and addressed the issue of what happens when a robot faces its camera at a featureless area such as a wall. Odometry

---

[1] https://www.robocuphumanoid.org/qualification/2018/AdultSize/NimbRo/tdp.
pdf.

and IMU data was used to provide a motion prior that estimates where the tracked features have moved to since the last frame. The odometry and IMU data was then fused with the results of the SLAM algorithm. ElasticFusion is a SLAM technique that tracks pixel intensities as opposed to tracking features like ORB-SLAM and PTAM. As mentioned in Sect. 1, the RoboCup team NimbRo reported trialing DSO and SVO, however they found the lack of long term reliability of these purely visual odometry techniques leads to unreliable results or complete loss of tracking.

Monocular or Binocular ORB-SLAM has been implemented on other platforms such as Micro-aerial Vehicles (MAVs) and image datasets from wheeled ground vehicles, but not on humanoids to the best of our knowledge. Using a ground station, Garcia et al. [4] combined LSD-SLAM [2] (which is another featureless, pixel tracking SLAM method) and ORB-SLAM (feature tracking based) in a complementary way, along with IMU data to provide pose and map data which could then be used by the ground station to provide path planning commands to the MAV. Song et al. [9] collected binocular ORB-SLAM data, along with IMU, GPS, and barometric data, which was then processed offline. For ground based vehicles, Mur-Artal et al. [6] who are the creators of ORB-SLAM, used wheeled ground based vehicle datasets of cars and smaller indoor wheeled robots, as well as quadrotors to benchmark their results against other SLAM algorithms.

2.2 Porting ORB-SLAM

ORB-SLAM, which is available for open source download[2], relies on OpenCV, as well as two third party libraries which come included in the download. The first is DBoW2 which is a Bags of Words library, and the second is g2o which handles the bundle adjustments and optimizations.

The NUbots team uses a framework called NUClear [5], which required some reorganizing of ORB-SLAM. The source code was mostly able to stay untouched, except that the threading had to be modified to work in NUClear, as it manages its own threading. The two third party libraries needed to be compiled separately and included into NUClear's libraries.

3 Methodology

3.1 NUbots iGus Humanoid Robot

The iGus humanoid robot used in this paper is a modified version of the NimbRo robot[3]. It is 90 cm tall and contains a Point Grey Flea3-U3-13E4 Global shutter cameras with fisheye lenses, an IMU, and an Intel NUC7i7BNH (core i7-7567U) 3.5 GHz processor. The current foot configuration does not include pressure sensors, so the odometry data is purely based off servo measurements. It is worth mentioning that the swaying motion that occurs when walking can potentially assist monocular depth perception.

---

[2] https://github.com/raulmur/ORB_SLAM2.
[3] http://nimbro.net/Humanoid/robots.html.

3.2 Data Collection

The data collection focused on recording the keyframe trajectory produced by ORB-SLAM, timing data, and truth data from an infrared camera based Motion Capture system set up in the lab. In the first experiment, the iGus walked in a 3 m by 2 m rectangular path, performing a loop closure once the rectangle was complete. In the second experiment, the iGus walked forwards for 2 m, then was picked up by the robot handler and moved rapidly back to a position a little to the left of the starting position (also received a 360° rotation), where it walks forward a little distance. This procedure is to simulate handling of the robot during a soccer match and tests the ability of ORB-SLAM to handle the kidnapped robot problem where a robot is lifted and moved to an unknown new location.

4 Results

With our walk engine running, ORB-SLAM ran on the iGus at an average frame rate of 20 frames/second (standard deviation of 1.7) before an initial map had been created, and an average of 26 frames/second (standard deviation of 5.2) afterwards (see Fig. 1). When the keyframe trajectory data is compared to the truth data, ORB-SLAM tracks the movement of the robot with a level of accuracy which is acceptable for a robot soccer application (see Fig. 2). In the kidnapped robot experiment (see Fig. 3), ORB-SLAM was able to realize it had been placed down in a familiar location. While ORB-SLAM was not able to track the trajectory of the carried segment, as soon as it was put down, it was able to recognize its location and resume tracking.

5 Discussion

The results demonstrated that a medium sized humanoid robot with a NUC7i7 processor is capable of running the current state-of-the-art ORB-SLAM in real

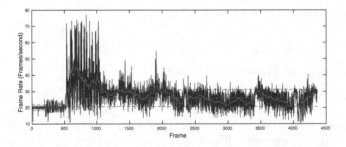

Fig. 1. Frame rate data from the first experiment (see Fig. 2). The blue line is the instantaneous frame rate of each frame, the bold red line is a 50 frame moving average, and the horizontal solid red lines bounded by dashed red lines show the average frame rate before and after map initialization, along with their standard deviations. (Color figure online)

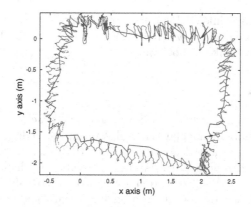

Fig. 2. First experiment trajectory as reported by ORB-SLAM keyframes in blue, and the motion capture system in red. The path walked is a 3 m by 2 m rectangle with a loop closure at the end. Notice the sway in the red trajectory, which represents the lateral movement of the robot's head as it walks. (Color figure online)

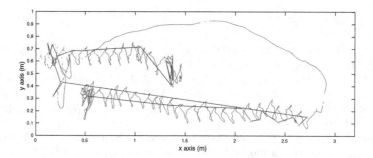

Fig. 3. Second experiment trajectory as reported by ORB-SLAM keyframes in blue, and the motion capture system in red. Occasional missing parts of the red trajectory are due to the robot handler temporarily blocking the view of the motion capture cameras. The robot first walked a straight line (0.5,0.3) to (2.7,0.15) before being picked up by handler and moved rapidly and disorientatingly to a new position (0.2,0.6) which was close to position it had seen before. (Color figure online)

time, was able to handle the swaying motion and could recover from a typical kidnapped robot situation. However several advantages and disadvantages that should be weighed before implementing ORB-SLAM onto a humanoid robot. An average frame rate of 20 fps was achieved before the initial map was created, rising to 26 fps afterwards, leaving plenty of computational resources for other system components to run.

Now that the basic reliability of ORB-SLAM has been observed, the authors intend to address some of the limitations of this visual SLAM method. The maps and trajectory ORB-SLAM produces are not referenced to the real world in any way, so for ORB-SLAM to be useful for localization in a known environment like RoboCup additional known feature extractors like goal detectors would need to be used. Additionally, while ORB-SLAM is resistant to objects moving within its environment, it is unknown how ORB-SLAM degrades when placed in crowded dynamic environments like RoboCup.

6   Conclusion

The objective of this research was to investigate the practicality of implementing the state-of-the-art monocular ORB-SLAM onto a medium sized humanoid robot. To the best of our knowledge, monocular ORB-SLAM has not been implemented on humanoid robots, with its unique locomotion challenges of swaying and jarring movements. We provided an evaluation of ORB-SLAM and detailed the process undertaken to port it onto an iGus humanoid robot intended for the robot soccer competition RoboCup and found that ORB-SLAM was able to run at 26 fps while the robot was walking. ORB-SLAM was able to successfully provide accurate localization to the robot during two experiments that tested for loop closure and relocalization.

References

1. Engel, J., Koltun, V., Cremers, D.: Direct sparse odometry. IEEE Trans. Pattern Anal. Mach. Intell. **40**(3), 611–625 (2018)
2. Engel, J., Schöps, T., Cremers, D.: LSD-SLAM: large-scale direct monocular SLAM. In: Fleet, D., Pajdla, T., Schiele, B., Tuytelaars, T. (eds.) ECCV 2014. LNCS, vol. 8690, pp. 834–849. Springer, Cham (2014). https://doi.org/10.1007/978-3-319-10605-2_54
3. Forster, C., Zhang, Z., Gassner, M., Werlberger, M., Scaramuzza, D.: SVO: semidirect visual odometry for monocular and multicamera systems. IEEE Trans. Robot. **33**(2), 249–265 (2017)
4. García, S., López, M.E., Barea, R., Bergasa, L.M., Gómez, A., Molinos, E.J.: Indoor SLAM for micro aerial vehicles control using monocular camera and sensor fusion. In: 2016 International Conference on Autonomous Robot Systems and Competitions (ICARSC), pp. 205–210, May 2016
5. Houliston, T., et al.: NUClear: a loosely coupled software architecture for humanoid robot systems. Front. Robot. AI **3**, 20 (2016). https://doi.org/10.3389/frobt.2016.00020
6. Mur-Artal, R., Montiel, J.M.M., Tardós, J.D.: ORB-SLAM: a versatile and accurate monocular SLAM system. IEEE Trans. Robot. **31**(5), 1147–1163 (2015)
7. Oriolo, G., Paolillo, A., Rosa, L., Vendittelli, M.: Humanoid odometric localization integrating kinematic, inertial and visual information. Auton. Robot. **40**(5), 867–879 (2016)
8. Scona, R., Nobili, S., Petillot, Y.R., Fallon, M.: Direct visual SLAM fusing proprioception for a humanoid robot. In: 2017 IEEE/RSJ International Conference on Intelligent Robots and Systems (IROS), pp. 1419–1426, September 2017
9. Song, Y., Nuske, S., Scherer, S.: A multi-sensor fusion MAV state estimation from long-range stereo, IMU, GPS and barometric sensors. Sensors **17**(1), 11 (2016)
10. Whelan, T., Salas-Moreno, R.F., Glocker, B., Davison, A.J., Leutenegger, S.: ElasticFusion: real-time dense SLAM and light source estimation. Int. J. Robot. Res. **35**(14), 1697–1716 (2016)

AI Applications and Innovations

Impact of Compression Ratio and Reconstruction Methods on ECG Classification for E-Health Gadgets: A Preliminary Study

Sophie Zareei$^{(\boxtimes)}$ and Jeremiah D. Deng

Information Science Department, University of Otago, Dunedin, New Zealand
sophie.zareei@postgrad.otago.ac.nz, jeremiah.deng@otago.ac.nz

Abstract. In IoT applications, it is often necessary to achieve an optimal trade-off between data compression and data quality. This study investigates the effect of Compressed Sensing and reconstruction algorithms on ECG arrhythmia detection using SVM classifiers. To neutralise the mutual effect of compression and reconstruction algorithms on one another, we consider each reconstruction algorithms with various compression ratios and vice versa. The employed reconstruction algorithms are Basis Pursuit (BP) and Orthogonal Matching Pursuit (OMP). We employ two steps: (a) identifying proper compression ratio that withholds essential information of ECG signals, (b) assessing the impact of two reconstruction algorithms and their exactness on quality of classification. The findings of this study are threefold: (a) Remarkably, the SVM classifier requires few samples to detect ECG arrhythmia. (b) The results indicate for compression ratios up to around 1:7 ECG signals are recovered then classified with the same quality for both algorithms. However, by increasing compression ratio BP outperforms OMP in terms of ECG arrhythmia detection. (c) Negative correlation between compression ratio and signal quality is observed, that is intuitive enough to realise the trade-off between them.

Keywords: Compressed sensing · OMP · BP · SVM classifier · ECG

1 Introduction

Internet of Things (IoT) is one of the promising approaches in interconnecting various devices via communication networks. IoT enables us to remotely monitor and collect data from individuals, and transmit them to data centres (e.g. cloud) wherein the data is analysed. Technological advances enable collecting various data from daily activities to biomedical information (e.g. wearable electrocardiogram (ECG/EKG) monitors which are easy to use and free of wires and patches [1]). In this work, we concentrate on ECG signals as an instance of biomedical data. One of the issues faced by IoT is producing vast amount

© Springer Nature Switzerland AG 2018
T. Mitrovic et al. (Eds.): AI 2018, LNAI 11320, pp. 85–97, 2018.
https://doi.org/10.1007/978-3-030-03991-2_9

of data collected by sensors mounted on different gadgets [2]. Another concern is energy management especially when IoT devices are powered by renewable sources. Energy consumption by sensors during data gathering and transmission introduces crucial concerns that need to be addressed. The problem is aggravated by using self-powered devices. Data compression is a promising method to decrease energy consumption in data transmission.

In this paper, our overall goal is to infer vital information from the big data gathered by biomedical sensors without a regular need of visiting a doctor. The utilisation of data mining gives a promising solution to reach this goal. There is a rich literature for classifying biomedical signals in past decades [3, 4]. In a recent study, Azariadi et al. focused on empirical implementation of classification methods for arrhythmia detection by building wearable gadgets [5]. While some studies proposed methods for classifiers to handle imbalanced data [6], others concentrate on improving classifier performance [7]. For more insights into different aspects of ECG arrhythmia detection using classifiers see [8].

To overcome energy constraints, various energy management techniques are proposed in the literature for example see [9]. There are different approaches that have been considered in energy management; some instances are: (a) enhancing harvester designs [10], (b) optimising buffer size for both energy and data storage [11], (c) decreasing data volume to be transmitted by compression [12]. This study focuses on data compression by Compressed Sensing technique. It is a promising method since it pushes heavy processing burdens to a decoder (e.g. cloud) considering limited computational capabilities of IoT devices [13,14].

Former studies investigated influence of data reduction or summarisation on classifier performance. Shen et al. [15] employed the idea of data reduction in web-page classification, for doing so, they used both summarised and pure data as input for the classifier. Their study indicated summaries provided either by human or machine help enhance web-page classification performance. Cosman et al. [16] assessed impact of compressing medical images on subjective (e.g. radiologist or physicians) diagnostic accuracy. The outcomes suggested the importance of training by same kind of images that subjects interpret. In other words, diagnosis made by physicians trained with slightly compressed (or compressed and then enhanced) images outperforms the one made by radiologists (specialists) without such training. These results trigger the idea of analysing how various compression ratios impact on ECG arrhythmia detection by classifiers. More precisely, ECG signals are compressed considering different compression ratios. Then, we reconstruct the signals employing two conventional algorithms, namely BP and OMP. These procedures are explained in Sect. 2. We use Discrete Wavelet Transform (DWT) for feature extraction and Synthetic Minority Oversampling Technique (SMOTE) to address class imbalance issue in ECG signals. Next, obtained features are fed to Support Vector Machine (SVM) classifier with Radial Basis Function (RBF) kernel as discussed in Sect. 3. In Sect. 4, we perform a statistical analysis to investigate influence of range of compression ratios on both precision and sensitivity of the classification result per algorithm (i.e. BP and OMP). We also apply Wilcoxon test to compare the effectiveness of reconstruction algorithms, BP and OMP on SVM classifier performance. Section 5 sums up the findings of the study and suggests future directions.

2   Overview of System and Analysis

The architecture of E-health monitoring system is illustrated in Fig. 1. This architecture is used for collecting and analysing all health-related information. In this research, we limit our study to ECG signals. The reason is essentially twofold: first, ECG provides vital health information and second, ECG signals are well-studied in various research [17], and we can use this rich literature as a solid foundation for our work.

As can be seen from Fig. 1, ECG signal is gathered by smart gadgets, compressed using Compressed Sensing Technique and sent to cloud. Cloud takes responsibility for reducing some burdens of sensors. One example is minimising processing that leads to energy efficiency, especially in green gadgets. In the cloud, original signals are recovered using reconstruction algorithm, (e.g. BP or OMP). After reconstructing the original signals, ECG arrhythmia detection is performed employing a classification algorithm. If any arrhythmia is detected, notification will be sent to both gadget user and hospital for further analysis.

2.1   Compressed Sensing Principles

In standard form, Compressed Sensing is an underdetermined inverse problem. Let $X \in \mathbb{R}^N$, in this context, be $N \times 1$ vector containing ECG signals. Basic Compressed Sensing measurement model is defined as [18]:

$$[Y]_{M,1} = [\Phi]_{M,N}[X]_{N,1}, \tag{1}$$

where $Y \in \mathbb{R}^M$ is a compressed ECG signal of length M and $\Phi \in \mathbb{R}^{M \times N}$ ($M < N$) is a fixed matrix known as sensing (or measurement) matrix that contains independently identically distributed (i.i.d) entries. The same version of this matrix is kept at decoder in order to enable reconstruction.

To fully recover the original signal, X needs to be sparse. In cases that X is not sparse in time domain, proper sparsifying dictionary, Ψ, is used in a way that X can be represented as sparse vector using Ψ:

$$[X]_{N,1} = [\Psi]_{N,P}[z]_{P,1}, \tag{2}$$

where z is sparse representation of X. Sparsifying dictionary, Ψ, is usually a basis, and it does not need to be of size $N \times P$. Number of columns, P, can be expanded above N to form overcomplete dictionary.

The purpose of signal reconstruction is to calculate z from Y as follows:

$$[Y]_{M,1} = [\Phi]_{M,N}[\Psi]_{N,P}[z]_{P,1}. \tag{3}$$

Then, X can be recovered employing (2). (3) is ill-conditioned since it consists of fewer equations (M) than unknown (N). However, it has been proven that, if signal is k-sparse in some domain, for proper $M > k$ and Φ, probability of finding suitable or exact solution of the equation is high [18,19].

Signal Recovery: Original signal is recovered employing the following convex optimization problem:

$$\min ||z||_1 \text{ subject to } Y = \Phi\Psi z. \tag{4}$$

This problem is solved utilising l_1-norm, also known as Basis Pursuit (BP) [20], which provides exact solution of the problem; or greedy algorithms, such as Orthogonal Matching Pursuit (OMP) [21,22], that has the advantage of low computational complexity.

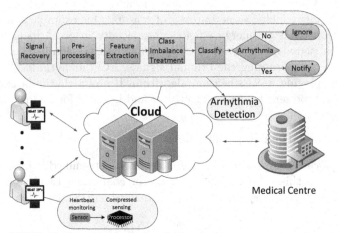

* Notification is sent to user and medical centre.

Fig. 1. Schematic overview of E-health monitoring system

Sensing Matrix Measurement: Sensing matrix, Φ, should be appropriately designed in order to guarantee robust and accurate signal recovery. A proper sensing matrix must satisfy Restricted Isometry Property (RIP) which is defined as:

$$(1 - \delta_k)||z||_2 \leq ||\Phi\Psi z||_2 \leq (1 + \delta_k)||z||_2, \tag{5}$$

where δ_k is the isometry constant of Φ. δ_k value must not be close to one. In other words, smaller values of δ_k guarantee exact reconstruction of signal with higher probability [19]. In practice, it is difficult to verify RIP. Alternatively, the concept of coherence is applied to sensing matrix Φ and sparsifying dictionary Ψ. Formally, coherence between the two, $\mu(\Phi, \Psi)$, is defined as follows [23,24]:

$$\mu(\Phi, \Psi) = \sqrt{N} \, max_{1 \leq k, j \leq N}|<\Phi_k, \Psi_j>|. \tag{6}$$

Ideally, $\mu(\Phi, \Psi)$ will be small (i.e. the matrices are incoherent). The most common choices for sensing matrix Φ are Gaussian or Bernoulli distribution.

3 ECG Arrhythmia Detection

This section presents steps of ECG analysis and arrhythmia detection.

3.1 Preprocessing

In preprocessing step, we normalise and standardise ECG signal to eliminate base and gain from raw signal. Next, R peaks (i.e. maximum amplitude in the ECG signal R wave) are located using beat-by-beat annotation file information. These locations are then employed to segment ECG signals into individual heartbeats. We choose 257 samples for the length of each heartbeat as suggested in [4]. Considering each R peak in the middle of a heartbeat, this length will cover the whole heartbeat waveform.

3.2 Feature Extraction

Feature extraction involves representing a large amount of data using only a few samples. Employing proper feature extraction method reduces the need for large memory storage capacity and computational power. Wavelet Transform (WT) is often used to extract features from ECG signals. Major concerns in using WT are choosing proper wavelet and number of signal decomposition levels. Daubechies wavelet [25] of order 2 is one of the best candidates for analysing ECG signal according to [3]. In this article, the employed decomposition level is four as suggested by the former study [4]. Each level of decomposition consists of two sets of coefficients, namely detail and approximation. Therefore, we obtained a total of eight sets of coefficients containing four sets of details (D1–D4) and four sets of approximation (A1–A4). To decide about the best coefficients to use, Azariadi et al. [5] performed a design space exploration for different combinations of the coefficients (i.e. level one to four detail and approximation). The best result was obtained by level four approximate coefficients. Therefore, approximation four is employed as the final feature vector to be fed to SVM classifier.

3.3 Class Imbalance Treatment

Any non-uniform distribution between classes is described as a class imbalance. Therefore, class imbalance negatively affects these algorithms [26]. In this article, we use SMOTE [27] to treat class imbalance problem. It is a popular technique which has been employed in many applications [6,28]. This algorithm creates artificial instances of existing minority samples instead of simply duplicating them. It selects k-nearest neighbours for a chosen target class. It then creates new samples based on feature combination of the target class and its neighbours. SMOTE is well-known for generating less specific decision region for minority classes.

3.4   Classification

In this article, SVM [29] is used to diagnose normal heartbeats from abnormal ones and to offer non-linear classification with adequate precision. The objective of SVM is finding an optimal hyperplane to distinguish classes of data. Generally, this idea takes place by identifying the hyperplane with the maximum margin between two classes. To find the best hyperplane, SVM utilises a kernel function to map identified patterns into high-dimensional space. Therefore, SVM classifier characteristics are twofold: linear from parameters aspect and non-linear in employed mapping attributes. Choosing suitable kernel function depends on the problem SVM is used for, and there is no straightforward technique on how to select a kernel function [29,30]. In this work, we applied *Radial Basis Function* (RBF) as the kernel function as it has been used in many studies for ECG classification [3,5,7].

4   Result

4.1   MIT-BIH Arrhythmia Database

To perform our experiments, we employ the MIT-BIH arrhythmia database [31] which has been used extensively for ECG related studies. This database contains half-hour ECG signals of 47 both inpatient and outpatient participants aged from 23 to 89 years. The recordings are divided to "100" and "200" series. The "100" series consists of more common arrhythmia while the "200" ones include rare arrhythmias that are clinically important. ECG signals were captured at 360 Hz with 11-bit resolution. Two independent cardiologists analysed the quality of each signal and annotated it. To investigate the performance of SVM in relation to different compression ratios of an ECG signal, we choose five participants namely 100, 106, 202, 205, and 208. A total number of heartbeats analysed in this article is 12095 including 9966 normal and 2129 abnormal beats. This data test set is selected from "100" and "200" series to ensure the performance was examined for common as well as rare arrhythmias. It is worth mentioning that in this work, we assume the smart gadget is customised for each user (i.e. the classifier is trained and tested by the same user's ECG data). Hence, there is no need of testing the SVM classifier with the data of patients who were not involved in training process.

4.2   Experiments Setup and Performance Metrics

We employ broadly accepted performance measures in Compressed Sensing and classification methods, namely, Compression Ratio (CR), Percentage Root-mean-squared Difference (PRD), Sensitivity (SE), and Precision (PR) to quantify functionality of compression algorithms coupled with SVM classification.

Compressed Sensing: To implement Compressed Sensing, we use Matlab functions written by [13]. In this implementation, sensing matrix, Φ, is a random matrix of i.i.d Gaussian entries. Moreover, sparsifying matrix, Ψ, is formed using nearly-perfect reconstruction cosine modulated filter banks [32]. After compressing ECG signals, it is encoded through scalar quantisation. What follows discuss measures associated with Compressed Sensing. Compression ratio is defined as follows:

$$CR = \frac{N \times bit_{orig}}{M \times bit_{rec}},$$ (7)

where N is the length of the signal processing window, and bit_{orig} is the sampling resolution. Also, M is the length of compressed signal regarding window size, and bit_{rec} is the resolution of compressed signal. In this article, a window size of $N = 1024$, compressed signal of length $M = 64 \times n(n = 1..9)$ bit sampling resolution, and 6 bit compressed signal resolution are used.

PRD is a measurement factor of the distortion or alteration from an original signal and defined as:

$$PRD = \sqrt{\frac{\sum_{i=1}^{N}(x_{orig}(i) - x_{rec}(i))^2}{\sum_{i=1}^{N}(x_{orig}(i))^2}} \times 100,$$ (8)

where x_{orig} and x_{rec} represent an original and reconstructed signal, respectively.

Classification: As mentioned before, approximation four of Daubechies Wavelet of order 2 is used to form feature vectors from the recovered signal with a specific compression ratio (i.e. 0 to 29.33). Next, SMOTE is applied to address the effect of class imbalance. The balanced classes are then fed to SVM classifier with RBF kernel (Weka interface of LIBSVM [33] is used to implement SVM). In SVM implementation, balanced classes are cross-validated employing 5-fold validation. In k-fold cross-validation, the original sample is divided into k subsamples. One subsample is kept for testing, and the rest are used as training data. The procedure is repeated for k times (k = number of folds). The benefit of this method is that all subsamples are used for both training and testing. We repeat SVM for ten seeds. The performance of SVM classifier is measured using sensitivity and precision factors. Sensitivity is the ratio between retrieved relevant instances (TP) and a total number of relevant cases as follows:

$$SE = \frac{TP}{TP + FN} \times 100,$$ (9)

where relevant cases include retrieved and missed instances ($TP+FN$). Precision is defined as the proportion of relevant instances over the retrieved ones:

$$PR = \frac{TP}{TP + FP} \times 100,$$ (10)

retrieved cases consist of relevant and irrelevant instances ($TP + FP$).

4.3   Experimental Results

First, we analyse a number of factors that influence quality of ECG classification including reconstruction algorithms and compression ratio. The impact of CR

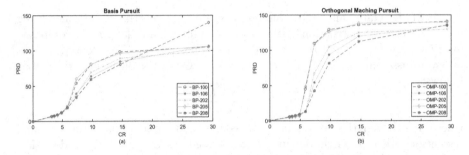

Fig. 2. Comparison between Basis Pursuit and Orthogonal Matching Pursuit. PRD as a function of CR for different ECG records. (a) Basis Pursuit (b) Orthogonal Matching Pursuit.

and PRD are presented in Fig. 2 for two reconstruction algorithms (i.e. BP and OMP). As can be seen, an increment in CR is followed by PRD growth which is intuitive as more compression leads to more distortion from the original signal. We also note from Fig. 2 that for most participants (i.e. 4 out of 5 instances), BP has a PRD less than 100 while OMP reaches a PRD over 140 when it becomes stable. For participant 208, even though BP algorithm has a strictly increasing trend for PRD, it still provides the same signal quality in relation to OMP in the worst case. Furthermore, participants 208 and 106 could not reach an entirely stable state for PRD in both BP and OMP.

Next, we present an analysis of SVM classification of the recovered signals using OMP and BP. Figure 3 depicts the decreasing trend of precision of SVM classifier with respect to CR for both OMP and BP algorithms. We use Wilcoxon Signed-Ranked test to investigate whether there is a difference between the precision of reconstructed signals for various CRs concerning employed algorithms. This test is used as a result of a limited number of participants and no evidence of normality of the data. According to Wilcoxon Signed-Ranked test for CR until 7.33, employed algorithms did not elicit a statistically significant change in precision. However, for compression rates from 7.33 BP and OMP are statistically different in a sense that BP outperforms OMP. We have repeated the same test to compare the sensitivity of SVM classifier for reconstructed signals by BP and OMP. Interestingly, the test shows no substantial difference between the sensitivity of the classifier regarding signal recovery methods. Table 1 shows the precision and sensitivity of SVM for five participants considering different CRs. As can be seen, there is a trade-off between CR and precision (sensitivity). In other words, a higher compression ratio leads to lower precision (sensitivity). However, this claim needs further investigations using statistical methods. Another important issue is deciding about reliable CR. From this table, we note that three out of five participants (100, 202, and 205) have precision and sensitivity more than 90% in CR 14.66 for both algorithms. From the same CR, OMP precision (sensitivity) declines to less than 90% for participants 106 and 208. The only case that has no issue either in understanding or measure of relevance in

CR 29.33 is participant 205. To statistically evaluate the trade-off between CR and precision (sensitivity), we employed Spearman's rank correlation test presented in table 2. We employ this test to examine both direction and strength of the relationship between CR and precision (sensitivity) monotonically. This table shows that regardless of fluctuations in data points, there is a negative correlation between them in 95% degree of confidence. Another essential criterion that needs more investigation is the strength of coefficient for BP and OMP. For precision in four out of five instances (i.e. all but 106) OMP has a stronger negative correlation to CR. This means the precision is aggravated faster by increasing CR. Similarly, the sensitivity of OMP for three out of five participants (100, 106, and 205) has the same behaviour. Despite the seemingly better performance of OMP for 106, 202, 208 in precision (sensitivity), the cost of it should be further evaluated. To do so, we use a measurement for OMP versus BP as $(CC_{BP}/CC_{OMP}) - 1$ for both precision and sensitivity. The measurement shows that a minor improvement in precision (sensitivity) leads to a significant deterioration in sensitivity (precision).

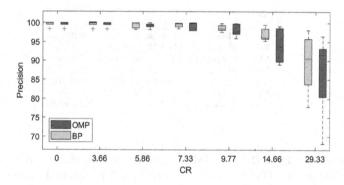

Fig. 3. Precision of classification associated with different compression ratios for all ECG records as recovered by BP and OMP.

5   Discussion

This study shed some lights on factors impact quality of ECG classification including reconstruction algorithms and compression ratio. What is most remarkable about the results is that arrhythmia detection has low sensitivity to intensity of signal recovery (i.e. a few samples represent important signal information). Put differently, ECG signals with compression ratios up to 9.77 can be classified with precision and sensitivity more than 90% for all participants employing both algorithms. Moreover, as discussed in [15,16], compression may improve precision of classifiers. This phenomenon is observed for some participants in our study (see Table 1).

Table 1. Performance measurements of five-fold SVM (mean ± standard deviation) for five ECG records based on different compression ratios.

CR	BP		OMP		BP		OMP	
	PR (%)	SE (%)	PR (%)	SE (%)	PR (%)	SE (%)	PR (%)	SE (%)
0	99.99±0.03	100±0	99.99±0.03	100±0	99.87±0.06	99.98±0.04	99.87±0.06	99.98±0.04
3.66	100±0	99.65±0.05	99.98±0.04	99.99±0.03	100±0	99.70±0.05	99.87±06	99.96±0.05
4.88	100±0	99.46±0.13	99.91±0.07	99.82±0.08	99.82±0.10	99.88±0.07	99.79±0.08	99.89±0.03
5.86	100±0	99.20±0.09	99.21±0.07	98.49±0.09	99.79±0.09	99.99±0.07	99.56±0.09	99.78±0.08
7.33	99.17±0.12	97.25±0.18	99.88±0.04	97.94±0.18	99.90±0	99.55±0.07	99.97±0.09	98.99±0.12
9.77	98.50±0.15	99.88±0.06	99.70±0.07	97.87±0.67	99.19±0.11	98.94±0.13	97.71±0.25	95.62±0.28
14.66	98.13±0.15	99.44±0.5	99.12±0.13	96.77±0.24	95.27±0.46	95.8±0.43	90.05±0.55	89.29±0.32
29.33	98.14±0.25	90.87±0.25	96.51±0.17	84.94±0.25	77.92±0.38	85.65±0.42	68.20±0.46	86.59±0.68

202					205			
0	99.87±0.01	98.85±0.05	99.87±0.01	98.85±0.05	100±0	99.71±0.07	100±0	99.71±0.07
3.66	99.81±0.09	98.87±0.17	99.81±0.09	98.87±0.17	100±0	99.64±0.06	100±0	99.75±0.09
4.88	99.88±0.04	98.70±0.18	99.76±0.10	98.54±0.03	100±0	99.64±0.05	99.99±0.03	99.62±0.08
5.86	98.84±0.21	98.58±0.14	99.37±0.32	98.76±0.08	99.98±0.04	99.57±0.05	100±0	99.21±0.09
7.33	99.75±0.07	98.22±0.15	97.97±0.07	97.95±07	99.79±0.19	99.35±0.21	99.96±0.05	99.54±0.05
9.77	98.35±0.09	96.96±0.14	97.52±0.06	96.8±0.16	99.82±0.08	98.93±0.13	99.87±0.05	99.07±0.13
14.66	96.11±0.15	92.39±0.2	93.77±0.26	97.40±0.21	99.51±0.11	98.55±0.14	98.5±0.15	97.26±0.16
29.33	90.60±0.19	84.13±0.42	92.15±0.34	75.31±0.4	95.06±0.20	94.20±0.18	91.68±0.2	95.59±0.2

208 CR	BP		OMP	
	PR (%)	SE (%)	PR (%)	SE (%)
0	98.36±0.13	98.29±0.06	98.36±0.13	98.29±0.06
3.66	98.42±0.16	98.17±0.11	98.41±0.13	98.31±0.018
4.88	98.29±0.09	98.1±0.05	98.32±0.14	98.02±0.1
5.86	98.21±0.23	97.15±0.14	98.26±0.14	98.23±0.13
7.33	98.52±0.9	97.00±0.15	97.97±0.2	96.06±0.22
9.77	97.54±0.11	93.86±0.24	95.95±0.32	92.52±0.27
14.66	96.04±0.2	91.22±0.22	89.1±0.37	84.02±0.42

As mentioned earlier, BP and OMP do not show a significant difference when it comes to sensitivity. What is more, the precision for both is the same for compression ratios up to 7.33, after that BP outperforms OMP. This observation expresses the idea that BP and OMP are interchangeable until a specific compression ratio. Hence, OMP is a proper choice for small compression ratios due to its lower time complexity [14]. An additional notable statement is regarding the quality of reconstructed signal when using SVM classifier. Consider, for example, compression ratio 9.77; the PRD ranges are roughly 55 to 80 and 80 to 125 for BP and OMP, respectively. Obtained PRDs are far more than suggested PRDs in the literature for high-quality signal recovery [12] (i.e. SVM classifier exploits limited information to identify heartbeat abnormality). The performance of SVM classifier with respect to individuals shows a general superiority of BP over OMP considering both precision and sensitivity irrespective of compression ratio. To be more precise, for three patients with slightly better performance in terms of precision (sensitivity) there is considerable drop in sensitivity (precision), see Table 2, participants 106, 202, 208. The results of SVM classification also indicate the negative correlation between compression ratio and precision as well as sensitivity for both algorithms. This observation can be explained as follows: regardless of minor fluctuations, losing data information leads to a reduction in

Table 2. Spearman's rank correlation coefficient test between compression ratio and (a) Precision and (b) Sensitivity.

	(a)				(b)		
Participant	BP	OMP	Index	Participant	BP	OMP	Index[2]
100 Cor.[1]	-0.657	-0.960	-31.6	100 Cor.	-0.673	-0.976	-31.0
100 Sig.	0.039	0.000		100 Sig.	0.033	0.000	
106 Cor.	-0.758	-0.730	3.8	106 Cor.	-0.782	-0.979	-20.1
106 Sig.	0.011	0.017		106 Sig.	0.008	0.000	
202 Cor.	-0.758	-0.985	-23.0	202 Cor.	-0.939	-0.867	8.3
202 Sig.	0.011	0.000		202 Sig.	0.000	0.001	
205 Cor.	-0.841	-0.899	-6.5	205 Cor.	-0.918	-0.939	-2.2
205 Sig.	0.002	0.000		205 Sig.	0.000	0.000	
208 Cor.	-0.661	-0.954	-30.7	208 Cor.	-0.985	-0.927	6.3
208 Sig.	0.038	0.000		208 Sig.	0.000	0.000	

[1] Correlation Coefficient $^2\ \frac{CC_{BP}}{CC_{OMP}} - 1\ (\%)$

the ability of the classifier to identify arrhythmia detection. It is now time to discuss the role played by severe heart disease. First, we need to know ratios of abnormal heartbeats for each participant. The ratios of abnormal to total (i.e. $RA = abnormal/(normal + abnormal)$) beats are $1.5, 26, 3.7, 3.4, 46.3$ per cent for participants $100, 106, 202, 205, 208$, respectively. On the one hand, in Table 1, patients 106 and 208 (with $RA > 25\%$) are the ones with precision (sensitivity) less than 90% regarding OMP. On the other hand, participants $106, 202, 208$ have $RA > 3.5\%$. These patients had misleading classification performances concerning OMP, see Table 2. These circumstances raise an important question. Does severity of heart disease have impacts on the functionality of SVM classifier? Admittedly, this question requires comprehensive investigation in terms of participants.

6 Conclusion

In this work, we performed an empirical study to identify acceptable compression ratios that hold crucial information of ECG signal. This is an efficient method for reducing data transmission cost in sensors. To recover the original signal, we applied two extensively used algorithms, namely BP and OMP. Next, we used SVM classification to assess the effect of both compression ratio and signal recovery methods on heartbeat arrhythmia detection. The results illustrated that the SVM classifier only needs sparsely sampled signals to identify ECG arrhythmia. Moreover, considering all of the participants, both OMP and BP have the same performance for compression ratios up to around 1:7, after that BP outperforms OMP with regard to ECG arrhythmia detection. For future works, one can consider mutual effects of other reconstruction algorithms and various classification methods on the acceptable interval of compression ratios. Another extension of this article is to investigate more patients and examine possible correlation between heart disease severity and classifier performance.

References

1. QardioCore. https://getqardio.com/qardiocore-wearable-ecg-ekg-monitor-iphone/. Accessed 09 Sept 2018
2. Zareei, S., Deng, J.D.: Energy harvesting modelling for self-powered fitness gadgets: a feasibility study. Int. J. Parallel Emergent Distrib. Syst., 1–17 (2017)
3. Übeyli, E.D.: ECG beats classification using multiclass support vector machines with error correcting output codes. Digit. Signal Process. **17**(3), 675–684 (2007)
4. Güler, İ., Übeyli, E.D.: ECG beat classifier designed by combined neural network model. Pattern Recognit. **38**(2), 199–208 (2005)
5. Azariadi, D., Tsoutsouras, V., Xydis, S., Soudris, D.: ECG signal analysis and arrhythmia detection on IoT wearable medical devices. In: 2016 5th International Conference on Modern Circuits and Systems Technologies (MOCAST), pp. 1–4, May 2016
6. Rajesh, K.N., Dhuli, R.: Classification of imbalanced ECG beats using re-sampling techniques and adaboost ensemble classifier. Biomed. Signal Process. Control **41**, 242–254 (2018)
7. Elhaj, F.A., Salim, N., Harris, A.R., Swee, T.T., Ahmed, T.: Arrhythmia recognition and classification using combined linear and nonlinear features of ECG signals. Comput. Methods Programs Biomed. **127**, 52–63 (2016)
8. da Silva Luz, E.J., Schwartz, W.R., Cámara-Chávez, G., Menotti, D.: ECG-based heartbeat classification for arrhythmia detection: a survey. Comput. Methods Programs Biomed. **127**, 144–164 (2016)
9. Zareei, S., Babaee, E., Salleh, R., Moghadam, S.: Employing orphan nodes to avoid energy holes in wireless sensor networks. Commun. Netw. **5**(03), 625 (2013)
10. Cao, J., Wang, W., Zhou, S., Inman, D.J., Lin, J.: Nonlinear time-varying potential bistable energy harvesting from human motion. Appl. Phys. Lett. **107**(14), 143904 (2015)
11. Zareei, S., Sedigh, A.H.A., Deng, J.D., Purvis, M.: Buffer management using integrated queueing models for mobile energy harvesting sensors. In: IEEE 28th Annual International Symposium on Personal, Indoor, and Mobile Radio Communications (PIMRC), pp. 1–5. IEEE (2017)
12. Mamaghanian, H., Khaled, N., Atienza, D., Vandergheynst, P.: Compressed sensing for real-time energy-efficient ECG compression on wireless body sensor nodes. IEEE Trans. Biomed. Eng. **58**(9), 2456–2466 (2011)
13. Carrillo, R.E., Polania, L.F., Barner, K.E.: Iterative algorithms for compressed sensing with partially known support. In: 2010 IEEE International Conference on Acoustics, Speech and Signal Processing, pp. 3654–3657, March 2010
14. Dixon, A.M.R., Allstot, E.G., Gangopadhyay, D., Allstot, D.J.: Compressed sensing system considerations for ECG and EMG wireless biosensors. IEEE Trans. Biomed. Circuits Syst. **6**(2), 156–166 (2012)
15. Shen, D., et al.: Web-page classification through summarization. In: Proceedings of the 27th Annual International ACM SIGIR Conference on Research and Development in Information Retrieval, SIGIR 2004, pp. 242–249. ACM (2004)
16. Cosman, P.C., Gray, R.M., Olshen, R.A.: Evaluating quality of compressed medical images: SNR, subjective rating, and diagnostic accuracy. Proc. IEEE **82**(6), 919–932 (1994)
17. Craven, D., McGinley, B., Kilmartin, L., Glavin, M., Jones, E.: Compressed sensing for bioelectric signals: a review. IEEE J. Biomed. Heal. Inform. **19**(2), 529–540 (2015)

18. Donoho, D.L.: Compressed sensing. IEEE Trans. Inf. Theory **52**(4), 1289–1306 (2006)
19. Candes, E.J., Romberg, J., Tao, T.: Robust uncertainty principles: exact signal reconstruction from highly incomplete frequency information. IEEE Trans. Inf. Theory **52**(2), 489–509 (2006)
20. Chen, S.S., Donoho, D.L., Saunders, M.A.: Atomic decomposition by basis pursuit. SIAM Rev. **43**(1), 129–159 (2001)
21. Pati, Y.C., Rezaiifar, R., Krishnaprasad, P.S.: Orthogonal matching pursuit: recursive function approximation with applications to wavelet decomposition. In: Proceedings of 27th Asilomar Conference on Signals, Systems and Computers, vol. 1, pp. 40–44, November 1993
22. Tropp, J.A., Gilbert, A.C.: Signal recovery from random measurements via orthogonal matching pursuit. IEEE Trans. Inf. Theory **53**(12), 4655–4666 (2007)
23. Tropp, J.A.: Just relax: convex programming methods for identifying sparse signals in noise. IEEE Trans. Inf. Theory **52**(3), 1030–1051 (2006)
24. Donoho, D.L., Huo, X.: Uncertainty principles and ideal atomic decomposition. IEEE Trans. Inf. Theory **47**(7), 2845–2862 (2001)
25. Daubechies, I.: The wavelet transform, time-frequency localization and signal analysis. IEEE Trans. Inf. Theory **36**(5), 961–1005 (1990)
26. He, H., Garcia, E.A.: Learning from imbalanced data. IEEE Trans. Knowl. Data Eng. **21**(9), 1263–1284 (2009)
27. Chawla, N., Bowyer, K., Hall, L., Kegelmeyer, W.: SMOTE: synthetic minority over-sampling technique. J. Artif. Intell. Res. **16**, 321–357 (2002). Cited By 3341
28. Thiam, P., Meudt, S., Palm, G., Schwenker, F.: A temporal dependency based multi-modal active learning approach for audiovisual event detection. Neural Process. Lett. **48**, 709–732 (2017)
29. Vapnik, V.: The Nature of Statistical Learning Theory. Springer, New York (1995). https://doi.org/10.1007/978-1-4757-2440-0
30. Cortes, C., Vapnik, V.: Support-vector networks. Mach. Learn. **20**(3), 273–297 (1995)
31. Moody, G.B., Mark, R.G.: The impact of the MIT-BIH arrhythmia database. IEEE Eng. Med. Biol. Mag. **20**(3), 45–50 (2001)
32. Blanco-Velasco, M., Cruz-Roldán, F., Moreno-Martínez, E., Godino-Llorente, J.-I., Barner, K.E.: Embedded filter bank-based algorithm for ECG compression. Signal Process. **88**(6), 1402–1412 (2008)
33. Chang, C.-C., Lin, C.-J.: LIBSVM: a library for support vector machines. ACM Trans. Intell. Syst. Technol. **2**(3), 27:1–27:27 (2011)

Intelligent Fault Detection of High-Speed Railway Turnout Based on Hybrid Deep Learning

Zhi Zhuang[1,2], Guohua Zhang[2(✉)], Wei Dong[2], Xinya Sun[2,3],
and Chuanjiang Wang[1]

[1] Shandong University of Science and Technology, Qingdao, China
[2] Beijing National Research Center for Information Science and Technology
(BNRist), Tsinghua University, Beijing, China
jsjrjl23@163.com
[3] Department of Automation, Tsinghua University, Beijing, China

Abstract. With the purpose of detecting the turnout fault without label data and fault data timely, this paper proposes a hybrid deep learning framework combining the DDAE (Deep Denoising Auto-encoder) and one-class SVM (Support Vector Machine) for turnout fault detection only using normal data. The proposed method achieves an accuracy of 98.67% on the real turn-out dataset for current curve, which suggests that this work realizes the purpose of detecting the fault with only normal data and provides a basis for the intelligent fault detection of turnouts.

Keywords: Fault detection · Deep Denoising Auto-encoder · DBSCAN
One-class SVM

1 Introduction

The high-speed railway in China has developed rapidly over the recent years, which has brought great convenient trips. However, there is also an increasing awareness of the train operation safety [1]. The turnout, as the most important infrastructure in the high-speed railway system, controls the position change of trains. Its current operation status shows characteristics of large quantity, frequent operation and harsh environment, which can easily cause the fault of the turnout and cause the hidden danger of the train operation safety [2–4]. It is paramount to detect fault of the turnout precisely in time for improving driving safety of the high-speed railway.

In the last decades, the research methods of fault detection for turnout mainly focus on two aspects: analytical model [5, 6] and traditional machine learning method [7–13]. Despite their success, they also have their own drawbacks. On the one hand, the analytical model-based detection system requires experts to establish the precise mathematical model which is difficult in practice. On the other hand, the fault detection based on traditional machine learning method relies heavily on the manual features extraction and data labeling which are exhausted works.

Compared to traditional machine learning techniques, Deep learning (DL), especially unsupervised DL algorithms [21], can eliminate the effect of manual feature and has been

© Springer Nature Switzerland AG 2018
T. Mitrovic et al. (Eds.): AI 2018, LNAI 11320, pp. 98–103, 2018.
https://doi.org/10.1007/978-3-030-03991-2_10

applied in the fault detection field [14]. Recently, as one of the effective DLs, DDAE was also first employed to automatically extract feature of the turnout data without expertise [17]. However, the work in [17] only focused on clustering analysis, not involving fault detection. As a special case of DL, the hybrid deep learning, which integrates DL with other classifiers to improve the classification accuracy [15, 16], has received an increasing attention in classification task [15, 20]. But such hybrid architectures have not been further studied in the field of fault detection, especially turnout fault detection.

This paper proposes a novel fault detection approach for high-speed railway turnout based on hybrid deep learning by integrating the DDAE with one-class SVM. In the proposed approach, DDAE is employed to extract features automatically instead of relying on artificial experience from unlabeled dataset composed of current curves of the turnout. The features are identified by the clustering algorithm and expert knowledge [18] to classify the normal and abnormal current curve of turnout. Then only the normal current curves are fed to one-class SVM model for detecting outliers. The experimental results confirm that the proposed method performs well on the real turnout dataset composed of more than 90,000 current curves of turnout provided by cooperative enterprise, which also suggests that this work realizes the purpose of intelligent detecting the turnout fault without label data and fault data.

This paper is organized as follows. In Sect. 2, an intelligent turnout fault detection method based on hybrid deep learning is proposed. This method is verified in real turnout data in Sect. 3. Finally, we conclude this paper in Sect. 4.

2　The Proposed Method

In this section, an intelligent fault detection method based on hybrid deep learning is proposed to solve the problem of turnout fault detection without labeled data. Figure 1 illustrates the procedure of the proposed method, which mainly composed of three steps: (1) data feature extraction, (2) normal data acquisition and (3) fault detection. Details of each step of the proposed method are described below.

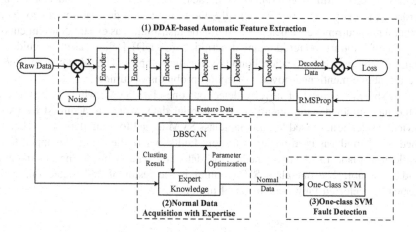

Fig. 1. Flow chart of proposed method.

DDAE-Based Automatic Feature Extraction - For fault detection of turnout, how to extract the features of the current curve is the key point. In the previous research on fault detection of turnout, the main way of feature extraction relies on artificial experience, which makes the result of extracted features very subjective and unreliable.

In order to get rid of the limitations of subjective artificial experience, we use a feature extraction method based on DDAE [22], which is a very important deep learning method that can extract features automatically. Specifically, Gaussian noise (Noise) is introduced on the basis of the original current curve (Raw Data), and then the high-dimension input data with Gaussian noise (X) is mapped to a low dimension encoding (Feature Data) by using an encoder (Encoder 1-Encoder n), finally the low dimension encoding is decoded to the reconstructed curve (Decoded Data) by the decoder (Decoder 1-Decoder n). The training process of DDAE is to minimize the mean square error function (Loss) between the original current curve and the reconstructed curve by root mean square prop (RMSprop).

Normal Data Acquisition with Expertise - The feature data without labels can't be used directly for the fault detection model training. So we propose a method of obtaining normal samples with expertise by clustering the feature data.

Density-Based Spatial Clustering of Applications with Noise (DBSCAN), as a well-known clustering method, is used to cluster feature data extracted by DDAE. The algorithm assumes that the clustering structure can be determined by the tightness of the distribution of the curve samples. By tuning the algorithm parameters, the clusters can be greatly different. To improve the process of the parameters tuning, the method of sensitivity analysis with expert knowledge is introduced. specifically, expert knowledge is employed as the decision fundament of sensitivity analysis. Based on this, two main parameters of DBSCAN algorithm (eps and MinPts), are jointly tuned by sensitivity analysis. The clusters that contain fault data are eliminated according to the expert knowledge. The process of data screening is unnecessary to label each data, so it can greatly reduce the workload of the fault data discrimination. And this process solves the problem that unlabeled data is difficult to apply to fault detection.

One-class SVM Fault Detection - Fault detection with normal data can be also regarded as novelty detection. Specifically, the turnout fault detection needs to decide whether a new current curve belongs to the same distribution as existing current curves. The idea of support vector domain description (SVDD) [19] is used to guide the training of compact classification boundary for the samples. This idea can be used to solve the above-mentioned novelty detection problems of turnout.

As a specific method of novelty detection, one-class SVM, which is inspired by SVDD, has attracted wide attention. The normal data, which is acquired by expert knowledge selection, is used to train one-class SVM model for fault detection. Then the trained SVM model is used to detect turnout faults, where the data are mapped to the classification plane to identify whether the detection data is inside the classification boundary or not. The one-class SVM output is the result of fault detection, which indicates the detected fault conclusion of turnout.

3   Experiments and Results

In this section, experimental results are presented to validate the proposed method, which is tested on the unlabeled datasets composed of more than 90,000 current curves of 128 S700K point machines. Due to the similar results obtained from the datasets of different point machines, the experimental results from one datasets including 1200 current curves are reported here.

The proposed method relies on unlabeled data while the existing turnout fault detection methods require labeled data, so there is no direct comparative experiment. For space limitation, the detailed experimental process is omitted. The paper only lists the key experimental steps as follows:

(1) All data are sorted in chronological order and normalized. Then stratified sampling is divided into two datasets: 3/4 of the data including 900 pieces as the training set and the rest 1/4 data including 300 pieces as the test set. The data of test set are labeled by expert knowledge.

(2) In order to better extract the feature automatically, the DDAE model is constructed. The Gaussian noise with average 0 and standard deviation 0.01 are added to the raw data so as to enhance the ability of denoising in feature extraction. The hidden layer size of DDAE is set as 200-128-64-32-16-8, which is determined by sensitivity analysis.

(3) The DBSCAN algorithm is used to cluster the 8 dimensions features, and two main parameters (eps and MinPts) are jointly tuned by sensitivity analysis. After clustering, the training set is divided into 14 clusters, and then the clusters that contain fault data are eliminated according to the expert knowledge. The data of remaining clusters are selected as the normal data for training fault detection model.

(4) The normal data acquired above is used to train fault detection model constructed by one-class SVM. And the sensitivity analysis method is used to determine the best parameters of the turnout fault detection model.

The experimental result is shown in the following table:

Table 1. The experiment result

Parameter	Value
Accurate rate (%)	98.67
Probability of false alarm (PFA, %)	1.33
Probability of missing alarm (PMA, %)	0

The detailed results displayed in Table 1 show that the accuracy of the proposed method in fault detection with unlabeled data is 98.67%, the probability of missing alarm is 0 and the probability of false alarm is 1.33%. This result has met the actual turnout fault detection needs of cooperative enterprise. The experimental result shows that the proposed method can give full play to the advantages of automatic feature extraction in deep learning, and uses hybrid deep learning to solve the problem of fault detection under the unlabeled data.

4   Conclusion

In this paper, a hybrid deep learning method combining deep learning and one-class SVM is proposed for the fault detection based on the actual situation of turnout operation and maintenance. The challenge of selecting normal data is addressed by taking inspiration from [17, 18]. The proposed method can be divided into three main steps: Firstly, in order to avoid obtaining subjective and unreliable features from manual extraction, a deep learning model is used to extract the features of the raw data automatically. Secondly, the clustering algorithm and expert knowledge are introduced so as to select normal data clusters. Finally, the normal data is fed to one-class SVM model for detecting the fault of turnout.

The evaluation of proposed method is carried out on the real turnout data, the fault detection accurate rate of the method reaches 98.67%. The result confirms that the proposed method can get rid of the dependence on manual feature extraction and overcome the limitations of requiring labeled data for fault detection, which is more flexible and practical. It is very interesting to combine deep learning and other traditional machine learning to detect the turnout fault. On the basis of this study, we plan to further study the small fault detection of turnout based on hybrid deep learning.

Acknowledgement. This work was supported by the National Key Research and Development Program of China under Grant 2017YFB1200700, the special fund of Suzhou-Tsinghua Innovation Leading Action under Grant 2016SZ0202, the Natural Science Foundation of China under Grants 61490701 and the Research and Development Project of Beijing National Railway Research & Design Institute of Signal & Communication Ltd.

References

1. Feng, L.: Turnout fault diagnosie by current analysis using computer monitor. Technol. Exch. **8**(1), 73–75 (2011)
2. Huang, B.: Fault analysis and countermeasures for turnout switching equipment of high-speed railway. Railw. Oper. Technol. **22**(1), 59–64 (2016)
3. Liu, X., Kuang, W., He, T.: The design of point switch simulator of high-speed turnout diagnostic apparatus. Railw. Stand. Des. **59**(12), 105–110 (2015)
4. Zhang, Y., Xie, Q.: A method of railway turnout detection based on machine vision. Comput. Appl. Softw. **32**(1), 225–228 (2015)
5. Bocaniala, C.D., Costa, J.S.D.: Application of a novel fuzzy classifier to fault detection and isolation of the DAMADICS benchmark problem. Control. Eng. Pract. **14**(6), 653–669 (2006)
6. Eker, O.F., Camci, F., Guclu, A., Yilboga, H., Sevkli, M., Baskan, S.: A simple state-based prognostic model for railway turnout systems. IEEE Trans. Industr. Electron. **58**, 1718–1726 (2011)
7. Zhang, K., Du, K., Ju, Y.: Algorithm of railway turnout fault detection based on PNN neural network. In: Seventh International Symposium on Computational Intelligence and Design, pp. 544–547. IEEE Computer Society (2014)

8. Zhang, K.: The railway turnout fault diagnosis algorithm based on BP neural network. In: IEEE International Conference on Control Science and Systems Engineering, pp. 135–138 (2015)
9. Zhou, F., Xia, L., Dong, W., et al.: Fault diagnosis of high-speed railway turnout based on support vector machine. In: IEEE International Conference on Industrial Technology, pp. 1539–1544. IEEE (2016)
10. He, Y.M., Zhao, H.B., Tian, J., Zhang, M.Q.: Railway turnout fault diagnosis based on support vector machine. Appl. Mech. Mater. **556-562**, 2663–2667 (2014)
11. Eker, O.F., Camci, F., Kumar, U.: SVM based diagnostics on railway turnouts. Int. J. Perform. Eng. **8**(8), 289–298 (2012)
12. Wang, S.M., Lei, Y.: Fault diagnosis of turnout control circuit based on LS-SVM. J. Lanzhou Jiaotong Univ. **29**(4), 1–5 (2010)
13. Vileiniskis, M., Remenyte-Prescott, R., Rama, D.: A fault detection method for railway point systems. Proc. Inst. Mech. Eng. Part F J. Rail Rapid Transit **230**(3), 18 (2016)
14. Shan, J.: Study on railway switches diagnosis system based on deep belief networks. Master's thesis, Shijiazhuang Tiedao University (2017). (in Chinese)
15. Wu, Z., Wang, X., Jiang, Y.G., Ye, H., Xue, X.: Modeling spatial-temporal clues in a hybrid deep learning framework for video classification. In: ACM International Conference on Multimedia, pp. 461–470 (2015)
16. Du, S., Li, T., Gong, X.: Traffic flow forecasting based on hybrid deep learning framework. In: International Conference on Intelligent Systems and Knowledge Engineering, pp. 1–6 (2018)
17. Wang, H., Dong, W., Ye, H., Yan, Y., Yan, X.: Clustering of S700K point machine's current curves based on reducing dimensions with denoising autoencoders and t-SNE. In: Chinese Automation Congress and Intelligent Manufacturing International Conference, pp. 742–747 (2017). (in Chinese)
18. Wuhan Railway Bureau: A Guide for Information Analysis of Signal Concentration Detection. China Railway Publishing House, Beijing (2015). (in Chinese)
19. Tax, D.M.J., Duin, R.P.W.: Support vector domain description. Pattern Recognit. Lett. **20**(11–13), 1191–1199 (1999)
20. Akhtar, S., Kumar, A., Ekbal, A., Bhattacharya, P.: A hybrid deep learning architecture for sentiment analysis. In: COLING (2016)
21. Sun, Y.A., Mao, H., Sang, Y.S., Zhang, Y.: Explicit guiding auto-encoders for learning meaningful representation. Neural Comput. Appl. **28**(3), 1–8 (2015)
22. Sun, Y.A., Xue, B., Zhang, M.J., Yen, G.G.: An experimental study on hyper-parameter optimization for stacked auto-encoders. In: IEEE Congress on Evolutionary Computation (2018, in press)

Uncovering Discriminative Knowledge-Guided Medical Concepts for Classifying Coronary Artery Disease Notes

Mahdi Abdollahi[1]([✉]), Xiaoying Gao[1], Yi Mei[1], Shameek Ghosh[2], and Jinyan Li[3]

[1] Victoria University of Wellington, Wellington, New Zealand
{mahdi.abdollahi, xiaoying.gao, yi.mei}@ecs.vuw.ac.nz
[2] Medius Health, Sydney, Australia
shameek.ghosh@mediushealth.org
[3] University of Technology Sydney, Sydney, Australia
Jinyan.Li@uts.edu.au

Abstract. Text classification is a challenging task for allocating each document to the correct predefined class. Most of the time, there are irrelevant features which make noise in the learning step and reduce the precision of prediction. Hence, more efficient methods are needed to select or extract meaningful features to avoid noise and overfitting. In this work, an ontology-guided method utilizing the taxonomical structure of the Unified Medical Language System (UMLS) is proposed. This method extracts concepts of appeared phrases in the documents which relate to diseases or symptoms as features. The efficiency of this method is evaluated on the 2010 Informatics for Integrating Biology and the Bedside (i2b2) data set. The obtained experimental results show significant improvement by the proposed ontology-based method on the accuracy of classification.

Keywords: Coronary artery disease notes · Text classification
Feature selection · Conceptualization · Ontology

1 Introduction

This paper proposes a method which applies ontology by referring to Unified Medical Language System (UMLS) [1] for entity recognition, and then aggregates frequent entities to create features. The proposed method is integrated with five common text classification methods to answer the following research questions:

1. Whether the proposed method can reduce the number of features and keep the meaningful features; and
2. Whether the proposed method can increase the accuracy in classification of the targeted clinical text.

© Springer Nature Switzerland AG 2018
T. Mitrovic et al. (Eds.): AI 2018, LNAI 11320, pp. 104–110, 2018.
https://doi.org/10.1007/978-3-030-03991-2_11

By analyzing the previous work, it is noticeable that the majority of disease-targeted systems have tended to develop static rule-based systems which require human interventions every time the model is updated with new features. Such systems are not scalable for practical machine learning purposes. Our system allows an easier and flexible selection of different types of medical concepts to enable automatic extraction of features or combinations and generation of a prediction model.

2   Proposed Ontology Based Approach

One of the important points in text classification problems is to investigate the domain of documents which should be classified and the domain of classes that documents should be labeled with. This can help to select only related features of the documents to the domain for training phase and improve the accuracy of prediction for unseen documents. In the clinic text classification task all of the documents are discharge notes of patients in medical domain. The candidate class is whether a disease such as that Coronary Artery Disease (CAD) is present or not. Our goal is to select features that have relations with the disease. In this case, the performance of the learned model can be improved.

To achieve the above goal, our proposed algorithm employs the knowledge in the 2010 Informatics for Integrating Biology and the Bedside (i2b2) data set [2] and UMLS library. For this purpose, the MetaMap tool is used to extract all the concepts of existing phrases for each document using the UMLS. As shown in Fig. 1, the concepts extraction step is employed on both the training and the test documents. Then, by considering the medical domain, the concept selection step is performed on the obtained concepts. As a first step, two concepts are selected among all the concepts: "Disease or Syndrome" and "Sign or Symptom". By following this way of concept selection, the meaningful concepts will be selected which will assist the training phase to learn better in order to increase the accuracy of classification.

2.1   Conceptualization

Two sentences are given below as a sample to show how MetaMap works on the input notes and what output it provides in classification process.

> *"Hyperlipidemia: The patient's Lipitor was increased to 80 mg q.d. A progress note in the patient's chart from her assisted living facility indicates that the patient has had shortness of breath for one day."*

Figure 2 shows a segment of the returned results from MetaMap. Table 1 summaries the extracted concepts of detected meaningful phrases from the sample sentences using MetaMap. As can be observed, the phrase "hyperlipidemia" belongs to "[Disease or Syndrome]" and "[Finding]" concepts. The phrase "shortest of breath" is allocated to the "[Sign or Symptom]", [Clinical Attribute] and

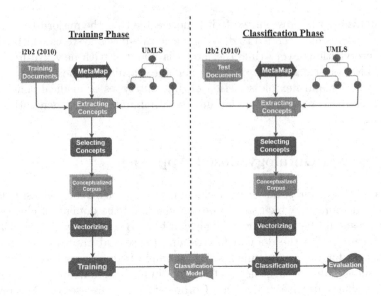

Fig. 1. The flowchart of the architecture of using MetaMap and UMLS for text classification.

"[Intellectual Product]" concepts. Considering the medical domain and the type of the classes in the selected data set, we choose concepts that appear in the "[Disease or Syndrome]" or "[Sign or Symptom]" categories. First we identify these two categories which are in square brackets, then the phrase that is within the round parentheses at the same line will be extracted as the main phrase. For example, the phrase "Dyspnea" is extracted in line 19 of Fig. 2 for the phrase "shortness of breath". After finishing the concept selection step, the obtained phrases will be used instead of the original documents in the binary classification problem. In order to give weights to the extracted terms of the documents, TF-IDF is applied in the vectorization step and each document is represented as a vector of weights based on the TF-IDF function.

```
1   --------------------------------------------------------------------------------
2   Phrase: hyperlipidemia .
3   >>>>> Phrase
4   hyperlipidemia
5   <<<<< Phrase
6   >>>>> Mappings
7   Meta Mapping (1000):
8      1000   Hyperlipidaemia, NOS (Hyperlipidemia) [Disease or Syndrome]
9   Meta Mapping (1000):
10     1000   Hyperlipidemia (Serum lipids high (finding)) [Finding]
11  <<<<< Mappings
12  Processing 00000000.tx.7: MEDICATIONS ON ADMISSION : Lipitor , Flexeril ,
13  hydrochlorothiazide and Norvasc .
14  --------------------------------------------------------------------------------
15  Phrase: shortness of breath
16  >>>>> Phrase
17  shortness of breath
18  <<<<< Phrase
19  >>>>> Mappings
20  Meta Mapping (1000):
21     1000   SHORTNESS OF BREATH (Dyspnea) [Sign or Symptom]
22  Meta Mapping (1000):
23     1000   Shortness of breath (shortness of breath:-;Point in time:^Patient:-) [Clinical Attribute]
24  Meta Mapping (1000):
25     1000   Shortness of breath (How Often Shortness of Breath) [Intellectual Product]
26  <<<<< Mappings
27  --------------------------------------------------------------------------------
```

Fig. 2. A segment of returned results of extracted concepts using MetaMap.

Table 1. The extracted concepts of example sentences using MetaMap.

Sentences	Detected phrases	Extracted concepts	Selected
First sentence	Hyperlipidaemia	[Disease or Syndrome]	✓
		[Finding]	×
	Patient	[Patient or Disabled group]	×
	Lipitor	[Organic Chemical, Pharmacologic Substance]	×
	80%	[Quantitative Concept]	×
	mg++ increased	[Finding]	×
Second sentence	Progress note	[Clinical Attribute]	×
		[Intellectual Product]	×
	Patient chart	[Manufactured Object]	×
	Assisted living facility	[Healthcare Related Organization, Manufactured Object]	×
	Patient	[Patient or Disabled group]	×
	Shortness of breath	[Sign or Symptom]	✓
		[Clinical Attribute]	×
		[Intellectual Product]	×
	One day	[Temporal Concept]	×

2.2   Data Preprocessing and Labelling

The idea of the paper is tested on the 2010 i2b2 data set. This paper focuses on binary classification, so all the documents are labeled based on whether or not the Coronary Artery Disease (CAD) is present. Each document in the original data set has three files consisting of "Concepts.con", "Relations.rel", and "Assertions.ast" which were provided by the i2b2 organization for Relations Challenge. We used the content of "Assertions.ast" file of each document to determine the label of it. As shown in Fig. 3, there are a number of problem names inside each Assertion file. To label all of the documents, at the first step, all the lines of the file is searched for the "Coronary Artery Disease" phrase. If the phrase is found by the search, the second step will be checking whether the disease is present or not. If the name of illness appears with the phrase "present" in the same line, we will consider that the document is in the CAD class. By following this rule, all of the labels of 170 training documents and 256 test documents are extracted.

Fig. 3. A subpart of the Assertions file.

3   Results and Discussions

The performance of the proposed method is assessed on the 2010 i2b2 data set. Among all the topics, class CAD is considered to form a binary classification.

Five popular classifiers are used in the experimental comparison. The classifiers are Naive Bayes, Linear Support Vector Machine (SVM), K-Nearest Neighbor (KNN), Decision Tree and Logistic Regression. The performance of the classifiers are evaluated based on three main metrics (Precision, Recall, F1-measure) using micro-average and macro-average.

Some of the parameters of these classifiers are turned to get better results. For this purpose, the number of the neighbors in the KNN is set to 28 for the "n_neighbors" parameter. In the Decision Tree classifier, the maximum depth of the tree and the random number generator are set to 14 for the "max_depth" and 11 for the "random_state" parameters, respectively. The inverse of regularization strength in the Logistic Regression is set to "1e1" for the "C" parameter. Furthermore, early stopping rule is selected to avoid overfitting in training Linear SVM and Logistic Regression classifiers. Other parameters of the classifiers are their default values.

Table 2 compares the obtained micro-average and macro-average results of the classifiers without using MetaMap and with using MetaMap. The best results are highlighted in the table. It can be concluded from the experimental results that the accuracies of all classifiers are increased significantly after applying the proposed method. In Table 2, K-Nearest Neighbor using MetaMap achieved better performance (with 94.86% accuracy) in comparison with the other classifiers in micro-average results (F1-measure metric).

Table 2. The obtained results for the 2010 i2b2 data set.

Method	Without MetaMap			With MetaMap		
	Precision	Recall	F1-measure	Precision	Recall	F1-measure
Micro-average results						
Naive Bayes	77.47	77.47	77.47	81.42	81.42	81.42
Linear SVM	**87.35**	**87.35**	**87.35**	93.28	93.28	93.28
KNN	84.98	84.98	84.98	**94.86**	**94.86**	**94.86**
Decision tree	85.77	85.77	85.77	90.12	90.12	90.12
Logistic regression	86.96	86.96	86.96	92.89	92.89	92.89
Macro-average results						
Naive Bayes	50.55	50.20	48.33	68.50	62.21	64.00
Linear SVM	84.44	70.66	74.67	91.07	86.28	88.41
KNN	85.33	62.01	65.08	91.92	91.24	**91.58**
Decision tree	77.17	**74.47**	**75.67**	82.78	**91.51**	85.93
Logistic regression	**86.39**	68.02	72.31	**92.38**	83.64	87.15

By analyzing the two F1-measure columns of micro-average results in Table 2 as the classification accuracy, Naive Bayes and Decision Tree classifiers are improved approximately 4% using the proposed method. Furthermore, Linear

SVM and Logistic Regression achieved 6% more precision. The biggest improvement is achieved by K-Nearest Neighbor (10%). Overall, all of the learned models by utilizing the concept of phrases instead of the original documents achieved on average a 6.1% improvement in classifying the 2010 i2b2 data set. Moreover, the number of features has been reduced from 7554 to 788 by the conceptualization approach, which is about 90% reduction.

To further evaluate our approach, instead of the original training-testing split given by the data set, we used 10-fold cross validation. We shuffle the documents and run the experiment 30 times, and each time is 10-fold cross validation. We did significance test using the experiment results of the 30 runs. Table 3 details the mean and the standard deviation of the suggested method with MetaMap and the method without MetaMap over the i2b2 data set. The classification accuracy is the average of 30 times 10-fold cross validation test. The Wilcoxon signed ranks test is applied to check whether the proposed method has made significant difference in classification accuracy. According to Table 3, "T" column shows the significance test of the without MetaMap method against the suggested method, where "+" implies the proposed technique is significantly more accurate, "=" implies no significant difference, and "−" implies significantly less accurate.

Table 3. Comparison of classification accuracy and standard deviation averages using 30 independent runs. The highlighted entries are significantly better (Wilcoxon Test, $\alpha = 0.05$)

Dataset	Classifier	Without MetaMap	Highest Mean (Lowest STD)	With MetaMap	Highest Mean (Lowest STD)	T
2010 i2b2	Naive Bayes	80.49 ± 0.055	81.34(0.036)	**84.26 ± 0.053**	85.64(0.029)	+
	Linear SVM	88.96 ± 0.046	89.49(0.031)	**92.56 ± 0.038**	93.08(0.016)	+
	KNN	86.76 ± 0.051	87.80(0.023)	**91.61 ± 0.039**	92.82(0.028)	+
	Decision Tree	90.36 ± 0.037	92.60(0.016)	89.14 ± 0.042	91.39(0.029)	=
	Logistic Regression	88.51 ± 0.047	89.02(0.027)	**92.63 ± 0.038**	93.32(0.021)	+

From Table 3, it can be concluded that the proposed method is able to achieve considerably higher classification accuracy than the other method. Our approach gains significantly better classification accuracy in four cases. Only in the case of Decision Tree classifier, the method shows not significantly difference of classification accuracy.

For further analyzing the methods, we checked the outputs and detected two documents with names "0101.txt" and "0302.txt" and label CAD which all the classifiers in the method without MetaMap have been labeled incorrectly, whereas all of the classifiers in the proposed method have been labeled correctly. By checking carefully the documents, we found two main reasons for this case. The first reason is that our work decreases the number of noisy data significantly. It assists classifiers to learn better. The second reason is that the new method maps phrases to their concepts which are meaningful and most of the time shorter than the original phrases. Since all the words in the documents stand alone as features, a phrase consists of more than one word will lose its meaning.

4   Conclusion and Future Work

The current study proposed a medical ontology driven feature engineering approach to reduce the number of features as well as persist with meaningful features. In conjunction with the MetaMap tool, we map meaningful phrases in medical text to specific UMLS medical concepts. The related concepts to the problem domain are selected as features. The number of features is reduced significantly by selecting "Disease or Syndrome" and "Sign or Symptom" concepts, which are the most important in the domain of clinical notes. Experimental and statistical results show that the suggested approach can accomplish significantly better classification accuracy.

As our future work, we will consider relations between diseases and symptoms, and include the ones that are interconnected as pairs [3]. Furthermore, we are planning to use concepts of sentences instead of phrases as features, hopefully to further reduce the number of features and increase the accuracy. We will find temporal relations between events to increase the classification accuracy. Finally, all of the suggested ideas will apply on other data sets for further analysis.

References

1. Unified Medical Language System (UMLS®). http://www.nlm.nih.gov/research/umls/. Last updated 20 April 2016
2. Uzuner, Ö.: Recognizing obesity and comorbidities in sparse data. J. Am. Med. Inf. Assoc. **16**(4), 561–570 (2009)
3. Ernst, P., Siu, A., Weikum, G.: KnowLife: a versatile approach for constructing a large knowledge graph for biomedical sciences. BMC Bioinform. **16**(1), 157–169 (2015)

A Multi-tree Genetic Programming Representation for Melanoma Detection Using Local and Global Features

Qurrat Ul Ain[✉], Harith Al-Sahaf, Bing Xue, and Mengjie Zhang

Victoria University of Wellington, P.O. Box 600, Wellington 6140, New Zealand
{Qurrat.Ul.Ain,Harith.Al-Sahaf,Bing.Xue,Mengjie.Zhang}@ecs.vuw.ac.nz

Abstract. Melanoma is the deadliest type of skin cancer that accounts for nearly 75% of deaths associated with it. However, survival rate is high, if diagnosed at an early stage. This study develops a novel classification approach to melanoma detection using a multi-tree genetic programming (GP) method. Existing approaches have employed various feature extraction methods to extract features from skin cancer images, where these different types of features are used individually for skin cancer image classification. However they remain unable to use all these features together in a meaningful way to achieve performance gains. In this work, Local Binary Pattern is used to extract local information from gray and color images. Moreover, to capture the global information, color variation among the lesion and skin regions, and geometrical border shape features are extracted. Genetic operators such as crossover and mutation are designed accordingly to fit the objectives of our proposed method. The performance of the proposed method is assessed using two skin image datasets and compared with six commonly used classification algorithms as well as the single tree GP method. The results show that the proposed method significantly outperformed all these classification methods. Being interpretable, this method may help dermatologist identify prominent skin image features, specific to a type of skin cancer.

Keywords: Genetic programming · Image classification
Feature extraction · Feature selection · Melanoma detection

1 Introduction

Skin cancer is the most common form of cancer, accounting for at least 40% of cases globally [19]. Australia and New Zealand have one of the highest rates of skin cancer incidence in the world, almost four times the rates registered in the United States, the UK and Canada [19]. The worldwide continuous increase in incidence of melanoma and other skin cancers in recent years, its high mortality rate, painful biopsy procedures and their huge medical cost have made its early diagnosis an important priority of public health. The advancements in the areas of computer vision and machine learning facilitate earlier diagnosis of various

© Springer Nature Switzerland AG 2018
T. Mitrovic et al. (Eds.): AI 2018, LNAI 11320, pp. 111–123, 2018.
https://doi.org/10.1007/978-3-030-03991-2_12

skin cancers that require no biopsy. For skin cancer image classification, important characteristics for distinguishing between different cancer types, are based on dermoscopy criteria; the Asymmetry, Border, Color, and Diameter (ABCD) rule [20] and the 7-point check-list method [4]. These are the key medical properties that help dermatologists diagnose various types of skin cancers.

Genetic programming (GP) is a domain-independent method that genetically breeds a population of computer programs (models or trees) to solve a particular problem [9]. Specifically, GP iteratively transforms a population of computer programs into a new generation of programs by applying analogues of naturally occurring genetic operations [9] such as crossover, mutation and reproduction. GP automatically evolves a computer program or candidate solution to a problem in a tree-like structure where terminal nodes consist of features and internal nodes consist of functions. As not all features are important for classification, GP (with its implicit feature selection ability) picks the most prominent features at its terminals, having high discriminating ability between classes in its evolved solutions, which significantly impacts on achieving good performance.

Different from single-tree GP (STGP) which evolves one tree in an individual, GP can evolve an individual having more than one trees to solve a particular problem, which is termed as multi-tree GP (MTGP) [17]. In the literature, MTGP has been explored for multi-class classification [15], self-assembling swarm robots [10], constructing new redundant features to create benchmark datasets for feature selection [11], and automatically evolving image descriptors [3]. Multi-tree approaches on non-image classification datasets have been studied in the literature [10,11,15], however, they have not been investigated for complex image classification tasks such as melanoma image classification, where different kinds of features (based on local and global as well as color and texture information) are necessary to be incorporated in the evolved solution. Hence, for having enough informative features in terminal set, various kinds of stated features need to be employed. Moreover, with advancements in technology, various optical instruments are in use to capture skin cancer images such as dermatoscope and standard cameras. Images captured from different instruments might have different visual properties such as illumination, scale, and reflection, therefore, which feature extraction methods are suitable for which type of images (captured from different instruments) is still an open question. In such a scenario, a multi-tree approach having multiple trees each evolved using a different type of informative features is more convenient (appropriate) to employ.

The existing methods [6,21] have used deep Convolutional Neural Networks (CNNs). Although these methods have shown very good performance, they are implemented as a black-box, hence, are not interpretable. In assisting a dermatologist, these methods cannot suggest which features are critical in classifying skin cancer images. Moreover, the performance of CNN is generally constrained by data and can only classify well when provided sufficient training examples which leads to long computation time and requires huge computing resources. Some existing approaches [7,18] rely on extracting various kinds of features from skin cancer images and compared the performance of these features for image classification using commonly used machine learning classification algorithms.

Goals: This work develops a new multi-tree GP method for skin cancer image classification. Different from most existing methods, the proposed method aims at evolving a GP individual based on different types of texture, color, border shape and geometrical information features for skin cancer images taken from different optical instruments (specialized dermatosocope and standard camera). As compared to evolving models using only one type of feature, each individual includes multiple trees each of which evolves one type of features. By doing so, the proposed method is expected to automatically evolve a classification model, using the best type of features for the images. This work aims to address the following research question:

- Which type of the features are most prominent in providing good classification performance and why?
- Whether multi-tree GP approach can provide better discriminating ability as compared to single-tree GP (STGP) approach across different datasets?
- Whether the proposed GP method can outperform the other non-GP classification algorithms?
- How well this new method works as compared to existing GP skin cancer image classification methods? and
- Whether all type of features are contributing equally to classification performance or a specific type of feature has more distinguishing ability for an image dataset captured using a specific instrument?

2   Feature Extraction

Feature extraction is used to extract the image features, similar to those visually detected by dermatologists, that can accurately characterize a melanoma lesion [7]. In this work, we capture local information from images using LBP image descriptor [16] and global information using lesion color variation [18], and border shape features [7,13]. We have employed various types of features in order to analyze which type of features are more prominent in providing good classification ability for which type of images (dermoscopy and standard camera).

2.1   Local Binary Patterns (LBP)

LBP is a dense image descriptor for feature extraction, developed by Ojala et al. [16]. LBP scans an image pixel-by-pixel, using a sliding window of fixed radius. The central pixel value is computed based on the intensity values of surrounding pixels lying on the radius as depicted in Fig. 1. LBP generates a histogram (i.e. feature vector) from the computed values. The LBP descriptor is defined as:

$$LBP_{p,r} = \sum_{i=0}^{p-1} K(s_i - s_c)2^i \tag{1}$$

where p is the number of neighboring pixels, r is the radius, s_i and s_c are the intensity values of the ith neighbor and central pixel, respectively. $K(x)$ returns 0 if $x < 0$ and 1 otherwise. The size of feature vector can be reduced from 2^p bins to $p(p-1)+3$ bins using only uniform codes and putting all non-uniform codes in one bin. In skin cancer images, uniform codes can help detect streaks (line ends) and blobs (flat regions) which may add to performance gains.

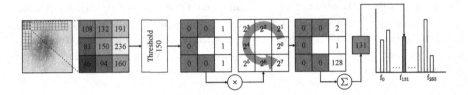

Fig. 1. The LBP process.

2.2 Lesion Color Variation

Color is an important characteristic often used by dermatologists to classify skin lesions as a significant component of the ABCD rule [20] and the 7-point checklist method [4]. Melanoma skin lesions are characterized by variation in color across the lesion area. This color variation induces high variance in the red, green, blue (RGB) color space. Therefore, features extracted from RGB color channels may have high discriminating ability between classes. To incorporate such global color features, the pixels in the segmented skin lesion of red, green and blue color channels are used. The mean (μ) and variance (σ) of each channel is calculated and represented as μR, μG, μB and σR, σG, σB. To capture complex non-uniform color distributions within the skin lesion region, mean ratios of the mean values are calculated, i.e., $\frac{\mu_R}{\mu_G}$, $\frac{\mu_R}{\mu_B}$, $\frac{\mu_G}{\mu_B}$. Variations in color of the skin lesion with respect to the surrounding skin is also considered. These features are calculated as $\frac{\mu_R}{\overline{\mu}_R}$, $\frac{\mu_G}{\overline{\mu}_G}$, $\frac{\mu_B}{\overline{\mu}_B}$, where $\overline{\mu}$ represents the mean value of surrounding/normal skin region. These features are adopted from [18].

2.3 Geometry-Based Features

Border information and geometrical properties of the shape of a lesion provide significant diagnostic information for detecting melanoma. According to the ABCD rule of dermoscopy [20], asymmetry is given the highest score among its four characteristics; asymmetry, border irregularity, color, and diameter. Here, we used some standard geometry features (area, perimeter, greatest diameter, circularity index, irregularity index A, irregularity index B, and asymmetry index) adopted from [13] complemented by others (shortest diameter, irregularity index C, irregularity index D, and major and minor asymmetry indices) adopted from [7]. Images within each dataset in this study have fairly similar spatial resolution; thus, there has been no scale issue for features such as area and perimeter. We extracted a set of 11 geometry-based features from each skin lesion image.

Several computer-aided diagnostic (CAD) systems [6,7,18,21] have been developed to help dermatologists in diagnosing *benign* and *malignant* skin lesions. However, these methods remain unable to design a way of using all these different type of features once, in order to get increased performance. Therefore, we become interested to formulate a method, which not only incorporates various types of features efficiently and effectively, but is also capable of evolving a classification model based on selecting prominent features.

3   The Proposed Method

The proposed method for melanoma detection from skin cancer images is described in this section. The overall structure is presented in Fig. 2.

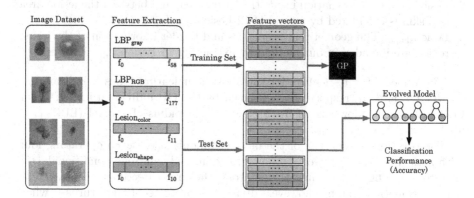

Fig. 2. The overall algorithm.

3.1   Representation

The images are first converted to feature vectors by employing the four feature extraction methods described in Sect. 2. These four types of features (LBP$_{gray}$, LBP$_{RGB}$, Lesion$_{color}$, and Lesion$_{shape}$) are fed into multi-tree GP method. Example of an individual in the proposed method is shown in Fig. 3. During the evolutionary process, the proposed method is designed in such a way that each tree can select from only one type of feature. In other words, our multi-tree GP method evolves an individual (model) which consists of four trees; one evolves using LBP$_{gray}$ features, second using LBP$_{RGB}$ features, third using Lesion$_{color}$ features and fourth using Lesion$_{shape}$ features as shown in Fig. 3.

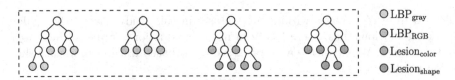

Fig. 3. An MTGP individual with different types of features at terminals of each tree.

3.2   Terminal Set and Function Set

The terminal set consists of four types of features, extracted from four different feature extraction methods as discussed in Sect. 2.

1. LBP_{gray}: A total of 59 LBP features are extracted from gray-level skin cancer images through the process shown in Fig. 1.
2. LBP_{RGB}: From each color channel (red, green, blue), 59 LBP features are extracted. These features are concatenated to make a total of 177 (= 59 LBP features × 3 channels) LBP_{RGB} features.
3. $Lesion_{color}$: Color variation inside the lesion area, and between the lesion area and skin is calculated by a total of 12 $Lesion_{color}$ features.
4. $Lesion_{shape}$: The geometrical properties and border information of the lesion region are included in our method by extracting 11 $Lesion_{shape}$ features.

The value of the ith feature for the above four feature types is indicated as Gi, Ri, Ci, and Si, respectively, as shown by the GP individual in Fig. 6. For LBP features, window size of 3×3 pixels and a radius of 1 pixel ($LBP_{8,1}$) is used.

The function set consists of the most commonly used seven operators; four arithmetic $\{+, -, \times, /\}$, two trigonometric $\{sin, cos\}$, and one conditional $\{if\}$ operator. Among the arithmetic operators, the first three operators have the same arithmetic meaning, however, division is protected that returns 0 when divided by 0. The *if* operator takes four inputs and returns the third input if the first input is greater than the second input; else, it returns the fourth input.

3.3   Crossover and Mutation

The genetic operators, such as crossover and mutation, are designed accordingly, which we call *same-index-crossover/mutation*. As presented in Fig. 4, the tree evolved from LBP_{RGB} features in Parent-1 can only crossover/mutate with the tree evolved from the same LBP_{RGB} features in Parent-2, and it cannot crossover/mutate with the other three trees evolved from LBP_{gray}, $Lesion_{color}$, $Lesion_{shape}$ features. At the end of the evolutionary process, the evolved GP individual consists of four trees each evolved using a single type of features.

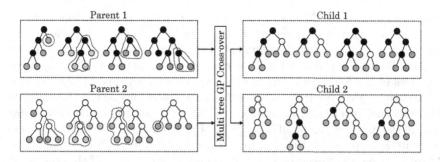

Fig. 4. The proposed same-index-crossover operator.

3.4 Fitness Function

For evaluating each individual in the proposed multi-tree GP approach, we have used a fitness function based on average of the classification accuracy of all the trees in one GP individual. The fitness is defined as

$$fitness = \frac{1}{m} \sum_{i=1}^{m} accuracy(T_i) \qquad (2)$$

$$accuracy(x) = \frac{1}{2} \left(\frac{TP_x}{TP_x + FN_x} + \frac{TN_x}{TN_x + FP_x} \right) \qquad (3)$$

where m shows the number of trees and T_i shows the ith tree in a GP individual and accuracy is the balanced accuracy among the two classes given by Eq. (3). TP refers to true positive, TN refers to true negative, FP refers to false positive, and FN refers to false negative. Using this fitness (Eq. (2)), we allow all the four trees to improve themselves during the evolutionary process, rather maximizing the accuracy of only one tree. When there is a class imbalance problem (different number of instances in different classes), it is more appropriate to use balanced accuracy rather than standard overall accuracy, defined as the ratio between correctly classified instances and total number of instances. After evolving a model on the training data, we know the different accuracies produced by each tree in a GP individual. Among these trees, we take the highest performing tree on the training set and test it on the test (unseen) data.

4   Experiment Design

For carrying out the experiments, the datasets are split by *10-fold cross validation*. Each dataset is divided into ten folds such that nine folds are used for training and the remaining one fold for testing. In our experiments, nine folds are used to evolve the model and one fold is used to test this evolved model for classification. The division of instances among the folds is random but it is ensured that the ratio of instances of each class in each fold is the same as in the original dataset. For our experiments, the number of GP runs is 30 and the results are reported in terms of the mean and standard deviation of the fitness values. For evolving an individual having four trees on the training data (9 folds), the fitness given in Eq. (2) is used, which computes the average of the accuracies of the four trees. This evolved model is then tested on the test data (1-fold) using only a single tree having the highest accuracy on the training data. This procedure is repeated 10 times to get the result for *10-fold cross validation* using all the different combinations of folds. Hence for the 30 GP runs, the above procedure is repeated 30 times to get 30 accuracy values each for training and test sets. In one set of experiments, the random seeds for each of the 30 runs are all different. The implementation of our multi-tree GP method is done using the Evolutionary Computing Java-based package [12].

4.1 Datasets

(a)   (b)

Fig. 5. Samples of (a) PH^2 dataset, and (b) Dermofit dataset.

PH^{2}Dataset: This dataset [14] contains dermoscopy images captured from a specialized instrument for skin cancer images called dermatoscope. Such high quality images are rich enough to investigate them for skin cancer classification. The dataset consists of 200 images that belong to three classes: common nevi (80 instances), atypical nevi (80 instances), and melanomas (40 instances). In dermatology, common nevi refers to non-disease lesion (mole), atypical nevi refers to a currently non-disease lesion, but may develop malignancy later, whereas melanoma is the diseased lesion. For our experiments on binary classification, 80 common nevi and 80 atypical nevi are used as *"benign"* class, and 40 melanoma are used as *"malignant"* class. Samples of the two classes are shown in Fig. 5(a).

***Dermofit* Dataset:** The Dermofit Image Library [5] is a collection of 1300 high quality skin lesion images collected under standardized conditions with internal color standards, captured from a standard camera. The lesions span across ten different classes, where each image has a gold standard diagnosis. Images consist of a snapshot of the lesion surrounded by normal skin. For evaluating our binary classification methods, we have used two classes; (1) Melanocytic Nevus (mole) with 331 images as *"benign"*, and (2) Malignant Melanoma with 76 images as *"malignant"*. Samples of the two classes are shown in Fig. 5(b).

4.2   GP Parameters

The parameter settings of our proposed multi-tree GP method are listed in Table 1. The evolutionary process keeps evolving until a maximum of 50 generations is reached or it stops when a perfect individual with accuracy 100% is found.

Table 1. Parameter settings of the GP method.

Parameter	Value	Parameter	Value	Parameter	Value
Generations	50	Crossover rate	0.80	Selection type	Tournament
Population size	1024	Mutation rate	0.19	Tournament size	7
Tree depth	2–6	Elitism	0.01	Initial population	Ramped half-and-half

4.3   Classification Methods for Comparison

To check the performance of our proposed multi-tree GP method on the test set, six classification methods are used: Naïve Bayes (NB), k-Nearest Neighbor (k-NN) where $k = 1$ (the closest neighbor), Support Vector Machines (SVMs), Decision Trees (J48), Random Forest (RF), and Multilayer Perceptron (MLP). These methods are implemented through the commonly used Waikato Environment for Knowledge Analysis (WEKA) package [8]. Similar to the existing approaches [1,2], we have used a Radial basis Function (RBF) kernel instead of the default linear kernel in WEKA. For MLP, the learning rate, momentum, training epochs and the number of hidden layers are set to 0.1, 0.2, 60, and 20, respectively. These parameters are specified empirically as they show the best performance amongst other settings.

5   Results and Discussions

5.1   Overall Results

The results of our experiments are presented in Table 2. Vertically, the table consists of three blocks where the first gives the results of the proposed multi-tree GP method (MTGP), the second shows results of other non-GP classification methods, and the third shows results of STGP methods each using one type of features. Horizontally, the table consists of 5 columns where first lists the classification algorithm, second and third show respectively the training and test performances for the PH^2 dataset, and fourth and fifth show these performances for the Dermofit dataset. The values of these results are represented as the mean and standard deviation of applying *10-fold cross validation* to the datasets. For all the GP methods (multi-tree and single-tree), the training and test processes are repeated 30 times, hence we get 30 accuracies for each method which are represented as mean and standard deviation ($\bar{x} \pm s$) in Table 2.

For making a clear comparison between the proposed method and other non-GP classification algorithms, and STGP methods, the results are also investigated using *Wilcoxon signed-rank test* with a significance level of 5%. This statistical test is applied on the test results to check which method has better ability to discriminate between benign and malignant classes. The symbols "+", "−" and "=" are used to represent significantly better, significantly worse and not significantly different performance, respectively, of the proposed MTGP method in comparison with other methods. For example, in case of the PH^2 dataset, the test performance of RF is represented as "76.56 ± 09.81", where the "+" sign represents that MTGP significantly outperformed the RF classification method. From the results of the statistical test, it has been observed that the proposed MTGP method not only outperformed all non-GP methods but also outperformed all STGP methods which proves the authenticity of our method.

Table 2. Comparison between the proposed Multi-tree GP method, the non-GP and single-tree GP Classification methods: Accuracy (%) on the training and test set of both datasets (represented in terms of mean accuracy and standard deviation ($\bar{x} \pm s$)).

		PH^2		Dermofit	
		Training	Test	Training	Test
MTGP		79.69 ± 1.35	**78.87 ± 2.92**	75.63 ± 0.99	**74.57 ± 1.86**
Non-GP methods	NB	93.85 ± 1.11	77.81 ± 08.44 +	86.42 ± 0.70	72.26 ± 11.62 +
	SVM	89.62 ± 1.37	70.00 ± 10.29 +	95.16 ± 0.84	70.02 ± 10.34 +
	KNN	100.0 ± 0.00	75.63 ± 14.71 +	100.0 ± 0.00	72.08 ± 09.52 +
	J48	97.05 ± 2.71	71.25 ± 11.08 +	97.09 ± 1.31	73.98 ± 10.65 +
	RF	100.0 ± 0.00	76.56 ± 09.81 +	99.93 ± 0.22	71.30 ± 09.80 +
	MLP	78.92 ± 1.23	78.44 ± 10.96 +	79.83 ± 1.95	73.00 ± 08.51 +
Single- tree GP	LBP$_{gray}$	82.84 ± 1.35	65.96 ± 3.96 +	73.41 ± 1.87	59.91 ± 3.57 +
	LBP$_{RGB}$	84.42 ± 1.43	73.87 ± 2.34 +	75.52 ± 1.62	63.26 ± 3.19 +
	Lesion$_{color}$	81.59 ± 2.31	65.70 ± 3.61 +	81.06 ± 1.31	74.13 ± 2.67 +
	Lesion$_{shape}$	78.06 ± 1.97	49.89 ± 5.34 +	74.74 ± 2.67	61.74 ± 7.06 +

In comparing the MTGP and STGP methods, we have seen that MTGP method has more potential to evolve good classification models that have more discriminating ability between classes. Moreover, among the two datasets, different types of features are prominent in playing the role of classification. For the PH^2 dataset, the LBP$_{RGB}$ features have shown highest performance (73.87 ± 2.34) among the four STGP methods. This shows that for images captured from specialized instruments (such as in PH^2 dataset), LBP$_{RGB}$ has the most potential to discriminate between "*benign*" and "*malignant*" classes. Whereas, for images captured from standard camera (such as in Dermofit dataset), the Lesion$_{color}$ feature has produced best results (74.13 ± 2.67) among the four type of features. Hence we can say that images captured from different instruments require different feature extraction methods to obtain information distinguishing between classes. We have also seen such a trend while evolving an individual using our multi-tree approach. Among all the four trees, on the PH^2 dataset LBP$_{\text{RGB}}$ features gave highest accuracy most of the time and in case of evolving an individual on the Dermofit dataset, the tree representing Lesion$_{\text{color}}$ features has the highest accuracy. We used the highest performing tree to check the performance on the unseen data. It is evident from the results of STGP methods for both datasets that selecting an appropriate feature extraction method is critical in evolving good classification models. The existing approaches to skin cancer image classification using GP [1,2] have used STGP methods and employed only a single dataset to test their performance. Our MTGP method has outperformed both of the existing methods in terms of classification performance.

5.2   Further Analysis

To see why our proposed MTGP method can achieve good performance, we show a good evolved GP individual (Fig. 6) with four trees evolved using the four types of features (a) LBP$_{\text{gray}}$, (b) LBP$_{\text{RGB}}$, (c) Lesion$_{\text{color}}$, and (d) Lesion$_{\text{shape}}$) having 80.32% accuracy on the test data. This individual is taken from the PH^2 experiments. In Fig. 6, white nodes represent functions and colored nodes represent terminals. While evolving this model on the training data, the individual accuracy values for LBP$_{\text{gray}}$ tree, LBP$_{\text{RGB}}$ tree, Lesion$_{\text{color}}$ tree, and Lesion$_{\text{shape}}$ tree are 76.74%, 77.08%, 70.49% and 65.63%, respectively. As discussed earlier in this section, for PH^2 dataset LBP$_{\text{RGB}}$ features have played the most prominent role in classification as compared to other feature types. This shows that for this dataset, local pixel-based features having color information can extract good information from images about the presence/absence of melanoma. Also the two feature types (Lesion$_{\text{color}}$ and Lesion$_{\text{shape}}$) which cover the global properties like color variation between lesion area and skin region, and border shape are not as good as LBP feature types which have the local pixel-based information.

From Fig. 6(a) in the LBP$_{\text{gray}}$ tree, the features $G50$ and $G12$ get selected 3 and 2 times, respectively, whereas the expression $G14$–$G10$ appears 2 times, which shows that these features have high discriminating ability. Among a total of 177 LBP$_{\text{RGB}}$ features, a tree (Fig. 6(b)) constructed from only four dominant features (R161, R79, R97, R31) has shown 77.08% accuracy on the training data. This is the highest performing tree among the four trees in this individual, hence applied on the test data and achieved an accuracy of 80.32%. In Lesion$_{\text{color}}$ tree (Fig. 6(c)), C6 and C11 (corresponding to $\frac{\mu_R}{\mu_G}$ and $\frac{\mu_B}{\bar{\mu}_B}$) showing the two ratios between mean of (1) red channel lesion area and green channel lesion area, and (2) blue channel lesion area and blue channel skin area, are significant. In Lesion$_{\text{shape}}$ tree (Fig. 6(d)), S2, S5, S7, S8, S9, and S10 are selected which corresponds to greatest diameter, irregularity indices A, C and D, minor and major asymmetry indices, and Asymmetry Index. These border shape features can provide significant knowledge to the dermatologist in making a diagnosis.

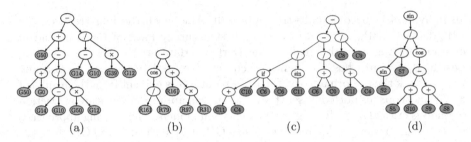

Fig. 6. A good evolved GP individual for PH^2 dataset using (a) LBP$_{\text{gray}}$, (b) LBP$_{\text{RGB}}$, (c) Lesion$_{\text{color}}$, and (d) Lesion$_{\text{shape}}$ features. (Color figure online)

6   Conclusions

This work has developed a novel method for skin cancer image classification using multi-tree Genetic Programming. The proposed method works by incorporating various types of local and global features extracted from skin cancer images that have information regarding pixel-based gray-level and RGB characteristics, variation in color across the image (inside and between the lesion and skin regions) and geometrical border shape properties. These four type of features are provided to multi-tree GP by designing *same-index-crossover/mutation* such that during the evolutionary process, same type of features undergo crossover/mutation in order to avoid mixing of different features in one tree. Our method has outperformed all the most commonly used classification algorithms and all the single-tree GP methods showing evidence of good discriminating ability between *"malignant"* and *"benign"* skin lesions. We have also found an interesting behavior for selecting a suitable feature extraction method for particular type of images captured from a specific instrument. The local pixel-based features have more potential for classifying dermoscopy images, however global color variation and geometrical shape features provide good discriminating ability between classes for skin cancer images captured from standard camera.

In the future, we would like to explore GP not only for performing classification but also employing feature extraction inside it's multi-tree individual directly from skin cancer images. Moreover, for real-world images, how to cope with reducing noise without losing informative features, is still an open issue.

References

1. Ain, Q.U., Xue, B., Al-Sahaf, H., Zhang, M.: Genetic programming for skin cancer detection in dermoscopic images. In: Proceedings of the 2017 Congress on Evolutionary Computation, pp. 2420–2427. IEEE (2017)
2. Ain, Q.U., Xue, B., Al-Sahaf, H., Zhang, M.: Genetic programming for feature selection and feature construction in skin cancer image classification. In: Geng, X., Kang, B.-H. (eds.) PRICAI 2018. LNCS (LNAI), vol. 11012, pp. 732–745. Springer, Cham (2018). https://doi.org/10.1007/978-3-319-97304-3_56

3. Al-Sahaf, H., Xue, B., Zhang, M.: A multitree genetic programming representation for automatically evolving texture image descriptors. In: Shi, Y. (ed.) SEAL 2017. LNCS, vol. 10593, pp. 499–511. Springer, Cham (2017). https://doi.org/10.1007/978-3-319-68759-9_41

4. Argenziano, G., Fabbrocini, G., et al.: Epiluminescence microscopy for the diagnosis of doubtful melanocytic skin lesions: comparison of the ABCD rule of dermatoscopy and a new 7-point checklist based on pattern analysis. Archiv. Dermatol. **134**(12), 1563–1570 (1998)

5. Ballerini, L., Fisher, R.B., Aldridge, B., Rees, J.: A color and texture based hierarchical k-NN approach to the classification of non-melanoma skin lesions. In: Celebi, M., Schaefer, G. (eds.) Color Medical Image Analysis. LNCVB, vol. 6, pp. 63–86. Springer, Heidelberg (2013). https://doi.org/10.1007/978-94-007-5389-1_4

6. Esteva, A., Kuprel, B., et al.: Dermatologist-level classification of skin cancer with deep neural networks. Nature **542**(7639), 115–118 (2017)

7. Garnavi, R., Aldeen, M., Bailey, J.: Computer-aided diagnosis of melanoma using border-and wavelet-based texture analysis. IEEE Trans. Inf. Technol. Biomed. **16**(6), 1239–1252 (2012)

8. Hall, M., Frank, E., et al.: The WEKA data mining software: an update. SIGKDD Explor. Newslett. **11**(1), 10–18 (2009)

9. Koza, J.R., Poli, R.: A genetic programming tutorial (2003)

10. Lee, J.H., Ahn, C.W., An, J.: An approach to self-assembling swarm robots using multitree genetic programming. Sci. World J. **2013**, 10 (2013)

11. Lensen, A., Xue, B., Zhang, M.: Generating redundant features with unsupervised multi-tree genetic programming. In: Castelli, M., Sekanina, L., Zhang, M., Cagnoni, S., García-Sánchez, P. (eds.) EuroGP 2018. LNCS, vol. 10781, pp. 84–100. Springer, Cham (2018). https://doi.org/10.1007/978-3-319-77553-1_6

12. Luke, S.: Essentials of Metaheuristics, 2nd edn. Lulu, Morrisville (2013). http://cs.gmu.edu/~sean/book/metaheuristics/

13. Maglogiannis, I., Doukas, C.N.: Overview of advanced computer vision systems for skin lesions characterization. IEEE Trans. Inf. Technol. Biomed. **13**(5), 721–733 (2009)

14. Mendonça, T., Ferreira, et al.: PH2-a dermoscopic image database for research and benchmarking. In: Proceedings of the 35th Annual International Conference of the IEEE Engineering in Medicine and Biology Society, pp. 5437–5440 (2013)

15. Muni, D.P., Pal, N.R., Das, J.: A novel approach to design classifiers using genetic programming. IEEE Trans. Evol. Comput. **8**(2), 183–196 (2004)

16. Ojala, T., Pietikäinen, M., Harwood, D.: A comparative study of texture measures with classification based on featured distributions. Pattern Recogn. **29**(1), 51–59 (1996)

17. Oltean, M., Dumitrescu, D.: Multi expression programming. J. Genetic Program. Evol. Mach. (2002). Kluwer, second tour of review

18. Satheesha, T., Satyanarayana, D., et al.: Melanoma is skin deep: a 3D reconstruction technique for computerized dermoscopic skin lesion classification. IEEE J. Transl. Eng. Health Med. **5**, 1–17 (2017)

19. Stewart, B.W., Wild, C.P., et al.: World cancer report 2014. Health (2017)

20. Stolz, W., Riemann, A., et al.: ABCD rule of dermatoscopy: a new practical method for early recognition of malignant-melanoma. Eur. J. Dermatol. **4**(7), 521–527 (1994)

21. Yu, L., Chen, H., Dou, Q., Qin, J., Heng, P.A.: Automated melanoma recognition in dermoscopy images via very deep residual networks. IEEE Trans. Med. Imaging **36**(4), 994–1004 (2017)

Impacts of Climate Change
and Socioeconomic Development
on Electric Load in California

Jie Shi and Nanpeng Yu[(✉)]

University of California Riverside, Riverside, CA 92501, USA
nyu@ece.ucr.edu

Abstract. In order to develop policies to mitigate the impacts of climate change on energy consumption, it is imperative to understand and quantify the impacts of climate change and socioeconomic development on residential electric load. This paper develops a feed-forward neural network to model the complex relationships among socioeconomic factors, weather, distributed renewable generation, and electric load at the census block group level. The influence of different explanatory variables on electric load is quantified through the layer-wise relevance propagation method. A case study with 4,000 census block groups in southern California is conducted. The results show that temperature, housing units, and solar PV systems have the highest influence on net electric load. The scenario analysis reveals that net electric load of disadvantaged communities are much more sensitive to rising temperature than the non-disadvantaged ones. Hence, they are much more vulnerable to climate change.

Keywords: Climate change · Disadvantaged community
Electric load · Layer-wise relevance propagation · Socioeconomic factors

1 Introduction

One of the most compelling evidences for global climate change is the rapid rise in global temperature. Around the world, people are already experiencing the effects of climate change. For example, the rise in temperature will lead to increased cooling need and electricity consumption from air conditioning systems. It is also expected that the disadvantaged communities will be disproportionately affected by climate change. In this paper, the impacts of climate change and socioeconomic development on residential net electric load in southern California are explored. In particular, we intend to answer questions such as whether electricity affordability will get worse for disadvantaged communities due to climate change and how income growth affects electricity consumption

The authors would like to thank Raymond Johnson from Southern California Edison for helpful discussions and supplying smart meter data.

for disadvantaged and non-disadvantaged communities. In addition, we are interested in modeling the relationships among socioeconomic factors, meteorological variables, renewable energy interconnection, and electric load.

Previous studies have shown that weather conditions significantly affect residential electric load [9]. The relationship between socioeconomic factors and residential electric load has been studied extensively in the past decades. A comprehensive review can be found in [5]. However, little work has been done to compare the impacts of climate change and socioeconomic development on electricity consumption of communities with different backgrounds. In addition, there has been no rigorous analysis to quantify the influence proportion of various input factors on residential electric load. Lastly, most of the previous works focus on studying sample data of individual households instead of electricity consumption at the community level such as census block groups (CBGs).

This work fills the knowledge gap by developing a feed-forward neural network (FNN) to capture the relationships among weather, socioeconomic variables, and net electric loads at the CBG level. The layer-wise relevance propagation (LRP) method is used to quantify the impacts of input factors on residential electric load. Finally, a comprehensive case study is conducted in southern California to analyze the impacts of climate change and socioeconomic development on electric loads of both poor and affluent communities.

The rest of this paper is organized as follows. Section 2 introduces our methodology to explore the relationships among climate change, socioeconomic factors, and electric load. Section 3 presents the case study with 4,000 CBGs in southern California. The conclusions are given in Sect. 4.

2 Methodology

To quantify the impacts of climate change and socioeconomic development on net electric load, we first establish a FNN to estimate the average electric loads of local communities based on census, weather, and distributed renewable generation data. The relative importance of each input feature is then measured by the LRP method [2].

2.1 Feed-Forward Neural Network

The proposed FNN is composed of four layers of neurons. The dimension of input layer is determined by the number of input features. The model output is the average electric load of a geographic region. Thus, the output layer's dimension is 1. There are two hidden layers with ReLU as activation functions. The dimension of each hidden layer is 200. We use Adam [6] optimizer to train the FNN. The early stopping procedure is adopted to avoid over-fitting.

2.2 Layer-Wise Relevance Propagation

The idea of LRP is to decompose the output value into a set of scores measuring input features' contributions to the output [2]. All neurons in each layer of FNN are assigned with relevance scores. Let $g(\cdot)$ be a trained FNN and x be the input features. The following equation needs to be satisfied for relevance propagation.

$$\sum_{p=1}^{L_1} R_p^1 = \sum_{n=1}^{L_2} R_n^2 = \cdots \sum_{i=1}^{L_k} R_i^k = \cdots = g(x) \tag{1}$$

where R_i^k is the relevance score of the ith neuron in the kth layer. L_k is the number of neurons in the kth layer. Let $R_{i \leftarrow j}^{k \leftarrow k+1}$ be the relevance score passed from the jth neuron in the $(k+1)$th layer to the ith neuron in the kth layer. Then, a sufficient but not necessary condition for Eq. (1) to be satisfied is $R_i^k = \sum_j R_{i \leftarrow j}^{k \leftarrow k+1}$ and $\sum_i R_{i \leftarrow j}^{k \leftarrow k+1} = R_j^{k+1}$. Specifically, $R_{i \leftarrow j}^{k \leftarrow k+1}$ is defined as follows

$$R_{i \leftarrow j}^{k \leftarrow k+1} = \begin{cases} \dfrac{x_i^k \omega_{i,j}^{k \rightarrow k+1}}{\sum_i x_i^k \omega_{i,j}^{k \rightarrow k+1} + b_j^{k+1} + \epsilon} \cdot R_j^{k+1}, & \sum_i x_i^k \omega_{i,j}^{k \rightarrow k+1} + b_j^{k+1} \geq 0 \\ \dfrac{x_i^k \omega_{i,j}^{k \rightarrow k+1}}{\sum_i x_i^k \omega_{i,j}^{k \rightarrow k+1} + b_j^{k+1} - \epsilon} \cdot R_j^{k+1}, & \sum_i x_i^k \omega_{i,j}^{k \rightarrow k+1} + b_j^{k+1} < 0 \end{cases} \tag{2}$$

where ϵ is a small value used to avoid excessively small denominator. x_i^k is the activated value of ith neuron in kth layer. $\omega_{i,j}^{k \rightarrow k+1}$ is the $\{i, j\}$ element of weight matrix $W^{k \rightarrow k+1}$. b_j^{k+1} is the jth element of bias vector b^{k+1}.

The interpretation of above formulation is stated as follows. The relevance score passed between two neurons in adjacent layers is in proportional to the previous-layer neuron's contribution on latter-layer neuron's pre-activated value. By iterating Eq. (2) and $R_i^k = \sum_j R_{i \leftarrow j}^{k \leftarrow k+1}$, we can finally transform the output value into relevance scores of input features. Note that these scores can be either positive or negative. Therefore, we introduce the influence proportion $I_d = |R_d^1| / \sum_{p=1}^{L_1} |R_p^1|$ to measure the impacts of different input features on output, where I_d is the influence proportion of the dth input feature.

3   Case Study of Southern California

In this section, a case study is conducted for southern California to investigate the impacts of climate change and social economic factors on residential electric load. The residential electric load and solar PV interconnection data are provided by Southern California Edison (SCE) and aggregated at the CBG level. The census and weather related data are gathered through the National Historical Geographic Information System (NHGIS) and the Weather Underground's website. The details of the data used in the case study will be discussed in Subsect. 3.1. The forecasting performance of the data-driven electric load model and the importance of input features are reported in Subsect. 3.2. Finally, scenario analysis is carried out in Subsect. 3.3 to investigate the impacts of climate change and socioeconomic factors on electric load.

3.1   Data Description

Three categories of input data are used in the case study: census data, weather data, and solar PV data. The subcategories and input features of the three data categories are shown in Table 1.

Census Data: The smallest geographic area for which the Census Bureau publishes sample data is CBG, which is the next level above census block in the geographic hierarchy. Hence, the latest census data from 2011 to 2015 at the CBG level is used in the case study. We extract 16 input features from 8 different subcategories of the raw data as presented in Table 1. The input features of Age, Income, Education, and Employment record the proportion of residents in corresponding ranges. For each subcategory of these four, the input features sum up to 1. Therefore, one input feature can be omitted for each subcategory to avoid redundancy.

Table 1. Final input features of FNN

Data category	Subcategory	Input features & Ranges
Census	Age	*Childhood age (5 yrs old and below)*
		School age (6 to 17 yrs old)
		Working age (18 to 61 yrs old)
		Retired age (62 yrs old and above)
	Income	*Low-income ($0-$34,999)*
		Middle-income ($35,000-$149,999)
		High-income ($150,000+)
	Education	*No college experience, College experience, Bachelor, Graduate*
	Employment	*Employed, Unemployed, Military service, Not in labor force*
	Housing units	*Number of housing units, Occupancy rate*
	Children	*Proportion of households with children under 18*
	Rooms	*Average number of rooms*
	Population	*Number of residents in CBG*
Weather	Temperature	*Average hourly temperature*
		Average daily peak temperature
		Proportion of cooling degree days
Solar PV	Solar PV	*Solar PV capacity, Solar installation rate*

Weather Data: The historical hourly temperature data of cities in southern California in 2015 are collected from Weather Underground. The temperature data are then mapped to all the CBGs. Three weather related features/variables

are extracted from the raw hourly temperature data. *Average hourly tempera-*
ture: The average hourly temperature of a CBG. *Average daily peak temperature*:
The average daily peak temperature of a CBG. *Proportion of cooling degree days*:
The proportion of cooling degree days of a CBG [1].

Electric Load and Solar PV Interconnection Data: The hourly electric
load data at the household level are collected by smart meters in SCE's service
territory in 2015. Note that for buildings which are equipped with solar PV
systems, the net electric loads are recorded by the smart meters. The electric
load data are then aggregated to the CBG level. For each CBG, the average
hourly electric load is calculated and used as the output data of FNN model.

The solar PV interconnection data as of the beginning of 2015 are gathered
by SCE for the residential customers in its service territory. The following two
input features are extracted from the raw data files. *Solar PV capacity*: The sum
of solar PV systems' capacities in a CBG. *Solar installation rate*: The proportion
of residential customers who installed solar PV systems in a CBG.

3.2   Model Performance and Feature Importance Analysis

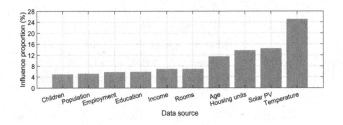

Fig. 1. The influence proportions of all data subcategories.

A FNN is trained to capture the relationships among census, temperature,
solar PV systems, and electric load data. The input layer of the neural network
consists of 16 input features from the census data, 3 input features from the
weather data, and 2 input features from the solar PV interconnection data as
shown in Table 1. The output variable is the average hourly electric load of a
CBG.

The entire dataset contains 4,000 CBGs in SCE's service territory. It is
divided into three datasets: training set (2,400 CBGs), validation set (600
CBGs), and testing set (1,000 CBGs). Early stopping procedure is carried out
by evaluating the generalization error for the validation set. Five different sets of
initial FNN weights are used as the starting points to train the FNN. The initial
weights are randomly generated using "Xavier" initialization [3]. The forecasting

---

[1] The cooling degree days are defined as the days with average temperature (highest
value plus lowest value divided by two) above 65 °F.

performance of the FNN is evaluated by measuring the model's prediction error for average electric loads of CBGs on the testing dataset. The mean absolute percentage error (MAPE) and the root mean square error (RMSE) of prediction are used as the evaluation metrics. The average MAPE across five fitted model is 14.88% and the average RMSE is 104.85 kWh. The prediction accuracy is decent given that the geographic area of a CBG is often small.

We select the model with the lowest MAPE for the testing set as the final model. The influence proportions of all input features are calculated via the LRP algorithm discussed in Sect. 2. The influence proportions of input features of the same data subcategory are merged together to measure its total influence and the results are depicted in Fig. 1. As shown in the figure, temperature, housing units, and solar PV interconnection data are three most important inputs which determine the average electric load in the CBG. Together, they account for nearly 60% of the total influence. Given that HVAC systems account for around 50% of the total building energy consumption [8] and there is a significant need for space-cooling during summer in southern California, it is not surprising to see that temperature related variables have the highest impact on the residential electric load. Similarly, it is intuitive to see that the number of housing units is directly related to the amount of electric load in a CBG. Lastly, solar PV system can generate significant amount of electricity to offset the electric load. Hence, it is also an important factor in determining the net load.

3.3   Scenario Analysis

In this subsection, we investigate the impacts of climate change and socioeconomic development on residential electricity consumption in California. In particular, we explore if the impacts are different for disadvantaged and non-disadvantaged communities using the FNN trained in Sect. 3.2.

Impacts of Household Income Growth on Electric Load: The U.S. gross median household income grew 46% between 1979 and 2011 after adjusting for inflation. To explore the impacts of income growth on electricity consumption, we gradually increase the average household income for each CBG by $30,000 in 30 steps from the current income level. The 4,000 CBGs in southern California are divided into two communities: disadvantaged communities (DACs) and non-disadvantaged communities (non-DACs). According to the definitions of the California Environmental Protection Agency (CalEPA) [1], DACs are communities burdened the most by environmental pollution, socioeconomic stress, and health issues. These areas typically possess concentrations of people with low income, high unemployment rate, and low education levels. 1,018 out of 4,000 CBGs in this study are DACs and the rest are non-DACs.

The impacts of income growth on electric load for both DACs and non-DACs are depicted in Fig. 2(a). As shown in the figure, the households of non-DACs on average consume more electricity than that of DACs. The electric loads of both DACs and non-DACs increase when the household income grows. The percentage change in electricity consumption for DACs is much higher than that of the non-DACs given the same amount of household income growth. This observation implies that the residents in DACs can afford to consume more electricity compared to the baseline consumption with the same income growth.

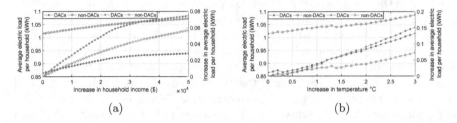

(a)   (b)

Fig. 2. Impacts of income growth and temperature rise on residential electricity consumption of DACs and non-DACs. (a) Income growth. (b) Temperature rise.

Impacts of Rising Temperature on Electric Load: Due to the global warming and urban heat island effect, the average temperature is expected to rise in California. It is projected that residents of California will, on average, face a 2.4 °C temperature increase by 2060s [7]. The coastal regions will likely experience less warming thanks to the moderating effect of ocean, while the residents of the inland areas, such as the Inland Empire, are expected to suffer summers that are more than 3 °C hotter. To study the impacts of rising temperature on net electric loads in different regions, the 4,000 CBGs in southern California are clustered by climate zones (CZs) defined by California Energy Commission (CEC) [4]. Based on average temperatures in summer and winter, CEC partitions California's territory into 16 distinct CZs. Each CZ has reasonably consistent weather and easily recognized boundaries. There are only 9 CZs in the study area of southern California. Hence, the 4,000 CBGs are separated into 9 clusters. CZ 5 is not included in the analysis due to its small number of CBGs. To explore the impact of rising temperature on electricity consumption, we gradually increase the average temperature by 3 °C in 30 steps from the current level. The changes in forecasted CBG electric loads in different CZs with the rising temperature are shown in Fig. 3(a) and (b). As shown in Fig. 3(a) the inland areas such as CZ 13, 14, and 15, have the highest electricity consumption per household. In addition, the electric loads in all CZs are expected to increase with rising temperature. As shown in Fig. 3(b), the increase in electricity usage for residents in inland areas are much higher than those in the coastal areas. Hence, they are more vulnerable to the climate change.

Similarly, the impacts of rising temperature on DACs and non-DACs are also evaluated separately for comparison purposes. As shown in Fig. 2(b), the electricity consumption of both DACs and non-DACs in California increase with temperature. Compared to the non-DACs, the electricity consumptions of DACs are, on average, much more sensitive to the change in temperature. There are two possible reasons why this is so. First, the insulations of buildings in DACs

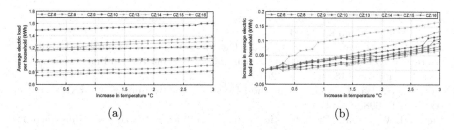

(a)   (b)

Fig. 3. Impact of temperature increase on electric loads of different climate zones.

are typically poorer than that of non-DACs. Second, low income communities typically have less vegetation coverage, thereby enduring a higher land surface temperature in summer. The poor insulation and vegetation coverage require longer running time for air conditioning units and lead to higher electricity consumption and bills. Given that the residents of low-income communities pay a much higher percent of their income on electricity bill, and the electricity consumptions of DACs are more sensitive to rising temperature, we can conclude that DACs are much more vulnerable to climate change and rising temperatures.

4   Conclusion

This paper models the nonlinear relationships among residential electric load, socioeconomic factors, weather variables, and distributed renewable generation with a FNN. The relative importance of explanatory variables in determining the electric load is estimated by the LRP method. A case study with 4,000 CBGs in southern California is conducted. The results show that temperature, housing units, and solar PV interconnection are the most influential determinants for net electric load at the CBG level. The scenario analysis demonstrates that the electricity consumption of poor Californian communities increases much faster than that of the affluent communities when temperature rises. Given that the residents of low-income communities pay a much higher percent of their income on electricity bill, they are much more vulnerable to climate change. Therefore, it is crucial for policy makers to make targeted investments in disadvantaged communities to mitigate the adverse effects of climate change.

References

1. Designation of disadvantaged communities pursuant to senate bill 535 (2017). https://calepa.ca.gov/envjustice/ghginvest
2. Bach, S., Binder, A., Montavon, G., Klauschen, F., Müller, K.R., Samek, W.: On pixel-wise explanations for non-linear classifier decisions by layer-wise relevance propagation. PloS One **10**(7), e0130140 (2015)
3. Glorot, X., Bengio, Y.: Understanding the difficulty of training deep feedforward neural networks. In: Proceedings of the Thirteenth International Conference on Artificial Intelligence and Statistics, pp. 249–256 (2010)

4. Hall, V.T., Deter, E.R.: California climate zone descriptions for new buildings. California Energy Commission (1995)
5. Jones, R.V., Fuertes, A., Lomas, K.J.: The socio-economic, dwelling and appliance related factors affecting electricity consumption in domestic buildings. Renew. Sustain. Energy Rev. **43**, 901–917 (2015)
6. Kingma, D., Ba, J.: Adam: A method for stochastic optimization. ArXiv Preprint ArXiv:1412.6980 (2014)
7. Pierce, D.W., et al.: Probabilistic estimates of future changes in California temperature and precipitation using statistical and dynamical downscaling. Clim. Dyn. **40**(3–4), 839–856 (2013)
8. Shi, J., Yu, N., Yao, W.: Energy efficient building HVAC control algorithm with real-time occupancy prediction. Energy Procedia **111**, 267–276 (2017)
9. Yan, Y.Y.: Climate and residential electricity consumption in Hong Kong. Energy **23**(1), 17–20 (1998)

Implementing Propositional Networks on FPGA

Cezary Siwek[1], Jakub Kowalski[1(✉)], Chiara F. Sironi[2],
and Mark H. M. Winands[2]

[1] Institute of Computer Science, Faculty of Mathematics and Computer Science,
University of Wrocław, Wrocław, Poland
`ave@cezar.info, jko@cs.uni.wroc.pl`
[2] Games and AI Group, Department of Data Science and Knowledge Engineering,
Maastricht University, Maastricht, The Netherlands
`{c.sironi,m.winands}@maastrichtuniversity.nl`

Abstract. The speed of game rules processing plays an essential role in
the performance of a General Game Playing (GGP) agent. Propositional
Networks (propnets) are an example of a highly efficient representation
of game rules. So far, in GGP, only software implementations of propnets have been proposed and investigated. In this paper, we present the
first implementation of propnets on Field-Programmable Gate Arrays
(FPGAs), showing that they perform between 25 and 58 times faster
than a software-propnet for most of the tested games. We also integrate
the FPGA-propnet within an MCTS agent, discussing the challenges of
the process, and possible solutions for the identified shortcomings.

Keywords: General Game Playing
Field-Programmable Gate Arrays · Propositional Networks
Monte Carlo Tree Search

1 Introduction

The aim of General Game Playing (GGP) [7] is to develop a program that can
play any arbitrary game at an expert level, given only its rules. Moreover, these
rules are previously unknown, and an agent has a limited time to process them
before the game begins. During the game, the time is also constrained, with
usually only a few seconds available to choose a move.

In GGP, it is impossible for the designers of the program to embed in the
agent existing knowledge about the game, as it is in the case of chess, checkers,
Go, and other standard AI challenges. As such, with the goal to create a universal
algorithm performing well in various situations and environments, the domain

J. Kowalski—Supported in part by the National Science Centre, Poland under project
number 2015/17/B/ST6/01893.
C. F. Sironi—Supported by the Netherlands Organisation for Scientific Research
(NWO) under the GoGeneral project, grant number 612.001.121.

T. Mitrovic et al. (Eds.): AI 2018, LNAI 11320, pp. 133–145, 2018.
https://doi.org/10.1007/978-3-030-03991-2_14

has been identified as a new grand challenge of Artificial Intelligence [6], and a special logic-based Game Description Language (GDL) has been designed to describe any deterministic, turn-based, finite game with perfect information [11].

Because of the generality, GGP benefits algorithms that are knowledge-free. As a result, the most successful approaches are based on the Monte Carlo Tree Search (MCTS) [4], the algorithm that apart from GGP [5] has proven itself in Go [17] and many other domains [3].

As the strength of game-playing search algorithms is usually closely correlated with their performance, it is crucial for the game reasoners to be as fast as possible. When in 1997 DEEP BLUE defeated Gary Kasparov, it was partially because of the hardware accelerators – Application Specific Integrated Circuits designed specifically for this system [9].

In GGP, as the quality of results obtained by MCTS depends on a number of performed simulations, much attention has been devoted to improving the speed of GDL resolution engines. This includes mainly fast, logically-optimized interpreters and compilers to low-level languages [10,19]. Propositional Networks (propnets) [14], are efficient representation of GDL reasoners, closely correlated to logic circuits. They can speed-up the state computation process by several orders of magnitude compared to non-optimized custom-made or Prolog-based GDL reasoners [18]; thus they are used by many successful GGP players.

In this paper, we present the first implementation of Propositional Networks on Field-Programmable Gate Arrays (FPGAs), the integrated circuits that can be reconfigured by the end-user. Thus, we were able to achieve performance impossible for the reasoners encoded as a software. Resulting FPGA-based reasoner computes game states mostly about 25–58 times faster than the optimized software propnet implementation described in [18].

To utilize this computational potential, we have implemented a working MCTS-based GGP player proof of concept, upon which we study and present shortcomings and effort required to construct a hardware-accelerated player.

2   Preliminaries

2.1   Game Description Language and Propositional Networks

GDL is a first order logic language proposed to represent game rules in GGP in a compact and modular format [11]. A state in GDL is represented as a set of true facts. Special keywords, described in Table 1, are used to define different game elements and the game dynamics. By processing the GDL game rules, a player is able to reconstruct the dynamics of a finite state machine for the game.

Propnets [14] are an alternative to GDL to represent the dynamics of a game, and any GDL game description can be converted into a propnet. Propnets are directed graphs where the components are either propositions or connectives. Each component has incoming arcs from its input components and outgoing arcs to its output components. The truth value of a component depends on the truth value of its inputs and is propagated to its outputs.

Table 1. Description of GDL keywords. $?f$ represents a fact.

Keyword	Description	Keyword	Description
$role(?r)$	$?r$ is a player in the game	$true(?f)$	$?f$ is true in current state
$init(?f)$	$?f$ is true in initial state	$next(?f)$	$?f$ is true in next state
$terminal$	current state is terminal	$does(?r, ?m)$	$?r$ plays move $?m$
$goal(?r, ?s)$	$?r$ gets score $?s$ in current state	$legal(?r, ?m)$	$?r$ can play move $?m$ in current state

There are four types of connectives: *and, or* and *not* logic gates, and *transitions*, identity gates that output their input value with one step delay. Propositions can be divided into three categories: *input*, that have no input components, *base*, that have one single *transition* as input, and all other propositions, identified as *view*. The truth values of *base* propositions represent the state of the game. Their input, the *transition*, controls their value for the next state. Having no inputs, *input* proposition have their value set by the game playing agent, that sets to true the one corresponding to the action he decides to play. *View* propositions express agents' goals, legal moves and terminality of game states.

A unique truth assignment to *base* propositions determines the unique truth values of *view* propositions. The combination of truth assignments to *base* and *input* proposition uniquely determines the truth assignment for the next state.

2.2 Monte Carlo Tree Search

MCTS [4] is a simulation-based search algorithm that incrementally builds a tree representation of the search space of the game. More precisely, it repeats the following four phases until a given search budget expires:

- Selection: the algorithm traverses the tree built so far. A *selection strategy* is used to choose which action to simulate in each visited node until a state not yet in the tree is reached. One of the most commonly used selection strategies is UCB1 [1], the same we use in our MCTS implementation.
- Expansion: the first visited state in the simulation that was not part of the tree yet, is added to the tree as a new node.
- Playout: starting from the state corresponding to the node added during expansion, a *playout strategy* is used to simulate the game until a terminal state or a certain depth is reached.
- Backpropagation: the result obtained at the end of the simulation is propagated back in the tree and used to update statistics about the visited moves.

2.3 Field-Programmable Gate Arrays

FPGAs are chips, whose logic is designed to be configured after they were manufactured or even embedded in the final product (hence *Field*). This allows fast prototyping of the Integrated Chips (ICs), creating small amounts of products with custom hardware, or even performing remote updates to the hardware in the end devices. FPGAs are made out of thousands of interconnected Universal

Logic Modules (ULMs), which can be individually programmed to perform simple logic operations and arbitrarily connected with each other. For specialized operations, this allows for a significant increase of computational speed and IO bandwidth against implementation in software.

Desired structure and behavior of the FPGA is usually written in a Hardware Description Language (HDL), like Verilog or VHDL. It resembles classic programming with expressions, statements and datatypes, but the execution flow is parallel rather than sequential, and there are explicit constructs to handle time.

FPGAs are used in many domains, including communication, image processing, control engineering, networks, cryptography, mathematics, neuro-computing, etc. A comprehensive survey on FPGA applications can be found in [13].

Related research, mostly concerns using FPGAs to implement game engines, especially board games [12], to accelerate computations and thus improve the performance of the agents. This includes FPGA-based approaches to play, e.g., chess [2], Othello [20], and Go [8].

3   Methodology

We present our approach, that given an arbitrary GDL game generates FPGA-based reasoner and embeds it into the MCTS algorithm. The entire random playout phase, has been implemented within a reasoner component. This significantly reduces the number of tree-to-reasoner calls, reducing the overhead, and improving the overall performance of the system.

We based our solution on Propositional Networks. They are a fast reasoning mechanism on their own, and because their structure consists mainly of standard logic gates, we can almost directly mirror their computational logic in a hardware chip. This approach can increase performance by orders of magnitude because of zero computational overhead and simultaneous propagation of signals. The latter is essential, as the simulation speed is dictated by the clock frequency, which is in turn constrained by the longest component path, not the total number of propnet components.

FPGAs are especially well suited to be used as a GGP reasoner because their reprogramming capability allows for switching between various (previously known) games on the fly. The Cyclone V chip we are using is even more up to the task because it integrates a dual core ARM computer running GNU/Linux operating system that can communicate with the FPGA through fast shared memory. We run the player search algorithm on this ARM computer, and the intense reasoning computations are delegated to the FPGA-part of the chip.

3.1   From GDL to Verilog

Our system generates ready-to-synthesize Verilog code. We use previously prepared Verilog modules that implement the behavior of the propnet component types, a template for a whole propnet module, and the project into which the propnet module will be injected. Now, given GDL rules of a new game, we generate software propnet using the code from [18]. Then, for every component in this propnet, we create new instance belonging to one of the before-mentioned modules and make it a new node in our hardware propnet. When all components are placed, we implement edges of the software propnet as wire connections in the HDL. We do this by BFS traversal of the underlying propnet graph.

The propnet meta-information contains information about the propnet structure (e.g. initial state, game state size) and describes game's legal moves, states, etc. We write this data to the propnet module and a separate XML file that will be later passed to the software side running on the ARM computer. Propnet graph and meta-information for the propnet controller logic are filled into the propnet module template, and resulting file is copied to the FPGA project.

Because of the complexity of the compilation process for the FPGA, and the fact that Intel's tools require to be run on an AMD64 PC, given GDL rules, our system waits until the image for the FPGA is provided from the computer controlled by a human. Thus, the current version cannot compete in a standard GGP match; however, the human does not make any contribution to the resulting image, and in principle, the process can be fully automated.

3.2 System Architecture

Figure 1 presents the overall architecture of our project. The ARM computer contains the high-level part of the system. It consists of GGP player, MCTS implementation, and driver library initialized with a game meta-information. It exchanges data with the FPGA board through the shared memory, containing four regions for communication with the propnet controller. Those are for: command queue (e.g., reset, execute n random simulations, set return context); sending next states; sending next legal moves; and sending scores of the players.

The information flow on FPGA is presented on the lower half of the figure. The main components are propnet driver, responsible for proper data transmission, and the propnet itself, programmed as described in Subsect. 3.1 and containing parts dedicated to communicating with the rest of the board.

3.3 MCTS Reasoner Implementation

Our goal is to implement a reasoner that can be effectively used by the MCTS algorithm. Thus, it needs to perform random simulations from an arbitrary game state to some terminal state, computing players' scores in this state.

The search algorithm works on the integrated ARM computer and interfaces with the FPGA via a driver library encoded in Java. For the FPGA to start playouts from a specific node, it has to switch context into the state corresponding to this node. Thus, we require from the MCTS tree implementation to store data representing the internal state of the FPGA propnet. This state is provided by the library during the MCTS expansion phase. The library exposes to MCTS three functions:

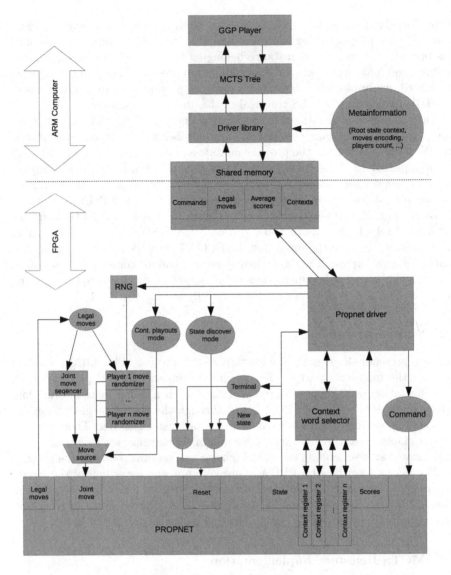

Fig. 1. System architecture.

- **FPGAState** *getRootState*(): returns game tree root in FPGA encoding.
- (**list<legalMoves>**, **list<(FPGAState, jointMove)>**) *getNextStates* (**FPGAState** *state*): returns for a given state the list of legal moves for each role, and all the children states and edges going to them.
- **list<long>** *getScores*(**FPGAState** *state*, **int** n): computes for each player the scores obtained during a batch consisting of n random simulations.

Calling reasoner to calculate a single playout, which is standard for software propnets, is very inefficient in our FPGA-based architecture, mainly because of communication costs. In order to reduce the number of read-write cycles, we only provide interface for scheduling batched playouts. When simulating, MCTS uses the *getScores* function to request a specific number of playouts (it is an MCTS initialization parameter) and backpropagates the summarized scores.

3.4   State Computation

Each transition node has assigned a unique number, and thus the game state is coded as a bit vector, where nth bit corresponds to the value stored in the nth transition node. Since this can grow up to a few kilobytes, it is divided into 128-bit words when loaded from or stored in the shared memory. Now, when the library issues new playouts, the propnet driver module loads every context word into an appropriate context register in the propnet. Propnet reset, and every new game state evaluation, takes place in one clock cycle.

We have three modes that we use to control the behavior of the propnet module: *state discovery*, *context switching*, and *continuous playout*.

In the state discovery mode, all legal joint actions are iterated over by the move sequencer. For each joint action, after calculating the next state, the propnet driver starts forwarding context words (state representation) and the corresponding joint move into the shared memory. This can be a multi-step process, as the memory may force to stall sending the state until it is ready.

In the context switching mode, the propnet driver queries requested place in the shared memory for the context words, which are then written to the propnet's context registers.

In the continuous playout mode, the players' actions are continuously taken from the modules generating legal random actions, until a terminal state is reached. When that happens, the propnet module signals scores to the propnet driver and resets the internal propnet to the previously set context. To ensure generated actions are uniformly distributed, for each player, we randomize a number i between 0 and the number of his legal actions, and loop through all his actions, reducing i on set bits, until the i-th legal action is found.

4   Experiments

To evaluate the performance of the FPGA implementation of propnets we carried out two types of experiments. Firstly, we compare the speed of our propnets with one of the fastest software propnets reasoners [18] and also with the Java-based Prover from the GGP-Base package [15] used as a baseline. Secondly, we investigate how the obtained speed-up translates to the performance of an MCTS agent, focusing on analysis of influence of batch size to the number of MCTS node expansions and software MCTS operations overhead.

In our experiments we use TerasIC DE1-SoC board containing the Altera's Cyclone V series SoC: 5CSEMA5F31C6. The GGP player, search algorithm and communication with the reasoner are run by a computer embedded in the before-mentioned SoC with ARM Cortex A9, Dual core @925 Mhz with 1 GB RAM, running Debian 9 Strech 32-bit. The FPGA project compilation is performed on Intel Core i5-4670 with 16 GB DDR3 @1600 Mhz RAM using Ubuntu 16.04 server 64-bit and Intel Quartus Prime Lite Edition 17.0 as FPGA compilation IDE. Software propnets and the GGP-Base Prover are tested on a Linux server consisting of 64 AMD Opteron 6174 2.2-GHz cores and 252 GB RAM.

4.1 Performance Comparison

To test the reasoner's performance, we use a Flat Monte Carlo Search, measuring the number of states visited during random playouts from the initial game state.

We compare results obtained for FPGA with other reasoners – software prop-nets and Prover. The overall results are presented in Table 2. They are based on 1 million simulations for FPGA, and more than 250 thousands simulations for the other reasoners (except 1000 simulations for Reversi). GDL descriptions of the games can be found in the Stanford Gamemaster repository [16].

Table 2. Comparison of reasoners based on running Flat Monte Carlo algorithm. FPGA speed is equivalent to the clock frequency, which is probed in 1.0Mhz steps. FPGA chip utilization is the space required to fit the propnet on the board.

Game	Speed (avg nodes/sec)			Initialization time		#Propnet components	FPGA chip utilization
	FPGA	Software	Prover	FPGA (min)	Software (sec)		
Horseshoe	8,500,000	192,583	3,812	4:20	0.45	350	7%
Connectfour	7,000,000	285,908	561	5:37	0.67	814	12%
Pentago	7,000,000	119,111	342	5:20	2.70	1,291	13%
Jointconnectfour	4,500,000	171,575	270	5:53	1.00	1,614	16%
Breakthrough	1,400,000	38,015	601	12:03	1.35	17,752	72%
Reversi	1,171,875	4,806	19	14:08	23.91	56,014	41%

As expected, the usage of hardware accelerator substantially increases the reasoner's efficiency. For all games except Reversi, the improvement factors are between 24.5 (Connect-Four) and 58 (Pentago). For Reversi, which produces the largest propnet among the tested games, FPGA-based reasoner computes states over 290 times faster. This example shows that smaller propnets do not necessarily imply smaller chip utilization.

The downside of moving from software to hardware is a considerable increase of initialization time. Instead of seconds it is about 5–6 min for small and medium games, and for large propnets it is almost a quarter. Such times exclude GGP players from being ready during their standard initialization clock. We discuss this issue in detail and present possible solutions in the next section.

4.2   MCTS Player Performance

Embedding an FPGA propnet reasoner into the MCTS involves delegating some computation time to the software responsible for managing the MCTS tree. The longer the time, the more overhead is observed, and the results are getting worse compared to the zero-overhead situation from the previous experiment.

Increasing batch size makes the evaluation of expanded nodes more reliable, yet significantly reduces their number. Reduced batches, instead, lead to more frequent calls to software part of the algorithm, increasing the overhead.

Figure 2 presents the data we gathered for Pentago (for other games the charts look similar). For both games we run 10 matches against the random player, considering only 10 first turns of each match. The number of node expansions obtained by the software player (using the same, yet non-batched MCTS, so number of playouts and node expansions are the same) is provided as a baseline.

Despite the overhead, it is possible to adjust batch so the FPGA player performs much more playouts than software-only agent. However, it is impossible to reach the same size of MCTS tree, which significantly influences the performance. This can be solved by implementing multithreaded MCTS, embedding MCTS in the FPGA, or using hardware with shorter communication latency.

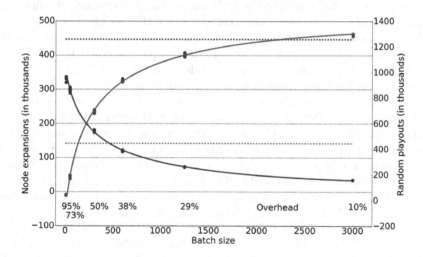

Fig. 2. Dependency between a batch size and the FPGA-based agent's performance measured by a number of nodes expansions, number of computed playouts, and the overhead (percent of time spent in an MCTS tree). Data was measured for batches of size 10, 50, 300, 600, 1500, and 3000; 10 runs for each test.

5   Discussion

Let us analyze the time-profile of an initialization process. The FPGA initialization time currently prevents the described solution to be embedded in a competition-ready GGP player. However, there are possibilities for reducing it significantly. The first phase is a software propnet construction. The exact times have been presented in Table 2. For generating Verilog propnet module, we use our own Java library, that requires up to 2 min and can be easily optimized. In our GGP player, the dynamic part of FPGA is a particular game's propnet, and the support structure remains constant. Preparing this support structure (compilation and fitting) requires 3 min, but can be reduced significantly using commercial tools, e.g., Intel Quartus Prime Pro, which allows caching part of the compilation process. The most time-consuming phase is propnet structure fitting, responsible for the physical placement of the logic modules on a chip. Its time depends mostly on the number of components, and requires solving computationally hard problems. Currently, it can take from 1 to about 30 min, depending on the game size.

Due to limited space on the FPGA chip, there is a hard limit on the game size we are able to handle. However, this size is not a direct result of the number of the propnet components, as it also heavily depends on the graph planarity and the optimizations performed by the synthesis toolchain. We can observe in Table 2 that for Reversi and breakthrough smaller initial propnet size lead to much higher chip utilization. Also, we would like to point out that the largest chip utilization we have observed is 72%, which allows to estimate the limit on the games we are able to hardware-accelerate using the described system.

We also have a limitation associated with memory block size that can be easily extended in the future. In the described implementation, the state size times number of legal joint moves in this state cannot exceed 32 KB.

There is also a number of significant optimization improvements we can apply. For example, during gameplay, clock frequency has to be low because of long signal propagation paths within the game propnet. However, after the result is calculated and information exchange between the shared memory and propnet driver starts, frequency can be temporarily increased by an order of magnitude. This will make the process of writing data to the memory several times faster.

The usage of a PCI-E equipped FPGA-board would allow pushing the ARM computer out of the loop, removing the need to handle propnet on two machines and allowing FPGA board to talk directly to the main, much powerful, computer (which is necessary to reduce the influence of the MCTS tree overhead).

Currently, when MCTS has control, the reasoner is idle, waiting for the next task. As the reasoner operates independently of the ARM computer, it is possible to remove those pauses, by scheduling tasks ahead. From the MCTS point of view it can be managed as multithreaded simulations, e.g., by using virtual loses [17].

Summarizing, it is possible to create a fully functional GGP player that can successfully participate in the GGP competitions, although it requires heavy optimizations and top-level hardware and software. Still, for some large games, there is no guarantee that the initialization will finish before the imposed start time. This can be partially solved by storing compiled FPGA projects for already known games, allowing their fast retrieval when the same game is detected.

5.1   Future Work

Although the hardware accelerators provide the highest computational efficiency, it comes with some drawbacks. However, as we have a complete implementation of the propnet in the Verilog, we can use the industrial-grade simulators and optimizers to run the propnet in software. This could lead to better optimized propnet structure and allow more straightforward embedding into the GGP player. To evaluate the usefulness of such simulated hardware propnets, we plan to implement them and compare their efficiency against the reference Java implementation and our FPGA-based reasoner.

Most MCTS implementations are based on the purely random playouts; however, multiple more sophisticated strategies have proven to be quite effective [5,17]. We would like to implement and test such non-random simulations on the FPGA. This will complicate the board architecture and slow down the reasoner. Yet, it may be the only possibility to overcome certain limitations, and tackle games that cannot be solved by even extremely efficient brute force search.

In particular, because FPGAs have memory distributed around the entire chip, it is possible to locally keep track of state changes. Thus, once a player wins, we can memorize which propositions contributed to this, and create a heuristic state evaluation function that improves over time, similarly to some simulation control learning algorithms presented in [5].

6   Conclusions

In this paper, we present the first attempt to encode propnets, a successful computational representation in GGP, on a hardware chip. Because a GGP player has to handle any game encoded in GDL, we based our system on FPGAs, which allow us to reprogram our hardware reasoners and quickly switch between previously encountered games.

This is preliminary work that opens a new branch of GGP research, parallel to the improvement of software-based reasoners, which has been worked on for nearly a decade [19]. The approach we described is able to achieve from 25 up to 290 times improvement over the software propnets when comparing the number of visited states per time unit. Moreover, the ratio is considerably better for large games, the ones that are especially problematic for all kinds of software-based reasoners – even GDL compilers. We may conclude that FPGA-propnets are a faster alternative to software propnets for reasoning on game descriptions.

We also integrate the FPGA-propnet within an MCTS agent and discuss the difficulties that this entails. Using Pentago, we show how the communication between the FPGA-propnet and the software that manages the search introduces a considerable overhead. Because of this, our FPGA-propnet MCTS agent is not ready to participate in a GGP competition yet. However, we discuss various improvements that can solve the current shortcomings. This, together with the successful performance of the FPGA-propnet with respect to the software propnet when tested on their own, indicates that this research direction is promising.

Moreover, although we plan to enhance our system to handle more sophisticated AI approaches, we think that merging vanilla MCTS with computation power of hardware raises an interesting question about a gameplay level that can be achieved by using sheer brute force.

References

1. Auer, P., Cesa-Bianchi, N., Fischer, P.: Finite-time analysis of the multiarmed bandit problem. Mach. Learn. **47**(2–3), 235–256 (2002)
2. Boulé, M., Zilic, Z.: An FPGA move generator for the game of chess. ICGA J. **25**(2), 85–94 (2002)
3. Browne, C.B., et al.: A survey of Monte Carlo tree search methods. IEEE TCIAIG **4**(1), 1–43 (2012)
4. Coulom, R.: Efficient selectivity and backup operators in Monte-Carlo tree search. In: van den Herik, H.J., Ciancarini, P., Donkers, H.H.L.M. (eds.) CG 2006. LNCS, vol. 4630, pp. 72–83. Springer, Heidelberg (2007). https://doi.org/10.1007/978-3-540-75538-8_7
5. Finnsson, H., Björnsson, Y.: Learning simulation control in general game playing agents. In: AAAI, pp. 954–959 (2010)
6. Genesereth, M., Love, N., Pell, B.: General game playing: overview of the AAAI competition. AI Mag. **26**, 62–72 (2005)
7. Genesereth, M., Thielscher, M.: General Game Playing. Morgan & Claypool, San Rafael (2014)
8. Haiying, G., Fuming, W., Wei, L., Yun, L.: Monte Carlo simulation of 9x9 Go game on FPGA. In: 2010 IEEE International Conference on Intelligent Computing and Intelligent Systems (ICIS), Haiying, vol. 3, pp. 865–869 (2010)
9. Hsu, F.H.: Chess hardware in deep blue. Comput. Sci. Eng. **8**(1), 50–60 (2006)
10. Kowalski, J., Szykuła, M.: Game description language compiler construction. In: Cranefield, S., Nayak, A. (eds.) AI 2013. LNCS (LNAI), vol. 8272, pp. 234–245. Springer, Cham (2013). https://doi.org/10.1007/978-3-319-03680-9_26
11. Love, N., Hinrichs, T., Haley, D., Schkufza, E., Genesereth, M.: General Game Playing: Game Description Language Specification. Technical report. Stanford Logic Group (2008)
12. Olivito, J., Resano, J., Briz, J.L.: Accelerating board games through hardware-/software codesign. IEEE TCIAIG **9**(4), 393–401 (2017)
13. Romoth, J., Porrmann, M., Rückert, U.: Survey of FPGA applications in the period 2000–2015, Technical report (2017)
14. Schkufza, E., Love, N., Genesereth, M.: Propositional automata and cell automata: representational frameworks for discrete dynamic systems. In: Wobcke, W., Zhang, M. (eds.) AI 2008. LNCS (LNAI), vol. 5360, pp. 56–66. Springer, Heidelberg (2008). https://doi.org/10.1007/978-3-540-89378-3_6
15. Schreiber, S.: The general game playing base package (2013). http://code.google.com/p/ggp-base/
16. Schreiber, S.: Stanford Gamemaster (2016). http://games.ggp.org/stanford/
17. Silver, D., et al.: Mastering the game of Go with deep neural networks and tree search. Nature **529**, 484–503 (2016)
18. Sironi, C.F., Winands, M.H.M.: Optimizing propositional networks. In: Cazenave, T., Winands, M.H.M., Edelkamp, S., Schiffel, S., Thielscher, M., Togelius, J. (eds.) CGW/GIGA -2016. CCIS, vol. 705, pp. 133–151. Springer, Cham (2017). https://doi.org/10.1007/978-3-319-57969-6_10

19. Waugh, K.: Faster state manipulation in general games using generated code. In: IJCAI Workshop on General Intelligence in Game-Playing Agents (2009)
20. Wong, C., Lo, K., Leong, P.H.W.: An FPGA-based Othello endgame solver. In: Conference on Field-Programmable Technology 2004, pp. 81–88 (2004)

A Genetic Programming Hyper-heuristic Approach for Online Resource Allocation in Container-Based Clouds

Boxiong Tan[(✉)], Hui Ma, and Yi Mei

Victoria University of Wellington, Wellington, New Zealand
{Boxiong.Tan,Hui.Ma,Yi.Mei}@ecs.vuw.ac.nz

Abstract. The popularity of container-based clouds is its ability to deploy and run applications without launching an entire virtual machine (VM) for each application. Container-based clouds support flexible deployment of applications and therefore brings the potential to reduce the energy consumption of data centers. With the goal of energy reduction, it is more difficult to optimize the allocation of containers than traditional VM-based clouds because of the finer granularity of resources. Little research has been conducted for applying human-design heuristics on balanced and unbalanced resources. In this paper, we first compare three human-design heuristics and show they cannot handle balanced and unbalanced resources scenarios well. We propose a learning-based algorithm: genetic programming hyper-heuristic (GPHH) to automatically generate a suitable heuristic for allocating containers in an online fashion. The results show that the proposed GPHH managed to evolve better heuristics than the human-designed ones in terms of energy consumption in a range of cloud scenarios.

Keywords: Cloud computing · Resource allocation
Energy consumption · Genetic programming · Hyper-heuristic

1 Introduction

A container-based cloud [1] is a promising new technology for both software and cloud computing industries. Containers are beneficial for cloud providers because they can potentially reduce the energy of data centers [2]. Energy reduction is achieved by deploying more applications in fewer physical machines (PMs).

Although container-based clouds have the potential of better energy efficiency, the complexity for allocating both containers and VMs is much higher than solely managing VMs. In a container-based cloud, a typical PM may host multiple VMs with different operating systems. Each VM hosts multiple containers. This box-inside-box structure forces us to break down the container allocation process into two levels: containers to VMs and VMs to PMs.

To address the high complexity, this work considers a simplified structure and focuses on the challenge of the container allocation problem. Many cloud

© Springer Nature Switzerland AG 2018
T. Mitrovic et al. (Eds.): AI 2018, LNAI 11320, pp. 146–152, 2018.
https://doi.org/10.1007/978-3-030-03991-2_15

providers (e.g. Amazon) skip VM level and deploy containers directly to PMs. Moreover, we consider an online container allocation in which the request come in real time, and the information of each request (e.g. CPU and memory demand) is unknown until the request arrives.

AnyFit-based algorithms with human-designed greedy rules such as *sub* and *sum* (detailed discussed in Sect. 2) are used by existing approaches [2]. We argue that the goal for resource allocation in clouds is to minimize the accumulated energy consumption instead of the cutting-point energy. It is critical to consider the order of creating new PMs when allocating containers [3]. Therefore, the container allocation problem can be treated as a scheduling task. Existing human-designed rules, therefore, may not be suitable for the scheduling task.

To address the drawbacks of human-design rules and the high design difficulty, we propose a learning algorithm: Genetic programming-based hyperheuristic (GPHH) to automatically design scheduling rules using the information of a data center. To apply GPHH in the container allocation problem, we need to define a terminal set and a fitness function to evaluate scheduling rules.

In this paper, our contributions are:

- We perform an experimental comparison of the widely used human-designed greedy rules: *sub*, *sum*, and *random* in online container allocation. This comparison provides an important insights of their limitations in flexibly handling different scenarios, and therefore motivate us to develop a learning algorithm to automatically generate rules to adapt all scenarios.
- We develop a GPHH for generating rules for online container allocation.

2 Background

Problem Description: The container allocation problem can be described as, for a given set of t containers, each container arrives at a time i, $0 <= i <= t$, the overall objective of container allocation is to allocate containers to physical machines so that during the period of time of allocation. These t number of containers to be allocated into p physical machines. Each container i has a CPU demand A_i and a memory occupation M_i. Each physical machine $j \in \{1, \cdots, p\}$ has a CPU capacity PA_j and a memory capacity PM_j. A physical machine can host multiple containers. We consider all physical machines have the same size of CPU capacity and memory.

The accumulated energy consumption of PMs $AE = \sum_{i=1}^{t} \sum_{j=1}^{p} E_j^i \cdot [u_{cpu}^i(j) > 0]$ are minimized where E_j^i is the energy consumption of a physical machine for allocating the container i. $[u_{cpu}^i(j) > 0]$ returns 1 if the CPU utilization $u_{cpu}^i(j) > 0$ (the physical machine is active), and 0 otherwise.

E_j^i is determined by a widely used energy model $E_j^i = \alpha \cdot E^{max} + (1 - \alpha) \cdot E^{max} \cdot u_{cpu}^i(j)$ [4]. The CPU utilization of a physical machine can be computed as $u_{cpu}^i(j) = \sum_{c=1}^{i} (x_j^c \cdot A_c)$. Where x_j^c is a binary value (e.g. 0 and 1) denoting whether a container c is allocated on a physical machine j when i containers have been allocated.

Constraints: A container can be allocated on a physical machine if and only if the physical machine has enough CPU and memory. The other constraint is that each container should be deployed exactly once.

Human-Designed Rules for Online Container Allocation: AnyFit algorithms [2] are greedy-based algorithms and use human-designed rules for evaluating an allocation. Mann [2] applied six rules (such as *sub*, *sum*, and *product*) for container allocation. However, the performance of these rules have not been shown. Therefore, it motivates us to explore the effectiveness of the most used rules – *sum* and *sub* – in solving the problem of the container allocation problem.

sum is the most commonly used rule in multi-dimensional bin packing. It can be represented as $resourceA + resourceB$ in the two-dimensional case. Resources A and B are the residual resources of a chosen bin after the item has been allocated. The smaller the function result, the better the candidate bin. This heuristic tries to minimize the residual resources in all dimensions. It is based on a simple assumption that less residual resource results in fewer number of used bins.

sub is designed to maintain the balance in a bin. It can be represented as $|resourceA - resourceB|$. Similar to the *sub*, it prefers a smaller function value. The *sub* rule tries to minimize the difference between the two resources. With the assumption of balanced resource allocation can lead to fewer bins.

In summary, the performance of these simple rules has not been well studied. Because of their simplicity, we believe they cannot fully capture the complex behavior of diverse resource requirements and temporal effect. Therefore, these two reasons motivate us to investigate a learning method: GPHH using the information from a data center to generate rules.

3   GPHH for Online Container Allocation

This section describes the overview of our GPHH approach, including a training process, function and terminal nodes, and a fitness function.

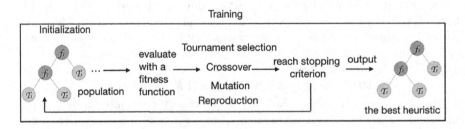

Fig. 1. The overview of GPHH training and testing process

Training and Testing: GPHH trains on the training set which includes the trace of resource requirement. GPHH iteratively improves the generated heuristics by the standard procedure [5] shown in Fig. 1. A testing process evaluates the generated rules from GPHH training with a test set and compare with human-designed rules in terms of the energy consumption (see details in Sect. 4).

Both training and testing rely on the simulation of container allocation for evaluating the quality of rules. The simulation includes two parts: data center initialization and container allocation. Data center initialization randomly initializes a data center with PMs and containers. Without initialization, allocation algorithms perform similarly. Container allocation process allocate containers to the PM according to a BestFit-based algorithm (see Algorithm 1). The rule decides the goodness of a candidate PM.

Algorithm 1. BestFit framework for the evolved rules

    Input   : container, A list of available PMs,
    Output: The best PM
1 $BestPM = nil$;
2 $bestFitness = nil$;
3 **while** PM_i *in PMs* **do**
4      $fitness =$Rule($container, PM_i$);
5   **if** $fitness > bestFitness$ **then**
6         $bestFitness = fitness$;
7         $BestPM = PM_i$;
8   **end**
9      $i = i + 1$;
10 **end**
11 return $BestPM$;

Function, Terminal Sets, and Fitness Function: Our function set is $\{+, -, \times\}$ and the protected $\div$ that returns 1 when divided by 0. Terminal set includes four features. The CPU and memory requirement of a container and the residual CPU and memory from a PM. Residual CPU and memory are calculated as the current PM's resources subtract the resource requirement of the container.

We calculate the fitness function $fitness = \frac{\sum_{k=1}^{N} \frac{AE_k}{t}}{N}$ where N is the number of training instances. The fitness value represents the average increase in energy consumption for allocating a container in all N number of training instances. Therefore, it is free from the bias of the randomize initial data center.

4 Experiments

We design three scenarios – unbalanced containers and PMs, balanced containers and unbalanced PMs, and balanced containers and PMs – for two objectives:

testing whether existing rules can work well in container allocation and evaluate the proposed GPHH.

Experiment Settings: Each of the three scenarios includes 100 of test instances. They are splitted equally into training and testing set. Each test instance consists of 200 containers to be allocated. The scenario with unbalanced containers and PMs is the most common scenario in the real world because of the diverse applications. We use a real-world dataset (AuverGrid trace [6]) to generate test instances of unbalanced container scenario.

For container generation, we randomly choose pairs of CPU and memory from the dataset with both resource requirement less than or equal to the maximum capacity. Balanced containers are generated from an exponential distribution with the rate $\lambda = 0.004$ in both CPU and memory. For initialization of a data center, we randomly generate 4 to 8 running PMs. Each VM will host at least one container. In addition, we use the corresponding dataset as the test cases for generating the initial containers in PMs. For the balanced PMs scenarios, we set the PM's CPU and memory as (3300 MHz, 3300 MBs) and for unbalanced PMs scenario, we set the PM's CPU and memory as (3300 MHz, 4000 MBs).

To compare the performance between *sub* and *sum*, we add a *random* rule. The *random* rule chooses a random available PM instead of the best one. We intend to compare *sub* and *sum* with the *random* rule as a baseline. Hence, we can identify which rule performs badly in which scenario.

We run GP 30 times to generate 30 rules with different random seeds. Each evolved rule is applied on the test instances. The accumulated energy of each test instance is then normalized with the result of the benchmark *sub*

Table 1. Real world scenarios

	evo	sub	sum	random
evo	NaN	49-0-1	30-0-20	45-0-5
sub	1-0-49	NaN	2-1-47	5-2-43
sum	20-0-30	47-1-2	NaN	40-4-6
random	5-0-45	43-2-5	6-4-40	NaN

rule with equation $normalized\ E_{evolve} = \frac{E_{evolve}}{E_{sub}}$. Then, for each instance, we calculate the average normalized accumulated energy from 30 runs. Lastly, we applied the paired Wilcoxon test to calculate the statistic significance between the evolved rules and the benchmark rules (*sub*, *sum*, and *random*).

For GPHH, we use the population size of 1024. The number of generation is 100. For crossover, mutation, and reproduction, we use 0.8, 0.1, and 0.1 respectively. We use tournament selection with the size of the tournament as 7.

Table 2. Unbalanced PMs

	evo	sub	sum	random
evo	NaN	44-0-6	41-0-9	43-0-7
sub	6-0-44	NaN	20-1-29	30-0-20
sum	9-0-41	29-1-20	NaN	33-1-16
random	7-0-43	20-0-30	16-1-33	NaN

Experiment Results: In all scenarios, the rules generated by GPH show significant advantages than other rules (Tables 1, 2 and 3). Table 1 shows the Win-Draw-Loss of the unbalanced containers and PMs dataset among four algorithms. The *sub* rule is significantly worse than all the other rules.

Evolved rules dominate the *sub* and *random* rules, and is better than the *sum* rule with a small margin.

In balanced containers and unbalanced PMs scenario (Table 2), there is no statistic difference between *sub*, *sum* and *random* rules. In balanced containers and PMs (Table 3), evolved rules dominate other rules. Both *sub* and *sum* are significantly better than the *random* rule.

Table 3. Balanced containers and PMs

	evo	sub	sum	random
evo	NaN	**43-0-7**	**38-0-12**	**46-0-4**
sub	7-0-43	NaN	23-0-27	32-0-18
sum	12-0-38	27-0-23	NaN	35-0-15
random	4-0-46	18-0-32	15-0-35	NaN

To explain the goodness of evolved rules, Fig. 2 shows the energy consumption of the data center while allocating 200 containers with four rules. The initial energy consumption are the same because of the same initialized data center. With the allocation processing, *random* rule (yellow) creates a new PM which incurs the sudden increase of energy while other rules can still allocate containers to the existing PMs. Similarly, *sub* and *sum* create new PMs earlier than the evolved rule. Although, in most cases, all four rules create the same number of PMs (not in this case), evolved rules always allocate more containers to the existing PMs.

5 Conclusion

In this paper, we first show that existing rules for container allocation do not perform well in dealing with real-world resource requirement and PM. Second, we develop a novel GPHH approach for container allocation to automatically generate rules using the information of data centers.

Experiments show that the evolved rules perform significantly better than human-designed rules in all scenarios. The proposed GPHH approach is effective for automatically generating rules for various container allocation scenarios in data centers. In future work, we

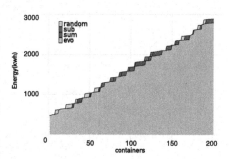

Fig. 2. The energy consumption of allocating 200 containers with four algorithms (from balanced VM dataset, run 15, test case 5)

will investigate the container allocation in a general architecture where multiple VMs are allocated in PMs.

References

1. Bernstein, D.: Containers and cloud: from LXC to docker to kubernetes. IEEE Cloud Comput. **1**(3), 81–84 (2014)
2. Mann, Z.Á.: Interplay of virtual machine selection and virtual machine placement. In: Aiello, M., Johnsen, E.B., Dustdar, S., Georgievski, I. (eds.) ESOCC 2016. LNCS, vol. 9846, pp. 137–151. Springer, Cham (2016). https://doi.org/10.1007/978-3-319-44482-6_9

3. Cauwer, M.D., Mehta, D., O'Sullivan, B.: The temporal bin packing problem: an application to workload management in data centres. In: 28th International Conference on Tools with Artificial Intelligence (ICTAI), pp. 157–164 (2016)
4. Fan, X., Weber, W.-D., Barroso, L.A.: Power provisioning for a warehouse-sized computer. ACM SIGARCH Comput. Archit. News **35**(June), 12–13 (2007)
5. Burke, E.K., et al.: Hyper-heuristics: a survey of the state of the art. J. Oper. Res. Soc. **64**(12), 1695–1724 (2013)
6. Shen, S., van Beek, V., Iosup, A.: Statistical characterization of business-critical workloads hosted in cloud datacenters. In: IEEE/ACM International Symposium on Cluster, Cloud and Grid Computing, pp. 465–474 (2015)

A Computational Framework
for Autonomous Self-repair Systems

Tran Nguyen Minh-Thai[1,4(✉)], Jagannath Aryal[2], Sandhya Samarasinghe[1],
and Michael Levin[3]

[1] Complex Systems, Big Data and Informatics Initiative (CSBII), Lincoln University,
Canterbury, New Zealand
tnmthai@cit.ctu.edu.vn, Sandhya.Samarasinghe@lincoln.ac.nz
[2] Discipline of Geography and Spatial Sciences, University of Tasmania,
Hobart, Australia
jagannath.aryal@utas.edu.au
[3] Allen Discovery Center, Tufts University, Boston, USA
Michael.Levin@tufts.edu
[4] College of ICT, Can Tho University, 3/2 Street, Can Tho City, Vietnam

Abstract. This paper describes a novel computational framework for
damage detection and regeneration in an artificial tissue of cells resembling living systems. We represent the tissue as an Auto-Associative Neural Network (AANN) consisting of a single layer of perceptron neurons
(cells) with local feedback loops. This allows the system to recognise its
state and geometry in a form of collective intelligence. Signalling entropy
is used as a global (emergent) property characterising the state of the
system. The repair system has two submodels - global sensing and local
sensing. Global sensing is used to sense the change in whole system state
and detect general damage region based on system entropy change. Then,
local sensing is applied with AANN to find the exact damage locations
and repair the damage. The results show that the method allows robust
and efficient damage detection and accurate regeneration.

Keywords: Self-repair · Multi-cellular structures · Regeneration
Auto-Associative Neural Network · Perceptron · Signalling entropy
Modeling

1 Introduction

Regeneration is an important phenomenon in nature; while it plays a key role
in living organisms that are capable of recovering a fully functional state from
diverse forms of injury, it is not completely understood [4]. Although molecular
mechanisms required for regeneration are being discovered, the algorithms sufficient for regeneration of complex anatomical structures represent a significant
knowledge gap that holds back progress in evolutionary developmental biology
and regenerative medicine. Currently, there is insufficient knowledge to mimic

© Springer Nature Switzerland AG 2018
T. Mitrovic et al. (Eds.): AI 2018, LNAI 11320, pp. 153–159, 2018.
https://doi.org/10.1007/978-3-030-03991-2_16

regeneration in living organisms, making it essential to analyze computational models of cell activity and communication dynamics that can implement complex structural repair. It is especially important to explore connectionist (neural-like) models in the control of regeneration to begin to formulate rigorous formalisms for pattern memory and decision-making during anatomical remodeling.

In software engineering, *self-repair systems* are not popular yet and often apply when working with agent-based systems or service-oriented architectures that are still the subject of intense research [7]. The term *self-repair* refers to automatic software repair which involves finding a solution to software faults without human interference. This is analogous to wound healing and regenerative repair in living organisms. In robotics, multi-robot systems have the ability to form patterns or configurations to achieve desired goals, such as detecting and recovering from faults [1,5]. However, great gains can be achieved in robotics and synthetic biology by advancing research in bio-inspired self-repair systems.

In this paper, we propose a concept for an autonomous self-repair system that has the capacity to sense, detect and regenerate missing cells in a simple tissue system (Fig. 1a) under any damage condition induced by injury in a simple way that resembles some related processes in biological systems.

2   Related Work

One of the key questions facing biology today is how cells in an organism collectively collaborate to maintain the normal state of the system. Several computational models have been proposed with regeneration capabilities. In [2,15], authors developed dynamic models for describing morphogenesis and regeneration of complex patterns assuming that cells communicate with each other by passing signals. The change in signal distribution is used for detecting damage and regenerating a tissue structure. However, the large amount of communication between cells reduces the computationally efficiency of the models. Research has continued to explore methods to bring the morphology back to correct form, in particular, by avoiding overgrowth, with limited success [9–12] with other methods such as nervous system communicating with non-neural cells [3], genetic algorithms [8] and agent-based models [6]. Some main challenges to current models are computational burden due to excessive cell communications and overgrowth; these can be improved for greater efficiency or biological realism.

In robotics, a swarm of robots has been programmed to construct and self-repair two-dimensional structures [1,13]. When robots suffer damage, the remaining robots may reconfigure and reorganize the same pattern but on a smaller scale and continue to function. This process to some extent is analogous to regeneration in biology. From a robotic perspective, how robots can learn to reorganise into new structural patterns need further research.

Thus there is great scope for models that are not only bio-realistic but also computationally efficient. This research attempts to make improvements towards efficient self-repair systems that completely and correctly regenerate their form that in a broad sense resemble biological systems.

3   Methodology

In this paper, we assume that an artificial tissue pattern (organism) consists of a stem cell surrounded by more than 2000 differentiated cells in a 2-dimensional plane (Fig. 1a). A cell is identified by polar coordinates $(radius, \theta)$ (Fig. 1a). The stem cell can divide in a way that makes a copy of itself and produces a differentiated cell. The tissue structure is described by a network of cells embedded in a medium similar to Extra Cellular Matrix (ECM) in a living tissue.

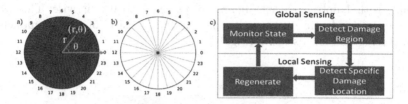

Fig. 1. (a) A stem cell at the centre surrounded by differentiated cells, (b) Tissue pattern divided into n segments (e.g, n = 24) and (c) Functional aspects of the framework

There are two types of communication in the tissue - local direct communications between neighbour cells and global diffusion of information through the tissue matrix - the form of communication between a stem cell and differentiated cells. Direct neighbourhood communication is facilitated by representing the tissue as an AANN consisting of a single layer of perceptrons (threshold neurons) that represent cells that are connected with local feedback loops (Fig. 2a). AANN are networks where neurons influence themselves through feedback loops that typically give rise to emergent systemic properties. Thus the tissue is represented as a locally recurrent dynamical system that collectively maintains tissue states. The global diffusion means that longer the distance the information travels the greater the uncertainty of its content so we use the concept of entropy to encode this information. Entropy has been used to identify signalling pathways, understand drug sensitivity profiles, and determine cancer stem-cell phenotypes [14]. In the context of a network of cells, it can measure overall uncertainty in a desired state, such as signaling entropy in the tissue. This model also considers stochasticity in cell position due to cell movement using Brownian motion and is approximated by white noise $\epsilon(\mu, \sigma)$ that adjusts cell position as $(r, \theta) \pm \epsilon(\mu, \sigma)$. The $\epsilon(\mu, \sigma)$ is assumed to be a Gaussian noise distribution with mean (μ) and standard deviation (σ) with a value determined heuristically.

Assume that a stem cell SC_i has k number of differentiated cells. Let d_{ij} be the distance between the stem cell SC_i and differentiated cell DC_j. We define a stochastic matrix P with components p_{ij} and signalling entropy E_i:

$$p_{ij} = \frac{d_{ij}}{\sum_{j=1}^{k} d_{ij}}; \quad E_i = -\gamma \sum_{j=1}^{k} p_{ij} log p_{ij}; \quad \gamma = \frac{1}{log k} \tag{1}$$

where $\sum_{j=1}^{k} d_{ij}$ denotes the total distance and γ is a positive constant. The stem cell estimates and stores the entropy of the cells in the 24 segments.

Normal System: System in its normal state establishes its global (original) entropy and tissue border. We assume that each interior cell has four neighbours while a boundary cell has only three neighbours with two-way communication (Fig. 2a) and the cell thus receives inputs from its neighbours. The perceptron computes the output from the received inputs and connection weights (Fig. 2b) (weights are fixed to 1.0 indicating cells communicate their presence to the neighbours precisely). Figure 2c presents a sample dataset showing that a perception responds with 1 only if all neighbours are present and 0 otherwise. This way, tissue border is identified. The self-repair system consists of two submodels - global sensing and local sensing (Fig. 1c)

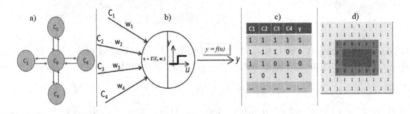

Fig. 2. (a) Two-way communication of a perceptron with its neighbours, (b) Computation in a Perceptron (c) Sample data showing perceptron response to inputs from neighbours and (d) Output of a damaged segment of AANN

Global Sensing: The stem cell can sense a change in the system due to damage anywhere within it. The stem cell scans the system by segments and the difference between the current and original entropy informs the segment(s) that have received damage.

Local Sensing: The stem cell initiates a local search for the exact location of damage in the already identified damage segments to be able to regenerate missing cells. Specifically, knowledge of the damaged segment(s) allows it to inform the cells in these segment(s) (corresponding part of the AANN) to process information through local feedback connections to assess any missing neighbours. The single layer perceptron outputs help the system identify the boundary of the damage (Fig. 2d). In order to regenerate, the stem cell moves along the shortest path to the damage location and then regenerates missing neighbours of each cell in the damage area. In the case of a damage extending to the original border, when a new cell is added next to a border neuron, the new cell becomes the marker for the next border cell and so on until the whole set of border cells is added and regeneration comes to completion with the renewal of the correct original form.

4   Results and Discussion

To determine the level of noise in the cell position the system can handle, we first perturbed the system by $\pm$ (2%, 5% and 10%) and calculated entropy. We observed only a relatively small increase in the absolute change in entropy for $\pm$2% and $\pm$5% perturbations but $\pm$10% introduces a significant change and disorder into the system producing random cell clusters. Further experimentation with entropy calculation with various cell deletions revealed that $\pm$5% perturbation introduces enough noise into the system but still keeps it sensitive to single cell deletions; therefore, $\pm$5% perturbation with corresponding noise distribution $\epsilon(0, 0.03)$ was selected to represent stochasticity in the tissue.

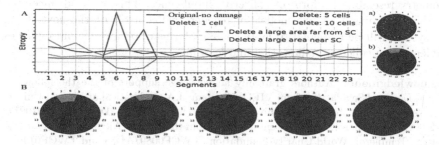

Fig. 3. (A) System entropy over the 24 segments of tissue for: original - no damage, and random deletions of 1, 5 and 10 cells in each segment (as in (a)), and 100 cells far from the stem cell (as in (b)); and (B) Progression of damage repair until correct completion (from left to right) for damage in A(b)

We start with $\pm$5% perturbed cell system and calculate its entropy over all 24 segments. Then we make six cases of damage with increasing damage intensity by randomly deleting 1, 5 and 10 cell(s) in each segment or a large area near the stem cell or far from it (Fig. 3A (a and b) show two cases). The system senses damage from the entropy recalculated for the whole system and the graphs in Fig. 3A show the degree of entropy change in relation to the intensity of the damage. As can be seen, entropy undergoes change due to even single cell deletions and the larger the number of cell deletions, the larger the change in entropy. The stem cell determined damaged segments from these changes in entropy. Then, local sensing activated the perceptrons in the portion of the AANN corresponding to the affected segments and found the exact location, size and the boundary of the damage. All damages and boundaries were identified correctly. To repair a damage, the stem cell moved to the nearest location of the damage and initiated regeneration of missing cells as shown in Fig. 3B for the case of 100-cell damage far from the stem cell (Fig. 3A(b)).

For performance discussion, we compare our method with several previous approaches. Global and local sensing in our model involving limited cell communications make our system more robust and computationally efficient in comparison to models in [2, 15]. Compared to models in [6], this model not only depends on much less communication between cells but also keeps minimal information - just the global entropy and state of neurons in the original system. De et al. model [3] does not recognise damage and generates and kills many cells before reaching a partially recovered form. In contrast, the current model detects damage and recovers the complete form using simpler and efficient computations.

5　Conclusions

In this paper, we propose a new model for damage detection and regeneration in multicellular tissues based on assumptions inspired by the biology of living tissues. This is achieved by enabling a cellular system to maintain its state and geometry resembling a form of collective intelligence. This work advances the effort of building ANN-like models of regenerative control. At the next stage, the system will be extended to more complex forms of organisms and damages implementing collective adaptation and learning.

Acknowledgments. Authors gratefully acknowledge support of the the following: TNM - Doctoral Scholarship from VIED, Vietnam; J.A.- Sabbatical at Lincoln University, New Zealand; S.S.- Lincoln University Research Fund; M.L.- DARPA (#HR0011-18-2-0022), the Allen Discovery Center award from the Paul G Allen Frontiers Group, and the Templeton World Charity Foundation (TWCF0089/AB55 and TWCF0140).

References

1. Arbuckle, D.J., Requicha, A.A.G.: Self-assembly and self-repair of arbitrary shapes by a swarm of reactive robots: algorithms and simulations. Auton. Robots **28**(2), 197–211 (2010)
2. Bessonov, N., Levin, M., Morozova, N., Reinberg, N., Tosenberger, A., Volpert, V.: On a model of pattern regeneration based on cell memory. PLOS ONE **10**(2), e0118091 (2015)
3. De, A., Chakravarthy, V.S., Levin, M.: A computational model of planarian regeneration. Int. J. Parallel Emerg. Distrib. Syst. **32**(4), 331–347 (2017)
4. Dinsmore, C.E.: A history of regeneration research: milestones in the evolution of a science. J. Hist. Biol. **26**(1), 156–158 (1993)
5. Edwards, C.: Self-repair techniques point to robots that design themselves. Commun. ACM **59**(2), 15–17 (2016)
6. Ferreira, G.B.S., Smiley, M., Scheutz, M., Levin, M.: Dynamic structure discovery and repair for 3D cell assemblages. In: Proceedings of the Fifteenth International Conference on the Synthesis and Simulation of Living Systems (ALIFEXV) (2016)
7. Frei, R., McWilliam, R., Derrick, B., Purvis, A., Tiwari, A., Di Marzo Serugendo, G.: Self-healing and self-repairing technologies. Int. J. Adv. Manuf. Technol. **69**(5), 1033–1061 (2013)
8. Gerlee, P., Basanta, D., Anderson, A.R.A.: Evolving homeostatic tissue using genetic algorithms. Prog. Biophys. Mole. Biol. **106**(2), 414–425 (2011)
9. Levin, M.: The wisdom of the body: future techniques and approaches to morphogenetic fields in regenerative medicine, developmental biology and cancer. Regen. Med. **6**(6), 667–673 (2011). pMID: 22050517

10. Levin, M.: Morphogenetic fields in embryogenesis, regeneration, and cancer: non-local control of complex patterning. Biosystems **109**(3), 243–261 (2012). Biological Morphogenesis: Theory and Computation
11. Lobo, D., Solano, M., Bubenik, G.A., Levin, M.: A linear-encoding model explains the variability of the target morphology in regeneration. J. Roy. Soc. Interface **11**(92), 20130918 (2014)
12. Mustard, J., Levin, M.: Bioelectrical mechanisms for programming growth and form: taming physiological networks for soft body robotics. Soft Robot. **1**(3), 169–191 (2014). Biological Morphogenesis: Theory and Computation
13. Rubenstein, M., Sai, Y., Chuong, C., Shen, W.: Regenerative patterning in swarm robots: mutual benefits of research in robotics and stem cell biology. Int. J. Dev. Biol. **53**(5–6), 869–881 (2009)
14. Teschendorff, A.E., Enver, T.: Single-cell entropy for accurate estimation of differentiation potency from a cell's transcriptome. Nat. Commun. **8**, 15599 (2017)
15. Tosenberger, A., Bessonov, N., Levin, M., Reinberg, N., Volpert, V., Morozova, N.: A conceptual model of morphogenesis and regeneration. Acta Biotheor. **63**(3), 283–294 (2015)

Investigation of Unsupervised Models for Biodiversity Assessment

KVSN Rama Rao, Saurabh Garg$^{(\boxtimes)}$, and James Montgomery

School of Technology, Environments and Design, University of Tasmania,
Hobart, Australia
saurabh.garg@utas.edu.au

Abstract. Significant animal species loss has been observed in recent decades due to habitat destruction, which puts at risk environmental integrity and biodiversity. Traditional ways of assessing biodiversity are limited in terms of both time and space, and have high cost. Since the presence of animals can be indicated by sound, recently acoustic recordings have been used to estimate species richness. Bioacoustic sounds are typically recorded in habitats for several weeks, so contain a large collection of different sounds. Birds are of particular interest due to their distinctive calls and because they are useful ecological indicators. To assess biodiversity, the task of manually determining how many different types of birds are present in such a lengthy audio is really cumbersome. Towards providing an automated support to this issue, in this paper we investigate and propose a clustering based approach to assist in automated assessment of biodiversity. Our approach first estimates the number of different species and their volumes which are used for deriving a biodiversity index. Experimental results with real data indicates that our proposed approach estimates the biodiversity index value close to the ground truth.

Keywords: Biodiversity · Unsupervised model · Bioacoustics

1 Introduction

Monitoring environmental health has become a critical need for governments and ecological agencies. Environment health can be monitored through several methods. Biodiversity is one such measure. Biodiversity can be assessed by measuring species richness at desired locations. The work described hear focuses on birds as an indicator of environmental health. A traditional method to determine species richness is by using the point-count method. In this method, an experienced and skilled expert has to physically visit the location, observe and hear bird sounds for a specified period and count them. Typically, experts observe during morning, noon and dawn/dusk for a specified time period and fixed number of days. Several point-count methods have been outlined in [1], however Wimmer et al. [2] mentioned that 20 min of observation, three times a day (morning,

© Springer Nature Switzerland AG 2018
T. Mitrovic et al. (Eds.): AI 2018, LNAI 11320, pp. 160–171, 2018.
https://doi.org/10.1007/978-3-030-03991-2_17

noon, dawn) for a specified number of days is considered as the typical convention. Though this method is traditional, we can clearly observe an obvious wastage of human effort in addition to time consumption and cost. Further, the bird expert is listening to only a small amount of time, which may affect their biodiversity assessment since the sample size is too small. Hence there is need of some kind of automated support to assist this manual task.

Since the advent of bioacoustics, recording devices have been installed in many locations to collect bird sounds, which dramatically reduces the need to visit sites at regular intervals for observation. These recordings will assist in several assessments such as species richness. Expert human labellers will listen to the audio and label sections, thus assessing species richness. However, the recent growth of technology in terms of hardware, recording devices and sensors has enabled researchers to collect massive recordings. Listening to such enormous volume of audio is cumbersome. Several automatic recognisers have been created to detect species using supervised methods, however the state of art cannot reliably detect species in many natural environments since the search space is so high and often the ground truth is not available. Consequently, unsupervised models are appropriate for such kind of problems. Seoane et al. [5] experimented and concluded that unsupervised methods are a better and more cost effective way to obtain species distributions. Further, with unsupervised learning, models can learn different sounds in an area which makes further classification easier. Hence through this unsupervised model, we propose to identify different birds present in the audio and thus assess biodiversity.

Several works have attempted to use unsupervised methods in the domain of bioacoustics. Eichinski et al. [3] used unsupervised models for selecting the richest parts in long recordings such that a human listener used their effort most effectively. The events are detected and clustered to estimate the amount of information present in a sample. Phillips et al. [4] has applied unsupervised modelling for revealing ecological content in long duration audio recordings. The whole audio content is reduced to vectors of acoustic indices and then clustered. To interpret and visualize the clusters, colour coding is used which enabled quicker identification and indexing of long duration audio recordings. Although these methods are robust, they are focusing on smart sampling, and so still rely on a human labeller to assessing species richness manually. Hence, here also there is some part of manual intervention. Further, it is a fact that most of the audio data collected may not have ground truth available. In such a scenario, computing biodiversity will be a challenge. To address this issue, we propose a novel clustering based approach to approximate biodiversity index in an automated manner. In our approach, we first investigated the best way to estimate the number of different species, which becomes the input to either *k-means* or *Gaussian mixture model (GMM)*. Then, we investigate the best clustering algorithm that categories different sounds in different clusters. These clusters then become the basis for estimating biodiversity.

This paper is organized as follows: Sect. 2 discusses several research works on traditional biodiversity approaches. In Sect. 3 the problem scenario is explained.

The proposed approach has been detailed in Sect. 4, and experimental results are presented in Sect. 5. Section 6 presents discussion and briefly concludes.

2 Related Work

Biodiversity assessment is important as it provides an indication of the number of varieties of animals living in that particular habitat. To analyse audio data and obtain a biodiversity assessment, several approaches have been found in the literature, however most of them have several manual steps and are therefore not scalable to large recordings.

Riede [6] has made use of the Shannon-Wiener statistic to estimate cricket diversity in the Amazon rainforest. The recordings are for a duration of two weeks at 10 different points twice a day. The Shannon-Wiener statistic is used to obtain an understanding of species and their abundance. Colwell et al. [7] applied extrapolation to estimate terrestrial biodiversity. They considered two important measures: *richness* to estimate species availability and *complementarity* to estimate species varieties. They utilized a species accumulation curve for richness or complementarity estimation. If these curves are stable and uniformly sampled, then extrapolation can be applied. To extrapolate, asymptotic and non-asymptotic functions are used to predict unknown values from known ones. Celis-Murillo et al. [8] proposed a Soundscape Recording System (SRS) that overcomes the limitations of point count methods. To obtain species richness estimation for the acoustic data, they still applied the manual hearing process.

In an attempt to address this automatically, several works have attempted the use of unsupervised models in bioacoustics. Thakur et al. [16] developed a two-pass approach to detect species. Agranat [17] has developed a bat call classification model using Hierarchical Mixture Models (HMM). Salamon et al. [18] used unsupervised feature learning motivated by their use in music retrieval systems by using spherical k means. Somervuo and Härmä [19] has applied SOM for analysing bird song syllables. Further, Eichinski et al. [3] and Phillips et al. [4] have developed unsupervised models for smart sampling of audio content that identifies the richest part where more species are present. The smart sampled audio part will be assessed by human labeller to measure species richness. In summary, these works focus more on developing unsupervised sampling techniques to reduce a human labeller's work. In contrast to these works, this paper's focus is on the applicability of unsupervised machine learning models for automating biodiversity estimation of a region.

3 Problem Definition and System Scenario

When attempting to assess biodiversity from long-duration environmental recordings automatically there will be several issues, including:

1. Ground truth may not be available.
2. Data will be recorded for several hours.

3. Data will be recorded for different days.
4. Data will be recorded in different regions.

In such a scenario, this paper proposes unsupervised models to automatically assess and approximate the biodiversity index. The proposed approach is to estimate the number of different species and their abundance through clustering methods. In order to do this, first the number of clusters will be estimated and then different samples in the recording will be allocated to clusters (using standard clustering algorithms). Based on the results of clustering algorithm, biodiversity is estimated. Specifically this paper focuses on investigating answers to the following questions:

1. How to decide on number of clusters and studying whether the same number of clusters can be used for any day/region.
2. Which method of clustering is appropriate?
3. Developing a biodiversity index to estimate species richness or biodiversity.

4 Proposed Methodology

Our methodology consists of several steps which are outlined in Fig. 1.

Fig. 1. Methodology

4.1 Data Collection and Preparation

Raw audio data is usually collected from habitats. Data collection and preparation is the first bioacoustic analysis activity. It involves gathering the data and further making it ready for analysis through several pre-processing methods.

4.2 Pre-processing

Since the raw data is not directly suitable for analysis, certain pre-processing activities are required. Sampling and normalization are several pre-processing activities. Noise removal also plays a major role in pre-processing. Filters such as band pass filters will be used to cut off unwanted sounds by using the high and low frequencies bounding an acoustic event.

4.3   Feature Extraction

To build our unsupervised learning model, we have considered Mel-frequency cepstral coefficients (MFCC) as features as they offer several advantages: they are simple, robust and computationally efficient. They have good accuracy, computation does not require any performance tuning and they have exceptional recognition rates irrespective of call type. MFCC features have wide applicability in human speech recognition. Cai et al. [10] argues that there are several similarities between humans and birds with regard to hearing, the vocal tract and auditory processing, which enables the usage of MFCCs across a diversified set of animals. Several authors have used MFCCs as features for frogs, crickets and bird sounds. However, Furui et al. [11] and Hanson et al. [12] have demonstrated that MFCCs combined with *delta* and *delta-delta* features will enhance accuracy. Hence we have considered delta and delta-delta features as well.

Delta features: These are obtained by computing the first order derivative of MFCC features. These features represent the change in cepstral features with respect to time. Each delta feature represents the change between frames and hence they typically represent temporal information.

Delta-Delta features: These are obtained by computing the derivative of delta features. These are referred as acceleration coefficients that will display the change in delta features with respect to time. These features have longer temporal context.

4.4   Estimation of Different Species (Clusters)

The goal of the clustering stage is to cluster audio samples containing the same species together. Ideally, the process results in one cluster for each species. One major task in clustering is to determine number of clusters. There are different approaches to decide the initial number of clusters.

1. Elbow method: This approach focuses on the variance change as the number of clusters increases. Model accuracy increases as the number of clusters increases, however after some point adding clusters will not yield a better model. The mean squared error is plotted against the number of clusters. The point where the graph tends toward being flat is considered to be optimal value of the number of clusters, which is referred as the elbow criterion.

2. BIC/AIC: In a clustering algorithm based on mixture models, the information criterion has been extensively used to determine a suitable number of clusters. Bayesian Information Criterion (BIC) and Akaike's Information Criterion (AIC) have been widely used. Mixture models allows the use of Bayes Factors for selecting the clustering method and number of clusters. Expectation maximization is used to find maximum likelihood, while twice the Bayes factor referred as BIC is a more reliable approximation. More details about AIC and BIC can be found in [13, 14].

4.5 Clustering Algorithm

After deciding on the best value of clusters, we perform clustering. To perform clustering, several algorithms exist. For this study, we investigate two well known clustering algorithms:k-*means* and *Gaussian mixture model (GMM)*. k-means has been chosen as it works well with large datasets and GMM since the cluster assignment is flexible which can accommodate clusters of different structures and sizes.

1. k-*means:* It is one of the simplest algorithm yet robust and fast algorithm that is used in clustering. It requires initial k centers to be specified. Then associate each dataset point to the nearest center. After assigning all points, re-compute k new centroids. Re-assign the points to the new centroids. The process is repeated until there are no changes.
2. *GMM:* Here, we consider clusters as Gaussian distributions. In this, finite mixture of distributions are considered where components of each mixture correspond to a separate group. Multi-variate Gaussian distribution is considered as typical component distribution model. Expectation- Maximization algorithm is used to estimate the number of finite mixture models. Further each observation is assigned to cluster based on model and its estimated parameters. Since we are using probabilities, GMM performs soft assignment of points to clusters rather than hard clustering as in k-means.

4.6 Computing Biodiversity Index

To assess biodiversity, species richness is typically evaluated. However species richness alone cannot determine biodiversity as it does not take into account the number of individuals of each species. Hence an appropriate measure of biodiversity should consider abundance of each species as well. For instance, consider the data of birds distributed in different regions A and B. In region A, sparrow and parrot richness and abundance may be the same, but in region B there may be only sparrows with no parrots. In this case, we can consider that region A biodiversity is high compared to region B, because region B is dominated by only one species.

To quantify species richness and evenness, Simpsons Index (D) is one of the prominent measures [20]:

$$D = 1 - \frac{\sum n_i(n_i - 1)}{N(N - 1)} \tag{1}$$

where n_i is the total number of observations of species i and N is the total number of observed individuals.

We compute the biodiversity index as follows:

1. Ground truth based biodiversity index ($Simpson - GT$): We consider the ground truth data for validating our result, using human expert labels of the dataset (see next Section for details). The data related to a specific date is

obtained and the samples belonging to a specific species counted which is referred as n_i. The total number of samples is considered as N. Using these two values, actual biodiversity is computed.

2. Clustering based biodiversity index ($Simpson - ClusEst$): Cluster output is considered to compute this index. The number of samples in a cluster is computed and referred as n_i. The count of all samples across all clusters gives N. Using these two values, we estimate the biodiversity.

These two values are computed for each day and each region. The error difference between these values is observed. If the error is minimal and the both trends are similar, then we consider our computed biodiversity index is close to ground truth value.

It may be noted that, like manual surveys, both the biodiversity indices are slight overestimates of the actual value. However, these will be good enough for estimating changes and trends in biodiversity.

5   Evaluation

5.1   Dataset

We have obtained data from the Samford Ecological Research Facility (SERF). This dataset's acquisition is well described in [15]: recordings were made continuously for five days from three different sites in bushland in the Brisbane city outskirts (North East (NE), North West (NW), South East (SE)). The audio data was labelled by human experts with bird calls for all five days. The number of labelled calls in each day's audio is summarised in Table 1.

Table 1. Summary of labels

Region	Day 1	Day 2	Day 3	Day 4	Day 5
NE	16025	7880	8095	3260	7890
NW	9565	9790	11140	4185	11100
SE	15275	10205	13980	2965	10385

5.2   Pre-processing

The collected audio is converted to mono channel (the original stereo recording is purely for redundancy; no spatial information is derived from it). The audio is then down sampled to 17,640 samples per second. This sampling rate is chosen in order to reduce computational load. To extract short audio clips of each species, the duration of the call was used. The call between event start and event end is extracted. The extracted short audio will be of different lengths. Further, a band pass filter is applied which will filter the frequencies below and above the given frequencies. For each day, the number of audio files that are used for clustering are as many as the label count (Table 1).

5.3   Experiments and Analysis of Results

Number of Clusters. The goal of the clustering stage is to associate calls by the same species together. Ideally, the process results in one cluster for each species. To determine the number of clusters or species, we experimented with three methods: Elbow, Bayesian information criterion (BIC) and Akaike's information criteria (AIC). Applying these to the data for Day 1 of the NE region suggested 30, 36 or 54 clusters, respectively. Given the actual number of species this suggests that the AIC value is more appropriate. In order to check that the number of clusters obtained is valid for any day in the NE region we repeated the above experiments on the remaining days. Results are shown in Fig. 2a. From the figure, we can observe that the values are different for each day. However, AIC continues to give values closer to ground truth than the other methods.

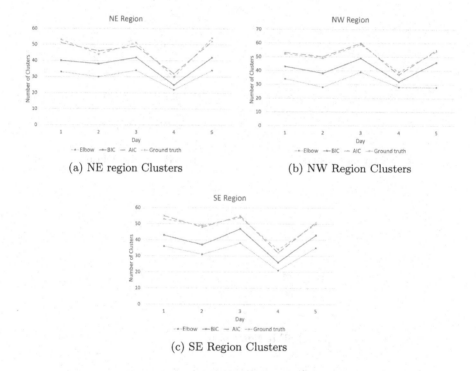

(a) NE region Clusters   (b) NW Region Clusters

(c) SE Region Clusters

Fig. 2. Estimation of number of clusters

We further investigated the other regions, NW and SE. Results are shown in Figs. 2b and c. Based on these experiments, we can infer that:

- The number of clusters/species are different each day
- Among the three methods, AIC gives the most realistic value.

In summary, since each consecutive day the cluster counts are different it indicates the amount of bird activity varies quite drastically, further supporting the need for an automated approach to this problem.

Clustering Methods and Different Regions. As discussed before, clustering is performed using k-means and Gaussian Mixture Models (GMM) using the Python Scikit-learn package. To determine the better clustering method, we applied these two algorithms on the NE region (across all five days). The clusters are evaluated by the external measure *purity*. Figure 3a shows the cluster purity obtained for NE region, and shows that both k-means and GMM performed similarly well. However, when compared with GMM, the k-means algorithm's performance is slightly better across all days in the NE region.

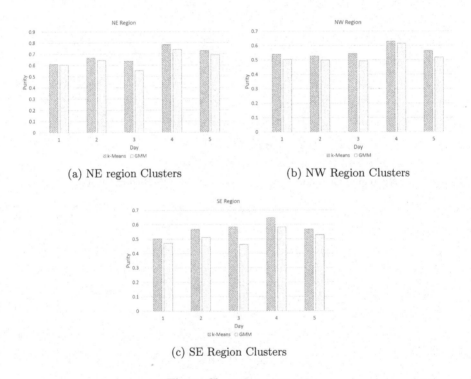

(a) NE region Clusters   (b) NW Region Clusters

(c) SE Region Clusters

Fig. 3. Clustering accuracy

To reaffirm this fact, the experiment is repeated for other the NW and SE regions, with results shown in Figs. 3b and c, respectively. These also show that k-means performed better than GMM. We also compared the performance of two algorithms using the internal measure of the silhouette index, which demonstrated that k-means' performance is better when compared with GMM. Hence, based on the above experiments, we concluded that k-means would be best algorithm as the basis for the estimated biodiversity index.

Computing Biodiversity Index. Our ultimate aim is to compute a biodiversity index that can estimate the bird activity using clustering results. Since k-means performed well in all regions of the dataset, we considered the cluster results of k-means and computed the estimated biodiversity index ($Simpson - ClusEst$). To evaluate this index, we computed the ground truth biodiversity index ($Simpson - GT$). These two indexes are plotted for all three regions, shown in Fig. 4. It can be observed that the trend of the estimated Simpson biodiversity index using our methodology and the actual value are quite similar. Even in terms of actual value, the proposed unsupervised approach resulted the biodiversity index which is very close to ground truth index. For example, for the NE region the difference between the two indices is 6–7% while for the other two regions it is just 3–4%.

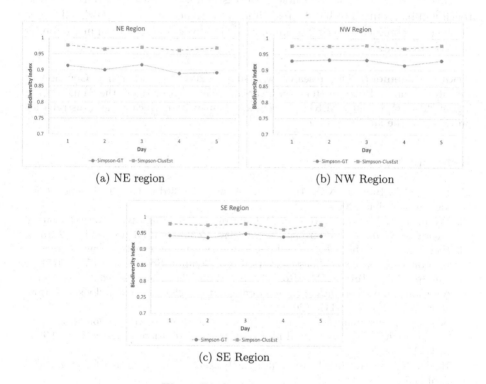

(a) NE region

(b) NW Region

(c) SE Region

Fig. 4. Biodiversity estimation

6   Conclusions and Future Work

Bioacoustics can be used to monitor sound-producing species in a variety of habitats. Analysing the sounds in a long-duration recording can enable an area's biodiversity to be assessed. As the use of bioacoustic recorders increases so does the volume of data needing to be analysed. While automated species recognisers are being developed, it is still generally required that human labellers inspect selections of the audio to reliably identify all species present (which can then support biodiversity assessments), but such an approach is too slow. This paper proposed an unsupervised approach to assess biodiversity. In our approach, after determining a suitable number of clusters using the AIC method, two clustering algorithms were evaluated. Results indicated that k-means algorithm performed better than GMM. Since it is a large dataset, k-means algorithm has shown better performance than GMM. Hence k-means algorithm output can be used to estimate biodiversity using the Simpson index. Estimated biodiversity index values indicated that our approach produces an estimate that is close to the ground truth.

However much of the data now a days is non-stationary, so a different approach will be required to handle real time data. Hence our future work will focus on the use of online clustering techniques for biodiversity estimation in streaming bioacoustics data.

Acknowledgement. This research was supported by an Australian Government Research Training Program (RTP) Scholarship. We sincerely thank the Samford Ecological Research Facility (SERF), Queensland University of Technology, Australia for providing us the labelled dataset.

References

1. Bibby, C.J., Burgess, N.D., Hill, D.A., Mustoe, S.: Bird Census Techniques. Elsevier, Amsterdam (2000)
2. Wimmer, J., Towsey, M., Roe, P., Williamson, I.: Sampling environmental acoustic recordings to determine bird species richness. Ecol. Appl. **23**, 1419–1428 (2013)
3. Eichinski, P., Sitbon, L., Roe, P.: Clustering acoustic events in environmental recordings for species richness surveys. Proc. Comput. Sci. **51**, 640–649 (2015)
4. Phillips, Y.F., Towsey, M., Roe, P.: Revealing the ecological content of long-duration audio-recordings of the environment through clustering and visualisation. PloS One **13**(3), e0193345 (2018)
5. Seoane, J., Bustamante, J., Daz-Delgado, R.: Effect of expert opinion on the predictive ability of environmental models of bird distribution. Conserv. Biol. **19**(2), 512–522 (2005)
6. Riede, K.: Monitoring biodiversity: analysis of Amazonian rainforest sounds. Ambio 546–548 (1993)
7. Colwell, R.K., Coddington, J.A.: Estimating terrestrial biodiversity through extrapolation. Philos. Trans. Roy. Soc. B: Biol. Sci. **345**(1311), 101–118 (1994)
8. Celis-Murillo, A., Deppe, J.L., Allen, M.F.: Using soundscape recordings to estimate bird species abundance, richness, and composition. J. Field Ornithol. **80**(1), 64–78 (2009)
9. BioDiversityGroup: Biodiversity Website (2017). http://www.bioacoustics.myspecies.info/en. Accessed May 2017
10. Cai, J., Ee, D., Pham, B., Roe, P., Zhang, J.: Sensor network for the monitoring of ecosystem: bird species recognition. In: 3rd International Conference on Intelligent Sensors, Sensor Networks and Information, ISSNIP 2007, pp. 293–298. IEEE (2007)

11. Furui, S.: Speaker-independent isolated word recognition using dynamic features of speech spectrum. IEEE Trans. Acoust. Speech Signal Process. **34**(1), 52–59 (1986)
12. Hanson, B., Applebaum, T.: Robust speaker-independent word recognition using static, dynamic and acceleration features: experiments with Lombard and noisy speech. In: 1990 International Conference on Acoustics, Speech, and Signal Processing, ICASSP-90. IEEE (1990)
13. Akaike, H.: Information theory and an extension of the maximum likelihood principle. In: Proceedings of the 2nd International Symposium on Information Theory, Tsahkadsor, Armenia, 28 September 1971
14. Schwarz, G.: Estimating the dimension of a model. Ann. Stat. **6**, 461–464 (1978)
15. Wimmer, J., Towsey, M., Roe, P., Williamson, I.: Sampling environmental acoustic recordings to determine bird species richness. Ecol. Appl. **23**, 1419–1428 (2013)
16. Thakur, A., Rajan, P.: Model-based unsupervised segmentation of birdcalls from field recordings. In: 2016 10th International Conference on Signal Processing and Communication Systems (ICSPCS), pp. 1–6. IEEE, December 2016
17. Agranat, I.: Bat species identification from zero crossing and full spectrum echolocation calls using hidden Markov models, fisher scores, unsupervised clustering and balanced winnow pairwise classifiers. In: Proceedings of Meetings on Acoustics ICA2013, vol. 19, no. 1, p. 010016. ASA, June 2013
18. Salamon, J., Bello, J.P.: Unsupervised feature learning for urban sound classification. In: 2015 IEEE International Conference on Acoustics, Speech and Signal Processing (ICASSP), pp. 171–175. IEEE, April 2015
19. Somervuo, P., Härmä, A.: Analyzing bird song syllables on the self-organizing map. In: Workshop on Self-Organizing Maps (WSOM 2003), September 2003
20. Peet, R.K.: The measurement of species diversity. Ann. Rev. Ecol. Syst. **5**(1), 285–307 (1974)

Field-Regularised Factorization Machines for Mining the Maintenance Logs of Equipment

Zhibin Li[1(✉)], Jian Zhang[1], Qiang Wu[1], and Christina Kirsch[2]

[1] University of Technology Sydney, Sydney, Australia
Zhibin.Li@student.uts.edu.au, {Jian.Zhang,Qiang.Wu}@uts.edu.au
[2] Sydney Trains-Operational Technology, Sydney, Australia
Christina.Kirsch@transport.nsw.gov.au

Abstract. Failure prediction is very important for railway infrastructure. Traditionally, data from various sensors are collected for this task. Value of maintenance logs is often neglected. Maintenance records of equipment usually indicate equipment status. They could be valuable for prediction of equipment faults. In this paper, we propose Field-regularised Factorization Machines (FrFMs) to predict failures of railway points with maintenance logs. Factorization Machine (FM) and its variants are state-of-the-art algorithms designed for sparse data. They are widely used in click-through rate prediction and recommendation systems. Categorical variables are converted to binary features through one-hot encoding and then fed into these models. However, field information is ignored in this process. We propose Field-regularised Factorization Machines to incorporate such valuable information. Experiments on data set from railway maintenance logs and another public data set show the effectiveness of our methods.

Keywords: Factorization Machines · Failure prediction
Categorical data

1 Introduction

Railway points are a kind of mechanical installations allowing railway trains to be guided from one track to another. They are among the key components of railway infrastructure. As a part of the signal equipment, points control the routes of trains at railway junctions, having a great impact on the reliability and punctuality of rail transport. Existing research on failure prediction of points mainly relies on additional sensors' data [1,6,7,15,22,26], e.g. voltages, currents and forces. Installation of sensors incurs costly labour and material expenses, as well as the possibility of sensor malfunction, which limits their implementation. Other research focuses on approximating the long-term degradation curve of equipment under certain maintenance strategy [11,12,18,21,23], rather than predicting failure of equipment in the near future.

© Springer Nature Switzerland AG 2018
T. Mitrovic et al. (Eds.): AI 2018, LNAI 11320, pp. 172–183, 2018.
https://doi.org/10.1007/978-3-030-03991-2_18

Maintenance logs of equipment contain formatted maintenance records, including maintenance type, components, finished time, etc. They can be of great value in failure prediction. These data often carry information of equipment status with timestamps. Compared to data collected by sensors, maintenance records are usually ready to hand with a specified format. They mainly consist of categorical variables and could be very sparse after commonly performed one-hot encoding. Besides, railway points consist of many components, and failures can be viewed as a result of their interactions. Domain knowledge regarding such interactions might be very limited and depends on equipment types. In order to predict failures with maintenance logs, the model needs to learn the complex interactions from such sparse data.

Aiming at this challenging task, we put forward Field-regularised Factorization Machines (FrFMs) for failure prediction of railway points. Factorization Machines (FMs) combine the advantages of Support Vector Machines (SVMs) with factorization models [19]. In contrast to SVM, FMs factorise all interactions between features into products of two low-rank matrices. In this way, they are likely to learn interactions which even do not appear in training data. Many variants of FMs have been proposed and achieved good performance. Locally Linear Factorization Machines [13] adopts locally linear coding scheme and jointly optimise FM models with anchor points. They are capable of learning complex non-linear data by exploring local coding technique. Wang et al. [24] propose Contextual and Position-Aware Factorization Machines targeted at sentiment analysis of texts. Inspired by the neural skip-gram model, Contextual and Position-Aware Factorization Machines limits interactions to a range of words. In addition, latent vectors are learned based on the relative position of words, which means that there will be several independent latent vectors for one word. FMs are usually limited to quadratic models, and related loss functions are non-convex. Many papers have focused on overcoming these two limitations. Neural Factorization Machines [9] take in the advantages of deep neural networks to modelling higher-order feature interactions. They firstly encode feature vectors by pre-training FMs and then train a neural network with these embedding vectors. DeepFM [8] is similar to Neural Factorization Machines, except that it is an end-to-end model that requires no pre-training. Unlike Neural Factorization Machines, DeepFM jointly learns the embedded vectors and the neural networks. Yamada et al. [25] reformulate the optimisation problem of FMs as a semi-definite programming problem. By introducing nuclear norm in FMs, their loss functions of FMs becomes convex.

The above-mentioned models focus less on the inherent properties of data carried by field information. Field-aware Factorization Machines (FFMs) [10] consider the field structure of data and learn pair-wise interactions with regard to each pair of fields. They are more complex than FMs in terms of the number of parameters and computational complexity. Field-weighted Factorization Machines [16] add additional coefficients to depict the interactions of fields, and reduce the number of model parameters compared to FFMs. These models treat features from different fields differently. In other words, they only consider inter-field information.

Existing models either ignore the field information or only consider the inter-field information. They neglect the **relationships among features inside each field**, which is going to be used in our models.

Our contributions could be shown in two aspects. Firstly, to the best of our knowledge, it is the first time that maintenance logs are used to predict the failure of railway points. Secondly, we propose FrFMs which leverage field information and develop a method to solve the related optimisation problems. Experiments on two data sets show that our methods can achieve better performance compared to some state-of-the-art methods.

2 Preliminaries

A degree-2 polynomial mapping can often effectively capture the information of feature conjunctions [2]. It learns a weight for each feature conjunction:

$$\phi_{Poly2}(W, \boldsymbol{x}) = \sum_{i=1}^{n} \sum_{j=i+1}^{n} w_{i,j} x_i x_j$$

$$W = (w_{i,j}) \in \mathbb{R}^{n \times n}, \boldsymbol{x} \in \mathbb{R}^n \tag{1}$$

where W is the learned weight matrix and $\boldsymbol{x}$ is the input vector of dimension n. Corresponding 2-way FMs can be written in following form:

$$\phi_{FM}(V, \boldsymbol{x}) = \sum_{i=1}^{n} \sum_{j=i+1}^{n} \langle \boldsymbol{v}_i, \boldsymbol{v}_j \rangle x_i x_j$$

$$V = \begin{bmatrix} \boldsymbol{v}_1 \\ \boldsymbol{v}_2 \\ \vdots \\ \boldsymbol{v}_n \end{bmatrix} \in \mathbb{R}^{n \times k}, \boldsymbol{x} \in \mathbb{R}^n \tag{2}$$

$\langle \cdot, \cdot \rangle$ stands for dot product of two vectors. $\boldsymbol{v}_i$ and $\boldsymbol{v}_j$ denote two row vectors of V with dimension k. $\boldsymbol{v}_i$ is referred to as **embedding vector** or **latent vector** for feature i. For simplicity of formulations, we omit linear terms and bias term following [10], but we include them in experiments.

Categorical data are highly sparse after one-hot encoding. Some pairs of $x_i x_j$ might even not appear in training data. In this case, for polynomial mapping some $w_{i,j}$ are not able to be learned. By factorizing weight matrix W into VV^T, FMs are able to learn interactions for rare feature pairs. Each row vector $\boldsymbol{v}_i$ in V stands for latent vector regarding feature x_i.

Table 1. A sample of maintenance records with failures to be predicted.

Failure	Maintenance type	Component
1	A	II
1	C	II
−1	B	VI

3   Field-Regularised Factorization Machines

3.1   Motivation

Table 1 presents some simple data constructed from maintenance records for failure prediction. 'Maintenance Type' and 'Component' are two different **fields**. A, B and C stand for different maintenance types that can probably be 'Routine Inspection', 'Corrective Maintenance' and so on. The field 'Component' shows the maintenance was performed over which component. '1' and '−1' in column 'Failure' stand for whether there was a fault occurred after this maintenance and before next planned maintenance.

FMs will learn latent vectors for A, B, C, II and VI respectively. In engineering practice, we anticipate different effects with different maintenance behaviours. Each field can be regarded as a classification criterion for maintenance work, and corresponding features in that field are the class labels. We would prefer diverse latent vectors in the same field because we could distinguish the effects caused by different maintenance work in this way. As a result, latent vectors for A, B and C should be diverse, as well as latent vectors for II and VI.

3.2   Methods

In this section, we propose the FrFMs for binary classification. For simplicity of formulations, we omit linear terms and bias term following [10], but we include them in experiments as they often improve the results. The loss function of FrFMs with logistic loss regarding one sample (y, x) is:

$$\mathcal{L}(V) = \log(1 + \exp(-y\phi_{FM}(V, x))) + \frac{\lambda_1}{2}\|V\|_F^2 + \frac{\lambda_2}{2}R(V) \qquad (3)$$

$\phi_{FM}(V, x)$ is defined in (2), as we share the same prediction function with FMs. $\|\cdot\|_F$ is the Frobenius norm for matrices. $y \in \{-1, 1\}$ is the ground truth label for sample x. The first term denotes the prediction loss compared to ground truth, and the second term forces the solution V sparse. $R(V)$ is a regulariser that measures the similarity of latent vectors in each field, and we prefer smaller similarity as discussed above. By introducing $R(V)$ into loss function, field information is included. λ_1, λ_2 are two non-negative parameters obtained by cross validation.

In order to capture the inherent properties come with fields of data, we construct a feature relation matrix A which will be included in $R(V)$:

$$A_{i,j} = \begin{cases} \frac{1}{N_{i,j}} & \text{if } x_i, x_j \text{ are in same field and } i \neq j, \\ 0 & \text{else.} \end{cases} \quad (4)$$

$N_{i,j}$ is the number of features in the field contains x_i and x_j. It is introduced to avoid deviation caused by different number of features in different fields. Each element in A stands for the relationship of two features. If they are in same field, then corresponding entries in A will be one divided by the number of features in this field. Otherwise they will be zeros.

Various metrics can be used to measure the similarity of latent vectors. In this work, we will present FrFM with Euclidean distance and cosine similarity.

FrFM-EUC. We refer to FrFM with Euclidean distance as FrFM-EUC. Euclidean distance is used to measure the similarity of two vectors in FrFM-EUC, and larger Euclidean distance indicates smaller similarity. Therefore, $R(V)$ has the following form:

$$R(V) = -\sum_{i=1}^{n} \sum_{j=i+1}^{n} A_{i,j} \|v_i - v_j\|_2^2 \quad (5)$$

$\|\cdot\|_2$ denotes l^2-norm for vectors. The loss function for FrFM-EUC is:

$$\mathcal{L}_{euc}(V) = \log(1 + \exp(-y\phi_{FM}(V, x))) + \frac{\lambda_1}{2}\|V\|_F^2 - \frac{\lambda_2}{2}\sum_{i=1}^{n}\sum_{j=i+1}^{n} A_{i,j}\|v_i - v_j\|_2^2 \quad (6)$$

FrFM-COS. FrFM-COS denotes FrFM with cosine similarity. $R(V)$ has the following form:

$$R(V) = \sum_{i=1}^{n}\sum_{j=1}^{n} A_{i,j} \frac{\langle v_i, v_j \rangle}{\|v_i\|_2 \|v_j\|_2} \quad (7)$$

Directly optimizing (3) with (7) is complicated. Rewriting rows of V into products of their direction vectors and lengths leads to:

$$V = \begin{bmatrix} w_1\hat{v}_1 \\ w_2\hat{v}_2 \\ \vdots \\ w_n\hat{v}_n \end{bmatrix} \in \mathbb{R}^{n \times k}, \quad \hat{v}_i = \frac{v_i}{\|v_i\|_2}, \quad w_i = \|v_i\|_2 \quad (8)$$

Then (7) equals to:

$$R(V) = \sum_{i=1}^{n}\sum_{j=1}^{n} A_{i,j} \hat{v}_i \hat{v}_j^T = tr(\hat{V}^T A \hat{V}) \quad (9)$$

Substitute V with $\hat{V}$ and $\boldsymbol{w}$ in formulation of FMs:

$$\phi_{FM}(\hat{V}, \boldsymbol{w}, \boldsymbol{x}) = \sum_{i=1}^{n} \sum_{j=i+1}^{n} \langle w_i \hat{\boldsymbol{v}}_i, w_j \hat{\boldsymbol{v}}_j \rangle x_i x_j \tag{10}$$

and finally we get loss function for FrFM-COS:

$$\mathcal{L}_{cos}(\hat{V}, \boldsymbol{w}) = \log(1 + \exp(-y\phi_{FM}(\hat{V}, \boldsymbol{w}, \boldsymbol{x}))) + \frac{\lambda_1}{2} \|\boldsymbol{w}\|_2^2 + \frac{\lambda_2}{2} tr(\hat{V}^T A \hat{V})$$

$$s.t. \; \|\hat{\boldsymbol{v}}_i\|_2 = 1, \forall i = 1, 2, \ldots, n. \quad \boldsymbol{w} \in \mathbb{R}_+^{1 \times n} \tag{11}$$

3.3 Optimization

Similar to FMs, our loss functions are non-convex. Gradient descent is used to find local minima of our loss functions. Stochastic Gradient Descent (SGD) is widely used in optimisation of FMs and its variants. It has shown its effectiveness. Mini-batch Gradient Descent also enjoys the advantages of SGD while it is more efficient. Thus we adopt Mini-batch Gradient Descent in optimisation. We apply AdaGrad [5] to determine the learning rate in each iteration for it has shown great power in similar problems [3,10]. To lessen over-fitting, we utilise early-stop strategy in training of FrFM-EUC and FrFM-COS. The best training epoch T will be decided based on a validation set.

FrFM-EUC. The gradient with regard to one sample $(y, \boldsymbol{x})$ is:

$$\frac{\partial \mathcal{L}_{euc}(V)}{\partial \boldsymbol{v}_i} = \frac{-y}{1 + \exp(y\phi_{FM}(V, \boldsymbol{x}))} (x_i \sum_{j=1}^{n} \boldsymbol{v}_j x_j - \boldsymbol{v}_i x_i^2)$$

$$+ (x_i \neq 0)(\lambda_1 \boldsymbol{v}_i - \lambda_2 \sum_{j=1}^{n} A_{i,j}(\boldsymbol{v}_i - \boldsymbol{v}_j)) \tag{12}$$

$(x_i \neq 0)$ in (12) indicates that gradients would be zero if corresponding features are zero. This strategy has been used in FFMs and performs well. We can update model parameters with adaptive learning rate in iteration l:

$$G_{i,f}^{(l+1)} = G_{i,f}^{(l)} + \left(\frac{\partial \mathcal{L}_{euc}(V)}{\partial v_{i,f}} \bigg|_{V=V^{(l)}} \right)^2 \tag{13}$$

$$v_{i,f}^{(l+1)} = v_{i,f}^{(l)} - \frac{\eta}{\sqrt{G_{i,f}^{(l+1)} + \epsilon}} \circ \frac{\partial \mathcal{L}_{euc}(V)}{\partial v_{i,f}} \bigg|_{V=V^{(l)}} \tag{14}$$

∘ denotes element-wise multiplication of vectors. G stores the accumulated square gradient for AdaGrad and ϵ is s a smoothing term that avoids division by zero (we set it to 10^{-8} in this paper). The training process for FrFM-EUC is presented in Algorithm 1.

Algorithm 1. Training FrFM-EUC by Mini-batch Gradient Descent

---

input Data matrix $D \in \mathbb{R}^{M \times n}$ contains M samples, feature relation matrix A, latent
dimension k, hyper-parameters λ_1, λ_2, learning rate η, batch size m, $G^{(0)} = \mathbf{0}$.
Randomly initialise $V^{(0)} \in \mathbb{R}^{n \times k}$ with values sampled from a uniform distribution
$[0, 1/\sqrt{k}]$. Calculate the number of batches $b = \lfloor \frac{M}{m} \rfloor$.
for $Epoch = 0$ to T **do**
    Shuffle the samples in D randomly.
    Split D into batches $X_1, X_2, ..., X_b \in \mathbb{R}^{m \times n}$.
    for $i \in \{1, 2, ..., b\}$ **do**
        Calculate the gradient of V by (12) for every sample in X_i and get the average.
        Update accumulated square gradient G by (13).
        Update V by (14).

FrFM-COS. The gradient with regard to one sample $(y, \boldsymbol{x})$ is:

$$
\frac{\partial \mathcal{L}_{cos}(\hat{V}, \boldsymbol{w})}{\partial \hat{\boldsymbol{v}}_i} = \frac{-y}{1 + \exp(y\phi_{FM}(\hat{V}, \boldsymbol{w}, \boldsymbol{x}))}(w_i x_i \sum_{j=1}^{n} \hat{\boldsymbol{v}}_j w_j x_j - \hat{\boldsymbol{v}}_i w_i^2 x_i^2)
$$
$$
+ (x_i \neq 0)\lambda_2 \sum_{j=1}^{n} A_{i,j} \hat{\boldsymbol{v}}_j
\tag{15}
$$

$$
\frac{\partial \mathcal{L}_{cos}(\hat{V}, \boldsymbol{w})}{\partial \boldsymbol{w}} = \frac{-y}{1 + \exp(y\phi_{FM}(\hat{V}, \boldsymbol{w}, \boldsymbol{x}))}((\boldsymbol{w} \circ \boldsymbol{x})(\hat{V}\hat{V}^T - diag(\hat{V}\hat{V}^T))) \circ \boldsymbol{x}
$$
$$
+ \lambda_1(\boldsymbol{x} \neq 0) \circ \boldsymbol{w}
\tag{16}
$$

$(\boldsymbol{x} \neq 0)$ is a binary row vector indicates non-zero indices of $\boldsymbol{x}$. Similarly, gradients
would be zero if corresponding features are zero. With gradient in hand, we can
train the model similar to Algorithm 1. Differences are that we need to project
$\hat{V}$ and $\boldsymbol{w}$ into feasible sets in each iteration.

4   Experiments

4.1   Data Set

POINTS-3 data set was generated from the maintenance logs of Sydney Trains'
railway points. For numerical features, they were simply transformed into features 'Zero' or 'Non-Zero'. As shown in Fig. 1, for one piece of equipment, we
selected three consecutive maintenance records: Maintenance 1, Maintenance 2
and Maintenance 3, to construct a sample and labelled the sample depending on
whether a failure occurred between Maintenance 3 and Maintenance 4. If there
was a failure record, then this sample was labelled with '1', otherwise '−1'.

Equipment details including equipment type, location and other features were
also concatenated to construct one data sample. We randomly split the data set
into 60% training set, 20% validation set and 20% test set.

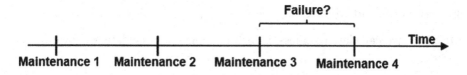

Fig. 1. An example for sample labelling in POINTS-3.

Phishing data set contains important features that have been proven to be sound and effective in predicting phishing websites [4]. We randomly split the data into 64% training set, 16% validation set and 20% test set.

Table 2 summarises the statistics of the data sets.

Table 2. Statistics of the data sets.

Data set	# Instances	# Features	# Fields
POINTS-3	55784	2226	52
Phishing	11055	68	30

4.2 Baselines and Hyper-parameter Tuning

We compare our models with three baselines.

LINEAR-LR denotes Logistic Regression with linear terms. It has been proven to be effective in classification tasks with sparse data. We implemented LINEAR-LR with Python library sklearn [17].

FM is the implementation of Factorization Machines defined in (2). We also included linear terms and bias term.

FFM is the implementation of Field-aware Factorization Machines. We also included linear terms and bias term.

FrFM-EUC and **FrFM-COS** stand for our methods proposed in this paper.

Both FM and FFM were implemented by xLearn [14] with AdaGrad and SGD optimizer. All hyper-parameters were chosen based on validation sets. The regularisation parameters were chosen from $\{10^{-6}, 10^{-5}, \ldots, 10^{6}\}$ for LINEAR-LR and $\{10^{-6}, 10^{-5}, \ldots, 10^{-1}\}$ for all other methods. Learning rates for AdaGrad were chosen from $\{0.02, 0.2\}$. Latent dimensions were chosen from $\{20, 40, \ldots, 100\}$ for FM and our method, and from $\{10, 20, \ldots, 50\}$ for FFM. Early-stop strategy was adopted for FM, FFM and our method to reduce overfitting. Batch size was set to 64 in training of FrFM-EUC and FrFM-COS.

4.3 Results and Metrics

Metrics. We calculated Logloss of each baseline on every data set. **Logloss** is given by:

$$\text{Logloss} = \frac{1}{M} \sum_{i=1}^{M} log(1 + \exp(-y_i \hat{y}_i)) \tag{17}$$

y_i and $\hat{y}_i$ are the label and model output for test sample i respectively. M is the total number of test instances.

AUROC and **AUPRC** stand for area under receiver operating characteristic curve and area under precision-recall curve respectively.

Results. Table 3 shows the results on different data sets, the best results are bold and second best are underlined. We trained and tested these models five times on each data set and reported the average results. POINTS-3 data set is an imbalanced data set with only 1701 positive samples out of 55784 samples, so AUPRC is more representative compared to AUROC according to [20]. AUPRC were calculated from $recall > 0.1$ for the reason that too low recall is meaningless in our case. Phishing data set is a balanced data set that won't show much difference between AUROC and AUPRC, so we only present the AUROC for it.

Table 3. Comparison of LINEAR-LR, FM, FFM, FrFM-EUC and FrFM-COS.

Method	POINTS-3			Phishing	
	AUROC	AUPRC (*recall* > 0.1)	Logloss	AUROC	Logloss
LINEAR-LR	0.7012	0.0641	0.1275	0.9886	0.1384
FM	0.6987	0.0622	0.1285	0.9911	0.1226
FFM	0.6974	0.0619	0.1291	0.9923	0.1134
FrFM-COS	<u>0.7090</u>	**0.0676**	<u>0.1271</u>	<u>0.9925</u>	<u>0.1120</u>
FrFM-EUC	**0.7108**	<u>0.0674</u>	**0.1270**	**0.9950**	**0.0919**

Experiment results show that our methods perform best on these two data sets. Precision-recall curves related to POINTS-3 data set for $recall > 0.1$ and $precision > 0.06$ are plotted in Fig. 2.

Figure 2 shows that FrFM-COS can also achieve the best F_1-score (0.165) compared to other methods. By appropriately setting threshold value for the classifier got from FrFM-EUC, we can get an overall **Accuracy: 90.99%**, with **Precision: 11.02%** and **Recall: 27.65%**. This may not be a perfect prediction but it is still acceptable considering that we didn't use any sensor data (e.g. current, voltage, force and so on). There are wrongly recorded data and failures that are caused by vandalism which makes some failures unpredictable. Outputs of the model could be used as references for maintenance plans.

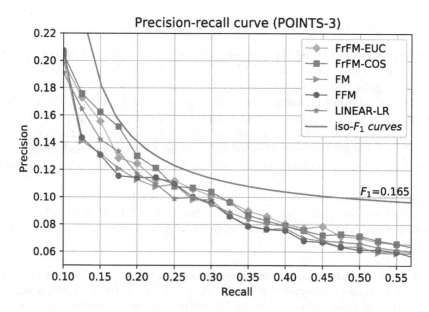

Fig. 2. Precision-recall curves with regard to POINTS-3.

Receiver operating characteristic curves with regard to Phishing data set are plotted in Fig. 3. Our method FrFM-EUC consistently outperforms other methods.

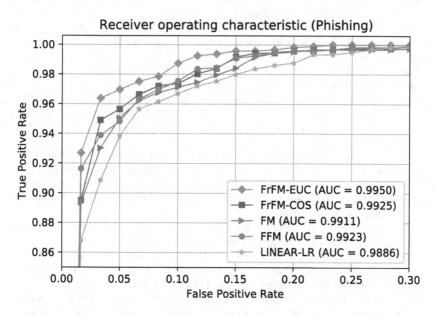

Fig. 3. Receiver operating characteristic curves with regard to Phishing.

5   Conclusion and Future Work

In this paper, we proposed the Field-regularised Factorization Machines for failure prediction of railway points. Field information is often ignored in many related methods. Especially for the inner-field relationships among features, there is little work concerning them. The key components of FrFMs are the regularisation terms that incorporate field information in the training process. Two forms of FrFMs: FrFM-EUC and FrFM-COS are presented. Experiment results showed that our models outperformed some state-of-the-art methods in predicting failure of railway points. We also achieved a better result on a public data set.

The predictions for points failure were not perfect but could be used as the reference for maintenance plans. Our following work will be focusing on combining data from other sources with maintenance data to improve the prediction results.

Acknowledgements. The authors greatly appreciate the financial support from the Rail Manufacturing Cooperative Research Centre (funded jointly by participating rail organisations and the Australian Federal Governments Business Cooperative Research Centres Program) through Project R3.7.2 - Big data analytics for condition based monitoring and maintenance.

References

1. Camci, F., Eker, O.F., Başkan, S., Konur, S.: Comparison of sensors and methodologies for effective prognostics on railway turnout systems. Proc. Inst. Mech. Eng. Part F: J. Rail Rapid Transit **230**(1), 24–42 (2016)
2. Chang, Y.W., Hsieh, C.J., Chang, K.W., Ringgaard, M., Lin, C.J.: Training and testing low-degree polynomial data mappings via linear SVM. J. Mach. Learn. Res. **11**(Apr), 1471–1490 (2010)
3. Chin, W.-S., Zhuang, Y., Juan, Y.-C., Lin, C.-J.: A learning-rate schedule for stochastic gradient methods to matrix factorization. In: Cao, T., Lim, E.-P., Zhou, Z.-H., Ho, T.-B., Cheung, D., Motoda, H. (eds.) PAKDD 2015. LNCS, vol. 9077, pp. 442–455. Springer, Cham (2015). https://doi.org/10.1007/978-3-319-18038-0_35
4. Dheeru, D., Taniskidou, E.K.: UCI machine learning repository (2017). http://archive.ics.uci.edu/ml
5. Duchi, J., Hazan, E., Singer, Y.: Adaptive subgradient methods for online learning and stochastic optimization. J. Mach. Learn. Res. **12**(Jul), 2121–2159 (2011)
6. García Márquez, F.P., Roberts, C., Tobias, A.M.: Railway point mechanisms: condition monitoring and fault detection. Proc. Inst. Mech. Eng. Part F: J. Rail Rapid Transit **224**(1), 35–44 (2010)
7. Guclu, A., Yilboga, H., Eker, Ö.F., Camci, F., Jennions, I.K.: Prognostics with autoregressive moving average for railway turnouts (2010)
8. Guo, H., Tang, R., Ye, Y., Li, Z., He, X.: DeepFM: a factorization-machine based neural network for CTR prediction. In: Proceedings of the 26th International Joint Conference on Artificial Intelligence, pp. 1725–1731. AAAI Press (2017)
9. He, X., Chua, T.S.: Neural factorization machines for sparse predictive analytics. In: Proceedings of the 40th International ACM SIGIR Conference on Research and Development in Information Retrieval, pp. 355–364. ACM (2017)

10. Juan, Y., Zhuang, Y., Chin, W.S., Lin, C.J.: Field-aware factorization machines for CTR prediction. In: Proceedings of the 10th ACM Conference on Recommender Systems, pp. 43–50. ACM (2016)
11. Kobayashi, K., Kaito, K., Lethanh, N.: A Bayesian estimation method to improve deterioration prediction for infrastructure system with Markov chain model. Int. J. Archit. Eng. Constr. **1**(1), 1–13 (2012)
12. Le Son, K., Fouladirad, M., Barros, A.: Remaining useful lifetime estimation and noisy gamma deterioration process. Reliab. Eng. Syst. Saf. **149**, 76–87 (2016)
13. Liu, C., Zhang, T., Zhao, P., Zhou, J., Sun, J.: Locally linear factorization machines. In: Proceedings of the 26th International Joint Conference on Artificial Intelligence, pp. 2294–2300. AAAI Press (2017)
14. Ma, C.: XLearn. https://github.com/aksnzhy/xlearn
15. Oyebande, B., Renfrew, A.: Condition monitoring of railway electric point machines. IEE Proc.-Electr. Power Appl. **149**(6), 465–473 (2002)
16. Pan, J., et al.: Field-weighted factorization machines for click-through rate prediction in display advertising. In: Proceedings of the 2018 World Wide Web Conference on World Wide Web, pp. 1349–1357. International World Wide Web Conferences Steering Committee (2018)
17. Pedregosa, F., et al.: Scikit-learn: machine learning in Python. J. Mach. Learn. Res. **12**, 2825–2830 (2011)
18. Rama, D., Andrews, J.D.: A reliability analysis of railway switches. Proc. Inst. Mech. Eng. Part F: J. Rail Rapid Transit **227**(4), 344–363 (2013)
19. Rendle, S.: Factorization machines. In: 2010 IEEE 10th International Conference on Data Mining, ICDM, pp. 995–1000. IEEE (2010)
20. Saito, T., Rehmsmeier, M.: The precision-recall plot is more informative than the ROC plot when evaluating binary classifiers on imbalanced datasets. PloS One **10**(3), e0118432 (2015)
21. Shafiee, M., Patriksson, M., Chukova, S.: An optimal age–usage maintenance strategy containing a failure penalty for application to railway tracks. Proc. Inst. Mech. Eng. Part F: J. Rail Rapid Transit **230**(2), 407–417 (2016)
22. Tao, H., Zhao, Y.: Intelligent fault prediction of railway switch based on improved least squares support vector machine. Metall. Min. Ind. **7**(10), 69–75 (2015)
23. Tsuda, Y., Kaito, K., Aoki, K., Kobayashi, K.: Estimating Markovian transition probabilities for bridge deterioration forecasting. Struct. Eng./Earthq. Eng. **23**(2), 241s–256s (2006)
24. Wang, S., Zhou, M., Fei, G., Chang, Y., Liu, B.: Contextual and position-aware factorization machines for sentiment classification. arXiv preprint arXiv:1801.06172 (2018)
25. Yamada, M., et al.: Convex factorization machine for toxicogenomics prediction. In: Proceedings of the 23rd ACM SIGKDD International Conference on Knowledge Discovery and Data Mining, pp. 1215–1224. ACM (2017)
26. Yilboga, H., Eker, Ö.F., Güçlü, A., Camci, F.: Failure prediction on railway turnouts using time delay neural networks. In: 2010 IEEE International Conference on Computational Intelligence for Measurement Systems and Applications, CIMSA, pp. 134–137. IEEE (2010)

Real-Time Collusive Shill Bidding Detection in Online Auctions

Nazia Majadi[1]([✉]) [iD], Jarrod Trevathan[1] [iD], and Neil Bergmann[2] [iD]

[1] Griffith University, Brisbane, QLD 4111, Australia
nazia.majadi@griffithuni.edu.au, j.trevathan@griffith.edu.au
[2] University of Queensland, Brisbane, QLD 4072, Australia
n.bergmann@itee.uq.edu.au

Abstract. Shill bidding is where a seller introduces fake bids into an auction to artificially inflate an item's final price, thereby cheating legitimate bidders. Shill bidding detection becomes more difficult when a seller involves multiple collaborating shill bidders. Colluding shill bidders can distribute the work evenly among each other to collectively reduce their chances of being detected. Previous detection methods wait until an auction ends before determining who the shill bidders are. However, if colluding shill bidders are not detected during the auction, an honest bidder can potentially be cheated by the end of the auction. This paper presents a real-time collusive shill bidding detection algorithm for identifying colluding shill bidders while an auction is running. Experimental results on auction data show that the algorithm can potentially highlight colluding shill bidders in real-time.

Keywords: Collusive shill bidding · Collusion score
Local outlier factor · Loopy belief propagation · Markov random field

1 Introduction

Participating in an online auction often requires bidders to trust an inherently adverse environment [9]. *Shill bidding* is a fraudulent practice where a seller introduces fake bids in his/her auction [8]. This forces legitimate bidders to pay more for the item. *Collusive shill bidding* is a strategy employed by a seller where multiple shill bidders work together to undertake price inflating behaviour [11]. Shill bidding detection becomes more difficult when shill bidders collaborate to distribute the work evenly among each other. This behaviour can collectively reduce the chance of colluding shill bidders being detected.

Researchers [3–6,13] have proposed various methods for shill bidding detection in real-time. However, there are few research proposals to identify colluding shill bidders in online auctions. For instance, Chau et al. [2] presented an algorithm for detecting collusive fraud based on *Markov Random Field* (MRF) to identify reputation inflation and non-delivery fraud [2]. Trevathan and Read [11] proposed a statistical reputation system algorithm for identifying colluding

© Springer Nature Switzerland AG 2018
T. Mitrovic et al. (Eds.): AI 2018, LNAI 11320, pp. 184–192, 2018.
https://doi.org/10.1007/978-3-030-03991-2_19

shill bidders in online auctions. Later, Zhang et al. [14] proposed a technique for detecting auction fraud based on *Loopy Belief Propagation* (LBP). Furthermore, Tsang et al. [7] introduced the *Score Propagation over an Auction Network* (SPAN) algorithm for detecting collaborative fraud in online auctions.

All of the aforementioned approaches work only when an auction ends which eventually cheated an innocent bidder. Therefore, it is essential to identify colluding shill bidders in real-time (i.e., while an auction is running). To our knowledge, there is no literature available on detecting collusive shill bidding in real-time. This paper introduces a real-time *Collusive Shill Bidding Detection* (CSBD) algorithm for identifying colluding shill bidders during a live auction. Our algorithm acts as a detection mechanism and a deterrent for colluding shill bidders. We implemented the algorithm and applied it on simulated and commercial auction datasets. Experimental results show the algorithm can potentially detect colluding shill bidders in real-time.

This paper is organised as follows: Sect. 2 illustrates the details of the real-time CSBD algorithm; Sect. 3 presents our experimental setup and preliminary results on simulated and commercial auction datasets. Finally, Sect. 4 provides concluding remarks and avenues for future work.

2   Real-Time Detection of Collusive Shill Bidding

This section presents a real-time CSBD algorithm for identifying colluding shill bidders while an auction is running. To limit the scope of what the algorithm is trying to achieve, we consider multiple live auctions hosted by a single seller (we are not considering concurrent auctions [12]). We assume there is no collusion amongst sellers and a seller is not using multiple accounts in an attempt to thwart the shill detection mechanism. We also assume that there are collusive shill bidders who are participating in the live auctions.

The algorithm splits an auction into a series of stages depending on the time elapsed (refer to [4,5,13]):

(a) *Early stage* - the first 25% of the auction duration;
(b) *Middle stage* - between 25.1% and 80% of the auction duration;
(c) *Late stage* - the next 15% (between 80.1% and 95%) of the auction duration; and
(d) *Final stage* - the last 5% of the auction duration.

Figure 1 shows the operation of the real-time CSBD algorithm. The algorithm consists of the following processes:

(a) **Data transformation.** An auction dataset is represented as an auction network (referred to as a *collusion graph*). The interactions between bidders in the auction network are indicated as a weighted graph. The collusion graph is denoted as $G = (V, E)$. V is the set of bidders, and E is the set of edges where each edge between two bidders indicates they have both participated in the same auction. Consider two bidders, $v_i \in V$, $v_j \in V$,

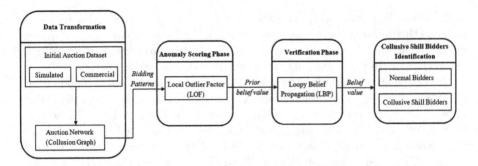

Fig. 1. The functional components of the real-time CSBD algorithm.

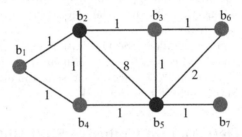

Fig. 2. Example of a collusion graph containing seven bidders.

where $i \neq j$, that submitted bids in the same auction. An edge $e_{i,j}$ is added to E that connects these two bidders together and the weight of the edge, $w(e_{i,j})$, indicates the number of auctions they participated in together.

Figure 2 illustrates an example of a collusion graph. Bidders b_2 and b_5 have an edge weighting of 8. This indicates they have participated in 8 auctions together and may be involved in collusive shill bidding.

(b) **Selection of collusive shill bidding patterns.** We selected the following three bidding behaviours which may indicate potential colluding shill bidding behaviour:

- **Alpha rating (α rating)** - A shill bidder usually submits bids in auctions run by a particular seller [8]. Two bidders can be considered as colluding shill bidders if their α ratings are approximately the same. The α ratings are also typically higher than legitimate bidders.
- **Collusion rating (η rating)** - A shill bidder usually has the most number of edges (i.e., highest degree), and higher edge weightings compared to legitimate bidders [11]. Two bidders are potentially involved in collusive shill bidding if the η ratings of the bidders are approximately the same. In general, colluding shill bidders will have similar η ratings and these will be higher than honest bidders.
- **Bind rating (λ rating)** - Colluding shill bidders have approximately the same number of bids (β rating [8]) [11]. The bind rating of two bidders i and j, $\lambda_{i,j}^{\beta}$, gives both bidders values between 0 and 1 depending on

how similar their β ratings are [11]. A bind rating of 1 indicates a high likelihood of collusive shill bidding, whereas 0 indicates a low likelihood.

(c) **Anomaly score calculation.** We calculate a *Local Outlier Factor* (LOF) [1] of each behaviour pair over multiple k values in parallel, and select the maximum value as the best performance for the behaviour pair. We choose LOF because the interpretation of its score is easy and it has the ability to capture outliers that were previously unseen by the global approaches. So, the anomaly score for bidder i can be calculated as follows:

$$Score_i = \max_p(\max_k(LOF_i(p, k)))$$

where k denotes the distance to be used to calculate LOFs and p indicates the selected behaviour pairs. In general, the anomaly score for a shill bidder will be higher than that for a legitimate bidder.

(d) **Verification.** This phase is used to verify the anomaly score for each bidder found in the anomaly score calculation step. We use a *Markov Random Field* (MRF) to model our auction network. A bidder i can have two states: (i) honest state (b_i^h); or (ii) shill state (b_i^s). The beliefs for bidder i sum to 1. That is, $b_i^h + b_i^s = 1$. We use the anomaly score found for bidder i, $o_i^{'}$, in the anomaly score calculation step as the observed state of bidder i in the MRF. As the anomaly score for bidder i is a positive value, we normalise the value to keep it between 0 and 1 which is denoted by o_i^s. The honest belief for bidder i is calculated as: $o_i^h = 1 - o_i^s$; where $0 \leq o_i^h \leq 1$. In general, the shill belief of a shill bidder will be higher than that of a legitimate bidder. We applied *Loopy Belief Propagation* (LBP) on the auction network for detecting collusive shill bidding. To implement LBP, we need to define the two types of potential functions: (i) *Prior belief function* (denoted by $\phi()$) defines the prior knowledge (probabilities) of auction network nodes belonging to each class (e.g., honest or shill); (ii) *Compatibility function* (denoted by $\psi()$) represents the compatibility of two bidders with a given pair of nodes being connected. Table 1 shows a sample instantiation of the compatibility matrix.

A default value of ϵ_0 is 0.2 suggested by [2] which is a heuristic. We found a wide range of $\epsilon_0 \in [0.05, 0.2]$ yields desired results through the analysis of the real-time CSBD algorithm. Therefore, we have selected $\epsilon_0 = 0.2$ for the real-time CSBD algorithm.

(e) **Collusive shill bidders identification.** When the LBP converges, the nodes (bidders) are ranked according to their beliefs for the shill state. The set of bidders is divided into potential shill and honest bidders by setting a threshold value. We choose a threshold value, $\xi = 0.75$, depending on two factors: (a) the relative misclassification cost for honest and shill bidders; and (b) the ratio of honest and shill bidders in the auction dataset [7].

Table 1. Compatibility matrix (ψ).

Neighbour state	Node belief	
	Shill	Honest
Shill	$1 - \epsilon_0$	ϵ_0
Honest	ϵ_0	$1 - \epsilon_0$

3   Experimental Results

3.1   Simulated Auctions

We first tested the real-time CSBD algorithm on a simulated auction dataset using a shill bidding agent [10]. We applied the algorithm on a dataset which consisted of 5 sellers, 50 bidders, and 3 shill bidders. Each of these 5 sellers generated a random number of auctions. We selected the smallest size of the dataset to easily visualise how the real-time CSBD algorithm performs. We considered one auction as a live auction (i.e., Auction ID: 5 posted by *seller_a*) and the rest as past auctions.

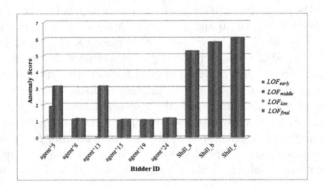

Fig. 3. Anomaly score for each bidder in different stages of Auction ID: 5.

Figure 3 shows the anomaly score for each bidder in Auction ID: 5. Figure 3 suggests that *Shill_a*, *Shill_b*, and *Shill_c* exhibit anomalous behaviour compared to other bidders as they have the highest LOF values. Table 2 shows that *Shill_a*, *Shill_b*, and *Shill_c* achieved the highest *prior shill belief* (o_i^s) during AuctionID: 5.

We then applied the LBP on our simulated data using the prior function (ϕ) and compatibility function (ψ) for each bidder. Figure 4 shows that the shill belief values of *Shill_a*, *Shill_b*, and *Shill_c* remain the highest throughout the auction duration compared to other legitimate bidders. This indicates that *Shill_a*, *Shill_b*, and *Shill_c* are potential colluding shill bidders.

Table 2. Prior belief function of each bidder in different stages of Auction ID: 5.

Bidder ID	Early stage $o^s_{i_{early}}$	Middle stage $o^s_{i_{middle}}$	Late stage $o^s_{i_{late}}$	Final stage $o^s_{i_{final}}$
agent^5	0.17	0.41	0.41	0.41
agent^8	0.01	0.02	0.02	0.02
agent^13	0.00	0.41	0.41	0.41
agent^15	0.00	0.01	0.01	0.01
agent^19	0.00	0.00	0.00	0.00
agent^24	0.02	0.02	0.02	0.02
Shill_a	**0.84**	**0.84**	**0.84**	**0.84**
Shill_b	**0.95**	**0.95**	**0.95**	**0.95**
Shill_c	**1.00**	**1.00**	**1.00**	**1.00**

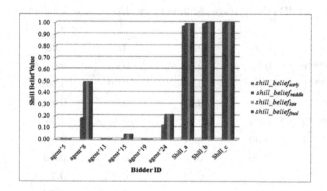

Fig. 4. Shill belief value of each bidder in different stages of Auction ID: 5.

3.2 Commercial Auctions

We applied the algorithm on a commercial auction dataset obtained from the website http://www.modelingonlineauctions.com/datasets. Since we do not have a ground truth label for any of the bidders, we employed the algorithm in a general fashion to work completely unsupervised. We considered an auction listing for Palm Pilot PDAs because of its popularity. We randomly selected Auction ID: 3025373736 as a live auction and the other auctions are considered as past auctions.

Figure 5 shows the anomaly score for each bidder during Auction ID: 3025373736. Table 3 shows the prior belief function of each bidder during the auction. We found $r{***}h$, $c{***}am$, and $d{***}n$ achieved the highest prior shill belief consistently in each of the four stages during the auction (see Table 3).

We applied the LBP on Auction ID: 3025373736 using the prior belief and compatibility function. Figure 6 shows the shill belief values for each bidder. We observed that $c{***}am$, $d{***}n$, and $r{***}h$ consistently show the highest shill

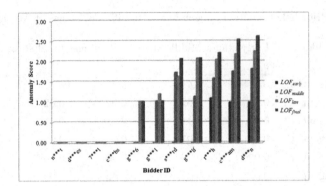

Fig. 5. Anomaly score for each bidder in different stages of Auction ID: 3025373736.

Table 3. Prior belief function for each bidder in Auction ID: 3025373736.

Bidder ID	Early stage $o^s_{i_{early}}$	Middle stage $o^s_{i_{middle}}$	Late stage $o^s_{i_{late}}$	Final stage $o^s_{i_{final}}$
n***t	0.00	0.00	0.00	0.00
d***es	0.00	0.00	0.00	0.00
7***l	0.00	0.00	0.00	0.00
c***bs	0.00	0.00	0.00	0.00
g***6	0.00	0.00	0.45	0.39
g***1	0.00	0.57	0.53	0.39
s***rd	0.00	**0.95**	0.72	**0.79**
g***lf	0.00	0.63	**0.92**	**0.79**
r***h	**1.00**	0.87	0.91	0.84
c***am	**0.91**	**0.97**	**0.97**	**0.97**
d***n	**0.91**	**1.00**	**1.00**	**1.00**

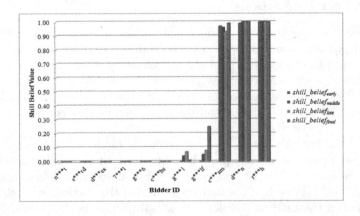

Fig. 6. Shill belief value of each bidder in different stages of Auction ID: 3025373736.

belief value during the auction, which indicates they could be potential colluding shill bidders. Note that, some legitimate bidders (e.g., $s{***}rd$, $g{***}lf$) achieve a high value of prior shill belief during the auction (see Table 3). The bidders' shill belief values are minimised after applying the LBP (see Fig. 6). This indicates the verification process is able to improve the detection accuracy.

4 Conclusion

This paper proposed a real-time collusive shill bidding detection (CSBD) algorithm for detecting colluding shill bidders during a live auction. We calculated the anomaly score for each bidder using LOF based on collusive bidding behaviour of the bidder. Finally, we verified the anomaly score for the bidder acquired from the anomaly score calculation step based on their interactions with other bidders to improve the detection accuracy.

We applied the algorithm on simulated and commercial datasets. Experimental results show that the real-time CSBD algorithm was able to highlight potential colluding shill bidders during a live auction. However, it is difficult to determine the detection accuracy as we do not have a ground truth label for any of the bidders in the commercial auction dataset. The algorithm acts as a detection mechanism and deterrent to potential colluding shill bidders. Future work involves detecting collusive seller shill bidding behaviour where a colluding seller can spread the risk between the various sellers to reduce suspicion on the individual shill bidders.

References

1. Breunig, M.M., Kriegel, H.P., Ng, R.T., Sander, J.: LOF: identifying density-based local outliers. ACM Sigmod Rec. 29(2), 93–104 (2000)
2. Chau, D.H., Pandit, S., Faloutsos, C.: Detecting fraudulent personalities in networks of online auctioneers. In: Fürnkranz, J., Scheffer, T., Spiliopoulou, M. (eds.) PKDD 2006. LNCS (LNAI), vol. 4213, pp. 103–114. Springer, Heidelberg (2006). https://doi.org/10.1007/11871637_14
3. Ford, B.J., Xu, H., Valova, I.: A real-time self-adaptive classifier for identifying suspicious bidders in online auctions. J. Comput. 56(5), 646–663 (2013)
4. Majadi, N., Trevathan, J.: A real-time detection algorithm for identifying shill bidders in multiple online auctions. In: Proceedings of the 51st Hawaii International Conference on System Sciences, pp. 3831–3840. IEEE Press, USA (2018)
5. Majadi, N., Trevathan, J., Gray, H.: A run-time algorithm for detecting shill bidding in online auctions. J. Theor. Appl. Electron. Commer. Res. 13(3), 17–49 (2018)
6. Sadaoui, S., Wang, X.: A dynamic stage-based fraud monitoring framework of multiple live auctions. Appl. Intell. 46(1), 1–17 (2016)
7. Tsang, S., Koh, Y.S., Dobbie, G., Alam, S.: SPAN: finding collaborative frauds in online auctions. Knowl.-Based Syst. 71, 389–408 (2014)
8. Trevathan, J., Read, W.: Detecting shill bidding in online english auctions. In: Handbook of Research on Social and Organizational Liabilities in Information Security, vol. 46, pp. 446–470. IGI Press (2009)

9. Trevathan, J.: Getting into the mind of an in-auction fraud perpetrator. Comput. Sci. Rev. **27**, 1–15 (2018)
10. Trevathan, J., Read, W.: A simple shill bidding agent. In: Proceedings of the 4th International Conference on Information Technology-New Generations, pp. 933–937. IEEE Press, USA (2007)
11. Trevathan, J., Read, W.: Investigating shill bidding behaviour involving colluding bidders. J. Comput. **2**(10), 63–75 (2007)
12. Xu, H., Cheng, Y.T.: Model checking bidding behaviors in internet concurrent auctions. Int. J. Comput. Syst. Sci. Eng. **22**(4), 179–191 (2007)
13. Xu, H., Bates, C.K., Shatz, S.M.: Real-time model checking for shill detection in live online auctions. In: Proceedings of International Conference on Software Engineering Research and Practice, pp. 351–358. CSREA press, USA (2009)
14. Zhang, B., Zhou, Y., Faloutsos, C.: Toward a comprehensive model in internet auction fraud detection. In: Proceedings of the 41st Hawaii International Conference on System Sciences, pp. 79–88. IEEE Press, USA (2008)

OHC: Uncovering Overlapping Heterogeneous Communities

Ranran Bian[1,2]([✉]), Yun Sing Koh[1], Gillian Dobbie[1], and Anna Divoli[2]

[1] The University of Auckland, Auckland, New Zealand
rbia002@aucklanduni.ac.nz
[2] Pingar, Auckland, New Zealand

Abstract. A heterogeneous correlation network represents relationships (edges) among source-typed and attribute-typed objects (nodes). It can be used to model an academic collaboration network, describing connections among authors and published papers. To date, there has been little research into mining communities in heterogeneous networks. The objective of our research is to discover overlapping communities that include all node and edge types in a heterogeneous correlation network. We describe an algorithm, OHC, that detects overlapping communities in heterogeneous correlation networks. Inspired by a homogeneous community scoring function, Triangle Participation Ratio (TPR), OHC finds target heterogeneous communities then expands them recursively with triangle-forming nodes. Experiments on different real world networks demonstrate that OHC identifies heterogeneous communities that are tightly connected internally according to two traditional scoring functions. Additionally, analyzing the top ranking heterogeneous communities in a case study, we evaluate the results qualitatively.

Keywords: Heterogeneous community detection
Academic collaboration network mining · Algorithm

1 Introduction

A homogeneous network represents relationships between one object type. A wide variety of methods for detecting communities in homogeneous networks have been proposed [1,8,14]. Researchers in the fields of Computer Science [6,16] and Physics [5,8] describe such communities as sets of nodes with high density of internal edges and low density external edges. In contrast, a heterogeneous network represents relationships (edges) between multiple types of interacting objects (nodes). To date, there has been limited research that detects communities in heterogeneous networks. Existing homogeneous community detection techniques cannot be used to detect communities that retain the complex

Funded by New Zealand Callaghan Innovation and Pingar, under an R&D Student Fellowship Grant (Contract Number: PTERN1502).

T. Mitrovic et al. (Eds.): AI 2018, LNAI 11320, pp. 193–205, 2018.
https://doi.org/10.1007/978-3-030-03991-2_20

characteristics of heterogeneous networks, such as multi-dimensional information [10]. The motivation of our work is to find a group of objects which interact
significantly on multi-dimensional information of a heterogeneous network. For
example, in an academic collaboration network, we identify sets of authors who
relate to other authors with significant relationships on papers.

Network schemas have been used to represent the metastructure of heterogeneous networks. Various schemas have been proposed, including: Multi-relation
with single-typed object schema [17], Bipartite schema [7], Star schema [11] and
Correlation schema [4]. We constrain our work to correlation schemas, where
objects can be categorized as either Source Type (ST) or Attribute Type (AT).
Figure 1 presents a bibliographic heterogeneous correlation network H_1, where
authors are the source-typed objects (nodes) and papers are the attribute-typed
objects (nodes) (represented by circles and rectangles respectively). The rectangles with a striped pattern represent papers that share a common theme, namely
they are about texture spaces. The co-authorship relationship between authors
is denoted by solid lines. The relationship weighting represents the number of
papers the pair of authors have co-published together. Relationships between
authors and papers denoted by dashed lines, indicate the authors of a paper.

Applying heterogeneous community detection techniques on H_1, we can identify communities of authors that publish together, and the papers that are
most significant in this community. Our Overlapping Heterogeneous Community detection algorithm, OHC, detects one heterogeneous community, denoted
by the dotted boundary in Fig. 1: {Lawrence M. Brown, Riza Erturk, Senol Dost,
Murat Diker, Paper 1, Paper 2, Paper 3, Paper 6, Paper7}. The authors were
shown to have a common interest in the field of texture spaces (as highlighted by
the papers with stripped patterns in Fig. 1). This example illustrates that OHC
can detect communities of authors that are interested in a particular research
sub-field.

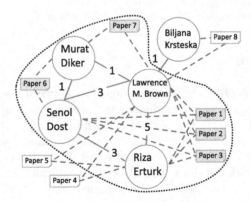

Fig. 1. Sample heterogeneous correlation network H_1

The main contributions of our research are: (1) We propose a novel algorithm, OHC, that detects communities which contain multi-typed objects (nodes) and relationships (edges) in heterogeneous correlation networks. Evaluation experiments and case studies on real world datasets validate the effectiveness of the algorithm. (2) We demonstrate that traditional metrics can be used to evaluate the quality of detected heterogeneous communities.

We define overlapping heterogeneous communities as subgraphs of a given heterogeneous network, where each community contains nodes of all object types and edges of all relationship types that exist in the network. The aim of our research is to identify heterogeneous communities with dense internal connections and loose external connections in a heterogeneous correlation network.

2   Related Work

We introduce existing community detection methods for homogeneous and heterogeneous networks.

Community Detection Methods in Homogeneous Networks. In recent years, community detection in homogeneous networks has been researched widely from various perspectives. Some methods focus on identifying disjoint communities while others focus on overlapping communities [14]. Newman and Girvan [8] proposed that modularity can be used as a measure to divide the homogeneous network into a set of graph partitions. This idea has been influential in later community detection techniques, such as [1].

Speaker-listener Label Propagation Algorithm (SLPA) [14] has been shown empirically to be one of the best performing algorithms for both overlapping and disjoint homogeneous communities [3,15]. The algorithm propagates all labels in each iteration to identify community membership between nodes of a given network. Louvain [1] is a popular homogeneous community detection algorithm based on modularity-optimization. This parameter-free algorithm is able to analyze a network with millions of nodes within seconds.

Homogeneous Community Scoring Functions. A homogeneous community scoring function assesses a group of nodes' connectivity level for representing a network community structure [16]. Triangle Participation Ratio (TPR) is a scoring function based on internal connectivity, which measures the fraction of nodes in a community that belong to a triad [6,13,16]. The value range of TPR is [0, 1], where a higher ratio represents better internal connectivity and a value of 1 indicates a highly interconnected community. TPR has been widely recognized as a useful metric for measuring community density and cohesion. Furthermore, Yang and Leskovec's [16] experiments with 230 large real-world networks highlighted TPR's high accuracy in identifying ground-truth homogeneous communities.

Fraction Over Median Degree (FOMD) is another community scoring function based on internal connectivity [16]. This metric calculates the proportion of nodes in a community that have internal degree greater than the median degree of all nodes in the network. FlakeODF is a community scoring function that combines internal and external connectivity [2,16] by calculating the fraction of nodes in a community that have fewer edges pointing inside than outside the community.

Community Detection Methods in Heterogeneous Networks. The existing techniques for detecting communities in heterogeneous networks were developed for multi-relation with single-typed object schema [17], bipartite schema [7] or star schema [11]. Many of these techniques find communities that contain only a single type of object with one or more types of relationships. None of the existing techniques produce heterogeneous communities that contain multiple-typed objects and relationships.

3   OHC: Overlapping Heterogeneous Community Detection Algorithm

In this section, we present our greedy community detection technique, OHC. Details of OHC and how it transforms our example heterogeneous network shown in Fig. 1 into a heterogeneous community are provided. Java source code for the OHC algorithm and experiment datasets are available for download at http://bit.ly/2vEfOQU.

Three Phases of OHC. Our proposed approach is composed of three main phases. Phase One processes the input data and generates a set of seed communities. Inspired by Triangle Participation Ratio (TPR) scoring function [13,16] described in Sect. 2, Phase Two produces a set of heterogeneous communities by adding triangle-forming source-typed nodes with associated attribute-typed nodes to each seed community. The output of Phase Two is fed into Phase Three, where we remove the duplicate and subset heterogeneous communities. Figures 1 and 2 demonstrate outcomes of OHC's third phase and the first two phases respectively. The data presented in these figures is a subset of real-world datasets used in our experiments.

Phase One. The heterogeneous network processed by OHC in the initial phase is composed of a homogeneous network that contains relationships among source type (ST) nodes and a heterogeneous network containing relationships between both ST nodes and attribute type (AT) nodes. For example, the heterogeneous network processed by OHC in Fig. 1, is constructed from an author-collaboration homogeneous network, containing co-authorship relationships between authors and an authorship heterogeneous network, which contains the author-to-paper relationships. This phase generates a list of heterogeneous seed communities based on a set of distinct and interconnected source-typed nodes. Each of the seed communities must contain more than one ST node, at least one commonly linked node of AT, and the corresponding relationship edges. Seed communities with solo ST nodes are eliminated due to their inability of forming triangles in the next phase. When applied to the heterogeneous network shown in Fig. 1, Phase One produces the set of seed communities, C_{seeds}, denoted by the dotted boundaries in Fig. 2(1).

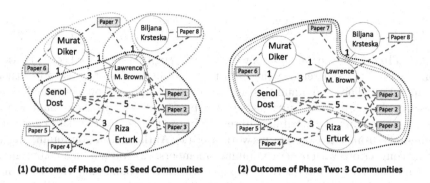

(1) Outcome of Phase One: 5 Seed Communities   **(2) Outcome of Phase Two: 3 Communities**

Fig. 2. Outcome of OHC's first two phases (identified (seed) communities denoted by the dotted boundaries)

Phase Two. When expanding an individual seed community, C_{a_seed} in C_{seeds}, OHC takes a depth-first search approach to iterate through all pairs of ST (Source Type) nodes (ST_x, ST_y) in the original and expanded C_{a_seed}, and recursively finds all triangle-forming triads (ST_x, ST_y, ST_z) in an exhaustive manner by examining all other seed heterogeneous communities generated from Phase One. The expansion process introduces the eligible triangle-forming ST nodes, the associated AT (Attribute Type) nodes, and the corresponding relationship edges that do not already exist to C_{a_seed}. The recursive process for each pair of ST nodes continues until no further triangle-forming ST nodes can be found. The expansion processes for seed communities are independent and deterministic. Additionally, resulting communities that have fewer than three AT nodes or do not form triangles with any ST nodes will be removed from the outcome of Phase Two.

To become a triangle-forming ST node, a node must have at least one distinct edge with each member of the pair (ST_x, ST_y). The triangle-forming ST node, ST_z, with the associated AT nodes will be added to C_{a_seed} if they are not already present. In the situation where ST_z is not included in the initial set of nodes of C_{a_seed}, ST_z forms two new pairs (ST_z, ST_x) and (ST_z, ST_y) with each member of the original pair. The recursive process starts on each of the new pairs to find further triangle-forming ST nodes. While in the situation where ST_z is included in the initial set of nodes of C_{a_seed}, OHC will explore further triangle-forming ST nodes using the pairs (ST_z, ST_x) and (ST_z, ST_y) only when both ST_x and ST_y are not included in the initial set of nodes of C_{a_seed}.

To better illustrate the mechanisms of this phase, we refer to the seed community, s, {Lawrence M. Brown, Murat Diker, Paper 7} in Fig. 2(1) as an example, with the author pair (Lawrence M. Brown, Murat Diker) being a pair of ST nodes. OHC detects that Senol Dost has one distinct edge with Lawrence M. Brown (due to the associated AT nodes: Paper 1, Paper 2, Paper 3) and another distinct edge with Murat Diker (resulted from Paper 6), therefore, Senol Dost is a triangle-forming ST node for s, which expands s into the community {Lawrence

M. Brown, Murat Diker, Paper 7, Senol Dost, Paper 1, Paper 2, Paper 3, Paper 6}. The outcome of Phase Two is denoted by the dotted boundaries in Fig. 2(2).

Phase Three. For the final phase, we iterate through the expanded communities from Phase Two and remove the ones that are duplicates or subsets of other communities. These communities are removed as information contained in a subset or duplicate community has already been replicated in their counterpart superset communities. Attributes observed in the OHC-detected heterogeneous community from our example network are: (1) Authors in a community have strong connections with other community members. (2) Authors in a community are more likely to be interested in a paper within the community that they did not co-publish than the authors outside of the community.

In our running example, the seed community, {Lawrence M. Brown, Riza Erturk, Senol Dost, Paper 1, Paper 2, Paper 3} expanded to {Lawrence M. Brown, Riza Erturk, Senol Dost, Paper 1, Paper 2, Paper 3, Murat Diker, Paper 6, Paper 7}. This results in the two duplicated sub-communities removed from OHC's final output. The final result is denoted by the dotted boundaries in Fig. 1.

Time Complexity Analysis of OHC. To analyze the complexity of the proposed algorithm we use $|x|$ ST nodes, $|y|$ AT nodes and $|s|$ seed communities. Here we first analyze the best case performance of OHC. Based on a set of distinct and interconnected ST nodes, Phase One iterates through $|y|$ AT nodes to generate qualified seed communities with $O(|y| \times |x|)$ runtime. The best case for Phase Two is when only one pair of ST nodes needs to be processed in all the seed communities and none of them have triangle-forming ST nodes, which leads to a runtime of $O(|s|^2)$. During Phase Three, a linear execution time of $O(|s|)$ is required when the communities produced from the previous phase can all be merged into one superset community. Pulling runtime of the three phases all together we have a complexity of $O(|y| \times |x| + |s|^2 + |s|)$. Values of $|x|$, $|y|$ and $|s|$ are data dependent, in our experiments, $|x|$ and $|y|$ are normally orders of magnitude higher than $|s|$. In which case the best case runtime of OHC reduces to $O(|y| \times |x| + |s|^2)$.

In a rare case where all ST nodes are processed in every seed community, Phase Two's runtime becomes $O(|x|^2 \times |s|^2)$. Execution time of the worst case in the third phase is $(|s|^2)$ where no duplicate or subset communities can be eliminated. As a result, OHC's worst case performance is $O(|y| \times |x| + |x|^2 \times |s|^2 + |s|^2)$, which can be reduced to $O(|x|^2 \times |s|^2)$.

Conditions of OHC. Our proposed approach works for a given heterogeneous network H, which satisfies the following three conditions:

1. The meta-structure of H is correlation schema based.
2. H contains two or more different types of nodes.
3. H is a static heterogeneous network.

4   Experiments and Results

To study the effectiveness of OHC, we conducted experiments on various publicly accessible real-world heterogeneous networks. All the experiments were performed on a computer with 3.40 GHz i7 CPU, 8 GB RAM and Windows 10 operating system.

Datasets. Bibliographic data is widely used in heterogeneous network experiments in the existing literature. For our experiments, we analyzed the ACL Anthology Network (**AAN**) dataset [9] and the following five bibliographic datasets from ArnetMiner [12]: Data Mining database information retrieval (**DM**) dataset, Software Engineering (**SE**) dataset, Computer Graphics Multimedia (**CGM**) dataset, Artificial Intelligence (**AI**) dataset and Interdisciplinary Studies (**IS**) dataset. Statistics of the six datasets are shown in Table 1. For each dataset, we constructed an author-collaboration network and authorship network. In the author-collaboration network, authors are represented as nodes while the number of edges between two nodes indicates the number of papers that the corresponding authors have co-published. For the authorship network, there exist two types of nodes: author and paper nodes, an edge between these two types of nodes represents that the author had published the paper. We define author nodes to be our source type (ST) nodes while the paper nodes are described as attribute type (AT) nodes.

Benchmark Techniques. We are unable to compare OHC with existing heterogeneous community detection techniques because they were designed for a different purpose (as described in Sect. 2). Hence, we build benchmark techniques based on two state-of-the-art homogeneous community detection algorithms: SLPA and Louvain. For simplicity, we notate the SLPA-based method as **SLPAh** and the Louvain-based method as **Louvainh**. SLPAh is built on top of SLPA [14], where SLPA is initially applied to the author-collaboration network to detect homogeneous communities of the ST nodes. Appropriate AT nodes are then appended to each of these detected homogeneous communities. In our experiments, the number of iterations T was set to 100 to guarantee SLPA's stable performance and the threshold r, which affects the number of detected overlapping communities, was varied: 0.01, 0.25 and 0.45. The construction process of Louvainh is similar as SLPAh with the exception of Louvain [1] being the community detection technique for the Louvain-based method. Both Louvain and SLPA are non-deterministic heuristics, therefore, we repeated our experiments twenty times for both techniques. For SLPAh, we repeated this for each threshold, r.

Evaluation Metrics. Without ground-truth heterogeneous communities and particular metrics for evaluating heterogeneous communities available, we adopt the homogeneous community scoring functions, FOMD and Flake-ODF, to measure the inter and intra connectivity of the communities. Edge (relationship) weightings are used for calculating FOMD and FlakeODF scores. The value range of FOMD is [0, 1], where a higher FOMD score represents better internal

Table 1. Statistics of datasets used

Dataset	No. of authors	No. of papers	Average node degree*
DM	5856	2640	3.35
SE	8127	3923	3.82
CGM	25961	16599	4.41
AI	41478	27596	4.43
IS	46097	18583	7.64
AAN	14464	18041	8.24

* Measured based on author-collaboration network

connectivity and a value of 1 indicates a highly interconnected community. The value range of FlakeODF is [0, 1] as well. As the FlakeODF score approaches 0, this indicates that a community is highly connected internally while being more disconnected from the rest of the network. For our evaluations, we aim to find heterogeneous communities with high FOMD score and low FlakeODF score.

Community Quality. In our experiments, we evaluated the performance of benchmark algorithms, SLPAh and Louvainh, and compared them with OHC. We calculate the minimum, maximum, median and average values for FOMD and FlakeODF for the 6 datasets and collated them in Tables 2 and 3 respectively, with the best results highlighted for each dataset. As SLPAh and Louvainh are non-deterministic, we present their best results from multiple runs.

Notice in Table 2 that Louvainh and SLPAh despite having the same maximum value as OHC, their median FOMD value of 0. This indicates that at least half of their communities scored very poorly resulting in an overall lower average. On the other hand, OHC's positive results were reinforced by its higher median and lower standard deviation values, indicating the distribution between their communities was less volatile. The average FOMD values for OHC communities were approximately five times higher than the other two techniques. Table 3 shows that the median FlakeODF score for Louvainh and SLPAh is either 0 or 1, indicating the communities produced by these algorithms have FlakeODF scores at either extreme. The average FlakeODF score for OHC communities are considerably lower than other techniques, particularly in the AAN dataset.

Figure 3 presents the distributions of FOMD and FlakeODF value ranges across different heterogeneous community detection heuristics. From the results of the three datasets presented, we identify common trends that underline the performances of OHC, SLPAh and Louvainh. From Fig. 3a to c, we see that both SLPAh and Louvainh have a larger percentage of communities in the lowest value range (0–0.2). This indicates that most of SLPAh and Louvainh's resulting communities have low internal connectivity. On the other hand, OHC's result presents a more normal distribution curve, with the majority of communities scoring between 0.4 and 0.6, indicating that OHC produces communities with denser internal connectivity on average. The FlakeODF value ranges in Fig. 3d to f again indicate favorable results for OHC. The results from SLPAh and

Table 2. FOMD results

Method-dataset	Min	Max	Median	Average ± SD
OHC-DM	**0.19**	1	**0.50**	**0.57 ± 0.17**
SLPAh-DM	0	1	0	0.19 ± 0.39
Louvainh-DM	0	1	0	0.07 ± 0.25
OHC-SE	**0.18**	1	**0.50**	**0.55 ± 0.15**
SLPAh-SE	0	1	0	0.17 ± 0.37
Louvainh-SE	0	1	0	0.08 ± 0.26
OHC-CGM	**0.11**	1	**0.40**	**0.48 ± 0.16**
SLPAh-CGM	0	1	0	0.13 ± 0.33
Louvainh-CGM	0	1	0	0.06 ± 0.22
OHC-AI	**0.12**	1	**0.40**	**0.48 ± 0.16**
SLPAh-AI	0	1	0	0.13 ± 0.32
Louvainh-AI	0	1	0	0.07 ± 0.24
OHC-IS	0	1	**0.4**	**0.48 ± 0.19**
SLPAh-IS	0	1	0	0.09 ± 0.29
Louvainh-IS	0	1	0	0.05 ± 0.22
OHC-AAN	**0.09**	1	**0.50**	**0.44 ± 0.15**
SLPAh-AAN	0	1	0	0.13 ± 0.33
Louvainh-AAN	0	1	0	0.08 ± 0.26

Louvainh communities form clusters on the value ranges of both extremes, indicating around half of the communities have poor quality. Whereas the trend from OHC presents a sharp negative slope, with the majority of communities in the 0 to 0.4 value ranges.

Due to SLPAh and Louvainh's non-deterministic nature, we ran both of them multiple times and record the average and standard deviation values for FOMD and FlakeODF. There were minor variation in the average values obtained from each run, indicating both SLPAh and Louvainh had fairly stable performance.

In SLPAh and Louvainh we appended papers which were published by all authors within a community. However, this methodology does not include papers that have been authored by a subset of authors within a community. We produced two additional sets of results, firstly adding all papers that were authored by one or more authors within a community and secondly adding all papers that were authored by two or more authors within a community. In both cases, OHC retains higher minimum, median and average FOMD values across all datasets. However, the modified SLPAh and even Louvainh slightly outperform OHC in some cases in terms of FlakeODF scores. The results indicate that when adding papers that require at least two internal authors, the modified SLPAh and Louvainh produce a more tightly internally bound community and more loosely externally connected community as compared to adding papers of each author, likely due to the decrease in loosely connected papers.

Table 3. FlakeODF results

Method-dataset	Min	Max	Median	Average $\pm$ SD
OHC-DM	**0.67**	0	0.10	**0.18 $\pm$ 0.15**
SLPAh-DM	1	0	**0**	0.28 $\pm$ 0.45
Louvainh-DM	1	0	1	0.79 $\pm$ 0.40
OHC-SE	**0.86**	0	0.20	**0.24 $\pm$ 0.16**
SLPAh-SE	1	0	**0**	0.34 $\pm$ 0.47
Louvainh-SE	1	0	1	0.75 $\pm$ 0.43
OHC-CGM	**0.78**	0	0.19	**0.21 $\pm$ 0.15**
SLPAh-CGM	1	0	**0**	0.41 $\pm$ 0.49
Louvainh-CGM	1	0	1	0.70 $\pm$ 0.45
HC-AI	**0.89**	0	0.20	**0.22 $\pm$ 0.15**
SLPAh-AI	1	0	**0**	0.43 $\pm$ 0.49
Louvainh-AI	1	0	1	0.69 $\pm$ 0.46
OHC-IS	**0.93**	0	0.30	**0.34 $\pm$ 0.19**
SLPAh-IS	1	0	**0**	0.43 $\pm$ 0.49
Louvainh-IS	1	0	1	0.61 $\pm$ 0.48
OHC-AAN	**0.89**	0	**0.10**	**0.22 $\pm$ 0.14**
SLPAh-AAN	1	0	1	0.52 $\pm$ 0.49
Louvainh-AAN	1	0	1	0.60 $\pm$ 0.47

Case Study. The purpose of the case study is to evaluate the results qualitatively. For each dataset, we examined the top five heterogeneous communities with the highest FOMD and lowest FlakeODF scores generated by OHC, SLPAh and Louvainh and found: (1) By analyzing common keywords across the paper titles of a community, OHC was often able to identify additional information such as the research sub-field that the community focused on, (2) OHC clusters authors that frequently publish in the same field of research despite there being no co-publication between all of these authors, (3) Regardless of the paper appending methodology used, the vast majority of the top five scoring communities identified by SLPAh and Louvainh do not have these two properties.

We illustrate our findings further by analyzing the Top-1 AAN heterogeneous community detected by OHC which achieved a FOMD score of 1 and a FlakeODF score of 0. The common keyword across the five paper titles in this Top-1 community is "metaphor". In addition, by examining the AAN dataset, we found that the authors in this community had not published any papers together and only partial co-authorship exists among them. To reduce bias, we evaluated

SLPAh and Louvainh communities that contain one or more nodes in the Top-1 OHC community and found that the same property was not demonstrated in these communities.

To present our findings in a systematic way, we analyze the top five AAN communities detected by each of OHC, SLPAh and Louvainh. Each of the top five

Table 4. Run time of algorithms in seconds

Dataset	OHC	SLPAh	Louvainh
DM	11	7	2
SE	26	9	3
CGM	492	62	23
AI	535	200	58
IS	658	254	69
AAN	12860	20	9

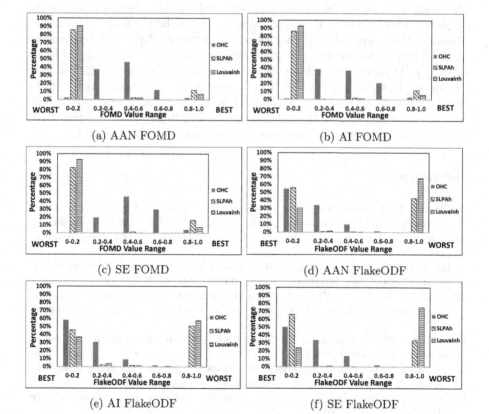

(a) AAN FOMD

(b) AI FOMD

(c) SE FOMD

(d) AAN FlakeODF

(e) AI FlakeODF

(f) SE FlakeODF

Fig. 3. Distributions for FOMD and FlakeODF value

OHC communities have common keywords across their paper titles. In contrast, for both SLPAh and Louvainh, only one of the top communities had common keywords. Additionally, for all of the SLPAh and Louvainh top five communities, there are only authors that have published the same papers together, which differs substantially from OHC. Overall, based on our analysis of the top scoring communities, OHC clusters authors with papers for a specific research sub-field despite the authors not being fully interconnected.

Run Time. Table 4 shows the execution time of each technique across various datasets. As expected, OHC consumed more time than both SLPAh and Louvainh. The difference increased with the size of dataset. As an example, OHC took 12860 s (3.5 h) to detect heterogeneous communities in the AAN dataset, which we suspect was caused by high overlapping density and high overlapping diversity of the dataset as indicated in Table 1.

5   Conclusions and Future Work

This research identifies heterogeneous communities by integrating and utilizing multiple node-to-node relationships that exist in heterogeneous correlation networks. The proposed OHC algorithm uncovers overlapping heterogeneous communities and has been shown to outperform benchmark techniques through higher FOMD values. In addition, by analyzing the top scoring communities in our case study, OHC clustered authors for specific research topics with indirect authorships more effectively. Future work will include improving OHC's efficiency by limiting depth of the recursive process in Phase Two, adapting OHC to find an evolution of communities in dynamic heterogeneous networks.

References

1. Blondel, V.D., Guillaume, J.L., Lambiotte, R., Lefebvre, E.: Fast unfolding of communities in large networks. J. Stat. Mech.: Theory Exp. **10**, P10008 (2008)
2. Flake, G.W., Lawrence, S., Giles, C.L.: Efficient identification of web communities. In: KDD, pp. 150–160 (2000)
3. Harenberg, S., et al.: Community detection in large-scale networks: a survey and empirical evaluation. Interdiscip. Rev. Comput. Stat. **6**(6), 426–439 (2014)
4. Kong, X., Cao, B., Yu, P.S.: Multi-label classification by mining label and instance correlations from heterogeneous information networks. In: KDD, pp. 614–622 (2013)
5. Lancichinetti, A., Fortunato, S.: Community detection algorithms: a comparative analysis. Phys. Rev. E **80**, 056117 (2009)
6. Leskovec, J., Lang, K.J., Mahoney, M.: Empirical comparison of algorithms for network community detection. In: WWW, pp. 631–640 (2010)
7. Long, B., Zhang, Z.M., Yu, P.S.: Co-clustering by block value decomposition. In: KDD, pp. 635–640 (2005)
8. Newman, M.E.J., Girvan, M.: Finding and evaluating community structure in networks. Phys. Rev. E **69**(2), 026113 (2004)

9. Radev, D.R., Muthukrishnan, P., Qazvinian, V., Abu-Jbara, A.: The ACL anthology network corpus. Lang. Resour. Eval. **47**(4), 919–944 (2009)

10. Shi, C., Li, Y., Zhang, J., Sun, Y., Yu, P.S.: A survey of heterogeneous information network analysis. IEEE TKDE **29**(1), 17–37 (2017)

11. Sun, Y., Yu, Y., Han, J.: Ranking-based clustering of heterogeneous information networks with star network schema. In: KDD, pp. 797–806 (2009)

12. Tang, J., Zhang, J., Yao, L., Li, J., Zhang, L., Su, Z.: Arnetminer: extraction and mining of academic social networks. In: KDD, pp. 990–998 (2008)

13. Watts, D.J., Strogatz, S.H.: Collective dynamics of 'small-world' networks. Nature **393**(6684), 440 (1998)

14. Xie, J., Szymanski, B.K., Liu, X.: SLPA: uncovering overlapping communities in social networks via a speaker-listener interaction dynamic process. In: ICDM Workshops, pp. 344–349 (2011)

15. Xie, J., Kelley, S., Szymanski, B.K.: Overlapping community detection in networks: the state-of-the-art and comparative study. ACM Comput. Surv. **45**(4), 43:1–43:35 (2013)

16. Yang, J., Leskovec, J.: Defining and evaluating network communities based on ground-truth. Knowl. Inf. Syst. **42**(1), 181–213 (2013)

17. Zhong, E., Fan, W., Zhu, Y., Yang, Q.: Modeling the dynamics of composite social networks. In: KDD, pp. 937–945 (2013)

Computer Vision

A Genetic Programming Approach for Constructing Foreground and Background Saliency Features for Salient Object Detection

Shima Afzali[✉], Harith Al-Sahaf, Bing Xue, Christopher Hollitt,
and Mengjie Zhang

School of Engineering and Computer Science, Victoria University of Wellington,
Wellington, New Zealand
{shima.afzali,harith.al-sahaf,bing.xue,
christopher.hollitt,mengjie.zhang}@ecs.vuw.ac.nz

Abstract. Salient Object Detection (SOD) methods have been widely investigated in order to mimic human visual system in selecting regions of interest from complex scenes. The majority of existing SOD methods have focused on designing and combining handcrafted features. This process relies on domain knowledge and expertise and becomes increasingly difficult as the complexity of candidate models increases. In this paper, we develop an automatic feature combination method for saliency features to relieve human intervention and domain knowledge. The proposed method contains three phases, two Genetic Programming (GP) phases to construct foreground and background features and a spatial blending phase to combine those features. The foreground and background features are constructed to complement each other, therefore one can improve other's shortcomings. This method is compared with the state-of-the-art methods on four different benchmark datasets. The results indicate the new automatic method is comparable with the state-of-the-art methods and even improves SOD performance on some datasets.

Keywords: Salient object detection · Foreground · Background
Genetic programming

1 Introduction

Visual saliency detection is a fundamental research and real life problem in neuroscience, psychology, and computer vision [7]. Salient Object Detection (SOD) is a process of identifying and localizing regions including objects that attract more attention than other parts of an image when examined by a human viewer [7].

In the past two decades, various types of saliency features have been designed for the SOD task by domain experts. Using the existing collection of features

© Springer Nature Switzerland AG 2018
T. Mitrovic et al. (Eds.): AI 2018, LNAI 11320, pp. 209–215, 2018.
https://doi.org/10.1007/978-3-030-03991-2_21

saves us from designing similar or redundant features. However, manually selecting features from the existing features and combining them is not an efficient way and not guarantee the optimal combination. Liu et al. [7] developed some well-known SOD features including local, regional, and global features. However, their proposed method loses its performance in some challenging images due to lack of more informative features and a suitable combination method. Lin et al. [6] proposed a method to detect salient object by extracting multiple features such as local contrast, global contrast, and background prior. They refined local and global contrasts by object center priors and then combined the refined features to salient region detection, and the feature combination part has been manually designed by the authors.

In order to have a more precise saliency map, saliency features are required to complement each other. Some features can complement each other, while some others may corrupt others' efficacy. A good feature combination method explores complementary characteristics of features and finds an optimal way to combine these features. However, in the literature, authors often have not paid attention to the complementary characteristic of features.

The aforementioned issues motivates us to develop a method which can automatically explore a set of the different features, select informative ones, consider their complementary characteristic and combine them suitably. Genetic Programing (GP) [5] is a search strategy to automatically evolve solutions (programs) by automatically exploring different possible combinations of features. GP has a flexible tree-based representation which also allows searching the space of various integration operations to combine different features. Thus, the aforementioned capabilities of GP make it suitable choice to develop a GP-based automatic feature combination method to address the aforementioned issues.

The overall goal of this study is to develop an automatic method to combine features to construct two new informative features. We propose a new method which focuses on two important parts of the image, foreground objects and background. In the proposed method, two GP-based foreground and background feature construction phases are developed. The GP-based foreground feature mainly targets the foreground object, while the GP-based background feature focuses on suppressing background. Specifically, this paper aims to fulfill the following objectives:

Develop new automatic feature combination method to construct two new informative features; and

Design two new fitness functions to evaluate the evolved solutions (individuals) by GP method.

2   The Proposed Method

In this paper, the overall process contains three phases, two GP-based feature construction phases to build foreground (FG) and background (BG) features, respectively, and a spatial blending phase to combine the constructed features. GP is utilized to find a good combination of the input features to construct

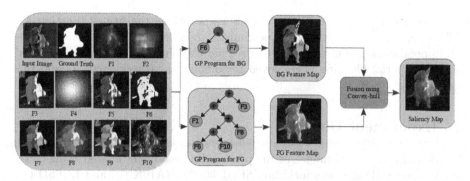

Fig. 1. Scheme of the proposed method.

FG and BG features. The process of the complete method is depicted in Fig. 1. For the first GP phase, GP-based foreground feature construction (GPFG), we focus on constructing the FG feature in order to effectively highlight foreground object(s). In this phase, GP takes a set of saliency feature maps as input and constructs FG feature as output that is a combination of those features. For the second GP phase, GP-based background feature construction (GPBG), GP is used to construct the BG feature to suppress background. GPBG takes saliency features and the function set as input to combine features, and returns a constructed feature as output. In contrast to GPFG, GPBG utilizes a different fitness function in constructing the BG feature (see details in Sect. 3.3). Fitness function for GPFG: saliency detection is a type of classification model that classifies pixels into, salient or non-salient groups. Since saliency detection is a Bernoulli distribution problem, binary entropy is chosen as the fitness measure. Here, binary entropy is employed to enhance precision of salient regions by decreasing the difference between the constructed feature and the ground truth.

$$H(p, q) = -p \log q - (1 - p) \log(1 - q) \tag{1}$$

where p is the ground truth value, q is the saliency value which is calculated by the GP program, and $H(p, q)$ is the entropy value between the ground truth and the saliency map. The fitness function is the average entropy of all the training images. The lower entropy shows the better fitness value for the GP program.

Table 1. GP parameters.

Population size	Generations	Mutation rate	Crossover rate
100	50	0.19	0.8
Elitism rate	Tree depth	Selection type	Tournament size
0.01	2–4	Tournament	7

Fitness function for GPBG: *recall* is employed as the fitness function for GP because recall operates as a pessimistic measure of saliency, so attempts to suppress background regions. For the final GP phase, an object center prior map and spatial blending is employed to combine the constructed FG and BG features [9].

3   Experiment Design

In this work, the performance of the proposed method is evaluated using three widely used SOD datasets including SED1 [4], MSRA10K [7], and ECSSD [4]. Each dataset is split into a training set (60%), a validation set (20%) and a test set (20%). Each of the GP methods were run 30 times on each dataset.

Similar parameter values are used for both GP methods, GPFG and GPBG. Table 1 summarizes the GP parameters. The parameter settings mostly follow the suggested values from the literature [3]. The initial population is created by the ramped half-and-half method. In this study, the population size is set to 100 to reduce the computational time. The tree depth was limited to 2–4, since it prevents individuals to growing inefficiently and becoming more complex. For the function set, both GP methods use a simple set of the commonly used arithmetic operations including addition, subtraction, and multiplication. Each function in the set $\{+, -, \times\}$, takes two saliency feature maps as input in 2D-array and returns another 2D-array saliency feature map as output. For the terminal set, different types of features is collected based on different characteristics of the saliency features from the literature. Here, nine saliency features are taken from the previous work [2], and the SUSAN edge detector is also added to the feature set [8]. The performance of the proposed method is evaluated using precision-recall (PR) curve, receiver operating characteristic (ROC) curve, and F-measure [4]. GPFBC is compared to seven other methods, five methods are selected from [4] including DRFI, GS, GMR, SF, RBD, and two other methods MSSS [1] and wPSO [2].

4   Results and Discussions

4.1   Quantitative Comparison

Based on the precision-recall curves in Fig. 2(a) and (b), GPFBC outperforms most other methods, but is slightly worse than RBD and DRFI. On the ECSSD dataset in Fig. 2(c), GPFBC performs better than RBD and also has a comparable result with wPSO. Based on the ROC curves in Figs. 3(a)–(c), GPFBC has the second best Area Under Curve (AUC) on all three data sets, where DRFI has the best AUC. GPFBC has a higher true positive rate in relation to false positive rate comparing to all the other methods apart from DRFI. Figure 4(a) shows that GPFBC has slightly lower average precision, recall, and F-measure to DRFI, RBD, and GS, but it has better performance than the other methods on the SED dataset. In Fig. 4(b), GPFBC has better results than most of the methods on the ASD dataset, while DRFI and RBD have slightly better results than GPFBC. On the ECSSD dataset, GPFBC has a slightly lower average precision than wPSO and DRFI, but a higher average recall than wPSO (Fig. 4(c)). The ECSSD dataset contain more complex images than the SED and ASD datasets. Although GPFBC performs well on the ASD and SED datasets, it has better performance on ECSSD regarding average precision, recall, and F-measure. Generally, GPFBC shows a comparable or even better performance compared to the other methods except for DRFI. Although the performance of the GPFBC method is not as good as the DRFI method, GPFBC uses only 10 features and DRFI employs a 93 dimensional feature vector.

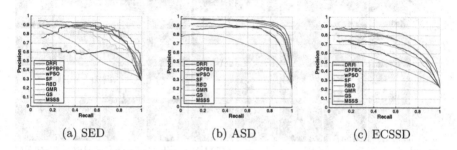

(a) SED   (b) ASD   (c) ECSSD

Fig. 2. Precision-recall curves of GPFBC compared to seven other methods.

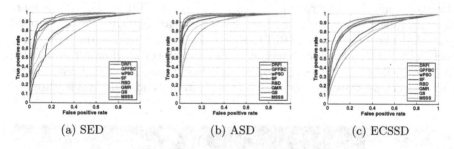

(a) SED   (b) ASD   (c) ECSSD

Fig. 3. ROC curves of GPFBC compared to seven other methods.

4.2   Qualitative Comparison

Some sample saliency maps are shown in Figs. 5 and 6 to illustrate the qualitative performance of GPFBC and the seven other methods. It can be seen that the performance of GPFBC is mostly good on the challenging and complex images, e.g., images having non-homogeneous foreground object (e.g., 4th row),

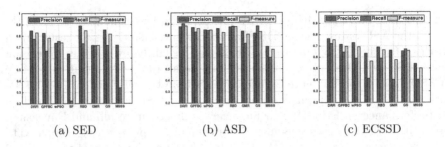

(a) SED   (b) ASD   (c) ECSSD

Fig. 4. Average precision, recall, and F-measure of GPFBC compared to seven other methods.

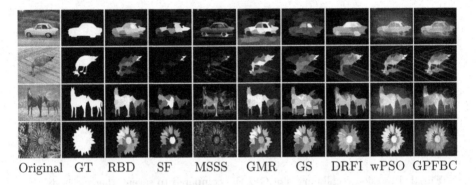

Original GT   RBD   SF   MSSS   GMR   GS   DRFI wPSO GPFBC

Fig. 5. Some visual examples of the new method and seven other SOD methods.

cluttered/complex background regions (e.g., 1st and 3rd rows), having more than one salient object (e.g., 3rd row), having similar color with the background (e.g., 2nd row). Generally, GPFBC shows the highest quality on suppressing background and completely detecting foreground object(s). However, it may fail in some challenging images (Fig. 6), since it has the lack of enough informative features such as shape information, texture features, and high-level features.

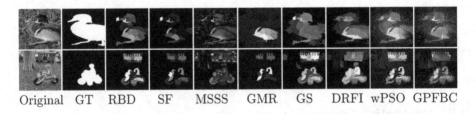

Original GT   RBD   SF   MSSS   GMR   GS   DRFI wPSO GPFBC

Fig. 6. Some visual examples of the new method and seven other SOD methods.

5   Conclusions

In this study, an automatic feature combination method is developed to construct two new informative features using GP to focus on the foreground object and the background, respectively. The first GP method takes input saliency features and generates a foreground feature, which is mainly good at highlighting foreground objects. The second GP method focuses on generating background feature, that mostly suppresses background for SOD. The results show that GP has a promising capability for exploring a large search space and finding a good way to combine different input saliency features. The findings motivate us to further explore GP for developing a fully automatic feature combination method in our future work that does not rely on the spatial blending approach in the third phase of the proposed method.

References

1. Achanta, R., Süsstrunk, S.: Saliency detection using maximum symmetric surround. In: Proceedings of the 17th IEEE International Conference on Image Processing, pp. 2653–2656. IEEE (2010)
2. Afzali, S., Xue, B., Al-Sahaf, H., Zhang, M.: A supervised feature weighting method for salient object detection using particle swarm optimization. In: Proceedings of the IEEE Symposium Series on Computational Intelligence, pp. 1–8 (2017)
3. Al-Sahaf, H., Al-Sahaf, A., Xue, B., Johnston, M., Zhang, M.: Automatically evolving rotation-invariant texture image descriptors by genetic programming. IEEE Trans. Evol. Comput. **21**(1), 83–101 (2017)
4. Borji, A., Cheng, M.M., Jiang, H., Li, J.: Salient object detection: a survey. arXiv preprint arXiv:1411.5878, pp. 1–26 (2014)
5. Koza, J.R.: Genetic Programming (1997)
6. Lin, M., Zhang, C., Chen, Z.: Predicting salient object via multi-level features. Neurocomputing **205**, 301–310 (2016)
7. Liu, T., et al.: Learning to detect a salient object. IEEE Trans. Pattern Anal. Mach. Intell. **33**(2), 353–367 (2011)
8. Smith, S.M., Brady, J.M.: SUSANA new approach to low level image processing. Int. J. Comput. Vis. **23**(1), 45–78 (1997)
9. Yang, C., Zhang, L., Lu, H.: Graph-regularized saliency detection with convex-hull-based center prior. IEEE Signal Process. Lett. **20**(7), 637–640 (2013)

Distinction Between Ships and Icebergs in SAR Images Using Ensemble Loss Trained Convolutional Neural Networks

Xiaocai Zhang[1], Yuansheng Liu[1], Yi Zheng[1], Zhixun Zhao[1], Jinyan Li[1(✉)], and Yang Liu[2]

[1] Advanced Analytics Institute, University of Technology Sydney, Sydney, Australia
{xiaocai.zhang,yuansheng.liu,yi.zheng-8,zhixun.zhao}@student.uts.edu.au,
jinyan.li@uts.edu.au
[2] Transportation Engineering College, Dalian Maritime University, Dalian, Liaoning, China
leoyoung0817@163.com

Abstract. With the phenomenon of global warming, more new shipping routes will be open and utilized by more and more ships in the polar regions, particularly in the Arctic. Synthetic aperture radar (SAR) has been widely used in ship and iceberg monitoring for maritime surveillance and safety in the Arctic waters. At present, compared with the object detection of ship or iceberg, the task of ship and iceberg distinction in SAR images is still in challenge. In this work, we propose a novel loss function called ensemble loss to train convolutional neural networks (CNNs), which is a convex function and incorporates the traits of cross entropy and hinge loss. The ensemble loss trained CNNs model for the distinction between ship and iceberg is evaluated on a real-world SAR data set, which can get a higher classification accuracy to 90.15%. Experiment on another real image data set also confirm the effectiveness of the proposed ensemble loss.

Keywords: Ship · Iceberg · Distinction
Synthetic aperture radar (SAR)
Convolutional neural networks (CNNs) · Ensemble loss

1 Introduction

With the rapid and observable global-scale warming of climate, more and more commercial, economic and environmental interests have been attracted in the polar regions, especially in the Arctic. One of those is the opening of more Arctic new shipping routes, which is directly arisen from the sea ice decline in recent 30 year. Actually, the Arctic shipping route is the shortest shipping network between North America, Europe and Northeast Asia, with the advantages of short distance, short duration of voyage, less congestion, no piracy. For example, the Northwest Passage would get a huge shortcut for shipping between

© Springer Nature Switzerland AG 2018
T. Mitrovic et al. (Eds.): AI 2018, LNAI 11320, pp. 216–223, 2018.
https://doi.org/10.1007/978-3-030-03991-2_22

the Northwest Atlantic Ocean and Pacific Ocean. In general, vessels must go through Panama Canal or even Cape Horn if they take transit between Northwest Atlantic and Pacific Ocean. However, navigating through Canadian Arctic would cut the normal voyage by more than 7,000 km.

The Arctic Passage's opening will present more and more vessel traffic flow, which also requires more accurate and efficient maritime surveillance approaches. SAR is a common and important instrument for oceanographic observation. For ship detection, ship-iceberg discrimination approach can be used to detect and surveille merchant ships or even other non-merchant ships. In addition, since the research conducted by Norwegian Defence Research Establishment in 2004 to insight the feasibility of space-based automatic identification system (SAIS) for ship monitoring in high sea, the research of SAIS has attracted more and more interests. At present, one emerging technology is the combination of SAR and SAIS to enhance maritime surveillance [6]. On the other hand, for iceberg detection, large drifting icebergs present huge threat to vessels, particularly for oil tanker, as well as human activities such as offshore oil platforms in the high latitude regions. Currently, many stakeholders use aerial reconnaissance and shore-based support to monitor icebergs and assess associated risks. However, these methods are not viable in remote sea areas or under particularly harsh weather conditions, and the only feasible option is via satellite.

Iceberg or ship detection in SAR image can be well implemented by adaptive threshold techniques [3], some papers [4,9] have addressed this issue. However, object recognition in SAR image is still challenging. Denbina et al. [5] conduct feature extraction before feeding into a support vector machine (SVM) classifier. Zakharov et al. [10] apply supervised learning after hand feature extraction from satellite altimetry. Howell et al. [7] detect the difference in the dominant scattering mechanism between the classes of iceberg and ship. However, it's only applicable for discrimination in multi-polarization SAR data, not suitable for single-polarization data. Bentes et al. [3] use CNNs to learn features from SAR image and classify ship or iceberg with a fully connected layer.

2   Ensemble Loss

In this section, we will present the details of the ensemble loss and how to prove its convexity. In machine learning, the most common loss function for classification task is cross entropy (CE). For binary classification, let y_i denote the ground truth class probabilities (also called as label), y_i are either 0 or 1. p_i refer to the predicted class probabilities, N defines the number of class.

$$J_{CE} = -\sum_{i=1}^{N} y_i \cdot log p_i \tag{1}$$

When applying CE for error calculation while training CNNs, the optimization objective is to minimize J_{CE}. On the other hand, to make the output probability p_i approach to 1 if the ground truth probability to this class is 1,

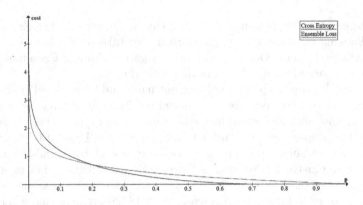

Fig. 1. Cost function for cross entropy and ensemble loss ($\varepsilon = 0.3$).

otherwise, to let it close to 0. However, for some outputs with relatively high probabilities (i.e. $p > 0.9$), it means the sum probabilities of the rest is quite low (i.e. less than 0.1). In that situation, the cost is still positive and the optimization process will still be proceeding to minimize the cost (i.e. to drive p from 0.9 to 1). However, this optimization mechanism means a waste of capacity [8], as the outputs with high probabilities is with enough evidences for classification.

To avoid such case, we propose an ensemble loss (EL) function. The inspiration comes from the hinge loss function (Eq. (2)) used in SVM.

$$J_{HL} = \max(0, 1 - \hat{y} \cdot (\mathbf{w}^T \cdot \mathbf{x} + b)) \tag{2}$$

where $\hat{y}$ is the ground truth label, $\hat{y} = \pm 1$ for classification. $\mathbf{w}$ and b is the weight and bias of hyperplane $\mathbf{w}^T \cdot \mathbf{x} + b$.

We introduce the multiplication of cross entropy loss and hinge loss, and set a marginal value ε to avoid the problem of capacity wastage.

The proposed EL function is defined as Eqs. (3) and (4), and the plot is displayed in Fig. 1. Equation (4) is derived from Softmax layer on the top of network.

$$J_{EL} = -\sum_{i=1}^{N} y_i \cdot \log p_i \cdot \max(0, 1 - (2y_i - 1) \cdot (2 \cdot (p_i + \varepsilon) - 1)) \tag{3}$$

$$\sum_{i=1}^{N} p_i = 1, 0 < p_i < 1 \tag{4}$$

where ε is a small non-negative marginal value, $0 \leqslant \varepsilon < 0.5$, y_i are either 0 or 1.

Let

$$L(p) = -y \cdot \log p \cdot \max(0, 1 - (2y - 1) \cdot (2 \cdot (p + \varepsilon) - 1)) \tag{5}$$

Thus we can get,

$$\frac{\partial L}{\partial p} = \begin{cases} 0, & p \geqslant \frac{y}{2y-1} - \varepsilon \\ (4y^2 - 2y) \cdot (1 + \log p) + \frac{(4y^2 - 2y)\varepsilon - 2y^2}{p}, & p < \frac{y}{2y-1} - \varepsilon \end{cases} \tag{6}$$

$$\frac{\partial^2 L}{\partial p^2} = \begin{cases} 0, & p \geqslant \frac{y}{2y-1} - \varepsilon \\ \frac{(4y^2-2y)(p-\varepsilon)+2y^2}{p^2}, & p < \frac{y}{2y-1} - \varepsilon \end{cases} \tag{7}$$

From Eqs. (3) to (7), y is either 1 or 0, we can derive,

$$\frac{\partial^2 L}{\partial p^2} \geqslant 0 \tag{8}$$

Therefore, it is proved that the constructed EL function $L(p)$ and J_{EL} are convex. So that EL loss could get rid of the problem of multiple local minimums when introducing stochastic gradient descent (SDG) for optimization.

3 Experiments and Results

We conduct experiments on a real SAR data set generated from Sentinel-1 satellite. Moreover, in order to validate the effectiveness and robustness of our loss function, we also conduct experiments on a real optical satellite image data set.

3.1 Data Set

SAR Image Data Set: It comes from Sentinel-1 satellite carrying C-band SAR instrument [1]. It contains 1604 groups of data, each group includes two channel images: HH (transmit/receive horizontally) and HV (transmit horizontally and receive vertically), both are with size of 50 × 50 pixels. The labels of each image are either ship or iceberg. Figure 2(a) gives an example of one group SAR images.

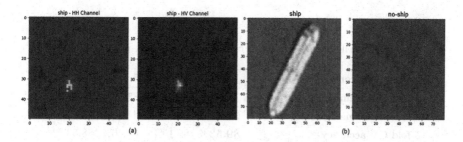

Fig. 2. (a) SAR image of a ship. (b) Ship and non-ship labeled images.

Optical Image Data Set: These satellite images are captured by satellite Planet [2]. It covers 2800 80 × 80 pixels RGB images with label of ship or no-ship. Figure 2(b) illustrates the ship and no-ship labeled images.

3.2 Architecture

There are some parameters that we need to determine before network training, such as size of each convolution and fully connected layer, kernel size in convolution and max-polling layers, ε in the proposed EL loss function (Eq. (3)) and so on. We use a greedy strategy to find the optimal network architecture. First of all, We choose a default architecture and then conduct a five-fold cross-validation on the training and validation sets with different parameter one by one. From Tables 1, 2 and 3 give the process of searching the optimal architecture of CNNs for ships and icebergs classification task. Note that in SAR images, we use the component of HH, HV and the mean of HH and HV channels as the input.

Table 1. Layer size selection

Layer size	10-20-40-60	**20-40-60-80**	40-60-80-100	60-80-100-120	80-100-120-140
5-fold CV accuracy	87.03%	**89.53%**	86.66%	88.34%	88.90%

Table 2. Fully connected layer size and parameter ε selection

Neurons	200	300	**400**	500	1000
5-fold CV accuracy	88.53%	89.40%	**89.53%**	89.21%	88.79%
ε	0	0.1	0.2	**0.3**	0.4
5-fold CV accuracy	88.15%	89.34%	88.53%	**89.53%**	88.59%

Table 3. Kernel size selection in convolution and max-pooling layers

Kernel size (convolution layers)	1×1	3×3	5×5	7×7
5-fold CV accuracy	76.37%	**89.53%**	87.84%	87.53%
Kernel size (max-pooling Layers)	2×2	3×3	4×4	5×5
5-fold CV accuracy	**89.53%**	89.15%	89.40%	88.53%

3.3 Convergence

We use the augmented SAR images as the inputs with the aforementioned optimal architecture. Both CE and EL are conducted with a five-fold cross-validation. The mean validation accuracy in the training process is displayed in

Fig. 3. Note that all variables in both experiments are initialized with the same initializer. Analyzing the curves, accuracy in both methods does not differ much at the earlier stage. After the turning point, observably, EL gets higher accuracy than CE. Among the last 10 training epochs, the mean validation accuracy of EL is 87.59%, which is better than 87.06% of CE.

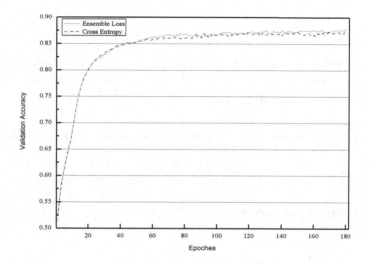

Fig. 3. Mean accuracy on validation data (SAR image data set).

3.4   Results

We compare EL trained CNNs (CNNs-EL) with CE trained CNNs and CNNs without data augmentation, PCA+SVM [3] and human labeling with testing set. For PCA+SVM, firstly, we extract 60 principle components via PCA and then feed them into a SVM classifier. We also conduct human labeling experiment to explore the ability of human brain for this task, 20 volunteers are participated in this experiment. They are divided into 5 groups randomly with different labeling tasks from fold 1 to 5. Then, they are required to learn SAR images with labels in the training set by themselves. After completing independent learning stage, they are asked to give the labels for unlabeled images in the testing set.

Table 4 presents the accuracy of CNNs-EL compared with other baselines. CNNs-EL performs better than CE trained CNNs, as it employs the notion of a margin like hinge loss. The employment of data augmentation in CNNs also improves the accuracy by more than 3% as it has better generative ability. The human performance is just at 63.77%, which is quite below our CNNs-EL, which reflects the restriction of human ability on the task of SAR image distinction.

We also conduct experiments on an optical image data set for task of ship and no-ship classification. From Table 5, overall, all methods can get much higher

Table 4. Accuracy comparison with different models on SAR image data set

Model	Fold 1	Fold 2	Fold 3	Fold 4	Fold 5	Mean
CNNs-EL	**89.38%**	**91.59%**	**91.28%**	87.86%	**90.65%**	**90.15%**
CNNs [3]	88.75%	89.72%	90.34%	**89.41%**	88.78%	89.40%
CNNs without data augmentation	87.50%	83.80%	85.05%	88.16%	86.60%	86.22%
PCA+SVM [3]	68.75%	78.82%	81.93%	73.83%	82.24%	77.11%
Human labeling	58.12%	65.73%	66.09%	63.55%	65.34%	63.77%

classification accuracy compared with ship-iceberg classification task, as the patterns of ship and no-ship classes in optical images can be well recognized. CNNs-EL also improves the performance compared with CE trained CNNs.

Table 5. Accuracy comparison with different models on optical image data set

Model	Fold 1	Fold 2	Fold 3	Fold 4	Fold 5	Mean
CNNs-EL	**100%**	**100%**	**99.82%**	**100%**	**99.64%**	**99.89%**
CNNs	100%	100%	99.29%	100%	98.93%	99.64%
CNNs without data augmentation	100%	100%	98.39%	100%	98.93%	99.46%

4   Conclusion and Future Work

This paper builds a ship and iceberg classification model for SAR images based on CNNs, which employs a novel ensemble loss for optimization. We evaluate the performance of the proposed model on a real-world SAR image data set and compare it with cross entropy trained CNNs, CNNs without data augmentation, PCA+SVM and human labeling, and the results show that the proposed model can get more accurate classification performance than the competing methods. Besides, classification experiments conducted on an optical satellite image data set also confirm the effectiveness of the proposed ensemble loss.

In future our plan is to develop multi-label classifier for this problem and conduct more experiments to test the effectiveness of ensemble loss.

References

1. Kaggle: https://www.kaggle.com. Accessed 10 Jan 2018
2. Planet: https://www.planet.com. Accessed 1 Jul 2018
3. Bentes, C., Frost, A., Velotto, D., Tings, B.: Ship-iceberg discrimination with convolutional neural networks in high resolution SAR images. In: Proceedings of 11th European Conference on Synthetic Aperture Radar, pp. 1–4 (2016)
4. Collins, M.J., Denbina, M., Atteia, G.: On the reconstruction of quad-pol SAR data from compact polarimetry data for ocean target detection. IEEE Trans. Geosci. Remote Sens. **51**(1), 591–600 (2013)

5. Denbina, M., Collins, M.J., Atteia, G.: On the detection and discrimination of ships and icebergs using simulated dual-polarized radarsat constellation data. Canadian J. Remote Sens. **41**(5), 363–379 (2015)
6. Eriksen, T., Høye, G., Narheim, B., Meland, B.J.: Maritime traffic monitoring using a space-based AIS receiver. Acta Astronaut. **58**(10), 537–549 (2006)
7. Howell, C., Youden, J., Lane, K., Power, D., Randell, C., Flett, D.: Iceberg and ship discrimination with ENVISAT multipolarization ASAR. In: Proceedings of 2004 IEEE International Geoscience and Remote Sensing Symposium, pp. 113–116 (2004)
8. Jin, J., Fu, K., Zhang, C.: Traffic sign recognition with hinge loss trained convolutional neural networks. IEEE Trans. Intell. Transp. Syst. **15**(5), 1991–2000 (2014)
9. Zakharov, I., Power, D., Howell, M., Warren, S.: Improved detection of icebergs in sea ice with RADARSAT-2 polarimetric data. In: Proceedings of 2017 IEEE International Geoscience and Remote Sensing Symposium, pp. 2294–2297 (2017)
10. Zakharov, I., Puestow, T., Fleming, A., Deepakumara, J., Power, D.: Detection and discrimination of icebergs and ships using satellite altimetry. In: Proceedings of 2017 IEEE International Geoscience and Remote Sensing Symposium, pp. 882–885 (2017)

Shark Detection from Aerial Imagery Using Region-Based CNN, a Study

Nabin Sharma[1]([⊠]), Paul Scully-Power[2], and Michael Blumenstein[1]

[1] School of Software, Center for Artificial Intelligence, University of Technology
Sydney, Broadway, NSW 2007, Australia
{Nabin.Sharma,Michael.Blumenstein}@uts.edu.au
[2] The Ripper Group Pty. Ltd., 50 York Street, Sydney, NSW 2000, Australia
psp@littleripper.com

Abstract. Shark attacks have been a very sensitive issue for Australians
and many other countries. Thus, providing safety and security around
beaches is very fundamental in the current climate. Safety for both
human beings and underwater creatures (sharks, whales, etc.) in general is essential while people continue to visit and use the beaches heavily for recreation and sports. Hence, an efficient, automated and real-
time monitoring approach on beaches for detecting various objects (e.g.
human activities, large fish, sharks, whales, surfers, etc.) is necessary
to avoid unexpected casualties and accidents. The use of technologies
such as drones and machine learning techniques are promising directions
in such challenging circumstances. This paper investigates the potential
of Region-based Convolutional Neural Networks (R-CNN) for detecting
various marine objects, and Sharks in particular. Three network architectures namely Zeiler and Fergus (ZF), Visual Geometry Group (VGG16),
and VGG_M were considered for analysis and identifying their potential.
A dataset consisting of 3957 video frames were used for experiments.
VGG16 architecture with faster-R-CNN performed better than others,
with an average precision of 0.904 for detecting Sharks.

Keywords: Faster R-CNN · Marine animal detection · Deep learning

1 Introduction

Sharks and other marine animals have a significant contribution in the maintenance of healthy marine ecosystems. Beach recreation involve extensive use
of ocean and humans are vulnerable to shark attacks. Australian Shark attack
statistics for 2015 [26] recorded 33 unprovoked cases, with 23 injured and 2 were
fatal. In 2016 [27], total number of shark attack reported were 26, with 2 fatal
and 16 injured. The statistics clearly reveal the risk involved while entering the
ocean. Thus, providing safety and security around beaches is very fundamental
in the current climate. Safety for both human beings and marine life (e.g. sharks,
dolphins, etc.) in general is essential while people continue to visit and use the

© Springer Nature Switzerland AG 2018
T. Mitrovic et al. (Eds.): AI 2018, LNAI 11320, pp. 224–236, 2018.
https://doi.org/10.1007/978-3-030-03991-2_23

beaches heavily for recreation and sport. Hence, an efficient, automated and real-time monitoring approach on the beaches for detecting shark in particular is necessary to avoid unexpected casualties and accidents.

Manned aircrafts with trained onboard crew has been used of conducting aerial surveys [1] and beach monitoring for more than a decade. This process is quite expensive, time-consuming, requires specialized skills and prone to human error. Hence, automation of the process is an inevitable choice considering the high degree of risk involved and the high precision required. Recent advancements in the Unmanned Aerial Vehicle (UAV) technology have produced low-priced drones/UAVs. Availability for sophisticated drones/UAVs with high definition digital cameras have made them a popular choice for aerial surveys and beach monitoring, in the recent past. Drones/UAVs can be explicitly used for beach monitoring, combined with an intelligent system which analyses the video stream to identify the presence of shark or potential threats.

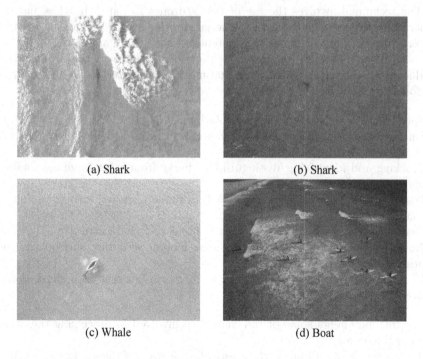

(a) Shark   (b) Shark

(c) Whale   (d) Boat

Fig. 1. Sample aerial images of shark, whale and boats.

Increase in the global shark encounters are mainly due to the increase in population and number of people using the ocean [4]. A number of shark control program [3,5–8] have been adopted around the world with the aim of decreasing the risk by removing/restricting the sharks from areas used for recreation purposes. This programs in general do not discriminate sharks from other marine life, which results in the interference with marine ecosystem and can be harmful

[9,10]. Hence, there is need for exploring alternate solutions which facilitates the co-existence of marine life and humans, without compromising the safety.

In order to ensure safety for beach/ocean users, personal shark deterrents (e.g. Shark Shield) were created and are commercially available to mitigate the risk from Sharks. This shark deterrents usually creates strong non-lethal electric fields which repels sharks. The study presented by Kempster et al. [2], shows that Shark Shield can reduce interactions between white sharks and static-bait under test conditions. It also suggests that further studies are required to test the device on different shark species by varying the discharge frequency. Although, the shark deterrents are effective, it still has a hidden risk involved as there are various shark species available and some may not respond to the pre-defined frequency. Moreover, the devices are invasive in the context that they are wearable and the discharge frequencies can be harmful to both human and sharks or marine life in general. Hence, a study of non-invasive technique to ensure safety for ocean users is presented in this paper.

The technique involves the use of UAVs/drones to patrol beaches and the camera attached to them captures the aerial view for real-time analysis to detect the presence of shark or identifying potential risks. There are many challenges involved in the automatic processing of the video streams. Initial investigation conducted for the development of an automatic shark detection system, reveals the following challenges:

- Speed of UAV, altitude, camera resolution.
- Unconstrained lighting conditions while capturing real-time videos of beaches using the UAV/drone.
- Tracking and identifying/distinguishing sharks from other large fish/marine life.
- Distinguishing sharks from other objects namely, surfer, swimmers, drone shadows, etc.
- Detecting potentially unusual activities indicating shark attacks.
- Noisy backgrounds dues to ocean waves, human activities, surf boards and other objects.
- Real-time alarms for Surf lifesaving clubs/teams in case of a shark detection/attack.

Figure 1 highlights some of the challenges involved in processing the aerial video of the ocean.

In this paper, we proposed to investigate the state-of-the-art Deep Convolutional Neural Networks for detection of various marine animal and object namely, Shark, Whale, Surfer, Largefish, and Boat. Specifically, we analyze the potential of Faster Region-based Convolutional Neural Networks (R-CNN) [19] for the detection of the areas-of-interest and adapt it to the current problem. Three different network architectures namely Zeiler and Fergus (ZF) [20], Visual Geometry Group (VGG16) [21] and VGG_CNN_M_1024(VGGM) [22] were used in the study. The primary intension of the present study is to model region segmentation task for shark detection, as a standard object detection problem. The study explores object detection methods which can detect shark at real-time, in a single pipeline and can eventually be used for beach monitoring/surveillance. To the best of our knowledge, this is the first study which considers the use of Deep CNNs for detecting Shark and other marine animals from aerial imagery capture using UAV/drone patrolling Australian beaches.

The paper is organized as follows. The related works on marine life detection and the Deep CNN based object detection methods are discussed in Sect. 2. The proposed approach in presented in Sect. 3. In Sect. 4, experimental analysis and result are discussed. Finally, the paper is concluded in Sect. 5.

2   Related Works

In this section, the recent works on automated marine animal detection and the current state-of-the-art methods for object detection using Deep Convolutional Neural Networks (CNN) are discussed in Subsects. 2.1 and 2.2, respectively. In particular, a brief overview of Region-based Convolutional Neural Networks (R-CNN) [18], Fast R-CNN [17], and Faster R-CNN [19] is presented in Subsect. 2.2.

2.1   Automated Marine Animal Detection

Not much work has been reported in the literature to address the problem of automatic marine animal detection in general, and shark detection [11,12] in particular. Among the recent work, Mejias et al. [14] presented tow algorithms to detect marine species automatically. They focus on detecting dugongs from aerial images, in order to automate the aerial surveys. They proposed two algorithms. The first algorithm used morphological operations and combined colour analysis for blob detection. The second algorithm uses a shape profiling method on saturation channel from HSV colour space. The reported result had a very low precision rate and high false-positives.

Maire et al. [13] also presented an algorithm for detecting dugongs from aerial imagery. Their approach consist of two stages. Regions-of-interest are determined in the first stage using colour and morphological filter. In the second stage, shape analysis is performed on the candidate blobs identified from the first stage. A template matching technique is used for finalizing detection results. The system performed better when the sea surface was calm, but the performance degraded as the sea surface became rough.

Shrivakshan [15] presented an analysis of Sobel and Gabor filters for classifying different shark types. The analysis shows that Gabor filters performed better than Sobel filter. Use of multi-spectral imaging for automatic detection of marine animals was studied by Lopez et al. [16].

To summarize, although global shark attacks in the recent years were quite high, not many works have been reported toward the automation of the detection process, as compared to the severity of the consequences. Most of the works found in the literature used traditional machine learning approach and were quite slow with unacceptable precision. To the best of our knowledge, no work has been reported in the literature considering the Deep Learning methodologies for shark detection or marine animal detection, in general.

2.2 Deep CNN-Based Object Detection Methods

Recent advances in object detection techniques presented the community with Region-Based Convolutional Neural Network (R-CNN) and its successors (Fast and Faster R-CNN). R-CNN [18] uses Selective Search (SS) to compute ($\approx 2k$) object proposals of different scales and positions. For each of these proposals, image regions are warped to fixed size (227 × 227) pixels. The warped image regions are then fed to the CNN for detections. The proposed network architecture uses classification head for classifying region into one of the classes. The SS does not necessarily provide perfect proposals. Therefore, to make up for the slightly wrong object proposals, regression head uses linear regression to map predicted bounding boxes to the ground-truth bounding boxes. R-CNN is very slow at test time where every individual object proposals are passed through CNN. The feature extracted are cached to the disk. Finally, a classifier such as SVM is trained in an offline manner. Therefore, the weights of the CNN did not have the chance to update itself in response to these offline part of the network. Moreover, the training pipeline of the R-CNN is complex.

In Fast R-CNN [17] the order of the extracting region of proposals and running the CNN is exchanged. In this architecture whole image is passed once through the CNN and the regions are now extracted from convolutional feature map using ROI pooling. This change in architecture reduces the computation time by sharing the computation of convolutional feature map between region proposals. The region proposals are projected to the corresponding spatial part of convolutional feature volume. Finally, fully connected layer expects the fixed size feature vector and therefore the projected region is divided into grid and Spatial Pyramid Pooling (SPP) is performed to get fixed size vector. SPP deals with the variable window size of pooling operation and thus end-to-end training of the network is very hard. The generation of the region proposals is the bottle neck at the test time. In above mentioned approaches, CNN was used only for regression and classification. The idea was further extended to use CNN also for region proposals. The latest offspring from the R-CNN family, the Faster R-CNN [19] proposed the idea of small CNN network called Region Proposal Network (RPN), build on top of the convolutional feature map. A sliding window is placed over feature map in reference to the original image. The notion of anchor box is used to capture object at multiple scales. The center of the anchor box having different aspect ratio and size coincide with the center of sliding window. RPN generates region proposals of different sizes and aspect ratios at various spatial locations. RPN is a two layered network which does not add to the computation of overall network. Finally, regression provides finer localization with the reference to the sliding window position.

Although R-CNN and its predecessors perform well with high accuracy, they are computationally very expensive and time consuming, making them undesirable for real-time applications. Faster-R-CNN works at a rate of 7 frames per second, while maintaining high accuracy.

Based on the brief investigation of the state-of-the-art, Faster R-CNN was considered in this study for experiments on shark detection. Different CNN architectures were used with Faster R-CNN for analysis.

3   Proposed Approach

3.1   Dataset Preparation

The aerial images for the current work have been collected from live streaming video captured from the trial runs of drones on popular Australian beaches. Video streams were saved in high definition mode and later down sampled to 720p. The frames where extracted from the videos for preparing the dataset for experiments. For training Faster R-CNN, ground truth/annotation were created for frames/images as per PASCAL VOC XML format [25]. Specifically, Shark, Surfer, Whale, Boat and LargeFishes were considered for annotation. Boat is generic category which represents various types of boats namely, paddle boat, kayak boat, etc. Whereas, Largefish is generic category which represents large fish/marine animals which could pose potential risk to the safety of ocean users. Due to the availability of a smaller number of samples for various large marine animals and lack of ground truth information, the generic categories was defined in order to reduce the confusion with sharks. Missing ground truth information was due many reasons namely, low resolution resulting in unclear shape, glitter, speed of UAV, etc. A sample video frame and its corresponding XML annotation is shown in Fig. 2.

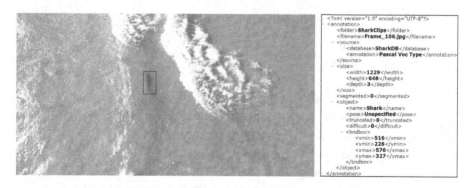

Fig. 2. Sample aerial image of a shark (marked in red) with annotation (Color figure online)

3.2   Approach

Faster R-CNN [19] with Caffe [24] deep learning library was considered for our experiments. The Caffe-based pre-trained models are publically available for most of the object detectors. There are less number of images in the dataset for a deep learning system to learn from scratch. Hence, to take full advantage of network architectures, transfer learning technique from ImageNet [23] was used to fine-tune our models. The fine-tuning process helps our system to converge faster and perform better. We have used various network architectures such as ZF [20], VGG16 [21], and VGG_CNN_M_1024 [22] to train the system and evaluate the performance on the dataset. ZF is a 8 layered architecture containing 5 convolutional layers and 3 fully-connected layers. Whereas, VGG16 is a much deeper layered architecture with 16 layers, comprising 13 convolutional layers and 3 fully connected layers.

4   Results and Discussion

The dataset used for experiments comprises of 3856 aerial video frames/images. The dataset consists of videos from UAV trials conducted on popular Australian beaches. The dataset was divided in three subsets, for training, validation, and testing, with random sampling. The train set consist of 60% for total dataset, whereas validation and test set consist of 10% and 30% of the total samples, respectively. Three different network architectures namely, ZF, VGG_CNN_M_1024 (VGGM in short), and VGG16 were used for experiments. Implementations details, and the detection results are discussed in the subsections given below.

Table 1. Performance of various network architectures on test dataset.

Class	ZF	VGG16	VGG_M
Shark	0.903	**0.904**	0.895
Surfer	**0.905**	0.904	0.901
LargeFish	0.886	**0.894**	0.737
Whale	0.989	**0.991**	0.901
Boat	0.776	**0.811**	0.685
mAP	0.892	**0.901**	0.824
Iterations	60 K	50 K	70 K
Time (per image)	0.044 s	0.130 s	0.048 s

4.1 Implementation Details

We trained our models with Nvidia Quadro P6000 GPU, 24 GB, on a Ubuntu server (Core i7 processor, 64 GB RAM) with a learning rate of 0.001 and batch size of 128. The RPN batch size is kept constant at 128 for region-based proposal networks (RPN). Regions proposal networks were trained end-to-end using back-propagation and stochastic gradient descent (SGD). In order reduce redundancies arising from RPN proposals, non-maximum suppression (NMS) was applied to the proposals based on the class scores. Performance of each network architecture at different iterations was also analysed. In the training phase, the snapshot of trained models were saved at an interval of $10k$ iterations. Detections with

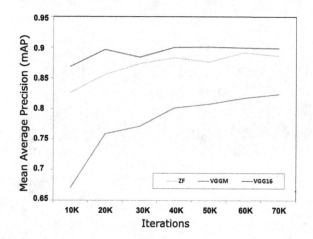

Fig. 3. Mean average precision analysis at different iterations

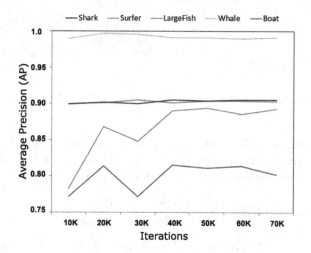

Fig. 4. AP analysis of each class using VGG16

(a) Shark   (b) Shark

(c) Surfers and Boat

(d) Whale   (e) Boat

Fig. 5. Sample detection results obtained using VGG16 trained model

overlap greater than the 50% Intersection Over Union (IOU) threshold with the corresponding ground-truth bounding box are considered as true positive and all other detections as false positive as shown in Eq. 1 [25].

$$IOU = \frac{area\left(BBox_{pred} \cap BBox_{gt}\right)}{area\left(BBox_{pred} \cup BBox_{gt}\right)} \tag{1}$$

where, $BBox_{pred}$ and $BBox_{gt}$ denotes predicted bounding box and ground truth bounding box respectively. The ground truth box with no matching detection are considered false negative detection. To evaluate the detection performance, we use Average Precision (AP) calculated from the area under the Precision-Recall (PR) curve [25]. While, mean Average Precision (mAP) is used for a set of detections and is the mean over classes, of the interpolated AP for each class.

4.2 Detection Results

The detection results of different object are detailed in Table 1. The results obtained considering the different architectures are given in the respective columns of the table. Among all the iterations, best results obtained for each network architectures are reported in Table 1. The Table 1 shows that VGG16 performed better than ZF and VGGM. Mean average precision of 0.892 (60 K iterations), 0.901 (60 K iterations) and 0.824 (70 K iterations) were obtained for ZF, VGG16 and VGG_M, respectively. Average time taken for processing each image for detection was 0.044 s, 0.130 s and 0.048 s, for ZF, VGG16 and VGG_M, respectively. For shark detection, VGG16 performed better with an average precision of 0.904. Lower precision for the detection of boat was due to the unconstrained nature and confusion with surfer/surf-boards. On the contrary, performance of whale detection was better than other objects and this is due to its size, shape and clear image samples. The performance of Largefish category detection was also comparable with an average precision of 0.894. High precision obtained for LargeFish class, justifies its creation for representing a generic class of marine animals which are quite large in size and could of potential risk to surfers/swimmer and beach recreation in general. This also helped in reducing the confusion/miss-classification with shark and whale. Although, there was small improvement in the accuracy using VGG16 network compared to ZF, but the processing time for ZF is significantly better than VGG16.

An analysis of mAP obtained at an interval of $10K$ iterations for each Deep CNN architectures is given in the graph shown in Fig. 3. Figure 4 shows the average precision obtained for each class using VGG16 model at 50 K iterations. VGG16 was chosen for averge precision analysis, as it out performed other architectures. Sample detection results obtained from VGG16 trained model are shown in Fig. 5.

5 Conclusion

Shark attacks have been a very sensitive issue in Australia as well as globally. In spite of various shark management programs implemented globally, the risk of shark attacks is still high and a serious risk to beach recreation. Moreover, the existing programs are invasive in nature and interferes with the marine ecosystem. Although non-lethal shark deterrents are commercially available, they are not extensively tested on all spices of sharks and other marine animals, which can still pose potential risk to ocean users. In this paper, the potential of the state-of-the-art Deep CNN-based object detection methods are investigated to identify their potential in real-time shark and marine animal detection from aerial imagery. To the best of our knowledge, this is the first study which considers Deep CNN based object detection for the detection of sharks and other marine animals/objects. Faster-R-CNN was considered in the study and three different CNN architectures were used in the experiments. Experimental results are very promising and a high precision of 0.904 was obtained for detecting sharks using VGG16 architecture. Whereas, the mean average precision (mAP) of 0.901 was obtained considering five different categories, namely shark, whale, surfer, boat and largefish. The average processing time per frame was 0.130 s, which also satisfies the real-time processing requirement.

To summarize, the study reveals that Deep CNN has a huge potential in the development of a real-time shark/marine animal detection system, with various applications such as real-time beach surveillance, shark detection and conducting automatic marine surveys, to mention a few. Future research work includes customizing the CNN architectures for optimal performance which best suites the problem of marine animal detection and development of a large annotated dataset which include various shark spices, dolphins, stingrays, dugongs, swimmers, different type of boats etc. This will facilitate further research in this area, realizing the intention of making beach recreation much safer.

Acknowledgement. The authors would like to thank the Ripper Group for providing the data samples for the experiments. The Ripper Group operates the Westpac Little Ripper Lifesaver UAV/drones at beaches in NSW in conjunction with Surf Life Saving NSW. This research was funded by The Ripper Group under Research Contract with The University of Technology Sydney (UTS).

References

1. Robbins, W.D., Peddemors, V.M., Kennelly, S.J., Ives, M.C.: Experimental evaluation of shark detection rates by aerial observers. PLOS ONE **9**(2), e83456 (2014). https://doi.org/10.1371/journal.pone.0083456
2. Kempster, R.M., Egeberg, C.A., Hart, N.S., Ryan, L., Chapuis, L., et al.: How close is too close? The effect of a non-lethal electric shark deterrent on white shark behaviour. PLOS ONE **11**(7), e0157717 (2016). https://doi.org/10.1371/journal.pone.0157717
3. Muter, B.A., Gore, M.L., Gledhill, K.S., Lamont, C., Huveneers, C.: Australian and US news media portrayal of sharks and their conservation. Conserv. Biol. **27**, 187–196 (2013). pmid:23110588
4. West, J.: Changing patterns of shark attacks in Australian waters. Mar. Freshw. Res. **62**, 744–754 (2011)
5. Wetherbee, B.M., Lowe, C., Christopher, G.: A review of shark control in hawaii with recommendations for future research. Pac. Sci. **4**, 95–115 (1994)
6. House, D.: Western Australian Shark Hazard Mitigation Drum Line Program 2014–17: Public Environmental Review. Western Australia: The Department of the Premier and Cabinet, 85 p (2014)
7. Reid, D., Robbins, W., Peddemors, V.: Decadal trends in shark catches and effort from the New South Wales, Australia, Shark meshing program 1950–2010. Mar. Freshw. Res. **62**, 676–693 (2011)

8. Dudley, S.F.J.: A comparison of the shark control programs of New South Wales and Queensland (Australia) and KwaZulu-Natal (South Africa). Ocean. Coast. Manag. **34**, 1–27 (1997)

9. Cliff, G.: Sharks caught in the protective gill nets off Kwazulu-Natal, South Africa. 8. The great hammerhead shark Sphyrna mokarran (Ruppell). S. Afr. J. Mar. Sci. **15**, 105–114 (1995)

10. Cliff, G., Dudley, S., Jury, M.: Catches of white sharks in KwaZulu-Natal, South Africa and environmental influences. In: Great White Sharks, the Biology of Carcharodon Carcharias, pp. 351–362 (1996)

11. Gururatsakul, S., Gibbins, D., Kearney, D.: A simple deformable model for Shark recognition. In: Canadian Conference on Computer and Robot Vison, pp. 234–240 (2011)

12. Gururatsakul, S., Gibbins, D., Kearney, D., Lee, I.: Shark detection using optical image data from a mobile aerial platform. In: 25th International Conference of Image and Vision Computing New Zealand (IVCNZ) 2010, pp. 1–8 (2010)

13. Maire, F., Mejias, L., Hodgson, A., Duclos, G.: Detection of dugongs from unmanned aerial vehicles. In: IEEE/RSJ International Conference on Intelligent Robots and Systems (2013)

14. Mejias, L., Duclos, G., Hodgson, A., Maire, F.: Automated marine mammal detection from aerial imagery. In: MTS/IEEE OCEANS, San Diego, USA (2013)

15. Shrivakshan, G.T.: An analysis of SOBEL and GABOR image filters for identifying fish. In: 2013 International Conference on Pattern Recognition, Informatics and Mobile Engineering, pp. 115–119 (2013)

16. Lopez, J., Schoonmaker, J., Saggese, S.: Automated detection of marine animals using multispectral imaging. In: 2014 Oceans - St. John's, St. John's, NL, pp. 1–6 (2014)

17. Girshick, R.: Fast R-CNN. In: Proceedings of the IEEE International Conference on Computer Vision, pp. 1440–1448 (2015)

18. Girshick, R., Donahue, J., Darrell, T., Malik, J.: Rich feature hierarchies for accurate object detection and semantic segmentation. In: Proceedings of the IEEE Conference on Computer Vision and Pattern Recognition, pp. 580–587 (2014)

19. Ren, S., He, K., Girshick, R., Sun, J.: Faster R-CNN: towards real-time object detection with region proposal networks. In: Advances in Neural Information Processing Systems, pp. 91–99 (2015)

20. Zeiler, M.D., Fergus, R.: Visualizing and understanding convolutional networks. In: Fleet, D., Pajdla, T., Schiele, B., Tuytelaars, T. (eds.) ECCV 2014. LNCS, vol. 8689, pp. 818–833. Springer, Cham (2014). https://doi.org/10.1007/978-3-319-10590-1_53

21. Simonyan, K., Zisserman, A.: Very deep convolutional networks for large-scale image recognition. In: International Conference on Learning Representations (ICLR) (2014)

22. Chatfield, K., Simonyan, K., Vedaldi, A., Zisserman, A.: Return of the devil in the details: delving deep into convolutional nets. In: British Machine Vision Conference (BMVC) (2014)

23. Deng, J., Dong, W., Socher, R., Li, L.-J., Li, K., Fei-Fei, L.L: ImageNet a large-scale hierarchical image database. In: IEEE Conference on Computer Vision and Pattern Recognition 2009, pp. 248–255. IEEE (2009)

24. Jia, Y., et al.: Caffe: convolutional architecture for fast feature embedding. In: Proceedings of the 22nd ACM International Conference on Multimedia, pp. 675–678. ACM (2014)

25. Everingham, M., et al.: The pascal visual object classes challenge: a retrospective. Int. J. Comput. Vis. **111**, 98–136 (2015)
26. https://taronga.org.au/conservation/conservation-science-research/australian-shark-attack-file/2015
27. https://taronga.org.au/conservation/conservation-science-research/australian-shark-attack-file/2016

A Hybrid Differential Evolution Approach to Designing Deep Convolutional Neural Networks for Image Classification

Bin Wang[✉], Yanan Sun, Bing Xue, and Mengjie Zhang

School of Engineering and Computer Science, Victoria University of Wellington,
PO Box 600, Wellington 6140, New Zealand
wangbin@myvuw.ac.nz, {yanan.sun,bing.xue,mengjie.zhang}@ecs.vuw.ac.nz

Abstract. Convolutional Neural Networks (CNNs) have demonstrated their superiority in image classification, and evolutionary computation (EC) methods have recently been surging to automatically design the architectures of CNNs to save the tedious work of manually designing CNNs. In this paper, a new hybrid differential evolution (DE) algorithm with a newly added crossover operator is proposed to evolve the architectures of CNNs of any lengths, which is named DECNN. There are three new ideas in the proposed DECNN method. Firstly, an existing effective encoding scheme is refined to cater for variable-length CNN architectures; Secondly, the new mutation and crossover operators are developed for variable-length DE to optimise the hyperparameters of CNNs; Finally, the new second crossover is introduced to evolve the depth of the CNN architectures. The proposed algorithm is tested on six widely-used benchmark datasets and the results are compared to 12 state-of-the-art methods, which shows the proposed method is vigorously competitive to the state-of-the-art algorithms. Furthermore, the proposed method is also compared with a method using particle swarm optimisation with a similar encoding strategy named IPPSO, and the proposed DECNN outperforms IPPSO in terms of the accuracy.

Keywords: Differential evolution · Convolutional Neural Network
Image classification

1 Introduction

Convolutional Neural Networks (CNNs) have proved their dominating spot in various machine learning tasks, such as speech recognition [1], sentence classification [6] and image classification [7]. However, from the existing efforts taken by researchers such as LeNet [9,10], AlexNet [7], VGGNet [14] and GoogLeNet [19], it can be found that designing CNNs for specific tasks could be extremely complicated.

Since the difficulties of manually designing the architectures of CNNs have been raised more frequently in recent years, exploiting evolutionary computation

© Springer Nature Switzerland AG 2018
T. Mitrovic et al. (Eds.): AI 2018, LNAI 11320, pp. 237–250, 2018.
https://doi.org/10.1007/978-3-030-03991-2_24

(EC) algorithms to generate deep neural networks [18] has come into the spotlight to resolve the issues. Interested researchers have accomplished promising results on the automatic design of the architectures of CNNs by using Genetic Programming (GP) [17] and Genetic Algorithms (GAs) [21]. However, the computational cost of the existing algorithms is very expensive, so more research tends to focus on improving the efficiency by developing new algorithms.

Deferential Evolution (DE) has been proved to be an efficient heuristic for global optimisation over continuous spaces [16], but it has never been used to evolve deep CNNs. The IP-Based Encoding Strategy (IPES) [20] has demonstrated its powerfulness in particle swarm optimisation for evolving deep CNNs, but it has a critical drawback which is that the maximum depth of the CNN architectures has to be set before the commencement of the evolutionary process. Therefore, the encoding strategy is refined in the proposed algorithm to break the constraint of the predefined maximum length.

Goals: The overall goal of this paper is to explore the ability of DE for automatically evolving the structures and parameters of deep CNNs. The goal will be achieved by designing an effective encoding scheme, new mutation and crossover operators of DE, and a second crossover operator. The proposed method named DECNN will be examined and compared with 12 state-of-the-art methods on six widely-used datasets of varying difficulty. The specific objectives are

- refine the existing effective encoding scheme used by IPPSO [20] to break the constraint of predefining the maximum depth of CNNs;
- design and develop new mutation and crossover operators for the proposed DECNN method, which can be applied on variable-length vectors to conquer the fixed-length limitation of the traditional DE method;
- design and integrate a second crossover operator into the proposed DECNN to produce the children in the next generation representing the architectures of CNNs whose lengths differ from their parents.

2   Background and Related Work

2.1   CNN Architecture

A typical Convolutional Neural Network (CNN) is constituted of four types of layers - convolution layer, pooling layer, fully-connected layer and output layer. The output layer depends only on the specific classification problem. For the example of image classification, the number of classes decides the size of the output layer. Therefore, when designing an architecture of CNNs, the output layer is fixed once the specific task is given. However, to decide the other three types of layers, first of all, the depth of the CNN architecture has to be decided; Then, the type of each layer needs to be chosen from convolution layer, pooling layer and fully-connected layer ; Last but no least, since there are different sets of attributes for different types of layers - filter size, stride size and feature maps for the convolution layer; kernel size, stride size and pooling type enclosing max-pooling or average pooling for the pooling layer; and the number of neurons for the fully-connected layer, the attributes of each layer have to be tuned based on its layer type in order to accomplish a CNN architecture that can obtain good performance.

2.2 Differential Evolution

Differential Evolution (DE) is a population-based EC method which searches for the optimal solutions of a problem. It has been proved to be a simple and efficient heuristic method for global optimisation over continuous spaces [16]. Overall, there are four major steps in a DE algorithm, which are initialisation, mutation, crossover and selection [12]. First of all, a population of candidate vectors are randomly initialised. Secondly, mutation is applied according to Formula (1), where $\mathbf{v}_{i,g}$ means the ith temporary candidate vector of the gth generation; $\mathbf{x}_{r0,g}$, $\mathbf{x}_{r1,g}$ and $\mathbf{x}_{r2,g}$ indicate three randomly picked candidates of the gth generation; and F is the differential rate, which is used to control the evolution rate. Thirdly, the crossover is performed based on Formula (2), where $u_{j,i,g}$ represents the jth dimension of the ith candidate at the gth generation. At the beginning of the crossover process for each candidate, a random number j_{rand} is generated, and then for each dimension of each candidate vector, another random number $rand_j$ is generated, which then is compared with the crossover rate Cr and j_{rand} as shown in Formula (2) to decide whether the crossover applies on this dimension. After applying the DE operators, a trial vector $\mathbf{u}_{i,g}$ is produced, which is then compared with the parent vector to select the one that has a better fitness. By iterating the steps of mutation, crossover and selection until the stopping criterion is met, the best candidate can be found.

$$\mathbf{v}_{i,g} = \mathbf{x}_{r0,g} + F \times (\mathbf{x}_{r1,g} - \mathbf{x}_{r2,g}) \tag{1}$$

$$u_{j,i,g} = \begin{cases} v_{j,i,g} & \text{if } rand_j(0,1) < Cr \text{ or } j = j_{rand} \\ x_{j,i,g} & \text{otherwise} \end{cases} \tag{2}$$

2.3 Related Work

Recently, more and more research has been done using EC methods to evolve the architectures of CNNs. Genetic CNN [21] and CGP-CNN [17] are two of the most recent proposed methods that have achieved promising results in comparison with the state-of-the-art human-designed CNN architectures.

Genetic CNN uses a fixed-length binary string to encode the connections of CNN architectures in a constrained case. It splits a CNN architecture into stages. Each stage is comprised of numerous convolutional layers which may or may not connect to each other, and pooling layers are used between stages to connect them to construct the CNN architecture. Due to the fixed-length binary representation, the number of stages and the number of nodes in each stage have to be predefined, so a large fraction of network structures are not explored by this algorithm. Other than that, the encoding scheme of Genetic CNN only encodes the connections, i.e. whether two convolutional layers are connected or not; while the hyperparameters of the convolutional layers, e.g. the kernel size, the number of feature maps, and the stride size, are not encoded, so Genetic CNN does not have the ability to optimise the hyperparameters.

CGP-CNN utilises Cartesian Genetic Programming (CGP) [11] because the flexibility of CGP's encoding scheme is suitable to effectively encode the complex CNN architectures. CGP-CNN employs a matrix of N_r rows and N_c columns to represent the layers of a CNN architecture and their connections, respectively, so the maximum number of layers is predefined. In addition, as six types of node functions called ConvBlock, ResBlock, max pooling, average pooling, concatenation and summation are prepared, CGP-CNN is confined to explore the limited types of layers of CNN architectures. Last but not least, from the experimental results, the computational cost of CGP-CNN is quite high because training CNNs in fitness evaluation is time-consuming.

In summary, manually design of CNN architectures and parameters is very challenging and time-consuming. Automatically evolving the architectures of deep CNNs is a promising approach, but their potential has not been fully explored. DE has shown as an efficient method in global optimisation, but has not been used to evolve deep CNNs. Therefore, we would like to investigate a new approach using DE to automatically evolve the architectures of deep CNNs.

3   The Proposed Algorithm

The proposed DECNN method uses DE as the main evolutionary algorithm, and a second crossover operator is proposed to generate children whose lengths differ from their parents to fulfil the requirement of evolving variable-length architectures of CNNs.

3.1   DECNN Algorithm Overview

The overall procedure of the proposed DECNN algorithm is written in Algorithm 1.

Algorithm 1. Framework of IPDE

    $P \leftarrow$ Initialise the population elaborated in Sect. 3.3;
    $P\_best \leftarrow empty$;
    while termination criterion is not satisfied **do**
        Apply the refined DE mutation and crossover described in Sect. 3.5;
        Apply the proposed second crossover to produce two children, and select the best between the two children and their parents illustrated in Sect. 3.6;
        evaluate the fitness value of each individual;
        $P\_best \leftarrow$ retrieve the best individual in the population;
    end while

3.2   Adjusted IP-Based Encoding Strategy

The proposed IP-Based Encoding Strategy is to use one IP Address to represent one layer of Deep Neural Networks (DNNs) and push the IP address into a sequence of interfaces, each of which bears an IP address and its corresponding subnet, in the same order as the order of the layers in DNNs. Taking CNNs as an example, the typical CNNs are composed of three types of layers - convolutional layer, pooling layer and fully-connected layer. The first step of the encoding is to work out the range that can represent each attribute of each type of the CNN layer. There are no specific limits for the attributes of CNN layers, but in order to practically apply optimisation algorithms on the task, each attribute has to be given a range which has enough capacity to achieve an optimal accuracy on the classification problems. In this paper, the constraints for each attribute are designed to be capable of accomplishing a relatively low error rate. To be specific, for the convolutional layer, there are three attributes, which are filter size ranging from 1 to 8, number of feature maps from 1 up to 128, and the stride size with the range from 1 to 4. As the three attributes need to be combined into one number, a binary string with 12 bits can contain all the three attributes of the convolutional layer, which are 3 bits for filter size, 7 bits for the number of feature maps, and 2 bits for the stride size. Following the similar way, the pooling layer and fully-connected layer can be carried in the binary strings with 5 bits and 11 bits, respectively. The details of the range of each attribute are listed in Table 1.

Table 1. The ranges of the attributes of CNN layers - convolutional, pooling, fullly-connected layer

Layer type	Parameter	Range	# of bits
Conv	Filter size	[1,8]	3
	# of feature maps	[1,128]	7
	Stride size	[1,4]	2
	Total		12
Pooling	Kernel size	[1,4]	2
	Stride size	[1,4]	2
	Type: 1(maximal), 2(average)	[1,2]	1
	Total		5
Fully-connected	# of neurons	[1,2048]	11
	Total		11

Once the number of bits of the binary strings has been defined, a specific CNN layer can be easily translated to a binary string. Suppose a convolutional layer with the filter size of 2, the number of feature maps of 32 and the stride size of 2 is given, the corresponding binary strings of [001], [000 1111] and [01] can be calculated by converting the decimal numbers[1] to the corresponding binary numbers. The final binary string that stands for the given convolutional layer is [001 000 1110 01] by joining the binary strings of the three attributes together. The details of the example are shown in Fig. 1.

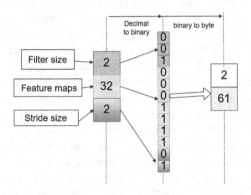

Fig. 1. An example of how to encode a convolutional layer using a byte array

Similar like network engineering where the subnet has to be defined before allocating an IP address to an interface, i.e. a laptop or desktop, the IP-Based Encoding Strategy needs to design a subnet for each type of CNN layers. Since the number of bits of each layer type decides its size of the search space, and the pooling layer takes much fewer bits than the other two, the chances of a pooling layer being chosen would be much smaller than the other two. In order to balance the probability of each layer type being selected, a place-holder of 6 bits is added to the binary string of the pooling layer to make it 11 bits, which brings the odds of picking a pooling layer the same as that of a fully-connected layer. As there are three types of layers with the maximum bits of 12, a 2-byte binary string has sufficient capacity to bear the encoded CNN layers. Starting with the convolutional layer of 12 bits, as this is the first subnet, the 2-byte binary representation of the starting IP address would be [0000 0000 0000 0000], and the finishing IP address would be [0000 1111 1111 1111]; The fully-connected layer of 11 bits starts from the binary string [0001 0000 0000 0000] by adding one to the last IP address of the convolutional layer, and ends to [0001 0111 1111 1111]; And similarly, the IP range of the pooling layer can be derived - from [0001 1000 0000 0000] to [0001 1111 1111 1111]. The IP ranges of the 2-byte style for each subset are shown in Table 2, which are obtained by converting the aforementioned binary strings to the 2-byte strings. Now it is ready to encode a CNN layer into an IP address, and the convolutional layer detailed in Fig. 1 is taken as an example. The binary representation of the IP address is [0000

---

[1] Before the conversion, 1 is subtracted from the decimal number because the binary string starts from 0, while the decimal value of the attributes of CNN layers begins with 1.

0010 0011 1001] by summing up the binary string of the convolutional layer and the starting IP address of the convolutional layer's subnet, which can be converted to a 2-byte IP address of [2.61]. Figure 2 shows an example vector encoded from a CNN architecture with 2 convolutional layers, 2 pooling layers and 1 fully-connected layer.

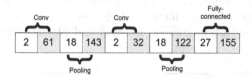

Fig. 2. An example of the encoded vector of a CNN architecture

Table 2. Subnets distributed to the three types of CNN layers and the disabled layer

Layer type	IP range
Convolutional layer	0.0–15.255
Fully-connected layer	16.0–23.255
Pooling layer	24.0–31.255

3.3 Population Initialisation

As the individuals are required to be in different lengths, the population initialisation starts by randomly generating the lengths of individuals. In the proposed DECNN, the length is randomly sampled from a Gaussian distribution with a standard deviation ρ of 1 and a centre μ of a predefined length depending on the complexity of the classification task as shown in Eq. (3). After obtaining the candidate's length, the layer type and the attribute values can be randomly generated for each layer in the candidate. By repeating the process until reaching the population size to accomplish the population initialisation.

$$P(x) = \frac{1}{\sigma\sqrt{2\pi}}e^{-(x-\mu)^2/2\sigma^2} \tag{3}$$

3.4 Fitness Evaluation

The fitness evaluation process is illustrated in Algorithm 2. First of all, four arguments are taken in by the fitness evaluation function, which are the candidate solution which represents an encoded CNN architecture, the training epoch number for training the model decoded from the candidate solution, the training set which is used to train the decoded CNN architecture, and the fitness evaluation dataset on which the trained model is tested to obtain the accuracy used as the fitness value. Secondly, the fitness evaluation process is pretty straightforward by using the back propagation to train the decoded CNN architecture on the training set for a fixed number of epochs, and then obtaining the accuracy on the fitness evaluation set, which is actually used as the fitness value. For the purpose of reducing computational cost, the candidate CNN is only trained on a partial dataset for a limited number of epochs, which are controlled by the arguments of the fitness function - k, D_train and $D\_fitness$.

Algorithm 2. Fitness Evaluation

Input: The candidate solution c, the training epoch number k, the training set D_train, the fitness evaluation dataset $D\_fitness$;

Output: The fitness value $fitness$;

Train the connection weights of the CNN represented by the candidate c on the training set D_train for k epochs;

$acc \leftarrow$ Evaluate the trained model on the fitness evaluation dataset $D\_fitness$

$fitness \leftarrow acc$;

return $fitness$

3.5 DECNN DE Mutation and Crossover

The proposed DECNN operations are similar to the standard DE mutation and crossover as described in Sect. 2.2, but it introduces an extra step to trim the longer vectors before applying any operation because the DECNN candidates have different lengths and the traditional DE operations in Eqs. (1) and (2) only apply on fixed-length vectors. To be specific, the three random vectors for the mutation are trimmed to the shortest length of them, and during the crossover, if the trial vector generated by the mutation is longer than the parent, it will be trimmed to the length of the parent.

3.6 DECNN Second Crossover

Similar as the crossover of GAs, each individual of the two parents is split into two parts by slicing the vector at the cutting points, and swap one part with each other. The cutting point is chosen by randomly finding a position based on Gaussian distribution with the middle point as the centre and a hyperparameter ρ as the standard deviation to control the variety in the population. The flow of the second crossover is outlined in Fig. 3.

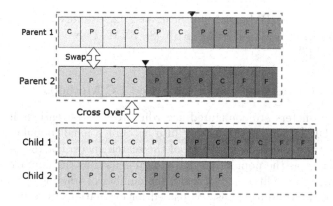

Fig. 3. Second crossover of the proposed DECNN algorithm

4 Experiment Design

4.1 Benchmark Datasets

In the experiments, six widely-used benchmark datasets[2] [3] are chosen to examine the proposed algorithm, which are the datasets of MNIST Basic (MB), MNIST with a black and white image as the Background Image (MBI), MNIST Digits Rotated with a black and white image as the Background Image (MDRBI), MNIST with a Random Background (MRB), MNIST with Rotated Digits (MRD), and CONVEX. The MB benchmark dataset and its four variants, the MBI, MDRBI, MRB and MRD datasets, consist of handwritten digits and the corresponding labels from 0 to 9, and each of the datasets is composed of a training set of 12,000 instances and a test set of 5,000 instances; while convex images and non-convex images with the corresponding labels constitute the CONVEX dataset, which is split into a training set of 8,000 examples and a test set of 5,000 examples. Each image in these benchmark datasets has 28×28 pixels. The reason for picking the six aforementioned datasets is to fulfil the purpose of thoroughly testing the proposed algorithms because both multi-class classification tasks for MB and its variants and the binary classification tasks for CONVEX are included in the selected datasets, and the complexity of MB and its variants differ from each other where MB is the simplest one; while MDRBI is the most complicated.

4.2 State-of-the-Art Competitors

Six state-of-the-art methods are reported to have achieved promising results on the aforementioned benchmark datasets in the literature [3]. Therefore, they are picked as the peer competitors of the proposed algorithm, which are CAE-2

---

[2] Download URL: http://www.iro.umontreal.ca/~lisa/twiki/bin/view.cgi/Public/MnistVariations.

[13], TIRBM [15], PGBM+DN1 [5], ScatNet-2 [2], RandNet-2 [3], PCANet-2 (softmax) [3], LDANet-2 [3], SVM+RBF [8], SVM+Poly [8], NNet [8], SAA-3 [8] and DBN-3 [8].

4.3 Parameter Settings of the Proposed EC Methods

All of the parameters are configured according to the conventions in the communities of DE [4] along with taking into account a small population to safe computation time and the complexity of the search space. For the evolutionary process, 30 is set as the population size and 20 is used as the number of generations; In regard to the fitness evaluation, the number of training epochs is set to 5 and 10% of the training dataset is passed for evaluation; In terms of the DE parameters, 0.6 and 0.45 are used as the differential rate and the crossover rate, respectively; The hyperparameter ρ of second crossover is set to 2, and μ of the population initialisation is set to 10; 30 independent runs is performed by the proposed DECNN on each of the benchmark dataset.

5 Results and Analysis

Since DE is stochastic, statistical significance test is required to make the comparison result more convincing. When comparing the proposed DECNN with the state-of-the-art methods, One Sample T-Test is applied to test whether the results of DECNN is better; when the comparison of error rates between DECNN and the peer EC competitor named IPPSO [20] is performed, Two Sample T-test is utilised to determine whether the difference is statistically significant or not. Table 3 shows the comparison results between the proposed DECNN and the state-of-the-art algorithms; Table 4 compares DECNN with IPPSO.

5.1 DECNN vs. State-of-the-Art Methods

The experimental results and the comparison between the proposed DECNN and the state-of-the-art methods are shown in Table 3. In order to clearly show the comparison results, the terms (+) and (−) are provided to indicate the result of DECNN is better or worse than the best result obtained by the corresponding peer competitor; The term (=) shows that the mean error rate of DECNN are slightly better or worse than the competitor, but the difference is not significant from the statistical point of view; The term − means there are no available results reported from the provider or cannot be counted.

It can be observed that the proposed DECNN method achieves encouraging performance in terms of the error rates shown in Table 3. To be specific, the proposed DECNN ranks the fifth on both the CONVEX and MB benchmark datasets; for the MBI benchmark, DECNN beats all of the state-of-the-art methods; for the MDRBI dataset, the mean error rate of DECNN is the fourth best, but the P-value of One Sample T-Test between DECNN and the third best is 0.0871, which indicates that the significance difference is not supported from the statistical point of view, so DECNN ties the third with PGBM+DN-1; for the MRB benchmark, the mean error rate of DECNN is smaller than all other methods, but the difference between DECNN and the second best algorithm is not significant given the calculated P-value of 0.1053, so DECNN ties the first with PGBM+DN-1; for the MRD benchmark, DECNN outruns the state-of-the-arts method apart from TIRBM. In addition, by looking at the best results of DECNN, DECNN achieves the smallest error rates on five out of the six datasets compared with the 12 state-of-the-art methods, which are 1.03% on MB, 5.67% on MBI, 32.85% on MDRBI, 3.46% on MRB and 4.07% on MRD. This shows that DECNN has the potential to improve the state-of-the-art results.

Table 3. The classification errors of DECNN against the peer competitors

classier	CONVEX		MB		MBI		MDRBI		MRB		MRD	
CAE-2		–	2.48	(+)	15.50	(+)	45.23	(+)	10.90	(+)	9.66	(+)
TIRBM		–		–		–	35.50	(-)		–	4.20	(-)
PGBM+DN-1		–		–	12.15	(+)	36.76	(=)	6.08	(=)		–
ScatNet-2	6.50	(-)	1.27	(-)	18.40	(+)	50.48	(+)	12.30	(+)	7.48	(+)
RandNet-2	5.45	(-)	1.25	(-)	11.65	(+)	43.69	(+)	13.47	(+)	8.47	(+)
PCANet-2 (soft-max)	4.19	(-)	1.40	(-)	11.55	(+)	35.86	(-)	6.85	(+)	8.52	(+)
LDANet-2	7.22	(-)	1.05	(-)	12.42	(+)	38.54	(+)	6.81	(+)	7.52	(+)
SVM+RBF	19.13	(+)	30.03	(+)	22.61	(+)	55.18	(+)	14.58	(+)	11.11	(+)
SVM+Poly	19.82	(+)	3.69	(+)	24.01	(+)	54.41	(+)	16.62	(+)	15.42	(+)
NNet	32.25	(+)	4.69	(+)	27.41	(+)	62.16	(+)	20.04	(+)	18.11	(+)
SAA-3	18.41	(+)	3.46	(+)	23	(+)	51.93	(+)	11.28	(+)	10.30	(+)
DBN-3	18.63	(+)	3.11	(+)	16.31	(+)	47.39	(+)	6.73	(+)	10.30	(+)
DECNN(best)	7.99		1.03		5.67		32.85		3.46		4.07	
DECNN(mean)	11.19		1.46		8.69		37.55		5.56		5.53	
DECNN(standard deviation)	1.94		0.11		1.41		2.45		1.71		0.45	

5.2 DECNN vs. IPPSO

In Table 4, it can be observed that by comparing the results between DECNN and IPPSO, the mean error rates of DECNN are smaller across all of the six benchmark datasets, and the standard deviations of DECNN is less than those of IPPSO on five datasets out of the six, so the overall performance of DECNN is superior to IPPSO. The second crossover operator improves the performance of DECNN because it performs a kind of local search between the two children and their parents both in terms of the depth of CNN architectures and their parameters.

5.3 Evolved CNN Architecture

After examining the evolved CNN architectures, it is found that DECNN demonstrates its capability of evolving the length of the architectures. When the evolutionary process starts, the lengths of individuals are around 10; while the lengths

Table 4. Classification rates of DECNN and IPPSO

	CONVEX	MB	MBI	MDRBI	MRB	MRD
DECNN(mean)	11.19	1.46	8.69	37.55	5.56	5.53
DECNN(standard deviation)	1.94	0.11	1.41	2.45	1.71	0.45
IPPSO(mean)	12.65	1.56	9.86	38.79	6.26	6.07
IPPSO(standard deviation)	2.13	0.17	1.84	5.38	1.54	0.71
P-value	**0.01**	**0.01**	**0.01**	0.26	0.10	**0.001**

of evolved CNN architectures drop to 3 to 5 depending on the complexity of the datasets, which proves that DECNN has the ability of effectively evolving CNN architectures of any lengths.

6   Conclusions and Future Work

The goal of this paper is to develop a novel DE-based algorithm to automatically evolve the architecture of CNNs for image classification without any constraint of the depth of CNN architectures. This has been accomplished by designing and developing the proposed hybrid differential evolution method. More specifically, three major contributions are made by the proposed DECNN algorithm. First of all, the IP-Based Encoding Strategy has been improved by removing the maximum length of the encoded vector and the unnecessary disabled layer in order to achieve a real variable-length vector of any length; Secondly, the new DE operations - mutation, crossover are developed, which can be applied to candidate vectors of variable lengths; Last but not least, a novel second crossover is designed and added to DE to produce children having different lengths from their parents. The second crossover plays an important role to search the optimal depth of the CNN architectures because the two children created through the second crossover have different length from their parents - one is longer and the other is shorter, and during the selection from the two children and the two parents, the candidate with a better fitness survives to the next generation, which indicates that the length of the remaining candidate tends to be better than the other three.

The proposed DECNN has achieved encouraging performance. By comparing the performance of DECNN with the 12 state-of-the-art competitors on the six benchmark datasets, it can be observed that DECNN obtains a very competitive accuracy by ranking the first on the MBI and MRB datasets, the second and the third on the MRD and MDRBI datasets, respectively, and the fifth on the MB and CONVEX datasets. In a further comparison with the peer EC competitor, the best results are achieved by DECNN on five out of the six datasets.

There are a couple of potential future works that can be done based on the proposed DECNN. As can been seen, the DECNN method gains much better accuracy on the most complex benchmark among all of the six benchmark datasets, which implies DECNN is very likely to perform well on large and complex datasets, so it is worthy investigating the DECNN algorithm on larger and more complex datasets in order to obtain an insight of how it will perform for industrial usage.

References

1. Abdel-Hamid, O., Deng, L., Yu, D.: Exploring convolutional neural network structures and optimization techniques for speech recognition. In: Interspeech 2013. ISCA, August 2013. https://www.microsoft.com/en-us/research/publication/exploring-convolutional-neural-network-structures-and-optimization-techniques-for-speech-recognition/
2. Bruna, J., Mallat, S.: Invariant scattering convolution networks. IEEE Trans. Pattern Anal. Mach. Intell. **35**(8), 1872–1886 (2013). https://doi.org/10.1109/tpami.2012.230
3. Chan, T.H., Jia, K., Gao, S., Lu, J., Zeng, Z., Ma, Y.: PCANet: a simple deep learning baseline for image classification? IEEE Trans. Image Process. **24**(12), 5017–5032 (2015). https://doi.org/10.1109/tip.2015.2475625
4. Gamperle, R., Muller, S.D., Koumoutsakos, A.: A parameter study for differential evolution. In: NNA-FSFS-EC 2002, vol. 10, pp. 293–298 (2002)
5. Sohn, K., Zhou, G., Lee, C., Lee, H.: Learning and selecting features jointly with point-wise gated boltzmann machines, June 2013. https://dl.acm.org/citation.cfm?id=3042918
6. Kim, Y.: Convolutional neural networks for sentence classification. In: Proceedings of the 2014 Conference on Empirical Methods in Natural Language Processing (EMNLP) (2014)
7. Krizhevsky, A., Sutskever, I., Hinton, G.E.: ImageNet classification with deep convolutional neural networks. Commun. ACM **60**(6), 84–90 (2017). https://doi.org/10.1145/3065386
8. Larochelle, H., Erhan, D., Courville, A., Bergstra, J., Bengio, Y.: An empirical evaluation of deep architectures on problems with many factors of variation. In: Proceedings of the 24th International Conference on Machine Learning - ICML 2007 (2007). https://doi.org/10.1145/1273496.1273556
9. LeCun, Y., et al.: Backpropagation applied to handwritten zip code recognition. Neural Comput. **1**(4), 541–551 (1989). https://doi.org/10.1162/neco.1989.1.4.541
10. Lecun, Y., Bottou, L., Bengio, Y., Haffner, P.: Gradient-based learning applied to document recognition. Proceed. IEEE **86**(11), 2278–2324 (1998). https://doi.org/10.1109/5.726791
11. Miller, J., Turner, A.: Cartesian genetic programming. In: Proceedings of the Companion Publication of the 2015 Annual Conference on Genetic and Evolutionary Computation, GECCO Companion 2015, pp. 179–198. ACM, New York (2015). https://doi.org/10.1145/2739482.2756571
12. Price, K.V., Storn, R.M., Lampinen, J.A.: Differential Evolution: A Practical Approach to Global Optimization, pp. 37–42. Springer, Heidelberg (2005). Chapter 2
13. Rifai, S., Vincent, P., Muller, X., Glorot, X., Bengio, Y.: Contractive autoencoders: explicit invariance during feature extraction, June 2011. https://dl.acm.org/citation.cfm?id=3104587

14. Simonyan, K., Zisserman, A.: Very deep convolutional networks for large-scale image recognition, April 2015. https://arxiv.org/abs/1409.1556
15. Sohn, K., Lee, H.: Learning invariant representations with local transformations, June 2012. https://arxiv.org/abs/1206.6418
16. Storn, R., Price, K.: Differential evolution a simple and efficient heuristic for global optimization over continuous spaces (1997). https://doi.org/10.1023/A:1008202821328
17. Suganuma, M., Shirakawa, S., Nagao, T.: A genetic programming approach to designing convolutional neural network architectures. CoRR abs/1704.00764 (2017). http://arxiv.org/abs/1704.00764
18. Sun, Y., Yen, G.G., Yi, Z.: Evolving unsupervised deep neural networks for learning meaningful representations. IEEE Trans. Evol. Comput. (2018). https://doi.org/10.1109/TEVC.2018.2808689
19. Szegedy, C., et al.: Going deeper with convolutions. In: 2015 IEEE Conference on Computer Vision and Pattern Recognition (CVPR), pp. 1–9, June 2015
20. Wang, B., Sun, Y., Xue, B., Zhang, M.: Evolving deep convolutional neural networks by variable-length particle swarm optimization for image classification. In: IEEE Congress on Evolutionary Computation (July 2018, to appear). https://arxiv.org/abs/1803.06492
21. Xie, L., Yuille, A.: Genetic CNN. In: 2017 IEEE International Conference on Computer Vision (ICCV), pp. 1388–1397, October 2017. https://doi.org/10.1109/ICCV.2017.154

A Gaussian Filter-Based Feature Learning Approach Using Genetic Programming to Image Classification

Ying Bi$^{(\boxtimes)}$, Bing Xue, and Mengjie Zhang

School of Engineering and Computer Science, Victoria University of Wellington,
Wellington 6140, New Zealand
{Ying.Bi,Bing.Xue,Mengjie.Zhang}@ecs.vuw.ac.nz

Abstract. To learn image features automatically from the problems being tackled is more effective for classification. However, it is very difficult due to image variations and the high dimensionality of image data. This paper proposes a new feature learning approach based on Gaussian filters and genetic programming (GauGP) for image classification. Genetic programming (GP) is a well-known evolutionary learning technique and has been applied to many visual tasks, showing good learning ability and interpretability. In the proposed GauGP method, a new program structure, a new function set and a new terminal set are developed, which allow it to detect small regions from the input image and to learn discriminative features using Gaussian filters for image classification. The performance of GauGP is examined on six different data sets of varying difficulty and compared with four GP methods, eight traditional approaches and convolutional neural networks. The experimental results show GauGP achieves significantly better or similar performance in most cases.

Keywords: Feature learning · Genetic programming
Image classification · Gaussian filter · Evolutionary computation
Feature extraction

1 Introduction

Image classification is an important task in computer vision [1]. The task is to assign class labels to images based on the content in images. It is a challenging task due to image variations, such as scale, illumination and rotation variations. Generally, image features, e.g., shape and texture, are employed to feed classification algorithms such as support vector machines (SVMs) to perform classification [3]. But most existing approaches require domain experts to extract features. Feature learning is to learn informative features from raw data without human intervention for visual tasks [7]. However, to learn discriminative features from the raw pixel values for effective classification is difficult due to the variations and high dimensionality of the image data. The state-of-the-art

© Springer Nature Switzerland AG 2018
T. Mitrovic et al. (Eds.): AI 2018, LNAI 11320, pp. 251–257, 2018.
https://doi.org/10.1007/978-3-030-03991-2_25

convolutional neural networks (CNNs) have achieved significant success in feature learning and image classification [7]. But deep CNNs often require a large number of training instances and computing resources.

In contrast to CNNs, genetic programming (GP), as an evolutionary computation (EC) technique, can evolve solutions with good interpretability [11]. GP aims at evolving computer programs to solve problems without the assumption of solution structures [6]. The commonly used tree-based GP has very flexible structure and is able to integrate different functions and terminals into feasible solutions [6]. Image operators/descriptors, such as histogram equalisation, Sobel and Laplacian, are employed in GP to learn discriminative features for classification [2,11]. However, there are many advanced image-related operators, which can be employed as GP functions to facilitate feature learning.

The Gaussian filter is a well-known and widely used filter in image processing and computer vision. e.g., in the edge and blob detection operator Laplace of Gaussian. The derivatives of the Gaussian filter are important for salient feature detection, such as in the Canny edge detector. This work integrates Gaussian filter and its derivatives in GP to achieve feature learning for image classification.

2 Proposed Method

Program Structure. GauGP is based on strongly typed GP (STGP). An example program of GauGP is shown in Fig. 1, where an input image goes through region detection, filtering, max-pooling, and feature concatenation process. Region detection functions, i.e., *Region_R* and *Region_S*, are employed to find the discriminative rectangle and square regions from the input image. Then the detected regions are processed by filtering functions, i.e., *GauD* and *Gau*, and max-pooling functions, i.e. *Max-poolingf*. Finally, a feature vector is generated using feature concatenation functions as the final output of GauGP.

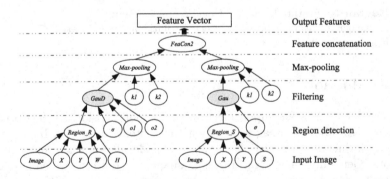

Fig. 1. An example program of GauGP.

Function Set. Table 1 lists all the functions employed in the GauGP method. *Region_S* and *Region_R* are to detect a square and rectangle region from the

Table 1. Function set

Functions	Input	Output	Function description
Root	2 vectors	1 vector	Concatenate two vectors to a vector
FeaCon2	2 images	1 vector	Concatenate two images into a vector
FeaCon3	3 images	1 vector	Concatenate three images into a vector
Max-pooling	1 image, k_1, k_2	1 image	Conduct max-pooling to the input image
Gau	1 image, σ	1 image	Gaussian filter with standard deviation σ
GauD	1 image, σ, o_1, o_2	1 image	The derivatives of Gaussian filter
Mix_Add	2 images	1 image	Add two images with different sizes
Mix_Sub	2 images	1 image	Subtract two images with different sizes
Mix_Mul	2 images	1 image	Multiply two images with different sizes
Mix_Div	2 images	1 image	Protected division on two images with different sizes
Region_S	1 images, X, Y, S	1 image	Detect a square region from the input image
Region_R	1 images, X, Y, W, H	1 image	Detect a rectangle region from the input image

input image, respectively. *Gau* is the Gaussian filter with the standard deviation σ. *GauD* takes an image and three parameters, as input and returns an image, where o_1 and o_2 represent the orders of derivative along the X axis and the Y axis. Four arithmetic functions, i.e., *Mix_Add*, *Mix_Sub*, *Mix_Mul*, and *Mix_Div*, are employed to deal with two images. These four functions take two images with different sizes as input and return an image by performing the corresponding arithmetic operation to the images after cutting them. Max-pooling function takes an image and kernel size i.e., k_1 and k_2 as input and returns a smaller image. *FeaCon2*, *FeaCon3* and *Root* are feature concatenate functions, which can be used to form the root node of GauGP. These functions are to concatenate two or three images or vectors to a feature vector.

Terminal Set. The terminals used in GauGP include *Image*, *X*, *Y*, *S*, *W*, *H*, k_1, k_2, σ, o_1, and o_2. Table 2 lists the description of all these terminals.

Table 2. Terminal set

Terminals	Type	Description
Image	Image	The input grey-scale image after normalisation
X, Y	Integer	The coordinates of the top left point of a detected region. They are in range [0, $Image_{width} - 20$] or [0, $Image_{height} - 20$]
S, W, H	Integer	The size or width/height of a square/rectangle region in *Region_S*/ *Region_R* functions. They are in range [20, 50]
k_1, k_2	Integer	The kernel size of the *Max-pooling* function. They are in range [2, 10] with a step of 2
σ	Integer	The standard deviation of the Gaussian filter in the *Gau* and *GauD* functions. It randomly initialized from range [1, 3]
o_1, o_2	Integer	The order of Gaussian derivatives. They are randomly initialised from range [0, 2]

Overall Process. The overall learning and testing process of GauGP on feature learning and classification is shown in Fig. 2. A training set is employed for GauGP to learn a set of discriminative features for image classification. In GauGP, each program can be considered as a feature extraction approach and evaluated using linear SVM with 5-fold cross-validation on the training set. The mean accuracy of the 5-fold are employed as the fitness function for GauGP. At the final stage of learning, the best program is returned and tested on the test set, as shown in Fig. 2. The classification accuracy on the test set is reported.

Fig. 2. The overall process of the proposed GauGP for image classification.

3   Experiment Design

Data Sets. To examine the performance of the proposed method, six different data sets of varying difficulty are employed for conducting experiments. They are JAFFE [9], YALE [5], FEI_1 [12], FEI_1 [12], SCENE [4], and TEXTURE [10]. The data sets are binary classification and have gray-scale images. More details of these data sets, e.g. image size and class label, are listed in Table 3.

Table 3. Data set properties

Name	Size	Class labels	Training set	Test set
JAFFE	128×128	*Happy/surprised*	20/20	10/10
YALE	128×128	*Happy/sad*	20/20	10/10
FEI_1	130×180	*Smile/natural*	75/75	25/25
FEI_2	130×180	*Smile/natural*	75/75	25/25
SCENE	128×128	*Highway/streets*	195/219	65/73
TEXTURE	100×100	*Cork/brown bread*	324/324	108/108

Baseline Methods. A number of advanced approaches are implemented for comparisons, including four GP-based approaches, eight traditional approaches and a CNN approach. The four GP-based approaches are 2TGP, DIF + GP, Histogram + GP, and uLBP + GP [2]. The eight traditional approaches extract image features using domain independent feature (DIF), Histogram, grey-level co-occurrence matrix (GLCM), Gabor bank features (Gabor), SIFT, HOG, local binary patterns (LBP), and uniform LBP (uLBP) methods, respectively, and employ linear SVM kernel for classification. The CNN method is the famous LeNet [8] with ReLU as activation function and softmax for classification.

Parameter Settings. GauGP and four GP methods are implemented in Python based on the *DEAP (Distributed Evolutionary Algorithm Package)* package. The number of generations is 50 and the population size is 500. The crossover rate is 0.8, the mutation rate is 0.19 and the elitism rate is 0.01. Tournament selection is employed and the size is 7. *Ramped half-and-half* is used for population generation and the tree depth is 2–6. In the four GP methods, the fitness function is the classification accuracy. Experiments of GP methods and eight traditional methods on each data set run 30 times independently. Experiments of LeNet run 10 times due to the high computation cost.

4   Results and Discussions

This section compares and discusses the results obtained by GauGP and 13 baseline methods. Table 4 lists the maximum classification accuracy, mean accuracy and standard deviation on each data set. The Wilcoxon signed-rank test with a 5% significance level is used to compare the GauGP method with a baseline method. The symbols "+", "=" and "−" in Table 4 denote the GauGP method is significantly better, similar or significantly worse than the competitor.

From Table 4, it is obvious that GauGP obtains good performance on the six different data sets, especially on JAFFE, YALE, FEI_1, and FEI_2. Compared with the four GP-based methods, GauGP achieves significantly better or similar results in all the comparisons. Compared with the eight feature extraction methods, GauGP obtains significantly better or similar performance in 44 cases out of the total 48 cases. Compared with LeNet, the GauGP method achieves significantly better results in 1 case and similar results in 4 cases on the six data sets. In the total 78 ($13 \times 6 = 78$) comparisons, GauGP performs significantly better in 65 cases, similar in 8 cases and significantly worse in 5 cases.

These results illustrate that GauGP is able to learn discriminative features from the input image with good classification accuracy. Especially, the learnt features by GauGP are very powerful for facial expression classification. The experiments confirm the difficulty of feature extraction by the traditional approaches as they perform differently on different data sets. For example, the HOG method performs well on the face image data sets, the SIFT method performs well on the scene data set, and the LBP and uLBP methods perform well on the texture data set. This also reveals that feature learning approaches are more powerful and adaptive than these existing feature extraction approaches.

Table 4. Classification accuracy (%) of the proposed GauGP method and the baseline methods on the six data sets

Algorithms	Max	Mean ± St.D	Max	Mean ± St.D	Max	Mean ± St.D
Data sets	JAFFE		YALE		FEI_1	
2TGP	95.00	68.83 ± 13.64+	95.00	74.67 ± 13.66+	96.00	88.13 ± 6.22+
DIF + GP	90.00	75.83 ± 7.20+	75.00	60.33 ± 9.74+	80.00	56.67 ± 6.88+
Histogram + GP	80.00	53.33 ± 11.13+	80.00	54.50 ± 11.57+	70.00	48.93 ± 7.22+
uLBP + GP	75.00	50.33 ± 9.99+	65.00	49.17 ± 9.84+	66.00	50.87 ± 7.48+
DIF + SVM	90.00	85.17 ± 5.24+	85.00	74.50 ± 7.89+	74.00	61.13 ± 4.89+
Histogram + SVM	60.00	51.17 ± 2.79+	55.00	50.00 ± 2.24+	54.00	48.13 ± 3.38+
GLCM + SVM	70.00	54.50 ± 6.50+	55.00	50.33 ± 1.25+	50.00	49.67 ± 0.75+
Gabor + SVM	100.0	96.17 ± 5.87+	75.00	60.50 ± 6.50+	82.00	71.60 ± 7.87+
SIFT + SVM	80.00	80.00 ± 0.00+	75.00	75.00 ± 0.00+	82.00	82.00 ± 0.00+
HOG + SVM	90.00	90.00 ± 0.00+	85.00	85.00 ± 0.00+	94.00	94.00 ± 0.00+
LBP + SVM	75.00	74.33 ± 1.70+	80.00	78.00 ± 3.32+	68.00	62.47 ± 3.49+
uLBP + SVM	80.00	73.17 ± 5.08+	85.00	76.00 ± 5.54+	64.00	56.87 ± 5.18+
LeNet	100.0	100.0 ± 0.00−	90.00	85.50 ± 2.69+	**98.00**	94.40 ± 1.96=
GauGP	100.0	99.17 ± 1.86	100.0	**92.17 ± 4.60**	**98.00**	**94.67 ± 2.09**
Data sets	FEI_2		SCENE		TEXTURE	
2TGP	**94.00**	85.47 ± 5.98+	93.48	87.85 ± 2.20+	86.11	79.40 ± 3.42+
DIF + GP	72.00	60.33 ± 8.38+	89.13	85.22 ± 2.24+	88.43	84.46 ± 2.54+
Histogram + GP	60.00	48.80 ± 6.14+	84.06	79.98 ± 1.83+	92.13	87.36 ± 2.15+
uLBP + GP	72.00	48.73 ± 7.87+	95.65	91.79 ± 2.98=	96.76	93.89 ± 2.01=
DIF + SVM	72.00	62.80 ± 6.10+	87.68	81.09 ± 6.87+	86.11	80.93 ± 6.74+
Histogram + SVM	54.00	50.13 ± 2.53+	59.42	56.74 ± 3.09+	52.31	52.31 ± 0.00+
GLCM + SVM	54.00	50.13 ± 0.72+	93.48	90.56 ± 6.73=	88.89	73.60 ± 11.13+
Gabor + SVM	74.00	65.67 ± 5.14+	82.61	75.14 ± 7.98+	50.93	50.17 ± 0.30+
SIFT + SVM	78.00	78.00 ± 0.00+	97.10	**97.10 ± 0.00−**	85.19	85.19 ± 0.00+
HOG + SVM	88.00	88.00 ± 0.00+	91.30	90.17 ± 0.40+	75.46	72.71 ± 1.26+
LBP + SVM	66.00	57.60 ± 3.56+	95.65	94.49 ± 1.05−	**99.54**	**99.09 ± 0.08−**
uLBP + SVM	56.00	51.93 ± 2.34+	**97.83**	94.15 ± 2.79=	**99.54**	98.72 ± 3.29−
LeNet	**94.00**	**90.80 ± 1.83=**	94.93	92.90 ± 1.77=	96.76	81.67 ± 20.77=
GauGP	**94.00**	90.27 ± 2.41	95.65	92.37 ± 1.92	97.69	94.66 ± 1.53

5   Conclusions

The goal of this paper has been successfully achieved by proposing a GauGP method with a new program structure, a new function set and a new terminal set, and examining it on six different data sets. The GauGP method was able to detect small regions from the input image, evolve Gaussian-based filters and max-pooling functions for feature learning, and produce a set of discriminative features for classification. The experimental results demonstrated that the proposed GauGP method was able to achieve significantly better or similar results in the majority cases than the 13 state-of-the-art competitors. In the future, the GauGP method will be further improved for feature learning to multi-class classification tasks.

References

1. Atkins, D., Neshatian, K., Zhang, M.: A domain independent genetic programming approach to automatic feature extraction for image classification. In: IEEE Congress on Evolutionary Computation, pp. 238–245 (2011)
2. Bi, Y., Xue, B., Zhang, M.: An automatic feature extraction approach to image classification using genetic programming. In: Sim, K., Kaufmann, P. (eds.) EvoApplications 2018. LNCS, vol. 10784, pp. 421–438. Springer, Cham (2018). https://doi.org/10.1007/978-3-319-77538-8_29
3. Bi, Y., Zhang, M., Xue, B.: Genetic programming for automatic global and local feature extraction to image classification. In: IEEE Congress on Evolutionary Computation, pp. 1–6 (2018)
4. Fei-Fei, L., Perona, P.: A Bayesian hierarchical model for learning natural scene categories. In: IEEE Computer Society Conference on Computer Vision and Pattern Recognition, vol. 2, pp. 524–531 (2005)
5. Georghiades, A., Belhumeur, P., Kriegman, D.: Yale face database, vol. 2. Center for Computational Vision and Control at Yale University (1997). http://cvc.yale.edu/projects/yalefaces/yalefa
6. Koza, J.R.: Genetic Programming: On the Programming of Computers by Means of Natural Selection. MIT Press, Cambridge (1992)
7. LeCun, Y., Bengio, Y., Hinton, G.: Deep learning. Nature **521**, 436–444 (2015)
8. LeCun, Y., Bottou, L., Bengio, Y., Haffner, P.: Gradient-based learning applied to document recognition. Proc. IEEE **86**(11), 2278–2324 (1998)
9. Lyons, M., Akamatsu, S., Kamachi, M., Gyoba, J.: Coding facial expressions with Gabor wavelets. In: The Third IEEE International Conference on Automatic Face and Gesture Recognition, pp. 200–205 (1998)
10. Mallikarjuna, P., Targhi, A.T., Fritz, M., Hayman, E., Caputo, B., Eklundh, J.O.: The KTH-TIPS2 database. Computational Vision and Active Perception Laboratory, Stockholm, Sweden (2006)
11. Shao, L., Liu, L., Li, X.: Feature learning for image classification via multiobjective genetic programming. IEEE Trans. Neural Netw. Learn. Syst. **25**(7), 1359–1371 (2014)
12. Thomaz, C.E.: FEI face database (2012). http://fei.edu.br/~cet/facedatabase.html

Image Up-Sampling for Super Resolution with Generative Adversarial Network

Shohei Tsunekawa$^{(\boxtimes)}$, Katsufumi Inoue, and Michifumi Yoshioka

Osaka Prefecture University, Osaka, Japan
tsunekawa@sig.cs.osakafu-u.ac.jp,
{inoue,yoshioka}@cs.osakafu-u.ac.jp

Abstract. In case, we carry out single image Super Resolution (SR) utilizing deep learning, we utilize bicubic interpolation for up-sampling of low resolution images before input them into SR methods. In the pre-processing, these basic interpolation methods cause blur and noise effects for after processed images. These noise images may affect the SR results. In this research, by focusing on this point, we propose a new image up-sampling method utilizing Generative Adversarial Network (GAN). In this work, we improve an image evaluation criterion in generator part of GAN by combining Multi-Scale Structural Similarity (MS-SSIM) and L1 norm. From experiments, we have confirmed that our method allows us to create more qualitatively up-sampling images. As the quantitative results, our proposed method have achieved 0.90 [dB] of average PSNR, 3.35 [%] of average SSIM, and 1.28 [%] of average MS-SSIM improvement using Set 5 and Set 14 dataset compared with bicubic interpolation.

Keywords: Image up-sampling · GAN · Super resolution

1 Introduction

Nowadays, a demand to enlarge images from High Definition size is increasing by rises of 4K TV. Therefore, "Super Resolution (SR)" techniques [1] have been actively studied. There are a lot of kinds of SR. For example, filter-based SR [2,3], edge-based SR [4,5] and database-based SR methods [6,7] are famous. We focus on the fillter-based approach, which achieves the highest quality [8,9].

In these days, filter-based SR method using Convolutional Neural Network (CNN) [8,9] has been reported as one of the most effective methods to make high-definition SR images. There are two typical methods in such methods.

For the first method, it is represented by Super Resolution with Convolutional Neural Network (SRCNN) [8]. This type utilizes up-sampled images, which processed by bicubic interpolation, for inputting SR function. Besides, bicubic interpolation has problems. In the case of the image expansion except the multiple of two, this method cannot utilize base image pixels for outputs. Besides, bicubic interpolation sometimes makes ringing noises in images. These up-sampled images may affect output images made from SR methods. From this

© Springer Nature Switzerland AG 2018
T. Mitrovic et al. (Eds.): AI 2018, LNAI 11320, pp. 258–270, 2018.
https://doi.org/10.1007/978-3-030-03991-2_26

information, we consider that outputting super resolution images may become higher quality by utilizing higher quality input images.

On the other hand, for the second method, it is represented by Gradual Up-sampling Network (GUN) [10]. This type method performs image expansion processing and super resolution processing sequentially. In this approach, we can process super resolution and gradually image expansion utilizing bicubic interpolation by designing the convolution layer and the up-sampling layer in network structure. Therefore, we can take less affection for images when we expand images by bicubic interpolation. Nevertheless, because it is necessary to perform down-sampling during back propagation, some information is lost, and there is possibility that most suitable model for super resolution is not produced.

In this research, we improve image up-sampling method for adopting SRCNN. To accomplish this, we focus on Generative Adversarial Network (GAN) [11], which is an image generation model. GAN is the machine learning model to learn the distribution of generated image accords with the distribution of input image. In recent researches [11,12], GAN can make high quality forgery images. Super Resolution with Generative Adversarial Network (SRGAN) [12], which utilizes GAN, is one of the highest quality image generation method and known as a state of the art method. We focus on SRGAN and utilize it for our proposed image up-sampling method. This method have problems in loss function. SRGAN utilizes VGG19 [13] and Mean Squared Error (MSE) loss for evaluating similarity between images. However, VGG19 loss is not enough to evaluate similarity of image. This is because VGG19 is used for image recognition and recognize image by unique way unlike human [14]. Moreover, MSE sometimes produces splotchy artifacts in output images. Therefore, we improve loss function of SRGAN by combining Multi-Scale Structural Similarity (MS-SSIM) [15] and L1 norm. We adopt our loss criteria for SRGAN and get high quality up-sampled images.

From experimental results with public data sets, Set5 and Set14, we have confirmed that our proposed method allows us to create more qualitatively images compared with SRGAN and bicubic interpolation. In addition, as the quantitative results, our proposed method have achieved 0.90 [dB] of average PSNR, 3.35 [%] of average SSIM, and 1.28 [%] of average MS-SSIM improvement compared with bicubic interpolation. Moreover, we adopt our up-sampled images for SR method to improve PSNR and SSIM score.

2   Related Work

In this research, we focus on GAN [11] to make up-sampled images for inputting SR model. GAN is one of the generative model, which can make image from scratch. In this section, we explain basic image generative models and GAN.

There are many image generative models using deep learning, e.g. "Variational Auto-Encoding" [16] and "Pixel Recurrent Neural Network" [17]. However, those methods have problems for adopting to SR. Variational Auto-Encoding have to add noise and blur for last part of image generation. As a result, output generated images have blurs and noises. Therefore, this model is not good for image up-sampling. Pixel Recurrent Neural Network needs long time for generating images. This method suppose best pixels for image generation, to every pixel. Therefore, computational cost is high. Moreover, in case, this model generate images, we cannot calculate the supposing pixels in parallel [17]. This is why, this method does not suit for image up-sampling.

GAN can make clear output images and need few seconds for generating output images. GAN has generator part and discriminator part in model. Generator part makes image from scratch, and discriminator judges what input image is similar to original image or not. In this model, learning process is carried out in turn. First, generator optimizes the model until discriminator cannot recognize the output image is made by generator part or not. After that, discriminator starts optimizing for being able to recognize input images. By iterating these processes, generator creates images like true images, and discriminator judges that input image is forgery or not. Finally, generator can make high quality forgeries which discriminator cannot recognize generated images or ground truth images.

Ledig utilizes GAN technology for making high resolution image from input images; "Super Resolution with Generative Adversarial Network" [12]. In this case, generator is optimized for making edges and denoising. Therefore input images become high quality images. We select SRGAN as a conventional method. As the previous section, this conventional method has the problems in loss function. SRGAN utilizes VGG19 and MSE loss in generator model to evaluate image similarity and generate images. We consider that VGG19 and MSE are not enough for these roles. VGG19 recognizes images by unique way unlike human, and, MSE produces noises in generated images. Therefore, we adopt new evaluation loss to overcome the problems. In this research, we improve a loss function criteria of SRGAN to obtain higher quality up-sampled images.

3   Conventional Method

In this section, we explain Super Resolution with Generative Adversarial Network (SRGAN), which is base of our proposed method. This method is known as state of the art image generation method calculated by Mean Opinion Score.

3.1   Structure

Figure 1 shows the structure of SRGAN, which has two models; generator and discriminator. These models are constructed by Residual Block [18] which has convolution layer, batch normalization layer and relu layer. Generator model creates output images which are similar to input images. Discriminator model judges whether input images are created by generator model or not. Utilizing these two models, SRGAN outputs high quality up-sampled images.

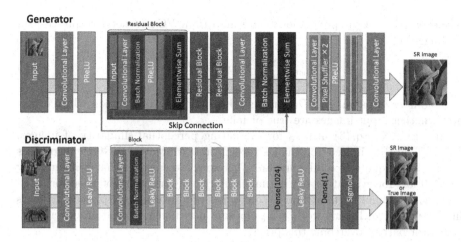

Fig. 1. Structure of SRGAN

3.2 Loss Function

In SRGAN, generator model employs Eq. (1) as the loss function l^{SR}, which is different from usual GAN.

$$l^{\mathrm{SR}} = l^{\mathrm{SR}}_{\mathrm{MSE}} + l^{\mathrm{SR}}_{\mathrm{VGG}} + 10^{-3} l^{\mathrm{SR}}_{\mathrm{Gen}} \tag{1}$$

$l^{\mathrm{SR}}_{\mathrm{MSE}}$, $l^{\mathrm{SR}}_{\mathrm{VGG}}$, $l^{\mathrm{SR}}_{\mathrm{Gen}}$ are shown as Eq. (2) - Eq. (4). $l^{\mathrm{SR}}_{\mathrm{MSE}}$ calculates mean square error between generated image and true image corresponding to generated image. $l^{\mathrm{SR}}_{\mathrm{VGG}}$ evaluates the differences between feature maps of generated images and feature maps of true images from VGG19 network. $l^{\mathrm{SR}}_{\mathrm{Gen}}$ means discrimination accuracy of input image which is evaluated by discriminator model.

$$l^{\mathrm{SR}}_{\mathrm{MSE}} = \frac{1}{r^2 W H} \sum_{x=1}^{rW} \sum_{y=1}^{rH} (I^{\mathrm{HR}}_{x,y} - G(I^{\mathrm{LR}})_{x,y})^2 \tag{2}$$

I^{LR}, I^{HR} are low resolution (LR) image and true high resolution (HR) image (true image) corresponding to LR image, respectively. W, H are image width and height, respectively, r is down-sampling factor, and $G(p)$ is an image processing function produced by generator model.

$$l^{\mathrm{SR}}_{\mathrm{VGG}/i,j} = \frac{1}{W_{i,j} H_{i,j}} \sum_{x=1}^{W_{i,j}} \sum_{y=1}^{H_{i,j}} (\phi_{i,j}(I^{\mathrm{HR}})_{x,y} - \phi_{i,j}(G(I^{\mathrm{LR}}))_{x,y})^2 \tag{3}$$

$W_{i,j}, H_{i,j}$ describe the dimensions of the respective feature maps within the VGG19 network. We separate VGG19 model into five stages by Maxpooling layer. Here, i means No.i stage, j means No.j convolution layer in i stage. $\phi_{i,j}(p)$

is the function of sampling the feature map from VGG19 network pre-trained by ImageNet.

$$l_{\text{Gen}}^{\text{SR}} = \sum_{n=1}^{N} -\log D(G(I^{\text{LR}})) \tag{4}$$

N is number of patch, and $D(p)$ means the discriminator function which evaluates whether input images are true or fake.

In SRGAN, Eq. (3) utilizes for evaluating perceptual similarity of images. VGG 19 are optimized for image recognition. Moreover, VGG19 recognizes images by unique way unlike human. Therefore, we consider that utilizing only VGG19 loss for evaluating perceptual similarity of images is not good for satisfying with human. Further, Eq. (2) sometimes produces visible splotchy artifacts in output images.In this work, we propose a new image evaluation criterion in generator part to overcome this point.

4   Proposed Method

In this research, we propose a new image criterion for a loss function of generator model utilizing Hang Zhao's criterion [19] which includes Multi Scale-Structural Similarity (MS-SSIM) and the L1 norm. MS-SSIM can evaluate the change of a brightness level and the image structure, which people utilize. Moreover, we can suppress the outbreak of the noise while obtaining an image processing effect similar to MSE by incorporating L1 norm in a loss function. We consider that we can perform the image expansion that we make use of a characteristic of GAN with maintaining structure information.

4.1   Structural Simirality

MS-SSIM is an image evaluation function based on Structural Similarity (SSIM) [20]. Equation (5) shows that SSIM utilizes pixel average values and image standard deviation. This is why, SSIM can evaluate differences of brightness, contrast, and image structure.

$$\text{SSIM} = \underbrace{\frac{(2\mu_x\mu_y + c_1)}{(\mu_x^2 + \mu_y^2 + c_1)}}_{l} \cdot \underbrace{\frac{(\sigma_{xy} + c_2)}{(\sigma_x^2 + \sigma_y^2 + c_2)}}_{cs} \tag{5}$$

where x, y are SR and true image, μ_x, μ_y are pixel average values, σ_x^2, σ_y^2 are standard deviation and σ_{xy} is covariance. Further $c_1 = (k_1 L)^2$, $c_2 = (k_2 L)^2$, we utilize $k_1 = 0.01$, $k_2 = 0.03$, $L = 255$ which are the same as reference [19].

4.2   MS-SSIM

In the case that we utilize SSIM for loss function of a deep learning model, σ in SSIM has an impact on the quality of the processed results of a network [19].

To solve this problem, we select MS-SSIM. This has the structure which changes scale of image. Moreover, MS-SSIM are calculated by average SSIM score of all scale changed images. Equation (6) shows loss function using MS-SSIM.

$$l^{\text{MS-SSIM}} = [l_M]^{\alpha_M} \cdot \prod_{j=0}^{M} [cs_j]^{\beta_j} \tag{6}$$

where l, cs are defined in Eq. (5). M means the total number of scale and α_M, β_j are weight for l, cs. We utilize $M = 5$, $(\alpha_M, \beta_j) = (1, 1)$ which is the same as reference [19].

4.3 L1 Norm

We employ L1 norm instead of MSE, which produces splotchy artifacts in SR images [19]. Equation (7) shows that we utilize Manhattan distance for L1 norm.

$$l^{L1}(P) = \frac{1}{N} \sum_{p \in P} |x_p - y_p| \tag{7}$$

where x,y are SR and true image, N means the total number of patches. p is index of pixel, and P is patch.

Table 1. Experimental condition for comparison of up-sampled images.

OS	Ubuntu16.04
CPU	Intel core i7-7700K 4.20 GHz
GPU	GeForceGTX 1080Ti
Memory	64 GB
Platform	Tensorflow
Test dataset	Set 5,14
Training data	800 images

4.4 Proposed Criterion

Utilizing $l^{\text{MS-SSIM}}$ and $l^{L1}(P)$, Hang Zhao's evaluation criteria for image super resolution is constructed. Equation (8) is our criteria.

$$l^{\text{SR}}_{\text{MSL}} = 0.84 \cdot (1 - l^{\text{MS-SSIM}}) + 0.16 \cdot l^{L1}(P). \tag{8}$$

0.84 and 0.16 are already defined in reference [19]. This criteria can evaluate structure similarity of input images and less noises than using mean square error for deep learning.

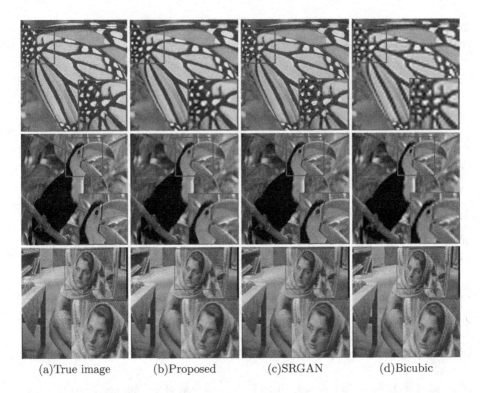

(a)True image   (b)Proposed   (c)SRGAN   (d)Bicubic

Fig. 2. The qualitative comparison among the proposed method and conventional methods. Images made by our propose method are higher quality than Bicubic method and conventional SRGAN method.

We make the new loss function model, which can generate clear expansion image unless changing an image structure, using Eq. (8). Equation (9) shows our new criterion.

$$l^{\text{Prop}} = l^{\text{SR}}_{\text{MSL}} + l^{\text{SR}}_{\text{VGG}} + 10^{-3} l^{\text{SR}}_{\text{Gen}}. \tag{9}$$

Conventional SRGAN utilizes VGG19 for evaluating perceptual loss, and MSE for evaluating pixel similarity of images. In our new criteria, we utilize L1 norm instead of MSE, and MS-SSIM for structural similarity. L1 norm can control noises which are produced in output images. And MS-SSIM is able to evaluate images quantitatively. Therefor, we delete $l^{\text{SR}}_{\text{MSE}}$ from conventional loss function to adopt our new criteria $l^{\text{SR}}_{\text{MSL}}$. We still employ $l^{\text{SR}}_{\text{VGG}}$ as perceptual loss. This is because MS-SSIM works other role what $l^{\text{SR}}_{\text{VGG}}$ does.

By utilizing the above criterion, we finally can obtain clear up-sampled images, which controlled occasion of blur and noise, and contrast of color, by utilizing our criteria for loss function in Generator model of SRGAN.

5   Experiment

In this research, we qualitatively and quantitatively evaluated upsampled images made by bicubic interpolation, SRGAN and our proposed method. Besides, we would like to prove that our up-sampled images can be useful for utilizing as input image of super resolution methods. Therefore, we selected SRCNN, which basically utilized bicubic interpolated images for input, and qualitatively and quantitatively evaluated super resolution images made from our proposed images and bicubic interpolated images.

5.1   Comparison of Up-Sampled Images Created by Our Proposed and Conventional Methods

We set our experiment condition as Table 1. In this experiment, we utilized 18 test images, Set5 and Set 14, which are used in [12], for super resolution. We scaled up images 2.5 times after scaled down 0.4 times for inputting model. We trained SRGAN and our proposed model for 2000 iteration. Other environment was same as [12].

We show images in Fig. 2 which are up-sampled Bird and Barbara images made by each method. We can see that our proposed images are less noises and blur than other conventional methods. This means that our propose method makes high quality up-sampled images compared with bicubic interpolation and SRGAN. And, in Tables 2, 3 and 4, we show PSNR [21], SSIM, and MS-SSIM

Table 2. Evaluation of Set 5 and Set 14 dataset by PSNR (dB)

Image	Baboon	Baby	Barbara	Bird	Bridge	Butterfly	Coastguard	Comic	Face
Bicubic	21.01	30.96	23.81	28.76	23.27	21.41	24.11	21.32	27.29
SRGAN	16.64	28.30	22.73	28.90	22.08	23.60	23.49	18.72	26.37
Proposed	19.93	31.34	24.18	30.28	23.73	24.53	24.50	19.90	29.24
	Flowers	Foreman	Lenna	Man	Monarch	Pepper	PPT3	Woman	Zebra
Bicubic	22.40	26.07	25.25	24.42	25.93	24.15	21.48	20.34	23.40
SRGAN	21.70	26.26	26.01	24.30	27.72	26.53	21.37	22.90	24.35
Proposed	22.55	27.05	26.53	24.48	28.88	24.42	21.42	23.79	24.95

Table 3. Evaluation of Set 5 and Set 14 dataset by SSIM (%)

Image	Baboon	Baby	Barbara	Bird	Bridge	Butterfly	Coastguard	Comic	Face
Bicubic	43.92	85.42	68.05	86.23	58.55	76.06	52.28	65.42	67.18
SRGAN	24.99	77.99	64.96	83.88	49.86	79.48	45.02	52.97	67.80
Proposed	44.11	85.93	70.27	88.23	59.54	84.79	52.92	62.21	71.17
	Flowers	Foreman	Lenna	Man	Monarch	Pepper	PPT3	Woman	Zebra
Bicubic	66.33	83.36	74.61	67.98	85.13	79.38	81.41	83.34	71.15
SRGAN	62.15	84.53	56.32	63.81	86.75	86.23	84.79	84.04	74.32
Proposed	67.90	87.91	75.21	71.27	91.08	90.69	89.55	87.77	75.32

Table 4. Evaluation of Set 5 and Set 14 dataset by MS-SSIM (%)

Image	Baboon	Baby	Barbara	Bird	Bridge	Butterfly	Coastguard	Comic	Face
Bicubic	89.81	95.23	93.34	97.76	92.10	95.32	87.24	84.92	94.21
SRGAN	82.13	95.26	91.80	97.34	88.74	97.24	83.12	85.73	93.78
Proposed	87.42	97.14	93.59	98.02	92.23	97.91	87.41	88.32	95.54
	Flowers	Foreman	Lenna	Man	Monarch	Pepper	PPT3	Woman	Zebra
Bicubic	91.32	97.30	91.30	94.21	95.78	82.84	95.42	96.84	92.84
SRGAN	89.51	97.62	86.77	93.10	97.76	87.45	96.81	97.18	80.45
Proposed	91.64	98.23	91.86	94.96	98.31	89.32	97.50	97.81	93.65

score of each images. From these result, our method can make high quality images compared with other methods. This model has similar functions as GAN and can make less noise images than GAN.

Some evaluation scores of our proposed up-sampled images are not better than bicubic interpolation ones. There are two reasons. First, GAN is generation model. Therefore, images, which have many thin lines, are very affected by gap of generation part. Second, we utilized L1 norm for the loss function instead of L2 norm. L2 norm utilizes square for modifying error of images. This is why L2 norm can more strongly revise images than L1 norm. In this research, we selected L1 norm to control occasion of noise and blur. Therefore, we loss strong revise power like L2 norm. In future work, we have to make better loss function to accomplish making high quality images.

(a)Butterfly   (b)Foreman   (a)Baboon   (b)Comic

Fig. 3. Images are improved by our proposed up-sampling method

Fig. 4. Images are not improved by our proposed up-sampling method

Figures 3 and 4 show that what images are very effective for our method, and not good for our method, respectively. From experimental result, our propose method tends to become little flat images. This is because, we utilize L1 norm instead of MSE. L1 norm weakly revises images compared with MSE. Therefore, baby and butterfly, which have few edges and do not need strong revise, become very high quality. On the other hands baboon and comic, which have many micro lines and need strong revise, are not improved. It is evident from experimental result that our proposed method is more skillful at up-sampling images, which have few edges in these structures.

5.2 Adopting for Super Resolution Method

In this research, we adopted our up-sampled images for super resolution method to evaluate the usability of our method. We selected SRCNN as SR method. SRCNN is the most basic super resolution method. This super resolution method utilizes bicubic interpolation images as input images to make up-sampled low resolution images. Figure 5 shows structure of SRCNN.

We set our experimental condition as Table 5. Most of all other experiment condition was the same as reference [8]. We prepared two type training data sets, up-sampled by bicubic interpolation and our propose method. For bicubic images, we scaled up images 2.5 times after scaled down 0.4 times for input model. Our proposed up-sampled images also made by scaled down 0.4 times images. Finally, we prepared two SRCNN networks which trained by those two training datasets.

We show images in Fig. 6 which are super resolution images made by bicubic interpolated images and our propose up-sampled images. We can see that the super resolution image made by our proposed method is a higher quality image compared with bicubic interpolated one and only up-sampled one. As we mentioned above, our propose up-sampled images are little flat ones. If we utilize super resolution method for those, we can get sharpness and clear images from them.

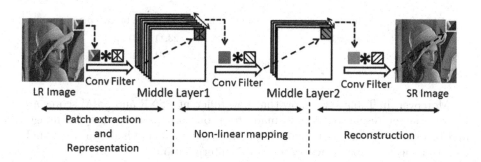

Fig. 5. Structure of SRCNN

Table 5. Experimental Condition for SRCNN

OS	Ubuntu16.04
CPU	Intel core i7-7700K 4.20 GHz
GPU	GeForceGTX 1080Ti
Memory	64 GB
Platform	Tensorflow
Test dataset	Set 5,14
Training data	91 images

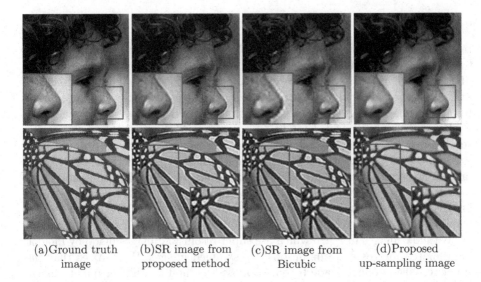

(a)Ground truth   (b)SR image from   (c)SR image from   (d)Proposed
    image   proposed method   Bicubic   up-sampling image

Fig. 6. The qualitative comparison of the super resolution images with SRCNN by changing the input images created by our proposed method and the conventional method, and our proposed up-sampling image

Table 6. Evaluation of Set5 and 14 dataset by SRCNN

Input image	SR image by propose up-sampled image	SR image by Bicubic image
Ave. PSNR	23.56 (dB)	23.11 (dB)
Ave. SSIM	68.93 (%)	68.31 (%)

Moreover, in Table 6, we show that how different PSNR and SSIM scores are between super resolution images made from our proposed up-sampled images and bicubic interpolation images. From this result, our method can make high quality images compared with the bicubic interpolation.

6   Conclusion

In this study, we improved image evaluation criterion for generator part of SRGAN. As a result, we can obtain higher quality up-sampled image compared with bicubic interpolation and SRGAN. Moreover, we adopted our up-sampled images for SRCNN to confirm our method was useful for conventional SR method. From experimental result, we have confirmed that our proposed method can adopt for other SR methods which are utilized bicubic interpolated images as input images.

Our up-sampled images become flatter than SRGAN. This is because, we utilize L1 norm for loss function instead of L2 norm. Further consideration will be needed to yield any findings about investigating more optimal evaluation criteria for solving this problem.

As a future work, we would like to make one end to end SR method including our up-sample part. Further we adopt our up-sampled images for other SR methods [22,23] to confirm our method's versatility.

References

1. Irani, M.: Improving resolution by image registration. CVGIP: Graph. Model. Image Process. **53**, 231–239 (1991)
2. Elad, M., Feuer, A.: Superresolution restoration of an image sequence: adaptive filtering approach. IEEE Trans. Image Process. **8**(3), 387–395 (1999)
3. Cruz, C., Mehta, R., Katkovnik, V., Egiazarian, K.O.: Single image super-resolution based on wiener filter in similarity domain. CoRR abs/1704.04126 (2017)
4. Wang, L., Xiang, S., Meng, G., Wu, H., Pan, C.: Edge-directed single-image super-resolution via adaptive gradient magnitude self-interpolation. IEEE Trans. Circuits Syst. Video Technol. **23**(8), 1289–1299 (2013)
5. Fattal, R.: Upsampling via imposed edges statistics. ACM Transactions on Graphics **26**(3) (2007). (Proceedings of SIGGRAPH 2007)
6. Freeman, W., Jones, T., Pasztor, E.: Example-based super-resolution. IEEE Comput. Graph. Appl. **22**(2), 56–65 (2002)
7. Sun, J., Zheng, N.N., Tao, H., Shum, H.Y.: Image hallucination with primal sketch priors. In: 2003 IEEE Computer Society Conference on Computer Vision and Pattern Recognition, Proceedings, vol. 2, pp. II-729-736 (2003)
8. Dong, C., Loy, C., He, K., Tang, X.: Image super-resolution using deep convolutional networks. IEEE Trans. Pattern Anal. Mach. Intell. **38**(2), 295–307 (2016)
9. Dong, C., Loy, C.C., He, K., Tang, X.: Learning a deep convolutional network for image super-resolution. In: Fleet, D., Pajdla, T., Schiele, B., Tuytelaars, T. (eds.) ECCV 2014. LNCS, vol. 8692, pp. 184–199. Springer, Cham (2014). https://doi.org/10.1007/978-3-319-10593-2_13
10. Zhao, Y., et al.: GUN: gradual upsampling network for single image super-resolution. CoRR abs/1703.04244 (2017)
11. Goodfellow, I., et al.: Generative adversarial nets. In: Ghahramani, Z., Welling, M., Cortes, C., Lawrence, N.D., Weinberger, K.Q. (eds.) Advances in Neural Information Processing Systems, vol. 27, pp. 2672–2680. Curran Associates, Inc. (2014)
12. Ledig, C., et al.: Photo-realistic single image super-resolution using a generative adversarial network. CoRR abs/1609.04802 (2016)
13. Simonyan, K., Zisserman, A.: Very deep convolutional networks for large-scale image recognition. CoRR abs/1409.1556 (2014)
14. Nguyen, A.M., Yosinski, J., Clune, J.: Deep neural networks are easily fooled: High confidence predictions for unrecognizable images. CoRR abs/1412.1897 (2014)
15. Wang, Z., Simoncelli, E.P., Bovik, A.C.: Multiscale structural similarity for image quality assessment. In: The Thrity-Seventh Asilomar Conference on Signals, Systems Computers, vol. 2, pp. 1398–1402, November 2003
16. Cai, L., Gao, H., Ji, S.: Multi-stage variational auto-encoders for coarse-to-fine image generation. CoRR abs/1705.07202 (2017)
17. van den Oord, A., Kalchbrenner, N., Kavukcuoglu, K.: Pixel recurrent neural networks. CoRR abs/1601.06759 (2016)
18. He, K., Zhang, X., Ren, S., Sun, J.: Deep residual learning for image recognition. In: 2016 IEEE Conference on Computer Vision and Pattern Recognition (CVPR), pp. 770–778, June 2016

19. Zhao, H., Gallo, O., Frosio, I., Kautz, J.: Loss functions for image restoration with neural networks. IEEE Trans. Comput. Imaging **3**(1), 47–57 (2017)
20. Wang, Z., Bovik, A., Sheikh, H., Simoncelli, E.: Image quality assessment: from error visibility to structural similarity. IEEE Trans. Image Process. **13**(4), 600–612 (2004)
21. Gonzalez, R.C., Woods, R.E.: Digital Image Processing. Prentice Hall, Upper Saddle River (2007)
22. Kim, J., Lee, J.K., Lee, K.M.: Accurate image super-resolution using very deep convolutional networks. CoRR abs/1511.04587 (2015)
23. Lim, B., Son, S., Kim, H., Nah, S., Lee, K.M.: Enhanced deep residual networks for single image super-resolution. CoRR abs/1707.02921 (2017)

A Model for Learning Representations of 3D Objects Through Tactile Exploration: Effects of Object Asymmetries and Landmarks

Xiaogang Yan[✉], Alistair Knott, and Steven Mills

University of Otago, Dunedin, New Zealand
{yanxg,alik,steven}@cs.otago.ac.nz

Abstract. In this paper, we develop a neural network model that learns representations of 3D objects via tactile exploration. The basic principle is that the hand is considered as an autonomous 'navigating agent', traveling within the 'environment' of a 3D object. We adapt a model of hippocampal place cells, which learns the structure of a 2D environment by exploiting constraints imposed by the environment's boundaries on the agent's movement, and perceptual information about landmarks in the environment. In the current paper, our focus is on 3D analogues of these 2D information sources. We systematically investigate the information about object geometry that is provided by navigation constraints in a simple cuboid, and by tactile landmarks. We find that an asymmetric cuboid conveys more information to the navigator than a symmetric cuboid (i.e., a cube) – and that landmarks convey additional information independently from asymmetry.

Keywords: Hippocampal place cells · 3D object representation
Tactile exploration · Landmarks · Recurrent self-organizing map

1 Introduction

When a human being enters an environment, hippocampal place cells develop a cognitive map of the environment. While the person reaches one location in the environment, one place cell or multiple place cells fire simultaneously, which represents such a location in the navigation environment. The process of hippocampal cells encoding spatial locations by the integration of linear and angular self motions is called 'path integration' or 'dead reckoning' [10,11].

Even though the exploring agent's movements are defined in an 'egocentric' reference frame, as are the perceptual stimuli it receives, the hippocampus can derive from this egocentric information an 'allocentric' or 'environment-centered' representation of its location in the environment [3,5]. In our current paper, we explore a 3D analogue of this navigation scenario, where the agent's hand is construed as traveling around the environment of a 3D object. Here again, information about the hand's movements and about landmarks arrive in an

© Springer Nature Switzerland AG 2018
T. Mitrovic et al. (Eds.): AI 2018, LNAI 11320, pp. 271–283, 2018.
https://doi.org/10.1007/978-3-030-03991-2_27

egocentric reference frame. We will focus on tactile information, which is more direct than visual information [6]. The egocentric information in this case is defined in a 'hand-centered' coordinate system. From this egocentric information, the agent can construct an allocentric (i.e., object-centered) representation of the object's geometry.

For concreteness, we can visualize the 'agent' traveling around the cube as a snail, as shown in Fig. 1. The agent can move by translation (forward, back, left or right), or can change its orientation by rotating on its current plane. It can detect when it crosses onto a different plane of the cube. It can also sense tactile landmarks that it is sliding over (the colored dots). From these egocentric (snail-centered) cues, the agent can derive an environment-centered (i.e., object-centered) representation of the cube.

It is not yet understood how this is done. However, as a starting point, we can consider models of the 2D place cells system, which is one of the most studied and best understood structures in the brain [2,4]. The place cells model we will adopt is one that uses a biologically plausible self-organizing map (SOM) [8]: specifically, a SOM is modified to take recurrent input, called a modified SOM (MSOM) [12]. Note that we are not suggesting that hippocampal place cells are involved in haptic object exploration; there is good evidence that object representations derived from touch are developed in the parietal cortex [1,13]. However, we suggest that the parietal circuitry for learning haptic object representations might be isomorphic in some way to the hippocampal circuitry for learning 2D environment representations. Based on this assumption, we investigate what allocentric information about object geometry can be provided by constraints on hand navigation, and by tactile landmarks.

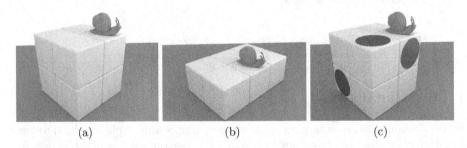

(a)   (b)   (c)

Fig. 1. By executing 'egocentric' movements, an agent (here a snail) learns the 'allocentric' representation of the explored object, i.e, (a) a cube, (b) a cuboid, and (c) a cube with landmarks.

The organization of this paper is summarized as follows. Section 2 presents the background knowledge, which consists of MSOM, the relationship between constrained action sequences and the object topography and a revisit of a existing MSOM model activated by translative movements (T-MSOM) for 3D object representations shown in [14] with its drawbacks pointed out. The proposed translative and orientational movements activated MSOM (TO-MSOM) model and the landmarks together with translative and orientational movements activated

MSOM (L-TO-MSOM) model are presented in Sect. 3. Section 4 shows simulative results of the proposed models for learning representations of two typical 3D objects. Finally, Sect. 5 concludes the paper with final remarks. The main contributions of this paper are highlighted as follows.

- Based on the authors' knowledge, this is the first time to present a neural network model for learning representations of 3D object via tactile exploration by executing both translative and orientational movements.
- Simulative results based on a 3D cube and cuboid demonstrate the effectiveness of the proposed models for learning representations of 3D objects. More importantly, the statistics and systematic analysis verify that the models are more accurate to learn a representation of a cuboid than a cube, which is owing to the contributive asymmetrical topography of a cuboid.
- The positive effect of landmarks is verified by the statistics analysis of simulative results of the models representing the cube and cuboid.

2 Background

In this section, we present the background knowledge for the proposed models. Specifically, the detailed description of MSOM algorithm is firstly presented. Then, the constraint of object topographies placed on action sequences for exploration is identified. After that, for comparison and for showing the contribution of this paper, drawbacks of the existing T-MSOM model are pointed out.

2.1 Modified Self-Organizing Map (MSOM)

Owing to the added previous state input, MSOM comes to learn frequently occurring input *sequences*, which is different from SOM learning the frequently occurring input *patterns* [2]. Regarding an input $x(t) \in \mathcal{R}^m$ at time instance t, the activity of unit i of a MSOM $\mathcal{M} \in \mathcal{R}^{n \times n}$ at that time instance is defined as

$$a_i(t) = \exp(-\eta d_i(t)), \tag{1}$$

where $i \in 1, 2, \cdots, n^2$, $\eta > 0$ is a design parameter, and $d_i(t)$ is a distance function, which is defined as a weighted sum of two parts. The first part is $\|x(t) - w_i(t)\|_2^2$ with $\|\cdot\|_2$ denoting the 2-norm of a matrix or vector, which is to evaluate the distance between the input $x(t)$ and the weight $w_i(t)$ of unit i (for simplicity, we name it as regular weight); and the second part is $\|c(t) - c_i(t)\|_2^2$, which is to evaluate the distance between the context weight $c(t)$ for the map $\mathcal{M}$ at time instance t and the individual context weight $c_i(t)$ of unit i. By introducing a weight factor $\xi \in (0, 1)$ to adjust the effect of such two parts on $d_i(t)$, the distance function $d_i(t)$ is formulated as

$$d_i(t) = (1 - \xi)\|x(t) - w_i(t)\|_2^2 + \xi\|c(t) - c_i(t)\|_2^2. \tag{2}$$

The context weight $c(t)$ for the map $\mathcal{M}$ in (2) is defined as

$$c(t) = (1 - \kappa)w^*(t - 1) + \kappa c^*(t - 1), \kappa \in (0, 1), \tag{3}$$

where $w^*(t-1)$ and $c^*(t-1)$ denote the regular weight and context weight of the unit in MSOM with the maximal activity $a_i(t)$ at previous time instance $t-1$, respectively. By norming the activities of all MSOM units shown in (1),

$$p_i(t) = \frac{a_i(t)}{\sum_{j=1}^{n^2} a_j(t)}, \tag{4}$$

which denotes the activity probability of unit i for the current input at time instance t. During training, the regular weight $w_i(t)$ is updated as

$$w_i(t+1) = w_i(t) + \mathcal{L}(t)\mathcal{H}(i, f(x(t)))(t)(x(t) - w_i(t)), \tag{5}$$

and the individual context weight $c_i(t)$ is changed as

$$c_i(t+1) = c_i(t) + \mathcal{L}(t)\mathcal{H}(i, f(x))(t)(c(t) - c_i(t)), \tag{6}$$

where $\mathcal{L}(t)$ and $\mathcal{H}(i, f(x(t)))(t)$ are a time-varying decreasing learning rate function and neighbourhood function respectively with $f(x)$ denoting the index of the unit in MSOM with the maximal activity for the current input $x(t)$. At the beginning of training, the regular weight $w_i(0) \in (0,1)$ is randomly selected and the context weight $c_i(0) = 0$. The process of MSOM is shown in Algorithm 1.

Algorithm 1. MSOM

Input: Input data $x(t) \in \mathcal{R}^m$
Output: A convergent MSOM $\mathcal{M} \in \mathcal{R}^{n \times n}$
1: Randomly initialize all m-dimensional regular weights $w_i(0) \in (0,1)$ and set all context weights $c_i(0) = \mathbf{0} \in \mathcal{R}^m$, $i = 1, 2, \ldots n^2$
2: **while** feature map is not convergent **do**
3:    Sampling: draw sample input $x(t) \in \mathcal{R}^m$
4:    Competition: find best matching unit based on a distance discriminant function:

$$f(x(t)) = \underset{i}{\arg\min} \ (1-\xi)\|x(t) - w_i(t)\|_2^2 + \xi\|c(t) - c_i(t)\|_2^2,$$

   where $c(t) = (1-\kappa)w_{f(x(t-1))}(t-1) + \kappa c_{f(x(t-1))}(t-1)$, $\xi \in (0,1)$ $\kappa \in (0,1)$
5:    Cooperation: select $f(x(t))$ neuron's neighbourhood neurons defined by a time-varying decreasing neighbourhood function $\mathcal{H}(i, f(x))(t)$
6:    Adaptation: update regular weights and context weights of all selected neurons:

$$w_i(t+1) = w_i(t) + \mathcal{L}(t)\mathcal{H}(i, f(x(t)))(t)(x(t) - w_i(t)),$$

$$c_i(t+1) = c_i(t) + \mathcal{L}(t)\mathcal{H}(i, f(x))(t)(c(t) - c_i(t)),$$

   where $\mathcal{L}(t)$ is a time-varying decreasing learning rate function.
7: **end while**
8: **return** $\mathcal{M}$

2.2 Action Sequences Constrained by Object Topographies

To lay a basis for further investigation, in this subsection, we present the relationship (more specifically, the constraint relationship) between navigation action sequences and object's topographies. Regarding the constraint on action sequences played by object topographies, we can refer to a cube shown in Fig. 2. Assuming a navigation agent starts in location 'L1' facing Right, after moving directly forward, it reaches location 'L2' facing Right. Then, the agent could reach location 'L3' by moving forward over the edge or could get location 'L4' by moving right over the edge. Thus, from the same starting exploration position and orientation, different action sequences lead the navigation agent to different locations. Different object topographies support different exploration action sequences and thus, constrained action sequences implicitly contain object topography information. Relationships among action sequences, the object topography plus navigation location and the MSOM are illustrated in Fig. 3.

Fig. 2. Geometrical description of a cube with four locations L1, L2, L3 and L4.

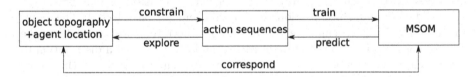

Fig. 3. Schematic showing analorelationships among object topography and agent location, action sequences and the MSOM.

Without performing orientational movements, starting from 'L2' facing Right, after moving forward over the edge to reach 'L3', moving right over the edge to reach 'L4' and moving back over the edge to go to 'L2', the agent is back in its starting location – but importantly, it is now facing a different direction than it did when it started. This highlights an important geometrical property of navigation in 3D space – the 'non-commutativity of rotations' (a good discussion is given in [7]). For our purposes, the key point about this property is that our navigating agent needs the ability to rotate in its current plane, as well as to translate, to make the task of returning to a given state tractable. We begin by presenting a model with translative movements but no rotational movements (i.e., T-MSOM model), and then introduce a model including orientational movements as well (i.e., TO-MSOM model).

2.3 T-MSOM

A basic model T-MSOM to learn representations of 3D objects based on translative movements and surface information is presented in the previous work [14,15].
Since orientational movements of a navigation agent are normally performed in
practice and without such kind of movements, an agent could not go back to the
start position with the same orientation, an improved and more practical model
with orientational movements considered is of significance. Meanwhile, because
objects generally do not have the differences among surfaces, to be more realistic,
the surface information included in T-MSOM model should be left out. What's
more, [14] presented the informal one test result about the effect of object asymmetry on the model's performance, while in the current paper, we present a
statistics and more systematic study of the effect and extend the analysis to
consider the effect of tactile landmarks on the object's surface.

3 Proposed Models

In this section, the proposed TO-MSOM and L-TO-MSOM model are presented.

3.1 TO-MSOM Model

By deleting the not always-existed surface difference information in T-MSOM
model and considering widely-performed orientational movements, TO-MSOM
model is developed and its architecture is shown in a blue frame in Fig. 4. As
illustrated in the figure, TO-MSOM model mainly consists of four parts: the
input, MSOM units, next action distribution and action selected. The input
to MSOM units is to simulate the circuit of object representations from the
somatosensory cortex to the parietal cortex, and the next action distribution to
action selected is to imitate the circuit from the premotor cortex to the motor
system. The details of such four parts are illustrated as below.

Algorithm 2. TO-MSOM model

Input: Constrained action sequences of the object to be explored and represented
Output: A representation of the object explored
  1: Randomly initialize the exploration starting position and orientation of the agent
  2: **while** training steps are not finished **do**
  3:    Input: input the executed constrained action
  4:    MSOM units: activate MSOM units to be responsive to the current input
  5:    Next action distribution: predict next possible actions allowed by the object
  6:    Action selected: select the most possible action allowed by the object and perform
  7: **end while**
  8: **return**

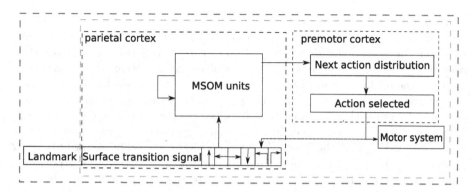

Fig. 4. Architectures of TO-MSOM model and L-TO-MSOM model for learning to represent 3D objects via translative movements (↑: move forward; ←: move left; →: move right and ↓: move back) and orientational movements (↰: rotate 90° counterclockwise and ↱: rotate 90° clockwise) together with the surface transition signal, where the blue frame shows the architecture of TO-MSOM model and the red frame illustrates the architecture of L-TO-MSOM model. (Color figure online)

Input. The input of TO-MSOM model is composed of the constrained action sequences, which is comprised of translative and orientational movements. Note that the bit of surface translation signal is to encode the difference between the movement of moving directly (that is, moving forward, left, right, back directly) and moving over the edge (that is, moving forward, left, right, back over the edge). The input part is to encode and simulate the obtained sensorimotor information from the peripheral sensors.

MSOM Units. The units in MSOM are driven to learn the frequently occurring action *sequences*, which are constrained by the object's topography. As pointed out above, starting from the same location and orientation, the navigation agent can lead to different locations and/or orientation by executing different action sequences. Therefore, with regard to one starting exploration location, each unit in MSOM comes to be responsive to one/many particular location(s) on the object via learning constrained action sequences. After training, given a particular MSOM activity pattern, the learning model could reconstruct or say predict the navigation agent's position owing to the learnt representation of such an object. Note that this MSOM units part aims to imitate neurons involved in the circuit of object representations fulfilled in the parietal cortex.

Next Action Distribution. Regarding each input at one time instance, there is an activity pattern in the MSOM, which denotes one particular location on the object. Based on the learnt representation of such an object, the model attempts to predict the next action possibly available to be preformed. In this model, the MSOM activity pattern is the input to a network, which is implemented by a multiple layer perceptron (MLP), and the output of MLP is the probability distribution of all actions predicted to be possibly performed.

Action Selected. After obtaining the possible action's probability distribution, the next action to be executed is then selected, which is based on the Boltzmann selection. Note that the selection procedure can be regulated by setting the selection decision policy involved in the Boltzmann selection. Regarding this model, if the navigation agent fails to execute one action to reach a new location for perceiving object's information, the probability of such an action is set to be zero, which implies that it cannot be selected for the next action to be performed. Moreover, in the model, for expediting the learning process, the navigation agent is commanded to find the boundary of the object as quickly as possible and therefore, the probability of the moving forward action is increased by a positive reinforced bias number. This part is to simulate the circuit of action selection performed in the premotor cortex.

After the next action to be performed is selected, an encoded signal of such an action is transferred to the motor system to perform. The performed action then leads the navigation agent to a different location, which gives rise to an update of the sensory information about the object and contributes to represent such an object. The flow diagram of the model is shown in Algorithm 2.

3.2 L-TO-MSOM Model

Landmarks in an environment are reported to have an effect on a navigation agent for exploring the environment, such as leading to remapping of the same environment and speeding up finishing a navigation task [9]. To investigate the effect of tactile landmarks on object representations, L-TO-MSOM model is developed with its architecture illustrated in the red frame in Fig. 4. Differing from TO-MSOM model, L-TO-MSOM model is not only activated by the constrained action sequences but also the landmarks on the object to be explored. The landmark in L-TO-MSOM model mainly denotes tactile landmarks, such as the temperature and texture differences among locations on the object. Since the implementation flow diagram of L-TO-MSOM model is similar to that of TO-MSOM model, it is omitted in the paper.

4   Simulation Results and Comparisons

To evaluate the effectivenesses of the proposed models and investigate effects of object asymmetries and landmarks on representing objects, two typical 3D objects–a $2 \times 2 \times 2$ cube and a $3 \times 2 \times 1$ cuboid–are assigned to be represented.

4.1   Effects of Object Asymmetries

To validate the effectiveness of TO-MSOM model for representing 3D objects as well as investigate the effect of encoding approach for the translative movements over the edge on the model, three kinds of TO-MSOM models, named TO-MSOM-1, TO-MSOM-2 and TO-MSOM-3, are assigned to explore the cube and cuboid with a random initial exploration position. Specifically, TO-MSOM-1 is the model using one bit of surface transition signal together with the four directly translative movement bits to denote the four translative over the edge movements (i.e., moving forward, left, right and back over the edge); TO-MSOM-2 is the model by utilizing four independent bits to denote such four translative over the edge movements, and TO-MSOM-3 is the model by using four bits of surface translation signal and four directly translative movement bits. Note that each model is to explore such two three objects for 30 sampled random tests/paths. Each test has 20 epochs and each epoch contains 100 exploration steps. The following results are based on statistics analysis of sampled 30 tests.

Table 1. Probability distribution of P_{max}, represented as $P_{max} \sim \mathcal{N}(\mu, \sigma^2)$ with μ and σ denoting the mean and standard deviation respectively, for TO-MSOM-1, TO-MSOM-2 and TO-MSOM-3 models when representing a cube and cuboid

Model	TO-MSOM-1	TO-MSOM-2	TO-MSOM-3
#Cube	$(6.59\%, 0.90\%^2)$	$(6.47\%, 0.66\%^2)$	$(6.63\%, 0.72\%^2)$
#Cuboid	$(11.19\%, 1.10\%^2)$	$(11.72\%, 1.20\%^2)$	$(11.26\%, 1.58\%^2)$

Table 2. 95% confidence interval of P_{max} for TO-MSOM-1, TO-MSOM-2 and TO-MSOM-3 models when representing a cube and cuboid

Model	TO-MSOM-1	TO-MSOM-2	TO-MSOM-3
#Cube	$[4.75\%, 8.43\%]$	$[5.12\%, 7.82\%]$	$[5.16\%, 8.10\%]$
#Cuboid	$[8.94\%, 13.44\%]$	$[9.27\%, 14.17\%]$	$[8.03\%, 14.49\%]$

To evaluate effectivenesses of the proposed model, a criterion P_{max} is introduced, which is defined as

$$P_{max} = \frac{T(\alpha = \beta)}{\phi}, \qquad (7)$$

where ϕ denotes a fixed size of a sliding window, $T(\cdot)$ denotes how many times a given event happened in a given window in the sliding window series, α denotes the probability of the actual agent position in the reconstructed probability distribution and β denotes the maximal value in the reconstructed probability distribution. Furthermore, another criterion $D_{geodesic}$ is also developed and defined as

$$D_{geodesic} = \sum_{i=1}^{m} \sum_{j=1}^{4} g(i, \delta) p_{ij}, \qquad (8)$$

where $g(i, \delta)$ denotes the geodesic distance between position i and the actual
agent position δ, m denotes the number of available exploration positions on
the object; $j = 1, 2, 3, 4$ is used to respectively denote North South East West
orientations; and p_{ij} denotes the probability of the agent being in location i and
with the particular j orientation in the reconstruction distribution. Regarding
details about such two criteria, please refer to [14, 15].

When exploring the cube and cuboid, the models' statistics probability dis-
tributions of $P_{\max} \sim \mathcal{N}(\mu, \sigma^2)$, with μ and σ denoting the mean and standard
deviation respectively, are illustrated in Table 1. From the table, we can see that
(1) the models have advantages in representing the cuboid over the cube, which
is owing to the additional asymmetry topography information of the cuboid; (2)
the models are effective on representing 3D objects; and (3) the encoding technique for translating over the edge movements does not make a difference on the
model's representing ability. Corresponding t-based 95% confidence intervals and
statistics means of $P_{\max}$ are shown in Table 2 and Fig. 5 respectively, which suggests the positive effect of asymmetry topography on TO-MSOM model's representing ability. Corresponding statistics probability distributions of D_{geodesic} for
TO-MSOM models are illustrated in Table 3, which further verifies the contributive effect of the asymmetry geometry. Note that the accuracy of TO-MSOM
model could be improved by adding other perceptual information, such as tactile landmarks (discussed later) and surface information (presented in [14]) or
by making the navigation agent articulated, which is more like mammals' hands
and can perceive and detect information on different surfaces of the object in
parallel.

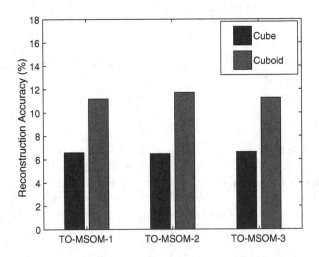

Fig. 5. Statistics means of $P_{\max}$ of TO-MSOM-1, TO-MSOM-2 and TO-MSOM-3 models when representing a cube and cuboid.

Table 3. Probability distribution of D_{geodesic}, represented as $D_{\text{geodesic}} \sim \mathcal{N}(\mu, \sigma^2)$ with μ and σ denoting the mean and standard deviation respectively, for TO-MSOM-1, TO-MSOM-2 and TO-MSOM-3 models when representing a cube and cuboid

Model	TO-MSOM-1	TO-MSOM-2	TO-MSOM-3
#Cube	$(2.48, 1.45\%^2)$	$(2.48, 1.18\%^2)$	$(2.48, 1.39\%^2)$
#Cuboid	$(2.39, 1.73\%^2)$	$(2.39, 1.81\%^2)$	$(2.38, 2.02\%^2)$

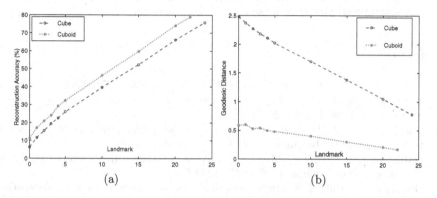

(a)   (b)

Fig. 6. Statistics means of $P_{\max}$ and D_{geodesic} for L-TO-MSOM model when representing a cube and cuboid.

4.2 Effects of Landmarks and Object Asymmetries

To investigate the effect of landmarks, L-TO-MSOM model is commanded to explore and represent the cube and cuboid. Similarly, each model with different numbers of landmarks explores such two 3D objects for 30 random tests/paths and the following results are based on the statistics analysis.

The statistics means of $P_{\max}$ and D_{geodesic} when L-TO-MSOM represents a cube and cuboid are illustrated in Fig. 6. As we can see from the figure, we can draw the conclusion that the simulation result validates (1) the effectiveness of the model for representing 3D objects; (2) the positive effect of landmarks on the model's learning representations ability; and (3) the superiority of a cuboid to a cube for representation due to the asymmetry topography of the cuboid.

5 Conclusion and Future Work

In the paper, TO-MSOM model activated by translative and orientational movements has been proposed to learn representations of 3D objects. To investigate the effect of landmarks as well as object asymmetries, L-TO-MSOM model activated by landmarks together with translative and orientational movements has been developed. Statistics simulative results of TO-MSOM model and L-TO-MSOM model for learning representations of two typical 3D objects– a $2 \times 2 \times 2$ cube and a $3 \times 2 \times 1$ cuboid–demonstrate that (1) the proposed models are effective on learning representations of 3D objects; (2) object asymmetries have a positive effect on representations; (3) landmarks also positively contribute to learn representations. Future work is to design a more realistic and practical model to learn representations of 3D objects with an articulated agent, which is to simulate human beings' hands and consists of multiple independently moving 'fingers' to compete and coordinate for achieving a task.

Acknowledgment. The authors would like to thank Martin Takac for the earlier work on a SOM-based navigation model.

References

1. Chafee, M.V., Averbeck, B.B., Crowe, D.A.: Representing spatial relationships in posterior parietal cortex: single neurons code object-referenced position. Cereb. Cortex **17**(12), 2914–2932 (2007)
2. Dar, H., Knott, A.: Learning and representing the spatial properties of objects via tactile exploration. Technical report OUCS-2018-01 (2018)
3. Ferbinteanu, J., Shapiro, M.L.: Prospective and retrospective memory coding in the hippocampus. Neuron **40**(6), 1227–1239 (2003)
4. Grossberg, S., Pilly, P.K.: How entorhinal grid cells may learn multiple spatial scales from a dorsoventral gradient of cell response rates in a self-organizing map. PLoS Comput. Biol. **8**(10), e1002648 (2012)
5. Ito, H.T., Zhang, S.J., Witter, M.P., Moser, E.I., Moser, M.B.: A prefrontal-thalamo-hippocampal circuit for goal-directed spatial navigation. Nature **522**(7554), 50 (2015)
6. Jamali, N., Ciliberto, C., Rosasco, L., Natale, L.: Active perception: building objects' models using tactile exploration. In: 2016 IEEE-RAS 16th International Conference on Humanoid Robots (Humanoids), pp. 179–185. IEEE (2016)
7. Jeffery, K.J., Wilson, J.J., Casali, G., Hayman, R.M.: Neural encoding of large-scale three-dimensional space–properties and constraints. Front. Psychol. **6**, 927 (2015)
8. Kohonen, T.: Self-organized formation of topologically correct feature maps. Biol. Cybern. **43**(1), 59–69 (1982)
9. Lozano, Y.R., Page, H., Jacob, P.Y., Lomi, E., Street, J., Jeffery, K.: Retrosplenial and postsubicular head direction cells compared during visual landmark discrimination. Brain Neurosci. Adv. **1** (2017). https://doi.org/10.1177/2398212817721859
10. McNaughton, B., Chen, L., Markus, E.: "Dead reckoning," landmark learning, and the sense of direction: a neurophysiological and computational hypothesis. J. Cogn. Neurosci. **3**(2), 190–202 (1991)
11. McNaughton, B.L., Battaglia, F.P., Jensen, O., Moser, E.I., Moser, M.B.: Path integration and the neural basis of the 'cognitive map'. Nat. Rev. Neurosci. **7**(8), 663–678 (2006)
12. Strickert, M., Hammer, B.: Merge SOM for temporal data. Neurocomputing **64**, 39–71 (2005)
13. Uchimura, M., Nakano, T., Morito, Y., Ando, H., Kitazawa, S.: Automatic representation of a visual stimulus relative to a background in the right precuneus. Eur. J. Neurosci. **42**(1), 1651–1659 (2015)

14. Yan, X., Knott, A., Mills, S.: A neural network model for learning to represent 3D objects via tactile exploration. In: Proceedings of the 40th Annual Conference of the Cognitive Science Society (2018)
15. Yan, X., Knott, A., Mills, S.: A neural network model for learning to represent 3D objects via tactile exploration: technical appendix. Technical report OUCS-2018-05 (2018)

Cyclist Trajectory Prediction Using Bidirectional Recurrent Neural Networks

Khaled Saleh[⊠], Mohammed Hossny, and Saeid Nahavandi

Institute for Intelligent Systems Research and Innovation (IISRI), Deakin University, Geelong, Australia
{kaboufar,mohammed.hossny,saeid.nahavandi}@deakin.edu.au

Abstract. Predicting a long-term horizon of vulnerable road users' trajectories such as cyclists become an inevitable task for a reliable operation of highly and fully automated vehicles. In the literature, this problem is often tackled using linear dynamics-based approaches based on recursive Bayesian filters. These approaches are usually challenged when it comes to predicting long-term horizon of trajectories (more than 1 sec). Additionally, they also have difficulties in predicting non-linear motions such as maneuvers done by cyclists in traffic environments. In this work, we are proposing two novel models based on deep stacked recurrent neural networks for the task of cyclists trajectories prediction to overcome some of the aforementioned challenges. Our proposed predictive models have achieved robust prediction results when evaluated on a real-life cyclist trajectories dataset collected using vehicle-based sensors in the urban traffic environment. Furthermore, our proposed models have outperformed other traditional approaches with an improvement of more than 50% in mean error score averaged over all the predicted cyclists' trajectories.

1 Introduction

Recently, the problem of intent and trajectory prediction of vulnerable road users (VRUs) has got more attention from the Advanced Driver Assistance Systems (ADAS) research community [8,10,18]. Furthermore, with the increased rate of testing highly and fully automated vehicles on our roads nowadays, the necessity for trustworthy predictive models that can deeply understand VRUs behaviors become inevitable [17]. Most of the work that has been done on the intent and trajectory prediction problem of VRUs were focused mainly on pedestrians. Other VRUs such as cyclists have not got the same attention because of their challenging behaviors which are hard to model especially from a moving vehicle. Until recently, there were almost no available datasets of cyclists observed from moving vehicles in a traffic environment, which was another hurdle for having such predictive models for cyclists. However, with the recent benchmark dataset for cyclist detection [11], it opened the way for the research community to build upon it for the trajectory prediction problem of the cyclists [13]. In the literature, the problem of intent and trajectory prediction of pedestrians in urban

© Springer Nature Switzerland AG 2018
T. Mitrovic et al. (Eds.): AI 2018, LNAI 11320, pp. 284–295, 2018.
https://doi.org/10.1007/978-3-030-03991-2_28

traffic environments was commonly approached through an explicit modeling of the dynamical motions done by the VRUs in the scene [8,18]. To this end, an initial motion model of the pedestrian is firstly classified and based on it a Bayesian recursive filtering stage is done accordingly for a short-term prediction of pedestrians' trajectories. Recently, data-driven approaches such as artificial neural networks have been also explored for the VRUs intent and trajectory prediction problem [5,16,20].

Unlike motion dynamics based approaches, data-driven approaches do not assume an explicit prior knowledge about the underlying motion done by the VRUs. However, they approach the problem in a rather holistic end-to-end fashion which was shown to be capable of generalizing across a wide range of traffic scenarios [16]. Thus, in this work we will be adopting the data-driven approach, in specific we will be utilizing a recurrent neural network (RNN)-based model for the cyclist trajectory prediction problem. Our proposed model will be exploiting the expressiveness of RNNs when it comes to model sequence-based data such as cyclists' trajectories. Given a short-time horizon of the cyclists' trajectories, it will infer their intentions by forecasting a long-term horizon of their future trajectories. The rest of this paper is organized as follows. In Sect. 2 a brief description of the work done in the literature related to the intent prediction will be described. A thorough description and discussion of our methodology will be covered in Sect. 3. Later, in Sect. 4, the experimental results of our proposed model against other baseline models will be presented. Finally, in Sect. 5, we summarize our paper.

2   Background

The intent and trajectory prediction problem of pedestrians has been studied in the literature. For the cyclists, however, the number of research that has been done on it is not as much as the pedestrians' work. In this section, we will give an overview of the work that has been done on the VRUs' trajectory prediction problem in general and its related work to our VRU of interest (i.e. cyclists).

2.1   Motion Modeling Approach

Most of the work on the VRUs intent and trajectory prediction were relying on modeling the dynamics of motion of VRUs in urban traffic environments. In [18], a dynamical motion model based on extended Kalman filter (EKF) was introduced for pedestrian trajectory prediction. In their proposed approach, given observed lateral positions of pedestrians from a vehicle-based stereo camera, they predict their trajectories over a short-term interval (less than 2 s). They relied in their approach on a various number of motion dynamics models such as constant acceleration (CA), constant velocity (CV) and constant turn (CT). In [10], another dynamical motion model was proposed as part of a dynamic Bayesian network (DBN). Their DBN incorporated prior information regarding the situational awareness of pedestrians of their surroundings as well as the contextual information of the traffic scene. Based on this prior information as a hidden variable on top of a switching linear dynamical system (SLDS), they can predict a short-term horizon of the pedestrians' trajectories in a specific traffic scenario. Their traffic scenario of interest was at a crossing where a pedestrian might intend to cross or continue walking beside the curb. Similar to [10], Pool et al. [13] recently pursued the same approach for the cyclist trajectory prediction problem using a stereo-based camera from a moving vehicle. They proposed two models; the first one is based on the standard Kalman filter (KF) with a CV underlying dynamical motion model for a linear cyclists' trajectory prediction. The other model is based on a mixture of five linear dynamical motion models based on KF as well.

2.2 Data-Driven Approach

On the other hand, Zernetsch et al. [20] proposed a data-driven approach based on multilayer perceptron neural network (MLP) in conjunction with a polynomial least-squares approximation. Their proposed model was able to forecast the future trajectory of cyclists in a traffic scene observed from a traffic camera mounted at an intersection. Their proposed MLP model consisted of one single layer and was trained using the approximated polynomials of different cyclists' movement types. In [16], another data-driven approach was also proposed for pedestrian trajectory prediction using the recurrent neural network architecture, long-short term memory (LSTM). Unlike traditional data-driven approaches based on MLP, the LSTM framework proposed in [16], was able to capture the temporal dependency exists in pedestrians' trajectories especially from a moving vehicle perspective. It provided a long-term prediction horizon (up to 4 secs) of the future pedestrians' trajectories. The LSTM approach achieved competitive small prediction errors in comparison to both the traditional MLP and the dynamical motion models approaches.

3   Proposed Methodology

Since the motion dynamics based approaches require an explicit modeling of the underlying motion model of the cyclists, thus it makes them more applicable only to specific scenarios. Moreover, motion dynamics based approaches were proved to be inefficient when it comes to predicting long-term horizons which are essential for a reliable fully and highly automated vehicles [17]. Given that, the data-driven approach becomes a more appealing approach for the cyclist trajectory prediction task.

3.1   Problem Formulation

The cyclists' trajectories are a series of consecutive measured positional information over a period of time $T_{1:N}$. Thus, we can formulate the cyclist's trajectory prediction problem as a sequence prediction task [2]. In this respective, given a few numbers of past positional observations of the cyclist trajectory at time t, a prediction of his/her position in the future from time $t + 1$ onward is to be inferred. The main advantage of such formulation is that it does not assume any underlying particular type of motion model of the cyclists. Additionally, in this formulation, longer prediction horizons can be reliably obtained [16]. In the following subsections, we will first go through one of the most successful data-driven approaches for predicting sequential-based tasks (i.e recurrent neural networks (RNN)). Then, we will discuss how we are utilizing one special variant of RNN for the task of cyclist trajectory prediction.

3.2 Predicting Sequential Data via RNN

Recently, a number of successful use cases for utilizing Recurrent Neural Networks (RNN) in sequence-based tasks were reported in the literature [1,3,6,15]. The main distinction between RNNs and traditional neural networks such as multilayer perceptron (MLP), is that RNNs can learn the temporal dependency exists in its sequential input data. RNNs can efficiently capture this dependency due to its internal feedback loop connection that makes it persist information over time. This internal feedback loop is called the hidden unit or the hidden state. Unfortunately, traditional RNNs can not memorize or keep track of its past hidden states for a much longer time. Thus, a number of enhanced RNN architectures were proposed in the literature to overcome the aforementioned problem [4]. One of the most commonly utilized RNN architectures is the Long Short-term Memory (LSTM) architecture [7]. The LSTM architecture replaces the basic hidden state of traditional RNNs with a base unit called memory block. Each memory block within LSTM can have one or more memory cells. For each memory cell, three gates (namely input, output and forget gates) are governing its operation. These three gates are commonly accessible by every memory cell inside the memory block of the LSTM. Each gate of the three gates is responsible for a certain task within the LSTM architecture. For instance, the input gate is responsible for updating the LSTM's memory state based on whether the input data have new information or not. While the forget gate is responsible for balancing the memory block load by throwing away non-useful information. On the other hand, the output gate is responsible for the final output from the LSTM's memory block based on the information from the input and the memory state. The following equations describe the operation of the LSTM's memory block (shown in Fig. 1) at each time step t:

$$f_t = sigm(W_{xf}x_t + W_{hf}h_{t-1} + W_{cf}c_{t-1} + b_f) \tag{1}$$

$$i_t = sigm(W_{xi}x_t + W_{hi}h_{t-1} + W_{ci}c_{t-1} + b_i) \tag{2}$$

$$c_t = f_t c_{t-1} + i_t \tanh(W_{xc}x_t + W_{hc}h_{t-1} + b_c) \tag{3}$$

$$o_t = sigm(W_{xo}x_t + W_{ho}h_{t-1} + W_{co}c_t + b_o) \tag{4}$$

$$h_t = o_t * \tanh(c_t) \tag{5}$$

where f_t, i_t, o_t and c_t are the activations for the forget, input, output and cell state gates at time t respectively. On the other hand, W_{*f}, W_{*i}, W_{*o}, W_{*c}, b_f, b_i, b_o, b_c are their respective weight matrices and variable biases. Additionally, x_t and h_t are the memory cell input and final output at time t.

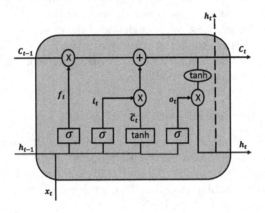

Fig. 1. LSTM memory block architecture (adopted from [12]).

It can be deduced from the previous equations, that the main basic building blocks governing all the operations of LSTM's memory block are comprised of a sigmoid layer with an element-wise multiplication operation. The sigmoid layer works in a way such as its input value is clipped into a value between [0, 1]. The lower bound value (i.e. 0) means the input data to it will not pass through. On the other hand, the upper bound (i.e. 1) means its input data will be passed through.

3.3 Bidirectional LSTM

The aforementioned architecture of LSTM with only one hidden unit (i.e. one memory block) is referred to in the literature as unidirectional LSTM (U-LSTM). There is another extension to this architecture and it is called bidirectional LSTM (B-LSTM) [19]. The main distinction between the two architectures is that in B-LSTM the input sequence data are processed in both forward and backward directions instead of the only forward direction of unidirectional LSTM. Thus, in B-LSTMs the two hidden layers from the two directions are connected to the same final output as shown in Fig. 2. The advantage of such two direction processing is that a higher level abstractions of sequential features can be learned as it was shown in [6]. Similar to U-LSTM, the output in B-LSTM is governed by the equations from (1)–(5). Whereas, the B-LSTM has two outputs, $\overrightarrow{h}$ for the forward layer and $\overleftarrow{h}$ for the backward layer. The final output from the B-LSTM memory block as shown in Fig. 2 at time step t is calculated according to the following:

$$y_t = \sigma(\overrightarrow{h_t}, \overleftarrow{h_t}) \tag{6}$$

where σ is a function to combine the output from the two inner LSTMs and it is usually implemented as a concatenation function.

3.4 Cyclist Trajectory Prediction via Stacked (B/U)-LSTM

The use of deep stacked LSTM layers (unidirectional or bidirectional) was shown recently in a number of sequence-based learning tasks to achieve higher accuracies in comparison to the shallow ones [1,3,6]. The reason for that is that the number of stacked hidden layers can build higher representation levels of understanding of the sequential data. As a result, it can be more effective in capturing the underlying temporal dependency of the sequence data. Thus, in this study, we will be adopting this paradigm for the cyclist trajectory prediction task. In this work, we are proposing two novel stacked LSTM models (B-LSTM and U-lSTM) for the task of cyclist trajectory prediction (shown in Fig. 3). The input sequence data to our two models will be a sequential positional data (lateral, longitudinal) u of the cyclists as observed from a vehicle-based stereo camera during the time period $T_{1:w}$. Where w is the windows size of the number of observations of the cyclists' positions. Given that as the input to our stacked models, a long-term prediction about the cyclists' future positions u from time T_w to time $T_{w+\delta}$ can be inferred. Where δ is the prediction horizon. Our proposed models will be consisting of two stacked LSTM layers (unidirectional & bidirectional) (as shown in Fig. 3).

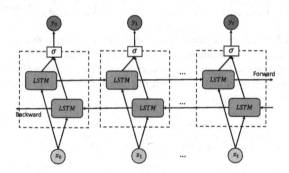

Fig. 2. Architecture of the bidirectional LSTM (B-LSTM) with its two inner forward and backward LSTM memory blocks unrolled over t time steps.

The input to these models is the aforementioned cyclists' sequential positions data. For the number of hidden units of the two stacked LSTM layers, we experimented with different parameters (32, 64, 128 and 256 respectively) using grid search and we found 128 to give the best performance. For the window size w of the sequential positional input, as a rule of thumb, the higher this number is the more the model will be able to capture the temporal dependency of the input data. However, since our predictive model is intended for predicting the future trajectories of cyclists from a moving vehicle perspective, therefore it needs to

provide an accurate prediction with the least possible number of sensor observations. Using grid search over parameters [1,3,5,8], we found that the effective
number of w to be 5. At the last layer of our proposed models, we have a fully
connected layer with one hidden unit that provides the next predicted position
of the cyclist at time T_{w+1}, given the past input position data from time $T_{1:w}$.
During the training, we are only using the next step ahead of the input position
sequential data as our target. However, at the testing/inference stage, we are
recursively predicting any variable prediction horizon δ determined at the inference time. Regarding the training of our proposed models, we were minimizing
the mean squared error (MSE) as our loss function during the training. The
MSE loss function is calculated according to the following:

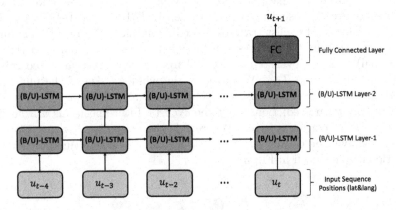

Fig. 3. Proposed framework for cyclist trajectory prediction based on stacked bidirectional LSTM (B-LSTM) or unidirectional (U-LSTM) architectures. The input to our
framework at time step t is five past observations $(u_{t-4:t})$ about cyclists' positions. The
output is the future cyclist position at the next time step ahead (u_{t+1}).

$$MSE = \frac{1}{N} \sum_{i=1}^{N} (\hat{Y}_i - Y_i)^2 \tag{7}$$

where N is the total number of training samples, $\hat{Y}_i$ and Y_i are the predicted
and target values for each training sample i, respectively. We utilized the Adam
algorithm [9] as our learning algorithm for optimizing the MSE loss function.
Adam is an extension of the traditional stochastic gradient descent algorithm [14]
but with less number of hyper-parameters which requires little tuning. As the
learning rate of Adam, we used value with 0.001. We trained proposed models
for total 500 epochs with a batch size of 64 training samples per each epoch.

4   Experiments

Throughout this section, we will first describe the dataset we used for training
and evaluating our proposed model. Then, we will give an overview of the prepa-

ration and preprocessing stage we have done on the data before feeding them as input to our models. Finally, we will compare the results of our models against a number of baseline approaches from the literature.

4.1 Data Description

In order to evaluate the performance of our proposed models, we utilized the recently published cyclist track dataset [13]. The dataset consists of cyclists tracks that were extracted at 5 fps from the TDC benchmark dataset [11]. Based on disparity maps and cyclists' bounding boxes annotations, the dataset creators obtained the sequence of lateral and longitudinal positions of the cyclists relative to the ego-vehicle. The dataset was further annotated with road topology which was used to determine the directions of the actual trajectories taken by the cyclists. There are five direction classes annotated in the dataset according to the cyclists' trajectory direction, namely: straight, 90°-right bend, 90°-left bend, 45°-right bend and 45°-left bend. Additionally, the extracted cyclists' tracks were also spatially aligned relative to the topology of the road and its intersections. The total number of cyclists tracks in the dataset are 119 trajectories (with 68 straight direction tracks, 17 90°-right, 16 90°-left, 10 45°-right and 8 45°-left). They further split all the trajectories in the dataset that have a straight direction label and last for more than 50 frames (10 s). As a result, the total number of the trajectories in the dataset becomes 134 trajectories in total.

Fig. 4. An example of annotated trajectories from the cyclist track dataset [13].

4.2 Data Preparation

Before feeding the extracted trajectories from the cyclist track dataset to our proposed framework. We firstly pre-process the trajectories to be in a format accessible by our stacked LSTM layers. Since the length distribution of the total 134 trajectories varies from 4 to 89 positional observations per trajectory. Thus, we firstly filtered out all trajectories with length less than 6 positional observations per trajectory, which resulted in a total number of 130 trajectories. Then, we run a sliding window of size 6 overall the trajectories. We chose a sliding window size of 6 because our proposed framework is expecting an input data of

Table 1. Performance of the different approaches over the cyclist track dataset according to the average mean error (in meters) evaluation metric. Our proposed approaches were evaluated over two different prediction horizons (5 or 15 steps ahead) of the cyclists' trajectories.

Approach	5 Steps Ahead (1 sec)					15 Steps Ahead (3 secs)				
	90° left	45° left	Straight	45° right	90° right	90° left	45° left	Straight	45° right	90° right
LDS [13]	1.75	1.15	1.19	1.23	2.36	-	-	-	-	-
U-MoLDS [13]	1.59	1.11	1.38	1.16	1.99	-	-	-	-	-
I-MoLDS [13]	1.51	1.10	1.20	1.08	1.88	-	-	-	-	-
MLP [20]	1.32	1.21	1.54	0.90	0.66	1.69	1.83	2.24	1.19	0.71
U-LSTM (proposed)	0.78	0.94	**0.78**	0.71	0.49	0.85	1.30	1.15	0.81	0.44
B-LSTM (proposed)	**0.41**	**0.91**	0.79	**0.36**	**0.24**	**0.67**	**1.13**	**1.15**	**0.69**	**0.40**

length (5) positional observations plus and an additional next (1) observation as our target data. The sliding window had an overlapping offset value of 1.

Given the small number of cyclists trajectories exist in the cyclist track dataset (only 130), we also similar to [13] adopted a Leave-One-Out (LOO) cross-validation technique to split training and testing data splits. In the LOO cross-validation, we train our proposed models on all the samples existing in the dataset except one sample we leave it for testing. We then iteratively, repeat the previous step by the number of the total samples (i.e 130), so that each sample in the dataset got tested by a model trained only on the unseen other samples of the dataset.

4.3   Results Analysis and Comparison

As we mentioned earlier, we used LOO as our cross-validation for evaluating the performance of our proposed models. In order to quantify the effectiveness of our proposed models, we used the average mean error similar to [13] as our evaluation metric over all the cyclists' trajectories. In Table 1, we present the results of our proposed two models (U-LSTM and B-LSTM) for the cyclist trajectory prediction task categorized based on the direction of the trajectories. We evaluated our models over two different prediction horizons, namely short-term one (1 sec or 5 steps ahead) and long-term one (3 secs or 15 steps ahead).

Furthermore, we compared the results of our proposed models against a number of baseline approaches that was utilized for trajectory prediction of VRUs in the literature. The first baseline model is the linear dynamical system (LDS) that was proposed in [13] for cyclist trajectory prediction. LDS is essentially a constant-velocity based Kalman filter similar to the one used in [18] for pedestrian trajectory prediction. The LDS estimates the Gaussian distribution of the future positions of the cyclists by recursively executing Kalman filter's predict step without its update step. As the name implies, LDS can only capture linear dynamics of motions done by the cyclists and will have harder times with non-linear motions.

The second baseline model is another model proposed by [13], which is referred to as an uninformed mixture of LDS (U-MoLDS). The U-MoLDS is combining 5 LDS models with different underlying dynamics according to the five directions labeled in the cyclist track dataset. The U-MoLDS approach is casting the motion direction of the cyclists as a latent variable with a uniform prior distribution that they are trying to estimate online. Hence, the name uninformed. At the inference time, both distributions of the cyclist's position and the direction latent variable are estimated based on past observations.

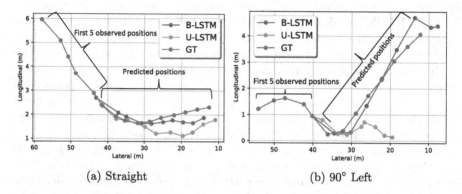

(a) Straight   (b) 90° Left

Fig. 5. Lateral and longitudinal future positions prediction of our proposed stacked LSTM models (B-LSTM&U-LSTM) over two different sample trajectories from the cyclist track dataset [13] in comparison to the ground truth (GT) trajectories. The prediction horizon of the predicted trajectories is 15 steps ahead (3 secs), however since the GT trajectories themselves have length less than 15, thus the predictions are clipped to match the GT length.

The third baseline approach, was also another model proposed in [13] and it achieved the best scores in their experiments, and it is referred to as Informed MoLDS (I-MoLDS). The I-MoLDS model is similar to U-MoLDS but with the exception that it relies on a prior information regarding the road topology (i.e. which direction existent in the cyclist trajectory). Thus, the prior distribution over the direction of the cyclist is set to zero for road directions that are not available in the topological labels of the cyclist's trajectories. On the other hand, the other directions have an equal distribution. Using this prior distribution with the past observations about the cyclists' trajectories, a mixture of Gaussians is estimated according to the 5 different LDS models.

The last baseline approach we are comparing against is a data-driven approach based on MLP. We implemented this model to mimic the one utilized in [20] for the cyclist trajectory prediction from observations of a surveillance camera at an intersection. Their MLP was consisting of only two layers with 20 hidden units in the first layer and 10 hidden units in the second layer.

As it is shown in Table 1, the four baseline approaches results are outlined in terms of the average mean error (in meters) of the predicted trajectories over two different prediction horizons (5 steps ahead and 15 steps ahead). It is worth noting here, that the results of the first three baseline approaches were adopted as they were reported in the author's paper in [13]. We have made sure that we are testing on their similar splits using the same technique for the cross-validation (i.e. LOO). For the MLP baseline approach, we implemented it with the same model specifications described in the author's paper in [20].

From Table 1, it can be shown that our proposed models (specifically the B-LSTM model) have achieved resilient results in terms of lower average mean error and longer prediction horizons (up to 3 secs ahead). Moreover, our proposed models have also outperformed both the motion dynamics based approaches (namely, LDS, U-MoLDS, and I-MoLDS) as well as other data-driven approaches (i.e. MLP) with significant margins. Our models have also shown higher accuracy in predicting the non-linear type of cyclists' trajectories (right/left 45/90), while on the contrary linear dynamics-based motion models were having a lot of challenges in predicting them. It is also worth mentioning that the best performing dynamics-based motion models (i.e. U-MoLDS and I-MoLDS) were having a prior information regarding the road topology while our proposed models did not have such information during training or testing phases.

Additionally, in order to show the prediction capabilities of our proposed models in Fig. 5 we are presenting the lateral and longitudinal predictions of the future trajectories of two sample cyclists trajectories over two different directions (straight and 90° left). As it can be seen, from the figures the B-LSTM model have more robust results in comparison to the U-LSTM model especially in the 90° left case. This is due to the expressiveness of bidirectional LSTM when it comes to modeling complex non-linear sequential data as we discussed in Sect. 3.3.

5   Conclusion

In this work, we have proposed two models based on stacked LSTM recurrent neural networks for the cyclist trajectory prediction task in urban traffic environments. The proposed models have shown resilient results in terms of long-term prediction horizons and lower mean prediction errors when evaluated on real cyclist trajectory dataset. Additionally, the proposed models have been compared against a number of the baseline approaches that have been proposed in the literature for VRUs trajectory prediction. Our models have shown significant improvements over these baseline approaches with more than 50% in mean error score averaged over all the tested cyclists' trajectories. Future directions would be to investigate adding more input information to our B-LSTM model such as semantic contextual information and inspect its performance.

References

1. Alahi, A., Goel, K., Ramanathan, V., Robicquet, A., Fei-fei, L., Savarese, S.: Social LSTM: human trajectory prediction in crowded spaces. In: CVPR (2016)
2. Clegg, B., Digirolamo, G., Keele, S.: Sequence learning. Trends Cogn. Sci. 2(8), 275–281 (1998)

3. Fragkiadaki, K., Levine, S., Felsen, P., Malik, J.: Recurrent network models for human dynamics. In: Proceedings of the IEEE International Conference on Computer Vision, pp. 4346–4354 (2015)
4. Gers, F.A., Schmidhuber, J., Cummins, F.: Learning to forget: continual prediction with LSTM. Neural Comput. **12**(10), 2451–2471 (2000)
5. Goldhammer, M., Köhler, S., Doll, K., Sick, B.: Camera based pedestrian path prediction by means of polynomial least-squares approximation and multilayer perceptron neural networks. In: SAI Intelligent Systems Conference (IntelliSys), 2015, pp. 390–399. IEEE (2015)
6. Graves, A.: Generating sequences with recurrent neural networks. arXiv preprint arXiv:1308.0850 (2013)
7. Hochreiter, S., Schmidhuber, J.: Long short-term memory. Neural Comput. **9**(8), 1735–1780 (1997)
8. Keller, C.G., Gavrila, D.M.: Will the pedestrian cross? A study on pedestrian path prediction. IEEE Trans. Intell. Transp. Syst. **15**(2), 494–506 (2014)
9. Kingma, D., Ba, J.: Adam: a method for stochastic optimization. arXiv preprint arXiv:1412.6980 (2014)
10. Kooij, J.F.P., Schneider, N., Flohr, F., Gavrila, D.M.: Context-based pedestrian path prediction. In: Fleet, D., Pajdla, T., Schiele, B., Tuytelaars, T. (eds.) ECCV 2014. LNCS, vol. 8694, pp. 618–633. Springer, Cham (2014). https://doi.org/10.1007/978-3-319-10599-4_40
11. Li, X., et al.: A new benchmark for vision-based cyclist detection. In: Intelligent Vehicles Symposium (IV), pp. 1028–1033. IEEE (2016)
12. Olah, C.: Understanding LSTM networks (2015). http://colah.github.io/posts/2015-08-Understanding-LSTMs/
13. Pool, E.A., Kooij, J.F., Gavrila, D.M.: Using road topology to improve cyclist path prediction. In: Intelligent Vehicles Symposium (IV), pp. 289–296. IEEE (2017)
14. Rumelhart, D.E., Hinton, G.E., Williams, R.J.: Learning representations by backpropagating errors. Nature **323**(6088), 533 (1986)
15. Saleh, K., Hossny, M., Nahavandi, S.: Driving behavior classification based on sensor data fusion using LSTM recurrent neural networks. In: 2017 IEEE 20th International Conference on Intelligent Transportation Systems (ITSC). IEEE (2017)
16. Saleh, K., Hossny, M., Nahavandi, S.: Intent prediction of vulnerable road users from motion trajectories using stacked LSTM network. In: 2017 IEEE International Conference on Intelligent Transportation Systems Conference (ITSC). IEEE (2017)
17. Saleh, K., Hossny, M., Nahavandi, S.: Towards trusted autonomous vehicles from vulnerable road users perspective. In: 2017 Annual IEEE International on Systems Conference (SysCon), pp. 1–7. IEEE (2017)
18. Schneider, N., Gavrila, D.M.: Pedestrian path prediction with recursive Bayesian filters: a comparative study. In: Weickert, J., Hein, M., Schiele, B. (eds.) GCPR 2013. LNCS, vol. 8142, pp. 174–183. Springer, Heidelberg (2013). https://doi.org/10.1007/978-3-642-40602-7_18
19. Schuster, M., Paliwal, K.K.: Bidirectional recurrent neural networks. IEEE Trans. Signal Process. **45**(11), 2673–2681 (1997)
20. Zernetsch, S., Kohnen, S., Goldhammer, M., Doll, K., Sick, B.: Trajectory prediction of cyclists using a physical model and an artificial neural network. In: Intelligent Vehicles Symposium (IV), pp. 833–838. IEEE (2016)

Constraints and Search

Diversified Late Acceptance Search

Majid Namazi[1,2], Conrad Sanderson[2,3(✉)], M. A. Hakim Newton[1],
Md Masbaul Alam Polash[1], and Abdul Sattar[1]

[1] Griffith University, Brisbane, Australia
[2] Data61, CSIRO, Sydney, Australia
conrad.sanderson@data61.csiro.au
[3] University of Queensland, Brisbane, Australia

Abstract. The well-known Late Acceptance Hill Climbing (LAHC) search aims to overcome the main downside of traditional Hill Climbing (HC) search, which is often quickly trapped in a local optimum due to strictly accepting only non-worsening moves within each iteration. In contrast, LAHC also accepts worsening moves, by keeping a circular array of fitness values of previously visited solutions and comparing the fitness values of candidate solutions against the least recent element in the array. While this straightforward strategy has proven effective, there are nevertheless situations where LAHC can unfortunately behave in a similar manner to HC. For example, when a new local optimum is found, often the same fitness value is stored many times in the array. To address this shortcoming, we propose new acceptance and replacement strategies to take into account worsening, improving, and sideways movement scenarios with the aim to improve the diversity of values in the array. Compared to LAHC, the proposed Diversified Late Acceptance Search approach is shown to lead to better quality solutions that are obtained with a lower number of iterations on benchmark Travelling Salesman Problems and Quadratic Assignment Problems.

Keywords: Local search · Late Acceptance · Diversification

1 Introduction

Local search algorithms are typically efficient and scalable approaches to solve large instances of real world optimisation problems [9,13]. Such algorithms use the following overall approach: starting from an *initial solution*, iteratively move from one solution to another, with the aim to eventually arrive at a good solution. The initial solution is often generated randomly or by using a specialised method. Then, in each iteration, a *candidate solution* is obtained by modifying the *current solution* using a *perturbation method*. If the candidate solution in a given iteration satisfies a given *acceptance criterion*, it is used as the starting point for the next iteration. Otherwise, the current solution in the given iteration becomes the starting point for the next iteration. The traditional Hill Climbing (HC) approach is a local search method that strictly uses a greedy strategy as its

© Springer Nature Switzerland AG 2018
T. Mitrovic et al. (Eds.): AI 2018, LNAI 11320, pp. 299–311, 2018.
https://doi.org/10.1007/978-3-030-03991-2_29

acceptance criterion [3]. HC accepts the candidate solution only if its fitness value is better (smaller in minimisation problems and larger in maximisation problems) than that of the current solution. This greedy strategy typically leads the search to quickly being trapped in a local optimum.

An important challenge in designing a local search algorithm is to find a good balance between interleaving *diversification* and *intensification* phases during search [13]. *Diversification* means exploring the solution space as widely as possible, with the intent of ideally finding a globally optimum solution. In contrast, *intensification* means improving the current solution in order to converge to the best local solution as quickly as possible. The perturbation method as well as the acceptance criterion need to take this balancing issue into account. As HC does not explore solutions that are worse than the current solution in each iteration, HC uses a very high level of intensification at the cost of very low level of diversification. Overall, the HC algorithm converges quickly to a local optimum, but the quality of its solutions is often not high [6,7]. Diversification strategies are hence necessary to provide better solutions.

There are well-studied acceptance criteria that, with the aim to avoid or escape local optima, also accept worsening moves, rather than simply accepting only better candidate solutions. Simulated Annealing (SA) [14] uses a stochastic acceptance criterion, where worsening moves are accepted with a probability based on the difference in the fitness values of the current solution and the candidate solution, with the probability exponentially diminishing over time. Threshold Acceptance (TA) [11] is a deterministic acceptance criterion, which accepts worsening moves if the difference in the fitness values of the current and the candidate solution is below a given threshold. The Great Deluge Algorithm (GDA) [10,16,17] accepts worsening moves if the fitness value of the candidate solution is below a given level. Each of the above acceptance criteria has a parameter whose *initial value* and a *variation schedule* must be defined beforehand. Unfortunately, obtaining a suitable initial value and variation schedule is difficult to achieve, and is often problem domain dependent and/or problem instance dependent [5,7,16]. This can make practical use of SA, TA and GDA quite finicky.

In contrast to the above approaches, Late Acceptance Hill Climbing (LAHC) search [6,7] is a relatively straightforward technique which deterministically accepts worsening moves and has no complicated parameters. An array with a predefined length stores the fitness values of previously visited solutions. Fitness values of candidate solutions are compared against the least recent element in the array. Since the fitness values from previous iterations can be worse than that of the current solution, a candidate solution that is worse than the current solution can be accepted. As the search progresses, the array is deterministically updated with fitness values of new solutions. The use of the fitness array thus brings about search diversity. The larger the length of the array, the better the diversity level. Overall, LAHC exhibits better diversification in terms of the explored solutions and provides solutions which typically have higher quality than HC [6,7]. Moreover, LAHC has been successful in several optimisation competitions [2,19], and has been used in real world applications [18].

Despite the promising aspects of LAHC, in this work we observe that there are situations where LAHC can unfortunately behave in a similar manner to HC, even when using a large fitness array. For example, when the same fitness value is stored many times in the array, particularly when a new local optimum is found. In this case, the fitness values in the array are iteratively replaced with the new local optimum fitness value, thereby reducing diversity.

To address the above shortcoming, we propose a new search approach termed Diversified Late Acceptance Search (DLAS). With the aim to improve the overall diversity of the search, the approach uses: (i) a new acceptance strategy which increases diversity of the accepted solutions, and (ii) a new replacement strategy to improve the diversity of the values in the fitness array by taking worsening, improving, and sideways movement scenarios into account.

Section 2 overviews the LAHC algorithm and discusses its problems. Section 3 presents the proposed DLAS algorithm. Section 4 provides comparative evaluations on benchmark Travelling Salesman Problems (TSPs) and Quadratic Assignment Problems (QAPs). The main findings are summarised in Sect. 5.

2 Late Acceptance Hill Climbing

Local search algorithms start from an *initial solution* S_0. The current solution S_k in each iteration k is then modified by a given perturbation method M to generate a new candidate solution $S_k' = M(S_k)$. Next, using a given *acceptance criterion* $\mathcal{A}$, the candidate solution S_k' is either accepted or rejected, meaning either $S_{k+1} = S_k'$ if $\mathcal{A}(k) = $ true, or $S_{k+1} = S_k$ if $\mathcal{A}(k) = $ false. Assume F_k and F_k' denote the fitness values of solutions S_k and S_k', respectively. For convenience, we assume *minimisation problems*, where one solution is *better* than the other if fitness value of the former is less than that of the latter. In HC, $\mathcal{A}(k) = $ true iff $F_k' \leq F_k$, and so $F_k \geq F_{k+1}$ for all $k \geq 0$. Hence HC accepts only non-worsening moves, i.e., sideways moves or improving moves.

The most recent version of LAHC [7] accepts candidate solution S_k' if its fitness value F_k' is better than or equal to the fitness value F_k of the current solution S_k, as in HC. Furthermore, for a given *history length* L, candidate solution S_k' is accepted if its fitness value F_k' is better than the fitness value F_{k-L} of the then current solution S_{k-L} at iteration $k - L \geq 0$. In other words, $\mathcal{A}(k) = F_k' \leq F_k$ or $F_k' < F_{k-L}$ for $k \geq L$. Since F_{k-L} is usually (not always as in HC) greater than F_k, the candidate solution S_k' can be accepted at iteration $k \geq L$, even if $F_k' > F_k$. LAHC thus accepts worsening moves like TA and GDA and thereby aims to avoid or escape from local minima. Overall, LAHC exhibits better diversification level with a larger L [4, 7], as this allows comparison with further earlier solutions which are most likely further worse as well.

Figure 1 shows the pseudo code for LAHC. To achieve memory efficiency, a circular *fitness array* Φ of size L stores fitness values of previous L solutions. Initially all values in Φ are set to the initial F, i.e., F_0 (line 4). Note that F, F', S and S' at each iteration k in Fig. 1 correspond to F_k, F_k', S_k and S_k', respectively. A candidate solution S' is accepted if $F' \leq F$ or $F' < \Phi[l]$ where $l = k \bmod L$ (lines 9–10). The value in $\Phi[l]$ is replaced by F whenever $F < \phi[l]$ (lines 13–14).

2.1 Problems with LAHC

We have empirically observed that for some problems LAHC unfortunately behaves in a similar manner to HC and does not accept worsening moves. Figures 3 and 4 show typical search progress trend while solving the benchmark U1817 TSP instance (see Sect. 4 for TSP details). A similar pattern is seen in other benchmark instances. For a small value of L, LAHC is quickly trapped in a local optimum, leading to poor quality solutions. Even using restart techniques may not help to obtain higher quality solutions [4,7]. For larger values of L the search is less prone to trapping, but this comes at the cost of slow convergence speed; the solution quality can be poor if not enough time is allotted. This characteristic of LAHC makes it less useful for applications in time-constrained systems where a high-quality solution must be found quickly.

The poor performance of LAHC is due to the following reasoning. Consider the LAHC algorithm in Fig. 1. Assume that in a given iteration, all the values in the fitness array Φ are equal to the fitness value F_* of a newly found best solution S_*, where S_* is a hard-to-improve or a local optimum solution. This happens when a new overall best solution S_* with fitness value F_* is found and F remains to be equal to F_* for at least L consecutive iterations. In this case, no worsening moves with larger fitness values than F_* will be accepted anymore,

```
1  proc LAHC
2    Initialise curr solution S, compute F
3    Specify length L for fitness array Φ
4    forall l ∈ [0, L), Φ[l] ← F
5    k ← 0, S* ← S, F* ← F        // best S*
6    while termination-criteria    // iter k
7      S' ← M(S), compute F'  // perturb
8      l ← k mod L
9      if F' ≤ F or F' < Φ[l]
10        S ← S', F ← F'           // accept
11       if F < F*
12          S* ← S, F* ← F       // new best
13       if F < Φ[l]
14          Φ[l] ← F             // replace in Φ
15     k ← k + 1
16   return S*, F*
```

```
1  proc DLAS
2    Initialise curr solution S, compute F
3    Specify length L for fitness array Φ
4    forall l ∈ [0, L), Φ[l] ← F
5    Φmax ← F, N ← L
6    k ← 0, S* ← S, F* ← F        // best S*
7    while termination-criteria    // iter k
8      F⁻ ← F                     // previous
9      S' ← M(S), compute F' // perturb
10     l ← k mod L
11     if F' = F or F' < Φmax
12        S ← S', F ← F'          // accept
13      if F < F*
14         S* ← S, F* ← F        // new best
15      if F > Φ[l]
16         Φ[l] ← F              // replace in Φ
17      else if F < Φ[l] and F < F⁻
18         if Φ[l] = Φmax
19            N ← N - 1          // decrement
20         Φ[l] ← F              // replace in Φ
21         if N = 0
22            compute Φmax, N  // recompute
23     k ← k + 1
24   return S*, F*
```

Fig. 1. Late Acceptance Hill Climbing (LAHC) algorithm, adapted from [7].

Fig. 2. Proposed Diversified Late Acceptance Search (DLAS).

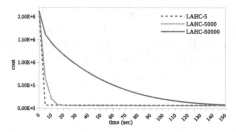

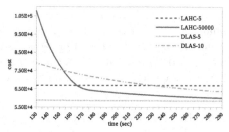

Fig. 3. Search progress for the first 150 s while solving the benchmark U1817 TSP instance via LAHC with $L \in \{5, 5000, 50000\}$. Further progress is shown in Fig. 4. (To aid clarity, results for DLAS are not shown as they effectively cover LAHC with $L=5$ at the given scale.)

Fig. 4. Search progress of LAHC and DLAS with various L values in later iterations of solving the U1817 instance. LAHC with $L=5$ converges quicker than LAHC with $L=50000$, but obtains a worse solution. DLAS with $L=5$ obtains a better solution than LAHC. Furthermore, DLAS with $L=5$ converges much quicker than LAHC with $L=50000$.

and if S_* is a local optimum then the search is trapped in that solution. Clearly, this is the situation HC reaches when it is trapped in a local optimum. In Sect. 4 we show that even when using a large value for L, LAHC behaves like HC in solving many problems in a large proportion of the iterations.

3   Proposed Diversified Late Acceptance Search

We propose a new search approach that aims to obtain high diversity level and high convergence speed, all while not suffering from the abovementioned drawbacks of LAHC. We have termed the proposed method as Diversified Late Acceptance Search (DLAS). We overview the approach as follows. We aim to keep or obtain larger fitness values in the fitness array when the search encounters non-improving moves (diversification). Furthermore, we cautiously replace large fitness values with small values when the search accepts improving moves (intensification). Lastly, our acceptance criterion is more relaxed than LAHC (diversification).

3.1   Acceptance Strategy

Comparing the fitness values of the candidate solutions with a larger value than $\Phi[l]$ (with $l = k \bmod L$) arguably increases diversity of accepted solutions. Our acceptance strategy is to compare the fitness value F' of the candidate solution S' in each iteration k with the maximum fitness value in the fitness array Φ, instead of comparing it just with $\Phi[l]$. The new candidate solution S' would be accepted if $F' = F$ or $F' < \Phi_{\max}$, i.e., the maximum value in the fitness array Φ. The first condition allows accepting new candidate solutions with fitness values equal to $\Phi_{\max}$ when all the values in Φ are the same, especially in the initial and final iterations of the search. Accepting candidate solutions with smaller fitness values than $\Phi_{\max}$ in other iterations increases the level of acceptable worsening moves and thereby increases the diversity level of the search. Section 3.3 shows how to efficiently find and maintain the maximum value in Φ.

3.2   Replacement Strategy

Our proposed replacement strategy has two parts. In the first part, if the fitness value F of the new current solution S is larger than $\Phi[l]$, the value in $\Phi[l]$ is always replaced by F. Such a replacement is avoided in the most recent version of LAHC to increase intensification of the search. However, this replacement increases the probability of accepting more worsening moves in future iterations and thereby can result in better final solutions. In the second part, if F is smaller than $\Phi[l]$, the replacement must be done just when F is smaller than the previous value of F as well. Such a replacement strategy avoids replacing other large values in the fitness array in a series of consecutive steps if the search falls in a plateau or local optimum.

We note that the combination of the above two replacement approaches is new and is different from replacing just in acceptance or just in improving moves. An illustration of the proposed method, especially the replacement strategy, is given in Sect. 3.4.

3.3   Diversified Late Acceptance Search

Figure 2 shows the pseudo code for the proposed method using the above acceptance and replacement strategies. Variables $\Phi_{\max}$ and N in Fig. 2 are respectively always equal to the maximum value in the fitness array and the number of occurrences of that value in the array. In line 5, $\Phi_{\max}$ and N are initialised by F and L. In every iteration in line 8, F^- holds the previous value of F. In line 11, new candidate solution S' is accepted if $F' = F$ or $F' < \Phi_{\max}$. In line 15, if $F > \Phi[l]$, replacement is made. Otherwise, in line 17, if $F < \Phi[l]$ and $F < F^-$, replacement is made. However, before making the replacement this time, if $\Phi[l]$ is equal to $\Phi_{\max}$, N is decremented by one. In line 21, if N is zero, the values of $\Phi_{\max}$ and N are recomputed by checking all the values in the fitness array.

3.4   DLAS Replacement Scenarios

Figure 5 shows eight possible combinations of values of F, F^- and $\Phi[l]$ compared to each other and corresponding replacement rules.

Worsening Moves. In cases (1)–(3) in Fig. 5, worsening moves take place. In case (1), the fitness value of the new current solution F is still smaller than $\Phi[l]$. In this case, contrary to LAHC, replacement is not allowed in the proposed DLAS method. This avoidance of replacement actually preserves the large values

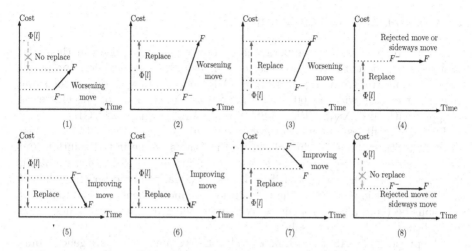

Fig. 5. All possible combinations of values of F, F^- and $\Phi[l]$ compared to each other and corresponding replacement rules in the proposed DLAS approach. See the text for details.

in the fitness array Φ when DLAS does not improve the current solutions in some consecutive iterations, and at the same time the fitness values of the new worse solutions are not larger than the corresponding values in the fitness array Φ. In cases (2) and (3), the fitness value of the new current solution F is greater than $\Phi[l]$. In both these cases, contrary to LAHC, replacement is allowed in DLAS to increase diversity of values in the fitness array Φ.

Improving Moves. In cases (5)–(7), improving moves take place. In cases (5) and (6), the fitness value of the new current solution F is smaller than $\Phi[l]$. In both these cases, as in LAHC, replacement is allowed to optimistically increase the intensification of the search. In case (7), the fitness value of the new current solution F is still greater than $\Phi[l]$. Contrary to LAHC, replacement is allowed in DLAS to increase diversity of values in the fitness array.

Sideways Moves or Rejected Moves. In cases (4) and (8), there are two possible outcomes: a candidate solution is not accepted, or a sideways move occurs. In case (4), the fitness values of the previous and the new current solutions, i.e., F^- and F, are greater than $\Phi[l]$. In this case, contrary to LAHC, replacement is allowed in DLAS to increase diversity of the accepted solutions in future iterations. In case (8), the fitness values of the previous and the new current solutions are smaller than $\Phi[l]$. In this case, contrary to LAHC, replacement is not allowed in DLAS. This avoidance of replacement actually avoids replacing all the values in the fitness array Φ in consecutive iterations when DLAS falls in a plateau or local optimum.

4   Comparative Evaluation

In this section we evaluate the performance of the proposed DLAS method, the most recent version of LAHC (as described in Sect. 2), and the recently proposed Step Counting Hill Climbing (SCHC) [8]. All experiments were ran on the same computing cluster with a 500 Mb memory limit. Each node of the cluster is equipped with Intel Xeon CPU E5-2670 processors running at 2.6 GHz.

In SCHC a fitness bound and a counter limit are used instead of a fitness array. The fitness bound is initialised by the fitness of the initial solution and the counter limit is similar to the length of the fitness array. In each iteration, a candidate solution is accepted if its fitness is equal to or better than that of the current solution or better than the fitness bound. Whenever the number of iterations becomes a factor of the counter limit, the fitness bound is made equal to the fitness of the current solution.

The proposed DLAS algorithm, as well as LAHC and SCHC, are general purpose local search algorithms for solving any optimisation problem. Hence, we use sets of Travelling Salesman Problems (TSPs) and Quadratic Assignment Problems (QAPs) just to compare the relative performance of the three algorithms, and not to improve the best known solutions for the individual problems.

4.1   Time Cutoff and Fitness Array Length

To provide a fair comparison, we use time cutoff as the stopping condition. However, as each instance has its own size and complexity level, we decided to solve all of them first with LAHC using a reasonably large fitness array size L. We initially performed 50 runs of the LAHC algorithm (with L=50000) on each instance, with the stopping condition as getting trapped in a local optimum for at least 10% of the total running time. Then we took the longest running time across the 50 runs as the cutoff time for each instance. We then ran all three algorithms with just the cutoff time as the stopping condition 50 times for each unique value for L.

The reported results in the following subsections are the averages of 50 runs on each instance using the best performing value for L. For example, Fig. 4 compares LAHC and DLAS algorithms in the later steps of solving U1817 TSP instance using various values for L. The figure shows that given 290 s as the cutoff time for this instance, L=50000 and L=5 are the best values for LAHC and DLAS algorithms, respectively.

4.2   Experiments on TSP Instances

Every TSP instance includes a set of cities or points on a map. The cities are all connected with each other by symmetric roads of given distances or lengths. The goal of solving such a TSP instance is to find the shortest closed tour that includes all the cities such that every city is visited exactly once. We took all the symmetric Euclidean distance TSP instances with 1,000 to 10,000 cities from the well-known TSPLIB benchmark dataset at http://comopt.ifi.uni-heidelberg.de/

Table 1. Results on TSP instances for LAHC and SCHC with L=50000, and DLAS with L=5. In the first column, the size of each instance is the number in the name of the instance, which indicates the number of cities. The 2nd column is the best known solution cost reported in the literature. The 3rd column is the time cutoff value used by all methods. The 4th column shows the deviations of the best solution cost from the best known solution cost. The 5th column shows the time spent by each algorithm to find the best solution. The 6th column shows percentage of iterations in which each algorithm undesirably behaves like HC. Shading denotes winning numbers where the differences are statistically significant.

Instance name	Best known sol. cost	Time cutoff	Dev. from the best known solution			Time to find the last best sol.			% of iterations behaving like HC		
			LAHC	SCHC	DLAS	LAHC	SCHC	DLAS	LAHC	SCHC	DLAS
Dsj1000	18659688	100	924536	705626	**339555**	80	66	52	21	36	0
Pr1002	259045	120	6265	6552	**4795**	78	63	51	37	47	0
U1060	224094	150	4560	5647	**4193**	84	68	55	45	54	0
Vm1084	239297	155	**5884**	6593	5927	79	65	51	51	60	0
Pcb1173	56892	160	1910	2118	**1306**	81	77	49	52	52	0
D1291	50801	165	2612	1856	**1404**	111	88	93	35	49	0
Nrw1379	56638	177	2024	2159	**1180**	117	93	90	37	51	0
Fl1400	20127	180	**290**	324	901	116	92	33	43	57	0
U1432	152970	200	3513	4139	**2022**	125	114	176	45	55	0
Fl1577	22249	250	**466**	524	634	153	139	108	50	57	0
D1655	62128	270	2424	2464	**1550**	153	120	160	43	59	0
Vm1748	336556	280	10328	11009	**8967**	163	125	173	45	59	0
U1817	57201	290	2320	2461	**1450**	189	146	244	41	59	0
D2103	80450	309	5846	6137	**2660**	194	161	279	39	47	0
U2152	64253	320	2598	2956	**1350**	211	198	292	46	51	0
U2319	234256	350	3625	3837	**2557**	258	228	347	45	56	0
Pr2392	378032	370	19557	16025	**9003**	238	167	274	40	58	0
Pcb3038	137694	521	6530	7118	**3116**	324	267	384	42	51	0
Fl3795	28772	1110	1542	1547	**1202**	802	769	666	65	72	0
Fnl4461	182566	1150	9607	10558	**3978**	454	419	940	62	69	0
Rl5915	565530	1200	36974	39929	**19232**	718	613	1198	48	59	0
Rl5934	556045	1320	35718	38535	**34863**	812	664	814	46	60	0
Pla7397	23260728	2545	962561	990251	**916947**	1926	1818	2542	59	70	0

software/TSPLIB95/. We used the same source code and the same perturbation heuristic provided by the authors of [7] for solving the TSP instances. The perturbation heuristic randomly divides a given tour into two parts and then reverses one part [15].

Table 1 shows the results on TSP instances using LAHC and SCHC with L=50000 and DLAS with L=5. The size of each instance is the number in the name of the instance, which indicates the number of cities. In 20 out of 23 instances, the proposed DLAS method with L=5 has found better solutions than both LAHC and SCHC with L=50000. In 17 of those instances the differences are statistically significant based on t-test with the confidence level of 0.95. The results also show that in small instances (with small number of cities), DLAS finds better solutions in less time, while in large instances it does not get trapped in a local optimum quickly and continues to search for a better solution. For

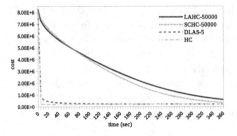 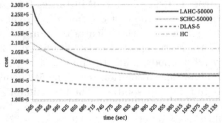

Fig. 6. Search progress for the first 360 s while solving the benchmark Fnl4461 TSP instance via HC, LAHC and SCHC with L=50000, and DLAS with L=5.

Fig. 7. As per Fig. 6, but in later iterations. The proposed DLAS approach obtains a better solution than HC, LAHC and SCHC. Furthermore, DLAS converges quicker than LAHC.

example, for the largest instance in the last line of the table with the time cutoff of 2545 s, LAHC and SCHC are quickly trapped in a local optimum and cannot improve their last found solutions. In contrast, the proposed DLAS method continues to improve its solutions until almost the end of the cutoff time.

The results also show that even when using a very large value for L in LAHC and SCHC, in about half of the iterations (especially for large instances), LAHC and SCHC undesirably behave like HC. This includes iterations in which the maximum value in the fitness array in LAHC and the fitness bound in SCHC are equal to the last found best solution. In contrast, the percentage of iterations in which DLAS behaves like HC is zero. In other words, even when using very small fitness arrays, there is always room for worsening moves to be accepted by DLAS. This indicates that the combination of the new acceptance and replacement strategies in DLAS is more effective in increasing the diversity level of the search than just increasing the length of the fitness array.

Figures 6 and 7 show that DLAS with L=5 has a high convergence speed (due to the small fitness array size) and converges almost as fast as HC. It also shows that DLAS with L=5 ends up with a better solution than LAHC and SCHC with L=50000, and HC for the Fnl4461 instance.

4.3 Experiments on QAP Instances

Every QAP instance includes two same-size sets of locations and facilities. The locations are all connected with each other by symmetric links of given distances or lengths. There is a flow between every pair of facilities with a given weight. The goal of solving such a QAP instance is assigning each facility to a location such that the sum of weights of flows between every two facilities multiplied by the distances between their assigned locations is minimised.

We took all QAP instances with at least 80 locations and facilities from the well-known QAPLIB benchmark dataset at http://anjos.mgi.polymtl.ca/qaplib/. We used the same source code and the same perturbation heuristic provided in http://mistic.heig-vd.ch/taillard/ for solving the QAP instances. The

Table 2. Results on QAP instances for LAHC and SCHC with L=50000, and DLAS with L=10. The size of each instance is the number in the name of the instance, which indicates the number of locations or facilities. Explanations for the other columns are as per Table 1.

Instance name	Best known sol. cost	Time cutoff	Dev. from the best known solution			Time to find the last best sol.			% of iterations behaving like HC		
			LAHC	SCHC	DLAS	LAHC	SCHC	DLAS	LAHC	SCHC	DLAS
Lipa80a	253195	20	1607	1564	**1411**	14	11	8	1.3	0.3	**0.0**
Tai80a	13499184	21	330957	354263	**264177**	15	12	15	0.5	0.0	**0.0**
Lipa80b	7763962	26	39769	190699	**0**	22	17	8	8.0	28.5	**0.0**
Tai80b	818415043	27	4227835	**3574665**	979737	20	17	6	8.1	16.8	**0.0**
Sko81	90998	24	222	178	**113**	19	16	5	4.7	14.8	**0.0**
Lipa90a	360630	23	2045	2024	**1893**	19	15	13	0.0	1.0	**0.0**
Lipa90b	12490441	36	51015	20709	**0**	29	22	11	15.0	33.2	**0.0**
Dre90	1838	35	1575	1615	**1450**	16	12	8	0.0	6.3	**0.0**
Sko90	115534	28	321	310	**219**	26	21	8	1.2	10.0	**0.0**
Sko100a	152002	40	**190**	239	218	32	25	11	4.6	16.8	**0.0**
Tai100a	21052466	35	460894	486157	**378092**	23	18	29	0.0	0.9	**0.0**
Sko100b	153890	52	175	173	**160**	30	24	10	9.3	16.0	**0.0**
Tai100b	1185996137	55	**2711882**	2823207	5124004	34	29	13	12.6	38.3	**0.0**
Sko100c	147862	42	147	132	**121**	32	26	11	6.6	15.6	**0.0**
Sko100d	149576	42	**241**	246	245	30	24	10	10.7	23.8	**0.0**
Sko100e	149150	42	**150**	165	156	31	25	10	5.8	19.7	**0.0**
Sko100f	149036	42	237	232	**204**	33	26	11	7.7	16.9	**0.0**
Wil100	273038	35	**149**	171	241	32	26	10	2.5	12.8	**0.0**
Dre110	2264	37	2031	2057	**1782**	25	19	18	1.7	4.9	**0.0**
Esc128	64	21	0	0	0	6	5	0.3	70.0	77.0	**0.0**
Dre132	2744	65	2522	2543	**2140**	39	30	39	4.7	10.8	**0.0**
Tai150b	498896643	105	**1511339**	1669639	2641722	73	61	56	9.2	22.8	**0.0**
Tho150	8133398	130	9615	9282	**6894**	80	65	79	14.1	23.8	**0.0**
Tai256c	44759294	60	**128527**	132333	134885	35	27	54	16.9	30.9	**0.0**

perturbation heuristic randomly selects two locations and swaps their assigned facilities.

Table 2 shows the results on QAP instances using LAHC and SCHC with L=50000 and DLAS with L=10, respectively. In 15 out of 24 instances, the proposed DLAS method with L=10 found better solutions than both LAHC and SCHC with L=50000. In 10 of those instances the differences are statistically significant based on t-test with the confidence level of 0.95. Notably, the results also show that in most of the instances, especially small ones, DLAS finds better solutions in considerably less time. The last column shows that even using a very large value for L, in about 10% of the iterations LAHC behaves like HC. For SCHC, it is about 20%. In contrast, the percentage of iterations in which DLAS behaves like HC is zero.

5 Main Findings

The well-known Late Acceptance Hill Climbing (LAHC) search algorithm strives to escape or avoid local optima by deterministically accepting worsening moves.

LAHC stores fitness values of a predefined number of previous solutions in a fitness array and compares fitness values of candidate solutions against the least recent element in the array, rather than simply against the fitness value of the current solution. The fitness values stored in the array are deterministically replaced as the search progresses. Unfortunately, the behaviour of LAHC can become similar to that of traditional Hill Climbing search (i.e., getting trapped in a local minimum) when the same fitness value is stored many times in the fitness array, particularly when a new local optimum is found.

To address the above issue, we have proposed: **(i)** a new acceptance strategy which increases diversity of the accepted solutions, and **(ii)** a new replacement strategy to improve the diversity of the values in the fitness array by taking worsening, improving, and sideways movement scenarios into account. These strategies improve the overall diversity of the search.

The proposed Diverse Late Acceptance Search (DLAS) method is shown to outperform the current state-of-the-art LAHC method on benchmark Travelling Salesman Problems and Quadratic Assignment Problems. The combination of the new acceptance and replacement strategies in DLAS is more effective in increasing the diversity of the search than just increasing the length of the fitness array, and can lead to better quality solutions that are obtained with a lower number of iterations (i.e., less time).

Future avenues of exploration include comparative evaluation of DLAS against other LAHC variants [1], as well as evaluation on other optimisation problems such as high-school timetabling [5,12].

References

1. Abuhamdah, A.: Experimental result of late acceptance randomized descent algorithm for solving course timetabling problems. Int. J. Comput. Sci. Netw. Secur. **10**(1), 192–200 (2010)
2. Afsar, H.M., Artigues, C., Bourreau, E., Kedad-Sidhoum, S.: Machine reassignment problem: the ROADEF/EURO challenge 2012. Ann. Oper. Res. **242**(1), 1–17 (2016)
3. Appleby, J., Blake, D., Newman, E.: Techniques for producing school timetables on a computer and their application to other scheduling problems. Comput. J. **3**(4), 237–245 (1961)
4. Bazargani, M., Lobo, F.G.: Parameter-less late acceptance hill-climbing. In: Genetic and Evolutionary Computation Conference, pp. 219–226 (2017)
5. Burke, E., Bykov, Y., Newall, J., Petrovic, S.: A time-predefined local search approach to exam timetabling problems. IIE Trans. **36**(6), 509–528 (2004)
6. Burke, E.K., Bykov, Y.: A late acceptance strategy in hill-climbing for examination timetabling problems. In: Conference on the Practice and Theory of Automated Timetabling (2008)
7. Burke, E.K., Bykov, Y.: The late acceptance hill-climbing heuristic. Eur. J. Oper. Res. **258**(1), 70–78 (2017)
8. Bykov, Y., Petrovic, S.: A step counting hill climbing algorithm applied to university examination timetabling. J. Sched. **19**(4), 479–492 (2016)

9. Curtin, R.R., Bhardwaj, S., Edel, M., Mentekidis, Y.: A generic and fast C++ optimization framework. arXiv 1711.06581 (2017)
10. Dueck, G.: New optimization heuristics: the great deluge algorithm and the record-to-record travel. J. Comput. Phys. **104**(1), 86–92 (1993)
11. Dueck, G., Scheuer, T.: Threshold accepting: a general purpose optimization algorithm appearing superior to simulated annealing. J. Comput. Phys. **90**(1), 161–175 (1990)
12. Fonseca, G.H., Santos, H.G., Carrano, E.G.: Late acceptance hill-climbing for high school timetabling. J. Sched. **19**(4), 453–465 (2016)
13. Hoos, H.H., Stützle, T.: Stochastic Local Search: Foundations and Applications. Elsevier, Amsterdam (2004)
14. Kirkpatrick, S., Gelatt, C.D., Vecchi, M.P.: Optimization by simulated annealing. Science **220**(4598), 671–680 (1983)
15. Lin, S., Kernighan, B.W.: An effective heuristic algorithm for the traveling-salesman problem. Oper. Res. **21**(2), 498–516 (1973)
16. McMullan, P.: An extended implementation of the great deluge algorithm for course timetabling. In: Shi, Y., van Albada, G.D., Dongarra, J., Sloot, P.M.A. (eds.) ICCS 2007. LNCS, vol. 4487, pp. 538–545. Springer, Heidelberg (2007). https://doi.org/10.1007/978-3-540-72584-8_71
17. Obit, J., Landa-Silva, D., Ouelhadj, D., Sevaux, M.: Non-linear great deluge with learning mechanism for solving the course timetabling problem. In: Metaheuristics International Conference (2009)
18. Smet, G.D., et al.: OptaPlanner User Guide. Red Hat and the community. http://www.optaplanner.org
19. Wauters, T., Toffolo, T., Christiaens, J., Van Malderen, S.: The winning approach for the verolog solver challenge 2014: the swap-body vehicle routing problem. In: Belgian Conference on Operations Research (ORBEL) (2015)

Hyper-heuristic Based Local Search
for Combinatorial Optimisation Problems

Ayad Turky[1]([⊠]), Nasser R. Sabar[2], Simon Dunstall[3], and Andy Song[1]

[1] RMIT University, Melbourne, VIC 3000, Australia
{ayad.turky,andy.song}@rmit.edu.au
[2] La Trobe University, Melbourne, VIC 3086, Australia
nasser.sabar@latrobe.edu.au
[3] CSIRO Data 61, Docklands, Australia
Simon.Dunstall@data61.csiro.au

Abstract. Combinatorial optimisation is often needed for solving real-world problems, which are often NP-hard so exact methods are not suitable. Instead local search methods are often effective to find near-optimal solutions quickly. However, it is difficult to determine which local search with what parameter setting should be optimal for a given problem. In this study two complex combinatorial optimisation are used, Multi-capacity Bin Packing Problems (MCBPP) and Google Machine Reassignment Problem (GMRP). Our experiments show that no single local search method could consistently achieve the best. They are sensitive to problem search space and parameters. Therefore we propose a hyper heuristic based method, which automatically selects the most appropriate local search during the search and tune the parameters accordingly. The results show that our proposed hyper-heuristic approach is effective and can achieve the overall best on multiple instances of both MCBPP and GMRP.

1 Introduction

Combinatorial optimisation problems (COPs) appear in a wide range of real world scenarios for example resource allocation, job scheduling and journey planning. COPs are often NP-hard hence not suited for exact methods which are to find the actual optimal solution. Instead approximation or heuristic algorithms that can obtain near-optimal solutions quickly are far more practical especially when the problem instance is sizeable. Various local search algorithms have been introduced for COPs in the literature [8,9,11–16]. They are effective on a variety of problems. However there is no single local search algorithm that can perform the best across different types of COPs.

Different local search algorithms are designed based on different mechanisms which might be more suitable for some kind of scenarios over others. It is difficult to determine which local search should be the optimal for a given problem. Furthermore local search algorithms often have their own components and parameters that can affect the search process and the final outcome. Selecting

© Springer Nature Switzerland AG 2018
T. Mitrovic et al. (Eds.): AI 2018, LNAI 11320, pp. 312–317, 2018.
https://doi.org/10.1007/978-3-030-03991-2_30

and tuning these components and parameters to reach the optimal combination could be challenging as well. To illustrate the aforementioned phenomenon, we study two well-known complex COPs: Multi-capacity Bin Packing Problems (MCBPP) and Google Machine Reassignment Problem (GMRP). A range of local search methods with different parameters were applied aiming to search for the best combination which may consistently perform the best on all instances on these two problems.

Furthermore we propose a hyper-heuristic method which adaptively select local search algorithms and adjust parameters. The aim is to establish a more generic yet effective approach which introduces auto-selection and tuning for COPs. It is an evolutionary hyper-heuristic approach, which selects local search and sets parameters by two levels of hyper-heuristics. An adaptive diversity strategy is introduced to guide the search at both levels. Two levels of hyper-heuristic interact with each other through a sharing mechanism so high-quality solutions can be shared. To test the generality, consistency and performance of the proposed methodology, two typical combinatorial optimisation problems, MCBPP and GMRP, used in this study. For more details about these two MCBPP and GMRP, please refer to [2, 6, 7, 10].

The remainder of the paper is organised as follows: Local search methods are given is Sect. 2. The details of the proposed algorithm are given in Sect. 3. Then Sect. 4 explains our experimental setup, while Sect. 4.2 shows and discusses the results. The conclusions were presented in Sect. 5.

2   Local Search Methods

In this work, five local search methods are commonly used in various combinatorial optimisation problems. For the MCBPP and GMRP, they are selected as good candidate algorithms. These are Simulated Annealing (SA) [4], Iterated Local Search (ILS) [5], Late Acceptance Hill Climbing (LAHC) [1], Great Deluge (GD) [3] and Steepest Descent (SD).

3   Hyper Heuristic Method

Selecting the most suitable local search and tuning the setting are non-trivial as the choices depend on factors like problems characteristics, constraints and environment changes. Hence a population based hyper-heuristic approach is proposed which aims to automate the selection and tuning local search as a single search method can not guarantee optimal for different problems and different instances of a same problem.

Hyper-heuristic is to find problem-solving methods rather than problem solutions. A typical hyper-heuristic methodology often accomplishes this task through a high-level strategy and low-level heuristics. The high-level strategy is problem independent and involves two key components, heuristic selection strategy and acceptance criterion. The low-level heuristic is problem dependent and consists of various set of operators that work directly on the solution space of the given problem. The high-level strategy selects and determines which low-level heuristic should be used to generate a new solution.

The hyper-heuristic method proposed in this study also follows the above principle. It has two main component where the first one focuses on local search selection while the second on the internal components of the selected search. They are denoted as HH_LS and HH_OP respectively, which stand for Local Search and Operation Components. Both use the aforementioned two-level hyper heuristic structure. Both use roulette wheel as the selection mechanism. HH_LS to select a local search while HH_OP to select components for a local search.

3.1 HH_LS

The candidate low level heuristics are the five local searches: Simulated Annealing (SA), Iterated Local Search (ILS), Late Acceptance Hill Climbing (LAHC), Great Deluge (GD) and Steepest Descent (SD).

3.2 HH_OP

For this component, the low level heuristics are a range of operators that can generate neighbourhood solutions. New solutions are reached by modifying the current solution, while observing all constraints. These operators are Single swap, Double swap, Single move, Double move, Swap-Move, Move-Swap and Big process (item).

3.3 Population of Heuristics

Our hyper heuristic search is population based. Initial solutions are randomly created and the feasible ones are used to fill the initial population for both HH_LS and HH_OP. Similar to other evolutionary search methods, this is to take advantage of population to better cover the search space hence better explore different areas so a better solution could be found.

4 Experiments

This section is divided into two subsections. The first subsection presents the parameters settings of local search. The second subsection is to evaluate the proposed hyper-heuristic method against local search algorithms. Experiments are evaluated on size 25 class 6 and a1_3 instances from MCBPP and GMRP, respectively.

4.1 Settings

The proposed hyper-heuristic relies on some parameters. The values of these parameters were carefully selected based on our preliminary experiments over both problems. In our preliminary experiments, we tested the proposed algorithm

30 independent runs with different parameters combination using different values for each parameter. The values of these parameters are determined one by one through manually changing the value of one parameter, while fixing the others. Then, the best values for all parameters are recorded. The maximum execution time fixed to 5 min for each instance. After a series of experiments, the final parameter values of each local algorithm are settled and presented in Table 1. It can be seen that large effort is needed to this type of tasks. Also when instance changes, there is no guarantee that these parameters would still remain the most suitable setting. Therefore an automated approach to fill the gap would more be high desirable. This is the motivation of the proposed hyper-heuristic method and the sequent study in the next part.

Table 1. Optimal parameter settings of the LS algorithms based on the experiments

Parameter	Tested range	Suggested value
Initial temperature (t) for SA	10^6–10^{10}	10^8
α for SA	0.6–0.8	0.7
Local search termination criterion for ILS	5–20	10
Perturbation size for ILS	2%–10%	5%
List size (L_{size}) for LAHC	10–25	20
Iteration counter (I) for LAHC	5–15	10
Number of iterations NI for GD	500–1500	1000
Number of iterations NI for SD	5–15	10

4.2 HH Results and Comparison

Our proposed method is denoted as **HH**, which is compared with local search LAHC, SA, GD, ILS and SD. To ensure a fair comparison the initial solution, number of runs, stopping condition and computer resources are the same for all instances and all algorithms. All algorithms (LAHC, SA, GD, ILS and SD) have been executed 31 independent runs over instances from MCBPP and GMRP. The best results of LAHC, SA, GD, ILS and SD on MCBPP and GMRP instances are presented in Tables 2 and 3 respectively. On these two tables, the best result which is the lowest on that row is highlighted in bold. Some rows have multiple cells in bold as several methods achieved the same best. In addition, the best result among the five local search algorithms, LAHC, SA, GD, ILS and SD, excluding HH is marked in italic font and with a pair of square brackets.

From the two tables, we can clearly see that when using a single local search algorithm, there is no single method can consistently perform better than others. All these five algorithms achieved 2 best results on MCBPP. Similarly on GMRP, these methods also achieved the best on different instance, except SD. The results

Table 2. Comparing LAHC, SA, GD, ILS, SD and HH on MCBPP instances

Size	Class	LAHC	SA	GD	ILS	SD	HH
25	1	107	105	112	[97]	112	**79**
25	6	130	[128]	134	132	139	**118**
25	7	130	128	[126]	[126]	140	**109**
25	9	116	110	[106]	111	124	**88**
24	10	[116]	125	118	117	129	**91**
50	1	202	[197]	213	204	218	**169**
50	6	390	398	401	[382]	499	**309**
50	7	[224]	237	236	228	230	**205**
50	9	199	194	[188]	191	[188]	**159**
51	10	209	209	213	216	[204]	**189**

Table 3. Comparing LAHC, SA, GD, ILS, SD and HH on GMRP instances

	LAHC	SA	GD	ILS	SD	HH
a1_1	**44,306,501**	**44,306,501**	44,307,107	44,306,874	44,306,805	**44,306,501**
a1_2	777,533,321	**777,533,313**	821,045,884	788,073,130	830,249,792	777,533,332
a1_3	583,006,901	583,416,998	[583,006,826]	583,009,451	583,416,992	**583,005,861**
a1_4	**251,015,641**	251,015,653	280,990,927	260,693,289	328,814,634	**244,875,916**
a1_5	727,579,557	727,579,558	727,579,618	**727,578,369**	727,579,212	727,578,396

are based on prior tuned parameters which are optimal for these algorithms. Problem instances affect their performance.

On the other hand, the proposed HH method performed very well. It consistently achieved the best on all MCBPP instances. On GMRP instances HH achieved the best on 3 out of 5. HH's results on a1_2 and a1_5 are not the best, but just marginally behind the best results. Its overall perform on GMRP is still the best.

5   Conclusion

In this study we investigated the effectiveness of different local search algorithms on combinatorial optimisation problems, namely Multi-capacity Bin Packing Problems (MCBPP) and Google Machine Reassignment Problem (GMRP). Through our experiments it can be seen that the performance of a local search is affected by its parameters. Different local search may cope with different problem instances, e.g. different search space, differently. Hence there is a big advantage in establishing an adaptive method which can automatically select the most appropriate local search during the search and tune the parameters. The experimental results show that our proposed hyper-heuristic approach is effective and can achieve the overall best on multiple instances of both MCBPP and GMRP.

References

1. Burke, E.K., Bykov, Y.: A late acceptance strategy in hill-climbing for exam timetabling problems. In: PATAT 2008 Conference, Montreal, Canada (2008)
2. Caprara, A., Toth, P.: Lower bounds and algorithms for the 2-dimensional vector packing problem. Discret. Appl. Math. **111**(3), 231–262 (2001)
3. Dueck, G.: New optimization heuristics: the great deluge algorithm and the record-to-record travel. J. Comput. Phys. **104**(1), 86–92 (1993)
4. Kirkpatrick, S., Gelatt, C.D., Vecchi, M.P., et al.: Optimization by simulated annealing. Science **220**(4598), 671–680 (1983)
5. Lourenço, H.R., Martin, O., Stützle, T.: A beginners introduction to iterated local search. In: Proceedings of MIC, pp. 1–6 (2001)
6. Monaci, M., Toth, P.: A set-covering-based heuristic approach for bin-packing problems. INFORMS J. Comput. **18**(1), 71–85 (2006)
7. ROADEF: ROADEF/EURO challenge 2012: machine reassignment. http:// challenge.roadef.org/2012/en/
8. Sabar, N.R., Song, A.: Grammatical evolution enhancing simulated annealing for the load balancing problem in cloud computing. In: Proceedings of the 2016 on Genetic and Evolutionary Computation Conference, pp. 997–1003. ACM (2016)
9. Sabar, N.R., Song, A., Zhang, M.: A variable local search based memetic algorithm for the load balancing problem in cloud computing. In: Squillero, G., Burelli, P. (eds.) EvoApplications 2016. LNCS, vol. 9597, pp. 267–282. Springer, Cham (2016). https://doi.org/10.1007/978-3-319-31204-0_18
10. Spieksma, F.C.R.: A branch-and-bound algorithm for the two-dimensional vector packing problem. Comput. Oper. Res. **21**(1), 19–25 (1994)
11. Turky, A., Sabar, N.R., Sattar, A., Song, A.: Parallel late acceptance hill-climbing algorithm for the Google machine reassignment problem. In: Kang, B.H., Bai, Q. (eds.) AI 2016. LNCS (LNAI), vol. 9992, pp. 163–174. Springer, Cham (2016). https://doi.org/10.1007/978-3-319-50127-7_13
12. Turky, A., Sabar, N.R., Sattar, A., Song, A.: Evolutionary learning based iterated local search for Google machine reassignment problems. In: Shi, Y., et al. (eds.) SEAL 2017. LNCS, vol. 10593, pp. 409–421. Springer, Cham (2017). https://doi.org/10.1007/978-3-319-68759-9_34
13. Turky, A., Sabar, N.R., Sattar, A., Song, A.: Multi-neighbourhood Great Deluge for Google machine reassignment problem. In: Shi, Y., et al. (eds.) SEAL 2017. LNCS, vol. 10593, pp. 706–715. Springer, Cham (2017). https://doi.org/10.1007/978-3-319-68759-9_57
14. Turky, A., Sabar, N.R., Song, A.: An evolutionary simulating annealing algorithm for Google machine reassignment problem. In: Leu, G., Singh, H.K., Elsayed, S. (eds.) Intelligent and Evolutionary Systems. PALO, vol. 8, pp. 431–442. Springer, Cham (2017). https://doi.org/10.1007/978-3-319-49049-6_31
15. Turky, A., Sabar, N.R., Song, A.: Cooperative evolutionary heterogeneous simulated annealing algorithm for Google machine reassignment problem. Genet. Program. Evolvable Mach. **19**(1–2), 183–210 (2018)
16. Turky, A., Sabar, N.R., Song, A.: Neighbourhood analysis: a case study on Google machine reassignment problem. In: Wagner, M., Li, X., Hendtlass, T. (eds.) ACALCI 2017. LNCS (LNAI), vol. 10142, pp. 228–237. Springer, Cham (2017). https://doi.org/10.1007/978-3-319-51691-2_20

Distributed Model Predictive Control of Linear Systems with Coupled Constraints Based on Collective Neurodynamic Optimization

Zheng Yan[(✉)], Jie Lu, and Guangquan Zhang

Centre for Artificial Intelligence, Faculty of Engineering and IT,
University of Technology Sydney, Broadway, Ultimo, NSW 2007, Australia
{yan.zheng,jie.lu,guangquan.zhang}@uts.edu.au

Abstract. Distributed model predictive control explores an array of local predictive controllers that synthesize the control of subsystems independently yet they communicate to efficiently cooperate in achieving the closed-loop control performance. Distributed model predictive control problems naturally result in sequential distributed optimization problems that require real-time solution. This paper presents a collective neurodynamic approach to design and implement the distributed model predictive control of linear systems in the presence of globally coupled constraints. For each subsystem, a neurodynamic model minimizes its cost function using local information only. According to the communication topology of the network, neurodynamic models share information to their neighbours to reach consensus on the optimal control actions to be carried out. The collective neurodynamic models are proven to guarantee the global optimality of the model predictive control system.

Keywords: Collective neurodynamic optimization
Recurrent neural networks · Distributed optimization
Model predictive control

1 Introduction

Model predictive control (MPC) is a popular optimization-based control technique. It iteratively predicts and optimizes control performances based on a system model. Dynamic feedback control actions are computed by solving online sequential optimization problems. As MPC can naturally deal with multivariable control problems and can explicitly take account of system constraints, it has been attracting much attention in many areas in recent years [11,20].

Many real-world control plants such as chemical reactors and smart grid usually consist of linked units that can be grouped into subsystems [16]. These

The work was supported by the Australian Research Council (No. DP150101645).

T. Mitrovic et al. (Eds.): AI 2018, LNAI 11320, pp. 318–328, 2018.
https://doi.org/10.1007/978-3-030-03991-2_31

subsystems are connected through a network and each subsystem can transmit certain local information to the others. As a result, the control technology can be implemented in a distributed fashion which takes the advantage of the plant structure to improve reliability and reduce cost. In distributed control, each subsystem computes its control action by considering its local plant information as well as the effect of local control actions on all subsystems in the network [17]. Correspondingly, a distributed optimization problem arises in the setting of distributed MPC [4]. A challenging issue is distributed MPC lies in constraint satisfaction of coupled subsystems where local constraints are affected by the network topology.

The success and performance of an MPC system are largely determined by the deployed optimization algorithm. Real-time optimization is a significant issue for MPC implementation. Conventional optimization methods may not be sufficiently efficient for real time MPC implementation for problems with very large dimensions and fast sampling frequency. In the past two decades, neurodynamic optimization using recurrent neural networks (RNNs) emerged as a promising computational approach to real time optimization [19]. The essence of neural optimization lies in its inherent nature of parallel and distributed information processing and the availability of hardware implementation. Various RNN models have been presented for solving constrained optimization problems, such as the one-layer neural network with a hard-limiting activation function [13], the improved dual network [7], the finite-time convergent neural network [14], the neural network for nonsmooth optimization [15], the neural network for pesudoconvex optimization [6], the neural network for invex optimization [12], the collective neural networks for global optimization [22], and the neural network for distributed optimization [10]. These RNNs have shown good performance in terms of global convergence and low model complexity.

Neural networks have demonstrated advantages to the design and analysis of MPC methods. Due to their capabilities to approximate any continuous function mapping, many studies on incorporating neural networks with MPC synthesis have been carried out. Generally speaking, the use of neural networks fall into three categories: (1) using neural networks for system identification and modeling [21], (2) using neural networks for real time optimization [3], (3) using neural networks for off-line control law approximation [1]. In these works, distinct advantages of neural networks are exploited in MPC design.

In this paper, a distributed MPC scheme is proposed for linear systems with coupled constraints. The distributed MPC problem is formulated to distributed convex optimization with globally coupled constraints. The overall performance index to be minimized is the summation of local convex objectives. Cooperative neurodynamic models are applied to collectively solve the distributed optimization problems in real-time. One salient feature this work is that the optimization algorithm is designed by exploring the characteristics of the control problem, which greatly improves the scalability and reduces the computational cost. The rest of this paper is organized as follows. Section 2 discusses some preliminaries. Section 3 describes the distributed MPC formulation. Section 4 presents a collective neurodynamic optimization approach. Section 5 provides simulation results. Finally, Sect. 6 concludes this paper.

2   Preliminaries

In this section, some basic concepts and results from the algebraic graph theory are introduced [5].

Let a triplet $\mathcal{G} = (\mathcal{V}, \xi, \mathcal{A})$ denote a graph, where $\mathcal{V} = \{\nu_1, ..., \nu_m\}$ denotes a set of vertexes of order m. Each vertex corresponds to an agent, $\xi \subseteq \mathcal{V} \times \mathcal{V}$ denotes a set of edges, and $\mathcal{A} = \{a_{ij}\}$ is a nonnegative $m \times m$ matrix called the adjacency matrix satisfying $a_{ij} > 0$ if and only if ν_i and ν_j are connected, i.e., $(\nu_i, \nu_j) \in \xi$. If $a_{ij} > 0$, then it indicates that the two corresponding agents can exchange information. The graph $\mathcal{G}$ is undirected if

$$\forall \nu_i, \nu_j \in \mathcal{V} : (\nu_i, \nu_j) \in \xi \leftrightarrow (\nu_j, \nu_i) \in \xi.$$

Correspondingly, $\mathcal{A}$ becomes a symmetric matrix. Moreover, an undirected graph $\mathcal{G}$ is connected if for any pair of vertexes ν_i and ν_j, $i, j = 1, ..., m$, there is a path. In this paper, the following assumption holds.

Assumption 1. The graph $\mathcal{G} = (\mathcal{V}, \xi, \mathcal{A})$ is undirected and connected. Moreover, no self-connection exists in the graph; i.e., $a_{ii} = 0, i = 1, ..., m$.

Given a graph $\mathcal{G} = (\mathcal{V}, \xi, \mathcal{A})$, a diagonal matrix $D = \{\deg(\nu_1), ..., \deg(\nu_m)\} \in \Re^{m \times m}$ is called the degree matrix where $\deg(\nu_i) = \sum_{j=1, j \neq i}^m a_{ij} (i = 1, ..., m)$. In view of it, the Laplacian matrix of the graph is defined as $L = D - \mathcal{A}$. According to the Assumption 1, the Laplacian matrix has the following properties [16]:

1. L is positive semidefinite and symmetric.
2. 0 is a simple eigenvalue of L.

3   Problem Formulation

Consider a network of M discrete-time subsystems where each subsystem is described as follows:

$$x^i(k+1) = f^i(x^i(k), u^i(k)) + g^i(u), \tag{1}$$

where $x^i \in \Re^n$ is the state vector of the ith subsystem, $x = [x^1; \cdots; x^m]$ is the state vector of the network, $u^i \in \Re^m$ is the input vector of the ith subsystem, $u = [u^1; \cdots; u^m]$ is the input vector of the network, f^i is the model of the ith subsystem, and g^i denotes the coupling effects on the subsystem i caused by inputs of its neighbouring systems in the network.

In (1), $x^i(k), u^i(k)$ are required to fulfill the following constraints:

$$x^i(k) \in \mathcal{X}^i, u^i(k) \in \mathcal{U}^i, \forall k \geq 0, \tag{2}$$

where $\mathcal{X}^i$ and $\mathcal{U}^i$ are closed compact convex sets. It is assumed that both $\mathcal{X}^i$ and $\mathcal{U}^i$ contain the origin as an interior point. In addition, the control system (1) is sometimes subject to coupling constraints which denote communication structures and requirements among subsystems [17]:

$$\phi^i(x^i, x^j, u^i, u^j) \leq 0. \tag{3}$$

An MPC law is supposed to optimize a performance index iteratively over a predicted future horizon via the explicit use of the system model (1). In MPC, the control inputs are obtained by solving a constrained optimization problem during each sampling interval, using the current state as an initial state. For each subsystem i, the following performance index is considered:

$$
\begin{aligned}
J^i(u^i(k)) = & \sum_{q=0}^{N-1} x^i(k+q|k)^T Q^i x^i(k+q|k) \\
& + \sum_{q=0}^{N-1} u^i(k+q|k)^T R^i u^i(k+q|k) \\
& + x^i(k+N|k)^T P^i x^i(k+N|k)
\end{aligned}
\tag{4}
$$

where $x^i(k+q|k)$ denotes the predicted state vector, $u^i(k+q|k)$ denotes the predicted input vector, N is the prediction horizon, Q^i, R^i are weighting matrices with compatible dimensions, and P^i is designed for closed-loop stability.

In many distributed MPC settings, each subsystem i independently minimizes the performance index (4) subject to its local constraints (1)–(3) to obtain the optimal control input $u^{i*}(k)$. In this paper, we consider a performance index of the overall control system as follows:

$$J(u(k)) = \sum_{i=1}^{M} J^i(u^i(k)), \tag{5}$$

where $J^i(u^i(k))$ is defined as (4). Correspondingly, the MPC problem is formulated as follows:

$$
\begin{aligned}
\min_{u^1(k),\cdots,u^M(k)} J = & \sum_{i=1}^{M} J^i(u^i(k)) \\
= & \sum_{i=1}^{M} \sum_{q=0}^{N-1} x^i(k+q|k)^T Q^i x^i(k+q|k) \\
& + \sum_{i=1}^{M} \sum_{q=0}^{N-1} u^i(k+q|k)^T R^i u^i(k+q|k) \\
& + \sum_{i=1}^{M} x^i(k+N|k)^T P^i x^i(k+N|k)
\end{aligned}
$$

$$\text{s.t.} \quad x^i(k+1) = f^i(x^i(k), u^i(k)) + g^i(u), i = 1, \cdots, M$$
$$x^i(k) \in \mathcal{X}^i, u^i(k) \in \mathcal{U}^i, \forall k \geq 0, i = 1, \cdots, M,$$
$$\phi^i(x^i, x^j, u^i, u^j) \leq 0, i = 1, \cdots, M. \tag{6}$$

The optimization problem (6) offers a framework for subsystems to cooperatively solve the MPC problem in a distributed manner. It differs from centralized MPC in that all parameters in (6) are designed based on the structures and characteristics of the corresponding subsystems. As a result, the objective functions $J^1, \cdots, J^M$ in optimization problem (6) are separable, which makes it suitable to be tackled by distributed optimization methods. However, it is worth noting that the presence of coupling effects $g(u)$ and $\phi(x, u)$ result in globally coupling constraints, which posts challenges for the design and implementation of distributed optimization algorithms. In this paper, we focused our attention on a special case of (6).

3.1   Linear Systems with Coupled Constraints

For each subsystem i it is assumed that its state space model independent of other subsystem j in the network, however, the states and control inputs are required to satisfy coupled constraints [18].

$$x^i(k+1) = A^i x^i(k) + B^i u^i(k),$$
$$\phi^i(x, u) \leq 0. \tag{7}$$

Assumption 2. The constraint $\phi^i(x, u)$ is convex and linearly separable, i.e., $\phi^i(x, u) = \sum \phi^i_j(x^j, u^j)$.

This assumption is valid in many scenarios, especially when $\phi^i(x, u)$ is linear, i.e., $\phi^i(x, u) = C^i x + D^i u \leq 0$, it is convex and linearly separable.

Denote the following vectors as the predicted system information:

$$\bar{x}^i(k) = [x^i(k); x^i(k+1); \cdots; x^i(k+N)];$$
$$\bar{u}^i(k) = [u^i(k); u^i(k+1); \cdots; u^i(k+N)];$$
$$\Delta \bar{u}^i(k) = [\Delta u^i(k); \Delta u^i(k+1); \cdots; \Delta u^i(k+N)];$$

where $u^i(k) = u^i(k-1) + \Delta u^i(k)$

Using (7) as the prediction model, the predicted states and control inputs of the subsystem i can be obtained

$$\bar{x}^i(k+1) = S^i x^i(k) + M^i \Delta \bar{u}^i(k) + V^i u(k-1), \tag{8}$$

where

$$S^i = \begin{bmatrix} A^i; \\ A^{i^2} \\ \vdots \\ A^{i^N} \end{bmatrix} \in \Re^{Nn \times n}, \ V = \begin{bmatrix} B^i \\ (A^i + I)B^i \\ \vdots \\ (A^{i^{N-1}} + \ldots + I)B \end{bmatrix} \in \Re^{Nn \times m},$$

$$M = \begin{bmatrix} B^i & \ldots & 0 \\ (A^i + I)B^i & \ldots & 0 \\ \vdots & \ddots & \vdots \\ (A^{i^{N-1}} + \ldots + I)B^i & \ldots & B^i) \end{bmatrix} \in \Re^{Nn \times Nm},$$

The corresponding distributed MPC problem can be correspondingly formulated as follows

$$\min_{\Delta \bar{u}(k)} J = \sum_{i=1}^{M} \|S^i x^i(k) + M^i \Delta \bar{u}^i(k) + V^i u(k-1))\|_{Q_i}^2 + \|\Delta \bar{u}^i(k)\|_{R_i}^2$$

$$\text{s.t. } u_{\min}^i \le M^i(\Delta \bar{u}^i(k) + V^i u(k-1)) \le u_{\max}^i,$$

$$\sum_i^M C^i(S^i x^i(k) + M^i \Delta \bar{u}^i(k) + V^i u(k-1)) + D^i(\Delta \bar{u}^i(k) + V^i u(k-1)) \le 0$$

$$\Delta u_{\min}^i \le \Delta \bar{u}^i(k) \le \Delta u_{\max}^i \qquad (9)$$

The optimization problem (9) is a distributed convex program, whose solution provides optimal control increments for all subsystems. Equivalently, (9) can be put into a compact form as follows:

$$\min_{\Delta \bar{u}} J = \sum_{i=1}^{M} \frac{1}{2} \Delta \bar{u}^{i^T} W^i \Delta \bar{u}^i + p^{i^T} \Delta \bar{u}^i$$

$$\text{s.t. } \sum_i^M E^i \Delta \bar{u}^i + b^i \le 0,$$

$$\sum_i^M H^i \Delta \bar{u}^i + q^i \le 0, \ H^{j \ne i} = 0, \ q^{j \ne i} = 0, \ j = 1, \ldots i, \ldots, M,$$

$$\Delta u_{\min}^i \le \Delta \bar{u}^i \le \Delta u_{\max}^i, \qquad (10)$$

where $W^i = 2M^{i^T} Q M^i + R^i$, $p^i = 2M^{i^T} Q^i(S^i x^i(k) + +V^i u(k-1))$, $E^i = C^i M^i + D^i$, $b^i = C^i(S^i x^i(k) + V^i u(k-1)) + D^i(V^i u(k-1))$, $H^i = [M^i; -M^i]$, $q^i = [M^i V^i u(k-1) - u_{\max}^i; u_{\min}^i - M^i V^i u(k-1)]$.

4   Collective Neurodynamic Optimization Model

In this section, we propose a collective neurodynamic optimization model described by cooperative recurrent neural networks to solve the optimization problem (10) in a fully distributed fashion. Each recurrent neural network is employed by a subsystem to minimize its local cost function. Their collective efforts, guided by the topology of the network, enforce satisfaction of coupled constraints. The recurrent neural networks share information if and only if the two subsystems are connected. For each subsystem i, the corresponding recurrent neural network is modeled as follows:

$$\frac{d}{dt}\beta_i = \text{Prog}_{\Omega^i}(\beta^i - W^i\beta^i - p^i - [E^i; H^i]^T\lambda^i) - \beta^i$$

$$\frac{d}{dt}\lambda^i = (\lambda^i + [E^i\beta^i + b^i; H^i\beta^i + q^i] - \sum_{j\in\mathscr{E}^i}(\gamma^i - \gamma^j + \lambda^i - \lambda^j))^+ - \lambda^i$$

$$\frac{d}{dt}\gamma^i = \sum_{j\in\mathscr{E}^i}(\lambda^i - \lambda^j) \tag{11}$$

At each time instant k, the output of the neurodynamic model in its equilibrium state β^{i*} is equal to the optimal control increment vector $\Delta\bar{u}^i(k)$. The optimal control input at k is obtained by implementing the first control action of the predicted vector: $u^i(k) = u^i(k-1) + \Delta u^i(k)$.

Intuitively, the neurodynamic model (11) exploits local information of each subsystem to reach consensus with the help of information sharing over the network. Denote $\mathscr{E}^i$ as the vertex set of the neighbors of the subsystem i. It can be viewed that λ^i is driven toward the average of λ^j by a proportional-integral controller $\sum_{j\in\mathscr{E}^i}\int(\lambda^i - \lambda^j)$. Thereafter, $(\lambda^i - \lambda^j)$ is expected to converge to 0. Next, we proceed to show that λ^i is equivalent to the Lagrange multiplier vector of (10).

Let β denote $[\Delta\bar{u}^1; \cdots; \Delta\bar{u}^M]$ and $\phi(\beta) = [\sum_i^M E^i\Delta\bar{u}^i + b^i; \sum_i^M H^i\Delta\bar{u}^i + q^i]$ for simplicity. The following lemma can be obtained.

Lemma 1. β^* *is an optimal solution to* (10) *if and only if there exists* λ^* *such that*

$$\beta^* = \text{Prog}_{\Omega}(\beta^* - (W\beta^* + p) - [E; H]^T\lambda^*)$$
$$\lambda^* = (\lambda^* + [E\beta^* + b; H\beta^* + q])^+.$$

Proof. It can be seen that the optimization (10) is convex since the objective is a convex function and the feasible domain is a convex set. According to the KKT conditions, variational equality conditions, and projection theorems [9], under the complementary conditions [2], β^* is an optimal solution to (10) if and only if there exist (β^*, λ^*) such that

$$\beta^* = \text{Prog}_{\Omega}(\beta^* - (\nabla J(\beta^*) + \nabla\phi^T(\beta^*)\lambda^*)), \ \beta^* \in \Omega \tag{12}$$

$$\phi^T(\beta^*) \le 0, \ \lambda^* \ge 0, \ \lambda^{*T}\phi(\beta^*)\lambda^* = 0. \tag{13}$$

where $\Omega = \{\mu \in \mathscr{R}^n : l_k \le \mu_k \le h_h\}$ and

$$\text{Prog}_{\Omega}(\mu) = \begin{cases} l_k, & \mu_k < l_k; \\ \mu_k, & l_k \le \mu_k \le h_k; \\ h_k, & \mu_k > h_k; \end{cases}$$

Moreover, (13) can be equivalently put into $\lambda^* = (\lambda^* + \phi(\beta^*))^+$, where

$$(\mu_k)^+ = \begin{cases} 0, & \mu_k \leq 0; \\ \mu_k, & \mu_k > 0. \end{cases}$$

Therefore, it is shown that λ in (11) is equal to the Lagrange multiplier.

The distributed MPC approach based on the collective neurodynamic optimization models is summarized as follows:

1. Let $k = 1$. Set MPC parameters including the control time terminal T, prediction horizon N, sampling period t, weight matrices Q and R.
2. Compute parameters of the optimization model including W, p, E, b, H, q.
3. Solve the distributed optimization problem using the proposed neurodynamic models to obtain the optimal control increment vector $\Delta \bar{u}(k)$.
4. Compute and implement the optimal control action $u(k)$.
5. If $k < T$, let $k = k + 1$, go to Step 2; otherwise terminate.

5   Simulation Results

In this section, the formation control of flying robots which aim to form and maintain desired relative position and orientation is considered. The coupled constraints arise due to the considerations for collision and obstacles avoidance [8]. For each mobile robot i, its state space model is

$$\begin{bmatrix} x^i(k+1) \\ y^i(k+1) \\ \dot{x}^i(k+1) \\ \dot{y}^i(k+1) \end{bmatrix} = \begin{bmatrix} 1 & 0 & 0.2 & 0 \\ 0 & 1 & 0 & 0.2 \\ 0 & 0 & 1 & 0 \\ 0 & 0 & 0 & 1 \end{bmatrix} \begin{bmatrix} x^i(k) \\ y^i(k) \\ \dot{x}^i(k) \\ \dot{y}^i(k) \end{bmatrix} + \begin{bmatrix} 0 & 0 \\ 0 & 0 \\ 0.2 & 0 \\ 0 & 0.2 \end{bmatrix} \begin{bmatrix} u_x^i(k) \\ u_y^i(k) \end{bmatrix} \qquad (14)$$

where $[x^i, y^i]$ denotes the position coordinates of the robot i, $[\dot{x}^i, \dot{y}^i]$ denotes a vector of velocity components along x-axis and y-axis, and $[u_x^i, u_y^i]$ denotes a vector of acceleration components along x-axis and y-axis.

The distributed MPC of the flying mobiles seeks the solution to the problem (6) via the neurodynamic model (11) based on the formulation (9). The linear constraints on states and inputs of every flying robots are $|x| \leq [100; 100; 24; 24]$ and $|u| \leq [2; 2]$. The coupled constraints are introduced to ensure flying robots cannot enter protection zones of each other, and they are represented as $\|(x^{i^2} + y^{i^2}) - (x^{j^2} + y^{j^2})\|_\infty \leq d_{min}^2$.

We consider a scenario of three flying robots formed a formation in a structure shown in Fig. 1. The initial conditions of the three robots are $x^1(0) = [1; -3; 0; 0]$, $x^2(0) = [10; -3; 0; 0]$, $x^3(0) = [15; -3; 0; 0]$. The final conditions are $x^1(T) = [6; 5; 0; 0]$, $x^2(T) = [11; 5; 0; 0]$, $x^3(T) = [3; 5; 0; 0]$. The protection zone of each robot is 0.3 m. The controlled result is depicted in Fig. 2. The control inputs are shown in Figs. 3 and 4. It is shown that flying robots can effectively form the desired formation with guaranteed input and safety constraints satisfaction.

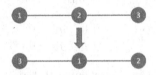

Fig. 1. Formation structure of three robots

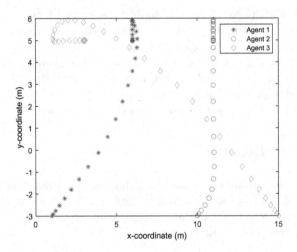

Fig. 2. Formation trajectory

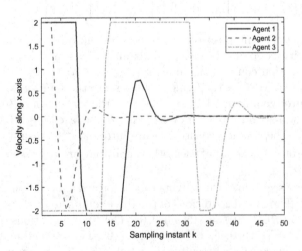

Fig. 3. Velocity along x-axis

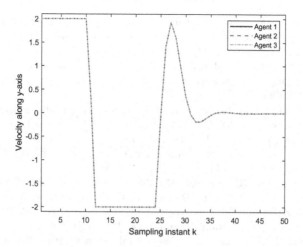

Fig. 4. Velocity along y-axis

6 Conclusion

This paper presented a model predictive control approach to linear systems with coupled constraints in a fully distributed fashion. The global cost function took an additive form of each local cost functions. The model predictive controllers of each subsystem were designed based on local information only, and were computed by using a neurodynamic model in real time. The collective efforts of neurodynamic models forced the local controllers to reach consensus at the global optimal control with theoretically guaranteed optimality. optimality were given. An illustrative example on the formation control of flying robots was provided to demonstrate the effectiveness of the approach. Future research will be directed to nonlinear systems and more complex network topologies.

References

1. Akesson, B., Toivonen, H.: A neural network predictive controller. J. Process Contr. **16**, 937–946 (2006)
2. Bazaraa, M.S., Sherali, H.D., Shetty, C.M.: Nonlinear Programming: Theory and Algorithms. Wiley, Hoboken (2013)
3. Cheng, L., Hou, Z., Tan, M.: Constrained multi-variable generalized predictive control using a dual neural network. Neural Comput. Appl. **16**(6), 505–512 (2007)
4. Christofides, P.D., Scattolini, R., de la Pena, D.M., Liu, J.: Distributed model predictive control: a tutorial review and future research directions. Comput. Chem. Eng. **51**, 21–41 (2013)
5. Godsil, C., Royle, G.F.: Algebraic Graph Theory. GTM, vol. 207. Springer, New York (2013). https://doi.org/10.1007/978-1-4613-0163-9
6. Guo, Z., Liu, Q., Wang, J.: A one-layer recurrent neural network for pseudoconvex optimization subject to linear equality constraints. IEEE Trans. Neural Netw. **22**(12), 1892–1900 (2011)

7. Hu, X., Wang, J.: An improved dual neural network for solving a class of quadratic programming problems and its k-winners-take-all application. IEEE Trans. Neural Netw. **19**(12), 2022–2031 (2008)
8. Keviczky, T., Borrelli, F., Balas, G.J.: A study on decentralized receding horizon control for decoupled systems. In: Proceedings of the American Control Conference, pp. 4921–4926 (2004)
9. Kinderlehrer, D., Stampacchia, G.: An Introduction to Variational Inequalities and Their Applications, vol. 31. SIAM, Philadelphia (2000)
10. Le, X., Chen, S., Yan, Z., Xi, J.: A neurodynamic approach to distributed optimization with globally coupled constraints. IEEE Trans. Cybern. **48**(11), 3149–3158 (2018). https://doi.org/10.1109/TCYB.2017.2760908
11. Lezana, P., Aguilera, R., Quevedo, D.: Model predictive control of an asymmetric flying capacitor converter. IEEE Trans. Ind. Electron. **56**(6), 1894–1905 (2009)
12. Li, G., Yan, Z., Wang, J.: A one-layer recurrent neural network for constrained nonsmooth invex optimization. Neural Netw. **50**, 79–89 (2014)
13. Liu, Q., Wang, J.: A one-layer recurrent neural network with a discontinuous hard-limiting activation function for quadratic programming. IEEE Trans. Neural Netw. **19**(4), 558–570 (2008)
14. Liu, Q., Wang, J.: Finite-time convergent current neural network with hard-limiting activation function for constrained optimization with piecewise-linear objective functions. IEEE Trans. Neural Netw. **22**(4), 601–613 (2011)
15. Liu, Q., Wang, J.: A one-layer recurrent neural network for constrained nonsmooth optimization. IEEE Trans. Syst., Man Cybern. B Cybern **40**(5), 1323–1333 (2011)
16. Olfati-Saber, R., Fax, J.A., Murray, R.M.: Consensus and cooperation in networked multi-agent systems. Proc. IEEE **95**(1), 215–233 (2007)
17. Richards, A., How, J.P.: Robust distributed model predictive control. Int. J. Control **80**(9), 1517–1531 (2007)
18. Stewart, B.T., Venkat, A.N., Rawlings, J.B., Wright, S.J., Pannocchia, G.: Cooperative distributed model predictive control. Syst. Control Lett. **59**(8), 460–469 (2010)
19. Xia, Y., Feng, G., Wang, J.: A novel neural network for solving nonlinear optimization problems with inequality constraints. IEEE Trans. Neural Netw. **19**(8), 1340–1353 (2008)
20. Yan, J., Bitmead, R.: Incorporating state estimation into model predictive control and its application to network traffic control. Automatica **41**, 595–604 (2005)
21. Yan, Z., Wang, J.: Model predictive control of nonlinear systems with unmodeled dynamics based on feedforward and recurrent neural networks. IEEE Trans. Ind. Informat. **8**(4), 746–756 (2012)
22. Yan, Z., Fan, J., Wang, J.: A collective neurodynamic approach to constrained global optimization. IEEE Trans. Neural Netw. Learn. Syst. **28**(5), 1206–1215 (2017)

Constraint-Guided Local Search for Single Mixed-Operation Runway

Vahid Riahi[(✉)], M. A. Hakim Newton, and Abdul Sattar

Institute for Integrated and Intelligent Systems (IIIS), Griffith University,
Brisbane, Australia
vahid.riahi@griffithuni.edu.au,
{mahakim.newton,a.sattar}@griffith.edu.au

Abstract. Aircraft sequencing problem (ASP) is to schedule the operation times of departing and arriving aircraft such that their deviation from the desired operation times are minimised. There are two types of hard constraint which make this problem very challenging: time window constraint for the operation time of each aircraft, and minimum separation time between each pair of aircraft. ASP is known to be NP-Hard. Although some progress has been made in recent years in solving ASP, existing techniques still rely on generic algorithms that usually lack problem specific knowledge. This leads to either finding low quality solutions or scrambling with large-sized problems. In this work, we propose a constraint-guided local search algorithm that advances ASP search by injecting the specific knowledge of the problem into its different phases. In the intensification phase, we propose a greedy approach that gives more priorities to aircraft that are more problematic and create more delays. In the diversification phase, we employ a bounded-diversification technique that controls the new position of each selected aircraft and does not allow them to move very far away from their current positions. Computational results show that the proposed algorithm outperforms the existing state-of-the-art methods with considerable margin.

Keywords: Aircraft scheduling · Constraints · Local search

1 Introduction

Air transport has significantly developed over the last few decades with the increase of the demand for the air travelling and freight services. In Australia, 58.93 million passengers travelled by aircraft in 2016, which was 2.5% more compared to that in 2015 [1]. In this situation, air transport systems may face congestion and some have already reached their capacity limits; which causes many problems including flight delays. In Europe in March 2015, 7% more departing flights were delayed by about 4 more minutes compared to that in March 2014 [4].

To overcome such problems and to keep pace with this demand, one possible solution could be to increase the airport capacities by building more runways.

© Springer Nature Switzerland AG 2018
T. Mitrovic et al. (Eds.): AI 2018, LNAI 11320, pp. 329–341, 2018.
https://doi.org/10.1007/978-3-030-03991-2_32

However, this process needs availability of the space and more importantly, the huge investments. For example, Brisbane airport is constructing a new parallel runway; which is expected to take 8 years and AU$1.35 billion investment [2]. It has been showed that operational delays at a major US airport can be reduced up to four hours a day by optimising aircraft landing and takeoff sequences [8]. These results highlight the importance of the aircraft sequencing problem (ASP) and therefore ASP algorithms. By producing optimal or near-optimal sequences of aircraft, these scheduling algorithms will utilise the runways efficiently to increase the overall capacity of an airport and reduce the air traffic.

ASP contains a set of departing and arriving aircraft. Each aircraft belongs to a weight class (e.g. heavy, large, and small). Solving a given ASP instance with a single runway has two steps. The first step is sequencing the aircraft allocated to the runway. The second step is determining the operation times of each aircraft. These two steps must be carried out by satisfying constraints and optimising the objective. There are both **hard** and **soft** constraint in ASP. The hard constraints are *time window* and *minimum separation time*. The former forces each aircraft to be operated within a specified time window, while the latter forces each aircraft to have a minimum separation time with other aircraft. On the other hand, the soft constraint is *deviation of actual operation times from desired operation times*. All hard constraints must be satisfied in order to obtain a feasible schedule while soft constraints could be violated if necessary, but each instance of violation is penalised. The smaller the overall penalty value, the better the quality of the scheduling. An efficient aircraft sequencing technique can reduce flight times and fuel burn, thereby reduce traffic delays and increase airspace capacity. ASP has been classified as an NP-hard problem [7].

ASP recently has made some progress and a number of methods have been proposed for this problem including scatter search [10], simulated annealing (SA) with variable neighbourhood search (VNS) and variable neighbourhood descent (VND) [16], iterated local search (ILS) [15], and SA and metaheuristic for randomized priority search (Meta-RaPS) [6].

Nevertheless, existing scheduling algorithms take the typical way of using generic techniques that usually lack problem specific structural knowledge, i.e., they use random neighbourhood generation strategies rather than carefully crafted ones or use constraints only in the calculation of the objective function. In this paper, we design a search algorithm injecting the constraint awareness into different steps of the algorithm.

Our search algorithm, called Constraint-Guided Local Search (CGLS), includes two main steps: intensification and diversification. In the intensification phase, we use two neighbourhood operators with problem-specific aircraft selection procedure instead of the typical random one. The idea behind this procedure is that an aircraft with a higher objective value would have priority over an aircraft with a lower objective value (i.e., fix the more problematic part of a solution). In the diversification phase, a bounded-diversification technique is proposed that does not allow the selected aircraft to move very far away from its current position. The idea behind this is that because of the hard constraints, moving an aircraft at a position that is far from its current position might not be effective and reasonable.

In the rest of the paper, the problem is discussed in Sect. 2, the proposed CGLS technique is described in Sect. 3, computational results are provided in Sect. 4, and conclusions are presented in Sect. 5.

2 Problem Description

Assume there are N aircraft $\{1, \ldots, N\}$ either arriving or departing and one runway to perform the operations on. At any time, the runway can be used by only one aircraft. To solve ASP, we have to determine the *operation time OT_j* of the aircraft j. There are two generic constraint categories: **hard** and **soft** constraints that are to be satisfied to produce a feasible schedule. The aim is to satisfy all the hard constraints and attempt to accommodate the soft constraints as much as possible in order to produce a high-quality schedule.

2.1 Hard Constraints

- *Time window:* Because of several factors such as fuel restriction, airspeed, and possible manoeuvres, the operation time of each aircraft must lie within a specified time window. This time window is bounded by the *desired operation time DOT_j* and *latest operation time LOT_j* i.e. $OT_j \in [DOT_j, LOT_j]$.
- *Safety separation time:* Since each aircraft creates wake turbulence that the following aircraft need to avoid, a certain minimum separation time is required between any pair of aircraft. The separation times depend on the aircraft classes (heavy, large, and small) and the aircraft operation types (landing or takeoff). The separation times are determined by appropriate aviation authorities such as Federal Aviation Administration (FAA) in the United States or Civil Aviation Authority (CAA) in the United Kingdom [5]. Note that although the separation time constraints must hold between each pair of aircraft, it has been showed that using FAA standard, the separation times are automatically satisfied between two aircraft when there are three other aircraft in between [17].

2.2 Soft Constraints

Deviation from Desired Operation Times: For each aircraft j, DOT_j is its desired operation time; which means that operation at that time has no delays and extra fuel burn. However, because of the capacity limit of runways and the hard constraints mentioned, some flights cannot operate at their DOT_j. Therefore, the operation times of some flights are deferred from their desired times. If an aircraft j operates after its desired time DOT_j, it would be penalised by $(OT_j - DOT_j)$.

2.3 Objective Function

The objective function of ASP is to minimise total delay cost of the aircraft resulting from the deviation of their operation times from the respective desired times. However, the delay cost of all aircraft is not the same. So, a *penalty weight* w_j per unit time delay from DOT_j for aircraft j. This *penalty weight* depends on two priorities: *operation priorities* and *aircraft size priorities*. Based on the *operation priorities*, arriving aircraft have greater priorities than departing aircraft because of the higher average fuel burn and safety measures. On the other hand, based on the *size priorities*, heavier aircraft get more weights than the lighter ones owing to again higher average fuel burn and safety measures.

One of the main challenges is how to calculate the operation time OP_j of each aircraft j. Assume π is the current sequence, $[k]$ represents the aircraft at the position k, and $s(j, j')$ shows the separation time between aircraft j and j'. So the operation times of aircraft can be calculated as follows:

$$s([k], [k']) = 0, \ OP_{[k]} = 0 \qquad\qquad k < 1 \lor k' < 1 \qquad\qquad (1)$$

$$OP_{[k]} = \max\{DOT_{[k]}, OP_{[k-1]} + s([k-1], [k]),$$

$$OP_{[k-2]} + s([k-2], [k]), OP_{[k-3]} + s([k-3], [k])\} \qquad \forall k \in [2, n] \qquad (2)$$

The objective function is the total weighted tardiness of a schedule TWT $= \sum_{j=1}^{N} w_j(OT_j - DOT_j)$. This objective allows reduction of delays, maximisation of the runway capacity, and reduction of congestion at the airport [14].

3   Methodology

In order to solve this problem, we propose a Constraint-Guided Local Search (CGLS) algorithm. CGLS has two main steps: intensification and diversification. As the main contribution, unlike the most existing techniques in the literature, we use the specific knowledge of the problem to design our algorithm. In the following sections, each step is described in detail.

The proposed local search algorithm is given in Algorithm 1. It starts with an initial solution. The initial solution is then improved by the intensification method. The algorithm next goes through the loop in which the search restarts with the diversification method. The new solution would be considered as the current solution if it is better in terms of the objective value.

3.1   Solution Representation and Initial Solution

A single runway ASP solution is represented by a string of numbers containing a permutation of N aircraft, i.e., $\pi = \{[1], [2], \ldots, [N]\}$. The $[k]$ represents the aircraft at the kth position of the permutation. For example, for a problem with 7 aircraft, one possible solution is $\pi = \{3, 5, 4, 2, 7, 1, 6\}$; which means that aircraft 3 must be operated first, followed by aircraft 5, 4, 2, 7, 1 and aircraft 6.

Algorithm 1. Proposed CGLS Algorithm

1 $\pi \leftarrow$ Generate an initial solution
2 $\pi \leftarrow$ Use the intensification method on π
3 **while** *termination criteria not satisfied* **do**
4      $\pi' \leftarrow$ Use the diversification method on π
5      $\pi'' \leftarrow$ Use the intensification method on π'
6   **if** $TWT(\pi'') < TWT(\pi)$ **then** $\pi \leftarrow \pi''$
7 **return** π

As the initial solution, we use the simplest and the most common heuristic of aircraft sequencing, first-come-first-served (FCFS). In this method, the permutation of aircraft is based on a non-decreasing order of their *desired operation time*. Note that this very simple heuristic is still used in the air traffic control these days, e.g., in Doha International Airport [5]. However, it is not an efficient heuristic and can lead to the waste of resources and make the congestion in the terminal area severer [3]. Using this heuristic in the initialisation of the proposed algorithm can help find out how much improvement would be obtained by using the proposed method instead of the typical FCFS.

3.2   Intensification Method

To intensify the search, we propose an intensification method that is made up of two neighbourhood operators, instead of a single one. The reason is that different neighbourhood operators produce different landscapes and hence different local optima. We use insert and swap operators since they are widely used when solutions are represented as permutations e.g., in the flowshop scheduling problems [11,12] and the order scheduling problems [13].

Let π be a permutation of the given N aircraft. In the operator Insert(π, j, k), aircraft at position j is selected and then inserted at a different position k. In the Insert(π, j), aircraft at position j is inserted at all k ($k \neq j$). On the other hand, in the Swap(π, j, k) operator, an aircraft at position j is exchanged with another aircraft at position k. However, in the Swap(π, j) operator, an aircraft at position j is exchanged with all aircraft at positions k ($k \neq j$).

In this paper, we use Insert(π, j) and Swap(π, j) operators mentioned in an iterative procedure. It means that they would be applied for all N aircraft in the permutation π, one by one, in a given order and as soon as a better solution is found, it would be considered as the current solution and the procedure is restarted with the new solution. We refer them to Insert(π) and Swap(π).

Greedy Aircraft Selection: Our main contribution in the intensification method is to employ a greedy aircraft selection by using a constraint guidance. In the proposed greedy selection procedure, first, the weighted tardiness (WT$_j$) of each aircraft j in the current solution π is calculated. Then, the aircraft are sorted in a non-increasing order of WT$_j$ in a reference list $\pi^{\mathcal{L}}$. Next, in the Insert(π) and Swap(π) operators, the aircraft are selected based on their order in the reference list $\pi^{\mathcal{L}}$. For instance, suppose for a problem with 6 aircraft, the current sequence is $\pi = \{2, 3, 6, 4, 5, 1\}$ and the reference list is $\pi^{\mathcal{L}} = \{4, 2, 6, 1, 3, 5\}$. The Insert($\pi$) or Swap($\pi$) operator first selects aircraft 4 for insertion or swap process from the sequence π. Then, it selects aircraft 2 from the sequence π. This process is continued until all aircraft in the reference list $\pi^{\mathcal{L}}$ are selected. The idea behind this greedy procedure is that aircraft with higher objective values should get more priorities over aircraft with lower objective values. Our idea is to reschedule these aircraft and thus fix the sequence.

The proposed Insert(π) and Swap(π) operators with greedy aircraft selection are given in Algorithm 2. With the use of the Insert(π) and the Swap(π) operators, the proposed intensification method is shown in Algorithm 3. At each iteration, it first applies N_1 on the current solution π. If the new solution obtained by N_1 is better than the current solution, it would be considered as the current solution and the process is again continued with N_1; otherwise the algorithm moves to N_2. The current solution would be updated if the new solution obtained by N_2 is better and algorithm also goes back to N_1; otherwise intensification phase is finished. Note that, in the intensification method, Insert(π) and Swap(π) operators are selected as N_1 and N_2 respectively based on the results obtained in the literature [18].

Algorithm 2. Insert(π) and Swap(π) operators

1 Let π be the input solution
2 **foreach** aircraft j, calculate weighted tardiness WT_j, and sort them in the non-increasing order of WT_j to get a reference list $\pi^{\mathcal{L}} = (\pi_1^{\mathcal{L}}, \pi_2^{\mathcal{L}}, \ldots, \pi_N^{\mathcal{L}})$.
3 **for** $k = 1$ *to* N **do**
4     $\pi_j \leftarrow$ The position of the aircraft $\pi_k^{\mathcal{L}}$ in π
5   Apply Insert(π, π_j) or Swap(π, π_j) and take the permutation π' with the lowest total weighted tardiness.
6   if π' has a lower objective than π **then** let $\pi = \pi'$ and go to Step 1
7 **end**
8 **return** π as the output solution

Algorithm 3. Intensification Method

1 **Input:** sequence π
2 Set Insert(π) as N_1 and Swap(π) as N_2. Also $l = 1$
3 **while** $l \leq 2$ **do**
4   Find the best neighbor π' of π in $N_l(\pi)$.
5   if π' is better than π **then** Set $\pi = \pi'$ and $l = 1$
6   else $l = l + 1$
7 **end**
8 **Output:** sequence π

3.3   Diversification Method

The proposed algorithm uses a diversification method to avoid getting stuck and convergence towards local optima and also to explore new areas in the solution space. Diversification method helps the algorithm generate new solutions for the intensification method by modifying the current solution instead of a fully random solution. The diversification procedure includes a number of moves, diversification strength λ, that are applied to the current local optimum. In this paper the diversification method also used two neighbourhood operators: $\mathsf{Swap}(\pi, j, k)$ and $\mathsf{Insert}(\pi, j, k)$. In this phase, for each diversification move, with 50%–50% probabilities, we apply either $\mathsf{Swap}(\pi, j, k)$ or $\mathsf{Insert}(\pi, j, k)$ operators.

The value of the parameter λ is very important. A small λ may lead to the stagnation of the search and cycling among the previously visited solutions. On the other hand, a large λ may lead the algorithm to conduct like a random restart algorithm which in most cases generates low quality solutions. Therefore, we carefully calibrate the parameter λ which can be seen in Sect. 4.1.

Bounded-Diversification Technique: Unlike the typical diversification procedure that moves the selected aircraft to the completely randomly selected positions, we inject the problem specific knowledge into this method to find diverse as well as reasonable positions for the selected aircraft. As mentioned already, ASP has two types of hard constraint including *time window* constraint that forces each aircraft j to be operated within a window, i.e, $OT_j \in [DOT_j, LOT_j]$. Being operated the more closer to DOT_j leads to the less penalty value. Therefore, moving an aircraft to a position that is far from its current position could not be very effective and reasonable. Therefore, in this paper, we propose a bounded-diversification technique that does not allow a selected aircraft to move far away from its current position. To that end, we introduce a parameter γ that controls the position of each selected aircraft. In detail, when an aircraft at position j is selected for diversification, it could be moved just to the position k such that $\max(1, j - \gamma) \leq k \leq \min(N, j + \gamma)$. Similar to λ, this parameter is also carefully calibrated which can be seen in Sect. 4.1. The procedure of the proposed diversification method is given in Algorithm 4.

Algorithm 4. Proposed bounded diversification method

1 **Input:** Solution π, the diversification strength λ, the diversification bound γ.
2 **for** $h = 1$ *to* λ **do**
3 $\quad j \leftarrow$ pick a random position
4 $\quad k \leftarrow$ pick another random position from $[\max(1, j - \gamma), \min(N, j + \gamma)]$
5 $\quad$ **if** $\mathrm{rand}() \leq 0.5$ **then** $\pi \leftarrow \mathsf{Insert}(\pi, j, k)$ **else** $\pi \leftarrow \mathsf{Swap}(\pi, j, k)$
6 **end**
7 **return** π

---

4   Experimental Results

In order to evaluate the performance of the proposed algorithm, we use 20 well-known instances generated based on the Doha International Airport parameters [5]. These instances are made up of 50 aircraft and time windows of 30 min. We compare our algorithm with ILS algorithm [15] (called here as ILS-SK) as one of the leading algorithms for the single runway ASP. The ILS-SK algorithm uses a variant of FCFS as initialisation. In this paper, to have a fair comparison, we use the FCFS as initialisation of the ILS-SK as well. Both algorithms have been implemented in C++ language and on top of the constraint-guided local search system, Kangaroo [9]. The functions and the constraints are defined by using invariants in Kangaroo. Invariants are special constructs that are defined by using mathematical operators over the variables. Algorithms are also tested on the same computer.

To compare the performance of the algorithms, we use the relative percentage deviation $RPD = \frac{\text{TWT}^A - \text{TWT}^{BEST}}{\text{TWT}^{BEST}} \times 100$ where TWT^A is the total weighted tardiness obtained by algorithm A and TWT^{BEST} is the best total weighted tardiness achieved by any of the algorithms compared. We run each algorithm on each instance 5 times and compute average RPD (ARPD) over the 5 runs. We also compute a further average of RPDs or ARPDs over all instances in a benchmark set. As a stopping criterion, the algorithms were run for $20N$ ms CPU time.

4.1   CGLS Parameter Calibration

The proposed CGLS contains two parameters: the diversification strength λ, and the diversification bound γ. To analyse the effect of these two parameters, a full factorial design is used by considering 3 different values for each parameter: $\lambda \in \{10, 20, 30\}$ and $\gamma \in \{3, 4, 5\}$. For this experiment, we randomly select 8 instances from those 20 instances in our benchmark. Our algorithm is run 5 times for each of the $3 \times 3 = 9$ settings and for each instance with the same stopping criterion as already mentioned.

The 95% confidence interval plots of the parameters are shown in Fig. 1. The results of Fig. 1 says that CGLS algorithm is robust with respect to λ and γ as the tested values are statistically equivalent and each of them could be selected. However, since the λ and γ have lower ARPD in 20 and 4 respectively, these values are selected for further experiments.

4.2   Effectiveness of Multi Neighbourhood

The proposed intensification method includes two neighbourhoods N_1 and N_2. In this paper, we use insertion and swap operators with greedy aircraft selection, GI and GS respectively. In this section, we are to evaluate the efficiency of the greedy neighbourhoods against the random insertion and swap operators, RI and RS, and also to find the best order for the neighbourhood operators mentioned. To that end, the following four cases are considered:

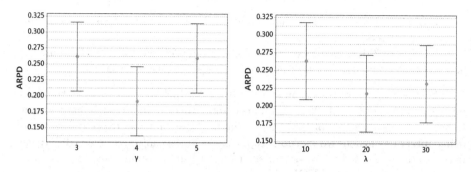

Fig. 1. Mean and 95% confidence intervals for parameters.

1. **Case 1:** Consider GI as N_1 and GS as N_2.
2. **Case 2:** Consider GS as N_1 and GI as N_2.
3. **Case 3:** Consider RI as N_1 and RS as N_2.
4. **Case 4:** Consider RS as N_1 and RI as N_2.

In this experiment, the proposed CGLS is tested by considering each of the cases mentioned as the intensification method on those 8 instances used already for parameter tuning. The 95% confidence interval plot for each case is given in Fig. 2. From this figure, it can be seen that cases 1 and 2 are significantly better than cases 3 and 4. It can be concluded that the proposed problem-dependent greedy strategies for Insertion and Swap moves statistically outperform the random cases. In addition, although cases 1 and 2 are statistically equivalent, we use case 1 for the intensification phase due to its lower ARPD.

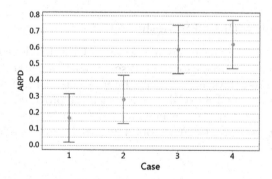

Fig. 2. 95% confidence intervals for CGLS with different neighbourhood cases.

4.3   Effectiveness of CGLS Components

CGLS has two main contributions: a new constraint based greedy aircraft selection in the neighbourhood operators of the intensification method, and a constraint based bounded-diversification procedure. To test the effectiveness of each component mentioned, we create three variants of CGLS as follows:

1. **CGLS:** Proposed CGLS that includes both greedy intensification and bounded-diversification.
2. **CGLS_R:** CGLS but greedy intensification is replaced by a random one.
3. **CGLS_NB:** CGLS but no bound in the diversification phase.

The algorithms are tested on the 8 instances which are the same as the ones for parameter tuning. A 95% confidence interval plot in Fig. 3 is carried out to show the effectiveness of the three variants. Note that non-overlapping confidence intervals of each two methods represent a statistically significant difference between them. From Fig. 3, we can see that both new components significantly affect the performance of CGLS. Among these two components, the bounded-diversification is more crucial as the algorithm obtained worse performance with the absence of this method.

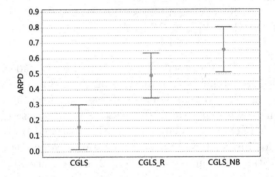

Fig. 3. 95% confidence interval for CGLS variants.

4.4   Comparison with FCFS Method

As mentioned before, the first-come-first-served (FCFS) heuristic is the simplest and the most common heuristic for aircraft sequencing, and is still applied in the air traffic control these days, e.g., in Doha International Airport [5]. As a result, comparing CGLS with FCFS can show how much the proposed CGLS improves over FCFS. The results are shown in Table 1. As can be seen from this table, CGLS hugely outperforms the FCFS obtaining ARPD of 0.157% compared to 99.353% of FCFS.

Table 1. Comparison of CGLS and FCFS algorithms.

Instance	1	2	3	4	5	6	7	8	9	10	11
FCFS	155.67	138.61	212.54	160.93	178.10	102.55	133.63	75.99	90.06	82.97	68.75
CGLS	0.29	0.60	0.26	0.14	0.39	0.00	0.07	0.20	0.23	0.00	0.23
Instance	12	13	14	15	16	17	18	19	20	Average	
FCFS	67.29	71.41	79.03	43.40	59.31	60.14	75.83	69.23	61.64	99.35	
CGLS	0.10	0.06	0.07	0.00	0.08	0.05	0.28	0.04	0.13	0.16	

4.5   Comparison with the State-of-the-Art Method

We compare the results of CGLS with the results of ILS-SK algorithm [15] shown in Table 2. In this table, besides the ARPD, we also show the number of times each algorithm finds the TWT^{BEST} (the best total weighted tardiness achieved by any of the tested algorithms) for each instance out of 5 runs. As can be seen, CGLS outperforms ILS-SK i.e., it achieves lower ARPD in 19 instances out of 20. In addition, except in instance 7, CGLS obtains the TWT^{BEST} in all instances at least once, while ILS-SK finds the TWT^{BEST} only in 6 instances out of the 20. To examine the difference of the algorithms statistically, we also perform a student t-test with significance level of $\alpha = 0.05$. Statistical results confirm a significant difference between CGLS and ILS-SK since p-value $= 0.00 < 0.05$.

Table 2. Comparison of CGLS and ILS-SK algorithms

Instance	CGLS		ILS-SK	
	ARPD	#best	ARPD	#best
1	**0.287**	3	3.222	0
2	**0.597**	1	1.119	0
3	**0.257**	3	1.427	0
4	**0.140**	2	1.440	1
5	**0.387**	2	4.230	0
6	**0.000**	5	0.361	1
7	**0.067**	0	0.149	2
8	**0.199**	2	0.668	0
9	**0.229**	1	1.415	0
10	**0.000**	5	0.641	0
11	0.225	2	**0.149**	1
12	**0.103**	1	1.117	0
13	**0.061**	2	0.240	0
14	**0.071**	2	0.150	1
15	**0.000**	5	0.207	0
16	**0.007**	3	0.292	0
17	**0.053**	1	0.244	1
18	**0.275**	2	0.431	0
19	**0.044**	2	0.751	0
20	**0.134**	1	0.355	0
Average	**0.157**		0.930	

5   Conclusion

In this paper, we proposed a Constraint-Guided Local Search (CGLS) for aircraft sequencing problem (ASP) with a single mixed-operation runway considering the total weighted tardiness as criterion. Unlike the other existing algorithms in the literature, CGLS injects the specific knowledge of the problem in its different phases. In the intensification phase, it uses a greedy approach that gives more priorities to aircraft that are more problematic and create more delays. In the diversification phase, it employs a bounded-diversification technique that controls the new position of each selected aircraft in this phase and do not allow aircraft to move very far away from their current position. The results show that the good performance of the proposed CGLS hugely depends on these two proposed main contributions. Moreover, the computational results show that CGLS significantly outperforms existing state-of-the-art methods.

References

1. BITRE: Bureau of Infrastructure, Transport and Regional Economics (2017). https://bitre.gov.au/
2. BNE: Brisbane Airport Corporation (2017). http://www.bne.com.au/
3. Caprì, S., Ignaccolo, M.: Genetic algorithms for solving the aircraft-sequencing problem: the introduction of departures into the dynamic model. J. Air Transp. Manag. 10(5), 345–351 (2004)
4. Eurocontrol: Eurocontrol - Driving excellence in ATM performance (2017). http://www.eurocontrol.int/
5. Farhadi, F., Ghoniem, A., Al-Salem, M.: Runway capacity management-an empirical study with application to doha international airport. Transp. Res. Part E: Logist. Transp. Rev. 68, 53–63 (2014)
6. Hancerliogullari, G., Rabadi, G., Al-Salem, A.H., Kharbeche, M.: Greedy algorithms and metaheuristics for a multiple runway combined arrival-departure aircraft sequencing problem. J. Air Transp. Manag. 32, 39–48 (2013)
7. Lawler, E.L., Lenstra, J.K., Rinnooy Kan, A.H.G.: Recent developments in deterministic sequencing and scheduling a survey. In: Dempster, M.A.H., Lenstra, J.K., Rinnooy Kan, A.H.G. (eds.) Deterministic and Stochastic Scheduling. ASIC, vol. 84, pp. 35–73. Springer, Dordrecht (1982). https://doi.org/10.1007/978-94-009-7801-0_3
8. Mehta, V., et al.: Airport surface traffic management decision support: perspectives based on tower flight data manager prototype. Technical report (2013)
9. Newton, M.A.H., Pham, D.N., Sattar, A., Maher, M.: Kangaroo: an efficient constraint-based local search system using lazy propagation. In: Lee, J. (ed.) CP 2011. LNCS, vol. 6876, pp. 645–659. Springer, Heidelberg (2011). https://doi.org/10.1007/978-3-642-23786-7_49
10. Pinol, H., Beasley, J.E.: Scatter search and bionomic algorithms for the aircraft landing problem. Eur. J. Oper. Res. 171(2), 439–462 (2006)
11. Riahi, V., Khorramizadeh, M., Newton, M.H., Sattar, A.: Scatter search for mixed blocking flowshop scheduling. Expert. Syst. Appl. 79, 20–32 (2017)
12. Riahi, V., Newton, M.H., Su, K., Sattar, A.: Local search for flowshops with setup times and blocking constraints. In: ICAPS, pp. 199–207 (2018)

13. Riahi, V., Polash, M.M.A., Hakim Newton, M.A., Sattar, A.: Mixed neighbourhood local search for customer order scheduling problem. In: Geng, X., Kang, B.-H. (eds.) PRICAI 2018. LNCS (LNAI), vol. 11012, pp. 296–309. Springer, Cham (2018). https://doi.org/10.1007/978-3-319-97304-3_23
14. Rodríguez-Díaz, A., Adenso-Díaz, B., González-Torre, P.L.: Minimizing deviation from scheduled times in a single mixed-operation runway. Comput. Oper. Res. **78**, 193–202 (2017)
15. Sabar, N.R., Kendall, G.: An iterated local search with multiple perturbation operators and time varying perturbation strength for the aircraft landing problem. Omega **56**, 88–98 (2015)
16. Salehipour, A., Modarres, M., Naeni, L.M.: An efficient hybrid meta-heuristic for aircraft landing problem. Comput. Oper. Res. **40**(1), 207–213 (2013)
17. Sherali, H., Ghoniem, A., Baik, H., Trani, A.: A combined arrival-departure aircraft sequencing problem. Manuscript, Grado Department of Industrial and Systems Engineering (0118), Virginia Polytechnic Institute and State University 250 (2010)
18. Soykan, B., Rabadi, G.: A tabu search algorithm for the multiple runway aircraft scheduling problem. In: Rabadi, G. (ed.) Heuristics, Metaheuristics and Approximate Methods in Planning and Scheduling. ISOR, vol. 236, pp. 165–186. Springer, Cham (2016). https://doi.org/10.1007/978-3-319-26024-2_9

Evolutionary Computation

A Hybrid GP-KNN Imputation for Symbolic Regression with Missing Values

Baligh Al-Helali[(✉)], Qi Chen, Bing Xue, and Mengjie Zhang

School of Engineering and Computer Science, Victoria University of Wellington,
PO Box 600, Wellington 6400, New Zealand
{baligh.al-helali,Qi.Chen,Bing.Xue,Mengjie.Zhang}@ecs.vuw.ac.nz

Abstract. In data science, missingness is a serious challenge when dealing with real-world data sets. Although many imputation approaches have been proposed to tackle missing values in machine learning, most studies focus on the classification task rather than the regression task. To the best of our knowledge, no study has been conducted to investigate the use of imputation methods when performing symbolic regression on incomplete real-world data sets. In this work, we propose a new imputation method called GP-KNN which is a hybrid method employing two concepts: Genetic Programming Imputation (GPI) and K-Nearest Neighbour (KNN). GP-KNN considers both the feature and instance relevance. The experimental results show that the proposed method has a better performance comparing to state-of-the-art imputation methods in most of the considered cases with respect to both imputation accuracy and symbolic regression performance.

Keywords: Symbolic regression · Genetic programming
Incomplete data · Imputation

1 Introduction

Symbolic Regression (SR) is a crucial machine learning field the task of which is to construct a mathematical model that best fits a given data set. Different from traditional regression, no priori assumption is required in SR. This means many benefits to real-world applications, especially when dealing with multivariate data from unknown systems, such as real-time forecasting and physical model integration [1]. Genetic Programming (GP) is an evolutionary computation technique which is inspired by the biological evolution analogy. It creates new solutions from the current ones using mutation and crossover processes with the expectation to find a good solution in the evolution process. SR problems have been typically solved via GP [13].

Many real-world data sets have instances with missing values due to some common reasons such as unfilled survey fields and sensor failures. When analyzing the regression data sets in the UCI machine learning repository [6], among

© Springer Nature Switzerland AG 2018
T. Mitrovic et al. (Eds.): AI 2018, LNAI 11320, pp. 345–357, 2018.
https://doi.org/10.1007/978-3-030-03991-2_33

about the 80 available data sets, more than 20 data sets are annotated as having missing values.

There are three main types of missing data: missing completely at random (MCAR), missing at random (MAR), and missing not at random (MNAR) [8]. MCAR implies that the events that lead to any missing value happen independently of both unobservable parameters and observable variables of interest, i.e. no relationship presents between the missingness of values and other values, observed or missing. In MAR, the missingness is related to some observed data rather than to the missing data itself. MNAR means that the missingness is related to the reason it's missing (neither MAR nor MCAR).

Imputation is the process of filling missing values with plausible ones and it can be categorized into single imputation and multiple imputation [8]. Single imputation provides a specific value in place of the missing data directly. While multiple imputation selects such imputed value from several possible responses based on the variance/confidence interval analysis. Some methods are widely used for imputation. K-nearest neighbour (KNN) is used to impute the missing values with the average of the k most similar instances. Classification and regression trees (CART) is used for imputation by employing decision trees to predict the missing values based on the non-missing ones. Another method adopting the decision trees approach is random forest (RF). It starts from replacing the missing data with the average of the corresponding complete values and then iteratively improves the missing imputation using proximity. One of the most flexible and powerful imputation methods is multivariate imputation by chained equations (MICE). MICE is an iterative method based on chained equations that generates an imputation model for each feature and involves other features as predictors.

GP-based imputation has been investigated on the classification tasks and has shown better performance than some popular imputation methods. In [17], GP-based multiple imputation method is introduced. This method utilizes the robust SR method to predict the missing values in classification data sets. In [18], the GP-based imputation is separated into two stages: the training process and the imputation process. In the training process, imputation regression functions are constructed using chunks of training instances. The imputation process is performed on individual instances by applying the constructed predictors. In [19], multiple imputation and GP are combined to evolve classifiers on data with missing values. Common patterns of missing values are firstly extracted and GP is then used to construct a classifier for each pattern.

The existing research on dealing with missing values mainly focus on the classification tasks. The impact of missing values when performing traditional regression has been considered in several studies [11,12,14]. In SR research, the most common strategy to deal with incomplete data is to delete the instances having missing values [5,7,9]. The only studies that consider imputation for SR are [3,15]. However, they have some limitations. [3] considered only artificial functions, while in [15], missing values are simply replaced with corresponding feature values from other instances. Therefore, how to deal with missing values in SR is still an open issue.

In this work, we aim to develop a new imputation method to handle missing values for SR. This implies conducting SR research with incomplete data. Specific objectives include:

1. developing a new hybrid imputation method to utilize two existing approaches: KNN and GPI;
2. investigating whether the proposed method can outperform state-of-the-art imputation methods on obtaining a small imputation error; and
3. investigating whether the proposed method can outperform state-of-the-art imputation methods on achieving a good regression performance.

2   The Proposed Method

In this section, a new imputation method is proposed. An overall structure of the imputation treatment is firstly introduced and the proposed method is then presented and described.

2.1   The Overall Structure and Evaluation Measures

The framework of imputation for incomplete data is shown in Fig. 1. The first step is to divide a data set into the training and test sets by ratios (70:30). After that the imputation method is performed on the incomplete training and test data sets independently and the imputed complete sets are then fed into the evaluation process. Usually, two measures are used for evaluating the performance of the imputation methods: the imputation error and the regression performance.

For measuring the imputation error, complete regression data sets are used to produce incomplete data sets by generating different percentages of missing values. These synthetic incomplete data sets are then imputed and the imputation error is measured by the difference between the original complete data sets and the imputed ones. In this work, the relative squared error (RSE) shown in the following equation, is used to measure the imputation error:

$$RSE = \frac{\sum_{i=1}^{n}(y_i - t_i)^2}{\sum_{i=1}^{n}(t_i - \bar{t})^2} \tag{1}$$

where n is number of instances, y_i is the ith predicted value, t_i is the ith desired value, and $\bar{t}$ is the average of the desired values t_i, $i = 1, 2, 3 \ldots, n$.

In addition to the synthetic incomplete data sets, real-world regression data sets with missing values are also used in the experiments, where the regression performance is used in both cases to evaluate the imputation methods. The imputed complete training data sets are fed to GP-based SR to build the regression model and the obtained model is evaluated on the unseen test data sets. RSE (Eq. 1) is used as the fitness function.

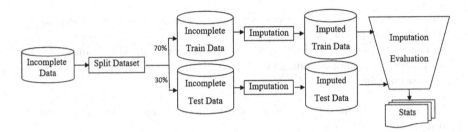

Fig. 1. Incomplete data sets treatment using imputation methods.

2.2   The Proposed GP-KNN Imputation

GPI methods are adopted for classification with missing values in [17–19]. The main idea is to consider each feature having missing values as the target variable while using other features as predictive variables. Instances with complete corresponding feature values are used to build the regression functions and these functions are then used to predict the missing values. This method has the advantage of not requiring any presumptions. However, it performs the regression on all instances regardless of the potential variation. Such variation might due to the imbalanced distribution of certain features. GPI might use some instances that are irrelevant to the instance to be imputed. On the other hand, KNN imputation replaces the missing value with the weighted average (weighted based on distance) of the 'k' closest instances [2]. Although KNN clearly takes the instance-based relevance into account, it ignores the feature-based relevance.

To overcome the limitations of GPI and KNN imputation by taking both instance-based and feature-based relevance into consideration, this work proposes a new imputation method named GP-KNN. The proposed method is formed by combining the two methods GPI and KNN to handle the missing values. The main idea is that, instead of using all instances to build the SR regression functions for features having missing values, only k nearest instances are used to build such predictors for the missing values. This modification is to get the benefits of both GPI and KNN. It firstly explores the instance-based similarity to extract k closest instances and then employs the feature-based predictability power of GPI to impute the missing value. This method considers the variance in each feature to be imputed. More specifically, one feature might require more than one imputation regression function according to the distances between the corresponding instances.

Without loss of generality, the main steps of the proposed method assuming that the input data $\mathcal{X}$ has a missing value at the position i, j (the ith instance and the jth feature) are described as follows:

1. From the ith instance, extract the non-missing values to form a complete instance $V_{i,j}$.
2. Obtain a sub data set $\mathcal{X}_{i,j}^{T}$ by excluding the features that are not included in $V_{i,j}$.

3. Form a complete sub data set $\mathcal{X}_{i,j}$ by removing instances having missing values from $\mathcal{X}_{i,j}^T$.
4. Get k nearest instances to $V_{i,j}$ from $\mathcal{X}_{i,j}$ and put them in a new matrix $\mathcal{X}_{i,j}^k$.
5. Build an SR function $f_{i,j}$ using $\mathcal{X}_{i,j}^k$ considering the corresponding j^{th} feature of $\mathcal{X}$ as a target variable.
6. Impute the missing value $\mathcal{X}[i,j]$ using the prediction value obtained by applying the constructed function $f_{i,j}$ on the ith instance $V_{i,j}$, i.e. $\mathcal{X}^C[i,j] = f_{i,j}(V_{i,j})$, where $\mathcal{X}^C$ is the output compete imputed data.

An illustrative example for the main steps of the proposed method is presented (see supplementary Example S1 that can be found online at: http://ecs.victoria.ac.nz/foswiki/pub/Groups/ECRG/OnlineSupplimentaryMaterials/GPKNN_AI2018.pdf).

The above is a high level introduction of the proposed method. The psoduecode of the proposed method is shown in Algorithm 1 and more detailed description of this procedure is given below.

Algorithm 1. Modified GP-KNN Imputation

Input   : Data set $\mathcal{X}$ with missing values
Output: Complete data set $\mathcal{X}^C$

1 Let $F = \phi$ $R = \phi$ $D = \phi$, where F: regression functions set, R: instance-based references set, D: the corresponding distance thresholds set;
2 **foreach** *missing value* $\mathcal{X}[i,j]$ **do**
3   From the ith instance, extract the non-missing values to form a complete instance $V_{i,j}$;
4   **if** $\exists V_{\hat{i},j} \in R$ *s.t distance*$(V_{\hat{i},j}, V_{i,j}) \leq d_{\hat{i},j}$ **then**
5     $\mathcal{X}^C[i,j] \leftarrow f_{\hat{i},j}(V_{i,j})$
6   **else**
7   Extract a sub data set $\mathcal{X}_{i,j}^T$ by excluding the features that are not included in $V_{i,j}$;
8   Obtain $\mathcal{X}_{i,j}$ as the non-missing sub matrix of $\mathcal{X}_{i,j}^T$;
9     $k \leftarrow min(max(|J_{i,j}|, |I_{i,j}|/3), |I_{i,j}|)$, where $I_{i,j}$ and $J_{i,j}$ are the instance and feature indexes of $\mathcal{X}_{i,j}$;
10    $\mathcal{X}_{i,j}^k \leftarrow KNN(\mathcal{X}_{i,j}, V_{i,j}, k)$;
11    $d_{i,j} \leftarrow max(distance(V, V_{i,j})), \forall V_{i,j}$ an instance in $\mathcal{X}_{i,j}^k$;
12   **for** $r = 1$ *to* N **do**
13     $f_r \leftarrow SR(\mathcal{X}_{i,j}^k, \mathcal{X}[I_{i,j}^k, j])$, where $I_{i,j}^k$ is the instance indexes of $\mathcal{X}_{i,j}^k$;
14   **end**
15    $\hat{r} \leftarrow arg(\min_{r=1,...N} f_r)$;
16    $f_{i,j} \leftarrow f_{\hat{r}}$;
17    $\mathcal{X}^C[i,j] \leftarrow f_{i,j}(V_{i,j})$;
18   Append $f_{i,j}, d_{i,j}, V_{i,j}$ to F, D, R, respectively
19   **end**
20 **end**

Step 1. Initialize empty sets F, R, and D. These sets are used to store the necessary parameters during the imputation process. The set F contains the constructed imputation SR regression functions. R is a reference set formed by extracting complete samples from the instances having missing values. D is a set of distance thresholds representing the neighborhood diameter of the processed missing values.

Step 2. Extract the non-missing values from the ith instance forming a complete instance $V_{i,j}$.

Step 3. Compare $V_{i,j}$ with the existing imputed instances, if there is already a similar one $V_{\hat{i},j}$ then use the corresponding stored imputation function $f_{\hat{i},j}$ to impute $\mathcal{X}[i,j]$ directly, i.e. $\mathcal{X}^C[i,j] = f_{\hat{i},j}(V_{i,j})$. The similarity is measured by the Euclidean distance.

Step 4. Obtain a sub data set $\mathcal{X}_{i,j}^T$ by excluding features having missing values at the ith instance and instances having missing values at the jth feature. After that, delete incomplete instances forming a complete sub data set $\mathcal{X}_{i,j}$.

Step 5. Instead of using all instances in $\mathcal{X}_{i,j}$ to build the regression function as in GPI, the KNN method is employed to extract $\mathcal{X}_{i,j}^k$ which contains the k nearest instances of $\mathcal{X}_{i,j}$ to $V_{i,j}$. For the selection of k, the lower bound is set to the number of features in $V_{i,j}$ ($|J_{i,j}|$) to avoid the curse of dimensionality problem. The upper bound is chosen empirically as one-third of the number of the instances ($|I_{i,j}|/3$). However, if these constraints can not be satisfied, i.e. small complete sub set, the whole set is used ($|I_{i,j}|$). k is selected by the following equation.

$$k = min(max(|J_{i,j}|, |I_{i,j}|/3), |I_{i,j}|) \tag{2}$$

Step 6. The sub-data set $\mathcal{X}_{i,j}^k$ is then used to build N regression functions $\{f_r\}_{r=1}^N$ via SR where the jth feature is the target variable. The value of N is set to 10 empirically.

Step 7. The best constructed SR function (the one having the least fitness value), $f_{i,j}$, is used to predict (impute) the value of $\mathcal{X}[i,j]$ and put it in $\mathcal{X}^C[i,j]$, i.e. $\mathcal{X}^C[i,j] = f_{i,j}(V_{i,j})$. The fitness function is computed using Eq. 1.

Step 8. To avoid the time consuming process of performing GP-KNN imputation for each missing value, the maximum distance $d_{i,j}$ of the returned k nearest instances is computed and stored. This distance can be seen as the diameter of this set of samples w.r.t $V_{i,j}$. It is used to compare the new missing values with the previously imputed ones to check whether the already stored functions can be used directly.

3   Experimental Setup

A set of the experiments has been conducted to evaluate the performance of the proposed imputation method and compare it with state-of-the-art imputation methods, i.e. MICE, KNN, CART, RF, and GPI, using two measures: the imputation error and the SR performance.

As mentioned above, the first evaluation approach requires the complete data sets as ground truth. Table 1 shows the statistics of the complete data sets used in this work. The instances having missing target values are deleted and some non-numerical features are ignored. For each data set, 30 data sets of five instance MAR missingness probabilities (10, 20%, 30%, 40%, 50%) are generated on 40% of the features, i.e. 150 incomplete data sets are obtained. The imputation and missing imposing methods are implemented using R packages: mice [4] and simsem [16] with the default settings. After applying the imputation method, the statistics are aggregated to evaluate the performance. However, to validate the proposed method on reality, real-world data sets with different probabilities of missing values are used. The information of these data sets are shown in Table 2. More details on the used data sets can be found in the UCI repository [6].

Table 3 shows the parameters for the GP runs that used for both imputation (GPI) and regression (SR). They are common settings in GP research. For each experiment, 30 independent GP runs are performed and the implementation is carried out under the GP framework provided by distributed evolutionary algorithms in python (DEAP) [10].

Table 1. Statistics of the used complete data sets

Data set	#Features	#Instances
Yacht-hydrodynamics	7	308
Forestfires	13	517
ENB2012	8	768
Concrete	9	1030
Airfoil-self-noise	6	1503

Table 2. Statistics of the used incomplete data sets

Data set	#Features	#Instances	#Instances with missing	% Missing
SkillCraft1	19	3395	57	1.68
Imports-85	15	205	54	26.34
Auto-mpg	7	398	6	1.58
CCN	122	1994	1676	84.05

4   Results and Analysis

This section shows the experimental results of the proposed GP-KNN imputation method, CART, KNN, MICE, RF, and GPI. The comparisons are carried out in terms of both the imputation error and the regression performance. The

Table 3. The used values for GP parameters

Parameter	Value
Generations	100
Population size	512
Crossover rate	0.9
Mutation rate	0.1
Elitism	5
Selection method	Tournament
Tournament size	7
Maximum depth	17
Initialization	Ramped-half and half
Function set	$+, -, *$, protected %
Terminal set	features and constants $\in (-1, 1)$

Wilcoxon non-parametric statistical significance test with a significance level of 0.05 has been used to compare the imputation methods with the proposed method. The means of RSEs achieved by the best-of-run GP programs on the imputed test sets using the examined imputation methods are shown.

4.1   Imputation Performance

The imputation performance with different missingness probabilities are shown in Fig. 2(a). It can be seen that the proposed method has the best performance among the examined methods on four of the five data sets with respect to almost all considered missingness probabilities. The differences are all significant on the data sets Yacht, Concrete, and Airfoil. On the Forestfires data set, CART achieves a similar imputation performance to GP-KNN. However, CART and MICE have smaller imputation errors than other imputation methods on ENB2012.

One of the most important advantages of GP-KNN is that it mostly performs well even if one of the two underlying methods, i.e. GPI and KNN, has an undesirable performance. This is indicated by the results on Yacht, Forestfires, and Concrete. On these data sets, using KNN results in the worst imputation while GP-KNN has the best performance. On airfoil data set, the good performance of GPI along with acceptable performance of KNN leads to a highly preferred GP-KNN performance. However, the extremely low performance of KNN on ENB2012 data set seems to affect the overall performance of GP-KNN negatively. On this data set, GPI advances KNN significantly which indicates that the correlation between features might be higher than that between instances. However, it is difficult for GP-KNN to advance GPI notably in this case.

Considering the comparison between the other imputation methods, the GPI method performs better than the rest and the CART method comes next. And

KNN method has the worst imputation performance on the five data sets. A common pattern among all the imputation methods is that the higher probability of the missingness the worse imputation error as there will be less useful data to predict the missing values properly.

4.2 SR Performance on Synthetic Incompleteness

The symbolic regression errors on these synthetic incomplete data sets are shown in Fig. 2(b).

Similar to the pattern on the imputation evaluation, the proposed GP-KNN method achieves the best performance except for the ENB2012 data set. However, the agreement between the imputation performance and the regression performance is not as high as expected. Such agreement can be seen in the Concrete data set with the corresponding results. However, on the Forestfires data set, although CART achieves a similar imputation performance comparing to GP-KNN, the best regression results are obtained by GP-KNN. This is an indicator of the applicability of the proposed method when performing SR.

Unlike the corresponding imputation performance results, the regression errors' curves are not monotonically increasing w.r.t the missingness probabilities. The functionality can be noticed when comparing the mean error obtained on 10% missingness and that on 20% missingness on Airfoil data set. The reason is that the regression models are trained on the imputed data and the regression errors are evaluated on imputed data as well which means the error depends on the modeling process regardless of the missingness itself.

4.3 SR Performance on Real-World Incompleteness

To validate the applicability of the proposed method, real-world incomplete data sets are considered. In this section, four real-world data sets having different ratios of missing values are examined.

As the data sets are incomplete, it is impossible to measure the imputation error. Hence, the regression performance will be the only criterion to compare the imputation methods. The SR performance results on the imputed test data sets are shown in Table 4. The mean, standard deviation and the significant test sign of RSEs achieved by the best-of-run programs on test sets are shown. ST refers to the results of the significance test (Wilcox) against the proposed GP-KNN method where "+" means GP-KNN is significantly better, "−" means GP-KNN is significantly worse, and "=" indicates no significant difference.

GP-KNN achieves the best regression performance on Imports-85, Skill, and CCN while on Auto-mpg, the best results are obtained by the CART method. This may be due to the low percentage of missing values in the Auto-mpg data set. The GP-based imputation methods are not the worst in any of the used data sets. The worst reported results are obtained when using KNN on Auto data, RF on Imports-85 data, and MICE on both Skill and CNN data sets.

The main limitation of the proposed method is the imputation time complexity. This problem is due to the need to go through all missing values. It is also

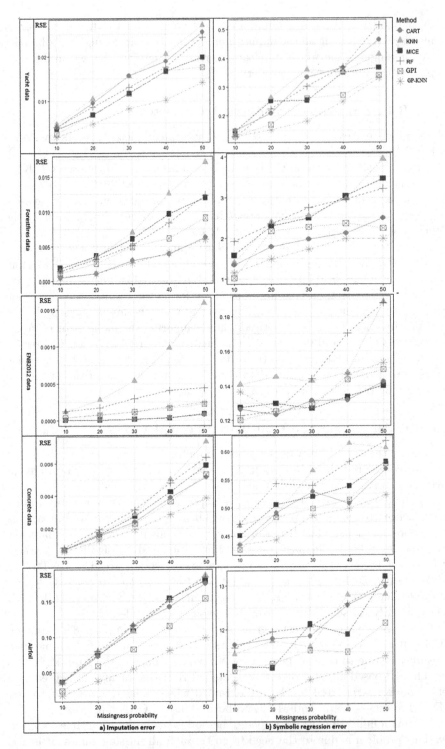

Fig. 2. The experimental results on synthetic incomplete data sets, where the x-axis represents the missingness probability and the y-axis is the RSE error.

required to apply the KNN method and then construct the regression function using SR which means an extra load.

Table 4. The test results of SR error on real incomplete data sets with different imputation methods.

Method	Measure	Auto	Imports-85	Skill	CCN
MICE	Mean	0.248889	0.346285	<u>0.646367</u>	<u>0.546712</u>
	Std	0.05624	0.038141	0.024561	0.056658
	ST	=	+	+	+
KNN	Mean	<u>0.276211</u>	0.33792	0.635711	0.539296
	Std	0.071383	0.042548	0.032341	0.049915
	ST	+	+	+	+
CART	Mean	**0.240706**	0.335545	0.640299	0.509417
	Std	0.046465	0.045827	0.026141	0.038756
	ST	−	+	+	=
RF	Mean	0.24339	<u>0.373118</u>	0.649879	0.517652
	Std	0.058325	0.040726	0.028141	0.028572
	ST	=	+	+	+
GPI	Mean	0.242211	0.331869	0.635089	0.533547
	Std	0.036748	0.031374	0.28758	0.0458
	ST	=	+	+	+
GP-KNN	Mean	0.24411	**0.327196**	**0.633138**	**0.504164**
	Std	0.042643	0.0303757	0.02848	0.033821

5 Conclusions and Future Directions

This work proposed a new genetic programming-based imputation method which combines KNN and GPI. The performance of this method is evaluated from two aspects: the imputation error and the symbolic regression performance. The proposed method has been compared with state-of-the-art imputation methods. The experimental results show that the proposed GP-KNN method significantly outperforms the other methods in most considered cases.

For future work, more experimental work should be done to investigate the impact of generating incomplete data sets with more ratios and different missingness kinds. Moreover, various data sets from different applications should be used. The use of the imputation methods can be then studied and analyzed with more statistical evidences. Another plan is to deal with the incompleteness issue in big data such as data sets with high dimensional features. However, this should be done along with handling the problem of time-complexity which represents the main limitation of the proposed method.

References

1. Austel, V., et al.: Globally optimal symbolic regression. arXiv preprint arXiv:1710.10720 (2017)
2. Beretta, L., Santaniello, A.: Nearest neighbor imputation algorithms: a critical evaluation. BMC Med. Inform. Decis. Mak. **16**(3), 74 (2016). https://doi.org/10.1186/s12911-016-0318-z
3. Brandejsky, T.: Model identification from incomplete data set describing state variable subset only - the problem of optimizing and predicting heuristic incorporation into evolutionary system. In: Zelinka, I., Chen, G., Rössler, O., Snasel, V., Abraham, A. (eds.) Nostradamus 2013: Prediction, Modeling and Analysis of Complex Systems. AISC, vol. 210, pp. 181–189. Springer, Heidelberg (2013). https://doi.org/10.1007/978-3-319-00542-3_19
4. van Buuren, S., Groothuis-Oudshoorn, K.: mice: multivariate imputation by chained equations in R. J. Stat. Softw. **45**, 1–68 (2010)
5. Chen, Q., Zhang, M., Xue, B.: Feature selection to improve generalization of genetic programming for high-dimensional symbolic regression. IEEE Trans. Evol. Comput. **21**(5), 792–806 (2017). https://doi.org/10.1109/TEVC.2017.2683489
6. Dheeru, D., Karra Taniskidou, E.: UCI machine learning repository (2017). http://archive.ics.uci.edu/ml
7. Dick, G.: Bloat and generalisation in symbolic regression. In: Dick, G., et al. (eds.) SEAL 2014. LNCS, vol. 8886, pp. 491–502. Springer, Cham (2014). https://doi.org/10.1007/978-3-319-13563-2_42
8. Donders, A.R.T., van der Heijden, G.J., Stijnen, T., Moons, K.G.: Review: a gentle introduction to imputation of missing values. J. Clin. Epidemiol. **59**(10), 1087–1091 (2006)
9. Eggermont, J., et al.: Data mining using genetic programming: classification and symbolic regression. Institute for Programming research and Algorithmics, Leiden Institute of Advanced Computer Science, Faculty of Mathematics & Natural Sciences, Leiden University (2005)
10. Fortin, F.A., Rainville, F.M.D., Gardner, M.A., Parizeau, M., Gagné, C.: DEAP: evolutionary algorithms made easy. J. Mach. Learn. Res. **13**(Jul), 2171–2175 (2012)
11. Haitovsky, Y.: Missing data in regression analysis. J. R. Stat. Soc. Ser. B (Methodol.) **30**, 67–82 (1968)
12. Horton, N.J., Kleinman, K.P.: Much ado about nothing: a comparison of missing data methods and software to fit incomplete data regression models. Am. Stat. **61**(1), 79–90 (2007)
13. Koza, J.R.: Genetic programming as a means for programming computers by natural selection. Stat. Comput. **4**(2), 87–112 (1994)
14. Loh, P.L., Wainwright, M.J.: High-dimensional regression with noisy and missing data: provable guarantees with non-convexity. In: Advances in Neural Information Processing Systems, pp. 2726–2734 (2011)
15. Pennachin, C., Looks, M., de Vasconcelos, J.: Improved time series prediction and symbolic regression with affine arithmetic. In: Riolo, R., Vladislavleva, E., Moore, J. (eds.) Genetic Programming Theory and Practice IX. GEVO, pp. 97–112. Springer, New York (2011). https://doi.org/10.1007/978-1-4614-1770-5_6
16. Pornprasertmanit, S., Miller, P., Schoemann, A., Quick, C., Jorgensen, T., Pornprasertmanit, M.S.: Package 'simsem' (2016)
17. Tran, C.T., Zhang, M., Andreae, P.: Multiple imputation for missing data using genetic programming. In: Proceedings of the 2015 Annual Conference on Genetic and Evolutionary Computation, pp. 583–590. ACM (2015)

18. Tran, C.T., Zhang, M., Andreae, P.: A genetic programming-based imputation method for classification with missing data. In: Heywood, M.I., McDermott, J., Castelli, M., Costa, E., Sim, K. (eds.) EuroGP 2016. LNCS, vol. 9594, pp. 149–163. Springer, Cham (2016). https://doi.org/10.1007/978-3-319-30668-1_10
19. Tran, C.T., Zhang, M., Andreae, P., Xue, B.: Multiple imputation and genetic programming for classification with incomplete data. In: Proceedings of the Genetic and Evolutionary Computation Conference, pp. 521–528. ACM (2017)

Adaptive Reference Point Generation for Many-Objective Optimization Using NSGA-III

Atiya Masood[✉], Gang Chen, Yi Mei, and Mengjie Zhang

Victoria University of Wellington, Wellington, New Zealand
{masoodatiy,aaron.chen,yi.mei,mengjie.zhang}@ecs.vuw.ac.nz

Abstract. In Non Dominated Sorting Genetic Algorithm-III (NSGA-III), the diversity of solutions is guided by a set of uniformly distributed reference points in the objective space. However, uniformly distributed reference points may not be efficient for problems with disconnected and non-uniform Pareto-fronts. These kinds of problems may have some reference points that are never associated with any of the Pareto-optimal solutions and will become useless reference points during evaluation. The existence of these useless reference points in NSGA-III significantly affects its performance. To address this issue, a new reference points adaptation mechanism is proposed that generates reference points according to the distribution of the candidate solutions. The use of this proposed adaptation method improves the performance of evolutionary search and promotes population diversity for better exploration. The proposed approach is evaluated on a number of unconstrained benchmark problems and is compared with NSGA-III and other reference point adaptation approaches. Experiment results on several benchmark problems clearly show a prominent improvement in the performance by using the proposed reference point adaptation mechanism in NSGA-III.

Keywords: Many-objective optimization · Genetic programming
Reference points · Evolutionary computation

1 Introduction

Non Dominated Sorting Genetic Algorithm-III (NSGA-III) [4] is one of the prominent and effective algorithms in the field of many-objective optimization. It is an extension of NSGA-II [5] which uses the widely distributed reference points for preserving diversity. Therefore, the obtained Pareto-optimal solutions are also likely to be widely distributed on the Pareto-optimal front. Previous studies have shown [4,9] that NSGA-III performs better on 3 to 15 objectives of constrained and unconstrained optimization problems.

Even though NSGA-III has successfully solved various practical many- objective optimization problems, it still has challenges when applying the algorithm on real-world problems such as engineering problem. These real-world problems

T. Mitrovic et al. (Eds.): AI 2018, LNAI 11320, pp. 358–370, 2018.
https://doi.org/10.1007/978-3-030-03991-2_34

usually have non-uniform and irregular Pareto-fronts and the adoption of uniformly distributed reference points affect the performance of NSGA-III adversely [8,9]. This is because many of these reference points are never associated with any of the optimal solutions and become useless reference points. Evidently, useless reference points will also notably affect the performance of NSGA-III [8,9].

Particularly, in problems with irregular, non-uniform and disconnected Pareto-fronts, useful reference points are associated with more than one optimal solutions in their closest proximity. Selecting some of these popular reference points with a number of solutions may not help to span all solutions uniformly over the entire Pareto-fronts [9]. This may reduce the solution diversity of current and future population evolved by NSGA-III.

To address this key issue of useless reference points in NSGA-III, the main goal of this study is to develop a new *effective mechanism for reference point generation*. This mechanism will improve the association between reference points and the Pareto-fronts during evaluation. Further, a *proposed algorithm* will discover well-distributed solutions on the Pareto-optimal fronts. Guided by this goal, we will develop an adaptation mechanism by using a modelling technique and accurately approximates the Pareto-fronts based on evolved solutions. In particular, we introduce a *density-based model* that estimates the density of solutions from each defined sub-location in a whole objective space. Using distribution density information, we can further identify the distribution of candidate solutions in each generation and generate reference points in more promising regions. Furthermore, reference points in each partition are generated uniformly at that specific location. Therefore, associated solutions of these reference points are also well-distributed over the Pareto-fronts. Consequently, the proposed algorithm will decrease the existence of useless reference points for the close match between reference points and the evolved Pareto-front. Moreover, well distributed solutions over the entire Pareto-fronts will enhance the solution's diversity.

Driven by the goal of reducing the useless reference points and promoting the solution diversity, this paper is organized as follow. Section 2 presents the problem definition and related works in the literature for adaptive reference points approaches. Section 3 provides the technical description of the proposed algorithm. Section 4 outlines the experimental design and parameter setting. Section 5 analyses the experimental studies on very well known many-objective test problems and finally our conclusion in Sect. 6.

2   Research Background

This section briefly introduces many-objective optimization problems and then discusses in more detail s several adaptive reference points approaches that have been proposed previously in the literature [8,9].

2.1   Problem Definition

Without losing generality, Many-Objective Optimization Problems (MaOPs) involve four or more objectives [1] which often conflict with each other. In general, an MaOPs can be formulated as follows:

$$min \quad \overrightarrow{f(x)} = \{f_1(\overrightarrow{x}) \ldots f_m(\overrightarrow{x})\} : s.t. \quad \overrightarrow{x} \in X \quad f \in Y \qquad (1)$$

Given two solutions x_1 and x_2, it is said that x_1 *dominates* x_2 if and only if

$$\forall i, 1 \leq i \leq D, f_i(x_1) \leq f_i(x_2) : where\, D \geq 4$$

and

$$\exists i, f_i(x_1) < f_i(x_2).$$

Moreover, a solution x^* is said to be Pareto-optimal if there does not exist another solution x_1 that dominates it.

2.2   Related Works

Several experimental and analytical studies [7,11] have shown that Evolutionary Multi-Objective (EMO) algorithms were vulnerable when handling many-objective (four or more objective) problems due to the lack of adequate selection pressure toward the Pareto-fronts.

To cope with many-objective issues, reference points based approach is one of the state-of-the-art approaches that plays an important role for selecting well diversified solutions during evaluation [4,10,14]. These points are used to guide the solutions toward targeted locations. Therefore, the reference points based approach has been used in several EMO algorithms for handling many-objective optimization problems.

As an effective reference point based version of NSGA-II [5], NSGA-III [4] is one of the most effective many-objective optimization algorithm which works on uniformly distributed reference points. Although NSGA-III performs better on a number of problems with uniformly distributed Pareto-fronts such as DTLZ1 problem, uniformly distributed reference points NSGA-III has an issue when it is applied on non-uniform and irregular Pareto-front problems such as DTLZ7 problem. This limitation is also highlighted by Deb and Jain [9]. They have witnessed in several many-objective problems that some reference points can never be associated with a well-dispersed Pareto-optimal set while others are associated with more than one candidate solutions. Several adaptive extensions have been proposed [8,15] in the literature for alleviating an issue of NSGAIII.

Reference Points based Evolutionary Algorithms for Many objective Optimization (REPA) [12] is one of the extension of NSGA-III which adaptively generates a series of reference points. These points are generated by adopting a series of local ideal points. Later individuals are selected by calculating the euclidean distance between the reference points and individuals in the environmental selection process.

ANSGA-III [9] is one of the well-known adaptive extension of NSGA-III. This extension of NSGA-III relocates the reference points adaptively. Further, relocation of the reference points adopt the distribution of candidate solutions on current generation. This relocation of reference points is carried out by two major operations: inclusion and exclusion. In the inclusion procedure, m-objective reference points are added around the j-th reference points in form of $m - 1$ dimensional simplex. Moreover, the j-th reference points are kept as a centroid and the side length of the simplex is equal to the distance between two existing closest reference points. Unfortunately, this inclusion procedure requires adding the reference points outside the simplex, if new reference points introduces around the vertices of simplex. Due to this reason, ANSGA-III is not able to fully relocate the reference points and may fail to guide the evolution of a well-distributed set of Pareto-optimal solutions.

One of our earlier work, Density Model based Reference Point Adaptation (NSGA-III-DRA) [13] demonstrates the potential usefulness of the density model. In addition, this algorithm estimates the density of solutions in each sub location. NSGA-III-DRA generates reference points according to the average distance between selected solution and the centroid of all the existing solutions in the location. Random distribution of reference points does not allow to achieve an ideal association, thus the algorithm still has the issue of useless reference points.

Our proposed algorithm overcomes the limitations of NSGA-III and previously proposed adaptive approaches. Our proposed algorithm enables close match between reference points and the Pareto-front.

In addition, our algorithm generates reference points that distribute Pareto-optimal points uniformly across the entire Pareto-front, thus alleviating the issue of randomness in NSGA-III-DRA. Moreover, our approach does not add any extra reference points during evolution and it is easy to implement regardless of the number of optimization objectives under consideration.

3   Proposed Algorithm

Our proposed adaptive algorithm is inspired by a density-based model that estimates the density of solutions at each sub location $\hat{w}$. Building this density-based probabilistic model consists of two steps. First, the whole objective space is decomposed into several sub-locations $\hat{w}_1, \hat{w}_2, \hat{w}_3 \ldots, \hat{w}_k \in W$. This decomposition uses Das and Dennis's [3] systematic approach. Then the number of the associated solutions with $\hat{w}$ is recorded in archive $E(\hat{w})$ where $E(\hat{w})$ preserves the index of associated individuals. The association between each solution $\hat{s}$ with $\hat{w}$ is obtained by a perpendicular distance ($\perp$). As a result, a solution is associated with a sub-location where the perpendicular distance between the two reaches the minimum. Lastly, solutions in $E(\hat{w})$ are divided by the total of the non-dominated solutions ($\| S \|$) so far. Then the algorithm calculates the density of solutions of each sub-simplex locations $\hat{w}$. The density-based probabilistic model is defined as

$$P(D|\hat{w} \in W) = \frac{\| \sum(argmin_{s \in S} d^\perp(s, w)) \|}{\| S \|} \tag{2}$$

Previous efforts on improving the adaptiveness of reference points in NSGA-III focused mainly on adapting uniformly distributed reference points, guided implicitly by the distribution of solutions (i.e. no distribution models are explicitly constructed and utilized to adjust reference point locations). However, in our proposed algorithm, we emphasize clearly on the importance of using modelling techniques to obtain a more accurate approximation of the Pareto-fronts. Accordingly, our algorithm is capable of generating references points that matches closely with the distribution model. Furthermore, with the help of a new technique that generates reference points around the centroids of associated solutions, our algorithm can effectively handle solutions in close proximity to the simplex vertices. Additionally improvements have also been made to ensure even distribution of reference points around any solutions that fall well inside the simplex. Therefore, our algorithm has the ability to improve the diversity of solutions in NSGA-III.

3.1   Reference Point Adaptation

The basic framework of our proposed work is shown in Algorithm 1. In this framework, the density model is built first. This formation of the density model is shown in Algorithm 2. Next, a new adaptive procedure (see **line 15** of Algorithm 1) is introduced into Algorithm 3.

Algorithm 1. The framework of NSGA-III-DRAU.

Input   : Parent population P_g
Output: A set of non-dominated solutions

1 Initialize the population P_0;
2 evaluate the population P_0;
3 Generate the W that partition the Objective Space into sub-simplex locations;
4 Set $g \leftarrow 0$;
5 **while** $g < g_{\max}$ **do**
6 | Generate the offspring population Q_g using the crossover, mutation and reproduction;
7 | **foreach** $Q \in Q_g$ **do** Evaluate Q;
8 | $R_g \leftarrow P_g \cup Q_g$;
9 | Apply non-dominated sorting on (R_g) and find $(F_1, F_2 \ldots)$;
10 | Normalize the population members :$\overline{S_g} = ObjectiveNormalization(S_g)$;
11 | **foreach** $w \in W$ **do**
12 | | identify member of $\overline{S_g}$ associated with w;
13 | | Assign $(E(\hat{w}), D(\hat{w})) = Associatew(\overline{S_g}, W)$;
14 | **end**
15 | Assign $Z_g^* = Generate(E(\hat{w}), D(\hat{w}), \overline{S_g}, W)$;
16 | Construct the new population P_{g+1} by the $NSGA - III$ association and Niching;
17 | $g \leftarrow g + 1$;
18 **end**
19 **return** *The non-dominated individuals* $P^* \subseteq P_{g_{\max}}$;

Algorithm 2. $Associatew(\overline{S_g}, W)$

Input : $\overline{S_g}, W$
Output: $E(\hat{w})$ (individuals at $\hat{w}$) & $D(\hat{w})$ (solution's density at $\hat{w}$)
1 **foreach** $w \in W$ **do**
2 | $E(w) = \phi$;
3 **end**
4 **foreach** $s \in \overline{S_g}$ **do**
5 | **foreach** $w \in W$ **do**
6 | | compute $d^\perp(s, w)$;   // perpendicular distance of each solution from $\hat{w}$
7 | **end**
8 | Assign $\hat{w} = argmin_{s \in S} d^\perp(s, w)$;   // associate the solution with the sub-location
9 | Save s in $E(\hat{w})$;
10 **end**
11 **foreach** $s \in E(\hat{w})$ **do**
12 | Calculate the number of associated solutions with $\hat{w}$ and store in $A(\hat{w})$;
13 **end**
14 **while** $i \leq \| A(\hat{w}) \|$ **do**
15 | Assign $P(D|\hat{w}) = \| A(\hat{w}) \| \div \| S \|$;   // probability of the associated solution
16 | Assign $D(\hat{w}) = \| P(\hat{w}) \|$*length of reference points;   // return solution's density
17 | set i=i+1;
18 **end**
19 **return** $E(\hat{w})$ & $D(\hat{w})$;

Algorithm 3. $Generate(E(\hat{w}), D(\hat{w}), \overline{S_g}, W)$

Input : $E(w), P(w), D(w), \overline{S_g}, W$
Output: Z_g^*
1 **foreach** $\hat{w} \in W$ **do**
2 | set nref= $\| D(\hat{w}) \|$;   // number of reference points required at location $\hat{w}$
3 | Assign $Z^r = \hat{w}$;   // set $\hat{w}$ as a first reference point
4 | **if** $Z^r != Vertex\ Points$ **then**
5 | | Assign $Z_g^* = IntermediatePoints(E(\hat{w}), D(\hat{w}), nref, \overline{S_g}, W, Z^r)$;   // call
  | | intermediate points method
6 | **end**
7 | **if** $Vertex\ points$ **then**
8 | | Assign $Z_g^* = VertexPoints(E(\hat{w}), D(\hat{w}), nref, \overline{S_g}, W, Z^r)$;   // call vertex
  | | points method
9 | **end**
10 **end**
11 **return** Z_g^*;

3.2 Reference Point Generation

Our proposed algorithm is broken into two parts: (1) handling references points on the vertex and (2) dealing with the intermediate points.

References Points on the Vertex. The first method of the proposed algorithm handles the issue of ANSGA-III. This issue relates to the generation of the reference points around the vertices of simplex. In this method, the reference points are generated from the centroid location of the associated solutions and these reference points are always generated inside a simplex location. In this procedure we have used the following steps:

1. Obtain the centre location from existing solutions in the sub-simplex $\hat{w} \in W$, where $\hat{w}$ is one of the vertices of the hyperplane.
2. Calculate the perpendicular distance from the centroid to associated solutions of $\hat{w}$.
3. Select a solution s based on a minimum perpendicular distance.
4. Calculate a mid-point value between the selected solution and the centroid for generating a corresponding reference point. This mid-point of each dimension is considered as one of the reference points around the vertices.
5. Repeat steps 1 to 4 until the required number of reference points are generated.

Intermediate Points. The generation of reference points at any intermediate location is described in Algorithm 4. Consider the situation in $M = 3$ objective case where M points are generated around any of the intermediate locations on the simplex. This example is shown in Fig. 1. In this example, $\{Z^1, Z^2, Z^3\}$ reference points are generated using the following two equations:

$$points^i = Z^r - (Interval)/M \tag{3}$$

$$Z^i_{new} = Z^i_{new}/div + points^i \tag{4}$$

where the interval is the difference between two consecutive reference points on the hyperplane and the division(div) is the total number of partitions on the original simplex.

Algorithm 4. $IntermediatePoints(E(\hat{w}), D(\hat{w}), nref, \overline{S}_g, W, Z^r)$

Input : $E(\hat{w}), D(\hat{w}), nref, \overline{S}_g, W, Z^r$
Output: Z^*_g

```
 1 foreach ŵ ∈ W do
 2 |   associate(Z^r, s ∈ E(ŵ)) ;        // associate solutions with the reference point
 3 |   if ρ(Z^r) = 1 then
 4 |   |   Assign Z_g = Z^r : nref=nref-1;
 5 |   end
 6 |   while nref ≥ 0 do
 7 |   |   foreach z^r ∈ Z^r do
 8 |   |   |   if ρ(Z^r) ≥ 2 and Flag(Z^r) = 0 then
 9 |   |   |   |   while i ≤ M do
10 |   |   |   |   |   Z^r = Z^r - interval ÷ M;
11 |   |   |   |   |   Z_new = Z_new ÷ div + Z_r ;        // generate new reference point
12 |   |   |   |   |   i=i+1;
13 |   |   |   |   end
14 |   |   |   |   while i ≤ M do
15 |   |   |   |   |   associate(Z^i_new, s ∈ E(ŵ)) ;    // associate the solutions with the
           |   |   |   |   |   new reference point
16 |   |   |   |   |   if ρ(Z^i_new) ≠ 0 then
17 |   |   |   |   |   |   set Flag(Z_new)=0;
18 |   |   |   |   |   |   if already − exist(Z^i_new) = FALSE and Z^i_new lie in first quadrant
           |   |   |   |   |   |   then
19 |   |   |   |   |   |   |   Assign Z^r = Z^i_new ∪ Z_r;
20 |   |   |   |   |   |   end
21 |   |   |   |   |   end
22 |   |   |   |   |   i=i+1;
23 |   |   |   |   end
24 |   |   |   |   foreach z^r ∈ Z^r do
25 |   |   |   |   |   if ρ(z^r) = 1 then
26 |   |   |   |   |   |   Z_g = z^r : set Flag(z_r)=1;
27 |   |   |   |   |   |   nref=nref-1;
28 |   |   |   |   |   end
29 |   |   |   |   |   if ρ(z^r) = 0 then
30 |   |   |   |   |   |   remove(z^r) ;                  // remove reference point
31 |   |   |   |   |   end
32 |   |   |   |   end
33 |   |   |   end
34 |   |   end
35 |   end
36 end
37 return Z^*_g;
```

These newly generated reference points can be inserted in the reference points archive called Z^r if they satisfy the two main conditions: (i) a reference point must be inside the boundary of entire simplex; (ii) duplication is not allowed and reference points must be unique. Once new reference points are added into archive Z^r, then the association between existing members of Z^r and solutions in $E(\hat{w})$ must be checked. If the i-th reference point from Z^r still has $\rho_i \geq 2$, reference points are generated around i-th reference points but this time a parameter value of interval is set to half of the current value and the division(div) is set to be double its existing value. This process is also shown in Fig. 1. Figure 1 demonstrates that the i-th reference point is kept as a centroid location for newly generated reference points and the reference points are generated as a layer approach. These layers are also shows into the Fig. 1 with two different colours. Thus, we named this method a centroid layer approach.

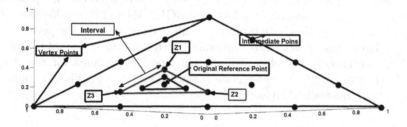

Fig. 1. Generate reference points until $M - 1$ times

4   Experimental Setup

4.1   Test Problems

In order to verify the quality of the proposed algorithm, we have compared the performance of NSGA-III-DRAU with NSGA-III, ANSGA-III and NSGAIII-DRA on benchmark problems with three to eight objectives. We selected four many-objective test problems, DTLZ and Inverted DTLZ (IDTLZ), introduced by Deb et al. [6]. The characteristics of DTLZ and IDTLZ problems [2] are mentioned in Table 1.

Table 1. The characteristics of DTLZ problems

Problems	No. of obj(m)	n	Characteristics
$IDTLZ1$	3, 5, 8	m + 4	Linear, multi-model, inverted
$IDTLZ2$	3, 5, 8	m + 9	Concave, inverted
$DTLZ5$	3, 5, 8	m + 9	Concave, degenerate
$DTLZ7$	3, 5, 8	m + 19	Mixed, disconnected, multi model

4.2 Parameter Setting

The number of decision variables for DTLZ and inverted DTLZ test problems are set as recommended in [6]. The population size of all compared algorithms are set to 92 for the three-objective, 212 for the five-objective and 156 for eight-objective. The size of reference points are also kept same as the population size. 91 reference are supplied to all compared algorithms for three-objective case, 210 for five-objective case and 156 for eight-objective case. The crossover and the mutation parameters of NSGA-III are kept identical in the proposed algorithm. In order to maintain a consistent and fair comparison the parameter settings of compared algorithms are kept the same in all experiments.

4.3 Performance Measures

To evaluate the performance of the all proposed algorithm on DTLZ problems, we used the Inverted Generational Distance (IGD) [16] and Hyper-Volume (HV) [17]. These two indicators have been commonly used to evaluate the performance of EMO algorithms. In this study, the exact Pareto-optimal surface of DTLZ test problems are known. Therefore, we use the true Pareto-fronts for calculating IGD. In the case of HV the nadir point is set as $(1, 1, 1, \ldots 1)$. The HV values in this study are normalized to $[0, 1]$.

5 Results and Discussions

In the experiment, for each algorithm, 30 independent runs are carried out. Then, the mean and the standard deviation of HV and IGD values are reported. The best value for each problem is marked in boldface.

5.1 Overall Results

Table 2 presents the mean and standard deviation of the four compared algorithms on DTLZ problems. The Wilcoxon rank sum test with the significance level of 0.05 is carried out on both HV and IGD values.

IDTLZ1 fitness landscape contains a large number of local optima which may require better exploration. Therefore, a higher degree of population diversity plays an important role for more exploration in this multi-model test problem. Table 2 shows that adaptively relocating reference points NSGAIII-DRA, NSGAIII-DRAU and ANSGA-III have better HV and IGD values because they can generate higher population diversity than the predefined uniformly distributed reference points in NSGA-III. Furthermore, the result also reveals that NSGAIII-DRAU performs significantly better than NSGA-III and NSGAIII-DRA but is competitive with ANSGA-III. This can also be seen in Fig. 2. Figure 2 also demonstrates that the NSGAIII-DRA has random distribution of solutions and some area of the plane do not have any of the solution. Thus, the NSGAIII-DRA plot indicates that reference points are not widely distributed in the objective space.

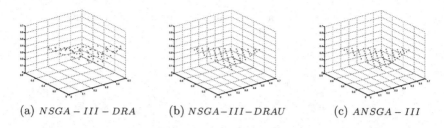

(a) $NSGA-III-DRA$ (b) $NSGA-III-DRAU$ (c) $ANSGA-III$

Fig. 2. Approximate Pareto-front for 3-objective Inv-IDTLZ1 problem

Table 2. The mean and standard deviation over the average HV values on M-objectives inverted $DTLZ1$, inverted $DTLZ2$, $DTLZ5$ and $DTLZ7$ problems. The significantly better results are shown in bold.

Function	M	NSGAIII	ANSGA-III	NSGAIII-DRA	NSGAIII-DRAU
HV $Mean\,(std)$					
Inv-DTLZ1	3	1.07e−1(4.0e−3)	1.30e−1(2.8e−3)	1.19e−1(4.7e−3)	1.31e−1(2.0e−3)
	5	7.91e−4(4.2e−4)	2.05e−3(3.0e−4)	2.75e−3(2.9e−4)	**3.62e−3(2.0e−4)**
	8	2.62e−4(3.8e−5)	**9.10e−3(1.5e−3)**	1.35e−4(4.3e−5)	1.58e−4(4.3e−4)
Inv-DTLZ2	3	4.14e−1(1.7e−2)	4.47e−1(4.0e−3)	4.35e−1(6.74e−3)	**4.54e−1(4.1e−3)**
	5	6.30e−2(2.4e−3)	6.89e−2(5.9e−3)	8.53e−2(3.1e−3)	**2.85e−1(1.1e−2)**
	8	6.62e−3(6.8e−4)	9.37e−3(1.1e−4)	7.92e−3(8.8e−4)	**1.25e−2(7.9e−4)**
DTLZ5	3	8.19e−2(1.7e−2)	**8.54e−2(6.3e−4)**	8.41e−2(1.2e−3)	8.45e−2(2.3e−3)
	5	2.28e−1(2.6e−1)	7.12e−1(4.2e−1)	4.5e−1(4.7e−2)	**7.21e−1(3.5e−2)**
	8	6.03e−1(1.9e−2)	6.92e−1(2.2e−2)	6.44e−1(5.4e−2)	**6.96e−1(2.2e−2)**
DTLZ7	3	3.10e−1(7.9e−3)	3.15e−1(1.4e−2)	2.99e−1(5.5e−3)	**3.19e−1(1.2e−2)**
	5	2.240e−1(3.8e−3)	3.23e−1(6.3e−3)	2.75e−2(2.7e−3)	**3.25−1(4.3e−3)**
	8	3.08e−1(4.8e−3)	3.25e−1(6.3e−3)	2.23e−3(1.7e−2)	**3.28e−1(6.2e−3)**
IGD $Mean\,(std)$					
Inv-DTLZ1	3	3.22e−2(5.0e−3)	2.37e−2(7.7e−3)	2.82e−2(2.5e−3)	2.34e−2(1.8e−3)
	5	8.62e−2(3.8e−3)	5.53e−2(8.3e−3)	4.47e−2(6.8e−3)	**3.11e−2(3.9e−3)**
	8	9.62e−2(8.8e−3)	7.13e−2(9.2e−3)	6.17e−2(9.9e−3)	**5.49e−2(8.9e−3)**
Inv-DTLZ2	3	6.80e−2(8.3e−3)	6.39e−2(4.6e−3)	6.38e−2(4.2e−3)	**6.19e−2(4.6e−3)**
	5	2.33e−1(1.2e−2)	2.03e−1(1.2e−2)	1.61e−1(1.2e−2)	**1.23e−1(1.4e−2)**
	8	2.62e−1(3.8e−2)	3.53e−1(2.3e−2)	2.78e−1(3.5e−2)	**2.39e−1(3.4e−2)**
DTLZ5	3	2.18e−2(2.5e−3)	**1.35e−2(1.5e−3)**	1.99e−2(3.7e−3)	1.39e−2(2.84e−3)
	5	2.70e−1(5.16e−2)	1.99e−1(5.7e−2)	3.57e−1(8.4e−2)	**1.85e−1(5.4e−2)**
	8	4.04e−1(8.8e−2)	4.01e−1(7.2e−2)	4.57e−1(8.9e−2)	**3.95e−1(9.14e−2)**
DTLZ7	3	9.6e−2(5.07e−3)	8.60e−2(6.8e−3)	9.57e−2(1.6e−3)	**8.37e−2(6.43e−3)**
	5	4.54e−1(2.2e−2)	**3.44e−1(2.4e−2)**	3.68e−1(2.7e−2)	3.60e−1(2.6e−2)
	8	7.89e−1(3.7e−2)	7.61e−1(2.7e−2)	8.83e−1(5.5e−2)	**7.54e−1(7.9e−2)**

For the IDTLZ2 problem, Table 2 shows that our proposed algorithm NSGAIII-DRAU significantly outperformed NSGAIII, ANSGA-III and NSGAIII-DRA in terms of HV and IGD. To verify this result, we plotted the Pareto-fronts of our proposed algorithm and ANSGA-III. Fig. 3a and b show

that the proposed algorithm has generated more diversified solutions on the
hyperplane than ANSGA-III for this problem.

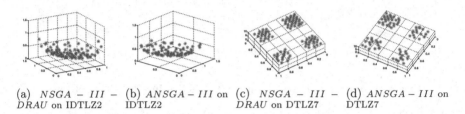

(a) $NSGA - III -$ (b) $ANSGA - III$ on   (c) $NSGA - III -$ (d) $ANSGA - III$ on
$DRAU$ on IDTLZ2   IDTLZ2 $DRAU$ on DTLZ7   DTLZ7

Fig. 3. Approximate Pareto-front for 3-objective Inv-IDTLZ2 and DTLZ7 test problems

DTLZ5 has a degenerated Pareto-front, i.e., the Pareto-front is always a curve
regardless of the dimensionality of the objective space. For DTLZ5 problem,
Fig. 4a and b show that the solutions obtained by NSGAIII-DRAU are well
distributed around Pareto-fronts, thus achieving better diversity than ANSGA-
III. For the five-and-eight objective test problems, Table 2 shows that NSGAIII-
DRAU significantly outperforms NSGAIII, ANSGA-III and NSGAIII-DRA.

Similar observations can be made from the results on DTLZ7 with three
to eight objectives as well. DTLZ7 has a disconnected Pareto-front. Due to this
feature, some algorithms that rely on uniformly distributed reference points cannot perform well on this problem. Hence, the algorithms having adaptive reference points eventually have significantly better performance. Figure 4c and d
show that NSGAIII-DRAU can converge faster than ANSGA-III. For the three-
objective test problem, ANSGA-III apparently failed to cover some location on
the Pareto-fronts. This can be seen in Fig. 3c and d.

For the eight-objective test problems, Table 2 shows that NSGAIII-DRAU
significantly outperforms NSGAIII, ANSGA-III and NSGAIII-DRA on most of
the test problems.

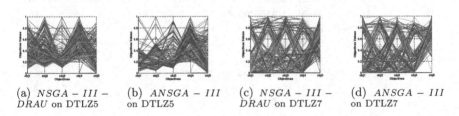

(a) $NSGA - III -$ (b) $ANSGA - III$ (c) $NSGA - III -$ (d) $ANSGA - III$
$DRAU$ on DTLZ5   on DTLZ5 $DRAU$ on DTLZ7   on DTLZ7

Fig. 4. Parallel coordinate plot for the e fitness values of the population on 5-objective
DTLZ5 and DTLZ7 problems.

6   Conclusion

In this paper, we proposed a new adaptive generation strategy NSGA-III-DRAU for reference points in the recently proposed many-objective NSGA-III. NSGA-III-DRAU addresses a key research issue of using uniformly distributed reference points NSGA-III on many-objective irregular and disconnected Pareto-front problems and attempted to alleviates the limitations of recently proposed adaptive approaches. The proposed algorithm is applied to a number of unconstrained three to eight-objective optimization problems. We compared our proposed algorithm with NSGA-III and previously proposed reference points adaptive approaches. Experimental results on the benchmark problems show that NSGA-III-DRAU reduces the useless reference points and provides a better distribution of Pareto- optimal solutions on the entire Pareto-fronts. Further, a better distribution of reference points also helps improve the diversity of the solutions that can be observed visually and in terms of HV and IGD. This finding leads us believe that our algorithm NSGA-III-DRAU is capable of handling many-objective problems with non-uniformly distributed Pareto-front effectively.

This study opens up a substantial research direction for many-objective optimization problems. It is still in exploration phase and more studies are required in future. Thus, we have a plan to do more analytical and experimental studies to know in detail about the behavior of the solutions in term of non-uniform and irregular Pareto-fronts.

References

1. Chand, S., Wagner, M.: Evolutionary many-objective optimization: a quick-start guide. Surv. Oper. Res. Manag. Sci. **20**(2), 35–42 (2015)
2. Cheng, R., et al.: A benchmark test suite for evolutionary many-objective optimization. Complex Intell. Syst. **3**(1), 67–81 (2017)
3. Das, I., Dennis, J.E.: Normal-boundary intersection: a new method for generating the Pareto surface in nonlinear multicriteria optimization problems. SIAM J. Optim. **8**(3), 631–657 (1998)
4. Deb, K., Jain, H.: An evolutionary many-objective optimization algorithm using reference-point-based nondominated sorting approach, part I: solving problems with box constraints. IEEE Trans. Evol. Comput. **18**(4), 577–601 (2014)
5. Deb, K., Pratap, A., Agarwal, S., Meyarivan, T.: A fast and elitist multiobjective genetic algorithm: NSGA-II. IEEE Trans. Evol. Comput. **6**, 182–197 (2002)
6. Deb, K., Thiele, L., Zitzler, E.: Scalable multi-objectove optimization test problems. In: IEEE Congress on Evolutionary Computation, pp. 825–830. IEEE (2002)
7. López Jaimes, A., Coello Coello, C.A.: Many-objective problems: challenges and methods. In: Kacprzyk, J., Pedrycz, W. (eds.) Springer Handbook of Computational Intelligence, pp. 1033–1046. Springer, Heidelberg (2015). https://doi.org/10.1007/978-3-662-43505-2_51
8. Jain, H., Deb, K.: An improved adaptive approach for elitist nondominated sorting genetic algorithm for many-objective optimization. In: Purshouse, R.C., Fleming, P.J., Fonseca, C.M., Greco, S., Shaw, J. (eds.) EMO 2013. LNCS, vol. 7811, pp. 307–321. Springer, Heidelberg (2013). https://doi.org/10.1007/978-3-642-37140-0_25

9. Jain, H., Deb, K.: An evolutionary many-objective optimization algorithm using reference-point based nondominated sorting approach, part II: handling constraints and extending to an adaptive approach. IEEE Trans. Evol. Comput. 18(4), 602–622 (2014)
10. Jiang, S., Yang, S.: A strength Pareto evolutionary algorithm based on reference direction for multiobjective and many-objective optimization. IEEE Trans. Evol. Comput. 21(3), 329–346 (2017)
11. Li, B., Li, J., Tang, K., Yao, X.: Many-objective evolutionary algorithms: a survey. ACM Comput. Surv. (CSUR) 48(1), 13 (2015)
12. Liu, Y., Gong, D., Sun, X., Zhang, Y.: A reference points-based evolutionary algorithm for many-objective optimization. In: Proceedings of the Companion Publication of the 2014 Annual Conference on Genetic and Evolutionary Computation, pp. 1053–1056. ACM (2014)
13. Masood, A., Chen, G., Mei, Y., Zhang, M.: Reference point adaption method for genetic programming hyper-heuristic in many-objective job shop scheduling. In: Liefooghe, A., López-Ibáñez, M. (eds.) EvoCOP 2018. LNCS, vol. 10782, pp. 116–131. Springer, Cham (2018). https://doi.org/10.1007/978-3-319-77449-7_8
14. Masood, A., Mei, Y., Chen, G., Zhang, M.: Many-objective genetic programming for job-shop scheduling. In: IEEE WCCI 2016 Conference Proceedings. IEEE (2016)
15. Masood, A., Mei, Y., Chen, G., Zhang, M.: A PSO-based reference point adaption method for genetic programming hyper-heuristic in many-objective job shop scheduling. In: Wagner, M., Li, X., Hendtlass, T. (eds.) ACALCI 2017. LNCS (LNAI), vol. 10142, pp. 326–338. Springer, Cham (2017). https://doi.org/10.1007/978-3-319-51691-2_28
16. Zhang, Q., Zhou, A., Zhao, S., Suganthan, P.N., Liu, W., Tiwari, S.: Multiobjective optimization test instances for the CEC 2009 special session and competition. Technical report, University of Essex, Colchester, UK and Nanyang Technological University, Singapore, Special Session on Performance Assessment of Multi-objective Optimization Algorithms, pp. 1–30 (2008)
17. Zitzler, E., Thiele, L., Laumanns, M., Fonseca, C.M., Da Fonseca, V.G.: Performance assessment of multiobjective optimizers: an analysis and review. IEEE Trans. Evol. Comput. 7(2), 117–132 (2003)

Improving Representation
in Benchmarking of Binary PSO
Algorithms

Shinichi Yamada$^{(\boxtimes)}$ and Kourosh Neshatian

Department of Computer Science and Software Engineering,
University of Canterbury, Christchurch, New Zealand
shinichi.yamada@pg.canterbury.ac.nz

Abstract. Binary PSO algorithms are extensions of the PSO algorithm that enjoy some of the social intelligence properties of the original algorithm. The intensive local search ability is one of the most important characteristics of PSO. In this paper, we argue that, when evaluating binary PSO algorithms against common real-value benchmark problems—a common practice in the literature—the representation of the search space can have a significant effect on the results. For this purpose we propose the use of *reflected binary code*, which is a minimal change ordering representation for mapping a binary genotype space to a real phenotype space, while preserving the notion of locality in the phenotype space.

Keywords: Binary particle swarm optimization
Reflected binary code · Minimal change ordering · Representation
Benchmarking

1 Introduction

Particle swarm optimization (PSO) is a population-based optimization method that produces computational intelligence through social interaction [1]. In the algorithm, each particle has a memory of the best performance by itself and by the swarm and is attracted to those best points. In the later stages of the optimization process, particles swarm around the best points and those areas are intensively explored. Eventually the particles gather around the best point found by the swarm. This mechanism of intensive search around the optimal points is the reason for the excellent performance of PSO.

The PSO algorithm was originally developed for continuous spaces, but many real-world problems are defined in discrete spaces. Kennedy and Eberhart [2] introduced a discrete binary version of PSO for discrete optimization problems. In the binary PSO, the positions of particles are restricted to the vertices of hyper-cubes and the velocities are interpreted as the probability that particles move from the current vertices to other vertices.

© Springer Nature Switzerland AG 2018
T. Mitrovic et al. (Eds.): AI 2018, LNAI 11320, pp. 371–383, 2018.
https://doi.org/10.1007/978-3-030-03991-2_35

An alternate version of binary PSO, a probability-based binary PSO—was introduced by Zhen et al. [3]—in which the positions of particles represent the probabilities of assuming the value of 1 and the binary outcomes are stochastically generated based on these probabilities. In this model, the update rules of the velocity and position vectors are identical to those in the continuous PSO. Therefore, the theories developed for the continuous PSO can be applied to the analysis of this version of binary PSO.

It is a common practice to use benchmark functions to test the performance of new PSO algorithms. For binary PSO, the common practice is to use a binary representation for the domain (search space) of a benchmark function and then operate the algorithm. The most commonly-used binary representation is based on lexicographical ordering. In this paper, we will argue that this representation does not preserve *locality*: two close points in the domain of the function may have binary representations that are far apart from one another. For instance, the integers $\{0, 1, 2, 3, 4, 5, 6, 7\}$ are represented as $\{000, 001, 010, 011, 100, 101, 110, 111\}$ in the binary system. The distance between 3 and 4 is one but the Hamming distance between 011 and 100 is three. A better choice for the transformation of real solutions is Reflected Binary Code (RBC), which is also known as Gray code. There are some debates about RBC versus binary encoding in the field of genetic algorithm (GA) (Chakraborty et al. [4]). Since the movement of particles in PSO exclusively relies on the geometrical information in spaces, the preservation of relative distance is crucial for PSO. The purpose of this article is to verify this claim experimentally.

This paper is organized as follows. In Sect. 2, we review variants of continuous and binary versions of PSO. In Sect. 4, we discuss the shortcomings in the current representation used for binary PSO and present the proposed representation. In Sect. 5, we conduct experiments to test the alternate representation and discuss the results. We conclude the paper in Sect. 6.

2   Background and Review

In this section, we review major variants of continuous and binary-valued particle swarm optimization.

2.1   Particle Swarm Optimization (PSO)

The goal of continuous PSO is to solve the following optimization problem:

$$\text{minimize:} \quad F(\mathbf{x}), \quad \mathbf{x} = (x_1, \ldots, x_d) \in S \subseteq \mathbb{R}^d \tag{1}$$

where the search space S is a hyper-cube in $\mathbb{R}^d$,

$$l_j \leq x_j \leq u_j, \quad l_j, u_j \in \mathbb{R}, \quad j = 1, \ldots, d. \tag{2}$$

PSO is a population-based algorithm where the individuals in the population (or swarm) are called "particles". For each particle i, at time t and along dimension j, $x_{i,j}^t$ represents the current *position*, $v_{i,j}^t$ represents the current velocity, and $p_{i,j}^t$ represents the best position seen so far (**pbest**). The algorithm also keeps track of the best position seen by the swarm thus far (**gbest**), which is, at time t and along dimension j, denoted by g_j^t.

Standard PSO. The original form of the PSO algorithm was first introduced by Kennedy and Eberhart [1], with the following update equations for the elements of the velocity and position vectors, respectively:

$$v_{i,j}^{t+1} = v_{i,j}^t + c_1 \, r_{1,i,j}^t \left(p_{i,j}^t - x_{i,j}^t\right) + c_2 \, r_{2,i,j}^t \left(g_j^t - x_{i,j}^t\right); \tag{3}$$

$$x_{i,j}^{t+1} = x_{i,j}^t + v_{i,j}^{t+1}, \tag{4}$$

for $i \in \{1, \ldots, n\}$ and $j \in \{1, \ldots, d\}$, where $r_{1,i,j}^t$ and $r_{2,i,j}^t$ are random numbers distributed uniformly in $[0,1]$ for each i, j and t; and c_1 and c_2 are constant values. The d-dimensional **pbest** and **gbest** vectors are then updated as follows:

$$\mathbf{p}_i^{t+1} = \begin{cases} \mathbf{x}_i^{t+1}, & \text{if } F(\mathbf{x}_i^{t+1}) < F(\mathbf{p}_i^t) \\ \mathbf{p}_i^t, & \text{otherwise;} \end{cases} \tag{5}$$

$$\mathbf{g}^{t+1} = \operatorname{argmin}_i F(\mathbf{p}_i^{t+1}), \tag{6}$$

where, $\mathbf{x}_i^t = (x_{i,1}^t, \ldots, x_{i,d}^t)$ and $\mathbf{p}_i^t = (p_{i,1}^t, \ldots, p_{i,d}^t)$, for $i \in \{1, \ldots, n\}$.

Shi and Eberhart [5] introduced the inertia weight ω in the velocity update formula, which controls the effect of the velocity in the previous iteration, such that:

$$v_{i,j}^{t+1} = \omega \, v_{i,j}^t + c_1 \, r_{1,i,j}^t \left(p_{i,j}^t - x_{i,j}^t\right) + c_2 \, r_{2,i,j}^t \left(g_j^t - x_{i,j}^t\right). \tag{7}$$

This is the most popular form of PSO, which is often referred to as standard PSO (SPSO).

2.2 Binary Variants of PSO

The search space in binary PSO is $\{0,1\}^b$. The goal is to find a bit string of length b that minimizes a given objective function. In this section, we review the original version of binary PSO followed by two improved versions which will be used in our experiments.

Original Binary PSO. The first extension of PSO for discrete problems was introduced by Kennedy and Eberhart [6]. In binary PSO, the positions of particles are restricted to the vertices's of hyper-cubes, which are represented by binary values 0 or 1. They interpret the velocity $v_{i,j}^t$ as the probability of $x_{i,j}^t$ taking the value 1. The velocity update equation has the same form as that of (3). Since the velocity is a probability, it is constrained to the interval $[0,1]$.

Using a sigmoid function $\Lambda(v) = \frac{1}{1+e^{-v}}$, the position update rule is defined as follows:

$$x_{i,j}^{t+1} = \begin{cases} 1, & \text{if } r < \Lambda(v_{i,j}^{t+1}) \\ 0, & \text{otherwise} \end{cases} \qquad (8)$$

where r is a random number generated uniformly from the interval $[0,1]$.

Khanesar's Binary PSO (KBPSO). An improvement of BPSO was proposed by Khanesar et al. [7], where like the original (continuous) PSO, the velocity vector determines the rate of change. They introduced two vectors $\mathbf{v}_{0,i}^t$ and $\mathbf{v}_{1,i}^t$, which can be interpreted as the probability of the bits of particles changing to 0 and 1 respectively, conditional on the current values of the bits in the particle. The velocity is then defined as

$$v_{i,j}^t = \begin{cases} v_{0,i,j}^t, & \text{if } x_{i,j}^t = 1 \\ v_{1,i,j}^t, & \text{if } x_{i,j}^t = 0. \end{cases}$$

The idea is that if the j-th element of **pbest** (or **gbest**) is 1, then $v_{1,i,j}$ is increased and $v_{0,i,j}$ is decreased, and similarly, if the j-th element of **pbest** (or **gbest**) is 0, then $v_{0,i,j}$ is increased and $v_{1,i,j}$ is decreased. Based on the velocity update rule of SPSO, given in (7), they formulate the velocity update rules as follows:

$$v_{0,i,j}^{t+1} = w\, v_{0,i,j}^t + d_{0,1,i,j}^t + d_{0,2,i,j}^t;$$
$$v_{1,i,j}^{t+1} = w\, v_{1,i,j}^t + d_{1,1,i,j}^t + d_{1,2,i,j}^t,$$

where

$$d_{0,1,i,j}^t = -c_1 r_{1,i,j}^t, \quad d_{1,1,i,j}^t = c_1 r_{1,i,j}^t, \quad \text{if } p_{i,j}^t = 1$$
$$d_{0,1,i,j}^t = c_1 r_{1,i,j}^t, \quad d_{1,1,i,j}^t = -c_1 r_{1,i,j}^t, \quad \text{if } p_{i,j}^t = 0,$$

and

$$d_{0,2,i,j}^t = -c_2 r_{2,i,j}^t, \quad d_{1,2,i,j}^t = c_2 r_{2,i,j}^t, \quad \text{if } g_j^t = 1$$
$$d_{0,2,i,j}^t = c_2 r_{2,i,j}^t, \quad d_{1,2,i,j}^t = -c_2 r_{2,i,j}^t, \quad \text{if } g_j^t = 0.$$

The update rule for position is defined as follows:

$$x_{i,j}^{t+1} = \begin{cases} \bar{x}_{i,j}^t, & \text{if } r < \Lambda(v_{i,j}^{t+1}) \\ x_{i,j}^t, & \text{otherwise} \end{cases}$$

where $\bar{}$ is a complement operator, such that, $\bar{x}_{i,j}^t = 0$, if $x_{i,j}^t = 1$, and $\bar{x}_{i,j}^t = 1$, if $x_{i,j}^t = 0$. The matlab code provided in (Khanesar [8]) uses $w = 0.5$ and $c_1 = c_2 = 1$. In our experiments we denote this model as KBPSO.

Probability-Based Binary PSO (PBPSO). Zhen et al. [3], who view the departure of BPSO from the continuous PSO and its theories as a weakness, proposed a probability-based binary PSO (PBPSO), in which "the value of each bit is determined by its corresponding probability of being 1, while this probability is updated according to the information share mechanism of PSO" [3]. The position vector (representing probabilities in this method) is initialized as follows:

$$\mathbf{\dot{x}}_i^0 = \left(\dot{x}_{i,1}^0, \ldots, \dot{x}_{i,b}^0\right) = \left(\frac{1}{2}, \ldots, \frac{1}{2}\right).$$

All the update equations are identical to those in the original continuous PSO. That is, the elements of the velocity and position vectors are updated according to (3) and (4) respectively, in which x is replaced with $\dot{x}$.

The actual outcome of a particle is obtained stochastically as follows:

$$x_{i,j}^t = \begin{cases} 1, & \text{if } r < \dot{x}_{i,j}^t \\ 0, & \text{otherwise,} \end{cases}$$

where r is a uniformly generated random number. The **pbest** and **gbest** vectors are updated according to (5) and (6) respectively.

In order to avoid premature convergence, the authors also propose a mutation operator that with a probability P_m (set to 0.08 in their experiments) flips the bits in the outcome as follows:

$$x_{i,j}^{t+1} = \begin{cases} \bar{x}_{i,j}^t, & \text{if } r < P_m \\ x_{i,j}^t, & \text{otherwise.} \end{cases} \tag{9}$$

3   Reflected Binary Code

We present a brief review of the basics of Reflected Binary Code (RBC) proposed by Frank Gray (Gray [9]). RBC is minimal change ordering of bit strings where successive strings differ by a single bit. An n-bit RBC code $G(n)$ consists of 2^n n-bit strings $G_{n,0}, \ldots, G_{n,2^n-1}$.

$$G(n) = \begin{pmatrix} G_{n,0} \\ G_{n,1} \\ \vdots \\ G_{n,2^n-1} \end{pmatrix}$$

where $G_{n,k} = (g_{k,n-1}, \ldots, g_{k,0})$ for $g_{k,j} \in \{0,1\}$, $k \in \{0,1,\ldots,2^n-1\}$, and $j \in \{0,1,\ldots,n-1\}$. The code can be constructed recursively. The basis is

$$G(1) = \begin{pmatrix} 0 \\ 1 \end{pmatrix}$$

and the recurrence is

$$G(n+1) = \begin{pmatrix} 0G_{n,0} \\ 0G_{n,1} \\ \vdots \\ 0G_{n,2^n-1} \\ 1G_{n,2^n-1} \\ 1G_{n,2^n-2} \\ \vdots \\ 1G_{n,0} \end{pmatrix}.$$

In RBC, $G(n+1)$ consists of a copy of $G(n)$ with a "0" attached to each bit string and a copy of $G(n)$ in reverse order with a "1" attached to each string. For instance,

$$G(2) = \begin{pmatrix} 00 \\ 01 \\ 11 \\ 10 \end{pmatrix}$$

$$G(3) = \begin{pmatrix} 000 \\ 001 \\ 011 \\ 010 \\ 110 \\ 111 \\ 101 \\ 100 \end{pmatrix}$$

The common binary encoding, $B(n)$ of n-bit strings is

$$B(n) = \begin{pmatrix} B_{n,0} \\ B_{n,1} \\ \vdots \\ B_{n,2^n-1} \end{pmatrix}$$

where $B_{n,k} = (b_{k,n-1}, \ldots, b_{k,0})$ for $b_{k,i} \in \{0,1\}$, $k \in \{0,1,\ldots,2^n-1\}$ and $i \in \{0,1,\ldots,n-1\}$. It can be recursively constructed with

$$B(1) = \begin{pmatrix} 0 \\ 1 \end{pmatrix}$$

and the following recurrence

$$B(n+1) = \begin{pmatrix} B_{n,0}0 \\ B_{n,0}1 \\ B_{n,1}0 \\ B_{n,1}1 \\ \vdots \\ B_{n,2^n-1}0 \\ B_{n,2^n-1}1 \end{pmatrix} \quad (10)$$

For instance,

$$B(2) = \begin{pmatrix} 00 \\ 01 \\ 10 \\ 11 \end{pmatrix}$$

$$B(3) = \begin{pmatrix} 000 \\ 001 \\ 010 \\ 011 \\ 100 \\ 101 \\ 110 \\ 111 \end{pmatrix}$$

Lemma 1 *(Reingold et al. [10]). Suppose the bit string $B_{n,k} = (b_{k,n-1}, \dots, b_{k,0})$ is expressed as $B_{n,k} = (b_{k,n}, b_{k,n-1}, \dots, b_{k,0})$ with $b_{k,n} = 0$. Then,*

$$g_{k,j} = (b_{k,j} + b_{k,j+1}) \mod 2 \quad (11)$$

$$b_{k,j} = \sum_{i=j}^{n-1} g_{k,i} \mod 2 \quad (12)$$

for $k = 0, \dots, 2^n - 1$, $j = 0, \dots, n-1$

4   Representation of the Search Space

Most binary PSO algorithms are evaluated in a "classical testbed", where a particle in a multi-dimensional binary space $\{0,1\}^b$ is mapped to a point in a real space $S \subset \mathbb{R}^d$ with the goal of solving (1) [1,3,7]. In evolutionary computation terms, $\{0,1\}^b$ is the *genotype* space and S is the *phenotype* space. This means that the search happens in the genotype space while the objective function is evaluated on a point in the phenotype space. Thus the goal is to

$$\text{minimize:} \quad F(\Psi(\mathbf{x})), \quad \mathbf{x} \in \{0,1\}^b, \quad \Psi : \{0,1\}^b \to S$$

where the mapping Ψ is the *representation*. A good representation can lead to a "smooth" *fitness landscape* which increases the chance of finding a good solution.

The most common way of mapping a binary string to a number in the real space is using a floating-point representation. The most widely-used floating point representation standard is the IEEE 754 standard [11], which is very efficient because it is implemented at the hardware level in most modern computers. This representation, however, is not appropriate for searching binary spaces. This is because small changes in the parts of the bit string that are related to sign and exponent (i.e. small changes in the genotype space) can lead to drastic changes in the phenotype space.

The other alternative is using a fixed-point representation in which the interval $[l_j, u_j]$ (the j-th dimension of S) is meshed by a number of equi-distant points. If b_j is the number of bits dedicated to the j-th dimension, then the distance between the points on the mesh is $\frac{u_j - l_j}{2^{b_j}}$.

A *ranking function* $\rho(x_1, \ldots, x_{b_j})$ takes a binary vector and returns an integer in $\{0, 1, \ldots, 2^{b_j} - 1\}$ which determines the rank (or order) of the points on the mesh that the binary vector maps to. If $r = \rho(x_1, \ldots, x_{b_j})$, then the vector $(x_1, \ldots, x_{b_j})$ is mapped onto points in the interval $[l_j, u_j]$ as follows:

$$\psi_j(r) = l_j + \frac{r(u_j - l_j)}{2^{b_j}}. \tag{13}$$

If we view the vector $\mathbf{x} \in \{0,1\}^b$ as a bit string of length b, which has been divided into d consecutive substrings such that the j-th substring is b_j bits long, then the overall representation function can be defined as follows:

$$\Psi(\mathbf{x}) = \begin{bmatrix} \psi_1(\rho(x_1, \ldots, x_{b_1})) \\ \vdots \\ \psi_d(\rho(x_{b-b_d}, \ldots, x_b)) \end{bmatrix}$$

where $\sum_{j=1}^d b_j = b$.

The choice of the ranking function ρ is important because it affects the fitness landscape. Although the literature does not use the terminology we introduced here, the most common choice of representation (for instance, those used in [1,3,7]) is effectively equivalent to choosing a ρ_l defined as

$$\rho_l(x_1, \ldots, x_{b_j}) = \sum_{i=1}^{b_j} x_i 2^{(i-1)}.$$

This is the usual way of converting a binary string to an unsigned integer—binary strings in *lexicographical order* are mapped to consecutive integers.

When PSO is trying to "fine-tune" a solution, the closest points on the left and on the right of some point $\psi(r)$ in the interval $[l_j, u_j]$ are $\psi(r-1)$ and $\psi(r+1)$ respectively. Ideally this notion of locality must also be presented in the binary vector $(x_1, \ldots, x_{b_j})$ but this is not always the case when using a ranking function like ρ_l and this can cause undesired hurdles in the search process. For example, while the rankings 3 and 4 are next to each other, their conventional binary representations, namely 0011 and 0100, have a Hamming distance of 3 between them. In other words, the locality in the phenotype space is not preserved in the genotype space. The problem becomes more acute when the size of the binary vector increases.

In order to preserve locality, neighbourhood in the phenotype space must imply neighbourhood in the genotype space. We address this point using a *minimal change ordering* [12] instead of the lexicographical ordering imposed by ρ_l.

More formally, we use a function ρ_m such that

$$|\rho_m(\mathbf{x}) - \rho_m(\mathbf{x}')| = 1 \implies \sum_i |x^i - x'^i| = 1. \tag{14}$$

In other words, the Hamming distance between two points $\mathbf{x}$ and $\mathbf{x}'$ in the genotype space being 1 is a necessary condition for their corresponding points in the phenotype space being adjacent.

One option when defining such a ranking function is to interpret the sequence $x_1, \ldots, x_{b_j}$ as RBC, and define ρ_m as

$$\rho_m(x_1, \ldots, x_{b_j}) = \sum_{i=1}^{b_j} \left(\left(\sum_{k=i}^{b_j} x^k \right) \mod 2 \right) 2^{(i-1)}. \tag{15}$$

This ranking function meets the criterion set in (14). The relationship between the domains (inputs) of ρ_m and ρ_l is specified by (11) and (12).

5   Experiments

In this section, we conduct experiments in order to test our hypothesis that a 'smoother' representation of the search space, obtained by using reflected binary code, improves the performance of binary PSO algorithms.

5.1   Experimental Design

We use the following two binary PSO algorithms in our experiments:

1. **PBPSO:** We follow the parameter specifications in Zhen et al. [3]. We set $(c_1, c_2) = (2, 2)$ in (7). However, we adaptively adjust the parameter P_m in (9): we start with 0.1 in the first iteration and end at 0.05 in the last iteration.
2. **KBPSO:** We follow the parameter specification in (Khanesar et al. [7], Khanesar [8]). We set $(\omega, c_1, c_2) = (0.5, 1, 1)$, and the maximum of the velocity we set to 4.

We use these two algorithms because they represent two main ideas of binary PSO. In PBPSO the positions of particles are interpreted as the underlying probabilities which generate the binary responses. The update equations of PBPSO are compatible with those of the continuous PSO. In KBPSO the velocities of particles are interpreted as the probabilities which change the positions of particles.

We use benchmark functions commonly used in the literature to evaluate binary PSO algorithms [1, 3, 7]. Table 1 lists the benchmark functions from CEC 2005 [13] that we use in our experiments. The domain of all the functions is $\mathbb{R}^d$ and their range is $\mathbb{R}$. We experiment with values of d taken from $\{3, 6, 9\}$. The optimal points for all the functions is at zero.

Table 1. Basic and CEC 2005 benchmark functions [13]

ID	Name	Mode
S1	Sphere	Unimodal
S2	Rosenbrock	Multi-modal
S3	Griewangk	Multi-modal
S4	Rastrigin	Multi-modal
F1	Shifted Sphere Function	Unimodal
F2	Shifted Schwefel's Problem 1.2	Unimodal
F4	Shifted Schwefel's Problem 1.2 with Noise in Fitness	Unimodal
F5	Schwefel's Problem 2.6 with Global Optimum on Bounds	Unimodal
F6	Shifted Rosenbrock's Function	Multi-modal
F9	Shifted Rastrigin's Function	Multi-modal
F10	Shifted Rotated Rastrigin's Function	Multi-modal
F11	Shifted Rotated Weierstrass Function	Multi-modal
F12	Schwefel's Problem 2.13	Multi-modal
F14	Shifted Rotated Expanded Scaffer's F6	Multi-modal

In the experiments, each real dimension in the input vector is represented by 20 bits of code:

$$b_j = 20 \quad \forall j \in \{1, \ldots, d\}.$$

Thus $b = 20 \times d$; that is, the dimensionality of the binary space in our experiments will be 60, 120 and 180.

For each of the benchmark functions S1, S2, S3, S4, F1, F2, F4, and F5, we set the size of the population to $\frac{100d}{3}$ and the number of iterations to $\frac{200d}{3}$. For each of the multi-modal benchmark functions F6, F9, F10, F11, F12, and F14, we set the size of the population to $100d$ and the number of iterations to $\frac{500d}{3}$. The experiments are repeated 100 times for each function.

5.2   Results

The results of our experiments are presented in Table 2. For each method of PBPSO and KBPSO we compare the RBC representation with the common

Table 2. Optimal solutions for the benchmark functions

Func.	d	PBPSO	PBPSO (RBC)	NBPSO	NBPSO (RBC)
S1	3	**6.82e−09** ± 8.31e−24	**6.82e−09** ± 8.31e−24	4.49e−07* ± 7.5e−07	1.07e−06 ± 1.9e−06
	6	**2.79e−05** ± 1.87e−05	3.27e−05 ± 2.56e−05	0.00239 ± 0.00357	**0.00178** ± 0.00129
	9	**0.00524** ± 0.00281	0.00531 ± 0.00271	0.0905 ± 0.0547	**0.0734*** ± 0.042
S2	3	**6.6** ± 10.7	7.2 ± 9.42	7.02 ± 11.2	**5.77** ± 8.99 6
	6	29.6 ± 62.4	**8.03*** ± 10.3	36.4 ± 82.4	**9.86*** ± 10.2
	9	60.7 ± 131	**20.2*** ± 19.4	106 ± 189	**63.1*** ± 44.2
S3	3	**0.0102*** ± 0.00759	0.0149 ± 0.0143	0.0115 ± 0.009	**0.0102** ± 0.00955
	6	**0.0276** ± 0.014	0.0305 ± 0.0159	0.0414 ± 0.0232	**0.0408** ± 0.0233
	9	0.0705 ± 0.0356	**0.0682** ± 0.0281	0.122 ± 0.0489	**0.0931*** ± 0.0331
S4	3	**0.0428*** ± 0.209	1.63 ± 0.794	**0.0943*** ± 0.288	1.3 ± 0.84 6
	6	**0.78*** ± 0.891	3.69 ± 1.17	4.02 ± 2.48	**3.86** ± 1.06
	9	7.87 ± 3.63	**6.39*** ± 1.37	19 ± 6.02	**9.49*** ± 2.43
F1	3	3.09 ± 5.69	**4.9e−09*** ± 4.08e−09	1.14 ± 3.69	**2.3e−06*** ± 5.2e−06
	6	3.15 ± 5.58	**8.43e−05*** ± 6.23e−05	4.13 ± 5.86	**0.00584*** ± 0.00542
	9	16.7 ± 33.3	**0.0146*** ± 0.00786	23.6 ± 36.7	**0.21*** ± 0.141
F2	3	5.35 ± 15.4	**1.46e−07*** ± 2.51e−07	3.49 ± 12.3	**5.54e−05*** ± 0.000125
	6	16.5 ± 22.6	**0.00438*** ± 0.00476	17.5 ± 20.9	**0.126*** ± 0.14
	9	18.6 ± 20.9	**0.393*** ± 0.38	43.2 ± 31.4	**3.85*** ± 2.61
F4	3	8.95 ± 18.4	**5.61e−07*** ± 1.12e−06	1.17 ± 6.23	**0.00011** ± 0.000217
	6	19 ± 23.4	**0.00997*** ± 0.0146	21.3 ± 28.5	**0.278*** ± 0.371
	9	30.1 ± 27.9	**0.809*** ± 0.675	48 ± 41	**7.25*** ± 7.19
F5	3	**0.0404*** ± 0.0743	0.932 ± 1.37	**0.613*** ± 0.702	3.12 ± 3.85
	6	14.5 ± 36.9	**4.23*** ± 1.89	19.5* ± 25.3	26.3 ± 17.2
	9	394 ± 166	**42.5*** ± 22.8	424 ± 221	**157*** ± 80
F6	3	21.8 ± 20	**6.75*** ± 11.4	16.5 ± 19.1	**5.9*** ± 10.5
	6	1.48e+03 ± 2.07e+03	**8.6*** ± 17.9	1.26e+03 ± 1.98e+03	**11.9*** ± 16.4
	9	1.78e+04 ± 7.23e+04	**13.9*** ± 33.1	1.33e+04 ± 5.11e+04	**52.5*** ± 65
F9	3	0.114 ± 0.262	**0.0398*** ± 0.196	0.0565 ± 0.184	**0.00995*** ± 0.0995
	6	0.297 ± 0.426	**0.259** ± 0.482	0.448 ± 0.552	**0.389** ± 0.598
	9	**0.945** ± 0.844	1.03 ± 1.02	2.64 ± 1.26	**1.64*** ± 1.1
F10	3	1.06 ± 1.3	**0.916** ± 0.783	0.688 ± 0.663	**0.56** ± 0.603
	6	5.26 ± 2.86	**4.92** ± 2.37	5.58 ± 2.46	**4.61*** ± 2.21
	9	11.1 ± 4.46	**10.7** ± 4.52	12.7 ± 4.92	**12.2** ± 5.34
F11	3	0.198 ± 0.175	**0.129*** ± 0.15	0.145 ± 0.124	**0.092*** ± 0.105
	6	1.25 ± 0.758	**0.868*** ± 0.769	1.26 ± 0.67	**1.03*** ± 0.698
	9	2.8 ± 1.09	**1.73*** ± 0.938	3.31 ± 1.04	**2.73*** ± 1.2
F12	3	**0.558** ± 3.68	1.31 ± 5.72	0.37 ± 2.67	**0.0334** ± 0.0991
	6	**25.3** ± 44.8	28.4 ± 40.4	**39.4** ± 54.5	55.5 ± 76.3
	9	498 ± 721	**346** ± 573	**628*** ± 770	1.01e+03 ± 744
F14	3	0.149 ± 0.229	**0.0851*** ± 0.166	0.111 ± 0.17	**0.0455*** ± 0.0358
	6	1.21 ± 0.401	**1.08*** ± 0.545	1.1 ± 0.401	**1.06** ± 0.494
	9	**2.14** ± 0.409	2.25 ± 0.395	2.37 ± 0.326	**2.29** ± 0.357

binary representation. The better results are emphasized in boldface. We conduct the two-tailed t-test with unequal variance for each comparison. If the results of two representations are significantly different (p-values < 0.05), (*) is shown beside the number in the column of the better representation.

Table 2 report the results of the experiments carried out on the three different dimensions on the 14 benchmark functions. For PBPSO, 23 out of 42 solutions using RBC representation are significantly better ($p < 0.05$) than those using the binary representation and 4 solutions using RBC representation are significantly worse than those using the binary representation. For KBPSO, 24 out of 42 solutions using RBC representation are significantly better ($p < 0.05$) than those using the binary representation and 5 solutions using RBC representation are significantly worse than those using the binary representation. In some cases (for instance, the F1, F2, F4, F6 functions), the difference is quite large. In this experiment the computing time for the RBC representation was not different from that for the binary representation.

6   Conclusion

When benchmark functions with real domains are used to evaluate binary PSO algorithms—as is the case in the literature—the representation (or encoding) of numbers can influence the results. A good representation should be able to preserve the notion of neighbourhood across the binary search space (where the search happens) and the real space (where the functions are evaluated). We proposed a representation based on minimal change ordering. Our experiments on benchmark problems showed that state-of-the-art binary PSO algorithms significantly benefit from this new representation. It implies that the proposed encoding scheme provides more accurate means to test the new binary PSO methods using the benchmark functions.

References

1. Kennedy, J., Eberhart, R.C.: Particle swarm optimization. In: Proceedings of the 1995 IEEE International Conference on Neural Networks, Perth, Australia, vol. 4, pp. 1942–1948. IEEE Service Center, Piscataway (1995)
2. Kennedy, J., Eberhart, R.C.: A discrete binary version of the particle swarm algorithm. In: Proceedings of the IEEE International Conference on Systems, Man, and Cybernetics, Washington, DC, USA, vol. 5, pp. 4104–4108, IEEE Computer Society, October 1997
3. Zhen, L., Wang, L., Wang, X., Huang, Z.: A novel PSO-inspired probability-based binary optimization algorithm. In: 2008 International Symposium on Information Science and Engineering, vol. 2, pp. 248–251, December 2008
4. Chakraborty, U.K., Janikow, C.Z.: An analysis of gray versus binary encoding in genetic search. Inf. Sci. **156**(3–4), 253–269 (2003)
5. Shi, Y., Eberhart, R.C.: A modified particle swarm optimizer. In: Proceedings of IEEE International Conference on Evolutionary Computation, Washington, DC, USA, pp. 69–73. IEEE Computer Society, May 1998
6. Kennedy, J., Eberhart, R.C.: A discrete binary version of the particle swarm algorithm. In: 1997 IEEE International Conference on Systems, Man, and Cybernetics, Computational Cybernetics and Simulation. vol. 5, pp. 4104–4108, October 1997
7. Khanesar, M.A., Teshnehlab, M., Shoorehdeli, M.A.: A novel binary particle swarm optimization. In: 2007 Mediterranean Conference on Control Automation, pp. 1–6, June 2007

8. Khanesar, M.A.: Binary particle swarm optimization (2013)
9. Gray, F.: Pulse code communication. US Patent 2,632,058 (1953)
10. Reingold, E.M., Nievergelt, J., Deo, N.: Combinatorial Algorithms: Theory and Practice. Prentice Hall College Div, Englewood Cliffs (1977)
11. IEEE: IEEE standard for floating-point arithmetic. Standard, IEEE Computer Society, August 2008
12. Kreher, D.L., Stinson, D.R.: Combinatorial Algorithms: Generation, Enumeration, and Search. CRC Press, Boca Raton (1998)
13. Suganthan, P.N., et al.: Problem definitions and evaluation criteria for the CEC 2005 special session on real-parameter optimization. Technical report, Nanyang Technological University, Singapore (2005)

Investigation of a Simple Distance Based Ranking Metric for Decomposition-Based Multi/Many-Objective Evolutionary Algorithms

Hemant Kumar Singh[1]($\boxtimes$), Kalyan Shankar Bhattacharjee[1], Tapabrata Ray[1], and Sanaz Mostaghim[2]

[1] University of New South Wales, Canberra, Australia
{h.singh,t.ray}@adfa.edu.au, k.bhattacharjee@student.adfa.edu.au
[2] Otto von Guericke University, Magdeburg, Germany
sanaz.mostaghim@ovgu.de

Abstract. Multi-objective problems with more than three objectives, more commonly referred to as *many-objective problems*, have lately been a subject of significant research interest. Decomposition of the objective space is one of the most widely used approaches, where the original problem is decomposed into several single-objective sub-problems and solved collaboratively. The sub-problems are defined using reference vectors, to which candidate solutions are assigned based on some proximity measures (e.g. perpendicular distance/angle etc.). The individuals attached to a given reference vector can thus be considered as a sub-population trying to solve that sub-problem. To create selection pressure among the members of the sub-population, several measures have been proposed in the past; such as weighted sum, penalty boundary intersection, achievement scalarizing function, Tchebycheff, etc. While being competitive, some of them require parameters or reference points for implementation, which is far from ideal. The aim of this study is to investigate an alternative, less explored avenue - the use of *distance based ranking* with a decomposition based algorithm. Towards this end, we propose an improved version of an existing distance based metric and embed it within a decomposition based evolutionary algorithm (DBEA-MDR). We characterize its performance through a comprehensive benchmarking on a range of regular and inverted DTLZ/WFG problems. While the performance of DBEA-MDR based on conventional benchmarking practice (quality of solutions of the *final populations*) is not competitive with existing state-of-the-art algorithms, selection of a diverse set of solutions (of same size as the population) from the archive significantly improves its performance which in a number of cases supersedes the performance of other algorithms. Based on these observations, apart from highlighting the scope of improvement in the presented strategy, the study also emphasizes the need to look into existing benchmarking practices further. In particular, instead of the performance judged by the final population, a better approximation set could be found from the archive and performance judged on such sets would be more reflective of the true performance of the algorithms.

© Springer Nature Switzerland AG 2018
T. Mitrovic et al. (Eds.): AI 2018, LNAI 11320, pp. 384–396, 2018.
https://doi.org/10.1007/978-3-030-03991-2_36

Keywords: Multi-objective optimization · Decomposition
Distance based ranking

1   Introduction

Real-world design problems often require simultaneous optimization of multiple conflicting objectives, referred to as multi-objective optimization problems (MOP). Problems with more than three objectives are further sub-categorized as *many-objective* optimization problem (MaOP) due to their unique set of challenges. It is now well established in literature that traditional dominance-based methods that have been quite successful in solving 2/3-objective MOPs tend to not scale well for MaOPs [10]. This deterioration in performance is primarily attributed to loss in adequate selection pressure, since most of the solutions in the population become non-dominated (and hence indistinguishable in terms of convergence). Additional challenges include diversity maintenance for large number of objectives, visualization, decision making, etc. [2]. Consequently, several proposals have been put forward in the past decade to overcome the associated challenges and it still remains an active area of interest. Some of the prominent approaches to deal with MaOPs include use of secondary ranking measures, dimensionality reduction, indicator based approaches and decomposition based approaches.

A particular class of methods which have been widely reported builds upon the principle of *decomposition*. The motivation of the approach is to incorporate ideas from classical optimization into evolutionary methods for solving MOP/MaOPs. This is accomplished by decomposing the objective space of the original problem into several single-objective problems (or occasionally simpler multi-objective problems); and solving them co-cooperatively through an evolving population. Multi-objective evolutionary algorithm based on decomposition (MOEA/D) [21] is among the most well-known algorithm in this class; although some other prior studies along this line also exist [16]. The strengths of decomposition particularly in overcoming selection pressure has been widely recognized. A number of further developments have leveraged this idea [19], often incorporating decomposition in conjunction with other enhancements.

The decomposition of the problem is typically done based on a set of uniformly distributed points generated using systematic sampling [4] on a unit hyperplane (i.e. a plane with an intercept of 1 on each objective axis). Lines joining the ideal point to the above sampled set of points yield the set of reference vectors that are used to define the sub-problems. The solution(s) in the population or under consideration are assigned/attached to the reference vector(s) based on their proximity (based e.g. on angle or distance measures). This translates to each sub-problem being solved by evolving a sub-population, in collaboration with other sub-populations. Evidently, selection measures are required to rank the solutions within each sub-population. Some of the frequently used selection measures include penalized boundary intersection (PBI) [21], achievement scalarizing function (ASF) [14,20], Tchebychev, angle penalized distance

(APD) [3] etc. A range of studies have shown their effectiveness in use within optimization frameworks based on decomposition; but at the same time have also revealed some of their shortcomings. For example, some of these techniques require a parameter to balance the convergence and diversity, e.g., PBI and APD, which could require some tuning depending on the nature of the problem. Weighted sum is known to be ineffective for locating non-convex regions of the Pareto front. The formulation of ASF requires a reference point to be set, and has issues in ranking the weakly dominated solutions.

In this paper, we aim to conduct investigations on the use of an alternate, non-parametric, distance-based measure to rank members of a sub-population. The inspiration for this study comes from reflecting on some of the earlier attempts for secondary ranking for solving MaOPs using *dominance* based methods. By default, the dominance based algorithms incorporate a density estimation based measure for ranking solutions within a given non-dominated front. In the widely used non-dominated sorting genetic algorithm (NSGA-II) [7], this is done by assigning each solution a "crowding distance" value, and sorting them in a decreasing order; thereby ranking the relatively sparse solutions higher in the list. In [12], four "substitute distance" based secondary ranking methods were proposed for NSGA-II in lieu of crowding distance. The idea was that since crowding distance measure does not work well for density estimation in higher dimensions, it could be replaced by a ranking measure that could differentiate between the solutions that are non-dominated to each other. In the process, these secondary ranking measures could be chosen that promote both convergence and diversity (in lieu of diversity alone in case of crowding distance). The methods include epsilon-dominance, sub-vector dominance, fuzzy Pareto dominance and sub-objective dominance count [12,17]. However, to the authors' knowledge, the potential of such measures in the context of decomposition based algorithms has not been studied. Towards this end, we examine an existing distance-based measures and propose an enhancement to overcome its limitation. The resulting modified distance ranking (MDR) is integrated within a decomposition based evolutionary algorithm (DBEA); referred to hereafter as DBEA-MDR. Thereafter, we study the performance on a range of conventional and inverted versions of the commonly studied DTLZ and WFG test problems with up to 10 objectives, and compare the results with those reported in the literature. Further, we observe the performance of the DBEA-MDR in two scenarios - one where the final population is used for calculating the performance metric (hypervolume), and one where a different set (of same size as population) is picked instead from the archive of evaluated non-dominated solutions. We present the comparisons of both versions with the results reported for state-of-the-art algorithms in the literature and conclude with some additional observations about the benchmarking practices and potential future improvements.

The remainder of this paper is organized as follows. In Sect. 2, we provide a brief background of the distance measure adopted in this study. Thereafter, we describe the decomposition based framework in Sect. 3, followed by numerical experiments in Sect. 4. Concluding remarks are presented in Sect. 5.

2 Distance Based Ranking

In this study, we focus on modifying existing distance based ranking measure discussed previously in [15] in the context of particle swarm optimization. The distance based ranking (DR) proposed in [15] simply accounts for the sum of absolute differences in the objective values between the two solutions, irrespective of the domination status (i.e. how many and which objectives are better for one solution over other and vice versa). In order to calculate DR for any given set of solutions, first the distance vectors between each solution pair $\mathbf{x}_i$ and $\mathbf{x}_j$ are calculated as shown in Eq. 1.

$$d_{ij} = \{|f_1(\mathbf{x}_i) - f_1(\mathbf{x}_j)|, |f_2(\mathbf{x}_i) - f_2(\mathbf{x}_j)|, \ldots |f_m(\mathbf{x}_i) - f_M(\mathbf{x}_j)|\} \qquad (1)$$

Thereafter, DR for each solution $\mathbf{x}_i$ is calculated as shown in Eq. 2.

$$DR(\mathbf{x}_i) = \sum_{k=1}^{M} \sum_{j=1, j \neq i}^{N} d_{ij}^k, \quad \text{where} \quad d_{ij}^k = |f_k(\mathbf{x}_i) - f_k(\mathbf{x}_j)| \qquad (2)$$

A predecessor of DR, known as average ranking (AR) was also discussed in [15], which was calculated simply based on how many objectives one is better than compared to the other, irrespective of the magnitude of the differences in the objective values. For a simple illustration, let us consider two non-dominated solutions A and B for a three objective problem with objective values $\{0, 5, 10\}$, and $\{7, 5, 0\}$ respectively. Thus, for the given two points, the values of AR and DR for the two solutions can be summarized as shown in Table 1.

Table 1. AR and DR metrics

Metric	A	B
AR	9	9
DR	17	17

It can be seen that among the two solutions, A is better than B in one objective (f_1) and vice versa in f_3, while they are equal in the remaining objective (f_2). However, A is better than B by a smaller amount (7 units) in f_1 and B is better than A in f_3 (10 units). Therefore, B should ideally have a preference over A in the ranking. However, neither AR or DR can capture this preference; as both the points are indistinguishable by either of the measures. In fact, owing to this, they are not suitable to be used within a decomposition-based framework, mainly because (a) AR can not quantify the scale of difference since it only captures number of objectives, and (b) DR value will be the same irrespective of whether a solution is dominating or dominated by another solution since it only captures the absolute differences.

In order to overcome this limitation, we propose a simple modification of DR in the following way. Instead of taking absolute difference between the objective values (Eq. 2), we observe the difference between the raw objective values, and the summation considers only the objectives in which one solution is better than the others. Without loss of generality, we consider all objectives in a minimization sense. Thus, the formulation can be written as shown below, where a lower MDR indicates a preferred solution.

$$MDR(x_i) = \sum_{k=1}^{M} \sum_{j=1, j \neq i}^{N} min((f_k(\mathbf{x}_i) - f_k(\mathbf{x}_j), 0) \tag{3}$$

Note that with this simple change, the information about the amount of domination could be integrated into the ranking process. Revisiting the above two points, A will get an MDR value of -7, whereas B will get a value of -10; making the latter a more preferred solution. An example of the computation of this metric for a larger set of $(N_p = 6)$ solutions is given next. Consider a set of non-dominated points (A–F) shown in Table 2 which could be a set of solutions identified in a sub-population during the search corresponding to a particular sub-problem. Based on Eq. 3, their MDR and ranking are shown in the last two columns. The solution A is best in this case, followed by solution C, E, D, F and B.

Table 2. Objective values for an assumed sub-population

Solutions	f_1	f_2	f_3	MDR	Rank
A	10.25	8	7	-16.55	1
B	9	9	9	-9.25	6
C	8	10	7	-15.85	2
D	7	11	9	-14.25	4
E	9.2	10.2	6.3	-14.75	3
F	11.1	7.2	10.5	-12.2	5

The key idea in this paper is to use this MDR within a DBEA to improve ranking within a sub-population. Some of the potential advantages of a distance based approach include:

- Unlike AR and DR, it takes into account of the objectives where the performance is better along with its amount. Thus it creates a better and more complete ordering of solutions, while promoting solutions with more desired dominance characteristics.
- Based on above, the integration of proposed MDR in a DBEA could also be thought of as combining the advantages of dominance and decomposition.
- The proposed ranking does not involve choice of any additional parameters or reference points, unlike some of the existing measures such as PBI, APD, ASF, etc.
- It is simple to implement and easily scalable with the number of objectives.

- It has no conceptual limitation in handling non-convex Pareto fronts (as opposed to weighted sum).

Having discussed the basic idea and motivation behind the proposed approach, we move on to discuss the decomposition-based framework used for this study.

3 Overview of the Framework

A generic unconstrained multi/many-objective optimization problem can be defined as shown in Eq. 4.

$$\text{Minimize } f_i(\mathbf{x}); i = 1, 2, ...M, \quad \text{Subject to } \mathbf{x}^L \leq \mathbf{x} \leq \mathbf{x}^U, \quad (4)$$

Here, $f_1(\mathbf{x})$ to $f_M(\mathbf{x})$ are the M objective functions. The upper and lower bounds of the variables are denoted as $\mathbf{x}^U$ and $\mathbf{x}^L$. The ideal vector (Z^I) can be constructed by identifying minimum value of each of the M objectives. Similarly, the nadir vector Z^N can be constructed using the maximum values of each objective in a given non-dominated set.

The proposed algorithm (DBEA-MDR) follows the general structure of the Reference Vector guided Evolutionary Algorithm (RVEA) [3] with variations in some components. It is based on a ($\mu + \lambda$) evolutionary model, where μ parents are recombined to generate λ offspring and the *best* μ solutions are selected as parents for the next generation. The pseudo-code of the proposed method is presented in Algorithm 1 and the details of its key components (highlighted in bold) are outlined below.

Algorithm 1. DBEA-MDR

Input: Gen_{max} (Max. generations), N (Population size), CR, F (DE crossover parameters), η_c, η_m, p_c, p_m (SBX/Polynomial mutation parameters)

1: $Gen = 0, j = 0$;
2: $Archive = \{\}$ { to store all evaluated solutions}
3: **Generate** W reference points using Normal Boundary Intersection.
4: Construct W reference directions by joining origin and W reference points
5: $P^j =$ **Initialize**(), $|P^j| = N_I$
6: **Evaluate** every objective function of P^j; Update $Archive$
7: $W_m =$ **UpdateRef**(W, P^j)
8: $P^j =$ **Assign**(W_m, P^j)
9: **while** ($Gen \leq Gen_{max}$) **do**
10:     $C =$ **CreateOffspring**(P^j), $|C| = N$
11:     **Evaluate** each objective function of C; Update $Archive$
12:     $W_m =$ **UpdateRef**($W, P^j \cup C$)
13:     $P^{j+1} =$ **Assign**($W_m, P^j \cup C$)
14:     $Gen = Gen + 1$
15: **end while**

- **Generate:** A structured set of W reference points is generated using the method of systematic sampling (normal boundary intersection) as outlined in [4]. The approach generates W points on the hyperplane in M-objective space with a uniform spacing of $\delta = 1/H$ with H unique sampling locations along each objective axis. The reference directions are formed by joining the ideal point (origin in the scaled space) to each of these reference points. For 8 or more objectives, a two-layered approach is commonly used in the field (and adopted here), which limits the number of reference points from growing exponentially.
- **Initialize:** N solutions are initialized within the variable bounds $\mathbf{x}^L$ and $\mathbf{x}^U$ using Latin Hypercube Sampling based on "maximin" criterion.
- **Evaluate:** In this stage, the objective functions are evaluated for all the solutions generated above.
- **UpdateRef:** In this stage, the ith reference direction W^i is modified to W_m^i based on the ideal vector (Z^I) and nadir vector (Z^N) of the combined parent and child population using Eq. 5. Take note that the proposed approach uses the nadir point of the combined parent and child population as opposed to maximum value of each objective function of parent and child population in the RVEA. This stage is necessary to achieve a decent distribution of solutions in the objective space irrespective of the scale of objectives.

$$(W_m^i)_j = (W^i)_j \times (Z^N - Z^I)_j, \forall\, 1 \leq j \leq M \tag{5}$$

- **Assign:** In this stage, solutions are assigned to the reference directions. A sub-population with respect to a reference direction is constructed using the solutions which are closest to that reference direction based on angle measure as described in [3]. If no solutions belong to a sub-population, it is considered empty and all solutions in the existing population are made available to the sub-population in this scenario. A modified distance based ranking scheme is used to select the best solution in each sub-population to assign to the reference direction and subsequently carry forward as parent for the next generation.
- **CreateOffspring:** In our approach, each solution is selected as a base parent and its partner is randomly chosen from the rest. Such a scheme offers opportunity to all solutions to act as base parents for generating offspring. We capitalize on the advantages of two commonly used recombination schemes, i.e., differential evolution (DE) crossover [5] and simulated binary crossover (SBX) [7]. In each generation both types of crossover and polynomial mutation are employed for each of the base parents attached to each reference direction, i.e., if at the first generation, the first reference direction uses DE crossover, the second reference direction would use SBX and this will be reversed in the second generation. The intent behind such an alternation is to remove the bias induced by the specific operators, and possibly gain advantages of exploratory behaviors of both DE and SBX.

4 Numerical Experiments

4.1 Test Problems and Experimental Settings

The most commonly studied benchmarks in the field of MaOPs are DTLZ series [8] and WFG [9] series problems, both of which are scalable in terms of decision variables as well as objectives. Both the series share one common property that makes them conducive use of traditional decomposition based methods. Most of the problems in these series have linear/quadratic PFs which are oriented such that they can be mapped well by the traditional way of generating reference vectors on a hyperplane. It has been revealed and discussed in-depth in some of the recent papers [1,11] that the performance of the decomposition based approaches strongly depends on the shape of the PF, and hence testing them on the regular problems alone may form an incomplete picture of an algorithm's performance. A series of problems with so called "inverted" PFs was therefore proposed in [11], which are referred to as the "minus" problems. Therefore, in this study, even though no active mechanism is employed for adaptation of the reference vectors for irregular fronts, a more diverse set of test problems from both the original (DTLZ1–DTLZ7, WFG1–WFG9) and the minus sets (DTLZ1^{-1}–DTLZ4^{-1}, WFG1^{-1}–WFG9^{-1}) is used for a more comprehensive evaluation. The detailed description of the problems and the difficulties in solving them can be found in [11]. Up to 10 objectives are considered for each problem in the experiments.

For a fair comparison, we adopt the same settings as in [11], including the population size and generations (hence, the number of function evaluations are same). The performance of DBEA-MDR is benchmarked against some state-of-the-art algorithms such as NSGA-III [6], θ-DEA [20], MOEA/DD [13], MOEA/D-PBI [21]. The results obtained by the listed algorithms are taken from [11].

A probability of crossover of 1 and a probability of mutation of $\frac{1}{n}$ (n is the number of variables) [6] was used for all problems studied in the paper. The distribution index of crossover was set to 30 and the distribution index of the mutation was set to 20 for all problems [6]. The DE crossover rate (CR) and scaling factor (F) are set to 1 and 0.5 respectively [5]. 21 independent runs were conducted for all problems to observe the statistical behavior. The performance metric used for comparison is hypervolume (HV), which is widely used in the literature for benchmarking. The procedure of HV computation is consistent with the recent works, e.g. [11] which can he referred to for more details. Comparisons are also done using the inverted generational distance (IGD) metric and reflect the same relative performance as the HV metric. Therefore, for brevity, only HV results are presented in the following subsection.

4.2 Preliminary Results and Discussion

The HV statistics across 21 runs for regular DTLZ and WFG problems are shown in Table 3, while the same for minus problems is shown in Table 4. The last four

Table 3. Mean HV statistics for DTLZ and WFG series problems

Problem	M	DBEA-MDR	DBEA-MDR(A)	DBEA-ASF	NSGA-III	θ-DEA	MOEA/DD	MOEA/D-PBI
DTLZ1	3	0.87768	1.11642	0.860	1.11508	1.11767	**1.11913**	1.11711
	5	1.24519	1.56026	1.095	1.57677	1.57767	**1.57794**	1.57768
	8	1.77964	2.10287	1.546	2.13770	**2.13788**	2.13730	2.13620
	10	2.20918	2.54055	1.851	**2.59280**	2.59272	2.59260	2.59220
DTLZ2	3	0.72644	0.74064	0.736	0.74336	0.74390	**0.74445**	0.74418
	5	1.27645	1.29126	1.278	1.30317	1.30679	**1.30778**	1.30728
	8	1.94691	1.89669	1.919	1.96916	1.97785	**1.97862**	1.97817
	10	2.48903	2.42884	2.456	2.50878	2.51416	**2.51509**	2.51500
DTLZ3	3	0.54073	**0.74369**	0.573	0.73300	0.73642	**0.73944**	0.73654
	5	0.88550	1.27828	0.874	1.29894	1.30376	**1.30638**	1.30398
	8	1.60912	1.69096	1.629	1.95007	1.96849	**1.97162**	1.74240
	10	2.31720	1.99442	2.239	2.50727	2.51279	**2.51445**	2.50933
DTLZ4	3	0.72755	0.73290	0.722	0.73221	0.71077	**0.74484**	0.48232
	5	1.25023	1.28020	1.286	1.30839	**1.30878**	1.30876	1.20680
	8	1.92917	1.87871	1.917	1.98025	1.98078	**1.98083**	1.86439
	10	2.49688	2.43674	2.433	2.51524	**2.51539**	2.51532	2.43536
WFG1	3	0.45018	0.47148	0.523	0.65088	**0.70151**	0.69393	0.67291
	5	0.67352	0.69421	0.668	0.85608	1.14844	1.23809	**1.34797**
	8	0.89056	0.90596	0.847	1.36206	1.88297	**1.91925**	1.73875
	10	1.09117	1.10279	1.061	2.22078	**2.38349**	2.37705	1.78435
WFG2	3	1.20802	1.22187	1.203	1.22359	**1.22945**	1.22193	1.11888
	5	1.53911	1.57338	1.536	**1.59770**	1.59708	1.55672	1.52205
	8	2.02956	2.11305	2.047	**2.13629**	2.12442	2.04619	2.01678
	10	2.49843	2.56934	2.512	**2.58890**	2.57778	2.48332	2.45715
WFG3	3	**0.93175**	**0.97330**	0.961	0.81929	0.81556	0.77295	0.75364
	5	1.28885	**1.38442**	1.299	1.01000	1.02782	0.95386	0.89357
	8	1.26601	**1.70179**	1.795	1.21146	1.11348	1.15306	0.74674
	10	1.60113	**2.14605**	2.269	1.55771	1.55919	1.37737	0.55186
WFG4	3	0.69821	0.70282	0.702	0.72867	**0.72949**	0.72031	0.68710
	5	1.11140	1.18648	1.124	1.28496	**1.28736**	1.26067	1.15695
	8	1.17570	1.75340	1.620	1.96402	**1.96426**	1.83751	1.19841
	10	1.53370	2.28334	2.155	2.50322	**2.50376**	2.22383	1.43393
WFG5	3	0.66558	0.67785	0.667	0.68658	**0.68706**	0.67698	0.65668
	5	1.07398	1.17637	1.073	1.22187	**1.22209**	1.18965	1.11627
	8	1.26872	1.76605	1.510	1.84995	**1.85027**	1.71196	1.27483
	10	1.58990	2.26602	1.979	2.34640	**2.34644**	2.07711	1.53615
WFG6	3	0.65969	0.66651	0.671	0.68696	**0.68698**	0.67923	0.65655
	5	1.04261	1.14185	1.043	1.21978	**1.22284**	1.19424	1.04043
	8	1.01886	1.58509	1.372	**1.84625**	1.84330	1.69055	0.71742
	10	1.19848	1.97188	1.789	2.32660	**2.32759**	2.01837	0.82027
WFG7	3	0.71442	0.72140	0.720	0.72894	**0.73099**	0.72126	0.61145
	5	1.13161	1.23049	1.140	1.29190	**1.29548**	1.25983	1.07723
	8	1.25180	1.78232	1.613	1.97138	**1.97353**	1.82024	0.83439
	10	1.50651	2.25390	2.140	2.50754	**2.50858**	2.25713	0.95972
WFG8	3	0.63015	0.63452	0.642	0.66560	**0.66687**	0.65741	0.62986
	5	0.99859	1.07245	1.019	1.18225	**1.18354**	1.15376	0.95660
	8	0.58597	1.13586	1.321	1.75970	**1.76647**	1.70621	0.30471
	10	0.90617	1.57374	1.771	2.28203	**2.28502**	2.10729	0.27470
WFG9	3	0.66160	0.67438	0.660	0.67519	**0.67978**	0.67146	0.57864
	5	1.05117	1.14811	1.053	1.21058	**1.22122**	1.15493	1.02426
	8	1.21164	1.67194	1.460	1.80911	**1.83678**	1.60407	0.97800
	10	1.49998	2.14480	1.914	2.34332	**2.36516**	1.92977	1.15138

columns in the tables denote the HV corresponding to the final populations obtained using four of the widely reported algorithms in the current literature, namely NSGA-III [6], θ-DEA [20], MOEA/DD [13] and MOEA/D-PBI [21]. The first two columns denote the two ways in which the solutions from DBEA-MDR are chosen for benchmarking:

- The first column shows the results for the conventional approach, i.e., the computing the HV of the final population delivered by the algorithm.
- The second column (DBEA-MDR(A)) shows results for a diverse subset of solutions chosen from the archive of all solutions evaluated using DBEA-MDR. The subset selection method here is the slightly modified version of the one proposed in [18]. The selection process starts by picking a random solution from the non-dominated solutions of the archive, followed by progressively selecting the non-dominated solutions furthest from the currently selected point(s). The scheme is designed to pick a diverse set of solutions and make use of all information encountered during the search instead of relying only on the final population.

Lastly, the third column in Tables 3 and 4 denotes a more commonly used measure, namely ASF, in lieu of MDR in DBEA so it can be directly compared with MDR in exactly same framework.

The first prominent observation from the tables is that the performance of the DBEA-MDR is inferior to the compared state-of-the-art methods both for most of the regular (except MOEA/D-PBI for WFG2-9) and inverted problems. Secondly, the performance of DBEA-ASF is better than DBEA-MDR. Thus, even though MDR has some conceptually desirable properties as discussed in Sect. 2, it still does not seem to be well-suited to a decomposition based framework. The apparent reason for this is that MDR is not able to enforce explicit selection pressure towards alignment of solutions to the reference vectors that is done in other methods through penalized distance or reference point specification.

However, an interesting behavior is observed when the performance of DBEA-MDR(A) is considered relative to other algorithms. It can be seen that the performance of DBEA-MDR(A) is always better than DBEA-MDR (with a few exceptions). Moreover, DBEA-MDR(A) is also better than DBEA-ASF for most of the instances. This observation is noteworthy since it confirms that there exists a subset of solutions with much better HV than final population within the archive of solutions evaluated during the DBEA-MDR run. In-fact, the DBEA-MDR(A) results are also better than the other four algorithms for 5 instances in the regular problems (Table 3), and as many as 28 instances in the minus problems (Table 4). For the remaining instances, the differences in performance are less than those observed for the case of DBEA-MDR. Consequently, the output of the algorithm could potentially be presented as this set instead of the final population for the benchmarking. This is equally applicable to other algorithms in the table. The full archives of the other algorithms are not available to be included in this study, but in principle, the results reported for the other algorithms are also potentially under-reported given that final populations are used by default in the current benchmarking practices.

Given the above observations, an interesting and timely research direction in the field of MaOP could therefore be to design strategies to pick the solutions with the best possible output metric. In this regard, the closest related work is on the so called *hypervolume subset selection problem*, which involves selecting K solutions out of N_0 such that HV is maximized. Such methods are, however,

Table 4. Mean HV statistics for $DTLZ^{-1}$ and WFG^{-1} series problems

Problem	M	DBEA–MDR	DBEA–MDR(A)	DBEA–ASF	NSGA–III	θ–DEA	MOEA/DD	MOEA/D–PBI
DTLZ1⁻¹	3	0.23731	**0.29074**	0.255	**0.27258**	0.25057	0.24887	0.26146
	5	0.00531	**0.01769**	0.006	0.01265	0.00898	0.00972	**0.01739**
	8	4.241E–06	3.676E–05	1.327E–05	**5.227E–05**	4.499E–05	0.881E–05	0.598E–05
	10	4.38E–08	6.72E–07	1.887E–07	**1.185E–06**	0.451E–06	0.100E–06	0.079E–06
DTLZ2⁻¹	3	0.67037	**0.71027**	0.682	0.68986	0.69303	0.68912	0.69439
	5	0.12781	**0.20580**	0.119	0.13957	0.13496	0.08794	0.15984
	8	4.809E–03	**7.194E–03**	0.004	4.454E–03	3.406E–03	2.690E–03	**5.978E–03**
	10	0.00048	**0.00073**	3.723E–04	**6.308E–04**	5.541E–04	1.836E–04	5.199E–04
DTLZ3⁻¹	3	0.66738	**0.70867**	0.679	0.69251	0.69468	0.68990	0.69609
	5	0.12557	**0.20106**	0.112	0.12951	0.13273	0.08190	0.15902
	8	4.455E–03	**6.888E–03**	0.004	0.00414	0.00401	0.00255	**0.00596**
	10	0.00046	**0.00071**	3.568E–04	0.00054	**0.00059**	0.00018	0.00052
DTLZ4⁻¹	3	0.67785	**0.71193**	0.689	0.69397	0.69546	0.68942	0.59319
	5	0.12599	**0.18504**	0.125	0.12326	0.11428	0.07242	0.12296
	8	1.492E–03	1.793E–03	3.618E–03	**4.582E–03**	3.921E–03	2.198E–03	2.020E–03
	10	0.00016	0.00014	2.994E–04	6.065E–04	**6.409E–04**	2.569E–04	2.333E–04
WFG1⁻¹	3	0.07936	0.09848	**0.115**	0.10955	0.08936	0.08475	0.03944
	5	0.00107	**0.00242**	1.208E–03	0.00221	0.00155	0.00094	0.00033
	8	8.395E–07	**3.371E–06**	1.180E–06	1.835E–06	1.401E–06	1.028E–06	0.126E–06
	10	8.84E–09	**4.82E–08**	1.060E–08	1.891E–08	1.524E–08	0.962E–08	0.149E–08
WFG2⁻¹	3	0.37024	0.38323	0.378	**0.38373**	0.38347	0.38123	0.37769
	5	0.00540	**0.01121**	0.006	0.01067	0.00805	0.00611	0.00500
	8	3.792E–06	**1.375E–05**	4.975E–06	0.784E–05	0.638E–05	0.383E–05	0.368E–05
	10	3.61E–08	1.37E–07	5.044E–08	**0.795E–07**	0.569E–07	0.441E–07	0.378E–07
WFG3⁻¹	3	0.21564	0.24638	0.233	**0.26507**	0.24959	0.23184	0.25481
	5	0.00662	**0.01363**	0.007	0.01279	0.00912	0.00388	0.00459
	8	5.388E–06	1.538E–05	1.347E–05	**3.666E–05**	1.415E–05	0.262E–05	0.417E–05
	10	5.49E–08	1.83E–07	1.873E–07	**6.673E–07**	2.511E–07	0.250E–07	0.483E–07
WFG4⁻¹	3	0.66790	**0.70742**	0.681	0.66343	0.68880	0.66140	0.68582
	5	0.06909	**0.15952**	0.088	0.12711	0.14416	0.10758	0.13711
	8	7.145E–04	3.229E–03	3.964E–03	5.007E–03	**5.123E–03**	0.255E–03	0.602E–03
	10	2.82E–05	0.00023	2.837E–04	**5.475E–04**	2.537E–04	0.039E–04	0.239E–04
WFG5⁻¹	3	0.64977	**0.69642**	0.673	0.66841	0.68748	0.67405	0.68567
	5	0.05195	**0.14725**	0.070	0.12789	0.12399	0.12320	0.13919
	8	5.847E–04	4.260E–03	3.146E–03	0.00421	**0.00436**	0.00062	0.00080
	10	3.82E–05	0.00043	2.533E–04	**0.00046**	0.00025	0.00002	0.00003
WFG6⁻¹	3	0.66472	**0.70203**	0.678	0.68331	**0.69235**	0.67553	0.68534
	5	0.04747	0.13408	0.072	0.13628	0.12549	0.12332	**0.13846**
	8	5.633E–04	3.300E–03	4.227E–03	**0.00450**	0.00382	0.00075	0.00076
	10	3.76E–05	0.00027	3.446E–04	**0.00053**	0.00022	0.00002	0.00003
WFG7⁻¹	3	0.66821	**0.70673**	0.681	0.65101	0.68135	0.65126	0.67742
	5	0.04916	0.12707	0.074	0.11727	0.11857	0.11268	**0.13727**
	8	5.633E–04	2.841E–03	3.351E–03	**0.00441**	0.00382	0.00049	0.00054
	10	3.02E–05	0.00024	1.857E–04	**0.00047**	0.00023	0.00002	0.00002
WFG8⁻¹	3	0.67247	**0.71039**	0.686	0.68958	**0.69311**	0.67910	0.68517
	5	0.06124	**0.15807**	0.091	0.13845	0.12755	0.12962	0.13872
	8	7.538E–04	3.968E–03	3.624E–03	**0.00460**	0.00405	0.00129	0.00090
	10	4.57E–05	0.00032	3.169E–04	**0.00055**	0.00023	0.00005	0.00003
WFG9⁻¹	3	0.65629	**0.69861**	0.671	0.67193	0.68446	0.64574	0.66636
	5	0.05504	**0.16321**	0.082	0.13747	0.12627	0.11905	0.13411
	8	6.451E–04	4.164E–03	3.117E–03	**0.00478**	0.00431	0.00088	0.00073
	10	3.10E–05	0.00043	2.317E–04	**0.00048**	0.00026	0.00003	0.00003

time consuming and have mostly been restricted to low values of K and N_0. In the context of MaOPs, given that several thousands of solutions are evaluated, new strategies are needed that can scale up the capability of selection process for large sets. The method of picking diverse solutions above improves the results over the final population, but certainly there remains a potentially large scope for research in improving the selection methods.

5   Conclusions and Future Work

In this study, we propose and conduct an initial assessment of a distance based metric, MDR, for its use within a decomposition-based framework. The main motivation of studying this was from the earlier attempts of using similar metrics in dominance-based frameworks. Although the measure has some conceptual advantages, its performance was observed to be inferior with other state-of-the-art algorithms in the literature; as well as with ASF as a measure within the same framework when HV was calculated based on the final population. However, when a different subset (of same size as the population) was chosen from archive of all evaluated solutions using DBEA-MDR instead of the final population, the performance showed notable improvements. The results of utilizing all information from the archive in the selection scheme clearly improved the performance of the approach. Such a scheme in principle is likely to improve the performance of all existing algorithms and could provide significant new insights in the context of performance assessment and benchmarking. A related research direction would be to devise computationally efficient ways of selecting prescribed number of solutions from large archives for performance assessment. A more in-depth investigation of the distance based metric itself could also be conducted to understand and improve its performance.

Acknowledgment. The authors would like to acknowledge the Australia-Germany Joint Research Cooperation Scheme for supporting this work.

References

1. Asafuddoula, M., Singh, H., Ray, T.: An enhanced decomposition based evolutionary algorithm with adaptive reference vectors. IEEE Trans. Cybern. (2017, in press)
2. Bhattacharjee, K.S., Singh, H.K., Ray, T.: A novel decomposition-based evolutionary algorithm for engineering design optimization. J. Mech. Des. **139**(4), 041403 (2017)
3. Cheng, R., Jin, Y., Olhofer, M., Sendhoff, B.: A reference vector guided evolutionary algorithm for many-objective optimization. IEEE Trans. Evol. Comput. **20**(5), 773–791 (2016)
4. Das, I., Dennis, J.E.: Normal-boundary intersection: a new method for generating the pareto surface in nonlinear multicriteria optimization problems. SIAM J. Optim. **8**(3), 631–657 (1998)
5. Das, S., Suganthan, P.N.: Differential evolution: a survey of the state-of-the-art. IEEE Trans. Evol. Comput. **15**(1), 4–31 (2011)
6. Deb, K., Jain, H.: An evolutionary many-objective optimization algorithm using reference-point-based nondominated sorting approach, part I: solving problems with box constraints. IEEE Trans. Evol. Comput. **18**(4), 577–601 (2014)
7. Deb, K., Pratap, A., Agarwal, S., Meyarivan, T.: A fast and elitist multiobjective genetic algorithm: NSGA-II. IEEE Trans. Evol. Comput. **6**(2), 182–197 (2002)

8. Deb, K., Thiele, L., Laumanns, M., Zitzler, E.: Scalable test problems for evolutionary multiobjective optimization. In: Abraham, A., Jain, L., Goldberg, R. (eds.) Evolutionary Multiobjective Optimization: Theoretical Advances and Applications. AI&KP, pp. 105–145. Springer, London (2005). https://doi.org/10.1007/1-84628-137-7_6
9. Huband, S., Hingston, P., Barone, L., While, L.: A review of multi-objective test problems and a scalable test problem toolkit. IEEE Trans. Evol. Comput. 10(5), 477–506 (2006)
10. Ishibuchi, H., Tsukamoto, N., Nojima, Y.: Evolutionary many-objective optimization: a short review. In: IEEE Congress on Evolutionary Computation, pp. 2419–2426 (2008)
11. Ishibuchi, H., Setoguchi, Y., Masuda, H., Nojima, Y.: Performance of decomposition-based many-objective algorithms strongly depends on Pareto front shapes. IEEE Trans. Evol. Comput. 21(2), 169–190 (2017)
12. Köppen, M., Yoshida, K.: Substitute distance assignments in NSGA-II for handling many-objective optimization problems. In: Obayashi, S., Deb, K., Poloni, C., Hiroyasu, T., Murata, T. (eds.) EMO 2007. LNCS, vol. 4403, pp. 727–741. Springer, Heidelberg (2007). https://doi.org/10.1007/978-3-540-70928-2_55
13. Li, K., Deb, K., Zhang, Q., Kwong, S.: An evolutionary many-objective optimization algorithm based on dominance and decomposition. IEEE Trans. Evol. Comput. 19(5), 694–716 (2015)
14. Miettinen, K.: Nonlinear Multiobjective Optimization, vol. 12. Springer, Heidelberg (2012)
15. Mostaghim, S., Schmeck, H.: Distance based ranking in many-objective particle swarm optimization. In: Rudolph, G., Jansen, T., Beume, N., Lucas, S., Poloni, C. (eds.) PPSN 2008. LNCS, vol. 5199, pp. 753–762. Springer, Heidelberg (2008). https://doi.org/10.1007/978-3-540-87700-4_75
16. Murata, T., Ishibuchi, H., Gen, M.: Specification of genetic search directions in cellular multi-objective genetic algorithms. In: Zitzler, E., Thiele, L., Deb, K., Coello Coello, C.A., Corne, D. (eds.) EMO 2001. LNCS, vol. 1993, pp. 82–95. Springer, Heidelberg (2001). https://doi.org/10.1007/3-540-44719-9_6
17. Singh, H.K., Isaacs, A., Ray, T., Smith, W.: A study on the performance of substitute distance based approaches for evolutionary many objective optimization. In: Li, X., et al. (eds.) SEAL 2008. LNCS, vol. 5361, pp. 401–410. Springer, Heidelberg (2008). https://doi.org/10.1007/978-3-540-89694-4_41
18. Tanabe, R., Ishibuchi, H., Oyama, A.: Benchmarking multi-and many-objective evolutionary algorithms under two optimization scenarios. IEEE Access 5, 19597–19619 (2017)
19. Trivedi, A., Srinivasan, D., Sanyal, K., Ghosh, A.: A survey of multi-objective evolutionary algorithms based on decomposition. IEEE Trans. Evol. Comput. 21, 440–462 (2017)
20. Yuan, Y., Xu, H., Wang, B., Yao, X.: A new dominance relation-based evolutionary algorithm for many-objective optimization. IEEE Trans. Evol. Comput. 20(1), 16–37 (2016)
21. Zhang, Q., Li, H.: MOEA/D: a multiobjective evolutionary algorithm based on decomposition. IEEE Trans. Evol. Comput. 11(6), 712–731 (2007)

Hierarchical Learning Classifier Systems for Polymorphism in Heterogeneous Niches

Yi Liu, Will N. Browne$^{(\boxtimes)}$, and Bing Xue

Victoria University of Wellington, Wellington 6140, New Zealand
liuyi4@myvuw.ac.nz, Will.Browne@vuw.ac.nz, bing.xue@ecs.vuw.ac.nz

Abstract. Learning classifier systems (LCSs) have been successfully adapted to real-world domains with the claim of human-readable rule populations. However, due to the inherent rich characteristic of the employed representation, it is possible to represent the underlying patterns in multiple (polymorphic) ways, which obscures the most informative patterns. A novel rule reduction algorithm is proposed based on ensembles of multiple trained LCSs populations in a hierarchical learning architecture to reduce the local diversity and global polymorphism. The primary aim of this project is to interrogate the hidden patterns in LCSs' trained population rather than improve the predictive power on test sets. This enables successful visualization of the importance of features in data groups (niches) that can contain heterogeneous patterns, i.e. even if different patterns result in the same class the importance of features can be found.

Keywords: Learning classifier systems · Pattern visualization
Hierarchical learning

1 Introduction

The proposed work is inspired by the concept of *convergent evolution* [1], where similar traits arise in different species when they live in a similar environment. As the species adapt to similar ecological niches, certain structures will be evolved. It is hypothesised that by analyzing multiple LCSs' rule populations trained on the same environment (problem) the optimum structure of patterns will be observable.

Previously, the Razor Cluster Razor (RCR) Boolean [2] was proposed to search for the global optimal solutions in Boolean domains based on analyzing a set of LCSs' trained populations. RCR-Boolean compacts rulesets for any such domain that LCSs can completely solve. This work aims to determine whether the convergent evolution phenomenon helps in real-valued domains, which are inherently unlikely to be completely solvable by any classification technique due to their imprecise decision boundaries. It proposes RCR-real, which is tailored to the most common representation used in real domains, i.e. upper and lower

© Springer Nature Switzerland AG 2018
T. Mitrovic et al. (Eds.): AI 2018, LNAI 11320, pp. 397–409, 2018.
https://doi.org/10.1007/978-3-030-03991-2_37

bounds rather than the ternary alphabet of Boolean domains. An LCSs-based hierarchy learning architecture is also proposed to extract the common ruleset for LCSs' non-completely solvable domains. The first objective is to create a method to extract a common ruleset for an ensemble of LCSs that have separately explored the domain. Second, then estimate each involved attribute's distinguishability. Finally, visualise a problem's detected underlying heterogeneous patterns. Ten varied UCI datasets are used as benchmarks to visualise learnt knowledge. Note, we do not seek to improve LCSs' prediction capability, thus the system's performance is estimated by the training result only where overfitting is to be detected through the visualisation. The proposed work is based on XCS (a reinforcement-learning LCS) as it forms a complete map of inputs to outputs. The main alternative, UCS (a supervised-learning LCS) [3] forms a best-action map, which lacks the consistent incorrect information of the observed domain needed to calculate attribute importance.

2   Background

Learning Classifier System (LCS). An LCS represents a Michigan approach rule-based agent, where each rule in a population consists of a fixed length condition that combine to form the solution. Environmental features are encoded, e.g. in an upper and lower boundary e.g. [*upper, lower*] [4], and a mapping learnt to one of a set of plausible actions. Learning is achieved through evolutionary computing [5] incorporating Q-learning [6] to explore and then exploit the given environment. XCSs [7] are accuracy based LCSs, where consistency in the reward has more import than the reward itself.

Seven parameters are also introduced to assist the evolutionary process. The *numerosity* indicates the number of duplicates of a rule, the *experience* relates to a rule's training time, the *prediction* is a recency weighted sum of the environmental rewards gained, *prediction error* shows by how much this prediction is incorrect, *accuracy* is a function of this error, *fitness* shows a rule's potential performance calculated from the previous parameters and *action set size* shows a rule's approximate niche size.

There is an ongoing interest in visualizing data mining results, e.g. interacting attributes [8]. Although LCSs' results are readable, visualizing the importance of attributes to the optimum rule set is difficult due to the inherent rich characteristics of the representation. Previously, rule compaction algorithms were merely removing irrelevant and redundant rules based on diversity [9]. As a result, it is difficult to compact LCSs' results into the optimized form [10].

Razor Cluster Razor in Boolean. RCR [2] stands for razor in micro, rule cluster, and razor in macro, which is a rule reduction [9] algorithm applied in sequence. RCR seeks to simplify multiple LCSs' outputs applied to the same problem as much as possible, but no simpler, so a single common solution can be discovered. Razor in micro aims to reduce complexity in diversity level through removing poor performance rules in each individual population. Subsequently, remaining rules in all populations are gathered together to be clustered according to the number of specified attributes in each rule, thus a bridge between diversity and polymorphism is found. Lastly, razor in macro is introduced, which seeks the underlying single common morphism by reducing complexity by considering these clusters at each polymorphic level.

Removing poor rules when 100% performance is possible and counting specified attributes in the ternary alphabet for Boolean problems is straightforward, but in real domains with rich alphabets neither is easy.

Benchmark Problems. Ten UCI datasets for continuous real domains are studied, six basic datasets are selected to interrogate the proposed work's correctness, including Iris, Sonar, Wine, Australian, German, Wisconsin Breast Cancer Diagnostic (WBCD), and four other complex domains to investigate the novel method's limitations are selected due to high dimensionality e.g. lung cancer, artificial problem e.g. hill and valley, and multiple actions with low number of instances e.g. Zoo, and natural domains, e.g. Ionosphere [11]. As the aim is not to test LCSs capability in dealing with missing data, all the instances that contain missing data have been removed to avoid this confounding variable rather than a lack of capability in LCSs.

3   The Proposed Method

This section includes three novel parts. Firstly, the Razor Cluster Razor is adapted for real domains. Secondly, two formulas are proposed that estimate any involved attributes' distinguishability by its contribution to constructing the representation space. Lastly, a hierarchical learning architecture is introduced to enable the ability to completely represent a target domain.

3.1   Razor Cluster Razor (RCR) in Real Domains

Since XCSs employ different representations for Boolean and real domains, the implementation between RCR-Boolean and RCR-Real is different, and the only commonality between them is the basic philosophy, which is that "entities are not to be multiplied without necessary, i.e. Occam's razor" [12]. The RCR-Real process is shown in Fig. 1.

Razors in Micro. In XCS, the training population is larger than the optimal number of final rules to guarantee that XCS is capable of exploring multiple competing hypotheses simultaneously. Thus, a high diversity of rules is introduced to the actual final population. As a result, the quality of evolved rules is varied. In certain domains, the majority of rules are redundant for representing the task's patterns. Moreover, a few rules may even make a negative contribution. Hence, this pre-processing phrase is needed to remove the inferior individuals in a population.

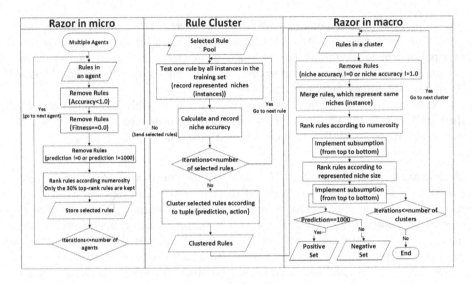

Fig. 1. The graph for the RCR-Real process.

Generally, an inferior individual can be described by three factors; inadequate training, inconsistent prediction behavior, and no contribution to represent the task. Any such rule in the final populations should be deleted. The whole process is split into four steps. Firstly, remove any rules where accuracy is less than maximum. In an XCS, a rule's accuracy reaching to maximum only becomes apparent when a rule has been trained sufficiently and the prediction behavior is consistent. Secondly, no rule with minimum fitness should be kept, as a rule's fitness indicates its potential performance in representing the ideal solution. Hence, when a rule's fitness falls decreases to the minimum this rule is actually completely irrelevant to the representation. Thirdly, if a rule's prediction is equal to neither maximum nor minimum, then it ought to be removed. This is only true in a classification task. Lastly, all the remaining rules will be ranked according to their numerosity size, and only the 30% top-ranked individuals will be retained. This strategy is supported by empirical evidence from the previous experiment of Boolean domains, where XCSs tend to offer the most important individuals a higher numerosity value compared with the redundant ones. By implementing this strategy, the majority of the redundant diversity will be eliminated.

Rule Cluster. XCSs commonly employ the upper and lower bounds representation in real domains [[$attribute_0$ *high boundary*, $attribute_0$ *low boundary*], [$attribute_1$ *high boundary*, $attribute_1$ *low boundary*]], which offer rules both precision and generality. However, due to the rich representation style, a rule's explicitly represented niches cannot be observed directly in the condition part, which hampers efforts to detect the target's unique morphism.

In this implementation, the rule cluster has two stages. In stage one, each selected rule reviews the training set, whilst recording the matched niches (instances) and the correctly represented niches. Subsequently, each rule's niche accuracy can be calculated by dividing the size of correct niches by the size of matched niches. In the second stage, all the pre-processed rules will be clustered according to the prediction, action tuple, since after pre-processing all the remaining rules' prediction can only be either the maximum or minimum value. Thus, the number of clusters is equal to double the number of actions. Moreover, if a rule's prediction is associated with the maximum, then it is a correct rule, otherwise, the rule is an incorrect one. As XCSs naturally seek to form complete maps it consists of correct and incorrect rules where the inherent patterns of each can be different, especially in multi-action domains. Thus, without the clustering process, the effort of identifying the underlying patterns from trained populations cannot make progress, since important patterns are mixed together.

Razor in Macro. XCSs aim to form a complete map to represent the explored domains. However, due to the XCS' rich representation, extremely diverse rules are generated, which obscures the discovered patterns. Razor in macro is designed to compact the XCS's trained populations to their single common state by reducing the populations' polymorphism. Three processes are involved, including error detection, rules merging, and two-level subsumption. The error detection aims to eliminate all the remaining over-general individuals by interrogating each rules' niche accuracy. For any correct rule, its niche accuracy reaches the maximum and for any incorrect rule, its niche accuracy ought to decrease to the minimum. Otherwise, the rule must be over-general.

The rule merging method focuses on merging rules within the same niche. During the merging process, attributes will be merged one by one, and only the common overlap interval will remain. Therefore, the final merged rule will approximate the target, which successfully removes any unsupported attribute interval. Merged rules' numerosity will be summed.

In XCSs, subsumption focuses on addressing the over-specific rules problem. In RCR, a novel two-level subsumption is implemented. The first level ranks all the remaining rules according to their numerosity, and invokes subsumption from top to bottom. Each rule will be compared with all their peers that have a lower rank. If a lower-rank rule can be subsumed, it will be deleted. In the second level, all the rules will be ranked according to their represented niche size, then subsumption is reactivated to ensure that the output set is as general as possible. Eventually, all the selected individuals will be stored into a positive set or a negative set, depending on whether prediction is maximum or minimum.

3.2 Attribute Importance Equation

Traditionally, an attribute's importance is estimated by its generality level [8]. Here the attribute importance is estimated by analyzing each attribute independent distinguishability by comparing each attribute's represented non-overlap space for each action between the RCR produced positive set and negative set. Assume a problem, which has an action set M, $M = [Act_0, Act_1...Act_m]$ and an attributes set N, $N = [Att_0, Att_1, ...Att_n]$, and for an action m ($m \in M$), it associates a support rule set I_m, $I_m = [P_{m0}, P_{m1}...P_{mi}]$ and an opposite rule set J_m, $J_m = [N_{m0}, N_{m1}...N_{mj}]$, in i ($i \in I$) positive ruleset or j ($j \in J$) negative ruleset, for any related attribute n, ($n \in N$), its represented range is defined as $PSize_{nmi}$ and $NSize_{nmj}$. The overlap between i positive rule and j negative rule for attribute n is defined as $PNsize_{nmij}$, $N_{mlength}$ response for the number of negative rules for action m ($m \in M$), then the attribute n's influence for action m $AInf_{nm}$ can be estimated by Eq. (1). Afterward, the attribute k ($k \in N$) importance to action m $AImp_{nm}$ can be calculated by normalizing the attribute influence as shown in Eq. (2).

$$AInf_{nm} = \frac{\sum_{i=m0}^{i=mi} \frac{(\sum_{j=m0}^{j=mj}(PSize_{nmi}+NSize_{nmj}-2*PNSize_{nmij}))}{N_{mlength}}}{\sum_{i=m0}^{i=mi} PSize_{nmi} + \sum_{j=m0}^{j=mj} NSize_{nmj}} \tag{1}$$

$$AImp_{km} = \frac{AInf_{km}}{\sum_{att=0}^{att=n} AInf_{attm}} \tag{2}$$

3.3 Hierarchical Learning Classifier System

The Hierarchical Learning Classifier System (HLCS) is proposed (Fig. 2) to visualize underlying patterns in data. It utilizes homologues of ensemble learning, such as bagging and boosting [13]. The principles are also influenced by population-based incremental learning (PBIL), where learning is "adapted to new data without forgetting the existing knowledge" [14]. In HLCS, all layers' components are exactly same, except for the first one, which lacks a data filter. The number of introduced layers for HLCS is flexible since the HLCS will automatically create new layers until the observed dataset can be represented completely.

In each layer, an HLCS has five sequential modules; data filter, training, rule compact, rule importance analyze, and attribute importance visualization. The first module selects un-represented instances from the observed dataset, and this module is formed by the RCR produced positive set in the previous layer. Hence, the initial layer's data filter is empty. After selecting the subset from the dataset, the training module is invoked, which is a bagging style structure and employs multiple standard XCSs to explore the input dataset synchronously. Two benefits are achieved from this architecture; firstly, any deviations caused by the XCS's stochastic search can be avoided. Secondly, this architecture naturally splits computation into multiple tasks with progressively less, but harder to classify, examples. Thus, the computation in HLCS only introduces around 20% additional execution time than standard XCS.

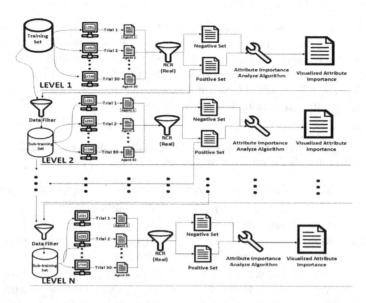

Fig. 2. The architecture of the Hierarchical Learning Classifier System (HLCS). The number of layers will automatically be extended until the HLCS completely represents the observed dataset. Each layer consist of five modules, a data filter based on the RCR compacted positive set, a bagging based training process, RCR, attribute importance analysis, and attribute importance visualization.

4   Results

In all the conducted experiments here, the system uses the common parameter values in [7] learning rate $\beta = 0.2$; fitness fall-off rate $\alpha = 0.1$; prediction error threshold $\theta_0 = 10$; fitness exponent $v = 5$; threshold for GA application in the action set $\theta_{GA} = 25$; two-point crossover with probability $\chi = 0.8$; mutation probability $\mu = 0.04$; experience threshold for classifier deletion $\theta_{del} = 20$; fraction of mean fitness for deletion $\delta = 0.1$; classifier experience threshold for subsumption $\theta_{sub} = 20$; Scale range in covering is $[-1.0, 1.0]$; Scale range in mutation is $[-1.0, 1.0]$; reduction of the fitness $= 0.1$; and the selection method is tournament selection with tournament size ratio 0.4. Only GA subsumption is activated. The size of the population is set as 3000 and the number of training iterations is 50,000, The reward scheme used is 1000 for a correct classification and 0 otherwise. All the experiments have been repeated 30 times with a known different seed in each run. Each result reported in this work is average of the 30 runs.

Among all the ten explored datasets, HLCS achieves 100% training accuracy, whereas standard XCS failed in four of them (see Table 1). For all the domains, more than 90% of the introduced rules are removed. After the RCR-Real compaction process, a stable performance agent that consists of a unique rule set is obtained. Importantly, the LCSs' performance can be interrogated not only by the accuracy but also its generality/overfitting. For example, the visualization for the Lung cancer and Sonar problems indicate the most specific rule sets (Lung cancer is a high-dimension problem and Sonar is a difficult domain). Surprisingly, a very general rule set is produced for the Zoo dataset, which contains seven actions. Traditionally, LCSs are not systems that have good performance for the high number of actions but low instances tasks.

Table 1. RCR results VS XCS results VS HLCS results in number of rules and training accuracy, where [low, high] values or average over 30 runs are presented.

Domain	Size	XCS_Rule	RCR_Rule	XCS_Acc	RCR_Acc	HLCS_Acc
Iris	150	[1557, 1675]	9	[99.5%, 100%]	100%	100%
wine	178	[2736, 2813]	13	[100%, 100%]	100%	100%
Australian	680 + 10	[2611, 2714]	115 + 9	[93.9%, 97.2%]	98.56%	100%
sonar	208	[2924, 2958]	208	[99%, 100%]	100%	100%
Zoo	101	[2756, 2834]	12	[100%, 100%]	100%	100%
BCWD	683	[2576, 2653]	37	[99.6%, 100%]	100%	100%
Ionosphere	351	[2764, 2848]	154	[97.5%, 100%]	100%	100%
German	940 + 60	[2642, 2745]	242 + 14	[78.5%, 86.8%]	94%	100%
Lung Cancer	18 + 9	[2944, 2963]	18 + 9	[63.1%, 70.3%]	66.66%	100%
Hill Valley	559 + 47	[2981, 2994]	267 + 31	[79.7%, 86.8%]	92.24%	100%

The training plot (Fig. 3) shows that there is a limitation on the ability to comprehend a pattern in LCSs, without the edition of the method to add hierarchies. Level 0 is essentially a standard LCS where a clear steady-state error range exists, regardless of how many additional iterations are introduced. This can be caused by overlapping niches suited to polymorphic rule sets, where the LCS identifies multiple main patterns. Hierarchically removing the main pattern and associated data enables the LCS to discover the next most important patterns and so forth. Each such pattern can contain epistatic relationships between features, unlike decision trees where each hierarchy level focusses on an individual feature. Ultimately, the last hierarchy could consist of the hard to classify outlier data points where no generality is possible, giving rise to specific rules. These can be identified through equal importance being given to each attribute (feature).

After the HLCS splits the problem domain into successive comprehensive parts, the completely represented solutions are obtained. Thus, it is practicable for LCSs to completely represent domains. The training map for the German domain exhibits how LCS's population is dominated by over-general rules in the first stage of training (level 0) as when they form performance drops. This does not occur for the Australia dataset, which suggests specific rules are formed.

4.1   Attribute Importance

Generally, HLCS offers a fine-grained level of feature ranking and assessment of the relationships between condition attributes according to their support for a given action. The Iris dataset is easy to understand, so is selected to interrogate the feature selection of HLCS, see Table 2 and Fig. 3. It is compared with three traditional attribute ranking and selection algorithms, i.e. Principal components analysis (PCA), Relief, and Consecution based feature selection (CFS), which are implemented in WEKA [15].

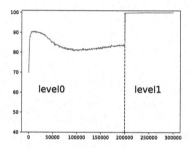 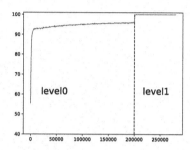

Fig. 3. HLCS' training performance for German and Australia dataset problems.

In all actions, HLCS identifies that petal length and petal width that are the most important attributes, which is supported by PCA and CFS. Moreover, HLCS also points out that petal length and petal width having similar attribute importance. Meanwhile, sepal width and sepal length having similar attribute importance. This discovery can also be found by using Relief. The Iris domain indicates that although HLCS is based on investigating the LCS produced rules, the novel proposed system obtains a common attribute importance with traditional statistics-based algorithms, but displays the achievement in a much clearer manner.

Table 2. RCR vs traditional feature rankers' results for iris problem.

Attribute Ranker	Attribute Importance
HLCS species1	Petal length, Petal Width: 50%, Sepal length, Sepal width: 0%
HLCS species2	Petal length: 32.8%, Petal Width: 31%
	Sepal width: 18.3%, Sepal length:17.9%
HLCS species3	Petal Width:29.4%, Petal length: 28.9%
	Sepal length:21.3%, Sepal width: 20.4%
PCA	Petal length, petal width
relief	Petal width, petal length, sepal width, sepal length
CFS	Petal length, petal width

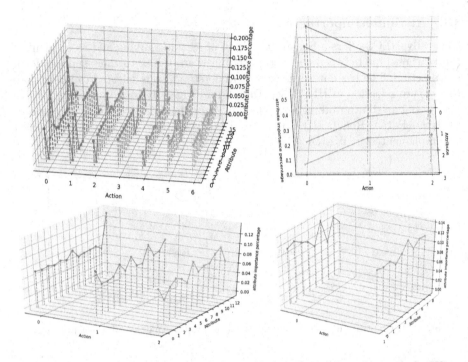

Fig. 4. First line the result for Zoo and Iris problems. Second line the result for Wine and WBCD problems

5   Discussion

Once the output is known, the solution can be interrogated, such that over-fitting can be tested, i.e., the discovered patterns can be observed. It appears that LCSs learns some strange patterns, e.g. in the Zoo dataset (see Table 3: the *feather* attribute is not important to classify birds, but *milk* is. LCSs consider birds are animals that can be distinguished by [not] drinking milk, laying eggs, and [not] having hair. *Mammals* need to seriously consider their fins, where this is an excellent example of a heterogeneous niche. To distinguish all the animal classes, *milk* is really important. Amphibian contain fewer species, which does not distract HLCS as it identifies that *backbone type* and the *number of tails* are important to categories these species. Also, [not] *feathers* has the same importance level as *fin* for identifying fishes.

If LCSs' detected underlying patterns are directly compared with human's knowledge, there is obviously a huge gap between human' and LCS' comprehension of the world. However, if the training dataset of learnt knowledge is further investigated, interesting patterns emerge. Firstly, Zoo is a typically unbalanced dataset, where mammals occupy around 41% of the dataset. This indicates that identifying differentiating common attributes for the mammals class is the most important task, and among all the species, only mammals drink milk. Moreover, due to the involvement of sea mammals, only mammals have an non-consistent fin number. That is the main reason why LCSs identify *fin* and *milk* as the most important attributes to distinguish mammals from others. Meanwhile, birds only get 20% of the dataset, and the *feathers* only could be used for birds, such that this attribute's function can be replaced by a combination from the first ten attributes. Thus, the *feather* is a redundant attribute in this case, e.g. CFS removes *feather*, and in Relief, *feather* gets a low rank, which is 10th. Not only bird, but the mammal, amphibian, and reptile also note *feather* is redundant. Fish and bird do have a similar attribute importance distribution. Therefore, to distinguish these two species, certain discriminative attributes need to be considered. Thus, in fish support rules the *feather* attribute is considered (Fig. 4).

Table 3. RCR highlighting mammal and fish classes vs traditional feature rank results for Zoo problem.

Attribute ranker	Attribute importance
HLCS Mammal	Milk: 17.4%, fins: 17.1%, hair: 8.8%, tail: 8.5%, airborne: 5.8% Eggs, toothed, backbone, breathes, venomous, domestic: 4.4% Legs, catesize: 4.3%, aquatic: 4.2%, predictor 3.4%, feathers: 0%
HLCS Fish	Hair, feathers, eggs, milk, airborne, aquatic, predator, toothed, backbone, fins, legs, tail, domestic: 7.3%, Venomous, catesize: 2.4% breathes: 0%
PCA	Feathers, eggs, milk, airborne, aquatic, predator, toothed, backbone, breathes, venomous
relief	Venomous, breathes, tail, milk, backbone, domestic, predator, eggs, fins, airborne, feathers, legs, aquatic, toothed, catesize
CFS	Airborne, breathes, venomous, fins, domestic, catesize

In the Wine domain, HLCS identifies *proline, color intensity*, and *OD280/OD315* of diluted wines as the most important attributes for class0, class1, and class2, respectively. *Flavanoids* need to be considered for all the classes. The HLCS identifies that the most important attributes for WBCD are *Bare Nuclei* and *Normal Nucleoli* in both actions. Generally, as WBCD only contains two actions the results for each action's attribute importance distribution become very similar. However, the attributes' potential range is still different, which is why these two distributions are not exactly same.

The result shows that compared with humans LCSs have an advantage, which is to get rid of the primacy effect. LCSs are impartial to the underlying patterns for the domains. Therefore, by visualizing these hidden patterns humans could understand the patterns in the dataset better as prejudice can be avoided. In contrast with standard attribute rank algorithms, the proposed HLCS offers a fine-grained level ranked attributes, which helps research not only know which attributes are important but also hints about why these attributes are important.

6   Conclusions

The overall aim to develop the LCS technique to construct a single common rule-set for real domains was successful. Moreover, the LCSs' potential to completely represent a target domain is also explored, where the results show that despite the different representation style, RCR is capable of identifying different underlying patterns for attributes. That is, for Boolean domains, LCSs can employ the ternary representation to detect the inherent natural structure [16], and for real domains, LCSs can now utilize higher and lower bounds, where underlying patterns can be visualised. This includes heterogeneous patterns and epistatic relationships at different levels of hierarchical patterns. This avoids problems with polymorphic rules in previous LCSs. The result shows the convergent evolution phenomenon appears in all the explored domains.

Further work is required to implement this approach in attribute list knowledge representation (ALKR) [17] for synthetic datasets [18]. It is also important to discover whether the same phenomenon will happen in the rich alphabet based LCS, such as XCSCFA [19] or XCSCFC [20]. It is plausible that the relationship between different attributes can be visualized by the inherent methods presented here.

References

1. Partha, R., et al.: Subterranean mammals show convergent regression in ocular genes and enhancers, along with adaptation to tunneling. eLife **6**, e25884 (2017)
2. Liu, Y., Browne, W.N., Xue, B.: Adapting bagging and boosting to learning classifier systems. In: Sim, K., Kaufmann, P. (eds.) EvoApplications 2018. LNCS, vol. 10784, pp. 405–420. Springer, Cham (2018). https://doi.org/10.1007/978-3-319-77538-8_28
3. Orriols-Puig, A., Bernadó-Mansilla, E.: Revisiting UCS: description, fitness sharing, and comparison with XCS. In: Bacardit, J., Bernadó-Mansilla, E., Butz, M.V., Kovacs, T., Llorà, X., Takadama, K. (eds.) IWLCS 2006-2007. LNCS (LNAI), vol. 4998, pp. 96–116. Springer, Heidelberg (2008). https://doi.org/10.1007/978-3-540-88138-4_6
4. Stone, C., Bull, L.: For real! XCS with continuous-valued inputs. Evol. Comput. **11**(3), 299–336 (2003)
5. Fogel, D.B.: Evolutionary Computation: Toward a New Philosophy of Machine Intelligence, vol. 1. Wiley, Hoboken (2006)
6. Dayan, P., Watkins, C.J.C.H.: Q-learning. Mach. Learn. **8**(3), 279–292 (1992)
7. Urbanowicz, R.J., Browne, W.N.: Introduction to Learning Classifier Systems. Springer, Heidelberg (2017). https://doi.org/10.1007/978-3-662-55007-6
8. Urbanowicz, R.J., Granizo-Mackenzie, A., Moore, J.H.: An analysis pipeline with statistical and visualization-guided knowledge discovery for Michigan-style learning classifier systems. IEEE Comput. Intell. Mag. **7**(4), 35–45 (2012)
9. Nakata, M., Lanzi, P.L., Takadama, K.: Rule reduction by selection strategy in XCS with adaptive action map. Evol. Intell. **8**(2–3), 71–87 (2015)
10. Butz, M.V., Lanzi, P.L., Wilson, S.W.: Function approximation with XCS: hyper-ellipsoidal conditions, recursive least squares, and compaction. IEEE Trans. Evol. Comput. **12**(3), 355–376 (2008)

11. Cervante, L., Xue, B., Zhang, M., Shang, L.: Binary particle swarm optimisation for feature selection: a filter based approach. In: 2012 IEEE Congress on Evolutionary Computation, pp. 1–8 (2012)
12. Iacca, G., Neri, F., Mininno, E., Ong, Y.-S., Lim, M.-H.: Ockham's Razor in memetic computing: three stage optimal memetic exploration. Inf. Sci. **188**, 17–43 (2012)
13. Quinlan, J.R., et al.: Bagging, boosting, and C4.5. In: AAAI/IAAI, vol. 1, pp. 725–730 (1996)
14. Baluja, S.: Population-based incremental learning. A method for integrating genetic search based function optimization and competitive learning. Technical report, Department of Computer Science, Carnegie Mellon University in Pittsburgh, Pennsylvania (1994)
15. Hall, M., Frank, E., Holmes, G., Pfahringer, B., Reutemann, P., Witten, I.H.: The WEKA data mining software: an update. ACM SIGKDD Explor. Newsl. **11**(1), 10–18 (2009)
16. Liu, Y., Xue, B., Browne, W.N.: Visualisation and optimisation of learning classifier systems for multiple domain learning. In: Shi, Y., et al. (eds.) SEAL 2017. LNCS, vol. 10593, pp. 448–461. Springer, Cham (2017). https://doi.org/10.1007/978-3-319-68759-9_37
17. Bacardit, J., Burke, E.K., Krasnogor, N.: Improving the scalability of rule-based evolutionary learning. Memetic Comput. **1**(1), 55–67 (2009)
18. Calian, D.A., Bacardit, J.: Integrating memetic search into the BioHEL evolutionary learning system for large-scale datasets. Memetic Comput. **5**(2), 95–130 (2013)
19. Iqbal, M., Browne, W.N., Zhang, M.: Learning overlapping natured and niche imbalance Boolean problems using XCS classifier systems. In: 2013 IEEE Congress on Evolutionary Computation, pp. 1818–1825 (2013)
20. Alvarez, I.M., Browne, W.N., Zhang, M.: Reusing learned functionality to address complex Boolean functions. In: Dick, G. (ed.) SEAL 2014. LNCS, vol. 8886, pp. 383–394. Springer, Cham (2014). https://doi.org/10.1007/978-3-319-13563-2_33

A Cooperative Coevolutionary Algorithm for Real-Time Underground Mine Scheduling

Wesley Cox, Tim French, Mark Reynolds, and Lyndon While[✉]

Computer Science and Software Engineering, The University of Western Australia,
Perth, Australia
{wesley.cox,tim.french,mark.reynolds,lyndon.while}@uwa.edu.au

Abstract. We apply a cooperative coevolutionary algorithm for the real-time evolution of schedules in underground mines. The algorithm evolves simultaneously both truck dispatching and traffic light schedules for one-lane roads. The coevolutionary approach achieves high production with fewer trucks than both the widely-used DISPATCH algorithm, and commonly-used greedy heuristics.

Keywords: Evolutionary algorithms · Coevolution · Mine scheduling

1 Introduction

In underground mines, access to the orebody is often via an angled decline which is traversed by trucks that move ore from the shovels, operating at the orebody at various depths, to the crusher, situated at the surface. The expensive nature of the decline [6] means that the majority is usually only one lane wide with occasional passing points. When a truck finishes unloading ore at the crusher, the dispatcher tells it which shovel to service next. Poor scheduling choices can result in high truck waiting times, either at shovels or at passing points. To solve this problem, automated scheduling methods can be used to optimise the throughput of a mine. Truck haulage typically represents 50–60% of mining costs [1,23], so a scheduling method should minimise the number of trucks required to achieve good throughput. Access to one-lane sections is managed by traffic lights, adding a further scheduling opportunity.

We apply a coevolutionary algorithm (CEA) to evolve schedules in real-time for truck dispatching and traffic light switching [3,27]. We test our approach on an abstract model of an underground mine, using a discrete event simulator based on timed automata [7]. We compare its performance against common greedy heuristics and against an adaptation of DISPATCH [17,25,26]. The coevolutionary approach for combined truck and traffic light scheduling is shown to achieve high production with fewer trucks than the alternative approaches, although with varying results depending on the exact choice of fitness function.

© Springer Nature Switzerland AG 2018
T. Mitrovic et al. (Eds.): AI 2018, LNAI 11320, pp. 410–418, 2018.
https://doi.org/10.1007/978-3-030-03991-2_38

Section 2 describes previous work on real-time dispatching. Section 3 describes our approach to scheduling and the model used. Section 4 describes the experiments and discusses the results. Section 5 concludes the paper.

2 Literature Review

There is much previous work on truck dispatching in mining [1,7,18]. Here we describe strategies relevant to our approach and to underground mining.

Greedy heuristics for truck dispatching attempt to optimise some heuristic for each truck alone [22]. Common choices are to dispatch to the shovel

- from which the truck is expected to return soonest (MTCT);
- where the truck is expected to wait the least time (MTWT);
- where the truck is expected to be serviced in the least time (MTST);
- that has been waiting longest, or will be available soonest (MSWT).

DISPATCH is a two-stage plan-driven approach [25,26]. In the offline stage the desired truck haulage rates along the available routes are determined using linear programming (LP). In the online stage routing creates a series of temporary schedules from which only the first assignment in the schedule is deployed; the remainder of the schedule is discarded. A DISPATCH system for underground mines is available [17], but any improvements are not publicly available.

[14] also produces a plan using LP, then dispatching is performed by greedily choosing the shovel with the highest ratio between the time since its last dispatch and the optimal inter-arrival times. The current state of the mine is ignored, thus there is no compensation for excessive queueing. [7] uses an EA to evolve cyclic finite automata for truck dispatching, avoiding traffic contention by selective routing. A simulation model inspired by a network of timed automata is used.

The literature on underground scheduling primarily deals with long-term decisions [19]. [10] presents a graph-based approach, extending earlier work [12,13,24] with automated guided vehicles. Nodes represent locations and orientations of the trucks at each time step, and edge weights are based on the desired objective. [4] extends this for multiple trucks per assignment using an enumeration algorithm. [21] investigates a model where the positions of the mining points change in the short-term, and discuss some basic collision-avoidance, truck dispatching, and drawpoint selection strategies.

3 Approach

3.1 Problem Description

Figure 1 shows the topology of our model of an underground mine. Trucks travel continuously between the shovels and the crusher. Horizontal crosscuts allow two-way traffic. Overtaking is not possible. Trucks are homogeneous, but shovels are heterogeneous; their average filling rates differ and they are at different depths. Shovels and the crusher can each service only one truck a time.

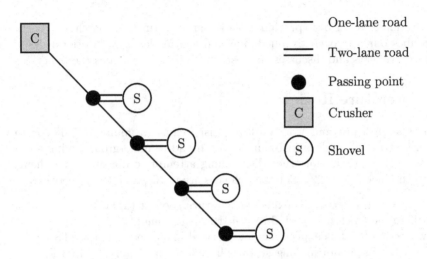

Fig. 1. The road network used in the test problem.

Each one-lane section is managed by a pair of traffic lights, which may be managed by greedy rules or by a timer. The greedy rules make a light green iff no trucks are travelling or waiting in the opposite direction. The timer assigns a light a fixed amount of time to stay green.

We want to optimise the schedule for a mine to maximise total production. A schedule determines the outgoing destination for each truck leaving the crusher, and also manages the timing of the traffic lights. Production is measured in total truckloads unloaded at the crusher per shift. The model assumes that we always know the location of all trucks.

To compare dispatching algorithms we use a simulator based on a network of timed automata (TA) [2,7]. The TA for a truck includes states for travelling between shovels and the crusher, waiting in various queues, and waiting at traffic lights. The clocks in the TA limit the times at which the truck can transition between certain states. The traffic lights are represented by separate TA. Additionally, at any point in time a separate simulation can be initiated to test the performance of a schedule from the current state of the mine [7].

3.2 Evolutionary Algorithm

There are four potential methods using EAs. We could evolve truck dispatching schedules alone, or we could evolve traffic light schedules alone, or we could evolve both together. In this paper we focus on the last option, which we label CEA-RTL. The EA is run to produce a temporary schedule; periodically, this schedule is discarded and the EA is rerun using updated information to ensure that the schedule remains useful over time under variable real-time conditions. Schedule updates are fifteen minutes apart in simulation time.

The population size is set to 100, and in each generation 100 offspring are produced. Survival is solely by elitism, from both parents and offspring. Reproduction selection is by stochastic roulette-wheel selection [15]. A run terminates if 0.5% improvement in fitness is not observed in 100 generations. All parameters were chosen based on early experimentation.

Two separate populations are maintained, one for each type of schedule. A truck schedule is represented by a list of shovel IDs of length H/Cr, for time horizon H and crusher service rate Cr. We use single-point crossover and three independent mutations; either mutate a gene, or insert/delete a gene into/from a random position. A light schedule is represented by a real-encoded list for each one-lane section, representing the lengths of green lights, in minutes, alternating in direction. We use blended crossover [9] and normally-distributed mutation.

The fitness function runs the stochastic simulator, using the current position of each truck. Fitness is assigned using the parallel shuffling method [16]. In each generation, each chromosome is assessed by randomly pairing it with one from the other population, evaluating this pairing twenty times, and taking the average. The fitness of the chromosome is that of the best pairing it has ever participated in. The final output is the best observed pairing of schedules.

There is a discrepancy in the timeframe between what the fitness function can practically measure and the overall goal of the problem. The overall goal is to maximise the number of truckloads of ore unloaded into the crusher over a long time period, but measuring this directly presents at least five difficulties:

- the simulation-based evaluations limit the period that can be considered;
- longer periods exacerbate the stochastic nature of the simulations;
- the effects of dispatching decisions on production are often delayed;
- longer periods require larger genotypes, making the search space bigger;
- the discreteness of the objective could limit the effectiveness of an EA.

A discounting scheme would address some but not all of these issues. We consider instead two alternative proxy metrics.

Minimise total truck waiting time (MTTWT) returns the total waiting time for all trucks in all queues. MTTWT allows some effects of decisions to be observed immediately, enabling a shorter time horizon.

Minimise average truck cycle time (MATCT) returns the average cycle time for all trucks that finish unloading at the crusher in the simulation window. As an average, MATCT can operate with a flexible time horizon.

For both MTTWT and MATCT, H was set to be the longest expected cycle time on all routes. On our test instances, H ranges from 56 to 72 min.

3.3   Cyclic Truck Scheduling and Cyclic Light Scheduling

Cyclic truck schedules are derived using LP, based on expected travel times and using Monte Carlo simulation to estimate expected clear times for each one-lane road. With these flow rates a fixed schedule can be produced, henceforth referred to as flow-based cyclic scheduling (FCS).

In cyclic light scheduling, each traffic light is assigned a pair of values which denote the length of green lights in each direction. These values are produced by running an EA with a real-valued chromosome and most of the same parameters as described in Sect. 3.2. The fitness function evaluates a set of timers by simulating whole shifts using FCS for truck dispatching (determined by LP).

4   Results and Discussion

4.1   Methodology

Testing was performed in a discrete event simulator, as described in Sect. 3.1, implemented in Java [8]. We used six instances of the problem in Fig. 1, with randomly-generated set-ups: distances between passing points vary from 400–600 m; lengths of crosscuts vary from 150–250 m; and filling rates for shovels vary from 9–17 min per truck, and always sum to the emptying rate at the crusher (3 min per truck). Empty trucks average 15 km/hr, and full trucks average 12 km/hr on the flat and 6 km/hr uphill [20].

The EA approach was compared with greedy heuristics, FCS, and DISPATCH, each with greedy (GL) and cyclic light scheduling (CL). Our adaptation of DISPATCH has only a single LP [7], with unused constraints [25] removed. All algorithms were implemented in Java by the authors; LPs were solved with *lpsolve* [5]. Figures 2 and 3 show the algorithms' performance, measured in the average number of truckloads unloaded in a 500-min shift. Each data point is the average of 25 shifts, for a fixed number of trucks.

The greedy algorithms calculated their heuristics using 20 simulations. Two versions of MTCT were used: MTCT minimises the complete cycle time of the next truck, while MTRT excludes time spent at the crusher. Three versions of MTWT were used: MTSWT minimises time spent queueing at the shovel for the next truck, while MTTWT(1S) includes time spent queueing at passing points on the way to the shovel, and MTTWT(2S) includes all waiting time in both directions. Results for all seven heuristics are combined into an algorithm portfolio [11] called Best-H. For each number of trucks, the performance of the portfolio is that of the best-performing heuristic for that number.

4.2   Basic Algorithms and Simple Light Schedules

Figure 2 shows for two typical instances, the performance of Best-H, DISPATCH, and FCS, with both GL and CL. Best-H almost always outperforms DISPATCH and FCS. Section 4.3 compares CEA-RTL with Best-H alone.

Among the greedy heuristics, MTSWT and MTTWT(1S) perform best, although MTSWT sometimes suffers in undertrucked systems. MTCT and MTRT consistently perform much worse than all other heuristics. Greedy application of MTCT results in trucks being over-dispatched to closer shovels; long-term, this results in excessive shovel queues. MTTWT(2S) tries to minimise the waiting times of one truck at the expense of trucks in opposing traffic. These

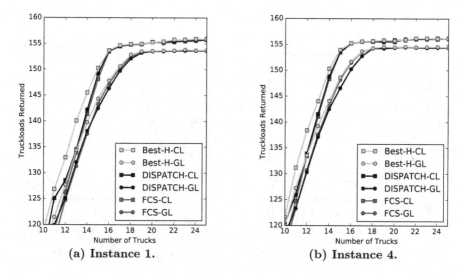

Fig. 2. Typical comparisons of Best-H, DISPATCH, and FCS.

effects will not occur when considering an entire schedule rather than individual trucks. MTSWT works well in this case, as minimising shovel queueing time for one truck does not affect trucks that have already been dispatched.

DISPATCH being outperformed has been discussed in [7]: it primarily performs well in multi-crusher systems, the real-time version over-dispatches on long routes, and the variation in actual waiting times limits its success. CL consistently beats GL, providing up to a 1.5% increase in production and allowing Best-H to achieve over 99% of its peak production with 1–3 fewer trucks.

4.3 Coevolution

Figure 3 shows two typical comparisons of the performance of CEA-RTL against Best-H-CL. CEA-RTL with MATCT outperforms Best-H on undertrucked systems, while MTTWT slightly overtakes MATCT for overtrucked systems.

Table 1 shows the minimum number of trucks required for each method to achieve at least 99% of the observed peak performance. CEA-RTL with MTTWT can achieve this with one fewer truck than Best-H on all but one instance; while this may seem small, the significance of minimising truck use has already been mentioned [1]. It corresponds broadly to a 6% reduction in haulage costs, or approximately 3–4% of whole-mine costs. Additionally, while it may be unlikely that a real-world mine would ever deliberately operate undertrucked, the better results in undertrucked systems of CEA-RTL over Best-H indicates increased reliability against sudden changes in mine conditions.

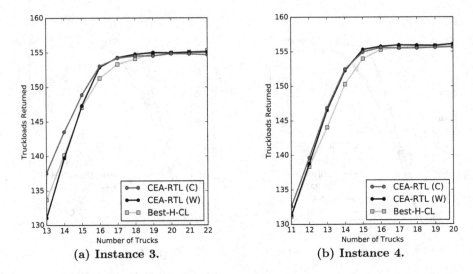

(a) Instance 3.   (b) Instance 4.

Fig. 3. Typical comparisons of Best-H-CL and CEA-RTL.

Table 1. The minimum number of trucks required for Best-H-CL and CEA-RTL to achieve at least 99% of the observed peak performance on each problem instance.

Instance	Best-H-CL	CEA-RTL (W)	CEA-RTL (C)
1	17	17	17
2	18	17	17
3	18	17	17
4	16	15	15
5	17	16	16
6	18	17	18

5   Conclusion

We have used a cooperative coevolutionary algorithm to evolve short-term schedules for underground mines in real-time. The CEA was compared with common greedy heuristics and the DISPATCH algorithm, using a discrete event simulator based on timed automata. Two proxy fitness metrics were used as alternatives to the overall objective of maximising production: minimising average truck cycle time generally performed well on undertrucked systems, and was slightly outperformed by minimising total truck waiting time otherwise. The CEA performed best, especially in achieving good performance with fewer trucks.

Future work will investigate continuous evolution alongside production, and allowing for limited communication underground.

Acknowledgements. The authors would like to thank Ivan Zelina of Micromine Pty. Ltd. for his input.

References

1. Alarie, S., Gamache, M.: Overview of solution strategies used in truck dispatching systems for open pit mines. Int. J. Surf. Min., Reclam. Environ. **16**(1), 59–76 (2002)
2. Alur, R., Dill, D.L.: A theory of timed automata. TCS **126**(2), 183–235 (1994)
3. Bäck, T., Fogel, D.B., Michalewicz, Z.: Evolutionary Computation 1: Basic Algorithms and Operators, vol. 1. CRC Press, Boca Raton (2000)
4. Beaulieu, M., Gamache, M.: An enumeration algorithm for solving the fleet management problem in underground mines. Comput. Oper. Res. **33**(6), 1606–1624 (2006)
5. Berkelaar, M., Eikland, K., Notebaert, P.: lpsolve (2006–2016). https://sourceforge.net/projects/lpsolve/
6. Brazil, M., Grossman, P., Lee, D., Rubinstein, J., Thomas, D., Wormald, N.: Decline design in underground mines using constrained path optimisation. Min. Technol. **117**(2), 93–99 (2008)
7. Cox, W., French, T., Reynolds, M., While, L.: A genetic algorithm for truck dispatching in mining. In: 3rd GCAI, vol. 50, pp. 93–106 (2017)
8. Cox, W., While, L., French, T., Reynolds, M.: CEA-TA mine scheduling (2017). https://github.com/wesleycox/CEA-TA-Mine-Scheduling
9. Eshelman, L.J., Schaffer, J.D.: Real coded genetic algorithms and interval-schemata. FOGA **2**, 187–202 (1993)
10. Gamache, M., Grimard, R., Cohen, P.: A shortest-path algorithm for solving the fleet management problem in underground mines. EJOR **166**(2), 497–506 (2005)
11. Gomes, C.P., Selman, B.: Algorithm portfolios. AI **126**(1–2), 43–62 (2001)
12. Kim, C.W., Tanchoco, J.M.: Conflict-free shortest-time bidirectional AGV routing. IJPR **29**(12), 2377–2391 (1991)
13. Krishnamurthy, N.N., Batta, R., Karwan, M.H.: Developing conflict-free routes for automated guided vehicles. Oper. Res. **41**(6), 1077–1090 (1993)
14. Li, Z.: A methodology for the optimum control of shovel and truck operations in open-pit mining. Min. Sci. Technol. **10**(3), 337–340 (1990)
15. Lipowski, A., Lipowska, D.: Roulette-wheel selection via stochastic acceptance. Phys. A: Stat. Mech. Appl. **391**(6), 2193–2196 (2012)
16. Luke, S., Sullivan, K., Abidi, F.: Large scale empirical analysis of cooperative coevolution. In: GECCO, pp. 151–152. ACM (2011)
17. Modular Mining Systems: DISPATCH (2017). www.modularmining.com/product/. Accessed 20 Sept 2017
18. Munirathinam, M., Yingling, J.C.: A review of computer-based truck dispatching strategies for surface mining operations. Int. J. Surf. Min., Reclam. Environ. **8**(1), 1–15 (1994)
19. Newman, A.M., Rubio, E., Caro, R., Weintraub, A., Eurek, K.: A review of operations research in mine planning. Interfaces **40**(3), 222–245 (2010)
20. Rupprecht, S.: Mine development-access to deposit. In: 5th International Platinum Conference, pp. 101–121 (2012)
21. Saayman, P., Craig, I., Camisani-Calzolari, F.: Optimization of an autonomous vehicle dispatch system in an underground mine. J. South. Afr. Inst. Min. Metall. **106**(2), 77–86 (2006)
22. Tan, S., Ramani, R.V.: Evaluation of computer truck dispatching criteria. In: Proceedings of the SME/AIME Annual Meeting and Exhibition, pp. 192–215 (1992)
23. Upadhyay, S., Askari-Nasab, H.: Truck-shovel allocation optimisation: a goal programming approach. Min. Technol. **125**(2), 82–92 (2016)

24. Vagenas, N.: Dispatch control of a fleet of remote-controlled/automatic load-haul-dump vehicles in underground mines. IJPR **29**(11), 2347–2363 (1991)

25. White, J.W., Olson, J.P.: Computer-based dispatching in mines with concurrent operating objectives. Miner. Eng. **38**(11) (1986)

26. White, J.W., Olson, J.P., Vohnout, S.I.: On improving truck/shovel productivity in open pit mines. CIM Bull. **86**, 43–43 (1993)

27. Wiegand, R.P.: An analysis of cooperative coevolutionary algorithms. Ph.D. thesis, George Mason University, Virginia (2003)

Particle Swarm Optimization for Feature Selection with Adaptive Mechanism and New Updating Strategy

Ke Chen[1], Fengyu Zhou[1(✉)], and Bine Xue[2]

[1] School of Control Science and Engineering, Shandong University,
Jinan 250061, Shandong, China
{chenke_zixf,fyzhou_sdu}@163.com
[2] School of Engineering and Computer Science, Victoria University of Wellington,
Wellington 6140, New Zealand
bing.xue@ecs.vuw.ac.nz

Abstract. Feature selection is an important data preprocessing technique in the emerging field of artificial intelligence and data mining which aims at finding a small set of features from the original dataset with predetermined targets. Particle swarm optimization (PSO) has been widely used to address feature selection problems because of its easy implementation, efficiency and simplicity. However, in high-dimensional problems, selecting the discriminative features with a higher correct classification rate is limited. To solve the issue above, a particle swarm optimization method with adaptive mechanism and new updating strategy is proposed to choose best features to improve the correct classification rate. The proposed approach, named as EPSO, is verified and compared with other three meta-heuristic algorithms and four recent PSO-based feature selection methods. The experimental results and statistical tests have proved the efficiency and feasibility of the EPSO approach in obtaining higher classification accuracy along with smaller number of features. Therefore, the proposed EPSO algorithm can be successfully used as a novel feature selection strategy.

Keywords: Feature selection · Particle swarm optimization
Classification · Adaptive mechanism · New updating strategy

1 Introduction

The goal of feature selection is to eliminate the irrelevant and redundant features without sacrificing the classification correct rate and find an optimal feature subset from the original dataset. In recent years, feature selection techniques have

Supported by The National Key R & D Program of China (Grant No. 2017YFB1302400), National Natural Science Foundation of China (Grant No. 61773242 and 61803227), Key Program of Scientific and Technological Innovation of Shandong Province (Grand No. 2017CXGC0926), Key Research and Development Program of Shandong Province (Grant No. 2017GGX30133).

T. Mitrovic et al. (Eds.): AI 2018, LNAI 11320, pp. 419–431, 2018.
https://doi.org/10.1007/978-3-030-03991-2_39

been successfully applied to solve many real-world problems such as text categorization [1], face recognition [2] and recommender systems [3]. Therefore, feature selection attracts more and more attention from specialists and researchers.

Feature selection is a challenging problem because there may exist mutual influence among features. In other words, a single relevant feature can become redundant or less useful when combined with other features, vice versa. Therefore, an optimal feature subset from the original dataset should be a set of complementary features that span different attributes of the classes to correctly distinguish them. According to the evaluation indicator, feature selection approaches can be divided into two types [4,5]: filter approaches and wrapper approaches. In filter approaches, a feature subset is assessed by the performance of simple auxiliary criteria such as mutual information, distance, relief and correlation, or consistence measures to verify the quality of the selected feature subset. Meanwhile, wrapper approaches evaluate the feature subset's classification performance in an independent way of a specific learning algorithm, such as a neural network, support vector machines and K-nearest neighbor classifier. Compared with filter approaches, wrapper methods are usually more superior in terms of classification accuracy. Furthermore, wrapper methods consider interactions among a group of features, which is difficult to discover in the filter approaches [6]. Therefore, in this study, a wrapper method is adopted to assess the selected feature subsets.

So as to better accomplish feature selection tasks, a strong and efficient search algorithm is desired. Swarm intelligence optimization algorithms are famous for their strong global search capability. Particle swarm optimization (PSO) is a comparatively recent population-based search algorithm in the optimization techniques family. Similar to the evolutionary algorithm (EA) and the genetic algorithm (GA), PSO is a meta-heuristic stochastic optimization approach, which searches for the global optima based on the generation number update. In last two decades, several PSO-based feature selection techniques have been proposed in the literature, such as the feature selection approach based on momentum BPSO (SBPSO) [7], the approach based on GA and PSO (HGAPSO) [8], the method based on PSO and genetic operators (CMPSO) [9], and the approach based on a novel local search strategy and hybrid PSO (HPSO-LS) [10]. Although these feature selection approaches have better classification performance and smaller number of features than the traditional PSO algorithm, the performance of robustness, universality and trade-off between the exploitation and exploration is still unsatisfactory for solving complex data mining problems with different characteristics.

In this paper, a particle swarm optimization algorithm with adaptive mechanism and new updating strategy is developed to further solve feature selection problems. The proposed improved version of PSO is named as enhance particle swarm optimization (EPSO). In EPSO, there are two major modifications. Firstly, an adaptive parameter update mechanism is proposed to tune or control the fly velocity v_{id}^{t+1}. Secondly, a new position update strategy is developed to improve the solution quality. A wrapper feature selection approach is proposed by using EPSO as the search method and K-nearest neighbor to measure the quality of the feature subsets. Eight well-known classification datasets and two groups of contrast experiments are used to evaluate the feasibility and validity of the EPSO-based feature selection approach. The experimental results indicate that the proposed method achieves higher classification correct rate and employs fewer features than other feature selection approaches.

2 Particle Swarm Optimization

Particle swarm optimization (PSO) is a stochastic global optimization technique proposed by Kennedy and Eberhart in the 1995 [11]. PSO simulates the sociological behaviors of bird flocking and fish schooling in a swarm. In PSO, each particle represents a potential candidate solution in the search space. To search the global optimal solution, each particle adjusts its forward direction based on its own best previous position and the current best position of all other particles. During the search phase, the previous location of particle i is denoted by a vector $x_i = (x_{i1}, x_{x2}, \cdots, x_{xd})$, where d indicates the dimensionality of the problem space. The fly velocity of the particle i is denoted as $v_i = (v_{i1}, v_{i2}, \cdots, v_{id})$, and the range of v_{id} is $[-V_{\max}, V_{\max}]$, where the $V_{\max}$ is defined as the maximum fly velocity to control the value within a reasonable range. Moreover, the best currently location of the particle i is recorded as $pbest_i = [pbest_{i1}, pbest_{i2}, \cdots, pbest_{id}]$, the best location achieved by the entire population is recorded as $gbest = [gbest_1, gbest_2, \cdots, gbest_d]$. The PSO method searches for the global optimal solution by updating the location and the fly velocity of each particle in the swarm according to the following formulas:

$$v_{id}^{t+1} = v_{id}^t + c_1 \times r_{1i} \times \left(pbest_{id} - x_{id}^t\right) + c_2 \times r_{2i} \times \left(gbest_d - x_{id}^t\right) \quad (1)$$

$$x_{id}^{t+1} = x_{id}^t + v_{id}^{t+1} \quad (2)$$

where c_1 and c_2 are position constants, called acceleration coefficient, usually set as $c_1 = c_2 = 2$; r_{1i} and r_{2i} are two random values between 0 and 1; t denotes t-th iteration in the search process.

3 New Approach for Feature Selection

A novel thinking of the new approach for feature selection is achieved from the original PSO and proposes an innovative PSO method called enhanced particle swarm optimization (EPSO) in terms of the idea. The presented EPSO is an excellent and effective approach for solving feature selection problems. In the following subsection, we describe the EPSO method first and construct the new approach later to address feature selection tasks.

3.1   Proposed Method - Enhanced Particle Swarm Optimization

PSO has been proved to widely optimize a wide range of real-world optimization problems. However, PSO exists insufficient with premature convergence, inefficient in tradeoff global search capability and local search capability. Therefore, an enhanced particle swarm optimization called EPSO is presented to improve the search performance of the original PSO method. In EPSO, there are two major modifications, which are described in detail as follows:

Firstly, an adaptive mechanism is proposed to control or adjust the fly velocity v_{id}^{t+1}. From Eq. (2), we can see that v_{id}^{t+1} is used to control the direction and distance of particle motion during the search process. Therefore, v_{id}^{t+1} plays an important role to obtain a high quality particle position in the problem space. Generally, in a population-based optimization method, we hope that the particle can wander through the entire solution space in the early search process. Furthermore, in the later stage of search process, it is very important to increase the capability of local search, for finding out the global optimal position efficiently. Since PSO was introduced in 1995, some strategies are introduced to balance the early stage's global search and the latter stage's local search capabilities, such as inertia weight [12], constriction factor [13]. Although these strategies have better control capabilities than the traditional version of PSO, the performance of trade-off between the exploitation and exploration is still unsatisfactory for solving complex optimization problems with different characteristics. In order to better control particle's trajectory and further improve the search performance of PSO, in this paper, an adaptive mechanism is introduced to tune the fly velocity v_{id}^{t+1}, which can effectively control the PSO's convergence tendencies in the search process. In this improvement, the adaptive mechanism is designed as a nonlinear decreasing function to maintain the diversity of the search process. Mathematically, the modified fly velocity update strategy can be rewritten as follows:

$$v_{id}^{t+1} = \Re(t) \times \left[v_{id}^t + c_1 \times r_{1i} \times \left(pbest_{id} - x_{id}^t \right) + c_2 \times r_{2i} \times \left(gbest_d - x_{id}^t \right) \right] \tag{3}$$

$$\Re(t) = \rho \times \exp\left(-\alpha \times \left(\frac{t}{t_{\max}} \right)^\beta \right) \tag{4}$$

where t and t_{max} represent the current iteration and the maximum iteration, respectively.

From experience, the value of ρ set as 1.5. Furthermore, simulation was carried out with Ackley function to find out the best parameter values for α and β. Results are shown in Table 1. A modified optimum solution for Ackley function was observed when α and β are equal to 2. So $\Re(t)$ decreased from 1.5 to 0.2 with iteration.

Secondly, a new position update strategy is proposed to generate particle position of next generation, which can effectively improve the particle quality

Table 1. The experimental for parameter selection

α	β				
	1.0	1.5	2.0	2.5	3.0
1.0	7.31E−05	2.01E−03	1.39E−04	1.22E−04	5.84E−04
1.5	5.41E−05	6.43E−05	9.86E−05	1.39E−04	2.87E−04
2.0	5.54E−05	6.37E−05	2.47E−05	7.36E−05	1.57E−04
2.5	6.98E−05	8.19E−05	1.01E−04	9.36E−05	1.35E−04
3.0	7.29E−05	1.03E−04	1.59E−04	1.19E−04	1.11E−04

in the search process. As seen from Eq. (2), we can see that the position of the next generation particle depends primarily on the current position x_{id}^t and the fly velocity v_{id}^{t+1}. This may weaken the capability of searching the neighborhood around the known optimal solution in the search process. Considering this problem, we present three major improvements by introducing two contraction factors and the previous best position to update the next generation particle position with these two parts. Especially, this modified position update strategy not only can strengthen the ability of global search around the known optimal position but also can accelerate the global convergence by introducing the previous best position. Furthermore, two contraction factors are used to control the maximum step size. In this paper, two contraction factors are defined as a linear function with iteration. The update strategy of the modified PSO, described in Eq. (5), provides more opportunities to the dense search region with many local optimal solutions and thus gives more chances to find the global optimal solution during the search process. The position of each particle in the population is generated depended on the following equation:

$$x_{id}^{t+1} = \chi(t) \times x_{id}^t + \chi'(t) \times gbest_d + v_{id}^{t+1} \tag{5}$$

$$\chi(t) = 1 - \frac{t}{t_{\max}} \tag{6}$$

$$\chi'(t) = 1 - \chi(t) \tag{7}$$

3.2 EPSO for Feature Selection

Feature selection is an important data pre-processing technique, which is executed before classification and it can effectively remove irrelevant and redundant features from the entire feature set. Feature selection approaches minimize the feature subset dimension and maximize the classification accuracy, whilst it chooses the discriminative features. In this paper, a novel wrapper-based feature selection method using EPSO has been proposed and the working of this approach is described in the following part.

In the EPSO approach, a particle represents a feature subset. The dimension of the swarm denotes the number of available feature of the dataset. In the original dataset, each feature corresponds to a dimension and each variable is fixed within the range $[0, 1]$. The solution will be better when the number of selected features is minimal and the classification accuracy is higher. The position of the particle determines the reservation and rejection of the features. If the position value is within $(0.5, 1]$, it represents the reservation decision on of the respective feature and if not, it represents the rejection [14]. Each position is assessed by the developed fitness function, which includes two objectives: the accuracy achieved by the K-nearest neighbor (KNN) model and the number of determined features. In this study, the fitness function is described as follows:

$$Fitness_{\min} = \alpha \times \gamma_R (D) + \beta \times \frac{|S|}{|N|} \tag{8}$$

where $\gamma_R (D)$ denotes the classification error rate of feature set R relative to the decision D; Furthermore, $|S|$ represents the number of the selected features and $|N|$ represents the total number of the available features in the dataset. α and β are two parameters corresponding to the relative importance of classification accuracy and selected feature subset size. $\alpha \in [0, 1]$ and $\beta = 1 - \alpha$ achieved from [15]. The pseudo-code of EPSO is shown in Algorithm 1.

Algorithm 1: Pseudo-code of EPSO for feature selection

---

begin
    divide the instances into a Training set and a Test set;
    uniformly randomly initialize each particle position in the swarm;
    generate the initial fly velocity for each particle randomly;
    while $t{<}t_{\max}$ **do**
        evaluate the fitness value of each particle on the Training set using Eq. (8);
        for i=1 **to** populationsize **do**
            update the *pbest* of particle *i*;
            update the *gbest* of particle *i*;
        end
        for i=1 **to** populationsize **do**
            for i=1 **to** dimension **do**
                update the fly velocity of particle *i* using Eq. (3);
                update the position of particle *i* using Eq. (5);
            end
        end
    end
    calculate the classification accuracy of the selected feature subset on the Test set;
    return the position of gbest (the selected feature subset);
    return the training and test classification accuracies
end

---

4 Experimental Results and Discussions

4.1 Experimental Design

To examine the effectiveness and feasibility of the proposed EPSO method, a series of simulation experiments have been executed on eight well-known classification datasets, which are obtained from the UCI machine learning repository [16] and can be seen in Table 2. As can be seen from Table 2, these eight classification datasets have different features, classes, instances and characteristics. Therefore, they are adopted as representative examples of the classification problems that the proposed EPSO approach will be examed on. On each dataset, 70% of instances were selected as the training examples randomly and the remaining 30% of instances are adopted as the testing examples.

The K-nearest neighbor (KNN) technique is the most simple and effective approach and one of the researcher's leading options for a classification research. Especially, the set of samples is small or no prior knowledge about the data distribution is available. In this paper, a wrapper-based EPSO method has been presented in which KNN has been used as a learning algorithm. In order to simplify the assessment process, we set K = 5 in KNN. We implement the proposed EPSO method and 5NN for feature selection in Matlab. In addition, using five cross-validation to avoid feature selection bias in the training stage. The computer is Intel(R) Core(TM) i5-7400, 3.00 GHz, 16 GB RAM and the operating system is Windows 10 Professional Edition.

The detailed parameters of EPSO are set as follows: the size of the population is 20, and the maximum iteration is set to 100 for all test datasets. Other control parameters of the PSO approach are available from Ref. [17]. In this paper, the fully connected topology is used. For each dataset, the experiments are executed 30 times to ensure the feature selection performance of each approach. Furthermore, in the view of illustrating the significant difference of the proposed EPSO algorithm with other feature selection approaches for each dataset, a test namely the nonparametric Wilcoxon rank-sum has been conducted at a significance level of 0.05. The results of Wilcoxon rank-sum test are described in Tables 3 and 4. In Tables 3 and 4, when the proposed EPSO algorithm significantly outperforms other contrast algorithms, + mark was used. Otherwise, − mark was used. ≈ means that they are similar.

4.2 Results and Discussions

The results are mainly shown in two Experiments: (a) Comparisons of EPSO and other meta-heuristic methods, and (b) Comparison of EPSO and other existing PSO-based methods. Furthermore, the average execution time (E.T.) and comparison via Wilcoxon rank-sum test (T-test) are recorded to verify the effectiveness and efficiency of the proposed EPSO approach.

Experiment 1: Comparisons of EPSO and Other Meta-heuristic Methods. Table 3 shows the simulation experimental results of PSO, Differential

Table 2. Datasets used for experimentation

Dataset	#Features	#Class	#Instances	#Characteristics
Wine	13	3	178	Real, Integer
Zoo	16	7	101	Categorical, Integer
Spect	22	2	267	Categorical
Ionosphere	34	2	351	Real, Integer
Sonar	60	2	208	Real
Hillvalley	100	2	606	Real
Musk 1	166	2	476	Integer
Multiple features	649	15	2000	Real, Integer

Evolution (DE), Artificial Bee Colony (ABC) and EPSO through the 30 independent runs in terms of average classification correct rate (AveCR) along with their chosen number of features. "All" indicates that all of the available features are adopted for classification. The tabulated results of Table 3 show that the EPSO method has obtained the best classification performance for six out of the eight datasets. For example, datasets such as Zoo, Spect, Sonar, Hillvalley, Musk 1 and Multiple feature datasets have the best average classification correct rate with the reduced feature subset. Inferences illustrate that the proposed EPSO method outperforms the other three approaches and KNN using all the available features in terms of average classification accuracy for the before-mentioned six datasets. However, for Wine and Ionosphere datasets, the original PSO method has obtained the best classification accuracy.

For all datasets, the reduction in the number of features is quite significant, which is a remarkable capability of the proposed EPSO method. For example, in case of the Zoo dataset, the EPSO approach has achieved the average classification accuracy of 100% with 3.83 features. Hence, one can conclude that the optimal feature subset has been achieved by the EPSO approach for most datasets. On an overall view, when comparing EPSO with DE, ABC, basic PSO and using all available features, we speculate that the EPSO method seems to execute well in obtaining the higher average classification accuracy and the better feature subset for almost all classification datasets. From Table 3, we can see that the EPSO algorithm has the best average computation time in comparison to other seven approaches on 9 datasets. Furthermore, four groups of the Wilcoxon rank-sum test results are also recorded. The Wilcoxon rank-sum test is adopted to compare two related approaches. From Table 3, we can clearly see that the performance of HPSO-SSM is better than other four approaches. Figure 1 shows the feature selection process of the proposed EPSO method for the Ionosphere and Musk 1 datasets. Figure 1 also illustrates the relationship between the obtained classification correct rate and the number of the chosen feature. It can be known that, from Fig. 1, elimination of irrelevant and redundancy features benefits classification correct rate.

Table 3. Comparisons of proposed approach and other meta-heuristic methods

Dataset	Approach	Size	E.T.	AveCR ± S.D.	T-test
Wine	All	13		74.07	+
	PSO	3.30	2.60	98.15 ± 0.28	≈
	DE	3.00	5.67	96.30 ± 0.64	+
	ABC	5.20	2.84	97.78 ± 0.49	≈
	EPSO	5.10	2.47	98.02 ± 0.47	
Zoo	All	16		96.77	+
	PSO	6.63	2.57	99.11 ± 0.14	+
	DE	5.80	5.31	96.13 ± 0.96	+
	ABC	7.60	2.80	100 ± 0.00	≈
	EPSO	3.83	3.40	100 ± 0.00	
Spect	All	22		67.90	+
	PSO	10.93	2.78	76.30 ± 1.81	+
	DE	11.00	5.46	76.30 ± 1.92	+
	ABC	12.20	2.87	77.04 ± 1.84	+
	EPSO	9.73	2.76	79.63 ± 1.61	
Ionosphere	All	34		83.02	+
	PSO	9.30	2.95	94.87 ± 1.53	≈
	DE	11.80	6.59	94.53 ± 1.47	≈
	ABC	16.00	3.10	92.64 ± 1.68	+
	EPSO	9.57	2.50	94.47 ± 1.30	
Sonar	All	60		88.89	+
	PSO	25.87	2.61	95.08 ± 1.77	+
	DE	24.96	6.57	96.37 ± 1.56	+
	ABC	25.94	3.58	96.89 ± 0.95	+
	EPSO	20.53	3.48	99.68 ± 0.77	
Hillvalley	All	100		58.24	+
	PSO	45.23	6.67	65.57 ± 1.91	+
	DE	38.20	12.82	61.10 ± 1.58	+
	ABC	49.40	7.87	65.27 ± 1.73	+
	EPSO	41.77	6.56	66.36 ± 1.28	
Musk 1	All	166		83.22	+
	PSO	76.63	6.82	92.31 ± 1.52	+
	DE	70.00	13.76	95.38 ± 1.37	+
	ABC	82.03	8.01	88.11 ± 1.96	+
	EPSO	72.90	7.06	96.60 ± 1.06	
Multiple features	All	649		95.33	+
	PSO	310.80	397.08	98.00 ± 0.57	≈
	DE	334.00	721.23	95.83 ± 0.96	+
	ABC	321.00	443.37	96.17 ± 0.74	+
	EPSO	298.87	394.84	98.49 ± 0.18	

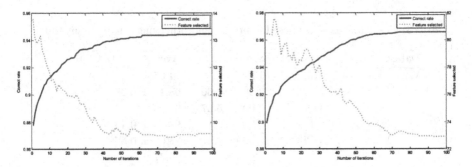

Fig. 1. Iteration times versus the classification correct rate and the number of features selected for Ionosphere (the left one) and Musk 1 (the right one) based on average of the 30 runs

As a conclusion, for most classification datasets, EPSO achieves the best classification performance, selects fewer features and obtains higher classification accuracy than other three algorithms and KNN using all available features.

Experiment 2: Comparison of EPSO and Other Existing PSO-Based Methods. To further examine the performance of the proposed EPSO approach, we compare its classification ability with other four feature selection methods, called Gaussian PSO (GPSO) [18], Gaussian PSO based Representation (GPSOR) [19], PSO based Representation (PSOR) [20] and Corossover-Mutation PSO (CMPSO) [9]. The four feature selection approaches used datasets with a relatively small number of features. Therefore, we adopt only the five classification datasets that are used in both our experiments, and the results of the feature selection approaches in Table 4 is found in [9].

From Table 4, in terms of average classification accuracy, the proposed EPSO method owns the best performance on four out of the five datasets. Only on the Multiple features, EPSO achieves the average classification correct rate of 98.49%, which is only 0.56% lower than the best average classification accuracy, achieve by CMPSO. Furthermore, as per the results in Table 4, on the small datasets, the EPSO method chooses a similar number of features in comparison with other four PSO-based feature selection approaches. However, on the large datasets, the proposed EPSO method tends to choose more features to retain higher classification accuracy. In addition, according to the results of the Wilcoxon rank-sum test (T-test), the performance of EPSO is different from other four algorithms. Therefore, the EPSO approach are more suitable for classification datasets including different numbers of original features than other existing PSO-based methods.

Table 4. Comparisons of proposed approach and existing PSO-based methods

Dataset	Approach	Size	AveCR ± S.D.	T-test
Wine	GPSO	5.40	96.59 ± 2.76	+
	GPSOR	4.60	97.70 ± 2.52	≈
	PSOR	4.75	96.70 ± 3.10	+
	CMPSO	4.70	97.24 ± 2.89	+
	EPSO	5.10	98.02 ± 0.47	
Ionosphere	GPSO	7.66	89.50 ± 1.68	+
	GPSOR	3.17	86.89 ± 1.80	+
	PSOR	9.70	88.63 ± 1.68	+
	CMPSO	3.77	87.94 ± 2.00	+
	EPSO	9.57	94.47 ± 1.30	
Sonar	GPSO	17.64	78.19 ± 4.14	+
	GPSOR	10.17	78.25 ± 2.95	+
	PSOR	14.33	78.94 ± 4.02	+
	CMPSO	11.60	79.42 ± 2.48	+
	EPSO	20.53	99.68 ± 0.77	
Musk 1	GPSO	39.64	84.95 ± 2.73	+
	GPSOR	38.93	83.29 ± 2.48	+
	PSOR	35.03	83.12 ± 3.41	+
	CMPSO	39.93	85.06 ± 2.49	+
	EPSO	72.90	96.60 ± 1.06	
Multiple features	GPSO	91.40	99.01 ± 0.13	+
	GPSOR	51.00	98.86 ± 0.17	≈
	PSOR	51.07	98.84 ± 0.18	≈
	CMPSO	110.77	99.05 ± 0.01	-
	EPSO	298.87	98.49 ± 0.18	

5   Conclusions and Future Work

In this paper, a new feature selection algorithm, named enhanced PSO (EPSO), is presented and successfully used to address feature selection tasks. This method extends the idea of the traditional PSO to feature selection problems with a new adaptive mechanism and new updating strategy. By compared with those existing results achieved by other three meta-heuristic algorithms and four PSO-based feature selection methods. The experimental results show that the proposed EPSO method has strong abilities in reducing the size of the feature subset, improving the classification correct rates, and low computational complexity. In addition, the results of Wilcoxon rank-sum test display the statistical robustness of the EPSO method. Therefore, the EPSO method can be employed as an effective and efficient preprocessing approach to address feature selection problems.

In the future, we would like to apply the proposed EPSO method to solve other feature selection in other tasks like pattern recognition and image processing.

References

1. Bhopale, A.-P., Kamath, S.-S., Tiwari, A.: Concise semantic analysis based text categorization using modified hybrid union feature selection approach. In: 4th International Conference on Recent Advances in Information Technology, pp. 1–7. IEEE (2018)
2. Lin, S.-D., Wang, D.-E.: Features selection and statistical classification for pose-invariant face recognition. In: 10th International Conference on Advanced Computational Intelligence, pp. 23–27. IEEE (2018)
3. Ragone, A., Tomeo, P., Magarelli, C., Noia, T.-D.: Schema-summarization in linked-data-based feature selection for recommender systems. In: Proceedings of the Symposium on Applied Computing, pp. 330–335. ACM (2017)
4. Xue, B., Cervante, L., Shang, L., Browne, W.-N., Zhang, M.-J.: A multi-objective particle swarm optimisation for filter-based feature selection in classification problems. Connect. Sci. **24**(2–3), 91–116 (2012)
5. Kohavi, R., John, G.-H.: Wrappers for feature subset selection. Artif. Intell. **97**(1–2), 273–324 (1997)
6. Nguyen, H.B., Xue, B., Andreae, P.: Mutual information estimation for filter based feature selection using particle swarm optimization. In: Squillero, G., Burelli, P. (eds.) EvoApplications 2016. LNCS, vol. 9597, pp. 719–736. Springer, Cham (2016). https://doi.org/10.1007/978-3-319-31204-0_46
7. Nguyen, B.H., Xue, B., Andreae, P.: A novel binary particle swarm optimization algorithm and its applications on knapsack and feature selection problems. In: Leu, G., Singh, H.K., Elsayed, S. (eds.) Intelligent and Evolutionary Systems. PALO, vol. 8, pp. 319–332. Springer, Cham (2017). https://doi.org/10.1007/978-3-319-49049-6_23
8. Ghamisi, P., Benediktsson, J.-A.: Feature selection based on hybridization of genetic algorithm and particle swarm optimization. IEEE Geosci. Remote Sens. Lett. **12**(2), 309–313 (2015)
9. Nguyen, H.-B., Xue, B., Andreae, P., Zhang, M.-J.: Particle swarm optimisation with genetic operators for feature selection. In: CEC 2017, pp. 286–293. IEEE (2017)
10. Moradi, P., Gholampour, M.: A hybrid particle swarm optimization for feature subset selection by integrating a novel local search strategy. Appl. Soft Comput. **43**, 117–130 (2016)
11. Kennedy, J., Eberhart, R.: Particle swarm optimization. In: IEEE International Conference on Neural Networks, pp. 1942–1948. IEEE (1995)
12. Shi, Y., Eberhart, R.: A modified particle swarm optimizer. In: IEEE World Congress on Computational Intelligence, pp. 69–73. IEEE (1998)
13. Clerc, M., Kennedy, J.: The particle swarm-explosion, stability, and convergence in a multidimensional complex space. IEEE Trans. Evolut. Comput. **6**(1), 58–73 (2002)
14. Sindhu, R., Ngadiran, R., Yacob, Y.-M., Zahri, N.-A.-H., Hariharn, M.: Sine–cosine algorithm for feature selection with elitism strategy and new updating mechanism. Neural Comput. Appl. **28**(10), 2947–2958 (2017)

15. Hancer, E., Xue, B., Zhang, M.-J., Karaboga, D., Akay, B.: Pareto front feature selection based on artificial bee colony optimization. Inf. Sci. **422**, 462–479 (2018)
16. Newman, S.-H.-D.-J., Blake, C.-L., Merz, C.-L.: UCI Repository of Machine Learning Databases (1998). http://archive.ics.uci.edu/ml/index.php
17. Rezaee, J.-A., Jasni, J.: Parameter selection in particle swarm optimisation: a survey. J. Exp. Theor. Artif. Intell. **25**(4), 527–542 (2013)
18. Lane, M.C., Xue, B., Liu, I., Zhang, M.: Gaussian based particle swarm optimisation and statistical clustering for feature selection. In: Blum, C., Ochoa, G. (eds.) EvoCOP 2014. LNCS, vol. 8600, pp. 133–144. Springer, Heidelberg (2014). https://doi.org/10.1007/978-3-662-44320-0_12
19. Nguyen, H.B., Xue, B., Liu, I., Andreae, P., Zhang, M.: Gaussian transformation based representation in particle swarm optimisation for feature selection. In: Mora, A.M., Squillero, G. (eds.) EvoApplications 2015. LNCS, vol. 9028, pp. 541–553. Springer, Cham (2015). https://doi.org/10.1007/978-3-319-16549-3_44
20. Nguyen, H.B., Xue, B., Liu, I., Zhang, M.: PSO and statistical clustering for feature selection: a new representation. In: Dick, G., et al. (eds.) SEAL 2014. LNCS, vol. 8886, pp. 569–581. Springer, Cham (2014). https://doi.org/10.1007/978-3-319-13563-2_48

An Improved Genetic Programming Hyper-Heuristic for the Uncertain Capacitated Arc Routing Problem

Jordan MacLachlan[1(✉)], Yi Mei[1], Juergen Branke[2], and Mengjie Zhang[1]

[1] Victoria University of Wellington, Kelburn 6140, New Zealand
{maclacjord,yi.mei,mengjie.zhang}@ecs.vuw.ac.nz
[2] The University of Warwick, Coventry CV4 7AL, UK
Juergen.Branke@wbs.ac.uk

Abstract. This paper uses a Genetic Programming Hyper-Heuristic (GPHH) to evolve routing policies for the Uncertain Capacitated Arc Routing Problem (UCARP). Given a UCARP instance, the GPHH evolves feasible solutions in the form of decision making policies which decide the next task to serve whenever a vehicle completes its current service. Existing GPHH approaches have two drawbacks. First, they tend to generate small routes by routing through the depot and refilling prior to the vehicle being fully loaded. This usually increases the total cost of the solution. Second, existing GPHH approaches cannot control the extra repair cost incurred by a route failure, which may result in higher total cost. To address these issues, this paper proposes a new GPHH algorithm with a new No-Early-Refill filter to prevent generating small routes, and a novel Flood Fill terminal to better handle route failures. Experimental studies show that the newly proposed GPHH algorithm significantly outperforms the existing GPHH approaches on the *Ugdb* and *Uval* benchmark datasets. Further analysis has verified the effectiveness of both the new filter and terminal.

Keywords: Arc routing · Hyper-heuristic · Genetic programming

1 Introduction

The Capacitated Arc Routing Problem (CARP) [9] is an important optimisation problem with many real-world applications such as city waste collection [1] and winter gritting [10,11]. With the intention of accurately aligning CARP with reality, risk was introduced by [16] in presenting the Uncertain CARP (UCARP). At a high level, this consists of a set of vehicles which generate a number of routes (cycles) from a depot node, serving a number of edge-tasks at minimal cost subject to some constraints, e.g. the total demand of a route cannot exceed the vehicle's finite capacity.

In UCARP, some information such as travel time and task demand is unknown, and can only be estimated prior to arrival at the edge in question.

© Springer Nature Switzerland AG 2018
T. Mitrovic et al. (Eds.): AI 2018, LNAI 11320, pp. 432–444, 2018.
https://doi.org/10.1007/978-3-030-03991-2_40

Therefore, preplanned solutions can fail and need to be adjusted in real time. For example the actual demand of a task can be greater than expected, and exceed the remaining capacity of the vehicle, or an edge along the planned path becomes impassable and the vehicle has to plan a detour. Traditional optimisation approaches (e.g. [22,23]) that obtain a (robust) solution cannot handle this well, as they usually have high computational complexity, and cannot adjust the preplanned solution efficiently. *Routing policies* (e.g. [14,17,24]), on the other hand, are a promising strategy in making real-time decisions due to their low time complexity. A routing policy does not require any preplanned solution; instead, it models the UCARP as an online *decision making process*, where the routes are built over time by assigning the routes their next task at each step.

Manually designing effective routing policies is very time consuming, and requires a high level of domain expertise. To combat this, Genetic Programming Hyper-Heuristic (GPHH) can be applied to automatically evolve routing policies without the need of a human expert. The GP-evolved routing policy has shown great success in UCARP, and managed to achieve state-of-the-art solutions on many UCARP benchmark instances [14,17].

However, the existing studies on GPHH for evolving routing policies are still preliminary, and most problem-specific characteristics have been neglected. As a result, the performance of existing GPHH methods are not satisfactory, having two main drawbacks. First, in the decision making process, a route tends to return to the depot early (i.e. with remaining capacity), which generates many small cycles and leads to a large total cost. The existing methods are not intelligent enough to recognise and exclude this case. Second, the existing GPHH approaches cannot handle *route failure* (incurred when the actual demand of a task is larger than the vehicle's remaining capacity) well, often leading to a large repair cost. This paper aims to propose new approaches to tackle the above two drawbacks, and develop an improved GPHH to evolve more effective routing policies. Specifically, the paper has the following research goals.

- Develop a *new decision making process* that explicitly prevents the routes from going back to the depot too early.
- Design a *new feature* to handle the route failure more effectively.
- Propose a new GPHH algorithm with the new decision making process and feature as a terminal.
- Examine the effectiveness of the newly proposed GPHH algorithm.

2   Background

2.1   Uncertain Capacitated Arc Routing Problem

In a UCARP instance, a graph $G(V, E)$ is given, and a set of vehicles with capacity Q are located at the depot $v_0 \in V$. Each edge $e \in E$ has a positive *random* deadheading cost $dc(e)$, non-negative *random* demand $d(e)$ and a non-negative *deterministic* serving cost $sc(e)$. These represent e's non-serving traversal cost, the demand to serve and the serving traversal cost, respectively. If $d(e) > 0$, then *e* is called a *task*, and needs to be served. The goal is for the vehicles to serve all tasks with the least total cost (sum of the serving and deadheading cost of all edges in each route) subject to the following constraints:

- Each route starts and ends at the depot. Due to the route failures, the service of a task can be interrupted. A vehicle can therefore stop to replenish capacity early, before returning to complete the remaining service.
- Between two visits of the depot, the total demand served by the route cannot exceed the vehicle's capacity.

A *sampled* UCARP instance is a realised instance where each random variable has a sampled value. In a sampled UCARP instance, the sampled (actual) demand of a task is unknown until the vehicle completes its service. The actual deadheading cost of an edge is known exactly after the vehicle has traversed it. One can generate an arbitrary number of different sampled UCARP instances (e.g. using different random seeds) based on the same UCARP instance.

The objective of a UCARP instance is to find a solution (e.g. a predefined robust solution in proactive approaches or a routing policy in reactive approaches) that minimises the expected total cost across all the possible sampled UCARP instances based on that UCARP instance. In practice, it is impossible to enumerate all the possible sampled UCARP instances. Therefore, we will test our solution on a test set consisting of a large number of sampled UCARP instances.

2.2   Related Work

Solutions to static CARP, where costs of travel and task demand are known in full, range from exact mathematical methods on small instances [5], to tabu search methods [6,12], memetic algorithms (MA) [13,15] and Edge Based Histogram (EBH) methods [20]. A number of simple heuristics, such as Path-Scanning [13], Augment-Merge [9] and Ulusoy's single tour splitting method [21], have also been proposed to generate reasonably good solutions in a very short time. These heuristics can be used to generate initial solutions for the more advanced search algorithms.

To simulate the uncertain real world better, a variety of stochastic CARP models have been introduced, such as the CARP with stochastic demand [7], CARP with collaborating depots [19], and UCARP [16]. In [7], a genetic algorithm was proposed which took advantage of the concept of a 'slack' in determining the next task. In [4], a Branch-and-Price algorithm was proposed to consider the same stochastic task demand. UCARP was proposed in [16], considering four different stochastic factors to simulate the reality as closely as possible. There have been a number of studies for solving UCARP, including proactive approaches (e.g. [22,23]) that optimise a robust solution, and reactive approaches that use Genetic Programming Hyper-Heuristics (GPHH) to evolve routing policies (e.g. [14,17,24]). Wang et al. proposed an Estimation of Distribution Algorithm with Stochastic Local Search (EDASLS) [22] that encompasses the work by [20]. They build routes for the static CARP instance using a path scanning heuristic [8] then construct an edge based histogram matrix on a template individual whenever a mutation operation occurs, per [20]. Further, they then perform a novel SLS method to manipulate the route string in an attempt to develop a better individual. To the best of our knowledge, EDASLS is the current state-of-the-art proactive approach in solving UCARP.

GPHH has achieved great success in solving dynamic combinatorial optimisation problems [2,3,18]. Based on the idea in [24], Liu et al. [14] proposed a GPHH to evolve routing policies for UCARP, and achieved promising results on the benchmark instances designed in [16]. In [14], a UCARP instance is modelled as a decision making process, where a routing policy is used for deciding the next task whenever a vehicle completes its current service. Then they use GP to evolve the routing policy. When route failure occurs, the vehicle simply returns to the depot in the middle of the service to refill, then returns to resume the interrupted service. When an edge failure occurs, the vehicle finds a detour using the updated graph topology. The work in [14] contains two contributions. First, it proposes a filter method to select a small set of candidate tasks at each decision point, improving the accuracy of the decisions made by the routing policy. Second, it designs a set of promising features to represent the current state, leading to better and more meaningful policies.

Mei et al. [17] extend the proactive approaches [14,24] from a single-vehicle case to the general multi-vehicle case, developing a new meta-algorithm that generates routes simultaneously.

3   Proposed Algorithm

The standard framework of GPHH is described as follows.

1. Initialise a population of GP trees, each a routing policy (heuristic).
2. **Evaluate** the fitness of each GP tree using a training set.
3. Generate a new population by crossover/mutation/reproduction.
4. If stopping criteria is met, stop. Otherwise, go back to Step 2.

The evaluation of a GP tree on a training instance is essentially a decision making process with that tree as the routing policy. The fitness of the GP tree is set to the average total cost of the generated solutions on the training instances. A decision making process is described as follows.

1. Initially, all the vehicles are at the depot, and all the tasks are unserved.
2. Whenever a vehicle becomes idle (at either the beginning or upon task completion), a set of candidate tasks Ω are selected from all the unserved tasks by a *filter* method.
3. The GP tree is a priority function, applied to each candidate task to calculate their relative priority. The task with the smallest heuristic value is selected to be served next.

4. If all the tasks have been served, return to depot and end the simulation. Otherwise, go back to Step 2.

Using the terminals from Table 1, consider each variable in the oversimplified heuristic below. A lower CFH value decreases the output of the heuristic, making the task of a higher priority. Using similar logic, we can say that this heuristic prioritises tasks that are close to the vehicle's location (CFH) and the depot (CTD) and that have a low task demand to vehicular capacity ratio (/ DEM RQ).

$$(+ \ (+CFH \ CTD) \ (/DEM \ RQ))$$

In the existing GPHH approaches, the filter method identifies the candidate tasks as those expected to be feasible, i.e. their expected demand does not exceed the remaining capacity. In this paper we design a new decision making process by proposing a new filter method called the No-Early-Refill filter.

3.1   The New No-Early-Refill Filter

Algorithm 1 describes the new No-Early-Refill filter. The difference between this and the standard existing filter is that it excludes the tasks where the depot is on the expected shortest path to the task (lines 4–6) to avoid automatic, premature refilling. $\delta(a1, a2)$ represents the cost of the fastest route between arcs $a1$ & $a2$.

Algorithm 1. The new No-Early-Refill Filter

1: $\Omega \leftarrow \emptyset$;
2: **for each** unserved task t **do**
3:     **if** $\hat{d}(t) \leq \hat{Q}$ **then**   ▷ Remaining demand is less than remaining capacity
4:         **if** $\delta(\text{currNode}, t) \ != \delta(\text{currNode}, \text{depot}) + \delta(\text{depot}, t)$ **then**
5:             $\Omega \leftarrow \Omega \cup t$;
6:         **end if**
7:     **end if**
8: **end for**
9: **Return** Ω;

Figure 1 shows an example where the depot is v_0 and all the edges are undirected and all except (v_1, v_2) are tasks. Each edge is associated with a number denoting its deadheading cost. Suppose a vehicle has served (v_0, v_1) and is therefore located at v_1. In this state, (v_2, v_3), (v_0, v_3) and (v_0, v_4) are yet to be served. The existing filter considers all the three tasks and tends to prioritise (v_0, v_3) or (v_0, v_4) to serve next as they are closest to the vehicle's current location. The proposed No-Early-Refill filter on the other hand only considers (v_2, v_3), and can therefore serve (v_0, v_1), (v_2, v_3) and (v_3, v_0) in a single route, followed by (v_0, v_4). In doing so the new filter reduces the noise introduced by these misleading tasks, making it more capable of generating solutions with smaller total cost.

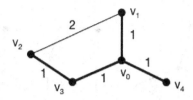

Fig. 1. An example to show the difference between filters.

3.2   The New Flood Fill Feature Terminal

It is important to efficiently handle potential route failures, limiting the cost of the recourse action. Intuitively, route failures occur toward the end of routes and the incurred extra cost is smaller if they occur on a task close to the depot. Therefore, given the same expected route cost, it is more desirable to serve tasks closer to the depot at the end of the route.

An example is given in Fig. 2, where v_0 is the depot, all 9 edges are tasks with an expected demand of 1, and vehicle capacity is 4. As depicted in this example, the routes R and R' have the same expected cost. However, R should be preferred over R', since route failures (premature vehicular capacity exhaustion) in R tend to occur at the end of the route (i.e. on (v_5, v_0)), which is closer to the depot than (v_3, v_2) in R', resulting in a lower recourse cost of returning to the depot.

Existing GPHH approaches cannot recognise this relationship. In the provided example, the GP-evolved policies tend to generate R' more often than R by preferring nearest neighbours. To address this issue, we design a new feature called *Flood Fill* (**FF**) to reflect the ability of a task to be served towards the end of the route to save the extra cost caused by the route failure.

FF borrows the concept of water flow dynamics, considering each edge as a pipe. When pouring water into the depot node until all the edge-pipes are uniformly full, the edges that pass a higher volume of water are easier to get to from the depot. Following this idea, we calculate the shortest path from the depot to the end of each unserved task using Djikstra's Algorithm. Then, for each task, **FF** is defined as the number of these shortest paths the task is a member of. Therefore, a smaller **FF** should be preferred.

The calculation for **FF** is performed in three situations: first in the preprocessing stage, then again on the realisation of route and edge failures. Specifically, for each task t, we store a set of tasks $\Theta(t)$, which is defined as follows.

$$\Theta(t) = \{t' | either\ direction\ of\ t\ is\ on\ the\ shortest\ path\ from\ the\ depot\ to\ t'\}$$

For all the tasks, **FF** is calculated as $\mathrm{FF}(t) = |\Theta(t)|$. As task t' is served during the decision making process, each $\Theta(t)$ is updated as $\Theta(t) \setminus t'$.

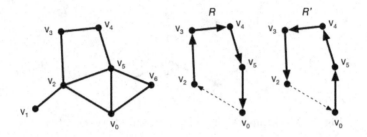

Fig. 2. An example to show the effectiveness of the new feature.

4   Experimental Studies

To verify the effectiveness of the proposed No-Early-Refill filter and Flood Fill feature, we compare the following four algorithms on the *Ugdb* and *Uval* instances [16].

- GPHH [17]: the baseline GPHH algorithm with the standard filter and terminal set (given by Table 1).
- GPHH-NER: with the No-Early-Refill filter and standard terminal set.
- GPHH-FF: with the standard filter and the *extended* terminal set, which contains the standard terminals and the new **FF** feature.
- GPHH-NF: with both the No-Early-Fill filter and extended terminal set.

In the experiment, each random variable follows a truncated normal distribution, where μ is set as the value given by the static instance, and $\sigma = 0.2\mu$. For each UCARP instance, 500 sampled instances were generated independently to be the test set. A separate training set of 5 sampled instances per generation, was generated as well for the GP training process.

Table 1 gives the terminal set used in the GPHH [17]. The extended terminal set used by GPHH-FF and GPHH-NF contains **FF** as well. The function set is $\{+, -, \times, /, \max, \min\}$ (the "/" is protected, returning 1 if divided by 0). In all the compared algorithms, the population size is set to 1024, and the maximal generations is 51. The crossover/mutation/reproduction rates are set to 80%/15%/5% and the maximal depth is set to 8. All the compared algorithms were run 30 times independently, and Wicoxon rank sum test with significance level of 0.05 was conducted to test the statistical significance. This follows standard experimental norms [14,16,24].

4.1   Experimental Results

Table 2 summarises the results of the compared algorithm, and shows the mean and standard deviation of the normalised total cost of the compared algorithms on the *Ugdb* and *Uval* datasets. These datasets are conventional for this problem

Table 1. The terminals used in the GPHH.

Terminal	Description
CFH	Estimated cost from here (the current node) to the candidate task
CFR1	Estimated cost from the alternative closest route to the task
CR	Estimated cost to refill (from the current node to the depot)
CTD	Estimated cost from the candidate task to the depot
CTT1	Estimated cost from the candidate task to its closest remaining Task
DEM	The estimated DEMand of the candidate task
DEM1	The estimated DEMand of the closest unserved task to this candidate
FRT	The fraction of the remaining tasks (unserved)
FUT	The fraction of the unassigned tasks
FULL	The FULLness of the route (current load over capacity)
RQ	The remaining capacity of the route
RQ1	The remaining capacity for the closest alternative route
SC	The serving cost of the candidate task
ERC	A random constant number

Table 2. The mean and standard deviation (in brackets) of the normalised total cost of the compared algorithms over the *Ugdb* and *Uval* datasets.

	GPHH [17]	GPHH-NER	GPHH-FF	GPHH-NF
Ugdb	0.928 (0.057)	0.925 (0.061)	0.927 (0.059)	**0.925** (0.061)
Uval	0.828 (0.048)	0.828 (0.051)	0.828 (0.048)	**0.825** (0.051)

and range from 2 to 10 vehicles serving between 11 and 97 tasks of varying average demands. For normalisation, the total cost for each test instance is divided by the total cost obtained by the Path-Scanning 5 (PS5) [13] benchmark policy.

From Table 2, it can be seen that all the three newly proposed GPHH algorithms obtained better normalised total cost than GPHH. Whilst GPHH-NER performed better on the smaller *Ugdb* dataset, GPHH-FF did so on the larger *Uval* dataset with more vehicles. Finally, GPHH-NF performed the best.

For a more comprehensive statistical comparison, Table 3 shows the win-draw-lose results of the pairwise comparisons over the total 57 (23 *Ugdb* plus 34 *Uval*) instances. For example, the row-3-column-2 entry (10-44-3) shows that under the rank sum test with significance level of 0.05, GPHH-NF performed significantly better than GPHH-NER on 10 instances, and significantly worse on 3 instances. There is no statistical difference between the two algorithms on 44 instances. From the results, it is obvious that all the three newly proposed algorithms significantly outperformed the baseline GPHH on many instances. This demonstrates the effectiveness of the new No-Early-Refill filter and the FF feature. Note that GPHH-NER was never significantly worse than GPHH. When being used alone, the No-Early-Refill filter obtained relatively better performance than FF. GPHH-NER won over GPHH-FF on more instances (15 versus 6), and showed significantly better performance than GPHH on more instances than GPHH-FF (18 versus 7). Moreover, when using the new No-Early-Refill filter and FF simultaneously, GPHH-NF achieved much better results; significantly outperforming GPHH-NER on 10 instances, and GPHH-FF on 17 instances.

Note that EDASLS is the current state-of-the-art algorithm for UCARP. However, it made an impractical assumption that the actual demand of a task is known before it is served, which is not directly comparable to our problem, which assumes the demand of a task is unknown until it is served. For this reason, we do not compare against EDASLS.

Table 3. The win-draw-lose results of the pairwise comparisons over the 57 UCARP instances.

	GPHH [17]	GPHH-NER	GPHH-FF
GPHH-NER	18-39-0	—	—
GPHH-FF	7-49-1	6-36-15	—
GPHH-NF	24-29-4	10-44-3	17-37-3

4.2 Analysis on No-Early-Refill Filter

To further analyse the effectiveness of the newly proposed No-Early-Refill Filter, we first observe how it changes the size of the candidate task set during the decision making process. Against the standard filter, the No-Early-Refill filter is stronger as it removes tasks in addition to the standard filter. Therefore, the No-Early-Refill filter tends to obtain smaller candidate tasks during the decision making process. To verify this, we observed the decision making process of GPHH, GPHH-NER and GPHH-NF on *Ugdb23*. For each of GPHH, GPHH-NER and GPHH-NF, we arbitrarily selected one run, and applied the best rule to a randomly sampled instance. For each decision making process, the candidate set size is recorded for each time the routing policy is called.

Figure 3 shows the curves of the candidate set size of GPHH, GPHH-NER and GPHH-NF. We have examined other GP-evolved policies and other scenarios, and observed similar patterns. From the figure, it is obvious that the curve of GPHH is very smooth. This is because GPHH tends to generate early-refill routes that almost always have sufficient remaining capacity. Thus, all the unserved tasks are expected to be feasible at most decision points. The curves of GPHH-NER and GPHH-NF are below the curve of GPHH, demonstrating the effectiveness of the new filter in reducing the candidate set size. In addition, the valleys of the GPHH-NER and GPHH-NF curves show that there are usually a large fraction of candidate tasks being removed. GPHH therefore has a much higher chance of generating early-refill routes by not excluding such tasks. Finally, when averaging this across the final generation the curve of GPHH-NF is smoother than that of GPHH-NER. This demonstrates that using the No-Early-Refill filter and FF simultaneously can further improve the performance.

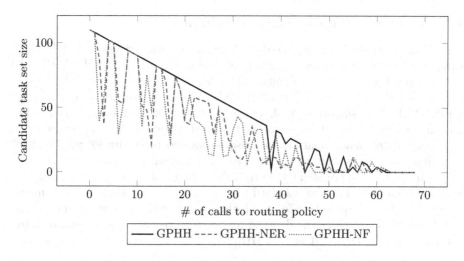

Fig. 3. Candidate task set size.

4.3 Analysis on the Flood Fill Terminal

To ensure FF is used to construct policies, basic high-level frequency analysis was used. This simply counted the frequency of each feature in the best policy of each generation. FF accounted for 7.19% of the terminals used in the *Ugdb* dataset and 6.77% on the *Uval* dataset. Whilst most other features were uniformly decreased to accompany FF, the rate of CFH use increased by 6.39% (relatively) over GPHH, suggesting the two terminals are most useful in tandem. It is worth noting that the average policy size does not significantly change between the two algorithms.

To determine whether or not FF was used as expected, individual analysis was performed. Presented below is an exemplary policy on the *Ugdb2* instance.

$$(+ \ (\max \ (* \ CFH \ SC) \ (+ \ FUT \ (+ \ (- \ CR \ CTD) \ (+ \ (* \ FUT \ (* \ FUT \ SC)) \ (+ \ FUT \ FF))))) \ (+ \ (+ \ CTT1 \ CTT1) \ (\max \ FF \ CFH)))$$

The above policy uses FF in two places. In both uses, a smaller FF will decrease the priority value, making the task more desirable. It is then not surprising that this policy has exceptional training and test performance in relation to its peers. This use trend is continued across most policies that perform well on both the training and test sets. There are policies that have an excellent training fitness yet use FF inverse to how we would expect. This tends to result in a disproportionately poor test fitness, showing that the GP process is not always able to appropriately utilise FF.

A way of improving the performance of policies using FF is to recalculate the flood fill map as frequently as new instance data is realised. For example, whenever the exact deadheading cost of an edge is determined. A balance between instance fidelity and computational efficiency must be struck, however.

4.4   Analysis on the Integrated Algorithm

Candidate set analysis was repeated to ensure the positive effects of GPHH-NER carried over. One may expect similar pool sizes in GPHH-NER and GPHH-NF, however per Fig. 3, they are significantly different. When averaging this graph across all decision processes, the GPHH-NF plot is significantly smoother than GPHH-NER. This smoothing makes logical sense when considering the effect FF has on the simulation, where smoother traversal of the graph is encouraged.

Terminal frequency analysis was also performed to ensure FF was used in a similar manner to that of GPHH-FF. This was mostly true, with GPHH-NF utilising the feature slightly more; 7.01%. Figure 4 shows the terminal use variance from GPHH on the standard terminal set (i.e. algorithm % value minus GPHH % value). A notable difference is the usage of CFH, showing the new filter in GPHH-NER decreases the demand for the feature - a concept reinforced by comparison of GPHH-NER and GPHH.

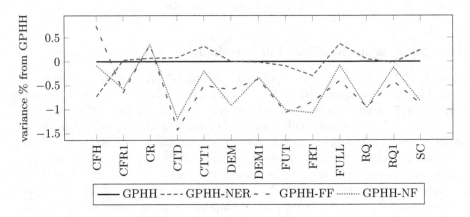

Fig. 4. Standard terminal use variation on GPHH

5   Conclusions and Future Work

Our motivations with this paper have been to ensure vehicle capacity is wholly utilised before replenishment and to encourage the prioritisation of hard to access tasks. This paper has presented two new techniques to meet these motivations and improve the performance of the GPHH method. Firstly, a filtering method that removes tasks from the possible selection pool if the fastest route to said task passes the depot was shown to significantly outperform the standard GPHH benchmark on 18 of the 57 tested instances. Secondly, the introduction of a new flood fill value to the possible terminal set improved on 7 of the tested instances. Additionally, when used together, these improvements further increased the performance over the benchmark of [14] on 24 of the tested instances. Note that improvement of this merged algorithm was not limited or restricted to the instances on which the two sub-algorithms performed well - together, the two parts became a distinct whole.

Analysis was done on the terminal use and pool-size in relation to the GPHH benchmark, highlighting some important anomalies between instance performance. This highlighted the need for further research into the effects algorithms have on particular instance characteristics. From this research, it is clear that very particular algorithms react, often erratically, to the specific nature of the instance in question. Discovering what exactly these critical topological features are, and deciding which algorithmic features to use in each given environment is certainly an interesting area for future research we believe worth exploring.

References

1. Amponsah, S., Salhi, S.: The investigation of a class of capacitated arc routing problems: the collection of garbage in developing countries. Waste Manag. **24**(7), 711–721 (2004)
2. Branke, J., Nguyen, S., Pickardt, C.W., Zhang, M.: Automated design of production scheduling heuristics: a review. IEEE Trans. Evol. Comput. **20**(1), 110–124 (2016)
3. Burke, E.K., Hyde, M., Kendall, G., Woodward, J.: A genetic programming hyper-heuristic approach for evolving 2-D strip packing heuristics. IEEE Trans. Evol. Comput. **14**(6), 942–958 (2010)
4. Christiansen, C., Lysgaard, J., Wøhlk, S.: A branch-and-price algorithm for the capacitated arc routing problem with stochastic demands. Oper. Res. Lett. **37**(6), 392–398 (2009)
5. Defryn, C., Sörensen, K., Cornelissens, T.: The selective vehicle routing problem in a collaborative environment. Eur. J. Oper. Res. **250**(2), 400–411 (2015)
6. Eglese, R.W., Li, L.Y.O.: A tabu search based heuristic for arc routing with a capacity constraint and time deadline. In: Osman, I.H., Kelly, J.P. (eds.) Meta-Heuristics: Theory and Applications, pp. 633–649. Springer, Boston (1996). https://doi.org/10.1007/978-1-4613-1361-8_38
7. Fleury, G., Lacomme, P., Prins, C., Ramdane-Chérif, W.: Improving robustness of solutions to arc routing problems. J. Oper. Res. Soc. **56**(5), 526–538 (2005)
8. Golden, B., Dearmon, J., Baker, E.: Computational experiments with algorithms for a class of routing problems. Comput. Oper. Res. **10**, 47–59 (1983)
9. Golden, B., Wong, R.: Capacitated arc routing problems. Networks **11**(3), 305–315 (1981)
10. Handa, H., Chapman, L., Yao, X.: Dynamic salting route optimisation using evolutionary computation. In: IEEE Congress on Evolutionary Computation, pp. 158–165 (2005)
11. Handa, H., Chapman, L., Yao, X.: Robust route optimization for gritting/salting trucks: a CERCIA experience. IEEE Comput. Intell. Mag. **1**(1), 6–9 (2006)
12. Hertz, A., Laporte, G., Mittaz, M.: A tabu search heuristic for the capacitated arc routing problem. Oper. Res. **48**, 129–135 (2000)
13. Lacomme, P., Prins, C., Ramdane-Cherif, W.: Competitive memetic algorithms for arc routing problems. Ann. Oper. Res. **131**(1), 159–185 (2004)
14. Liu, Y., Mei, Y., Zhang, M., Zhang, Z.: Automated heuristic design using genetic programming hyper-heuristic for uncertain capacitated arc routing problem. In: Proceedings of GECCO, pp. 290–297. ACM (2017)

15. Mei, Y., Tang, K., Yao, X.: Improved memetic algorithm for capacitated arc routing problem. In: IEEE Congress on Evolutionary Computation, pp. 1699–1706 (2009)
16. Mei, Y., Tang, K., Yao, X.: Capacitated arc routing problem in uncertain environments. In: IEEE Congress on Evolutionary Computation, pp. 1–8 (2010)
17. Mei, Y., Zhang, M.: Genetic programming hyper-heuristic for multi-vehicle uncertain capacitated arc routing problem. In: ACM Genetic and Evolutionary Computation Conference (GECCO) (2017)
18. Nguyen, S., Mei, Y., Zhang, M.: Genetic programming for production scheduling: a survey with a unified framework. Complex Intell. Syst. **3**(1), 41–66 (2017)
19. Speranza, M., Fernandez, E., Roca-Riu, M.: The shared customer collaboration vehicle routing problem. Eur. J. Oper. Res. **265**(3), 1078–1093 (2016)
20. Tsutsui, S., Wilson, G.: Solving capacitated vehicle routing problems using edge histogram based sampling algorithms. In: Proceedings of the 2004 Congress on Evolutionary Computation, vol. 1, pp. 1150–1157 (2004)
21. Ulusoy, G.: The fleet size and mix problem for capacitated arc routing. Eur. J. Oper. Res. **22**(3), 329–337 (1985)
22. Wang, J., Tang, K., Lozano, J.A., Yao, X.: Estimation of the distribution algorithm with a stochastic local search for uncertain capacitated arc routing problems. IEEE Trans. Evol. Comput. **20**(1), 96–109 (2016)
23. Wang, J., Tang, K., Yao, X.: A memetic algorithm for uncertain capacitated arc routing problems. In: 2013 IEEE Workshop on Memetic Computing, pp. 72–79 (2013)
24. Weise, T., Devert, A., Tang, K.: A developmental solution to (dynamic) capacitated arc routing problems using genetic programming. In: Proceedings of GECCO, pp. 831–838. ACM (2012)

Uncovering Performance Envelopes
Through Optimum Design of Tests

Tapabrata Ray, Ahsanul Habib, Hemant Kumar Singh$^{(\boxtimes)}$, and Michael Ryan

School of Engineering and Information Technology,
The University of New South Wales, Canberra, Australia
{t.ray,a.habib,h.singh,m.ryan}@adfa.edu.au

Abstract. Test and evaluation is a process that is used to determine if a product/system satisfies its performance specifications across its entire operating regime. The operating regime is typically defined using factors such as types of terrains/sea-states/altitudes, weather conditions, operating speeds, etc., and involves multiple performance metrics. With each test being expensive to conduct and with multiple factors and performance metrics under consideration, design of a test and evaluation schedule is far from trivial. Design of experiments (DOE) still continues to be the most prevalent approach to derive the test plans, although there is significant opportunity to improve this practice through optimization. In this paper, we introduce a surrogate-assisted optimization approach to uncover the performance envelope with a small number of tests. The approach relies on principles of decomposition to deal with multiple performance metrics and employs bi-directional search along each reference vector to identify the best and worst performance simultaneously. To limit the number of tests, the search is guided by multiple surrogate models. At every iteration the approach delivers a test plan involving at most K_T tests, and the information acquired is used to generate future test plans. In order to evaluate the performance of the proposed approach, a set of scalable test functions with various Pareto front characteristics and objective space bias are introduced. The performance of the approach is quantitatively assessed and compared with two popular DOE strategies, namely Latin Hypercube Sampling (LHS) and Full Factorial Design (FFD). Further, we also demonstrate its practical use on a simulated catapult system.

Keywords: Design of tests · Performance envelope
Multi-objective optimization

1 Background

The origin of most products can be traced back to a need/capability/requirement that advances through concepts, prototypes and ultimately to the product. Many of the technologies deployed in a product might be new or the product itself might be operating in a new environment. Both these aspects might adversely

© Springer Nature Switzerland AG 2018
T. Mitrovic et al. (Eds.): AI 2018, LNAI 11320, pp. 445–457, 2018.
https://doi.org/10.1007/978-3-030-03991-2_41

affect the intended performance of the product. Operational test and evaluation (OT&E) is typically carried out to ascertain that the product meets its performance metrics across its entire operational regime. Testing is an expensive process and operational tests should be conducted using enough samples across a wide range of plausible scenarios to derive statistically sound information for decisions [10]. Since the operational regime involves multiple factors and there is often a hard limit on the number of tests (budget and scheduling constraints), biased test plans are commonly used, i.e., the product is tested with a combination of factors that are more likely to occur than others. Such an approach however provides very little information on the performance when it is at its limits, i.e., less common environments which might lead to non-performance or even failures. Since the overall objective of any test and evaluation exercise is to identify, reduce and potentially eliminate risk, it is important to establish the boundaries of operation [13]. In the current context, we refer to the boundaries of the performance space as the *performance envelope*. The notion of strategically varying factors have been suggested in OT&E literature [10] but such methods still do not exploit state-of-the-art developments in the field of optimization.

From a user's perspective, one is interested in either of the two possible scenarios (a) what are the operating conditions where the performance of the product is the best and/or (b) what are the operating conditions where the performance is the worst. Theoretically, it would mean assessing the performance of the product at all possible combinations of factors, which is practically untenable. For example, 5^{10} tests would be needed to evaluate 10 factors with 5 levels each. Thus, it is important to address the following fundamental questions in any test design (a) how many tests to conduct, (b) what combinations of factors to test, (c) in which order should the tests be conducted, and finally (d) how to derive meaningful conclusions from such data. In addition to these, a few other practical considerations need to be acknowledged. The first relates to the error in performance measures which can be reduced through use of replicates and/or use of more precise instrumentation. In the case where historical data is used to augment the test plan, particular attention needs to be paid to the level of these errors as they may vary significantly across batches and over time. Secondly, tests need to be scheduled, e.g. a day/week ahead plan to conduct K_T tests. While conventional full factorial/partial factorial designs create the test plan in one shot, there is an opportunity to update the test plans based on observations, i.e., feedback. It is also important to take note that while an FFD creates uniform and structured sampling locations across the factor space, the resulting solutions in the performance space may have significant bias. For example, 125 points sampled using FFD in the factor space with 3 factors is presented in Fig. 1(a) along with its corresponding performance space defined using two metrics f_1 and f_2 in Fig. 1(b). Throughout this paper, performance is considered in a *minimization* sense, i.e., lower values of f_1 and f_2 are preferred. Its clear from Fig. 1(b) that even an FFD sampling will yield identification of operating conditions that are more preferable as opposed to those where the performance is at its worst. Such a scenario might be helpful in the event the user is interested to identify favorable operating conditions. However, if one is interested to uncover operating conditions that are unfavorable, i.e., stressed operations, the results will be of little use. This simple illustration clearly highlights the need for more efficient sampling strategies and particularly optimal strategies that learn through feedback with an intent to deliver best and worst operating conditions simultaneously with minimum number of tests. Figure 1(c) presents the crux of proposal of this paper - to search efficiently for the best and worst performance along a set of uniformly sampled search directions to uncover the performance envelope.

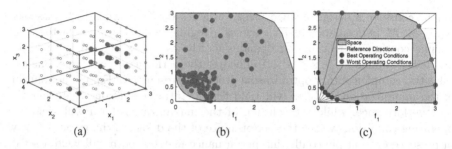

(a)   (b)   (c)

Fig. 1. (a) Sampling locations; (b) Performance at full factorial sampling locations; (c) Underlying principle of the approach

Optimization methods are regularly used to uncover designs with good performance metrics. Although there is vast amount of literature on application of optimization methods for design, there is very limited effort directed towards its use to develop optimal test plans. The underlying optimization method must however be able to deal with multiple performance metrics (two or more) and navigate potentially highly nonlinear performance landscapes. *Decomposition*-based algorithms [14] have attracted significant interest in recent times as their performance scales relatively well for problems more than 3 objectives (also referred to as *many*-objective problems). Decomposition based approaches typically operate by dividing the problem into a set of single-objective problems along a set of reference vectors and solve them collaboratively. However, since such algorithms evolve a population, they require evaluation of numerous solutions during the course of search. Thus if the number of evaluations (tests) are limited, e.g., in the current context the optimal test plan design or optimization involving computationally expensive evaluations, the algorithms cannot be used in their native form. In such cases, surrogates-assisted optimization is typically used, where computationally cheap approximation/meta-models are used to guide the underlying optimizer in lieu of expensive evaluations/tests [8]. Surrogate-assisted optimization strategies have been used to solve a number of practical, single and multi-objective optimization problems involving computationally expensive simulations [1]. Surrogate assisted *many*-objective optimization is currently in its infancy and its full potential is yet to be realized [2,3,11]. Such algorithms however share some common threads. Firstly, they all use a set of reference vectors generated via systematic sampling to guide the search. Secondly, all of them use surrogates to approximate the responses (performance metrics in the current case). Thirdly, they all use local search based on surrogates to improve candidate solutions before evaluation, and lastly they rely on surrogate model updates through feedback and evaluate solutions in batches. All the above developments align well with the challenges faced in design of optimal test plans, which forms the key motivation of this work.

2   Approach

Let us consider a design defined using variables $\mathbf{d}$ which needs to be assessed based on M performance metrics across a regime defined using n factors. We assume continuous rectangular domains for the factors $\mathbf{x}$ defined using upper and lower bounds $\mathbf{x}^L \leq \mathbf{x} \leq \mathbf{x}^U$. To uncover the performance envelope, one can solve two complementary optimization problems presented in Eq. 1. The solution of the minimization problem will yield the operating conditions that offer the best performance, while the solution of the maximization form will yield the operating conditions where the performance of the design is the worst. Clearly, in presence of multiple conflicting performance metrics, both will yield a set of trade-off solutions.

$$\text{Minimize } f_i(\mathbf{d}, \mathbf{x}); i = 1, 2, \ldots\ldots M$$
$$\text{Maximize } f_i(\mathbf{d}, \mathbf{x}); i = 1, 2, \ldots\ldots M \tag{1}$$

Here, $f_1(\mathbf{d}, \mathbf{x})$ to $f_M(\mathbf{d}, \mathbf{x})$ are the M performance metrics (considered to be minimized in a general sense). Such an approach would attempt to simultaneously locate the best and worst operating conditions as schematically presented in Fig. 1(c).

The general optimization framework is presented in Algorithm 1 and the details of the key components (highlighted in bold) are outlined below.

- **_Initialize_**: N_I candidate sampling locations (combinations of factors) are initialized using the variable bounds $\mathbf{x}^L$ and $\mathbf{x}^U$ using the space-filling Latin Hypercube Sampling (LHS) based on *maximin* criterion. This can be an unbiased coarse sampling and a mapping might be required if the factor space is non-continuous or non-rectangular.
- **_Build_**: This process involves building the surrogate models that can predict the performance metrics of the design at any given operating condition. Different types of surrogates are used for this purpose and include Radial Basis Function, Kriging and Response Surface Methodology of 1st and 2nd order. Training of the surrogate models use 80% data selected based on "k-medoid" clustering (scaled between 0 and 1 using the bounds $\mathbf{x}^L$ and $\mathbf{x}^U$) and the remaining data are used for validation. Mean squared error (MSE) based on the validation set is used to choose the most appropriate surrogate model for each performance metric.

Algorithm 1. Optimal Design of Tests

Input: T_{max} (Total number of tests permitted), N_I (Initial number of tests), N (Population size during evolution i.e. μ), K_T (Maximum number of tests in each batch), K (Maximum number of tests for best or worst operating conditions $K = K_T/2$).

1: $T = 0$, $j = 1$, Archive of sampling locations and performance metrics $\mathscr{A} = \emptyset$
2: **Generate** initial reference vector set W using Systematic Sampling [4]
3: $P^I = $ **Initialize**(), $|P^I| = N_I$; One can use a coarse DOE for this purpose
4: Conduct tests at sampling sites P^I, Update T, $\mathscr{A}$
5: **Build** global surrogate models for each of the performance metrics $f_1, \ldots, f_M$
6: $W_m = $ **UpdateRef**(W,$\mathscr{A}$)
7: $PB^j = $ **Assign**(W_m,P^I); Select set of best performing operating conditions.
8: $PW^j = $ **Assign**(W_m,P^I); Select set of worst performing operating conditions.
9: **while** ($T \leq T_{max}$) **do**
10:    $CB = $ **CreateOffspring**(PB^j), $|CB| = N$
11:    $CW = $ **CreateOffspring**(PW^j), $|CW| = N$
12:    **Approximate** performance of the design at the set of sampling sites CB and CW
13:    $CB_K = $ **Identify**(PB^j,CB,$\mathscr{A}$), $|CB_K| \leq K$
14:    $CW_K = $ **Identify**(PW^j,CW,$\mathscr{A}$), $|CW_K| \leq K$
15:    Conduct tests at sampling sites CB_K and CW_K, Update T, $\mathscr{A}$
16:    **Build** global surrogate models for each of the performance metrics $f_1, \ldots, f_M$
17:    **Approximate** performance of the design at the set of sampling sites $(CB \cup CW) \setminus (CB_K \cup CW_K)$
18:    $W_m = $ **UpdateRef**(W,$PB^j \cup CB_K \cup CB \setminus CB_K$)
19:    $PB^{j+1} = $ **Assign**(W_m,$PB^j \cup CB_K \cup CB \setminus CB_K$)
20:    $PW^{j+1} = $ **Assign**(W_m,$PW^j \cup CW_K \cup CW \setminus CW_K$)
21:    $j = j + 1$
22: **end while**

- **_UpdateRef_**: In this stage, the ith reference direction W^i is modified to W_m^i based on the ideal vector (Z^I) and nadir vector (Z^N) using Eq. 2. The *ideal* vector Z^I comprises the minimum values of f_1 to f_M and Z^N comprises the maximum values among the non-dominated set of solutions of the presented set.

$$(W_m^i)_j = (W^i)_j \times (Z^N - Z^I)_j, \forall \ 1 \leq j \leq M \qquad (2)$$

- **_Assign_**: In this stage, the candidate sampling locations are assigned to the reference directions. The performance metrics of the design at a sampling location **x** are represented using a vector **f** of size M. The vector is translated using $f_j - Z_j^I \forall j = 1, \ldots M$. The acute angle between this translated vector and all reference vectors W_m^i are computed and the sampling location is assigned to the reference vector with the minimum angle. This process creates *sub-populations* of candidate sampling sites corresponding to a reference direction. A reference direction is considered to be non-empty if there is at least a sampling site assigned to it. For the non-empty reference directions, one can identify the best and the worst operating conditions using the scaled

Euclidean Distance (ED) in the performance space as a measure. For the empty reference directions, the best and worst selection is based on performance measures at all sampling locations. The above process will result in two sets of sampling sites, PB and PW, denoting the best and worst performing operating conditions respectively along each reference direction.

- **CreateOffspring**: Recombination is carried out among the members of PB via simulated binary crossover (SBX)[5] and polynomial mutation (PM) [5] or differential evolution (DE) [12]to yield a set of offspring sampling sites. Similarly, the same recombination process is also applied within the members of PW to yield yet another set of offspring sampling sites. It is important to highlight that all the members of PB (or PW) participate in recombination with mating partners selected at random. Furthermore, DE and SBX operation is selected with equal probability.

- **Identify**: This step of the algorithm is aimed at identifying at most K candidate sampling sites each for best and worst operating conditions. The sampling sites PB and PW identified at the end of the **Assign** stage are each clustered into K clusters via k-medoid clustering. In each of the clusters, the sampling site with the best metric, i.e., minimum ED for PB and maximum ED for PW is identified along with its assigned reference direction. Thereafter, a surrogate assisted local search is initiated from each of these sampling sites with an aim to minimize ED (for PB) or maximize ED (for PW) subject to an angle constraint. The angle constraint ensures that the angle between any sampling site explored during local search and the reference direction associated with it is always less than the minimum angle between that reference direction and its neighboring reference directions; to ensure diversity. Out of these K solutions obtained after local search from each of PB and PW, the ones that are not already members of the archive ($\mathscr{A}$) are used as new test sites for evaluation.

3   Scalable Test Problems for Benchmarking

In order to mathematically illustrate the effect of bias due to non-linearity of the objective functions, we systematically construct a set of test problems, referred to here as SOT problems. The SOT problems are constructed through the modification of scalable DTLZ2 problem [6] which is widely used in literature for benchmarking of multi/many-objective evolutionary algorithms. The mathematical formulation of a M-objective DTLZ2 problem is shown in Eq. 3. The variables used here in Eq. 3 represent the operating conditions in the current context. The design variables **d** are held constant and therefore not shown in Eq. 3 for brevity.

Minimize $f_1(\mathbf{x}) = r(\mathbf{x}_M) \cos(\pi x_1/2) \cdots \cos(\pi x_{M-2}/2) \cos(\pi x_{M-1}/2)$,

$\qquad f_2(\mathbf{x}) = r(\mathbf{x}_M) \cos(\pi x_1/2) \cdots \cos \pi (x_{M-2}/2) \sin(\pi x_{M-1}/2)$,

$\qquad f_3(\mathbf{x}) = r(\mathbf{x}_M) \cos(\pi x_1/2) \cdots \sin(\pi x_{M-2}/2)$,

$$\vdots$$

$\qquad f_{M-1}(\mathbf{x}) = r(\mathbf{x}_M) \cos(\pi x_1/2) \sin(\pi x_2/2)$,

$\qquad f_M(\mathbf{x}) = r(\mathbf{x}_M) \sin(\pi x_1/2)$,

where $\qquad r(\mathbf{x}_M) = 1 + g(\mathbf{x}_M) = 1 + \sum_{x_i \in \mathbf{x}_M} (x_i - 0.5)^2$,

$\qquad 0 \le x_i \le 1$, for $i = 1, 2, \ldots, n$.

$$(3)$$

The total number of variables involved in the problem is $n = M + k - 1$. The set of last k variables (i.e. $x_M, x_{M+1}, \ldots x_n$) is collectively referred to as *distance variables*. They are denoted using $\mathbf{x}_M$ and as evident from Eq. 3, they control the radial distance $r(\mathbf{x}_M)$ of a solution from the origin in the objective space. The Pareto optimal solutions of the problem correspond to $\mathbf{x}_M^* = 0.5$, since the term $r(\mathbf{x}_M)$ achieves its lowest value of 1 when $g(\mathbf{x}_M) = 0$. In the objective space, the Pareto front corresponds to a ball of radius 1 in the positive orthant, i.e., $\sum_{i=1}^{M} f_i^2 = 1, f_i \ge 0$ for $i = 1, 2, \ldots, M$. The Pareto Front is non-convex in nature. The maximum possible value of $r(\mathbf{x}_M)$ can also be similarly deduced; as it would occur when $g(\mathbf{x}_M)$ is at its maximum value. This value will correspond to $g(\mathbf{x}_M) = k \times 0.5^2$, since given the range of the variables ($[0, 1]$), each term in $g(\mathbf{x}_M)$ can be a max of 0.5. Thus, the worst case performance will be bounded by a ball of radius $r(\mathbf{x}_M) = 1 + k \times 0.5^2$. For example, for $k = 2$, the radius will be 1.5, and thus the best and worst performances are bounded by $r = 1$ and 1.5 respectively.

The proposed SOT problem is constructed by introducing a bias in the above DTLZ2 formulation. This is achieved through a mapping of the original distance variables $\mathbf{x}_M$ to intermediate distance variables $\mathbf{x}_M'$ as follows: $x_i' = ((x_i - 0.5)^a/0.5^a + 1)/2 \quad \forall x_i \in \mathbf{x}_M$. Thereafter, $\mathbf{x}_M$ is replaced by $\mathbf{x}_M'$ in Eq. 3 to yield the SOT problem. This mapping function simply translates a large portion of the original variables towards 0.5, i.e., close to the Pareto front (best performance). Consequently, when the variables (in this case the parameters of the scenarios) are sampled uniformly in the original search space using structured techniques such as LHS or Full Factorial Design (FFD), the distribution of the points become non-uniform in the mapped space $\mathbf{x}_M'$, and subsequently in the objective (performance) space itself. Furthermore, the exponent a (an odd positive integer) can be used to control the severity of bias. With $a = 1$, the problem is identical to the original DTLZ2, whereas it gets increasingly more biased as the value of a increases. The mapping for different values of a is shown in Fig. 2.

The impact of introducing the bias discussed above can be visualized from Fig. 3. The left column of subfigures show 1000 solutions generated using LHS in the variable space, with increasing values of a. For $a = 1$, SOT problem behaves exactly like original DTLZ2 problem, with the designs reasonably uniformly spread within the performance envelope. However, a clear increase in density towards the best case performance can be observed as the value of a increases. This implies that for $a > 1$, if the envelope of design performance is estimated

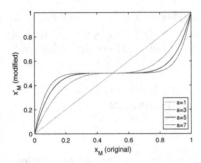

Fig. 2. Mapping of $\mathbf{x}_M$ to $\mathbf{x}'_M$ to introduce different levels of bias

using LHS, much of the region near the worst case performance would remain unexplored. The consequences of this can be potentially catastrophic as the worst-case performance of the design is not apparent from the initial sampling (of possible scenarios), even though a large number of scenarios were evaluated. On the right column of subfigures, the same is illustrated for scenarios sampled using FFD with 10 levels (1000 points for a 3-variable problem). A very similar behavior is apparent, i.e., increasing number of points fall closer to the best case performance as a is increased. However, additional to this *radial* bias, one can also observe the *lateral* bias. As the value of a increases, the coverage of the best and worst case performance boundaries become less diverse; and the objective values become concentrated only along certain directions.

As evident, the above described SOT problem has a *non-convex* Pareto front. In order to also investigate the performance for problems with *convex* Pareto fronts, we introduce another problem, referred to as the SOT^{-1} problem. In SOT^{-1} problem, all the response functions and mappings remain exactly the same as SOT problem, but instead of minimizing the objective $f(\mathbf{x})$ of SOT, the minimization of $-f(\mathbf{x})$ is undertaken. This simple negation inverts the shape of the performance envelope, where both best case and worst case fronts become convex in nature. Also, instead of the bias of performance values along the best-case performance, it is now directed towards the worst case performance. The corresponding plots for $a = 3$ are shown in Fig. 4. The general concept of generating a 'minus' problem through negation of objectives is inspired from a recent work by Ishibuchi et al. [7].

4   Numerical Experiments

In order to objectively assess the performance of the proposed approach we use 6 test problems: SOT2, SOT3, SOT5 and their minus counterparts SOT2^{-1}, SOT3^{-1} and SOT5^{-1} involving 2, 3 and 5 performance metrics respectively (suffix denotes the number of objectives in this case). We use $k = 2$ for all versions, implying that the number of operating parameters is $M+1 = 3, 4$, and 6 respectively. For creating the bias in objective values, we use $a = 3$ for all cases.

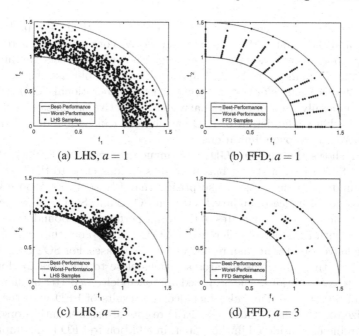

Fig. 3. LHS and FFD samplings for SOT problem (non-convex) with $a = 1, 3$.

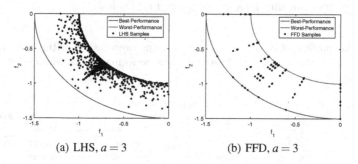

Fig. 4. LHS and FFD samplings for SOT^{-1} problem (convex) with $a = 3$.

The population size was set equal to the number of reference vectors, i.e., 100, 105 and 210 for 2, 3 and 5 objective problems. It was evolved over 100 generations in all cases where at any generation at most $K_T = 10$ solutions can be evaluated. For recombination, the probability of SBX crossover was set to 1 and the probability of polynomial mutation was set to 0.1. The distribution index of SBX crossover was set to 30 while the distribution index of polynomial mutation was set to 20. For DE based recombination a differential weight of 0.5 and a crossover probability of 1.0 was used. The average number of evaluations across 31 runs was computed for each of the problems and listed in Table 1. We used LHS to generate 100, 105 and 210 initial sampling locations for 2, 3 and 5 objective problems respectively. The performance of the approach was assessed against two reference sets, i.e., on the theoretical best performance boundary and the worst performance boundary. We construct two reference sets for this purpose using systematic sampling. The reference sets contain 3000, 5050 and 20475 points for the 2, 3 and 5 objective problems. The proximity to these reference sets is quantified using inverted generational distance (IGD), which is commonly used in evolutionary multi-objective optimization literature for benchmarking. The details of IGD calculations can be found in [1] and are omitted here due to page limitations.

Table 1 shows the median IGD performance comparison. Problems SOT2, SOT3 and SOT5 have a strong bias towards solutions close to the best performance boundary. Hence it is not surprising that LHS delivers good estimates of the best performance boundary (better in SOT2 and SOT3). However, LHS struggles to deliver good estimates of the worst performance boundary (worse in all of them with an order of difference in SOT2). Take note that our proposed approach delivers better median results in 4 out of 6 cases. For SOT2^{-1}, SOT3^{-1} and SOT5^{-1}, there is a bias towards solutions close to the worst performance boundary (easy to obtain). The proposed approach delivers better median results in 6 out of 6 cases. We have also included the results of FFD with the closest sample size (on the higher side). The FFD results are significantly worse off for the test problems considered in this paper, in addition to FFD being impractical for higher number of factors due to exponential increase in sample size. The overall numbers of evaluations are compared in Table 2.

Table 1. Comparison of IGD metric obtained using proposed algorithm with LHS and FFD sampling methods. For both best and worst performance boundaries, lower values of IGD is preferable.

Probs.	Objs.	Proximity to the best performance boundary								
		SOT				LHS				FFD
		Best	Worst	Mean	Median	Best	Worst	Mean	Median	
SOT2	2	0.0145	0.0267	0.0189	0.0184	0.0116	0.0204	0.0150	**0.0147**	0.1302
SOT3	3	0.0790	0.1155	0.0932	0.0906	0.0718	0.1051	0.0845	**0.0827**	0.2131
SOT5	5	0.1967	0.2863	0.2387	**0.2390**	0.2563	0.3057	0.2864	0.2870	0.3313
SOT2^{-1}	2	0.1092	0.2432	0.1887	**0.1859**	0.1631	0.2156	0.1857	0.1864	0.1204
SOT3^{-1}	3	0.1272	0.3011	0.2270	**0.2312**	0.2852	0.3289	0.3045	0.3043	0.2623
SOT5^{-1}	5	0.3660	0.5166	0.4634	**0.4712**	0.4945	0.5513	0.5234	0.5237	0.4938
		Proximity to the worst performance boundary								
SOT2	2	0.0272	0.0793	0.0517	**0.0514**	0.2014	0.2838	0.2530	0.2568	0.1954
SOT3	3	0.1112	0.2489	0.1469	**0.1413**	0.3053	0.3507	0.3285	0.3282	0.3050
SOT5	5	0.2946	0.4190	0.3626	**0.3602**	0.4970	0.5469	0.5299	0.5332	0.4938
SOT2^{-1}	2	0.0037	0.0065	0.0045	**0.0043**	0.0048	0.0069	0.0058	0.0058	0.0803
SOT3^{-1}	3	0.0568	0.0771	0.0658	**0.0658**	0.0592	0.0768	0.0677	0.0672	0.1829
SOT5^{-1}	5	0.2130	0.2981	0.2601	**0.2697**	0.2420	0.2995	0.2780	0.2768	0.3313

Table 2. Average number of function evaluations in 31 independent runs for the SOT algorithm, and corresponding number of samples for LHS and FFD

Probs.	Avg. evals	LHS samples	FFD samples	Probs.	Avg. evals	LHS samples	FFD samples
SOT2	196.6	197	216	SOT2^{-1}	805.1	806	1000
SOT3	381.5	382	625	SOT3^{-1}	628.8	629	1296
SOT5	599.4	600	729	SOT5^{-1}	656.2	657	729

5   Illustrative Example: Catapult Operation

Having shown consistently favorable performance of the proposed approach on mathematical benchmarks, we now illustrate its practical use using a catapult example [9]. Let us assume a catapult is available as a weapon to launch projectiles on an even land towards an enemy territory (Figure 5(a)). The catapult can use various projectiles of mass varying between 1 and 20 kg and projectiles can be launched with different settings of arm lengths between 2.5 and 3.4 m. From a combat perspective, projectiles with larger ranges and with shorter time of flight are preferred. The user involved in test and evaluation is interested to uncover the performance envelope with minimum number of tests. Since there are 2 factors (mass and arm length), we first construct a 100×100 FFD sampling plan and present the true performance envelope in Fig. 5. One can observe that the vast majority of the sampled solutions do not correspond to either best or worst operating conditions.

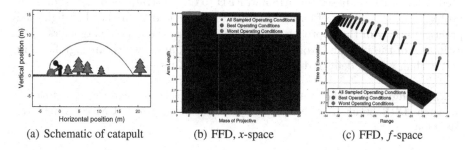

(a) Schematic of catapult   (b) FFD, x-space   (c) FFD, f-space

Fig. 5. FFD sampling locations corresponding performance (10,000 solutions)

Now let's say the user has limited resources for testing and is allowed to only test at 64 sampling locations. The outcome from an FFD is presented in Fig. 6. It is clear that the user will have a good estimate of best performance but extremely poor estimates of worst performance. The same problem is solved using the proposed approach with 20 reference directions (all remaining parameters are the same as used for the previous experiments) with only 49 tests, including 9 LHS samples used for initialization. The results presented in Fig. 6(c) clearly indicate that the proposed approach delivers a more complete performance envelope compared to FFD.

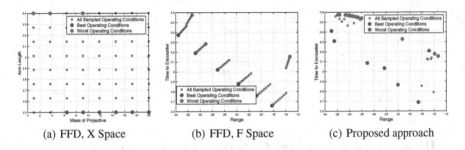

(a) FFD, X Space   (b) FFD, F Space   (c) Proposed approach

Fig. 6. Performance of FFD (64 solutions) and proposed approach (49 solutions)

6 Summary and Conclusions

In this paper, we introduced a surrogate-assisted optimization approach to uncover the performance envelope, i.e., best and worst performance boundaries simultaneously using minimum number of tests. The approach relies on principles of decomposition to deal with multiple performance metrics and employs bi-directional search along each reference vector to identify best and worst operating conditions simultaneously. At every iteration, the approach delivers a test plan involving at most K_T tests, the information of which is used to recursively update future test plans. In order to evaluate the performance of the proposed approach, we introduced scalable test functions with various bias characteristics. The performance of the proposed approach is compared with commonly used DOE practices based on LHS and FFD to demonstrate its benefits for such problems. A case-study of catapult system is presented to further highlight the practical utility of the approach. With only 49 tests, the approach delivers good estimates of the best and worst performance boundaries, which are significantly better than results delivered by FFD even with 64 tests.

Acknowledgments. The authors would like to acknowledge Defence Related Research (DRR) grant from the University of New South Wales (UNSW), Canberra, Australia.

References

1. Bhattacharjee, K.S., Singh, H.K., Ray, T.: Multi-objective optimization with multiple spatially distributed surrogates. J. Mech. Des. **138**(9), 091401 (2016)
2. Bhattacharjee, K.S., Singh, H.K., Ray, T.: Multiple surrogate-assisted many-objective optimization for computationally expensive engineering design. J. Mech. Des. **140**(5), 051403 (2018)
3. Chugh, T., Jin, Y., Meittinen, K., Hakanen, J., Sindhya, K.: A surrogate-assisted reference vector guided evolutionary algorithm for computationally expensive many-objective optimization. IEEE Trans. Evol. Comput. **22**(1), 129–142 (2018)
4. Das, I., Dennis, J.E.: Normal-boundary intersection: a new method for generating the Pareto surface in nonlinear multicriteria optimization problems. SIAM J. Optim. **8**(3), 631–657 (1998)

5. Deb, K., Pratap, A., Agarwal, S., Meyarivan, T.: A fast and elitist multiobjective genetic algorithm: NSGA-II. IEEE Trans. Evol. Comput. **6**(2), 182–197 (2002)
6. Deb, K., Thiele, L., Laumanns, M., Zitzler, E.: Scalable test problems for evolutionary multiobjective optimization. In: Proceedings of the International Conference on Evolutionary Multiobjective Optimization, pp. 105–145 (2005)
7. Ishibuchi, H., Yu, S., Hiroyuki, M., Yusuke, N.: Performance of decomposition-based many-objective algorithms strongly depends on Pareto front shapes. IEEE Trans. Evol. Comput. **21**(2), 169–190 (2017)
8. Jin, Y.: A comprehensive survey of fitness approximation in evolutionary computation. Soft Comput. - Fusion Found. Methodol. Appl. **9**(1), 3–12 (2005)
9. Kelly, M.: Simple catapult simulation. https://au.mathworks.com/matlabcentral/fileexchange/56469-simple-catapult-simulation?focused=6163843&tab=function
10. Lillard, V.B.: Science of test: improving the efficiency and effectiveness of DoD test and evaluation (2014). http://fs.fish.govt.nz/Page.aspx?pk=7&sc=SUR
11. Pan, L., He, C., Tian, Y., Wang, H., Zhang, X., Jin, Y.: A classification based surrogate-assisted evolutionary algorithm for expensive many-objective optimization. IEEE Trans. Evol. Comput. (2018). https://ieeexplore.ieee.org/document/8281523
12. Storn, R., Price, K.: Differential evolution - a simple and efficient heuristic for global optimization over continuous spaces. J. Glob. Optim. **11**(4), 341–359 (1997). https://doi.org/10.1023/A:1008202821328
13. Stuber, M.D.: Evaluation of process systems operating envelopes. Ph.D. thesis, Massachusetts Institute of Technology (2013)
14. Trivedi, A., Srinivasan, D., Sanyal, K., Ghosh, A.: A survey of multi-objective evolutionary algorithms based on decomposition. IEEE Trans. Evol. Comput. **21**(3), 440–462 (2017)

Towards Fully Automated Semantic Web Service Composition Based on Estimation of Distribution Algorithm

Chen Wang[1(✉)], Hui Ma[1], Gang Chen[1], and Sven Hartmann[2]

[1] School of Engineering and Computer Science, Victoria University of Wellington,
Wellington, New Zealand
{chen.wang,hui.ma,aaron.chen}@ecs.vuw.ac.nz
[2] Department of Informatics, Clausthal University of Technology,
Clausthal-Zellerfeld, Germany
sven.hartmann@tu-clausthal.de

Abstract. Web service composition has been a challenging research area, where many researchers have been working on a composition problem that optimizes Quality of service and/or Quality of semantic matchmaking of composite solutions. This NP-hard problem has been successfully handled by many Evolutionary Computation techniques with promising results. Estimation of Distribution has shown its initial promise in solving fully automated service composition, and its success strongly relies on distribution models and sampling techniques. Our recently published work proposed a Node Histogram-Based approach to fully automated service composition. However, many services presented in sampled optimized queues does not contribute to decoded solutions of the queue. Therefore, efforts should be made to focus on learning distributions of component services in solutions. Consequently, we aim to learn more suitable distributions considering services satisfying service dependency in the solutions and use the Edge Histogram Matrix to learn restricted sampled outcomes satisfying the dependency. Besides that, we proposed effective sampling techniques with high efficiency in a straightforward implementation. Our experimental evaluation using benchmark datasets shows our proposed EDA-based approach outperforms two recent approaches regarding both efficiency and effectiveness.

Keywords: Web service composition · QoS optimization
Combinatorial optimization

1 Introduction

Web services are reusable components of web applications, and can be published, discovered, and invoked on the Web, providing services to users or other software [1]. *Web service composition* aims to loosely couple web services to provide more complicated functionalities since one atomic web service does not always satisfy users' complex requirement completely. *Fully automated service composition*

© Springer Nature Switzerland AG 2018
T. Mitrovic et al. (Eds.): AI 2018, LNAI 11320, pp. 458–471, 2018.
https://doi.org/10.1007/978-3-030-03991-2_42

constructs a composition of services without strictly obeying any specific service workflow [7]. As the number of web service with similar functionalities has significantly increased, web service composition challenges many researchers to find composition solutions with the best overall *Quality of Service* (QoS) within polynomial-time. Apart from optimizing QoS, *Quality of Semantic Matchmaking* (QoSM) is often optimized simultaneously that creates more challenges for researchers [14].

Many Evolutionary Computation (EC) techniques have been widely used to achieve QoS-aware web service composition in a fully automated way [4,5,8,10,14–17]. Often, conventional EC techniques [4,8,15,17] rely on domain-dependent genetic operators to generate new candidate solutions. Estimation of Distribution Algorithm (EDA) is different from most conventional EC-based techniques because a probabilistic model is learned based on the distribution of superior subpopulation, and further used for sampling new candidate solutions. EDA has been widely used in many problem domains, such as portfolio management and cancer chemotherapy optimization, achieving better results compared to conventional EC-based techniques [2], and it has been used for solving semi-automated service composition, where service composition workflow is given in advance. Learning distribution over a pre-defined structure of a workflow is relatively less challenging. To support learning distributions over uncertain structures of candidate composite solutions in fully automated web service composition, our recently published work [16] proposed a Node Histogram-Based work for fully automated service composition with the aim to find composition solutions with optimized QoS and QoSM. The algorithm has been demonstrated to achieve higher effectiveness and efficiency than one PSO-based approach [14].

Despite the initial success in EDA for solving fully automated service composition problems. A more suitable distribution model over superior subpopulation needs further studies. Therefore, opportunities still exist to further investigate the potential use of other distribution models for supporting fully automated service composition and propose effective sampling algorithms to support sampling composition solutions from these distribution models.

The overall goal of this paper is to *propose an effective EDA-based approach to fully automated semantic web service composition*, where QoS and QoSM are jointly optimized. We achieve three objectives in this work.

1. To learn more suitable distributions that can naturally capture the most essential ingredients for building effective service composition solutions, we consider dependencies of components services in composite solutions and using Edge Histogram Matrix (EHM) to learn a distribution of restricted sampled outcomes satisfying the service dependencies. To achieve that, we will develop an ontology-based querying technique for efficiently querying the dependencies and a way of using EHM to learn those dependencies for service compositions.
2. To easily achieve high efficiency in a straightforward implementation, and to effectively sample candidate composition solutions of high quality and validity

from EHM directly, we will propose a guided edge histogram-based backward graph sampling algorithm.

3. To demonstrate the effectiveness of our overall EDA-based approach, we conduct experiments to compare it against two recent works [14,16] that solve the same problem in semantic web service composition.

2   The Semantic Web Service Composition Problem

We consider a *semantic web service* (*service*, for short) as a tuple $S = (I_S, O_S, QoS_S)$ where I_S is a set of service inputs that are consumed by S, O_S is a set of service outputs that are produced by S, and $QoS_S = \{t_S, c_S, r_S, a_S\}$ is a set of non-functional attributes of S. The inputs in I_S and outputs in O_S are parameters modeled through concepts in a domain-specific ontology $\mathcal{O}$. The attributes t_S, c_S, r_S, a_S refer to the response time, cost, reliability, and availability of service S, respectively, which are four commonly used QoS attributes [18].

A *service repository* $\mathcal{SR}$ is a finite collection of services supported by a common ontology $\mathcal{O}$. A *service request* (or *composition task*) over a given $\mathcal{SR}$ is a tuple $T = (I_T, O_T)$ where I_T is a set of task inputs, and O_T is a set of task outputs. The inputs in I_T and outputs in O_T are parameters that are semantically described by concepts in the ontology $\mathcal{O}$. We use two special services $Start = (\emptyset, I_T, \emptyset)$ and $End = (O_T, \emptyset, \emptyset)$ to account for the input and output requirements of a given composition task T, and add them to $\mathcal{SR}$.

A *composite service* (or *composition solution*) is represented as a directed acyclic graph (DAG). Its nodes correspond to those services in $\mathcal{SR}$ (also called *component services*) that are used in the composition, including $Start$ and End.

In this paper, we are concerned with the *Semantic Web Service Composition Problem* where we aim to jointly optimize QoS and QoSM. In previous work [14–16] we have proposed and explored a comprehensive quality model for evaluating these quality aspects. The comprehensive quality of a composition solution can be evaluated based on a weighted sum of all quality criteria in QoS and QoSM using the fitness function in Eq. (1):

$$Fitness = w_1 \hat{MT} + w_2 \hat{SIM} + w_3 \hat{A} + w_4 \hat{R} + w_5 (1 - \hat{T}) + w_6 (1 - \hat{C}) \quad (1)$$

with $\sum_{k=1}^{6} w_k = 1$. This objective function aggregates the quality criteria of semantic matching type $\hat{MT}$, semantic similarity $\hat{SIM}$, availability $\hat{A}$, reliability $\hat{R}$, time $\hat{T}$, and cost $\hat{C}$. $\hat{T}$ and $\hat{C}$ are offset by 1, so that higher scores correspond to better quality. We refer to [14–16] for details on the calculation of each quality criterion. Therefore, the goal of our semantic web service composition is to maximize the objective function in Eq. (1) to find the best solution.

3   Our EDA-Based Approach for Service Composition

In this section, we introduce our EDA-based approach for fully automatic semantic web service composition. We first outline our EDA-based service composition approach in Sect. 3.1. Subsequently, we discuss three ideas behind this approach: the first one is a proposed ontology-based querying technique for querying service dependency in Sect. 3.2; the second one is an application of EHM for learning service dependency in Sect. 3.3; the third one is a proposed sampling technique for building composite solutions in Sect. 3.4.

As the success of EDA strongly relies on its distribution model, especially when the number of outcomes (i.e., component services) sampled from a distribution is huge, we aim to learn a suitable distribution model. Our recent work [16] learns the distribution of each service in $\mathcal{SR}$ at each absolute position of a service queue. However, many services presented in sampled optimized queues does not contribute to decoded solutions of the queue. Therefore, efforts should be made on learning distributions of the component services that contribute to composite solutions. Therefore, we aim to learn distributions restricted by the dependencies among component services in DAG-based solutions, and this distribution can be easily presented in EHM. To achieve that, we proposed an ontology-based querying technique for querying dependencies of services in $\mathcal{SR}$. This technique provides a set of outcomes, whose distributions are to be learned in EHM, and we will demonstrate an application of EHM by mapping DAG-based solutions and dependencies.

Furthermore, to easily achieve high efficiency in a straightforward implementation, and to sample component services satisfying services dependencies that contribute to composition solutions with high quality and validity, we proposed a Guided Edge Histogram-Based Backward Graph-Sampling Algorithm. This algorithm builds a DAG-based composition from *End* to *Start* using guided information of services dependencies, and service layers, see details in Sect. 3.4.

Algorithm 1. Our EDA-based method for service composition.

Input   : composition task T, service repository $\mathcal{SR}$ and $g \leftarrow 0$
Output: an optimal composition solution $\mathcal{G}^{opt}$
1: discovery task-related web services and layers $\mathcal{L}_p$ (where $p = 0, \ldots, q$) ;
2: label $\mathcal{O}$ with task-related web services using Algorithm 2;
3: initialize $\mathcal{P}^g$ with m valid DAG-based solutions, each solution represented as a $\mathcal{G}_k^g$ (where $k = 1, \ldots, m$);
4: evaluate each solution in $\mathcal{P}^g$ using Eq. 1;
5: generate $\mathcal{EHM}^g$ from the top $\frac{1}{2}$ of best solutions in $\mathcal{P}^0$;
6: **while** $g <$ *maximum number of generations* **do**
7:    sample m solutions $\mathcal{G}_k^{g+1}$ sampled from $\mathcal{EHM}^g$ using Algorithm 3;
8:    populate $\mathcal{P}^{g+1}$ with newly sampled solutions ;
9:    evaluate each solution in $\mathcal{P}^{g+1}$ using Eq. 1;
10:    generate $\mathcal{EHM}^{g+1}$ from the top $\frac{1}{2}$ of the best solutions in $\mathcal{P}^{g+1}$;
11:    set $g \leftarrow g + 1$;
12: let $\mathcal{G}^{opt}$ be the best solution in $\mathcal{P}^g$;

3.1   Outline of Our EDA-Based Method

We outline our proposed algorithm in Algorithm 1. We start with filtering task-relevant services with respect to any specific composition task, utilizing a simple discovery algorithm from [11] to identify all relevant services and their layers $\mathcal{L}_p$ from $Start$ (where $p = 0, \ldots, q$ and q is the number of layers). Basically, the first layer contains services that can be immediately executed by using I_T, and the second layer contains the remaining services that can be executed by using I_T and outputs provided by services in the previous layers. Other layers can be discovered in the similar way, see details in [11]. After that, we label $\mathcal{O}$ with task-related web services using Algorithm 2, which enables us to identify non-zero entries in EHM for setting bias, see details in Sect. 3.3. Next, we initialize a population $\mathcal{P}^0$ with m DAG-based candidate solutions by a greedy search algorithm over randomly sorted $\mathcal{SR}$ [14] for building graphs. Those candidate solutions are evaluated using Eq. 1. Then, the top half best-performing solutions are used to generate a $\mathcal{EHM}^g$ (where $g = 0$), see details in Sect. 3.3. The following steps (Step. 5 to Step. 9) will be repeated until the maximum number of generations is reached: we sample m new valid candidate solutions from $\mathcal{EHM}^g$ using our proposed Guided Edge Histogram-Based Graph-sampling Algorithm. These newly sampled candidate solutions form the next population $\mathcal{P}^{g+1}$ and will be evaluated and selected to learn $\mathcal{EHM}^{g+1}$.

In summary, we propose a way of learning EHM from high-quality solutions discovered by EDA so far and a novel sampling technique for building valid solutions from EHM.

3.2 Discovery of Service Dependency

Service dependency represents a relationship between two services (i.e., one service S_j and its predecessor S_i) that are determined by the existence of robust causal links [14] between these two services. In other words, one service can be either partially or fully satisfied by its predecessor, denoted as $S_i \rightarrow S_j$.

To identify service dependencies regarding each service, we proposed an ontology-based querying technique to efficiently find their predecessor services in $\mathcal{SR}$. We first create labels for concept nodes of a taxonomy tree in $\mathcal{O}$ with task-related services using Algorithm 2. In this Algorithm, we mark each tree node with two sets of services, i.e., O_C and I_C, where robust causal links can be ensured from services in O_C and services in I_C. We can query the predecessors of one service S by a union of O_C from concept nodes with respect to input-related concepts of S. We will demonstrate this technique in Example 1.

Example 1. Suppose we have a service repository $\mathcal{SR}$ consisting of a single service $S_0 = (\{c, d\}, \{e\}, QoS_{S_0})$. Let us consider the *service request* $T = (\{a, b\}, \{i\})$. The two special services $Start = (\emptyset, \{a, b\}, \emptyset)$ and $End = (\{i\}, \emptyset, \emptyset)$ are defined by the given composition task T. Concepts related to a, b, c, d, e, and i are Dog, Artificial Data, Data, Canine, Animal Robot and Robot respectively. These concepts are represented and labeled with services in an taxonomy tree in Fig. 1. The predecessor of End is S_0, which is a service in O_{Robot} of concept $Robot$ related to i. The predecessor of S_0 is $Start$, which is a service in an union of O_{Data} and O_{Canine} related to c and d respectively.

Algorithm 2. Labeling services on taxonomy tree in $\mathcal{O}$

Input : $\mathcal{SR}$ and $\mathcal{O}$
Output: a labeled $\mathcal{O}$
1: **foreach** *concept C in taxonomy tree in $\mathcal{O}$* **do**
2:    label two empty service set I_C and O_C in relation to inputs and output;
3: **foreach** *S in $\mathcal{SR}$* **do**
4:    **foreach** *I_S of S* **do**
5:      find concepts C of I_S on taxonomy tree in $\mathcal{O}$;
6:      **foreach** *C in $C \cup$ its child concepts* **do**
7:        put S to I_C of C;
8:    **foreach** *O_S of S* **do**
9:      find concepts C of O_S on taxonomy tree in $\mathcal{O}$;
10:      **foreach** *C in $C \cup$ its parent concepts* **do**
11:        put S to O_C of C;
12: **return** labeled $\mathcal{O}$;

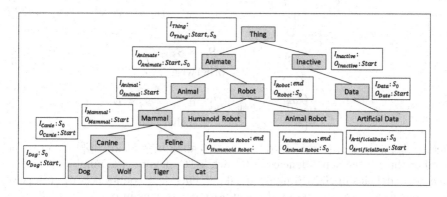

Fig. 1. An example of labeled $\mathcal{O}$

3.3 Application of Edge Histogram Matrix

Let $\mathcal{D} = \{S_i \rightarrow S_j\}$ be the set of all existing service dependencies among all possible pairs of services in $\mathcal{SR}$. Let $\mathcal{G}$ be a DAG-based composition solution consisting of a set of service dependencies, satisfying $\mathcal{G} \subset \mathcal{D}$. Consequently, $\mathcal{G}_k^g$ represents the kth ($0 \leq k < m$) DAG-based composite solution, and $\mathcal{P}^g = [\mathcal{G}_0^g, \ldots, \mathcal{G}_k^g, \ldots, \mathcal{G}_{m-1}^g]$ is represented as a population of solutions of generation g.

Example 2. Suppose we have a service repository $\mathcal{SR}$ consisting of five services $S_0 = (\{c, d\}, \{e\}, QoS_{S_0})$, $S_1 = (\{a\}, \{f, g\}, QoS_{S_1})$, $S_2 = (\{a, b\}, \{h\}, QoS_{S_2})$, $S_3 = (\{f, h\}, \{i\}, QoS_{S_3})$ and $S_4 = (\{a\}, \{f, g, h\}, QoS_{S_4})$. Let us consider the *service request* $T = (\{a, b\}, \{i\})$ as in Example 1.

The initial population $\mathcal{P}^0$ may consist of m composition solutions for T, given by their DAG-representations, such as follows (note that $m = 6$ in this example):

$$\mathcal{P}^0 = \begin{bmatrix} \mathcal{G}_0^0 \\ \mathcal{G}_1^0 \\ \mathcal{G}_2^0 \\ \mathcal{G}_3^0 \\ \mathcal{G}_4^0 \\ \mathcal{G}_5^0 \end{bmatrix} = \begin{bmatrix} \{Start \rightarrow S_1, Start \rightarrow S_2, S_1 \rightarrow S_3, S_2 \rightarrow S_3, S_3 \rightarrow End\} \\ \{Start \rightarrow S_0, S_0 \rightarrow End\} \\ \{Start \rightarrow S_0, S_0 \rightarrow End\} \\ \{Start \rightarrow S_4, S_4 \rightarrow S_3, S_3 \rightarrow End\} \\ \{Start \rightarrow S_4, S_4 \rightarrow 3, S_3 \rightarrow End\} \\ \{Start \rightarrow S_1, Start \rightarrow 2, S_1 \rightarrow S_3, S_2 \rightarrow S_3, S_3 \rightarrow End\} \end{bmatrix}$$

The *edge histogram matrix at generation* g (denoted by $\mathcal{EHM}^g$) is a matrix with entries $e_{i,j}^g$ (where $i, j = Start, 0, 1, \cdots, m - 1, End$) as follows:

$$e_{i,j}^g = \begin{cases} \sum_{k=0}^{m-1} \delta_{i,j}(\mathcal{G}_k^g) + \varepsilon_{i,j} & \text{if } i \neq j \\ 0 & \text{otherwise} \end{cases} \qquad (2)$$

$$\delta_{i,j}(\mathcal{G}_k^g) = \begin{cases} 1 & \text{if } S_i \rightarrow S_j \in \mathcal{G}_k^g \\ 0 & \text{otherwise} \end{cases} \qquad (3)$$

$$\varepsilon_{i,j} = \begin{cases} \frac{b_{ratio}}{|\mathcal{D}|} \sum_{k=0}^{m-1} |\mathcal{G}_k^g| & \text{if } S_i \rightarrow S_j \in \mathcal{D} \\ 0 & \text{otherwise} \end{cases} \qquad (4)$$

Herein, b_{ratio} is a predetermined constant (called bias ratio), $|\mathcal{G}_k^g|$ denotes the number the service dependencies in $\mathcal{G}_k^g$, while $|\mathcal{D}|$ denotes the number of all service dependencies in $\mathcal{SR}$. Roughly speaking, entry $e_{i,j}^g$ counts how often service dependency $S_i \rightarrow S_j$ occurs in all composition solutions in population $\mathcal{P}^g$.

3.4 A Guided Edge Histogram-Based Backward Graph-Sampling Algorithm

The sampling algorithm is proposed based on an Edge Histogram-Based Sampling Algorithm [13]. By providing the distribution information of predecessors of each service in EHM, it is then possible to build up a composition graph from the dependencies. Some useful information is used to guide the sampling to produce only restricted outcomes, which makes this algorithm more effective: only row indexes of non-zero entries in $\mathcal{EHM}^g$ are to be sampled, and layer information is used to verify sampled predecessors for preventing cycles in solutions. This algorithm builds a DAG in a backward way. It has been suggested in [11] that backward graph building has its advantage over the forward graph building since it does not create dangling services. This sampling algorithm is summarized in Algorithm 3.

In Algorithm 3, we first initialize a DAG-based solution $\mathcal{G}$ with an empty set of service dependencies, and a set of service $SerSet$, whose inputs satisfactions required to be checked, with End. The following steps are repeated if $SerSet$ does not only contains $Start$ or any service in $SerSet$ are not fully satisfied (Step.

Algorithm 3. Guided Edge Histogram-Based Backward Graph-Sampling Algorithm

---

Input : $\mathcal{EHM}^g$
Output: a composition solution $\mathcal{G}$
1: initial $\mathcal{G} = \{\ \}$ and $SerSet = \{End\}$;
2: **foreach** S_j *in SerSet* **do**
3:　　**if** *SerSet does not only contains start and S_j is not fully satisfied* **then**
4:　　　　identify $\mathcal{L}_p$ *s.t.* $S_j \in \mathcal{L}_p$;
5:　　　　determine a set SC of row indexes for non-zero entries in $\{e^g_{\cdot,j}\}$;
6:　　　　**while** *inputs of S_j is not fully satisfied and SC is not empty* **do**
7:　　　　　　sample one predecessor x with probability $\dfrac{e^g_{x,j}}{\sum_{i \in SC} e^g_{i,j}}$;
8:　　　　　　identify $\mathcal{L}_{p'}$ *s.t.* $S_x \in \mathcal{L}_{p'}$;
9:　　　　　　**if** $p' \le p$ *and any unsatisfied input of S_j is fulfilled by S_x* **then**
10:　　　　　　　　put $S_x \rightarrow S_j$ into $\mathcal{G}$;
11:　　　　　　　　**foreach** $S_{j\star}$ *in SerSet* **do**
12:　　　　　　　　　　identify $\mathcal{L}_{p\star}$ *s.t.* $S_{j\star} \in \mathcal{L}_{p\star}$;
13:　　　　　　　　　　**if** $p' \le p^\star$ *and any unsatisfied input of $S_{j\star}$ is fulfilled by S_x* **then**
14:　　　　　　　　　　　　put $S_x \rightarrow S_{j\star}$ into $\mathcal{G}$;
15:　　　　　　add S_x to $SerSet$;
16:　　　　　　remove x from SC;
17:　　　　remove S_j from $SerSet$;
18: **return** $\mathcal{G}$;

---

2 to Step. 17): for each service S_j in $SerSet$, we identify its layer $\mathcal{L}_p$. Meanwhile, we initialize a set, SC, consisting of row indexes of non-zero entries in $\{e^g_{\cdot,j}\}$. Afterward, another repeated sampling process is used to produce predecessors of S_j until S_j is fully satisfied (Step. 6 to Step. 16). During the sampling, let S_x be the corresponding service of sampled service index x, if the layer that contains S_x is ahead of or the same to that of S_j, and any unsatisfied inputs of S_j can be fulfilled by S_x (Step. 9), we create a dependency $S_x \rightarrow S_j$ and put it into $\mathcal{G}$ (Step. 10). Meanwhile, to create a more compacted DAG, we also check the satisfaction of other services in $SerSet$ in the similar way that we create the dependency with S_j (Step. 11 to Step. 14). Later on, the sampled predecessor S_x is added to $SerSet$ and sampled x is removed from SC. Once S_j is fully satisfied, we remove it from $SerSet$, and repeat creating dependencies for newly added services in $SerSet$ until the stop conditions are met (Step. 2 to Step. 17). Then, a $\mathcal{G}$ is returned.

4　Experimental Evaluation

We experimentally evaluate the performance of our proposed EDA-based approach (named as EHM-EDA). In particular, we compared it to two recent works [14,16] (named NHM-EDA and PSO respectively) that were conducted to solve the same problem. Two Web Service composition Challenge (WSC) benchmarks, i.e., WSC-08 and WSC-09 extended with QoS attributes are utilized for the experiment. These two benchmarks are widely used in recent service composition research, e.g. in [4,8,10,14–17].

The same number of evaluation times are ensured to conduct a fair comparison. In particular, we set the population size as 200, the number of generations as 300, and b_{ratio} as 0.0002. We run 30 independent repetitions for all the competing approaches. We set the weights in the fitness function Eq. (1) to balance the QoSM and QoS, following the existing work [14–16], i.e., w_1 and w_2 are set to 0.25, and w_3, w_4, w_5 and w_6 to 0.125. We set the parameter p for the plugin match 0.75 as recommended in [3]. Additional experiments are also conducted with other weights and parameters, where the same behavior is usually observed.

4.1   Comparison of the Fitness

We utilize an independent-sample T-test to test the significant difference in mean fitness and mean execution time over 30 repetitions of the three methods. In particular, a significant level 5% is established for all pairwise comparisons over the composition tasks in WSC-08 and WSC-09. We highlight the top performance with its related fitness value and standard deviation in Table 1, while the pairwise comparisons of fitness are summarized in Table 2. In pairwise comparisons, *win/draw/loss* shows frequencies one method outperforms, equals or is outperformed by another method.

Table 1. Mean fitness values for our approach in comparison to NHM-EDA [16] and PSO [14] (Note: the higher the fitness the better)

Task	EHM-EDA	NHM-EDA [16]	PSO [14]
WSC-08-1	0.5326 ± 0	0.504916 ± 0.010355	0.522621 ± 0.00283
WSC-08-2	0.614333 ± 0	0.614333 ± 0	0.614333 ± 0
WSC-08-3	0.456083 ± 0.000194	0.455118 ± 6.8e−05	0.454343 ± 0.000531
WSC-08-4	0.463066 ± 0.001054	0.464498 ± 0.000117	0.464511 ± 0.000133
WSC-08-5	0.474222 ± 0.000414	0.469205 ± 0.000245	0.468536 ± 0.001148
WSC-08-6	0.472665 ± 0.000382	0.474322 ± 9.9e−05	0.472942 ± 0.000736
WSC-08-7	0.488584 ± 0.000527	0.480765 ± 0	0.479235 ± 0.000502
WSC-08-8	0.462254 ± 0.00017	0.46182 ± 0	0.461478 ± 0.000371
WSC-09-1	0.604377 ± 0.00429	0.569929 ± 0.005625	0.568493 ± 0.009659
WSC-09-2	0.471123 ± 0.000234	0.471164 ± 1.2e−05	0.4711 ± 0.000283
WSC-09-3	0.551159 ± 0	0.551159 ± 0	0.551159 ± 0
WSC-09-4	0.471059 ± 0.000404	0.472804 ± 0.000227	0.471512 ± 0.000904
WSC-09-5	0.47269 ± 0.000104	0.470408 ± 0	0.470132 ± 0.000304

Tables 1 and 2 show that the two EDA-based methods outperform the PSO-based method [14]. This observation agrees with the findings in our previous work [16] that learning the distributions of the superior subpopulation can help to find

Table 2. Summary of the statistical significance tests for fitness, where each column shows the win/draw/loss score of one method against a competing one for all tasks of WSC-08 and WSC-09.

Dataset	Method	EHM-EDA	NHM-EDA [16]	PSO [14]
WSC-08 (8 tasks)	EHM-EDA	-	2/1/5	2/1/5
	NHM-EDA [16]	5/1/2	-	1/2/5
	PSO [14]	5/1/2	5/2/1	-
WSC-09 (5 tasks)	EHM-EDA	-	1/2/2	0/2/3
	NHM-EDA [16]	2/2/1	-	0/2/3
	PSO [14]	3/2/0	3/2/0	-

higher-quality composition solutions. For the two EDA-based methods, EHM-EDA appears to be more effective. This corresponds well with our expectations that taking the services dependencies into account can enhance the competency of EDA for improving the quality of composition solutions.

It has been discussed in the examples of composition solutions analyzed in [14,15], a small improvement of fitness that measures QoS and QoSM can make a significant difference in the practical use of the computed composition service.

4.2 Comparison of the Execution Time

Tables 3 and 4 show the mean execution time with standard deviation over 30 repetitions and the frequencies of pairwise comparisons respectively.

Table 3 shows that two EDA-based approaches require less execution time consistently over PSO [14]. For the two EDA-based approaches, our EDA-based approach requires significantly and consistently less execution time than the competing EDA-based approach [16]. These correspond well with our assumptions: on the one hand, although useful services are more likely to be put in front of sampled service queue for the decoding algorithm in NHM-EDA [16], improvements on the efficiency may not be outstanding; on the other hand, our proposed sampling technique achieves outstanding efficiency with a straightforward implementation.

4.3 Comparison of the Convergence Rate

To investigate the effectiveness of our EDA-based approach, we use WSC-08-05 and WSC-08-08 as examples for demonstrating the convergence rate of fitness over 30 independent runs. Note that WSC-08-08 is a more challenging task than WSC08-05 as it involves more service dependencies and results in larger composite services.

Figures 2a and b show the mean fitness of the best solutions found by EHM-EDA, NHM-EDA [16] and PSO [14] over 300 generations for the two composition tasks. In Fig. 2a, for the less challenging composition task (WSC08-5), we

Table 3. Mean execution time in seconds for our approach in comparison to NHM-EDA [16] and PSO[14] (Note: the lower the execution time the better)

Task	EHM-EDA	NHM-EDA [16]	PSO [14]
WSC-08-1	20 ± 1	152 ± 7	200 ± 130
WSC-08-2	13 ± 1	89 ± 12	130 ± 79
WSC-08-3	104 ± 4	1753 ± 87	4786 ± 1471
WSC-08-4	29 ± 1	86 ± 4	353 ± 109
WSC-08-5	50 ± 2	833 ± 141	4241 ± 1712
WSC-08-6	231 ± 7	18436 ± 1043	48215 ± 13973
WSC-08-7	96 ± 2	1351 ± 205	5482 ± 3277
WSC-08-8	204 ± 5	1267 ± 87	5890 ± 1534
WSC-09-1	18 ± 2	136 ± 11	284 ± 196
WSC-09-2	135 ± 11	2306 ± 283	6419 ± 1786
WSC-09-3	126 ± 4	782 ± 46	2273 ± 1007
WSC-09-4	733 ± 29	71932 ± 4370	105568 ± 31797
WSC-09-5	535 ± 20	6692 ± 565	19266 ± 5840

Table 4. Summary of the statistical significance tests for execution time, where each column shows the win/draw/loss score of one method against a competing one for all tasks of WSC-08 and WSC-09.

Dataset	Method	EHM-EDA	NHM-EDA [16]	PSO [14]
WSC-08 (8 tasks)	EHM-EDA	-	0/0/8	0/0/8
	NHM-EDA [16]	8/0/0	-	0/0/8
	PSO [14]	8/0/0	8/0/0	-
WSC-09 (5 tasks)	EHM-EDA	-	0/0/5	0/0/5
	NHM-EDA [16]	5/0/0	-	0/0/5
	PSO [14]	5/0/0	5/0/0	-

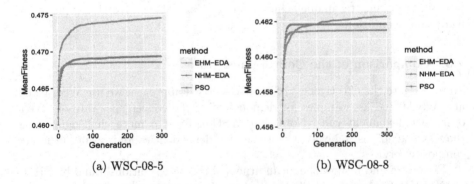

(a) WSC-08-5   (b) WSC-08-8

Fig. 2. Mean fitness values of best solutions over generations

observe that our EDA-based converges much faster against the two competing methods while the two competing methods reach a plateau in their early stages. In Fig. 2b, for the more challenging composition task (WSC-08-08), the two competing methods happen to converge fast in the early stage, but our EDA-based method eventually outperforms them. It can be inferred from those observations that EHM-EDA is less prone to premature convergence to local optima, but it may suffer from low convergence rate in more complex datasets, such as WSC08-8.

5   Related Work

AI planning and EC techniques have been acquired in web service composition to compute solutions automatically. AI planning is a commonly used technique to handle dynamic scenarios with agents in constructing composition plans, but combinatorial optimization is not a focus [12]. EC techniques have been widely used for optimizing QoS and/or QoSM in fully automated service composition [4,5,8–10,14–17]. These EC-based works can be categorized into two groups: conventional EC-based and model learning-based approaches.

Conventional EC techniques have been used to breed candidate solutions for an optimization purpose. Genetic Programming (GP) employs genetic operators directly on tree-based solutions, and it allows the evolution of composition structure as well as services for exploration and exploitation. [8] proposed a context-free grammar for initializing tree-based candidate solutions, while [17] randomly initialized tree-based candidate solutions without ensuring structures of composite solutions, but they proposed a general adaptive rule of crossover and mutation for improving quality of computed composite solutions. These two works present a low convergence rate since their population always consists of invalid candidate solutions that are required to be penalized by the fitness functions. To increase the convergence rate, a random greedy search algorithm was utilized in [4,10] to construct DAG-based valid candidate composite solutions for each population, and two different tree conversion algorithms were proposed to allow a straightforward application of GP. However, their tree-based representation allows replicas of subtrees that potentially build up huge trees. To eliminate these replicas, a tree-like representation was proposed in [15]. Other conventional EC techniques, like swarm intelligence, such as Particle Swarm Optimization was utilized to optimize the order of a queue of services, and each service is corresponding to the position of a particle, a decoding algorithm [14] are developed to decode the queue into DAG-based solutions.

Despite some successes in conventional EC techniques, some efforts have been made to investigate model learning-based algorithms, such as EDA. Two works [5,6] proposed EDA-based approaches to semi-automated services composition, but their distributions models can hardly support fully automated service composition. One recent work [16] proposed a novel representation that allows a Node Histogram Matrix to learn the distributions from composite solutions structured in different composition workflows. However, opportunities still exist to propose more effective approaches by proposing more suitable distributions, and sampling techniques from that distribution also remain to be developed.

6   Conclusion

In this paper, we proposed an effective EDA-based approach, which learns suitable distributions by considering service dependencies, and efficiently samples high-quality solutions. The advantages of this approach have been experimentally illustrated by comparing it with NHM-EDA [16] and PSO [14]. In the future, we will study its scalability for more challenging datasets as scalability is a common difficulty faced by most algorithms, and develop local search strategies to enhance its searching ability.

References

1. Curbera, F., Nagy, W., Weerawarana, S.: Web services: why and how. In: Workshop on Object-Oriented Web Services-OOPSLA (2001)
2. Hauschild, M., Pelikan, M.: An introduction and survey of estimation of distribution algorithms. Swarm Evol. Comput. 1(3), 111–128 (2011)
3. Lécué, F.: Optimizing QoS-aware semantic web service composition. In: Bernstein, A., et al. (eds.) ISWC 2009. LNCS, vol. 5823, pp. 375–391. Springer, Heidelberg (2009). https://doi.org/10.1007/978-3-642-04930-9_24
4. Ma, H., Wang, A., Zhang, M.: A hybrid approach using genetic programming and greedy search for QoS-aware web service composition. In: Hameurlain, A., Küng, J., Wagner, R., Decker, H., Lhotska, L., Link, S. (eds.) Transactions on Large-Scale Data- and Knowledge-Centered Systems XVIII. LNCS, vol. 8980, pp. 180–205. Springer, Heidelberg (2015). https://doi.org/10.1007/978-3-662-46485-4_7
5. Peng, S., Wang, H., Yu, Q.: Estimation of distribution with restricted Boltzmann machine for adaptive service composition. In: IEEE ICWS, pp. 114–121 (2017)
6. Pichanaharee, K., Senivongse, T.: QoS-based service provision schemes and plan durability in service composition. In: Meier, R., Terzis, S. (eds.) DAIS 2008. LNCS, vol. 5053, pp. 58–71. Springer, Heidelberg (2008). https://doi.org/10.1007/978-3-540-68642-2_5
7. Rao, J., Su, X.: A survey of automated web service composition methods. In: Cardoso, J., Sheth, A. (eds.) SWSWPC 2004. LNCS, vol. 3387, pp. 43–54. Springer, Heidelberg (2005). https://doi.org/10.1007/978-3-540-30581-1_5
8. Rodriguez-Mier, P., Mucientes, M., Lama, M., Couto, M.I.: Composition of web services through genetic programming. Evol. Intell. 3(3–4), 171–186 (2010)
9. Sadeghiram, S., Ma, H., Chen, G.: Cluster-guided genetic algorithm for distributed data-intensive web service composition. 2018 IEEE Congress on Evolutionary Computation (CEC) (2018)
10. da Silva, A.S., Ma, H., Zhang, M.: Genetic programming for QoS-aware web service composition and selection. Soft Comput. 20, 1–17 (2016)
11. da Silva, A.S., Mei, Y., Ma, H., Zhang, M.: Evolutionary computation for automatic web service composition: an indirect representation approach. J. Heuristics 24, 1–32 (2017)

12. Tong, H., Cao, J., Zhang, S., Li, M.: A distributed algorithm for web service composition based on service agent model. IEEE Trans. Parallel Distrib. Syst. **22**(12), 2008–2021 (2011)
13. Tsutsui, S., Pelikan, M., Goldberg, D.E.: Node histogram vs. edge histogram: a comparison of PMBGAs in permutation domains. MEDAL Report (2006009) (2006)
14. Wang, C., Ma, H., Chen, A., Hartmann, S.: Comprehensive quality-aware automated semantic web service composition. In: Peng, W., Alahakoon, D., Li, X. (eds.) AI 2017. LNCS (LNAI), vol. 10400, pp. 195–207. Springer, Cham (2017). https://doi.org/10.1007/978-3-319-63004-5_16
15. Wang, C., Ma, H., Chen, A., Hartmann, S.: GP-based approach to comprehensive quality-aware automated semantic web service composition. In: Shi, Y., et al. (eds.) SEAL 2017. LNCS, vol. 10593, pp. 170–183. Springer, Cham (2017). https://doi.org/10.1007/978-3-319-68759-9_15
16. Wang, C., Ma, H., Chen, G., Hartmann, S.: Knowledge-driven automated web service composition—an EDA-based approach. In: International Conference on Web Information Systems Engineering. Springer (2018)
17. Yu, Y., Ma, H., Zhang, M.: An adaptive genetic programming approach to QoS-aware web services composition. In: IEEE CEC, pp. 1740–1747 (2013)
18. Zeng, L., Benatallah, B., Dumas, M., Kalagnanam, J., Sheng, Q.Z.: Quality driven web services composition. In: Proceedings of the 12th International Conference on World Wide Web, pp. 411–421. ACM (2003)

Genetic Programming with Multi-tree Representation for Dynamic Flexible Job Shop Scheduling

Fangfang Zhang$^{(\boxtimes)}$, Yi Mei, and Mengjie Zhang

School of Engineering and Computer Science, Victoria University of Wellington,
PO BOX 600, Wellington 6140, New Zealand
{fangfang.zhang,yi.mei,mengjie.zhang}@ecs.vuw.ac.nz

Abstract. Flexible job shop scheduling (FJSS) can be regarded as an optimization problem in production scheduling that captures practical and challenging issues in real-world scheduling tasks such as order picking in manufacturing and cloud computing. Given a set of machines and jobs, FJSS aims to determine which machine to process a particular job (by routing rule) and which job will be chosen to process next by a particular machine (by sequencing rule). In addition, dynamic changes are unavoidable in the real-world applications. These features lead to difficulties in real-time scheduling. Genetic programming (GP) is well-known for the flexibility of its representation and tree-based GP is widely and typically used to evolve priority functions for different decisions. However, a key issue for the tree-based representation is how it can capture both the routing and sequencing rules simultaneously. To address this issue, we proposed to use multi-tree GP (MTGP) to evolve both routing and sequencing rules together. In order to enhance the performance of MTGP algorithm, a novel tree swapping crossover operator is proposed and embedded into MTGP. The results suggest that the multi-tree representation can achieve much better performance with smaller rules and less training time than cooperative co-evolution for GP in solving dynamic FJSS problems. Furthermore, the proposed tree swapping crossover operator can greatly improve the performance of MTGP.

Keywords: Multi-tree representation · Flexible job shop scheduling
Dynamic changes · Genetic programming

1 Introduction

The rapid development of globalization and information technologies has made our world a Global Village, where the interest of countries is interconnected. The core of the connection highly relies on international trade. Thus, it brings more opportunities and also thrives competition among companies. The study of allocating the jobs to machines and determining the order of processing the allocated jobs on each machine to optimize criteria such as flowtime, tardiness

© Springer Nature Switzerland AG 2018
T. Mitrovic et al. (Eds.): AI 2018, LNAI 11320, pp. 472–484, 2018.
https://doi.org/10.1007/978-3-030-03991-2_43

or customer satisfaction will benefit the companies by increasing their efficiency, profit or reputation.

Flexible job shop scheduling (FJSS) is an extension to classical job shop scheduling (JSS). The FJSS task, as its name suggests, assumes a more flexible situation. It reflects a production environment where it is possible to run an operation on more than one machine. This special trait causes the problem to become more complicated than classical JSS because we not only have to decide where to allocate jobs, but also need to decide which job to be processed next simultaneously. FJSS is NP-hard [2].

In addition, dynamic changes are inevitable in the real-world applications. For example, it is obvious that job orders are unpredicted or cannot be accurately predicted for companies, especially taking uncertain factors such as price impact, asymmetric information, rush hours and indefinite events into consideration. That is to say, we could not know job information until the job arrives. Dynamic flexible job shop scheduling (DFJSS) was born for considering this situation.

All these characteristics make DFJSS much more challenging than standard JSS and FJSS. Thus, the exact optimization methods such as mathematical programming [15] are often inapplicable, especially to large scale instances. Under this circumstance, heuristic search methods such as tabu search [14], genetic algorithm [16], simulated annealing [18] become more and more popular. These methods can get better performance in achieving reasonable solutions in less time. However, the biggest drawback is their lack of capability to adapt to the dynamic environmental change.

In order to reduce computational complexity and cope with dynamic changes, dispatching rules (DRs) have been widely applied [6,10,13]. When a machine becomes idle and has waiting operations in its queue, DRs will be triggered to select the operation with highest priority to be processed next. In this way, computation is carried out only at each decision point and decisions can be made efficiently.

However, lots of DRs are designed manually [17] and manual design has its inherent weaknesses. For instance, it highly relies on domain knowledge and it is very demanding on labour and time. Fortunately, genetic programming (GP) has been proven to be an effective hyper-heuristic method, which can automatically design DRs for scheduling [1,9,10,12] that are much better than the manually designed ones. However, the existing works mainly focus on evolving the *sequencing rule* (the rule to select which waiting operation will be processed next when a machine becomes idle) without considering the *routing rule* (the rule to select which machine will be chosen to allocate the ready operations).

For DFJSS, a crucial issue is how it can evolve both routing and sequencing rules simultaneously. The representation is the crux of the applicable algorithm. There are two main reasons. Firstly, an appropriate representation is definitely a rudimentary factor for an algorithm to build a solution. Secondly, the representation determines the size of the search space and there is a clear trade-off between the complexity of the representation and the ability of GP to explore the search space. These two facts foster the motivation to propose a more suitable representation for DFJSS. To the best of our knowledge, cooperative co-evolution (CC) was firstly embedded into GP to evolve routing and sequencing rules together [19]. The proposed CCGP in [19] is the current state-of-the-art algorithm of DFJSS. However, the CC approach cannot fully capture the interaction between the routing and sequencing rules. Research in this area is still in a very early stage and little work has been reported on this important aspect. Dealing with multiple interdependent decisions, especially in dynamic environment, is always difficult but also creates opportunities to find the real global optimal solution. This is particularly challenging when multiple decisions need to be made at the same time.

In this paper, GP with multi-tree representation is introduced to evolve routing and sequencing rules together and a novel tree swapping crossover operator is proposed to evolve more effective rules. We aim to find more effective routing and sequencing rules for DFJSS based on GP with a multi-tree representation. In particular, we have the following research objectives.

- Introduce GP with multi-tree representation (MTGP) for evolving the routing and sequencing rules simultaneously.
- Propose a novel tree swapping crossover operator for the MTGP algorithm according to the feature of the DFJSS problem. The MTGP with the newly proposed tree swapping crossover is denoted as sMTGP.
- Compare the performance of MTGP, sMTGP and CCGP to verify the effectiveness of the multi-tree representation and the novel tree swapping crossover operator.
- Analyse the rules evolved by MTGP, sMTGP and CCGP.

2   Background

2.1   Dynamic Flexible Job Shop Scheduling

In the basic version of the job shop scheduling problem, n jobs need to be processed by m machines. Each job consists of a sequence of operations and a machine can process at most one operation at a time. For each operation, it can be processed at a specified machine. In essence, the JSS problem is based on the assumption that only one machine is able to run a particular operation.

FJSS breaks through the constraints of resources uniqueness: each operation can be processed by more than one machine and its processing time depends on the machine that processes it. Thus, FJSS can improve the production efficiency, shorten the ordering cycle and increase the rate of orders delivered on time.

In real life, industry is in a dynamic environment, for instance, in terms of a factory, the orders will arrive over time. Actually, there are some methods to predict the information of incoming jobs to reduce uncertainty, thus to improve the accuracy of decisions. However, the gap between prediction and reality is always inevitable and sometimes they have a very wide difference. It is indicated that when dealing with the real-world applications, dynamic changes should be taken into consideration.

2.2   Rules for Dynamic Flexible Job Shop Scheduling

This paper aims to evolve two kinds of rules for DFJSS, which are routing and sequencing rules, to make decisions at decision points. A routing rule is triggered when a new job arrives or when an operation is completed and its next operation becomes ready to be processed to allocate ready operation to a particular machine. When a machine is free and there are operations waiting, an operation in its queue will be chosen by a sequencing rule to be processed next.

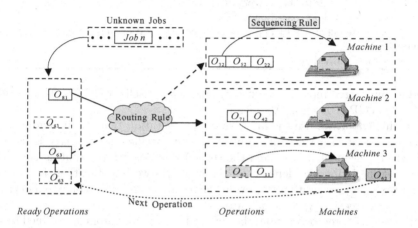

Fig. 1. An example of decision process of DFJSS.

Figure 1 shows an example of decision process of DFJSS. In the figure, the solid lines stand for what is happening and the dotted lines indicate what will happen. There are three machines in the job shop and each job can be processed by any machine. Each job consists of several operations in a certain order. In the current system state, the operations (O_{32}, O_{52}, O_{22}, O_{71}, O_{42}, O_{62} and O_{11}) have been allocated to different machines by the routing rule. Then, each machine uses the sequencing rule to decide the next operation to be processed, e.g. *machine* 3 selects O_{62}. When O_{62} processing is completed, its subsequent operation O_{63} becomes ready, and will be allocated by the routing rule.

3   Genetic Programming with Multi-tree Representation

The choice of which representation to use when dealing with a problem using GP is vital. Tree-based GP is a popular way in previous research and multi-tree representation [7] as a special structure has been applied to classifier design [3,11] and feature manipulation [8].

In multi-tree representation, each individual is represented as a list trees. Taking advantage of this feature to solve the DFJSS problems, routing and sequencing rules can be denoted by different trees in one individual. According

---

Algorithm 1. Pseudo-code of MTGP

// Initialization
1 **while** N_{ind} < Popsize **do**
2   **foreach** individual
3   **Initialize each tree** //Randomly initialize each tree by ramp half-and-half
4 **end**
// Evolution
5 **while** *Stopping criteria not met* **do**
6   Evaluate the individuals
7   Copy the elites to the new population
8   Select individuals based on fitness value
9   Generate offsprings by applying **crossover**/mutation/reproduction operators
10 **end**
11 return best individual

---

to this, multi-tree representation naturally lends itself to DFJSS. The pseudo-code of MTGP is given in Algorithm 1.

In this paper, we use the multi-tree representation that one individual contains two trees to match our problem. To be specific, the first tree is used to indicate the sequencing rule and the second tree denotes the routing rule. The fitness of one individual depends on the two trees working together. In the case of multi-tree representation, the evolutionary algorithm must come to a decision as to which trees the genetic operator will be applied.

In multi-tree representation, the classical genetic operators are defined to act upon only one tree in an individual at a time. Other trees are unchanged and copied directly from the parents to the offsprings. Genetic operators are limited to a single type of trees at a time in the expectation that this will reduce the extent to which they disrupt "building blocks" of useful code. However, when coping with DFJSS, such a crossover operator has the following issues.

Firstly, the crossover operation only happens between one type of trees of the parents, therefore, the offsprings generated might not be substantially different from their parents. Thus, the population will lose its diversity and the ability of exploration will decrease.

Secondly, the crossover operation cannot improve the diversity of the combinations of routing and sequencing rules. In DFJSS, a good rule cannot be "good" by itself, but should behave well when collaborating with the other rule. Thus, the diversity of combinations is an important factor for achieving good solutions.

In order to overcome these shortcomings and make the algorithm more in line with the properties of DFJSS, a new tree swapping crossover operator is proposed. Figure 2 shows the tree swapping crossover operator, which shares the same process with the classical crossover operator except that the unselected trees (the same type) are also swapped with each other. To be specific, two parents ($parent_1$ and $parent_2$) are selected to generate offsprings and the second type (T_2) of trees is selected for crossover. The dotted circles mean that the subtrees are chosen and will be swapped. The standard crossover operator will

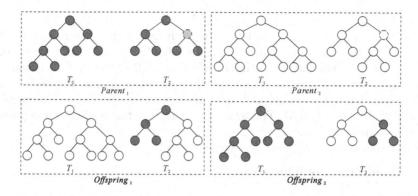

Fig. 2. Tree swapping crossover operator for multi-tree representation.

stop here. But for the tree swapping crossover operator, the other type of trees is also swapped. Thus, two offsprings ($Offspring_1$ and $Offspring_2$) are generated.

This will bring two benefits. The first is that useful blocks are not easily broken. The second is more possible pairs or combinations of routing and sequencing rules will be examined in sMTGP. That is to say, the population of sMTGP will become more diverse compared with MTGP. More importantly, this point matches well with the characteristics of the DFJSS problems.

4 Experiment Design

4.1 Parameter Settings

In our experiment, time-invariant terminals in [10], were adopted. The details are shown in Table 1. Six functions $\{+, -, *, /, max, min\}$ are selected in the function set, in which "/" is the protected division that returns the largest double positive number if divided by 0. All of them take two operands.

Table 1. The terminal set.

	Notation	Description
Machine-related	NIQ	The number of operations in the queue
	WIQ	Current work in the queue
	MWT	Waiting time of a machine
	PT	Processing time of an operation on a specified machine
Job-related	NPT	Median processing time for the next operation
	OWT	The waiting time of an operation
	WKR	Median amount of work remaining for a job
	NOR	The number of operations remaining for a job
	W	Weight of a job
System-related	TIS	Time in system

For fair comparison, the parameters in MTGP and sMTGP are the same as in [19]. The population size is 1024 and the maximize depth of programs is 8. The crossover, mutation and reproduction rates are 0.80, 0.15 and 0.05, respectively. The rates of terminal and non-terminal selection are 0.10 and 0.90. Tournament selection was set as parent selection method with a tournament size of 7.

The learning process continued until the generation met the maximum generation, which was set to 51. The 30 independent runs test results were reported as the system performance.

4.2   Simulation Configuration

For dynamic simulation, the configuration is given in Table 2, which has been commonly used in existing studies [5,10]. In order to improve the generalization ability of the evolved rules, the seeds used to stochastically generate the jobs were rotated in the training process at each generation.

Table 2. Dynamic simulation configuration.

Parameter	Value
Number of machines	10
Number of jobs	5000
Number of warmup jobs	1000
Number of operations per job	Uniform discrete distribution between 1 and 10
Available machines per operation	Uniform discrete distribution between 1 and 10
Job arrival process	Poisson process
Utilization level	0.85, 0.95
Processing time	Uniform discrete distribution between 1 and 99
Job weights	weight 1 (20%), weight 2 (60%), weight 4 (20%)

4.3   Comparison Settings

In our research, three algorithms were involved. CCGP [19] is built on GP with cooperative co-evolution and MTGP is the proposed algorithm that introduces GP with multi-tree representation to evolve routing and sequencing rules together. sMTGP is the improved MTGP with the tree swapping crossover. Moreover, a typical performance indicator for JSS is the flowtime, i.e., the sum of the total waiting time and the total processing time for one job. In this paper, we used three different kinds of variations of flowtime to measure the performance of the proposed algorithms, namely Max-Flowtime, Mean-Flowtime and Mean-weighted-Flowtime. Different scenarios were used to measure their robustness.

For the DFJSS problem, in our case, it is impossible to get the best known (lower bound) objective value of the instances. So, benchmark routing rule

(LWIQ, Least Work in Queue, select the machine with the least work in its queue) and sequencing rules (SPT, Shortest Processing Time, choose the job with shortest processing time, for mean-flowtime; FCFS, First Come First Serve, the job comes first will be processed firstly, for max-flowtime and mean-weighted-flowtime) [4], were applied to get a baseline objective value for each instance. The reason for choosing them is that they show better performance than others in previous work [6] and often be chosen as benchmark rules [19]. Here, the relative performance ratio was defined as the average normalized objective value obtained by evolved rules over the counterpart got by benchmark rules. Thus, in our case, the smaller the fitness, the better.

5   Results and Discussions

5.1   Optimization Performance

In our experiment, six scenarios were set to test the performance of MTGP, sMTGP and CCGP. The best pair of rules of the last generation was tested on test data set to measure its performance. The test data set consists of 50 dynamic simulations with different random seeds. In addition, Wilcoxon signed rank test at the 5% level was used for comparison between the three algorithms. First of all, MTGP and sMTGP were compared with CCGP respectively to measure the feasibility of multi-tree based GP. Then, sMTGP and MTGP were compared for analysing the effectiveness of proposed tree swapping crossover operator.

All the mean value obtained by MTGP and sMTGP are better than CCGP and all the standard deviation value are smaller than the counterparts. Wilcoxon signed rank test results show that sMTGP is significantly better than CCGP only in two scenarios (Max-Flowtime-0.85, Mean-Flowtime-0.85). It is interesting that MTGP got better mean value than CCGP, but none of the instances of MTGP is significantly better than CCGP.

When further looking into the boxplot in Fig. 3, one can see that CCGP has many more outliers than MTGP and sMTGP. This is because CCGP cannot handle well the interactions between routing and sequencing rules directly, thus can be stuck into poor local optima more often. The reason why there is no statistical significance between MTGP and CCGP is that the two algorithms showed very similar performance except the outliers. Figure 3 clearly shows that multi-tree representation managed to dramatically reduce the probability of outliers.

According to these observations, the performance of GP with the multi-tree representation is more stable than GP with cooperative co-evolution. Also, Wilcoxon signed rank test results show that sMTGP is significantly better than MTGP in four scenarios, which are Max-Flowtime-0.85, Mean-Flowtime-0.85, Mean-weighted-Flowtime-0.85/0.95. It means that the proposed tree swapping crossover operator can effectively improve the performance of MTGP.

Figure 4 shows that the sizes of evolved best sequencing rules by sMTGP and MTGP are obviously and dramatically smaller than the best rules evolved by CCGP. Also, Fig. 5 shows that the best routing rule sizes got by sMTGP and

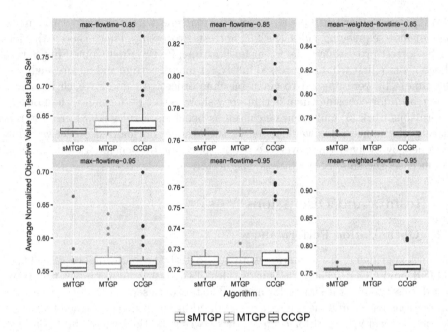

Fig. 3. The boxplot of average normalized objective value obtained by sMTGP, MTGP and CCGP on test data set.

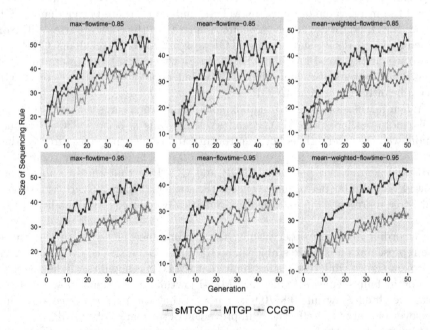

Fig. 4. The convergence curves of the average best sequencing rule size (30 runs) obtained by sMTGP, MTGP and CCGP at each generation.

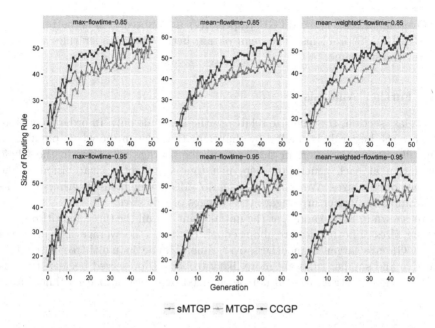

Fig. 5. The convergence curves of the average best routing rule size (30 runs) obtained by sMTGP, MTGP and CCGP at each generation.

Table 3. The average training time for each run of the three algorithms.

Index	Scenario	Training time (seconds)		
		sMTGP	MTGP	CCGP
1	Max-Flowtime-0.85	4459.9	4267.1	4642.8
2	Max-Flowtime-0.95	5057.2	4790.3	5144.9
3	Mean-Flowtime-0.85	4184.5	4278.0	4538.5
4	Mean-Flowtime-0.95	4667.6	4721.3	4849.9
5	Mean-weighted-Flowtime-0.85	4348.1	4181.7	4458.4
6	Mean-weighted-Flowtime-0.95	4585.7	4680.3	4957.0

MTGP are smaller than that of CCGP. However, there is not so much difference compared with the changes of sequencing rule sizes. These observations confirm the potential of using multi-tree based GP to achieve smaller size rules.

From Table 3, it is clear that sMTGP and MTGP can evolve rules with lower time complexity than CCGP in all scenarios. In addition, for sMTGP, less training time is needed as compared to MTGP in three situations (scenario 3, 4, 6). This is a promising finding that GP with multi-tree representation is computationally cheaper than GP via cooperative co-evolution for DFJSS.

Overall, MTGP and sMTGP (especially) undoubtedly show better ability to solve DFJSS problems. They can obtain better and smaller rules within a shorter training time.

5.2   Further Analysis

In the last section, the rule size relates to the best rule only. In order to explore whether the best rule is smaller by chance or the rules in the whole population generally become smaller, in this section, the average rule sizes in the whole population at each generation were investigated to get a clear vision of the changes of rule sizes. We took the scenario (Mean-Weighted-Flowtime-0.95) as an example to further investigate the changes of rule sizes.

As shown in Figs. 6 and 7, at the initial point, for all the three algorithms, the average sizes of both rules are about equal. However, the average sizes obtained by CCGP are larger than others over time. Maybe in multi-tree based GP, effective and smaller rules are more likely to be well preserved because there is at least one rule structure will not be changed by operator at each time during

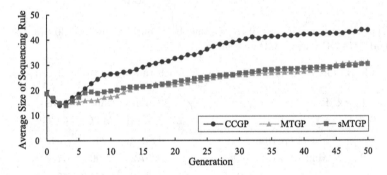

Fig. 6. The convergence curves of average sequencing rule size (30 runs) obtained by CCGP, MTGP and sMTGP in population at each generation.

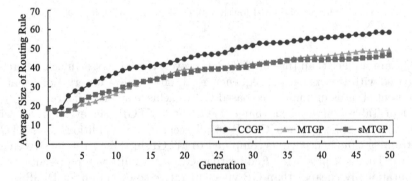

Fig. 7. The convergence curves of average routing rule size (30 runs) obtained by CCGP, MTGP and sMTGP in population at each generation.

the evolution process. In addition, the average sizes obtained by MTGP and sMTGP show the same trend basically and routing rule sizes are bigger than sequencing rules. This is consistent with the observation in the last section.

6 Conclusions and Future Work

This paper tried to evolve routing and sequencing rules based on GP with multi-tree representation simultaneously, which is one of the very first piece of work in this field. From the experimental results, we got some interesting findings. Firstly, in addition to performance, both the routing and sequencing rules evolved by MTGP and sMTGP are much smaller than that of CCGP. MTGP and sMTGP also take less training time. This is an important merit because high training time is a big limitation of GP. Secondly, the proposed tree swapping crossover operator can enhance the ability of MTGP from the perspective of performance, rule size and training time in general. Thirdly, for average normalized objective values on test data set, there are more outliers obtained by CCGP. That is to say, the assumption in CCGP that routing and sequencing rules are independent and can be involved separately, might be not true. This suggests that when we evolve two rules at the same time, we would better to take the interaction into consideration. In the future, the reason why the average rule size in the whole population becomes smaller will be further explored in the future.

References

1. Branke, J., Nguyen, S., Pickardt, C.W., Zhang, M.: Automated design of production scheduling heuristics: a review. IEEE Trans. Evol. Comput. **20**(1), 110–124 (2016)
2. Brucker, P., Schlie, R.: Job-shop scheduling with multi-purpose machines. Computing **45**(4), 369–375 (1990)
3. Cordelia, L., De Stefano, C., Fontanella, F., Marcelli, A.: Genetic programming for generating prototypes in classification problems. In: 2005 IEEE Congress Evolutionary Computation, vol. 2, pp. 1149–1155 (2005)
4. Haupt, R.: A survey of priority rule-based scheduling. Oper.-Res.-Spektrum **11**, 3–16 (1989)
5. Hildebrandt, T., Branke, J.: On using surrogates with genetic programming. Evol. Comput. **23**(3), 343–367 (2015)
6. Holthaus, O., Rajendran, C.: Efficient dispatching rules for scheduling in a job shop. Int. J. Prod. Econ. **48**(1), 87–105 (1997)
7. Langdon, W.B.: Genetic Programming and Data Structures: Genetic Programming + Data Structures = Automatic Programming!, vol. 1. Springer, New York (2012). https://doi.org/10.1007/978-1-4615-5731-9
8. Lensen, A., Xue, B., Zhang, M.: Generating redundant features with unsupervised multi-tree genetic programming. In: Castelli, M., Sekanina, L., Zhang, M., Cagnoni, S., García-Sánchez, P. (eds.) EuroGP 2018. LNCS, vol. 10781, pp. 84–100. Springer, Cham (2018). https://doi.org/10.1007/978-3-319-77553-1_6

9. Mei, Y., Nguyen, S., Xue, B., Zhang, M.: An efficient feature selection algorithm for evolving job shop scheduling rules with genetic programming. IEEE Trans. Emerg. Top. Comput. Intell. 1(5), 339–353 (2017)
10. Mei, Y., Nguyen, S., Zhang, M.: Evolving time-invariant dispatching rules in job shop scheduling with genetic programming. In: McDermott, J., Castelli, M., Sekanina, L., Haasdijk, E., García-Sánchez, P. (eds.) EuroGP 2017. LNCS, vol. 10196, pp. 147–163. Springer, Cham (2017). https://doi.org/10.1007/978-3-319-55696-3_10
11. Muni, D.P., Pal, N.R., Das, J.: A novel approach to design classifiers using genetic programming. IEEE Trans. Evol. Comput. 8(2), 183–196 (2004)
12. Nguyen, S., Mei, Y., Zhang, M.: Genetic programming for production scheduling: a survey with a unified framework. Complex Intell. Syst. 3(1), 41–66 (2017)
13. Nguyen, S., Zhang, M., Johnston, M., Tan, K.C.: A computational study of representations in genetic programming to evolve dispatching rules for the job shop scheduling problem. IEEE Trans. Evol. Comput. 17(5), 621–639 (2013)
14. Nowicki, E., Smutnicki, C.: A fast taboo search algorithm for the job shop problem. Manag. Sci. 42(6), 797–813 (1996)
15. Papadimitriou, C.H., Steiglitz, K.: Combinatorial Optimization: Algorithms and Complexity. Courier Corporation, North Chelmsford (1998)
16. Pezzella, F., Morganti, G., Ciaschetti, G.: A genetic algorithm for the flexible job-shop scheduling problem. Comput. Oper. Res. 35(10), 3202–3212 (2008)
17. Sels, V., Gheysen, N., Vanhoucke, M.: A comparison of priority rules for the job shop scheduling problem under different flow time-and tardiness-related objective functions. Int. J. Prod. Res. 50(15), 4255–4270 (2012)
18. Van Laarhoven, P.J., Aarts, E.H., Lenstra, J.K.: Job shop scheduling by simulated annealing. Oper. Res. 40(1), 113–125 (1992)
19. Yska, D., Mei, Y., Zhang, M.: Genetic programming hyper-heuristic with cooperative coevolution for dynamic flexible job shop scheduling. In: Castelli, M., Sekanina, L., Zhang, M., Cagnoni, S., García-Sánchez, P. (eds.) EuroGP 2018. LNCS, vol. 10781, pp. 306–321. Springer, Cham (2018). https://doi.org/10.1007/978-3-319-77553-1_19

Knowledge Representation and
Reasoning

Adaptive Inference on Probabilistic Relational Models

Tanya Braun[(⊠)] and Ralf Möller

Institute of Information Systems, University of Lübeck, Lübeck, Germany
{braun,moeller}@ifis.uni-luebeck.de

Abstract. Standard approaches for inference in probabilistic relational models include lifted variable elimination (LVE) for single queries. To efficiently handle multiple queries, the lifted junction tree algorithm (LJT) uses a first-order cluster representation of a model, employing LVE as a subroutine in its steps. Adaptive inference concerns efficient inference under changes in a model. If the model changes, LJT restarts, possibly unnecessarily dumping information. The purpose of this paper is twofold, (i) to adapt the cluster representation to incremental changes, and (ii) to transform LJT into an adaptive version, enabling LJT to preserve as much computations as possible. Adaptive LJT fast reaches the point of answering queries again after changes, which is especially important for time-critical applications or online query answering.

1 Introduction

A common task in many applications is repeated inference on variations of a model. Variations range from conditioning on a new set of observed events to updating a probability distribution given observations or adapting a model structure while optimising a model representation. Applications include risk analysis where most likely explanations are of interest with changing sets of events coming in regularly [14]. When learning a model structure given data, one approach, called structural expectation-maximisation, alternates between minimally changing a model structure and updating distributions in a model to optimise the representation of the given data. The approach involves changing a model w.r.t.structure and distributions as well as repeated inference when computing the probability of the observed data in the altered model [11].

In a naive way, one incorporates the changes in a model or evidence and performs inference. Adaptive inference, however, aims at performing inference more efficiently when changes in a model or evidence occur. Research exists for adaptive inference on propositional models [1,10]. But, modelling realistic scenarios yields large probabilistic relational models, requiring exact and efficient reasoning about sets of individuals.

Research in the field of lifted inference has lead to efficient algorithms for relational models. Lifted variable elimination (LVE), first introduced in [16] and expanded in [13,17,20], saves computations by reusing intermediate results for

© Springer Nature Switzerland AG 2018
T. Mitrovic et al. (Eds.): AI 2018, LNAI 11320, pp. 487–500, 2018.
https://doi.org/10.1007/978-3-030-03991-2_44

isomorphic subproblems when answering a query. The lifted junction tree algorithm (LJT) sets up a first-order junction tree (FO jtree) to handle multiple queries efficiently [4] using LVE as a subroutine. Van den Broeck et al. apply lifting to weighted model counting and knowledge compilation [8], with newer work on asymmetrical models [7]. To scale lifting, Das et al. use graph databases storing compiled models to count faster [9]. Lifted belief propagation (BP) provides approximate solutions to queries, often using lifted representations, e.g. [2]. But, to the best of our knowledge, research for adaptive inference on relational models is limited. In relational models, changes can also affect the sets of individuals over which one reasons or on which one conditions on. How to handle such incremental changes correctly and efficiently is not obvious.

Nath and Domingos as well as Ahmadi et al. provide approximate algorithms based on BP for lifted, adaptive inference for changing evidence [3,15]. They reuse results from previous algorithm runs and propagate messages only in affected regions or adapt their lifted representations to the changed evidence. We focus on *exact* inference for multiple queries and present an efficient algorithm for *adaptive inference* based on LJT, called aLJT, handling changes in model and evidence. This paper includes two main contributions, (i) procedures for adapting an FO jtree to incremental changes for its underlying model and (ii) an algorithm, aLJT, preserving as much computations as possible under changes in a model. aLJT handles changes ranging from new evidence to extending a model with new factors. aLJT fast reaches the point of answering queries again, which is especially important for time-critical or online query answering.

The remainder of this paper is structured as follows: First, we introduce basic notations and recap LJT. Then, we show how to adapt an FO jtree to changes and present aLJT, followed by a discussion. We conclude with upcoming work.

2   Preliminaries

This section specifies notations and recaps LJT. Based on [17], a running example models the interplay of natural or man-made disasters, an epidemic, and people being sick, travelling, and being treated. Parameters represent disasters, people, and treatments.

2.1   Parameterised Probabilistic Models

Parameterised models compactly represent models by using logical variables (logvars) to parameterise randvars, abbreviated PRVs.

Definition 1. *Let* $\mathbf{L}$, Φ, *and* $\mathbf{R}$ *be sets of logvar, factor, and randvar names respectively. A PRV* $R(L_1, \ldots, L_n)$, $n \geq 0$, *is a syntactical construct with* $R \in \mathbf{R}$ *and* $L_1, \ldots, L_n \in \mathbf{L}$ *to represent a set of randvars. For PRV* A, *the term* $range(A)$ *denotes possible values. A logvar* L *has a domain* $\mathcal{D}(L)$. *A constraint* $(\mathbf{X}, C_{\mathbf{X}})$ *is a tuple with a sequence of logvars* $\mathbf{X} = (X_1, \ldots, X_n)$ *and a set* $C_{\mathbf{X}} \subseteq \times_{i=1}^{n} \mathcal{D}(X_i)$ *restricting logvars to values. The symbol* $\top$ *marks that no restrictions* *apply and may be omitted. For some P, the term $lv(P)$ refers to its logvars, the term $rv(P)$ to its PRVs with constraints, and the term $gr(P)$ to all instances of P, i.e. P grounded w.r.t. constraints.*

For the epidemic scenario, we build the boolean PRVs $Epid$, $Sick(X)$, and $Travel(X)$ from $\mathbf{R} = \{Epid, Sick, Travel\}$ and $\mathbf{L} = \{X\}$, $\mathcal{D}(X) = \{alice, eve, bob\}$. $Epid$ holds if an epidemic occurs. $Sick(X)$ holds if a person X is sick, $Travel(X)$ holds if X travels. With $C = (X, \{eve, bob\})$, $gr(Sick(X)_{|C}) = \{Sick(eve), Sick(bob)\}$. $gr(Sick(X)_{|\top})$ also contains $Sick(alice)$. Parametric factors (parfactors) combine PRVs. A parfactor describes a function, identical for all argument groundings, mapping argument values to real values (potentials), of which at least one is non-zero.

Definition 2. *Let $\mathbf{X} \subseteq \mathbf{L}$ be a set of logvars, $\mathcal{A} = (A_1, \ldots, A_n)$ a sequence of PRVs, built from $\mathbf{R}$ and $\mathbf{X}$, C a constraint on $\mathbf{X}$, and $\phi : \times_{i=1}^{n} range(A_i) \mapsto \mathbb{R}^+$ a function with name $\phi \in \Phi$, identical for all $gr(\mathcal{A}_{|C})$. We denote a parfactor g by $\forall \mathbf{X} : \phi(\mathcal{A})_{|C}$. We omit $(\forall \mathbf{X} :)$ if $\mathbf{X} = lv(\mathcal{A})$ and $|\top$. A set of parfactors forms a model $G := \{g_i\}_{i=1}^n$.*

We define a model G_{ex} as our running example. Let $\mathbf{L} = \{D, W, M, X\}$, $\Phi = \{\phi_0, \phi_1, \phi_2, \phi_3\}$, and $\mathbf{R} = \{Epid, Nat, Man, Sick, Travel, Treat\}$. We build three more boolean PRVs. $Nat(D)$ holds if a natural disaster D occurs, $Man(W)$ if a man-made disaster W occurs. $Treat(X, T)$ holds if a person X is treated with treatment T. The other domains are $\mathcal{D}(D) = \{earthquake, flood\}$, $\mathcal{D}(W) = \{virus, war\}$, and $\mathcal{D}(T) = \{vaccine, tablet\}$. The model reads $G_{ex} = \{g_i\}_{i=0}^3$, $g_0 = \phi_0(Epid)$, $g_1 = \phi_1(Epid, Nat(D), Man(W))_{|\top}$, $g_2 = \phi_2(Epid, Sick(X), Travel(X))_{|\top}$, and $g_3 = \phi_3(Epid, Sick(X), Treat(X, T))_{|\top}$. Parfactors g_1 to g_3 have eight input-output pairs, g_0 has two (omitted here). Figure 1 depicts G_{ex} as a graph with six variable nodes for the PRVs and four factor nodes for the parfactors with edges to arguments.

Evidence displays symmetries if observing the same value for n instances of a PRV [20]. In a parfactor $g_E = \phi_E(P(\mathbf{X}))_{|C_E}$, a potential function ϕ_E and constraint C_E encode the observed values and instances for PRV $P(\mathbf{X})$. Assume we observe the value $true$ for ten randvars of the PRV $Sick(X)$. The corresponding parfactor is $\phi_E(Sick(X))_{|C_E}$. C_E represents the domain of X restricted to the 10 instances and $\phi_E(true) = 1$ and $\phi_E(false) = 0$. A technical remark: To *absorb* evidence, we split all parfactors g_i that cover $P(X)$, called shattering [17], restricting C_i to those tuples that contain $gr(P(X)_{|C_E})$ and a duplicate of g_i to the rest. g_i absorbs g_E (cf. [20]).

The *semantics* of a model G is given by grounding and building a full joint distribution P_G. With Z as the normalisation constant, G represents $P_G = \frac{1}{Z} \prod_{f \in gr(G)} f$. The query answering (QA) problem asks for a marginal distribution of a set of randvars or a conditional distribution given events, which boils down to computing marginals w.r.t. a model's joint distribution, eliminating non-query terms. Formally, $P(\mathbf{Q}|\mathbf{E})$ denotes a query with $\mathbf{Q}$ a set of grounded PRVs and $\mathbf{E} = \{E_i = e_i\}_{i=1}^n$ a set of events. An example query for G_{ex} is $P(Epid|Sick(eve) = true)$. Next, we look at LJT, a lifted QA algorithm, which seeks to avoid grounding and building a full joint distribution.

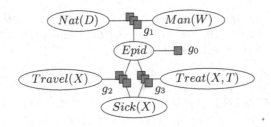

Fig. 1. Parfactor graph for G_{ex}

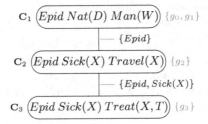

Fig. 2. FO jtree for G_{ex}

2.2 Lifted Junction Tree Algorithm

LJT answers queries for probability distributions. It uses an FO jtree to efficiently answer a set of queries, with LVE as a subroutine. We briefly recap LJT.

LJT answers a set of queries $\{\mathbf{Q}_i\}_{i=1}^m$ given a model G and evidence $\mathbf{E}$. The main workflow is: (i) Construct an FO jtree J for G. (ii) Enter $\mathbf{E}$ into J. (iii) Pass messages in J. (iv) Compute answers for $\{\mathbf{Q}_i\}_{i=1}^m$. LJT first constructs a minimal FO jtree with parameterised clusters (parclusters) as nodes, which are sets of PRVs connected by parfactors, both defined as follows.

Definition 3. *Let $\mathbf{X}$ be a set of logvars, $\mathbf{A}$ a set of PRVs with $lv(\mathbf{A}) \subseteq \mathbf{X}$, and C a constraint on $\mathbf{X}$. Then, $\forall \mathbf{X}: \mathbf{A}_{|C}$ denotes a parcluster. We omit $(\forall \mathbf{X}:)$ if $\mathbf{X} = lv(\mathbf{A})$ and $|\top$. An FO jtree for a model G is a cycle-free graph $J = (V, E)$, where V is the set of nodes, i.e., parclusters, and E the set of edges. J must satisfy three properties: (i) $\forall \mathbf{C}_i \in V: \mathbf{C}_i \subseteq rv(G)$. (ii) $\forall g \in G: \exists \mathbf{C}_i \in V$ s.t. $rv(g) \subseteq \mathbf{C}_i$. (iii) If $\exists A \in rv(G)$ s.t. $A \in \mathbf{C}_i \wedge A \in \mathbf{C}_j$, then $\forall \mathbf{C}_k$ on the path between $\mathbf{C}_i$ and $\mathbf{C}_j$: $A \in \mathbf{C}_k$ (running intersection property). An FO jtree is minimal if by removing a PRV from any parcluster, the FO jtree ceases to be an FO jtree, i.e., it no longer fulfils at least one of the three properties. The parameterised set $\mathbf{S}_{ij}$, called separator of edge $\{i, j\} \in E$, is defined by $\mathbf{C}_i \cap \mathbf{C}_j$. The term $nbs(i)$ refers to the neighbours of node i, defined as $\{j|\{i, j\} \in E\}$. Each $\mathbf{C}_i \in V$ has a local model G_i and $\forall g \in G_i: rv(g) \subseteq \mathbf{C}_i$. The G_i's partition G.*

In a minimal FO jtree, no parcluster is a subset of another parcluster. Figure 2 shows a minimal FO jtree for G_{ex} with parclusters $\mathbf{C}_1$ =

Algorithm 1. Adapting an FO jtree $J = (V, E)$

procedure ADD(FO jtree J, parfactor g')	**procedure** ADJUST(FO jtree J, PRVs **A**)

procedure ADD(FO jtree J, parfactor g')
  Let $\mathbf{A}^{old}$ known, $\mathbf{A}^{new}$ new PRVs in g'
  ADJUST(J, $\mathbf{A}^{old}$) to get $\mathbf{C}_i$ with $\mathbf{A}^{old} \subseteq \mathbf{C}_i$
  if $\mathbf{A}^{new} = \emptyset$ **then**
    $G_i \leftarrow G_i \cup \{g'\}$, mark $\mathbf{C}_i$
  else if $\mathbf{A}^{old} = \mathbf{C}_i$ **then**
    $\mathbf{C}_i \leftarrow \mathbf{C}_i \cup rv(g'), G_i \leftarrow G_i \cup \{g'\}$, mark $\mathbf{C}_i$
  else
    New $\mathbf{C}_k \leftarrow rv(g')$, $G_k \leftarrow \{g'\}$, mark $\mathbf{C}_k$
    Add $\{i, k\}$ to E

procedure DELETE(FO jtree J, parfactor g)
  Get $\mathbf{C}_i \in V$ where $g \in G_i$
  $G_i \leftarrow G_i \setminus \{g\}$
  MIN(J, $\mathbf{C}_i$, $rv(g) \setminus rv(G_i)$), mark $\mathbf{C}_i$

procedure MIN(FO jtree J, node $\mathbf{C}_i$, PRVs **A**)
  for PRV $A \in \mathbf{A}$ **do**
    if $\forall j, k \in nbs(i) : A \notin \mathbf{S}_{ij} \wedge A \notin \mathbf{S}_{ik}$ **then**
      $\mathbf{C}_i \leftarrow \mathbf{C}_i \setminus \{A\}$, mark $\mathbf{C}_i$
  if $\mathbf{C}_i$ marked $\wedge$ $\exists j \in nbs(i) : \mathbf{C}_i \subseteq \mathbf{C}_j$ **then**
    MERGE(J, $\mathbf{C}_i$, $\mathbf{C}_j$)

procedure ADJUST(FO jtree J, PRVs **A**)
  Extract set of nodes N s.t. $\mathbf{A} \subseteq rv(N)$
  while $|N| > 1$ **do**
    Get $\mathbf{C}_i, \mathbf{C}_j \in N$
    $P \leftarrow$ path betw. i, j without i, j, mark P
    $\mathbf{C}' := \mathbf{C}_i, \mathbf{C}'' := \mathbf{C}_j$, $lst \leftarrow |P| - 1$
    MERGE(J, $\mathbf{C}_i$, $\mathbf{C}_j$), remove $\mathbf{C}_j$ from N
    while $lst > 0$ **do**
      if $\exists k, l \in P : \mathbf{S}_{kl} \subseteq \mathbf{C}' \wedge \mathbf{S}_{kl} \subseteq P[lst]$
        $\vee \mathbf{S}_{kl} \subseteq \mathbf{C}'' \wedge \mathbf{S}_{kl} \subseteq P[0]$ **then**
        Remove $\{k, l\}$ from E
        break
      $\mathbf{C}' := P[0], \mathbf{C}'' := P[lst]$
      MERGE(J, $P[0]$, $P[lst]$), update N
      $P \leftarrow P[1 \ldots lst - 1]$, $lst \leftarrow |P| - 1$

procedure MERGE(FO jtree J, nodes $\mathbf{C}_i, \mathbf{C}_j$)
  $\mathbf{C}_i \leftarrow \mathbf{C}_i \cup \mathbf{C}_j$, $G_i \leftarrow G_i \cup G_j$
  Remove $\mathbf{C}_j$ from V
  for each $k \in nbs(j)$ **do**
    Remove $\{j, k\}$, add $\{i, k\}$, $k \neq i$, in E

$\{Epid, Nat(D), Man(W)\}$, $\mathbf{C}_2 = \{Epid, Sick(X), Travel(X)\}$, and $\mathbf{C}_3 = \{Epid, Sick(X), Treat(X, T)\}$. $\mathbf{S}_{12} = \{Epid\}$ and $\mathbf{S}_{23} = \{Epid, Sick(X)\}$ are the separators. Parfactor g_0 appears at $\mathbf{C}_1$ but could be in any local model as $rv(g_0) = \{Epid\} \subset \mathbf{C}_i \forall i \in \{1, 2, 3\}$.

During construction, LJT assigns the parfactors in G to local models (cf. [4]). LJT enters $\mathbf{E}$ into each parcluster $\mathbf{C}_i$ where $rv(\mathbf{E}) \subseteq \mathbf{C}_i$. Local model G_i at $\mathbf{C}_i$ absorbs $\mathbf{E}$ as described above. Message passing distributes local information within the FO jtree. Two passes from the periphery to the center and back suffice [12]. If a node has received messages from all neighbours but one, it sends a message to the remaining neighbour (*inward* pass). In the *outward* pass, messages flow in the opposite direction. Formally, a *message* m_{ij} from node i to node j is a set of parfactors, with arguments from $\mathbf{S}_{ij}$. LJT computes m_{ij} by eliminating $\mathbf{C}_i \setminus \mathbf{S}_{ij}$ from G_i and the messages of all other neighbours with LVE. A minimal FO jtree enhances the efficiency of message passing. Otherwise, messages unnecessarily copy information between parclusters. To answer a query $\mathbf{Q}_i$, LJT finds a subtree J' covering $\mathbf{Q}_i$, compiles a submodel G' of local models in J' and messages from outside J', and sums out all non-query terms in G' using LVE.

Currently, LJT partially handles *adaptive inference*. LJT assumes a constant G for which it builds an FO jtree J, reusing J for varying $\mathbf{E}$ and $\mathbf{Q}$. If G or $\mathbf{E}$ change, LJT restarts with construction or evidence entering. However, changes do not necessarily mean a completely new model or evidence set. LJT may preserve J, local models, or messages in parts. Before presenting aLJT, we show how to adapt an FO jtree.

3   Adapting an FO Jtree to Model Changes

Changes may yield a structure change in a model G, which may cause a structure change in an FO jtree J. All actions towards adapting J need to ensure that J continues to be a minimal FO jtree and that local models still partition G. This section looks at adding, deleting, or replacing a parfactor and ends with an example.

Adding a parfactor g' to G requires adding g' to a local model to partition $G \cup \{g'\}$. Algorithm 1 includes pseudocode for adding g' to $J = (V, E)$. It contains marking instructions relevant for aLJT. We assume that g' contains at least one PRV from V to yield one FO jtree. If the arguments in g' appear in a parcluster $\mathbf{C}_i$, we add g' to G_i. But, if g' contains new PRVs $\mathbf{A}^{new}$ or if the old, known PRVs in g', $\mathbf{A}^{old} \leftarrow rv(g') \cap rv(V)$, do not appear in a single parcluster, there is no parcluster $\mathbf{C}_i$ s.t. $rv(g') \subseteq \mathbf{C}_i$. Thus, we adjust J until $\mathbf{A}^{old} \subseteq \mathbf{C}_i$ for some i and handle $\mathbf{A}^{new}$ appropriately.

Procedure ADJUST in Algorithm 1 arranges that $\mathbf{A}^{old} \subseteq \mathbf{C}_i$ for some i in J. ADJUST finds a set of parclusters N that cover the PRVs in $\mathbf{A}^{old}$ and merges N into a single parcluster to fulfil $\mathbf{A}^{old} \subseteq \mathbf{C}_i$ by successively merging parclusters $\mathbf{C}_i, \mathbf{C}_j \in N$. Merging is a union of parclusters, local models, and neighbours. Since J is acyclic, there exists a unique path P from $\mathbf{C}_i$ to $\mathbf{C}_j$ without i and j, which forms a cycle if $|P| > 1$, which ADJUST resolves: It searches for a separator $\mathbf{S}_{kl}$ of two parclusters $\mathbf{C}_k, \mathbf{C}_l$ on P s.t.

$$\mathbf{S}_{kl} \subseteq \mathbf{C}' \wedge \mathbf{S}_{kl} \subseteq P[lst] \vee \mathbf{S}_{kl} \subseteq \mathbf{C}'' \wedge \mathbf{S}_{kl} \subseteq P[0] \tag{1}$$

where $\mathbf{C}'$ and $\mathbf{C}''$ are $\mathbf{C}_i$ and $\mathbf{C}_j$ in the beginning, i.e., information on $\mathbf{S}_{kl}$ reaches $\mathbf{C}_k$ from one end and $\mathbf{C}_l$ from the other end. If $\mathbf{S}_{kl}$ exists, ADJUST deletes the edge $\{k, l\}$ to break the cycle, which keeps the parclusters on P small. Otherwise, it continues along P, merging parclusters at the path ends if the search for a separator fulfilling Eq. 1 fails. For details, see Algorithm 1.

After adjusting J, there is a parcluster $\mathbf{C}_i$ s.t. $\mathbf{A}^{old} \subseteq \mathbf{C}_i$. If g' contains only $\mathbf{A}^{old}$, procedure ADD adds g' to local model G_i at $\mathbf{C}_i$. If g' contains new PRVs, it distinguishes between $\mathbf{A}^{old} \subset \mathbf{C}_i$ and $\mathbf{A}^{old} = \mathbf{C}_i$. In the former case, PRVs in $\mathbf{C}_i$ do not appear in $rv(g)$ and vice versa. ADD adds a new node $\mathbf{C}_k \leftarrow rv(g')$ with $G_k \leftarrow \{g'\}$ as a neighbour to i. In the latter case, $\mathbf{C}_i$ is a strict subset of the PRVs in g. ADD adds the new PRVs to $\mathbf{C}_i$ and g' to G_i. Now, the local models partition G'.

Deleting a parfactor g from G requires removing g from the local model G_i in which g appears. Afterwards, the local models partition $G \setminus \{g\}$. Algorithm 1 contains pseudocode for deleting g from J. After removing g from G_i, it minimises $\mathbf{C}_i$ w.r.t. $\mathbf{A}^{del} \leftarrow rv(g) \setminus rv(G_i)$. The procedure deletes a PRV $A \in \mathbf{A}^{del}$ from $\mathbf{C}_i$ if no two separators contain A, i.e., $\forall j, k \in nbs(i) : A \notin \mathbf{S}_{ij} \wedge A \notin \mathbf{S}_{ik}$. If now $\mathbf{C}_i \subseteq \mathbf{C}_j$ for a neighbour $\mathbf{C}_j$, MIN merges $\mathbf{C}_i$ and $\mathbf{C}_j$ to keep J minimal.

Replacing a parfactor g with a parfactor g' in G boils down to adding g' and then deleting g. If $rv(g) = rv(g')$, adding g' and deleting g does not touch J. If $rv(g) \subseteq rv(g')$, adding g' yields J', followed by deleting g from J', which does not change J'. First deleting g may lead to removing PRVs and superfluously merging parclusters. If $rv(g') \subseteq rv(g)$, adding g' before deleting g uses that there exists a parcluster $\mathbf{C}_i$ with $rv(g') \subseteq \mathbf{C}_i$ as $rv(g) \subseteq \mathbf{C}_i$. If the arguments of g and g' overlap otherwise, first adding g' and then deleting g avoids unnecessarily deleting PRVs and merging parclusters for the overlap PRVs. If both parfactors do not share any PRVs, replacing g with g' naturally decomposes into adding g' and deleting g.

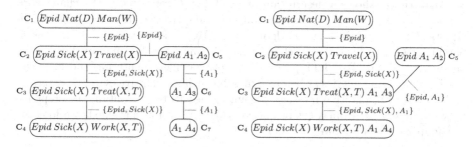

Fig. 3. Adapted and extended FO jtree   **Fig. 4.** Adjusted FO jtree

To illustrate adaption, consider the FO jtree in Fig. 2. We add the parfactor $g_4 = \phi_4(Epid, Sick(X), Work(X))$ to G_{ex}, where PRV $Work(X)$ holds if a person X works. For g_4, the known PRVs are $Epid$ and $Sick(X)$ which appear in $\mathbf{C}_2$ and $\mathbf{C}_3$. Assume Algorithm 1 chooses $\mathbf{C}_3$, which contains a PRV not in g_4, $Treat(X, T)$, while g_4 contains a new PRV, $Work(X)$. Thus, Algorithm 1 adds a parcluster $\mathbf{C}_4 = \{Epid, Sick(X), Work(X)\}$, $G_4 = \{g_4\}$. The left column of parclusters in Fig. 3 shows the result.

Next, we replace g_2 with a parfactor $g'_2 = \phi'_2(Travel(X), Sick(X))$ in G_{ex}, which means adding g'_2 to $\mathbf{C}_2$ and deleting g_2. After removing g_2 from G_2, $Epid$ no longer appears in G_2. But, $Epid$ appears in both its separators and as such, has to remain in $\mathbf{C}_2$ to connect the appearance of $Epid$ from $\mathbf{C}_1$ to $\mathbf{C}_3$. If $g'_2 = \phi'_2(Epid, Travel(X))$, Algorithm 1 would delete $Sick(X)$ as $Sick(X)$ appears only in one separator. If $g'_2 = \phi'_2(Epid, Sick(X))$, Algorithm 1 would delete $Travel(X)$ and merge $\mathbf{C}_2$ with $\mathbf{C}_3$.

To illustrate adjusting an FO jtree, let the adapted FO jtree have three more parclusters with PRVs A_1, A_2, A_3, and A_4, shown in Fig. 3. We add a parfactor $g' = \phi'(A_4, Work(X))$. ADJUST merges $\mathbf{C}_4$ and $\mathbf{C}_7$ into $\mathbf{C}'_4$, causing a cycle. $P[0]$ and $P[lst]$ are $\mathbf{C}_3$ and $\mathbf{C}_6$, i.e., the neighbours of 4 and 7 on the cycle/path. No separator appears in $\mathbf{C}_4$ and $\mathbf{C}_6$ or $\mathbf{C}_7$ and $\mathbf{C}_3$ (Eq. 1 not fulfilled). ADJUST merges $\mathbf{C}_3$ and $\mathbf{C}_6$ into $\mathbf{C}'_3$. Separator $\mathbf{S}_{25} = \{Epid\}$ appears in $\mathbf{C}'_3$ and $\mathbf{C}_5$. ADJUST deletes edge $\{2, 5\}$, forming an acyclic FO jtree as seen in Fig. 4. At $\mathbf{C}'_4$, Algorithm 1 adds g' to the local model.

4 LJT for Adaptive Inference

The extended algorithm aLJT performs adaptive inference for more efficient QA than by restarting from scratch. aLJT basically still consists of the steps construction, evidence entering, and message passing before it answers queries. Each step proceeds in an adaptive manner w.r.t. changes in input model G or in evidence $\mathbf{E}$ given an FO jtree J. Without an FO jtree, the steps are identical to the LJT steps.

Algorithm 2 shows a description of aLJT for J, referring to the changes in G and $\mathbf{E}$ by Δ_G and $\Delta_{\mathbf{E}}$. Line 1 contains the adaptive construction step, which adapts J to Δ_G according to Algorithm 1. To track changes, aLJT marks a parcluster $\mathbf{C}_i$ if a local model changes s.t. the messages become invalid. Based on the marks and $\Delta_{\mathbf{E}}$, aLJT performs adaptive evidence entering and message passing, answering queries as before. Lines 2 to 4 show adaptive evidence entering and lines 5 to 9 adaptive message passing. Lines 10 to 12 contain the steps to answer a query $\mathbf{Q}_i$ from a set of queries $\{\mathbf{Q}_i\}_{i=1}^m$, as in LJT. Next, we look at the adaptive steps, followed by an example.

Construction: aLJT handles changes Δ_G as in Algorithm 1 with J as input and Δ_G referring to parfactors to add, delete, or replace. When adding a parfactor g, aLJT marks the parcluster $\mathbf{C}_i$ that receives g. If adjusting J for known PRVs, aLJT marks all parclusters on the cycle between two parclusters $\mathbf{C}_i, \mathbf{C}_j$ that it merges. The merged parcluster $\mathbf{C}_i'$ has two messages m_{xi}, m_{yj} from its neighbours on the cycle with both information about the parclusters on the cycle and with information from G_i (in m_{yj}) and G_j (in m_{xi}), which is already contained in $G_i' \leftarrow G_i \cup G_j$. A similar situation occurs for all cycle parclusters, requiring new messages. Merging adjacent parclusters does not require a mark since messages between them are no longer considered and all other messages remain valid. When deleting a parfactor from the local model of $\mathbf{C}_i$, aLJT marks $\mathbf{C}_i$. aLJT replaces a parfactor by adding and deleting, which includes marks.

For changes in potentials, ranges, or constraints, aLJT replaces parfactors. For domain changes of a logvar X, aLJT marks a parcluster $\mathbf{C}_i$ if $X \in lv(\mathbf{C}_i)$ and its constraint w.r.t. X is $\top$. After incorporating all changes, parclusters are properly marked.

Evidence Entering: Adaptive entering deals with evidence at marked parclusters and changes $\Delta_{\mathbf{E}}$ in evidence. In the first case, marked parcluster only need evidence entering if new parfactors or domain changes affect it. If evidence does not change, only new parfactors or parfactors affected by domain changes need to absorb evidence.

In the second case, aLJT enters evidence at all parclusters $\mathbf{C}_i$ affected by $\Delta_{\mathbf{E}}$, which refers to changes in the form of additional or retracted evidence or new observed values. For additional evidence, aLJT uses the current local model G_i and enters the additional evidence. For retracted evidence, aLJT resets parfactors where the evidence no longer appears, which may require reentering evidence if evidence for a PRV is partially retracted. For new values, aLJT resets parfactors that have absorbed the original evidence. These parfactors absorb the new values. If $\Delta_{\mathbf{E}}$ leads to changes in G_i, aLJT marks $\mathbf{C}_i$.

Message Passing: aLJT maintains the same two-pass scheme starting at the periphery going inward and returning to the periphery outward. Inward, if a parcluster has received messages from all neighbours but one, it sends a message to the remaining neighbour. Outward, after a parcluster has received a message from the remaining neighbour, it sends messages to all other neighbours. The scheme preserves the ability for an automatic execution. After message passing, aLJT starts answering queries.

The adaptive part occurs during message calculation. A parcluster $\mathbf{C}_i$ calculates a new message if messages have become invalid during adjusting or if $\mathbf{C}_i$ has to distribute changes in its local model or received messages, else, it sends an empty message. The receiver replaces the old message with the new message and marks it changed (if not empty) or marks the old message as unchanged. Formally, $\mathbf{C}_i$ calculates a message m_{ij} for neighbour $\mathbf{C}_j$ if $\mathbf{C}_i$ itself is marked or if a message from a neighbour is marked as changed. Then, $\mathbf{C}_i$ computes m_{ij} using LVE with $G' \leftarrow G_i \cup \bigcup_{k \in nbs(i), k \neq j} m_{ki}$ as model (messages irregardless of whether they are marked changed) and $\mathbf{S}_{ij}$ as query.

Algorithm 2. LJT for adaptive inference answering queries $\{\mathbf{Q}_i\}_{i=1}^{m}$ given an FO jtree J and changes Δ_G for model G and $\Delta_{\mathbf{E}}$ for evidence $\mathbf{E}$

1: Adapt J to Δ_G according to Alg.1   ▷ marks parclusters
2: **for** each parcluster $\mathbf{C}_i$ in J **do**
3:     **if** $\mathbf{C}_i$ marked or affected by $\Delta_{\mathbf{E}}$ **then**
4:         Handle evidence at $\mathbf{C}_i$, mark $\mathbf{C}_i$
5: **while** $\exists \mathbf{C}_i$ ready to send message m_{ij} to $\mathbf{C}_j$ in J **do**
6:     **if** $\mathbf{C}_i$ marked or has marked message **then**
7:         Send newly computed m_{ij}, mark m_{ij} at $\mathbf{C}_j$ as changed
8:     **else**
9:         Send empty message, mark m_{ij} at $\mathbf{C}_j$ as unchanged
10: **for** each query $\mathbf{Q}_i$ **do**
11:     Extract submodel G' from subtree J' that covers $\mathbf{Q}_i$
12:     Answer $\mathbf{Q}_i$ on G' using LVE

As an example, consider the FO jtree in Fig. 4 with all its changes. All parclusters are marked except $\mathbf{C}_1$. Thus, the only empty message is m_{12}. After message passing, aLJT can answer queries for any randvar in $gr(rv(G))$. Next, assume we add evidence about $Nat(D)$ at $\mathbf{C}_1$, which leads aLJT to mark $\mathbf{C}_1$. With no further changes, aLJT only needs to distribute the updated information in G_1. Thus, messages m_{53} and m_{43} from $\mathbf{C}_5$ and $\mathbf{C}_4$ to $\mathbf{C}_3$ are empty as well as the messages from $\mathbf{C}_3$ over $\mathbf{C}_2$ to $\mathbf{C}_1$ as no change occurs in local models. Message m_{12} from $\mathbf{C}_1$ to $\mathbf{C}_2$ is new. The new message received by $\mathbf{C}_2$ leads to new messages from $\mathbf{C}_2$ to $\mathbf{C}_3$ and from $\mathbf{C}_3$ back to the leaf nodes $\mathbf{C}_4$ and $\mathbf{C}_5$. After sending all messages, aLJT can answer queries again.

Theoretical Discussion: aLJT and LJT have a *runtime complexity* linear in domain sizes, which also holds for other lifted algorithms [6,19]. The speedup comes in form of a factor as aLJT can avoid handling evidence for up to all parclusters and save calculating up to half of the messages after a change. Next, we argue why aLJT is sound.

Theorem 1. *aLJT is sound, i.e., computes a correct result for a query* $\mathbf{Q}$ *on an FO jtree J after adapting to changes in input model G and evidence* $\mathbf{E}$.

Proof sketch. We assume that LJT is correct, yielding an FO jtree J, fulfilling the FO jtree properties, which allows for local computations [18]. Further, we assume that LVE is correct, ensuring correct local computations during evidence entering, message passing, and query answering. aLJT first adapts J, which consists of adding, deleting and replacing parfactors. We briefly sketch how to prove that adapting J outputs an FO jtree again: we follow the changes in J showing that J remains an FO jtree. For the changes regarding adding, extending, or deleting a parcluster, it is straightforward to see that J' still fulfils the properties. The main part concerns the ADJUST procedure, which relies on J being acyclic and thus, causing at most one cycle between two parclusters. Breaking the cycle then ensures the FO jtree properties. Thus, adaptive construction outputs an FO jtree with marked parclusters. Adaptive evidence entering enters the new evidence version at all parclusters covering evidence and re-enters evidence at parclusters with changed local models, ensuring a correct evidence handling at all parclusters. Adaptive message passing distributes updated information whenever changed information arrives or local information has changed. With messages and local models updated, aLJT uses local models and messages to correctly answer $\mathbf{Q}$ using LVE.   □

5   Empirical Evaluation

We have implemented prototypes of (a) LJT, named `ljt` and `aljt` here. Taghipour provides an LVE implementation (https://dtai.cs.kuleuven.be/software/lve), named `lve`. We fixed some lines in `lve` for queries with more than one grounded logvar. We do not include ground algorithms as we have already shown the speed-up by lifting (e.g., [5]).

The evaluation has two parts. First, we look at runtimes for G_{ex} under changes, focussing on how fast the programs provide answers again after consecutive changes. Second, we look at runtimes for the individual steps of LJT and aLJT for varying models G of sizes $|G|$ ranging from 2 to 1024 under a model change (adding a parfactor) and an evidence change (adding new evidence).

5.1   Consecutive Changes

This first part concerns three consecutive changes and two queries each. As input, we use G_{ex} with random potentials. We set $|\mathcal{D}(X)| = 1,000$ and $|\mathcal{D}(.)| = 100$ for the other logvars, yielding $|gr(G_{ex})| = 111,001$. Evidence occurs for 200 instances of $Sick(X)$ with the value *true*. There are two queries, $Sick(x_{1000})$ and $Treat(x_1, t_1)$. The consecutive changes for G_{ex}, based on the adaption examples, are (i) adding parfactor $\phi(Epid, Sick(X), Work(X))$ (referred to as model G^1_{ex}), (ii) replacing g_2 with parfactor $\phi(Sick(X), Travel(X))$ (referred to as model G^2_{ex}), and (iii) adding as evidence $Work(X) = true$ for 100 instances of X (referred to as model G^3_{ex}). The X values are a subset of the X values in the $Sick(X)$ evidence. After each change, the programs answer both queries again. We compare runtimes for inference averaged over five runs. Runtimes for ljt and aljt include construction, evidence entering, message passing, and query answering. Runtimes for lve consist of query answering.

Figure 5 shows runtimes in seconds [s] accumulated over all four models for lve (square), ljt (triangle), and aljt (circle). The vertical lines indicate when the programs have answered both queries, after which lve and ljt proceed with the next model, while aljt starts with adaption. For a model, the points on the ljt and aljt lines mark when an individual step is finished. lve takes longer than both LJT versions, showcasing the advantage of using an FO jtree. After only two queries, ljt and aljt have already offset their overhead and provide answers faster than lve.

For G_{ex}, ljt and aljt have the same runtimes since their runs are identical. As G_{ex} incrementally changes, aljt displays its advantage of adaptive steps in contrast to ljt. Starting with G^1_{ex}, aljt provides answers faster than ljt. Before ljt has completed message passing, aljt has already answered both queries. Especially message passing is faster as aljt does not need to compute half of the messages ljt computes. Construction is slightly faster. Evidence entering does not take long for both programs. But, evidence usually leads to longer runtimes for query answering compared to no evidence for LVE and LJT as the necessary splits lead to larger models. Since G^3_{ex} contains more evidence, all runtimes increase compared to the previous models.

aljt fast reaches the point of answering queries again, providing answers more timely than the other two programs. As each change provides the possibility for aljt to save computations, leading to savings in runtime, the savings add up over a sequence of changes. Thus, performing adaptive inference pays off.

5.2   Step-Wise Performance

This second part looks at runtimes of the individual steps of LJT and aLJT given models of varying size. The model sizes start at 2 and double until they reach 1,024. The first model is $G_2 \cup G_3$ from the FO jtree of G_{ex}. The second model is G_{ex}. For the other models, we basically duplicated the current G, starting with G_{ex}, renamed the PRVs and logvars of the duplicate, and connected the original part with the copied part through a parfactor. The largest model has 1,024 parfactors and logvars and 3,072 PRVs, resulting in an FO jtree with 770 parclusters. The largest parcluster contains 256 PRVs. Technical remark: The maximum parcluster size is larger than need be due to the heuristic the construction is based on. The largest parcluster contains all PRVs without parameters, because the heuristic leads the (a)LJT implementations to handle all parfactors

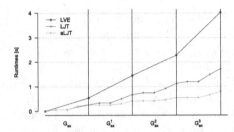 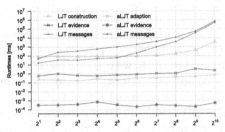

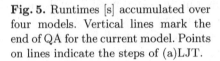

Fig. 5. Runtimes [s] accumulated over four models. Vertical lines mark the end of QA for the current model. Points on lines indicate the steps of (a)LJT.

Fig. 6. Runtimes [ms] of the (a)LJT steps. X-axis: increasing $|G|$ from 2 to 1,024. Both axes appear on log scale. Points are connected for readability.

without logvars separately at the beginning, resulting in one large parcluster as the parameterless PRVs also appear in all other parts of the model.

The domain sizes for all logvars are set to 1,000, leading to grounded model sizes, ranging from 1,001,000 to 513,256,256. A part of the model receives evidence for 50% of the instances of one PRV. We compare runtimes of the corresponding LJT and aLJT step for the following settings: (i) Add a parfactor with a new PRV. (ii) Enter new evidence to an unchanged model. (iii) Pass messages after changes in a model. Reentering known evidence after changes in a model and passing messages after changes in evidence have shown similar runtimes to settings (ii) and (iii).

Figure 6 shows runtimes in milliseconds [ms] of `ljt` and `aljt` averaged over five runs for the three settings. The triangles and crosses mark `ljt`, while the circles and stars mark `aljt`. The hollow marks refer to construction/adaption, the cross and star marks to evidence entering, and the filled marks to message passing. In all three settings, `aljt` is faster than `ljt` and both performing similar given larger models. The curves have a similar shape but are on a different level if domain sizes are different to 1,000.

For construction (hollow marks), `aljt` is two to three orders of magnitude faster than `ljt` (0.0024 in average). For evidence entering (cross/star marks), the savings are even higher: `aljt` is faster than `ljt` by more than three orders of magnitude (0.0004 in average). Evidence handling appears to be constant in this setup. Since LVE has to perform one split per evidence PRV independent of the domain sizes and the evidence is restricted to one part of the model, evidence handling does not depend on the model size. Message passing (filled marks) shows only a clear speedup for smaller models. The first half of the models allows for `aljt` to be one order of magnitude faster than `ljt` (0.0955 in average). For the larger models, the factor of the speedup lays between 0.25 and 0.79. Concerning providing an answer to a query after a change, runtimes are basically a sum of the previous steps plus the time for answering a query, which takes around 100 ms. Since message passing dominates in the overall performance of (a)LJT with only one query, the overall runtimes resemble the runtimes of message passing.

Overall, `aljt` runtimes are faster by a factor ranging from 0.003 and 0.5 for such models. In the first two steps, aLJT is two orders of magnitude faster with changes in evidence and model restricted to certain parts of an FO jtree. Considering the first part of the evaluation, savings add up given frequent changes. In summary, performing adaptive inference pays off as `aljt` is able to provide a faster online QA than `ljt`.

6   Conclusion

We present aLJT, an adaptive version of LJT, which incorporates incremental changes in its input model or evidence efficiently. We specify how to adapt an FO jtree when deleting, adding, or replacing parts of a model. We formalise under which conditions evidence entering and new messages are necessary. Given the adaptive steps, aLJT reduces its static overhead for construction, evidence entering, and message passing under gradual changes compared to LJT. aLJT allows for fast online inference for answering multiple queries, minimising the lag in query answering when inputs change.

We currently work on learning lifted models, where we use aLJT as a subroutine. Other interesting algorithm extensions include parallelisation, construction using hypergraph partitioning, and different message passing strategies. Additionally, we look into areas of application to see its performance on real-life scenarios.

References

1. Acar, U.A., Ihler, A.T., Mettu, R.R., Sümer, Ö.: Adaptive inference on general graphical models. In: Proceedings of the 24th Conference on Uncertainty in AI, UAI 2008, pp. 1–8 (2008)
2. Ahmadi, B., Kersting, K., Mladenov, M., Natarajan, S.: Exploiting symmetries for scaling loopy belief propagation and relational training. Mach. Learn. **92**(1), 91–132 (2013)
3. Ahmadi, B., Kersting, K., Sanner, S.: Multi-evidence lifted message passing, with application to Pagerank and the Kalman filter. In: Proceedings of the 22nd International Joint Conference on AI, IJCAI 2011, pp. 1152–1158 (2011)
4. Braun, T., Möller, R.: Lifted junction tree algorithm. In: Friedrich, G., Helmert, M., Wotawa, F. (eds.) KI 2016. LNCS (LNAI), vol. 9904, pp. 30–42. Springer, Cham (2016). https://doi.org/10.1007/978-3-319-46073-4_3
5. Braun, T., Möller, R.: Counting and conjunctive queries in the lifted junction tree algorithm. In: Croitoru, M., Marquis, P., Rudolph, S., Stapleton, G. (eds.) GKR 2017. LNCS (LNAI), vol. 10775, pp. 54–72. Springer, Cham (2018). https://doi.org/10.1007/978-3-319-78102-0_3
6. van den Broeck, G.: On the completeness of first-order knowledge compilation for lifted probabilistic inference. Adv. Neural Inf. Process. Syst. **24**, 1386–1394 (2011)

7. van den Broeck, G., Niepert, M.: Lifted probabilistic inference for asymmetric graphical models. In: Proceedings of the 29th Conference on AI, AAAI 2015, pp. 3599–3605 (2015)

8. van den Broeck, G., Taghipour, N., Meert, W., Davis, J., Raedt, L.D.: Lifted probabilistic inference by first-order knowledge compilation. In: Proceedings of the 22nd International Joint Conference on AI, IJCAI 2011 (2011)

9. Das, M., Wu, Y., Khot, T., Kersting, K., Natarajan, S.: Scaling lifted probabilistic inference and learning via graph databases. In: Proceedings of the SIAM International Conference on Data Mining, pp. 738–746 (2016)

10. Delcher, A.L., Grove, A.J., Kasif, S., Pearl, J.: Logarithmic-time updates and queries in probabilistic networks. In: Proceedings of the 11th Conference on Uncertainty in AI, UAI 1995, pp. 116–124 (1995)

11. Friedman, M.: The Bayesian structural EM algorithm. In: Proceedings of the 14th Conference on Uncertainty in AI, UAI 1998, pp. 129–138 (1998)

12. Lauritzen, S.L., Spiegelhalter, D.J.: Local computations with probabilities on graphical structures and their application to expert systems. J. Royal Statist. Soc. Ser. B: Methodol. **50**, 157–224 (1988)

13. Milch, B., Zettelmoyer, L.S., Kersting, K., Haimes, M., Kaelbling, L.P.: Lifted probabilistic inference with counting formulas. In: Proceedings of the 23rd Conference on AI, AAAI 2008, pp. 1062–1068 (2008)

14. Muñoz-González, L., Sgandurra, D., Barrère, M., Lupu, E.C.: Exact inference techniques for the analysis of Bayesian attack graphs. IEEE Trans. Depend. Secur. Comput. **PP**(99), 1–14 (2017)

15. Nath, A., Domingos, P.: Efficient lifting for online probabilistic inference. In: Proceedings of the 24th AAAI Conference on AI (2010)

16. Poole, D.: First-order probabilistic inference. In: Proceedings of the 18th International Joint Conference on AI, IJCAI 2003 (2003)

17. de Salvo Braz, R., Amir, E., Roth, D.: Lifted first-order probabilistic inference. In: Proceedings of the 19th International Joint Conference on AI, IJCAI 2005 (2005)

18. Shenoy, P.P., Shafer, G.R.: Axioms for probability and belief-function propagation. Uncertain. AI **4**(9), 169–198 (1990)

19. Taghipour, N., Fierens, D., van den Broeck, G., Davis, J., Blockeel, H.: Completeness results for lifted variable elimination. In: Proceedings of the 16th International Conference on AI and Statistics, pp. 572–580 (2013)

20. Taghipour, N., Fierens, D., Davis, J., Blockeel, H.: Lifted variable elimination: decoupling the operators from the constraint language. J. AI Res. **47**(1), 393–439 (2013)

Reinterpretation with Systems of Spheres

Özgür Lütfü Özçep[✉]

Institute of Information Systems (IFIS), University of Lübeck, Lübeck, Germany
oezcep@ifis.uni-luebeck.de

Abstract. Communicating agents in open environments such as the semantic web face the problem of inter-ontological ambiguity, i.e., the problem that some agent uses a (constant, role or concept) name differently than another agent. In this paper, we propose a strategy for online ambiguity resolution relying on the ideas of belief revision and reinterpretation. The data structures guiding the conflict resolution are systems of spheres, which, in particular, allow to select a resolution result amongst other potential results. The paper defines operators for (iterated) reinterpretation based on systems of spheres and shows that they fulfill some desirable set of properties (postulates).

Keywords: Belief revision · Spheres · Ontology · Ambiguity

1 Introduction

Ambiguous use of words is a typical phenomenon of natural languages (next to others such as vagueness, anaphora etc.) that may cause misunderstandings within communicating humans. Similar problems occur also within artificial agents communicating in open environments such as the semantic web. Though artificial agents usually rely on formal languages one cannot assume that they rely on the same ontology. Hence, instead of following the unrealistic aim of one ontology for all agents, agents should be equipped with an online mechanism for identifying and resolving conflicts caused by ambiguous use of symbols.

In this paper we consider the situation of two communicating agents, where a receiver agent holds an ontology and receives (one-after-one) bits of information from a sender agent, holding a different but kindred ontology. We consider a class of operators that use the idea of reinterpretation for the resolution of logical conflicts [2,4,6]: The meaning of the symbol as used in the ontology is changed by broadening or weakening its extension such that the conflict is resolved, and the different meanings are interrelated by bridging axioms.

The possible ways in which the receiver's ontology could be changed has to be constrained declaratively such that only "rational" types of changes results. This idea was one of the corner-stones of the rationality postulates for revision operators as developed in the pioneering work of AGM (Alchourron, Gärdenfors, Makinson) on belief revision [1]. One rationality postulate requires that the outcome of the change deviates only minimally from the original knowledge

© Springer Nature Switzerland AG 2018
T. Mitrovic et al. (Eds.): AI 2018, LNAI 11320, pp. 501–506, 2018.
https://doi.org/10.1007/978-3-030-03991-2_45

base. In case of AGM the knowledge base is a logically closed set of sentences called belief set, in this paper the knowledge base is an ontology.

Usually, there is more than a single "minimal" change result, hence the change has to be supported by some data structure that allows to select a unique result. In the literature different forms of such structures have been considered, e.g., epistemic entrenchment relations, preference orders over models, selections functions in partial meet operators etc. The kind of data structure that was considered in [4]—and that is also in the focus of this paper—are systems of spheres as introduced by Grove [3] and used in prototype revision in [8].

In this paper we build on the general idea of [4] using *systems of spheres* for changing concepts by reinterpretation and we extend the operators of [4] to deal with *iterated reinterpretation*. We show that (iterated) sphere-based reinterpretation operators enjoy most of the properties one would expect from a rational semantic integration operator by considering the classical AGM-postulates [1] as well as other postulates that fit the integration scenario mentioned above.

A longer version of this paper can be found at https://tinyurl.com/y8n3p6zo.

2   Example

Here and in the following we assume familiarity with description logics (DLs). A receiver agent is the owner of the following ontology $\mathcal{O} = \langle O, \mathcal{V}_p, \mathcal{V}_i \rangle$ where O is a set of tbox and abox axioms over $\mathcal{V}_p \cup \mathcal{V}_i$, $\mathcal{V}_p$ is a public vocabulary, in which agents communicate, and $\mathcal{V}_i$ is the internal vocabulary of the receiver agent.

$$O = \{Student \sqsubseteq \neg Researcher, Researcher(peter)\} \qquad \alpha = Student(peter)$$

O says that no student is a researcher and that Peter is a researcher. The information α, stemming from a trustworthy sender, has to be integrated into $\mathcal{O}$. It says that Peter is a student. Information α leads to a logical conflict with the ontology. And hence a change of the ontology is triggered.

Reinterpretation traces back the conflict between $\mathcal{O}$ and α to different readings of the concept symbol *Student* or the constant *peter*. We consider only the reinterpretation of concept symbols, hence *Student* has to be reinterpreted.

The outcome of sphere-based reinterpretation is given in the following:

$$O \odot_S \alpha = \{Student' \sqsubseteq \neg Researcher, Researcher(peter)\} \cup \tag{1}$$
$$\{Student' \sqsubseteq Student\} \cup \tag{2}$$
$$\{Student \sqsubseteq Student' \sqcup Researcher\} \cup \tag{3}$$
$$\{Student(peter)\} \tag{4}$$

As the receiver trusts the sender, it adopts the sender's reading of "student" and hides its own reading in the internal vocabulary as *Student'*. As the notions are assumed to be similar, they are related by two bridging axioms: the first (line (2)) is an upper bound for *Student'*, stating that *Student'* is a subconcept of *Student*. The second one (line (3)) is an upper bound for *Student*.

In order to motivate the second bound let us write it the equivalent form {*Student* ⊓ ¬*Researcher* ⊑ *Student'*}. This axiom says that a *Student* (student in the sender's sense) is a *Student'* (student in the receiver's sense) except for the case that it is also a researcher. The concept *Researcher* which expresses the exception and hence the difference between *Student* and *Student'* is found by exploiting the ontology for a compatible conceptual representation for the constant *peter* involved in the conflict. In order to find this conceptual representation the reinterpretation operator extracts the *most specific concept* $msc_O(peter)$ for *peter* and than does a form of concept contraction based on spheres: it weakens the original concept *Student* in the ontology such that it does not contain one of the conflicting properties of peter, mentioned in $msc_O(peter)$, anymore. That is, the student concept is contracted with the negation of $msc_O(peter)$. The result of this is exactly the upper bound *Student'* ⊔ *Researcher* for *Student*.

3 Revision and Contraction of Concepts

The reinterpretation operators considered in this paper are based on the revision and contraction of (atomic or complex) DL concepts as defined in [4].

Let $\mathcal{O} = \langle O, \mathcal{V}_p, \mathcal{V}_i \rangle$ be an ontology. Let $\mathcal{V}_{rel} \subseteq \mathcal{V}_i \cup \mathcal{V}_p$ be a subset of the whole vocabulary, called the relevant vocabulary. It is possible to define a Tarskian consequence operator $C_{\mathcal{O}}^{\Uparrow} = (C)_{\mathcal{O}, \mathcal{V}_{rel}}^{\Uparrow}$ on the set of concepts C over $conc(\mathcal{V}_{rel})$. (See long version of this paper.) A set $X \subseteq conc(\mathcal{V}_{rel})$ is called *consistent* iff $\bot \notin X$. $X \subseteq conc(\mathcal{V}_{rel})$ is *maximally* $(\mathcal{O}, \mathcal{V}_{rel})$-*consistent* iff X is consistent, $(\mathcal{O}, \mathcal{V}_{rel})$-closed and inclusion maximal with this property. The set of maximally $(\mathcal{O}, \mathcal{V}_{rel})$-consistent sets X is denoted $M_{\mathcal{O}, \mathcal{V}_{rel}}$. Let $M_{\mathcal{O}} = M_{\mathcal{O}, (\mathcal{V}(\mathcal{O}) \cap \mathcal{V}_i) \cup \mathcal{V}_p}$. Intuitively, $M_{\mathcal{O}}$ denotes the set of all "possible objects" in ontology $\mathcal{O}$. The "dynamics" of possible objects under changing axioms, vocabularies, resp. are captured by the following propositions.

Proposition 1. *Let $\mathcal{O}_1 = \langle O_1, \mathcal{V}_p, \mathcal{V}_i \rangle$, $\mathcal{O}_2 = \langle O_2, \mathcal{V}_p, \mathcal{V}_i \rangle$ and $\mathcal{V} \subseteq \mathcal{V}_p \cup \mathcal{V}_i$. Then $O_1 \subseteq O_2$ entails $M_{\mathcal{O}_2, \mathcal{V}} \subseteq M_{\mathcal{O}_1, \mathcal{V}}$.*

Proposition 2. *Let $\mathcal{O} = \langle O_1, \mathcal{V}_p, \mathcal{V}_i \rangle$ be an ontology, $\mathcal{V}_1, \mathcal{V}_2 \subseteq \mathcal{V}_p \cup \mathcal{V}_i$ be vocabularies and assume that the consequence operator $(\cdot)_{\mathcal{O}, \mathcal{V}_i \cup \mathcal{V}_p}^{\Uparrow}$ fulfills the interpolation property. If $\mathcal{V}_1 \subseteq \mathcal{V}_2$, then for the injective function $F_{\mathcal{O}, \mathcal{V}_1, \mathcal{V}_2} :$ $M_{\mathcal{O}, \mathcal{V}_1} \xrightarrow{inj} \mathcal{P}(M_{\mathcal{O}, \mathcal{V}_2}); X \mapsto F_{\mathcal{O}, \mathcal{V}_1, \mathcal{V}_2}(X) = \{Y \in M_{\mathcal{O}, \mathcal{V}_2} \mid Y \supseteq X\}$ it holds that $M_{\mathcal{O}, \mathcal{V}_2} = \biguplus_{X \in M_{\mathcal{O}, \mathcal{V}_1}} F_{\mathcal{O}, \mathcal{V}_1, \mathcal{V}_2}(X)$.*

For concept representation $\underline{C}$, i.e., a set of concepts, let $[\underline{C}]^{\mathcal{O}} = \{X \in M_{\mathcal{O}} \mid \underline{C} \subseteq X\}$ be the set of possible objects $X \in M_{\mathcal{O}}$ that are not in conflict with $\underline{C}$. This adapts Grove's model bracket [3]. For a concept C we let $[C]^{\mathcal{O}}$ abbreviate $[C_{\mathcal{O}}^{\Uparrow}]^{\mathcal{O}}$. With this machinery we recapitulate the notion of a system of spheres of [4].

Definition 1 ([4]). *For an ontology $\mathcal{O} = \langle O, \mathcal{V}_p, \mathcal{V}_i \rangle$ and a subset $\mathcal{W} \subseteq M_{\mathcal{O}}$ a family of sets $\mathcal{S} \subseteq \mathcal{P}(M_{\mathcal{O}})$ is called a* system of spheres *(for short SoS) for $\mathcal{W}$ in $\mathcal{O}$ iff the following conditions are fulfilled: 1. $\mathcal{S}$ is totally ordered w.r.t. set* *inclusion; 2. $\mathcal{W}$ is inclusion minimal in $\mathcal{S}$; 3. $M_{\mathcal{O}}$ is inclusion maximal in $\mathcal{S}$; for all concepts C the following holds: If there is a sphere $S \in \mathcal{S}$ with $[C]^{\mathcal{O}} \cap S \neq \emptyset$, then there is an inclusion minimal sphere $S_{min} \in \mathcal{S}$ with $[C]^{\mathcal{O}} \cap S_{min} \neq \emptyset$. Let $c_{\mathcal{S}}$ denote the function that selects for each $[C]^{\mathcal{O}}$ the minimal sphere with non-empty intersection with $[C]^{\mathcal{O}}$ (which must exist due to condition 4.) One sets $c_{\mathcal{S}}(\emptyset) = M_{\mathcal{O}}$. Furthermore, let $f_{\mathcal{S}}([C]^{\mathcal{O}}) = c_{\mathcal{S}}([C]^{\mathcal{O}}) \cap [C]^{\mathcal{O}}$.*

For each SoS $\mathcal{S}$ one can define a dual chain of concept representations $T_{\mathcal{S}} = \{\bigcap S \mid S \in \mathcal{S}\}$. Because in the following examples concept representations $\bigcap S \in T_{\mathcal{S}}$ are equivalently describable by concepts C_S due to $((\bigcap S)^{\Uparrow}_{\mathcal{O}} = (K_S)^{\Uparrow}_{\mathcal{O}})$, we will describe a SoS by the set of concepts $\{C_S \mid S \in \mathcal{S}\}$. Sphere-based revision and contraction of concepts in an ontology are defined as follows.

Definition 2. *Let $\mathcal{O} = \langle O, \mathcal{V}_p, \mathcal{V}_i \rangle$ be an ontology, $\underline{C}$ be an $\mathcal{O}$-closed concept representation and D a concept from $conc((\mathcal{V}(\mathcal{O}) \cap \mathcal{V}_i) \cup \mathcal{V}_p)$. Furthermore let $\mathcal{S}$ be a SoS for $[\underline{C}]^{\mathcal{O}}$ in $\mathcal{O}$. Then sphere-based revision of $\mathcal{O}$-closed concept representations $@_{\mathcal{S}}$ and sphere-based contraction of $\mathcal{O}$-closed concept representations $\ominus_{\mathcal{S}}$ are defined by $\underline{C} @_{\mathcal{S}} D = \bigcap (f_{\mathcal{S}}([D]^{\mathcal{O}}))$, $\underline{C} \ominus_{\mathcal{S}} D = (\underline{C} @_{\mathcal{S}} \neg D) \cap \underline{C}$, resp. Revision and contraction of single concepts are defined by $C @_{\mathcal{S}} D = C^{\Uparrow}_{\mathcal{O}} @_{\mathcal{S}} D$, $C \ominus_{\mathcal{S}} D = C^{\Uparrow}_{\mathcal{O}} \ominus_{\mathcal{S}} D$ resp.*

As the $\mathcal{O}$-closure operator $(\cdot)^{\Uparrow}_{\mathcal{O}}$ is a Tarskian consequence operator, one can prove that $@_{\mathcal{S}}$ and $\ominus_{\mathcal{S}}$ fulfill exactly those properties—adapted from sentences to concepts—that are fulfilled by the operators of [3].

4   Sphere-Based Reinterpretation

Using $\ominus_{\mathcal{S}}$ we now formally define sphere-based reinterpretation operators. Their input is an ontology and a trigger information, that is a *concept-based literal*, i.e. has the form $K(a)$ or $\neg K(a)$ for an atomic concept symbol K, for short: the form $\hat{K}(a)$. Their output is a new ontology. The input ontology $\mathcal{O}$ is equipped with a family of many SoS: For all concept symbols $K \in \mathcal{V}_p$ there is a SoS $[K]^{\mathcal{O}}$, and a SoS $[\neg K]^{\mathcal{O}}$ for its negation.

Definition 3. *A collection of systems of spheres $\mathbb{S}$ of $\mathcal{O} = \langle O, \mathcal{V}_p, \mathcal{V}_i \rangle$ for concept-based literals over $\mathcal{V}_p$, for short $\langle \mathbb{S}(\hat{K}) \rangle_{\hat{K} \in CLit(\mathcal{V}_p)}$, is a family of SoS for each set of models $[\hat{K}]^{\mathcal{O}}$ of a concept literal $\hat{K}$ over $\mathcal{V}_p$. A pair $\langle \mathcal{O}, \mathbb{S} \rangle$ of an ontology $\mathcal{O}$ and a collection of SoS for $\mathcal{O}$ is called structured ontology.*

$\langle \mathcal{O}_1, \mathbb{S}^1 \rangle$ and $\langle \mathcal{O}_2, \mathbb{S}_2 \rangle$ are called equivalent, for short $\langle \mathcal{O}_1, \mathbb{S}_1 \rangle \stackrel{\cong}{=} \langle \mathcal{O}_2, \mathbb{S}_2 \rangle$ iff $\mathcal{O}_1 \equiv \mathcal{O}_2$ and additionally the collections of SoS are identical, $\mathbb{S}_1 = \mathbb{S}_2$.

The definition of sphere-based reinterpretation operators (Definition 4) relies on *weak operators* for reinterpretation defined in [2] as follows:

$$O \otimes K(a) = \begin{cases} O \cup \{K(a)\} & \text{if } O \cup \{K(a)\} \text{ is consistent,} \\ O_{[K/K']} \cup \{K(a), K' \sqsubseteq K\} & \text{else} \end{cases}$$

$$O \otimes \neg K(a) = \begin{cases} O \cup \{\neg K(a)\} & \text{if } O \cup \{\neg K(a)\} \text{ is consistent,} \\ O_{[K/K']} \cup \{\neg K(a), K \sqsubseteq K'\} & \text{else} \end{cases}$$

Definition 4. *Let* $\langle \mathcal{O}, \mathbb{S} \rangle$ *be a structured ontology.* Sphere-based reinterpretation $\odot_{\mathbb{S}}$ *for concept-based literals is defined by*

$$O \odot_{\mathbb{S}} \hat{K}(a) = \begin{cases} O \cup \{\hat{K}(a)\} & \text{if } O \cup \{\hat{K}(a)\} \text{ is consistent,} \\ O \otimes \hat{K}(a) \cup \{\hat{K} \sqsubseteq C \mid C \in (\hat{K} \ominus_{\mathbb{S}(\hat{K})} \neg msc_O(a))_{[K/K']}\} & \text{else} \end{cases}$$

The properties of these operators are listed in the following theorem. Some of the postulates have already been discussed by [1] for belief revision. Other postulates (such as the postulate RI-right preservation) are postulates that express desirable properties for semantic integration scenarios (see [5] for a discussion).

Theorem 1. *For structured ontologies* $\langle \mathcal{O}, \mathbb{S} \rangle$, $\langle \mathcal{O}_1, \mathbb{S}_1 \rangle$, *and* $\langle \mathcal{O}_2, \mathbb{S}_2 \rangle$ *and concept-based literals* α *and* β *the following holds:*

1. *If* $\langle \mathcal{O}_1, \mathbb{S}_1 \rangle \stackrel{\sim}{=} \langle \mathcal{O}_2, \mathbb{S}_2 \rangle$ *then* $(O_1 \odot_{\mathbb{S}_1} \alpha) \equiv (O_2 \odot_{\mathbb{S}_2} \alpha)$.   *(RI-left extensionality)*
2. *If* $\alpha \equiv \beta$, *then* $(O \odot_{\mathbb{S}} \alpha) \equiv (O \odot_{\mathbb{S}} \beta)$.   *(RI-right extensionality)*
3. $O \odot_{\mathbb{S}} \alpha = O \cup \{\alpha\}$ *iff* $O \cup \{\alpha\} \not\models \bot$.   *(RI-vacuity)*
4. $\alpha \in O \odot_{\mathbb{S}} \alpha$ *(RI-success)*
5. *There is a substitution* σ *s.t.* $O\sigma \subseteq O \odot_{\mathbb{S}} \alpha$.   *(RI-left preservation)*
6. *There is a substitution* σ *s.t.* $\alpha\sigma \in O \odot_{\mathbb{S}} \alpha$.   *(RI-right preservation)*
7. *There is a substitution* σ *s.t.* $O \subseteq (O \odot_{\mathbb{S}} \alpha)\sigma$.   *(RI-left recoverability)*
8. *There is a substitution* σ *s.t.* $\alpha \in (O \odot_{\mathbb{S}} \alpha)\sigma$.   *(RI-right recoverability)*
9. $O \odot_{\mathbb{S}} \alpha \models \bot$ *iff* $O \models \bot$.   *(RI-consistency)*

As collections of SoS $\mathbb{S}$ are defined for a specific ontology $\mathcal{O}$, they are not necessarily also proper collections for the reinterpretation result $\mathcal{O} \odot_{\mathbb{S}} \alpha$. In the following we mitigate this problem by proposing an iterated sphere-based reinterpretation operator $\odot_{\mathbb{S}}$. We require SoS to fulfill a condition called (SW) that strengthens the fourth condition on SoS according to Definition 1, requiring it to be well-ordered. Adapting the terminology of [7], we call a collection of systems of spheres *well-behaved* if it contains only well-ordered systems of spheres.

Let $O_{res} = O \odot_{\mathbb{S}} \alpha$ be the result of reinterpretation with $\alpha = \hat{K}(a)$ according to the one-step sphere-based reinterpretation. The main challenge in defining the follow-up sphere collection is the change of the vocabulary: some of the symbols of the receiver's ontology become private. In order to handle this vocabulary dynamics we use function $DynP(M_{\mathcal{O}}) \longrightarrow P(M_{\mathcal{O}_{res}})$; $S \mapsto Dyn(S) = \bigcup F[S_{[K/K']}] \cap M_{\mathcal{O}_{res}}$ relying on the function F from Proposition 2.

Definition 5. *For* $\mathcal{O} = \langle O, V_p, V_i \rangle$ *and* $\alpha = \hat{K}(a)$, *let* $V_1 = (\mathcal{V}(O_{[K/K']}) \cap V_i) \cup V_p \setminus \{K\}$ *and* $V_2 = (\mathcal{V}(O_{[K/K']}) \cap V_i) \cup V_p$ *and* $F = F_{\mathcal{O},V_1,V_2}$ *be the function* $F(X) = \{Y \in M_{\mathcal{O}_{res},V_2} \mid Y \supseteq X\}$ *defined in Proposition 2. Further assume that* $\mathbb{S}$ *is a well-behaved collection of SoS w.r.t.* $\mathcal{O}$ *for concept-based literals over* V_p. *The follow-up collection of spheres of* $O_{res} = O \odot_{\mathbb{S}} \alpha$ *is defined as follows: If* $O \cup \{\alpha\} \not\models \bot$, *then for all concept literals* $\hat{L}$ *with* $L \in V_p$ *the follow-up SoS is defined as* $\mathbb{S}'(\hat{L}) = \{S \cap M_{\mathcal{O}_{res}} \mid S \in \mathbb{S}(\hat{L})\}$. *If* $O \cup \{\alpha\} \models \bot$ *and if* $L \neq K$, *then one sets* $\mathbb{S}'(\hat{L}) = \{Dyn(S) \mid S \in \mathbb{S}(\hat{L})\}$. *If* $O \cup \{\alpha\} \models \bot$ *and* $L = K$, *then:* $\mathbb{S}'(\overline{\hat{K}}) = \{[\hat{K}]^{O_{res}}\} \cup \{Dyn(S) \mid S \in \mathbb{S}(\hat{K})\}$ *and* $\mathbb{S}'(\hat{K}) =$

$\{[\hat{K}]^{\mathcal{O}_{res}}\} \cup \{Dyn(\hat{K} \ominus_{\mathbb{S}(\hat{K})} \neg msc_O(a))\} \cup \{Dyn(S) \mid S \in \mathbb{S}(\hat{K}) \text{ and } Dyn(S) \supseteq$
$Dyn(\hat{K} \ominus_{\mathbb{S}(\hat{K})} \neg msc_O(a))\}$. (Here we use the notation $\overline{\hat{K}} = \neg K$ if $\hat{K} = K$ and
$\overline{\hat{K}} = K$ if $\hat{K} = \neg K$.)

The follow-up collection of systems of spheres $\mathbb{S}'$ of Definition 5 are well-behaved.

An iterated operator is called *stable* [2] if after some step the outcomes of the operator do not change anymore—assuming that the set of triggers in the input sequence is finite. (Triggers may be sent more than once.) Sphere-based revision reinterpretation is strong in the sense that it does not forget about the reinterpretation history—and hence stability is not guaranteed.

Theorem 2. *Iterated sphere-based reinterpretation operators are not stable.*

For the proof one may use the same example as in [2, Theorem 7.15].

5   Conclusion

Following the general idea of reinterpretation for resolving conflicts caused by inter-ontological ambiguities, this paper defined iterable reinterpretation operators that rely on the preference structure of systems of spheres and showed (at least for the single-step case) that it fulfills some desirable properties.

Questions for future work are: What is a full characterization of iterated sphere-based reinterpretation operators via postulates? What is the best way to extend the approach to handle not only concept-based literals but also whole triggering ontologies—using still systems of spheres?

References

1. Alchourrón, C.E., Gärdenfors, P., Makinson, D.: On the logic of theory change: partial meet contraction and revision functions. J. Symb. Log. **50**, 510–530 (1985)
2. Eschenbach, C., Özçep, Ö.L.: Ontology revision based on reinterpretation. Log. J. IGPL **18**(4), 579–616 (2010)
3. Grove, A.: Two modellings for theory change. J. Philos. Log. **17**, 157–170 (1988)
4. Özçep, Ö.L.: Ontology revision through concept contraction. In: Artemov, S., Parikh, R. (eds.) Proceedings of the Workshop on Rationality and Knowledge at ESSLLI-06, pp. 79–90 (2006)
5. Özçep, Ö.L.: Towards principles for ontology integration. In: Eschenbach, C., Grüninger, M. (eds.) FOIS. Frontiers in Artificial Intelligence and Applications, vol. 183, pp. 137–150. IOS Press (2008)
6. Özçep, Ö.L.: Iterated ontology revision by reinterpretation. In: Kern-Isberner, G., Wassermann, R. (eds.) Proceedings of the 16th International Workshop on Non-Monotonic Reasoning, NMR-2016, pp. 105–114 (2016)
7. Peppas, P.: The limit assumption and multiple revision. J. Log. Comput. **14**(3), 355–371 (2004)
8. Wassermann, R., Fermé, E.: A note on prototype revision. Spinning Ideas. Electronic Essays Dedicated to Peter Gärdenfors on his 50th Birthday (1999). http://www.lucs.lu.se/spinning/

Sparse Approximation for Gaussian Process with Derivative Observations

Ang Yang[✉], Cheng Li, Santu Rana, Sunil Gupta, and Svetha Venkatesh

Center for Pattern Recognition and Data Analytics, Deakin University,
Geelong, Australia
{leon.yang,cheng.l,santu.rana,sunil.gupta,svetha.venkatesh}@deakin.edu.com

Abstract. We propose a sparse Gaussian process model to approximate full Gaussian process with derivatives when a large number of function observations t and derivative observations t' exist. By introducing a small number of inducing point m, the complexity of posterior computation can be reduced from $\mathcal{O}((t+t')^3)$ to $\mathcal{O}((t+t')m^2)$. We also find the usefulness of our approach in Bayesian optimisation. Experiments demonstrate the superiority of our approach.

Keywords: Sparse Gaussian process model
Bayesian optimisation · Derivative-based

1 Introduction

Gaussian process (GP) has been widely used for regression and classification tasks. It is a Bayesian method which specifies a prior distribution on the latent functions. Generic Gaussian process focuses on the observations of the function. Recent works have shown that the model accuracy can be improved by not only the function observations but also the derivative observations [1–6]. It is straightforward to use GP to model the combination of function observations and derivative observations due to the fact that the derivative of GP is still a GP [3].

A practical limitation of GP with derivative observations is that its computation expense increases rapidly with the size of training set. We shall recall that each derivative observation is a vector and each entry is a separate observation for GP. So the number of total observations also scales with the dimension. Generally, GP with derivatives requires $\mathcal{O}((t + t')^3)$ time to compute the Cholesky decomposition of a $(t+t') \times (t+t')$ covariance matrix, where t is the number of function observations and t' is the number of derivative observations. Therefore, it becomes very difficult to apply GP with derivative observations to large scale data sets. Similar limitation can also be found in the generic GP [7–11].

The focus of this paper is on deriving an efficient sparse GP model to approximate the full GP with derivative observations while preserving its predictive accuracy. We use a set of inducing variables, which contains the number of m inducing points and $m \leq t$. Firstly, we assume that the function observations and

© Springer Nature Switzerland AG 2018
T. Mitrovic et al. (Eds.): AI 2018, LNAI 11320, pp. 507–518, 2018.
https://doi.org/10.1007/978-3-030-03991-2_46

derivative observations are conditionally independent by giving a set of inducing variables. Then the conditional distribution for a test point can be obtained by integrating out the inducing variables. To further decrease the costly computation, we introduce the fully independent conditional approximation where function observations, derivative observations and test points have no any deterministic relation on the inducing variables, so that we can ignore the covariance but remain the variance. This work is the first to develop a sparse GP model to approximate the full GP with derivative observations. The resultant sparse GP model is named sparse Gaussian process with derivatives, requiring the time $\mathcal{O}((t + t')m^2)$ for posterior computation. We have applied the proposed model in regression and Bayesian optimisation [12] on large scale datasets. The experimental results show the effectiveness of our proposed model.

2   Background

2.1   Gaussian Process

Gaussian processes [13] is a strategy of specifying prior distributions over the space of smooth functions. The property of the Gaussian distribution allows us to compute the predictive mean and variance in the closed form. A GP is specified by its mean function $\mu(\boldsymbol{x})$ and covariance function $k(\boldsymbol{x}, \boldsymbol{x}')$. A sample from a Gaussian process is a function given as

$$f(\boldsymbol{x}) \sim \mathcal{N}(\mu(\boldsymbol{x}), k(\boldsymbol{x}, \boldsymbol{x}'))$$

where $\mathcal{N}$ is a Gaussian distribution and $\boldsymbol{x}$ denotes a D-dimensional vector. Without any loss in generality, the prior mean function can be assumed to be a zero function making the Gaussian process fully defined by the covariance function. A popular choice of kernel is the squared exponential function,

$$(\boldsymbol{x}, \boldsymbol{x}') = \sigma_f^2 exp(-\frac{1}{2}\frac{\|\boldsymbol{x} - \boldsymbol{x}'\|^2}{\rho_l^2})$$

where ρ_l is the length scale, and σ_f is the amplitude.

Given a set of observations $\mathcal{D} = \{\boldsymbol{x}_i, \boldsymbol{f}_i\}_{i=1}^{t}$, the joint distribution of observations $\mathcal{D}$ and a new point $\{\boldsymbol{x}_{t+1}, f_{t+1}\}$ in GP is a multivariate Gaussian distribution

$$\begin{bmatrix} \boldsymbol{f}_{1:t} \\ f_{t+1} \end{bmatrix} \sim \mathcal{N}\left(\boldsymbol{0}, \begin{bmatrix} K & \mathbf{k} \\ \mathbf{k}^T & k(\boldsymbol{x}_{t+1}, \boldsymbol{x}_{t+1}) \end{bmatrix}\right)$$

where $\boldsymbol{f}_{1:t} = \{f(\boldsymbol{x}_i)\}_{i=1}^{t}$, $\mathbf{k} = [k(\boldsymbol{x}_{t+1}, \boldsymbol{x}_1)\ k(\boldsymbol{x}_{t+1}, \boldsymbol{x}_2) \ldots k(\boldsymbol{x}_{t+1}, \boldsymbol{x}_t)]$, and K is the kernel matrix given by

$$K = \begin{bmatrix} k(\boldsymbol{x}_1, \boldsymbol{x}_1) \ldots k(\boldsymbol{x}_1, \boldsymbol{x}_t) \\ \vdots \quad \ddots \quad \vdots \\ k(\boldsymbol{x}_t, \boldsymbol{x}_1) \ldots k(\boldsymbol{x}_t, \boldsymbol{x}_t) \end{bmatrix}$$

Then the predictive distribution of f_{t+1} can be computed as

$$P(f_{t+1}|\mathcal{D}_{1:t}, \boldsymbol{x}_{t+1}) = \mathcal{N}(\mu(\boldsymbol{x}_{t+1}), \sigma^2(\boldsymbol{x}_{t+1}))$$

with the predicted mean and variance

$$\mu(\boldsymbol{x}_{t+1}) = \mathbf{k}^T K^{-1} \boldsymbol{f}_{1:t}$$
$$\sigma^2(\boldsymbol{x}_{t+1}) = k(\boldsymbol{x}_{t+1}, \boldsymbol{x}_{t+1}) - \mathbf{k}^T K^{-1} \mathbf{k}.$$

If the observation is a noisy estimation of the actual function value

$$y = f(\boldsymbol{x}) + \xi$$

where $\xi \sim \mathcal{N}(0, \sigma^2_{noise})$, the predicted mean and variance can be computed as

$$\mu(\boldsymbol{x}_{t+1}) = \mathbf{k}^T [K + \sigma^2_{noise} I]^{-1} \boldsymbol{y}_{1:t}$$
$$\sigma^2(\boldsymbol{x}_{t+1}) = k(\boldsymbol{x}_{t+1}, \boldsymbol{x}_{t+1}) - \mathbf{k}^T [K + \sigma^2_{noise} I]^{-1} \mathbf{k}.$$

GP is prohibitive for large data sets because its training requires $\mathcal{O}(t^3)$ time due to the inversion of the covariance matrix, where t is the number of function observations.

2.2   Sparse Gaussian Process

In sparse Gaussian process [9], it introduces a set of inducing observations $\mathcal{D}_u = \{\mathbf{M}_i, \mathbf{u}_i\}_{i=1}^m$ where $\mathbf{u} = \{\mathbf{u}_i\}_{i=1}^m$ contains values of the function at the points $\mathbf{M} = \{\mathbf{M}_i\}_{i=1}^m$, knowing as inducing points. Given prior distribution $p(\mathbf{u}) = \mathcal{N}(\mathbf{u} \mid \mathbf{0}, \boldsymbol{K}_{m,m})$, the training conditional distribution of $\boldsymbol{f}_{1:t}$ given $\mathbf{u}$ can be written as

$$p(\boldsymbol{f}_{1:t} \mid \mathbf{u}) = \mathcal{N}(\boldsymbol{f}_{1:t} \mid \boldsymbol{K}_{t,m} \boldsymbol{K}_{m,m}^{-1} \mathbf{u}, \ \boldsymbol{K}_{t,t} - \boldsymbol{Q}_{t,t}), \tag{1}$$

where $\boldsymbol{K}_{t,m}$ is the covariance matrix between all observations and inducing points and $\boldsymbol{K}_{m,m}$ is the covariance matrix between all inducing points. Besides, a shorthand notation $\boldsymbol{Q}_{a,b} = \boldsymbol{K}_{a,m} \boldsymbol{K}_{m,m}^{-1} \boldsymbol{K}_{m,b}$ is also introduced. Since $\mathbf{u}$ plays the role of observations so that the posterior mean is written as $\boldsymbol{K}_{t,m} \boldsymbol{K}_{m,m}^{-1} \mathbf{u}$. The covariance matrix has the form of the $\boldsymbol{K}_{t,t}$ minus a non-negative definite matrix $\boldsymbol{Q}_{t,t}$ which gives the measurement of how much information that $\mathbf{u}$ provides in $\boldsymbol{f}_{1:t}$. The test conditional $p(f_{t+1} \mid \mathbf{u})$ is formed the same way with Eq. (1) as

$$p(f_{t+1} \mid \mathbf{u}) = \mathcal{N}(f_{t+1} \mid \boldsymbol{K}_{t+1,m} \boldsymbol{K}_{m,m}^{-1} \mathbf{u}, \ \boldsymbol{K}_{t+1,t+1} - \boldsymbol{Q}_{t+1,t+1}), \tag{2}$$

where f_{t+1} is a test point and $\boldsymbol{K}_{t+1,m}$ is the covariance matrix between the test point and inducing points.

To recover $p(\boldsymbol{f}_{1:t}, f_{t+1})$ we can simply integrating out $\mathbf{u}$ from the joint GP prior $p(\boldsymbol{f}_{1:t}, f_{t+1}, \mathbf{u})$ as

$$p(\boldsymbol{f}_{1:t}, f_{t+1}) = \int p(\boldsymbol{f}_{1:t}, f_{t+1}, \mathbf{u}) \, d\mathbf{u} = \int p(\boldsymbol{f}_{1:t}, f_{t+1} \mid \mathbf{u}) p(\mathbf{u}) d\mathbf{u}$$

In the first stage of approximation, we make the assumption that $\boldsymbol{f}_{1:t}$ and f_{t+1} are conditionally independent given $\mathbf{u}$, so the joint distribution of them can be written as

$$p(\boldsymbol{f}_{1:t}, f_{t+1}) \approx q(\boldsymbol{f}_{1:t}, f_{t+1}) = \int q(\boldsymbol{f}_{1:t} \mid \mathbf{u})q(f_{t+1} \mid \mathbf{u})p(\mathbf{u})d\mathbf{u}$$

The sparse approximation is then derived by making additional assumptions about the $q(\boldsymbol{f}_{1:t} \mid \mathbf{u})$ and $q(f_{t+1} \mid \mathbf{u})$.

2.3 Gaussian Process with Derivative Observations

The joint distribution of a function observation and a derivative observation is analytically tractable as the derivatives of a Gaussian process is still a GP [3]. The joint distribution is given as

$$\begin{bmatrix} f \\ \nabla f \end{bmatrix} \sim \mathcal{N}\left(\mathbf{0}, \begin{bmatrix} k_{[f,f]} & k_{[f,\nabla f]} \\ k_{[\nabla f,f]} & k_{[\nabla f,\nabla f]} \end{bmatrix}\right) \tag{3}$$

In terms of the squared exponential covariance function, the covariance between function values and partial derivatives can be written as [1]

$$cov(f^i, \frac{\partial f^j}{\partial x_g^{(j)}}) = \sigma_f^2 exp(-\tfrac{1}{2}\textstyle\sum_{b=1}^{D} \rho_l^{-2}(x_b^{(i)} - x_b^{(j)})^2) \times (\rho_l^{-2}(x_g^{(i)} - x_g^{(j)}))$$

and covariance between partial derivatives is given as

$$cov(\frac{\partial f^j}{\partial x_g^{(i)}}, \frac{\partial f^j}{\partial x_h^{(j)}}) =$$
$$\sigma_f^2 exp(-\tfrac{1}{2}\textstyle\sum_{b=1}^{D} \rho_l^{-2}(x_b^{(i)} - x_b^{(j)})^2) \times \rho_l^{-2}(\delta_{gh} - \rho_l^{-2}(x_h^{(i)} - x_h^{(j)})(x_g^{(i)} - x_g^{(j)}))$$

where $\delta_{gh} = 1$ if $g = h$, and $\delta_{gh} = 0$ if $g \neq h$.

Suppose we have extra derivative observations upon giving function observations $\mathcal{D}$ and we denote the set as $\mathcal{D}' = \{\boldsymbol{x}_j, \nabla \boldsymbol{f}_j\}_{j=1}^{t'}$, where $\nabla \boldsymbol{f}_{1,t'} = \{\nabla f(\boldsymbol{x}_j)\}_{j=1}^{t'}$. Now using GP we can derive the posterior over a new function value f_{t+1} at $\boldsymbol{x}_{t+1}$ when given a set of observations of the function values and a set of derivative information. We use $\bar{K}_{[f_{1:t}, \nabla f_{1:t'}]}$ to denote the joint covariance matrix over a set of observations of function values and the derivatives. Then the new joint distribution for $[\boldsymbol{f}_{1:t}, \nabla \boldsymbol{f}_{1:t'}, f_{t+1}]$ is showing as

$$\begin{bmatrix} \boldsymbol{f}_{1:t} \\ \nabla \boldsymbol{f}_{1:t'} \\ f_{t+1} \end{bmatrix} \sim \mathcal{N}\left(\mathbf{0}, \begin{bmatrix} \bar{K}_{[f_{1:t}, \nabla f_{1:t'}]} & \bar{\mathbf{k}} \\ \bar{\mathbf{k}}^T & k(\boldsymbol{x}_{t+1}, \boldsymbol{x}_{t+1}) \end{bmatrix}\right) \tag{4}$$

3 Proposed Framework

Full GP with derivative observations becomes prohibitive when a large number of function observations and derivative observations exist due to the high computational cost. We propose a sparse model to approximate the full GP with derivative observations while preserving the desirable properties of it. Firstly, we derive our model named sparse Gaussian process with derivatives (SGPD). Then we apply the proposed sparse method as the probabilistic model in Bayesian optimisation.

3.1   Sparse Gaussian Process with Derivatives for Regression

Similar with sparse GP, we induce a set of variables $\mathbf{u}$ and use the same notations as before. We can easily get the following equation by marginalizing out $\mathbf{u}$

$$p(\boldsymbol{f}_{1:t}, \nabla\boldsymbol{f}_{1:t'}, f_{t+1}) = \int p(\boldsymbol{f}_{1:t}, \nabla\boldsymbol{f}_{1:t'}, f_{t+1} \mid \mathbf{u})p(\mathbf{u})\mathrm{d}\mathbf{u} \qquad (5)$$

Further we make the assumption that function observation, derivative observations and test points only depend on the inducing variables $\mathbf{u}$. Then we can rewrite the Eq. (5) as

$$p(\boldsymbol{f}_{1:t}, \nabla\boldsymbol{f}_{1:t'}, f_{t+1}) = \int p(\boldsymbol{f}_{1:t} \mid \mathbf{u})p(\nabla\boldsymbol{f}_{1:t'} \mid \mathbf{u})p(f_{t+1} \mid \mathbf{u})p(\mathbf{u})\mathrm{d}\mathbf{u} \qquad (6)$$

Therefore we next show how to compute the conditional distributions $p(\boldsymbol{f}_{1:t} \mid \mathbf{u})$, $p(\nabla\boldsymbol{f}_{1:t'} \mid \mathbf{u})$ and $p(f_{t+1} \mid \mathbf{u})$ using both exact expressions and approximate expressions.

Given the prior $p(\mathbf{u}) = \mathcal{N}(\mathbf{u} \mid \mathbf{0}, \boldsymbol{K}_{m,m})$, the exact expression for $p(\boldsymbol{f}_{1:t} \mid \mathbf{u})$ can be computed as

$$p(\boldsymbol{f}_{1:t} \mid \mathbf{u}) = \mathcal{N}(\boldsymbol{f}_{1:t} \mid \boldsymbol{K}_{t,m}\boldsymbol{K}_{m,m}^{-1}\mathbf{u}, \boldsymbol{K}_{t,t} - \boldsymbol{Q}_{t,t}) \qquad (7)$$

where we recall $\boldsymbol{Q}_{a,b} = \boldsymbol{K}_{a,m}\boldsymbol{K}_{m,m}^{-1}\boldsymbol{K}_{m,b}$. Similarly, the conditional distribution for a test point $\{\boldsymbol{x}_{t+1}, f_{t+1}\}$ is

$$p(f_{t+1} \mid \mathbf{u}) = \mathcal{N}(f_{t+1} \mid \boldsymbol{K}_{t+1,m}\boldsymbol{K}_{m,m}^{-1}\mathbf{u}, \boldsymbol{K}_{t+1,t+1} - \boldsymbol{Q}_{t+1,t+1}) \qquad (8)$$

and the conditional distribution for derivative observations is

$$p(\nabla\boldsymbol{f}_{1:t'} \mid \mathbf{u}) = \mathcal{N}(\nabla\boldsymbol{f}_{1:t'} \mid \boldsymbol{K}_{t',m}\boldsymbol{K}_{m,m}^{-1}\mathbf{u}, \boldsymbol{K}_{t',t'} - \boldsymbol{Q}_{t',t'}) \qquad (9)$$

It is noted that $\boldsymbol{K}_{t',m}$ is the covariance matrix between derivative observations $\nabla\boldsymbol{f}_{1:t'}$ and inducing variables $\mathbf{u}$ and $\boldsymbol{Q}_{t',t'} = \boldsymbol{K}_{t',m}\boldsymbol{K}_{m,m}^{-1}\boldsymbol{K}_{m,t'}$.

There are several methods to approximate conditional distributions in Eqs. (7, 8 and 9) and Joaquin and Carl [9] have provided a unifying view of them. In our framework, we use the fully independent conditional (FIC) approximation where training function observations, derivative observations and test points are fully independent on $\mathbf{u}$.

Now we can derive the approximate expression of $p(\boldsymbol{f}_{1:t} \mid \mathbf{u})$ as

$$q(\boldsymbol{f}_{1:t} \mid \mathbf{u}) = \mathcal{N}(\boldsymbol{K}_{t,m}\boldsymbol{K}_{m,m}^{-1}\mathbf{u}, diag[\boldsymbol{K}_{t,t} - \boldsymbol{Q}_{t,t}]) \qquad (10)$$

where $diag[\boldsymbol{K}_{t,t} - \boldsymbol{Q}_{t,t}]$ is a diagonal matrix whose elements match the diagonal of $\boldsymbol{K}_{t,t} - \boldsymbol{Q}_{t,t}$ so that we only keep the variance information of function observations themselves and ignore covariance between function observations and inducing points. Then $\boldsymbol{f}_{1:t}$ have no any deterministic relation on $\mathbf{u}$. Likewise, the approximate expression for $p(f_{t+1} \mid \mathbf{u})$ can write as

$$q(f_{t+1} \mid \mathbf{u}) = \mathcal{N}(\boldsymbol{K}_{t+1,m}\boldsymbol{K}_{m,m}^{-1}\mathbf{u}, \; diag[\boldsymbol{K}_{t+1,t+1} - \boldsymbol{Q}_{t+1,t+1}]) \qquad (11)$$

and the approximated format for $p(\nabla \boldsymbol{f}_{1:t'} \mid \mathbf{u})$ is

$$q(\nabla \boldsymbol{f}_{1:t'} \mid \mathbf{u}) = \mathcal{N}(\boldsymbol{K}_{t',m}\boldsymbol{K}_{m,m}^{-1}\mathbf{u}, \; diag[\boldsymbol{K}_{t',t'} - \boldsymbol{Q}_{t',t'}]) \qquad (12)$$

By substituting Eqs. (10, 11 and 12) into Eq. (6) we can give the FIC approximate joint distribution

$$q(\boldsymbol{f}_{1:t}, \nabla \boldsymbol{f}_{1:t'}, f_{t+1}) = \mathcal{N}\left(\mathbf{0}, \begin{bmatrix} \boldsymbol{KQ}_t & \boldsymbol{Q}_{t,t'} & \boldsymbol{Q}_{t,t+1} \\ \boldsymbol{Q}_{t',t} & \boldsymbol{KQ}_{t'} & \boldsymbol{Q}_{t',t+1} \\ \boldsymbol{Q}_{t+1,t} & \boldsymbol{Q}_{t+1,t'} & \boldsymbol{KQ}_{t+1} \end{bmatrix}\right) \qquad (13)$$

where $\boldsymbol{KQ}_t = \boldsymbol{Q}_{t,t} + diag[\boldsymbol{K}_{t,t} - \boldsymbol{Q}_{t,t}]$, $\boldsymbol{KQ}_{t'} = \boldsymbol{Q}_{t',t'} + diag[\boldsymbol{K}_{t',t'} - \boldsymbol{Q}_{t',t'}]$ and $\boldsymbol{KQ}_{t+1} = \boldsymbol{Q}_{t+1,t+1} + diag[\boldsymbol{K}_{t+1,t+1} - \boldsymbol{Q}_{t+1,t+1}]$.
The posterior distribution of the test point $\{\boldsymbol{x}_{t+1}, f_{t+1}\}$ is a Gaussian distribution

$$f(\boldsymbol{x}_{t+1}) \sim \mathcal{N}(\tilde{\mu}(\boldsymbol{x}_{t+1}), \tilde{\sigma}^2(\boldsymbol{x}_{t+1}))$$

with mean and variance as

$$\tilde{\mu}(\boldsymbol{x}_{t+1}) = \boldsymbol{Q}_{t+1,tt'}\boldsymbol{K}_{t,t'}^{FIC-1}[\boldsymbol{f}_{1:t}, \nabla \boldsymbol{f}_{1:t'}]$$

$$\tilde{\sigma}^2(\boldsymbol{x}_{t+1}) = \boldsymbol{K}_{t+1,t+1} - \boldsymbol{Q}_{t+1,tt'}\boldsymbol{K}_{t,t'}^{FIC-1}\boldsymbol{Q}_{tt',t+1}$$

where $\boldsymbol{K}_{t,t'}^{FIC} = \begin{bmatrix} \boldsymbol{Q}_{t,t} + diag[\boldsymbol{K}_{t,t} - \boldsymbol{Q}_{t,t}] & \boldsymbol{Q}_{t,t'} \\ \boldsymbol{Q}_{t',t} & \boldsymbol{Q}_{t',t'} + diag[\boldsymbol{K}_{t',t'} - \boldsymbol{Q}_{t',t'}] \end{bmatrix}$,
$\boldsymbol{Q}_{t+1,tt'} = [\boldsymbol{Q}_{t+1,t}, \boldsymbol{Q}_{t+1,t'}]$ which combines $\boldsymbol{Q}_{t+1,t}$ and $\boldsymbol{Q}_{t+1,t'}$ into one matrix and $\boldsymbol{Q}_{tt',t+1} = \boldsymbol{Q}_{t+1,tt'}^T$.
If the function observation is a noisy estimation of the actual function value, the predicted mean and variance can be computed as

$$\tilde{\mu}(\boldsymbol{x}_{t+1}) = \boldsymbol{Q}_{t+1,tt'}[\boldsymbol{K}_{t,t'}^{FIC} + [\begin{smallmatrix} \sigma_{noise}^2 \\ 0 \end{smallmatrix}]I]^{-1}[\boldsymbol{y}_{1:t}, \nabla \boldsymbol{f}_{1:t'}]$$

$$\tilde{\sigma}^2(\boldsymbol{x}_{t+1}) = \boldsymbol{K}_{t+1,t+1} - \boldsymbol{Q}_{t+1,tt'}[\boldsymbol{K}_{t,t'}^{FIC} + [\begin{smallmatrix} \sigma_{noise}^2 \\ 0 \end{smallmatrix}]I]^{-1}\boldsymbol{Q}_{tt',t+1}$$

Complexity Analysis. In full GP with derivatives the computational complexity for training is $\mathcal{O}((t + t')^3)$ where t is the number of function observations and t' is the number of derivative observations. The proposed method which introduced a set of inducing points $\mathbf{u}$, bring the complexity down to $\mathcal{O}((t+t')m^2)$, where m is the number of inducing points and $m \leq t$.

3.2   Application to Bayesian Optimisation

Bayesian optimisation (BO) has two main components [14]. The one is to model the latent function using Gaussian process as a prior. The other component is to search the next point where to perform the experiment. The search for the next point is guided by a surrogate function, called acquisition function. Acquisition functions are designed to trade off exploitation and exploration. High exploitation means the areas where the mean prediction for function values are high. High exploration means the areas where the epistemic uncertainty about the function values is high. There are different types of acquisition functions. Popular ones include EI [15], PI [16] and UCB [17]. In this paper, we use EI as the criteria.

Bayesian optimisation using Gaussian process as a prior can be extremely costly when there is a large number of function observations and derivative observations and it is because the size of the covariance matrix is too large. Therefore, we replace the modeling part with our method SGPD so that the time taken during optimisation will not increase regardless of the increasing number of function and derivative observations. The proposed algorithm is showing in Algorithm 1.

Algorithm 1. Bayesian Optimisation Using SGPD

Input data: $\mathcal{D} = \{\boldsymbol{x}_i, \boldsymbol{f}_i\}_{i=1}^t$, $\mathcal{D}' = \{\boldsymbol{x}_j, \nabla \boldsymbol{f}_j\}_{j=1}^{t'}$ and $\mathcal{D}_u = \{\mathbf{M}_i, \mathbf{u}_i\}_{i=1}^m$
1: **for** $n = 1, 2,...$ **do**
2:       Model SGPD using input data.
2:       Find $\boldsymbol{x}_{t+1}$ by optimizing the acquisition function $EI(\boldsymbol{x}|\mathcal{D})$:
          $\boldsymbol{x}_{t+1} = argmax_x EI(\boldsymbol{x}|\mathcal{D})$
3:       Evaluate the objective function: $y_{t+1} = f(\boldsymbol{x}_{t+1}) + \xi$
4:       Augment the observation set $\mathcal{D} = \mathcal{D} \cup (\boldsymbol{x}_{t+1}, y_{t+1})$,
          $\mathcal{D}' = \mathcal{D}' \cup \{\boldsymbol{x}_{1:t+1'}, \boldsymbol{f}_{1:t+1'}\}$
5: **end for**

---

4   Experiments

We evaluate our method on regression tasks and application of Bayesian optimisation. We compare the proposed method SGPD with the following baselines for regression:

- Standard Gaussian process (StdGP)
- Sparse Gaussian process (SGP)
- Gaussian process with derivatives (GPD)

In Bayesian optimisation tasks, we only compare with StdGP and GPD. For all GPs we use the SE kernel with the hyperparameters - the isotropic length scale $\rho_l = 0.8$, signal variance $\sigma_f^2 = 1$ and noise variance $\sigma_{noise}^2 = (0.01)^2$. In terms of the inducing variables selection, we use a randomly selected subset of function observations as inducing points in all of our experiments.

We visualise the results for 1D function in Fig. 1. We use 30 function observations ($t = 30$) and their derivatives ($t' = 30$) as training data and use 450 points for testing. We randomly select 70% of t (21 points) as inducing points (Derivative observations will not be used as inducing points in all of our cases), then compare our method with StdGP and GPD. The mean functions of 3 methods look similar but the variance of our method SGPD has a very close format with GPD.

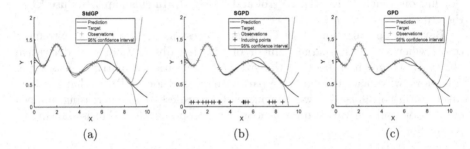

Fig. 1. The visualisation of 3 methods for regression on 1D function (a) standard Gaussian process (b) sparse Gaussian process with derivatives and (c) Gaussian process with derivatives.

4.1   Regression on Benchmark Functions

In regression tasks, we run each algorithm 50 trials with different initialisation and report the mean square error (MSE). Within each trial of SGP and SGPD, we run 50 times on randomly selecting subset to calculate the average MSE of each trial. We test our algorithm on five benchmark functions below:

1. Function with multiple local optima-1D (1D).
2. Branin function-2D (2D).
3. Hartmann-3D (3D).
4. Hartmann-4D (4D).
5. Hartmann-6D (6D).

For different functions, we use the number of training and test data referring to Table 1. The number of function observations t shows in column 2 while column 3 indicates the number of derivative observations t'. We use derivative observations at each dimension so that t' is equal to $D * t$, where D is the dimensional of the input space. We set the number of inducing points m as 70% of function observations (t) for 1D and 2D functions while setting 50% for 3D, 4D and 6D functions. We also set up an experiment to discover how our method performs if we use all function observations as inducing points ($m = t$). We summarise the MSE of each algorithm in Table 2. For all experiments, GPD has shown the best result since function observations and derivatives observations are fully used. Our method SGPD closely approximates the GPD and shows a better result than SGP as well as StdGP in all regression tasks. Besides, the setting of $m = t$ with our method achieves very comparable performance to GPD while requiring less computational complexity. While requires less computational complexity, the setting of $m = t$ in SGPD achieves very comparable performance to GPD. For example, GPD requires 300 function observations plus 1800 derivative observations in 6D case, but SGPD ($m = t$) only incorporates 300 function observations.

Table 1. Functions for regression

	Function observations	Derivative observations	Test points
1D	30	30	450
2D	200	400	800
3D	200	600	800
4D	300	1200	900
6D	300	1800	900

Table 2. Comparison of MSE results among each method for regression tasks.

	StdGP	SGP	GPD
1D	$4.81e\text{-}5 \pm 1.23e\text{-}4$	$6.20e\text{-}5 \pm 1.51e\text{-}4$ $(0.7t)$	$4.54e\text{-}6 \pm 1.19e\text{-}5$
2D	0.0164 ± 0.0200	0.0397 ± 0.0408 $(0.7t)$	$6.80e\text{-}4 \pm 0.0014$
3D	0.0786 ± 0.0145	0.0787 ± 0.0145 $(0.5t)$	0.0319 ± 0.0051
4D	0.0453 ± 0.0064	0.0473 ± 0.0066 $(0.5t))$	0.0106 ± 0.0024
6D	0.0176 ± 0.0038	0.0177 ± 0.0026 $(0.5t))$	0.0053 ± 0.0016
	SGPD	SGPD $(m = t)$	
1D	$4.68e\text{-}5 \pm 2.12e\text{-}4$ $(0.7t)$	$8.00e\text{-}6 \pm 2.92e\text{-}5$	
2D	0.0114 ± 0.0145 $(0.7t)$	0.0014 ± 0.0022	
3D	0.0368 ± 0.0072 $(0.5t)$	0.0338 ± 0.0052	
4D	0.0401 ± 0.0079 $(0.5t)$	0.0131 ± 0.0030	
6D	0.0162 ± 0.0019 $(0.5t)$	$0.0092 \pm \pm 0.0015$	

4.2   Experiments with Bayesian Optimisation

We apply our method on Bayesian optimisation for two benchmark functions:

1. Hartmann-3D, where $x^* = (0.1146, 0.5556, 0.8525)$ is the global minimum location with function value of $f(x^*) = -3.8628$.

2. Hartmann-4D, where $x^* = (0.1873, 0.1906, 0.5566, 0.2647)$ is the global minimum location with function value of $f(x^*) = -3.1355$.

We use EI as acquisition function and DIRECT [18] as optimiser to optimise EI. We run each algorithm 30 trials with different initialisation and report the simple regret and standard errors at the end. Simple regret is defined as $r = f(x^*) - f(x^+)$ where $f(x^*)$ is the global optimum and $f(x^+) = max_{x \in \{x_{1:t}\}} f(x)$ which is the current best value. Figure 2 plots the simple regret vs iteration for all experiments. BO with GPD performs the best in all three algorithms. It is easy to explain since all function observations and derivative observations have been incorporated in the algorithm. In Fig. 2a, BO with our method SGPD using 100% function observations as inducing points outperforms BO with StdGP along the entire process. Figure 2b demonstrates the result of using 50% function observation as inducing points. Although our method performs similar to StdGP at the beginning, but jump ahead after 23 iterations as more information come into SGPD. But we should emphasize that the computational cost of SGPD is less than both GPD and StdGP in this case. We also receive similar results for Hartmann-4D, and illustrate in Figs. 2c and d respectively.

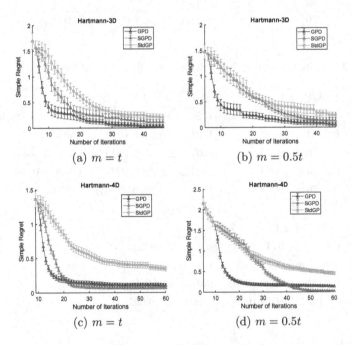

Fig. 2. Simple regret vs iterations for (a) Hartmann-3D using 100% t as inducing points (b)Hartmann-3D using 50% t as inducing points (c) Hartmann-4D using 100% t as inducing points(d) Hartmann-4D using 50% t as inducing points.

5   Conclusion

We propose a novel method for speeding up Gaussian process with derivatives in the case of a large number of function observations and derivatives observations. We also investigate the usability of our method in large scale Bayesian optimisation. For all experiments, our proposed approach closely approximate full Gaussian process with derivatives. In future, we consider to automatically estimate locations and number of inducing points and extend to other applications.

Acknowledgment. This research was partially funded by the Australian Government through the Australian Research Council (ARC). Prof Venkatesh is the recipient of an ARC Australian Laureate Fellowship (FL170100006).

References

1. Riihimäki, J., Vehtari, A.: Gaussian processes with monotonicity information. In: Proceedings of the Thirteenth International Conference on AIStat (2010)
2. Siivola, E., Vehtari, A., Vanhatalo, J., González, J.: Bayesian optimization with virtual derivative sign observations. arXiv preprint arXiv:1704.00963 (2017)
3. Solak, E., Murray-Smith, R., Leithead, W.E., Leith, D.J., Rasmussen, C.E.: Derivative observations in Gaussian process models of dynamic systems. In: NIPS (2003)
4. Jauch, M., Peña, V.: Bayesian optimization with shape constraints. arXiv preprint arXiv:1612.08915 (2016)
5. Li, C., Rana, S., Gupta, S., Nguyen, V., Venkatesh, S.: Bayesian optimization with monotonicity information (2017)
6. Yang, A., Li, C., Rana, S., Gupta, S., Venkatesh, S.: Efficient Bayesian optimisation using derivative meta-model. In: Geng, X., Kang, B.-H. (eds.) PRICAI 2018. LNCS (LNAI), vol. 11013, pp. 256–264. Springer, Cham (2018). https://doi.org/10.1007/978-3-319-97310-4_29
7. Snelson, E., Ghahramani, Z.: Sparse gaussian processes using pseudo-inputs. In: Advances in Neural Information Processing Systems, pp. 1257–1264 (2006)
8. Snelson, E., Ghahramani, Z.: Variable noise and dimensionality reduction for sparse Gaussian processes. arXiv preprint arXiv:1206.6873 (2012)
9. Quiñonero-Candela, J., Rasmussen, C.E.: A unifying view of sparse approximate Gaussian process regression. J. Mach. Learn. Res. **6**(Dec), 1939–1959 (2005)
10. Li, C., Gupta, S., Rana, S., Nguyen, V., Venkatesh, S., Shilton, A.: High dimensional Bayesian optimization using dropout. arXiv preprint arXiv:1802.05400 (2018)
11. Rana, S., Li, C., Gupta, S., Nguyen, V., Venkatesh, S.: High dimensional Bayesian optimization with elastic gaussian process. In: International Conference on Machine Learning, pp. 2883–2891 (2017)
12. Jones, D.R., Schonlau, M., Welch, W.J.: Efficient global optimization of expensive black-box functions. J. Glob. Optim. **13**(4), 455–492 (1998)
13. Rasmussen, C.E., Williams, C.K.: Gaussian Processes for Machine Learning. MIT press, Cambridge (2006)
14. Brochu, E., Cora, V.M., De Freitas, N.: A tutorial on bayesian optimization of expensive cost functions, with application to active user modeling and hierarchical reinforcement learning. arXiv preprint arXiv:1012.2599 (2010)

15. Mockus, J.: Application of Bayesian approach to numerical methods of global and stochastic optimization. J. Glob. Optim. **4**(4), 347–365 (1994)
16. Kushner, H.J.: A new method of locating the maximum point of an arbitrary multipeak curve in the presence of noise. J. Basic Eng. **86**(1), 97–106 (1964)
17. Srinivas, N., Krause, A., Kakade, S.M., Seeger, M.: Gaussian process optimization in the bandit setting: no regret and experimental design. arXiv preprint arXiv:0912.3995 (2009)
18. Finkel, D.E.: Direct optimization algorithm user guide. CRSC **2**, 1–14 (2003)

Counterfactual Inference with Hidden Confounders Using Implicit Generative Models

Fujin Zhu[1,2(✉)], Adi Lin[1], Guangquan Zhang[1], and Jie Lu[1]

[1] Centre for Artificial Intelligence, School of Software, FEIT,
University of Technology Sydney, Sydney, NSW 2007, Australia
{Fujin.Zhu,Adi.Lin}@student.uts.edu.au,
{Guangquan.Zhang,Jie.Lu}@uts.edu.au
[2] School of Management and Economics, Beijing Institute of Technology,
Beijing 100086, China

Abstract. In observational studies, a key problem is to estimate the causal effect of a treatment on some outcome. Counterfactual inference tries to handle it by directly learning the treatment exposure surfaces. One of the biggest challenges in counterfactual inference is the existence of unobserved confounders, which are latent variables that affect both the treatment and outcome variables. Building on recent advances in latent variable modelling and efficient Bayesian inference techniques, deep latent variable models, such as variational auto-encoders (VAEs), have been used to ease the challenge by learning the latent confounders from the observations. However, for the sake of tractability, the posterior of latent variables used in existing methods is assumed to be Gaussian with diagonal covariance matrix. This specification is quite restrictive and even contradictory with the underlying truth, limiting the quality of the resulting generative models and the causal effect estimation. In this paper, we propose to take advantage of implicit generative models to detour this limitation by using black-box inference models. To make inference for the implicit generative model with intractable likelihood, we adopt recent implicit variational inference based on adversary training to obtain a close approximation to the true posterior. Experiments on simulated and real data show the proposed method matches the state-of-art.

Keywords: Causal effect · Counterfactual inference · Latent variable models

1 Introduction

The problem of estimating the treatment effect of some intervention on the outcome is fundamental across many domains [1, 2]. In biology, scientists conduct randomized experiments to discover and measure the effect of genes on certain phenotypes; in healthcare, patients need to known the effect of the medication on their health to decide whether to take a particular medication or not; in economics, policy makers debate the possible effect of job training on employees' earning; and in marketing, what ad companies are really interested is the causal effect of an online advertisement on customers' purchasing habits. Due to the widespread accumulation of data in these fields, causal inference from observational data is gaining increasing research interest in the data science and machine learning community.

© Springer Nature Switzerland AG 2018
T. Mitrovic et al. (Eds.): AI 2018, LNAI 11320, pp. 519–530, 2018.
https://doi.org/10.1007/978-3-030-03991-2_47

Denote the treatment space by $\mathcal{T}$, the set of contexts by $\mathcal{X}$, and the set of possible outcomes by $\mathcal{Y}$. For example, for an employee with covariates $x \in \mathcal{X}$, the set of treatments $\mathcal{T}$ might be whether she joined a specific training program and the set of outcomes might be $\mathcal{Y} = [0, 10K]$ indicating her monthly salary in dollars. For an individual x (e.g., an employee), let $Y_t(x) \in \mathcal{Y}$ be the potential outcome of x under the treatment $t \in \mathcal{T}$. The fundamental problem of causal inference is that only one of potential outcomes $Y_t(x), t \in \mathcal{T}$ is observed for a given individual x. In the machine learning literature, this kind of partial feedback is often called "bandit feedback" [3, 4].

Without loss of generality, we consider the case of a binary treatment set, i.e., $\mathcal{T} = \{0, 1\}$, where $t = 1$ indicates the individual is allocated into the "treated" group and $t = 0$ the "control" group. In this setting, the *individual treatment effect* $ITE(x) = Y_1(x) - Y_0(x)$ for individual x is of high interest. Knowing this quantity enables us to choose the best treatment options and to give personalized recommendations. Based on ITE, the *average treatment effect*, $ATE = \mathbb{E}_{x \sim p(x)}[ITE(x)]$ for a population with distribution $p(x)$ quantifies the average treatment effect difference between the two actions. Sometimes, we are only interested in the ATE for the treated group, i.e., the *average treatment effect on the treated*, $ATT = \mathbb{E}_{x \sim p(x)}[ITE(x)|t = 1]$.

The problem of causal effect estimation from observational data has been studied extensively in the literature [5–9]. One of the most widely used approaches is counterfactual inference, also known as potential outcome modelling. The main idea is: given n samples $\mathcal{D}_{obs} = \{(x_i, t_i, y_i)\}_{i=1}^n$, where the observed "factual" outcome $y_i = t_i Y_1(x_i) + (1 - t_i) Y_0(x_i)$, if we can unbiasedly learn the potential outcome model $Y_t(x) = h(x, t)$ using the observed data, the estimated ITE is then

$$\widehat{ITE}(x_i) = \begin{cases} y_i - h(x_i, 0), t_i = 1 \\ h(x_i, 1) - y_i, t_i = 0 \end{cases} \tag{1}$$

Therefore, the key is to learn the potential outcome function $h(x, t)$. In the literature, $Y_0(x) = h(x, 0)$ and $Y_1(x) = h(x, 1)$ are also called the response surfaces. As a learning problem, this is different from classic learning in that we never see the individual-level treatment effect in the observations. For each unit, we only observe her response to one of the possible treatments – the one she actually receives. This is called *the fundamental problem of causal inference* and is known in the machine learning literature as "counterfactual learning" [5, 6] and "learning from logged bandit feedback (LFBF)" [3, 4] where we do not have access to the treatment assignment model of the observed data. Because of the existence of unobserved confounders that affect both the treatment assignment and the outcome, naively fitting the outcome model from observational data is subject to confounding bias [1, 2].

To handle the confounding bias, recently, [7, 8] make a connection between covariate shift and counterfactual inference and propose to learn a balanced representation for the explicitly observed covariates. Specifically, they introduce a balancing regularization using integral probability metric distance between the treatment and control distributions. Alternatively, in this paper, we regard counterfactual inference as a Bayesian latent-variable modeling problem, modeling the potential outcome model and the treatment assignment mechanism simultaneously to handle the confounding bias. Moreover, the proposed latent-variable modelling framework takes advantage of recent advance in deep generative modelling to model causal mechanisms with deep neural networks. Compared with the balancing scheme, the proposed method avoids the trivial derivation of generalization bounds as well as cross validation for hyper-parameter tuning.

While adapting deep generative models for counterfactual inference has recently been studied by [9], their method is based on VAEs, the posterior of latent variables used in these methods is usually assumed to be a Gaussian distribution with diagonal covariance matrix. This kind of inference model is quite restrictive and even contra-dictory with the underlying truth, limiting the estimation of the causal coefficients as well as the causal effects. To tackle this limitation, in this paper, we propose to take advantage of implicit generative models to detour this limitation by using a black-box inference model.

The reminder of this paper is organized as follows: in Sect. 2, we firstly introduce preliminary knowledge on causal models and implicit models; details of the proposed method are presented in Sect. 3; Sect. 4 illustrates our experiments on two benchmark datasets; lastly, we conclude this paper and discuss further works in Sect. 5.

2 Preliminaries

In this section, we introduce two basic components of our proposed method introduced in the next section: the structural causal models and implicit generative models.

2.1 Structural Causal Models

Structural causal models [10], or functional causal models, defined in Definition 1, represent variables as deterministic functions of their parents and exogenous noises. They take advantages of the functional causal semantics of structural equation models (SEMs) [11] and the representation and reasoning power of Bayesian networks [12].

Definition 1 (structural causal model, SCM) [10]. A structural causal model $\mathcal{M}$ is a tuple $(V, U, F, P(u))$ that consists of (i) a set of observed endogenous variables $V = \{V_1, \cdots, V_n\}$; (ii) a set of unobserved background (or exogenous) variables U; (iii) a set of causal mechanisms $F = \{f_1, \cdots, f_n\}$ that determines the endogenous variables V; and (iv) the joint distribution $P(u)$ over the background variables U. Each causal mechanism f_i tells us the value of $V_i \in V$ given the value of all other variables, i.e., $V_i \leftarrow f_i(PA_i, U), U \sim P(u)$, where $PA_i \subseteq V \setminus V_i$ is called the parents of V_i.

In this definition, endogenous variables V are regarded as deterministic functions of other variables and randomness comes from unobserved exogenous variables U. Together with Pearl's *do*-calculus and counterfactual notations [10], it permits us to answer intervention and counterfactual questions. In this paper, we consider causal models with the observed set V including a treatment variable t, an outcome variable y, and some evidence variables x that act as proxies of the unobserved confounders z. The corresponding causal graph (or data-generating process) is illustrated as in Fig. 1(a). In this setting, Theorem 1 in [9] gives the identifiability condition of causal effect.

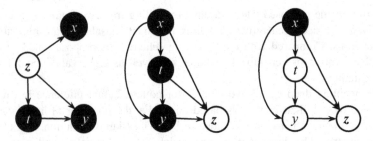

Fig. 1. Panel (a) shows the underlying causal model (the generative model). Panel (b) the inference model for within-sample observations. Panel (c) the inference model for out-of-sample data. Solid nodes are observed and hollow nodes are unobserved.

2.2 Implicit Generative Models

Implicit models (aka implicit generative models, IGMs) [13] [14] capture an unknown distribution by hypothesizing about its data-generating process. For a distribution $p(x)$ of observations x, we define a function g that takes in noise $\epsilon \sim p(\epsilon)$ and output x given parameters θ (including possible null set of parents),

$$x = g(\epsilon|\theta), \epsilon \sim p(\epsilon) \tag{2}$$

The induced implicit density of $x \in S$ given θ is

$$p(x \in S) = \int_{\{g(\epsilon|\theta)=x\in S\}} p(\epsilon)d\epsilon \tag{3}$$

In an implicit generative model, the function g is usually a deep neural network that is a universal approximator to any continuous function. By separating randomness (*noise* ϵ) from the transformation (function g), implicit generative models imitate the structural invariance of causal models [15]. A weakness of IGMs is that the integral in Eq. (3) is typically intractable and does not admit a tractable likelihood, making the inference of the parameters very difficult.

In its general form, an SCM $\mathcal{M}$ defined in Definition 1 is a non-parametric causal model, and each structural equation in F is a nonlinear, nonparametric generalization of the linear structural equation models (SEMs) [11, 16]. SCMs work regardless of the type of equations, linear or nonlinear, parametric or non-parametric. That means, SCMs provide us a framework to conduct causal modeling and reasoning. Existing simple parametric models apply simple nonlinearities such as polynomials, hand-engineered low order interactions between variables, and assume additive interactions with Gaussian noise. Deep neural networks provide us rich models to encode the causal mechanisms in high-dimensional complex causal systems. Recently, [15] proposed to use implicit causal models (ICMs). Analogous to the well known *approximator theorem* of feedforward neural networks [17], they present a similar universal approximation theorem for using implicit models to approximate causal models, as formally described in Theorem 2.

Theorem 2 (Universal Approximation). In an SCM $\mathcal{M} = (V, U, F, s(u))$, assume each causal mechanism is a continuous function on the n-dimensional unit cube $f \in \mathcal{C}([0,1]^n)$. Let σ be a non-constant, bounded, and monotonically increasing continuous function. For each causal mechanism f and any error $\delta > 0$, there exist parameters $\theta = (\alpha, \beta, b)$ for a H layer neural network, where $\alpha_h, b_h \in \mathbb{R}$ and $\beta_h \in \mathbb{R}^n$, $h = 1, 2, \ldots, H$, such that the following function approximates f:

$$\forall v \in [0,1]^n \quad g(v|\theta) = \sum_{h=1}^{H} \alpha_h \sigma\big(\beta_h^T v + b_h\big), \quad |g(v|\theta) - f(v)| < \delta$$

Besides the universal approximation property of deep implicit models for causal mechanisms, recent advances in the machine learning community, for example, approximate Bayesian computation [18], adversarial training [19, 20], and probabilistic programming [21], permit us to use fast algorithms for their Bayesian inference of the parameters.

3 Counterfactual Inference Using IGMs

In this section, we firstly introduce our proposed counterfactual inference method using implicit models. The lower bound objective and implicit variational inference method based on adversary training are then presented.

3.1 Latent Variable Modelling for Causal Models

As discussed in Sect. 1, we need to learn the potential outcome function $Y_t(x) = h(x, t)$. If the latent confounders are available, we can estimate the potential outcome by the following adjustment formula [2, 10]

$$Y_t(x) = h(x, t) = \mathbb{E}[Y_t|x] = \mathbb{E}[y|z, t] \tag{4}$$

Therefore, we need to obtain the posterior of the latent confounders, $p_\theta(z|x, t, y)$. Learning confounders for causal inference has its root from the "*abduction-action-prediction*" procedure for counterfactual inference (see Chap. 4 in [22]). Instead of such a multi-stage induction process, in this paper, we propose to jointly learn the response surfaces and latent confounder space. This is analogous to deep generative models which learn the "generative" and "inference" models jointly. The generative and inference models for our proposed method are illustrated in Fig. 1. For an observed triple (x_i, t_i, y_i), the log-likelihood is

$$\log p(x_i, t_i, y_i) = \int \log p_\theta(x_i, t_i, y_i|z_i) p(z_i) \, dz_i \tag{5}$$

where θ denotes the generative parameters. The generative model for each component in the triple (x_i, t_i, y_i) is

$$x_i \sim p_\theta(x|z_i) \tag{6}$$

$$t_i \sim p_\theta(t|z_i) \tag{7}$$

$$y_i \sim p_\theta(y|t_i, z_i) \tag{8}$$

We put Gaussian priors on the latent confounders z_i, i.e., $z_i \sim \mathcal{N}(z|0, I_M)$ where M is the dimension of z_i, and the implicit inference network (encoder) for z_i is

$$z_i = z_\phi(x_i, t_i, y_i, \epsilon), \epsilon \sim s(\cdot) \tag{9}$$

where ϕ denotes the variational parameters. Based on Eq. (3), the induced implicit density is denoted as $q_\phi(z|x, t, y)$. According to the generative models in Eqs. (6) (7) (8), we have the decoder from latent variables z_i to the observed tuple (x_i, t_i, y_i) as

$$\log p_\theta(x_i, t_i, y_i|z_i) = \log p_\theta(y_i|t_i, z_i) + \log p_\theta(t_i|z_i) + \log p_\theta(x_i|z_i) \tag{10}$$

How can this joint learning framework account for the confounding bias? This is because the posterior of the latent confounders z, $q_\phi(z|x, t, y)$, depends on both the outcome y and the treatment t. Moreover, the learning of latent confounders z are tailored to good generative models for the outcome y and the treatment t. This joint learning process will hopefully extract information from the observations to learn a good representation of the latent confounder that will account for the confounding bias. Such a philosophy is also discussed in [9] and [15].

3.2 Lower Bound Objective

To maximize the log-likelihood of the observed data

$$\ell = \sum_{(x,t,y) \in \mathcal{D}_{obs}} \mathbb{E}[\log p(x, t, y)] \tag{11}$$

variational inference minimizes the KL divergence from the variational approximation $q_\phi(z|x, t, y)$ to the posterior $p_\theta(z|x, t, y)$, $KL[q_\phi(z|x, t, y)||p_\theta(z|x, t, y)]$. This is equivalent to maximizing the *evidence lower bound*

$$\text{ELBO} = \sum_{(x,t,y) \in \mathcal{D}_{obs}} \mathbb{E}_{q_\phi(z|x,t,y)}[\log p_\theta(z, x, t, y) - \log q_\phi(z|x, t, y)] \tag{12}$$

Note that in observational causal effect estimation, the treatment assignment t and corresponding outcome y required for inferring $q_\phi(z|x,t,y)$ are not observed for new test samples. For this reason, we need to take two auxiliary approximation models into consideration in our variational lower bound.

$$t_i \sim q_\phi(t|x_i), \quad y_i \sim q_\phi(y|x_i,t_i) \tag{13}$$

This is first recognized in [9] and formalized as the following causal effect lower bound

$$\mathcal{L}^{CE} = \text{ELBO} + \sum_{i=1}^{n} \left(\log q_\phi\left(t_i^*|x_i\right) + \log q_\phi\left(y_i^*|x_i,t_i^*\right) \right) \tag{14}$$

Where $\left(x_i, t_i^*, y_i^*\right)$ are the observed values in the training set. We try to maximize this causal effect lower bound to learn the generative parameters θ and the variational parameters ϕ for counterfactual inference via Eq. (4).

3.3 Inference

Notice that the ELBO in Eq. (12) can be written as

$$\text{ELBO} = \sum_{(x,t,y) \in \mathcal{D}_{obs}} \mathbb{E}_{q_\phi(z|x,t,y)} \left[\log p_\theta(x,t,y|z) - \log \frac{q_\phi(z|x,t,y)}{p(z)} \right] \tag{15}$$

When we have an explicit representation $q_\phi(z|x,t,y)$ such as the neural network parameterized Gaussian distribution used in VAE [23] and the CEVAE, the ELBO $\mathcal{L}$ can be maximized using the reparameterization trick [23] and stochastic gradient descent. Unfortunately, when we use black-box approximation families, the implicit density $q_\phi(z|x,t,y)$ becomes intractable. In this paper, we follow [24] and define the log density ratio (or *prior contrastive*) $r(z,x,t,y,\phi) = \log \frac{q_\phi(z|x,t,y)}{p(z)}$. Then we have

$$\text{ELBO} = \mathbb{E}_{q_\phi(z|x,t,y)}[\log p_\theta(x,t,y|z) - r(z,x,t,y,\phi)] \tag{16}$$

Moreover, introducing the following objective for the discriminator $D(z,x,t,y;\psi)$

$$\max_\psi \quad \mathbb{E}_{q_\phi(z|x,t,y)}[\log \sigma(D(z,x,t,y;\psi))] + \mathbb{E}_{p(z)}[\log(1 - \sigma(D(z,x,t,y;\psi)))]$$

where $\sigma(\cdot)$ is the sigmoid activation function. The following proposition indicates that we can obtain the value of the prior contrastive via optimizing the discriminator.

Proposition 3. For fixed generative model $p_\theta(x,t,y|z)$ and inference model $q_\phi(z|x,t,y)$, the optimal discriminator parameter ψ^* is given by

$$D(z, x, t, y; \psi^*) = r(z, x, t, y, \phi) = \log q_\phi(z|x, t, y) - \log p(z)$$

Proof. The proof is analogous to the proof of Proposition 1 in [19].

As we get the optimal discriminator $D(z, x, t, y; \psi^*)$, Proposition 3 allows us to use it as a proxy of the log density ratio $r(z, x, t, y, \phi)$ and the ELBO

$$\text{ELBO} = \mathbb{E}_{q_\phi(z|x, t, y)}[\log p_\theta(x, t, y|z) - D(z, x, t, y; \psi^*)] \quad (17)$$

Substitute Eq. (17) into Eq. (14), we get the causal effect lower bound objective

$$\mathcal{L}^{CE} = \sum_{i=1}^{n} \left(\mathbb{E}_{q_\phi(z_i|x_i, t_i, y_i)}[\log p_\theta(x_i, t_i, y_i|z_i) - D(z_i, x_i, t_i, y_i; \psi^*)] + \log q_\phi(t_i^*|x_i) + \log q_\phi(y_i^*|x_i, t_i^*) \right)$$

$$(18)$$

4   Experiments

Evaluating causal inference methods using observational data is always challenging because we do not have access to the ground-truth for the target causal effects. Common evaluation approaches include creating synthetic or semi-synthetic datasets, where real data is modified in a way that allows us to know the true causal effect. In this section, we firstly introduce several metrics and baseline methods used for comparison. Experiment performances on two existing benchmark datasets, IHDP (continuous outcomes) and Jobs (binary outcomes), are then discussed to validate the proposed method. Our experiments are conducted using the TensorFlow [25] platform. The noise distributions $s(\epsilon)$ used in implicit inference networks are standard multivariate Gaussians.

4.1   Evaluation Metrics and Baselines

For causal inference evaluation, the absolute error of the ATE estimator, ϵ_{ATE}, is defined as

$$\epsilon_{ATE} = \left| \widehat{ATE} - ATE \right| = \left| \frac{1}{n} \sum_{i=1}^{n} (\hat{y}_1(x_i) - \hat{y}_0(x_i)) - \frac{1}{n} \sum_{i=1}^{n} (Y_1(x_i) - Y_0(x_i)) \right| \quad (19)$$

where $\hat{y}_t(x_i) = h(x_i, t), t = 0, 1$. Analogously, the absolute error of the ATT estimator, ϵ_{ATT}, is defined as

$$\epsilon_{ATT} = \left| \widehat{ATT} - ATT \right| = \left| \frac{1}{n_1} \sum_{t_i=1} (\hat{y}_1(x_i) - \hat{y}_0(x_i)) - \frac{1}{n_1} \sum_{t_i=1} (Y_1(x_i) - Y_0(x_i)) \right| \quad (20)$$

where n_1 is the number of units that are in the treatment group.

To evaluate the ITE estimation, when the underlying ground truth are known, the metric *precision in estimation of heterogeneous effect* (PEHE) [26] is defined in Eq. (21). We will report its square root.

$$PEHE = \frac{1}{n}\sum_{i=1}^{n}[(\hat{y}_1(x_i) - \hat{y}_0(x_i)) - (Y_1(x_i) - Y_0(x_i))]^2 \tag{21}$$

When the true ITEs are unknown, we can not calculate PEHE. Alternatively, the policy risk defined in Eq. (22) can be used as a proxy to the ITE performance

$$R_{pol}(\pi) = 1 - (p(\pi(x) = 1) \cdot \mathbb{E}[Y_1|\pi(x) = 1] + (1 - p(\pi(x) = 1)) \cdot \mathbb{E}[Y_0|\pi(x) = 0]) \tag{22}$$

where the induced policy $\pi(x)$ using the fitted outcome model $\mathbb{E}[Y_1|x]$ and $\mathbb{E}[Y_0|x]$ is to treat, $\pi(x) = 1$, if $\mathbb{E}[Y_1|x] > E[Y_0|x]$, and not to treat $\pi(x) = 0$ otherwise.

Since our method is based on implicit generative models, we call it CEIGM. Baseline methods used for comparison include Ordinary Least Squares (OLS-1, for continuous outcomes)/Logistic Regression (LR1 for binary outcomes) with treatment as feature, Ordinary Least Squares (OLS-2, for continuous outcomes)/Logistic Regression (LR2 for binary outcomes) with separate regressors for each treatment, k-nearest neighbor (k-NN), the double robust method Targeted Maximum Likelihood Estimation (TMLE) [27], Bayesian Additive Regression Trees (BART) estimator [26, 28], Random Forest (Rand. For.) [29, 30], Causal Forest (Caus. For.) [31], Balancing Linear Regression (BLR) and Balancing Neural Network (BNN) by [7], and CEVAE [9]. Following [7] and [9], we report both the within-sample and out-of-sample results.

4.2 Simulated Outcome: IHDP

The benchmark dataset IHDP was first compiled by [26] based in the Infant Health and Development Program, which aims at studying the effect of high-quality child care and home visits on future cognitive test scores. The dataset consists of 747 subjects (139 treated and 608 control), each represented by 25 covariates measuring aspects of children and their mothers. For the sake of comparison, we follow [9] and use the noiseless outcome to compute the true effects. The results are presented in Table 1.

The results shows that the proposed CEIGM method gets the lowest within-sample and out-of-sample PEHE errors. This indicates CEIGM fits both response surfaces $\mathbb{E}[Y_0|x]$ and $\mathbb{E}[Y_1|x]$ quite well. Unfortunately, CEIGM gets the highest errors for estimating the ATE. This is beyond our expectation. One possible reason is that, though the two response surfaces are well fitted, they differ from the underlying true response surfaces in opposite directions. For example, the fitted potential outcomes for the control $\mathbb{E}[Y_0|x]$ tend to be smaller than the true control outcomes, while the fitted potential outcomes for the treated $\mathbb{E}[Y_1|x]$ tend to be larger than the true treated outcome. As a result, even though both of them have small errors, the average of their difference may induce a relatively large error.

Table 1. Within-sample and out-of-sample results on IHDP dataset

	$\sqrt{\epsilon_{PEHE}^{within-s.}}$	$\epsilon_{ATE}^{within-s.}$	$\sqrt{\epsilon_{PEHE}^{out-of-s.}}$	$\epsilon_{ATE}^{out-of-s.}$
OLS1	5.8 ± .3	.73 ± .04	5.8 ± .3	.94 ± .06
OLS2	2.4 ± .1	.14 ± .01	2.5 ± .1	.31 ± .02
BLR	5.8 ± .3	.72 ± .04	5.8 ± .3	.93 ± .05
k-NN	2.1 ± .1	.14 ± .01	4.1 ± .2	.79 ± .05
TMLE	5.0 ± .2	.30 ± .01	–	–
BART	2.1 ± .1	.23 ± .01	2.3 ± .1	.34 ± .02
Rand. For.	4.2 ± .2	.73 ± .05	6.6 ± .3	.96 ± .06
Caus. For.	3.8 ± .2	.18 ± .01	3.8 ± .2	.40 ± .03
BNN	2.2 ± .1	.37 ± .03	2.1 ± .1	.42 ± .03
CEVAE	2.7 ± .1	.34 ± .01	2.6 ± .1	.46 ± .02
CEIGM	2.0 ± .1	1.1 ± .2	2.0 ± .2	1.2 ± .2

Table 2. Within-sample and out-of-sample results on Jobs dataset

	$R_{pol}^{within-s.}$	$\epsilon_{ATT}^{within-s.}$	$R_{pol}^{out-of-s.}$	$\epsilon_{ATT}^{out-of-s.}$
LR1	.22 ± .0	.01 ± .00	.23 ± .0	.08 ± .04
LR2	.21 ± .0	.01 ± .01	.24 ± .0	.08 ± .03
BLR	.22 ± .0	.01 ± .01	.25 ± .0	.08 ± .03
k-NN	.02 ± .0	.21 ± .01	.26 ± .0	.13 ± .05
TMLE	.22 ± .0	.02 ± .01	–	–
BART	.23 ± .0	.02 ± .00	.25 ± .0	.08 ± .03
Rand. For.	.23 ± .0	.03 ± .01	.28 ± .0	.09 ± .04
Caus. For.	.19 ± .0	.03 ± .01	.20 ± .0	.07 ± .03
BNN	.20 ± .0	.04 ± .01	.24 ± .0	.09 ± .04
CEVAE	.15 ± .0	.02 ± .01	.26 ± .0	.03 ± .01
CEIGM	.22 ± .0	.02 ± .00	.23 ± .0	.05 ± .01

4.3 Real World Outcome: Jobs

We also validate the proposed CEIGM method using the Jobs dataset, which combines a randomized study $\mathcal{R}$ based on the National Supported Work (NSW) program with observational data $\mathcal{O}$ to form a larger dataset. For more details of the data, refer[1]. Instead of the ATE, the NSW program aims at estimating the effect of job training on employment after training, i.e., the true average treatment effect on the treated (ATT). Since all the treated individuals come from the randomized study $\mathcal{R}$, we can easily estimate ATT by $ATT := \frac{1}{|T|}\sum_{i \in T}(Y_1(x_i) - Y_0(x_i)) = \frac{1}{|T|}\sum_{i \in T} y_i - \frac{1}{|C \cap \mathcal{R}|}\sum_{i \in C \cap \mathcal{R}} y_i = ATE$, where T and C are the treated and control group in the full dataset. Following [8] and [9], we use the NSW experimental sample (297 treated and 425 control) and the PSID

---

[1] http://users.nber.org/~rdehejia/data/nswdata2.html

comparison group (2490 control) and report the $\epsilon_{ATT} = \left| \widehat{ATT} - ATT \right|$. For evaluating ITE estimation, we use the policy risk R_{pol}. The results are list in Table 2.

For this dataset, our proposed CEIGM method has lower out-of-sample ATT error and policy risk than most of the benchmarks. Specifically, CEIGM gets the second smallest values for both the out-of-sample policy risk and ATT error. Compared with CEVAE, our proposed CEIGM method has lower out-of-sample policy risk but higher ATT error. The result validate again that the proposed CEIGM method is able to learn better potential outcome functions because the implicit posteriors are theoretically able to approximate arbitrarily complex distributions.

5 Conclusions and Discussion

In this paper, we model the causal mechanisms in a causal model by implicit generative models, which are proved universal approximators for the underlying causal mechanisms. The proposed CEIGM method is a generalization of the CEVAE method proposed in [9]. Specifically, we generalize the Gaussian inference model of latent confounders used in CEVAE to general black box inference models parameterized by deep neural networks. To tackle the intractability of implicit inference model, we adopt an adversary training scheme using a discriminator to learn the parameters. Experiments on two benchmark datasets validate our proposed method.

However, both experiments indicate that the proposed method tend to learn better potential outcome functions with opposite error directions, leading to better ITE estimation but worse ATE/ATT estimation. This issue is out of our expectation and we leave it as future investigation. We also notice that recent research [32, 33] on implicit model inference indicate that discriminator-based adversary training may lead to noisy gradients and thus unstable results. In future work, more implicit variational inference algorithms will be investigated to realize methods that are more robust.

References

1. Imbens, G.W., Rubin, D.B.: Causal Inference in Statistics, Social, and Biomedical Sciences. Cambridge University Press, Cambridge (2015)
2. Hernán, M.A., Robins, J.M.: Causal Inference. Chapman & Hall/CRC, Boca Raton (2018, forthcoming)
3. Swaminathan, A., Joachims, T.: Batch learning from logged bandit feedback through counterfactual risk minimization. J. Mach. Learn. Res. 16, 1731–1755 (2015)
4. Swaminathan, A., Joachims, T.: Counterfactual risk minimization: learning from logged bandit feedback. In: ICML, pp. 814–823 (2015)
5. Bottou, L., et al.: Counterfactual reasoning and learning systems: the example of computational advertising. J. Mach. Learn. Res. 14, 3207–3260 (2013)
6. Swaminathan, A., Joachims, T.: The self-normalized estimator for counterfactual learning. In: NIPS, pp. 3231–3239 (2015)
7. Johansson, F.D., Shalit, U., Sontag, D.: Learning representations for counterfactual inference. In: ICML (2016)

8. Shalit, U., Johansson, F.D., Sontag, D.: Estimating individual treatment effect: generalization bounds and algorithms. In: ICML, vol. 1050, p. 28 (2017)
9. Louizos, C., Shalit, U., Mooij, J., Sontag, D., Zemel, R., Welling, M.: Causal effect inference with deep latent-variable models. In: NIPS (2017)
10. Pearl, J.: Causality: Models, Reasoning and Inference. Cambridge University Press, Cambridge (2000)
11. Ullman, J.B., Bentler, P.M.: Structural equation modeling. In: Handbook of Psychology, 2nd Edn (2012)
12. Pearl, J.: Probabilistic Reasoning in Intelligent Systems: Networks of Plausible Inference. Morgan Kaufmann, San Francisco (1988)
13. Mohamed, S., Lakshminarayanan, B.: Learning in implicit generative models. arXiv preprint arXiv:1610.03483 (2016)
14. Tran, D., Ranganath, R., Blei, D.: Hierarchical implicit models and likelihood-free variational inference. In: NIPS, pp. 5527–5537 (2017)
15. Tran, D., Blei, D.M.: Implicit causal models for genome-wide association studies. In: ICLR (2018)
16. Pearl, J.: An introduction to causal inference. Int. J. Biostat. **6**(2) (2010). Article 7
17. Cybenko, G.: Approximation by superpositions of a sigmoidal function. Math. Control Sig. Syst. **2**, 303–314 (1989)
18. Izbicki, R., Lee, A.B., Pospisil, T.: ABC-CDE: towards approximate bayesian computation with complex high-dimensional data and limited simulations. arXiv:1805.05480 [stat.ME] (2018)
19. Goodfellow, I., et al.: Generative adversarial nets. In: Advances in Neural Information Processing Systems, pp. 2672–2680 (2014)
20. Jethava, V., Dubhashi, D.: GANs for LIFE: generative adversarial networks for likelihood free inference. arXiv preprint arXiv:1711.11139 (2017)
21. Tran, D., Hoffman, M.D., Saurous, R.A., Brevdo, E., Murphy, K., Blei, D.M.: Deep probabilistic programming. In: ICLR (2017)
22. Pearl, J., Glymour, M., Jewell, N.P.: Causal Inference in Statistics: A Primer. Wiley, Hoboken (2016)
23. Kingma, D.P., Welling, M.: Auto-encoding variational bayes. arXiv preprint arXiv:1312.6114 (2013)
24. Mescheder, L., Nowozin, S., Geiger, A.: Adversarial variational bayes: unifying variational autoencoders and generative adversarial networks. arXiv preprint arXiv:1701.04722 (2017)
25. Abadi, M., et al.: TensorFlow: large-scale machine learning on heterogeneous distributed systems. arXiv preprint arXiv:1603.04467 (2016)
26. Hill, J.L.: Bayesian nonparametric modeling for causal inference. J. Comput. Graph. Stat. **20**, 217–240 (2011)
27. Van der Laan, M.J., Rose, S.: Targeted Learning: Causal Inference for Observational and Experimental Data. Springer Science & Business Media, New York (2011). https://doi.org/10.1007/978-1-4419-9782-1
28. Chipman, H.A., George, E.I., McCulloch, R.E.: BART: Bayesian additive regression trees. Ann. Appl. Stat. **4**, 266–298 (2010)
29. Breiman, L.: Random forests. Mach. Learn. **45**, 5–32 (2001)
30. Athey, S., Tibshirani, J., Wager, S.: Generalized random forests. Ann. Stat. (2018, forthcoming)
31. Wager, S., Athey, S.: Estimation and inference of heterogeneous treatment effects using random forests. J. Am. Stat. Assoc. **113**, 1228–1242 (2018)
32. Huszár, F.: Variational inference using implicit distributions. arXiv preprint arXiv:1702.08235 (2017)
33. Shi, J., Sun, S., Zhu, J.: Kernel implicit variational inference. In: ICLR (2018)

On the Use of Matrix Based Representation to Deal with Automatic Composer Recognition

Izaro Goienetxea[1]([✉]) [ID], Iñigo Mendialdua[2] [ID], and Basilio Sierra[1] [ID]

[1] Department of Computer Science and Artificial Intelligence,
University of the Basque Country UPV/EHU, San Sebastian, Spain
{izaro.goienetxea,inigo.mendialdua,b.sierra}@ehu.eus
[2] Department of Computer Languages and Systems,
University of the Basque Country UPV/EHU, San Sebastian, Spain

Abstract. In this article the use of a matrix based representation of pieces is tested for the classification of musical pieces of some well known classical composers. The pieces in two corpora have been represented in two ways: matrices of interval pair probabilities and a set of 12 global features which had previously been used in a similar task. The classification accuracies of both representations have been computed using several supervised classification algorithms. A class binarization technique has also been applied to study how the accuracies change with this kind of methods. Promising results have been obtained which show that both the matrix representation and the class binarization techniques are suitable to be used in the automatic composer recognition problem.

Keywords: Matrices · Pairwise classification · Composer recognition

1 Introduction

Automatic music classification is a task within the field of Music Information Retrieval (MIR) which is getting more attention with the growth of the available information, thanks to the digital media. When dealing with automatic composer recognition it is important to choose the features that will be used to represent the pieces. Global feature sets, n-grams and string methods have been used to represent folk song collections [11], as well as event models [10]. Other works represent the pieces with multiple viewpoints [1] or discover patterns within collections of pieces, to find melodic families [7,12] within them. Herremans et al. [9] use a 12 global feature set to classify pieces of three classical composers, and Dor and Reich [3] manually extract some pitch based features and use a classifier tool named CHECKUP to discover more features that they then use to classify pieces of nine composers.

After the pieces are represented using one of the methods above, a classifier is built, which is first trained with a set of pieces with a known composer, and will

© Springer Nature Switzerland AG 2018
T. Mitrovic et al. (Eds.): AI 2018, LNAI 11320, pp. 531–536, 2018.
https://doi.org/10.1007/978-3-030-03991-2_48

predict a class for new pieces with no composer information. Since usually the classifier has to distinguish among several classes (composers), class binarization techniques can also be applied, to decompose the original multi-class (more than two classes) classification problem into multiple binary sub-problems [5].

In this work the automatic composer recognition problem is studied, using two corpora of symbolic representation of pieces of well known composers. A corpus of pieces of three composers, Bach, Beethoven and Haydn, similar to the one used in [9], is created, and a matrix based representation presented in the classification method of [6] is used to characterize the pieces. A matrix representation is tested to compare the classification accuracies obtained with it to the results obtained with a global feature set presented in [9], which achieves a promising accuracy. A binarization method is also applied, to see the effect that it has on the classification accuracies. Finally, the corpus is extended with the pieces of two more composers, Mozart and Vivaldi, and their classification accuracies are also computed, in order to observe the effect that the increase of classes has on the accuracies when applying class-binarization techniques.

2   Corpora

The two corpora used in this work have been downloaded from the KernScores website [14], which was developed by the Center for Computer Assisted Research in the Humanities (CCARH), at Stanford University, to organize musical scores.

The first corpus, which from this point will be referenced as $corpus_3$ includes pieces of the composers Bach, Beethoven and Haydn, similar to the corpus used in [9]. It has a total number of 1138 pieces, and the distribution of the composers and pieces can be seen in the top part of Table 1.

The second corpus, referenced as $corpus_5$, is an extension of the first one, but it also includes pieces of Mozart and Vivaldi. It contains 1586 pieces, and its composer/piece number distribution can be seen in Table 1. All the pieces used in the corpora are polyphonic MIDI files.

Table 1. Number of pieces of each composer used in this work. The central part shows the composers and piece numbers of corpus $composers_3$. The two composers of the right extend the first corpus to $corpus_5$.

Composer	Bach	Beethoven	Haydn	Mozart	Vivaldi
Instances	694	190	254	313	135

3   Methods

The method presented in this work has two main steps; representation and classification. A matrix-based melody representation presented in [6] is tried and the its classification accuracies are compared to the results of a global feature set used in [9], which obtained acceptable accuracy in a similar classification task.

3.1 Representation

The matrix representation of the pieces intends to capture some of their features that ideally would be able to characterize them well enough to be used in the classification process. To create the matrices of the pieces of the corpora, first they are represented using viewpoints. A viewpoint τ is a function that maps an event sequence $e_1, \ldots, e_l$ to a more abstract sequence $\tau(e_1), \ldots, \tau(e_l)$ [2]. In this work an interval viewpoint has been chosen to represent the voices in the pieces; intpc, which computes the pitch class interval (modulo 12). In Fig. 1 the first two bars of the first voice of a Bach chorale included in the corpora can be seen, along with their viewpoint representation.

intpc   ⊥   5   7   2   10   10   11   0

Fig. 1. First two bars the first voice of a Bach chorale and its viewpoint representation.

Once the viewpoint representation of the scores is made, the matrix$_{intpc}$ matrices are built, which are 12×12 matrices that describe the probabilities of the transitions between all the pitch class interval pairs that occur in each piece.

From every piece of the corpora a matrix$_{intpc}$ has been built and linked to its composer in a *arff* file that is then used by Weka in the classification process. In order to compare the classification results obtained with the matrix representation to the results of the global feature set presented in [9] the jSymbolic feature extractor is used [13]. The used feature collection will be referenced as global$_{12}$.

3.2 Class Binarization

Class binarization is composed of two main steps; decomposition and combination. In the decomposition step the original problem is divided into several binary sub-problems, for what two main techniques have been developed; One versus All (OVA) and One versus One (OVO). In the classification step, each binary classifier returns a prediction, which need to be combined. When a new instance is being classified using this method all the sub-problems give a prediction of its class, and all these outputs need to be combined. To do so, there are several strategies, but in this work the majority vote strategy [4] is used, where each sub-problem returns a vote, and the class with the largest amount of votes is predicted.

4   Experiments and Results

4.1 Experimental Setup

To test the suitableness of the matrix based representation two experiments have been performed, for which the two corpora (corpus$_3$ and corpus$_5$) presented in

Sect. 2 have been used. The pieces in the corpora have been represented with global$_{12}$ and matrix$_{intpc}$ representations. We have applied a stratified 10 fold cross-validation in each classification process, and used different base classifiers to study their accuracies, both in multi-class and binarized classifications.

Seven base classifiers from the machine learning software Weka [8] have been used in the classification steps: J48, SMO, JRip, Naive Bayes (NB), Bayesian Network (BNet), Random Forest (RF) and Multilayer Perceptron (MP).

4.2 Results

corpus$_3$. The classification accuracies of corpus$_3$ with all the base classifiers, with and without OVO, are presented in Table 2.

Table 2. Accuracy results of the classifications with each single classifier and OVO technique for corpus$_3$.

	J48	J48-OVO	SMO*	JRIP	JRIP-OVO	NB	NB-OVO
global$_{12}$	84.007	83.568	86.028	82.074	83.655	66.784	66.872
matrix$_{intpc}$	81.459	82.1617	**89.982**	81.986	82.162	80.668	80.580

	BNet	BNet-OVO	RF	RF-OVO	MP	MP-OVO	Mean	Mean-OVO
global$_{12}$	78.647	78.735	87.171	87.786	87.346	87.434	*81.722*	*82.011*
matrix$_{intpc}$	82.513	81.986	86.907	88.401	**89.982**	89.631	*84.559*	*84.986*

The best results are obtained with the matrix$_{intpc}$ representation and SMO or Multilayer Perceptron classifier. Even if this representation obtains the best classification accuracy, that does not happen for J48, JRip and Random Forest. The mean accuracies show that overall, better results are obtained with the matrix$_{intpc}$ representation and OVO technique.

The choice of the classifier that is used has a great impact on the obtained accuracies. Depending on the classifier that is used, the accuracies can vary from 66.8% to 87.3% in the case of the global$_{12}$ representation.

corpus$_5$. The classification accuracies of corpus$_5$ with all the base classifiers, with and without OVO, are presented in the Table 3.

The best accuracy is again obtained with the matrix$_{intpc}$ representation and a Multilayer Perceptron classifier, which achieves an accuracy of 80.7%. The results obtained with the matrix$_{intpc}$ representation are better than the ones obtained with the global$_{12}$ representation for every classifier but J48. It can be seen that the difference for some classifiers, such as SMO, is significant.

4.3 Statistical Results

We have applied Wilcoxon signed-rank test in order to detect statistical differences between global$_{12}$ and matrix$_{intpc}$ representations. The result of the statistical analysis rejects the null hypothesis that both methods are equivalent, since

Table 3. Accuracy results of the classifications with each single classifier and OVO technique for the five composers $corpus_5$.

	J48	J48-OVO	SMO*	JRIP	JRIP-OVO	NB	NB-OVO
$global_{12}$	71.402	75.126	73.864	70.328	72.980	56.692	56.692
$matrix_{intpc}$	70.266	72.917	80.556	72.033	72.854	71.970	71.843

	BNet	BNet-OVO	RF	RF-OVO	MP	MP-OVO	Mean	Mean-OVO
$global_{12}$	65.530	67.361	77.904	79.104	74.432	76.641	**70.022**	**71.681**
$matrix_{intpc}$	72.096	73.106	79.419	80.556	**80.682**	80.177	**75.289**	**76.001**

the p-value (0.0014) returned by the Wilcoxon test is lower than our α-value (0.01).

We have also carried out another statistical analysis in order to detect statistical differences between OVO and single classifier, in this case we have also applied Wilcoxon signed-rank test. Again, the obtained results rejects the null hypothesis since the p-value (0.0039) returned is lower than our α-value (0.01).

5   Conclusions

In this work the use of a matrix based representation is tested to be used for the automatic recognition of some well known composers. The classification accuracies of the interval matrices with several different base classifiers have been compared to the accuracies obtained with a global feature set which had already been used in a similar classification task with acceptable results. The application of binarization techniques in classification is also proposed, and their effect is studied.

The best accuracies have been achieved with the $matrix_{intpc}$ representation in both corpora, and even if the accuracy obtained with this representation does not improve the $global_{12}$ representation for every classifier, its mean accuracy is better in both corpora. The statistical analysis has also shown that there are significant differences between the results obtained with $matrix_{intpc}$ representation and the ones obtained with $global_{12}$ representation.

The application of OVO binarization technique has proven beneficial to the classification accuracies in general, even if in this work the best accuracies were obtained with single classifiers. Its effects are more noticeable when it is used on $corpus_5$ with five possible target classes, where the results with OVO are better for almost all the classifiers. The results of the statistical test also show that there are statistical differences between $global_{12}$ and $matrix_{intpc}$ representations and between single classifiers and OVO classifications.

Considering that the use of interval based matrices have obtained promising accuracies, more complex viewpoints should be considered to build the matrices, to study how the classification can be improved with more complex information.

Acknowledgements. This work has been partially supported by the Basque Government Research Teams grant (IT900-16) and the Spanish Ministry of Economy and Competitiveness. TIN2015-64395-R (MINECO/FEDER).

References

1. Conklin, D.: Multiple viewpoint systems for music classification. J. New Music Res. **42**(1), 19–26 (2013)
2. Conklin, D., Witten, I.H.: Multiple viewpoint systems for music prediction. J. New Music Res. **24**, 51–73 (1995)
3. Dor, O., Reich, Y.: An evaluation of musical score characteristics for automatic classification of composers. Comput. Music J. **35**(3), 86–97 (2011)
4. Fürnkranz, J.: Round robin classification. J. Mach. Learn. Res. **2**, 721–747 (2002)
5. Galar, M., Fernández, A., Barrenechea, E., Bustince, H., Herrera, F.: An overview of ensemble methods for binary classifiers in multi-class problems: experimental study on one-vs-one and one-vs-all schemes. Pattern Recognit. **44**(8), 1761–1776 (2011)
6. Goienetxea, I., Martínez-Otzeta, J.M., Sierra, B., Mendialdua, I.: Towards the use of similarity distances to music genre classification: a comparative study. PLOS ONE **13**(2), 1–18 (2018)
7. Goienetxea, I., Neubarth, K., Conklin, D.: Melody classification with pattern covering. In: 9th International Workshop on Music and Machine Learning (MML 2016), Riva del Garda, Italy (2016)
8. Hall, M., Frank, E., Holmes, G., Pfahringer, B., Reutemann, P., Witten, I.H.: The weka data mining software: an update. SIGKDD Explor. Newsl. **11**(1), 10–18 (2009)
9. Herremans, D., Sörensen, K., Martens, D.: Classification and generation of composer-specific music using global feature models and variable neighborhood search. Comput. Music J. **39**(3), 71–91 (2015)
10. Hillewaere, R., Manderick, B., Conklin, D.: Global feature versus event models for folk song classification. In: Proceedings of the 10th International Society for Music Information Retrieval Conference, Kobe, Japan, pp. 729–733 (2009)
11. Hillewaere, R., Manderick, B., Conklin, D.: String methods for folk tune genre classification. In: Proceedings of the 13th International Society for Music Information Retrieval Conference, Porto, Portugal (2012)
12. van Kranenburg, P., Conklin, D.: A pattern mining approach to study a collection of Dutch folk-songs. In: Proceedings of the 5th International Workshop on Folk Music Analysis (FMA 2016), Dublin, pp. 71–73 (2016)
13. Mckay, C., Fujinaga, I.: jsymbolic: a feature extractor for midi files. In: Proceedings of the International Computer Music Conference, pp. 302–305 (2006)
14. Sapp, C.S.: Online database of scores in the humdrum file format. In: ISMIR 2005, Proceedings of 6th International Conference on Music Information Retrieval, 11–15 September 2005, London, UK, pp. 664–665 (2005)

Flood-Fill Q-Learning Updates
for Learning Redundant Policies in Order
to Interact with a Computer Screen
by Clicking

Nathaniel du Preez-Wilkinson$^{(\boxtimes)}$, Marcus Gallagher, and Xuelei Hu

School of Information Technology and Electrical Engineering,
The University of Queensland, Brisbane, QLD 4072, Australia
{uqndupre,marcusg,xuelei.hu}@uq.edu.au

Abstract. We present a specialisation of Q-learning for the problem of training an agent to click on a computer screen. In this problem formulation the agent sees the pixels of the screen as input, and selects a pixel as output. The task of selecting a pixel to click on involves selecting an action from a large discrete action space in which many of the actions are completely equivalent in terms of reinforcement learning state transitions. We propose to exploit this by performing simultaneous Q-learning updates for equivalent actions. We use the flood fill algorithm on the input image to determine the action (pixel) equivalence.

1 Introduction

We consider the problem of training an agent to interact with a computer screen by clicking. The agent sees the pixels of the screen as input, and selects a pixel as output. The computer reacts to the selected pixel as if a human user had clicked on it. We use reinforcement learning [1] to solve this problem. Reinforcement learning has gained a lot of attention in recent years due to the record breaking performance of deep reinforcement learning on Atari video games [2] and in the game of Go [3]. An important difference between these examples and our work is the action space. The Atari games that were used are environments with 4 to 18 independent actions, depending on the game. The game of Go has an action space of 19×19 board positions that are similarly independent from each other. By contrast, even a conservative monitor resolution of 800×600 pixels creates a very large action space with many actions that are completely equivalent. Clicking on any pixel that is part of an object on the screen registers as clicking on the object, resulting in the same state transition. We propose to perform simultaneous learning updates for these equivalent actions.

2 Background

In reinforcement learning an agent learns to interact with an environment through trial and error [1]. The environment can take on one of a finite number

© Springer Nature Switzerland AG 2018
T. Mitrovic et al. (Eds.): AI 2018, LNAI 11320, pp. 537–542, 2018.
https://doi.org/10.1007/978-3-030-03991-2_49

of *states*, $s \in S$, and the agent interacts with the environment through *actions*, $a \in A$, that transition the environment from the current state, s_t, to a new state, s_{t+1}. After an agent's action changes the state of the environment, the agent receives feedback in the form of a *reward*, $r_t = r(s_t, a_t, s_{t+1})$, that indicates how desirable the choice of that action was while in that state. The goal of reinforcement learning is to develop an optimal *policy*, $\pi : S \rightarrow A$, a mapping from states to actions, for a given problem. An optimal policy is one which maximises the total cumulative reward, R:

$$R = \sum_{t=0}^{T} \gamma^t r(s_t, a_t, s_{t+1}) \tag{1}$$

where T is the total time the agent interacts with the environment; and γ is a discount factor applied to future rewards.

The type of reinforcement learning we use in this paper is *Q-learning*. In Q-learning, each state-action pair is represented by a Q-value, $Q(s, a)$, that represents the expected total reward resulting from taking action a in state s. After taking action a in state s, the Q-value, $Q(s, a)$, is modified according to the following update rule:

$$Q(s_t, a_t) \leftarrow (1 - \alpha)Q(s_t, a_t) + \alpha(r_t + \gamma \times max_a Q(s_{t+1}, a)) \tag{2}$$

where α is a learning rate parameter.

3   Related Work

There has been some research focused on large discrete action spaces in reinforcement learning [4]. However, there has been very little work that uses pixels as both the input (state) space and the output (action) space. The work that is most relevant to ours, from an application perspective, involves the *World of Bits* [5] environment which was designed to allow for training agents to interact with websites. It contains several web-related tasks, such as form filling and page navigation. The environment provides images of the screen and the Document Object Model (DOM) of the web page as the state. The actions it accepts are primitive mouse movements and keyboard presses.

Aside from the application perspective, there is work that is similar to ours in terms of methodology. The idea of an agent that learns multiple policies has been considered implicitly since the early days of reinforcement learning in the form of stochastic policies [1] (a stochastic policy can be considered a weighted combination of deterministic policies). However, this is not often the focus of the research that uses these methods, as the environments (e.g. Atari and Go) are often solvable with deterministic policies. The idea of explicitly ensuring an agent learns multiple policies has recently been explored by Haarnoja et al. with their energy-based deep reinforcement learning [6]. They add an entropy term to the loss function that the agent is minimising in order to prevent over committing to a single policy.

4   Flood-Fill Q-Learning Updates

We assume that the input images are simple enough that the flood-fill algorithm can be used to segment an object from the rest of an image. Consider the conventional Q-learning update Eq. (2), which only updates the Q-value for the state-action pair that was just involved in obtaining the reward the agent received. This implicitly assumes no correlation between different states/actions, and that they should all be updated independently. Our proposed modification can be written as follows:

$$Q(s_t, a') \leftarrow (1 - \alpha)Q(s_t, a') + \alpha(r_t + \gamma \max_a Q(s_{t+1}, a)) \ \forall a' \in A_t \quad (3)$$

where A_t is the set of all actions that are equivalent to action a_t. We consider two actions to be equivalent if, when applied to the same state, they receive the same reward and result in the same state transition. For the problem that we consider (clicking pixels on a computer screen) we use a modified version of the flood-fill algorithm to determine which actions belong in A_t. Instead of colouring nodes on a graph, our modified flood-fill algorithm adds actions/pixels to a set in the main loop, and then returns that set upon completion. Algorithm 1 shows our modified version of Q-learning that makes use of this flood-fill algorithm.

Algorithm 1. Q-Learning with Flood Fill Q-Value Updates

Initialise $Q(s, a)$
Initialise s_t
for $t \leftarrow 1$ **to** T **do**
    Choose action a_t according to an action selection policy (e.g. ϵ-greedy)
    Take action a_t, observe reward r_t and new state s_{t+1}
    $A_t \leftarrow FLOOD\_FILL(s_t, a_t)$
    for all $a' \in A_t$ **do**
        $Q(s_t, a') \leftarrow (1 - \alpha)Q(s_t, a') + \alpha(r_t + \gamma \max_a Q(s_{t+1}, a))$
    end for
    $s_t \leftarrow s_{t+1}$
    if s_t is terminal **then**
        Reset the environment and receive new s_t
    end if
end for

---

5   Experimental Setup

For our experiments we designed our own example problem called *Click Black*. The agent is presented with an 120×120 greyscale image containing 25 squares arranged in a 5×5 grid. One of these squares is black, and the remaining 24 squares are white. The task is to click on the black square. The black square starts at the top left position of the board. After every click/action the black square advances left to right, top to bottom, until it reaches the bottom right position. The episode ends after 25 clicks. For each interaction, the agent receives a reward of +1 if it clicks on the black square, and a reward of 0 otherwise.

In our experiments we evaluate both the conventional Q-learning update and our flood-fill update[1], in order to compare the two. We investigated the effects of the different update mechanisms on two different agent model types: (1) a tabular Q-learning agent; and (2) a neural network. For the neural network we used a single fully connected layer with 14400 inputs and 14400 outputs. The 14400 inputs correspond to a flattened 1D representation of the 120×120 input image. The 14400 outputs represent the network's predicted Q-values for the corresponding pixels.

In all experiments the tabular agents were trained for 300 iterations, and the neural network agents were trained for 400 iterations. During training all agents used the ϵ-greedy exploration strategy. The value of ϵ was annealed from 1 to 0.01 over the course of training. The value of the learning rate parameter in (2) was 0.01 for the tabular agents, and 0.00025 for the neural network agents. For the neural network agents we used double Q-learning [7], with a target network and memory replay buffer as described by [2]. To tune the weights of the neural network we used the Adam optimisation algorithm with the mean squared error (MSE) loss function, and a learning rate of 0.00025.

To gauge the sample efficiency of the different Q-learning update mechanisms we measured the testing performance of the agents for a fixed number of training iterations. To gauge the robustness of the agents, we measured testing performance under the condition that the agent's preferred action was unavailable. i.e. instead of testing the agents using the action of their highest learned Q-value, we tested them using the action corresponding to the second highest Q-value, or lower.

For the testing procedure, the agent played a fresh copy of the game from start to finish; resulting in a maximum possible score of 25. During testing the agents acted greedily according to their learned Q-values, and the agent models were not updated.

6   Results and Discussion

The results of the sample efficiency experiment are shown in Fig. 1. For both model types the agent using the flood fill Q-learning update converges faster, and to a higher testing reward. This demonstrates that using the flood fill Q-learning update can yield more efficient training even when learning a single policy.

---

[1] For the problem described in this paper all pixels of the same colour are also part of the same shape. Thus, for efficiency reasons, the flood fill algorithm was not actually implemented in this case. Instead we used the simpler method of updating the Q-values of all pixels with same colour.

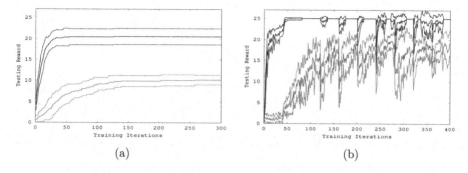

Fig. 1. Testing reward of different Q-learning update mechanisms while learning to play Click Black: (a) tabular agent; (b) neural network agent. Blue lines show agents using flood fill Q-learning; red lines show agents using conventional Q-learning. Solid lines represent mean values over 10 runs; dashed lines represent standard deviations. (Color figure online)

The results of the initial robustness experiment are shown in Fig. 2. In this experiment the agents used the action corresponding to their second highest Q-value during testing. This is equivalent to asking the agent to act in a constrained environment where a *single* specific pixel can not be clicked on. While the agents using the conventional Q-learning update suffer a heavy performance hit under these conditions, the agents trained with the flood fill Q-learning update obtain results almost identical to Fig. 1.

To investigate robustness further we repeated the experiment using the n-th maximum Q-value, with n varying from 1 to 10 (i.e. we repeated the experiment using the action corresponding to the 3rd, 4th, 5th, etc. maximum Q-values). For each value of n, we recorded the testing performance at the end of the training period. Figure 3 shows how this testing reward varies with the different values of n. In both the tabular and fully connected cases, the performance of the conventional Q-learning update plummets dramatically with increasing n, while the flood fill Q-learning update suffers no noticeable performance hit. This indicates that using the flood-fill Q-learning update can enable agents to learn redundant policies that can help make them robust to changes in the environment.

In summary, we have presented a specialisation of Q-learning for the problem of training an agent to click on a computer screen. Our method makes use of the flood-fill algorithm to simultaneously update all actions that are equivalent to the one selected by the agent at each time step. We performed experiments using a tabular Q-learning agent and a fully connected neural network layer as the agent models. Results for both models indicate that using our flood-fill Q-learning update improves the sample efficiency of the algorithm, and the robustness of the trained agents.

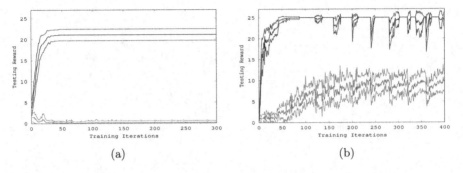

Fig. 2. Testing reward of different Q-learning update mechanisms, with the preferred agent action disabled: (a) tabular agent; (b) neural network agent. Blue lines show agents using flood fill Q-learning, and red lines show agents using conventional Q-learning. Solid lines represent mean values over 10 runs; dashed lines represent standard deviation. (Color figure online)

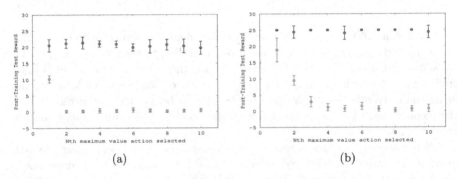

Fig. 3. Post-training test reward of different Q-learning update mechanisms, with multiple preferred actions disabled: (a) tabular agent; (b) neural network agent. Blue points show agents using flood fill Q-learning; red points show agents using conventional Q-learning. Circles represent mean values over 10 runs; error bars represent standard deviations. (Color figure online)

References

1. Sutton, R.S., Barto, A.G.: Reinforcement Learning: An Introduction, vol. 1. MIT Press, Cambridge (1998)
2. Mnih, V., et al.: Human-level control through deep reinforcement learning. Nature **518**, 529–533 (2015)
3. Silver, D., et al.: Mastering the game of Go with deep neural networks and tree search. Nature **529**(7587), 484–489 (2016)
4. Pazis,J., Parr, R.: Generalized value functions for large action sets. In: ICML, pp. 1185–1192 (2011)
5. Shi, T., et al.: World of bits: an open-domain platform for web-based agents. In: ICML (2017)
6. Haarnoja, T., et al.: Reinforcement learning with deep energy-based policies. In: ICML (2017)
7. Van Hasselt, H., Guez, A., Silver, D.: Deep reinforcement learning with double Q-learning. In: AAAI (2016)

Answering Multiple Conjunctive Queries with the Lifted Dynamic Junction Tree Algorithm

Marcel Gehrke[(⊠)], Tanya Braun, and Ralf Möller

Institute of Information Systems, University of Lübeck, Lübeck, Germany
{gehrke,braun,moeller}@ifis.uni-luebeck.de

Abstract. The lifted dynamic junction tree algorithm (LDJT) answers *filtering* and *prediction* queries efficiently for probabilistic relational temporal models by building and then reusing a first-order cluster representation of a knowledge base for multiple queries and time steps. We extend LDJT to answer conjunctive queries over multiple time steps by avoiding eliminations, while keeping the complexity to answer a conjunctive query low. The extended version of saves computations compared to an existing approach to answer multiple lifted conjunctive queries.

1 Introduction

Areas like healthcare and logistics involve probabilistic data with relational and temporal aspects and need efficient exact inference algorithms. These areas involve many objects in relation to each other with changes over time and uncertainties about object existence, attribute value assignments, or relations between objects. More specifically, healthcare systems involve electronic health records (relational) for many patients (objects), streams of measurements over time (temporal), and uncertainties [21] due to, e.g., missing information caused by data integration. Probabilistic databases (PDBs) can answer queries for relational temporal models with uncertainties [5,6]. However, each query possibly contains redundant information, resulting in huge queries. In contrast to PDBs, we build more expressive and compact models including behaviour (offline) enabling efficient answering of more compact queries (online). For query answering, our approach performs deductive reasoning by computing marginal distributions at discrete time steps. In this paper, we study the problem of exact inference for answering multiple conjunctive queries in temporal probabilistic models.

We propose the lifted dynamic junction tree algorithm (LDJT) to exactly answer multiple *filtering* and *prediction* queries for multiple time steps efficiently [7]. LDJT combines the advantages of the interface algorithm [13] and the lifted junction tree algorithm (LJT) [2]. Specifically, this paper presents $LDJT^{con}$ to

This research originated from the Big Data project being part of Joint Lab 1, funded by Cisco Systems Germany, at the centre COPICOH, University of Lübeck.

© Springer Nature Switzerland AG 2018
T. Mitrovic et al. (Eds.): AI 2018, LNAI 11320, pp. 543–555, 2018.
https://doi.org/10.1007/978-3-030-03991-2_50

answer multiple conjunctive queries efficiently. In the static case, LJT answers conjunctive queries by merging a subtree of a first-order junction tree (FO jtree), which contains all query terms. For the temporal case, merging multiple time steps, increases the complexity to answer multiple conjunctive query. Therefore, we propose to avoid eliminations of query terms to answer multiple conjunctive queries efficiently. Answering multiple conjunctive queries over different time steps can be used to perform probabilistic complex event processing (CEP) [25]. CEP is a hard problem and also for healthcare, a series of events is of interest.

The remainder of this paper has the following structure: We begin by recapitulating parameterised probabilistic dynamic models (PDMs) as a representation for relational temporal probabilistic models and LDJT. Afterwards, we present how LJT answers static conjunctive queries and propose an approach to answer temporal conjunctive queries. Lastly, we evaluate the computational savings of our approach and conclude by looking at possible extensions.

2   Related Work

We take a look at inference for propositional temporal models, relational static models, and give an overview about research on relational temporal models.

For exact inference on propositional temporal models, a naive approach is to unroll the temporal model for a given number of time steps and use any exact inference algorithm for static, i.e., non-temporal, models. Murphy [13] proposes the interface algorithm consisting of a forward and backward pass using temporal d-separation to apply static inference algorithms to the dynamic model.

First-order probabilistic inference leverages the relational aspect of a static model. For models with known domain size, it exploits symmetries in a model by combining instances to reason with representatives, known as lifting [16]. Poole [16] introduces parametric factor graphs as relational models and proposes lifted variable elimination (LVE) as an exact inference algorithm on relational models. Further, de Salvo Braz [18], Milch et al. [11], and Taghipour et al. [20] extend LVE to its current form. Lauritzen and Spiegelhalter [9] introduce the junction tree algorithm. To benefit from the ideas of the junction tree algorithm and LVE, Braun and Möller [2] present LJT, which efficiently performs exact first-order probabilistic inference on relational models given a set of queries.

To handle inference for relational temporal models most approaches are approximative. Additional to being approximative, these approaches involve unnecessary groundings or are not designed to handle multiple queries efficiently. Ahmadi et al. [1] propose lifted (loopy) belief propagation. From a factor graph, they build a compressed factor graph and apply lifted belief propagation with the idea of the factored frontier algorithm [12], which is an approximate counterpart to the interface algorithm. Thon et al. [22] introduce CPT-L, a probabilistic model for sequences of relational state descriptions with a partially lifted inference algorithm. Geier and Biundo [8] present an online interface algorithm for dynamic Markov logic networks (DMLNs), similar to the work of Papai et al. [15]. Both approaches slice DMLNs to run well-studied MLN inference algorithms [17] on each slice. Two ways of performing online inference using particle filtering are described in [10,14]. Vlasselaer et al. [23,24] introduce an exact approach for relational dynamic models, but perform inference on a ground knowledge base.

However, by using efficient inference algorithms, we calculate exact solutions for relational temporal models. Therefore, we extend LDJT, which leverages the well-studied LVE and LJT algorithms, to answer multiple conjunctive queries.

3   Parameterised Probabilistic Models

Based on [4], we present parameterised probabilistic models (PMs) for relational static models. Afterwards, we extend PMs to the temporal case, resulting in PDMs for relational temporal models, which, in turn, are based on [7].

3.1   Parameterised Probabilistic Models

PMs combine first-order logic with probabilistic models, representing first-order constructs using logical variables (logvars) as parameters. Let us assume, we would like to remotely infer the condition of patients with regards to water retaining. To determine the condition of patients, we use the change of their weights. An increase in weight could either be caused by overeating or retaining water. Additionally, we use the change of weights of people living with the patient to reduce the uncertainty to infer conditions. In case both persons gain weight, overeating is more likely, while otherwise retaining water is more likely. If a water retention is undetected, it can be an acute life-threatening condition.

Definition 1. *Let* **L** *be a set of logvar names,* Φ *a set of factor names, and* **R** *a set of random variable (randvar) names. A parameterised randvar (PRV)* $A = P(X^1, \ldots, X^n)$ *represents a set of randvars behaving identically by combining a randvar* $P \in$ **R** *with* $X^1, \ldots, X^n \in$ **L**. *If* $n = 0$, *the PRV is parameterless. The domain of a logvar* L *is denoted by* $\mathcal{D}(L)$. *The term range(A) provides possible values of a PRV* A. *Constraint* $(\mathbf{X}, C_{\mathbf{X}})$ *allows to restrict logvars to certain domain values and is a tuple with a sequence of logvars* $\mathbf{X} = (X^1, \ldots, X^n)$ *and a set* $C_{\mathbf{X}} \subseteq \times_{i=1}^{n} \mathcal{D}(X^i)$. $\top$ *denotes that no restrictions apply and may be omitted. The term* $lv(Y)$ *refers to the logvars in some element* Y. *The term* $gr(Y)$ *denotes the set of instances of* Y *with all logvars in* Y *grounded w.r.t. constraints.*

To model our scenario, we use the randvar names C, LT, S, and W for Condition, LivingTogether, ScaleWorks, and Weight, respectively, and the logvar names X and X'. From the names, we build PRVs $C(X)$, $LT(X, X')$, $S(X)$, and $W(X)$. The domain of X and X' is $\{alice, bob, eve\}$. The range of $C(X)$ is $\{normal, deviation, retains water\}$. $LT(X, X')$ and $S(X)$ have range $\{true, false\}$ and $W(X)$ has range $\{steady, falling, rising\}$. With $\kappa = (X, \{alice, bob\})$, $gr(C(X)|\kappa) = \{C(alice), C(bob)\}$. $gr(C(X)|\top)$ also contains $C(eve)$.

Definition 2. *We denote a parametric factor (parfactor) g with $\forall \mathbf{X} : \phi(\mathcal{A}) \,|C$. $\mathbf{X} \subseteq \mathbf{L}$ being a set of logvars over which the factor generalises and $\mathcal{A} = (A^1, \ldots, A^n)$ a sequence of PRVs. We omit $(\forall \mathbf{X} :)$ if $\mathbf{X} = lv(\mathcal{A})$. A function $\phi : \times_{i=1}^n range(A^i) \mapsto \mathbb{R}^+$ with name $\phi \in \Phi$ is defined identically for all grounded instances of $\mathcal{A}$. A list of all input-output values is the complete specification for ϕ. C is a constraint on $\mathbf{X}$. A PM $G := \{g^i\}_{i=0}^n$ is a set of parfactors and semantically represents the full joint probability distribution $P_G = \frac{1}{Z} \prod_{f \in gr(G)} f$ where Z is a normalisation constant.*

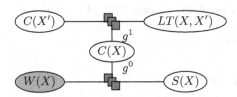

Fig. 1. Parfactor graph for G^{ex}

Fig. 2. FO jtree for G^{ex} (local models in grey)

Now, we build the model G^{ex} of our example with the parfactors:

$$g^0 = \phi^0(C(X), S(X), W(X))|\top \text{ and } g^1 = \phi^1(C(X), C(X'), LT(X, X'))|\kappa^1$$

We omit the concrete mappings of ϕ^0 and ϕ^1. Parfactor g^0 has the constraint $\top$, meaning it holds for *alice*, *bob*, and *eve*. The constraint κ^1 of g^1 ensures that $X \neq X'$ holds. Figure 1 depicts G^{ex} as a parfactor graph and shows PRVs, which are connected via undirected edges to parfactors, with $W(X)$ being observable.

The semantics of a model is given by grounding and building a full joint distribution. In general, queries ask for a probability distribution of a randvar using a model's full joint distribution and fixed events as evidence.

Definition 3. *Given a PM G, a ground PRV Q, and grounded PRVs with fixed range values $\mathbf{E} = \{E^i = e^i\}_i$, the expression $P(Q|\mathbf{E})$ denotes a query w.r.t. P_G.*

3.2 Parameterised Probabilistic Dynamic Models

We define PDMs based on the first-order Markov assumption, i.e., a time slice t only depends on the previous time slice $t - 1$. Further, the underlying process is stationary, i.e., the model behaviour does not change over time.

Definition 4. *A PDM is a pair of PMs $(G_0, G_\rightarrow)$ where G_0 is a PM representing the first time step and $G_\rightarrow$ is a two-slice temporal parameterised model representing $\mathbf{A}_{t-1}$ and $\mathbf{A}_t$ where $\mathbf{A}_\pi$ is a set of PRVs from time slice π.*

Figure 3 shows how the model G^{ex} behaves over time. $G^{ex}_\rightarrow$ consists of G^{ex} for time step $t - 1$ and for time step t with inter-slice parfactors for the behaviour over time. In this example, g^{LT}, g^C, and g^S are the inter-slice parfactors.

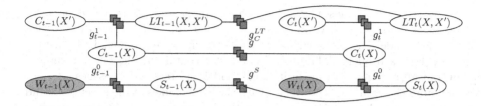

Fig. 3. $G_{\rightarrow}^{ex}$ the two-slice temporal parfactor graph for model G^{ex}

Definition 5. *Given a PDM G, a ground PRV Q_t, and grounded PRVs with fixed range values $\mathbf{E}_{0:t} = \{E_t^i = e_t^i\}_{i,t}$, $P(Q_t|\mathbf{E}_{0:t})$ denotes a query w.r.t. P_G.*

The problem of answering a marginal distribution query $P(A_\pi^i|e_{0:t})$ w.r.t. the model is called *prediction* for $\pi > t$ and *filtering* for $\pi = t$.

4   Lifted Dynamic Junction Tree Algorithm

In this section, we recapitulate LJT [3] to answer queries for PMs and LDJT [7] a *filtering* and *prediction* algorithm to answer queries for PDMs.

4.1   Lifted Junction Tree Algorithm

LJT provides efficient means to answer queries $P(Q^i|\mathbf{E})$, with $Q^i \in \mathbf{Q}$ a set of query terms, given a PM G and evidence $\mathbf{E}$, by performing the following steps: (i) Construct an FO jtree J for G. (ii) Enter $\mathbf{E}$ in J. (iii) Pass messages (iv) Compute answer for each query $Q^i \in \mathbf{Q}$.

We first define an FO jtree and then go through each step. To define an FO jtree, we define parameterised clusters (parclusters), nodes of an FO jtree.

Definition 6. *A parcluster $\mathbf{C}$ is defined by $\forall \mathbf{L} : \mathbf{A}|C$. $\mathbf{L}$ is a set of logvars, $\mathbf{A}$ is a set of PRVs with $lv(\mathbf{A}) \subseteq \mathbf{L}$, and C a constraint on $\mathbf{L}$. We omit $(\forall \mathbf{L}:)$ if $\mathbf{L} = lv(\mathbf{A})$. A parcluster $\mathbf{C}^i$ can have parfactors $\phi(\mathcal{A}^\phi)|C^\phi$ assigned given that (i) $\mathcal{A}^\phi \subseteq \mathbf{A}$, (ii) $lv(\mathcal{A}^\phi) \subseteq \mathbf{L}$, and (iii) $C^\phi \subseteq C$ holds. We call the set of assigned parfactors a local model G^i.*

An FO jtree for a PM G is $J = (\mathbf{V}, \mathbf{P})$ where J is a cycle-free graph, the nodes $\mathbf{V}$ denote a set of parclusters, and $\mathbf{P}$ is a set of edges between parclusters. J must satisfy the following properties: (i) A parcluster $\mathbf{C}^i$ is a set of PRV from G. (ii) For each parfactor $\phi(\mathcal{A})|C$ in G, $\mathcal{A}$ must appear in some parcluster $\mathbf{C}^i$. (iii) If a PRV from G appears in two parclusters $\mathbf{C}^i$ and $\mathbf{C}^j$, it must also appear in every parcluster $\mathbf{C}^k$ on the path connecting nodes i and j in J (running intersection). The separator $\mathbf{S}^{ij}$ of edge $i-j$ is given by $\mathbf{C}^i \cap \mathbf{C}^j$ containing shared PRVs.

LJTconstructs an FO jtree using a first-order decomposition tree, enters evidence in the FO jtree, and to distribute local information of the nodes through the FO jtree, passes messages through an *inbound* and an *outbound* pass. To compute a message, LJT eliminates all non-separator PRVs from the parcluster's local model and received messages. After message passing, LJT answers queries. For each query, LJT finds a parcluster containing the query term and sums out all non-query terms in its local model and received messages.

Figure 2 shows an FO jtree of G^{ex} with the local models of the parclusters and the separators as labels of edges. During the *inbound* phase of message passing, LJT sends messages from $\mathbf{C}^1$ to $\mathbf{C}^2$ and for the *outbound* phase a message from $\mathbf{C}^2$ to $\mathbf{C}^1$. If we would like to know whether $S(bob)$ holds, we query $P(S(bob))$ for which LJT can use parcluster $\mathbf{C}^1$. LJT sums out $C(X)$, $W(X)$, and $S(X)$ where $X \neq bob$ from $\mathbf{C}^1$'s local model G^1, $\{g^0\}$, combined with the received messages.

4.2   LDJT: Overview

LDJT efficiently answers queries $P(Q_\pi^i | \mathbf{E}_{0:t})$, with $Q_\pi^i \in \mathbf{Q_t}$ and $\mathbf{Q_t} \in \{\mathbf{Q_t}\}_{t=0}^T$, given a PDM G and evidence $\{\mathbf{E}_t\}_{t=0}^T$, by performing the following steps: (i) Construct offline two FO jtrees J_0 and J_t with *in-* and *out-clusters* from G. (ii) For $t = 0$, enter $\mathbf{E}_0$ in J_0, pass messages, answer each query term $Q_\pi^i \in \mathbf{Q}_0$, and preserve the state in message α_0. (iii) For $t > 0$, instantiate J_t for the current time step t, recover the previous state from α_{t-1}, enter $\mathbf{E}_t$ in J_t, pass messages, answer each query term $Q_\pi^i \in \mathbf{Q}_t$, and preserve the state in message α_t.

Next, we show how LDJT constructs the FO jtrees J_0 and J_t with *in-* and *out-clusters*, which contain a minimal set of PRVs to m-separate the FO jtrees. M-separation means that information about these PRVs render FO jtrees independent from each other. Afterwards, we present how LDJT connects the FO jtrees for reasoning to solve the *filtering* and *prediction* problems efficiently.

4.3   LDJT: FO Jtree Construction for PDMs

LDJT constructs FO jtrees for G_0 and $G_\rightarrow$, both with an incoming and outgoing interface. To be able to construct the interfaces in the FO jtrees, LDJT uses the PDM G to identify the interface PRVs $\mathbf{I}_t$ for a time slice t.

Definition 7. *The forward interface is defined as* $\mathbf{I}_t = \{A_t^i \mid \exists \phi(\mathcal{A}) | C \in G : A_t^i \in \mathcal{A} \wedge \exists A_{t+1}^j \in \mathcal{A}\}$, *i.e., the PRVs which have successors in the next slice.*

For $G_\rightarrow^{ex}$, which is shown in, PRVs $C_{t-1}(X)$, $LT_{t-1}(X, X')$, and $S_{t-1}(X)$ have successors in the next time slice, making up $\mathbf{I}_{t-1}$. To ensure interface PRVs $\mathbf{I}$ ending up in a single parcluster, LDJT adds a parfactor g^I over the interface to the model. Thus, LDJT adds a parfactor g_0^I over $\mathbf{I}_0$ to G_0, builds an FO jtree J_0 and labels the parcluster with g_0^I from J_0 as in- and out-cluster. For $G_\rightarrow$, LDJT removes all non-interface PRVs from time slice $t - 1$, adds parfactors g_{t-1}^I and g_t^I, constructs J_t, and labels the parcluster containing g_{t-1}^I as *in-cluster* and the parcluster containing g_t^I as *out-cluster*.

The interface PRVs are a minimal required set to m-separate the FO jtrees. LDJT uses these PRVs as separator to connect the *out-cluster* of J_{t-1} with the *in-cluster* of J_t, allowing to reusing the structure of J_t for all $t > 0$.

4.4   LDJT: Proceeding in Time with the FO Jtree Structures

Since J_0 and J_t are static, LDJT uses LJT as a subroutine by passing on a constructed FO jtree, queries, and evidence for time step t to handle evidence entering, message passing, and query answering using the FO jtree. Further, for proceeding to the next time step, LDJT calculates an α_t message over the interface PRVs using the *out-cluster* to preserve the information about the current state. Afterwards, LDJT increases t by one, instantiates J_t, and adds α_{t-1} to the *in-cluster* of J_t. During message passing, α_{t-1} is distributed through J_t.

Figure 4 depicts how LDJT uses the interface message passing between time step three to four. First, LDJT sums out the non-interface PRVs from $\mathbf{C}_3^2$'s local model and the received messages and saves the result in message α_3. After increasing t by one, LDJT adds α_3 to the *in-cluster* of J_4, $\mathbf{C}_4^3$. α_3 is then distributed by message passing and accounted for during calculating α_4.

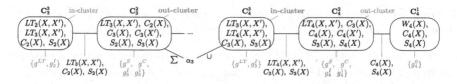

Fig. 4. Forward pass of LDJT without $\mathbf{C}_3^1$ (local models and labeling in grey)

5   Conjunctive Queries

We begin with recapitulating how LJT answers conjunctive queries in the static case [4]. Afterwards, we introduce LDJT^{con} to efficiently answer multiple conjunctive queries with query terms from different time steps.

5.1   Conjunctive Queries in LJT

We extend Definition 3 to allow for multiple query terms in a static query.

Definition 8. *Given a PM G, grounded PRVs $\mathcal{Q}$ and grounded PRVs with fixed range values* $\mathbf{E} = \{E^i = e^i\}_i$, *the expression $P(\mathcal{Q}|\mathbf{E})$ denotes a query w.r.t. $P(G)$.*

Each query of the set of queries $\mathbf{Q}$ that LJT answers can be a conjunctive query. Since the query terms are not necessarily contained in a single parcluster, LJT builds for that conjunctive query a parcluster containing all query terms to leverage its default query answering behaviour. Therefore, LJT identifies a subtree containing all query terms. LJT merges the subtree into one parcluster to answer the query. Further, LJT can still use the messages calculated during the initial message pass, which enter the subtree from the outside. Thus, after merging the subtree, LJT can directly use LVE on the local model of the merged subtree with the messages to answer a conjunctive query.

5.2 Conjunctive Queries in LDJT

Now, we introduce LDJT^{con} to answer multiple conjunctive queries. In case LDJT answers conjunctive *filtering* queries, meaning that all query terms are from the same time step, LDJT can just use LJT's merging approach. However, in case the query terms of a conjunctive query are from time step t up to time step $t + \delta$, LDJT would need to instantiate FO jtrees for δ time steps and identify a subtree for the combination of δ FO jtrees. The subtree contains at least $(\delta - 2) \times m + 2$ parclusters, where m is the number of parclusters on the path between *in-* and *out-cluster*. Thus, merging the parclusters of the subtree, leads to a parcluster with many PRVs. Further, the asymptotic complexity of LVE is exponential in the number of PRVs [19]. Hence, we propose an approach to answer temporal conjunctive queries, which merges fewer PRVs in a parcluster. First, we extend Definition 5 to allow for multiple query terms in a temporal query.

Definition 9. *Given a PDM G, grounded PRVs $\mathcal{Q}_t$ and grounded PRVs with fixed range values $\mathbf{E}_{0:t} = \{E_t^i = e_t^i\}_{i,t}$, $P(\mathcal{Q}_t | \mathbf{E}_{0:t})$ denotes a query w.r.t. $P(G)$.*

Now, each query that LDJT^{con} answers can be a conjunctive query. To answer a conjunctive query, LDJT^{con} needs a parcluster containing all query terms. We construct this parcluster without over-approximating the number of PRVs as much as merging a subtree. Thus, we develop an approach to avoid eliminations of query terms to obtain one parcluster with all query terms. To send a message from parcluster $\mathbf{C}^1$ to $\mathbf{C}^2$, LDJT eliminates all PRVs from $\mathbf{C}^1$ that are not included in the separator $\mathbf{S}^{12}$. Hence, LDJT extends separators with query terms. A PRV is in a separator iff the PRV is contained in both parclusters, which the separator connects. Therefore, to avoid the elimination of a PRV, LDJT^{con} adds the PRV to all parclusters on the path from the parcluster, where the PRV would be eliminated, to a designated parcluster. By extending parclusters with the query PRVs, LDJT can avoid the elimination of the query terms to answer conjunctive queries by leveraging LDJT's behaviour to answer a query.

A naive approach to extend parclusters is to add the query PRVs to all parclusters of the relevant time steps. Unfortunately by over-approximating the extension of parclusters, LDJT increases the number of PRVs in each parcluster. However, the complexity of LVE depends on the PRVs parclusters. Thus, we propose to add the query PRVs on demand, which is outlined in Algorithm 1. Basically, LDJT adds all query PRVs to a designated parcluster. Therefore, the number of PRVs in parclusters is only extended by the necessary number of PRVs.

Using Algorithm 1 LDJT^{con} ensures that one parcluster contains all query terms. Then, LDJT performs a message pass, and answers the conjunctive query $\mathcal{Q}$. To answer a conjunctive query, LDJT^{con} instantiates FO jtree $\mathcal{J}$ for the time steps t to $t + \delta$ of $\mathcal{Q}$. From $\mathcal{J}$ LDJT^{con} selects a *root* parcluster, which contains most of the query terms from $\mathcal{Q}$ and is from the last time step of $\mathcal{J}$, as designated receiver of all query PRVs. Now, LDJT^{con} needs to avoid the elimination of the query terms of $\mathcal{Q}$ to the *root* parcluster. Therefore, starting

---

Algorithm 1. Answer Conjunctive Query for Unrolled FO Jtrees for Time Steps t to $t + \delta$ $\mathcal{J}$ and Conjunctive Query $\mathcal{Q}$

---

procedure ANSWERCONJUNCTIVEQUERY($\mathcal{J}, \mathcal{Q}$)
    $root :=$ Parcluster with the most query terms from time step $t + \delta$
    for all Leaf parcluster $p \in \mathcal{J}$ **do**
        $current := p$
        while $current \neq root$ **do**
            $qt := \mathcal{Q} \cap current$
            $next :=$ next parcluster on the path to $root$
            $next := next + qt$
            $current := next$
    $\mathcal{J} :=$ LJT.PassMessages($\mathcal{J}$)
    LVE.AnswerQuery($root, \mathcal{Q}$)

---

from each leaf parcluster, LDJT^{con} traverses the path to the $root$ parcluster. As FO jtrees are cycle-free graphs, there is exactly one path from each leaf parcluster to the $root$ parcluster. While traversing the paths, LDJT^{con} checks whether a parcluster contains query PRVs and adds the query PRVs to all parclusters on the path to the $root$ parcluster. Thereby, LDJT avoids the elimination of query terms to the $root$ parcluster. Another way of interpreting the extension of the $root$ parcluster is to add all the query terms of $\mathcal{Q}$ to the $root$ parcluster and then to ensure the running intersection property of an FO jtree. After $root$ is extended, LDJT^{con} has to repeat a message pass, as the PRVs in parclusters changed. Lastly, LDJT^{con} can use LVE to answer the conjunctive query with the $root$ parcluster's local model, which contains at least the query terms, and the incoming messages.

Unfortunately, by avoiding eliminations of query terms, LDJT needs to perform an extra message pass as outlined in Algorithm 1. Nonetheless, the approach is still advantageous over identifying a subtree and merge the subtree into one parcluster for conjunctive queries over multiple time steps. Even though the work to answer one conjunctive query is the same, our approach is parallelisable and the search space for the elimination order is smaller. Further, for a second conjunctive query with the same query PRVs but different grounding, the work of the message pass can be reused and thereby redundant computations prevented.

To perform CEP, events from different time steps are queried. For example, we are interested whether there is an influence from $LT_t(x_1, x_2)$, $C_{t+2}(x_1)$, and $C_{t+2}(x_2)$. Figure 4 shows our example model unrolled for time step 3 and 4, without parcluster $\mathbf{C}_3^1$. Assuming, we have the conjunctive query $P(LT_2(eve, bob), C_4(bob), C_4(eve))$, then LDJT^{con} can apply the steps of Algorithm 1 to answer the query. First, LDJT^{con} selects $\mathbf{C}_4^1$ as $root$ parcluster, because $\mathbf{C}_4^1$ is from the latest time step and is a parcluster containing most of the query terms. Afterwards, LDJT^{con} extends the parclusters on the path from the leaf parclusters $\mathbf{C}_3^1$ and $\mathbf{C}_3^3$ to $root$. $\mathbf{C}_3^3$ includes the query term $LT_2(eve, bob)$. Hence, LDJT adds $LT_2(X, X')$ to all parclusters on the path to the $root$ parcluster, namely $\mathbf{C}_3^2$, $\mathbf{C}_4^3$, $\mathbf{C}_4^2$, and to the $root$ parcluster $\mathbf{C}_4^1$. No additional parcluster on the path from $\mathbf{C}_3^3$ to *root* contain any query terms. The same holds for the path from $\mathbf{C}_3^1$ to *root*. Second, LDJT^{con} performs a message pass on the extended FO jtree. Last, LDJT^{con} uses *root* to answer the conjunctive query. LDJT^{con} increases the maximum number of PRVs in a parcluster from 6 to 7, allowing us to efficiently answer multiple conjunctive query, e.g., also for *alice* and *bob*. By performing merging, all parclusters would be merged in a parcluster with 12 PRVs.

Theorem 1. *LDJT^{con}'s answering of conjunctive queries is correct.*

Proof. While extending a parcluster P to contain at least all query terms, LDJT ensures the running intersection property of FO jtrees. Thus, after the extension, the FO jtree is still valid, only with a changed elimination order. Further, LDJT performs a complete message pass after the FO jtree structure is changed to distribute information. Therefore, LDJT still has a valid FO jtree with P containing all query terms and the local model of P received the incoming messages. Hence, given that LVE is correct, using LVE to answer the conjunctive query with P's local model produces a correct answer to the conjunctive query.

Algorithm 1 still has room for improvement, e.g., currently, in case paths to the *root* parclusters merge, they are traversed multiple times. Further, LDJT could directly perform the message passing, while extending the parclusters and in case one only wants to use the unrolled FO jtree to answer conjunctive query with different grounding of the query PRVs, an *inbound* pass to the *root* parcluster would suffice to answer the conjunctive query. Furthermore, instead of unrolling FO jtrees, LDJT could also always only instantiate an FO jtree for one time step and proceed in time as described in Sect. 4.4, and one could increased parclusters to prevent groundings [3]. Nonetheless, Algorithm 1 in the current form allows for answering conjunctive queries from time step $t - \pi$ to $t + \delta$ in case one extends LDJT to answer *hindsight* queries by performing *smoothing*.

6   Evaluation

For the evaluation, we use the example model G^{ex} and evaluate computations LDJT^{con} can save. Therefore, we compare the maximum number of PRVs in a parcluster for LDJT^{con} against merging a subtree containing all query terms. We evaluate the influence the number of PRVs and the time interval in a conjunctive query have on the maximum number of PRVs in a parcluster. An example query is $P(W_{t-\delta}(eve), C_t(eve))$, which has two PRVs and the time interval is δ.

Figure 5 shows the maximum number of PRVs in a parcluster for different time intervals dependent on the maximum number of PRVs queried in a time step. The line for 2 PRVs (filled diamond) shows the parcluster size for conjunctive queries with at most 2 different PRVs queried in a time step, analogous for 1,3, 4, and 5. For example our query $P(W_{t-\delta}(eve), C_t(eve))$ has 1 PRV in each time step, relating to the 1 PRV line.

In Fig. 5 the 5 PRVs line (filled triangle) correspond to merging a subtree. Further, with merging one merges all time step in the time interval. Therefore,

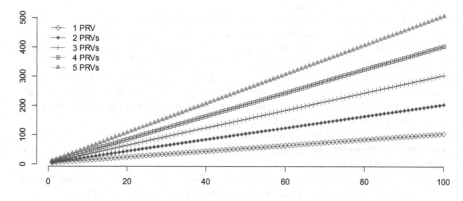

Fig. 5. Y-axis: maximum number of PRVs in a parcluster, x-axis: δ

for our example query with a δ of 10, the size of the maximum parcluster grows to 55 PRVs. For $LDJT^{con}$ there are only two different time steps involved with only one PRV for each time step involved. Therefore, the size of the largest parcluster only grows from 5 to 6 PRVs. Overall the size of the largest parcluster is always smaller by using $LDJT^{con}$ compared to merging a subtree.

We desire small parclusters, as the complexity of LVE is exponential to the number of PRVs [19]. For example with our query, with $LDJT^{con}$, the largest parcluster has 6 PRVs and with merging a subtree has 55 PRVs. Further, performing CEP could lead to asking the same conjunctive query at least for a subset of our individuals. Hence, starting with a second query only with different groundings, $LDJT^{con}$ saves the elimination of 49 PRVs, by reusing the computations performed during message passing by $LDJT^{con}$.

7 Conclusion

We present how $LDJT^{con}$ answers conjunctive queries by avoiding eliminations. To avoid eliminations, $LDJT^{con}$ increases parclusters with query PRVs until all query PRVs are in one parcluster. Results show that extending significantly reduces computations for multiple conjunction queries compared to merging.

We are currently working on extending LDJT to also calculate the most probable explanation. Other interesting future work includes a tailored automatic learning for PDMs, parallelisation of LJT, and improved evidence entering.

References

1. Ahmadi, B., Kersting, K., Mladenov, M., Natarajan, S.: Exploiting symmetries for scaling loopy belief propagation and relational training. Mach. Learn. **92**(1), 91–132 (2013)
2. Braun, T., Möller, R.: Lifted junction tree algorithm. In: Friedrich, G., Helmert, M., Wotawa, F. (eds.) KI 2016. LNCS (LNAI), vol. 9904, pp. 30–42. Springer, Cham (2016). https://doi.org/10.1007/978-3-319-46073-4_3

3. Braun, T., Möller, R.: Preventing groundings and handling evidence in the lifted junction tree algorithm. In: Kern-Isberner, G., Fürnkranz, J., Thimm, M. (eds.) KI 2017. LNCS (LNAI), vol. 10505, pp. 85–98. Springer, Cham (2017). https://doi.org/10.1007/978-3-319-67190-1_7

4. Braun, T., Möller, R.: Counting and conjunctive queries in the lifted junction tree algorithm. In: Croitoru, M., Marquis, P., Rudolph, S., Stapleton, G. (eds.) GKR 2017. LNCS (LNAI), vol. 10775, pp. 54–72. Springer, Cham (2018). https://doi.org/10.1007/978-3-319-78102-0_3

5. Dignös, A., Böhlen, M.H., Gamper, J.: Temporal alignment. In: Proceedings of the 2012 ACM SIGMOD International Conference on Management of Data, pp. 433–444. ACM (2012)

6. Dylla, M., Miliaraki, I., Theobald, M.: A temporal-probabilistic database model for information extraction. Proc. VLDB Endow. **6**(14), 1810–1821 (2013)

7. Gehrke, M., Braun, T., Möller, R.: Lifted dynamic junction tree algorithm. In: Chapman, P., Endres, D., Pernelle, N. (eds.) ICCS 2018. LNCS (LNAI), vol. 10872, pp. 55–69. Springer, Cham (2018). https://doi.org/10.1007/978-3-319-91379-7_5

8. Geier, T., Biundo, S.: Approximate online inference for dynamic markov logic networks. In: Proceedings of the 23rd IEEE International Conference on Tools with Artificial Intelligence (ICTAI), pp. 764–768. IEEE (2011)

9. Lauritzen, S.L., Spiegelhalter, D.J.: Local computations with probabilities on graphical structures and their application to expert systems. J. Roy. Stat. Soc. Ser. B (Methodol.) **50**(2), 157–224 (1988)

10. Manfredotti, C.E.: Modeling and inference with relational dynamic Bayesian networks. Ph.D. thesis, Ph.D. dissertation, University of Milano-Bicocca (2009)

11. Milch, B., Zettlemoyer, L.S., Kersting, K., Haimes, M., Kaelbling, L.P.: Lifted probabilistic inference with counting formulas. In: Proceedings of AAAI, vol. 8, pp. 1062–1068 (2008)

12. Murphy, K., Weiss, Y.: The factored frontier algorithm for approximate inference in DBNs. In: Proceedings of the Seventeenth Conference on Uncertainty in Artificial Intelligence, pp. 378–385. Morgan Kaufmann Publishers Inc. (2001)

13. Murphy, K.P.: Dynamic Bayesian networks: representation, inference and learning. Ph.D. thesis, University of California, Berkeley (2002)

14. Nitti, D., De Laet, T., De Raedt, L.: A particle filter for hybrid relational domains. In: Proceedings of the IEEE/RSJ International Conference on Intelligent Robots and Systems (IROS), pp. 2764–2771. IEEE (2013)

15. Papai, T., Kautz, H., Stefankovic, D.: Slice normalized dynamic Markov logic networks. In: Proceedings of the Advances in Neural Information Processing Systems, pp. 1907–1915 (2012)

16. Poole, D.: First-order probabilistic inference. In: Proceedings of IJCAI, pp. 985–991 (2003)

17. Richardson, M., Domingos, P.: Markov logic networks. Mach. Learn. **62**(1), 107–136 (2006)

18. de Salvo Braz, R.: Lifted first-order probabilistic inference. Ph.D. thesis, Ph.D. dissertation, University of Illinois at Urbana Champaign (2007)

19. Taghipour, N., Davis, J., Blockeel, H.: First-order decomposition trees. In: Proceedings of the Advances in Neural Information Processing Systems, pp. 1052–1060 (2013)

20. Taghipour, N., Fierens, D., Davis, J., Blockeel, H.: Lifted variable elimination: decoupling the operators from the constraint language. J. Artif. Intell. Res. **47**(1), 393–439 (2013)

21. Theodorsson, E.: Uncertainty in measurement and total error: tools for coping with diagnostic uncertainty. Clin. Lab. Med. **37**(1), 15–34 (2017)
22. Thon, I., Landwehr, N., De Raedt, L.: Stochastic relational processes: efficient inference and applications. Mach. Learn. **82**(2), 239–272 (2011)
23. Vlasselaer, J., Van den Broeck, G., Kimmig, A., Meert, W., De Raedt, L.: TP-compilation for inference in probabilistic logic programs. Int. J. Approx. Reason. **78**, 15–32 (2016)
24. Vlasselaer, J., Meert, W., Van den Broeck, G., De Raedt, L.: Efficient probabilistic inference for dynamic relational models. In: Proceedings of the 13th AAAI Conference on Statistical Relational AI, AAAIWS'14-13, pp. 131–132. AAAI Press (2014)
25. Wang, Y., Cao, K., Zhang, X.: Complex event processing over distributed probabilistic event streams. Comput. Math. Appl. **66**(10), 1808–1821 (2013)

Preventing Unnecessary Groundings in the Lifted Dynamic Junction Tree Algorithm

Marcel Gehrke$^{(\boxtimes)}$, Tanya Braun, and Ralf Möller

Institute of Information Systems, University of Lübeck, Lübeck, Germany
{gehrke,braun,moeller}@ifis.uni-luebeck.de

Abstract. The lifted dynamic junction tree algorithm (LDJT) answers *filtering* and *prediction* queries efficiently for probabilistic relational temporal models by building and then reusing a first-order cluster representation of a knowledge base for multiple queries and time steps. Unfortunately, a non-ideal elimination order can lead to groundings. We extend LDJT (i) to identify unnecessary groundings and (ii) to prevent groundings by delaying eliminations through changes in a temporal first-order cluster representation. The extended version of LDJT answers multiple temporal queries orders of magnitude faster than the original version.

1 Preventing Groundings in LJT

The elimination order in the lifted dynamic junction tree algorithm (LDJT) can lead to unnecessary groundings [2]. In this paper, we propose an approach to prevent unnecessary groundings and use the examples and definitions from [2].

A lifted solution to a query given a model means that we compute an answer without grounding a part of the model. Unfortunately, not all models have a lifted solution because lifted variable elimination (LVE), the basis for lifted junction tree algorithm (LJT), requires certain conditions to hold. Therefore, these models involve groundings with any exact lifted inference algorithm. Grounding a logical variable (logvar) is expensive and, during message passing, may propagate through all nodes. LJT has a few approaches to prevent groundings for a static first-order junction tree (FO jtree). On the one hand, some approaches originate from LVE. On the other hand, LJT has a fuse operator to prevent groundings, occurring due to a non-ideal elimination order [1].

1.1 General Grounding Prevention Techniques from LVE

One approach to prevent groundings is to perform lifted summing out. The idea is to compute VE for one case and exponentiate the result for isomorphic instances. Another approach in LVE to prevent groundings is count-conversion,

This research originated from the Big Data project being part of Joint Lab 1, funded by Cisco Systems Germany, at the centre COPICOH, University of Lübeck.

© Springer Nature Switzerland AG 2018
T. Mitrovic et al. (Eds.): AI 2018, LNAI 11320, pp. 556–562, 2018.
https://doi.org/10.1007/978-3-030-03991-2_51

which exploits that all random variables (randvars) of a parameterised randvar (PRV) A evaluate to a value v of $range(A)$. LVE forms a histogram by counting for each $v \in range(A)$ how many instances of $gr(A)$ evaluate to v.

Definition 1. $\#_{X \in C}[P(\mathbf{X})]$ *denotes a counting randvar (CRV) with PRV $P(\mathbf{X})$ and constraint C, where $lv(\mathbf{X}) = \{X\}$. Its range is the space of possible histograms. If $\{X\} \subset lv(\mathbf{X})$, the CRV is a parameterised CRV (PCRV) representing a set of CRVs. Since counting binds logvar X, $lv(\#_{X \in C}[P(\mathbf{X})]) = \mathbf{X} \setminus \{X\}$. We count-convert a logvar X in a parametric factor (parfactor) $g = \mathbf{L} : \phi(\mathcal{A})|C$ by turning a PRV $A^i \in \mathcal{A}$, $X \in lv(A^i)$, into a CRV $A^{i'}$. In the new parfactor g', the input for $A^{i'}$ is a histogram h. Let $h(a^i)$ denote the count of a^i in h. Then, $\phi'(...,a^{i-1}, h, a^{i+1}, ...)$ maps to $\prod_{a^i \in range(A^i)} \phi(...,a^{i-1}, a^i, a^{i+1}, ...)^{h(a^i)}$.*

One precondition to count-convert a logvar X in g, is that only one input in g contains X. To perform lifted summing out PRV A from parfactor g, $lv(A) = lv(g)$. For the complete list of preconditions for both approaches, see [3].

1.2   Preventing Groundings During Intra FO Jtree Message Passing

During message passing, LJT tries to eliminate PRVs by lifted summing out. However, the messages LJT passes via the separators restrict the elimination order, which can lead to groundings. LJT has three tests whether groundings occur during message passing, namely: (i) check whether LJTcan apply lifted summing out, (ii) check whether count-conversion can prevent groundings, and (iii) check that count-converting will not lead to groundings in another parcluster.

A parcluster $\mathbf{C}^i = \mathcal{A}^i|C^i$ sends a message m^{ij} containing the PRVs of the separator $\mathbf{S}^{ij}$ to parcluster $\mathbf{C}^j$. To calculate the message m^{ij}, LJT eliminates the PRVs not part of the separator, i.e., $\mathbf{E}^{ij} := \mathcal{A}^i \setminus \mathbf{S}^{ij}$, from the local model and all messages received from other nodes than j, i.e., $G' := G^i \cap \{m^{il}\}_{l \neq j}$. To eliminate a PRV from G', LJT has to eliminate the PRV from all parfactors of G'. By combining all these parfactors, LJT only has to check whether a lifted summing out is possibile to eliminate the PRV. To eliminate $E \in \mathbf{E}^{ij}$ by lifted summing out from G', we replace all parfactors $g \in G'$ that include E with a parfactor $g^E = \phi(\mathcal{A}^E)|C^E$ that is the lifted product of these parfactors. Let $\mathbf{S}_E^{ij} := \mathbf{S}^{ij} \cap \mathcal{A}^E$ be the set of randvars in the separator that occur in g^E. For lifted message calculation, it necessarily has to hold $\forall S \in \mathbf{S}_E^{ij}$,

$$lv(S) \subseteq lv(E). \tag{1}$$

Otherwise, E does not include all logvars in g^E. LJT may induce Eq. (1) for a particular S by count-conversion if S has an additional, count-convertible logvar:

$$lv(S) \setminus lv(E) = \{L\}, \text{ L count-convertible in } g^E. \tag{2}$$

In case Eq. (2) holds, LJT count-converts L, yielding a (P)CRV in m^{ij}, else, LJT grounds. Unfortunately, a (P)CRV can lead to groundings in another parcluster. Hence, count-conversion helps in preventing a grounding if all following messages can handle the resulting (P)CRV. Formally, for each node k receiving S as a (P)CRV with counted logvar L, it has to hold for each neighbour n of k that

$$S \in \mathbf{S}^{kn} \vee \text{L count-convertible in } g^S. \tag{3}$$

LJT fuses two parclusters to prevent groundings if Eqs. (1) to (3) checks determine unnecessary groundings would occur by message passing between these parcluster.

2 Preventing Groundings in LDJT

LDJT has an intra and inter FO jtree message passing phase. Intra FO jtree message passing takes place inside of an FO jtree. Inter FO jtree message passing takes place between two FO jtrees. In both cases unnecessary groundings can occur. To prevent groundings during intra FO jtree message passing, LJT successfully proposes to fuse parclusters. Additionally, LDJT performs inter FO jtree message passing using two instantiations of an FO jtree structure. Unfortunately, having two FO jtrees, LDJT cannot fuse parclusters from different FO jtrees. Hence, LDJT requires a different approach to preventing unnecessary groundings during inter FO jtree message passing. In the following, we present how LDJT prevents grounding and discuss preventing of groundings during intra and inter FO jtree message passing as well as the implications for a lifted run.

2.1 Preventing Groundings During Inter FO Jtree Message Passing

As we desire a lifted solution, LDJT also needs to prevent unnecessary groundings induced during inter FO jtree message passes. Therefore, LDJT's *expanding* performs two steps: (i) check whether inter FO jtree message pass induced groundings occur, (ii) prevent groundings by extending the set of interface PRVs, and prevent possible intra FO jtree message pass induced groundings.

Checking for Groundings. To determine whether an inter FO jtree message pass induces groundings, LDJT also uses Eqs. (1) to (3). For the forward pass, LDJT applies the equations to check whether the α_{t-1} message from J_{t-1} to J_t leads to groundings. More precisely, LDJT needs to check for groundings for the inter FO jtree message passing between J_0 and J_1 as well as between two temporal FO jtree copy patters, namely J_{t-1} to J_t for $t > 1$.

Thus, LDJT checks all PRVs $E \in \mathbf{E}^{ij}$, where i is the *out-cluster* from J_{t-1} and j is the *in-cluster* from J_t, for groundings. In case Eq. (1) holds, no additional checks for E are necessary as eliminating E does not induce groundings. In case Eq. (2) holds, LDJT has to test whether Eq. (3) holds in J_t at least on the path from *in-cluster* to *out-cluster*. Hence, if Eqs. (2) and (3) both hold, eliminating E does not lead to groundings, but if Eq. (2) or Eq. (3) fail groundings occur.

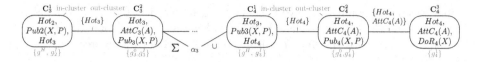

Fig. 1. Forward pass of LDJT without $\mathbf{C}_3^3$ (local models and labeling in grey)

Expanding Interface Separators. In case eliminating E leads to groundings, LDJT delays the elimination to a point where the elimination does no longer lead to groundings. Therefore, LDJT adds E to the *in-cluster* of J_t, which results in E also being added to the inter FO jtree separator. Hence, LDJT does not need to eliminate E in the *out-cluster* of J_{t-1} anymore. Based on the way LDJT constructs the FO jtree structures, the FO jtrees stay valid. Lastly, LDJT prevents groundings in the extended *in-cluster* of J_t as described in Sect. 1.2.

Let us now have a look at Fig. 1 to understand the central idea of preventing inter FO jtree message pass induced groundings. Figure 1 shows J_t instantiated for time step 3 and 4. Using these instantiations, LDJT checks for groundings during inter FO jtree message passing for the temporal copy pattern. To compute α_3, LDJT eliminates $AttC_3(A)$ from $\mathbf{C}_3^2$'s local model. Hence, LDJT checks whether the elimination leads to groundings. In this example, Eq. (1) does not hold, since $AttC_3(A)$ does not contain all logvars, X and P are missing. Additionally, Eq. (2) is not applicable, as the expression $lv(S) \setminus lv(E) = \{X, P\} \setminus \{C\} = \{X, P\}$, which contains more than one logvar and therefore is not count-convertible.

As eliminating $AttC_3(A)$ leads to groundings, LDJT adds $AttC_3(A)$ to the parcluster $\mathbf{C}_4^1$. Additionally, LDJT also extends the inter FO jtree separator with $AttC_3(A)$ and thereby changes the elimination order. By doing so, LDJT does not need to eliminate $AttC_3(A)$ in $\mathbf{C}_3^2$ anymore and therefore calculating α_3 does not lead to groundings. However, LDJT has to check whether adding the PRV leads to groundings in $\mathbf{C}_4^1$. For the extended parcluster $\mathbf{C}_4^1$, LDJT needs to eliminate the PRVs Hot_3, $AttC_3(A)$, and $Pub3(X, P)$. To eliminate $Pub3(X, P)$, LDJT first count-converts $AttC_3(A)$ and then Eq. (1) holds for $Pub3(X, P)$. Afterwards, it can eliminate the count-converted $AttC_3(A)$ and the PRV Hot_3 as Eq. (1) holds for both of them. Thus, by adding the PRV $AttC_{t-1}(A)$ to the *in-cluster* of J_t and thereby to the inter FO jtree separator, LDJT can prevent unnecessary groundings. Additionally, as LDJT uses this FO jtree structure for all time steps $t > 0$, i.e., the changes to the structure also hold for all $t > 0$.

Theorem 1. *LDJT's expanding is correct and produces a valid FO jtree.*

Proof. In the initial FO jtree structures, the separator between FO jtree J_{t-1} and J_t consists of exactly $\mathbf{I}_{t-1}$. Thus, by taking the intersection of the PRVs contained in J_{t-1} and J_t, we get the set of PRVs from $\mathbf{I}_{t-1}$. While LDJT calculates α_{t-1}, it only needs to eliminate PRVs $\mathbf{E}$ not contained in the separator and thereby $\mathbf{I}_{t-1}$. Therefore, all $E \in \mathbf{E}$ are not contained in any parcluster of J_t. Hence, by adding E to the *in-cluster* of J_t, LDJT does not violate any FO jtree properties. Further, LDJT does not even have to validate properties like the running intersection property, since it could not have been violated in the first place. Additionally, LDJT extends the set of interface PRVs, resulting in an over-approximation of the required PRVs for the inter FO jtree communication to be correct.

2.2   Discussion

In the following, we start by discussing workload and performance aspects of the intra and inter FO jtree message passing. Afterwards, we present model constellations where LDJT cannot prevent groundings.

Performance. The additional workload for LDJT introduced by handling unnecessary groundings is moderate. In the best case, LDJT checks Eqs. (1) to (3) for calculating two messages, namely for the α_{t-1} message and for the message LDJT passes from in *in-cluster* of J_t in the direction of the *out-cluster* of J_t. In the worst case, LDJT needs to check $1 + (m - 1)$ messages, where m is the number of parclusters on the path from the *in-cluster* to the *out-cluster* in J_t.

From a performance point of view, increasing the size of the α messages and of a parcluster is not ideal, but always better than the impact of groundings, which would result in ground calculations for each time step. By applying the intra FO jtree message passing check, LDJT may fuse the *in-cluster* and *out-cluster*, which most likely results in a parcluster with many model PRVs. Increasing the number of PRVs in a parcluster, increases LDJT's workload for query answering. But even with the increased workload a lifted run is faster than grounding. However, in case the checks determine that a lifted solution is not obtainable, using the initial model with the local clustering is the best solution.

First, applying LJT's *fusion* is more efficient since fusing the *out-cluster* with another parclusters could increase the number of its PRVs. In case of changed PRVs, LDJT has to rerun the *expanding* check. Therefore, LDJT first applies the intra and then the inter FO jtree message passing checks.

Groundings LDJT Cannot Prevent. Fusing the *in-cluster* and *out-cluster* due to the inter FO jtree message passing check is one case for which LDJT cannot prevent groundings. In this case, LDJT cannot eliminate E in the *out-cluster* of J_{t-1} without groundings. Thus, LDJT adds E to the *in-cluster* of J_t. The checks whether LDJT can eliminate E on the path from the *in-cluster* to the *out-cluster* of J_t fail. Thereby, LDJT fuses all parclusters on the path between the two parclusters and LDJT still cannot eliminate E. Even worse, LDJT cannot eliminate E from time step $t - 1$ and t in the *out-cluster* to calculate α_t. In theory, for an unrolled model, a lifted solution might be possible, but with many PRVs in a parcluster, since, in addition to other PRVs, one parcluster contains E for all time steps. Depending on the domain size and the maximum number of time steps, either grounding or using the unrolled model is advantageous.

If S occurs in an inter-slice parfactor for both time steps, then another source of groundings is a count-conversion of S to eliminate E. In such a case, LDJT cannot count-convert S in the inter-slice parfactor, which leads to groundings.

3   Evaluation

For the evaluation, we use the example model G^{ex} with the set of evidence being empty, for $|\mathcal{D}(X)| = 10$, $|\mathcal{D}(P)| = 3$, $|\mathcal{D}(C)| = 20$, and the queries $\{Hot_t, AttC_t(c_1), DoR_t(x_1)\}$ for each time step. We compare the runtimes on commodity hardware with 16 GB of RAM of the extended LDJT version against the original version and then also against LJT for multiple maximum time steps.

Figure 2 shows the runtime in seconds for each maximum time step. We can see that the runtime of the extended LDJT (diamond) and the original LDJT (filled triangle) is, as expected, linear, while the runtime of LJT (cross) roughly is exponential, to answer queries for changing maximum number of time steps. Further, we can see how crucial preventing groundings is. Due to the FO jtree construction overhead, the extended version is about a magnitude of three faster for first time steps, but the construction overhead becomes negligible with more time steps. Overall, the extended LDJT is up to four orders of magnitude faster.

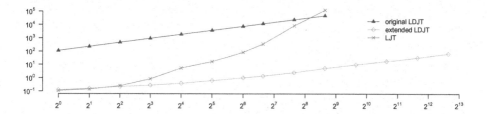

Fig. 2. Y-axis: runtimes [seconds], x-axis: maximum time steps, both in log scale

Additionally, we see the runtimes of LJT. LJT is faster for the initial time steps, especially in case grounding are prevented by unrolling. Nonetheless, after several time steps, the size of the parclusters becomes a big factor, which also explains the exponential behaviour [3]. To summarise the evaluation results, on the one hand, we see how crucial the prevention of groundings is and, on the other hand, how crucial the dedicated handling of temporal aspects is.

4   Conclusion

We present how LDJT can prevent unnecessary groundings by delaying eliminations to the next time step and thereby changing the elimination order. To delay eliminations, LDJT increases the *in-cluster* of the temporal FO jtree structure and the separator between *out-cluster* and *in-cluster* with PRVs, which lead to the groundings. First results show that the extended LDJT significantly outperforms the orignal version and LJT if unnecessary groundings occur.

We currently work on extending LDJT to calculate the most probable explanation. Other interesting future work includes a tailored automatic learning for parameterised probabilistic dynamic models and parallelisation of LJT.

References

1. Braun, T., Möller, R.: Preventing groundings and handling evidence in the lifted junction tree algorithm. In: Kern-Isberner, G., Fürnkranz, J., Thimm, M. (eds.) KI 2017. LNCS (LNAI), vol. 10505, pp. 85–98. Springer, Cham (2017). https://doi.org/10.1007/978-3-319-67190-1_7
2. Gehrke, M., Braun, T., Möller, R.: Towards preventing unnecessary groundings in the lifted dynamic junction tree algorithm. In: Trollmann, F., Turhan, A.Y. (eds.) KI 2018. LNCS, pp. 38–45. Springer, Cham (2018). https://doi.org/10.1007/978-3-030-00111-7_4
3. Taghipour, N.: Lifted probabilistic inference by variable elimination. Ph.D. thesis, KU Leuven (2013)

Machine Learning and Data Mining

Feature Standardisation in Symbolic Regression

Caitlin A. Owen$^{(\boxtimes)}$ⓘ, Grant Dickⓘ, and Peter A. Whighamⓘ

Department of Information Science, University of Otago, Dunedin, New Zealand
{caitlin.owen,grant.dick,peter.whigham}@otago.ac.nz

Abstract. While standardisation of variables is a common practice for many machine learning algorithms, it is rarely seen in the literature on genetic programming for symbolic regression. This paper compares the predictive performance of unscaled and standardised genetic programming, using artificial datasets and benchmark problems. Linear scaling is also applied to genetic programming for these problems. We show that unscaled genetic programming provides worse predictive performance than genetic programming augmented by linear scaling and/or standardisation as it is highly sensitive to the magnitude and range of explanatory or response variables. While linear scaling does provide better predictive performance on the simple artificial datasets, we attribute much of its success to an implicit standardisation within the predictive model. For benchmark problems, the combination of linear scaling and standardisation provides greater stability than only applying linear scaling to genetic programming. Also, for many of the simple artificial datasets, unscaled genetic programming produces larger individuals, which is undesirable in the search for parsimonious models.

Keywords: Genetic programming · Standardisation · Linear scaling

1 Introduction

Symbolic regression is the process of fitting mathematical models to observations through searching for arbitrary equations rather than pre-defining a fixed form. Though there are many ways to potentially search the space of equations in symbolic regression, the majority of research has focused upon using methods based upon genetic programming (GP) [9]. Indeed, symbolic regression has become almost synonymous with GP, with indications that as much as a third of all research into GP is dedicated to using or improving symbolic regression [17]. However, the baseline symbolic regression performance of *canonical* GP as defined by Koza has been shown to be quite poor [3], and a large body of work has introduced new search operators, selection methods, and fitness functions to improve upon this performance. Almost all of this work has focused upon internal factors of GP itself: factors relating to the nature of the data provided to GP for training remain largely unexplored. This is in contrast to many other types of

© Springer Nature Switzerland AG 2018
T. Mitrovic et al. (Eds.): AI 2018, LNAI 11320, pp. 565–576, 2018.
https://doi.org/10.1007/978-3-030-03991-2_52

machine learning, such as neural networks, where it is well-understood that data must be adequately preprocessed (e.g., through standardising variables) prior to training to best exploit the learning method's behaviour [10].

Given that GP typically evolves solutions that involve multiple interactions between numerous variables, there is a need to properly understand the impact that variable scale, and more importantly removing the scale of variables through standardisation, has on GP performance. This paper explores the impact of standardisation of GP on a range of symbolic regression problems, and compares the resulting behaviour to that of GP augmented with linear scaling. The results suggest that the success of linear scaling at improving GP performance can largely be attributed to an explicit translation and rotation of the predictive model. We also demonstrate that standardisation of variables prior to evolution has a positive effect on the size on individuals relative to canonical GP and GP using linear scaling. Exploiting this knowledge, we explore the behaviour of a GP variant that utilises both standardisation and linear scaling, and demonstrate that this variant offers the lowest error with increased stability over a range of benchmark problems. Given that it demands almost no cost in terms of computational effort, we argue that all future investigations using GP for symbolic regression adopt standardisation of variables.

The remainder of this paper is structured as follows: Sect. 2 provides a background review of the methods used to improve the performance of GP (including linear scaling), Sect. 3 outlines the process involved in performing standardisation, Sect. 4 presents the method and experimental results for simple artificial datasets, Sect. 5 presents the method and experimental results for the benchmark datasets, and Sect. 6 presents the conclusions and suggestions for future work.

2   Background

There have been many previous attempts to improve the baseline performance of GP for symbolic regression: these include the use of gradient descent to optimise coefficients [15], interval arithmetic to increase reliability [4,7], special crossover methods to accelerate search [16], and semantic methods such as geometric semantic GP (GSGP) [11]. In all these cases, the emphasis is on the underlying algorithms used by GP: there is little emphasis on exploring the behaviour of GP in response to the nature and scale of the data used for training. As data used for modelling is typically supplied in arbitrary scales, dimensions and formats, this has many practical implications for genetic programming. The units used to record the state of a variable may have significant impact in the way that they interact with other variables in the problem. For example, recording an elapsed time in hours will produce values several orders of magnitude smaller than the same quantity recorded in seconds, and this would produce considerably different behaviour if this variable was used within a ratio computation. To cope with this, canonical GP using raw *unscaled variables* needs to rely on the use of ephemeral random constants, and possibly adjusting their magnitude, in order to appropriately scale variables within the evolved model. However, the search mechanisms in canonical GP do not lend themselves well to searching for optimal coefficient values [7].

2.1 Linear Scaling

Earlier work, particularly that of Keijzer et al., introduced extensions to GP that attempt to acknowledge the scale and nature of the variables used for modelling [7,8]. Of particular interest to the work in this paper is the concept of *linear scaling*: this involves calculating the slope and intercept for a regression of the actual values on the fitted values for the set of outputs of a GP system, resulting in the scaled formula $a + b\hat{y}$, where $\hat{y}$ is the prediction/output of the GP system. The slope (b) and intercept (a) are calculated using the formulas:

$$b = \frac{\sum[(y - \bar{y})(\hat{y} - \bar{\hat{y}})]}{\sum[(\hat{y} - \bar{\hat{y}})^2]} \tag{1}$$

$$a = \bar{y} - b\bar{\hat{y}} \tag{2}$$

where y is the actual response, $\bar{y}$ is the mean actual response, $\hat{y}$ is the prediction/output of the GP system and $\bar{\hat{y}}$ is the mean prediction/output. As linear scaling calculates two coefficients that would otherwise have to be evolved explicitly by GP, this means that GP is "free to search for that expression whose shape is most similar to that of the target function" [7, p. 7]. Implicit in this is the notion that the scale of input variables and their impact on the resulting GP function will be standardised when wrapped in a linear model. However, no standardisation of variables was done by Keijzer et al., so linear scaling was effectively tasked with both shifting the search space and correcting the shape of the evolved GP function.

3 Standardisation of Variables

Standardising variables is a common practice in machine learning. The motivation for this is that all variables are initially treated with equal importance in a predictive model. For example, variables are standardised for k-nearest neighbour methods so that a variable captured in an arbitrarily small unit does not dominate other variables when measuring Euclidean distance. Standardisation is a preferred preprocessing method compared to normalisation because the distribution of a variable with standardised values more closely follows a normal distribution and standardisation reduces the effect of outliers. A variable y is converted into its standardised form y_{ST} using the equation:

$$y_{ST} = \frac{y - \bar{y}}{SD(y)} \tag{3}$$

where $\bar{y}$ is the sample mean value of y and $SD(y)$ is the sample standard deviation of y. The predictor variables can be standardised in the same way. Typically, once a model using standardised inputs has been trained, any predictions are also in a standardised space, and so a reverse transformation is typically applied to the prediction to restore the value back into the original scale of the response.

4   Initial Comparisons of Standardisation in GP

Though it appears to be essentially overlooked, the concept of standardisation can be easily applied to GP. This is an important concept to explore, as the scale of the response in relation to its predictor variables is likely to have an effect on the performance of a predictive model. If a model is produced to predict the outcomes from an underlying data generating process that involves a reasonably large intercept, for example, then the individuals evolved in GP may have difficulty in capturing random constants that capture the magnitude of the underlying intercept. Therefore, the importance of standardisation for GP needs to be investigated.

We adopt a simple model of standardisation: after performing GP, the predicted value is converted back into its normal range using the equation:

$$\hat{y}_* = \bar{y} + SD(y) * GP(X_{ST}) \tag{4}$$

where $GP(X_{ST})$ is the output value from the GP system, using standardised predictors (we call this full standardisation). Alternatively, only the response variable could be standardised, which would be converted back into its normal range using the equation:

$$\hat{y}_* = \bar{y} + SD(y) * GP(X) \tag{5}$$

where $GP(X)$ is the output value from the GP system, using unstandardised predictors (we call this partial standardisation).

An initial controlled experiment was set up to compare unscaled GP, fully standardised GP, partially standardised GP, linear scaled GP and the combination of fully standardised and linear scaled GP (see Eq. 8). These variations of GP all operated with the function set $\{+, -, *, AQ\}$, where AQ is the analytic quotient defined by [12] as:

$$AQ(x_1, x_2) = \frac{x_1}{\sqrt{1 + x_2^2}} \tag{6}$$

where x_1 and x_2 are real numbers. The analytic quotient has similar properties to that of the division operator but without the need for protection. This is important in terms of operator closure as Koza argues that an operation on a real number should always map to another real number [9]. Operators often used by Koza, including sin, cos, log_e and exp, have not been included in this function set as they can be approximated by polynomial combinations of arithmetic operators in a GP tree and often require protection. The possible terminal nodes consist of the explanatory variables in the dataset as well as ephemeral random constants (ERCs) drawn from the uniform distribution [-1,1). GP was performed using the

ECJ library in Java. To avoid bias, the sample mean and standard deviation of all variables was established using training data, and the same values were then used for subsequent testing.

The predictive performance of different versions of GP was determined using root relative squared error (RRSE), which is calculated using the formula:

$$RRSE = \sqrt{\frac{\sum_i (y_i - \hat{y}_i)^2}{\sum_i (y_i - \bar{y})^2}} \tag{7}$$

where i denotes the index of an instance in the data set. For standardised GP, $\hat{y}$ is replaced by $\hat{y}_*$ (see Eqs. 3 to 5) and by $a + b\hat{y}$ for linear scaled GP (see Eqs. 1 and 2). In addition to RRSE, we measure and compare the size of models produced by the different variations of GP.

Unscaled GP, fully standardised GP, partially standardised GP, and linear scaled GP were compared using a number of artificial datasets, all of which use the same underlying data generating process:

$$y = Bx_1x_2 + C + U(-0.05, 0.05) \tag{8}$$

where x_1 and x_2 are drawn from the uniform distribution [-1,1). Given that this generating function involves a single interaction of only two variables, we could naïvely assume that GP would find this a trivial problem to search. However, previous research has indicated that GP struggles on functions of this form when B and C become large [7]. In order to determine how the methods perform based on the magnitude of coefficient B and magnitude of intercept C, the data were produced for B and C equal to 1, 2, 4, 8, 16 and 32 (i.e. 36 different datasets). Each dataset was generated with 100 observations and was split into training (90 observations used to train GP) and test sets (10 observations) using 10-fold cross-validation that was repeated 10 times. For these datasets, GP was performed using the default parameters in ECJ.

4.1 Results

The testing RRSE (averaged over the different cross-validation folds) for the best individual in the population is shown in Fig. 1. The RRSE values in the range [0,1] are plotted on the vertical axis; only the unscaled GP provides RRSE values greater than one. The training RRSE values (not shown) exhibit similar behaviour, although with smaller RRSE values for the initial population. For small B and C, the four methods provide similar predictive performance, particularly after approximately 10 generations. As with the training RRSE, linear scaling provides better performance for the initial population, staying relatively constant during the evolutionary process. As the magnitude of C increases, the test RRSE associated with unscaled GP increases while the test RRSE of the three other methods remains relatively constant. This strongly suggests the importance of standardisation or linear scaling in GP providing good predictive performance. As the magnitude of B increases, unscaled GP provides a higher RRSE for the initial population and a slower decrease in RRSE. Also, the test RRSE associated with linear scaled GP decreases as B increases, providing better predictive performance than the other methods. This shows that linear scaling provides better generalisation performance than standardisation for large scale coefficients in a simple data generating process. Fully standardised GP and partially standardised GP provide similar predictive performance, although fully standardised GP does provide slightly better generalisation performance for the initial population.

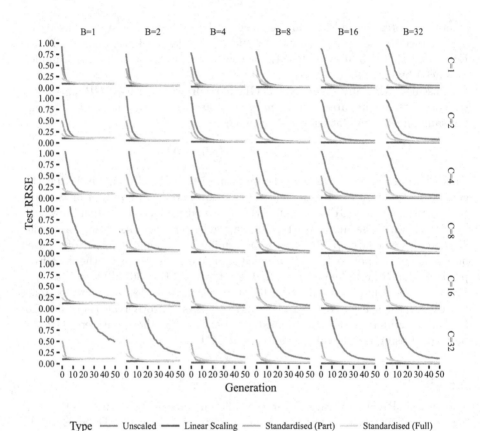

Fig. 1. Test RRSE of best individual averaged over cross validation folds

The mean tree size (averaged over the different cross-validation folds) is shown in Fig. 2. For small B and C, unscaled GP provides the smallest increase in tree size and linear scaling provides the largest increase. This may be due to linear scaling protecting good solutions from disruption due to crossover operations, in order to maintain good predictive performance [13]. As the magnitude of B or C increases, the size of trees generated by unscaled GP increase faster than for the other methods. This suggests that unscaled GP trees require more nodes than the other methods to try to capture the larger coefficient or intercept in the underlying data generating process as it is more difficult to evolve larger coefficients or intercepts without standardisation or linear scaling. The increase in tree size for unscaled GP is more pronounced for larger values of B and C.

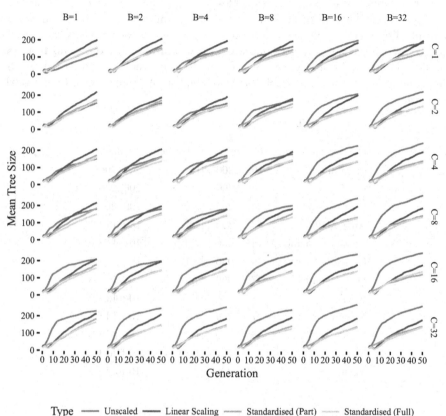

Fig. 2. Mean tree size averaged over cross validation folds

For these artificial datasets, linear scaled GP provides greater predictive performance than the other variations of GP. However, $y = Bx_1x_2 + C + U(-0.05, 0.05)$ is a simple underlying process, so it is not surprising that shifting the search space through linear scaling provides good predictive performance. Therefore, these methods should be examined using more complex datasets. Also, given that linear scaling appears to perform an implicit standardisation within the predictive model, a combination of fully standardised and linear scaled GP should be investigated to allow linear scaling to concentrate solely on its intended purpose.

5   Comparisons on Benchmark Data

All of the variations of GP examined in the previous section, with the additional combination of fully standardised and linear scaled GP, were compared using a number of artificial and real-world datasets, as shown in Table 1, where p is the number of explanatory variables and n is the number of observations. These datasets have been chosen as they are commonly used in the machine learning literature [5]. GP was repeated 100 times for each dataset: for Friedman 1–3 a different train/test split was drawn. For all other datasets, 10 trials of 10-fold cross-validation were used. The GP parameters used for these benchmark datasets are shown in Table 2 and are typical of those used in recent work [4,5,11].

Table 1. Benchmark datasets

Dataset	p	n	References	Train/Test
Friedman 1	10	2200	[1]	200, 2000
Friedman 2	4	2200	[1]	200, 2000
Friedman 3	4	2200	[1]	200, 2000
Auto MPG	7	392	[14]	10-fold CV
Boston Housing	13	506	[2,4,6]	10-fold CV
Concrete Strength	8	1030	[4,18]	10-fold CV
Dow Chemical	57	1066	[4]	10-fold CV
Energy	8	768	[4]	10-fold CV
Machine	7	209	[14]	10-fold CV
Ozone	8	330	[1]	10-fold CV
Servo	4	167	[1,14]	10-fold CV
Yacht	6	308	[4]	10-fold CV

Table 2. GP parameters for benchmark datasets

Parameter	Value
Population size	200
Number of generations	250
Probability of crossover	0.3
Probability of subtree mutation	0.7
Depth of subtree mutation	5
Elitism	Yes (1 individual)
Size of tournament	3

Training RRSE (averaged over the different cross-validation folds) for the best individual in the population is shown in Fig. 3, including the 95% confidence intervals for RRSE. The RRSE values in the range [0,1] are plotted on the vertical axis; only the unscaled GP provides RRSE values greater than one for the initial generations. For most of the datasets, unscaled GP and partially standardised GP provide the worst predictive performance. This is particularly the case for datasets that include explanatory variables with a much greater range and magnitude of values than the other explanatory variables in the dataset (e.g. the Dow Chemical dataset). As partially standardardised GP standardises only the response variable, the method does not affect the magnitude or range of explanatory variables. For some of the datasets, fully standardised GP provides worse predictive performance than unscaled GP or partially standardised GP after approximately 50 generations. This seems to be the case for datasets that have a response variable with a greater range and size of values than the explanatory values. As might be expected, standardising datasets that consist of explanatory variables with similar magnitudes and ranges results in performance largely equivalent to unscaled GP. However, linear scaled GP and the combination of standardised and linear scaled GP provide the best performance for all of the datasets. This shows that it is easier for GP to evolve desirable individuals when the search space is shifted, by calculating coefficient b for the predictions and intercept a. For many of the datasets, the combination of standardisation

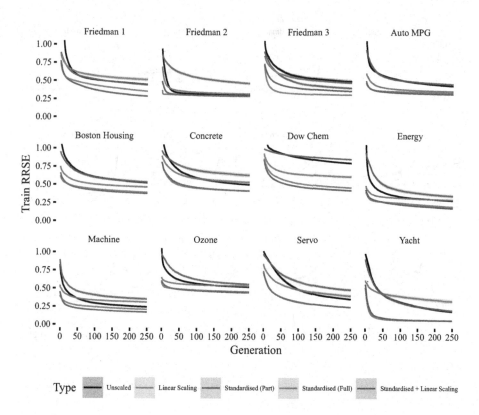

Fig. 3. Train RRSE of best individual averaged over cross validation folds

and linear scaling provides similar or better performance than linear scaling. This suggests that standardisation and linear scaling contribute in different ways and are therefore complementary in enhancing predictive performance.

The testing RRSE (averaged over the different cross-validation folds) for the best individual in the population is shown in Fig. 4, including the 95% confidence intervals for RRSE. Again, the RRSE values in the range [0,1] are plotted on the vertical axis; only unscaled GP and partially standardised GP provide RRSE values greater than one, mostly during the initial generations. The performance trends on the test and training data are similar. However, a number of the datasets (e.g. Machine and Ozone) exhibit more erratic behaviour in performance, particularly those that include explanatory variables with the largest magnitudes and/or ranges of values. For the Dow Chemical dataset, which has one explanatory variable with a very large range of values, unscaled GP and partially standardised GP provide large and erratic RRSE values. This shows the importance of standardising both the explanatory and response variables. Linear scaled GP provides more erratic predictive performance than combined standardised and linear scaled GP for some of the datasets, particularly those that include more than one variable with a large magnitude and range. This

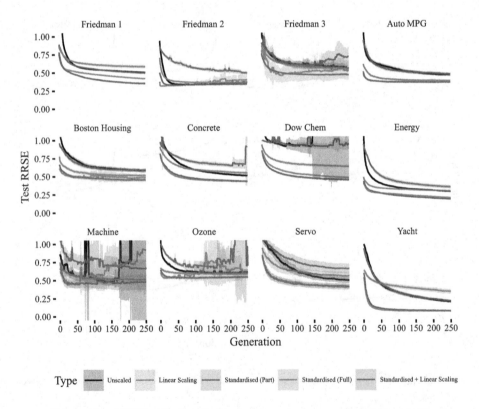

Fig. 4. Test RRSE of best individual averaged over cross validation folds

suggests that linear scaled GP does not generalise to unseen data as well as linear scaled and standardised GP combined. This may be because linear scaled GP shifts the search space based solely on information in the training data and so cannot manage the effects of outliers in the test set. In contrast, standardisation using statistics from the training data will have at least some effect on test outliers. For example, the Machine dataset includes one particularly large value for the fourth explanatory variable: if the observation associated with this value was included in the test data fold, it is unlikely to be represented by the search space shifted by linear scaling without standardisation. This observation may also contribute to the poor performance of unscaled GP, which provides very large mean test RRSE values (approximately 8) over the final 50 generations.

6   Conclusion

Standardisation of variables plays an important role in the performance of many machine learning methods. However, its effect on GP appears to be largely unexplored. This paper considers GP as a machine learning method, rather than systems identification, as GP is being used to approximate the unknown underlying function. This paper takes the first steps into exploring the importance of variable standardisation in GP and suggests that, like other methods that involve variable interactions, GP is highly sensitive to the scale in which variables are presented. Through a number of experiments, we have demonstrated that the performance of GP can be greatly improved simply through z-score standardisation of variables prior to training. Naturally, standardisation will have little effect if using GP to model a dataset that includes variables of similar scale. However, this process has positive effects on both error and size performance, typically resulting in models that were smaller and generalised better than using unscaled variables. Additionally, the process of standardisation had a positive effect on linear scaling, allowing it to concentrate on correcting the shape of the function evolved in GP and leaving standardisation to position the function within a promising region of the search space. The evidence presented in this paper strongly suggests that all future investigations into symbolic regression via genetic programming adopt a standardised variable approach.

The results reported in this paper are promising and suggest several areas of future investigation. While linear scaling is explicitly performing translation and rotation, the combination of linear scaled and standardised GP provides greater stability in predictive performance because it is more effective than implicitly dampening the oscillation between variables. Therefore, further investigation of how these variations of GP affect its predictive performance would be useful. This could be performed by decomposing the error associated with these methods. We also find that unscaled GP often produces larger individuals than standardised or linear scaled GP. Therefore, the models produced by these methods should be examined in order to test our hypothesis that unscaled GP produces large subtrees made up of ERCs in order to capture the magnitude or range of variables involved in the underlying data generating process.

References

1. Breiman, L.: Random forests. Mach. Learn. **45**(1), 5–32 (2001)
2. Breiman, L., Friedman, J., Stone, C.J., Olshen, R.A.: Classification and Regression Trees. CRC Press, Boca Raton (1984)
3. Dick, G.: Bloat and generalisation in symbolic regression. In: Dick, G., et al. (eds.) SEAL 2014. LNCS, vol. 8886, pp. 491–502. Springer, Cham (2014). https://doi.org/10.1007/978-3-319-13563-2_42
4. Dick, G.: Improving geometric semantic genetic programming with safe tree initialisation. In: Machado, P., et al. (eds.) EuroGP 2015. LNCS, vol. 9025, pp. 28–40. Springer, Cham (2015). https://doi.org/10.1007/978-3-319-16501-1_3
5. Dick, G., Owen, C.A., Whigham, P.A.: Evolving bagging ensembles using a spatially-structured niching method. In: Proceedings of the 2018 Annual Conference on Genetic and Evolutionary Computation. ACM (2018)
6. Harrison, D., Rubinfeld, D.L.: Hedonic housing prices and the demand for clean air. J. Environ. Econ. Manage. **5**(1), 81–102 (1978)
7. Keijzer, M.: Improving symbolic regression with interval arithmetic and linear scaling. In: Ryan, C., Soule, T., Keijzer, M., Tsang, E., Poli, R., Costa, E. (eds.) EuroGP 2003. LNCS, vol. 2610, pp. 70–82. Springer, Heidelberg (2003). https://doi.org/10.1007/3-540-36599-0_7
8. Keijzer, M., Babovic, V.: Dimensionally aware genetic programming. In: Proceedings of the 1st Annual Conference on Genetic and Evolutionary Computation, pp. 1069–1076. Morgan Kaufmann Publishers Inc., San Francisco (1999)
9. Koza, J.R.: Genetic Programming: On the Programming of Computers by Means of Natural Selection. MIT Press, Cambridge (1992)
10. LeCun, Y.A., Bottou, L., Orr, G.B., Müller, K.-R.: Efficient backprop. In: Montavon, G., Orr, G.B., Müller, K.-R. (eds.) Neural Networks: Tricks of the Trade. LNCS, vol. 7700, pp. 9–48. Springer, Heidelberg (2012). https://doi.org/10.1007/978-3-642-35289-8_3
11. Moraglio, A., Krawiec, K., Johnson, C.G.: Geometric semantic genetic programming. In: Coello, C.A.C., Cutello, V., Deb, K., Forrest, S., Nicosia, G., Pavone, M. (eds.) PPSN 2012. LNCS, vol. 7491, pp. 21–31. Springer, Heidelberg (2012). https://doi.org/10.1007/978-3-642-32937-1_3
12. Ni, J., Drieberg, R.H., Rockett, P.I.: The use of an analytic quotient operator in genetic programming. IEEE Trans. Evol. Comput. **17**(1), 146–152 (2013)
13. Nordin, P., Francone, F., Banzhaf, W.: Advances in genetic programming. In: Explicitly Defined Introns and Destructive Crossover in Genetic Programming, pp. 111–134. MIT Press, Cambridge (1996)
14. Quinlan, J.R.: Combining instance-based and model-based learning. In: Proceedings of the 10th International Conference on Machine Learning, pp. 236–243 (1993)
15. Topchy, A., Punch, W.F.: Faster genetic programming based on local gradient search of numeric leaf values. In: Proceedings of the 3rd Annual Conference on Genetic and Evolutionary Computation, pp. 155–162. Morgan Kaufmann Publishers Inc., San Francisco (2001)
16. Uy, N.Q., Hoai, N.X., O'Neill, M., McKay, R.I., Galván-López, E.: Semantically-based crossover in genetic programming: application to real-valued symbolic regression. Genet. Program. Evolvable Mach. **12**(2), 91–119 (2011)
17. White, D.R., et al.: Better GP benchmarks: community survey results and proposals. Genet. Program. Evolvable Mach. **14**(1), 3–29 (2013)
18. Yeh, I.C.: Modeling of strength of high-performance concrete using artificial neural networks. Cem. Concr. Res. **28**(12), 1797–1808 (1998)

Genetic Programming with Interval Functions and Ensemble Learning for Classification with Incomplete Data

Cao Truong Tran[(⊠)], Mengjie Zhang, Bing Xue, and Peter Andreae

School of Engineering and Computer Science, Victoria University of Wellington,
PO Box 600, Wellington 6140, New Zealand
{cao.truong.tran,mengjie.zhang,bing.xue,peter.andreae}@ecs.vuw.ac.nz

Abstract. Missing values are an unavoidable issue in many real-world datasets. Classification with incomplete data has to be addressed carefully because inadequate treatment often leads to a big classification error. Interval genetic programming (IGP) is an approach to directly use genetic programming to evolve an effective and efficient classifier for incomplete data. This paper proposes a method to improve IGP for classification with incomplete data by integrating IGP with ensemble learning to build a set of classifiers. Experimental results show that the integration of IGP and ensemble learning to evolve a set of classifiers for incomplete data can achieve better accuracy than IGP alone. The proposed method is also more accurate than other common methods for classification with incomplete data.

Keywords: Incomplete data · Classification · Genetic programming
Interval functions · Ensemble learning

1 Introduction

Classification is a major data mining task that predicts a class label for an instance based on feature values of the instance. Classification includes two main processes: a training process and an application (test) process. The goal of the training process is to use a classification algorithm on a training dataset to build a classifier. The goal of the application process is to use the built classifier to assign a class label to each instance. Classification has been widely applied to many areas such as computer science, engineering and medicine. However, there are still issues, one of which is incomplete data [1,6].

Missing values where the values of some features are unknown are a common example of incomplete data in many real-world datasets. For example, in the UCI machine learning repository [2], which is one of the most popular benchmarks for data mining, 45% of the datasets suffer from missing values. There are various causes of missing values. For example, in social surveys, respondents often refuse to answer some questions, so datasets collected from the surveys are incomplete.

© Springer Nature Switzerland AG 2018
T. Mitrovic et al. (Eds.): AI 2018, LNAI 11320, pp. 577–589, 2018.
https://doi.org/10.1007/978-3-030-03991-2_53

Medical datasets usually contain a large number of missing values because not all possible tests can be done on every patient [6].

Missing values cause serious problems for classification. One of the most serious problems is that the majority of classification algorithms do not work on datasets with missing values (incomplete datasets) [6]. For example, neural networks cannot directly work with incomplete data. Another problem is that missing values often lead to big classification error due to inadequate information for the training and application processes [10].

In classification tasks, discriminant functions are a popular method for representing classifiers. A discriminant function is a mathematical expression that represents a combination of the features of an instance which needs be classified. The value returned by the discriminant function determines the predicted class by using a single threshold (binary classification) or a set of thresholds (multi-class classification) [5].

Genetic programming (GP) is an evolutionary technique which constructs computer programs [9]. The capability of GP to learn the definition of a function from examples makes it a very good choice for constructing discriminant functions for classification tasks. Therefore, GP has been widely used to construct discriminant functions for classification tasks [5].

Although GP has been successfully used to construct classifiers, it has been mainly applied to complete data. To use traditional GP to construct classifiers for incomplete data, imputation methods which replaces missing values with plausible values [6] are required to transform incomplete data into complete data before using GP. To construct good classifiers, GP should be combined with sophisticated imputation methods such as multiple imputation by chained equations (MICE) [16]. Unfortunately, sophisticated imputation methods like MICE are only appropriate for batch imputation and are too computationally intensive to estimate missing values for individual incomplete instances in the unseen data [15].

In [14], interval GP (IGP) is proposed to directly construct classifiers for incomplete data without imputation requirement. Experimental results showed that IGP can evolve more effective and efficient classifiers than the combination of traditional GP and imputation. Moreover, IGP is more accurate than common classifiers able to directly classify incomplete data such as C4.5 and CART [17].

The overall goal of this paper is to improve the accuracy of IGP for classification with incomplete data. To achieve this goal, this paper proposes an integration of IGP and ensemble learning to construct an ensemble of classifiers for incomplete data. Specially, this paper will investigate:

- Whether a set of classifiers constructed by the proposed approach can achieve better classification accuracy than a single classifier constructed by IGP; and
- Whether a set of classifiers constructed by the proposed approach can achieve better classification accuracy than a set of classifier constructed by the combination of ensemble learning, imputation and traditional GP; and
- Whether a set of classifiers constructed by the proposed approach can achieve better classification accuracy than a set of classifiers constructed by the

combination of ensemble learning and classification algorithm that are able to directly work with incomplete data su such as C4.5/CART.

2 Related Work

This section outlines related work including approaches to classification with incomplete data, GP for classification and ensemble learning.

2.1 Approaches to Classification with Incomplete Data

There are three major approaches to classification with incomplete data: the deletion approach, the imputation approach, and directly classification with incomplete data [6].

- Deletion approach: this approach simply deletes all instances containing missing values. The benefit of this approach is that it provides complete data for classification. However, the deletion approach is only feasible for datasets with few missing values because this approach cannot provide enough information for training a classifier when a dataset has numerous missing values [1].
- Imputation approach: this approach uses imputation methods to transform incomplete data into complete data before building a classifier in the training process or classifying a new incomplete instance in the application process. This approach can provide complete data which then can be used by any classification algorithm. It also can deal with incomplete datasets with a large number of missing values. Therefore, imputation is the most popular approach to classification with incomplete data [6].
- Directly classification with incomplete data: this approach builds a model in the training process which can directly classify incomplete instances in the application process without requiring any imputation method. For example, C4.5 can directly classify incomplete datasets by using a probabilistic approach [17].

2.2 GP for Classification

GP has been widely applied to evolve classifiers. The basic idea of the application of GP for inducing classifiers is that each individual is made to represent a classifier or a part of a classifier, a fitness function is designed to score its quality and GP acts as a search technique to discover a high quality final classifier [5].

Discriminant functions are a common way to represent classifiers. A function is a mathematical expression where different types of operators are applied to the features of an instance that needs be classified. The value returned by the function determines the class predicted by using a threshold (binary classification) or set of thresholds (multiple classification) [5].

The obvious approach to evolving discriminant functions with GP is to have a population where each individual encodes one discriminant function. The function set in GP can be any type of operations and functions that can perform on the data. GP has been widely applied to evolve discriminant functions including binary discriminant functions and multiple discriminant functions [5].

GP has been mainly applied to evolve classifiers, but mainly for complete data. Therefore, to use GP for evolving classifiers for incomplete data, imputation methods are required to impute missing values before using GP. In order to evolve good classifiers, GP has to be combined with sophisticated imputation methods such as (MICE) [16]. However, sophisticated imputations such as MICE are computationally expensive. To deal with this problem, [14] proposed interval GP (IGP) to directly construct a classifier for each incomplete data. With the constructed classifier, each missing value is replaced by an interval that expresses the uncertainty associated with the missing value. Experimental results show that IGP can evolve effective and efficient classifiers for incomplete data.

2.3   Ensemble Learning

An important class of techniques for classification is ensemble learning which uses a set of classifiers instead of a single classifier. Ensemble techniques first build a set of classifiers, and then a new instance is classified by conducting a vote with decisions of the individual classifiers. Ensemble learning has proved capable of achieving better classification accuracy than any single classifier [13].

An ensemble of classifiers is good if the individual classifiers in the ensemble are accurate and diverse. Bagging is one of the most popular approaches to building accurate ensembles. Bagging use "resampling" techniques to manipulate the training data. Bagging manipulates the original training dataset by randomly drawing instances with replacement. Therefore, in the resulting training dataset, some of the original instances may appear multiple times while others might not appear. Bagging is often effective on "unstable" learning algorithms such as neural networks and decision trees where small changes in the training dataset can lead to major changes in predictions [13].

3   The Proposed Method

3.1   The Limitations of IGP

The problem with IGP [14] is that the output of a classifier constructed by IGP is an interval which can span more than one class boundary, but IGP determines a single class label by using the middle point of the output interval. This decision method does not select the highest probability class when the middle point belongs to one class region, but the biggest overlap with the output interval belongs to another class region. For example, in Fig. 1, the middle point belongs to *class 2*, but the highest overlap with the interval output is the region of *class 1*.

The decision method of IGP also makes an unjustified decision when there exist two or more class regions with the same or similar overlap with the interval output. For example, in Fig. 2, *class 2*, *class 3* and *class 4* have the same overlap with the interval, but IGP only outputs *class 3*.

Fig. 1. A potential failure example of IGP due to using the middle of interval output to decide a final class.

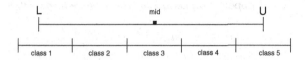

Fig. 2. A problem with IGP because of building only one classifier.

3.2   The Combination of Ensemble Learning with IGP

In order to overcome the limitations of IGP, this paper proposes algorithm, EnIGP, which integrates ensemble methods and IGP to construct a set of classifiers for incomplete data. To construct a set of classifiers, firstly, a training dataset is put into a resample procedure such as in bagging/boosting to build a set of training resampled datasets. After that, each training resampled dataset is used by IGP to build a single a classifier. As a result, a set of classifiers is generated. When a new instance needs be classified, each classifier in EIGP estimates the probability of the instance belonging to each class instead of determining a single class for the instance as IGP. After that, the final class of the instance is the class which achieves the highest total probability over all classifiers. The main steps of EnIGP are presented following steps:

Finding the Interval of a Feature: As IGP in [14], in order to make EnIGP able to directly work with missing values, we need to find an interval for each incomplete feature, and then replace missing values for the feature by the interval.

A feature interval is the range which covers a large majority of the actual values of the feature. The interval of a feature should be estimated from the distribution of the feature values. We used the method described in [12] which removes a fixed fraction of values from both the top and bottom of the range to find an interval for each feature. Experiments in [12] showed that this worked well for a range of distributions.

Interval Functions: Along with transforming incomplete data to interval data, we also need to build interval functions to work with interval data. We used the four interval arithmetic operations shown in [14]:

$$a + b = \begin{cases} lower : & a_l + b_l \\ upper : & a_u + b_u \end{cases}$$

$$a - b = \begin{cases} lower : & a_l - b_u \\ upper : & a_u - b_l \end{cases}$$

$$a * b = \begin{cases} lower : & min(a_l * b_l, a_l * b_u, a_u * b_l, a_u * b_u) \\ upper : & max(a_l * b_l, a_l * b_u, a_u * b_l, a_u * b_u) \end{cases}$$

$$a/b = \begin{cases} lower : & min(a_l/b_l, a_l/b_u, a_u/b_l, a_u/b_u) \\ upper : & max(a_l/b_l, a_l/b_u, a_u/b_l, a_u/b_u) \end{cases}$$

where a_l and a_u are lower and upper bounds of feature a; b_l and b_u are lower and upper bounds of feature b

Class Label Determination: Assuming $[l, u]$ is the output of a classifier constructed by GP with interval function, and $[T_{i-1}, T_i)$ is the class region of the ith class label, then the probability of the ith class label is chosen by the classifier is defined as followed:

$$prob([l, u] \in class_i) = \begin{cases} 0 : \text{if } u < T_{i-1} \quad or \quad Ti \leq l \\ \frac{min(u, T_i) - max(l, T_{i-1})}{u-l} : otherwise \end{cases}$$

where $T_1, T_2, ..., T_{n-1}$ are the pre-defined static class boundaries.

4   Experiment Design

4.1   The Comparison Methods

The experiments are designed to evaluate the proposed method to evolve a set of classifiers for incomplete data. To achieve this goal, the proposed method is compared to three benchmark methods:

- The first benchmark method is to use IGP to construct a single classifier. The purpose of this comparison is to figure out whether a set of classifiers constructed by the integration of ensemble learning and IGP can achieve better classification accuracy than a single classifier constructed by IGP alone.
- The second benchmark method is to combine imputation, ensemble learning and traditonal GP to construct a set of classifiers. The purpose of this comparison is to figure out whether a set of classifiers constructed by the integration of ensemble learning and IGP can achieve better classification accuracy than a set of classifier constructed by the combination of ensemble learning, imputation and traditional GP.

- The third benchmark method is to combine ensemble learning and classification algorithms able to directly work with incomplete data (C4.5/CART) to construct a set of classifiers. The purpose of this comparison is to figure out whether a set of classifiers constructed by the integration of ensemble learning and IGP can achieve better classification accuracy than a set of classifiers constructed by the combination of ensemble learning and classification algorithms able to directly work with incomplete data.

4.2   Datasets

The proposed method are evaluated and compared with other methods on a number of benchmark datasets. The datasets are chosen from the the UCI machine learning repository [2]. Table 1 shows the main characteristics of the chosen datasets: the number of instances, the number of features (Real/Integer/Nominal), the number of classes, the percentage of incomplete instances which contain at least one missing value, and the abbreviation of dataset.

Table 1. Datasets

Name	#Inst	#Features (R/I/N)	#Classes	Incomplete inst (%)	Abbrev
Breast cancer wisconsin	699	9(0/9/0)	2	2.29	Bre
Cleveland heart disease	303	13(13/0/0)	5	1.98	Cle
Cylinder bands	539	19(13/6/0)	2	32.28	Ban
Hepatitis	155	19(2/17/0)	2	48.39	Hep
Mammographic	961	5(0/5/0)	2	13.63	Mam
Marketing	8993	13(0/13/0)	9	23.54	Mar
Ozone	2536	73(73/0/0)	2	27.12	Ozo
Balance scale	625	4(0/4/0)	3	0	Bal
Diabetes	768	8(8/0/0)	2	0	Dia
Iris plants	150	4(4/0/0)	3	0	Iri
Liver disorders	345	6(1/5/0)	2	0	Liv
Statlog heart	270	13(13/0/0)	2	0	Sta

The first seven datasets suffer from missing values in a "natural" way. To evaluate the proposed method on datasets with various levels of missing values, from the last five complete datasets, some complete values are randomly removed to generate "artificial" incomplete datasets. Six levels of missing values: 5%, 10%, 15%, 20%, 25% and 30% are introduced into each complete dataset. Missing values are only introduced into important features which are selected by CFS [8]. Ten-fold cross-validation is used to divide these datasets into training sets and test sets.

4.3 Parameter Settings

ECJ package [11] is used to implement GP. Table 2 shows parameters of GP. The parameters of GP in imputation methods combined with GP are similar to the parameters of GP in the proposed methods, except using a normal function set and a normal terminal set instead of using the interval function set and interval terminal set.

Table 2. GP parameters.

Parameter	Value
Function set	Interval functions, $+$, $-$, $*$, $/$ (protected division)
Variable terminals	Interval of the original features $\setminus \{f_1, f_2, ..., f_n\}$
Constant terminals	Random float values
Population size	1024
Initialization	Ramped half-and-half
Generations	50
Crossover probability	60
Mutation probability	30
Reproduction rate	10
Selection type	Tournament (size $= 7$)

The experiments use two imputation methods to combine with GP are kNN-based imputation and MICE. For kNN-based imputation, the number of k is set 1; MICE in [3] with random forest is used to estimate missing values for incomplete features. Each incomplete feature is repeatedly regressed 20 times on other features. With each incomplete dataset, the multiple imputation is repeatedly done 5 times to generate 5 imputed datasets before averaging them to generate a final imputed dataset.

The proposed methods are compared with two decision trees which can directly classify incomplete data: C4.5 and CART [17]. WEKA [7] is used to implement the classification algorithms. For both the proposed method and the benchmark methods, bagging is used to build training resampled datasets. Following the suggestion in [13], the number of classifiers in ensemble learning evolving by the proposed method and the benchmark methods is set 25.

5 Results and Analysis

Table 3 presents the average of classification accuracy along with standard deviation of *EIGP* and the other benchmark methods on the first seven "natural" incomplete datasets. The average of classification accuracy in Table 3 is calculated on accuracies of each method on 30 times performing ten-fold cross-validation on each dataset. Table 4 shows the average of classification accuracy

Table 3. The comparison between EnIGP with the other benchmark methods on natural incomplete datasets.

Dataset	EnIGP	IGP	EnkNNGP	EnMICEGP	EnC4.5	EnCART
Ban	**72.15 ± 0.84**	69.97 ± 1.23 ↓	70.53 ± 0.77 ↓	70.74 ± 0.62 ↓	71.18 ± 1.26 ↓	70.10 ± 1.85 ↓
Bre	**96.69 ± 0.21**	96.33 ± 0.28 ↓	96.22 ± 0.28 ↓	96.30 ± 0.32 ↓	95.86 ± 0.31 ↓	95.84 ± 0.35 ↓
Cle	**59.85 ± 1.17**	58.12 ± 1.50 ↓	57.88 ± 0.84 ↓	57.69 ± 1.27 ↓	57.08 ± 1.29 ↓	57.73 ± 1.64 ↓
Hep	**82.39 ± 1.69**	81.05 ± 1.77 ↓	82.47 ± 1.84	82.85 ± 1.47	81.56 ± 1.63 ↓	81.27 ± 1.77 ↓
Mam	**83.44 ± 0.27**	83.13 ± 0.35 ↓	80.77 ± 0.54 ↓	80.77 ± 0.59 ↓	82.68 ± 0.50 ↓	81.63 ± 0.54 ↓
Mar	31.40 ± 0.28	30.74 ± 0.47 ↓	30.83 ± 0.39 ↓	30.89 ± 0.37 ↓	**31.56 ± 0.42**	31.26 ± 0.41
Ozo	97.09 ± 0.06	97.08 ± 1.42	**97.12 ± 0.01**	**97.12 ± 0.01**	97.05 ± 0.08	97.07 ± 0.09

along with standard deviation of *EIGP* and the other ensemble methods on the last five datasets with six levels of missing values. With each dataset and each level of missing values, the averages of classification accuracy in Table 4 is calculated on accuracies of each method on 30 generated incomplete datasets by using ten-fold cross-validation on each incomplete dataset.

In Tables 3 and 4, "EnIGP" refers to the proposed method combining bagging and interval GP to evolve a set of classifiers. "IGP" refers to the first benchmark method using interval GP to evolve a single classifier. "EnkNNGP" and "EnMICEGP" refer to the second benchmark method combining bagging, interval GP with kNN-based imputation and MICE to evolve a set of classifiers. "EnC4.5" and "EnCART" refer to the third benchmark method combining bagging and *C4.5* and *CART* to build a set of classifiers.

For each incomplete dataset, *Friedman* test [4], which is a non-parametric test for multiple comparisons, is used to statistical test the null hypothesis in classification accuracies at a 5% level of significant. The test shows that for all tasks, there is a significant difference in classification accuracies for the five methods, so null hypothesis rejected. Therefore, a post hoc multiple comparisons test using the *Holm* method [4] is used to determine the statistically significant differences between group means. In Tables 3 and 4, "↑" means that the benchmark method is significantly more accurate than the proposed method; and "↓" means that the benchmark method is significantly worse than the proposed method.

It is clear from Tables 3 and 4 that the classification accuracies of *EnIGP* are significantly better than *IGP* in almost all cases (significantly more accurate in 30 of the 36 cases). It means that ensemble learning helps to improve the accuracy of IGP for classifying incomplete data. The key reason is that by constructing a set of classifiers, ensemble learning can overcome the limitations of IGP as constructing a single classifier.

Tables 3 and 4 also show that the proposed method is significantly better than the combination of imputation, ensemble learning and traditional GP in most cases (significantly more accurate than both EnKnnGP and EnMICEGP in 23 of the 36 cases). The reason is that interval values can better reflect the uncertainty of missing values than a specific value estimated by imputation.

As also can be seen from Tables 3 and 4 that the proposed method is significantly better than the combination of ensemble learning and classification able

Table 4. The comparison between EnIGP with the other benchmark methods on artificial incomplete datasets.

Dataset	Missing values (%)	EnIGP	IGP	EnkNNGP	EnMICEGP	EnC4.5	EnCART
Bal	5	**98.98 ± 0.41**	98.61 ± 0.59	98.79 ± 0.41	98.92 ± 0.40	82.95 ± 0.77 ↓	82.51 ± 0.84 ↓
	10	**97.75 ± 0.64**	97.41 ± 0.71	97.70 ± 0.62	97.41 ± 0.57	82.66 ± 0.86 ↓	82.14 ± 0.80 ↓
	15	**97.10 ± 0.60**	96.63 ± 0.84	96.93 ± 0.72	96.73 ± 0.62	82.23 ± 0.94 ↓	81.95 ± 0.78 ↓
	20	**95.81 ± 0.53**	95.21 ± 0.65	95.32 ± 0.73	95.59 ± 0.50	81.69 ± 0.87 ↓	81.31 ± 0.95 ↓
	25	**94.95 ± 0.76**	94.20 ± 1.13	94.22 ± 0.90	94.65 ± 0.86	81.49 ± 1.10 ↓	80.82 ± 1.09 ↓
	30	**93.70 ± 0.71**	93.21 ± 0.99	92.87 ± 0.88	93.41 ± 0.81	81.02 ± 0.96 ↓	80.37 ± 0.96 ↓
Dia	5	**75.89 ± 0.88**	74.37 ± 0.78 ↓	67.37 ± 0.87 ↓	67.61 ± 0.79 ↓	74.86 ± 0.93	74.52 ± 0.80
	10	**75.20 ± 0.79**	73.16 ± 1.09 ↓	67.15 ± 1.00 ↓	67.36 ± 0.95 ↓	74.81 ± 0.72	73.71 ± 1.26
	15	**74.42 ± 0.68**	72.55 ± 1.04 ↓	66.87 ± 0.63 ↓	67.13 ± 0.85 ↓	74.34 ± 1.22	73.08 ± 1.09
	20	73.61 ± 0.98	71.99 ± 1.04 ↓	66.81 ± 0.80 ↓	66.93 ± 1.04 ↓	**73.62 ± 1.21**	72.37 ± 1.21
	25	73.08 ± 1.22	71.54 ± 1.40 ↓	66.61 ± 0.61 ↓	66.67 ± 0.95 ↓	**73.48 ± 0.96**	71.64 ± 1.24
	30	71.97 ± 1.16	70.19 ± 1.38 ↓	66.75 ± 0.86 ↓	67.13 ± 1.01 ↓	**72.24 ± 1.06**	70.88 ± 1.35
Iri	5	**96.06 ± 0.93**	94.73 ± 0.96 ↓	93.42 ± 1.58 ↓	93.77 ± 1.06 ↓	93.33 ± 1.24 ↓	94.17 ± 1.27 ↓
	10	**96.01 ± 0.93**	94.68 ± 1.45 ↓	92.11 ± 1.90 ↓	93.42 ± 1.35 ↓	93.17 ± 1.51 ↓	94.11 ± 1.46 ↓
	15	**95.19 ± 1.37**	93.68 ± 1.38 ↓	90.06 ± 2.22 ↓	92.11 ± 1.73 ↓	92.62 ± 1.73 ↓	93.06 ± 1.63 ↓
	20	**94.91 ± 1.48**	92.97 ± 1.85 ↓	87.91 ± 2.34 ↓	91.57 ± 1.80 ↓	91.20 ± 1.61 ↓	91.86 ± 1.81 ↓
	25	**94.51 ± 1.58**	92.42 ± 1.63 ↓	86.28 ± 2.43 ↓	90.24 ± 2.26 ↓	90.62 ± 1.95 ↓	90.57 ± 2.33 ↓
	30	**92.33 ± 2.20**	90.37 ± 2.91 ↓	84.91 ± 2.83 ↓	87.60 ± 2.62 ↓	88.24 ± 2.20 ↓	88.62 ± 1.87 ↓
Liv	5	**69.53 ± 1.62**	67.98 ± 1.95 ↓	69.24 ± 1.49	69.47 ± 1.62	69.12 ± 1.79	68.56 ± 1.72
	10	**69.05 ± 1.73**	67.87 ± 2.01 ↓	68.73 ± 1.54	68.96 ± 1.43	68.59 ± 1.93	68.07 ± 1.70
	15	68.54 ± 1.63	67.48 ± 1.89 ↓	68.21 ± 1.63	**68.65 ± 1.53**	68.10 ± 1.83	67.58 ± 1.73
	20	68.04 ± 1.72	66.97 ± 1.97 ↓	67.72 ± 1.55	**68.06 ± 1.42**	67.59 ± 1.92	67.07 ± 1.69
	25	67.53 ± 1.66	65.86 ± 1.86 ↓	67.22 ± 1.64	**67.66 ± 1.57**	67.12 ± 1.82	66.59 ± 1.72
	30	67.05 ± 1.74	64.98 ± 1.96 ↓	66.73 ± 1.56	**67.09 ± 1.43**	66.58 ± 1.97	66.03 ± 1.65
Sta	5	**83.04 ± 1.31**	81.02 ± 1.68 ↓	78.50 ± 1.63 ↓	78.46 ± 1.55 ↓	81.39 ± 1.25 ↓	80.49 ± 1.49 ↓
	10	**81.81 ± 1.70**	80.32 ± 1.59 ↓	77.60 ± 1.89 ↓	78.14 ± 1.56 ↓	80.04 ± 2.05 ↓	79.38 ± 1.54 ↓
	15	**81.45 ± 1.38**	79.56 ± 1.97 ↓	76.92 ± 1.40 ↓	77.71 ± 1.93 ↓	78.77 ± 1.67 ↓	78.70 ± 1.51 ↓
	20	**80.92 ± 1.83**	78.71 ± 1.77 ↓	76.46 ± 2.04 ↓	77.32 ± 2.13 ↓	79.06 ± 2.19 ↓	78.04 ± 1.75 ↓
	25	**80.22 ± 1.60**	78.45 ± 1.95 ↓	75.80 ± 1.66 ↓	76.80 ± 2.01 ↓	78.02 ± 1.96 ↓	77.12 ± 1.96 ↓
	30	**79.14 ± 1.51**	77.03 ± 2.45 ↓	74.67 ± 1.82 ↓	75.99 ± 1.98 ↓	77.35 ± 1.76 ↓	76.48 ± 1.65 ↓

to directly work with incomplete data such as C4.5 and CART (significantly more accurate than both EnC4.5 and EnCART in 23 of the 36 cases). The reason is that interval GP is able to better construct classifiers for incomplete data than C4.5 and CART.

In summary, the combination of ensemble learning and interval GP can achieve better accuracy than the benchmark methods for classification with incomplete data.

5.1 Analysis

To investigate how the proposed methods work, we further analysed trees generated by using interval GP on the *Diabetes* dataset. *Diabetes* is chosen because generated trees in this case are small enough to be analysed by humans. *Diabetes* is a binary classification problem (two classes: *tested_negative*,*tested_positive*), and it has eight features $\{f_1, f_2, ..., f_8\}$ and we put 10% missing values in four features $\{f_2, f_6, f_7, f_8\}$, which are selected by CFS [8].

In training process, the training data is firstly normalised. After that, the interval of each feature is estimated from complete values of the feature. Table 5 shows the interval of each feature in *Diabetes*. Subsequently, in the training data, each complete field is replaced by an interval where lower bound and upper bound are set the complete value, and each missing field is replaced by an interval of the feature containing the field. For example, from Table 5, if a field in f_2 is missing, it is replaced by $[-2.09, 2.40]$. Finally, the training data is put into interval GP to build a classifier. Figure 3 shows a tree generated by interval GP on *Diabetes*.

Table 5. Interval of features in *Diabetes* dataset.

	f_1	f_2	f_3	f_4	f_5	f_6	f_7	f_8
Lower	-1.14	-2.09	-3.44	-1.28	-0.68	-3.96	-1.17	-1.04
Upper	2.98	2.40	2.03	2.46	5.07	3.13	5.07	3.12

In application process, when an instance needs to be classified, it is firstly normalised, and then intervalised. For example, to classify an instance: *(5, 99, 9.74, 27, 0, ?, ?, ?)* (? means missing value), complete values are firstly normalised: *(0.34, −0.68, 0.25, 0.41, −0.69, ?, ?, ?)*. After that, each field is replaced by an interval: *([0.34, 0.34], [−0.68, −0.68], [0.25, 0.25], [0.41, 0.41], [−0.69, −0.69], [−3.96, 3.13], [−1.17, 5.07], [−1.04, 3.12])* (each missing field is replaced by an interval of corresponding feature). The interval instance is then put into a classifier such as shown in Fig.3 to result in an interval $[-9.42, 4.77]$. Subsequently, the middle point of the interval is calculated: $\frac{-9.42+4.77}{2} = -2.32$; therefore, the instance is classified into *tested_negative* class.

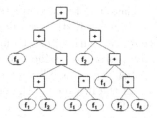

Fig. 3. The first tree generated by GP with interval. functions

In EnIGP, instead of constructing one classifier, a set of classifier is contructed and combined to classify new instances. For example, Fig. 4 shows another classifier generated by using interval GP on *Diabetes*. When the instance is put into the second classifier, the output is $[-7.28, -0.18]$. Instead of using middle point to decide class label, the proportion of the instance belonging to each class. For example, with the output $[-9.42, 4.77]$, $\frac{|-9.42|}{|-9.42|+4.77} * 100 = 66.38\%$ of the instance belongs $tested\_negative$ class, and $\frac{|4.77|}{|-9.42|+4.77} * 100 = 33.62\%$ belonging to the $tested\_positive$ class. With the output $[-7.28, -0.18]$, both lower bound and upper bound are less than zero; therefore, 100% of the instance belongs $tested\_negative$ class. As a result, if the two classifiers are used to classify an instance, on average, $\frac{66.38+100}{2} = 83.19\%$ of the instance belongs $tested\_negative$ class, and $\frac{33.62+0}{2} = 16.81\%$ of the instance belongs $tested\_positive$ class. Consequently, the instance is classified to the $tested\_negative$ class.

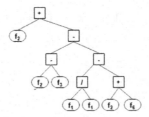

Fig. 4. The second tree generated by interval GP.

In summary, replacing missing values with intervals help reflect very well the uncertainty of incomplete data. Moreover, the combination of a set of classifiers generated by interval GP can improve the accuracy for classification with incomplete data.

6   Conclusions and Future Work

This paper proposed a method which combines interval GP with ensemble learning to directly evolve a set of classifiers for incomplete data. Ensemble learning methods such as bagging/boosting are firstly used to generate a set of training resampled datasets. After that, GP with interval functions uses each training resampled dataset to directly evolve a classifier. To classify a new instance, each evolved classifier calculates the probability of the instance belonging to each class, and the final class of the instance is the class achieving the highest total probability over all classifiers. Experimental results show that the proposed method helps to improve the accuracy of interval GP to evolve classifiers for incomplete data. The proposed method is also more accurate than other common methods for classification with incomplete data.

Along with bagging, boosting is one of the most popular ensemble methods. Therefore, in future work, we would like to investigate an integration of boosting and IGP for classification with incomplete data.

References

1. Acuna, E., Rodriguez, C.: The treatment of missing values and its effect on classifier accuracy. In: Banks, D., McMorris, F.R., Arabie, P., Gaul, W. (eds.) Classification, Clustering, and Data Mining Applications. Studies in Classification, Data Analysis, and Knowledge Organisation, pp. 639–647. Springer, Heidelberg (2004). https://doi.org/10.1007/978-3-642-17103-1_60
2. Asuncion, A., Newman, D.: UCI Machine Learning Repository (2013)
3. Buuren, S., Groothuis-Oudshoorn, K.: MICE: multivariate imputation by chained equations in R. J. Stat. Softw. **45**, 1–67 (2011)
4. Demšar, J.: Statistical comparisons of classifiers over multiple data sets. J. Mach. Learn. Res. **7**, 1–30 (2006)
5. Espejo, P.G., Ventura, S., Herrera, F.: A survey on the application of genetic programming to classification. IEEE Trans. Syst. Man Cybern. Part C (Appl. Rev.) **40**, 121–144 (2010)
6. García-Laencina, P.J., Sancho-Gómez, J.-L., Figueiras-Vidal, A.R.: Pattern classification with missing data: a review. Neural Comput. Appl. **19**, 263–282 (2010)
7. Hall, M., Frank, E., Holmes, G., Pfahringer, B., Reutemann, P., Witten, I.H.: The weka data mining software: an update. ACM SIGKDD Explor. Newsl. **11**, 10–18 (2009)
8. Hall, M.A.: Correlation-based feature selection for discrete and numeric class machine learning. In: Proceedings of the Seventeenth International Conference on Machine Learning, pp. 359–366 (2000)
9. Koza, J.R.: Genetic Programming III: Darwinian Invention and Problem Solving, vol. 3 (1999)
10. Liu, Y., Brown, S.D.: Comparison of five iterative imputation methods for multivariate classification. Chemom. Intell. Lab. Syst. **120**, 106–115 (2013)
11. Luke, S., et al.: A Java-based evolutionary computation research system, March 2004. http://cs.gmu.edu/~eclab/projects/ecj
12. Neshatian, K., Zhang, M., Andreae, P.: A filter approach to multiple feature construction for symbolic learning classifiers using genetic programming. IEEE Trans. Evol. Comput. **16**, 645–661 (2012)
13. Opitz, D.W., Maclin, R.: Popular ensemble methods: an empirical study. J. Artif. Intell. Res. (JAIR) **11**, 169–198 (1999)
14. Tran, C.T., Zhang, M., Andreae, P.: Directly evolving classifiers for missing data using genetic programming. In: 2016 IEEE Congress on Evolutionary Computation (CEC), pp. 5278–5285 (2016)
15. Tran, C.T., Zhang, M., Andreae, P., Xue, B., Bui, L.T.: An effective and efficient approach to classification with incomplete data. Knowl.-Based Syst. **154**, 1–16 (2018)
16. White, I.R., Royston, P., Wood, A.M.: Multiple imputation using chained equations: issues and guidance for practice. Stat. Med. **30**, 377–399 (2011)
17. Wu, X., Kumar, V., Quinlan, J.R., Ghosh, J., Yang, Q., Motoda, H., McLachlan, G.J., Ng, A., Liu, B., Philip, S.Y., et al.: Top 10 algorithms in data mining. Knowl. Inf. Syst. **14**(1), 1–37 (2008)

Stochastic Conjugate Gradient Descent Twin Support Vector Machine for Large Scale Pattern Classification

Sweta Sharma and Reshma Rastogi[(✉)]

Department of Computer Science, South Asian University, New Delhi, India
sharma.sweta.2007@gmail.com, reshma.khemchandani@sau.ac.in

Abstract. With the advent of technology, the amount of data available for learning is increasing day by day. However, machine learning algorithms such as Support Vector Machines (SVMs) are effective but slow in dealing with this huge inflow of information. Recent researches have largely focussed on increasing the scalability of machine learning algorithms including by using algorithmic level speed-ups such as TWSVM [10], LS-SVM [18] and training level speed-ups such as using Newton-Armijo method [12], Coordinate Descent Method [8] etc. Among these, recently proposed stochastic gradient based methods have attracted significant attention. However, these methods suffer from the inherent problems of stochastic gradient methodology such as ill-conditioning, slow convergence near minima etc. In this paper, we propose a Stochastic Conjugate Gradient Descent method based Twin Support Vector Machine (SCG-TWSVM) which improves upon the limitations of Stochastic Gradient Descent Support Vector Machine (SG-SVM) and Stochastic Gradient Twin Support Vector Machine (SG-TWSVM) and leads to a more robust, effective and generalizable classifier. We also extend our proposed classifier to non-linear case by using Kernel trick. We perform extensive experiments on a variety of machine learning benchmark datasets as well as real-world machine learning datasets which prove the efficacy of our proposed approach compared to related methods on large scale problems.

Keywords: Twin Support Vector Machine
Conjugate gradient method · Pattern classification
Large scale problem

1 Introduction

Support Vector Machines aims to separate two classes by maximizing the margin between the closest points from each class [5]. This simple idea of SVM has proved to be a breakthrough concept as the resulting convex optimization problem guarantee a global optima compared to other neural network based classifiers. The SVM model is well generalizable as well. However, SVM has proved to be a slow learner as the training time complexity for learning with n

© Springer Nature Switzerland AG 2018
T. Mitrovic et al. (Eds.): AI 2018, LNAI 11320, pp. 590–602, 2018.
https://doi.org/10.1007/978-3-030-03991-2_54

samples is $O(n^3)$. Thus, training an SVM is an expensive operation, especially for large n. However, many state-of-art methods have exclusively focused on this issue resulting into various faster variants such as LS-SVM [18], GEPSVM [14], Safe-screen SVM [22], CUDA-SVM [19] and TWSVM [10]. LS-SVM [18] introduce equality constraints in SVM optimization problem resulting into an unconstrained minimization problem whose solution can be obtained by solving a system of linear equations. Further, Catanzaro et al. [4] proposed an implementation of SVM on GPUs which resulted into an speed up of 5–32 times over the conventional SVM. Cao et al. [3] presented a variant of SMO where using parallel computations. A detailed review of large scale optimization methods can be found in [2].

Among the above-mentioned SVM based algorithms, Twin Support Vector Machine (TWSVM) is considered a innovative algorithmic approach. Unlike SVM, which is a parallel plane classifier, TWSVM is a binary non-parallel hyperplane based classifier which seeks two hyperplanes, each proximal to its corresponding class. It leads to two almost half-sized Quadratic Programming Problems (QPPs) resulting into approximately four-fold reduction in training time. Beside this, it shows excellent generalization performance as well. However, it is important to note that solving a QPP is still computationally expensive for large scale problems [16] as it requires $0(n^3)$ computational complexity if no. of training points n is extremely large. Hence, to further accelerate the learning process in SVM based scenarios, stochastic learning approaches have recently attracted attention [7,11,17,20]. Shavlev et al. [17] proposed Stochastic Gradient Support Vector Machine (SG-SVM) which partitions the learning problem into a series of sub-problems that are solved through iterative optimization using stochastic sampling. This approach resulted into a very fast classifier with a justifiable guarantee for convergence. On the similar lines, Wang et al. have recently proposed Stochastic Gradient Descent Twin Support Vector Machine (SG-TWSVM) [20]. SG-TWSVM selects a pair of samples randomly to construct a set of non-parallel hyperplanes. Unlike learning with entire data at a time, which usually involve extensive matrix computations, SG-TWSVM simply performs one matrix multiplication at a time. The main idea is to minimize the loss function specified in the objective function by moving α steps in the direction of descent obtained through a pair of points at a time. In an iterative process, the initial hyperplanes obtained are further improved upon by learning through stochastic samples until convergence is achieved. SG-TWSVM exhibits comparable performance to that with TWSVM [20]. However, it is well known that the gradient based approach is prone to inconsistency as an individual sample may deviate the algorithm from the global minima resulting into zig-zag behaviour which leads to instability in model training process. It is obviously not the optimal and fastest possible way. Further, this problem enhances the requirements for more training data to achieve convergence. This further increases the training time requirement of the model. Moreover, the diversion as well as ill-conditioning issue faced by stochastic gradient based approach may lead to poorly performing classifier model. Also, the success of SGD relies heavily on the setting of initial learning rate and decay strategy of learning rate [11].

In this regard, Conjugate Gradient Descent (CGD) method has inherent advantage over SGD method. Since CGD considers the structural information, it results into more stable and thus well generalizable solution compared to other methods. Moreover, effective theoretical guarantees can be established over convergence.

In this paper, in order to overcome the limitations of conventional gradient descent based approaches, we propose a stochastic Conjugate Gradient Descent methodology based Twin Support Vector Machine (termed as SCG-TWSVM) which can handle the above-mentioned issues by moving along conjugate gradient directions toward global optima while taking into consideration the useful information from data.

Thus, the key contributions of this paper can be summed up as follows:

1. We introduce stochastic framework to CGD method which enables it to deal with large data in stochastic manner while ensuring that the inherent idea of CGD prevails.
2. We further propose a novel Stochastic Conjugate Gradient Descent method based Twin Support Tensor Machine (SCG-TWSVM) classifier that seeks a pair of non-hyperplanes, each representative of its own class, by formulating related convex optimization problems in stochastic manner.
3. Experiments have been carried out on standard UCI benchmark datasets and popular human activity recognition application that establish the outperformance of our proposed algorithm over other stochastic approaches.

This paper is organized as follows: Sect. 2 gives a brief background of related work that forms the basis of our proposed algorithm. Section 3 introduces a general framework for the proposed classifier. Following this, Sect. 4 reports experimental results on machine learning benchmark datasets and human activity recognition dataset. Finally, Sect. 5 concludes the paper and highlights the future work.

2   Related Works

Consider a data set $\mathbb{D}$ in which l_1 data points belonging to class $+1$ are represented by matrix $A = \{x_1^+; \ldots; x_{l_1}^+\}$ while l_2 data points belonging to class -1 are represented by matrix $B = \{x_1^-; \ldots; x_{l_2}^-\}$. Therefore, the size of dataset D is $l = l_1 + l_2$ and $A \in \mathbb{R}^{n \times d}$, $B \in \mathbb{R}^{n \times d}$ respectively, where n is the dimension of feature space.

2.1   Twin Support Vector Machine

Twin Support Vector Machine [10] seeks two non-parallel hyperplanes given by $w_1^T x + b_1 = 0$ and $w_2^T x + b_2 = 0$ obtained by solving the following optimization problem:

$$\underset{w_1,b_1,\xi_2}{Min} \; \tfrac{1}{2}\sum_{i=1}^{l_1} f(x_i^+) + c_1 \sum_{j=1}^{l_2} L(x_j^-, y, f(x_j)), \tag{1}$$

and

$$\underset{w_2,b_2,\xi_1}{Min} \; \tfrac{1}{2}\sum_{i=1}^{l_2} f(x_i^-) + c_2 \sum_{j=1}^{l_1} L(x_j^+, y, f(x_j)), \tag{2}$$

where x_i^+ and x_j^- are points from class $+1$ and class -1 respectively. Also, $L(.)$ denotes the error function where the points of class -1 ($+1$) are less than unit distance from hyperplane of class $+1$ (-1). This eventually leads to following pair of quadratic programming problems:

$$(\text{TWSVM 1}) \quad \underset{w_1,b_1,\xi_2}{Min} \quad \frac{1}{2}||Aw_1 + e_1 b_1)||^2 + c_1 e_2{}^T \xi_2$$

$$\text{subject to} - (Bw_1 + e_2 b_1) + \xi_2 \geq e_2, \quad \xi_2 \geq 0, \tag{3}$$

and

$$(\text{TWSVM 2}) \quad \underset{w_2,b_2,\xi_1}{Min} \quad \frac{1}{2}||Bw_2 + e_2 b_2||^2 + c_2 e_1{}^T \xi_1$$

$$\text{subject to} \, (Aw_2 + e_2 b_2) + \xi_1 \geq e_1, \quad \xi_1 \geq 0, \tag{4}$$

where the constant $c_1 \geq 0$ ($c_2 \geq 0$) is trade-off factor between sum of error vector ξ_2 (ξ_1) due to samples of class -1 (class $+1$) and proximity of hyperplane towards its own class; and e_1 and e_2 are vectors of ones of appropriate dimensions.

The class label $\hat{y}$ of a new test point $\hat{x}$ is determined based on its proximity from the representative hyperplanes of the two classes.

2.2   Stochastic Gradient Twin Support Vector Machine

SG-TSVM [21] recast the QPP formulations similar to (3) and (4) into unconstrained minimization problems given as following:

$$(\text{SG-TSVM 1}) \; \underset{w_1,b_1}{\min} \; \frac{1}{2}(||w_1||^2 + b_1^2) + \frac{c_1}{2l_1}||Aw_1 + e_1 b_1||^2 + \frac{c_2}{l_2} e_2^T (e_2 + Bw_1 + e_2 b_1)_+,$$

$$\tag{5}$$

and

$$(\text{SG-TSVM 2}) \; \underset{w_2,b_2}{\min} \; \frac{1}{2}(||w_2||^2 + b_2^2) + \frac{c_1}{2l_2}||Bw_2 + e_2 b_2||^2 + \frac{c_2}{l_1} e_1^T (e_1 - Aw_2 - e_1 b_2)_+,$$

$$\tag{6}$$

where $c_1, c_2 \geq 0$ are trade-off factors and $(.)_+$ is the corresponding hinge-loss function which replaces the negative component of a vector with zero.

While solving (5) and (6) iteratively, SG-TSVM constructs a pair of momentary functions using sub-gradients with respect to w_1, b_1, w_2 and b_2 using a pair of samples $(x_t^+, +1)$ and $(x_t^-, -1)$ from two classes given as:

$$\nabla_{w_{1,t}} f_{1,t} = w_{1,t} + c_1(w_{1,t}^T x_t^+ + b_{1,t})x_t^+ + c_2 x_t^- sign(1 + w_{1,t}^T x_t^+ + b_{1,t})_+,$$

$$\nabla_{b_{1,t}} f_{1,t} = b_{1,t} + c_1(w_{1,t}^T x_t^+ + b_{1,t})x_t^+ + c_2 x_t^- sign(1 + w_{1,t}^T x_t^+ + b_{1,t})_+, \tag{7}$$

and

$$\nabla_{w_{2,t}} f_{2,t} = w_{2,t} + c_1(w_{2,t}^T x_t^- + b_{2,t})x_t^- - c_2 x_t^+ sign(1 - w_{2,t}^T x_t^+ + b_{2,t})_+,$$
$$\nabla_{b_{2,t}} f_{2,t} = b_{2,t} + c_1(w_{2,t}^T x_t^- - b_{2,t})x_t^- - c_2 x_t^+ sign(1 - w_{2,t}^T x_t^+ - b_{2,t})_+, \quad (8)$$

respectively. Finally, SG-TSVM iteratively updates $w_{1,t}$, $w_{2,t}$, $b_{1,t}$ and $b_{2,t}$ with some predefined step-size α. The process is stopped if some predefined termination criteria is reached. The label of a new test point $x \in \mathbb{R}^n$ is assigned similar to TWSVM.

Wang et al. showed that SG-TWSVM [20] algorithm will converge to an optimal solution but existence of any upper bound on the maximum number of iteration used is not known. Further, as discussed earlier, in stochastic process, an individual pair of points in iteration t may deviate the direction of descent and in order to compensate for that deviation, algorithm may require more iterations to converge. Moreover, similar to limitation in most of stochastic gradient methods, SG-TSVM is also prone to ill conditioning which adversely affect the convergence of the same [15].

3   Proposed Work

In this section, we describe our proposed Stochastic Conjugate Gradient Twin Support Vector Machine (SCG-TWSVM) in detail.

3.1   Linear SCG-TWSVM

On the lines of TWSVM [10], the proposed SCG-TWSVM also solves the following unconstrained optimization problem (as given in Eqs. (5) and (6))to obtain the requisite hyperplanes:

$$\min_{w_1,b_1} \frac{1}{2}(||w_1||^2 + b_1^2) + \frac{c_1}{2m_1}||Aw_1 + e_1b_1||^2 + \frac{c_2}{m_2}e_2^T(e_2 + B^T w_1 + e_2b_1)_+ \quad (9)$$

and

$$\min_{w_2,b_2} \frac{1}{2}(||w_2||^2 + b_2^2) + \frac{c_1}{2m_2}||Bw_2 + e_2b_2||^2 + \frac{c_2}{m_1}e_1^T(e_1 - A^T w_2 - e_1b_2)_+ \quad (10)$$

where $(.)_+$ denote the hinge loss function. The QPP problem in Eq. (9) (Eq. (10)) aims to find a hyperplane such that it is close to points of positive (negative) class and atleast one unit distance away from the points of other class. The optimization problem in Eq. (9) seeks to find a hyperplane which is proximal to samples from class A while simultaneously being at least unit distance away from the samples of other class. The first terms of the problem takes care of Structural Risk Minimization (SRM). Similar interpretation can be obtained for the hyperplane of class B using Eq. (10).

To model the above optimization problem in a stochastic manner, consider that at iteration t, we have a pair of samples $\theta_{1,t} = (x_t^+, +1)$ and $\theta_{2,t} = (x_t^-, -1)$ where $+1$ and -1 denotes the corresponding class labels. Thus, the stochastic objective functions drawn on these two distributions are, thus, given as:

$$f_{1,t}(w_1, b_1, \theta_{1,i}) = \frac{1}{2}(||w_{1,t}||^2 + b_{1,t}^2) + \frac{c_1}{2m_1}||x_t^+{}^T w_1 + b_1||^2 + \frac{c_2}{m_2}e_2^T(e_2 + x_t^-{}^T w_1 + e_2 b_1)_+, \quad (11)$$

and

$$f_{2,t}(w_2, b_2, \theta_{2,i}) = \frac{1}{2}(||w_{2,t}||^2 + b_{2,t}^2) + \frac{c_1}{2m_2}||x_t^- w_2 + b_2||^2 + \frac{c_2}{m_1}e_1^T(e_1 - x_t^+{}^T w_2 - b_2)_+, \quad (12)$$

where x_t^+ and x_t^- are selected randomly from A (points from class $+1$) and B (points from class -1).

To solve the above problems, while considering $A_t = [x_t^+ \quad 1]$, $B_t = [x_t^- \quad 1]$, $z_{1,t} = [w_{1,t} \quad b_{1,t}]$ and $z_{2,t} = [w_{2,t} \quad b_{2,t}]$, we equate the gradient of these strictly convex functions to zero as follows:

$$g_{1,t} = \frac{\partial f_{1,t}}{\partial z_{1,t}} = z_{1,t} + c_1(z_{1,t}^T A_t) + c_2 B_t^T sign(1 + z_{1,t}^T B_t) = 0 \quad (13)$$

$$g_{2,t} = \frac{\partial f_{2,t}}{\partial z_{2,t}} = z_{2,t} + c_1(z_{2,t}^T B_t) - c_2 A_t^T sign(1 - z_{2,t}^T A_t) = 0 \quad (14)$$

where A_t and B_t are augmented vectors of randomly selected points from class $+1$ and -1 respectively.

Comparing this with standard Conjugate Gradient form $\min_x \frac{1}{2}x^T Q x - x^T D$, we have two unconstrained minimization problem to be solved whose corresponding matrices to Q and d are given as:

$$Q_1 = c_1(e^T + A_t), \qquad D_1 = -c_2 B_t^T sign(1 + z_{1,t}^T B_t),$$
$$Q_2 = c_2(e^T + B_t), \qquad D_2 = c_2 A_t^T sign(1 + z_{2,t}^T A_t).$$

Now, in order to optimize the two problems given in (9) and (10), SCG-TWSVM seeks to minimize the objective function toward the conjugate directions. Let $r_{1,0} = g_{1,t}$ and $r_{2,0} = g_{2,t}$ be initial residual terms for class $+1$ and -1 respectively; and $p_{1,0} = -r_{1,0}$ and $p_{2,0} = -r_{2,0}$ be initial gradient directions in which objective functions is to be optimized. The length of step to be taken in the direction of minimization is given as follows:

$$\alpha_{1,t} = \frac{r_{1,t}^T r_{1,t}}{p_{1,t}^T Q_1 p_{1,t}}, \quad (15)$$

$$\alpha_{2,t} = \frac{r_{2,t}^T r_{2,t}}{p_{2,t}^T Q_2 p_{2,t}}. \quad (16)$$

The solution and residual terms are now updated while moving $\alpha_{1,t}$ and $\alpha_{2,t}$ steps in the gradient direction as follows:

$$z_{1,t+1} = z_{1,t} + \alpha_{1,t} p_{1,t}, \qquad z_{2,t+1} = z_{2,t} + \alpha_{2,t} p_{2,t}, \quad (17)$$

$$r_{1,t+1} = r_t + \alpha_{1,t} r_{1,t}, \qquad r_{2,t+1} = r_t + \alpha_{2,t} p_{2,t}. \quad (18)$$

At this new point, the search direction is updated as:

$$\beta_{1,t+1} = \frac{r_{1,t+1}^T r_{1,t+1}}{r_{1,t}^T r_{1,t}}, \qquad \beta_{2,t+1} = \frac{r_{2,t+1}^T r_{2,t+1}}{r_{2,t}^T r_{2,t}}, \tag{19}$$

$$p_{1,t+1} = -r_{1,t+1} + \beta_t p_t, \qquad p_{2,t+1} = -r_{2,t+1} + \beta_t p_t, \tag{20}$$

The above procedure for training a SCG-TWSVM model is summarized in Algorithm 1.

Algorithm 1 Stochastic Conjugate Gradient Twin Support Vector Machine (SCG-TWSVM)

Input : Parameter values c_1, c_2, σ; error tolerance (*tol*), maximum number of iterations (*max_iter*)

Output: Optimal hyperplane parameters $z_1 = [w_1; b_1]$, $z_2 = [w_2; b_2]$

1 Initialize $t = 0$, $diff\_w_1 = 0$, $diff\_w_2 = 0$
2 Acquire $\theta_{1,t} = \{(x_i^+, y_i^+) : y_i^+ = +1, i = 1, ...l\}$ and $\theta_{2,t} = \{(x_j^-, y_j^-) : y_j^- = -1, j = 1, ...l\}$.
3 Compute stochastic gradient $g_{1,t}$ and $g_{2,t}$ using (13) and (14) respectively.
4 Compute $r_{1,0} = g_{1,t}$ and $r_{2,0} = g_{2,t}$ as initial residual terms for class $+1$ and -1 respectively.
5 Initialize initial direction $p_{1,0} = -r_{1,0}$ and $p_{2,0} = -r_{2,0}$
6 **while** $(diff\_w_1 > tol$ & $diff\_w_2 > tol$) $\| t < max\_iter$ **do**
7 $\quad$ $t = t + 1$
8 $\quad$ Acquire $\theta_{1,t} = \{(x_i^+, y_i^+) : y_i^+ = +1, i = 1, ...l\}$ and $\theta_{2,t} = \{(x_j^-, y_j^-) : y_j^- = -1, j = 1, ...l\}$.
9 $\quad$ Compute stochastic gradient $g_{1,t}$ and $g_{2,t}$ using (13) and (14) respectively.
10 $\quad$ Calculate the step length using Eq. (15) and (16).
11 $\quad$ Update the solution $z_{1,t}$ and $z_{2,t}$ and the residual terms using Eq. (17) and (18).
12 $\quad$ Compute $diff\_z_1 = |z_{1,t+1} - z_{1,t}|$, $diff\_z_2 = |z_{2,t+1} - z_{2,t}|$.
13 **end**
14 $z_1^* = z_{1,t+1}$, $z_2^* = z_{2,t+1}$.
15 Separate (w_1, b_1) and (w_2, b_2) from z_1^* and z_2^*.
16 **return** (w_1, b_1) and (w_2, b_2).

---

4   Experimental Results

The experiments are performed in MATLAB version 8.0 under Microsoft Windows environment on a machine with 3.40 GHz CPU with 16 GB RAM.

4.1   Benchmark Datasets

In order to prove the competence of proposed work, we performed classification experiments on a variety of machine learning benchmark datasets including UCI datasets [1]. The training data has been normalized to the range [0,1] before experimentation. In our simulations, we performed experiments with Linear as well as Gaussian kernel.

We have used grid search method [9] to obtain the best values for the parameters c_1, c_2 and kernel parameter σ. For each dataset, a validation set comprising of 10% randomly selected samples from the dataset is used. For this work, we have selected values of c_1 and c_2 from the range $[2^{-3}; 2^{-2}, ..., 2^3]$. The value of

σ has been tuned in the range {0.1 to 1}. We also fixed the maximum number of iterations max_iter equals to the number of available training points. Mean of classification accuracy as well as the average training time has been determined using 10-fold cross validation [6].

Classification Results. In order to compare the performance of SCG-TWSVM, we have also implemented SG-SVM and SG-TWSVM. The experiments are conducted with all the algorithms using 10-fold cross validation [6] and the mean classification accuracy along with standard deviation has been reported. Further, average number of iterations required for convergence by each model has also been reported.

The classification results using Linear kernel is reported in Table 1. The bold values indicate best result and the mean accuracy (in %) across 10-folds. The table clearly demonstrates that SCG-TWSVM outperforms other SGD methods as it considers the structural information obtained through the use of residual information. Moreover, the as underlying number of training iterations for SCG-TWSVM is much less compared to SG-SVM and SGD-TWSVM so, the overall computational time is better despite a performing more computations per iterations. This establishes the resulting out performance of SCG-TWSVM in prediction accuracy and training time. The results with Gaussian kernel for SCG-TWSVM, SG-SVM and SGD-TWSVM are reported in Table 2. The table demonstrates similar trends as in the results obtained with Linear Kernel. Note that, here, we have used rectangular kernel technique [13] with just 10% of the data for kernel calculation. As the results show in Table 2 demonstrates, the mean accuracy is still better than other compared method.

4.2 Application to Activity Recognition

In this subsection, we compared the performance of our proposed algorithm on real-world activity recognition problem. Human activity recognition is an active area of research with varied practical applications in video surveillance, human-computer interaction, user interface design etc. The main challenges include presence of extreme noises due to inter-related classes and huge training time complexity because of large training data involved. We have used Weizmann dataset which consists of 93 low-resolution (180 × 144 pixels) video sequences of 10 activity sequence performed by 9 actors. We have used motion-context [6] features for activity representation. Please refer to [6] for details.

We used Leave One Actor Out (L1AO) cross-validation methodology for comparison of prediction performance. L1AO removes all sequences of one actor from the training set and measures prediction accuracy. We have reported here the prediction accuracy of video sequence based on the classification accuracy of each frame.

Results. For Human Activity Recognition, we choose radial basis function (RBF) kernel for our classifiers because of non-linear relationship between action

Table 1. Comparison of performance of different methods with Linear Kernel on UCI datasets

Dataset	SCG-TWSVM	SGD-TWSVM	SGD-SVM
	Training accuracy		
	Average training time (in $\times 10^{-3}$ s)		
Australian	**85.38 ± 3.82**	83.49 ± 3.01	84.95 ± 6.09
(690 × 14)	138.4	148.04	312.28
Compound	87.71 ± 5.88	**89.47 ± 2.87**	87.47 ± 0.10
(399 × 2)	79.42	64.04	137.93
Bupaliver	**71.08 ± 1.02**	59.45 ± 1.09	58.28 ± 1.48
(345 × 6)	115.2	83.84	183.88
Flame	**97.92 ± 2.20**	87.94 ± 7.59	84.91 ± 5.50
(240 × 2)	43.24	28.81	93.80
Heart-Statlog	80.37 ± 7.62	80.74 ± 1.15	**80.74 ± 2.69**
(270 × 13)	54.54	54.28	124.98
Ionosphere	**86.59 ± 6.40**	82.03 ± 6.61	81.15 ± 7.62
(351 × 34)	125.81	97.38	200.62
PimaIndian	**75.92 ± 3.85**	58.23 ± 4.89	70.70 ± 5.35
(768 × 8)	189.47	178.04	337.14
Sonar	**89.83 ± 6.18**	85.84 ± 4.05	86.46 ± 3.66
(208 × 16)	59.48	52.29	116.61
CMC	**66.8 ± 3.38**	54.65 ± 6.24	61.44 ± 2.80
(1433 × 10)	273.36	281.1	423.45
Titanic	**79.05 ± 2.43**	77.10 ± 3.07	77.60 ± 1.23
(2201 × 41)	655.2	642.51	886.50
Twonorm	**97.80 ± 0.51**	96.37 ± 0.65	97.77 ± 0.58
(7400 × 21)	1594.2	1425.74	1984.74
Ringworm	**98.51 ± 0.40**	97.39 ± 4.44	97.59 ± 1.74
(7400 × 21)	1501.2	1541.18	1970.8
Letter recognition	90.27 ± 1.34	95.26 ± 2.03	90.37 ± 1.51
(20,000 × 16)	4523.13	13271.34	18734.60
Credit Card	75.01 ± 0.81	75.35 ± 0.12	76.51 ± 1.59
(30,000 × 24)	5043.37	18147.31	23744.34
Skin	84.35 ± 3.25	85.15 ± 2.21	83.57 ± 2.29
(245,057 × 4)	32742.64	877843.37	107745.12

classes and histogrammed feature obtained in the descriptor. Optimal values of parameter c_1, c_2 and kernel parameter σ were obtained using grid search with a set comprising 10% of the frames from each video sequence.

Table 2. Comparison of performance of different methods with Gaussian Kernel on UCI datasets

Dataset	SCG-TWSVM	SGD-TWSVM	SGD-SVM
	Training accuracy		
	Average training time (in $\times 10^{-3}$ s)		
Australian	**86.96 ± 3.84**	84.23 ± 4.30	85.80 ± 3.11
(690 × 14)	172.90	175.04	240.54
Compound	**94.72 ± 4.54**	93.46 ± 3.68	92.72 ± 2.97
(399 × 2)	140.50	98.81	149.38
Bupaliver	**71.92 ± 7.59**	57.98 ± 0.88	57.98 ± 0.89
(345 × 6)	124.98	98.51	126.95
Flame	**98.32 ± 2.18**	94.77 ± 1.44	89.48 ± 5.83
(240 × 2)	78.94	63.71	92.99
Heart-Statlog	**83.33 ± 7.46**	80.37 ± 9.57	82.96 ± 6.10
(270 × 13)	91.75	72.44	77.74
Ionosphere	**94.62 ± 4.05**	92.64 ± 3.67	88.07 ± 3.99
(351 × 34)	89.36	89.21	120.59
PimaIndian	**76.05 ± 5.91**	72.80 ± 5.48	70.58 ± 3.34
(768 × 8)	211.04	191.54	253.79
Sonar	**89.60 ± 1.09**	88.46 ± 1.60	87.10 ± 2.71
(208 × 16)	65.79	58.04	75.89
CMC	**70.06 ± 1.90**	68.52 ± 4.92	63.07 ± 2.78
(1433 × 10)	414.95	382.21	477.22
Titanic	**80.05 ± 2.43**	79.30 ± 0.10	78.10 ± 1.67
(2201 × 41)	658.59	550.34	738.59
Twonorm	**97.82 ± 0.43**	97.80 ± 5.81	97.63 ± 0.31
(7400 × 21)	1598.10	1267.81	1740.12
Ringworm	**98.59 ± 0.35**	98.51 ± 0.05	96.78 ± 2.63
(7400 × 21)	1327.74	1271.53	1877.30

In order to implement activity recognition problem as a binary classification problem, we picked two activity classes at a time e.g. bend versus wave etc. and used them to evaluate our results. We performed the activity recognition task using SCG-TWSVM and SG-TWSVM and SG-SVM with given evaluation methodology.

The results using SG-SVM, SG-TWSVM and SCG-TWSVM classifiers have been summarised in Tables 3, 4 and 5 respectively. The results in Table 5 shows that SCG-TWSVM performs comparable to other approaches and for the more confusing classes such as skip and jump, SCG-TWSVM clearly outperforms which validates the robustness of the algorithm's ability to optimize the objective function well.

Table 3. Activity classification results on Weizmann dataset obtained using Stochastic SG-SVM

	Bend	Jack	Jump	PJump	Run	Side	Skip	Walk	Wave1	Wave2
Bend	-									
Jack	93.62	-								
Jump	94.67	99.18	-							
Pjump	92.33	90.06	99.40	-						
Run	95.05	99.79	88.27	99.27	-					
Side	90.23	89.11	96.10	95.06	86.04	-				
Skip	94.45	99.84	80.26	99.32	71.10	93.21	-			
Walk	93.84	98.35	95.42	89.59	74.67	94.98	86.09	-		
Wave 1	81.84	99.18	98.40	97.66	100	99.85	100	96.43	-	
Wave 2	91.44	83.22	99.16	88.35	99.69	97.48	99.38	98.90	91.00	-

Table 4. Activity classification results on Weizmann dataset obtained using SG-TWSVM

	Bend	Jack	Jump	PJump	Run	Side	Skip	Walk	Wave1	Wave2
Bend	-									
Jack	91.70	-								
Jump	99.52	100	-							
Pjump	96.88	86.18	100	-						
Run	99.05	99.90	86.40	100	-					
Side	98.25	100	87.12	100	92.98	-				
Skip	98.77	99.75	71.27	100	69.86	94.70	-			
Walk	99.88	100	88.38	100	87.35	76.45	86.09	-		
Wave 1	85.80	99.91	100	100	100	100	100	100	-	
Wave 2	92.59	98.69	99.91	99.02	99.69	100	99.64	100	88.95	-

Table 5. Activity classification results on Weizmann dataset obtained using SCG-TWSVM

	Bend	Jack	Jump	PJump	Run	Side	Skip	Walk	Wave1	Wave2
Bend	-									
Jack	99.74	-								
Jump	98.91	100	-							
Pjump	98.84	96.77	100	-						
Run	99.60	99.32	93.12	100	-					
Side	99.73	100	90.76	100	98.21	-				
Skip	99.40	100	76.55	100	74.02	92.50	-			
Walk	99.92	100	96.05	100	90.70	100	86.09	-		
Wave 1	99.46	100	100	100	99.71	100	100	100	-	
Wave 2	97.35	99.81	100	99.02	99.34	100	100	100	98.99	-

5   Conclusions

In this paper, we proposed a novel stochastic conjugate gradient method based TWSVM model, which has been termed as SCG-TWSVM. The proposed model can effectively handle ill-conditioning, slow convergence and instability related issues faced by traditional stochastic gradient descent methods such as SG-SVM and SG-TWSVM. The experimental results on diverse ML datasets as well as activity recognition datasets proves the efficacy of proposed method compared to related methods over large scale datasets. The main advantages of the SCG-TWSVM are- (1) it leads to faster convergence as it proceeds in the direction of conjugate gradient directions, (2) the generalization performance which is at par, if not better, with SG-SVM and SG-TWSVM.

In future, we aim to incorporate the structural information of each class in the objective function of each problem so that feature noise among inter-related classes can be taken care of.

References

1. Asuncion, A., Newman, D.: UCI machine learning repository (2007)
2. Bottou, L., Curtis, F.E., Nocedal, J.: Optimization methods for large-scale machine learning. SIAM Rev. **60**(2), 223–311 (2018)
3. Cao, L.J., et al.: Parallel sequential minimal optimization for the training of support vector machines. IEEE Trans. Neural Netw. **17**(4), 1039–1049 (2006)
4. Catanzaro, B., Sundaram, N., Keutzer, K.: Fast support vector machine training and classification on graphics processors. In: Proceedings of the 25th International Conference on Machine Learning, pp. 104–111. ACM (2008)
5. Cortes, C., Vapnik, V.: Support-vector networks. Mach. Learn. **20**(3), 273–297 (1995)
6. Duda, R.O., Hart, P.E., Stork, D.G.: Pattern Classification. Wiley, Hoboken (2012)
7. Gulcehre, C., Sotelo, J., Moczulski, M., Bengio, Y.: A robust adaptive stochastic gradient method for deep learning. In: 2017 International Joint Conference on Neural Networks (IJCNN), pp. 125–132. IEEE (2017)
8. Hsieh, C.J., Chang, K.W., Lin, C.J., Keerthi, S.S., Sundararajan, S.: A dual coordinate descent method for large-scale linear SVM. In: Proceedings of the 25th International Conference on Machine Learning, pp. 408–415. ACM (2008)
9. Hsu, C.W., Chang, C.C., Lin, C.J.: A practical guide to support vector classification. National Taiwan University (2003)
10. Jayadeva, Khemchandani, R., Chandra, S.: Twin support vector machines for pattern classification. IEEE Trans. Pattern Anal. Mach. Intell. **29**(5), 905–910 (2007)
11. Jin, X.B., Zhang, X.Y., Huang, K., Geng, G.G.: Stochastic conjugate gradient algorithm with variance reduction. arXiv preprint arXiv:1710.09979 (2017)
12. Kumar, M.A., Gopal, M.: Application of smoothing technique on twin support vector machines. Pattern Recognit. Lett. **29**(13), 1842–1848 (2008)
13. Mangasarian, O.L., Wild, E.W.: Proximal support vector machine classifiers. In: Proceedings KDD-2001: Knowledge Discovery and Data Mining. Citeseer (2001)
14. Mangasarian, O.L., Wild, E.W.: Multisurface proximal support vector machine classification via generalized eigenvalues. IEEE Trans. Pattern Anal. Mach. Intell. **28**(1), 69–74 (2006)

15. Mokhtari, A., Ribeiro, A.: A quasi-newton method for large scale support vector machines. In: 2014 IEEE International Conference on Acoustics, Speech and Signal Processing (ICASSP), pp. 8302–8306. IEEE (2014)
16. Omidvar, M.N., Li, X., Tang, K.: Designing benchmark problems for large-scale continuous optimization. Inf. Sci. **316**, 419–436 (2015)
17. Shalev-Shwartz, S., Singer, Y., Srebro, N., Cotter, A.: Pegasos: primal estimated sub-gradient solver for SVM. Math. Program. **127**(1), 3–30 (2011)
18. Suykens, J.A., Vandewalle, J.: Least squares support vector machine classifiers. Neural Process. Lett. **9**(3), 293–300 (1999)
19. Vanek, J., Michalek, J., Psutka, J.: A GPU-architecture optimized hierarchical decomposition algorithm for support vector machine training. IEEE Trans. Parallel Distrib. Syst. 1 (2017). https://doi.org/10.1109/tpds.2017.2731764
20. Wang, Z., Shao, Y.H., Bai, L., Li, C.N., Liu, L.M., Deng, N.Y.: Insensitive stochastic gradient twin support vector machines for large scale problems. Inf. Sci. (2018)
21. Wang, Z., Shao, Y.H., Bai, L., Liu, L.M., Deng, N.Y.: Stochastic gradient twin support vector machine for large scale problems. arXiv preprint arXiv:1704.05596 (2017)
22. Zhao, J., Xu, Y.: A safe sample screening rule for Universum support vector machines. Knowl.-Based Syst. **138**, 46–57 (2017)

A Novel Synthetic Over-Sampling Technique for Imbalanced Classification of Gene Expressions Using Autoencoders and Swarm Optimization

Maisa Daoud$^{(\boxtimes)}$ and Michael Mayo

University of Waikato, Hamilton, New Zealand
{mtdd1,michael.mayo}@waikato.ac.nz

Abstract. A new synthetic minority class over-sampling approach for binary (normal/cancer) classification of microarray gene expression data is proposed. The idea is to exploit a previously trained autoencoder in combination with the Particle Swarm Optimisation algorithm to generate new synthetic examples of the minority class for solving the class imbalance problem. Experiments using two different autoencoder representation sizes (500 and 30) and two base classifiers (Support Vector Machine and naïve Bayes) show that the proposed method is able to generate discriminating representations that outperformed state-of-the-art methods such as Synthetic Minority Class Over-sampling Technique and Density-Based Synthetic Minority Class Over-sampling Technique in many test cases.

Keywords: Class imbalance · Cancer prediction · Autoencoders
Classification

1   Introduction

A labeled dataset for classification purposes is considered imbalanced when samples are distributed unequally among different classes. This kind of dataset poses a challenge to machine learning classifiers as it becomes difficult to model the minority class samples.

The problem of imbalanced datasets exists in many real-world applications such as text classification [20], detection of fraudulent telephone calls [9], information retrieval and filtering tasks [19]. In this research we are interested in high dimensional cancer prediction applications where using a dimensionality reduction method such as an autoencoder is a necessity for reducing noise and increasing classification accuracy.

Microarrays produce high dimensional matrices consisting of thousands of gene expressions for only a few hundred samples. The shortage in the number of samples is a result of the cost and time needed for sequencing the biological samples. Microarray datasets are usually imbalanced, where cancer samples form

© Springer Nature Switzerland AG 2018
T. Mitrovic et al. (Eds.): AI 2018, LNAI 11320, pp. 603–615, 2018.
https://doi.org/10.1007/978-3-030-03991-2_55

the majority of the dataset, and have non-linearly separable classes [15]. The high dimensionality of the datasets is a major challenge to machine learning classifiers and reducing it would help in decreasing computational complexity and increasing classifier's accuracy [8].

Autoencoders are commonly used to reduce the dimensionality of data and to remove the noise. However, the suggested approach utilizes the representations learnt by a pre-trained autoencoder for generating new synthetic minority class data. To achieve this, we employed the Particle Swarm Optimisation (PSO) algorithm to optimize the generated data to be as much similar (close) to the original source data as possible. The aim of the approach is to find a variation of a desired minority class representation that will make a good synthetic example to be added to the dataset.

The approach was experimentally tested by training different autoencoders using the training split of the considered microarray datasets. We tried different number of hidden nodes, 500 and 30, in the network's bottleneck layers to test the suitability of the approach in generating representations with different dimensionalities. The approach showed promising results when compared to two other methods called Synthetic Minority Class Over-sampling Technique (SMOTE) and Density-Based Synthetic Minority Over-sampling Technique (DBSMOTE). We used naïve Bayes and Support Vector Machine (will be abbreviated by SMO after the Sequential Minimization Optimization algorithm which is used for training it) classifiers to classify the data generated by each oversampling method. Generally, naïve Bayes achieved the highest prediction accuracy overall when used with the suggested method's representations compared to SMO and other oversampling methods. However, the SMO classifier performed better with our method's 500D representations than SMOTE and DBSMOTE.

The rest of the paper is organized as follows. In Sect. 2 we present a basic background to autoencoders, PSO and the class imbalance problem. Section 3 presents our motivation, Sect. 4 shows the methodology, Sect. 5 discusses the experiments and results. Finally, the conclusion is presented in Sect. 6.

2   Background

This section presents a basic introduction to autoencoders, PSO and the class-imbalance problem.

2.1   Autoencoders

Autoencoders are neural network models that have been successfully used for extracting low dimensional representations from high dimensional data. In its simplest form, the autoencoder consists of two fully connected feedforward layers called the encoder and the decoder and this results in a three-layered network. In the general (deep) case, both the encoder and the decoder may have multiple layers. The number of outputs at every layer L_l equals the number of inputs at the next layer L_{l+1}, and the number of outputs from the encoder equals to the number of inputs to the decoder.

The autoencoder learns from examples $x_1, x_2, \ldots$ by feeding the training input vectors forward through the network to calculate the activation values of its neurons at every layer subsequent to the input layer. The activation values at the output layer are calculated and aggregated to get an output $O(x_i)$ for each x_i. Since the aim of an autoencoder is to reconstruct the input perfectly, then the difference between $O(x_i)$ and x_i is calculated using a predefined error function such as the Mean Squared Error (MSE). The network tries to minimize the objective function using a backpropagation learning algorithm which propagates the error derivatives back through the network to fine-tune the weights for optimal reconstruction.

Stacked Denoising Autoencoders (SDA) [18] are an improved variation of the ordinary stacked autoencoder which is trained to denoise corrupted versions of the inputs. Different methods can be used for corrupting the initial input such as Gaussian noise, mask noise, and salt-and-pepper noise [18]. SDAs use the same training algorithm that is used by normal autoencoders but achieve significant improvements over the latter as they are better able to learn useful structures of the data such as Gabor-like edge detectors from natural images [18].

2.2 Particle Swarm Optimization

PSO [16] is an optimization algorithm ideally used for optimizing continuous nonlinear functions. The algorithm can be simply implemented by randomly initializing the location (vector) and velocity (vector) for a number of particles in a flock. On each iteration of the algorithm, the fitness of each particle's position is evaluated using the problem's objective function. Each particle i updates its velocity based on its current position y_i and its previous best position p_i. The velocity is also influenced by the position p_i found by the best neighbor p_g. New points are found, for the subsequent iteration, by adding the velocity coordinates to y_i according to the following equations:

$$v_i = v_i + U(0, \phi_1) \times (p_i - y_i) + U(0, \phi_2) \times (p_g - y_i) \tag{1}$$

$$y_i = y_i + v_i \tag{2}$$

where $U(0, \phi_1)$ is a vector of random numbers generated for each particle at each iteration and uniformly distributed over $[0, \phi_i]$, ϕ_1 and ϕ_2 are acceleration factors and v_i has to be kept within the range $[V_{min}, V_{max}]$ [16].

Typically, PSO will continue iterating until either the best particle with the best position (representing a perfect solution) is found, or until a maximum number of iterations has been reached.

2.3 Class Imbalance

Different approaches have been suggested to improve the prediction accuracy of imbalanced test samples. Majority class random under-sampling is one of the direct and most straight forward suggested approaches [14]. Focused under-sampling, which targets the samples that are further away from the classes' borders, has been investigated by Japkowicz [13] who observed that using sophisticated under-sampling techniques did not add an advantage to the results in the considered domain.

Minority over-sampling, on the other hand, is a different approach that can be either applied using random duplication method or more sophisticated synthetic methods. SMOTE [5] is a synthetic over-sampling method which generates samples on the line segment joining a chosen minority class sample and its neighbors from the same class. DBSMOTE is a new variation of SMOTE that discovers an arbitrary shaped cluster and over-samples it. Majority Weighted Minority Over-sampling (MWMOTE) [2] is another synthetic over-sampling clustering-based technique which generates new samples from weighted minority class samples.

3   Motivation

Most of the suggested minority over-sampling methods are efficient and effective when generating synthetic samples, with the resulting datasets increasing classification accuracy [2,12]. However, we found that existing methods work ideally when the boundaries between the classes are not ambiguous, a situation that is not true for all kinds of datasets.

Real world datasets, especially medical datasets, are high dimensional, complex, noisy and often have limited number of samples [15]. In such kind of datasets, majority and minority class samples are not separable and they frequently overlap [15], see Fig. 1. Classifying high-dimensional datasets requires reducing the dimensionality of the data using either a dimensionality reduction method or a feature selection method to remove the noise. Both of these solutions depend on trial-and-error techniques for generating or selecting a number of discriminating features that increase the accuracy. Hence, reducing the dimensionality of the data does not necessarily solve the class overlap and borderline-ambiguity problems.

K-nearest neighbor-based methods such as SMOTE generate synthetic samples on the line segments between sample s and its K nearest neighbors. This tends to increase the density of the minority-class samples generated within the majority class region. For example, in Fig. 1, a synthetic sample (the red sample) is generated from two positive (white) examples. Since the synthetic example lies on the line between two positive examples, it ends up being very close to several negative (black) examples. As a consequence, the classifier's performance in discriminating both majority and minority samples may well decrease. The problem becomes more complicated if the minority class has small number of samples, the samples are very sparse or when the dimensionality of the data increases. Blagus and Lusa [3] demonstrated the poor performance of SMOTE in generating high-dimensional gene expression data.

Based on this observed weakness of the SMOTE family of algorithms, our proposed new method aims to overcome this problem by generating synthetic examples that are variations of a single real example as opposed to being a function of multiple real examples. In this way, the synthetic examples should in theory be better represent the true region of the feature space occupied by the minority class we are attempting to model. In Fig. 1, such an example is illustrated by green example.

Our approach is not a random oversampling-by-replication or duplication approach. Instead, we use an optimization method to utilize the trained decoder part of an autoencoder to generate a new representation that is similar to an existing minority class one. The autoencoder is trained on all of the training examples, both minority and majority, but the optimisation step focuses only on the minority class training samples since these are ones being generated. In this respect, our approach shares a commonality with SMOTE: both approaches consider all minority class training samples to generate the synthetic data. Therefore we chose SMOTE and a newer version DBSMOTE as suitable baseline methods for comparison.

Fig. 1. Border line ambiguity in 2-D space. white circle: minority class samples, black dots: majority class samples, red circle: SMOTE generated sample and green circle: a synthetic sample generated by the proposed approach. (Color figure online)

4 Minority Over-Sampling Using Autoencoder and Optimization

Our proposed approach integrates both the decoder part of a trained SDA and the PSO algorithm for generating synthetic minority class samples. The algorithm is presented in detail in the following two sub-sections.

4.1 Training the Autoencoder

We first configure the autoencoder by specifying the number of layers and their sizes where input and output layers must be fixed and equal to the dimensionality of the dataset. The size of the hidden layers, however, can be varied. We also select the network's learning parameters including the weight initialization method, a noising method, and an objective function to compute the difference between training examples (both minority and majority class examples) and their reconstructed versions. The optimization algorithm for minimising the reconstruction error must be also be specified.

After training the network (Fig. 2) for a set of iterations, the autoencoder is expected to learn the training data abstract representations. To generate a compact representation j with dimensionality M for data instance J with dimensionality N where $M << N$, we simply propagate J forward through the encoder and "read off" the final activations at the bottleneck layer which consists of M neurons. This process of encoding can be encapsulated as a function $j = Encoder(J)$.

Our approach uses a trained encoder to generate low-dimensional training and testing datasets, $R_{training}$ and $R_{testing}$ respectively, by activating the encoder part using the training and testing datasets. The generated compact training representations $R_{training}$, since they are labeled with the same classes as the original train-

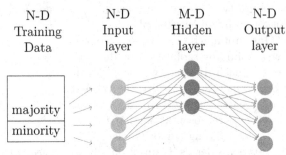

Fig. 2. Training a single layer autoencoder.

ing data, can be used for building a machine learning model for classification, while $R_{testing}$ is going to be used for evaluating the accuracy of the model.

4.2 Generating Optimized Representations

We used the decoder part of the trained autoencoder in combination with the PSO algorithm to generate new synthetic examples. This procedure is described in Algorithm 1 and by Fig. 3. Given one real minority class sample, multiple synthetic examples can be generated by repeatedly applying the algorithm.

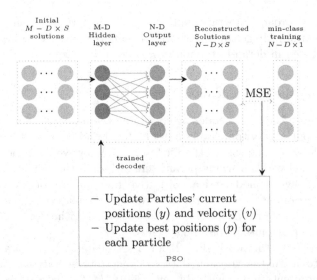

Fig. 3. Generating minority class over-sampling using trained decoder and PSO.

To generate a single optimized minority class representation, we randomly initialize the location and velocity (each of which is an M-D vector) for a swarm $y(t = 0)$ of S particles to small numbers between [0,1]. The algorithm iterates over the initial particles $y_1, y_2, ..., y_s$ to feed them separately through the decoder part of the trained autoencoder to generate $Y_1', Y_2', .., Y_s'$ at the output layer.

The MSE (difference) between each generated version Y_i' (at the output layer) and a desired minority training sample Y is computed to determine the particle's fitness. PSO determines each particle's p_g to update the positions and the velocities according to Eqs. 1 and 2. Updated particles are fed again through the decoder part for a subsequent iteration and the algorithm runs until a termination condition is satisfied. The algorithm returns the most fitted particle (representation) y whose inverse Y' is the most similar to the original sample Y.

Algorithm 1. Minority-Class Over-Sampling using PSO

---

1 $t = 0$;
2 $Y =$ target minority-class training sample;
3 $y(t) = y_1, y_2, .., y_S$ /*Swarm with S randomly initialized M-D particles*/ ;
4 $p_1, p_2, .., p_S = y_1, y_2, .., y_S$;
5 **while** *terminal condition is not satisfied* **do**
6   **for** $i = 1...S$ **do**
7   /*feed y_i through the trained decoder to generate the reconstructed versions */;
8          $Y_i' = $ decoder(y_i) ;
9   /* evaluate the fitness $f(y_i)$ */ ;
10         $f(y_i) = $ MSE(Y, Y_i') ;
11   **if** $f(y_i) < f(p_i)$ **then**
12            $p_i = y_i$;
13   **end**
14   determine p_g [16] ;
15   update y_i using Eq(1) and Eq(2);
16   **end**
17      $t = t + 1$;
18 **end**

---

5 Experiments

To experimentally test the proposed approach, we used 10 different datasets downloaded from[1] The Cancer Genome Atlas (TCGA) Data Portal. The datasets are genomic data made publicly available for researchers to improve the prevention, diagnosis, and treatment of cancer. An R/Bioconductor package called TCGAbiolinks [6] was used to download and prepare the RNA-seq gene expression data. Table 1 shows detailed characteristics of the experimental datasets which were chosen based on the number of samples and imbalance ratios.

---

[1] https://portal.gdc.cancer.gosv/.

Table 1. The microarray datasets and the distribution of the samples across normal and cancerous groups. "No" denotes normal samples and "Ca" cancer samples.

Dataset	Cancer type	No(train/test)	Ca(train/test)	Imb.ratio	length(N)
BLCA	Bladder Urothelial Carcinoma	15/4	326/82	0.047	31209
BRCA	Breast Invasive Carcinoma	90/13	877/218	0.094	3506
ESCA	Esophageal Carcinoma	8/3	147/37	0.060	4438
HNSC	Head & Neck Squamous Cell Carcinoma	35/9	416/102	0.085	3459
KICH	Kidney Chromophobe	13/5	73/18	0.198	4293
LUAD	Lung Adenocarcinoma	47/12	412/103	0.115	3849
LUSC	Lung Squamous Cell Carcinoma	40/11	401/101	0.102	5354
READ	Rectum Adenocarcinoma	8/2	75/19	0.106	3649
STAD	Stomach Adenocarcinoma	29/7	331/83	0.087	2439
THCA	Thyroid Carcinoma	48/13	400/100	0.122	2149

5.1   Experimental Setup

To build our proposed approach, we used an open source machine intelligence library called TensorFlow r.1.4 [1] to configure two different autoencoders as follows:

1. An $input - 1000 - 500 - 1000 - output$ autoencoder, with bottleneck layer size $M = 500$; and
2. An $input - 1000 - 30 - 1000 - output$ autoencoder, with bottleneck layer size $M = 30$.

We used the MSE as an objective function. The Stochastic Gradient Descent (SGD) [4] back propagation algorithm was used to optimise the network weights. The learning rate was set to 0.001, the batch size was 25 and the number of epochs was 250. We also attempted to train the autoencoder for more (500) and less (100) iterations but results were comparable to the 250 iteration case, so we only considered this number of iterations in our experiments.

For optimization, we used a python library called `pyswarm`[2] to generate synthetic samples from minority class representations by utilizing the decoder part of the trained autoencoder. The PSO library requires the user to specify the lower-bound and upper-bound vectors that bound the swarms' locations between them. Hence, we defined the lower-bound as an M-D vector of zeros, and the upper-bound as an M-D vector of ones. The number of particles have been experimentally specified and set to 200 and 2.

For the baseline comparison, we used SMOTE and DBSMOTE methods from an R package called `smotefamily` [17] to over-sample the minority-class representations extracted using the trained autoencoder. SMOTE method requires the user to specify K, the number of neighbors to be considered, which was set to 5 as indicated by the original paper [5].

---

[2] https://pythonhosted.org/pyswarm/.

Each of the configured autoencoders was separately trained and tested ten times per dataset so that the mean expected performance metrics of the algorithm could be calculated. In each run, we randomly selected 80% of the cancer samples and 80% of the normal samples to form a training set, and the remaining 20% were reserved for testing. After training, we extracted the training and testing datasets representations, and then over-sampled the minority class training representations to varying degrees. The exact amount of over-sampling was determined by the size of the majority class. We tried over-sampling the minority class until it was 25%, 35%, 50%, 75%, 85% or 100% of the majority class size. This was done for each of the ten repetitions per dataset, and was done using both our new proposed method (referred to hereafter as Opt/Decoder), SMOTE and DBSMOTE. Therefore three versions of each training dataset for each amount of over-sampling was generated. Finally, we built a classifier using the training samples and tested it using the testing representations.

5.2   Classification Algorithms

The goal of this research is to solve the class-imbalance problem which degrades the performance of classification algorithms. In order to evaluate this, we chose two classifiers naïve Bayes and SMO implemented by WEKA package [10] and trained using the extracted training representations, from both classes, and the appended generated minority-class samples.

The metric used for assessing the performance of each algorithm was Area Under the Receiver Operating Characteristics graph (AUROC, or alternatively ROC).

An AUROC value of close to 0.5 indicates random prediction performance while a value close to 1.0 indicates near-perfect prediction performance.

5.3   Results Using the TCGA Datasets

We compared the average AUROC (over 10 runs) of the SMO and naïve Bayes (NB) classifiers in classifying Opt/Decoder, SMOTE and DBSMOTE representations with different minority/majority class ratios (25%, 35%, 50%, 75%, 85%, 100%) and representation size $M = 500$ and $M = 30$ respectively.

A visual inspection, based on the number of winning cases per method, of the graphs shows that NB and Opt/Decoder (NB+Opt/Decoder) representations, indicated by the blue line, have generally achieved the highest AUROC for most datasets compared to other methods and classifiers.

Comparing the performance of the NB+Opt/Decoder with NB+SMOTE (Fig. 4) and NB+ DBSMOTE (Fig. 6) indicates that our method's 500D representations were better classified than SMOTE (500) and DBSMOTE (500) respectively. Another interesting point to note is the slight increase in the NB+ Opt/Decoder (500) AUROC with the increase in the number of generated minority samples (BLCA, ESCA, KICH, LUSC, READ). NB+Opt/Decoder (500) has also proved success in cases where the number of minority training samples is relatively small (BLCA, ESCA, HNSC, LUSCA, STAD). The NB+Opt/Decoder

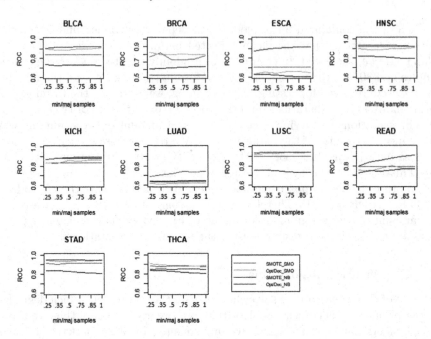

Fig. 4. AUROC results for SMOTE and Opt/Decoder (500D) using SMO and NB.

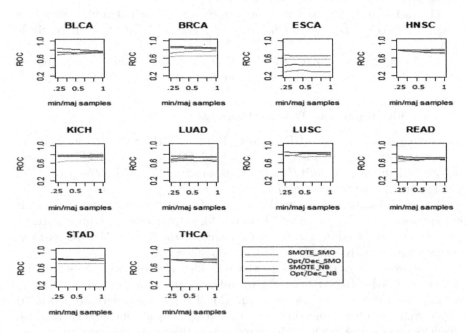

Fig. 5. AUROC results for SMOTE and Opt/Decoder (30D) using SMO and NB.

Table 2. Wilcoxon signed rank test for (Opt/Decoder v.s. each of the listed method) using the average AUROC over the 10 runs.

Method	Classifier	R+	R−	p-val
SMOTE30	SMO	587	1243	0.0080
SMOTE30	NB	1761	68	2.32E−10
SMOTE500	SMO	1797	32	4.59E−11
SMOTE500	NB	1645	184	3.93E−08
DBSMOTE30	SMO	375	1454	8.81E−05
DBSMOTE30	NB	1148	682	0.0870
DBSMOTE500	SMO	1203	627	0.0343
DBSMOTE500	NB	1728	101	2.42E−09

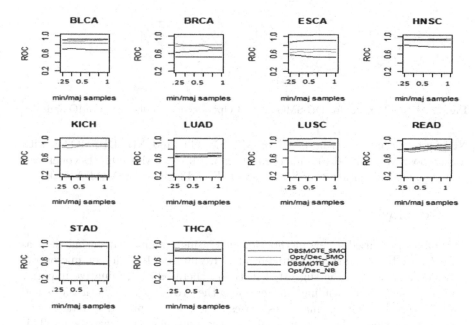

Fig. 6. AUROC results for DB-SMOTE and Opt/Decoder (500D) using SMO and NB.

(30) had a slight better performance than NB+SMOTE (30) (Fig. 5) and a comparable behavior to NB+DBSMOTE (30) (Fig. 7).

The performance of the SMO classifier, on the other hand, was generally lower than the NB. However, our method, represented by the green line, showed a slight improvement over SMO+SMOTE and SMO+DBSMOTE in the 500D case (Figs. 4 and 6 respectively). SMO classifier had better prediction accuracy to other methos 30D representations.

A statistical analysis across all the datasets was performed following the method described in [7] by applying Wilcoxon signed-rank test [11]. The test results represented in Table 2 indicate that the overall performance of the

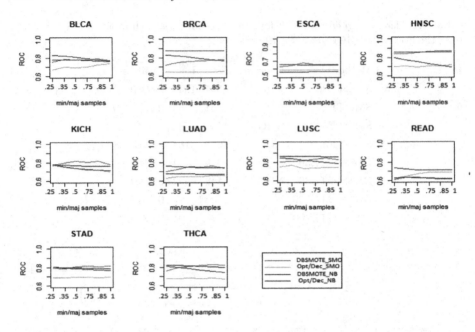

Fig. 7. AUROC results for DB-SMOTE and Opt/Decoder (30D) using SMO and NB.

NB+Opt/ Decoder was better than NB+SMOTE and NB+DBSMOTE with higher positive rank (R+) sum than other methods. SMO+Opt/Decoder had also a general advantage over SMO+SMOTE and SMO+DBSMOTE (500D).

6 Conclusion

This paper presented a new method for generating training data using the features learnt by a pre-trained autoencoder. Results on 10 different microarray datasets showed that the suggested method generated discriminative minority class representations, leading to increasing the AUCROC for both SMO and naïve Bayes classifiers in many test cases. The method proved a notable success in cases where the dimensionality of the representations was 500D. This leads to the question of whether SMOTE family of algorithm is suitable for high dimensional imbalanced datasets.

Several issues are left for future work, such as the consideration of other optimisation algorithms and applying this method to very small, imbalanced and multi-class datasets.

References

1. Abadi, M. et. al.: TensorFlow: Large-Scale Machine Learning on Heterogeneous Systems (2015). https://www.tensorflow.org/
2. Sukarna, B., Md Monirul, I., Xin, Y., Kazyuki, M.: MWMOTE-majority weighted minority oversampling technique for imbalanced data set learning. IEEE Trans. Knowl. Data Eng. **26**(2), 405–425 (2014)

3. Blagus, R., Lusa, L.: Evaluation of smote for high-dimensional class-imbalanced microarray data. In: 11th International Conference on Machine Learning and Applications (icmla), vol. 2, pp. 89–94. IEEE (2012)
4. Bottou, L.: Large-scale machine learning with stochastic gradient descent. In: Lechevallier, Y., Saporta, G. (eds.) Proceedings of COMPSTAT 2010, pp. 177–186. Springer, Heidelberg (2010). https://doi.org/10.1007/978-3-7908-2604-3_16
5. Chawla, N., Bowyer, K.W., Hall, L.O., Kegelmeyer, W.P.: SMOTE: synthetic minority over-sampling technique. J. Artif. Intell. Res. **16**, 321–357 (2002)
6. Antonio, C., et al.: TCGAbiolinks: an R/Bioconductor package for integrative analysis of TCGA data. Nucleic Acids Res. (2015). https://doi.org/10.1093/nar/gkv1507
7. Demšar, J.: Statistical comparisons of classifiers over multiple data sets. J. Mach. Learn. Res. **7**, 1–30 (2006)
8. Dong, Y., Du, B., Zhang, L., Zhang, L.: Dimensionality reduction and classification of hyperspectral images using ensemble discriminative local metric learning. IEEE Trans. Geosci. Remote Sens. **55**(5), 2509–2524 (2017)
9. Fawcett, T., Provost, F.: Adaptive fraud detection. Data Min. Knowl. Discov. **1**(3), 291–316 (1997)
10. Hall, M., Frank, E., Holmes, G., Pfahringer, B., Reutemann, P., Witten, H.I.: The WEKA data mining software: an update. ACM SIGKDD Explor. Newsl. **11**(1), 10–8 (2009)
11. Gibbons, J.D., Chakraborti, S.: Nonparametric statistical inference. In: Lovric, M. (ed.) International Encyclopedia of Statistical Science, pp. 977–979. Springer, Heidelberg (2011). https://doi.org/10.1007/978-3-642-04898-2
12. Han, H., Wang, W.-Y., Mao, B.-H.: Borderline-SMOTE: a new over-sampling method in imbalanced data sets learning. In: Huang, D.-S., Zhang, X.-P., Huang, G.-B. (eds.) ICIC 2005. LNCS, vol. 3644, pp. 878–887. Springer, Heidelberg (2005). https://doi.org/10.1007/11538059_91
13. Japkowicz, N.: The class imbalance problem: significance and strategies. In: Proceedings of the International Conference on Artificial Intelligence (2005)
14. Kubat, M., Matwin, S., et al.: Addressing the curse of imbalanced training sets: one-sided selection. In: ICML 1997, Nashville, USA (1997)
15. Lin, W.J., Chen, J.J.: Class-imbalanced classifiers for high-dimensional data. Brief. Bioinform. **14**(1), 13–26 (2012)
16. Poli, R., Kennedy, J., Blackwell, T.: Particle swarm optimization. Swarm Intell. **1**(1), 33–57 (2007)
17. Siriseriwan, W.: Smotefamily: A Collection of Oversampling Techniques for Class Imbalance Problem Based on SMOTE (2016)
18. Vincent, P., Larochelle, H., Lajoie, I., Bengio, Y., Manzagol, P.: Stacked denoising autoencoders: learning useful representations in a deep network with a local denoising criterion. J. Mach. Learn. Res. **11**, 3371–3408 (2010)
19. Weiss, G.M.: Mining with rarity: a unifying framework. ACM Sigkdd Explor. Newsl. **6**(1), 7–19 (2014)
20. Zheng, Z., Wu, X., Srihari, R.: Feature selection for text categorization on imbalanced data. ACM Sigkdd Explor. Newsl. **6**(1), 80–89 (2004)

Co-evolution of Novel Tree-Like ANNs and Activation Functions: An Observational Study

Damien O'Neill, Bing Xue[✉], and Mengjie Zhang

Victoria University of Wellington, P.O. Box 600, Wellington 6140, New Zealand
{Damien.Oneill,Bing.Xue,Mengjie.Zhang}@ecs.vuw.ac.nz

Abstract. Deep convolutional neural networks (CNNs) represent the state-of-the-art model structure in image classification problems. However, deep CNNs suffer from issues of interpretability and are difficult to train. This work presents new tree-like shallow ANNs, and offers a novel approach to exploring and examining the relationship between activation functions and network performance. The proposed work is examined on the MNIST and CIFAR10 datasets, finding surprising results relating to the necessity and benefit of activation functions in this new type of shallow network. In particular the work finds high accuracy networks for the MNIST dataset which utilise pooling operations as the only non-linearity, and demonstrate a certain invariance to the specific form of activation functions on the more complicated CIFAR10 dataset.

1 Introduction

Over recent years, deep convolutional Artificial Neural Networks (ANNs), have made great strides, particularly in tasks related to image classification [3,5,7]. Despite the success, they have been primarily designed by human experts, frequently with state-of-the-art networks taking strong structural inspiration from prior state-of-the-art networks [7,20]. Where the ANN design has been automatically explored, it has tended to either augment existing state-of-the-art networks [22,25,26], be highly computationally expensive and use only a few hand-picked operators [25], explore only a component of the network [22], or develop small networks without utilising gradient descent for training [21]. Because of the style of these explorations, and the use of previous state-of-the-art networks to guide manual ANN design, there are many open questions related to the necessity of size and optimality of operations used in these networks.

Motivations: several problems have been noted with regards to the training of deep networks. In particular, the vanishing gradient [2] and shattered gradients problems [1] have been demonstrated to have a severe and detrimental effect on the training in terms of both efficacy and final accuracy. Skip connections [7] and ReLU [4] activation functions have been used in manually designed ANNs to address the vanishing gradient problem and "looks linear" initialisation [1] to address the shattered gradients problem. However, little investigation

© Springer Nature Switzerland AG 2018
T. Mitrovic et al. (Eds.): AI 2018, LNAI 11320, pp. 616–629, 2018.
https://doi.org/10.1007/978-3-030-03991-2_56

has been done to see whether or not sufficiently well constructed novel architectures can achieve sufficient results while avoiding these two issues altogether. Further, the current state-of-the-art networks seem to be of ever increasing complexity, becoming deeper with each new discovery [4,7]. This complexity tends to decrease the interpretability of models, making their application difficult to problems where interpretability is considered of high importance. Work on increasingly deep ANNs also has yet to establish whether this additional complexity is strictly necessary to achieve the results that have been demonstrated.

Existing work on automatically discovering ANN architectures has the potential to answer this question, and tends to fall into 3 frameworks. Neuroevolution of Augmenting Topologies (NEAT) [19] and extensions [18,21] create small ANNs using EC methods. Generally these methods use a neuron level encoding scheme, where weights are also found by EC methods, rather than trained through back propagation, and tend to struggle on complex problems. Other styles of ANN architecture discovery utilise novel EC methods to encode fully connected layers, and the connections between layers, before training through back propagation [10,14,22]. While these methods can to evolve accurate classification networks, the ANNs are globally non-branching deep networks (i.e. [10,22] finds graph-like cells for use in a manually designed, globally linear, ANN structure, while [14] produces novel deep linear ANNs with skip connections), and the majority of searches through the architecture space take place solely through mutation [10,14], despite the efficacy of crossover in many traditional EC algorithms [15]. The last common framework for ANN architecture discovery utilises reinforcement learning to construct ANNs [24–26]. These algorithms tend to be more computationally expensive than their EC counterparts, and significantly limit the search space of possible ANNs, either using only one operator [25] or discovering novel 'blocks' for use in larger network structures inspired by existing hand designed ANNs [24,26].

Notably, in all prior works where large ANN architectures are discovered and trained by back propagation, accuracy improvement is the primary focus of ANN design, rather than a balance of complexity and accuracy, and no techniques have been introduced specifically to aid in the interpretability of models. A similar issue lies in the established use of ReLU [4] and ReLU-like (e.g. [3]) activation functions. Given the use of non-linear pooling layers in image classification networks it has not been demonstrated that activation functions are always necessary to introduce non-linearity to networks. Further, it has been previously noted that little work has been done to investigate whether ReLU-like activation functions are optimal for ANNs generally, or whether ANNs were developed to be optimal for ReLU-like activation functions [23].

Two notable works have looked at the automatic discovery of activation functions, utilising either EC methods [6] or reinforcement learning [13]. However, each work suffers from significant drawbacks. The work in [6] utilises a simple weighting of a few known activation functions within a NEAT framework for use with relatively simple datasets, whereas the work done in [13] sought to discover activation functions which improve accuracy in ReLU utilising networks, potentially biasing discovered activations towards ReLU-like functions.

Goals: this work aims to propose a novel Genetic Programming (GP) representation of ANNs, and utilises cooperative co-evolution [12] to concurrently evolve ANNs and activation functions. GP is an Evolutionary Computation (EC) technique which represents models as variably sized trees [9], utilising operations inspired by biological evolution (i.e. elitism, crossover, and mutation) to evolve populations through time, optimising fitness functions which are not required to be differentiable. Cooperative co-evolution is used in situations where two or more populations are desired, and the fitness of individuals within populations is partly determined by individuals within other populations [12]. Three key goals to be investigated are to:

- create a GP representation of tree-like ANNs, utilising branching to introduce complexity rather than depth and allowing crossover during evolution,
- utilise region selection to decrease the overall number of parameters in the network and increase the interpretability on image classification tasks, and
- create novel activation functions concurrently with the tree-like ANNs and examine the structure and variation of high performing activation functions.

The novel representation proposed will also allow automatic region selection on images, and utilise co-evolution to concurrently evolve ANNs and activation functions, where good individuals within one population should improve fitness within the other. Further, the novel GP representation allows for novel tree-like ANNs to be developed, with the tree-like structure naturally allowing for multiple regions of input images to be selected by the ANN, and allowing these different regions to be processed independently within the network. In this way it is hoped that tree-like ANNs will allow sufficiently complex, novel, low-depth, and interpretable ANNs to be discovered. Further, this approach provides a more thorough search of the space of possible ANNs and activation functions, providing interesting insights and generating relatively high-accuracy, quick training, shallow networks with fewer parameters than many state-of-the-art networks.

2   The Proposed Method

The overall method is based in cooperative co-evolutionary techniques. In particular, we define a GP encoding for ANNs and GP encoding for activation functions, create populations of each of these two types of GP tree, and evaluate the ANNs and activation functions with respect to each other. The GP trees are strongly typed to ensure that, within each branch of the tree structure, the following structure occurs: $RegionSelection \rightarrow ANN \rightarrow Softmax\ Output$. The novel method utilises validation loss as fitness during evolution, and provides constraints on the networks during training to reduce the required computation and provide evolutionary pressure towards networks with a small number of trainable parameters and converge to optima quickly.

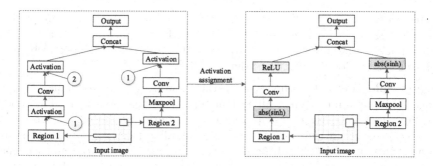

Fig. 1. Example activation function assignment

2.1 The Evolutionary Process

The novel method utilises cooperative co-evolution to develop novel ANN architectures and novel activation functions concurrently, where two GP populations are created, one of tree-like ANN structures and another of novel activation functions. Within the ANN structures, an activation function is taken from a subpopulation of activation functions, where the subpopulation is specified by a terminal integer input to the node. The final fitness value of the network is assigned to both the ANN structure and the activation functions used in it. An example of this process and a simple example tree-like ANN can be seen in Fig. 1. Note that this example does not show any parameters except for the activation function node, which demonstrates subpopulation specification. To ensure robustness, ANNs utilising activation functions are run 3 times, each time selecting a new activation function from the least used activation functions within the subpopulation, and the best fitness is used as the fitness of the networks and activation functions.

2.2 ANN Construction

ANN construction takes place from nodes which represent fully connected layers in an ANN. The novelty in the construction of these ANNs comes primarily from three specific nodes, the Region Selection node, the Activation node, and the Concatenation node. In general, nodes take as input another node and some relevant parameters (e.g. layer size, convolution size, etc.). The only nodes for which this is not true are Concatenation, which takes two nodes as input, and Region Selection, which takes the input images as input rather than other nodes.

Notation. Throughout the next section we denote the size of an input to a layer within the ANN as $BatchSize \times N \times M \times C$, and define output size in these terms, where N represents the size of the first variable input dimension, M represents the size of the second variable input dimension, and C the third. For example, the input images for the MNIST dataset have size $BatchSize \times 28 \times 28 \times 1$. We note that $BatchSize$ is always a function of the overall complexity of the network and is constant within a network.

Terminal Sets. The terminal set is {*input image, RandSmallFloat, RandFloatRandInt, RandInt*}, where *RandSmallFloat* and *RandSmallFloat* is a random float number from two float generators $U[0, 0.1]$ and $U[0, 1]$, respectively, and *RandInt* is a random int number from $U[1, 256]$.

Region Selection is the only layer in the network defined as taking the raw image as input, and as such all leaf nodes utilise this operation. This node also takes four integers, $x_1, x_2, y_1,$ *and* y_2, as input, all uniformly in the range $[1, SizeOfImage]$. It then crops the image according to these inputs. The start of the crop is then defined, in (x, y) as $(min(x_1, x_2), min(y_1, y_2))$ and the end of the crop as $(max(x_1, x_2), max(y_1, y_2))$, giving a rectangle of arbitrary size. The output is a Tensor with shape: $BatchSize \times (max(x1, x2) - min(x1, x2)) \times (max(y1, y2) - min(y1, y2)) \times \#InputChannels$.

Activation Nodes. Activation layers are the only time an activation function is used within the network. In particular, this layer specifies a subpopulation of activation functions to draw an activation function from through an integer input in $[1, \#Subpopulations]$. Within each utilisation of a network the same activation function will be used for each node specifying the same subpopulation.

Concatenation is the only 'true' branching operator available to the GP algorithm, as it accepts two nodes as inputs, and thus is the operator which allows the GP algorithm to avoid creating fundamentally linear feed-forward networks. Within this operation zero-padding is used to pad inputs to be the same shape. In particular, where N_1, M_1, and C_1 are the unique dimensions of the first input, and N_2, M_2, and C_2 the unique dimensions of the second input, the output size for this layer is: $BatchSize \times max(N_1, N_2) \times max(M_1, M_2) \times (C_1 + C_2)$.

Layer Nodes: *Dense* layers are standard fully connected linear layers, with bias but without an activation function. They output a layer of shape $BatchSize \times N \times M \times LayerSize$, where $LayerSize$ is an integer input parameter in $U[1, 256]$.

Layer Nodes: *Convolutional* layers are implemented with bias but without an activation function. They will run a $KernalSize \times KernalSize$ square kernal over the input Tensor, outputting a Tensor with different shapes depending on the padding type, stride, and number of filters chosen. In particular, where $NumberFilters$ is an integer input parameter in $U[1, 256]$, $KernalSize$, $Stride$ an integer input parameter in $U[1, 3]$, and $PaddingType$ a Boolean input:

- If the padding type is 0 then no padding is added, and the output shape is:
  $BatchSize \times \lfloor \frac{(N+1-KernalSize)}{Stride} \rfloor \times \lfloor \frac{(M+1-KernalSize)}{Stride} \rfloor \times NumberFilters$,
- If the padding type is 1 then padding will offset the KernalSize, giving the output shape: $BatchSize \times \lfloor \frac{N}{Stride} \rfloor \times \lfloor \frac{M}{Stride} \rfloor \times NumberFilters$.

To avoid errors, if the $KernalSize$ is greater than any input dimensions, the $KernalSize$ is reduced to this input dimensionality.

Pooling Nodes all share a similar structure and perform a similar function. They will run a square 'window' over the input returning the maximum or minimum value found within this window, and iterating over the input according to either a given stride or some real-valued chosen reduction in output size.

Maxpooling runs a $PoolSize \times PoolSize$ square window over the input Tensor, outputting the maximal value found in this window. In particular:

- If padding type is 0 then no padding is added, and the output shape is: $BatchSize \times \lfloor \frac{(N+1-PoolSize)}{Stride} \rfloor \times \lfloor \frac{(M+1-PoolSize)}{Stride} \rfloor \times C$,
- If padding type is 1 then padding will offset the KernalSize, giving the output shape: $BatchSize \times \lfloor \frac{N}{Stride} \rfloor \times \lfloor \frac{M}{Stride} \rfloor \times C$.

where $PoolSize$ and $Stride$ are integer parameters in $U[1,3]$ and $PaddingType$ is a Boolean parameter.

Minpooling is equivalent to maxpooling in terms of input parameters but will output the minimal value found in the pool.

Fractional Maxpooling layers return the maximum value found from a 2×2 window and iterating over the image pseudo-randomly such that the output is reduced by a specified ratio. The output shape is: $BatchSize \times \lfloor \frac{N}{Ratio} \rfloor \times \lfloor \frac{M}{Ratio} \rfloor \times C$. The value for ratio is a real-valued parameter in $[1,2]$. If N or $M < 2$ then the input is padded minimally such that $N \geq 2$ and $M \geq 2$.

Fractional Minpooling is equivalent to fractional maxpooling in terms of input parameters but will output the minimal value found in the pool.

Regularisation Nodes: the regularisation layer is an implementation of several regularisation techniques, with the specific regularisation technique chosen being determined by an input parameter. Each regularisation form chosen requires a single real-valued parameter, denoted $Rate$, and is taken from the range $[0,1]$. The possible regularisation techniques, and their description are as follows:

Dropout [17] sets each value in the input to 0 with probability $Rate$.
Gaussian Noise is specifically a form of additive Gaussian noise, such that each value in the input has a value from $\mathcal{N}(0, Rate)$ added to it.
Gaussian Dropout [17] is a form of multiplicative Gaussian noise. Specifically, inputs are multiplied with probability $Rate$ by a value drawn from $\mathcal{N}(0, \sqrt{\frac{Rate}{1-Rate}})$.

Batch Normalisation maintains the dimensionality of the input and has no parameters, simply enforcing that each element of the input is transformed to approximate a standard normal distribution with respect to the batch.

Repeat Nodes are designed to allow GP to more easily construct deep networks, which are beneficial within the constraints. In addition to a node, repeat layers take two integer inputs, *#Repetitions* and *Depth*, both drawn from $U[1,16]$. A repeat node will repeat all operations 'below' the repeat node up to *Depth*, excluding other repeat nodes and region selection operators, and do so *#Repetitions* times. Other repeat nodes are excluded from this operation to avoid compounding effects on the depth of the network, and region selection is excluded as it is only meaningful when to the input images.

Padding Nodes: zero-padding is included to allow networks to generate one form of sparsity within the network, or to counteract the gradual shrinking of layers that is encountered by repeated application of pooling and convolutional operators. Given a node and parameter $PadN$ in $U[1,3]$, the input is padded with $PadN$ zeros before and after the input, such that the original input is centred after the operation. Particularly, where $PadN$ is the selected padding size, the output size for this layer is: $BatchSize \times (N+2(PadN)) \times (M+2(PadN)) \times C$.

2.3 ANN Mutation Operations and Activation Construction

Mutation on these ANNs is chosen randomly from the followings:

Uniform Mutation selects a point in the tree at random and replaces it with a random tree where $depth \in U[1,4]$, to avoid generating over-sized trees.

Reroll Constants has a 50% chance to replace each terminal with a newly generated number from the same range.

Node Replacement will select a non-terminal node at random and replace it with another node with the same input types.

Insertion will pick a non-terminal node at random and insert a new node as its parent, selecting random terminals as needed as further children to this new parent to ensure that the node is complete.

Activation construction utilises a simpler set of function nodes and terminals:

Function name	Input types	Function name	Input types	Terminal name	Type
ReLU	Tensor	Abs	Tensor	Input	Tensor
Sigmoid	Tensor	Negative	Tensor	RandomFloat	Float, U[−4, 4]
Softmax	Tensor	Multiply	Tensor, Tensor		
Square	Tensor	Max	Tensor, Tensor		
Sin	Tensor	Min	Tensor, Tensor		
Cos	Tensor	Sub	Tensor, Tensor		
Sinh	Tensor	Add constant	Tensor, Float		
Cosh	Tensor	Scale	Tensor, Float		
Log	Tensor				

2.4 Computation Reduction Techniques

The proposed method utilises three key computation time reduction techniques. Firstly, the method evaluates all ANNs after only 10 epochs of training. This both limits training time, and provides evolutionary pressure towards networks which train quickly. Secondly, the novel method begins training on only subsets of CIFAR10. Namely, the first generations utilise only $\frac{1}{8}$ of the available training data, splitting this into the training and validation set, with this ratio doubling every 5 generations. Thirdly, the method estimates the maximal batch size that can be trained given memory constraints, and rejects networks that are unable to be trained with a batch size of at least 256. As this value is influenced heavily by the number of trainable parameters, it provides an implicit limit to model complexity.

3   Experimental Configuration

3.1   Parameter Settings

Adam is utilised as a the gradient descent technique, using parameters outlined in the original work [8], i.e. $\alpha = 0.001$, $\beta_1 = 0.9$, and $\beta_2 = 0.999$. Each network is trained to 10 epochs, returning the validation loss from the final epoch.

Network evolution utilises the following GP parameters:

Parameter name	Value - MNIST	Value - CIFAR10
Population size	100	200
Number generations	20	20
Crossover probability	0.5	0.5
Crossover type	Single point uniform	Single point uniform
Mutation probability	0.5	0.5
Mutation type	See Sect. 2.3	See Sect. 2.3
Selection type	Tournament	Tournament
Tournament size	5	5
Initalisation	Grow	Grow
Initalisation depth	$U[4, 8]$	$U[4, 8]$
Runs per activation network	3	3
Fitness function	Best validation loss	Best validation loss

Within the available nodes, network evolution has 50% chance of utilising the concatenation operation, with other operations having uniform chance of being selected. This is to give the tree-like ANNs an average branching factor of 1.5.

Activation Function Evolution parameters are as follows, where crossover and selection are applied only within subpopulations.

Parameter name	Value - MNIST	Value - CIFAR10
Population size	100	200
Number subpopulations	2	2
Subpopulation size	50	100
Number generations	20	20
Crossover probability	0.5	0.5
Crossover type	Single point uniform	Single point uniform
Mutation probability	0.5	0.5
Mutation type	Uniform	Uniform
Selection type	Tournament	Tournament
Tournament size	3	3
Initalisation	Grow	Grow
Initalisation depth	$U[1,4]$	$U[1,4]$
Fitness function	Best validation loss	Best validation loss

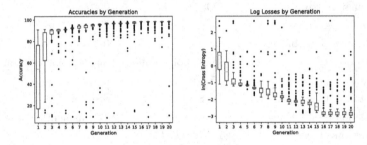

Fig. 2. Network performance by generation on MNIST

3.2   Benchmark Methods

The model from the final generation which minimises the Cross Entropy when applied to the validation set will be trained for 100 epochs, where the set of weights which minimise the validation Cross Entropy within this training is used to compare with other networks. In particular, we compare the results to work done by [5] for the unaugmented MNIST dataset and [16] for the unaugmented CIFAR10 dataset, although we note that the comparison is not perfect, as our goals are not strictly accuracy improvement.

4   Results and Discussions

4.1   MNIST

Overall validation accuracies and losses on MNIST for the ANNs considered by the novel algorithm are presented in Fig. 2.

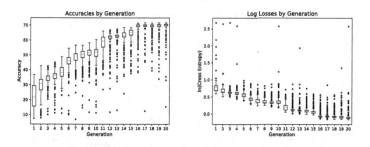

Fig. 3. Network performance by generation on CIFAR10

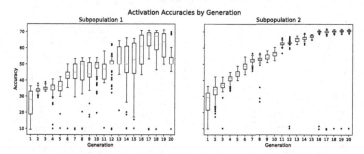

Fig. 4. Activation accuracies by generation

For MNIST the novel algorithm quickly converged to networks containing no activation functions, limiting the benefit of examining the efficacy of specific activation functions as many went unevaluated, thus graphs showing their respective performance are omitted for space. The final model selected for classification on the MNIST dataset reached a minimum validation loss at epoch 8, where the accuracies are 99.06%, 98.69%, and 98.89% on training, validation and test sets, respectively, while the losses are 0.0295, 0.0451 and 0.0727, respectively. The model selected a total of 17 regions from the inputs, had $\approx$ 1.2 M trainable weights, and the maximum number of layers with trainable parameters occurring within a single brach, prior to output layer, is 2 (a convolutional layer and a dense layer). Work done in [5] demonstrated higher accuracy on the same data, finding a test accuracy of 99.56 using $\approx$ 3.2 M trainable weights. The number of epochs used for training on MNIST in [5] is unspecified.

4.2 CIFAR10

Figure 3 shows the overall validation accuracies and losses on CIFAR10 for the ANNs considered by the novel algorithm. Activation function performance tends to mirror network performance, which is expected given the cooperative framework being utilised (Fig. 4).

The final model structure selected for classification on CIFAR10 reached a minimum validation loss at epoch 20, where the accuracies are 80.32%, 72.87%,

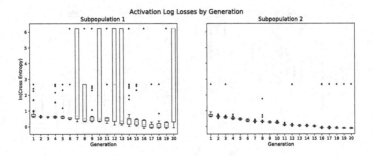

Fig. 5. Activation log losses by generation

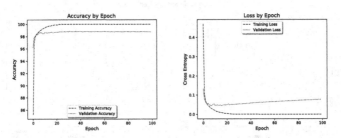

Fig. 6. Performance of best MNIST model during extended training

and 72.30% on training, validation and test sets, respectively, while the loss are 0.5651, 0.8505 and 0.8651, respectively. The model selected a total of 21 regions from the inputs, had ≈ 1.2 M trainable weights, and the maximum number of layers with trainable parameters occurring within a single branch, prior to the output, is 3 (a convolutional layer, a dense layer, and another convolutional layer). Work done in [16] demonstrated far higher accuracy on the same data, finding a test accuracy of 90.92 using ≈ 1.4 M trainable weights, although the network was designed with a training period of 350 epochs.

4.3   Analysis

MNIST: The overall results of the novel algorithm on MNIST show a highly accurate shallow network being developed. Interestingly the algorithm appears to find sufficient non-linearity in pooling operations, having top performing networks utilising no activation functions. It is further noted that the algorithm has found a network reaching a local optima within just 8 epochs that appears robust to overfitting during subsequent training, shown in Fig. 6. Note the evidence of overfitting throughout extended training when observing Cross Entropy, but the accuracy is effectively stable from an early epoch (Fig. 5).

CIFAR10: The overall results of the novel algorithm on CIFAR10, unlike on MNIST, showed drastically diminished test and validation accuracy from the final selected model when compared with published results from state-of-the-art networks [7], although results are in line with manually designed shallow networks which calculate weights exactly (i.e. do not perform gradient descent) and utilise some form of data augmentation [11]. In particular we note that the large number of regions selected indicates that fixed regions may not be appropriate for this dataset, i.e. unlike MNIST the same 'feature' may not always appear in a similar area of the image, possibly contributing to the relatively poor accuracy. Further, expanded training behaviour, seen in Fig. 7, indicates that this network is designed such that it can easily find a local optima for validation loss. We note that validation accuracy has effectively peaked by epoch 10, although training set accuracy continues to increase modestly through to epoch 100. In this way, we see a network tailoured exactly to the evolutionary environment in which we performed architecture discovery, indicating that a relaxing of these evolutionary pressures towards quick training may yield significantly better results.

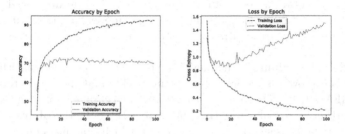

Fig. 7. Performance of best CIFAR10 model during extended training

Three observations have been found when examining the top activations from each activation subpopulation. Firstly, networks tended to utilise only activation functions from a single sub-population, indicating that networks which are homogeneous with respect to activation functions tend to perform somewhat better relative to those which are heterogeneous, which disagrees with a conclusion in [6]. This led to a behaviour where one activation sub-population became dominant during training, and several activation functions from the less used sub-population were not evaluated. In particular, by the final generation half of the non-dominant activation population went unevaluated. Secondly, we note that activation functions seem to remain relatively simple, agreeing broadly with an observation in [13]. Thirdly, and somewhat divergent with prior research, we also note a certain invariance with regards to activation functions, with no common themes appearing in what is considered optimal except for non-linearity and the aforementioned simplicity of functions. The top three activation functions from each sub-population are shown in Table 1 to demonstrate. Note that many of these are equivalent to simpler functions.

Table 1. Top 3 activations from CIFAR10

(a) Sub-population 1			(b) Sub-population 2		
Activation	ValLoss	ValAcc	Activation	ValLoss	ValAcc
$-softmax(x + x)$	0.938	69.12	$abs(max(ReLU(x), abs(x))$	0.850	71.46
$sinh(x + sigmoid(x + x))$	0.946	69.95	$(abs(-x) * x)^2$	0.858	71.73
$abs(softmax(x))$	0.960	68.91	$-ReLU(sinh(x) + x)$	0.859	71.47

5 Conclusions and Future Work

This work has demonstrated a novel tree-like ANN structure, and a GP based system to automatically explore and generate structures for specific problem instances, while concurrently discovering novel activation functions. The algorithm with computation reduction techniques found accurate models for the MNIST dataset, but failed to find a high-accuracy model for CIFAR10, although the results were similar to other manually designed shallow ANNs for this dataset.

Analysis of the training of the final CIFAR10 model indicates that the evolutionary pressure towards models which train quickly may have been too strong, pushing CIFAR10 models towards a relatively inaccurate, but easily tainable, optima. Further, particularly with regards to CIFAR10, the ability of region selection to reliably select parts of the input which contain similar information between images is unclear, as region selection in the presented form is not translation invariant, potentially contributing to the poor accuracy. Lastly we note that further evidence for the evolutionary pressure towards small networks being too high is seen in the very similar number of trainable parameters found in the two top models for significantly different datasets. As such, future work should focus on the development and implementation of more nuanced computation reduction techniques, which allow for models to train towards more robust optima, and should investigate translation invariant forms of region selection.

References

1. Balduzzi, D., Frean, M., Leary, L., Lewis, J., Ma, K.W.D., McWilliams, B.: The Shattered Gradients Problem: If resnets are the answer, then what is the question? arXiv preprint arXiv:1702.08591 (2017)
2. Bengio, Y., Simard, P., Frasconi, P.: Learning long-term dependencies with gradient descent is difficult. IEEE Trans. Neural Netw. 5(2), 157–166 (1994)
3. Clevert, D.A., Unterthiner, T., Hochreiter, S.: Fast and accurate deep network learning by exponential linear units (ELUs). arXiv preprint arXiv:1511.07289 (2015)
4. Glorot, X., Bordes, A., Bengio, Y.: Deep sparse rectifier neural networks. In: Proceedings of the Fourteenth International Conference on Artificial Intelligence and Statistics, pp. 315–323 (2011)
5. Graham, B.: Fractional max-pooling. arXiv preprint arXiv:1412.6071 (2014)

6. Hagg, A., Mensing, M., Asteroth, A.: Evolving parsimonious networks by mixing activation functions. In: Proceedings of the Genetic and Evolutionary Computation Conference, pp. 425–432. ACM (2017)
7. He, K., Zhang, X., Ren, S., Sun, J.: Deep residual learning for image recognition. In: Proceedings of the IEEE Conference on Computer Vision and Pattern Recognition, pp. 770–778 (2016)
8. Kingma, D.P., Ba, J.: Adam: a method for stochastic optimization. arXiv preprint arXiv:1412.6980 (2014)
9. Koza, J.R.: Genetic programming as a means for programming computers by natural selection. Stat. Comput. 4(2), 87–112 (1994)
10. Liu, H., Simonyan, K., Vinyals, O., Fernando, C., Kavukcuoglu, K.: Hierarchical representations for efficient architecture search. arXiv preprint arXiv:1711.00436 (2017)
11. McDonnell, M.D., Vladusich, T.: Enhanced image classification with a fast-learning shallow convolutional neural network. arXiv preprint arXiv:1503.04596 (2015)
12. Potter, M.A., Jong, K.A.D.: Cooperative coevolution: an architecture for evolving coadapted subcomponents. Evol. Comput. 8(1), 1–29 (2000)
13. Ramachandran, P., Zoph, B., Le, Q.V.: Searching for Activation Functions (2018). https://openreview.net/forum?id=SkBYYyZRZ
14. Real, E., et al.: Large-scale evolution of image classifiers. arXiv preprint arXiv:1703.01041 (2017)
15. Spears, W.M.: Adapting crossover in evolutionary algorithms. In: Evolutionary Programming, pp. 367–384 (1995)
16. Springenberg, J.T., Dosovitskiy, A., Brox, T., Riedmiller, M.: Striving for simplicity: the all convolutional net. arXiv preprint arXiv:1412.6806 (2014)
17. Srivastava, N., Hinton, G., Krizhevsky, A., Sutskever, I., Salakhutdinov, R.: Dropout: a simple way to prevent neural networks from overfitting. J. Mach. Learn. Res. 15(1), 1929–1958 (2014)
18. Stanley, K.O., D'Ambrosio, D.B., Gauci, J.: A hypercube-based encoding for evolving large-scale neural networks. Artif. Life 15(2), 185–212 (2009)
19. Stanley, K.O., Miikkulainen, R.: Evolving neural networks through augmenting topologies. Evol. Comput. 10(2), 99–127 (2002)
20. Szegedy, C., et al.: Going deeper with convolutions. In: Proceedings of the IEEE Conference on Computer Vision and Pattern Recognition, pp. 1–9 (2015)
21. Turner, A.J., Miller, J.F.: Recurrent Cartesian genetic programming of artificial neural networks. Genet. Program. Evolvable Mach. 18(2), 185–212 (2017)
22. Xie, L., Yuille, A.: Genetic CNN. arXiv preprint arXiv:1703.01513 (2017)
23. Xu, B., Wang, N., Chen, T., Li, M.: Empirical evaluation of rectified activations in convolutional network. arXiv preprint arXiv:1505.00853 (2015)
24. Zhong, Z., Yan, J., Liu, C.L.: Practical Network Blocks Design with Q-Learning, abs/1708.05552. CoRR (2017)
25. Zoph, B., Le, Q.V.: Neural architecture search with reinforcement learning. arXiv preprint arXiv:1611.01578 (2016)
26. Zoph, B., Vasudevan, V., Shlens, J., Le, Q.V.: Learning transferable architectures for scalable image recognition. arXiv preprint arXiv:1707.07012 2(6) (2017)

Lift-Per-Drift: An Evaluation Metric for Classification Frameworks with Concept Drift Detection

Robert Anderson$^{(\boxtimes)}$, Yun Sing Koh, and Gillian Dobbie

Department of Computer Science, University of Auckland, Auckland, New Zealand
rand079@aucklanduni.ac.nz, {ykoh,gill}@cs.auckland.ac.nz

Abstract. Data streams with concept drift change over time. Detecting drift allows remedial action, but this can come at a cost *e.g.* training a new classifier. Prequential accuracy is commonly used to evaluate the impact of drift detection frameworks on data stream classification, but recent work shows frequent periodic drift detection can provide better accuracy than state-of-the-art drift detection techniques. We discuss how sequentiality, the degree of consecutive matching class labels across instances, allows high accuracy without a classifier learning to differentiate classes. We propose a novel metric: lift-per-drift (*lpd*). This measures drift detection performance through its impact on classification accuracy, penalised by drifts detected in a dataset. This metric solves three problems: *lpd* cannot be increased by periodic, frequent drifts; *lpd* clearly shows when using drift detection increases classifier error; and *lpd* does not require knowledge of where real drifts occurred. We show how *lpd* can be set to be sensitive to the cost of each drift. Our experiments show *lpd* is not artificially increased through sequentiality; that *lpd* highlights when drift detection has caused a loss in accuracy; and that it is sensitive to change in true-positive drift and false-positive drift detection rates.

Keywords: Data streams · Concept drift · Evaluation · Classification

1 Introduction

Concept drifts in data streams cause a classification problem to change over time. Drift detectors monitor for changes (*e.g.* in classifier accuracy) to signal when drift occurs. Addressing drift can come at a cost of losing valid learning. Consider identifying intrusion attempts in a stream of network connections. If we restart the classifier whenever we detect drift, then the classifier will need to relearn what an intrusion attack looks like after each drift. Drift detection may help identify intrusion attempts faster when they change in nature, but poorly chosen drifts may lead to relearning the same rules that have just been forgotten. Prequential accuracy (classifying and then training on each instance) [1] is commonly used to measure improvement in classification provided by drift detection, but does not in itself prove that drift detection has improved accuracy. Bifet [2] shows

© Springer Nature Switzerland AG 2018
T. Mitrovic et al. (Eds.): AI 2018, LNAI 11320, pp. 630–642, 2018.
https://doi.org/10.1007/978-3-030-03991-2_57

that detecting drifts periodically can lead to better accuracy than the latest drift detection techniques. High sequentiality (the degree to which consecutive instances share a class label in a data stream) allows periodic drift detection to provide high accuracy despite a classifier lacking the ability to differentiate classes. When evaluating drift detection on real-world data where actual drifts are rarely known, accuracy is often used as a proxy for correct drift detection, though it is not suitable for this purpose.

Our contribution is a novel evaluation metric, lift-per-drift (lpd), which measures drift detector performance as the impact of drift detection on classification accuracy against the same framework without drift detection, penalised by the number of drifts detected. By measuring improvement over not using drift detection, it shows when drift detection reduces classifier error. It is not increased by periodic drift detection on datasets with high sequentiality. We distinguish sequentiality from class imbalance [3] and show how it can be tested for in a dataset. Five common real-world data streams used for drift detection evaluation are shown to have high sequentiality, suggesting it is prominent in real-world datasets. Finally, lpd does not require knowing where real drifts occur in a dataset so it can be used to evaluate drift detection on non-synthetic streams.

In Sect. 2, we describe current techniques and goals for drift detection evaluation. In Sect. 3, we define lpd. We discuss its characteristics and introduce a parameter, r, that allows control over its cost-sensitivity. We define sequentiality, contrast it to class imbalance, and provide a method to test the degree of sequentiality in a dataset given class imbalance. Section 4 details experimental results that support our claims about lpd. We show lpd is not artificially increased through sequentiality, that it highlights when drift detection has caused a loss in accuracy and that it is sensitive to change in true-positive drift and false-positive drift detection rates. We back these claims up by testing on real-world data. We suggest how our work can be extended and conclude this paper in Sect. 5.

2   Related Work

In a data stream, instances arrive one at a time, with no upper bound on the number that may arrive. Metrics that scale well in terms of cost in memory and time [4] are used as it is be infeasible to retain every prior classification/error. Incremental summary metrics are better suited to streams, requiring a set amount of memory over time to store. Metrics that measure performance against baseline approaches are an understood gap in available evaluation approaches [5]. At any point in the stream, prequential accuracy acc may be measured: of all instances seen, acc is the proportion that have been correctly classified at that point [1]. Concept drift refers to a change in the underlying data-generating distribution of a stream [6]: *real*, in which the relationship between classes and attributes change; and *virtual*, where the balance of classes change over time. Detecting drifts allows remedial action, such as switching to a new classifier [7]. This is the approach to drift detection we consider in this work. Drift detectors can have a tolerance specified for false positive drift detection *e.g.* [8]. When measuring drift detection quality, often true positive detection rate TP is compared against false positive detection rate FP. These can be combined with drift delay into a single measure, MTR [2]. In real-world data, where actual drift points are often unknown, these measures cannot be used. Adapting models comes at a cost, such as training a new classifier for scratch; metrics that can account for this cost are desirable for real-world applications [9].

Bifet [2] shows periodic drift detection (*i.e.* every n instances) can attain better accuracy than many highly regarded drift detection techniques. This is related to autocorrelation of class labels through a stream. Accuracy here is not related to successful drift detection. However, accuracy is commonly used to demonstrate the value of drift detection techniques on real-world datasets *e.g.* in [8]. Accuracy can be biased towards majority classes in imbalanced datasets. Kappa can be used to measure classification accuracy across classes compared to a chance classifier [10] instead. However, this measure can also be increased with periodic drift [2]. Temporal-Kappa [11] instead uses a baseline that classifies each instance by the class of the prior instance. This accounts for sequentiality, but leads to common negative scores and does not evaluate drift detection. The authors' proposed Combined metric combines both versions of Kappa, but is zero when either of the above baselines are better than the comparison technique, which is common in datasets with sequentiality. A metric for evaluating drift detector performance on real-world data with sequentiality is required.

3   Lift-Per-Drift (*lpd*) and Sequentiality

Lift-Per-Drift. Lift-per-drift (*lpd*) measures the impact of drift detection on classification accuracy against the same framework without drift detection, penalised by the number of drifts detected. It can be measured at any point in a data stream. It can: show whether drift detection has improved classification accuracy on a given dataset; compare drift detection frameworks on a given dataset; be used as a proxy to evaluate quality of drift detection where we do not know actual drift points. It is defined in Eq. 1, where acc_d is the accuracy when using a drift detection framework; $acc_{\not{d}}$ is the accuracy on the same data without drift detection; and $\#drifts \in \mathbb{W}$ is the number of drifts detected by drift detection. Here, $lpd \in \mathbb{R}$, and $-1 \leq lpd \leq 1$. Calculating lpd in real-time requires running a framework with and without drift detection in parallel. We propose the default version lpd. The user-set parameter r, described further below, allows cost-sensitive penalisation of drifts. By default $r = 1$.

$$
lpd = \begin{cases} \dfrac{acc_d - acc_{\not{d}}}{\#drifts}, & \text{if } \#drifts \geq 1 \text{ and } r = 1 \\[2ex] \dfrac{(acc_d - acc_{\not{d}})(1-r)}{(1 - r^{\#drifts})}, & \text{if } \#drifts \geq 1 \text{ and } 0 < r < 1 \\[2ex] 0 & \text{otherwise.} \end{cases}
\tag{1}
$$

In Fig. 1, using an example range of $0 \leq \#drifts \leq 20$ and $r = 1$, we show how absolute lpd varies over values of its numerator $(acc_d - acc_{\not{d}})$ and

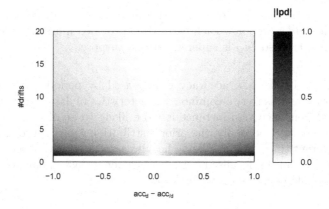

Fig. 1. Absolute value of *lpd* across potential range of $acc_d - acc_\beta$ and $0 \leq \#drifts \leq 20$

denominator $\#drifts$. When $acc_d < acc_\beta$ then *lpd* is negative; when $acc_d > acc_\beta$ then *lpd* is positive. Where $\#drifts = 0$, $lpd = 0$. Our metric is furthest from zero where we have fewer drifts and a larger numerator. The $|lpd|$ becomes smaller as acc_d approaches acc_β or when $\#drifts$ increases.

Example 1: Checking if drift detection improves accuracy over a framework without drift detection, we measure $acc_d = 85.0\%$, $acc_\beta = 90.0\%$ and $\#drifts = 100$ over a period of our stream. As $lpd = -0.05\%$, negative *lpd* shows that drift detection has caused a relative loss in classification accuracy over this period.

Example 2: Comparing two drift detectors, dd_A and dd_B, we measure *lpd* for both for the same period of a data stream. For dd_A, $\#drifts = 50$ and $acc_d = 75.0\%$. For dd_B, $\#drifts = 500$ and $acc_d = 80.0\%$. For both, $acc_\beta = 60.0\%$. On this sample, dd_A has $lpd = 0.30\%$ while dd_B has $lpd = 0.04\%$. On average, each drift in dd_A provides a better increase in classification accuracy than dd_B, and so it provides improved drift detection.

When $r = 1$, each drift must improve accuracy as much as the last to maintain *lpd*. Sometimes, incremental gains are more valuable then the cost of drift, so subsequent drifts should be less penalised. The user-set r parameter decides the proportional improvement in accuracy each subsequent drift must provide over the last (following a geometric progression) to maintain its *lpd*. For instance, a classifier with $acc_d - acc_\beta = 10\%$ with one drift would need $acc_d - acc_\beta = 15\%$ to maintain *lpd* if $r = 0.5$ but only $acc_d - acc_\beta = 12.5\%$ if $r = 0.25$. This allows a user to specify the relative improvement each drift must provide to be justified. Setting $r < 1$ penalises each subsequent drift less, so *lpd* is less able to penalise approaches relying on sequentiality and repeated drifts. Holding all else constant, lower r values lead to larger *lpd* values so the same r setting must be used for comparing drift frameworks.

Example 3: Comparing, dd_A and dd_B, we set $r = 0.5$ as we wish each drift to contribute at least half as much accuracy as the drift before it. For dd_A, with

100 drifts, $lpd = 0.005\%$ and for dd_B, with 150 drifts, $lpd = 0.008\%$. As dd_B has higher lpd than dd_A, we know each extra drift provided more accuracy relative to our set cost-ratio, so dd_B is superior for our purpose.

Sequentiality. Unlike lpd, accuracy is increased by periodic drift detection. Bifet [2] attributes this to two common characteristics of data streams. The first is temporal dependence - an instance is more likely to be of the same class as the previous instance. Secondly, the prior distribution evolves through a stream *e.g.* with different times of a day being heavily associated with electricity prices rising or falling, causing localised periods of extreme class imbalance, despite a stream as a whole being relatively balanced.

$$AAAAA|AAAAA|AAAAA|AABBB|BBBBB|AAAAA$$

Fig. 2. Example of sequential class labels with frequent drifts, denoted by '|'

In Fig. 2, drift is detected and the classifier replaced every five instances. Up until the third drift, only one class is seen by new classifiers and so the classifier will classify all instances as that class. After the third drift, the classifier may begin to learn how to distinguish class A from B. The fourth drift will interrupt this learning. However, the framework will continue to get high accuracy while an evidence-based drift detector may not detect drift as often but is likely to get worse accuracy. We define sequentiality as per Eq. 2. Here, n represents the number of instances seen in a stream, x_i refers to the ith instance, y_i refers to the index of the class label of the ith instance and y_{max} refers to the total number of class labels. It follows that $0 \leq seq \leq 1$ and $seq \in \mathbb{R}$.

$$seq = \frac{\sum_{i=1}^{n-1} g(x_i)}{n-1} \quad g(x_i) = \begin{cases} 1, & \text{if } y_i = y_{i+1} \\ 0, & y_i \neq y_{i+1} \end{cases} \text{ where } y \in (0, 1, \ldots, y_{max}) \quad (2)$$

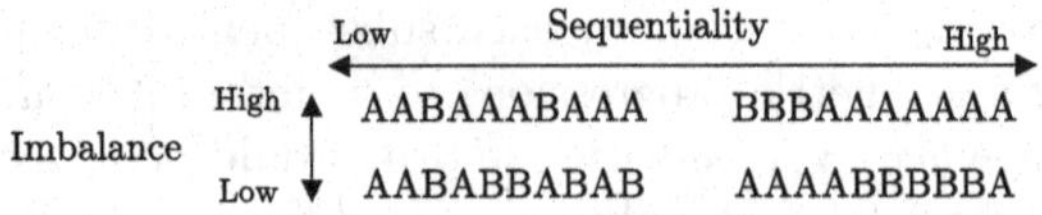

	Low	Sequentiality	High
High	AABAAABAAA		BBBAAAAAAA
Imbalance			
Low	AABABBABAB		AAAABBBBBA

Fig. 3. Contrast of imbalance and sequentiality in class labels of a dataset

$$P(seq) = 1 - I_{1-q}\big((n-1) - (k-1), 1 + (k-1)\big)$$

$$k = \sum_{i=1}^{n-1} g(x_i), q = \sum_{j=1}^{y_{max}} \frac{n_j}{n-1} \times \frac{n_j - 1}{n-2} \quad (3)$$

Table 1. Imbalance and sequentiality in commonly used real-world data streams

Dataset	n	y_{max}	Majority class %	seq	q	p-value
Airlines	539,383	2	55.5%	58.1%	50.6%	0
Covtype	581,012	7	48.8%	95.1%	37.7%	0
Elec	45,312	2	57.5%	85.3%	51.1%	0
Intrusion	494,021	23	56.8%	99.9%	40.9%	0
Poker	829,201	10	50.1%	74.5%	43.2%	0

*p-values less than $1.00 * 10^{-16}$

High class imbalance and high sequentiality are distinct traits for a dataset
e.g. Fig. 3. We can calculate the probability of randomly distributed classes given
class balance using Binomial probability (Eq. 3). The chance of seeing at least
that many sequential classes, $P(seq)$, is given by 1 minus the Binomial CDF
with $k - 1$ successes. The probability of a class being followed by another class
assuming random distribution for a given class balance, q, is calculated as the
sum of chances for each class being followed by the same class; here, n_j refers to
the total number of instances in the jth class, excluding the last instance in the
dataset. This gives us a p-value that indicates if the class is more sequential than
the class balance alone would explain. Table 1 shows five datasets regularly used
to evaluate drift detection. The proportion of instances in the majority class
indicates imbalance. Our test strongly shows that none of these datasets have
random distributions of classes given their imbalance. These common datasets
for evaluating drift detection techniques have sequentiality that may provide
misleading accuracy. There is a clear need for an alternative metric that will not
be increased by periodic detection when evaluating drift detection frameworks.

4   Experimental Results

In this section, we support our claims about *lpd* with experimental results. For
experiments shown, we use both synthetic dataset generators and real-world
datasets. We use dataset generators included in MOA. Each experiment was
repeated 30 times; we show mean results with a 95% confidence interval assuming a Normal distribution of results. Each stream had 500 drifts (unless otherwise stated) and seven distinct concepts. Real-world datasets used are available from http://moa.cms.waikato.ac.nz/datasets, except for Intrusion, available here: http://kdd.ics.uci.edu/databases/kddcup99/kddcup99.html. Experiment code is available from https://github.com/rand079/lpd. An incremental
Naïve Bayes classifier has been used in each experiment. We used *lpd* with $r = 1$
for experiments unless otherwise stated.

Streams with Varied Sequentiality. Here we support our claim that the
lpd metric is not increased by periodic drift detection on datasets with high

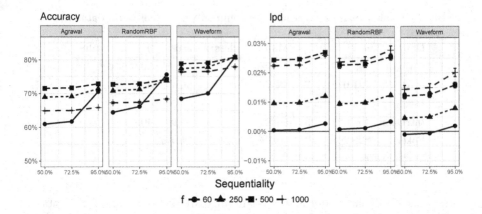

Fig. 4. Mean accuracy and *lpd* for three synthetic datasets with varied sequentiality

sequentiality. We detect drift and replace the classifier every f instances, where $f = \{60, 250, 500, 1000\}$ regardless of the data seen. Every concept drift occurs at 500 instances, so $f = 500$ is perfect drift detection, while $f = 250$ has additional false positive drifts. The detector with $f = 60$ matches the 'No-Change' periodic detector in [2]. Accuracy, as per Fig. 4, is always highest for the perfect drift detector with $f = 500$ and worst for the $f = 60$ detector when $seq = 50.0\%$. Accuracy for the $f = 60$ detector dramatically improves as seq increases, matching the perfect drift detector across datasets at $seq = 95.0\%$. However, the very frequent drift detector contributes very little accuracy per drift compared to other approaches. Its *lpd* is consistently poor and even sometimes negative for the 'No-Change' detector, substantiating our claim about *lpd*. It should be noted that for two of the three datasets, $f = 1000$ provides superior *lpd* to the perfect drift detector. When $f = 500$, the drift detector detects twice as many drifts as when $f = 1000$ so *lpd* is sometimes relatively lower. The *lpd* measure tends to be conservative due to its denominator; r allows the user to specify if they want a less conservative measure.

Streams with Virtual Drift. Here we support our claim that *lpd* indicates when drift detection reduces classifier error compared to a baseline without it. Accuracy does not, and can be misleading when presented as a sole metric for stream classification. In these experiments, we show accuracy and *lpd* for five synthetic streams. Only virtual drift is present *i.e* only the class balance changes when concept drift occurs. Each drift occurs after 250 instances. Classifiers learn how classes are related to attributes over time, and this learning is still relevant after virtual drift. However, frequent drifts can interrupt this learning. For this experiment, we use drift detectors that detect drift every $f = \{125, 250, 500\}$ instances. These represent over-reactive, perfect and under-active drift detectors. We introduce imbalance by generating up to 80% more of one class than others.

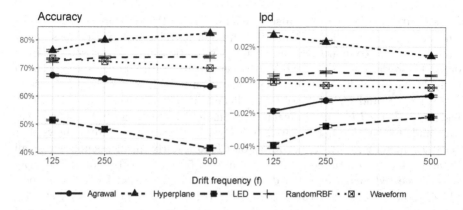

Fig. 5. Mean accuracy and *lpd* for five synthetic datasets with virtual drift and 250 instances between drifts

In Fig. 5, we can identify which value of f for a drift detector is getting the best classification accuracy. When presented with this plot, a reader may assume that the detector with the best f setting for each stream is worth using and provides a good accuracy. However, these have not been compared to the baseline approach with no drift detector. When we consider *lpd*, we can identify where drift detectors are not providing a genuine improvement in classification accuracy. Negative values of *lpd* for Agrawal (which has very particular classification rules), Waveform (with three classes) and LED (which has ten classes) show that using detectors with any f value will result in fewer correct classifications than using no drift detector. Even when $f = 250$ where drift is perfectly detected, the remedial action can cost more than taking no action. This is not the case with Hyperplane, which has a much simpler relationship between attributes and classes to learn.

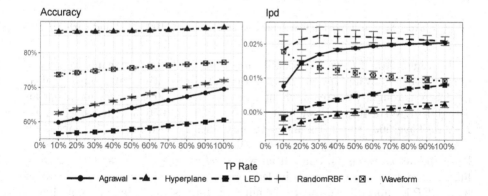

Fig. 6. Accuracy and *lpd* for five synthetic streams with varied TP and 0% FP

Sensitivity to True and False Positive Drift Rate. Here we show *lpd*'s suitability as a proxy for TP and FP through its relationship with these measures. First, we compare *lpd* and accuracy's relationship to TP over synthetic data. These datasets each have 500 concept drifts, with 500 instances between each. No sequentiality nor imbalance has been added, so accuracy is a useful proxy for TP and FP. We use an artificial drift detector that detects drift 30 instances after a TP drift (to include a realistic detection delay). We show accuracy and *lpd* across different levels of TP with $FP = 0\%$. Figure 6, shows that accuracy increases with higher levels of TP in a fairly linear fashion across all datasets. Every additional 10% TP results in 50 more drifts. For this reason, we can see *lpd* increasing at a decreasing rate for Agrawal, LED and Hyperplane, showing that the mean improvement per drift rises with higher TP. This is less clear with RandomRBF, and for Waveform, *lpd* drops with higher rates of TP. This suggests that there is enough similarity between concepts that regular drifts do not improve accuracy beyond the penalty for extra drifts, even though they are correct detections. With *lpd*, we also see that drift detection achieves worse accuracy than not using drift detection for low levels of TP on LED and Hyperplane.

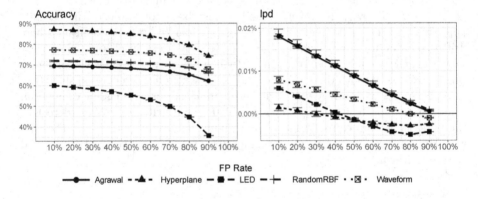

Fig. 7. Accuracy and *lpd* for five synthetic streams with 100% TP and varied FP

Keeping 100% TP we introduced false positive drifts to streams to see the impact on accuracy and *lpd*, as shown in Fig. 7. False positive drifts were signalled randomly through the stream, though never within 100 instances following an actual drift. With 10% FP, we have 500 true drifts and 56 false drifts; with 90% FP, we have 500 true drifts and 4500 false drifts. With higher FP, accuracy decreased at an increasing rate across all datasets. Higher levels of FP led to lower *lpd* across datasets, apart from when *lpd* was negative and FP was very high, as the drop in accuracy is divided by more drifts. The reduction in *lpd* with higher FP is almost linear due to the number of drifts increasing in a superlinear fashion with higher FP. The level of FP that results in lower accuracy than using no drift detection is very clear, with RandomRBF and Agrawal never performing worse than the baseline approach.

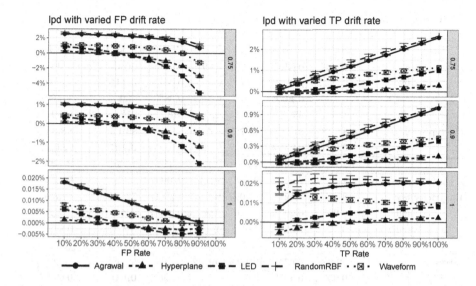

Fig. 8. Mean *lpd* with varied TP (with 0% *FP*) and varied *FP* rate (with 100% *TP*) where $r \in \{0.75, 0.9, 1.0\}$

This comparison of *lpd* and accuracy shows how the metrics differ and that they can both be useful proxies for drift detection quality when evaluating on real-world datasets. Our proposed metric generally increases with improved drift rate, and where *lpd* is positive, we know drifts are improving classification accuracy. As *lpd* is a trade-off between accuracy and drifts detected, we do not seek to have a perfect correlation with TP; *lpd* should only increase when each drift notably increases accuracy. When varying FP, we could see both accuracy and *lpd* dropping with higher FP. Across both experiments, negative *lpd* plainly shows where drift detection is not providing additional classification accuracy (Fig. 8).

Varying r with FP and TP Rate. When varying r, we see that *lpd* still drops with higher FP rate and increases with higher TP rate, making it a valid proxy for TP and FP. Increasing FP is associated with more drifts. When $r < 1$, *lpd* decreases more slowly than with $r = 1$. The more r is reduced, the less *lpd* penalises an approach for using many drifts. The range of *lpd* increases with higher r: only *lpd* scores with the same r should be compared with each other.

Real-World Datasets. Here, we show *lpd*'s usefulness for evaluating drift detectors on real-world data, mirroring the experiments by Bifet [2] which demonstrate increased accuracy through periodic drift (the 'No-Change' detector). We show accuracy, *lpd*, $lpd(r = 0.9)$ and the number of drifts for each experiment and detector. We use an incremental Naïve Bayes classifier and drift detectors use default parameters as per their implementation in MOA.

Table 2. Accuracy, *lpd* and number of drifts detected for real-world datasets

		ADWIN	CUSUM	DDM	EDDM	HDDMw	PageHinkley	NoChange
Airlines	*acc*	66.7%	**67.5%**	66.6%	64.9%	65.3%	67.0%	58.6%
	lpd	0.011%	0.083%	0.116%	0.009%	0.001%	**0.119%**	−0.001%
	lpd(r = 0.9)	0.21%	**0.30%**	0.25%	0.04%	0.08%	0.28%	−0.60%
	#*drifts*	195	35	18	42	613	21	8989
Covtype	*acc*	83.2%	81.5%	78.7%	85.1%	85.9%	80.1%	**88.4%**
	lpd	0.020%	0.074%	0.008%	0.011%	0.011%	**0.167%**	0.003%
	lpd(r = 0.9)	2.27%	2.10%	1.82%	2.46%	2.54%	1.95%	**2.79%**
	#*drifts*	1151	286	2185	2214	2290	117	9683
Electricity	*acc*	81.0%	79.2%	84.0%	**84.5%**	84.0%	78.0%	82.7%
	lpd	0.087%	0.209%	0.056%	0.057%	0.080%	**0.468%**	0.012%
	lpd(r = 0.9)	0.77%	0.62%	1.07%	**1.11%**	1.07%	0.72%	0.93%
	#*drifts*	88	28	192	196	133	10	755
Intrusion	*acc*	99.8%	99.7%	**99.9%**	**99.9%**	99.8%	99.6%	98.2%
	lpd	0.057%	0.455%	0.045%	0.166%	0.326%	**0.610%**	0.000%
	lpd(r = 0.9)	0.33%	0.61%	0.33%	0.38%	0.50%	**0.74%**	0.17%
	#*drifts*	58	7	74	20	10	5	8233
Poker	*acc*	73.7%	72.5%	66.5%	77.6%	77.0%	70.7%	**79.0%**
	lpd	0.010%	0.020%	0.007%	0.004%	0.008%	**0.023%**	0.001%
	lpd(r = 0.9)	1.41%	1.30%	0.69%	1.81%	1.74%	1.11%	**1.95%**
	#*drifts*	1388	659	958	4868	2263	489	13820

For the No-Change detector, we detected drift and replaced the classifier with an untrained classifier after every sixtieth instance.

Through accuracy alone, the No-Change detector appears competitive with other techniques as per Table 2. However when $r = 1$, *lpd* is lowest for the No-Change detector, penalising the approach for its extreme number of drifts. Page-Hinkley has the best *lpd*, partly due to the lower number of drifts detected. Compared to approaches like EDDM, Page-Hinkley has notably worse classification accuracy. As *lpd* rewards lift in accuracy per drift, it will generally value techniques with fewer drifts, unless the improvement in accuracy is dramatic. This is valid. However, if drifts do not come with a significant cost, then selecting a framework using both *lpd* and accuracy is a good option. CUSUM and ADWIN both seem to provide a balance of *lpd* and classification accuracy. Across all datasets, drift detection provides an improvement in accuracy compared to not using drift detection, as evidenced by usually positive *lpd*. The one negative case suggests that the No-Change detector does not improve classification accuracy on Airlines. This dataset provides the most difficult classification problem, and frequent drifts as per the No-Change detector may interrupt learning of more complex rules. Intrusion by contrast is much easier to classify correctly. In this dataset, 20 classes make up 1.8% of the dataset. Constantly replacing the classifier will forget what has been learnt about these rare minority classes.

The No-Change detector does best on Poker in terms of classification accuracy. In all of these cases, Page-Hinkley achieves the best lpd. When $r = 0.9$, No-Change appears best for Covtype and Poker, as each drift is penalised less than the prior one. However, lpd is less conservative, rewarding drift detectors more for accuracy and penalising less for increased drifts.

5   Conclusion and Future Work

High accuracy does not necessarily reflect well-chosen concept drifts; approaches with high accuracy can be worse than baseline approaches. The lpd metric measures the impact on accuracy of drift detection against the number of drifts detected. Unlike metrics such as FP, TP and MTR, lpd can be used on datasets even when we do not know where drift has genuinely occurred. Through the r parameter, lpd can account for the relative cost of drifts. Sequentiality can lead to significant increases in accuracy despite a classifier being unable to differentiate classes well. We have shown how to test for its presence in datasets while accounting for class imbalance. Our experiments show that our metric achieves the goals set out for it: lpd is not increased by periodic detection with high sequentiality. It measures improvement over a non-drift detecting framework, which shows when a drift detection framework actually reduces classifier error. On synthetic datasets, lpd is related to true positive and false positive drift detection so can work as a proxy for these measures. On real-world data, lpd does not require knowing where real drifts occurred. We have contrasted lpd to accuracy across real-world datasets and shown that it rewards well chosen drifts.

We have shown how to calculate lpd based upon accuracy. However, lpd could be based on other classification metrics. For instance, the Kappa metric κ [1] normalizes a classifier's accuracy by that of a chance predictor to evaluate how well a classifier performs across classes. For imbalanced data, where drifts may negatively impact classifications of minority classes, lpd_κ could be formulated to measure the impact on κ per-drift detected relative to having no drifts. It would also be of value to assess how lpd could be used in alternate frameworks such as ensemble approaches that handle concept drift in different ways.

References

1. Bifet, A., de Francisci Morales, G., Read, J., Holmes, G., Pfahringer, B.: Efficient online evaluation of big data stream classifiers. In: Proceedings of the 21st ACM SIGKDD International Conference on Knowledge Discovery and Data Mining, pp. 59–68. ACM (2015)
2. Bifet, A.: Classifier concept drift detection and the illusion of progress. In: Rutkowski, L., Korytkowski, M., Scherer, R., Tadeusiewicz, R., Zadeh, L.A., Zurada, J.M. (eds.) ICAISC 2017. LNCS (LNAI), vol. 10246, pp. 715–725. Springer, Cham (2017). https://doi.org/10.1007/978-3-319-59060-8_64
3. Hoens, T.R., Polikar, R., Chawla, N.V.: Learning from streaming data with concept drift and imbalance: an overview. Prog. Artif. Intell. 1(1), 89–101 (2012)

4. Gama, J., Sebastião, R., Rodrigues, P.P.: Issues in evaluation of stream learning algorithms. In: Proceedings of the 15th ACM SIGKDD International Conference on Knowledge Discovery and Data Mining, pp. 329–338. ACM (2009)
5. Krempl, G., et al.: Open challenges for data stream mining research. ACM SIGKDD Explor. Newsl. **16**(1), 1–10 (2014)
6. Tsymbal, A.: The problem of concept drift: definitions and related work, vol. 106. Computer Science Department, Trinity College Dublin (2004)
7. Gama, J., Medas, P., Castillo, G., Rodrigues, P.: Learning with drift detection. In: Bazzan, A.L.C., Labidi, S. (eds.) SBIA 2004. LNCS (LNAI), vol. 3171, pp. 286–295. Springer, Heidelberg (2004). https://doi.org/10.1007/978-3-540-28645-5_29
8. Frías-Blanco, I., del Campo-Ávila, J., Ramos-Jiménez, G., Morales-Bueno, R., Ortiz-Díaz, A., Caballero-Mota, Y.: Online and non-parametric drift detection methods based on Hoeffdings bounds. IEEE TKDE **27**(3), 810–823 (2015)
9. Žliobaitė, I., Budka, M., Stahl, F.: Towards cost-sensitive adaptation: when is it worth updating your predictive model? Neurocomputing **150**, 240–249 (2015)
10. Bifet, A., Frank, E.: Sentiment knowledge discovery in Twitter streaming data. In: Pfahringer, B., Holmes, G., Hoffmann, A. (eds.) DS 2010. LNCS (LNAI), vol. 6332, pp. 1–15. Springer, Heidelberg (2010). https://doi.org/10.1007/978-3-642-16184-1_1
11. Žliobaitė, I., Bifet, A., Read, J., Pfahringer, B., Holmes, G.: Evaluation methods and decision theory for classification of streaming data with temporal dependence. Mach. Learn. **98**(3), 455–482 (2015)

Genetic Programming Based on Granular Computing for Classification with High-Dimensional Data

Wenbin Pei[1(✉)], Bing Xue[1], Lin Shang[2], and Mengjie Zhang[1]

[1] School of Engineering and Computer Science, Victoria University of Wellington,
PO Box 600, Wellington 6140, New Zealand
{Wenbin.Pei,Bing.Xue,Mengjie.Zhang}@ecs.vuw.ac.nz
[2] State Key Laboratory for Novel Software Technology, Nanjing University,
Nanjing 210093, China
shanglin@nju.edu.cn

Abstract. Classification tasks become more challenging when having the curse of dimensionality issue. Recently, there has been an increasing number of datasets with thousands of features. Some classification algorithms often need feature selection to avoid the curse of dimensionality. Genetic programming (GP) has shown success in classification tasks. GP does not require to do feature selection because of its built-in capability to automatically select informative features. However, GP-based methods are often computationally intensive to achieve a good classification accuracy. Based on perspectives from granular computing (GrC), this paper proposes a new approach to linking features hierarchically for GP-based classification. Experiments on seven high-dimensional datasets show the effectiveness of the proposed algorithm in terms of saving training time and enhancing the classification accuracy, compared to baseline methods.

Keywords: High-dimensional data · Genetic programming
Granular computing · Classification

1 Introduction

Classification is one of the most important tasks of data mining, which refers to an algorithmic procedure to assign a given piece of input data into one of the given categories [15]. Classification has a wide range of applications, e.g. medicine, biology and education, etc. Many algorithms have been proposed for classification tasks, e.g. K-nearest neighbors (KNN) [4], Native bayes (NB) [9], decision tree (DT) [7], and support vector machines (SVMs) [6]. However, when having the curse of dimensionality issue, to enhance the classification performance is challenging. Recently, there has been an increase in the number of datasets with thousands to millions of features. To avoid the curse of dimensionality, some classification algorithms, e.g. KNN, often require to perform a pre-processing step, such as feature selection [3] or feature construction [16].

© Springer Nature Switzerland AG 2018
T. Mitrovic et al. (Eds.): AI 2018, LNAI 11320, pp. 643–655, 2018.
https://doi.org/10.1007/978-3-030-03991-2_58

Genetic programming (GP) [11,16] is a heuristic technique, inspired by biological evolution and nature selection. GP is effective for classification tasks [5], especially for binary classification. GP has been applied to pre-processing and post-processing steps of high-dimensional classification, such as feature selection [10] and feature construction [16,17], to enhance performance of different classification algorithms, e.g. KNN and NB. Furthermore, GP is often employed to construct classifiers by using different kinds of representations, e.g. rules [5,8]. GP-based methods do not require domain knowledge, human intervention, or statistical assumption or inference. Moreover, there is no requirement to do feature selection or other pre-processing steps before classification, because of its build-in capability to automatically select informative features during the classification process [17]. Another crucial advantage of GP-based methods is that GP is able to cope with different types of features.

However, GP-based methods are often time-consuming, which is a main disadvantage of GP. In standard GP, all the features are fed to the algorithm as terminals. For high-dimensional datasets, the search space is large, which often requires a large amount of training time. Moreover, it is not equally difficult to classify each instances in a dataset. Some instances are classified correctly by using only a small number of features, while some instances are difficult to be classified, requiring features with very good discrimination ability. In order to save training time and further enhance classification performance, this paper proposes a new strategy to organise features hierarchically by taking perspectives from granular computing (GrC) [1,18,20]. According to mechanisms from GrC, knowledge should be understood and organized hierarchically and spirally. Inspired by this, for high-dimensional datasets, the whole features are divided into several feature set linked hierarchically, to learn hierarchically and spirally, based on previous good feature knowledge.

Goals

In this paper, we focus on exploring the potential of GP in classification with high-dimensional data, based on the perspectives of GrC. The overall goal is to enhance the performance of GP-based methods, to save training time and improve the accuracy for classification with high-dimensional data. This goal is composed of the following three objectives.

- Proposes a new approach to link features hierarchically for GP-based methods.
- Investigate whether the proposed algorithm can effectively improve the accuracy, and save training time, compared to standard GP on classification tasks with high-dimensional data.
- Investigate whether the proposed algorithm can achieve significantly better or similar performance in classification with high-dimensional data, compared to other non-GP classification algorithms.

2 Background

2.1 Genetic Programming

Genetic programming [11] is a population-based evolutionary computation technique that aims at generating program automatically for addressing complex problems. It emphasizes on tree structure, which makes GP distinctive and more flexible to be applied widely [5]. When applying GP to solve problems, a terminal set and a function set need to be defined. In tree-based GP, the internal nodes of GP trees, called a function set, is the set of all possible operators or functions, e.g. arithmetic operators ($+$, $-$, $\times$ and $/$), or mathematics functions e.g. $\sin(x)$. All the possible arguments for internal nodes consist of a terminal set, or called leaf nodes of GP trees. Individuals are evaluated by a predefined fitness function for selection. New individuals are created by operators, e.g. crossover and mutation. The pseudo-code of GP [11] is shown as follows:

Algorithm 1. Tree-based Genetic Programming

Initialization:Individuals (trees or programs) of initial population are generated randomly;
repeat
    Evaluation: each individual is evaluated by a fitness function;
    Selection: One or two individuals are selected from the population with a probability based on its fitness;
    Evolution: new individuals are created by the following genetic operators with specific probabilities:
        Reproduction
        Crossover
        Mutation
until the stopping criterion is satisfied;
return best program or individual;

2.2 Granular Computing

Granular Computing (GrC) [20] is a systematic study of using granules (such as classes, clusters, intervals, groups, subsets, etc.) for solving complex problems. It suggests to use a hierarchical granular structure for a multi-layer understanding at multiple layers of varying granularity, and to use different granular structures to achieve a multi-view understanding from different angles [21]. Yao proposes a granular computing triangle: structured thinking within the philosophical perspective, structured problem solving within the methodological perspective, and structured information processing within the computational perspective. This paper adopts the reductionist thinking from structured granular thinking, which focuses on breaking a complex problem into relatively simpler parts and inferring properties of the whole by a summary of properties of its parts [21]. Yao explains the reductionist thinking according to *Discourse on the method of rightly conducting one's reason and seeking truth in the sciences* by Rene Descartes [21]:

– To divide each of the difficulties into as many parts as possible and as might be required in order to resolve them better;

- To direct thoughts in an orderly manner, by starting with the simplest and most easily known objects in order to move up gradually to knowledge of the most complex, and by stipulating some order even among objects that have no natural order of precedence;
- To make all enumerations so complete, and reviews so comprehensive.

To some extend, the methodology of GrC for classification is similar to methods used by human for classification. Human beings might solve problems, especially complex problems, in different granular worlds, and more importantly, they are likely to shift from a granular world to another quickly and easily [1,18]. In other words, human often solve problems with hierarchical knowledge in their mind, which seems to be an aspect of human intelligence [18]. For human, knowledge is often understood hierarchically and spirally. For example, when solving a complex classification problem, people usually tend to classify some instances that can be easily classified, based on their general knowledge, and then for some instances that are difficult to be classified, they have to use more specific knowledge to distinguish them.

3 The Proposed Approach

3.1 Hierarchical Feature Knowledge

In standard GP, all the features are fed to the algorithm as terminals. For high-dimensional datasets, the search space is large, which often consumes a large amount of training time. Furthermore, it is not equally difficult to classify each instance in a dataset. Some instances are easily classified, while some instances are difficult to be classified, requiring features with the good discrimination ability.

According to mechanisms from GrC, knowledge should be understood and organized hierarchically and spirally. It motivates us to divide features into different feature sets that are linked hierarchically to provide hierarchical knowledge for complex classification tasks. At different hierarchy layers, the discrimination ability of feature sets is different. Discrimination ability of features at the first feature layer is relatively low, in which only a small number of features are included, and then the discrimination ability of features in following feature layers would become better and better. This paper assumes that classification with more than a thousand is a complex classification problem.

When a number of features is more than a thousand, the whole feature space F is divided into five independent parts, with same number of features, namely $F1$, $F2$, $F3$, $F4$ and $F5$. First, a GP process is employed, using features in $F1$ only as its terminals, with a small population and a small number of generations for evolving a classifier. After this evolutionary learning process, the best individual is chosen as the first classifier. As mentioned previously, GP has a build-in capability to automatically select good-quality features during the evolutionary learning process. After the first GP process, the terminals of n top-ranked trees $(n = (\#population)^1 * 0.1)$ are selected to be a good feature set, denoted as

---

[1] # indicates cardinality.

$F1^*$ ($F1^*$ is expected to have the similar discrimination ability as original set $F1$). The second feature layer includes $F2$ and $F1^*$ to ensure its discrimination ability better than $F1$.

Similarly, the second GP process is employed to evolve the second classifier by using feature set $F2$ and $F1^*$, and then $F2^*$, the second good feature set is generated and transferred to the third feature layer, with new features from $F3$, to be fed to the next GP process. The similar processes continue until the fifth feature layer is generated by $F5$ and $F4^*$. It is worth of noticing that this hierarchical feature structure is generated during classification process.

3.2   Learning from Incorrectly-Classified Instances

After each learning process, some instances might not be classified correctly, which should be remained for further learning. The ideal situation is that all of the correctly-classified instances will continue to be classified correctly by classifiers that are evolved by the next GP processes at the following feature layers. However, some correctly-classified instances might become incorrectly-classified since the structure of the classifiers is different. Therefore, incorrectly-classified instances from different GP processes might be different. All of these incorrectly-classified instances are remained for learning by the sixth GP process using features at the sixth feature layer, in which all of high-quality features selected by previous five GP processes are included. Theoretically speaking, the discrimination ability of the feature set at the sixth layer should be better than other feature layers, because it is based on all of the good-quality features selected previously by five GP processes.

Moreover, correctly-classified instances by all of the five classifiers (five best individual from each GP process) are sampled randomly, with possibility 0.5, for learning at sixth layer. A reason is that some high-dimensional datasets have noisy data, so the sixth GP process should not consider incorrectly-classified instances only. Furthermore, because some datasets are unbalanced, it is possible that all of the incorrectly-classified instances have the same label. In that case, the final GP process does not know any information about another label, thereby making some mistakes.

As explained in Sect. 3.1, six GP processes are employed in total. Five GP processes are learning all of the instances in the training set, and the sixth GP process is learning incorrectly-classified instances and 50% of the correctly-classified instances. A multi-classifier system is built when constructing a hierarchical feature structure. Majority voting [2] is an effective and easy strategy, which also embodies multi-view from GrC because a single feature set is seen as one criterion taking one point of perspective. Therefore, for the testing process, the best individual of each GP process is chosen to be a classifier voting for a final decision, and their training accuracy as their weight of each classifier. The overall structure is shown by Fig. 1.

For multi-classifier systems, their robustness is often better than a single classifier to tolerate noise [12]. Moreover, this system is expected to save training time. Although six GP classifiers are involved, each of them only requires a subset

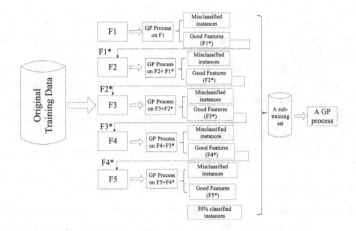

Fig. 1. The overall structure

of features, instead of using all of the features. Therefore, for each GP process, the search space is significantly reduced. Because of the reduced search space, it is reasonable to set a small population size and a smaller number of generations to save training time.

3.3   The Overall Algorithm

In GP, each individual is seen as a simple classifier. For binary classification, a threshold is set to separate two classes. If a program output of an instance is greater than this threshold, it is classified to $Class1$, otherwise it is classified to $Class2$. For c-classification, $c - 1$ values are used to separate c classes.

Fitness Function: For binary classification, the balanced accuracy is employed as the fitness function since many high-dimensional datasets are unbalanced. Therefore, the fitness function is defined as [16]:

$$fitness_b = 0.5 * \frac{TP}{TP + FN} + 0.5 * \frac{TN}{TN + FP} \tag{1}$$

where TP is true positive, TN is true negative, FP is false positive, and FN is false negative.

For c-class classification problems, the fitness function is [13]:

$$fitness_m = \frac{\sum_i^c \frac{TP_i + TN_i}{TP_i + TN_i + FP_i + FN_i}}{c} \tag{2}$$

where c is the number of classes.

Algorithm 2 shows the pseudo-code of the proposed method.

Algorithm 2. GrC_GP

Input: The (whole) training set and the test set
Output: Classification accuracy
 1. Initialization;
    $q \Leftarrow 1$;
    Good_features set, Incorrect_instance set $\Leftarrow \emptyset$;
 2. The whole feature space is divided into 5 feature sets;
 if $q \leq 5$ **then**
    Features in a feature set F_q are fed to the first GP process;
    Obtained a good feature set F_q^* is appended into next feature set F_{q+1} and Good_features set
    set;
    Misclassified instances are appended into Incorrect_instance set;
    $q \Leftarrow q + 1$;
 end if
 if $q = 6$ **then**
    Generate a new sub-training set by randomly sampling 50% of the correctly-classified
    instances and use all the instances from Incorrect_instance set, and feature set is from six
    Good_features set;
    Apply a GP process on this sub-training set;
 end if
 3. Classify unseen instances in the test set, best individuals from each GP process are chosen as
    classifiers voting for a final decision;
 4. Calculate accuracy;

---

4 Experiment Design

4.1 Datasets

Seven datasets[2] [23] with thousands of features are used to examine the performance of the proposed method in classification with high-dimensional data. Table 1 describes these datasets in details, including information about the number of features, instances, classes, and the proportions of instances in each class.

Table 1. Dataset description

Dataset	#Features	#Instances	#Classes	Class1	Class2	Class3
Colon	2,000	62	2	35%	65%	–
DBWorld e-mails	4,071	64	2	45%	55%	–
DLBCL	5,469	77	2	25%	75%	–
Leukemia (or ALL-AML)	7,129	72	2	35%	65%	–
Leukemia_3c (or ALL-AML-3)	7,129	72	3	13%	35%	53%
Ovarian	15,154	253	2	36%	64%	–
Breast	24, 481	97	2	47%	53%	–

For these datasets, they only contain a small number of instances, but are involved with thousands of features. Therefore, these datasets may suffer from the curse of dimensionality problem. Since some datasets are unbalanced, e.g.

---

[2] http://www.gems-system.org,
   http://csse.szu.edu.cn/staff/zhuzx/Datasets.html, and
   https://archive.ics.uci.edu/ml/datasets/DBWorld+e-mails.

DLBCL and Colon, when splitting a dataset into the training set and test set, the stratified sampling is employed to ensure instances in each class having the same the proportion in both training and test set, which is same as in the original whole set of data. Moreover, the majority of these datasets have noisy data [16]. In each dataset, the instances are divided into two sets: 70% as the training set and 30% as the test set.

4.2   Baseline Methods

In order to examine performance of the proposed method, the new method is compared with standard genetic programming (SGP) and non-GP methods, including 1-nearest neighbours (1NN), random forest (RF), gradient boosting decision tree (GBDT), SVMs, neural networks (NNs) and NB. They are representatives of different kinds of classification methods. KNN is a well-known instance-based classification method. SVMs [6] are a kernel based methods, which often achieve good classification performance. RF [14] and GBDT [19] are variants of decision tree (DT) methods that often use a tree-like representation, which often achieve better classification performance than DT. NNs are data-driven self-adaptive methods, which are able to approximate any function [22]. NB is the representative of probabilistic-based classification algorithms [9].

4.3   Parameter Settings

Table 2 shows the parameter settings for standard GP and GrC_GP.

Table 2. Parameters setting

Parameters	Values in SGP	Values of GrC_GP (each feature layer)
Population size	1024	256
Generations	50	33
Initial population	Ramped half-and-half	Ramped half-and-half
Maximum tree depth	17	17
Mutation rate	0.2	0.2
Crossover rate	0.8	0.8
Elitism	10	2
Selection method	Tournament (size = 6)	Tournament (size = 6)
Function set	$+, -, \times, \div$, sin, cos, neg	$+, -, \times, \div$, sin, cos, neg
Terminal set	Features of a dataset a random constant	Features at current layer a random constant

The function set includes four basic arithmetic functions ($+$, $-$, $\times$, and protected division $\div$), trigonometric functions (sin and cos) and *neg* function.

Protected division returns zero when dividing by zero, and sin (or cos) returns sin (or cos) value of an input. *Neg* returns the negative value of an input.

The population size of SGP is 1024 for 50 generations, which are common settings for GP. To ensure a relatively fair comparison with SGP, for GrC_GP, at each feature layer, the population size of each GP process is 256 for 33 generations so that the total number of evaluations (i.e. 256*33*6) in GrC_GP is similar to that in SGP (i.e. 1024*50). Both SGP and GrC_GP have been run for 30 times independently with different random seeds on each dataset. The results from 30 runs of SGP and GrC_GP are also compared using Wilcoxon statistical significance test, with the significance level of 0.05.

5 Results and Discussion

Comparison Between SGP and GrC_GP

GrC_GP is compared with SGP and the accuracies on the test set are reported in the Table 3. "+" means that the accuracy of GrC_GP is significantly better than SGP, "=" means that they are similar, and "−" means GrC_GP is significantly worse than SGP.

Table 3 shows that, in all datasets, the average classification accuracy of GrC_GP is improved, compared to SGP. According to Wilcoxon statistical significance test, for dataset Colon, DBWorld, DLBCL, Leukemia_3c, and Breast, the average accuracy is significantly better than SGP. For other two datasets, the accuracies are similar to that of SGP. It is worth noticing that dataset Leukemia_3c has 3 class labels, which is multi-classification, but the average accuracy of this dataset also improved 14.05%. Multi-classifier systems seem to be a possible method for multi-classification by GP.

Table 3. Comparison with standard GP

	Methods	Best	Mean ± StdDev	Average training time (s)
Colon	SGP	86.67	66.42 ± 0.11924+	366
	GrC_GP	95.14	81.82 ± 0.072892	83 (22.67%)
DBWorld e-mails	SGP	88.69	72.90 ± 0.08823+	791
	GrC_GP	87.71	80.22 ± 0.040453	184 (23.26%)
DLBCL	SGP	97.37	73.17 ± 0.109808982+	1,213
	GrC_GP	96.04	85.52 ± 0.0658	271 (22.34%)
Leukemia	SGP	93.33	79.07 ± 0.126652655=	962
	GrC_GP	100	85.96 ± 0.076838	124 (12.89%)
Leukemia_3c	SGP	86.96	58.41 ± 0.140070796+	858
	GrC_GP	95.65	72.46 ± 0.093267	184 (21.44%)
Ovarian	SGP	100	94.58 ± 0.04163=	6,881
	GrC_GP	100	95.98 ± 0.024394	1,247 (18.12%)
Breast	SGP	66.52	54.20 ± 0.07508+	4,722
	GrC_GP	76.72	61.27 ± 0.0762	635 (13.44%)

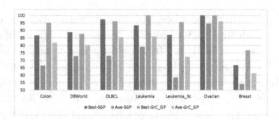

Fig. 2. The gap between the best and the average accuracies

According to the Fig. 2, except for dataset Breast, using GrC_GP, the gap between the best and average accuracies is narrower than those achieved using SGP. For example, the best result that SGP achieves on dataset Colon is 86.67%, which is 20.25% higher than its average accuracy 66.42%, while the gap is narrowed to 13.32% using GrC_GP (the best accuracy is 95.14% and the average accuracy is 81.82%). We also notice that datasets with a small number of instances, such as Colon (62 instances), have the relatively wider gap between the best and average accuracies, compared to datasets with a relatively large number of instances, such as Ovarian (253 instances). A possible reason is that with a small number of instances in a test set, one misclassified instance would significantly decrease the classification accuracies. For example, dataset Colon includes 18 instances in the test set, so one misclassified instance would cause 5.56% accuracy loss. However, for dataset Ovarian with 76 instances in the test set, a misclassified instance only cause 1.32% accuracy loss.

The average training time for all of these datasets is significantly reduced. For all of the datasets, the average training time of GrC_GP for the 30 runs only are 12.44%−22.67% of training time of SGP. The reason is that each GP process of GrC_GP only uses a part of features at their feature layer, and population size is 256 for 33 generations. This results would show that our goal is achieved in terms of saving training time and enhancing the classification accuracy.

Comparison Between Non-GP Methods and GrC_GP

GrC_GP is compared with non-GP methods, including 1NN, RF, GBDT, SVM, NNs and NB. For a relatively fair comparison, non-GP classification algorithms are also run 30 times and average accuracies are reported in Table 4.

According to average results of 30 runs, except for dataset Leukemia_3c, GrC_GP often achieves significantly better or similar accuracy, compared with other classification algorithms. The last column in Table 4 shows the best accuracy of GrC_GP on each dataset. The best accuracy by GrC_GP is often higher than other classification algorithms, except for dataset DBWorld e-mails (88.86% by NB, compared to 87.71% by GrC_GP). In three datasets, namely Colon, DLBCL and Breast, both the best accuracy and average accuracy of GrC_GP are higher than other methods. However, in Leukemia, Leukemia_3c and Ovarian, the best accuracy is higher than other methods, but their average accuracy

Table 4. Comparison with other non-GP methods

	1NN	RF	GBDT	SVM	NNs	NB	GrC_GP (Mean)	GrC_GP (Best)
Colon	74.58+	69.16+	74.26+	48.77+	53.65+	60.42+	**81.82**	95.14
DBWorld e-mails	60.41+	65.69+	78.46=	52.69+	84.76=	**88.86−**	80.22	87.71
DLBCL	78.28+	76.63+	78.93+	56.18+	62.43+	73.61+	**85.52**	96.04
Leukemia	88.04=	84.58=	87.40=	64.55+	61.47+	**98.08−**	85.96	100
Leukemia_3c	86.67−	75.12+	90.60−	51.50+	50.17+	**92.62−**	72.46	95.65
Ovarian	94.29=	94.63=	**97.09=**	88.11+	93.39=	88.64+	95.98	100
Breast	59.37=	58.94=	57.04+	55.05+	53.33+	49.60+	**61.27**	76.72

is not the highest. It is because GP is a stochastic search method, so the gap between the best and average accuracies is usually wider than non-GP methods.

According to results, NB is effective in many cases. The possible reason is that all of these algorithms maybe influenced by noise. It maybe true that probabilistic-based classification algorithms (e.g. NB) and algorithms involved with multi-classifiers are usually more robust to tolerate noise and alleviate overfitting. By NB, noise data would be averaged when estimating the conditional probabilities. It is a possible reason for the good performance of NB. Another reason is that NB only requires a small number of instances to evaluate parameters for classification. However, for the dataset Breast with 24,481 features, the accuracy of NB is lowest, compared to other classification algorithms. The possible reason is NB needs make a strict assumption that features are statistically independent, but if this assumption is not satisfied because of feature interactions or other reasons, the performance of NB would be degraded.

GrC_GP is involved with multiple classifiers to improve robustness. Furthermore, although our method does not require feature selection before classification, informative features are selected when constructing hierarchical feature layer. Therefore, some noisy features are possibly deleted.

6 Conclusions and Future Work

This paper investigates the use of GP for classification with high-dimensional data, which adopts ideas from GrC for GP to save the training time and enhance the classification accuracy. Experiments on seven high-dimensional datasets show that the proposed method significantly reduces the training time, and more importantly, the accuracy is increased, compare to the standard GP. This is probably because GrC_GP does not need to use all of the features at the same time, but use them hierarchically and spirally, based on previous useful feature knowledge. Since the search space is reduced, the training time is saved. The accuracy is improved because of the capability of the proposed method to alleviate overfitting. In this experiments, these high-dimensional datasets have a small number of instances, so the ratio of dimensionality and instance size is very high, which often results in evolved patterns being too specific, leading to overfitting. To learn features spirally for evolving multi-classifiers might alleviate overfitting to some extent.

Compared to non-GP classification algorithms, in most cases, the proposed method is able to achieve significantly better or similar accuracies in binary classification tasks, but this method was not able to achieve good performance for multi-classification. One piece of future work could focus on multi-classification by designing an effective classification strategy and a fitness function. Moreover, after the first evolutionary learning by a GP process, good GP individuals can be evolved. In order to reuse these good individuals, we will design a reinitialization strategy to initialize the new population of the next GP processes, so that they can start their evolutionary process based on good candidates, which is expected to enhance interpretability of GP individuals.

Acknowledgement. This work was supported in part by the Marsden Fund of New Zealand Government under Contracts VUW1209, VUW1509 and VUW1615, Huawei Industry Fund E2880/3663, Natural Science Foundation of Jiangsu, China BK20161406, and the University Research Fund at Victoria University of Wellington 209862/3580, and 213150/3662.

References

1. Bargiela, A., Pedrycz, W.: Granular computing. In: Handbook in Computational Intelligence. Fuzzy Logic, Systems, Artificial Neural Networks, and Learning Systems, vol. 1, pp. 43–66. World Scientific (2016)
2. Cao, J., Lin, Z., Huang, G.B., Liu, N.: Voting based extreme learning machine. Inf. Sci. **185**(1), 66–77 (2012)
3. Cervante, L., Xue, B., Shang, L., Zhang, M.: A dimension reduction approach to classification based on particle swarm optimisation and rough set theory. In: Thielscher, M., Zhang, D. (eds.) AI 2012. LNCS (LNAI), vol. 7691, pp. 313–325. Springer, Heidelberg (2012). https://doi.org/10.1007/978-3-642-35101-3_27
4. Deng, Z., Zhu, X., Cheng, D., Zong, M., Zhang, S.: Efficient knn classification algorithm for big data. Neurocomputing **195**, 143–148 (2016)
5. Espejo, P.G., Ventura, S., Herrera, F.: A survey on the application of genetic programming to classification. IEEE Trans. Syst. Man Cybern. Part C (Appl. Rev.) **40**(2), 121–144 (2010)
6. Fleury, A., Vacher, M., Noury, N.: SVM-based multimodal classification of activities of daily living in health smart homes: sensors, algorithms, and first experimental results. IEEE Trans. Inf. Technol. Biomed. **14**(2), 274–283 (2010)
7. Joshi, A., Dangra, J., Rawat, M.: A decision tree based classification technique for accurate heart disease classification and prediction. Int. J. Technol. Res. Manag. **3**, 1–4 (2016)
8. Luna, J.M., Pechenizkiy, M., del Jesus, M.J., Ventura, S.: Mining context-aware association rules using grammar-based genetic programming. IEEE Trans. Cybern. (2017)
9. Murphy, K.P.: Naive Bayes Classifiers. University of British Columbia (2006)
10. Nguyen, H.B., Xue, B., Andreae, P.: A hybrid GA-GP method for feature reduction in classification. In: Shi, Y., et al. (eds.) SEAL 2017. LNCS, vol. 10593, pp. 591–604. Springer, Cham (2017). https://doi.org/10.1007/978-3-319-68759-9_48
11. Poli, R., Langdon, W., McPhee, N.: A Field Guide to Genetic Programming (2008)

12. Sáez, J.A., Galar, M., Luengo, J., Herrera, F.: Tackling the problem of classification with noisy data using multiple classifier systems: analysis of the performance and robustness. Inf. Sci. **247**, 1–20 (2013)
13. Sokolova, M., Lapalme, G.: A systematic analysis of performance measures for classification tasks. Inf. Process. Manag. **45**(4), 427–437 (2009)
14. Svetnik, V., Liaw, A., Tong, C., Culberson, J.C., Sheridan, R.P., Feuston, B.P.: Random forest: a classification and regression tool for compound classification and QSAR modeling. J. Chem. Inf. Comput. Sci. **43**(6), 1947–1958 (2003)
15. Thearling, K.: An Introduction to Data Mining (2017)
16. Tran, B., Xue, B., Zhang, M.: Genetic programming for feature construction and selection in classification on high-dimensional data. Memetic Comput. **8**(1), 3–15 (2016)
17. Tran, B., Xue, B., Zhang, M.: Using feature clustering for GP-based feature construction on high-dimensional data. In: McDermott, J., Castelli, M., Sekanina, L., Haasdijk, E., García-Sánchez, P. (eds.) EuroGP 2017. LNCS, vol. 10196, pp. 210–226. Springer, Cham (2017). https://doi.org/10.1007/978-3-319-55696-3_14
18. Wang, G., Yang, J., Xu, J.: Granular computing: from granularity optimization to multi-granularity joint problem solving. Granul. Comput. **2**(3), 105–120 (2017)
19. Yang, H.J., Roe, B.P., Zhu, J.: Studies of stability and robustness for artificial neural networks and boosted decision trees. Nucl. Instrum. Methods Phys. Res. Sect. A: Accel. Spectrometers Detect. Assoc. Equip. **574**(2), 342–349 (2007)
20. Yao, J.: Novel Developments in Granular Computing: Applications for Advanced Human Reasoning and Soft Computation. IGI Global (2010)
21. Yao, Y.: A triarchic theory of granular computing. Granul. Comput. **1**(2), 145–157 (2016)
22. Zhang, G.P.: Neural networks for classification: a survey. IEEE Trans. Syst. Man Cybern. Part C (Appl. Rev.) **30**(4), 451–462 (2000)
23. Zhu, Z., Ong, Y.S., Dash, M.: Markov blanket-embedded genetic algorithm for gene selection. Pattern Recognit. **40**(11), 3236–3248 (2007)

Random-Sets for Dealing
with Uncertainties in Relevance Feature

Abdullah Semran Alharbi[1,2](✉) ⓘ, Md Abul Bashar[1] ⓘ, and Yuefeng Li[1] ⓘ

[1] School of EECS, Queensland University of Technology, Brisbane, QLD, Australia
{m1.bashar,y2.li}@qut.edu.au
[2] Department of Computer Science, Umm Al-Qura University, Makkah, Saudi Arabia
asaharbi@uqu.edu.sa

Abstract. Most relevance discovery models only consider document-level evidence, which may introduce uncertainties to relevance features. Research in information retrieval shows that adopting passage-level (i.e. paragraph-level) evidence can improve the performance of different models in various retrieval tasks. This paper proposes an innovative and effective relevance method based on paragraph evidence to reduce uncertainties in the relevance features discovered by existing models. The method exploits latent topics in the relevance feedback collection to estimate the implicit paragraph relevance. It uses random sets to effectively model the intricate relationships between paragraphs, topics and features to deal with the associated uncertainties. Experiments are conducted using the standard RCV1 dataset, its TREC filtering collections and six popular performance measures. The results confirm that the proposed Uncertainty Reduction (UR) method can significantly enhance the performance of 12 models for relevance feature selection.

Keywords: Relevance feature selection · Random set
Topic modelling · Feature re-ranking · User information needs
Uncertainty

1 Introduction

Relevance discovery aims to find and accurately weight useful features from a set of relevance feedback documents that describe user information needs [23]. Relevance is an essential concept in information filtering (IF) and information retrieval (IR). IR determines the relevance between a document and the user query while IF regards the documents' relevance to the user's long-term interests (e.g. their profile) [12]. Selecting relevant features that can be used to express what the user needs is crucial for many Web personalisation applications and has become a subject of study in areas such as data mining, web intelligence and machine learning, including IR and IF [3,12,24,31].

Relevance discovery models face challenges in identifying relevant text features from both an empirical and theoretical perspective [23]. One reason is the

© Springer Nature Switzerland AG 2018
T. Mitrovic et al. (Eds.): AI 2018, LNAI 11320, pp. 656–668, 2018.
https://doi.org/10.1007/978-3-030-03991-2_59

uncertainties associated with the relevance features. For example, a document can be labelled as relevant even if only a short part of it comprises relevant information. Using only the document-level evidence can select features from all parts of such a document, which can lead to uncertainties and scatter the focus because the features coming from nonrelevant parts do not represent user information needs. Therefore, the relevance of the corresponding part should be considered when selecting features from it. Many studies have been conducted to develop models of relevance feature discovery over the last few decades [12, 20, 23, 34, 35]. However, most of them consider only the document-level evidence for relevance feature discovery.

Research in IR shows that considering the evidence at the passage-level can improve document retrieval accuracy, especially when long documents discuss multiple subject areas [11, 25]. Generally, IR models' performance can dramatically improve depending on the amount of evidence available in each passage [11]. Most of the existing research used some query-similarity scores between fixed window-size passages as the passage-level evidence. However, the explicit query may not always be available as in the example of IF, which forbids the estimation of the query-similarity score [12]. In such a situation, it becomes very challenging to explicitly estimate a paragraph's relevance in a set of documents that describe user information needs. Therefore, an implicit mechanism is needed to utilise the paragraph-level evidence.

We propose a method to use paragraph relevance to reduce the uncertainties of the relevance features discovered by existing popular models (e.g. BM25 [30], Rocchio [32], RFD_2 [23], etc.). The method uses topics in the relevance feedback collection as an implicit mechanism to estimate the paragraph relevance. We call the user information needs specific subject matters as topics. For example, the user information needs of *global warming* may involve topics like *pollution*, *greenhouse gases*, and *ozone layer depletion*. We assume that frequent topics in relevance feedback collection are the relevant ones and use them to estimate the relevance of paragraphs. Latent Dirichlet Allocation (LDA) [9] is employed in this research to discover the topics of the collection.

LDA is a popular topic modelling algorithm that can probabilistically identify the subject matters of a text corpus in an unsupervised way [9]. LDA represents each discovered topic as a multinomial probability distribution over the set of features (i.e. terms) in the documents collection. It also represents any document or paragraph as a mixture over the discovered topics. As an unsupervised statistical generative model, LDA has been extensively adopted for text mining in a wide variety of applications such as machine translation, human exploration, information filtering, information retrieval, word sense disambiguation, multi-document summarisation and many more [8].

Given a relevance feedback collection that discusses user information preferences, the relationships between distinct entities in the collection, namely, its features, paragraphs, and topics, can be modelled as set-valued observations. The uncertainties is phenomena that can be observed and represented as multiple sets, not as exact points, can effectively be modelled using the mathematical tool random set [13]. Therefore, we developed multiple random sets to effectively model these complex relationships so they can be understood and the uncertainties be dealt with.

This paper makes three contributions: (a) it uses random set and paragraph relevance to reduce the uncertainty of relevance features; (b) it uses random set and topics of relevance feedback to estimate the paragraph relevance; and (c) it shows that topics discovered by LDA can effectively estimate paragraph relevance in the absence of an explicit user query.

The results of experiments conducted on the 50 assessed collections of documents from the standard RCV1 dataset and their TREC filtering collections show that the proposed Uncertainty Reduction (UR) method is highly effective. When applied to the suitable existing model, it significantly outperforms all the other state-of-the-art models in all evaluation metrics despite the kind of text features they utilise.

2   Related Work

In IR, there are a considerable number of methods that adopt the passage-level approach to locate relevant information [7,11,17,18,25]. Such an approach results in remarkable improvements compared to traditional document-wide techniques. However, in relevance discovery, and in the absences of a query, identifying relevant features from a set of documents that describe user information preferences is difficult mainly due to the problems of polysemy and synonymy [3,23]. Most existing methods are document-wide and utilise various text features, such as words (i.e. terms), phrases, patterns, topics, or mixtures of them. Term-based methods like TFIDF, Mutual Information (MI), Chi-Square (χ^2), BM25, Rocchio, LASSO, ranking SVM [16,20,30,32,36] are efficient and theoretically sound. Nevertheless, these methods suffer from synonymy and polysemy problems and ignore words order in documents [12,23,24]. Thus, they miss the semantic information between these words [3].

Phrase-based methods use phrases (e.g. n-grams) because they are semantically rich and more discriminative [24]. However, phrases can be redundant and noisy. Published phrase-based experiments do not consider the paragraph relevance. Therefore, they do not show encouraging results [28,33]. A pattern carries more semantic information than individual terms and is more frequent than phrases [24]. Nevertheless, general patterns suffer from noise and redundancy, and specific ones experience low frequency [3,23,38]. Overall, relevance models that use words, n-grams, patterns or even mixtures of them assume that users' information preferences can discuss a particular topic only. Statistical topic-modelling techniques such as pLSA [15] and LDA [9] can solve this problem by finding some topics that describe what users need.

The weighting scheme is the crucial component of the feature selection algorithm [23]. Utilising LDA terms' probabilistic weight to express the relevance of these terms is inadequate and does not show effective performance [2–6,12]. This applies to related models such as the pLSA [15]. For better performance, patterns have been integrated into LDA to identify discriminative topical features [12]. However, such a technique can be computationally complex and susceptive to the features-loss problem as it is challenging to select useful patterns. Random set (RS) has proven powerful in representing complicated relationships between different objects and interpreting them through a probability function (i.e. scoring function) [22]. Therefore, an RS-based method is used to calculate a more accurate weight for closed sequential patterns and helps in discovering specific patterns [1]. Nevertheless, selecting specific patterns from documents is difficult and may also result in feature loss.

3   Problem Formulation and Basic Definitions

In this paper, we assume that a given document d has a set of paragraphs, each paragraph is a bag of features, and each term in the paragraph is a feature. D is a set of training documents that describes user information needs (both relevant and irrelevant ones) [23,24] in which D^+ represents the relevant training set and D^- represents the irrelevant set, thus, $D = D^+ \cup D^-$.

Many models in relevance discovery assume that all paragraphs in relevance feedback documents are equally relevant [23,24,35,37], which might not be the case. People label a document as relevant because some of its paragraphs are relevant, even though others are not. Feature relevance estimated by assuming all paragraphs to be equally important increases uncertainties in representing users' information needs. For example, TFIDF calculated from a document can be less reliable for estimating feature relevance if most of the paragraphs in the document are irrelevant to users' information needs.

This research aims to develop a method that can estimate the relevance of paragraphs in a relevant document set D^+ and use the paragraph relevance to estimate feature relevance. The objective of the estimated feature relevance is to reduce the uncertainties induced in the feature set discovered by existing relevance discovery models. To discover the topics in relevance feedback D^+, this research uses LDA. The following subsection gives a brief description of LDA.

3.1   Latent Dirichlet Allocation

Let the collection $D^+ = \{d_1, d_2, ..., d_N\}$ consist of a set of N relevant documents that describe user information needs, which can discuss multiple topics. Each document d contains some paragraphs, and a bag of features represents each paragraph g. $G = \bigcup_{d \in D^+} \{g | g \in d\}$ is the set of paragraphs in D^+, and $\Omega = \{t_1, t_2, ..., t_V\}$ is the set of unique features in G, where $V = |\Omega|$. LDA observes features in each paragraph and generates collection-wide latent topics. The user specifies the number of latent topics, and, in this paper, it is considered to be fixed to T. LDA represents each latent topic z_j as a multinomial probability distribution over the V features as $\rho(t_i | z_j)$, where $1 \leq j \leq T$ and $\sum_i^V \rho(t_i | z_j) = 1$. LDA also describes a paragraph g as a probabilistic mixture of topics as $\rho(z_j | g)$. Therefore, the probability of the ith feature in a paragraph g can be calculated as $p(t_i|g) = \sum_{j=1}^{T} p(t_i|z_j) \times p(z_j|g)$. Thus, the only observable variable is $p(t_i|g)$ while $p(t_i|z_j)$ and $p(z_j|g)$ are hidden. This paper uses Gibbs sampling, a widely used statistical inference technique, to learn the hidden variables.

4   Feature Relevance Estimation

Let G be the set of paragraphs in the relevant documents D^+. We assume that the relevance of each paragraph $g_k \in G$ is defined by a probabilistic distribution over the features set Ω in D^+, which is modelled using the set-valued mapping $\Gamma_1(g_k)$. To estimate the feature relevance, we assume that a feature t_i relevance relies on a probabilistic mixture of G, which is modelled using the inverse set-valued mapping $\Gamma_1^{-1}(t_i)$.

The set G is the evidence space, and a set of features can represent the relevance of a paragraph g_k, but its relevance level to the entire space is unknown. Thus, the probability distribution Ψ_1 is defined on G to indicate this uncertainty. Ψ_1 is then used to estimate the relevance level of g_k to the features. Let the probability of a feature t_i be relevant to g_k be $p(t_i|g_k)$, where, for simplicity, we assume $p(t_i|g_k) = 1$ if $t_i \in g_k$ and $p(t_k|g_k) = 0$ if $t_i \notin g_k$.

The random set can be defined as an arbitrary entity that has values, which are a subset taken from a given space [27]. Given Ψ_1, as a probability distribution defined on G, we call the pair (Ψ_1, Γ_1) a random set [13,19,27]. Because each paragraph g_k is described by the probability distribution over the set Ω, we have the set-valued mapping of $\Gamma_1 : G \rightarrow 2^\Omega - \{\emptyset\}$; $\Gamma_1(g_k) = \{t_i \in \Omega | p(t_i|g_k) > \zeta\}$ to represent and describe the relationship between a set of features and a paragraph, where $\Gamma_1(g_k) \subseteq \Omega$ for all $g_k \in G$ and ζ is a user defined threshold assigned to $\zeta = 0$ in this research.

Because there is a need to identify the significance level of a feature t_i, the inverse set-valued mapping of Γ_1 is considered to estimate a representative distribution Ψ_1 on G. For all features $t_i \in \Omega$, the inverse of Γ_1 is defined as $\Gamma_1^{-1} : \Omega \rightarrow 2^G$; $\Gamma_1^{-1}(t_i) = \{g_k \in G | t_i \in \Gamma_1(g_k)\}$ to also represent and understand the relationships between a feature and a set of paragraphs. Therefore, the relevance weight $w_g(t_i)$ of a feature t_i to the user information needs can be estimated as follows:

$$\Psi_1(t_i) \propto w_g(t_i) \propto \sum_{g_k \in \Gamma_1^{-1}(t_i)} p(t_i|g_k) \times p(g_k) \qquad (1)$$

where $p(g_k)$ is the probability of g_k being relevant to what the user need.

As the paragraph g_k can discuss multiple topics or sub-topics, we assume that g_k is a probabilistic mixture of a set of latent topics Z in D^+, which is modelled using the set-valued mapping $\Gamma_2(g_k)$. Z is the evidence space in this case. The set Z can represent the relevance of g_k to the user information preferences. The more relevant topics a paragraph covers, the more the paragraph's relevance increases. This motivation implies the relevance of frequent topics (topics shared by many paragraphs). However, the relevance level of g_k is unknown. Similarly, as before, Ψ_2 is a probability distribution defined on Z to indicate this uncertainty, and

Ψ_2 is used to estimate the relevance level of g_k to Z. Let the probability of a paragraph g_k being relevant to a given topic z_j be $p(g_k|z_j)$.

The pair (Ψ_2, Γ_2) is also called a random set in this case. As each paragraph g_k is described by the probability distribution over the set Z of topics, there is a set-valued mapping of $\Gamma_2 : G \rightarrow 2^Z - \{\emptyset\}$; $\Gamma_2(g_k) = \{z_j \in Z | p(g_k|z_j) > \xi\}$, where $\Gamma_2(g_k) \subseteq Z$ for all $g_k \in G$ and ξ is another user-defined threshold assigned to $\xi = 0$ in this research. Thus, the relevance of g_k to D^+ can be estimated as follows:

$$\Psi_2(g_k) \propto p(g_k) \propto \sum_{z_j \in \Gamma_2(g_k)} p(g_k|z_j) \tag{2}$$

Using Eqs. 1 and 2, the relevance weight $w_g(t_i)$ of the feature t_i can be calculated as follows:

$$w_g(t_i) = \sum_{g_k \in \Gamma_1^{-1}(t_i)} \left\{ p(t_i|g_k) \times \sum_{z_j \in \Gamma_2(g_k)} p(g_k|z_j) \right\} \tag{3}$$

To find the latent topics in D^+, we use LDA that gives us $\rho(z_j|g_k)$, but we need $\rho(g_k|z_j)$. Therefore, by applying Bayes' theorem, we can get $\rho(g_k|z_j) = \frac{\rho(z_j|g_k) \times \rho(g_k)}{\rho(z_j)}$. Here, $\rho(g_k)$ is a prior distribution that can be ignored, and $\rho(z_j)$ is the marginal probability of z_j in G.

5   Relevance Feature Re-ranking

To effectively represent user information needs, we first need to select a set of features that are representative. To find such features, the Support Vector Machine (SVM) [14] is empirically used in this research. As a discriminative classifier, SVM finds a hyperplane that best separates the positive and the negative classes. The discrepancy between normal values and the hyperplane is used to weight and thus rank the features, and then a subset is empirically selected from these ranked features. Because SVM and other existing models consider a given document relevant if some parts of the document are relevant, some features selected by these models can come from irrelevant or less relevant parts of the document. Therefore, the selected features, their weights, and their ranks incorporate uncertainties. We want to reduce these uncertainties by effectively scaling the feature weights and re-ranking the features based on their relevance value estimated by Eq. 3.

Let the weight of a feature t_i estimated by a model (e.g. SVM) be $w_m(t_i)$ and its relevance estimated by Eq. 3 be $w_g(t_i)$. The re-ranking weight $w(t_i)$ of the feature is estimated by scaling $w_m(t_i)$ by $w_g(t_i)$, (i.e. $w(t_i) = w_m(t_i) \times w_g(t_i)$). Then, the features are re-ranked based on the new weight $w(t_i)$. When re-ranking is applied to the model (e.g. SVM), we call it the improved iModel (iSVM). An intuitive interpretation of $w(t_i)$ is that it combines the paragraph-level evidence of relevance with the document-level evidence of relevance, which is estimated by the existing models for reducing uncertainty. However, the sentence-level evidence is too specific, and our preliminary experiments showed that such evidence is not effective in our current relevance feature re-ranking framework.

6 Evaluation

The proposed UR method estimates paragraph relevance to user information needs. Then, it uses the estimated paragraph relevance to estimate feature relevance and re-rank the features discovered by existing models. The major objectives of the experiments are to show that: (a) our proposed paragraph relevance estimation method is effective, (b) paragraph relevance can effectively estimate feature relevance, and (c) feature relevance can effectively reduce the uncertainty of discovered features by scaling and re-ranking the feature weights. This research hypothesises that *paragraph relevance can effectively reduce uncertainties in relevance feature space*. As in [12,23,38], we use an IF system-based approach for evaluating the hypothesis.

6.1 Dataset

The standard dataset of Reuters Corpus Volume 1 (RCV1) [21] is used in this research. The TREC-10/2001 Filtering Track develops 100 collections of documents out of RCV1. The first 50 human-created assessor collections simulate the real user scenarios, and they are reliable and have high quality. Conversely, the second 50 artificially created intersection collections are not quite as good. Besides, Buckley et al. (2000) [10] support that 50 collections are stable and enough for controlling the correctness of the evaluation metrics. Hence, the assessor collections are used in this research. In RCV1, documents in each collection are provided with relevance judgements. Each collection has a set of training documents and a set of testing documents. In each of the training sets and the testing sets, the documents that are relevant to the collection specification are called positive document set D^+, and the documents that are not relevant to the collection specification are called negative document set D^-. In this research, the unsupervised models use the set D^+ of positive training documents, and the supervised models use $D = D^+ \cup D^-$, where D^- is the set of negative training documents. However, in the testing phase, both positive and negative documents in the testing sets are used. This research applies three pre-processing steps to all documents via the elimination of stop-words and meta-data, as well as the stemming of terms by Porter's suffix-stripping algorithm [29].

6.2 Baseline Models and Settings

Extensive experiments are conducted covering 12 major relevance feature discovery methods to assess the effectiveness of the proposed UR method. Most of these methods are used, and their experimental parameters are set as in [12,23,38]. We give a brief description of all these baseline models as follows: (1) RFD_2 [23,24] is a state-of-the-art supervised pattern-based model. It groups terms into positive specific, general and negative specific to represent information needs. (2) Rocchio [32] is a term-based relevance feedback model. It uses a centroid in a supervised way to identify user information needs' representation. (3) PDS [38] is another pattern-based model to discover relevance features in an unsupervised way. It uses pattern support in the paragraphs and feature frequency in the patterns to weight the features. (4) LDA [9] is the most widely used unsupervised topic modelling algorithm. It uses $p(t_i|g) = \sum_{j=1}^{T} p(t_i|z_j)p(z_j|g)$ to assign scores to each term. (5) SVM [14] is a supervised term-based learning model. It finds a hyperplane that best separates two classes. The discrepancy between normal values and the hyperplane is used to weight the features. (6) BM25 [30] is one of the best term-based supervised-learning algorithms for ranking documents in IR. (7) pLSA [15] is another unsupervised topic-based algorithm. It is the predecessor of LDA, but it is a nongenerative model. pLSA assigns scores to terms similar to LDA. (8) LASSO [36] is another supervised term-based method for relevance feature selection. (9) Pr is the most effective term-based probabilistic method reported in [38]. (10) MI and (11) χ^2 are two popular supervised and term-based methods for relevance feature selection. More details about MI and χ^2 can be found in [26]. (12) TFIDF [38] is a widely used term-based weighting technique in relevance feature selection.

6.3   Evaluation Measures

The proposed UR method is assessed by six standard measures of the IF track that are based on the relevance judgement. The measures are the Mean Average Precision (MAP), the average precision of the top 20 documents (P@20), the F_{score} measure (F_1), the Break-even Point (BP), interpolated precision averages at 11 standard recall points (11-point), and the 11-point Interpolated Average Precision (IAP). The larger the MAP, P@20, F_1, BP, and IAP of a system, the better the system performs. Each measure focuses on a different aspect of the system performance. Readers can refer to [26] for more details about these measures.

6.4   Experimental Design

For every new document from the testing set, the IF system has to determine whether the new document is relevant to the user information preferences. We use the set of discovered relevance features (i.e. relevant features and their estimated weights learned from the training set) as a query Q submitted to an IF system, as in the TREC Filtering Track [21,31]. The same procedure is used with each baseline model. If the IF results for the proposed UR method significantly surpass the baselines, we can claim that our proposed UR method reflects our hypothesis.

6.5 Experimental Results

The proposed UR method is applied to re-rank each relevance feature set discovered by the baseline models, which are trained on the RCV1 human-assessed collections. The measures described in Sect. 6.3 are used to evaluate each model's IF performance. Table 1 shows each feature set's performances before and after applying the UR method. The *imp%* row shows the percentage of improvement achieved by applying the UR method to the corresponding model's original feature set. The table clearly shows that re-ranking can significantly improve the performance of the feature set discovered by each model. Figure 1 shows the changes in MAP values with the percentage of feature numbers changed in each set. It is apparent from the figure that the re-ranked feature set performs significantly better at any percentage of features in the set, and usually, compared with the original feature set, requires less re-ranked features to obtain the highest performance.

Table 2 and Fig. 2 compare the performance of iSVM with all the baseline models. The *imp%* at the bottom of Table 2 shows the percentage of improvement achieved by iSVM against the best baseline model, RFD_2. The iSVM model outperforms all models in all five measures. The improvement of iSVM against the RFD_2 model is from a maximum of 13.710% to a minimum of 7.496% in all measures. The performance improvement against the most important measure for the IF system, MAP, is 13.344%, and the average improvement in all measures is 12.276%. The interpolated precision results of 11 standard recall levels in Fig. 2 show that iSVM consistently out-performs any baseline models. This means, when our re-ranking method is applied to suitable relevance

Table 1. Performance improvement to all models on all measures using the first 50 collections of documents in RCV1.

Model	P@20	BP	MAP	F1	IAP	Model	P@20	BP	MAP	F1	IAP
BM25	0.479	0.410	0.412	0.412	0.439	Pr	0.454	0.402	0.405	0.415	0.431
iBM25	0.594	0.505	0.533	0.490	0.550	iPr	0.591	0.491	0.523	0.484	0.541
imp%	+24.008	+23.198	+29.331	+18.992	+25.279	imp%	+30.176	+22.093	+29.139	+16.636	+25.350
LASSO	0.339	0.326	0.324	0.356	0.349	RFD_2	0.533	0.455	0.475	0.456	0.493
iLASSO	0.535	0.454	0.473	0.457	0.498	$iRFD_2$	0.558	0.476	0.499	0.472	0.520
imp%	+57.817	+39.118	+46.073	+28.198	+42.665	imp%	+4.690	+4.709	+5.071	+3.449	+5.453
LDA	0.496	0.432	0.448	0.443	0.475	Rocchio	0.501	0.440	0.458	0.445	0.477
iLDA	0.555	0.483	0.499	0.471	0.521	iRocchio	0.544	0.462	0.486	0.462	0.510
imp%	+11.895	+11.661	+11.266	+6.261	+9.744	imp%	+8.583	+5.141	+6.069	+3.631	+6.961
MI	0.329	0.315	0.316	0.350	0.341	SVM	0.492	0.415	0.435	0.436	0.462
iMI	0.539	0.464	0.473	0.459	0.498	iSVM	0.606	0.514	0.538	0.490	0.561
imp%	+63.830	+47.137	+49.677	+31.190	+46.133	imp%	+23.171	+23.854	+23.726	+12.587	+21.258
PDS	0.492	0.434	0.451	0.443	0.477	TFIDF	0.364	0.339	0.339	0.368	0.366
iPDS	0.584	0.487	0.523	0.482	0.544	iTFIDF	0.436	0.377	0.382	0.394	0.408
imp%	+18.699	+12.134	+16.036	+8.946	+13.968	imp%	+19.780	+11.350	+12.651	+7.114	+11.428
pLSA	0.434	0.380	0.383	0.388	0.405	χ^2	0.318	0.321	0.320	0.356	0.347
ipLSA	0.558	0.464	0.496	0.470	0.516	$i\chi^2$	0.503	0.445	0.451	0.446	0.474
imp%	+28.571	+22.095	+29.580	+21.101	+27.378	imp%	+58.176	+38.501	+40.978	+25.360	+36.292

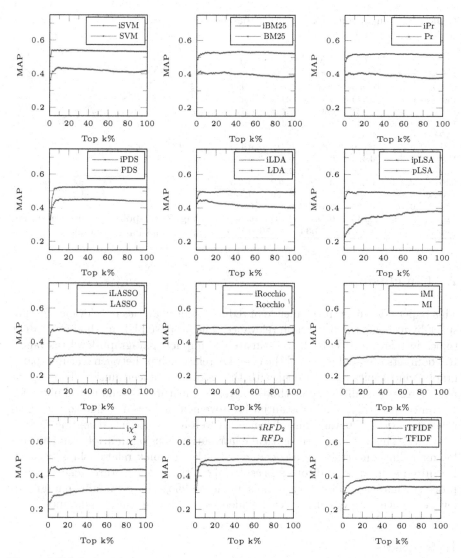

Fig. 1. MAP before and after uncertainty reduction for each model from 1% to 100% of the features space.

feature discovery model, the performance can be significantly better than existing models. All these results support our hypothesis that paragraph relevance can effectively reduce uncertainties in relevance feature space.

Table 2. Comparison of iSVM with baseline models

	P@20	BP	MAP	F1	IAP
iSVM	**0.606**	**0.514**	**0.538**	**0.490**	**0.561**
RFD_2	0.533	0.455	0.475	0.456	0.493
Rocchio	0.501	0.440	0.458	0.445	0.477
PDS	0.492	0.434	0.451	0.443	0.477
LDA	0.496	0.432	0.448	0.443	0.475
SVM	0.492	0.415	0.435	0.436	0.462
BM25	0.479	0.410	0.412	0.412	0.439
Pr	0.454	0.402	0.405	0.415	0.431
pLSA	0.434	0.380	0.383	0.388	0.405
TFIDF	0.364	0.339	0.339	0.368	0.366
LASSO	0.339	0.326	0.324	0.356	0.349
χ^2	0.318	0.321	0.320	0.356	0.347
MI	0.329	0.315	0.316	0.350	0.341
imp%	**+13.70**	**+13.13**	**+13.34**	**+13.70**	**+13.71**

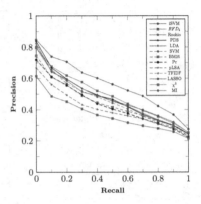

Fig. 2. 11-point results comparing iSVM and baseline models

7   Conclusion

This paper addresses the challenge of reducing uncertainties in relevance feature space by utilising the paragraph relevance. The proposed UR method uses latent topics in relevance feedback to estimate the implicit paragraph-level relevance. Random sets are used to model the complex relationships between features, paragraphs, and topics, and to deal with the associated uncertainties. The experimental results confirm the method's merit as a feature re-ranking technique for relevance discovery. The substantial improvement achieved is due to the effective estimation of paragraph relevance, as well as its use in estimating feature relevance. This research's theoretical contribution is using multiple random-sets for modelling uncertainties associated with the complex relationships between features, paragraphs, and topics as essential entities in the feature weight-scaling process. This study provides a promising methodology for combining paragraph-level evidence with document-level evidence to estimate feature relevance.

References

1. Albathan, M., Li, Y., Xu, Y.: Using extended random set to find specific patterns. In: WI 2014, vol. 2, pp. 30–37. IEEE (2014)
2. Alharbi, A.S., Li, Y., Xu, Y.: Enhancing topical word semantic for relevance feature selection. In: IJCAI-SML 2017, pp. 27–33. IJCAI (2017)
3. Alharbi, A.S., Li, Y., Xu, Y.: Integrating LDA with clustering technique for relevance feature selection. In: Peng, W., Alahakoon, D., Li, X. (eds.) AI 2017. LNCS (LNAI), vol. 10400, pp. 274–286. Springer, Cham (2017). https://doi.org/10.1007/978-3-319-63004-5_22
4. Alharbi, A.S., Li, Y., Xu, Y.: Topical term weighting based on extended random sets for relevance feature selection. In: WI 2017, pp. 654–661. ACM (2017)

5. Alharbi, A.S., Li, Y., Xu, Y.: An extended random-sets model for fusion-based text feature selection. In: Phung, D., Tseng, V.S., Webb, G.I., Ho, B., Ganji, M., Rashidi, L. (eds.) PAKDD 2018. LNCS (LNAI), vol. 10939, pp. 126–138. Springer, Cham (2018). https://doi.org/10.1007/978-3-319-93040-4_11

6. Bashar, M.A., Li, Y.: Random set to interpret topic models in terms of ontology concepts. In: Peng, W., Alahakoon, D., Li, X. (eds.) AI 2017. LNCS (LNAI), vol. 10400, pp. 237–249. Springer, Cham (2017). https://doi.org/10.1007/978-3-319-63004-5_19

7. Bendersky, M., Kurland, O.: Utilizing passage-based language models for document retrieval. In: Macdonald, C., Ounis, I., Plachouras, V., Ruthven, I., White, R.W. (eds.) ECIR 2008. LNCS, vol. 4956, pp. 162–174. Springer, Heidelberg (2008). https://doi.org/10.1007/978-3-540-78646-7_17

8. Blei, D., Carin, L., Dunson, D.: Probabilistic topic models. IEEE SPM **27**(6), 55–65 (2010)

9. Blei, D.M., Ng, A.Y., Jordan, M.I.: Latent dirichlet allocation. JMLR **3**, 993–1022 (2003)

10. Buckley, C., Voorhees, E.M.: Evaluating evaluation measure stability. In: SIGIR 2000, pp. 33–40. ACM (2000)

11. Callan, J.P.: Passage-level evidence in document retrieval. In: Croft, B.W., van Rijsbergen, C.J. (eds.) SIGIR 1994, pp. 302–310. Springer, London (1994). https://doi.org/10.1007/978-1-4471-2099-5_31

12. Gao, Y., Xu, Y., Li, Y.: Pattern-based topics for document modelling in information filtering. IEEE TKDE **27**(6), 1629–1642 (2015)

13. Goutsias, J., Mahler, R.P., Nguyen, H.T.: Random Sets: Theory and Applications, vol. 97. Springer, Heidelberg (2012)

14. Hearst, M.A., Dumais, S.T., Osuna, E., Platt, J., Scholkopf, B.: Support vector machines. IEEE Intell. Syst. Appl. **13**(4), 18–28 (1998)

15. Hofmann, T.: Unsupervised learning by probabilistic latent semantic analysis. Mach. Learn. **42**(1–2), 177–196 (2001)

16. Joachims, T.: Optimizing search engines using clickthrough data. In: KDD 2002, pp. 133–142. ACM (2002)

17. Kaszkiel, M., Zobel, J.: Passage retrieval revisited. In: ACM SIGIR Forum, vol. 31, pp. 178–185. ACM (1997)

18. Kaszkiel, M., Zobel, J.: Effective ranking with arbitrary passages. JAIST **52**(4), 344–364 (2001)

19. Kruse, R., Schwecke, E., Heinsohn, J.: Uncertainty and Vagueness in Knowledge Based Systems: Numerical Methods. Springer, Heidelberg (2012)

20. Lan, M., Tan, C.L., Su, J., Lu, Y.: Supervised and traditional term weighting methods for automatic text categorization. IEEE TPAMI **31**(4), 721–735 (2009)

21. Lewis, D.D., Yang, Y., Rose, T.G., Li, F.: Rcv1: a new benchmark collection for text categorization research. JMLR **5**(Apr), 361–397 (2004)

22. Li, Y.: Extended random sets for knowledge discovery in information systems. In: Wang, G., Liu, Q., Yao, Y., Skowron, A. (eds.) RSFDGrC 2003. LNCS (LNAI), vol. 2639, pp. 524–532. Springer, Heidelberg (2003). https://doi.org/10.1007/3-540-39205-X_87

23. Li, Y., Algarni, A., Albathan, M., Shen, Y., Bijaksana, M.A.: Relevance feature discovery for text mining. IEEE TKDE **27**(6), 1656–1669 (2015)

24. Li, Y., Algarni, A., Zhong, N.: Mining positive and negative patterns for relevance feature discovery. In: KDD 2010, pp. 753–762. ACM (2010)

25. Liu, X., Croft, W.B.: Passage retrieval based on language models. In: CIKM 2002, pp. 375–382. ACM (2002)

26. Manning, C.D., Raghavan, P., Schütze, H.: Introduction to Information Retrieval. Cambridge University Press, Cambridge (2008)
27. Molchanov, I.: Theory of Random Sets. Springer, Heidelberg (2006). https://doi. org/10.1007/1-84628-150-4
28. Moschitti, A., Basili, R.: Complex linguistic features for text classification: a comprehensive study. In: McDonald, S., Tait, J. (eds.) ECIR 2004. LNCS, vol. 2997, pp. 181–196. Springer, Heidelberg (2004). https://doi.org/10.1007/978-3-540-24752-4_14
29. Porter, M.F.: An algorithm for suffix stripping. Program **14**(3), 130–137 (1980)
30. Robertson, S., Zaragoza, H.: The Probabilistic Relevance Framework: BM25 and Beyond. Now Publishers Inc., Hanove (2009)
31. Robertson, S.E., Soboroff, I.: The TREC 2002 filtering track report. In: TREC, vol. 2002, p. 5 (2002)
32. Rocchio, J.J.: Relevance feedback in information retrieval. In: The Smart Retrieval System (1971)
33. Scott, S., Matwin, S.: Feature engineering for text classification. In: ICML, vol. 99, pp. 379–388. Citeseer (1999)
34. Song, Q., Ni, J., Wang, G.: A fast clustering-based feature subset selection algorithm for high-dimensional data. IEEE TKDE **25**(1), 1–14 (2013)
35. Tao, X., Li, Y., Zhong, N.: A personalized ontology model for web information gathering. IEEE TKDE **23**(4), 496–511 (2011)
36. Tibshirani, R.: Regression shrinkage and selection via the lasso. J. R. Stat. Soc. 267–288 (1996)
37. Zhao, Z., Wang, L., Liu, H., Ye, J.: On similarity preserving feature selection. IEEE TKDE **25**(3), 619–632 (2013)
38. Zhong, N., Li, Y., Wu, S.T.: Effective pattern discovery for text mining. IEEE TKDE **24**(1), 30–44 (2012)

Multiple-Task Learning and Knowledge Transfer Using Generative Adversarial Capsule Nets

Ancheng Lin[1], Jun Li[2], Lujuan Zhang[3], Zhenyuan Ma[3(✉)], and Weiqi Luo[4]

[1] School of Computer Sciences,
Guangdong Polytechnic Normal University, Guangzhou, China
cenbylin@163.com
[2] School of Software and Centre for Artificial Intelligence,
Faculty of Engineering and Information Technology,
University of Technology Sydney, POBox 123, Broadway, NSW 2007, Australia
Jun.Li@uts.edu.au
[3] School of Mathematics and System Sciences,
Guangdong Polytechnic Normal University, Guangzhou, China
ljzhangkan@163.com, mazy@gpnu.edu.cn
[4] College of Information Science and Technology,
Jinan University, Guangzhou, China
lwq@jnu.edu.cn

Abstract. It is common that practical data has multiple attributes of interest. For example, a picture can be characterized in terms of its content, e.g. the categories of the objects in the picture, and in the meanwhile the image style such as photo-realistic or artistic is also relevant. This work is motivated by taking advantage of all available sources of information about the data, including those not directly related to the target of analytics.

We propose an explicit and effective knowledge representation and transfer architecture for image analytics by employing Capsules for deep neural network training based on the generative adversarial nets (GAN). The adversarial scheme help discover capsule-representation of data with different semantic meanings in respective dimensions of the capsules. The data representation includes one subset of variables that are particularly specialized for the target task – by eliminating information about the irrelevant aspects. We theoretically show the elimination by mixing conditional distributions of the represented data. Empirical evaluations show the propose method is effective for both standard transfer-domain recognition tasks and zero-shot transfer.

Supported by National Natural Science Foundation of China (Grant No. 61877029); Science and Technology Program of Guangzhou (No. 201704030133), "A Knowledge-Connection and Cognitive-Style based Mining System for Massive Open Online Courses and Its Application" (UTS Project Code: PRO16-1300).

T. Mitrovic et al. (Eds.): AI 2018, LNAI 11320, pp. 669–680, 2018.
https://doi.org/10.1007/978-3-030-03991-2_60

1 Introduction

This work presents a image data representation framework based on the generative adversarial nets (GANs) [1] using Capsule network [2]. We are concerned with multiple-task learning scenarios, which is known to be beneficial to the particular target task [3]. The data are represented using entities discovered by Capsule Nets (CapsNet) [2] with the capsule elements being focused on different tasks. In practical image analytics, it is common that the samples are associated with multiple aspects. These aspects may or may not be the direct target of learning.

However, all attributes of a sample convey information and the information may be indirectly connected with the task target. For example, an image of a hand-written digit can has a tag of its identity as a digit "0~9". It can also be described by aspects such as "data source (URL or dataset)", "writing orientation: tilting left/right", etc. Those aspects may not be directly connected to the identity of the digit, but contribute to the raw observation of the pixels together with the identity. Our motivation is that the fact that some attribute affects the observation but is *not* the target is informative and can be helpful to the prediction of the target.

To classify the image content to "0~9" regardless the source of the data, it is likely to benefit the classification if we can (i) collect images from multiple data sources to make a richer dataset and (ii) represent samples from the different sources in such a way that the knowledge about the image identity (digit 0~9) and the image source are separated. In particular, we want to represent a sample x as z, where z has two groups of variables z^1 and z^2. In z^1, the data source information has been eliminated: it is difficult to find out where x comes from by inspecting z^1, but all information related to the identity of the data is preserved in z^1; z^2 is complementary to z^1, which is informative to the data source, but not to the identity.

Within the wide spectrum of transfer learning techniques [4–7], our focus is on data representation assisted by auxiliary tasks. We propose a adversarial deep capsule network scheme that represents data explicitly for transferring knowledge of multiple attributes. Given the task of classifying data with respect to one primary target aspect and taking into account of m auxiliary attributes, the framework contains one capsule net-based data encoder (the "generator" following convention in adversarial nets) and $m + 1$ discriminators. The generator produce capsule data representations that are fed to the discriminators, where one specialized group is particularly fit for the primary task. The generative adversarial framework is named MCGAN, due to it nature of multiple-task learning and capsule-based data representation.

In the rest of this paper, we discuss some related works in Sect. 2. Section 3 presents the MCGAN model. Section 4 reports empirical evaluation. Section 5 concludes the paper.

2 Background

The past decade has witnessed the renaissance of neural networks as generic function approximator in statistical learning and machine intelligence [8]. Effective training methods, massive data and heavily parallel and high speed computation hardware have catalyzed successful application of deep architectures of neural networks in a great variety of application areas [9–16]. Nonetheless, as new and increasingly more complex architectures keep being developed and ever more powerful high-performance computational facilities are built, the construction of large-scale annotated data to tune the complex models can hardly keep pace with the demand [17]. The need for the capability of sharing knowledge among different tasks has never been greater. Zheng et al. [18] investigated several empirical issues related to image search and classification in transfer learning for deep convolutional neural networks and found that simple combination of pooled features extracted across various CNN layers is effective for knowledge transfer.

More related to this work, in [7], Shen et al. proposed to adopt the generative adversarial nets (GAN) framework [1] to construct two-stage data analytic model for knowledge transfer between two domains. They trained an deep neural encoder to represent data, while employ one adversarial discriminator to make the encoder represent data in two domains indiscriminately. This work shares the motivation of making the theoretical advantage of the distribution metrics computed by the adversarial discriminator to improve data representation. However, the method proposed in this work naturally adopt multiple relevant or irrelevant aspects explicitly or implicitly annotated for knowledge transfer, which subsumes dual-domain data classification problem addressed in [7] as a special case.

As mentioned above, the theoretical foundation of the work is the link between distribution metrics and the adversarial discriminative net, which is due to Arjovsky et al. [19]. The Wasserstein distance motivated GAN has greatly improved the stability of training in GAN framework, which has been widely used in multiple application areas [1,6,20,21]. In Fu et al. [22], a transfer learning framework, MATGAN, has been proposed to address a similar problem. However, in MATGAN traditional deep neural networks are used in the generator G to generate a single data representation, while we use capsules to simultaneously generate multiple representations for all tasks.

CapsNet [2] represents an alternative visual information processing mechanism that addressing some above mentioned issues. The neurons are divided into small groups in each network layer, known as *capsules*. The capsules correspond to concepts in different levels of abstraction during the process of parsing visual information. The cross-layer association and the activation status of the capsules represent semantic analysis of the image data. Recently, CapsNet has undergone some developments such as Matrix Capsules [23] and has been employed in new application domains such as text classification [24].

3   Model

3.1   Multi-task Data Representation

We consider data with multiple categorical attributes. The data are distributed in the space $\mathcal{X} \times \mathcal{Y}_0 \times \mathcal{Y}_1 \times \mathcal{Y}_2 \times \cdots \times \mathcal{Y}_m$, where $\mathcal{X}$ is the space of observations and $\mathcal{Y}_0$ represent the primary target, $\mathcal{Y}_1, \ldots, \mathcal{Y}_m$ are m auxiliary tasks. For the convenience of discussion, we consider binary prediction tasks in this section, i.e. $\mathcal{Y}_i = \{0, 1\}$, and will discuss later that the binary setting does not harm generality. The ultimate goal is to learn a strong predictor on $\mathcal{Y}_0$. MCGAN adopts adversarial training to learn $m + 1$ groups of variables $\mathcal{Z}_0, \mathcal{Z}_1, \ldots, \mathcal{Z}_m$ to represent $\mathcal{X}$. Each group $\mathcal{Z}_i$ is focused on the information in $\mathcal{X}$ with respect to the corresponding goal $\mathcal{Y}_i$ while eliminating the information about other attributes $\{\mathcal{Y}_j\}_{j \neq i}^m$. Consider the affect on the classification task by one particular transfer attribute $\mathcal{Y}_1$. The motivation is that in an ideal representation, the distribution of $\mathcal{Z}$ with respect to $Y_1 = 0$ should be indistinguishable from the distribution of $\mathcal{Z}$ with respect to $Y_1 = 1$. Then $\mathcal{Z}$ is a form that mixes the subsets of $Y_1 = 0$ and $Y_1 = 1$, which integrates the knowledge about the target attribute $\mathcal{Y}_0$ represented by the samples in both subsets.

Formally, a data representor is a map G, $\mathcal{X} \overset{G}{\to} \mathcal{Z}$, and $\mathcal{Z}$ is the *representation space*. Given a probability distribution on $\mathcal{X}$, G induces a corresponding distribution on $\mathcal{Z}$. We consider the conditional distribution on $\mathcal{X}$ with respect to $\mathcal{Y}_i$, $X|Y_i = \xi$, where X and Y_i are variables in $\mathcal{X}$ and $\mathcal{Y}_i$, respectively, and $\xi \in \{0, 1\}$. The G-induced conditional distribution on $\mathcal{Z}$ is

$$P_{X|Y_i=\xi}(x) \overset{G}{\to} P^G_{Z|Y_i=\xi}(z) := \int_x P_{X|Y_i=\xi}(x)\delta(G(x), z)dx \qquad (1)$$

where the delta function $\delta(x, y) = 1$ if $x = y$ and 0 otherwise. For simplified math, we denote $P^G_{Z|Y_i=\{0,1\}}$ as $g^i_{\{0,1\}}$. Let $I(p, q)$ represent some distance metric between distributions. We can formulate the objective of being discriminative on $\mathcal{Y}_i$ and invariant to $\{\mathcal{Y}_j\}_{j \neq i}^m$ by

$$\min_G \left\{ \sum_{j=0, j \neq i}^m I(g^j_0, g^j_1) \; - \; I(g^i_0, g^i_1) \right\} \qquad (2)$$

where G is the data representor. Note that to train an entire framework of MCGAN, there are totally $m + 1$ equations in the form of (2), corresponding to tasks $i = 0, \ldots, m$.

In MCGAN, the metric I is the Wasserstein-1 (Earth-Mover, EM) distance

$$I \leftarrow W(p, q) := \inf_{\pi \in \prod(p, q)} \mathbf{E}_{(z, z') \sim \pi} \left[\|z - z'\| \right] \qquad (3)$$

where $\prod(p, q)$ represents the set of all joint distributions $\pi(z, z')$ with consistent marginal distributions: $\int_{z'} \pi(z, z')dz' = p(z)$ and $\int_z \pi(z, z')dz = q(z')$.

Kantorovich-Rubinstein duality [25] provides a feasible approach of computing the Wasserstein distance (3),

$$W(p,q) = \sup_{\|f\|_L \leq 1} \mathbf{E}_{z \sim p}[f(z)] - \mathbf{E}_{z' \sim q}[f(z')] \tag{4}$$

where f is any 1-Lipschitz function $\mathcal{Z} \to \mathbb{R}$. Combining (1–4), i.e. taking W as I and substituting g_0^j and g_1^j for p and q, the optimal data representation problem (1) can be formulated as a minimax game

$$\min_{G,D^i} \max_{\{D^j\}_{j=0,j\neq i}^m} \left\{ \sum_{j=0,j\neq i}^m \mathbf{E}_{x,y_j=1}[D^j\big(G(x)\big)] - \mathbf{E}_{x,y_j=0}[D^j\big(G(x)\big)] \right.$$
$$\left. + \mathbf{E}_{x,y_i=0}\left[D^i\big(G(x)\big)\right] - \mathbf{E}_{x,y_i=1}\left[D^i\big(G(x)\big)\right] \right\} \tag{5}$$

The discriminators $\{D^j\}_{j=0}^m$ are the 1-Lipschitz functions f in (4), which are implemented using deep neural networks. The data representation $G(x)$ within the expectation $\mathbf{E}_{x,y_j=\{0,1\}}[\cdot]$ realizes the expectation over the induced conditional distribution in the representation space $g_{\{0,1\}}^j$. As above mentioned, there are totally $m+1$ minimax games as defined in (5) for $m+1$ groups of data representation. The details of G and the representations are introduced in the following subsection.

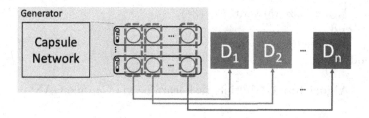

Fig. 1. Structure of the MCGAN Framework. The figure shows how the final layer capsules are organized into multiple groups of variables for data representation (boxes of broken lines in different colors). The discriminators take respective representation variable groups from the generator (shown in corresponding colors). (Color figure online)

3.2 Networks

Figure 1 sketches the overall structure of a MCGAN framework. We employ deep neural networks as the discriminators D and capsule networks for the generator G. The discriminator network D has a standard linear deep neural network structure. We propose a novel data representation scheme by employing capsule net [2] for the generator network G. The capsule nets transform an image into a number of vectors (capsules). The capsules embody semantic entities in the image, where the magnitude of the vector indicates the presence of the entity and the elements are specifying parameters of the entity [2]. The generator capsule net and the discriminator deep nets are chosen to suit particular applications. Example nets are sketched in a later figure in Sect. 4, Fig. 3.

To generate data representation specialized for different tasks, we make the final layer capsules $(m + 1)$-dimensional. Using respective dimensions in all the capsules, we can form data representation for the $m + 1$ tasks. For example, if in the final layer there are 64 capsules, and there are 2 auxiliary tasks plus the primary task, the final layer would contain 64×3 values. Taking the first dimension of the 64 capsules, we can have a 64D vector Z^1 as the data representation and will use Z^1 in the first minimax game as defined in (5). Similarly, the second/third minimax game is defined via Z^2/Z^3, which is collected taking the second/third dimension from each final layer capsule. Algorithm 1 lists the learning procedure of the networks under the proposed capsule-based adversarial framework.

> **input** : G: parameters $\boldsymbol{\theta}$
> **input** : D^j: parameters $\boldsymbol{w}^j$, $j = 0, \ldots, m$
> **input** : samples $\{(X, y^0, y^1, \ldots, y^m)\} \sim \mathcal{X} \times \mathcal{Y}^0 \times \mathcal{Y}^1 \times \cdots \times \mathcal{Y}^m$
> **output**: $\boldsymbol{\theta}$, $\boldsymbol{w}^j$, $j = 0, \ldots, m$
> **begin**
> > **while** θ *not converged* **do**
> > > compute capsules by $G(X)$
> > > **for** $j \in \{0, \ldots, m\}$ **do**
> > > > make Z^j
> > > > maximize (5) w.r.t. $D^j_{\boldsymbol{w}^j}(Z^j)$
> > > **end**
> > > minimize (5) w.r.t. $G_\theta(X)$
> > **end**
> **end**

Algorithm 1. Multiple task learning via Capsule GAN

4   Experiments

In our experiment, we apply the proposed multiple-task-transfer capsule GAN (MCGAN) to perform *different* learning tasks on hand-written digit datasets. We use the MNIST [26] and the USPS [27] dataset. The tests are designed to illustrate our motivation of learning designated aspects of data and verify the proposed model is effective for the task.

Model Training

We have implemented MCGAN according to the framework structure as shown in Fig. 1 and performed training as Algorithm 1. To stabilize training of GAN, we follow the technique proposed in [28].

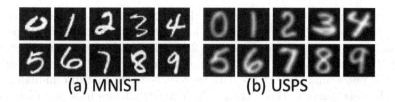

Fig. 2. Image samples from two hand-written datasets.

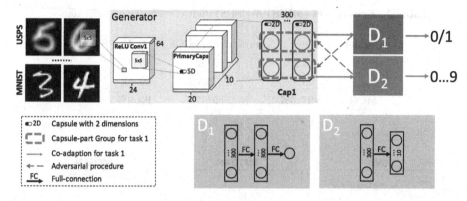

Fig. 3. Networks in MCGAN for handwritten digit recognition with data source transfer.

Effective Transfer with Capsule Nets

We first apply MCGANs on the commonly employed hand-written digit image recognition task. The test has been on two hand-written image datasets: MNIST and USPS. MNIST has 60,000 training/10,000 testing samples which are grayscale images. USPS has 7,291 grayscale images for training and 2,007 for testing. Figure 2 shows a few digit samples from both datasets.

As [22], we employ MCGANs and make advantage of its capability of transferring knowledge to classify images from two datasets using one data representation model. MCGANs are trained with respect to two kinds of objectives in this experiment. The first goal is to recognize the digits, "0~9". The second goal is to identify from which dataset an image is sampled. It is important to keep in mind that in practice the primary objective is semantic classification, i.e. the first goal of recognizing a digit to be one of "0~9". The auxiliary goal is introduced to assist training of the network, so a more reliable and versatile data representation can be found for the ultimate semantic recognition.

We construct the networks in MCGAN as shown in Fig. 3, which implements the framework introduced in Sect. 3.2 and displayed in Fig. 1. The representation net outputs a number of capsules for each data sample. As discussed in Sect. 3.1, the capsule representation is then re-organized into two groups, $H^{\{1,2\}}$. When H^1 is fed to discriminator D^1, D^1 is optimized to predict the digit identity $y \in \{0, \ldots, 9\}$. When H^2 is fed to D^1, the representations are formulated as non-informative samples for D^1's task, and the optimization objective is to confuse D^1 on H^2. Correspondingly, when H^2 is fed to discriminator D^2, D^2 predicts from which dataset a sample is drawn, 0 for MNIST and 1 for USPS. When H^1 is fed to D^2, the objective for H^1 is to be non-informative for D^2, which means H^1 should be indiscriminative to the data sources. Note the first discriminator D^1 is multi-class classifiers in this setting, which slightly differs from the formulation in Sect. 3 but does not change the fundamental architecture of MCGAN.

Table 1. Two-dataset (MNIST + USPS) digit classification performance

Mdoel	Overall accuracy	On MNIST	On USPS
CNN	75.2%	64.6%	85.9%
MATGAN	69.3%	79.5%	59.2%
MCGAN	**97.3%**	**98.7%**	**93.9%**

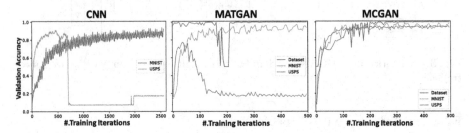

Fig. 4. Training processes on MNIST + USPS datasets. The figure shows three typical training process of CNN, MATGAN [22] and MCGAN on data from mixed two datasets of MNIST and USPS. The plots are optimization iteration steps versus model performance on *validation* data. When the training iterations exceeded certain numbers, both CNN and MATGAN had been dominated by MNIST and performed poorly on USPS.

Table 1 lists classification performance of MCGAN, standard CNN (similar to D^1) and a transfer framework using standard GAN, MATGAN [22]. The performance verifies the effectiveness of MCGAN. It is not surprising that GANs achieves superior performance over standard CNN considering the cross-dataset knowledge transfer. However, the performances of both MATGAN and CNN worth more investigation. In fact, we need to carefully tune the optimization, and adopt early stop using verification to prevent the training process of normal GAN from collapsing (despite employing the stabilizing technique for MATGAN [22]). With the training progressing, both MATGAN and CNN are seriously dominated by MNIST. However, the capsule nets have been remaining stable. A possible interpretation is that capsules can capture meaningful entities in the image and less prone to data source mixing. Figure 4 illustrates typical training processes for the three models.

Zero-Shot Transfer

MCGAN uses multiple groups of variables to represent data for distinctive prediction tasks. This design benefits transfer learning since the preceding layers must generate representation of the data that contains comprehensive information of all tasks. We test this attribute of MCGAN in this experiment where the network is required to classify new data population whose samples are unseen during the training. The experiment is also based on the MNIST + USPS datasets. Specifically, in addition to the auxiliary task of identifying the data source, we introduce geometric transformations of the images and each image has equal chance $(1/3)$ to be rotated by $\{-\frac{\pi}{4}, 0, +\frac{\pi}{4}\}$ as shown in Fig. 5. The challenge of zero-shot learning is posed in the following scheme. During the training stage, the models are given examples of MNIST *with* rotation and USPS *without* rotation, while during test, the models are required to classify USPS samples *with* rotation. Note during test, the models are only asked to produce a prediction of "0~9" about the digit in the image, and has no access to information about the data source of the image (USPS/MNIST) or whether/how the image has been rotated.

We address the challenge by explicitly modelling the geometrical rotation in MCGAN, and train an additional digit classifier using the penultimate layer capsules for data representation. The zero-shot transfer classifier is not to be confused with the digit identity classifier as a discriminator in MCGAN. More specifically, MCGANs are trained with respect to one more objective in this experiment. The first and the second goals are to recognize the digits as "0~9" and from MNIST or USPS as in the previous experiment. The third (new) goal is to estimate the rotation an image may undergo. The networks in MCGAN is similar to that is shown in Fig. 3. Note that the data representation for the final classifier in this experiment is not from the final layer of capsules, but from the penultimate capsule layer in the generator net.

During training MCGAN generates three groups of representation $H^{\{1,2,3\}}$ for three discriminators $D^{\{1,2,3\}}$, where the new D^3 outputs the prediction of the orientation of the images as 3 different rotation angles $\rho \in \{-\frac{\pi}{4}, 0, +\frac{\pi}{4}\}$. The objective function has totally 3×3 components:

$$+D^1(h^1) \; -D^1(h^2) \; -D^1(h^3)$$
$$-D^2(h^1) \; +D^2(h^2) \; -D^2(h^3)$$
$$-D^3(h^1) \; -D^3(h^2) \; +D^3(h^3)$$

where $h^{\{1,2,3\}}$ are instances of the variables $H^{\{1,2,3\}}$. The symbols indicate their respective contribution to the training objective. For example, h^1 should be a group of features that is distinctive with respect to the digits "0~9" and helpful to the first task $(+D^1(h^1))$, but invariant to the dataset and rotations $(-D^2(h^1)$ and $-D^3(h^1))$.

Table 2 shows the classification results on the rotated USPS data using the special classifier trained on MCGAN-generated representations, as well as standard CNN classifier fit to the same set of training samples as used by MCGAN. MCGAN achieved significant advantage in this zero-shot transfer task while

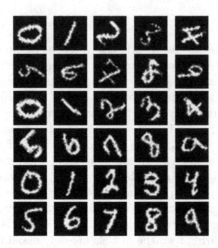

Fig. 5. Transformed hand-written image samples.

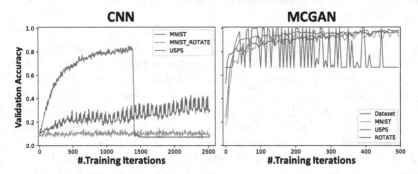

Fig. 6. Training processes on rotated MNIST + USPS datasets. The figure shows two typical training process of CNN and MCGAN on the zero-shot training task. The plots show classification accuracy on validation data (similar to Fig. 4). Note the classification tasks are different in standard CNN and those in MCGAN. MCGAN has auxiliary tasks of (i) classifying datasets (USPS/MNIST) and (ii) classifying rotations ($\{\pm\frac{\pi}{4}, 0\}$).

Table 2. Zero-shot classification on rotated USPS

Mdoel	On rotated USPS
CNN	13.4%
MCGAN	**72.6%**

CNN has failed to learn effective prediction model for data it has not seen. As aforementioned, MCGAN has also stabler training process than CNN on this task (Fig. 6).

5   Conclusion

We employ deep capsule nets to construct a knowledge transfer framework based on GAN. The proposed multitask capsule GAN (MCGAN) produces respective data representations for multiple tasks, and in the meanwhile achieve knowledge transfer from auxiliary tasks to improve the primary prediction task. Theoretically, we show that the data representor in MCGAN makes the representations of the data conditioned on the irrelevant aspects similar to each other, using the theory on the Wasserstein-1 distribution distances between populations produced by deep neural networks trained via an adversarial scheme [19]. Empirical study shows the capsule nets in MCGAN improve both model performance and training process.

References

1. Goodfellow, I.J., et al.: Generative adversarial nets. In: NIPS, pp. 2672–2680 (2014)
2. Sabour, S., Frosst, N., Hinton, G.E.: Dynamic routing between capsules. In: NIPS, pp. 3859–3869 (2017)
3. Odena, A., Olah, C., Shlens, J.: Conditional image synthesis with auxiliary classifier GANs. In: ICML, pp. 2642–2651 (2017)
4. Pan, S.J., Yang, Q.: A survey on transfer learning. IEEE Trans. Knowl. Data Eng. **22**(10), 1345–1359 (2010)
5. Long, M., Wang, J., Ding, G., Sun, J., Yu, P.S.: Transfer feature learning with joint distribution adaptation. In: ICCV, pp. 2200–2207 (2013)
6. Zhu, J., Park, T., Isola, P., Efros, A.A.: Unpaired image-to-image translation using cycle-consistent adversarial networks. In: ICCV, pp. 2242–2251 (2017)
7. Shen, J., Qu, Y., Zhang, W., Yu, Y.: Adversarial representation learning for domain adaptation, CoRR, abs/1707.01217 (2017)
8. Hinton, G.E., Salakhutdinov, R.R.: Reducing the dimensionality of data with neural networks. Science **313**(5786), 504–507 (2006)
9. Krizhevsky, A., Sutskever, I., Hinton, G.E.: Imagenet classification with deep convolutional neural networks. In: NIPS, pp. 1106–1114 (2012)
10. Dahl, G.E., Yu, D., Deng, L., Acero, A.: Context-dependent pre-trained deep neural networks for large-vocabulary speech recognition. IEEE Trans. Audio Speech Lang. Process. **20**(1), 30–42 (2012)
11. Zen, H., Senior, A.W., Schuster, M.: Statistical parametric speech synthesis using deep neural networks. In: ICASSP, pp. 7962–7966 (2013)
12. Jia, K., Gong, S.: Multi-modal tensor face for simultaneous super-resolution and recognition. In: ICCV, pp. 1683–1690 (2005)
13. Jia, K., Tao, D., Gao, S., Xu, X.: Improving training of deep neural networks via singular value bounding. In: CVPR, pp. 3994–4002 (2017)
14. Abdulnabi, A.H., Wang, G., Lu, J., Jia, K.: Multi-task CNN model for attribute prediction. IEEE Trans. Multimed. **17**(11), 1949–1959 (2015)
15. Tang, Z., Wang, D., Pan, Y., Zhang, Z.: Knowledge transfer pre-training, CoRR, abs/1506.02256 (2015)
16. Wang, H., Nie, F., Huang, H., Ding, C.H.Q.: Dyadic transfer learning for cross-domain image classification. In: ICCV, pp. 551–556 (2011)
17. LeCun, Y., Bengio, Y., Hinton, G.: Deep learning. Nature **521**(7553), 436 (2015)

18. Zheng, L., Zhao, Y., Wang, S., Wang, J., Tian, Q.: Good practice in CNN feature transfer, CoRR, abs/1604.00133 (2016)
19. Arjovsky, M., Chintala, S., Bottou, L.: Wasserstein GAN, CoRR, abs/1701.07875 (2017)
20. Chen, X., Duan, Y., Houthooft, R., Schulman, J., Sutskever, I., Abbeel, P.: Info-gan: interpretable representation learning by information maximizing generative adversarial nets. In: NIPS, pp. 2172–2180 (2016)
21. Choi, Y., Choi, M., Kim, M., Ha, J., Kim, S., Choo, J.: Stargan: unified generative adversarial networks for multi-domain image-to-image translation, CoRR, abs/1711.09020 (2017)
22. Fu, L., et al.: Utilizing information from task-independent aspects via GAN-assisted knowledge transfer. In: IJCNN (2018)
23. Hinton, G.E., Sabour, S., Frosst, N.: Matrix capsules with EM routing (2018)
24. Zhao, W., Ye, J., Yang, M., Lei, Z., Zhang, S., Zhao, Z.: Investigating capsule networks with dynamic routing for text classification, CoRR, abs/1804.00538 (2018)
25. Villani, C.: Optimal Transport: Old and New. Grundlehren der mathematischen Wissenschaften, vol. 338. Springer, Heidelberg (2008). https://doi.org/10.1007/978-3-540-71050-9
26. Cortes, C., LeCun, Y., Burges, C.J.: The MNIST database of handwritten digits (1998)
27. Hull, J.J.: A database for handwritten text recognition research. IEEE Trans. Pattern Anal. Mach. Intell. **16**(5), 550–554 (1994)
28. Gulrajani, I., Ahmed, F., Arjovsky, M., Dumoulin, V., Courville, A.C.: Improved training of wasserstein GANs. In: NIPS, pp. 5769–5779 (2017)

Link Prediction via Factorization Machines

Lile Li and Wei Liu[✉]

School of Software, Faculty of Engineering and Information Technology,
University of Technology Sydney, Sydney, Australia
Lile.Li@student.uts.edu.au, Wei.Liu@uts.edu.au

Abstract. Link prediction is the problem of predicting the existence of edges in a network. The link prediction problem is a fundamental research problem in graph mining and has numerous applications in social networks, bioinformatics, e-commerce, etc. A major challenge of link prediction problems is handling the fact that real-world networks are becoming extremely large. The large network size leads to huge sparsity in the network's adjacency matrix which most existing link prediction methods (such as matrix factorization) rely on. Moreover, when networks become very large, there exists a non-trivial link imbalance problem where the numbers of known present and known absent links are significantly different. Such sparsity and imbalance issues significantly impact and decrease the performance of existing link prediction methods. To address these challenges, in this research we propose a Balanced Factorization Machine (BFM) which performs link predictions on very sparse network via learning interactions among nodes and edges of the network in a supervised learning setting. Through extensive experiments on real-world network data sets, we show that our BFM method significantly outperforms other existing link prediction methods.

1 Introduction

Link prediction is a fundamental research problem in mining of graphs and networks. It has made wide and important impacts in social network analysis [9], bioinformatics [2], and e-commerce [8]. A major question that link prediction answers is how to estimate the structure of a network that is partially known: given the presence or absence of known links, how to predict the presence/absence of unknown ones? Solutions to this question can bring forward practical applications such as predicting following-behaviour in Twitter, suggesting friendship in Facebook, and inferring unknown interactions among proteins in protein-to-protein interaction networks [10].

Link prediction has been mostly viewed in the literature as an unsupervised learning problem and has been studied via different unsupervised methods including neighborhood-based approaches [10], matrix factorization [14], coupled tensor factorization [5], etc. But these unsupervised learning approaches are closely based on graph structure measures and adjacency matrices, while

© Springer Nature Switzerland AG 2018
T. Mitrovic et al. (Eds.): AI 2018, LNAI 11320, pp. 681–691, 2018.
https://doi.org/10.1007/978-3-030-03991-2_61

their performance have been shown to be limited to that of similarity based approaches [20]. There also has been research work that views link prediction as a supervised learning method [4,12]. This type of methods particularly focuses on deriving and extracting features from the graph data, and then use the extracted features for link prediction.

The existing supervised and unsupervised models are both challenged when dealing with very big networks. When the network becomes very large, the size of the adjacency matrix of the network increases exponentially to the increase of the number of nodes. This makes the adjacency matrix extremely sparse which non-trivially decreases the performance of unsupervised learning models [10]. Besides, the huge sparsity also means that there is significantly more known absent links than present ones. In other words, if we represent a network graph by $G = \{V, E\}$ and $E \in \{0, 1, ?\}$, where V denotes all vertices (nodes), E denotes all edges (links), 0 denotes a known absent link, 1 denotes a known present link, and ? denotes an unknown link whose status is to be predicted, then the huge sparsity means there are significantly more unknown ? entries than known 1 and 0 entries. Moreover, since the 0 and 1 entries are taken as class labels in supervised link prediction approaches, the frequently observed scenarios of having significantly more 0 entries than 1 ones result in a significant class imbalance issue which downgrades the performance of existing supervised learning approaches [23].

To address the above challenges, in this research we proposed an effective link prediction model called Balanced Factorization Machines (BFM). The BFM takes all pair-wise interactions among nodes, links, and all their properties into the training processes. It is a supervised learning model that is not reliant on the network's adjacency matrix and can handle network data with huge sparsity. Moreover, we design a balanced loss function for the BFM which is robust to the distribution of known link labels. Specifically, our main contributions in this paper are the following:

- We propose a factorization machine based model, named Balanced Factorization Machines (BFM), to address the sparsity issue in link prediction problems in a supervised learning approach. The BFM method models all interactions among nodes, edges, and their associated properties using both linear and second-order expressions among features, which ensures that the BFM can well handle the sparsity of the network.
- We design a quadratic-mean-based loss function for the BFM model to address the link label imbalance issue. The loss function of BFM is designed insensitive to distributions of labels in the training data and is thus robust to the imbalanced distribution of known links.
- We perform evaluations on several real-world network data sets. Results from our experiments demonstrate that the BFM model is significantly more accurate on link prediction tasks in comparisons to existing other models.

To the best of our knowledge, this paper is the first research that uses factorization machines to solve the link prediction problem and to address its inherent class label imbalance problem.

The structure of the rest of the paper is as follows. We provide a review of related work in Sect. 2. Section 3 introduces the formulation and design of the proposed BFM model. We empirically evaluate our model and analyze the experiment outcomes in Sect. 4. In Sect. 5, we provide conclusions of this research with our plan for future work.

2   Literature Review

In this section, we provide a review of related work from the perspectives of link prediction and factorization machines respectively.

2.1   Link Prediction

Link prediction has become an attractive field in graph and network mining [13]. Since many real-world data can be formulated as networks, the estimation of unknown connections among nodes in a network can provide a comprehensive understanding of the studied problem, and thus provide significant values to real-world applications. One type of solutions in link predictions is the neighbourhood-based approach [1,10]. In such approaches, similarity-based methods are used where it is assumed the nodes tend to have connections with other nodes with the highest similarity scores. More advanced approaches, such as factorization-based method [10,14], used the principles of collaborative filtering to make link predictions, which is a similar approach as building recommendation systems. In these methods, latent factors are learned from the adjacency matrix of a network, and the predictions of links are made by a product of the latent factors. Since these factorization based methods heavily rely on the adjacency matrix, their performance is impacted when the network becomes very large and the adjacency matrix becomes highly sparse. Another type of approach for link prediction is classification-based methods where the classification is for the two labels: presence and absence of the link. In the work of [1], different classification algorithms are empirically studied with respect to their effectiveness on link prediction. Besides, directed networks are particularly studied in [4] where random forests are found to be the most effective among other alternative ensemble methods. However, these classification-based methods all face a common challenge of class imbalance, as in real-world settings there is always extremely more absence than presence of known links [23].

2.2   Factorization Machines

Factorization machines (FM) [17] are a type of supervised learning model that improves linear classification models by incorporating second-order feature interactions into the modelling processes. After the initial publication of FMs, many researchers have improved the model theoretically from several perspectives. To integrate context information into modelling processes, [18] proposed Context-aware FMs which can integrate contextual data and user it to improve the training outcome. Besides, although FM was initially introduced as a method for building recommendation systems, it has also been applied to many other domains such as Click-Through Rate (CTR) prediction [7]. Specifically, the CTR prediction is made via an extended FM model named Field-aware Factorization Machines (FFMs).

Despite of the improvements and applications of FMs, the class imbalance problems for FM has not been addressed. Since the link prediction problem usually faces huge imbalance of class labels, the imbalance problem will nontrivially affect the performance of FM. In the next section, we explain how we design our new model to address the class imbalance problem.

3   Balanced Factorization Machines

In this section, we introduce how we model link prediction as a supervised learning problem that can be addressed by factorization machines. We will also introduce our Balanced Factorization Machine (BFM) model that is capable of handling class imbalance problems.

3.1   Feature Modelling for Link Prediction

To make link prediction a supervised learning problem, we extract several types of properties from the network and use them as feature vectors. In our modelling, each data sample represents a known absent or present link from the network where the label y is 0 or 1 respectively. The feature vector of a data sample is comprised of the properties associated with the corresponding link, such as which nodes the link connects, the degrees of the nodes, and what other nodes that the link's two ends connect to. An illustration of our feature modelling is presented in Fig. 1. In this figure, the first two blocks of features indicate the two nodes (denoted by N_1 and N_2) of each link, the third block stores the distance between the two nodes (such as random walk distance) or the weight of the link, the next two blocks are the degrees of N_1 and N_2, and the last two blocks have the other nodes that N_1 and N_2 are respectively connected to.

Our feature modelling is capable of handling many different types of link properties. When the network is directed, N_1 is modelled as the source node and N_2 is the target node. Our model also integrates in-degrees and out-degrees of nodes on directed network by adding extra in-degree and out-degree columns to the formulation.

3.2   Our Proposed BFM Model

The creation of factorization machines can be linked back to the fundamental model of linear supervised learners. Using bold font $\mathbf{x}$ to denote a data sample, $x_i(i \in \{1, ..., n\})$ to denote the ith feature value of $\mathbf{x}$, y to denote labels, and D

Feature vector x																				Link Label y	
0	1	0	...	1	0	0	...	11	2	16	0	0	1	...	0	0	0	...		1	$y^{(1)}$
1	0	0	...	0	1	0	...	25	9	6	1	1	0	...	0	0	1	...		0	$y^{(2)}$
...	...	...	...	...	...	...	...	...	...	...	...	...	...	...	...	...	...	...		...	
0	0	1	...	0	0	1	...	20	11	8	1	1	1	...	1	0	0	...		0	$y^{(n)}$
#1	#2	#3	...	#1	#2	#3	...	Dist/ Weight	N_1 Degree	N_2 Degree	#1	#2	#3	...	#1	#2	#3	...			
Node 1 (N_1)				Node 2 (N_2)							Other nodes linked to N_1				Other nodes linked to N_2						

Fig. 1. Network properties extracted as feature vectors. Each row represents a known presence (i.e., label y = 1) or absence (i.e., y = 0) of links. Node 1 and node 2 present the two ends of each link. When the network is directed, node 1 is the source and node 2 is the target (from node 1 pointing to node 2). When the network is undirected, the nodes 1 and 2 are arbitrarily two ends of each link.

to denote the training data, the formulation of a typical linear learning model is:

$$\min_{\mathbf{w}} \; Sqrt\{\frac{1}{|D|}\sum_{\forall x \in D}(y-\mathbf{w}^T\mathbf{x})^2\} + R(\mathbf{w}) \tag{1}$$

where $|D|$ represents the size of training data, $\mathbf{w}$ is the weight vector to be learned, $R(\mathbf{w})$ is the regularizer for $\mathbf{w}$ (such as L_2 norm), and $Sqrt$ represents the square root operation. Using the same notation, the optimization problem for a degree-2 polynomial learning model can be formulated as:

$$\min_{\mathbf{v}} \; Sqrt\{\frac{1}{|D|}\sum_{\forall x \in D}(y-\sum_{i,j}^{n}v_{i,j}x_i x_j)^2\} + R'(\mathbf{v}) \tag{2}$$

where $\mathbf{v}$ is a weight matrix of size $n \times n$, $v_{i,j}$ is an element of $\mathbf{v}$ at its ith row and jth column, and $R'(\mathbf{v})$ is the regularizer for $\mathbf{v}$ (such as matrix Frobenius norm). Factorization machines further improved the above two models by taking both linear and second-order feature interactions into its modelling process. Using the same notation above, factorization machines can be modelled as follows:

$$\min_{\mathbf{w},\mathbf{v}} \; Sqrt\{\frac{1}{|D|}\sum_{\forall x \in D}(y-(w_0+\sum_{i=1}^{n}w_i x_i+\sum_{i,j}^{n}<v_i,v_j>x_i x_j))^2\}+R(\mathbf{w})+R'(\mathbf{v}) \tag{3}$$

where $\mathbf{w}$ is the weight vector, $\mathbf{v}$ is the weight matrix of size $n \times k$ (where k is the length of a column vector of $\mathbf{v}$), and $< v_i, v_j >$ is the inner product (i.e., dot product) of the ith and jth column vectors of $\mathbf{v}$.

Since the factorization machine's loss function uses arithmetic mean (average of all errors), when the label is very imbalanced (e.g., when there is significantly more $y = 0$ than $y = 1$), Eq. 3 can be almost optimized by predicting all samples to be 0 since in this way it will generate very small error rates measured by the first term of Eq. 3. Consequently, the optimization of factorization machines will be biased towards the majority label in the training processes which will lead to low accuracy particularly on the minority label. The minority label is the presence of links in link prediction problems, the accuracy of which is vitally important and cannot be compromised. To address this label imbalance problem, we proposed a Balanced Factorization Machines (BFM) which uses the quadratic-mean of errors with respect to labels as its loss function. The overall formulation of our BFM model is as follows:

$$
\min_{\mathbf{w},\mathbf{v}} \; Sqrt\Bigg\{ \frac{\sum_{\forall x \in D+}(y - (w_0 + \sum_{i=1}^{n} w_i x_i + \sum_{i,j}^{n} < v_i, v_j > x_i x_j))^2}{|D^+|}
$$
$$
+ \frac{\sum_{\forall x \in D-}(y - (w_0 + \sum_{i=1}^{n} w_i x_i + \sum_{i,j}^{n} < v_i, v_j > x_i x_j))^2}{|D^-|} \Bigg\} + R(\mathbf{w}) + R'(\mathbf{v})
$$

(4)

where D^+ and D^- represent data samples in positive and negative labels (i.e., presence and absence of known links), respectively. The first term in Eq. 4 uses quadratic mean to measure the error loss of BFM. Now we introduce a lemma to show why our quadratic-mean-based loss function is theoretical more advantageous in learning from imbalanced data:

Lemma 1. $\forall \; err_1 \geq 0$, and $\forall \; err_2 \geq 0$, denote by $AM(err_1, err_2)$ and $QM(err_1, err_2)$ the arithmetic mean and quadratic mean of err_1 and err_2 respectively, then $QM(err_1, err_2) = \sqrt{AM(err_1, err_2) + (\frac{err_1 - err_2}{2})^2}$.

Proof. The lemma can be proved by the derivations below:

$$
QM(err_1, err_2) = \sqrt{\frac{err_1^2 + err_2^2}{2}}
$$
$$
= \sqrt{\frac{err_1^2 + err_2^2 + 2err_1 err_2}{4} + \frac{err_1^2 + err_2^2 - 2err_1 err_2}{4}}
$$
$$
= \sqrt{(\frac{err_1 + err_2}{2})^2 + (\frac{err_1 - err_2}{2})^2}
$$
$$
= \sqrt{AM(err_1, err_2) + (\frac{err_1 - err_2}{2})^2} \qquad \square
$$

The above lemma shows that conventional factorization machines (which use the AM) are optimized when the *sum of errors from all samples* are minimized, while our BFM model (which uses the QM) is optimized if only *the sum and the difference between errors of positive and negative samples* are both minimized. To further illustrate the significance of this difference between AM and QM, we provide the following example on error calculations:

Example 1. Consider a learning algorithm that has a classification performance shown in Table 1. Apparently the classification is biased towards the negative class (i.e., predicting almost all data to be negative). However, the AM-based error is as extremely low as 0.8% (i.e., $\frac{8+0}{10+990}$). On the contrary, the QM-based error is as high as 56.6% (i.e., $\sqrt{\frac{(8/10)^2 + (0/990)^2}{2}}$).

Table 1. Classification performance on an imbalanced data set for Example 1.

	Predicted positives	Predicted negatives	Sum
Actual positives	2	8	10
Actual negatives	0	990	990

This example illustrates that QM can detect the bias of the learning algorithm which AM cannot. This unique property of QM can effectively guide the optimization of our BFM model and make BFM robust to learning on imbalanced data sets.

4   Experiments and Analysis

We analyze and compare the performance of our BFM model against existing link prediction methods on real-world data sets. We compare our method with classical factorization machines (FM) [17], field-aware factorization machines (FFM) [7], graph-based link prediction method (GLP) [4], and matrix factorization based method (MF) [14]. We also include unsupervised learning based methods in the comparisons, such as non-negative matrix factorization (NNMF) [3] and Link Propagation (LP) [11]. We use the L_2 norm for $R(\mathbf{w})$ and use the Frobenius norm for $R'(\mathbf{v})$, and use graph random walk [6] as the distance between every pair of two nodes. In all our experiments, we use 5-fold cross validation to separate training and test data, conduct 10 repeated runs with different random seeds, and report the average results of the repeated runs. We use the AUC (i.e., the area under ROC curve) as our evaluation metric, which is more suitable than using the overall accuracy as the metric for imbalanced data.

4.1   Data Sets

We use six publicly available real-world network data sets in our experiments: protein-to-protein interaction networks (PPI) [21], NIPS co-authorship networks (NIPS) [19], email Eu-core network (Email) [24], UC Irvine messaging network (SMS) [16], adolescent health network (Health) [15], and US electric power grid network (PowerGrid) [22]. The details of all data sets are shown in Table 2.

4.2   Experimental Results

We compare BFM against the two most popular factorization machines, FM and FFM, by evaluating their responses to changes of parameter k (i.e., the length of the column vectors of $\mathbf{v}$). The experimental results are shown in Fig. 2. From the subfigures, we can clearly see that the performance of BFM is almost persistently better than that of FM and FFM by a large magnitude. Although the performances of FM and FFM are sometime indistinguishable (such as in the Email data set), the performance of our BFM model is always better than them.

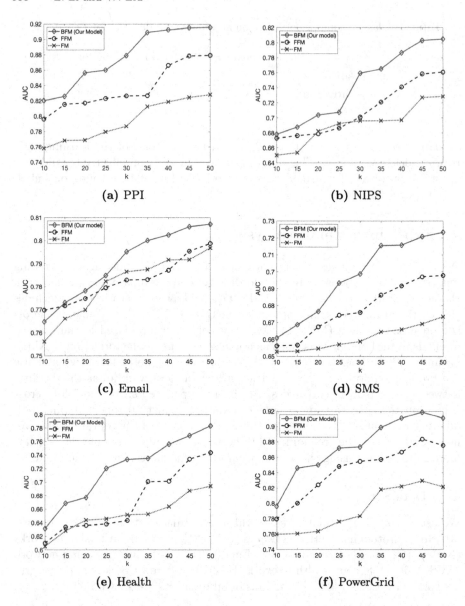

Fig. 2. Performance comparisons among factorization machines based methods.

This confirms that our QM-based loss function is significantly more effective on handling imbalanced data for link predictions problems.

We also compare our BFM model with other existing supervised and unsupervised link prediction methods. The detailed experimental results of these comparisons are presented in Table 3. In the table, we report the mean and variance values of 10 repeated runs for each algorithm on each data set. From the

Table 2. Details of data sets used in experiments.

Data sets	Type	Nodes	$|D^+|$	$|D^-|$	Pos:Neg
PPI	Undirected	2,617	23,710	6,824,979	1:287
NIPS	Undirected	2,865	9,466	8,198,759	1:866
Email	Directed	1,005	25,571	984,454	1:38
SMS	Directed	1,899	20,296	3,585,905	1:177
Health	Directed	2,539	12,969	6,433,552	1:496
PowerGrid	Undirected	4,941	13,188	24,400,293	1:1850

Table 3. Performance comparisons between BFM and other link prediction methods.

Data sets	AUC (Area Under ROC Curve)						
	GLP	MF	NNMF	LP	FM	FFM	BFM
PPI	.818 ± .008	.885 ± .006	.834 ± .005	.843 ± .004	.828 ± .007	.884 ± .008	**.907 ± .006**
NIPS	.699 ± .002	.778 ± .008	.744 ± .002	.763 ± .011	.728 ± .003	.760 ± .002	**.804 ± .002**
Email	.796 ± .006	.799 ± .005	.792 ± .003	.809 ± .009	.796 ± .006	.808 ± .006	**.821 ± .005**
SMS	.641 ± .004	.725 ± .009	.718 ± .008	.704 ± .004	.673 ± .006	.697 ± .005	**.724 ± .006**
Health	.687 ± .003	.762 ± .007	.731 ± .007	.734 ± .008	.694 ± .005	.743 ± .008	**.782 ± .003**
PowerGrid	.858 ± .021	.882 ± .017	.871 ± .019	.843 ± .016	.841 ± .025	.885 ± .018	**.919 ± .016**

table, we can observed that the performance of our BFM model is significantly better than all other alternative models.

5 Conclusions and Future Work

In this paper we propose to address the link prediction problem by using factorization machines. We extract graphical features from networks and use the features to training our model. Our modelling of the features can utilize information from both directed and undirected networks. More importantly, we designed a novel and effective loss function, which uses the quadratic mean of errors with respect to labels, to handle the label imbalance problems. Our experiment results on real-world data sets demonstrate that our BFM mode significantly outperforms other link prediction methods. In future, we plan to extend our model to address link prediction problems on temporal networks and graph streams.

References

1. Al Hasan, M., Chaoji, V., Salem, S., Zaki, M.: Link prediction using supervised learning. In: SDM06: Workshop on Link Analysis, Counter-Terrorism and Security (2006)
2. Barzel, B., Barabási, A.L.: Network link prediction by global silencing of indirect correlations. Nat. Biotechnol. **31**(8), 720 (2013)

3. Chen, B., Li, F., Chen, S., Hu, R., Chen, L.: Link prediction based on non-negative matrix factorization. PLoS ONE **12**(8), e0182968 (2017)
4. Cukierski, W., Hamner, B., Yang, B.: Graph-based features for supervised link prediction. In: The 2011 International Joint Conference on Neural Networks (IJCNN), pp. 1237–1244. IEEE (2011)
5. Ermiş, B., Acar, E., Cemgil, A.T.: Link prediction in heterogeneous data via generalized coupled tensor factorization. Data Min. Knowl. Discov. **29**(1), 203–236 (2015)
6. Hashimoto, T., Sun, Y., Jaakkola, T.: From random walks to distances on unweighted graphs. In: Advances in Neural Information Processing Systems (NIPS), pp. 3429–3437 (2015)
7. Juan, Y., Zhuang, Y., Chin, W.S., Lin, C.J.: Field-aware factorization machines for CTR prediction. In: Proceedings of the 10th ACM Conference on Recommender Systems, pp. 43–50. ACM (2016)
8. Kim, Y., Srivastava, J.: Impact of social influence in e-commerce decision making. In: Proceedings of the Ninth International Conference on Electronic Commerce, pp. 293–302. ACM (2007)
9. Liben-Nowell, D., Kleinberg, J.: The link-prediction problem for social networks. J. Assoc. Inf. Sci. Technol. **58**(7), 1019–1031 (2007)
10. Lichtenwalter, R.N., Lussier, J.T., Chawla, N.V.: New perspectives and methods in link prediction. In: Proceedings of the 16th ACM SIGKDD International Conference on Knowledge Discovery and Data Mining, pp. 243–252. ACM (2010)
11. Liu, J., Xu, B., Xu, X., Xin, T.: A link prediction algorithm based on label propagation. J. Comput. Sci. **16**, 43–50 (2016)
12. Lu, Z., Savas, B., Tang, W., Dhillon, I.S.: Supervised link prediction using multiple sources. In: 2010 IEEE 10th International Conference on Data Mining (ICDM), pp. 923–928. IEEE (2010)
13. Martínez, V., Berzal, F., Cubero, J.C.: A survey of link prediction in complex networks. ACM Comput. Surv. (CSUR) **49**(4), 69 (2017)
14. Menon, A.K., Elkan, C.: Link prediction via matrix factorization. In: Gunopulos, D., Hofmann, T., Malerba, D., Vazirgiannis, M. (eds.) ECML PKDD 2011. LNCS (LNAI), vol. 6912, pp. 437–452. Springer, Heidelberg (2011). https://doi.org/10.1007/978-3-642-23783-6_28
15. Moody, J.: Peer influence groups: identifying dense clusters in large networks. Soc. Netw. **23**(4), 261–283 (2001)
16. Panzarasa, P., Opsahl, T., Carley, K.M.: Patterns and dynamics of users' behavior and interaction: network analysis of an online community. J. Am. Soc. Inf. Sci. Technol. **60**(5), 911–932 (2009)
17. Rendle, S.: Factorization machines. In: 2010 IEEE 10th International Conference on Data Mining (ICDM), pp. 995–1000. IEEE (2010)
18. Rendle, S., Gantner, Z., Freudenthaler, C., Schmidt-Thieme, L.: Fast context-aware recommendations with factorization machines. In: Proceedings of the 34th International ACM SIGIR Conference on Research and Development in Information Retrieval, pp. 635–644. ACM (2011)
19. Roweis, S.: NIPS Conference Papers Vols 0-12. https://cs.nyu.edu/~roweis/data.html
20. Sarkar, P., Chakrabarti, D., Moore, A.W.: Theoretical justification of popular link prediction heuristics. In: International Joint Conference on Artificial Intelligence, vol. 22, p. 2722 (2011)
21. Tsuda, K., Noble, W.S.: Learning kernels from biological networks by maximizing entropy. Bioinformatics **20**(Suppl. 1), i326–i333 (2004)

22. Watts, D.J., Strogatz, S.H.: US Power Grid Network - KONECT, April 2017. http://konect.uni-koblenz.de/networks/opsahl-powergrid
23. Yang, Y., Lichtenwalter, R.N., Chawla, N.V.: Evaluating link prediction methods. Knowl. Inf. Syst. **45**(3), 751–782 (2015)
24. Yin, H., Benson, A.R., Leskovec, J., Gleich, D.F.: Local higher-order graph clustering. In: Proceedings of the 23rd ACM SIGKDD International Conference on Knowledge Discovery and Data Mining, pp. 555–564. ACM (2017)

Discovering Granger-Causal Features from Deep Learning Networks

Aneesh Sreevallabh Chivukula[1], Jun Li[2], and Wei Liu[1(✉)]

[1] Advanced Analytics Institute, University of Technology Sydney, Sydney, Australia
AneeshSrivallabh.Chivukula@student.uts.edu.au, Wei.Liu@uts.edu.au
[2] Centre for Artificial Intelligence, University of Technology Sydney,
Sydney, Australia
Jun.Li@uts.edu.au

Abstract. In this research, we propose deep networks that discover Granger causes from multivariate temporal data generated in financial markets. We introduce a Deep Neural Network (DNN) and a Recurrent Neural Network (RNN) that discover Granger-causal features for bivariate regression on bivariate time series data distributions. These features are subsequently used to discover Granger-causal graphs for multivariate regression on multivariate time series data distributions. Our supervised feature learning process in proposed deep regression networks has favourable F-tests for feature selection and t-tests for model comparisons. The experiments, minimizing root mean squared errors in the regression analysis on real stock market data obtained from Yahoo Finance, demonstrate that our causal features significantly improve the existing deep learning regression models.

1 Introduction

Causal inference is a central theme in computational sciences that construct mathematical models for causation. In statistics, causality is defined over conditional dependencies modelled between features in the data. Such conditional dependencies are used to construct data distributions linking causes with effects in causal relations defined on data features. Such causal relations are useful for feature discovery in machine learning. The impact and risk of including causal relations or causal features is validated by domain knowledge.

The Granger-Sargent statistic and the Granger-Wald statistic are commonly used to discover Granger-causal features on time-domain and frequency-domain formulations of Granger causality [1]. In this paper we discover Granger-causal features by measuring model improvement in deep networks. Our models are useful for simulating time-dependent observations in application domains with neural computations in deep learning.

Deep learning is a class of neural networks that learn hierarchical feature representations approximating non-linear functions. In data-driven analytics applications, deep learning has been used to visualize, store, process and predict

T. Mitrovic et al. (Eds.): AI 2018, LNAI 11320, pp. 692–705, 2018.
https://doi.org/10.1007/978-3-030-03991-2_62

information. In supervised deep learning, the information is typically modelled as statistical correlations and variable associations. Introducing causality methods into supervised deep learning creates analytics models for data-driven decision making in an application domain where causal features are separated from spurious features.

In computational learning theory, loss functions are mathematical functions mapping a complex data-driven event in complex systems to real numbers. In decision and estimation theory, loss functions relate empirical risk defined on actual data to expected risk defined on predicted output of an analytics model.

In this paper, we analyze time series data distributions with the help of deep learning networks to discover causal relations and causal graphs from Granger causality tests [2]. To derive data representations, the deep networks are trained to optimize squared error loss functions between actual data and predicted output. The corresponding analytics predictions are tested and validated with statistical significance tests on regression errors. We also extend unrestricted models in Granger causality for supervised feature discovery with bivariate regression as well as supervised causal inference with multivariate regression. Theoretically, the deep network architecture and its squared error loss function determine empirical risk in our regression models.

Following are the major contributions of this paper:

- We identify Granger-causal features using deep networks that improve bivariate regression predictions amongst temporal dependencies in time series distributions.
- We discover Granger-causal graphs in time series distributions to improve multivariate regression in deep networks.
- We evaluate our theoretical model on Yahoo Finance data to solve causal inference problems defining stochastic processes found in financial markets.

The paper starts with related work in Sect. 2 comparing the new approach with existing approaches. Algorithms and experiments for the proposed method are presented in Sect. 3 and Sect. 4 respectively. The paper ends with Sect. 5 which summarises current and future work.

2   Related Work

Causality is generally defined on logical formalizations of different classes of knowledge, reasoning and complexity in data. Causality also depends on features and representations, patterns and noise from ground truth data generated in an application domain. Depending on a particular definition of causality, causal relations identify causal features for machine learning.

2.1   Causal Inference in Deep Learning

Causality methods have been applied to deep learning problems such as semi-supervised learning and transfer learning. In these problems informed priors retrieved from other networks are used to center the weights in hybrid deep learning networks. Such networks then construct statistically significant hypotheses and corresponding data representation on actual data from complex systems. An analytics model employing causality methods can then validate such hypotheses against causal features discovering patterns, structure, context and content in actual data [3]. In general, the instance space for learning causal features in actual data consists of concept adapting data structures like strings, trees, networks and tensors.

Backpropagation learning algorithms for deep networks have been improved by incorporating ideas for training probabilistic graphical models typically used in causal inference. Such training is inherently Bayesian where prior distributions inform and constrain analytics models predicting posterior distributions [4]. The improved deep learning algorithms result in a predicted output informed by a causality graph.

2.2 Causal Inference in Time Series Analysis

In time series analysis, causal inference is identifies and classifies events in time series such that the events have either deterministic or probabilistic causal relations. Events are identified by mapping logic and structure of natural language to concept lattices and causal graphs [5]. Historically, causal reasoning in time series builds on statistical analysis of covariance or correlation between two or more events in time series. The calculated correlation strength is then used to predict causal relation between two events [6]. The disadvantage of this approach is that it cannot determine the direction and significance of causation. It also cannot discover hidden causes and patterns for which observed events are effects.

Granger causality is a simple learning mechanism that allows us to explore all preceding ideas about causality methods in deep learning for time series analysis [7]. Here, Granger causality does not empirically prove actual causation between events but acts as a stepping stone to explore the phenomenon relating two events participating in a cause-effect relationship. Granger-causal features have been discovered with rule-based analytics models [8] and feature-based analytics models [9]. Our approach to causal inference also builds a feature-based analytics model.

3   Our Proposed Algorithms

We predict stock prices in financial markets with Deep Neural Networks (DNNs) for discriminative learning based regression models and Recurrent Neural Networks (RNNs) for sequence learning based regression models. Outputs from bivariate regression models are used to search Granger-causal features in multivariate time series data.

3.1 Empirical Risk Training in Deep Learning Networks

Suppose a regression model for stock y having actual value $y(t)$ at time t predicts $\hat{y}(t; \boldsymbol{\alpha})$ parameterized by regression parameters $\boldsymbol{\alpha}$ belonging to parameter space A. In computational learning theory, the regression model is analyzed in terms of expected risk $E(L(\hat{y}(t; \boldsymbol{\alpha}), y(t)))$, which is defined as expected value of the loss function $L(\hat{y}(t; \boldsymbol{\alpha}), y(t))$, learning probability density function $P(\hat{y}(t; \boldsymbol{\alpha}), y(t))$ underlying the data [10]:

$$\text{Expected Risk}: E(L(\hat{y}(t; \boldsymbol{\alpha}), y(t))) = \int d(\hat{y}(t; \boldsymbol{\alpha})) d(y(t)) L(\hat{y}(t; \boldsymbol{\alpha}), y(t)) P(\hat{y}(t; \boldsymbol{\alpha}), y(t))$$

$$(1)$$

The expected risk $E(L(\hat{y}(t; \boldsymbol{\alpha}), y(t)))$ is posed as a regression model when loss function $L(\hat{y}(t; \boldsymbol{\alpha}), y(t))$ is defined on squared errors computed between $\hat{y}(t; \boldsymbol{\alpha})$ and $y(t)$. If the regression model defining $L(\hat{y}(t; \boldsymbol{\alpha}), y(t))$ is learning a training dataset of finite size m, then expected risk $E(L(\hat{y}(t; \boldsymbol{\alpha}), y(t)))$ is called empirical risk [11] $\hat{E}(L(\hat{y}(t; \boldsymbol{\alpha}), y(t)))$.

$$\text{Empirical Risk}: \hat{E}_{y(t) \sim P(\hat{y}(t; \boldsymbol{\alpha}), y(t))}(L(\hat{y}(t; \boldsymbol{\alpha}), y(t))) = \frac{\Sigma_{i=1}^{m} L(\hat{y}(t; \boldsymbol{\alpha})^{(i)}, y(t)^{(i)})}{m}$$

$$(2)$$

The computational complexity of empirical risk $\hat{E}(L(\hat{y}(t; \boldsymbol{\alpha}), y(t)))$ is determined by the computational complexity of $L(\hat{y}(t; \boldsymbol{\alpha}), y(t))$ which in turn is determined by the regression model's feature selection and model validation. Thus, our intuition is that introducing causal features into deep networks not only minimizes empirical risk but also minimizes regression error.

In our deep network based regression models, regression error is minimized by the weights $\boldsymbol{\alpha}$ learnt on Squared Error (SE) Loss function $L(\hat{y}(t; \boldsymbol{\alpha}), y(t))$ as in Eq. 3:

$$\text{SE Loss}: L(\hat{y}(t; \boldsymbol{\alpha}), y(t)) = (\hat{y}(t; \boldsymbol{\alpha}) - y(t))^2 \qquad (3)$$

$L(\hat{y}(t; \boldsymbol{\alpha}), y(t))$ is determined by the deep network's data representation $P(\hat{y}(t; \boldsymbol{\alpha}), y(t)))$ of actual data $y(t)$. For training data of size m, the total loss function $L_{MSE}(\hat{y}(t; \boldsymbol{\alpha}), y(t))$ is given in Eq. 4:

$$\text{MSE Loss}: L_{MSE}(\hat{y}(t; \boldsymbol{\alpha}), y(t)) = \frac{\Sigma_{i=1}^{m} L(\hat{y}(t; \boldsymbol{\alpha})^{(i)}, y(t)^{(i)})}{m} \qquad (4)$$

By training a deep network model, we use either a DNN or RNN to minimize empirical risk in Eq. 2. The backpropagation training algorithm solves for $\boldsymbol{\alpha}$ in Eq. 4 with a stochastic gradient descent procedure finding best model fit on $P(\hat{y}(t; \boldsymbol{\alpha}), y(t))$.

3.2   Granger Causality Testing in Deep Learning Networks

Causal features can be discovered by changing loss function $L(\hat{y}(t; \alpha), y(t))$ in Eq. 2 according to data representation $P(\hat{y}(t; \alpha), y(t))$ in deep learning networks conditioned on actual past data $y(t - j), j = 1, 2, \ldots, p$ with p lags. In the deep network, $P(\hat{y}(t; \alpha), y(t)) = P(\hat{y}(t; \alpha)|y(t - j))$ is the conditional probability of predicting regression value $\hat{y}(t)$ or it parameterized version $\hat{y}(t; \alpha)$ for stock y.

If another stock x at time point $x(t)$ with q lagged values $x(t - k), k = 1, 2, \ldots, q$, indicates the occurrence of $y(t)$ then we create a deep network conditioned on not only $y(t - j), j = 1, 2, \ldots, p$ but also $x(t - k), k = 1, 2, \ldots, q$. Then, $P(\hat{y}(t; \alpha; \beta), y(t)) = P(\hat{y}(t; \alpha; \beta)|y(t - j), x(t - k))$ is conditional probability of predicting regression value $\hat{y}(t)$ or it parameterized version $\hat{y}(t; \alpha; \beta)$ for stock y parameterized by regression parameters tensors α and β belonging to deep network parameter spaces A and B respectively.

From data representations $P(\hat{y}(t; \alpha), y(t))$ and $P(\hat{y}(t; \alpha; \beta), y(t))$ defined above, we devise following Granger causality test using Eq. 3 to predict $\hat{y}(t; \alpha)$ and $\hat{y}(t; \alpha; \beta)$ as dependent test variables for $y(t - j), x(t - k)$ as independent test variables.

$$\text{restricted model: } \hat{y}(t; \alpha) = L(P(\hat{y}(t; \alpha), y(t))) = L(P(\hat{y}(t; \alpha)|y(t - j))) \quad (5)$$

$$\begin{aligned} \text{unrestricted model: } \hat{y}(t; \alpha; \beta) &= L(P(\hat{y}(t; \alpha; \beta), y(t))) \\ &= L(P(\hat{y}(t; \alpha; \beta)|y(t - j), x(t - k))) \end{aligned} \quad (6)$$

The null hypothesis of no Granger causality is rejected if and only if $x(t - k)$ has been retained along with $y(t - j)$ in the $\hat{y}(t)$ regression according to an F-test on Root Mean Squared Errors (RMSEs) between $\hat{y}(t)$ and $y(t)$. The F-test in Definition 1 [2] determines the Granger causality relation between stocks x and y where RMSE is computed for unrestricted regression as $RMSE_{ur}$ and restricted regression as $RMSE_r$.

Definition 1. $F\text{-statistic} = \dfrac{\frac{RMSE_r - RMSE_{ur}}{q - p}}{\frac{RMSE_{ur}}{n - q}}$

To compute causal features over N multivariate time series $X = \{X(t)^u\}, u \in [1, N], t \in [1, n]$ selected from N stock prices at n time points in financial markets, we repeat the F-test for every pair of stocks x and y. In each F-test, the null hypothesis is that the sample means of predictions are equal and the regression parameters β are zero. The alternative hypothesis is that there is significant variation between the sample means of predictions for some non-zero α and β. The null hypothesis is rejected if p-value on F-test has a significance level less than 0.05. If the null hypothesis is rejected, deep network features $y(t - j)$ and $x(t - k)$ Granger cause predicted output $\hat{y}(t)$ with actual stock price $y(t)$. In experiments with deep learning networks, a Granger-causal feature is represented by the causal relation $x \to y$ for stocks x and y.

3.3   Multivariate Regression Validation with Deep Learning Networks

While we introduced theory to identify single Granger-causes in the previous subsection, in this subsection we explain the discovery of multiple Granger-causes for a given stock. Incorporating multiple Granger-causal features into the F-test allows us to improve deep learning with causal reasoning on multivariate time-dependent data.

Therefore, we discover multiple Granger-causal features with multivariate regression in an unrestricted model. The multiple Granger-causal features discovery process validates the single Granger-causal features and predictions. We extend the unrestricted model for bivariate regression in Eq. 6 to the unrestricted model for multivariate regression as in Eq. 7.

$$
\begin{aligned}
\text{multivariate unrestricted model: } \hat{y}(t; \{\boldsymbol{\alpha}^w\}) &= L(P(\hat{y}(t; \{\boldsymbol{\alpha}^w\}), y(t))) \\
&= L(P(\hat{y}(t; \{\boldsymbol{\alpha}^w\})|y(t-j), \{x(t-k)^w\}))
\end{aligned} \tag{7}
$$

Equation 7 predicts $\hat{y}(t)$ by discovering statistically significant Granger-causal features $\{x^w\} \rightarrow y$, $w \in [1, N]$ from multivariate regression. As detailed in Algorithm 2 in the next subsection, Granger causality test of Eq. 5 is applied to all pairs of restricted and unrestricted models that differ in one independent variable x^w discovered by bivariate regression. A feature selection procedure for multivariate regression searches candidate feature sets in the power set of the set $\{x^w\}$. The optimal feature set is determined by $\{\boldsymbol{\alpha}^w\}$ with minimum RMSE $RMSE_{mv}$.

In bivariate regression, the single Granger-causal features are discovered by a DNN-based and RNN-based regression model. In multivariate regression, multiple Granger-causal features are discovered by a DNN-based regression model.

3.4   Deep Learning Networks Based Regression Models

Algorithm 1 gives learning algorithm implementing Eqs. 5 and 6 for loss function in Eq. 4. The algorithm requires a multivariate time series $X = \{X(t)^u\}$ to predict regression model's causal graph G_{MSE} of Granger-causal features and corresponding regression errors $RMSE_r$, $RMSE_{ur}$, $RMSE_{mv}$ for the restricted model, the unrestricted model and the multivariate model participating in Granger causality.

Algorithm 1 executes from Line 1 to Line 16 for every pair of time series $y(t), x(t) \in X$ with lags p, q. Line 6 prepares crossvalidation data for training deep network on Line 8 which depends on the prediction $\hat{y}(t)$ from Granger causality models in Line 7. $\hat{y}(t)$ is predicted as a complex nonlinear combination of features $y(t - j)$ and $x(t - k)$ in Line 9. On Line 13 and Line 15, bivariate regression errors $RMSE_r$, $RMSE_{ur}$ are computed on actual time point $y(t)$ and predicted time point $\hat{y}(t)$. Line 11 applies F-test to discover Granger causality relations in Line 16. The null hypothesis of not finding Granger-causal

---

Algorithm 1. Discovery of Granger-causal features using deep learning networks

---

Input: Multivariate time series : $X = \{X(t)^u\}, u \in [1, N], t \in [1, n]$; Granger causality lags $p, q \in \mathbb{Z}$;
Output: Predictive model output : Bivariate Granger-causal features graph G_{MSE}; Multivariate Granger-causal features set C_{mv}; Bivariate regression errors $RMSE_r, RMSE_{ur}$ for restricted and unrestricted model; Multivariate regression errors $RMSE_{mv}$ for unrestricted model;
1: $G_{MSE} = C_{mv} = \Phi, RMSE_r = RMSE_{ur} = RMSE_{mv} = \Phi$
2: **for** $u \in [1, N]$ **do**
3:         $y(t) = X(t)^u$
4:         **for** $v \in [1, N]$ **and** $v \neq u$ **do**
5:                $x(t) = X(t)^v$
6:                Create preprocessed and lagged cross validation data $y(t - j), x(t - k)$ with lags p, q from time series $y(t), x(t), t \in [1, n]$
7:                Construct restricted and unrestricted regression model on actual data $y(t), x(t)$ according to Equation 5 and Equation 6.
8:                Construct MSE loss predictions $\hat{y}(t)$ from Equation 4 for DNN as well as RNN networks.
9:                Calculate regression errors $RMSE_r$ and $RMSE_{ur}$ for each $\hat{y}(t)$ and $y(t)$.
10:               From Definition 1, compute $F\text{-}statistic$ over $RMSE_r$ and $RMSE_{ur}$.

11:               **if** $F\text{-}statistic > 0.05$ **then**

12:                      **if** model is restricted **then**
13:                             Update bivariate regression error, $RMSE_r[u][v] = RMSE_r$, for restricted model
14:                      **else**
15:                             Update bivariate regression error, $RMSE_{ur}[u][v] = RMSE_{ur}$, for unrestricted model
16:                             Update Granger-causal features, $G_{MSE}[u] = G_{MSE}[u] \cup x(t) \rightarrow y(t)$, for bivariate regression
17: **for** $u \in [1, N]$ **do**
18:         $y(t) = X(t)^u$
19:         Retrieve bivariate Granger-causal features $\{x(t)^w\}$ for u from G_{MSE}
20:         $RMSE_{mv}[u], C_{mv}[u] = $ multivar_granger$(y(t), \{x(t)^w\}, RMSE_{ur})$ to compute multivariate regression outputs.
21: **return** $RMSE_r, RMSE_{ur}, RMSE_{mv}, G_{MSE}, C_{mv}$

---

features is rejected at 5% significance level. The corresponding Granger-causal graph G_{MSE} is searched on Line 19 to improve multivariate regression errors $RMSE_{mv}$ on Line 20. In Algorithm 1, while loop from Line 2 to Line 16 discovers single Granger-causal features G_{MSE} with bivariate regression, loop from Line 17 to Line 20 discovers multiple Granger-causal features C_{mv} with multivariate regression. Algorithm 1 ends on Line 21 by returning Granger-causal features G_{MSE}, C_{mv} as well as their regression errors $RMSE_r$, $RMSE_{ur}$ and $RMSE_{mv}$.

Algorithm 2 called on Line 20 of Algorithm 1 gives the search procedure implementing Eq. 7. Algorithm 2 requires unrestricted model error $RMSE_{ur}$ found for bivariate regression predicting $y(t)$ from single Granger-causal features $\{x(t)^w\}$. The causal relations discovered between $\{x(t)^w\}$ are in Granger-causal graph G_{MSE}. Algorithm 2 then returns unrestricted model error $RMSE_{mv}$ from multivariate regression as well as corresponding multiple Granger-causal features set c_{mv} discovered by multivariate regression network. For all predicted $\{X(t)^u\}$, Granger-causal feature sets C_{mv} stored on Line 20 are the optimal Granger-causal feature sets discovered across many multivariate regression networks. The loop from Line 4 to Line 19 in Algorithm 2 uses two sets of selected_causes and candidate_causes to generate and evaluate candidate Granger-causal feature sets for unrestricted model in multivariate regression. On Line 2, selected_causes are initialized to Granger-causal features $\{x(t)^w\}$ discovered in G_{MSE} of Algorithm 1. On Line 6, Cartesian product of selected_causes and bivariate Granger-causal features $\{x(t)^w\}$ generates candidate_causes. $Candidate\_RMSE_r$, $Candidate\_RMSE_{ur}$ are used to track regression errors of restricted and unrestricted models built from candidate_causes. On Line 10, initially a restricted model in multivariate regression is assumed to be the same as the unrestricted model in bivariate regression. Later as the loop from Line 4 to Line 19 crosses more than one iteration as tracked by counter $iter$, the restricted model is evaluated against Granger-causal features $c \setminus \{x(t)^w\}$ on Line 12 while the unrestricted model is evaluated against Granger-causal features c on Line 13. In any giver iteration $iter$, the restricted and unrestricted models differ by only one of the Granger-causal features present in $\{x(t)^w\}$. The multivariate regression error $Candidate\_RMSE_{ur}$ is computed for each candidate c at Lines 13–15. If the corresponding F-statistic is greater than a predefined threshold on Line 17, then the candidate c is found to be a legitimate Granger-causal feature for subsequent processing with multivariate regression. Such a c is updated to selected_causes on Line 18. For every new iteration $iter$, selected_causes are reset to the empty set on Line 7 immediately after being used to generate candidate_causes on Line 6. This loop convergence condition ensures that larger Granger-causal feature sets are generated across iterations. On convergence, no further selected_causes are available for processing. Algorithm 2 terminates the search procedure by returning the optimal Granger-causal feature set c_{mv} that minimizes multivariate regression error $RMSE_{mv}$.

Table 1. Companies listing

Abbreviation	Company name	Abbreviation	Company name
AAPL	Apple Inc.	MCD	McDonald's Corporation
ABT	Abbott Laboratories	MSFT	Microsoft Corporation
AEM	Agnico Eagle Mines Limited	ORCL	Oracle Corporation
AFG	American Financial Group, Inc.	WWD	Woodward, Inc.
APA	Apache Corporation	T	AT&T Inc.
CAT	Caterpillar Inc.	UTX	United Technologies Corporation

4 Experiments

In this section we discuss the empirical validation of Granger-causal features in deep learning networks regression models. Table 1 lists the stocks from different financial sectors in Standard & Poors 500 - a stock market index based on the market capitalizations of 500 large companies having common stock listed on the NYSE or NASDAQ. The stocks daily closing prices were obtained from Yahoo

---

Algorithm 2. Search procedure for constructing multivariate Granger-causal graphs

---

Input: Effect time series $y(t)$; Bivariate Granger-causal features $\{x(t)^w\}$; Bivariate Regression errors $RMSE_{ur}$ for unrestricted model
Output: Optimal Granger-causal feature set c_{mv} and multivariate regression error $RMSE_{mv}$ for unrestricted model
1: **function** MULTIVAR_GRANGER($y(t), \{x(t)^w\}, RMSE_{ur}$)
2:     Initialize selected_causes to Bivariate Granger-causal features $\{x(t)^w\}$
3:     $iter = 0, Candidate\_RMSE_r = Candidate\_RMSE_{ur} = \Phi$
4:     **while** selected_causes $\neq \Phi$ **do**
5:         $iter += 1$
6:         Generate candidate_causes, candidate_causes $= \{x(t)^w\} \times$ selected_causes, from previous iteration's selected_causes
7:         Reset selected_causes to Φ in current iteration
8:         **for** each candidate cause $c \in$ candidate_causes **do**
9:             **if** $iter == 1$ **then**
10:                 Set restricted model error $Candidate\_RMSE_r[c] = RMSE_{ur}[c]$
11:             **else**
12:                 Set restricted model error $Candidate\_RMSE_r[c] = Candidate\_RMSE_{ur}$ $[c \setminus \{x(t)^w\}]$
13:             Construct multivariate unrestricted regression model on actual data $y(t)$ and $\{x(t)^w\}$ according to Equation 7
14:             Construct MSE loss predictions $\hat{y}(t)$ from Equation 4 for DNN networks.
15:             Calculate regression error $Candidate\_RMSE_{ur}[c]$ for all $\hat{y}(t)$ and $y(t)$.
16:             From Definition 1, compute *F-statistic* over $Candidate\_RMSE_r[c]$ and $Candidate\_RMSE_{ur}[c]$.

17:             **if** *F-statistic* > 0.05 **then**
18:                 Update Granger-causal features: selected_causes = selected_causes $\cup$ c
19:     **end while**
20:     Among unrestricted models $Candidate\_RMSE_{ur}$, find optimal Granger-causal feature set c_{mv} with minimum multivariate regression error $RMSE_{mv}$
21:     **return** $RMSE_{mv}, c_{mv}$
22: **end function**

Finance website[1]. The data is obtained for a period of 21 years from 26-07-1996 to 25-07-2017.

The regression model's feature learning is determined by deep network structure weights α, β and $\{\alpha^w\}$ with MSE loss function. Deep network structure is designed to minimize bivariate/multivariate regression errors and maximize significant Granger causes in the unrestricted model. We treat the regression model as a time-dependent data-based model with causal lags p, q set to a default value of 200 days. 5285 days of time points are used to create the crossvalidation data. Each data record has delayed prices time series predicting current price of a given stock. For fair comparison of baseline models, we split 30% of crossvalidatiton data into testing data while remaining 70% of crossvalidatiton data is taken to be training data.

On bivariate data, we treat regression modelling problem as a discriminative learning problem in DNNs as well as a sequence learning problem in RNNs to show that discovered Granger-causal features are not specific to a given network structure. On multivariate data, we treat regression modelling problem as a discriminative learning problem in DNNs to validate generalization capability of proposed feature discovery procedure. The regression errors for discovering

---

[1] https://finance.yahoo.com/.

Granger-causal features are also compared with those from a Autoregressive Integrated Moving Average (ARIMA) regression model. A grid search procedure is used to select ARIMA training parameters. Number of training epochs in DNN is set to a default value 50 over a total of 12 stocks. The DNN has three hidden layers consisting of dense activation units and dropout regularization units. It is implemented in Keras[2] – a Tensorflow based API for deep learning. All time series are subject to min-max normalization before training.

We experiment with two variants of RNN with Long Short Term Memory (LSTM) and Gated Recurrent Unit (GRU) activation units. The number of training epochs in RNN is set to a default value 15. The LSTM has one hidden layer consisting of LSTM activation unit with 50 neurons. The GRU has three hidden layers consisting of GRU activation units with 25 neurons. Dropout units are the regularization units. LSTM as well as GRU state is reset after each training epoch. The LSTM and GRU are trained for 200 time steps - one record at a time - over lagged data. The time series data is differenced and scaled to a range of [-1,1]. For multivariate regression, all the identified single Granger-causal features are used as input. On multivariate testing data, regression values are predicted one time step at a time.

Table 2. RMSEs with MSE loss for bivariate regression. DNN is selected as the best network structure for Granger causality.

Abbreviation	ARIMA	LSTM	GRU	DNN
AAPL	0.807	1.449	1.475	0.504
ABT	0.748	0.461	0.469	0.626
AEM	1.643	1.115	1.107	0.143
AFG	0.795	0.580	0.588	0.485
APA	2.795	1.558	1.520	0.145
CAT	1.254	1.474	1.452	0.106
MCD	0.319	0.981	0.994	0.425
MSFT	1.555	0.597	0.606	0.361
ORCL	0.190	0.521	0.520	0.497
T	0.786	0.335	0.339	0.078
UTX	0.209	1.110	1.113	0.297
WWD	0.237	0.817	0.819	0.311
t-test	1.24×10^{-2}	2.21×10^{-4}	1.89×10^{-4}	Base

4.1   Single Granger-Causes Validation

For each company's price time series, autoregression models RMSEs are reported in Table 2. From t-test statistics in Table 2, we find DNN generally has better per-

---

[2] https://www.tensorflow.org/api_docs/python/tf/contrib/keras.

Table 3. RMSEs with MSE loss for Granger-causal feature discovery. The rows show causal relations with the restricted model and the unrestricted model RMSEs $RMSE_r$ and $RMSE_{ur}$ in bivariate regression with DNN.

Causal Relation	$RMSE_r$ Restricted model (DNN without causes)	$RMSE_{ur}$ Unrestricted model (our model with single cause)	Causal Relation	$RMSE_r$ Restricted model (DNN without causes)	$RMSE_{ur}$ Unrestricted model (our model with single cause)
AAPL → ABT	0.626	0.198	AAPL → AFG	0.485	0.293
AFG → ABT	0.626	0.191	WWD → AFG	0.485	0.396
APA → ABT	0.626	0.477	AAPL → MCD	0.425	0.315
CAT → ABT	0.626	0.372	AFG → MCD	0.425	0.418
MCD → ABT	0.626	0.261	UTX → MCD	0.425	0.365
MSFT → ABT	0.626	0.501	WWD → MCD	0.425	0.353
ORCL → ABT	0.626	0.362	ABT → MSFT	0.361	0.295
T → ABT	0.626	0.535	AFG → MSFT	0.361	0.249
UTX → ABT	0.626	0.271	UTX → MSFT	0.361	0.297
WWD → ABT	0.626	0.184	WWD → MSFT	0.361	0.183
WWD → UTX	0.297	0.219	UTX → ORCL	0.497	0.202
t-test	3.21×10^{-11}	Base	t-test	3.21×10^{-11}	Base

formance than competitive models. So we choose DNN as the regression model for discovering Granger-causal features with bivariate regression in Table 3 as well as multivariate regression in Fig. 1. For experimental validation of our algorithms, we also report Granger-causal features discovered by a GRU model in Table 4.

Tables 3 and 4 report RMSEs for restricted model $RMSE_r$ and unrestricted model $RMSE_{ur}$. $RMSE_{ur}$ is consistently lower than $RMSE_r$ for Granger causality models given in Eqs. 5 and 6 respectively. Each row in Tables 3 and 4 shows pairwise causal relations and their RMSEs. From t-test p-value statistic comparing RMSEs with and without Granger-causal features in Tables 3 and 4, we conclude that unrestricted model shows non-trivial reduction in RMSE compared to restricted model for any random pair of stocks involved in Granger causality. Figure 1(a) represents Granger-causal features discovered from bivariate regression as a causal graph between time series of stock prices represented by vertices where F-test statistics represented by edges show the strength of Granger causality.

Thus Tables 3 and 4 validate our proposal to use Granger causality in feature selection for deep networks based regression models. We also observe that the proposed feature discovery process and supervised learning process are robust to any particular deep network structure.

Table 4. RMSEs with MSE loss for Granger-causal feature discovery. The rows show causal relations with the restricted model and the unrestricted model RMSEs $RMSE_r$ and $RMSE_{ur}$ in bivariate regression with RNN.

Causal Relation	$RMSE_r$ Restricted model (RNN without causes)	$RMSE_{ur}$ Unrestricted model (our model with single cause)	Causal Relation	$RMSE_r$ Restricted model (RNN without causes)	$RMSE_{ur}$ Unrestricted model (our model with single cause)
ABT → AAPL	1.475	0.403	AFG → APA	1.529	0.788
AFG → AAPL	1.475	0.781	MCD → APA	1.571	0.944
MCD → AAPL	1.475	0.936	MSFT → APA	1.522	0.859
MSFT → AAPL	1.475	0.851	ORCL → APA	1.551	0.732
ORCL → AAPL	1.475	0.726	T → APA	1.527	0.741
T → AAPL	1.475	0.734	UTX → APA	1.522	1.021
UTX → AAPL	1.475	1.012	WWD → APA	1.526	0.846
WWD → AAPL	1.475	0.839	ABT → CAT	1.445	0.474
ABT → AEM	1.107	0.458	AFG → CAT	1.445	0.918
ABT → AFG	0.588	0.303	MSFT → CAT	1.445	1.001
ABT → APA	1.545	0.407	ORCL → CAT	1.444	0.853
ABT → MCD	0.994	0.382	T → CAT	1.445	0.863
ORCL → MCD	0.994	0.687	WWD → CAT	1.444	0.986
T → MCD	0.994	0.695	ABT → UTX	1.113	0.421
ABT → ORCL	0.521	0.257	ORCL → UTX	1.113	0.756
ABT → T	0.338	0.231	T → UTX	1.114	0.765
ABT → MSFT	0.606	0.256	ABT → WWD	0.821	0.397
t-test	3.21×10^{-11}	Base	t-test	3.21×10^{-11}	Base

4.2   Multiple Granger-Causes Validation

Figure 1(a) shows the Granger-causal graph with directed weighted edges that are outcomes of Definition 1. It indicates Granger-causal relations discovered for bivariate regression. The edge weights are F-test statistics for all the unrestricted models that reduce RMSEs in bivariate regression. For example, the causal relation $UTX \rightarrow ORCL$ indicates that UTX causes ORCL or ORCL is caused by UTX with F-test statistic 0.129. This relation has been selected in the Granger-causal graph because the unrestricted model including UTX prices in ORCL price prediction leads to a RMSE reduction from 0.497 to 0.202 according to Table 3. Figure 1(a) shows all the causalities identified on the training data. We do not assume causalities change at every time point. From Fig. 1(a), we not only can identify causal features but also indicate the strength of causality.

Figure 1(b) shows the top ranked Granger-causal features discovered by Algorithm 2 from Fig. 1(a). These causal features are suitable for multivariate regression. In Fig. 1(a), vertices like APA without Granger-causes, ORCL and MSFT with one and two Granger-causes result in no output from Algorithm 2. For

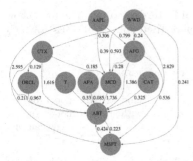

(a) Granger-causal graph with F-test statistics computed on RMSEs $RMSE_r, RMSE_{ur}$ in the restricted and unrestricted models for bivariate regression

(b) Two sets of Granger-causal features discovered by Algorithm 2 for predicting stock price ABT with multivariate regression. They reduce restricted model $RMSE_r$ from 0.626 to unrestricted model $RMSE_{mv}$ 0.141 and 0.178 respectively.

Fig. 1. Granger-causal features, F-statistics on RMSEs $RMSE_r, RMSE_{ur}$ and multivariate regression RMSEs $RMSE_{mv}$ for the unrestricted model with DNN. The edge directions indicate the causal relations between pairs of stocks and the edge weights show the corresponding F-test statistic given in Definition 1.

vertices like ABT with non-zero single Granger-causes, Algorithm 2 identifies multiple Granger-causes. For ABT, Algorithm 2 outputs a total of 69 Granger-causes which reduces RMSE $RMSE_{mv}$ in multivariate regression models from $RMSE_r = 0.626$ in the restricted model to $RMSE_{mv} \in [0.141, 0.541]$ in the unrestricted model. In Fig. 1(b), the multivariate Granger-cause {AAPL, AFG, APA, UTX} has regression error of $RMSE_{mv} = 0.141$ while {AAPL, CAT, MCD, MSFT, T} has regression error of $RMSE_{mv} = 0.178$ in the unrestricted model. Of the 69 causes, the longest but not optimal Granger-causes are found to be {AAPL, APA, CAT, MCD, ORCL, T, UTX, WWD} with $RMSE_{mv} = 0.162$ and {AAPL, APA, CAT, MCD, MSFT, T, UTX, WWD} with $RMSE_{mv} = 0.174$ in the unrestricted model. We also find two Granger-causes of length 8, six Granger-causes of length 7 and ten Granger-causes of length 6. From Fig. 1(b), we observe that multivariate regression on Granger-causal features results in a better unrestricted model than bivariate regression on Granger-causal features. In bivariate regression as well as multivariate regression, while F-test statistics on RMSEs validate our feature selection on regression errors, t-test statistics on RMSEs support our model validation on regression errors.

5   Conclusion and Future Work

We presented deep networks based regression models to augment and discover Granger-causal features analyzing multivariate time series data from finance domain. Our Granger-causal features are able to significantly improve multivariate regression performance. We also constructed Granger-causal graphs to capture temporal dependencies in multivariate data. On real stock market data we demonstrate that our theoretical model significantly outperforms existing deep learning regression models. As future work we shall combine multiple data sources to extract regularized features for cost sensitive concept learning and big data pattern detection.

Acknowledgements. This research is partially funded by The Capital Markets Cooperative Research Centre, Australia.

References

1. Guo, S., Ladroue, C.: Granger causality: theory and applications. Frontiers in Computational and Systems Biology. Computational Biology, vol. 15, pp. 83–111. Springer, London (2010). https://doi.org/10.1007/978-1-84996-196-7_5
2. Granger, C.W.: Investigating causal relations by econometric models and cross-spectral methods. Econ.: J. Econ. Soc. **37**, 424–438 (1969)
3. Mirowski, P., Ranzato, M., LeCun, Y.: Dynamic auto-encoders for semantic indexing. In: Proceedings of the NIPS 2010 Workshop on Deep Learning, pp. 1–9 (2010)
4. Spirtes, P., Glymour, C.N., Scheines, R.: Causation, Prediction, and Search. MIT Press, Cambridge (2000)
5. Keogh, E., Chu, S., Hart, D., Pazzani, M.: Segmenting time series: a survey and novel approach. Data Min. Time Ser. Databases **57**, 1–22 (2004)
6. Fu, T.: A review on time series data mining. Eng. Appl. Artif. Intell. **24**(1), 164–181 (2011)
7. Bahadori, M.T., Liu, Y.: An examination of practical granger causality inference. In: Proceedings of the 2013 SIAM International Conference on Data Mining, pp. 467–475. SIAM (2013)
8. Kleinberg, S.: Causal inference with rare events in large-scale time-series data. In: Proceedings of the 2013 International Joint Conference on Artificial Intelligence (2013)
9. Li, Z., Zheng, G., Agarwal, A., Xue, L., Lauvaux, T.: Discovery of causal time intervals. In: Proceedings of the 2017 SIAM International Conference on Data Mining, pp. 804–812. SIAM (2013)
10. Ancona, N., Marinazzo, D., Stramaglia, S.: Radial basis function approach to non-linear granger causality of time series. Phys. Rev. E **70**, 056221 (2004)
11. Goodfellow, I., Bengio, Y., Courville, A.: Deep Learning. MIT Press, Cambridge (2016). http://www.deeplearningbook.org

A New Family of Generative Adversarial Nets Using Heterogeneous Noise to Model Complex Distributions

Ancheng Lin[1], Jun Li[2], Lujuan Zhang[3], Lei Shi[4,5], and Zhenyuan Ma[3(✉)]

[1] School of Computer Sciences, Guangdong Polytechnic Normal University,
Guangzhou, China
cenbylin@163.com

[2] School of Software and Centre for Artificial Intelligence, Faculty of Engineering and
Information Technology, University of Technology Sydney, POBox 123, Broadway,
Sydney, NSW 2007, Australia
Jun.Li@uts.edu.au

[3] School of Mathematics and System Sciences,
Guangdong Polytechnic Normal University, Guangzhou, China
ljzhangkan@163.com, mazy@gpnu.edu.cn

[4] National Education Examinations Authority Ministry of Education of China,
Beijing 100084, China
shil@mail.neea.edu.cn

[5] School of Information Resource Management, Renmin University of China,
Beijing 100872, China

Abstract. Generative adversarial nets (GANs) are effective framework for constructing data models and enjoys desirable theoretical justification. On the other hand, realizing GANs for practical complex data distribution often requires careful configuration of the generator, discriminator, objective function and training method and can involve much non-trivial effort.

We propose an novel family of generative adversarial nets (GANs), where we employ both continuous noise and random binary codes in the generating process. The binary codes in the new GAN model (named BGANs) play the role of categorical latent variables helps improve the model capability and training stability when dealing with complex data distributions. BGAN has been evaluated and compared with existing GANs trained with the state-of-the-art method on both synthetic and practical data. The empirical evaluation shows effectiveness of BGAN.

1 Introduction

Generative adversarial nets (GANs) [9] have been shown effective in building generative data models. In particular, equipped with deep neural networks, GANs

Supported by Science and Technology Program of Guangzhou (No.201704030133), "A Knowledge-Connection and Cognitive-Style based Mining System for Massive Open Online Courses and Its Application" (UTS Project Code: PRO16-1300); Education Department Foundation of Guangdong Province 2017KTSCX112.

have achieved impressive success in representing the distributions of various image data populations [7]. There a wide range of applications, such as image and video analytics [5,15], image style conversion [6], image synthesis from natural language description [27].

Training GANs is equivalent to a two-player minimax game, where a generator G and a discriminator D compete with each other while being optimized for opposite objectives. G attempts to produce samples from the target distribution, namely the data population such as natural images, on the other hand, D is trained to distinguish "true" data samples from the training set and those generated by G. The two players reach the Nash equilibrium [22] of the game when G perfectly models the generative process of the data and D has an error rate of 50%. This basic setup of GANs is oriented to unsupervised learning, where the only knowledge about the data distribution is a set of presumably i.i.d. observed samples. On the other hand, structural knowledge of data population can be helpful to build models. For example, if corresponding labels are provided, i.e. samples in the form of (sample X, label Y), the labels Y can be employed to construct generative probabilistic models where latent variables have certain structures consistent with Y, which is beneficial to build high quality models for complex data such as images [25]. For example, one of the most straightforward extensions is to construct a generative model for each individual label [25].

However, labeled data samples are scarce compared to unlabeled ones. Moreover, in a practical dataset, labels are effectively the supervisors' decisions on using which attributes to characterize the data. The attributes may be relevant in the context for a particular task. But they are subject to human bias and error or limited by the scope of the task, and can be suboptimal to describe the latent structure of the data distribution.

In this paper, we consider a more general setting of GANs, where the generator accepts two sets of random variables as input. Input part one is a random vector Z drawn from multivariate normal distribution as in standard GANs. Input part two is a random binary vector C, elements drawn from independent Bernoulli distributions, which we call *generating code*. The motivation behind the design of $G(z, c)$ is as follows.

- The binary input C characterize the sample, while different code c_1 and c_2 can represent distinctive regions of the data distribution, such as images belonging to two different object categories or video recording of different types of events.
- The continuous input Z, through the mapping of G, spans a local variation of the data distribution, such as the viewing angle of an object, or geometrical or physical variations such as affine transforms or lighting conditions.

It is worthy noting that, unlike labels or latent variables associated to the training samples, the categorical attributes represented by C are not explicitly specified or inferred for the training samples. The training process of the propose binary GAN, BGAN, remains to be unsupervised. Instead, C participates the generative process as binary random noises (thus the name, generating code). The impose the constraint that C is corresponding to characteristic global structures of the distribution, we introduce a new set of neural networks and the corresponding training objectives in BGANs. It is required that the generating code C can be recognized from the generated samples. In our empirical evaluation of BGAN on complex data distributions, the codes C have been automatically aligned with underlying factors that are meaningful in forming the structure of the data distribution. In practical data, the automatically allocated code-sample association often reveals semantically significant attributes, such as object categories.

The rest of this paper is organized as follows. Section 2 reviews related works. In Sect. 3, we introduce the BGAN model. Section 4 reports empirical evaluation of BGAN on both synthetic and practical data. Section 5 concludes the paper.

2   Related Works

Deep neural networks have achieved impressive success in supervised tasks such as image recognition [11,30,35], object detection [21,28], natural language processing [34]. The learning of rich, distributed and hierarchical data representation is the key to the success [18]. The early works are mostly discriminative tasks, where the deep neural networks are adopted as powerful function approximator. The focus is effective learning of networks for accurate modelling of the associative map between an observation and the desired output [32].

On the other hand, deep generative models are useful to model the casual-effect relationship between interested underlying factors and observed data, while the intractable inference adds to the difficulty of model training [12,33]. Adversarial training strategy has been proposed to effectively tune a generative deep neural that models the sampling distribution of the data [9]. A discriminator is employed in the GAN framework as the critic on the output of the generator net: the discriminator attempts to differ the counterfeit samples produced by the generator from the genuine data samples. It has been theoretically verified that when the minimax game between the generator and the discriminator reaches the Nash equilibrium when the generator produces samples following the real data distribution and discriminator cannot make effective distinction. There are a growing number of practical applications of GAN in a wide range of AI tasks, including image generation [4,26], mode conversion [3,20,37], text-to-image translation [27], etc.

One concern of the GAN framework is that the lack of control over the sampling distribution – it is often desirable to sample from a subset of data distribution, e.g. given the observation of a low-resolution image, super-resolution task requires to produce a high-resolution image of the same content as the low-resolution input. Variational auto-encoder [16] is an alternative framework which models the posterior distribution of the latent variables. However, GAN has advantage over VAE in terms of the representative capability. Recently, various variants of GANs have been proposed to address the conditional generation given some external information [14,23], where the nets are provided with extra observation particular to individual samples.

Despite theoretical justification, empirical implementation of GAN often suffers from training difficulties. The optimization progress can fail to converge or the nets may collapse to undesirable trivial fixed point [7]. In particular, the generators can have difficult time in producing distributions of multiple modes. Previous efforts have been made to energy based models [8]. Explicit conditional GANs with categorical information (as opposed to side information on individuals as above) have been proposed [13,23,25]. However, the categorical codes must be provided during training, and the frameworks thus requires explicit supervision of sample labels. Instead, we randomly sample binary variables on which the continuous generating process is conditioned. Binary representation are also automatically inferred as code for image retrieval [31].

3   Model

We propose to incorporate binary noises in the inputs to the generator in the GANs architecture. The binary GANs, BGANs, are defined as follows. To produce one fake sample, x_{fake}, the generator G takes two sets of inputs, $c \in \{0,1\}^{k_c}$ and $z \in \mathbb{R}^{k_z}$,

$$c_i \sim \text{Bernoulli}(\eta), \ i \in 1 \dots k_c \tag{1}$$

$$z_j \sim \mathcal{N}(0, \sigma^2), \ j \in 1 \dots k_z \tag{2}$$

where the two noises are drawn as independent Bernoulli distributions and normal distributions, respectively. The η and σ are noise distribution parameters, which can be fixed to $\eta = 0.5$ and $\sigma = 1.0$ for most practical scenarios. The generated samples are

$$x_{fake} \leftarrow G(z, c) \tag{3}$$

Both x_{fake} and $x_{true} \sim p_{data}$ are taken by the discriminator D, which predicts the probability that the sample belonging to the ground-truth data distribution

---

input : G: parameters $\boldsymbol{\theta}$
input : D: parameters $\boldsymbol{w}^d$
input : I: parameters $\boldsymbol{w}^i$
input : samples x_{true}
output: $\boldsymbol{\theta}$, $\boldsymbol{w}^d$, $\boldsymbol{w}^i$
begin
    while $\boldsymbol{\theta}$ *not converged* **do**
        Sample binary c and z
        Produce x_{fake} sampled by $G(z,c)$
        minimize (7) and (8) w.r.t. $D_{\boldsymbol{w}^d}(x)$
        minimize (9) w.r.t. $I_{\boldsymbol{w}^i}(x)$
        minimize (9) but maximize (8) w.r.t. $G_{\boldsymbol{\theta}}(z,c)$
    end
end

Algorithm 1: BGAN

rather than the generated distribution. In BGAN, we introduce a new discriminator I, which examines the distinctiveness of the generated samples with respect to the generating codes c

$$d \leftarrow I(x_1^{fake}, x_2^{fake}) \tag{4}$$

I takes a pair of *generated* samples as its input. The output d is of the same dimension as the generating code c. The objective is designed such that I is trained to identify different bits in c_1 and c_2, where

$$x_1^{fake} = G(z_1, c_1) \tag{5}$$
$$x_2^{fake} = G(z_2, c_2) \tag{6}$$

i.e. c_1 and c_2 are the generating codes responsible for x_1^{fake} and x_2^{fake}, respectively.

During training, the objective function of BGAN consists of three parts,

$$L_T := \mathbf{E}_{x \sim p_{data}}[\log D(x)] \tag{7}$$
$$L_F := \mathbf{E}_{z \sim p_z, c \sim p_c}[\log (1 - D(G(z, c)))] \tag{8}$$
$$L_C := \mathbf{E}_{z_1, c_1, z_2, c_2}[D_B(\mathbf{1}[c_1 \neq c_2], I(G(z_1, c_1), G(z_2, c_2)))] \tag{9}$$

where the L_C measures the accuracy of identifying the differences in the generating codes of two fake samples. The indicator vector $\mathbf{1}[c_1 \neq c_2]$ is a binary vector of the same size as c_1 and c_2, each element representing the corresponding elements in c_1 and c_2 are different. For example, if $c_1 = [0, 0, 1, 0, 1]^T$ and $c_2 = [0, 0, 0, 0, 1]^T$, then the difference indicator vector would be $\mathbf{1}[c_1 \neq c_2] = [0, 0, 1, 0, 0]^T$. The metric D_B measures the divergence between two binary distributions, for example binary cross-entropy can be used to realize the definition in (9).

The training scheme of BGANs resemble the min-max game of the original GAN [9]. The discriminator D is trained to minimize the loss $L_T + L_F$. The difference identifier I is trained to optimize the loss L_C. A well trained I can help identify the differences in the generating codes behind two generated samples. The generator G is trained to minimize the loss $-L_F + L_C$. I.e. on one hand, G is required to generate samples sufficiently similar to the ones drawn from the true distribution that can fool D. On the other hand, the generating process must also respect the global structure induced in the codes c.

Training steps of BGAN was showed in Algorithm 1, and Fig. 1 illustrates the implementation of network structure.

4   Experiments

We train BGANs on both a toy dataset and practical image datasets of MNIST [36] and CIFAR-10 [17]. The MNIST dataset contains 70,000 grayscale images (size of 28×28, 60,000 for training and 10,000 for testing) of hand-written digits.

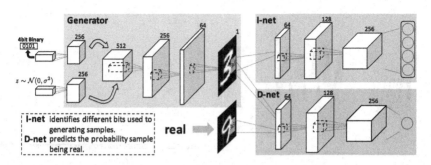

Fig. 1. BGAN Model Structure. The figure shows a typical workflow of BGAN on example image data. Binary noises and continuous noises are send to a transposed convolution structure, Generator, produce a sample more specifically an image. Standard convolution network is employed to construct both I-net and D-net. I-net receives sample pair and output distinctiveness with respect to their binary codes. D-net processes samples and output a single neuron corresponding to the probability sample belonging to the ground-truth data distribution.

The CIFAR-10 dataset consists of 10 classes samples having 60,000 32×32 color images in train set and 10,000 in test set.

In our implementation of BGANs, The generator G takes one m-dimensional continuous noise vector drawn from independent Gaussian distribution $\mathcal{N}(0, \sigma^2)$ and one n-dimensional binary noise vector drawn from independent Bernoulli distribution as (1). To generate an image of appropriate size, the noise vectors are concatenated and considered as a 1×1 image of $m + n$ channels. In one step of upsampling the noise signal, G uses a transposed convolutional layer [29] followed by rectifier linear activations [24]. The upsampling step is repeated several times with specific stride and dilution settings to have the output of G match that of the target images. The final layer of G has activation of sigmoid function. The discriminator D has a standard structure of convolutional nets [19]. In particular, we use 3 convolution layers followed by a full-connection layer. In terms of neural nets implementation, the code-identifier C is structurally similar to D. There are two noticeable differences: (i) C takes two concatenated images as input to identify the different bits in their respective generating code vectors, so the input of C is a 2-D image for the MNIST grayscale images and 6-D image for the CIFAR-10 color images. (ii) The output of C are of the same size 4 as the generating binary codes. Network structures adopted in the following experiments are similar to the model showed in Fig. 1.

4.1   Verification of Concept on Toy Data

To verify the idea of BGANs and easily visualize the BGAN model behavior, we construct a 2D point data and train BGANs on the synthetic data. The toy data is a mixture of 2D Gaussian distributions. Each component of the mixture is a simple isotropic 2D Gaussian differing from each other only by the mean

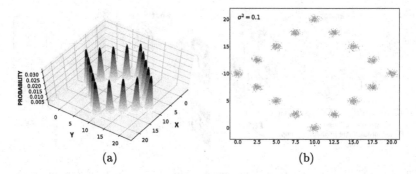

(a)   (b)

Fig. 2. Synthetic 2D data points. **(a)**: The probabilistic density of sampling distribution. **(b)**: 16,000 samples, 1000 from each of the 16 components of the Gaussian mixture.

$\mathcal{N}(\mu_1, \sigma^2 \cdot I_{2\times2}), \mathcal{N}(\mu_2, \sigma^2 \cdot I_{2\times2}), \dots$. In particular, we draw an example in Fig. 2, where the sampling distribution is a 16-Gaussian mixture with $\mu \in [0, 20]^2$ and $\sigma^2 = 0.1 \cdot I_{2\times2}$. Figure 2 shows the density of the Gaussian mixture and one set of 16, 000 training points. The task for the models is to generate points on the 2D plane that are distributed similarly to the mixture.

In this experiment, BGANs use 4 bits in the binary generating codes, and 2D Gaussian noise vectors. Our motivation is that we can represent up to 16 components by the 4-bit code and the data distribution is known to be in $\mathbb{R}^2$.

Figure 3 shows the points sampled from the generator nets trained with BGAN and Wasserstein GAN (WGAN) [10] respectively. Different panes represent different settings of the noise variance for z, in sufficiently trained models the results are not sensitive to z-variance. In the following experiment we will use $\sigma_z^2 = 0.1$. Simple visual inspection of the results show superior fitness of BGAN. which can be attributed to the binary code helping model spatially complex distribution. When the components of the mixture are arranged so that the density structure is spatially complex, BGANs can capture the complex structure more reliably. In Fig. 3, the points generated with different binary codes are plotted using respective colors. It is interesting to notice that the model automatically recognizes data clusters without explicit constraint on connection between z and generated points. In Fig. 7 (attached at the end of the paper on page 10), we plot points generated by different binary code separately, which clearly show the structure discovery and encoding capability of BGAN.

We also perform a quantitative evaluation of WGAN and BGAN on how they have modeled the data distribution. Although in this synthetic data experiment we have access to the ground-truth density function, we use a consistent evaluation criterion as used for the practical data. The details are introduced below. Briefly, we use the generated 16,000 points by BGAN and WGAN respectively (Fig. 3(a) and (d)), and fit a density estimator on the generated points. Then the likelihood of the training samples are computed. The higher the likelihood the better the model has fitted to the data distribution.

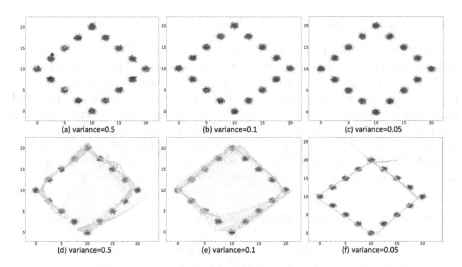

Fig. 3. Generated data points by BGAN and GAN. **(a–c)**: Samples produced by 4-bit BGAN with different continuous noise variance. The colors indicate different binary codes. See Fig. 7 for clearer demonstration on samples generated with different codes. **(d–f)**: Samples produced by GAN trained using the framework in [10] using the same noise variance as (a–c). (Color figure online)

Figure 4 shows the estimated probability using samples generated by trained BGAN and WGAN models respectively, along with the likelihood of the training samples. The plot shows the advantage of using generating codes when the structure of the distribution grows more complex, and especially when the distribution is *not* continuous in the raw observation space. The quantitative result

$$\log p_{BGAN}(Data) = -3.99 > \log p_{WGAN}(Data) = -4.35$$

shows effectiveness of BGAN.

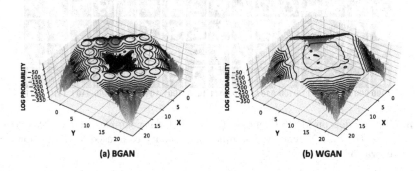

Fig. 4. Synthetic data probability modeled by BGAN and WGAN.

4.2 Modelling Distributions of Practical Image Datasets

We apply WGAN and BGAN to the MNIST [36] and CIFAR-10 datasets [17]. In the experiment, we have used 4 bits for c and $\sigma_z^2 = 0.1$ for both classes.

The learned probabilities are evaluated following the protocol as [1,2]. Specifically, as the ground-truth probability density is intractable for the practical image data, we generate samples using a learned model. Using a Gaussian Parzen window fitted to the generated samples, we can calculate the likelihood of the samples in the dataset under the learned probability. Higher likelihood indicates better learned probability distributions. Table 1 lists the likelihood of BGAN and WGAN, showing the binary codes improve the modelling of data distribution.

Table 1. Data average log-likelihood of BGAN and WGAN modeled distributions.

Data	BGAN	WGAN
MNIST	**−169.355**	−177.676
CIFAR-10	**−412.313**	−3097.502

The data samples, generated images using WGAN and BGAN on MNIST and CIFAR-10 are shown in Figs. 5 and 6, respectively. The generated samples from BGAN with different generating codes. It is noteworthy that BGAN are trained completely unsupervised as WGAN.

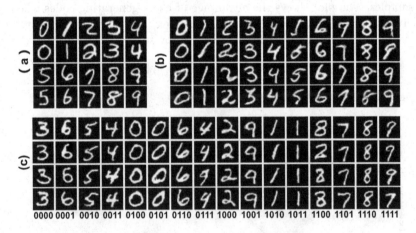

Fig. 5. GAN models on MNIST images. **(a)** MNIST data samples; **(b)** WGAN generated samples; **(c)** BGAN generated samples. The binary code used in BGAN for each sample generation is listed as well.

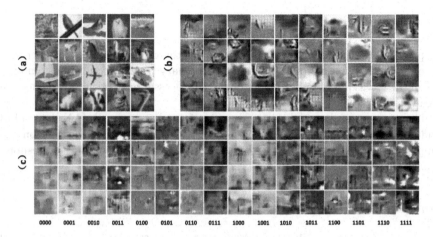

Fig. 6. GAN models on CIFAR-10 images. **(a)** Training data samples; **(b)** WGAN generated samples; **(c)** BGAN generated samples. The binary code for each sample generation is listed as well.

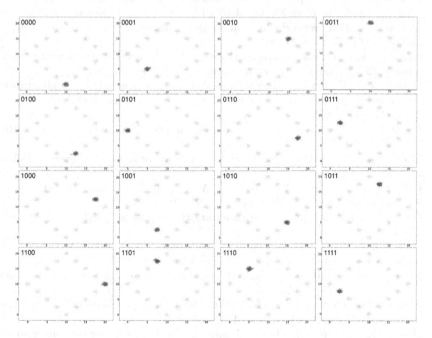

Fig. 7. Synthetic data generated by BGAN with different binary codes. Each plot in the figure shows samples from a particular binary code in the synthetic data experiment. (Color figure online)

5   Conclusion

We present a novel extension to GANs, where the generator takes into account not only continuous random noises, but also binary random code. The combination of the two types of underlying stochastic processes have been shown effective in capturing data distribution.

There are several straightforward yet useful extension to BGAN. Instead of randomly drawing the codes, one can have a few bits fixed and condition the sample generating process as $x \sim X|c_1, c_2, \ldots$. The known bits may correspond to partial knowledge of stochastic process modeled by BGAN.

References

1. Breuleux, O., Bengio, Y., Vincent, P.: Unlearning for better mixing. Technical Report 1349, Université de Montréal/DIRO (2010)
2. Breuleux, O., Bengio, Y., Vincent, P.: Quickly generating representative samples from an RBM-derived process. Neural Comput. **23**(8), 2058–2073 (2011)
3. Choi, Y., Choi, M., Kim, M., Ha, J.-W., Kim, S., Choo, J.: Stargan: unified generative adversarial networks for multi-domain image-to-image translation. arXiv preprint arXiv:1711.09020 (2017)
4. Denton, E.L., Chintala, S., Fergus, R., et al.: Deep generative image models using a laplacian pyramid of adversarial networks, pp. 1486–1494 (2015)
5. Garimella, S., Hermansky, H.: Factor analysis of auto-associative neural networks with application in speaker verification. IEEE Trans. Neural Netw. Learn. Syst. **24**(4), 522–528 (2013)
6. Gatys, L.A., Ecker, A.S., Bethge, M.: A neural algorithm of artistic style. CoRR, abs/1508.06576 (2015)
7. Goodfellow, I.J.: NIPS 2016 tutorial: generative adversarial networks. CoRR, abs/1701.00160 (2017)
8. Goodfellow, I.J., Mirza, M., Courville, A.C., Bengio, Y.: Multi-prediction deep Boltzmann machines. In: NIPS, pp. 548–556 (2013)
9. Goodfellow, I.J., et al.: Generative adversarial networks. CoRR, abs/1406.2661 (2014)
10. Gulrajani, I., Ahmed, F., Arjovsky, M., Dumoulin, V., Courville, A.C.: Improved training of wasserstein gans. In: NIPS, pp. 5769–5779 (2017)
11. He, K., Zhang, X., Ren, S., Sun, J.: Deep residual learning for image recognition. In: CVPR, pp. 770–778 (2016)
12. Hinton, G.E., Osindero, S., Teh, Y.W.: A fast learning algorithm for deep belief nets. Neural Comput. **18**(7), 1527–1554 (2006)
13. Hoang, Q., Nguyen, T.D., Le, T., Phung, D.: MGAN: training generative adversarial nets with multiple generators. In: ICLR, p. 24 (2018)
14. Isola, P., Zhu, J.Y., Zhou, T., Efros, A.A.: Image-to-image translation with conditional adversarial networks. In: CVPR, pp. 1125–1134 (2017)
15. Khosrowabadi, R., Quek, C., Ang, K.K., Wahab, A.: ERNN: a biologically inspired feedforward neural network to discriminate emotion from EEG signal. IEEE Trans. Neural Netw. Learn. Syst. **25**(3), 609–620 (2014)
16. Kingma, D.P., Welling, M.: Auto-encoding variational bayes. CoRR, abs/1312.6114 (2013)

17. Krizhevsky, A., Nair, V., Hinton, G.: The CIFAR-10 dataset (2014)
18. LeCun, Y., Bengio, Y., Hinton, G.E.: Deep learning. Nature **521**(7553), 436–444 (2015)
19. LeCun, Y., Bottou, L., Bengio, Y., Haffner, P.: Gradient-based learning applied to document recognition. Proc. IEEE **86**(11), 2278–2324 (1998)
20. Liu, M.Y., Breuel, T., Kautz, J.: Unsupervised image-to-image translation networks. In: NIPS, pp. 700–708 (2017)
21. Liu, W., et al.: SSD: single shot multibox detector. In: Leibe, B., Matas, J., Sebe, N., Welling, M. (eds.) ECCV 2016. LNCS, vol. 9905, pp. 21–37. Springer, Cham (2016). https://doi.org/10.1007/978-3-319-46448-0_2
22. Maskin, E.: Nash equilibrium and welfare optimality. Rev. Econ. Stud. **66**(1), 23–38 (1999)
23. Mirza, M., Osindero, S.: Conditional generative adversarial nets. CoRR, abs/1411.1784 (2014)
24. Nair, V., Hinton, G.E.: Rectified linear units improve restricted Boltzmann machines. In: ICML, pp. 807–814 (2010)
25. Odena, A., Olah, C., Shlens, J.: Conditional image synthesis with auxiliary classifier GANs. In: ICML, pp. 2642–2651 (2017)
26. Radford, A., Metz, L., Chintala, S.: Unsupervised representation learning with deep convolutional generative adversarial networks. CoRR, abs/1511.06434 (2015)
27. Reed, S., Akata, Z., Yan, X., Logeswaran, L., Schiele, B., Lee, H.: Generative adversarial text to image synthesis. In: ICML, pp. 1060–1069 (2016)
28. Ren, S., He, K., Girshick, R.B., Sun, J.: Faster R-CNN: towards real-time object detection with region proposal networks. In: NIPS, pp. 91–99 (2015)
29. Schwarz, B., Richardson, M.: Using a de-convolution window for operating modal analysis. In: Proceedings of the IMAC. Citeseer (2007)
30. Simonyan, K., Zisserman, A.: Very deep convolutional networks for large-scale image recognition. CoRR, abs/1409.1556 (2014)
31. Song, J., He, T., Gao, L., Xu, X., Hanjalic, A., Shen, H.T.: Binary generative adversarial networks for image retrieval. In: AAAI (2018)
32. Srivastava, N., Hinton, G.E., Krizhevsky, A., Sutskever, I., Salakhutdinov, R.: Dropout: a simple way to prevent neural networks from overfitting. J. Mach. Learn. Res. **15**(1), 1929–1958 (2014)
33. Sutskever, I., Hinton, G.E., Taylor, G.W.: The recurrent temporal restricted Boltzmann machine. In: NIPS, pp. 1601–1608 (2008)
34. Sutskever, I., Vinyals, O., Le, Q.V.: Sequence to sequence learning with neural networks. In: NIPS, pp. 3104–3112 (2014)
35. Szegedy, C., Ioffe, S., Vanhoucke, V., Alemi, A.A.: Inception-v4, inception-resnet and the impact of residual connections on learning. In: AAAI, pp. 4278–4284 (2017)
36. Cortes, C., LeCun, Y., Burges, C.J.C.: The MNIST database of handwritten digits (1998)
37. Zhu, J.Y., Park, T., Isola, P., Efros, A.A.: Unpaired image-to-image translation using cycle-consistent adversarial networks. In: ICCV (2017)

Twin Bounded Large Margin Distribution Machine

Haitao Xu[(✉)], Brendan McCane, and Lech Szymanski

Department of Computer Science, University of Otago, Otago 9016, New Zealand
{haitao,mccane,lechszym}@cs.otago.ac.nz

Abstract. In order to speed up the learning time of large margin distribution machine (LDM) and improve the generalization performance of twin bounded support vector machine (TBSVM), a novel method named twin bounded large margin distribution machine (TBLDM) is proposed in this paper. The central idea of TBLDM is to seek a pair of nonparallel hyperplanes by optimizing the positive and negative margin distributions on the base of TBSVM. The experimental results indicate that the proposed TBLDM is a fast, effective and robust classifier.

Keywords: Large margin distribution machine
Twin bounded support vector machine · Margin distribution
Margin mean · Margin variance

1 Introduction

Support vector machines (SVMs) [3,18] are powerful tools for pattern classification and regression. For the classical binary classification SVM, the optimal hyperplane can be obtained by maximizing a relaxed minimum margin, i.e., the smallest distance from data point to the classification boundary. This optimisation can be expressed as a quadratic programming problem (QPP). Margin theory [17] provides good theoretical support to the generalisation performance of SVMs and it has also been applied to many other machine learning approaches, such as AdaBoost [5]. There was, however, a long debate on whether margin theory plays a significant role in AdaBoost [2,14]. It had been believed that a single-data-point margin such as minimum margin is not crucial [13,19]. [6] ended the long debate and showed that margin distribution, characterized by margin mean and variance, is critical for generalisation in boosting. Inspired by these results, [23] first focused on the influence of the margin distribution for SVMs and proposed large margin distribution machine (LDM). The margin distribution heuristic can also be applied to clustering [24] and dimensionality reduction [9].

The twin support vector machine (TWSVM) proposed by [7] seeks for two nonparallel boundary hyperplanes and attempts to make each of the two hyperplanes close to one class and far from the other as much as possible. TWSVM solves two smaller size QPPs instead of a single large QPP. This results in

© Springer Nature Switzerland AG 2018
T. Mitrovic et al. (Eds.): AI 2018, LNAI 11320, pp. 718–729, 2018.
https://doi.org/10.1007/978-3-030-03991-2_64

TWSVM being faster than SVM. An improved version of TWSVM, called twin bounded support vector machine (TBSVM) was proposed by [16]. TBSVM implemented the structural risk minimisation principle by introducing a regularization term. Based on statistical learning theory, TBSVM can improve the performance of classification of TWSVM. Recently, many extensions of TWSVM have been proposed, for details, see [8,12,15,20,21].

In this paper, we propose the twin bounded large margin distribution machine (TBLDM). Similar to LDM, the margin distribution of TBLDM is characterised by first and second order statistics and optimizing the margin distribution is realized by maximizing the margin mean and minimizing the margin variance simultaneously. However, TBLDM tries to optimise the positive and negative margin distributions separately. This is different from LDM, which optimised the whole margin distribution for all training points.

To begin with, we will first provide a brief background on SVM, TWSVM and LDM in Sect. 2. Our novel approach TBLDM for classification problems will be introduced in Sect. 3. In Sect. 4, we will make numerical experiments to verify that our new model is very effective in classification. Discussions and conclusions will be summarized in Sect. 5.

2   Notation and Related Work

Given the dataset $T = \{(x_i, y_i)\}_{i=1}^{l}$, where $x_i \in R^n$ is the i-th input sample and $y_i \in \{\pm 1\}$ is the class label of x_i. Let l_1 and l_2 be the numbers of samples belonging to the positive and negative classes, respectively, such that $l = l_1 + l_2$. Denote $X = [x_1, \cdots, x_l] \in R^{n \times l}$, $A = [x_1^+, \cdots, x_{l_1}^+] \in R^{n \times l_1}$ and $B = [x_1^-, \cdots, x_{l_2}^-] \in R^{n \times l_2}$ as the entire, positive and negative sample matrices. Let $k : R^n \times R^n \to R$ be a kernel function with reproducing kernel Hilbert space (RKHS) $\widetilde{H}$ and nonlinear feature mapping $\phi : R^n \to \widetilde{H}$. Denote $\phi(A) = [\phi(x_1^+), \cdots, \phi(x_{l_1}^+)]$, $\phi(B) = [\phi(x_1^-), \cdots, \phi(x_{l_2}^-)]$ as the positive and negative mapped sample matrices, the kernel matrix $K = \phi(X)^T \phi(X)$ where $\phi(X) = [\phi(x_1), \cdots, \phi(x_l)]$, $K_A = \phi(A)^T \phi(X) \in R^{l_1 \times l}$, $K_B = \phi(B)^T \phi(X) \in R^{l_2 \times l}$, $K(x, X) = [k(x, x_1), \cdots, k(x, x_l)] \in R^{1 \times l}$, $\forall x \in R^n$. and $y = (y_1, \cdots, y_l)^T \in R^l$. $y_A = (y_1^+, \cdots, y_{l_1}^+)^T \in R^{l_1}$, $y_B = (y_1^-, \cdots, y_{l_2}^-)^T \in R^{l_2}$.

2.1   Support Vector Machine (SVM)

SVM tries to find a hyperplane $f(x) = w^T \phi(x) = 0$, where f is linear and $w \in \widetilde{H}$ is a linear predictor. According to [3] and [17], the margin of the individual sample (x_i, y_i) is defined as

$$\gamma_i = y_i w^T \phi(x_i), i = 1, \cdots, l. \tag{1}$$

In separable cases, all the γ_i will be non-negative. So we can get the geometric distance from each x_i to $w^T \phi(x) = 0$ by scaling each γ_i with $1/\|w\|$:

$$\hat{\gamma}_i = y_i \frac{w^T}{\|w\|} \phi(x_i), i = 1, \cdots, l.$$

For the separable case, SVM maximizes the minimum distance:

$$\max_{w} \hat{\gamma}$$
$$s.t. \quad \hat{\gamma}_i \geq \hat{\gamma}, i = 1, \cdots, l.$$

It can be written as

$$\max_{w} \frac{\gamma}{\|w\|}$$
$$s.t. \quad \gamma_i \geq \gamma, i = 1, \cdots, l.$$

We can simply set γ as 1 since it doesn't have influence on the optimisation. Note that maximizing $1/\|w\|$ is equivalent to minimizing $\|w\|^2$, we can get the classic formulation of hard-margin SVM as follows:

$$\min_{w} \frac{1}{2}\|w\|^2$$
$$s.t. \quad y_i w^T \phi(x_i) \geq 1, i = 1, \cdots, l.$$

For non-separable case, SVM can be written as

$$\max_{w,\xi_i} \gamma_0 - \bar{C} \sum_{i=1}^{l} \xi_i$$
$$s.t. \quad \gamma_i \geq \gamma_0 - \xi_i,$$
$$\xi_i \geq 0, i = 1, \cdots, l,$$

where γ_0 is a relaxed minimum margin, ξ_i is slack variable and $\bar{C}$ is the trading-off parameter. The above formula can be rewritten as

$$\max_{w,\xi_i} \gamma_0 - C \sum_{i=1}^{l} \xi_i$$
$$s.t. \quad y_i w^T \phi(x_i) \geq 1 - \xi_i,$$
$$\xi_i \geq 0, i = 1, \cdots, l,$$

where C is a trading-off parameter. We can see that SVMs for both separable and non-separable cases consider only single-data-point margins but not the whole margin distribution.

2.2   Twin Bounded Support Vector Machine (TBSVM)

Different from conventional SVM, TWSVM seeks for a pair of nonparallel hyperplanes $f_+(x) = w_+^T \phi(x) = 0$ and $f_-(x) = w_-^T \phi(x) = 0$. As an improved version of TWSVM, TBSVM consider the structural risk minimization principle by adding a regularization term. The training time of TBSVM is approximately four times faster than SVM. We introduce non-linear TBSVM in this subsection, for linear case and other details, see [7, 16]. The unknown vectors $w_+, w_- \in R^n$ of TBSVM can be obtained by solving the following two QPPs:

$$\min_{w_+, \xi_2} \frac{c_1}{2} ||w_+||^2 + \frac{1}{2} ||\phi(A)^T w_+||^2 + c_3 e_2^T \xi_2$$
$$s.t. \quad -\phi(B)^T w_+ + \xi_2 \geq e_2, \ \xi_2 \geq 0, \tag{2}$$

$$\min_{w_-, \xi_1} \frac{c_2}{2} ||w_-||^2 + \frac{1}{2} ||\phi(B)^T w_-||^2 + c_4 e_1^T \xi_1$$
$$s.t. \quad \phi(A)^T w_- + \xi_1 \geq e_1, \ \xi_1 \geq 0, \tag{3}$$

where $c_1, \cdots, c_4 > 0$ are trade-off parameters, $\xi_1 \in R^{l_1}, \xi_2 \in R^{l_2}$ are slack variable vectors and $e_1 \in R^{l_1}, e_2 \in R^{l_2}$ are vectors of ones. A new input $\tilde{x} \in R^n$ is assigned the class k depending on which of the two hyperplanes it is closer to. That is, the class label $y_{\tilde{x}}$ can be obtained by $y_{\tilde{x}} = \arg\min_{k=\pm} \frac{|f_k(\tilde{x})|}{||w_k||}$.

Similar to the definition of the margin of individual sample in (1), the positive and negative margin of individual sample can be formulated as

$$\gamma_j^+ = y_j^+ f_-(x_j^+) = y_j^+ w_-^T \phi(x_j^+), j = 1, \cdots, l_1, \tag{4}$$

$$\gamma_j^- = y_j^- f_+(x_j^-) = y_j^- w_+^T \phi(x_j^-), j = 1, \cdots, l_2, \tag{5}$$

respectively. We can see that TBSVM tries to maximize the minimal negative margin between the negative samples and positive decision hyperplane by (2) and maximize the minimal positive margin by (3).

2.3 Large Margin Distribution Machine (LDM)

LDM tries to achieve a strong generalization performance by optimizing the margin distribution of samples on the basis of soft-margin SVM. The margin distribution is characterized by first- and second-order statistics. Optimizing margin distribution is realized by maximizing the margin mean and minimizing the margin variance simultaneously. Based on (1), the margin mean $\bar{\gamma}$ and the margin variance $\hat{\gamma}$ can be calculated by $\bar{\gamma} = \frac{1}{l} \sum_{i=1}^{l} \gamma_i$ and $\hat{\gamma} = \frac{1}{l} \sum_{i=1}^{l} (\gamma_i - \bar{\gamma})^2$. The unknown $w \in \tilde{H}$ can be obtained by solving the following optimisation problem:

$$\min_{w, \xi_i} \frac{1}{2} w^T w + \lambda_1 \hat{\gamma} - \lambda_2 \bar{\gamma} + C \sum_{i=1}^{l} \xi_i$$
$$s.t. \quad y_i w^T \phi(x_i) \geq 1 - \xi_i, \ \xi_i \geq 0, i = 1, \cdots, l,$$

where $\lambda_1, \lambda_2 > 0$ are the parameters for trading-off the margin variance, the margin mean and the model complexity. It is obvious that LDM can be reduced to soft-margin SVM when $\lambda_1 = \lambda_2 = 0$.

3   Twin Bounded Large Margin Distribution Machine (TBLDM)

In this section, we will introduce our novel classification method named as twin bounded large margin distribution machine (TBLDM). Based on the concepts of positive margin and negative margin in (4) and (5), the positive margin mean $\bar{\gamma}^+$ and the positive margin variance $\hat{\gamma}^+$ can be calculated by $\bar{\gamma}^+ = \frac{1}{l_1}\sum_{j=1}^{l_1}\gamma_j^+ = \frac{1}{l_1}y_A^T\phi(A)^Tw_-$, and $\hat{\gamma}^+ = \frac{1}{l_1}\sum_{i=1}^{l_1}(\gamma_i^+ - \bar{\gamma}^+)^2 = w_-^T\phi(A)Q_1\phi(A)^Tw_-$ respectively. Here $Q_1 = \frac{l_1I_{l_1} - y_Ay_A^T}{l_1^2}$ is a symmetric matrix. Since $Q_1^2 = \frac{1}{l_1}Q_1$, it can be concluded that Q_1 is a symmetric nonnegative definite matrix. Similarly, we can get the negative margin mean $\bar{\gamma}^-$ and the negative margin variance $\hat{\gamma}^-$ by $\bar{\gamma}^- = \frac{1}{l_2}y_B^T\phi(B)^Tw_+, \hat{\gamma}^- = w_+^T\phi(B)Q_2\phi(B)^Tw_+$, where $Q_2 = \frac{l_2I_{l_2} - y_By_B^T}{l_2^2}$ is also a symmetric nonnegative definite matrix.

3.1   TBLDM

Specifically, TBLDM seeks a pair of unknown vectors $w_+, w_- \in \widetilde{H}$ by maximizing the positive and negative margin mean and minimizing the positive and negative margin variance simultaneously, that is, by considering the following two optimisation problems:

$$\min_{w_+,\xi_2} \frac{c_1}{2}\|w_+\|^2 + \frac{1}{2}\|\phi(A)^Tw_+\|^2 - \lambda_1\bar{\gamma}^- + \lambda_2\hat{\gamma}^- + c_3e_2^T\xi_2$$

$$s.t. \quad -\phi(B)^Tw_+ + \xi_2 \geq e_2, \ \xi_2 \geq 0, \tag{6}$$

$$\min_{w_-,\xi_1} \frac{c_2}{2}\|w_-\|^2 + \frac{1}{2}\|\phi(B)^Tw_-\|^2 - \lambda_3\bar{\gamma}^+ + \lambda_4\hat{\gamma}^+ + c_4e_1^T\xi_1$$

$$s.t. \quad \phi(A)^Tw_- + \xi_1 \geq e_1, \ \xi_1 \geq 0, \tag{7}$$

where $\lambda_1, \cdots, \lambda_4 > 0$ are the parameters for trading-off the margin variances, the margin means and the complexity of models. It is obvious that TBLDM can be reduced to the nonlinear TBSVM when $\lambda_1, \lambda_2, \lambda_3$ and λ_4 are equal to 0. Substituting $\bar{\gamma}^-$ and $\hat{\gamma}^-$ into the models (6), we can get the following:

$$\min_{w_+,\xi_2} \frac{c_1}{2}\|w_+\|^2 + \frac{1}{2}\|\phi(A)^Tw_+\|^2 - \frac{\lambda_1}{l_2}y_B^T\phi(B)^Tw_+ + \lambda_2w_+^T\phi(B)Q_2\phi(B)^Tw_+ + c_3e_2^T\xi_2$$

$$s.t. \quad -\phi(B)^Tw_+ + \xi_2 \geq e_2, \ \xi_2 \geq 0, \tag{8}$$

Due to $\widetilde{H} = \text{span}\{\phi(x_1), \cdots, \phi(x_l)\}$, we can let $w_+ = \phi(X)\beta_1$ and $w_- = \phi(X)\beta_2$, where $\beta_1, \beta_2 \in R^l$ are coefficient vectors, and then we can deduce that

$$\|w_+\|^2 = \beta_1^TK\beta_1, \qquad |w_-\|^2 = \beta_2^TK\beta_2,$$
$$\phi(A)^Tw_+ = K_A\beta_1, \qquad \phi(B)^Tw_+ = K_B\beta_1,$$
$$\phi(A)^Tw_- = K_A\beta_2, \qquad \phi(B)^Tw_- = K_B\beta_2,$$
$$f_+(x) = w_+^T\phi(x) = K(x,X)\beta_1, \ f_-(x) = w_-^T\phi(x) = K(x,X)\beta_2. \tag{9}$$

Substituting (9) into the models (8), we have

$$\min_{\beta_1,\xi_2} \frac{c_1}{2}\beta_1^T K\beta_1 + \frac{1}{2}\beta_1^T K_A^T K_A \beta_1 - \frac{\lambda_1}{l_2}y_B^T K_B \beta_1 + \lambda_2 \beta_1^T K_B^T Q_2 K_B \beta_1 + c_3 e_2^T \xi_2$$

$$s.t. - K_B\beta_1 + \xi_2 \geq e_2, \xi_2 \geq 0, \tag{10}$$

Let

$$G_1 = c_1 K + K_A^T K_A + 2\lambda_2 K_B^T Q_2 K_B \in R^{l \times l},$$
$$G_2 = c_2 K + K_B^T K_B + 2\lambda_4 K_A^T Q_1 K_A \in R^{l \times l}.$$

Obviously, G_1 and G_2 are symmetric nonnegative definite matrices. The models (10) can be rewritten as

$$\min_{\beta_1,\xi_2} \frac{1}{2}\beta_1^T G_1 \beta_1 - \frac{\lambda_1}{l_2}y_B^T K_B \beta_1 + c_3 e_2^T \xi_2$$

$$s.t. - K_B\beta_1 + \xi_2 \geq e_2, \xi_2 \geq 0, \tag{11}$$

Considering the Lagrangian function of the model (11)

$$L_1(\beta_1,\xi_2,\alpha_1,\delta_1) = \frac{1}{2}\beta_1^T G_1 \beta_1 - \frac{\lambda_1}{l_2}y_B^T K_B \beta_1 + c_3 e_2^T \xi_2 - \alpha_1^T(-K_B\beta_1 + \xi_2 - e_2) - \delta_1^T \xi_2,$$

where $\alpha_1, \delta_1 \in R^{l_2}$ are nonnegative Lagrangian multipliers vectors, and letting $\partial L_1/\partial \beta_1 = \partial L_1/\partial \xi_2 = 0$, we get

$$G_1\beta_1 = \frac{\lambda_1}{l_2}K_B^T y_B - K_B^T \alpha_1,$$

$$c_3 e_2 - \alpha_1 - \delta_1 = 0 \Rightarrow 0 \leq \alpha_1 \leq c_3 e_2. \tag{12}$$

Without loss of generality, we can assume that G_1 is an invertible matrix; otherwise, it can be regularized, that is, it can be replaced by the matrix $G_1 + t_1 I_l$, where $t_1 > 0$ is a small positive number called regularized coefficient. Consequently, it can be deduced from (12) that

$$\beta_1 = G_1^{-1}(\frac{\lambda_1}{l_2}K_B^T y_B - K_B^T \alpha_1). \tag{13}$$

Submitting (13) and (12) into the Lagrangian function, we can obtain the Wolfe dual form of the model (11):

$$\min_{\alpha_1} \frac{1}{2}\alpha_1^T H_1 \alpha_1 - (\frac{\lambda_1}{l_2}H_1 y_B + e_2)^T \alpha_1$$

$$s.t. \quad 0 \leq \alpha_1 \leq c_3 e_2, \tag{14}$$

where $H_1 = K_B G_1^{-1} K_B^T$. Similarly, we can get

$$\beta_2 = G_2^{-1}(\frac{\lambda_1}{l_1}K_A^T y_A + K_A^T \alpha_2), \tag{15}$$

and then the Wolfe dual form of the model (7) is:

$$\min_{\alpha_2} \frac{1}{2}\alpha_2^T H_2\alpha_2 + (\frac{\lambda_3}{l_1}H_2 y_A - e_1)^T \alpha_2$$

$$s.t. \quad 0 \le \alpha_2 \le c_4 e_1, \tag{16}$$

where $\alpha_2 \in R^{l_1}$ is a nonnegative Lagrangian multipliers vector and $H_2 = K_A G_2^{-1} K_A^T$. A new input $\tilde{x} \in R^n$ is assigned the class i ($i = 1, 2$ denotes the positive and negative classes, respectively) depending on which of the two hyperplanes is closer to, that is, label $(\tilde{x}) = \arg\min_{i=1,2} \frac{|K(\tilde{x},X)\beta_i|}{\sqrt{\beta_i K \beta_i}}$. The specific procedure is listed in Algorithm 1.

Algorithm 1. TBLDM

Input: Training set T, testing sample $\tilde{x}$, kernel function $k : R^n \times R^n \to R$, model
    parameters $\lambda_i, \cdots, \lambda_4$ and $c_i, \cdots, c_4$, regularized parameters t_1, t_2 and kernel
    parameters;
1: Solve the QPP (14) and obtain the optimal solution α_1^*;
2: Compute β_1^* by (13) with $\alpha_1 = \alpha_1^*$;
3: Solve the QPP (16) and obtain the optimal solution α_2^*;
4: Compute β_2^* by (15) with $\alpha_2 = \alpha_2^*$;
5: For $\tilde{x}$, predict its label by label $(\tilde{x}) = \arg\min_{i=1,2} \frac{|K(\tilde{x},X)\beta_i^*|}{\sqrt{\beta_i^* K \beta_i^*}}$.

3.2   TBLDM for Large Scale Datasets

It can be seen that we need to compute G_1^{-1} and G_2^{-1} and kernel matrix K, K_A, K_B before solving the dual problems (14) and (16). This is infeasible when the number of samples is significantly large both in terms of memory and computation. To effectively handle large scale problems, in this subsection, we first choose a kernel approximation method, Nyström method [22] to explicitly map features onto subspaces in the RKHS. In this case, the embedding features are obtained without constructing the complete kernel matrix for the data set. Given the kernel-specific embedding, we perform linear TBLDM. Because the inverse matrices of AA^T and BB^T still need to be computed to get the dual problem of linear TBLDM, we solve the primal problem of linear TBLDM here with stochastic gradient descent (SGD) algorithm.

Linear TBLDM is a special case of TBLDM with linear kernel function $k(u, v) = \langle u, v \rangle$ for any $u, v \in R^n$. In this case, the models (6) and (7) are reduced into the following two QPPs:

$$\min_{w_+, \xi_2} \frac{c_1}{2}\|w_+\|^2 + \frac{1}{2}\|A^T w_+\|^2 - \frac{\lambda_1}{l_2}y_B^T B^T w_+ + \lambda_2 w_+^T BQ_2 B^T w_+ + c_3 e_2^T \xi_2$$

$$s.t. \quad -B^T w_+ + \xi_2 \ge e_2, \; \xi_2 \ge 0, \tag{17}$$

$$\min_{w_-,\xi_1} \frac{c_2}{2}\|w_-\|^2 + \frac{1}{2}\|B^T w_-\|^2 - \frac{\lambda_3}{l_1}y_A^T A^T w_- + \lambda_4 w^T A Q_1 A^T w_- + c_4 e_1^T \xi_1$$

$$s.t. \quad A^T w_- + \xi_1 \geq e_1, \ \xi_1 \geq 0. \tag{18}$$

To solve formulas (17) and (18) in primal case, we express them equivalently as two unconstraint optimisation problems:

$$\min_{w_+,\xi_2} g_1(w_+) = \frac{c_1}{2}\|w_+\|^2 + \frac{1}{2}\|A^T w_+\|^2 - \frac{\lambda_1}{l_2}y_B^T B^T w_+ + \lambda_2 w_+^T B Q_2 B^T w_+$$

$$+ c_3 \sum_{i=1}^{l_2} \max\{0, 1 + w_+^T x_i^-\}, \tag{19}$$

$$\min_{w_-,\xi_1} g_2(w_-) = \frac{c_2}{2}\|w_-\|^2 + \frac{1}{2}\|B^T w_-\|^2 - \frac{\lambda_3}{l_1}y_A^T A^T w_- + \lambda_4 w_-^T A Q_1 A^T w_- +$$

$$c_4 \sum_{i=1}^{l_1} \max\{0, 1 - w_-^T x_i^+\}. \tag{20}$$

If examples (x_i^+, y_i^+), (x_j^+, y_j^+), (x_k^+, y_k^+) are randomly sampled from the positive training set and (x_i^-, y_i^-), (x_j^-, y_j^-), (x_k^-, y_k^-) are randomly sampled from the negative training set independently, it is straightforward to prove that

$$\nabla g_1(w_+, x_i^+, x_j^-, x_k^-) = c_1 w_+ + l_1 x_i^+ x_i^{+^T} w_+ + 2\lambda_2 x_j^- x_j^{-^T} w_+ - 2\lambda_2 x_j^- x_k^{-^T} w_+$$

$$+ \lambda_1 x_j^- + c_3 l_2 x_j^- \mathbb{I}(j \in I_1), \tag{21}$$

$$\nabla g_2(w_-, x_i^-, x_j^+, x_k^+) = c_2 w_- + l_2 x_i^- x_i^{-^T} w_- + 2\lambda_4 x_j^+ x_j^{+^T} w_- - 2\lambda_4 x_j^+ x_k^{+^T} w_-$$

$$- \lambda_3 x_j^+ - c_4 l_1 x_j^+ \mathbb{I}(j \in I_2). \tag{22}$$

are the unbiased estimation of $\nabla g_1(w_+)$ and $\nabla g_2(w_-)$ respectively. $\mathbb{I}(\cdot)$ is the indicator function that returns 1 when the argument holds, and 0 otherwise. I_1, I_2 are the index sets defined as $I_1 = \{j|w_+^T x_j^- > -1\}, I_2 = \{j|w_-^T x_j^+ < 1\}$. So we can update w_+, w_- by $w_+ \leftarrow w_+ - r_1 \nabla g_1(w_+, x_i^+, x_j^-, x_k^-)$ and $w_- \leftarrow w_- - r_2 \nabla g_2(w_-, x_i^-, x_j^+, x_k^+)$, r_1, r_2 are learning rates for each iteration of SGD algorithm. The detailed procedure is listed in Algorithm 2.

4   Experiments and Results Analysis

In order to demonstrate the effectiveness of TBLDM, a series of comparative experiments with SVM, TBSVM and LDM are performed. The experiments focus on the aspects of classification accuracy and computational time on sixteen regular scale datasets and four large-scale datasets. These datasets are taken

---

Algorithm 2. Nyström + linear TBLDM for large scale problems

Input: Positive training set A, negative training set B, testing sample $\widetilde{x}$, model parameters $\lambda_1, \cdots, \lambda_4$ and $c_1, \cdots, c_4$ and learning rates r_1, r_2;

1: Get data embedding A_e, B_e and $\widetilde{x}_e$ by Nyström method;
2: **while** w_+, w_- not converged **do**
3:     Randomly select a mini-batch $x_b^+ = \{x_i^+, x_j^+, x_k^+\}$ and a mini-batch $x_b^- = \{x_i^-, x_j^-, x_k^-\}$;
4:     **for** $x_b^+ \subset A_e$ and $x_b^- \subset B_e$ **do**
5:         Compute the gradient $\nabla g_1(w_+, x_i^+, x_j^-, x_k^-)$ by (21);
6:         Compute the gradient $\nabla g_2(w_-, x_i^-, x_j^+, x_k^+)$ by (22);
7:         $w_+ \leftarrow w_+ - r_1 \nabla g_1(w_+, x_i^+, x_j^-, x_k^-)$;
8:         $w_- \leftarrow w_- - r_2 \nabla g_2(w_-, x_i^-, x_j^+, x_k^+)$;
9:     **end for**
10: **end while**
11: For $\widetilde{x}$, predict its label by label $(\widetilde{x}) = \arg\min_{i=\pm} \frac{|w_i^T \widetilde{x}_e|}{\|w_i\|}$.

---

from UCI database [4] and real-world databases[1], respectively. All the computational time involved is the sum of the training time and the testing time and all the classification accuracy involved is the testing accuracy, that is, the classification accuracy on testing sets.

4.1   Experiments on Regular-Scale Datasets

The statistics of the regular-scale datasets are listed in the first four rows in Table 1, where l and n denote the number and the dimensionality of samples, respectively. Gaussian radial basis function (RBF) kernel $k(u, v) = \exp(-\|u - v\|^2/\gamma)$ for $u, v \in R^n$ is selected and SMO [11] algorithm is used for SVM, where $\gamma > 0$ is a kernel parameter. We use SOR solver [10] for fast training TBSVM; the source code of [23] for LDM; for TBLDM, the 'quadprog' toolbox in MATLAB [1] is used to solve QPPs (14) and (16). All the experiments are operated in MATLAB. For the convenience of computation, we take all the model parameters $C, c_1, c_2, c_3, c_4 = 1$, the kernel parameter γ and λ_1, λ_2 are chosen from $[2^{-6}, 2^6]$ by using 5-fold cross validation method. Experiments are repeated for 5 times with random data partitions to calculate the average accuracies and variances. The experimental results are listed in Table 2, from which we can see that for computational time, TBLDM is obviously faster than LDM except on spect and wpbc datasets, and faster than TBSVM on 12 datasets and similar on the remaining 4 datasets. For classification accuracy, TBLDM is higher than LDM on 11 datasets and same on wdbc data set, and is higher than TBSVM on 13 datasets. In addition, SVM only gets the highest classification accuracy on wdbc data set although its computational time is the fastest.

---

[1] https://www.csie.ntu.edu.tw/~cjlin/libsvmtools/datasets/.

Table 1. Statistics of datasets

Data set	l	n	Data set	l	n	Data set	l	n	Data set	l	n
Australian	690	14	Parkinsons	195	22	Bupa	345	6	Ringnorm	400	20
Ecoli	336	7	Sonar	208	60	German	1000	24	Spect	80	22
Haberman	306	3	Transfusion	748	4	Heart	270	13	Twonorm	400	20
Ionosphere	351	34	wdbc	569	30	Monks2	432	6	wpbc	198	32
cod-rna	216948	8	ijcnn1	141691	22	Skin	245057	3	w8a	64700	300

Table 2. Experimental results with regular size datasets

	SVM		TBSVM		LDM		TBLDM	
DATASETS	acc(mean±std)	time(s)	acc(mean±std)	time(s)	acc(mean±std)	time(s)	acc(mean±std)	time(s)
australian	0.8565±0.0262	0.0353	0.8574±0.0360	0.2015	0.8557±0.0258	1.4757	**0.8672±0.0194**	0.1500
bupa	0.6736±0.0591	0.0292	0.6986±0.0495	0.0818	0.6980±0.0542	0.1893	**0.7014±0.0366**	0.0820
ecoli	0.9637±0.0264	0.0189	0.9648±0.0331	0.0743	**0.9672±0.0232**	0.1785	0.9637±0.0175	0.0939
german	0.7224±0.0367	0.0611	0.7510±0.0211	0.5345	0.7590±0.0186	4.9356	**0.7724±0.0223**	0.4213
haberman	0.7333±0.0235	0.0241	0.7210±0.0203	0.1320	0.7353±0.0344	0.1337	**0.7380±0.0396**	0.0805
heart	0.8333±0.0367	0.0220	0.8356±0.0567	0.0577	0.8326±0.0461	0.0948	**0.8363±0.0464**	0.0491
ionosphere	0.9345±0.0327	0.0233	0.9248±0.0224	0.0688	**0.9441±0.0254**	0.2189	0.8872±0.0308	0.0511
monks2	0.7940±0.0450	0.0330	0.8065±0.0212	0.0595	0.8074±0.0391	0.3659	**0.8320±0.0448**	0.0509
parkinsons	0.9159±0.0387	0.0270	0.8995±0.0386	0.0399	0.9344±0.0421	0.0451	**0.9415±0.0378**	0.0358
ringnorm	0.9530±0.0273	0.0270	0.9560±0.0226	0.0594	**0.9675±0.0189**	0.3284	0.8485±0.0337	0.0448
sonar	0.8066±0.0460	0.0245	0.8489±0.0480	0.0467	0.8568±0.0519	0.0592	**0.8738±0.0449**	0.0296
spect	0.6900±0.1119	0.0217	0.6875±0.0633	0.0213	**0.7025±0.1094**	0.0038	0.7025±0.1033	0.0214
transfusion	0.7348±0.0262	0.0487	0.7628±0.0175	0.8928	**0.7939±0.0264**	1.8919	0.7839±0.0249	0.6641
twonorm	0.9725±0.0186	0.0195	0.9720±0.0158	0.0647	0.9695±0.0205	0.2988	**0.9730±0.0165**	0.0636
wdbc	**0.9761±0.0116**	0.0215	0.9708±0.0119	0.1345	0.9743±0.0146	0.8451	0.9743±0.0148	0.1185
wpbc	0.7627±0.0118	0.0306	0.7697±0.0176	0.0420	0.7988±0.0472	0.0428	**0.8002±0.0405**	0.0439

4.2   Experiments on Large-Scale Datasets

The statistics of the large-scale datasets are listed in the last row of Table 1. All of these four large-scale datasets are split into training and test parts. To compare with our method, we employ linear SVM, linear LDM and linear TBLDM after Nyström method. We choose Liblinear for linear SVM; the source code of [23] for linear LDM. A nonlinear SVM also runs directly on these large-scale datasets. For the convenience of computation, $C, c_1, c_2, c_3, c_4, \lambda_1, \lambda_2, \lambda_3, \lambda_4$ are all set to 1, γ that used for nonlinear SVM and Nyström method is set to the average squared distance between data points and the sample mean. The number of landmark points of Nyström method is chosen as $m = 50, 100$. Table 3 tells us that all linear classifiers running after the Nyström method can get a close classification accuracy result compared to nonlinear SVM, even with such small number of landmark points m. However, we can see from Table 4 that the running time of all linear classifier frameworks plus Nyström method are much faster than that of nonlinear SVM. Moreover, we can see that TBLDM is the fastest if we only compared the time running by three linear classifiers. In addition to nonlinear SVM, all classifiers labelled as SVM, LDM and TBLDM in Tables 3 and 4 are linear.

Table 3. Classification accuracy results on 4 large-scale datasets

Datasets	Nonlinear-SVM	m = 50			m = 100		
		SVM	LDM	TBLDM	SVM	LDM	TBLDM
cod-rna	0.8778	0.8650	0.8542	0.8536	0.8651	0.8618	0.8541
ijcnn1	0.9840	0.9138	0.9050	0.9050	0.9357	0.9203	0.9159
Skin	0.9756	0.9982	0.9972	0.9759	0.9985	0.9978	0.9807
w8a	0.9939	0.9696	0.9697	0.9698	0.9721	0.9709	0.9707

Table 4. Time (seconds) comparison on 4 large-scale data sets

Datasets	Nonlinear-SVM	m = 50				m = 100			
		Nyström	SVM	LDM	TBLDM	Nyström	SVM	LDM	TBLDM
cod-rna	358.88	0.41	0.50	0.49	**0.33**	0.71	0.55	0.53	**0.34**
ijcnn1	46.28	0.38	0.63	0.67	**0.12**	0.65	1.09	1.23	**0.15**
Skin	1357.9	0.86	0.99	1.64	**0.92**	1.45	1.49	2.42	**0.84**
w8a	533.02	1.39	0.30	0.40	**0.05**	1.77	0.54	0.73	**0.07**

5   Conclusions

Inspired by the idea of LDM and TBSVM, in this paper, we introduce the
notions of positive margin and negative margin of samples and then present a
novel classification method, TBLDM, by optimizing the positive and negative
margin distributions. The experimental results on sixteen regular scale datasets
and four large scale datasets indicate that, compared with SVM, TBSVM and
LDM, the proposed TBLDM is a fast, effective and robust classifier. From the
derivation process in Sect. 3, we can see that the technique used in this paper
has a certain commonality. Therefore, it will be interesting to generalize the idea
of TBLDM to regression models and other learning settings, which will be our
next work.

References

1. MATLAB version 9.2.0.538062 (R2017a). The Mathworks Inc., Natick, Massachusetts (2017)
2. Breiman, L.: Prediction games and arcing algorithms. Neural Comput. **11**(7), 1493–1517 (1999)
3. Cortes, C., Vapnik, V.: Support-vector networks. Mach. Learn. **20**(3), 273–297 (1995)
4. Dheeru, D., Karra Taniskidou, E.: UCI machine learning repository (2017). http:// archive.ics.uci.edu/ml
5. Freund, Y., Schapire, R.E.: A decision-theoretic generalization of on-line learning and an application to boosting. J. Comput. Syst. Sci. **55**(1), 119–139 (1997)
6. Gao, W., Zhou, Z.H.: On the doubt about margin explanation of boosting. Artif. Intell. **203**, 1–18 (2013)

7. Jayadeva, Khemchandani, R., et al.: Twin support vector machines for pattern classification. IEEE Trans. Pattern Anal. Mach. Intell. **29**(5), 905–910 (2007)
8. Khemchandani, R., Sharma, S.: Robust least squares twin support vector machine for human activity recognition. Appl. Soft Comput. **47**, 33–46 (2016)
9. Luo, X., Durrant, R.J.: Maximum margin principal components. arXiv preprint arXiv:1705.06371 (2017)
10. Mangasarian, O.L., Musicant, D.R.: Successive overrelaxation for support vector machines. IEEE Trans. Neural Netw. **10**(5), 1032–1037 (1999)
11. Platt, J., et al.: Sequential minimal optimization: a fast algorithm for training support vector machines (1998)
12. Rastogi, R., Sharma, S., Chandra, S.: Robust parametric twin support vector machine for pattern classification. Neural Process. Lett. **47**, 1–31 (2017)
13. Reyzin, L., Schapire, R.E.: How boosting the margin can also boost classifier complexity. In: Proceedings of the 23rd International Conference on Machine Learning, pp. 753–760. ACM (2006)
14. Schapire, R.E., Freund, Y., Bartlett, P., Lee, W.S.: Boosting the margin: a new explanation for the effectiveness of voting methods. Ann. Stat. **26**, 1651–1686 (1998)
15. Shao, Y.H., Chen, W.J., Wang, Z., Li, C.N., Deng, N.Y.: Weighted linear loss twin support vector machine for large-scale classification. Knowl.-Based Syst. **73**, 276–288 (2015)
16. Shao, Y.H., Zhang, C.H., Wang, X.B., Deng, N.Y.: Improvements on twin support vector machines. IEEE Trans. Neural Netw. **22**(6), 962–968 (2011)
17. Vapnik, V.: The Nature of Statistical Learning Theory. Springer, New York (2013). https://doi.org/10.1007/978-1-4757-3264-1
18. Vapnik, V.N., Vapnik, V.: Statistical Learning Theory, vol. 1. Wiley, New York (1998)
19. Wang, L., Sugiyama, M., Yang, C., Zhou, Z.H., Feng, J.: On the margin explanation of boosting algorithms. In: COLT, pp. 479–490. Citeseer (2008)
20. Xu, H., Fan, L., Gao, X.: Projection twin SMMs for 2D image data classification. Neural Comput. Appl. **26**(1), 91–100 (2015)
21. Xu, Y., Pan, X., Zhou, Z., Yang, Z., Zhang, Y.: Structural least square twin support vector machine for classification. Appl. Intell. **42**(3), 527–536 (2015)
22. Zhang, K., Kwok, J.T.: Clustered Nyström method for large scale manifold learning and dimension reduction. IEEE Trans. Neural Netw. **21**(10), 1576–1587 (2010)
23. Zhang, T., Zhou, Z.H.: Large margin distribution machine. In: Proceedings of the 20th ACM SIGKDD International Conference on Knowledge Discovery and Data Mining, pp. 313–322. ACM (2014)
24. Zhang, T., Zhou, Z.H.: Optimal margin distribution clustering (2018)

Concept Drift Detector Selection
for Hoeffding Adaptive Trees

Moana Stirling[1], Yun Sing Koh[1(✉)], Philippe Fournier-Viger[2],
and Sri Devi Ravana[3]

[1] The University of Auckland, Auckland, New Zealand
msti689@aucklanduni.ac.nz, ykoh@cs.auckland.ac.nz
[2] Harbin Institute of Technology Shenzhen, Shenzhen, China
philfv8@yahoo.com
[3] University of Malaya, Kuala Lumpur, Malaysia
sdevi@um.edu.my

Abstract. Dealing with evolving data requires strategies for detecting
and quantifying change, and forgetting irrelevant examples during the
model revision process. To design an adaptive classifier that is suitable
for different types of streams requires us to understand the characteristics
of the data stream. Current adaptive classifiers have built-in concept
drift detectors used as an estimator at each node. Our research aim is to
investigate the usage of different drift detectors for Hoeffding Adaptive
Tree (HAT), an adaptive classifier. We proposed three variants of the
proposed classifier, called HAT_{SEED}, HAT_{HDDM_A}, and HAT_{PHT}.

Keywords: Adaptive classifiers · Concept drift detectors
Data streams

1 Introduction

Data streams have numerous properties that are different from data found in stationary environments. They have continuous data that arrives indefinitely, thus,
storing all elements in memory is impossible. These differences mean that online
classification or decision tree algorithms acting on data streams have additional
constraints. Essentially these techniques should only process elements once. The
memory capacity and processing time for these techniques are limited. These
techniques must be able to provide predictions at anytime. The distribution of
the data may evolve over time. This is called concept drift. Concept drift may
render previously built models inaccurate as those previous models can no longer
be used to represent the current distribution. Responding to concept drifts is a
key challenge in building a successful data stream classification algorithm.

Existing adaptive classifiers [2] have been proposed to deal with evolving concept drift by using a specific concept drift detector. The decision to use a concept
drift detector against another is a crucial choice. A single specific drift detector is
unlikely to be the best choice for a given classifier. This research aims to identify

© Springer Nature Switzerland AG 2018
T. Mitrovic et al. (Eds.): AI 2018, LNAI 11320, pp. 730–736, 2018.
https://doi.org/10.1007/978-3-030-03991-2_65

concept drift detectors that are good choices for streams with specific character-istics. This would enable the appropriate concept drift detector to be selected for specific types of streams. The **main contribution** of our research is to investi-gate the usage of different drift detectors in a current state-of-the-art adaptive classifier, namely Hoeffding Adaptive Tree (HAT) [2]. In the process we develop three new variants of classifiers based on the original Hoeffding Adaptive Tree (HAT) which uses the ADWIN change detector. HAT_{ADWIN} is general decision tree algorithm with adaptive methodology for mining data streams with concept drift. Our proposed variants, called HAT_{SEED}, HAT_{HDDM_A}, and HAT_{PHT}, use three different concept drift detectors namely, SEED [8], $HDDM_A$ [6], and Page Hinkley Test (PHT) [9]. We note that this work is not to replace HAT but instead investigate the impact that different detectors have on HAT.

2   Related Work

The HAT algorithm [2] is an adaptive classification tree algorithm based upon the popular non-adaptive Hoeffding Tree algorithm [5]. HAT places instances of change detectors at every node. HAT features frequency statistic estimators at each node instead of maintaining sufficient statistic counters. The HAT_{ADWIN} [3] variant uses an ADWIN estimator. ADWIN [1] was selected as the detector of choice for HAT as it provides utility not only as a change detector but also simultaneously as a frequency statistic estimator.

Most drift detection approaches rely on well established test statistics for the difference between the true population and sample mean. Test statistics are based on bounds. Hoeffding's Inequality has been widely used in data stream mining [1]. We classify these drift detectors in three categories: (1) sequential analysis testing, (2) windowing schemes, and (3) hybrid of both statistical testing and windowing scheme. There are a large number of different drift detectors in the area of concept drift [7]. We chose three detectors named SEED [8], $HDDM_A$ [6], and Page-Hinkley Test [9] due to their specific nature. Each of these tests represent one of the drift detector categories aforementioned.

3   Hoeffding Adaptive Trees Beyond ADWIN

HAT_{ADWIN} is a efficient mechanism to build decision trees that is simpler to describe, adapt better to the data, perform better or much better, and use less memory than the ad-hoc designed CVFDT and VFDT mining algorithms [1].

The choice of change detector in HAT requires several important consider-ations. In terms of performance, maintaining an alternate sub-tree is a costly process and sub-trees should be swapped out as quickly as possible. However detecting change more frequently than it occurs will result in alternate trees being re-initialised unnecessarily. This further extends the time before the sub-tree becomes accurate enough to replace the original. Additionally failing to detect change at all detrimentally affects the accuracy of the model, as well as its usefulness for higher understanding of the data.

We chose to use the three different concept drift detectors due to two major factors. The selection criteria we consider are *diversity of the detectors* and *performance in dealing with various drift types*. In terms of diversity, each of the three different detectors belongs to one of the different detector categories. In terms of performance, these three drift detectors contains different characteristics when dealing with concept drifts differently. PHT is a memoryless technique, this means the memory needed would be relatively small. Both SEED and HDDM$_A$ are variants of the Hoeffding Bound techniques. SEED is shown to be effective in terms of memory and time for rather homogeneous data streams, whereas HDDM$_A$ has high accuracy. The impact of how each of these individual drift detectors handle changes may not be sufficient to determine how it translates to modelling and updating a classifier.

3.1   HAT Variants

The three variations of the HAT technique namely, HAT$_{SEED}$, HAT$_{HDDM_A}$, and HAT$_{PHT}$, has an instance of the specific change detector placed at every node as an estimator for the tree and the HAT-variant reacts to the detectors' alarmed in the same manner as HAT$_{ADWIN}$.

Algorithm 1 shows the process for HAT$_{SEED}$. Note that we outlined the difference (lines 3, 8, 15, and 16) to the original HAT. The main advantage of using SEED [8] as a change detector is its memory-efficiency when dealing with homogenous data streams without many drifts. SEED's boundary merging technique would be expected to perform well on homogeneous data, as the merging optimisation occurs frequently on consecutive blocks that are homogeneous in nature. Similar to ADWIN, SEED also does not maintain a window explicitly but has a compression mechanism.

Similar changes were carried out for HAT$_{HDDM_A}$, as per HAT$_{SEED}$ as shown in Algorithm 1. The estimator used in the variation is HDDM$_A$ instead of SEED. The HDDM$_A$ detector [6] maintains an adaptive sized window of instances and determines a cut point in the window. If the difference in the means of the two sub-windows either side of the cut point become sufficiently different, concept drift is determined to have occurred and the entire window is forgotten. Similarly to SEED, HDDM$_A$ maintains an uncompressed window. However the complete forgetting mechanism used in HDDM$_A$ means that for instances directly following the drift, HDDM$_A$ will use less memory. However this forgetting mechanism makes HDDM$_A$ less capable of adapting to abrupt drifts as instances that may be essential to establishing a distribution may be lost. An advantage of HDDM$_A$ as an estimator is it more suited to handling long drifts, where instances from each distribution may be interleaved for some time.

Similar changes were carried out for HAT$_{PHT}$, as per HAT$_{HDDM_A}$ as shown in Algorithm 1. The Page-Hinkley Test (PHT) [9] considers the variable m_t which is the cumulated difference between the observed values, x_t, and their mean at time t, where $x_t = \frac{1}{t} \sum_{l=1}^{t} x_l$, δ represents the allowed magnitude of change and α is a forgetting factor: $m_{t+1} = \alpha \sum_{1}^{t} (x_t - \bar{x}_t + \delta)$ The minimum value of m_t is

---

Algorithm 1. HAT$_{SEED}$ Algorithm

1: **function** HAT$_{SEED}$(*Stream*, δ)
2:    Let HT be a tree with a single leaf (root).
3:    Initialise SEED estimators at root.
4:    **for** each example x, y in Stream **do**
5:        HATGrow((x, y), HT, δ)
6: **function** HATGROW((x, y), HT, δ)
7:    Sort (x, y) to leaf l using HT.
8:    Update SEED estimators at leaf l and nodes traversed.
9:    **if** this node has an alternate tree T_{alt} **then**
10:        HATGrow((x, y), T_{alt}, δ)
11:    Compute information gain, G for each attribute.
12:    **if** G(Best Attribute) - G(Second Best Attribute) > ϵ **then**
13:        Split leaf on best attribute.
14:        **for** each branch of split **do**
15:            Start new leaf and initialise SEED estimators.
16:    **if** SEED drift detector has detected change **then**
17:        Create an alternate sub-tree if there is none.
18:    **if** existing alternate sub-tree is more accurate **then**
19:        Replace current node with alternate tree.

---

also recorded, $M_t = \min(m_t; t = 1, \ldots, t)$. Concept drift is determined to have occurred when $|M_t - m_t|$ exceeds a given threshold, λ.

4   Evaluation and Results

The new HAT variants are tested on both real and synthetic datasets. The algorithm implementations used are based upon the MOA [4] framework. The datasets and code are available at https://github.com/MoanaStirling/Concept-Drift-Detector-Selection-For-Hoeffding-Adaptive-Trees. All synthetic datasets are generated from modified MOA data stream generators. Four different stream generators are used: SEA, Agrawal, RBF, and Hyperplane.

Memory and Runtime. Table 1 displays the average memory and runtime performance along with the standard deviations in brackets. In terms of accuracy we measured the accuracy of the classifier for 10,000 instances after each subtree swap was carried out.

False Positive and True Positive Rates. Table 2 shows the true positive rate of correct HAT sub-tree switches and false positive rate of when there are incorrect sub-tree switches. This is measured as the average number of switches that occurred incorrectly per drift. This value should not be confused with concept drift detection of a model, which is normally higher. We are more interested in measuring whether an estimator at a node has triggered a warning. Table 2 shows the true positive rate and false positive rate at 10% and 40% noise level.

Table 1. Runtime(s) and model size (kB)

Stream	Detector/Noise	Runtime (s)		Memory (kB)	
		10%	40%	10%	40%
SEA, 100,000	HAT$_{ADWIN}$	$12.78 \pm (0.16)$	$17.2 \pm (1.87)$	$413 \pm (26)$	$981 \pm (272)$
	HAT$_{SEED}$	$\mathbf{8.52 \pm (0.29)}$	$22.43 \pm (2.34)$	$\mathbf{168 \pm (8)}$	$1,169 \pm (203)$
	HAT$_{HDDM_A}$	$10.22 \pm (0.35)$	$\mathbf{9.00 \pm (0.61)}$	$200 \pm (39)$	$\mathbf{157 \pm (103)}$
	HAT$_{PHT}$	$\mathbf{7.92 \pm (0.08)}$	$9.30 \pm (0.71)$	$217 \pm (8)$	$341 \pm (128)$
Agrawal, 100,000	HAT$_{ADWIN}$	$24.76 \pm (1.38)$	$40.35 \pm (8.28)$	$1,020 \pm (87)$	$965 \pm (421)$
	HAT$_{SEED}$	$23.29 \pm (1.45)$	$73.84 \pm (12.36)$	$\mathbf{768 \pm (52)}$	$4,025 \pm (1,394)$
	HAT$_{HDDM_A}$	$23.25 \pm (1.86)$	$\mathbf{27.51 \pm (6.12)}$	$793 \pm (212)$	$\mathbf{409 \pm (396)}$
	HAT$_{PHT}$	$23.31 \pm (1.48)$	$27.86 \pm (5.69)$	$827 \pm (39)$	$857 \pm (642)$
RBF, 100,000	HAT$_{ADWIN}$	$28.34 \pm (0.57)$	$28.03 \pm (0.78)$	$807 \pm (37)$	$809 \pm (22)$
	HAT$_{SEED}$	$\mathbf{21.65 \pm (0.55)}$	$\mathbf{22.63 \pm (1.43)}$	$\mathbf{551 \pm (52)}$	$\mathbf{550 \pm (20)}$
	HAT$_{HDDM_A}$	$23.20 \pm (0.90)$	$24.50 \pm (0.63)$	$561 \pm (159)$	$575 \pm (60)$
	HAT$_{PHT}$	$23.19 \pm (0.71)$	$26.05 \pm (1.67)$	$935 \pm (153)$	$623 \pm (109)$
Abrupt Hyperplane 100,000	HAT$_{ADWIN}$	$16.94 \pm (0.88)$	$14.91 \pm (0.22)$	$445 \pm (84)$	$449 \pm (42)$
	HAT$_{SEED}$	$16.25 \pm (1.06)$	$11.28 \pm (0.62)$	$\mathbf{244 \pm (35)}$	$236 \pm (7)$
	HAT$_{HDDM_A}$	$15.30 \pm (0.85)$	$\mathbf{10.39 \pm (0.37)}$	$309 \pm (29)$	$\mathbf{129 \pm (68)}$
	HAT$_{PHT}$	$\mathbf{13.9 \pm (0.96)}$	$10.55 \pm (0.25)$	$312 \pm (30)$	$269 \pm (32)$
Gradual Hyperplane, 100,000	HAT$_{ADWIN}$	$17.69 \pm (1.46)$	$54.00 \pm (9.37)$	$242 \pm (89)$	$3,638 \pm (1,339)$
	HAT$_{SEED}$	$15.68 \pm (1.42)$	$38.86 \pm (1.45)$	$\mathbf{169 \pm (78)}$	$2,294 \pm (290)$
	HAT$_{HDDM_A}$	$17.66 \pm (1.84)$	$\mathbf{15.75 \pm (2.33)}$	$205 \pm (118)$	$\mathbf{223 \pm (162)}$
	HAT$_{PHT}$	$\mathbf{14.94 \pm (1.44)}$	$25.27 \pm (8.22)$	$170 \pm (77)$	$1,125 \pm (814)$

Table 2. True positive rate and false positive rate

Stream	Detector/Noise	True Postive		False Positive	
		10%	40%	10%	40%
SEA, 100,000	HAT$_{ADWIN}$	$0.60 \pm (0.09)$	$0.21 \pm (0.10)$	$0.01 \pm (0.02)$	$0.04 \pm (0.09)$
	HAT$_{SEED}$	$\mathbf{0.73 \pm (0.1)}$	$\mathbf{0.55 \pm (0.08)}$	$0.00 \pm (0.00)$	$0.54 \pm (0.27)$
	HAT$_{HDDM_A}$	$0.55 \pm (0.13)$	$0.37 \pm (0.15)$	$0.02 \pm (0.05)$	$0.08 \pm (0.11)$
	HAT$_{PHT}$	$0.68 \pm (0.07)$	$0.14 \pm (0.06)$	$0.00 \pm (0.00)$	$0.0 \pm (0.02)$
Agrawal 100,000	HAT$_{ADWIN}$	$0.77 \pm (0.09)$	$0.33 \pm (0.08)$	$0.05 \pm (0.08)$	$0.04 \pm (0.06)$
	HAT$_{SEED}$	$\mathbf{0.82 \pm (0.07)}$	$0.25 \pm (0.12)$	$0.07 \pm (0.08)$	$0.06 \pm (0.12)$
	HAT$_{HDDM_A}$	$0.78 \pm (0.08)$	$\mathbf{0.44 \pm (0.13)}$	$0.83 \pm (0.74)$	$0.14 \pm (0.16)$
	HAT$_{PHT}$	$0.78 \pm (0.07)$	$0.37 \pm (0.1)$	$0.02 \pm (0.04)$	$0.01 \pm (0.03)$
RBF 100,000	HAT$_{ADWIN}$	$0.89 \pm (0.09)$	$0.89 \pm (0.09)$	$0.07 \pm (0.09)$	$0.19 \pm (0.13)$
	HAT$_{SEED}$	$\mathbf{0.92 \pm (0.09)}$	$\mathbf{0.97 \pm (0.05)}$	$0.05 \pm (0.07)$	$0.15 \pm (0.13)$
	HAT$_{HDDM_A}$	$0.84 \pm (0.11)$	$0.96 \pm (0.06)$	$0.40 \pm (0.28)$	$0.94 \pm (0.39)$
	HAT$_{PHT}$	$0.68 \pm (0.10)$	$0.69 \pm (0.15)$	$0.08 \pm (0.1)$	$0.39 \pm (0.27)$
Abrupt Hyperplane 100,000	HAT$_{ADWIN}$	$0.75 \pm (0.26)$	$1.0 \pm (0.02)$	$0.10 \pm (0.17)$	$0.04 \pm (0.05)$
	HAT$_{SEED}$	$0.74 \pm (0.27)$	$1.0 \pm (0.01)$	$0.10 \pm (0.19)$	$0.01 \pm (0.02)$
	HAT$_{HDDM_A}$	$0.69 \pm (0.29)$	$0.92 \pm (0.10)$	$0.13 \pm (0.17)$	$0.40 \pm (0.20)$
	HAT$_{PHT}$	$0.72 \pm (0.27)$	$1.00 \pm (0.01)$	$0.00 \pm (0.00)$	$0.00 \pm (0.02)$
Gradual Hyperplane 100,000	HAT$_{ADWIN}$	$0.28 \pm (0.17)$	$0.12 \pm (0.08)$	$0.04 \pm (0.07)$	$0.01 \pm (0.03)$
	HAT$_{SEED}$	$\mathbf{0.57 \pm (0.2)}$	$0.12 \pm (0.06)$	$0.30 \pm (0.25)$	$0.00 \pm (0.01)$
	HAT$_{HDDM_A}$	$0.49 \pm (0.18)$	$\mathbf{0.30 \pm (0.14)}$	$0.25 \pm (0.21)$	$0.06 \pm (0.09)$
	HAT$_{PHT}$	$0.24 \pm (0.15)$	$0.12 \pm (0.05)$	$0.03 \pm (0.07)$	$0.00 \pm (0.01)$

Note that 0.00 is a very small value > 0.

Table 3. Real datasets experimental results

Detector	Overall accuracy (percentage)	Kappa statistic	Model size (B)	Evaluation time (seconds)	Subtrees switched out
Forest covertype					
HAT_{ADWIN}	85.21	82.23	20,000	39.65	33.0
HAT_{SEED}	84.34	89.07	**18,000**	**36.0**	42.0
HAT_{HDDM_A}	83.59	**89.39**	19,000	70.66	8.0
HAT_{PHT}	**85.56**	87.33	72,000	40.10	41.0
Electricity					
HAT_{ADWIN}	84.49	69.88	42,000	1.40	3.0
HAT_{SEED}	84.47	**75.66**	37,000	**1.26**	4.0
HAT_{HDDM_A}	**84.71**	70.11	**10,000**	1.64	0.0
HAT_{PHT}	84.11	74.51	75,000	1.47	0.0

Real Datasets Case Study. Table 3 displays a summary of the results of the experiments on the real datasets from the MOA system [3].

5 Conclusion and Future Work

We proposed three additional variants of HAT namely HAT_{SEED}, HAT_{HDDM_A}, and HAT_{PHT}. We empirically showed that each of these versions has advantages over the others and previous techniques. We observed that the choice of a change detector can have different impact on data streams with different characteristics. This confirmed the idea that on streams with specific attributes certain change detectors have better performance.

In the future, we plan to learn the characteristics of the streams to enable us to automatically make a decision on the choice of change detector used in adaptive classifiers. Algorithmic identification of stream attributes would be an immensely powerful tool. This would enable dynamic switching of change detectors for a classifier as attributes are detected.

References

1. Bifet, A., Gavalda, R.: Learning from time-changing data with adaptive windowing. In: Proceedings of the 2007 SIAM International Conference on Data Mining, pp. 443–448. SIAM (2007)
2. Bifet, A., Gavaldà, R.: Adaptive learning from evolving data streams. In: Adams, N.M., Robardet, C., Siebes, A., Boulicaut, J.-F. (eds.) IDA 2009. LNCS, vol. 5772, pp. 249–260. Springer, Heidelberg (2009). https://doi.org/10.1007/978-3-642-03915-7_22

3. Bifet, A., Holmes, G., Kirkby, R., Pfahringer, B.: MOA: massive online analysis. J. Mach. Learn. Res. **11**, 1601–1604 (2010)
4. Bifet, A., Kirkby, R.: Data stream mining: a practical approach. Citeseer (2009)
5. Domingos, P., Hulten, G.: Mining high-speed data streams. In: Proceedings of the Sixth ACM SIGKDD International Conference on Knowledge Discovery and Data Mining, pp. 71–80. ACM (2000)
6. Frías-Blanco, I., del Campo-Ávila, J., Ramos-Jiménez, G., Morales-Bueno, R., Ortiz-Díaz, A., Caballero-Mota, Y.: Online and non-parametric drift detection methods based on hoeffdings bounds. IEEE Trans. Knowl. Data Eng. **27**(3), 810–823 (2015)
7. Gama, J., Žliobaitė, I., Bifet, A., Pechenizkiy, M., Bouchachia, A.: A survey on concept drift adaptation. ACM Comput. Surv. **46**(4), 441–4437 (2014)
8. Huang, D.T.J., Koh, Y.S., Dobbie, G., Pears, R.: Detecting volatility shift in data streams. In: 2014 IEEE International Conference on Data Mining, pp. 863–868. IEEE (2014)
9. Page, E.S.: Continuous inspection schemes. Biometrika **41**(1/2), 100–115 (1954)

Planning and Scheduling

Evolutionary Multitask Optimisation for Dynamic Job Shop Scheduling Using Niched Genetic Programming

John Park[1]([⊠]), Yi Mei[1], Su Nguyen[1,2], Gang Chen[1], and Mengjie Zhang[1]

[1] Evolutionary Computation Research Group, Victoria University of Wellington,
PO Box 600, Wellington, New Zealand
{John.Park,Yi.Mei,Aaron.Chen,Mengjie.Zhang}@ecs.vuw.ac.nz
[2] La Trobe University, Melbourne, Australia
p.nguyen4@latrobe.edu.au

Abstract. Dynamic job shop scheduling (DJSS) problems are combinatorial optimisation problems where dynamic events occur during processing that prevents scheduling algorithms from being able to predict the optimal solutions in advance. DJSS problems have been studied extensively due to the difficulty of the problem and their applicability to real-world scenarios. This paper deals with a DJSS problem with dynamic job arrivals and machine breakdowns. A standard genetic programming (GP) approach that evolves dispatching rules, which is effective for DJSS problems with dynamic job arrivals, have difficulty generalising over problem instances with different machine breakdown scenarios. This paper proposes a niched GP approach that incorporates multitasking to simultaneously evolve multiple rules that can effectively cope with different machine breakdown scenarios. The results show that the niched GP approach can evolve rules for the different machine breakdown scenarios faster than the combined computation times of the benchmark GP approach and significantly outperform the benchmark GP's evolved rules. The analysis shows that the specialist rules effective for DJSS problem instances with zero machine breakdown have different behaviours to the rules effective for DJSS problem instances with machine breakdown and the generalist rules, but there is also large variance in the behaviours of the zero machine breakdown specialist rules.

1 Introduction

Job shop scheduling (JSS) problems [1] are combinatorial optimisation problems with significant importance in operation research and artificial intelligence [2]. JSS also has applications to real-world manufacturing environments and production scheduling [3]. Because of this, JSS problems have been extensively studied over the past 60 years by both academics and industry experts [4]. A JSS problem instance consists of a *shop floor* with a limited number of *machine* resources that are used to process incoming *jobs* [1]. To process a job, a job's *operations* need to be processed in a specific sequence, and each operation requires a specific

© Springer Nature Switzerland AG 2018
T. Mitrovic et al. (Eds.): AI 2018, LNAI 11320, pp. 739–751, 2018.
https://doi.org/10.1007/978-3-030-03991-2_66

machine to process the operation. In addition, a machine can only process one operation at a time. The goal of JSS is to make intelligent decisions during processing to optimise a given *objective function*. Finally, in a real-world scenario, there are unforeseen events that can occur which can affect the properties of the shop floor [5]. JSS problems with unforeseen events are called *dynamic* JSS (DJSS) problems and have been studied extensively in the literature [5].

For this paper, we deal with a DJSS problem with the mean weighted tardiness (MWT) objective [1], dynamic job arrivals, and machine breakdowns [3,5]. This means that the jobs' properties are unknown they reach the shop floor, and unforeseen breakdowns of machines occur during processing where the machines need to be repaired for durations of times before they are available to process the jobs' operations. The most prominent method of handling DJSS problems with dynamic job arrivals is to evolve effective dispatching rules using evolutionary computation (EC) techniques such as genetic programming (GP) [2,3]. In general, the rules evolved by the EC techniques generally outperform the man-made dispatching rules [3] given that the training set used to evolve the GP rules is appropriate for the DJSS problem that the rules are applied to [6]. On the other hand, predictive-reactive approaches are extensively applied to DJSS problems with machine breakdowns and attempt to generate schedules that are as robust as possible to disruptions caused by machine breakdowns [5]. They often focus on small DJSS problem instances with a fixed number of job arrivals (e.g. up to 80 jobs [7]). Both dynamic job arrivals and machine breakdowns have been studied extensively in the literature, but there has only been a limited number of GP approaches to DJSS problems with both dynamic job arrivals and machine breakdowns [8].

By investigating the two types of dynamic events simultaneously, it is likely that we can extend the scope of research into DJSS problems, and better emulate real-world scenarios where large numbers of unforeseeable events are likely to occur. However, preliminary investigation by Park et al. [8] showed that it is too difficult for the evolved rules to generalise effectively over the different machine breakdown scenarios, and showed that the GP rules evolved using instances from all machine breakdown scenarios (i.e. "generalist" rules) were more biased towards the DJSS problem instances with no machine breakdowns than problem instances with machine breakdowns. Therefore, a GP approach that handles the DJSS problem by allowing the GP individuals to focus on the different machine breakdown scenarios as much as possible may be more effective than a standard GP approach. By focusing on specific machine breakdown scenarios, useful features can be discovered by the GP that can be shared during the GP process to improve the overall qualities of the output rules [9]. The idea of decomposing a problem to smaller subproblems has parallels to *multitask learning* [9], where multiple *tasks* are solved simultaneously. Evolutionary multitasking techniques [10] have been effectively applied to solve multiple optimisation problems concurrently [11], but they have not been applied to DJSS problems.

1.1 Goal

The goal of this paper is to develop a multitask GP approach that is able to cope with a DJSS problem with dynamic job arrivals and various severity of machine breakdowns that occur during processing. To do this, we propose a niched GP approach that evolves two types of rules: "generalist" rules that are effective over the entire DJSS problem and "specialist" rules that specifically handle the designated machine breakdown scenario that they are specialised for. Specialist rules are useful when the overall machine breakdown properties of the problems (e.g. the distribution of repair times [12]) are known in advance, and the generalist rules are useful otherwise. Compared to a standard GP approach that evolves GP rules for the different machine breakdown scenarios separately, a niched GP approach that evolves rules simultaneously has the potential to improve on the effectiveness of the evolved rules by sharing useful properties of rules effective on other machine breakdown scenarios, and have better performances overall than the standard GP approach. In addition, by analysing the rules evolved by the niched GP approach, e.g., by determining the behaviours of different specialist rules, we can observe the overlap between the machine breakdown scenarios based on the behaviours of the evolved specialist rules.

2 Niched GP Approach to Handling DJSS Problems with Machine Breakdown

This section covers the niched GP approach that is used to evolve a generalist rule and specialist rules for the different machine breakdown scenarios simultaneously. First, we give the framework of the niched GP process, then provide the details on the niched GP's representation, the terminal and the function sets.

2.1 Overall Framework

The niched GP approach in this paper is extended from a niched GP approach proposed by Mei et al. [13] used to evolve a diverse set of rules. The niched GP keeps track of the GP individuals that are the best for the different machine breakdown scenarios during training. By doing this, GP may be able to retain useful features from rules which may not have the best overall performance which can then be shared with other GP individuals.

For the niched GP process, the GP individuals are first randomly initialised and the set of specialist rule S is empty. For each generation when a GP individual p is being evaluated, the individual is first evaluated on the "general" training set T to calculate its fitness $f(p)$. The problem instances in training set T consist of N machine breakdown scenarios. If an individual p has the best performance for problem instances in niche n (i.e. under a specific machine breakdown scenario) in the training set T, then current generation niche individual t_I for niche n is updated to individual p. After all GP individuals in the current population have been evaluated, the current generation niched individuals $t_1, \ldots, t_N$ are then compared against the overall niched individuals $s_1, \ldots, s_N$. To compare

---

Algorithm 1. $\mathcal{S} \leftarrow$ NichedGP(G)

Output: The set of specialist rules $\mathcal{S}$ and the generalist rule g.
Initialise GP population $\mathcal{P}$;
Initialise specialist rule set $\mathcal{S} \leftarrow \{s_1, \ldots, s_N\}$ for the N niches;
for *gen* $\leftarrow$ 1 **to** G **do**
  Set $t_1, \ldots, t_N \leftarrow \varnothing$ and $f_1, \ldots, f_{|\mathcal{P}|} \leftarrow 0$;
  for *each individual p in GP population $\mathcal{P}$* **do**
    for *each problem instance I in the training set $\mathcal{T}$* **do**
      | Apply individual p to I to calculate normalised objective $Obj'(p, I)$;
    end
    Update $f(p)$ and g;
    Update t_n if p is better on problem instances in niche n;
  end
  for t_n *in* $t_1, \ldots, t_N$ **do**
    Apply t_n to problem instances in niched training set $\mathcal{V}_n$ and calculate
    the performance $f'(t_n)$ over the niched training set;
    Update $s_n \leftarrow t_n$ if $f'(t_n) < f'(s_n)$;
  end
  $\mathcal{P}' \leftarrow$ Clearing($\mathcal{P}, \mathcal{S}, \sigma, \kappa$);
  Apply the breeding procedure using $\mathcal{P}'$ and update the population $\mathcal{P}$;
end
Output the set of specialist GP rules $\mathcal{S}$ and the best overall GP rule g;

---

the current generation niched individuals t_n to overall niched individual s_n, the individuals are evaluated on a niched training set $\mathcal{V}_n$, separate from the general training set $\mathcal{T}$, that only consists of problem instances with the specific machine breakdown scenario (i.e. the niched training sets are validation sets specifically for the niched individuals). If the $f'(t_n)$ of the current generation niched individual t_n is better than the fitness $f'(s_n)$ of the overall niched individual s_n over the niched training set $\mathcal{V}_n$, then s_n is updated to the current generation's niche individual t_n. Otherwise, the individual t_n is kept the same.

After the set of niched individuals has been updated, the clearing algorithm (denoted as Clearing($\mathcal{P}, \mathcal{S}, \sigma, \kappa$)) is carried out before the individuals undergo the standard tournament selection procedure. The clearing algorithm is modified from the algorithm used by Mei et al. [13]. However, unlike Mei et al.'s clearing procedure, where all GP individuals have a niche radius, only the specialist GP rule from the rule set $\mathcal{S}$ (i.e., niched individuals that perform the best on the different machine breakdown scenarios) and the best individual found so far are used as the niches in our niched GP approach. Afterwards, the individuals with poor performances within distance σ from the best niched individuals are removed from the GP population if the niche has reached its capacity κ. This continues until the maximum number of generations has been reached. Finally, the algorithm reports the best overall rule as the generalist rule g and the set of specialist rules $\mathcal{S}$. The pseudocode that summarises the niched GP process is shown in Algorithm 1.

Table 1. Terminal set for GP, where a job j is waiting at the available machine m at a decision situation.

Terminal	Description	Terminal	Description
RJ	operation ready time of job j	SL	slack of job j
PT	operation processing time of job j	W	job's weight w_j
		NPT	next operation processing time of job j
RO	remaining number of operations of job j		
		NNQ	number of idle jobs waiting at the next machine
RT	remaining total processing times of job j		
		NQW	average waiting time of last 5 jobs at the next machine
RM	machine m's ready time		
WINQ	work in next queue for job j	AQW	average waiting time of last 5 jobs at all machines
DD	job's due date d_j		

Given that the same training set T is used, the niched GP approach will likely have a greater computation time than a standard GP approach that uses a single population because it further evaluates the niched individuals on the niched training sets on top of the standard evaluation procedure. When evolving dispatching rules for DJSS problems using GP, the evaluation procedure and the application of the individuals on the training instances is the most computationally intensive step of the GP process [2]. As the niched GP approach will have additional # *of niches* × *niched training sets sizes* simulation runs, the niched GP approach requires a total of $|\mathcal{P}| \times |T| + N \times |\mathcal{V}|$ simulation runs. However, the niched GP approach will still have significantly shorter computation time compared to evolving generalist and specialist rules using a standard GP separately, which requires $2 \times |\mathcal{P}| \times |T|$ simulation runs to evaluate all the GP individuals per generation.

2.2 GP Representation, Terminal Set and Function Set

The GP representation, terminals and function sets are adapted from the GP approach used by Park et al. [8] to investigate the DJSS problem with dynamic job arrivals and machine breakdowns. For the niched GP approach, the GP individuals are arithmetic function trees that are used to calculate the priorities of jobs waiting at an available machine m^* during a decision situation [3]. The terminals listed in Table 1 for a GP individual's tree correspond to job, machine and shop floor attributes. The non-terminals consist of arithmetic operators $+$, $-$, $\times$, protected $/$, binary operators max, min and a ternary operator if. Protected $/$ returns 1 if the denominator is zero, and returns the output of a standard division operator otherwise. if operator returns the value of the second child branch (representing the "then" condition) if the first child branch (representing the input into the "if" condition) is greater than or equal to zero, but returns the value of the third child branch (representing the "else" condition) otherwise.

2.3   Evaluation Procedure

The GP individual p is applied to the DJSS problem instances in the training sets as a *non-delay* [1] dispatching rule. The individual p is applied to a problem instance I to generate a schedule. Afterwards, the MWT value $Obj(p, I)$ of the schedule is normalised using a *reference rule* to reduce bias towards specific DJSS problem instances [14]. The reference rule R, which is the weighted apparent tardiness cost (wATC) rule [1], is applied to problem instance I to generate a schedule with $Obj(R, I)$. Afterwards, the normalised MWT value is calculated as $Obj'(p, I) = \frac{Obj(p,I)}{Obj(R,I)}$. From the normalised objective values, the fitness of individual p is given by $f(p) = \frac{1}{|T|} \sum_{I \in T} Obj'(p, I)$ after the individual has been applied to all problem instances in the training set T.

3   Experimental Design

This section describes the simulation model used to evaluate the specialised rules for the niched GP approach, followed by a description of benchmark GP used for comparison during evaluation. Afterwards, detailed parameter settings for GP and niching are provided.

3.1   DJSS Simulation Model

Discrete-event simulations are the standard method of simulating job shop scheduling problem instances [3]. A discrete-event simulation stochastically generates the dynamic events, i.e., the job arrivals and the machine breakdowns. The simulation model is adapted from the simulation model used by Park et al. [8], which is a modification of Holthaus's [12] simulation model. In the simulations, *machine breakdown level* (the proportion of simulation duration the machines are broken down [12]) and *mean machine repair time* parameters are used to stochastically generate machine breakdowns [12]. There are three different parameter values for machine breakdown level, three different values for mean times required to repair the machines, and two different values for the *due date tightness*. Due date tightness is a simulation parameter used to determine how the due date is generated for a job arrival [12]. Since the repair times are not a factor when the breakdown level is zero, i.e., there is no machine breakdown, the DJSS problem instances can be generated from $2 \times 3 \times 3 = 14$ different scenarios. There is no re-entry for the arriving jobs, i.e., a job has at most one operation on a machine [1]. These parameters are listed below in Table 2.

At each generation, the training set T simulates a DJSS problem instance from each simulation configuration scenarios (i.e. different combinations of due date tightness, breakdown level and mean repair time), resulting in a GP individual being applied to 14 DJSS problem instances. The simulations used in training set T are grouped up into the seven groups of two problem instances based on their breakdown level and mean repair time, e.g., a group with breakdown level of 2.5% and mean repair time of 25 is denoted as $\langle 2.5\%, 25 \rangle$. The

Table 2. The parameters used for simulating a DJSS problem instance.

Parameters		Value
Shop floor parameters	Number of machines	10
	Warm up jobs	500
	# completed jobs before simulation termination	2500
	Utilisation rate	90%
	Job arrival rate (λ)	$\lambda \sim Poisson(13.5)$
	Operation processing times (o_{ij})	$o_{ij} \sim Unif[1, 49]$
	# operations per job (N_j)	$N_j \sim Unif[2, 10]$
	Job weight	Random from 1, 2, 4 with probabilities 20%, 60%, 20%
	Due date tightness	3.0 or 5.0
Machine breakdown parameters	Breakdown level	0%, 2.5% or 5%
	Mean repair time	25, 125 or 250

group with no machine breakdowns (i.e. has a breakdown level of 0%) is simply denoted as $\langle 0 \rangle$. In other words, the seven groups are the "niches" that are filled up by GP individuals that perform the best for the different machine breakdown level and mean repair time parameter values (i.e. $N = 7$). The seed used to simulate the problem instances from the simulation configurations are rotated every generation to help improve the generalisation ability of the evolved rules [13].

After the current generation niched individuals have been found, they are further evaluated on the niched training sets to update the set of specialist GP rules S. A niched individual $t_{\langle b,r \rangle}$ from the current generation for the scenario $\langle b, r \rangle$ is applied to the niched training set $\mathcal{V}_{\langle b,r \rangle}$. The niched training set $\mathcal{V}_{\langle b,r \rangle}$ has the configurations with due date tightness of 3.0 or 5.0. In other words, a further two simulation runs are used per niched individuals. Finally, to ensure that the comparisons between the rules between different generations are kept consistent, the niched training sets are fixed over every generation for the niched GP.

3.2 GP Benchmarks

To evaluate the niched GP's evolved rules, we use a standard single-tree GP representation [2,3] with the same terminal and function set used by the niched GP for consistency (Table 1). Afterwards, the benchmark GP is applied to the machine breakdown scenarios independently to evolve the generalist and the specialist rules. The entire training set $\mathcal{T}$ is used to evolve the generalist rules from the benchmark GP approach. To evolve the specialist rules, instead of using the entire training set $\mathcal{T}$ described above, the benchmark GP only uses specific machine breakdown scenarios to evolve dispatching rules, e.g., a GP process is run with training instances being generated from $\langle 2.5\%, 25 \rangle$. Since there are two possible due date tightness parameters, an individual in the benchmark GP process is applied to two training problem instances during the evaluation procedure. The best individual of the last generation before the maximum number of generations is reached is the output dispatching rule for the benchmark GP process.

3.3 GP and Niching Parameters

The niched and the benchmark GP approaches follow parameters used by existing GP approaches for DJSS problems [8]. The GP population size is 1024, and the number of generations is 51. The crossover, mutation, and reproduction rates are 80%, 10% and 10% respectively. The maximum depth of the individuals during initialisation is 4, and 8 across all generations of the GP process. Tournament selection of size 7 for both the two GP approaches. For the clearing algorithm $\text{Clearing}(\mathcal{P}, \mathcal{S}, \sigma, \kappa)$ used by the niched GP approach, the two parameters niche radius σ and niche capacity κ are kept consistent as the parameters used by Mei et al. [13], i.e., $\sigma = 1$ and $\kappa = 1$. Finally, $k = 3.0$ is used for the wATC reference rule used for the fitness calculation (Sect. 2.3).

4 Experimental Results

To compare the two GP approaches, the GP process is run 30 times over each machine breakdown scenarios to obtain sets of independent rules for the different machine breakdown scenarios. The computation times of the runs are also recorded and compared against each other before comparing the performances of the generalist and the specialist rules. One GP approach is significantly better than the other GP approach either in terms of computation time or performance if it can be verified by the two-sided Student's t-test at $p = 0.05$. After the comparisons, we analyse the behaviours of the rules evolved by the niched GP approach.

4.1 Computation Costs

Both the niched and the benchmark GP approaches are implemented in a Java program ran on Intel(R) Core(TM) i7 CPU 3.60 GHz. The time required to evolve the rules is given in Table 3, where the computation time is measured in seconds. In the table, "Specialist Combined" denotes the sum of the times required to evolve the specialist rules with the benchmark GP approaches over the different machine breakdown scenarios. This is to compare the overall computation time required to evolve the specialist rules with the benchmark GP approach to the niched GP approach, as the niched GP approach evolves the generalist rule and the specialist rules simultaneously over a single run. "Total" denotes the sum of the time required to evolve the generalist and the specialist rules for the niched and the benchmark GP approaches. Since niched GP approach evolves the generalist and the specialist rules simultaneously, its time is only given in the "Total" category.

Table 3. Comparison of the computation time required to evolve the rules for the GP approaches (in seconds).

Approach		Computation time ($\times 10^4$ s)	
		GP	NGP
Generalist		2.17 ± 0.35	–
Specialist	$\langle 0\%, 0 \rangle$	0.20 ± 0.02	–
	$\langle 2.5\%, 25 \rangle$	0.25 ± 0.03	–
	$\langle 2.5\%, 125 \rangle$	0.30 ± 0.05	–
	$\langle 2.5\%, 250 \rangle$	0.26 ± 0.04	–
	$\langle 5\%, 25 \rangle$	0.31 ± 0.05	–
	$\langle 5\%, 125 \rangle$	0.42 ± 0.07	–
	$\langle 5\%, 250 \rangle$	0.37 ± 0.07	–
	Specialist combined	2.10 ± 0.15	–
Total		4.27 ± 0.39	2.32 ± 0.34

From the tables, compared to the combined amount of time required to evolve the specialist rules or the generalist rules individually using the benchmark GP approach, the niched GP approach takes a significantly longer amount of time. This is due to the additional evaluation required to further evaluate the niched individuals in the niched GP approach after the individuals have been evaluated over the training set. However, for evolving all rules, i.e., both the generalist and the specialist rules, the niched GP approach is significantly faster than the benchmark GP approach.

An interesting observation is that the additional computation time required by the niched GP approach does not exactly correspond with the theoretical amount of time required to further evaluate the niched GP individuals (Sect. 2.1). From the GP and the DJSS parameters, the number of simulation runs required per generation for each specialist rules for the benchmark GP approaches is the population size times the number of configurations per machine breakdown scenario, i.e., $1024 \times 2 = 2048$. Combined together, the total number of simulation runs required by the benchmark GP approach to evolve the specialist rules is $2048 \times 7 = 14336$. This is equivalent to the number of simulation runs required by the niched GP approach to evaluate the GP population minus the additional runs required to further evaluate the niched GP individuals, which requires $7 \times 2 = 14$ simulation runs. This means that the additional simulation runs should approximately add $14/14336 \times 100\% = 0.1\%$ overhead to the niched GP approach compared to evolving the specialist rules separately. However, the experiments show that the niched GP approach takes ~10% longer computation time to evolve the rules compared to the combined time required by the benchmark GP approach to evolve the specialist rules. Instead, the additional computation time is likely due to the fitness adjustments made to GP individuals that are close to the niched individuals in the clearing algorithm (Sect. 2.1).

It may also be likely that the evolved GP rules for the niched GP approach are also bigger, which results in longer computation time required to calculate the priorities of jobs during the simulation.

4.2   Performance Comparison of Evolved Rules

The performances of a set of rules are calculated by applying the evolved rules to simulation models generated from the simulation configurations provided in Sect. 3.1. A simulation model in the test set uses a new seed so that the exact times of the job arrivals and machine breakdowns (and their properties) that are generated by the simulation differs from the simulations during training. An evolved rule is applied to DJSS simulation model to generate a schedule and get a MWT objective value. This is then repeated 30 times with different seeds for the simulation model to get an average MWT performance of the evolved rule over the simulation configuration. The evolved generalist rules are applied to all simulation configurations, whereas the evolved specialist rules are applied to the machine breakdown scenarios they are designed for. The performances of the specialist and the generalist rules are given in Table 4. In the table, $\mu \pm \sigma$ for each set of rules denotes that the mean MWT performance is μ and the standard deviation is σ. In addition, $\langle b, r, h \rangle$ in the tables denotes that the particular simulation model has b breakdown level, r mean repair time and h due date tightness factor.

Table 4. Comparison showing the mean and the standard deviation of the MWT performances for the specialist and the generalist rules evolved by the niched and the benchmark GP approaches over the test simulation runs.

Approach		Specialist		Generalist	
		NGP	GP	NGP	GP
	$\langle 0\%, 0, 5 \rangle$	2.26 ± 0.44	1.94 ± 0.22	2.16 ± 0.13	2.21 ± 0.10
	$\langle 0\%, 0, 3 \rangle$	4.68 ± 1.35	3.43 ± 0.17	3.25 ± 0.06	3.29 ± 0.11
	$\langle 2.5\%, 25, 5 \rangle$	3.43 ± 0.21	3.55 ± 0.23	3.37 ± 0.12	3.46 ± 0.13
	$\langle 2.5\%, 25, 3 \rangle$	4.60 ± 0.21	4.72 ± 0.22	4.45 ± 0.06	4.52 ± 0.12
	$\langle 2.5\%, 125, 5 \rangle$	4.50 ± 0.10	4.69 ± 0.17	4.45 ± 0.13	4.54 ± 0.14
	$\langle 2.5\%, 125, 3 \rangle$	5.81 ± 0.08	6.10 ± 0.16	5.82 ± 0.08	5.93 ± 0.16
MWT	$\langle 2.5\%, 250, 5 \rangle$	6.12 ± 0.17	6.28 ± 0.15	6.06 ± 0.14	6.18 ± 0.20
$(\times 10^2)$	$\langle 2.5\%, 250, 3 \rangle$	7.55 ± 0.11	7.71 ± 0.15	7.51 ± 0.11	7.62 ± 0.18
	$\langle 5\%, 25, 5 \rangle$	4.50 ± 0.13	4.58 ± 0.19	4.40 ± 0.15	4.52 ± 0.21
	$\langle 5\%, 25, 3 \rangle$	6.50 ± 0.26	6.42 ± 0.18	6.33 ± 0.17	6.47 ± 0.27
	$\langle 5\%, 125, 5 \rangle$	6.40 ± 0.15	6.51 ± 0.20	6.42 ± 0.16	6.56 ± 0.26
	$\langle 5\%, 125, 3 \rangle$	8.42 ± 0.19	8.45 ± 0.26	8.55 ± 0.21	8.74 ± 0.35
	$\langle 5\%, 250, 5 \rangle$	8.77 ± 0.33	8.74 ± 0.35	8.95 ± 0.27	9.20 ± 0.46
	$\langle 5\%, 250, 3 \rangle$	11.20 ± 0.29	11.15 ± 0.30	11.43 ± 0.32	11.65 ± 0.46

From the tables, we can see that the niched GP approach generally outperforms the benchmark GP approach in terms of both the specialist rules performances and the generalist rules performances. The only configuration scenarios where the benchmark specialist rules significantly outperform the niched specialist rules are on the simulations with zero machine breakdowns. In addition, the benchmark specialist rules are slightly better than the niched specialist rules for the scenarios $\langle 5\%, 25, 3 \rangle$, $\langle 5\%, 250, 5 \rangle$ and $\langle 5\%, 250, 3 \rangle$, but the differences are not significant.

The table also shows that the generalist rules for the benchmark GP approach perform better than the specialist rules for a number of simulation configurations (from the simulation configuration $\langle 0\%, 0, 3 \rangle$ to the simulation configuration $\langle 2.5\%, 250, 3 \rangle$). This is likely attributed to the number of simulation runs each GP individual during the GP process undergoes during the evaluation procedure. The generalist rules are applied to 14 different simulation runs with different machine breakdown scenarios, whereas a specialist rule is only applied to two simulation runs over the specific machine breakdown scenario. In other words, the GP individuals in the benchmark GP process may not have had enough training instances to effectively evaluate the qualities of the individuals, resulting in underperforming specialist rules. To verify this, we ran additional experiments for the benchmark GP process where the GP individuals are applied to simulations under a specific machine breakdown scenario runs 14 times instead of two times, using different seeds for each simulation. The specialist rules evolved using the additional simulation runs for the GP individuals performs significantly better than the generalist rules.

4.3   Diversity Analysis

For the analysis procedure, the goal is to find differences in terms of the rules' behaviours that have been evolved using different machine breakdown scenarios. To do this, we calculate the phenotypic distances between the rules evolved by the niched GP approaches using the job rank distance measure proposed by Hildebrandt and Branke [14] and used by the clearing algorithm $\text{Clearing}(\mathcal{P}, \mathcal{S}, \sigma, \kappa)$ [13]. The distances between a single rule in a rule set are compared against the 30 rules of another rule set to obtain an average distance of the single rule to the rule set. The means and the standard deviations of the average distances of the rule for the generalist and the specialist rule sets are shown in Fig. 1. In the figure, we provide a heat map of the average distances of two sets of rules as visual aids.

Compared to the other scenarios, the specialist rules that specialise in the scenario with zero machine breakdown has a higher average distances from the specialist rules evolved on other machine breakdown scenarios and the generalist rules. This implies that the rules that are effective on DJSS problems with only dynamic job arrivals are very different from the rules that are effective on DJSS problems with both dynamic job arrivals and machine breakdowns. However, the large standard deviation in the average distances between the behaviours of the rules evolved on zero machine breakdown and the other sets of evolved rules mean that the differences in the distances are not statistically significant. Therefore, further experiments that isolate individual rules and analyse their behaviours may be required.

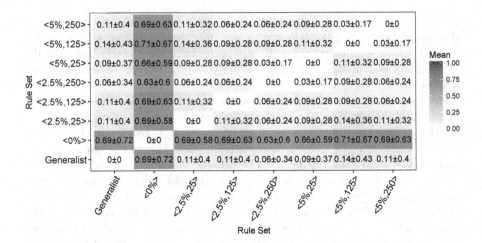

Fig. 1. Pairwise mean and standard deviations of the average distances between the rules evolved by the niched GP approach using Hildebrandt and Branke's ranked distance measure [14]. First table compares the specialist rule sets against each other, and the second table compares the generalist rule set against the specialist rule sets.

5   Conclusions and Future Work

This paper proposes a novel niched GP approach that incorporates multitasking [9] to evolve effective dispatching rules for a DJSS problem with dynamic job arrivals and machine breakdowns. The proposed niched GP approach evolves a generalist and multiple specialist rules for the different machine breakdown scenarios simultaneously. Evolving the generalist rules and the specialist rules for niched GP approach is significantly faster than sequentially evolving the rules using a benchmark GP approach. In addition, the evolved rules from the niched GP approach generally outperform the rules evolved by the benchmark GP approach.

For the future work, it may be promising to further investigate the behaviours of the rules evolved on the different machine breakdown scenarios, to determine why the rules evolved for the niched GP approach performs significantly better. The preliminary comparison shows that the rules that are effective for DJSS problem instances with no machine breakdowns behave differently than the rules that are effective for DJSS problem instances with machine breakdown, but the large variance in the behaviours of the rules means that this difference is not significant. In addition, further experiments that apply the rules to DJSS problem instances with unseen machine breakdown scenarios (e.g. a DJSS problem instance with machine breakdown level of 10%) may further be able to test generalisation ability of the generalist rules evolved by the niched GP approach.

References

1. Pinedo, M.L.: Scheduling: Theory, Algorithms, and Systems, 4th edn. Springer, Heidelberg (2012)
2. Nguyen, S., Mei, Y., Zhang, M.: Genetic programming for production scheduling: a survey with a unified framework. Complex Intell. Syst. **3**(1), 41–66 (2017)
3. Branke, J., Nguyen, S., Pickardt, C.W., Zhang, M.: Automated design of production scheduling heuristics: a review. IEEE Trans. Evol. Comput. **20**(1), 110–124 (2016)
4. Potts, C.N., Strusevich, V.A.: Fifty years of scheduling: a survey of milestones. J. Oper. Res. Soc. **60**(1), S41–S68 (2009)
5. Ouelhadj, D., Petrovic, S.: A survey of dynamic scheduling in manufacturing systems. J. Sched. **12**(4), 417–431 (2009)
6. Nguyen, S., Zhang, M., Johnston, M., Tan, K.C.: A computational study of representations in genetic programming to evolve dispatching rules for the job shop scheduling problem. IEEE Trans. Evol. Comput. **17**(5), 621–639 (2013)
7. Yin, W.J., Liu, M., Wu, C.: Learning single-machine scheduling heuristics subject to machine breakdowns with genetic programming. In: Proceedings of IEEE Congress on Evolutionary Computation (CEC 2003), pp. 1050–1055 (2003)
8. Park, J., Mei, Y., Nguyen, S., Chen, G., Zhang, M.: Investigating the generality of genetic programming based hyper-heuristic approach to dynamic job shop scheduling with machine breakdown. In: Wagner, M., Li, X., Hendtlass, T. (eds.) ACALCI 2017. LNCS (LNAI), vol. 10142, pp. 301–313. Springer, Cham (2017). https://doi.org/10.1007/978-3-319-51691-2_26
9. Pan, S.J., Yang, Q.: A survey on transfer learning. IEEE Trans. Knowl. Data Eng. **22**(10), 1345–1359 (2010)
10. Ong, Y.S., Gupta, A.: Evolutionary multitasking: a computer science view of cognitive multitasking. Cogn. Comput. **8**(2), 125–142 (2016)
11. Gupta, A., Ong, Y.S., Feng, L.: Multifactorial evolution: toward evolutionary multitasking. IEEE Trans. Evol. Comput. **20**(3), 343–357 (2016)
12. Holthaus, O.: Scheduling in job shops with machine breakdowns: an experimental study. Comput. Ind. Eng. **36**(1), 137–162 (1999)
13. Mei, Y., Nguyen, S., Xue, B., Zhang, M.: An efficient feature selection algorithm for evolving job shop scheduling rules with genetic programming. IEEE Trans. Emerg. Top. Comput. Intell. **1**(5), 339–353 (2017)
14. Hildebrandt, T., Branke, J.: On using surrogates with genetic programming. Evol. Comput. **23**(3), 343–367 (2015)

Autonomous Vehicle Constrained Path Planning Using Opal for Dynamic Networks

Kin-Ping Hui, Damien Phillips, Asanka Kekirigoda$^{(\boxtimes)}$,
and Alan Allwright

Defence Science and Technology (DST), Edinburgh, Australia
{kin-ping.hui, damien.phillips, asanka.kekirigoda,
alan.allwright}@dst.defence.gov.au

Abstract. Mobile communications networks may be required to operate in highly dynamic environments. We consider a communications network in an urban scenario where a UAV is used as a radio relay between mobile ground based nodes. The UAVs flight path is constrained by buildings such that ground based nodes will lose connectivity. We present the Opal system to generate, through multi-objective optimisation, network solutions for such a scenario. Opal is shown to develop novel behaviours which are effective in reducing network disconnection time.

Keywords: Constrained optimization · Dynamic networks
Survivable networks

1 Introduction

Contrary to typical experience communications challenges are everywhere in real world mobile networks. To the casual user such challenges are hidden due to the maturity and ongoing evolution of communications infrastructure. Mobile network challenges such as physical obstructions and restricted operating areas may be represented as planning constraints. We consider a mobile radio frequency (RF) communications exercise in an urban environment where it is necessary to deploy a network into an area without working communications infrastructure. For example, widespread infrastructure failure may result from Tsunami, flooding, or military or terrorist activity. Given the physical access and agility requirements of these operating environments, using autonomous Unmanned Aerial Vehicles (UAVs) as an RF communications relay is an attractive option.

In this paper, the authors present Opal [1–6], an autonomous, distributed agent based system developed by Defence Science and Technology (DST) Group, in a simulated urban scenario.

The communications environment in mobile scenarios is highly volatile and consequently the discretisation of the physical space is critical. To combat problems with state space exploration [7–9] Opal uses short-term prediction and adaptive constrained optimisation. These in combination produce novel behaviours that extend the communications range between autonomous vehicles. Such behaviours would not be anticipated under a conventional shortest path planning approach.

© Crown 2018
T. Mitrovic et al. (Eds.): AI 2018, LNAI 11320, pp. 752–758, 2018.
https://doi.org/10.1007/978-3-030-03991-2_67

This paper is organized as follows. Section 2 describes the constrained optimization technique used in Opal, Sect. 3 presents the simulation model. A discussion of results is provided in Sect. 4.

2   Constrained Planning Using Opal

2.1   Future State Predictions

In order to maintain/improve network connectivity in dynamic situations, Opal predicts the near term future state of the network such as the node positions, link qualities and noise levels. It then it directly optimises the UAV flight path in order to provide best connectivity of the network in the predicted future time frame. In this way Opal can foresee probable communications black-spots and propose trajectories to minimise disruption.

2.2   Optimisation Objective

The objective of the UAV radio relay path planning is to maximize the network quality represented by the Network Connection Level (NCL) [3], denoted as Q below within an arbitrary time interval $[T_1, T_2]$.

The scoring function of a trajectory of the network is described as

$$S = \int_{T_1}^{T_2} Q(G_j(t))dt, \tag{1}$$

where $Q(G_j(t))$ is the quality of the (dynamic) network G_j at time t, see [3] for details. The optimisation program is to find the trajectory j such that the induced network state trajectory $G_j(t)$ has the maximum score.

2.3   Optimisation Constraints

Assuming the UAV is required to fly at a fixed altitude due to an operational constraint, there are regions where the UAV is not allowed to enter (for example, to avoid collision). In population based optimisation processes, one approach is to generate candidates as if there were no restrictions and then reject those that violated the constraints before scoring. However, such an approach can be very inefficient. Alternatively, we discretise the UAV positions and remove those that fall inside the no-go zone (s). The discrete resolution can be as fine as we need, but should be as coarse as practical to reduce computational load.

The next step is to construct a Markov transition probability matrix M describing the possible next locations for the UAV within the location constraints and the speed limit. Then the Cross Entropy method [10] is employed to operate on M to find the transitions of the optimal UAV flight path. Note that due to the dynamic nature of the environment, measurements are collected continuously and future state predictions are updated regularly. Hence a new updated optimal path is generated at regular intervals to replace the previous one. Since all generated paths will not violate location or speed constraints, this process always produces a safe and correct flight path. Regardless of whether the optimisation process has converged or not, Opal can take the best candidate generated and execute the flight path.

2.4 Adaptive Warm Start Optimisation Cycle

Since Opal continuously receives measurement information from ground nodes and updates the future network states' prediction, the optimisation process needs to recalculate the optimal flight path at regular intervals in order to include the updates and extended horizon. One approach is to restart the optimisation from scratch each time; which is referred to as a cold start cycle. Opal, however, uses a warm start cycle to carry over what was learnt from the previous cycles and adapts to updated predictions. A warm start has the advantage of faster convergence than a cold start but has a disadvantage of higher risk of being "trapped" at local optimums.

If the environment has not changed significantly from the previous cycle, the predictions will be largely the same, and then the optimal matrix will be similar to those from the previous cycle. Alternatively if the environment has changed considerably, then the predictions will be changed accordingly. Opal uses an adaptive algorithm to dynamically adapt the degree of warm start as the mission progresses.

3 Simulation Scenario

We consider an example urban operation scenario where two ground nodes, for example, vehicles or dismounted personnel, (Node1 and Node2) are moving at 3 m/s on either side of a row of buildings as shown in Fig. 1. The buildings have heights of 8 m, 12 m and 40 m. The magenta arrows depict the radio links, while the cyan arrows show the travel paths for the mobile ground nodes. A small autonomous UAV controlled by Opal is deployed to support the communications between the two ground nodes, which have antennas 2 m above the ground. In order to avoid detection, the UAV is restricted to fly at a low altitude of 25 m above the ground, and at speeds of up to 8 m/s. The building map is known and pre-loaded onto Opal prior to operation. As a safeguard, the UAV is not allowed to fly within 4 m of obstructions. The scenario is arranged to challenge the path planning of the UAV due to the configuration of Building 2 (12 m high) and Building 4 (40 m high). If all buildings were as high as Building 1 (8 m high) a path that tracks the mid-point of Node 1 and Node 2 would be optimal. However, the relaying links of the mid-point tracking path are disrupted over building 2, and the mid-point path itself is physically disrupted by building 4.

The Opal prediction engine generates positions of the nodes during the scenario, in this case, using straight line vector extrapolation. It then uses radio simulation at those positions to calculate the link signal-to-noise ratio (SNR). The SNR is calculated from a propagation model incorporating nodes' positions, transmit signal strength, received noise, distance, and terrain obstructions. The process is repeated when a new set of measurements is passed to Opal to update the dynamics model (i.e. the next planning step).

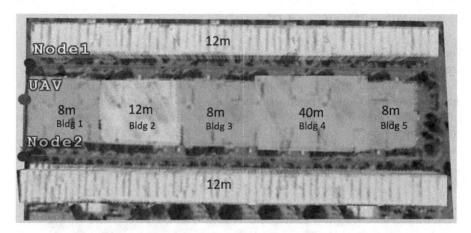

Fig. 1. The trajectories of Node1 and Node2, initial UAV position, and building heights.

This approach of iterative planning is particularly important when node positions diverge from prediction, since the candidate population must be steered to include the new information. Furthermore, this approach supports dynamic detection of flight obstructions.

In moving through the scenario depicted in Fig. 1, Opal will autonomously plan and conduct a solution in the context of maximising network connectivity, i.e. the total NCL in the forward predicted window. This is done by autonomously controlling a single UAV RF relay at a fixed altitude, whilst taking into account the effects of building obstructions to radio links as well as the UAV flight path.

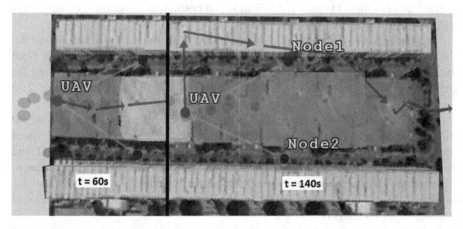

Fig. 2. Stages of the simulation scenario where the UAV stays back from the mobile nodes to extend the connection time. (Color figure online)

4 Simulation Results and Discussion

The tactical scenario was simulated using the same system as was used in [3–5]. Screen captures during simulation of the scenario are depicted in Figs. 2 and 3.

In these simulations, the solid blue circles represent ground nodes' positions at the time of capture with historic positions indicated as semi-transparent blue. Similarly, the UAV positions are indicated in red. The Opal planned trajectory vectors are depicted as green arrows.

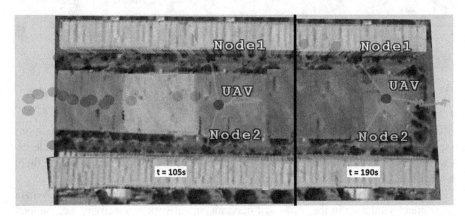

Fig. 3. Stages of the simulation scenario where the UAV speeds ahead of the mobile nodes to reconnect early. (Color figure online)

The UAV initially follows an approximately centre path, but exercises much more freedom of movement in speed (up to 8 m/s) and position in comparison to the ground nodes, as dictated by the planning horizon.

The first interesting behaviour is shown in Fig. 2 at time t = 60 s. Just before the UAV loses connectivity to the nodes due to the obstruction of building 2, Opal develops a solution by moving the UAV back from the ground nodes (increasing the glancing angle). This behaviour repeats before building 4, as shown in Fig. 2 at t = 140 s.

Once the radio links are lost, the UAV quickly moves to the other side of the building, anticipating the reconnection to the ground nodes. Subject to the speed constraint, the UAV moves to the other side ahead in time and waits for Node1 and Node2 to come back into communications range, then tracks them for the remainder of the mission. This behaviour is shown in Fig. 3 for building 2, at t = 105 s, and for building 4, at t = 190 s. In both cases, the UAV reconnects the ground nodes ahead of building edges by roughly 2 to 4 s.

With the adaptive and predictive optimisation techniques, Opal exhibits intelligent behaviour that reduces the disconnection time. It can be observed in the SNR graph plotted in Fig. 4 the two disconnection time windows are smaller than what would have been expected from a simple mid-point tracking algorithm. The total connection time "gain" is about 30 s.

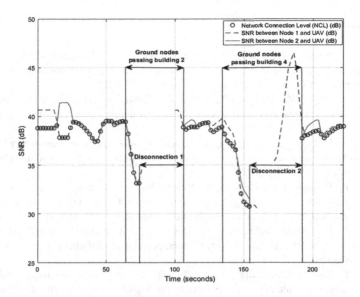

Fig. 4. SNR (dB) of the UAV network links against Time (seconds).

5 Conclusions and Future Work

In this paper, we have presented an adaptive optimisation approach to a range extension problem in an urban environment with Opal. The scenario comprised two mobile ground nodes and an autonomous UAV with planning constraints. This work demonstrated that optimising the Network Connection Level (NCL) in the context of planning constraints can improve the connectivity of a mobile communications network that would otherwise be disconnected. The use of network state prediction along a trajectory anticipates future requirements of that trajectory and minimises the downtime of communications in the near term. The autonomy of the UAV and the continuous optimisation enables high tempo support for communications in a highly dynamic mobile tactical radio network. Furthermore, Opal exhibits intelligent behaviour that reduced the disconnection time of the network.

Further work is planned to investigate the use of machine learning techniques to assist the candidate generation. At present, the RF model for links treats the edges of physical obstructions as hard edges; this can introduce positioning problems to the UAV. A more realistic model would consider the potential measurement errors in the vicinity of hard edges. Future models would include Gaussian or Raleigh distributions [11] to soften the edges and thereby produce more robust solutions. Similarly, we plan to use vectorization of the state space and parallel processing to reduce the granularity and increase the prediction interval.

References

1. Hui, K.-P., Pourbeik, P., George, P., Phillips, D., Magrath, S., Kwiatkowski, M.: OPAL - a survivability-oriented approach to management of tactical military networks. In: Military Communications Conference (MILCOM), pp. 1127–1132 (2011)
2. Hui K.-P., Elliot, M., Phillips, D., Fraser, B.: OPAL and HARLEQUIN - addressing survivability of tactical land networks through autonomy. In: Future Land Force Conference (2014)
3. Hui, K.-P., Phillips, D., Kekirigoda, A.: Beyond line-of-sight range extension with OPAL using autonomous unmanned aerial vehicles. In: Military Communications Conference (MILCOM), pp. 279–284 (2017)
4. Hui, K.-P., Phillips, D., Kekirigoda, A.: Beyond line-of-sight range extension in contested environments with OPAL using autonomous unmanned aerial vehicles. In: International Telecommunication Networks and Applications Conference (ITNAC), pp. 1–5 (2017)
5. Hui, K.-P., Phillips, D., Kekirigoda, A., Allwright, A.: Autonomous range extension using Opal in obstructed terrains. In: Military Communications and Information Systems (MilCIS) Conference (2018)
6. Hui, K.-P., Phillips, D., Kekirigoda, A., Allwright, A.: Range extension using Opal in open environments. In: International Conference on Signal Processing and Communication Systems (ICSPCS) (2018)
7. Roberts, M., et al.: Iterative goal refinement for robotics. In: International Conference on Automated Planning and Scheduling (ICAPS) (2014)
8. Damion, D.D., Charmane, V.C., Emmanuel, G.C., Oscar, C.: Motion planning for mobile robots via sampling-based model predictive optimization. In: Recent Advances in Mobile Robotics Andon Topalov, IntechOpen (2011). https://www.intechopen.com/books/recent-advances-in-mobile-robotics/motion-planning-for-mobile-robots-via-sampling-based-model-predictive-optimizationhttps://doi.org/10.5772/17790
9. Bobiti, R., Lazar, M.: Towards parallelizable sampling–based nonlinear model predictive control. In: International Federation of Automatic Control (IFAC)-Papers OnLine **50**(1), 13176–13181 (2017)
10. Rubinstein, R.Y., Kroese, D.P.: The Cross-Entropy Method. Springer, Heidelberg (2004). https://doi.org/10.1007/978-1-4757-4321-0
11. Rappaport, T.S.: Wireless Communications: Principles and Practice, 2nd (ed.) Pearson Education International (2002)

A Dynamic Planner for Object Assembly Tasks Based on Learning the Spatial Relationships of Its Parts from a Single Demonstration

Ahmed Abbas$^{(\boxtimes)}$, Frederic Maire, Sareh Shirazi, Feras Dayoub, and Markus Eich

Queensland University of Technology, Brisbane, Australia
ahmedkhodairabbas.abbas@hdr.qut.edu.au
{f.maire,s.shirazi,feras.dayoub,markus.eich}@qut.edu.au

Abstract. In this paper, we propose a general system for enabling robots to generate assembly plans for assisting people during assembly tasks. Such a plan is derived from a 3D occupancy grid that the system generates while observing a person performing an assembly task. Our proposed system uses the acquired 3D occupancy grid and a graph search to generate an assembly plan. This plan is used to guide users during assembly tasks to create a similar object. If the user deviates from the suggested plan, our system automatically validates whether the new state is solvable or not and reacts accordingly. Forward assembly planning is an NP-hard problem, but we introduce pruning methods for the search tree that make the approach practical.

1 Introduction

A primary challenge in robotics is to enable non-expert users to interact with robotic systems. Future robots will need to adapt to changing requirements to deliver personalized functionalities. A potential application of robotics is to assist users in assembly tasks. Several strategies have been proposed to address this problem. One of the most popular approaches is *Learning from Demonstration* (LfD) [7] which can be viewed as a way to transfer instructions from non-expert users to robots [1,4]. However, LfD does not generalise to new tasks.

Another common approach is to use *Computer-Aided Design* (CAD) models for generating assembly plans [2,8,9]. The limitation of this method is that a CAD model of each part of the object must be available beforehand and the geometric interference relations between each pair of parts are generated manually. Extracting sufficient visual information from observations, that can be used to help a user complete assembly tasks, cannot be achieved using available LfD approaches. Our key contributions are:

This work was supported by Thi Qar University, Iraq.

T. Mitrovic et al. (Eds.): AI 2018, LNAI 11320, pp. 759–765, 2018.
https://doi.org/10.1007/978-3-030-03991-2_68

- A system that computes assembly plans from a learned 3D occupancy grid.
- Pruning methods for the graph search used to generate assembly plans.
- Dynamic revision of the assembly plan.

Fig. 1. Workbench initialisation.

We demonstrate our system with the construction of 3D LEGO objects. Instead of using a CAD model, which must be provided beforehand, our system computes a 3D occupancy grid. This occupancy grid is a 3D array that encodes the spatial relationships of the components of the object. After creating the 3D occupancy grid of the assembled object, an assembly plan is generated by a depth-first graph search with pruning. Finally, the system can assist a user with the assembly of identical objects.

2   Related Work

Several approaches have been proposed for teaching assistant robots new skills. Most of these approaches are based on LfD, which provides the robot with the ability to learn tasks demonstrated by people [3]. A key problem in assembly task learning from demonstration is detecting accurate poses of each object in the scene during the demonstrations [4].

The most similar works to our approach is presented in [1]. Their work describes a simple model of spatial relationships. The only factor taken into account is the distance between each object and the robot. No assembly planning is done and the relationships between the objects are not taken into account. Our work offers more support to the user. Our system is observing, learning, identifying the workbench state, and recommending a next action based on a dynamic planner.

Another approach that can be used for assembly sequence generation is *reversed geometric planning*. Complete disassembly is the process of disassembling all the parts of an object. However, the disassembly sequence does not necessarily match the assembly plan used by a person as it is simply one among several possible solutions [6]. Most of the time, a complete disassembly sequence is not the optimal solution due to the different cost of the disassembly process [10]. In our work, reversed geometric planning is used for pruning the depth-first graph search.

3   System Description

Our system can be decomposed into three main modules *Workbench initialisation* (see Fig. 1), *Object structure induction* (see Fig. 2), and *Planning and guiding*. We call *a part*, either a single brick or a collection of connected bricks with their spatial relationships. Each brick is assigned a unique integer in the range $[1, n]$ where n is the number of bricks of the object. The value 0 codes empty space cells. Each non empty cell in the 3D occupancy grid corresponds to a stud of a LEGO brick.

3.1   Workbench Initialisation

The first frame f_0 of the observation video is used to identify the initial workbench state S_0. Abstractly, a (workbench) state is a set of parts. A state is represented with a dictionary of features of the present parts on the workbench.

Pixel Classifier. The part detector is based on a pixel classifier trained on images of the components (LEGO bricks) that form the assembled object. We extract 5D training vectors by stacking the pixel position and its RGB colour values. As a clustering method, we use the *density-based spatial clustering of applications with noise* (DBSCAN) [5]. However, DBSCAN is a slow algorithm, so we only use it to train a faster pixel classifier, namely a logistic regression classifier. We train the logistic regression classifier using only the RGB values.

3.2   Object Structure Induction

The 3D occupancy grid is built by tracking the LEGO parts during the assembly task. The pseudo-code of the object structure induction is given in Algorithm 1.

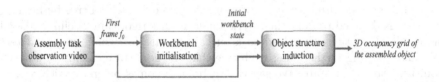

Fig. 2. Object structure induction.

3.3   Assembly Plan Generation and Guidance

During planning, the system relies on the extracted 3D occupancy grid to dynamically generate an assembly plan. The search space grows rapidly with the length of the sequence of actions, especially as we allow the user to swap equivalent parts. Two parts are considered *equivalent* if they have the same shape (they can have different colours). The interchangeability adds flexibility as the system can accept plan variations.

However, allowing these variations increases the size of the search tree of the planner. Let b denote the branching factor m the maximum depth v the maximum possible variations for assembling any two LEGO bricks, and n the number of the bricks. Considering the worst case scenario in the LEGO assembly problem, we have for a standard depth-first search (DFS), a space complexity

---

Algorithm 1. Object structure induction

---

    input : $\mathcal{V}$: video of the assembly of an object
    output: $\mathcal{S}_f$: final state of the workbench
1 **begin**
2    $\mathcal{S}_0$: initial workbench state
3   Initialize a foreground-background model
4    $\mathcal{S} = \mathcal{S}_0$ /* workbench current state */
5   **for** $t \in$ frame index range of $\mathcal{V}$ **do**
6       $\mathcal{H}_t$ = hands are visible   /* track hands */
7   **if** $\mathcal{H}_{t-1}$ **and not** $\mathcal{H}_t$ **then**
            /* Quiescent frame. A state transition has just been completed. A
               part $\mathcal{A}$ has been connected onto a part $\mathcal{B}$ */
8   Identify part $\mathcal{A}$ and part $\mathcal{B}$ from the last and the current quiescent
          frames.
9   Build the occupancy grid of the new part $\mathcal{C}$ by combining the
          occupancy grids of the old parts $\mathcal{A}$ and $\mathcal{B}$.
10   Update the state $\mathcal{S}$ by adding $\mathcal{C}$ and removing $\mathcal{A}$ and $\mathcal{B}$
11   Update the foreground-background model
12   **end**
13   **end**
14    $\mathcal{S}_f = \mathcal{S}$
15 **end**

---

of $O(bm)$ and a time complexity of $O(b^m)$. As $m = n - 1$ and $b = v$, a standard DFS planner would not scale well with the number of bricks.

In order to speed up the computation, we prune the search tree by filtering out actions doomed to fail. The filtering algorithm (Algorithm 2) eliminates all the candidate actions that lead to a successor state for which we can detect without exploring further the search tree that the goal state cannot be reached from that successor state. We say that a brick β comes before a brick γ with respect to the grid $\mathcal{O}$ if for all disassembly sequences, brick γ has to be removed before brick β. In this case, we write $\beta \prec \gamma$. For each brick β, we associate the set $\Gamma(\beta) = \{\gamma \mid \beta \prec \gamma\}$ of all the bricks γ that come after β.

The pruning dramatically speeds up the search algorithm at an additional cost of $O(n^2)$ for the generation of the candidate actions in a given state.

Figure 3 shows an example of a doomed state where backtracking is required. The two parts A and B (left) cannot physically be connected to create the goal part (middle) because the size of the studs prevents this action (right).

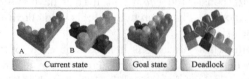

Fig. 3. Example of a doomed state.

Algorithm 2. Valid action generation

---

    input : $\mathcal{A}$: source part to move, $\mathcal{B}$: destination part to connect $\mathcal{A}$ to, $\mathcal{O}$:
               3D occupancy grid of the goal object
    output: $\mathcal{V}$: list of all valid actions $(\mathcal{A}, \mathcal{B}, d)$

1 **begin**
2   Compute $\Gamma(\beta)$ for each brick β in $\mathcal{O}$
3   eq($\mathcal{A}$) = set of all $\mathcal{A}$ equivalents in $\mathcal{O}$
4   eq($\mathcal{B}$) = set of all $\mathcal{B}$ equivalents in $\mathcal{O}$
5   **for** $(\tilde{\mathcal{A}}, \tilde{\mathcal{B}}) \in$ eq($\mathcal{A}$) $\times$ eq($\mathcal{B}$) **do**
6   **if** $\tilde{\mathcal{A}}$ is not connected to $\tilde{\mathcal{B}}$ in $\mathcal{O}$ **then**
7 | continue
8   **end**
9   d = the horizontal offset between $\tilde{\mathcal{A}}$ and $\tilde{\mathcal{B}}$ in $\mathcal{O}$
10        $\mathcal{C}$ = drop $\mathcal{A}$ onto $\mathcal{B}$ with offset d
            /* Check for potential obstructions   */
11        $C_b = \tilde{\mathcal{A}} \cup \tilde{\mathcal{B}}$
12   **for** $\gamma \in \left(\bigcup_{\beta \in C_b} \Gamma(\beta) \right) \setminus C_b$ **do**
13   **if** $\Gamma(\gamma) \cap C_b \neq \emptyset$ **then**
               /* γ will be obstructed by $\mathcal{C}$ */
14 | continue to next pair $(\tilde{\mathcal{A}}, \tilde{\mathcal{B}})$
15   **end**
16   **end**
17   **end**
18   Append $(\mathcal{A}, \mathcal{B}, d)$ to $\mathcal{V}$
19 **end**

---

4   Experimental Results

We have tested our object structure induction module by observing several LEGO assembly tasks of objects similar to those shown in Fig. 5. Our system has been tested on a standard stationary computer. In all the tests, the system did induce the correct 3D occupancy grids. The search tree is pruned dramatically thanks to the action filtering (detailed in Algorithm 2). The number of generated states can be as low as the number of bricks when no backtracking is required.

Table 1. Impact of action filtering on DFS running time

Exp. index	No. of parts	Execution time		No. of explored states	
		Filtering	No filtering	Filtering	No filtering
1	3	0.0952 s	3.9465 s	2	1737
2	4	0.1942 s	39.2 m	3	612874
3	5	0.3598 s	10 h	4	7122000
4	10	1.014 s	12 h+	27	3500000+

Table 1 shows the execution time and the number of the explored states in four different experiments. In each case of experiments 1–3, the goal is to assemble an object (State 3 in Fig. 4) that consists of 10 bricks but they start from different states. Experiment 4 provides an example where backtracking is required because the search comes across a situation similar to the case described in Fig. 3.

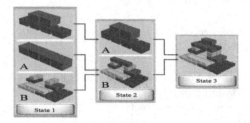

Fig. 4. Example of a solution generated by the planner.

The sequence of actions generated by the planner is used to guide a user to assemble an identical object. Figure 4 shows the last two actions of the assembly plan generated by the planner to reassemble the object shown in Fig. 5, state 3. At each state, the system suggests to move a part (A) onto a part (B) and shows the exact location to place A onto B. Figure 5 shows a user screen during the guiding stage. The system will revise its assembly plan if the user chooses another action.

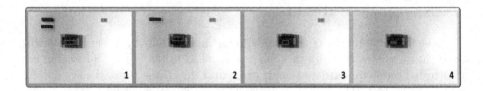

Fig. 5. Example of the guiding process.

5   Conclusion

In this paper, we have introduced a proactive assistant system for human assembly tasks. By observing the assembly of a single object, the system is capable of inducing a 3D occupancy grid of this object. Next, The planner generates on the fly an assembly plan, based on the current state and the goal state, and guides a user during the assembly of identical objects. The planner is fast because it uses ad hoc pruning techniques. The system can dynamically revise the plan, if the user deviates from it, and act accordingly.

We have started working on a prototype for IKEA pieces of furniture. The parts of these objects have more complex spatial relationships than LEGO bricks, but the same fundamental principles can be applied. Most of the presented module limitations will be addressed in this prototype.

References

1. Ahmadzadeh, S.R., Paikan, A., Mastrogiovanni, F., Natale, L., Kormushev, P., Caldwell, D.G.: Learning symbolic representations of actions from human demonstrations. In: Proceedings - ICRA, pp. 3801–3808 (2015)
2. Da Xu, L., Wang, C., Bi, Z., Yu, J.: Autoassem: an automated assembly planning system for complex products. IEEE Trans. Ind. Inf. **8**(3), 669–678 (2012)
3. Dillmann, R.: Teaching and learning of robot tasks via observation of human performance. Robot. Auton. Syst. **47**(2–3), 109–116 (2004)
4. Ekvall, S., Kragic, D.: Robot learning from demonstration: a task-level planning approach. Int. J. Adv. Robot. Syst. **5**(3), 223–234 (2008)
5. Ester, M., Kriegel, H.P., Sander, J., Xu, X., et al.: A density-based algorithm for discovering clusters in large spatial databases with noise. In: KDD, vol. 96, pp. 226–231 (1996)
6. Kongar, E., Gupta, S.M.: Disassembly sequencing using genetic algorithm. Int. J. Adv. Manuf. Technol. **30**(5–6), 497–506 (2006)
7. Kuniyoshi, Y., Inaba, M., Inoue, H.: Learning by watching: extracting reusable task knowledge from visual observation of human performance. IEEE Trans. Robot. Autom. **10**(6), 799–822 (1994)
8. Lee, K., Joo, S., Christensen, H.I.: An assembly sequence generation of a product family for robot programming. In: IROS. IEEE (2016)
9. Su, Q.: A hierarchical approach on assembly sequence planning and optimal sequences analyzing. Robot. Comput.-Integr. Manuf. **25**(1), 224–234 (2009)
10. Tang, Y., Zhou, M., Zussman, E., Caudill, R.: Disassembly modeling, planning, and application. J. Manuf. Syst. **21**(3), 200–217 (2002)

Surrogate-Assisted Genetic Programming for Dynamic Flexible Job Shop Scheduling

Fangfang Zhang$^{(\boxtimes)}$, Yi Mei, and Mengjie Zhang

School of Engineering and Computer Science, Victoria University of Wellington,
PO Box 600, Wellington 6140, New Zealand
{fangfang.zhang,yi.mei,mengjie.zhang}@ecs.vuw.ac.nz

Abstract. Genetic programming (GP) has been widely used for automatically evolving priority rules for solving job shop scheduling problems. However, one of the main drawbacks of GP is the intensive computation time. This paper aims at investigating appropriate surrogates for GP to reduce its computation time without sacrificing its performance in solving dynamic flexible job shop scheduling (DFJSS) problems. Firstly, adaptive surrogate strategy with dynamic fidelities of simulation models are proposed. Secondly, we come up with generation-range-based surrogate strategy in which homogeneous (heterogeneous) surrogates are used in same (different) ranges of generations. The results show that these two surrogate strategies with GP are efficient. The computation time are reduced by 22.9% to 27.2% and 32.6% to 36.0%, respectively. The test performance shows that the proposed approaches can obtain rules with at least the similar quality to the rules obtained by the GP approach without using surrogates. Moreover, GP with adaptive surrogates achieves significantly better performance in one out of six scenarios. This paper confirms the potential of using surrogates to solve DFJSS problems.

Keywords: Surrogate · Dynamic flexible job shop scheduling
Genetic programming

1 Introduction

Flexible job shop scheduling (FJSS) is an extension to classical job shop scheduling (JSS). However, in FJSS, one operation can be processed on more than one machine rather than a specified machine. In order to tackle the FJSS problem, two decisions, which are a machine-specific decision and a job-specific decision, have to be made. The machine-specific decision is to allocate a ready operation to an appropriate machine while the job-specific decision aims to select one operation as the next to be processed. FJSS is NP-hard [3].

In practice, the environment is usually dynamic and jobs arrive in the job shop over time without prior information. Dynamic job shop scheduling (DJSS)

© Springer Nature Switzerland AG 2018
T. Mitrovic et al. (Eds.): AI 2018, LNAI 11320, pp. 766–772, 2018.
https://doi.org/10.1007/978-3-030-03991-2_69

was proposed for considering this situation. Dispatching rules, as priority functions, have been widely adopted for solving DJSS problems [2,4], due to the ability to react in real time. A comprehensive comparison of dispatching rules can be found in [9]. Dynamic flexible job shop scheduling (DFJSS) considers both the characteristics of FJSS and DJSS. Naturally, two kinds of dispatching rules are needed in DFJSS, which are routing rule (machine-specific) and sequencing rule (job-specific), respectively. In this case, the quality of DFJSS schedule depends highly on how well the routing rule and the sequencing rule work together. However, dispatching rules are normally manually designed. That is, the design of dispatching rules is domain-dependent and time-consuming.

Genetic programming (GP) has been successfully applied to automatically evolve dispatching rules for JSS [5,7]. However, a challenge of using GP is the intensive computation time. Surrogate-assisted evolutionary computation with efficient computation models, known as surrogates, provides a promising means of handing complex applications [1,8]. The challenge is how to design appropriate surrogates with cheaper computation time that can represent the original models well.

1.1 Goals

To address the challenge above, this paper has the following research objectives.

- Propose adaptive surrogates for GP (ASGP) approach to operate linearly diverse surrogates with different fidelities in the search process.
- Design generation-range-based surrogates for GP (GSGP) that uses homogeneous (heterogeneous) surrogates in the same (different) predefined ranges of generations.
- Verify the effectiveness and efficiency of the proposed algorithms.
- Compare the learning processes of the proposed two algorithms with standard GP without surrogates.

2 The Proposed Surrogate Strategies

2.1 Adaptive Surrogates

In this section, adaptive surrogates are proposed for GP and the corresponding algorithm is named as ASGP. The basic idea is to deliberately enlarge accuracy of the surrogate models by building up a very simple surrogates at the early stage. As the evolutionary optimization proceeds, the accuracy of the surrogates increases gradually and smoothly expecting that the performance of approximated surrogate models is consistent with the original model.

Let N_{job} and N_{warmup} represent the number of jobs and warmup jobs, respectively. At the ith generation, the number of jobs and warmup jobs are denoted as $N_{job,i}$ and $N_{warmup,i}$. The expressions of $N_{job,i}$ and $N_{warmup,i}$ are shown as Eq. (1) and Eq. (2), respectively. In this way, the number of jobs and warmup jobs will increase linearly.

$$N_{job,i} = \begin{cases} N_{job} * \frac{1}{maxGen-1} & gen = 0 \\ N_{job} * \frac{Gen}{maxGen-1} & 1 \leq Gen < maxGen \end{cases} \tag{1}$$

$$N_{warmup,i} = \begin{cases} N_{warmup} * \frac{1}{maxGen-1} & gen = 0 \\ N_{warmup} * \frac{Gen}{maxGen-1} & 1 \leq Gen < maxGen \end{cases} \tag{2}$$

2.2 Generation-range-based Surrogates

For the ASGP, at each generation, different surrogate models are applied. In this section, generation-range-based surrogates is proposed for GP (GSGP) to explore whether a fixed interval change can be more efficient. In this paper, the number of jobs and warmup jobs of the original simulation model are set to 5000 and 1000, respectively. We set every ten generations into a range. The setting details of different surrogates used in different generations are shown in Table 1.

Table 1. The setting of generation-range-based surrogates.

Generation ranges	$N_{job,i}$	$N_{warmup,i}$
$[0, 10)$	500	100
$[10, 20)$	1000	200
$[20, 30)$	1500	300
$[30, 40)$	2500	500
$[40, 50]$	5000	1000

3 Experiment Design

In our experiment, the terminal and function sets in [6] are adopted. It is worth mentioned that "/" is the protected division that returns the largest double positive number if divided by 0. For dynamic simulation, commonly used configuration is adopted [10]. This paper presents the results obtained by the proposed two approaches and CCGP approach [10], which is the state-of-the-art algorithm for DFJSS, using three objectives, namely: (1) max-flowtime, (2) mean-flowtime, and (3) mean-weighted-flowtime. The smaller the result, the better.

4 Results and Analyses

The $(-, +)$ marks show whether our proposed approaches converge significantly better or poorer than CCGP approach in Wilcoxon rank sum test ($p \leq 0.05$), respectively. For the convenience of description, $< obj, uti >$ indicates the simulation scenarios, where obj and uti are the objective and the utilization level.

Table 2. The mean and deviation error of normalized objective value of the compared algorithms over 30 independent runs for six scenarios.

Index	Scenario	ASGP	GSGP	CCGP
1	$< tmax, 0.85 >$	0.640 (0.034)	0.638 (0.029)	0.642 (0.035)
2	$< tmax, 0.95 >$	0.571 (0.023)	0.565 (0.018)	0.568 (0.030)
3	$< tmean, 0.85 >$	0.772 (0.012)(-)	0.768 (0.008)	0.772 (0.015)
4	$< tmean, 0.95 >$	0.734 (0.023)	0.738 (0.022)	0.731 (0.015)
5	$< twt, 0.85 >$	0.778 (0.030)	0.772 (0.010)	0.774 (0.018)
6	$< twt, 0.95 >$	0.773 (0.023)	0.774 (0.024)	0.774 (0.037)

4.1 Test Performance of Evolved Rules

Table 2 shows that ASGP and GSGP algorithms are no significantly worse than CCGP in general. The mean value obtained by ASGP are about equal with the value obtained by CCGP in all scenarios. It is noted that ASGP significantly outperforms CCGP in scenario $< tmean, 0.85 >$. This clearly shows the potential of using surrogates to improve the performance of GP. It also indicates that the surrogates (approximation models) may not be always harm.

For GSGP, the mean value obtained are smaller than CCGP in four (scenario 1, 2, 3, 5) out of six scenarios. In addition, the variances obtained by GSGP are smaller than CCGP in five (scenario 1, 2, 3, 5, 6) out of six scenarios.

4.2 Training Time

Table 3 shows the computation time (reductions produced by surrogates compared with CCGP) of the three algorithms. Overall, ASGP and GSGP need less training computation times compared with CCGP. The average reductions produced by ASGP and GSGP are 25.7% and 34.4%, respectively.

The experimental results have confirmed that ASGP can reduce the computation time by at least 22.9% in six scenarios. In both scenario 2 and scenario 3, the computation time are reduced the most (27.2%). For GSGP, it is obvious that it can reduce more computation time (from 32.6% to 36.0%) than ASGP (from 22.9% to 27.2%). It is not surprising because the average fidelity of ASGP is higher than GSGP. In addition, the computation time is reduced the most (36.0%) in scenario 1 while the least (32.6%) in scenario 5.

4.3 Insight the Learning Process

The lines in Fig. 1 are the average normalized objective value from 30 independent runs. Although all GP methods start with the same population, the starting points are different because they use different surrogates. To be specific, CCGP get the value from surrogates with higher fidelities while ASGP and GSGP get the value from surrogates with lower fidelities.

Table 3. The average training time (reduction) of the compared algorithms over 30 independent runs for six scenarios.

Index	Scenario	Training time (seconds)		
		ASGP	GSGP	CCGP
1	$< tmax, 0.85 >$	3399.8 (26.8%)	2969.9 (36.0%)	4642.8
2	$< tmax, 0.95 >$	3743.6 (27.2%)	3326.2 (35.3%)	5144.9
3	$< tmean, 0.85 >$	3302.5 (27.2%)	2935.0 (35.3%)	4538.5
4	$< tmean, 0.95 >$	3635.3 (25.0%)	3220.2 (33.6%)	4849.9
5	$< twt, 0.85 >$	3436.2 (22.9%)	3004.4 (32.6%)	4458.4
6	$< twt, 0.95 >$	3725.7 (24.8%)	3282.7 (33.8%)	4957.0

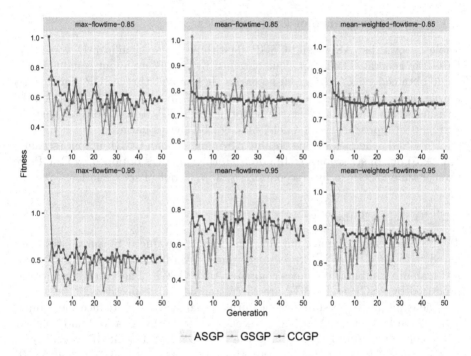

Fig. 1. The convergence curves of the fitness obtained by ASGP, GSGP and CCGP in training process.

It is noted that both ASGP and GSGP have higher fluctuations in all scenarios than CCGP, especially at the early stage of evolutionary process. For ASGP, the fidelities of surrogate models change smoothly to handle the learning process gradually. It is expected to meet the need of training. It is interesting that Fig. 1 shows that ASGP and GSGP have basically the same trends in six scenarios. This indicates that the predefined ranges and settings of simulations in GSGP are representative for the learning process. In addition, after generation

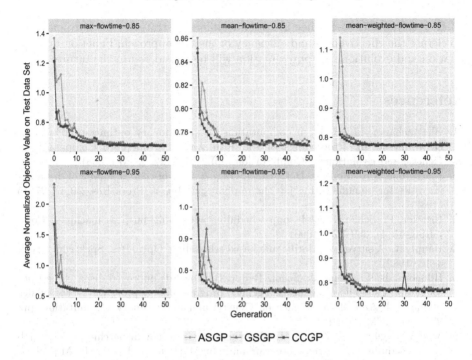

Fig. 2. The convergence curves of the normalized objective value obtained by ASGP, GSGP and CCGP in test process.

40, ASGP and GSGP can achieve almost the same learning ability as CCGP, although they use surrogates with lower fidelities at previous generations.

Figure 2 shows that CCGP can improve much faster at the beginning of the evolution in six scenarios. This benefits from the precise search with full simulations at the expense of computation time. However, after generation 10 approximately, the test performance between these three algorithms does not differ obviously.

Overall, taking the computation time and test performance into consideration, the proposed algorithms are more promising than CCGP.

5   Conclusions and Future Work

In order to tackle the intensive computation time of GP approach, this paper proposed two different kinds of strategies of surrogates for GP to automatically design dispatching rules for DFJSS. It is a preliminary attempt to apply surrogates into DFJSS. The results show that the two proposed surrogate strategies managed to reduce computation time without deteriorating the quality of the evolved rules. It also indicates that the proposed strategies have the potential to help GP to achieve more promising dispatching rules.

It is important to further investigate different strategies for surrogates to accelerate the effectiveness and efficiency of the GP approach. Function approximation and evolutionary approximation will be considered in the future.

References

1. Bhattacharya, M.: Reduced computation for evolutionary optimization in noisy environment. In: Proceedings of the 10th Annual Conference Companion on Genetic and Evolutionary Computation, pp. 2117–2122. ACM (2008)
2. Blackstone, J.H., Phillips, D.T., Hogg, G.L.: A state-of-the-art survey of dispatching rules for manufacturing job shop operations. Int. J. Prod. Res. **20**(1), 27–45 (1982)
3. Brucker, P., Schlie, R.: Job-shop scheduling with multi-purpose machines. Computing **45**(4), 369–375 (1990)
4. Haupt, R.: A survey of priority rule-based scheduling. Oper.-Res.-Spektrum **11**(1), 3–16 (1989)
5. Hildebrandt, T., Heger, J., Scholz-Reiter, B.: Towards improved dispatching rules for complex shop floor scenarios: a genetic programming approach. In: Proceedings of the 12th Annual Conference on Genetic and Evolutionary Computation, pp. 257–264. ACM (2010)
6. Mei, Y., Nguyen, S., Zhang, M.: Evolving time-invariant dispatching rules in job shop scheduling with genetic programming. In: McDermott, J., Castelli, M., Sekanina, L., Haasdijk, E., García-Sánchez, P. (eds.) EuroGP 2017. LNCS, vol. 10196, pp. 147–163. Springer, Cham (2017). https://doi.org/10.1007/978-3-319-55696-3_10
7. Nguyen, S., Zhang, M., Johnston, M., Tan, K.C.: A computational study of representations in genetic programming to evolve dispatching rules for the job shop scheduling problem. IEEE Trans. Evol. Comput. **17**(5), 621–639 (2013)
8. Ratle, A.: Accelerating the convergence of evolutionary algorithms by fitness landscape approximation. In: Eiben, A.E., Bäck, T., Schoenauer, M., Schwefel, H.-P. (eds.) PPSN 1998. LNCS, vol. 1498, pp. 87–96. Springer, Heidelberg (1998). https://doi.org/10.1007/BFb0056852
9. Sels, V., Gheysen, N., Vanhoucke, M.: A comparison of priority rules for the job shop scheduling problem under different flow time- and tardiness-related objective functions. Int. J. Prod. Res. **50**(15), 4255–4270 (2012)
10. Yska, D., Mei, Y., Zhang, M.: Genetic programming hyper-heuristic with cooperative coevolution for dynamic flexible job shop scheduling. In: Castelli, M., Sekanina, L., Zhang, M., Cagnoni, S., García-Sánchez, P. (eds.) EuroGP 2018. LNCS, vol. 10781, pp. 306–321. Springer, Cham (2018). https://doi.org/10.1007/978-3-319-77553-1_19

Virtual Roundabout Protocol
for Autonomous Vehicles

Jianglin Qiao[1(✉)], Dongmo Zhang[1], and Dave de Jonge[1,2]

[1] University of Western Sydney, Sydney, Australia
19469397@student.westernsydney.edu.au
[2] IIIA-CSIC, Barcelona, Spain
davedejonge@iiia.csic.es

Abstract. This paper investigates intersection management protocols under an environment in which all vehicles are autonomous and capable of communication. Three potential protocols for intersection control was considered and implemented as a multi-robot system under the Robot Operating System platform. Although these protocols mimic conventional control mechanisms for human-driving, their behaviour under environments of autonomous driving is different. We found that the virtual roundabout, a protocol under which all vehicles follow the real-world rule of roundabouts without a physical roundabout, is most effective among the three protocols with respect to traffic load, safety distance and traffic imbalances.

1 Introduction

Self-driving cars are becoming a tangible reality and will change our lives in more ways than we can imagine [1–4]. In a future when all cars are self-driving, traffic situations will be dramatically different and require different methods and infrastructure for control and management [5]. With the emergence of autonomous and connected vehicles (AVs and CVs), traffic facilities that were designed for human-driving such as traffic lights, stop signs and roundabouts would be replaced by less visible but more efficient algorithmic policies [6]. As such, the utilisation of new technologies with connected vehicles and intelligent traffic control for driverless cars has become one of the most important research topics for autonomous driving [7–12]. This paper aims to investigate the behaviour of AVs under different intersection control protocols.

There are three typical control mechanisms used almost anywhere in the world: *traffic signals, stop signs* and *roundabouts*. Traffic signals are considered the most efficient mechanism for intersections with heavy traffic, stop signs for intersections with light and unbalanced traffic and roundabouts built to accommodate for moderate traffic with balanced flow from all directions. These traffic control facilities were designed for human drivers. Despite new technologies such as smart intersections being developed to optimise traffic control [16,17], in the environments where all vehicles are fully connected and autonomous, these facilities are no longer necessary and efficient.

© Springer Nature Switzerland AG 2018
T. Mitrovic et al. (Eds.): AI 2018, LNAI 11320, pp. 773–782, 2018.
https://doi.org/10.1007/978-3-030-03991-2_70

In this paper we consider three potential protocols for intersection control and implement them as a multi-robot system based on the Robot Operating System (ROS) platform - traffic signals, first-in-first-out and virtual roundabout. Although these protocols mimic control mechanisms for human-driving, their behaviour under autonomous driving is different. Based on our results, the virtual roundabout outperformed the other two protocols in respect to average delays, safety distance and traffic load in addition to handling imbalanced traffic reasonably well.

The structure of this paper is as follows. Section 2 introduces the model algorithms of the three intersection protocols. Section 3 shows our simulation outcomes. Section 4 we summarise the paper with a discussion of related work and future directions.

2   Protocols for Intersection Control

As mentioned above, we will consider three protocols for intersection traffic flow controls. We will show how these protocols are implemented on the ROS platform.

2.1   The Model of Intersections

We consider an intersection as a four-way junction crossing over of two roads. An intersection is preset with an alert area, called the *intersection area* (see Fig. 1). Inside the intersection area exists a *stop line* on each road towards the intersection, a vehicle must stop before the stop line if the intersection is occupied by another vehicle or encountering a red light. The area between the stop lines is called the *central area* (see Fig. 1).

Vehicles on the road are assumed to possess valid software and hardware to follow the appropriate protocols and are capable of communicating with each other. Communication amongst the vehicles can be peer-to-peer or broadcast via the facilities of the intersection allowing vehicles to negotiate with each other. Whilst inside the intersection area, every vehicle will be aware of the status of other vehicles in the intersection area. For the purpose of simulations, the status include the following information:

- Vehicle id: an identification number to identify the vehicles inside the intersection area.
- Travel direction: the direction towards the intersection.
- Position: the current coordinates in the intersection area.
- State: used to determine whether the vehicle has or has not passed the intersection. It can be any of the following four values: *"before central area"*, *"waiting at stopping line"*, *"inside central area"*, *"after central area"*.
- Speed: current speed of the vehicle.

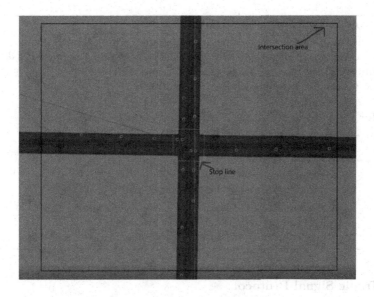

Fig. 1. The model of intersection

The state of a vehicle can be derived from its position and direction, however explicitly including the state allow for easier implementation of algorithm.

In this study, an intersection consists of four entrances: *east*, *west*, *south* and *north* with all cars entering the intersection proceeding straight without turning. *Road*1 consists of the two lanes running north-south separated by a solid line and similarly, *Road*2 the east-west lanes.

Consider an observation window period T. We let n denote the set of vehicles that are travelling through the intersection area during the period (excluding the vehicles that entered before the period or left after the period). Let W denote the width of the intersection area[1]. We assume that each vehicle $i \in n$ travels into and out of the *intersection area* with velocity V_i. Let s_i be the time it enters the *intersection area* and f_i be the time it leaves the *intersection area*. Then, the travel time $d_i = f_i - s_i$.

We define the *ideal travel time*, I_i, of a vehicle i to be the time it would take that vehicle to travel through the intersection at constant velocity V_i without stopping. Therefore, the ideal travel time $I_i = \frac{W}{V_i}$.

To test the efficiency of each intersection protocol, we compare the average delay against the ideal travel time. In this case, the average delay D^T of all vehicles in the observation period T can be calculated as

$$D^T = \frac{1}{n} \sum_{i=1}^{n} (d_i - I_i)$$

---

[1] For simplicity, we assume that the intersection is a square.

Algorithm 1. Traffic signal protocol

Input: The set of vehicles N and the array of states $\{state[i] : i \in N\}$
Output: Time record for each vehicle: the finish time f_i and time duration d_i
Function: *traffic_signals*()

1: **while** System is not shutdown **do**
2:     Get *Systemtime*;
3:     **for** $i \in N$ **do**
4:         **if** state[i] is *"after central area"* **then**
5:             Continue;
6:         **if** *Systemtime* in *phase*1, vehicle i in *Road*1 **then**
7:             Vehicle i crosses the intersection;
8:             state[i] changes to *"inside central area"*;
9:         **if** *Systemtime* in *phase*2, vehicle i in *Road*2 **then**
10:        Vehicle i crosses the intersection;
11:        state[i] change to *"inside central area"*;

2.2 Traffic Signal Protocol

From Algorithm 1 above, we divide the system time into two phases to replicate traffic signals. *Phase* 1 allows the vehicles on *Road* 1 to pass through whilst restricting vehicles on *Road* 2. In other words, *Phase* 1 means green light for *Road* 1 while *Road* 2 has the red light and vice versa for *Phase* 2. Instead of simulating yellow light, vehicles on one road do not enter the intersection until the vehicles on the other road have left the intersection.

2.3 FIFO Protocol

The second protocol follows the idea of first-in-first-out queues (FIFO), the earlier a vehicle enters the *intersection area*, the earlier it can pass through. Vehicles that arrived later must wait at the stop line until all the earlier vehicles have passed the intersection.

If we strictly follow FIFO, only a single vehicle can pass the intersection at any given time. In our implementation, we allow two consecutively arrived vehicles to pass the intersection at the same time if and only if they are on the same road (different directions).

2.4 Virtual Roundabout Protocol

From Algorithm 3 below, the virtual roundabout is implemented off FIFO. It is a protocol designed to mimic roundabouts without the need for a physical roundabout. If the central area is empty, the vehicle that arrived earliest is allowed to enter the intersection. However, if the central area is not empty, vehicles that are on the same road as the vehicle currently on the central area is allowed to enter the intersection. The difference between FIFO and the virtual roundabout protocol is the ability to allow multiple vehicles to cross the intersection regardless of arrival time.

Algorithm 2. FIFO Protocol

Input: The vector of vehicles N sorted by their arrived time and the array of states
$\{state[i] : i \in N\}$

Output: Time record for each vehicle: the finish time f_i and time duration d_i

Function: $fifo()$

1: **while** System is not shutdown **do**
2:     **for** $i = 1$ *to* $|N|$ **do**
3:         occupied=false;
4:         **if** $state[i]$ is *"inside central area"* **then**
5:             occupied=true;
6:     **for** $i = 1$ *to* $|N|$ **do**
7:         **if** state[i] is *"after central area"* **then**
8:             Continue;
9:         **if** Vehicles i and $i + 1$ are on *Road1* or *Road2*, $state[i]$ and $state[i + 1]$ are
10:            *"waiting at stop line"*, and !occupied **then**
11:                Vehicle i and vehicle $i + 1$ crosses the intersection;
12:                Set state[i] and state[i+1] to *"inside central area"*;
13:        **else if** state[i] is *"waiting at stop line"* and !occupied **then**
14:            Vehicle i crosses the intersection;
15:            Set state[i] to *"inside central area"*;

Algorithm 3. Virtual Roundabout Protocol

Input: The vector of vehicles N sorted by their arrived time and the array of states
$\{state[i] : i \in N\}$

Output: Time record for each vehicle: the finish time f_i and time duration d_i

Function: $roundabout()$

1: **while** System is not shutdown **do**
2:     occupied = false;
3:     **for** $i = 1$ *to* $|N|$ **do**
4:         **if** $state[i]$ is *"inside central area"* **then**
5:             occupied = true;
6:     **for** $i = 1$ to $|N|$ **do**
7:         **if** state[i] in *"after central area"* **then**
8:             Continue;
9:         **if** Vehicle i in the waiting state, and occupied **then**
10:            Vehicle i crosses the intersection;
11:            Set $state[j]$ to *"inside central area"*;
12:        **if** Vehicle i on *Road1* or *Road2*, $state[i]$ is *"inside central area"*,
13:            and !occupied **then**
14:            **for** $j = 1$ to $|N|$ **do**
15:                **if** $state[j]$ in *"after central area"* **then**
16:                    Continue;
17:                **else if** Vehicle j on same road with Vehicle i and
18:                    $state[j]$ is *"waiting at stop line"* **then**
19:                    Vehicle j crosses the intersection;
20:                    Set $state[j]$ to *"inside central area"*;

---

3   Simulation

In our simulations, we compare the throughput efficiency of the conventional traffic signal, FIFO, and the virtual roundabout protocol by measuring the average travel delay in each case. In order to simulate different traffic conditions, we repeat experiments with varying numbers of vehicles and safety distances. Furthermore, we varied the 'road balance' to examine the efficiency of the virtual roundabout under asymmetric traffic load.

3.1   Testing Environment

For our simulation environment, we used Gazebo, a simulator designed to simulate real world robots. The communication frequency was set to 10 Hz (vehicles broadcast a message 10 times a second). A unit of distance was defined to be exactly the width of the central area. The central area and intersection area was set to have 1×1 unit^2 and 10×10 unit^2 respectively with the speed in the intersection area to be 0.5 unit/s. With a scale of $1 : 30$, the central area is 30×30 m^2, the intersection area is 300×300 m^2, and the speed V_i inside the intersection area is 54 km/h. The start times s_i for each car was randomly generated. A screenshot of the simulation is shown in Fig. 1.

3.2   Results

In this section we analyse the results from our simulations and discuss the performance of the virtual roundabout against both the traffic light and FIFO protocol.

Varying Number of Vehicles. For each of the protocols, we measured the average delay time D^T for an increasing numbers of vehicles. Regardless of the protocol implemented, as the number of cars increased the average delay also increased (see Fig. 2). However, the growth rate of each protocol was different

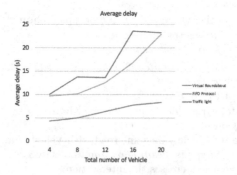

Fig. 2. Average delay

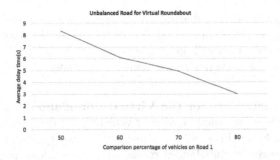

Fig. 3. Increased system efficiency as traffic load becomes imbalanced.

with the traffic signal showing a staggered growth, the FIFO with an exponential growth and the virtual roundabout showing a logarithmic growth.

As the traffic signal protocol was implemented with 30 s phases, traffic which exceeded the maximum number that can be processed in a single cycle must stop and wait resulting in a staggered growth. For FIFO protocol, the growth rate appears to increase at an exponential rate as each lane of traffic backs up at the stop line and must wait for cars that arrived at the central area first. For the virtual roundabout, the growth rate appears to increase at a logarithmic rate with an average delay 62% compared with the traffic lights and 56% of FIFO protocol.

Varying Safety Distance. In this section we analyse the influence of different safety distances on the vehicles' average delay times. We denote the vehicle body length by b and set the safety distance to $0.5b$, $1b$, $1.5b$ and $2b$.

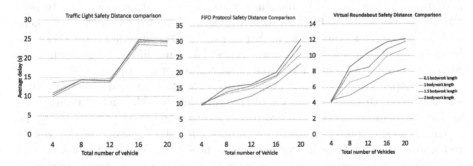

Fig. 4. Varying safety distance with traffic lights, FIFO and virtual roundabout.

In Fig. 4, we show the relationship between the average delays, the safety distance, and number of vehicles for the three protocols. It is apparent for FIFO and virtual round- about that as the safety distance increases so to does the average delay. Interestingly, for the traffic light protocol, it was found that the safety distance has no measurable impact on the average delay time. As discussed earlier, provided that the traffic load is able to pass in the allotted phase, the increase in safety distance will only have a measurable affect if the traffic load is unable to clear the cycle due to the increased distance.

Unbalanced Traffic Flow for the Virtual Roundabout Protocol. In the previous simulations, an equal number of vehicles pass through the central area from each direction. In this section, we present our experiments with the virtual roundabout protocol on unbalanced roads, i.e. more vehicles on one road than the other. Under realistic conditions, the ratio and direction of vehicles entering an intersection is not uniform.

In Fig. 3, as the intersection become increasingly imbalanced due to the composition of traffic load increasing on Road 1, the average delay decreases. Although beneficial for the intersection as an overall system, vehicles on the less congested roads suffer a penalty for taking the less congested path.

4   Related Work, Conclusion and Future Work

The rapid development of artificial intelligence and driverless cars has made intersection management an increasingly hot topic with two main approaches emerging for the management of intersections with AVs.

The first approach is implemented using a *centralized intersection management* system. Under this approach, AVs in the intersection area are under control of the central control unit. In this approach, there have been numerous approaches which includes Auction-based autonomous intersection management [9] and the first-come-first-served protocol [13].

The second approach is based on autonomous Multi-Agent Systems (MAS) and allows agents the ability negotiate with each other to decide when to pass the intersection [14,15]. In this scheme, AVs are regarded as one kind of agent and the intersection control as another agent [10]. Transportation networks can be made up of multiple Intersection Agents (IA), and different agreements can be reached by the AVs and IAs through several negotiation protocols.

This paper provides a new proposal to solve the management of an intersection for AVs by introducing the virtual roundabout. The virtual roundabout was tested against conventional protocols used to manage an intersection; traffic signal and FIFO protocol. From the simulations, the efficiency of the virtual roundabout drastically outperformed the traffic signals and FIFO protocol in all simulations with parameters such as traffic load and safety distance considered whilst performing well in imbalanced traffic conditions.

This research put forwards that the virtual roundabouts outperform standard protocols on intersections with four entries and vehicles all proceeding straight. In future research, we plan to examine the efficiency of the virtual roundabout with more complex traffic situations including intersections with more than 4 entries, multiple lanes, and the ability of vehicles to turn.

As the simulation environment was performed using ROS, our algorithms can be run directly on robots to replicate real world traffic. This is also the basis for applying the technology in practice as this protocol can be used with any vehicle with a communication device (level 3 AVs). Once the technology is ready for use, many benefits such as reduced fuel consumption, exhaust emissions, improvement of overall traffic efficiency, and safety is around the corner.

References

1. Thorpe, C., Herbert, M., Kanade, T., Shafer, S.: Toward autonomous driving: the CMU Navlab. I. Perception. IEEE Expert **6**(4), 31–42 (1991)
2. Bimbraw, K.: Autonomous cars: past, present and future a review of the developments in the last century, the present scenario and the expected future of autonomous vehicle technology. In: The 12th International Conference on Informatics in Control, Automation and Robotics (ICINCO), vol. 01, pp. 191–198 (2015)
3. Pettersson, I., Karlsson, I.C.M.: Setting the stage for autonomous cars: a pilot study of future autonomous driving experiences. IET Intell. Transp. Syst. **9**(7), 694–701 (2015)
4. Banerjee, T., Bose, S., Chakraborty, A., Samadder, T., Kumar, B., Rana, T.K.: Self driving cars: a peep into the future. In: 2017 8th Annual Industrial Automation and Electromechanical Engineering Conference, pp. 33–38 (2017)
5. Chan, C.Y.: Advancements, prospects, and impacts of automated driving systems. Int. J. Transp. Sci. Technol. **6**(3), 208–216 (2017)
6. Gruel, W., Stanford, J.M.: Assessing the long-term effects of autonomous vehicles: a speculative approach. Transp. Res. Procedia **13**, 18–29 (2016)
7. Fok, C.L., et al.: A platform for evaluating autonomous intersection management policies. In: Proceedings of the 2012 IEEE/ACM Third International Conference on Cyber-Physical Systems, pp. 87–96. IEEE Computer Society (2012)
8. Bashiri, M., Fleming, C.H.: A platoon-based intersection management system for autonomous vehicles. In: 2017 IEEE Intelligent Vehicles Symposium (IV), pp. 667–672 (2017)
9. Carlino, D., Boyles, S.D., Stone, P.: Auction-based autonomous intersection management. In: 16th International IEEE Conference on Intelligent Transportation Systems, pp. 529–534 (2013)
10. Hausknecht, M., Au, T.C., Stone, P.: Autonomous intersection management: multi-intersection optimization. In: 2011 IEEE/RSJ International Conference on Intelligent Robots and Systems (2011)
11. Lin, P., Liu, J., Jin, P.J., Ran, B.: Autonomous vehicle-intersection coordination method in a connected vehicle environment. IEEE Intell. Transp. Syst. Mag. **9**(4), 37–47 (2017)
12. Belkhouche, F.: Control of autonomous vehicles at an unsignalized intersection. In: 2017 American Control Conference (ACC), pp. 1340–1345 (2017)
13. Dresner, K., Stone, P.: Multiagent traffic management: a reservation-based intersection control mechanism. In: Proceedings of the Third International Joint Conference on Autonomous Agents and Multiagent Systems - Volume 2, pp. 530–537. IEEE Computer Society (2004)
14. Lamouik, I., Yahyaouy, A., Sabri, M.A.: Smart multi-agent traffic coordinator for autonomous vehicles at intersections. In: 2017 International Conference on Advanced Technologies for Signal and Image Processing (ATSIP), pp. 1–6 (2017)

15. Dresner, K., Stone, P.: A multiagent approach to autonomous intersection management. J. Artif. Intell. Res. **31**(1), 591–656 (2008)
16. Geng, Y., Cassandras, C.: Multi-intersection traffic light control with blocking. Discret. Event Dyn. Syst. **25**(1), 7–30 (2015)
17. Younis, O., Moayeri, N.: Employing cyber-physical systems: dynamic traffic light control at road intersections. IEEE Internet Things J. **4**(6), 2286–2296 (2017)

Multi-objective Container Consolidation in Cloud Data Centers

Tao Shi[✉], Hui Ma, and Gang Chen

School of Engineering and Computer Science, Victoria University of Wellington,
Wellington, New Zealand
{tao.shi,hui.ma,aaron.chen}@ecs.vuw.ac.nz

Abstract. In recent years, container-based clouds are becoming increasingly popular for their lightweight nature. Existing works on container consolidation mainly focus on reducing the energy consumption of cloud data centers. However, reducing energy consumption often results in container migrations which have big impact on the performance (i.e. availability) of applications in the containers. In this paper, we consider container consolidation as one multi-objective optimization problem with the objectives of minimizing the total energy consumption and minimizing the total number of container migrations within the certain period of time and present an NSGA-II based algorithm to find solutions for the container consolidation problem. Our experimental evaluation based on the real-world workload demonstrates that our proposed approach can lead to further energy saving and significant reduction of container migrations at the same time compared with some existing approaches.

Keywords: Container-based cloud · Energy consumption
Multi-objective · NSGA-II

1 Introduction

Cloud computing has been progressively gaining popularity in both industrial and academic worlds in the last decade for its elasticity, availability, and scalability. However, cloud data centers have to manage energy crisis due to the constraints from renewable or nonrenewable energy sources [10].

Fortunately, high energy efficiency can be achieved through virtualization-based approaches that implement multiple operating systems and applications on the same physical machines (PMs, also known as hosts in this paper) simultaneously. As the most widely used virtualization technique, hypervisor allows multiple operating systems to share one single PM through virtual machines (VMs) [2]. Another more flexible, scalable, and resource efficient solution, i.e. container is accelerated by the increasing popularity of Docker in recent years [1]. Compared with VMs, containers are lightweight in nature and enable high-density deployment, significantly reducing the thirst for large quantities of PMs. The aim of *container consolidation* is to consolidate multiple containers to a set

© Springer Nature Switzerland AG 2018
T. Mitrovic et al. (Eds.): AI 2018, LNAI 11320, pp. 783–795, 2018.
https://doi.org/10.1007/978-3-030-03991-2_71

of VMs which are then consolidated to a set of PMs so that the overall utilization of both VMs and PMs is maximized.

During the process of container consolidation, containers are often migrated among VMs to increase the utilization of VMs and PMs and therefore reduce the number of running PMs. However, container migrations lead to the startup delay because the migrations are implemented through shutting down the original PM's container and starting the same one on the destination PM. Naturally, the process impacts the performance of applications in cloud computing [15].

For the above reason, we regard the problem of container consolidation as one multi-objective optimization problem with two conflict objectives. On one hand, cloud data centers expect to consolidate containers to a smaller number of PMs to decrease energy consumption, which may cause a large number of container migrations. On the other hand, they would like to minimize container migrations to avoid service degradation derived from the container startup delay.

Existing works on container consolidation study the problem with different focuses. For example, Zhang et al. [19] model the container scheduling problem with the consideration of host energy consumption, network transmission cost, and container image pulling cost. They also deploy an integer linear programming (ILP) method to solve it. Piraghaj et al. [14] consider four metrics including energy consumption, Service Level Agreement (SLA) violations, container migrations rate and number of created virtual machines. In [9], Distance Based Evaluation (DBE) is used to orchestrate the four objectives as one ultimate value. However, this approach only suits to the situation when cloud providers have clear preference over different objectives.

In comparison to mathematical optimization techniques such as ILP, evolutionary multi-objective optimization (EMO) methodologies are ideal for solving multi-objective optimization problems, because they can find multiple Pareto-optimal solutions in one single run [5]. In particular, Non-dominated Sorting Genetic Algorithm II (NSGA-II) is one of the most widely used EMO methods that has shown its promises in solving combinatorial optimization problems. The algorithm can search well-spread solutions and usually converge quickly to the true Pareto-optimal front without specifying extra parameters [6]. The aim of this paper is to propose an NSGA-II based approach to produce a set of near optimal container consolidation solutions, to minimize energy consumption and the number of container migrations jointly.

The rest of the paper is organized as follows. Section 2 introduces the related work and background. Section 3 presents the objective functions and formulation of the container consolidation problem. Section 4 presents our NSGA-II based algorithm. Section 5 discusses the experiment results. Finally, Sect. 6 concludes the work.

2   Background

This section introduces the simulation environment we apply and NSGA-II for the problem we intend to solve.

2.1   ContainerCloudSim

ContainerCloudSim [15] is one simulation tool extended from the CloudSim simulation tookit [4]. It applies VM-Container configuration [14] as virtual environment and supports modeling and evaluating of container resource management techniques such as container scheduling, placement, and consolidation. The architecture of resource management in ContainerCloudSim is shown in Fig. 1. Concretely, the VM manager on the top of host sends the status of the host and the list of the containers required to be migrated to the consolidation manager. The consolidation manager running on a separate host decides the destination hosts of these containers and sends resource requests to them. There are two key modules involved in this process, i.e. container selection and host selection. The container selection module is implemented to select the candidate containers to migrate, and the host selection module is responsible for selecting the destination hosts for the migrated containers.

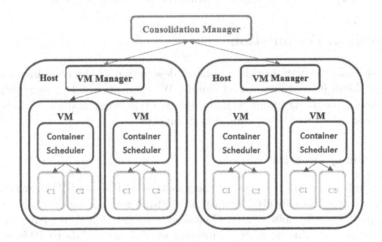

Fig. 1. The architecture of resource management in ContainerCloudSim [15].

Periodically, the container consolidation is triggered according to the status of hosts. If the CPU utilization of one host exceeds the predefined overload threshold or is lower than the under-load threshold, its status is set as Overloaded or Under-loaded correspondingly.

Overloaded Hosts Consolidation: Migrate the containers from the overloaded hosts until they are no longer overloaded by the container selection module and the host selection module. With regard to the container selection module, MaxUsage (MU) policy that selects the container with the biggest CPU utilization to migrate is proved to result in less energy consumption, fewer container migrations and SLA violations in [15]. Therefore, our study adopts this policy.

Under-Loaded Hosts Consolidation: For each under-loaded PM, all its containers will be migrated only if these containers can find the appropriate destination hosts by the host selection module. Our study focuses on this process since it has the potential for improvement by using NSGA-II and our new approach.

2.2 NSGA-II

NSGA-II is proposed in [6] to solve optimization problems with two or three objectives. It reduces the computational complexity of NSGA and also incorporates elitism. The algorithm can consider and control two attributes of each chromosome (e.g. container consolidation decision), i.e. non-domination rank and local crowding distance in the population to find the solutions near the true Pareto-optimal front. Instead of combining the conflicting objectives into one single fitness measure, NSGA-II generates solutions which provide a better trade-off taking all conditions into consideration. It has been used to solve many combinatorial optimization problems with the promising performance [18].

3   Problem Formulation

In this section, we first provide a general description of the container consolidation problem in container-based clouds. We then present the formulation of the problem, including assumptions, objective functions, and constraints that should be satisfied by the consolidation solutions.

3.1   Problem Description

Assume that in a cloud data center there is a set of PMs and VMs, which may have some containers allocated already, as the time going on new containers need to be deployed to the cloud center. Container consolidation aims to allocate new containers and migrate existing containers to VMs and VMs to PMs so that overall energy consumption of PMs is minimized while the container migration are also minimized.

3.2   Assumptions

The following assumptions are made in this paper.

- The major energy in data centers is consumed by CPU except the cooling devices [16], so we assume that the energy consumption of PMs only depend on the CPU utilization of PMs.
- Following the related work [14], the resources considered by PMs, VMs, and containers are CPU performance, memory, disk, and network bandwidth.
- We consider general situations where heterogeneous PMs, VMs, and containers have different configurations, i.e. CPU, memory.

3.3   Problem Formulation

Assume in a cloud data center, there are a set of physical machines $\mathbb{PM} = \{PM_1, \ldots, PM_m, \ldots, PM_p\}$ and a set of virtual machines $\mathbb{VM} = \{VM_1, VM_2, \ldots, VM_j, \ldots, VM_v\}$. Each physical machine PM_m has the capacities of CPU Pc_m, memory Pm_m, disk Pd_m and network bandwidth Pn_m, i.e. $PM_m(Pc_m, Pm_m, Pd_m, Pn_m)$. Similarly, for the virtual machine $VM_j \in \mathbb{VM}$, it has the corresponding capacities of resources, i.e. CPU, memory, disk, and network bandwidth. We describe them as $VM_j(Vc_j, Vm_j, Vd_j, Vn_j)$.

For a given set of applications, their CPU cost is defined as Million Instructions (MI). The cloud provider allocates each of the applications to a container which can be described as $C_i(Cc_i, Cm_i, Cd_i, Cn_i)$. During container consolidation, the list of containers that need to be allocated to the VMs on the corresponding PMs is denoted as $[C_1, \ldots, C_i, \ldots, C_c]$.

In order to minimize the power consumption of a data center, we formulate the first objective of the container consolidation problem as (1):

$$minimize\ E(t) = \sum_{m=1}^{p} P_m(t) \tag{1}$$

where $P_m(t)$ is the energy consumption of a physical machine PM_m at time t.

The energy consumption model of the physical machine PM_m we use is fully compatible with the VM-based energy model proposed by Blackburn [3]. The model is adopted widely by [11,17]. The power consumption is linearly related to the utilization of the CPU of the PMs, i.e., the power consumption of PM_m is determined by

$$P_m(t) = \begin{cases} P_m^{idle} + (P_m^{busy} - P_m^{idle}) \cdot pc_m(t), & if\ N_{vm} > 0 \\ 0, & if\ N_{vm} = 0 \end{cases} \tag{2}$$

where the CPU utilization at time t is $pc_m(t)$, P^{idle} and P^{busy} are the power consumption of the PM when its utilizations are 0% and 100% respectively, N_{vm} represents the total number of VMs being deployed in the PM.

Another objective of the container consolidation problem is to minimize the total number of container migrations, which is formulated in (3):

$$minimize\ TotalMigration = \sum_{m=1}^{p} Migration(P_m) \tag{3}$$

where $Migration(P_m)$ is the migration number of containers in a physical machine PM_m.

(4) shows the formula of calculating the CPU utilization of PM_m at time t. The Equation sums up the CPU utilization $vc_j(t)$ of VM_j. Similarly, its usages of memory, disk, and network bandwidth pm_m, pd_m and pn_m of PM_m are determined by (5), and N_{vm} represents the total number of VMs being deployed to PM_m.

$$pc_m(t) = \sum_{j=1}^{N_{vm}} vc_j(t) \tag{4}$$

$$pm_m = \sum_{j=1}^{N_{vm}} vm_j, \quad pd_m = \sum_{j=1}^{N_{vm}} vd_j, \quad pn_m = \sum_{j=1}^{N_{vm}} vn_j \tag{5}$$

Lastly, the CPU utilization at time t and the usages of memory, disk, and network bandwidth of VM_j can be calculated by (6) and (7). They are straightforward to sum up the relevant parameters of container C_i, and N_c represents the total number of containers being deployed to a VM_j.

$$vc_j(t) = \sum_{i=1}^{N_c} cc_j(t) \tag{6}$$

$$vm_j = \sum_{i=1}^{N_c} cm_i, \quad vd_j = \sum_{i=1}^{N_c} cd_i, \quad vn_j = \sum_{i=1}^{N_c} cn_i \tag{7}$$

3.4   Constraints

We consider resource constraints about VMs and PMs in (8). Generally speaking, VMs and PMs cannot process more CPU, memory, disk, and network bandwidth requirements than their capacities.

$$
\begin{aligned}
vc_j(t) &\leq Vc_j, & \forall j \in \{1...v\} \\
vm_j &\leq Vm_j, & \forall j \in \{1...v\} \\
vd_j &\leq Vd_j, & \forall j \in \{1...v\} \\
vn_j &\leq Vn_j, & \forall j \in \{1...v\} \\
pc_m(t) &\leq Pc_m, & \forall m \in \{1...p\} \\
pm_m &\leq Pm_m, & \forall m \in \{1...p\} \\
pd_m &\leq Pd_m, & \forall m \in \{1...p\} \\
pn_m &\leq Pn_m, & \forall m \in \{1...p\}
\end{aligned}
\tag{8}
$$

4   NSGA-II Algorithm for Container Consolidation

In this section we present our algorithm that involves non-overloaded hosts because they all have the potential to improve the utilization of PMs to decrease energy consumption by migrating containers. However, it is NP-hard to find the optimal consolidation solution. Consequently, we apply NSGA-II based algorithm to search non-dominated solutions that decide which non-overloaded hosts are attempted to migrate their containers at each time of reallocation. For each of these hosts, we apply the First-Fit (FF) policy to choose its containers' destination hosts. The strategy is widely used in existing works because of its reasonable computational time.

4.1 Chromosome Representation

Our approach uses a bit-string $[s_i]_{i=1}^{N}$ to represent all the non-overloaded hosts within a chromosome, where s_i is a binary value 1 or 0 to indicate whether the corresponding non-overloaded PM is considered for container migrations (see Fig. 2). In other words, the non-overloaded hosts whose corresponding binary values are 0 can be regarded as the destination hosts for the migrated containers.

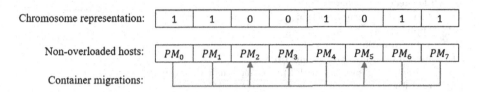

Fig. 2. An example chromosome representation.

4.2 Genetic Operators

As one discrete problem, we apply the binary crossover and mutation operators of Genetic Algorithm [12]. With respect to the selection operator, we use the tournament selection to choose the best individuals from candidates for further genetic processing [8].

4.3 NSGA-II Based Algorithm for Container Consolidation

In this section we present the process of NSGA-II based container consolidation as Algorithm 1. First of all, we initialize our non-dominated pool with the solution generated by Correlation Thresh-old Host Selection (CorHS) algorithm, which shows good performance in combination with MU policy [14] (step 1). Then we regard the non-overloaded hosts as the chromosome population, each of which represents which non-overloaded hosts are ready to migrate (step 2–4), the population are evolved with a predefined number of generations by NSGA-II to achieve the final non-dominated solutions pool (step 6–17). In the end, we decide one non-dominated solution according to practical requirement (e.g. the balance strategy between energy consumption and container migrations) and return its corresponding migration map to the simulator.

During the evolution, we calculate two objective functions of one solution by Algorithm 2, i.e. energy consumption and container migrations of the data center in line with (1) and (3). Firstly, we determine the destination host list (step 1–6). Subsequently, for each container in one host ready to migrate, we apply the FF policy to find the first host in the destination host list that meets the resource requirement as its destination host (step 9–17). If all the containers in the host can be migrated successfully, which means this host can be shut down, we subtract its energy consumption and accumulate the container number, otherwise we add the host to the list of destination hosts.

Algorithm 1. NSGA-II for container consolidation

Input: overloadedHostList and activeHostList
Output: ContainersToMigrateMap
1: Initialize the Nondominated Pool with the solution from CorHS
2: $Non\_overloadedHostList(NHL) \leftarrow activeHostList.removeAll(overloadedHostList)$
3: $L \leftarrow NHL.length()$
4: Initialize a population of chromosome with L random binary values
5: Evaluate population with fitness functions (Algorithm 2)
6: **while** predefined generation **do**
7:     Apply Tournament Selection
8:     Apply Crossover
9:     Apply Mutation
10:     **for all** offspring chromosome **do**
11:         Evaluate population with fitness functions (Algorithm 2)
12:     **end for**
13:     Non-dominated sort and assign a ranking to each chromosome
14:     Calculate the crowding distance of each chromosome
15:     Recombination and selection
16:     Update the Nondominated Pool with the current Nondominated solutions
17: **end while**
18: Decide one Nondominated solution from Nondominated Pool
19: Return ContainersToMigrateMap corresponding to the solution

5 Experiments

To evaluate the performance of our proposed NSGA-II based approach, we compare the energy consumption and the amount of container migrations with the recently developed CorHS algorithm and Least Full Host Selection (LFHS) algorithm [14]. Concretely, in the host selection module CorHS algorithm selects the most irrelevant host based on workload history between the container and the host, while LFHS algorithm chooses the host that has the least CPU utilization. They both have state-of-the-art performance with less computational overhead.

5.1 Simulation Setup

We use the containerized cloud simulation toolkit, i.e. ContainerCloudSim [15] to model our problem. The data center is simulated with 300 heterogeneous PMs, 500 heterogeneous VMs and 2500 heterogeneous containers (see Table 1). The number of applications is also 2500 (modeled as Cloudlet in ContainerCloudSim), each application is allocated to one container. We employ 80% and 70% as overload and under-load thresholds following the relevant research works in [14]. To conduct statistics analysis, for each algorithm, we perform 30 independent runs.

We use the workload traces from PlanetLab [13]. The workload are simulated as the containers' CPU utilization measured every 5 min.

We implemented the NSGA-II based approach based on the jMetal framework [7], and set parameters as follow. The population size is 100, and the maximum number of generations is 50. We decided the crossover probability

---

Algorithm 2. The process of calculating the fitness functions

---

Input: $Non\_overloadedHostList(NHL)$ and chromosome S
Output: ContainersToMigrateMap and two fitness values, i.e. energy consumption
    (E) and number of container migration (M)
1: $destinationHostList \leftarrow null$
2: **for all** bit s_i in S **do**
3:    **if** $s_i == 0$ **then**
4:        $destinationHostList.add(NHL_i)$
5:    **end if**
6: **end for**
7: $E \leftarrow current\_energy\_consumption, M \leftarrow 0$
8: **for all** bit s_i in S **do**
9:    **if** $s_i == 1$ **then**
10:        $containerList \leftarrow NHL_i.getContainerList()$
11:        **for all** container C_i in $containerList$ **do**
12:            **for all** host PM_m in $destinationHostList$ **do**
13:                **if** C_i fits in VM_j in the PM_m **then**
14:                    $tempMigrationList.add(\{C_i, VM_j, PM_m\})$
15:                **end if**
16:            **end for**
17:            $containerList.remove(C_i)$
18:        **end for**
19:        **if** $containerList.size() == 0$ **then**
20:            $ContainersToMigrateMap.addALL(tempMigrationList)$
21:            $E \leftarrow E - NHL_i.getPower()$
22:            $M \leftarrow M + tempMigrationList.size()$
23:        **else**
24:            $destinationHostList.add(NHL_i)$
25:        **end if**
26:    **end if**
27: **end for**
28: Return ContainersToMigrateMap, E, and M

---

and mutation probability are 80% and 20% respectively, since the combination can produce good results. In addition, the tournament size is 2.

5.2   Result

The energy consumption and the container migrations of our experimental evaluation are shown in Tables 2 and 3. With our proposed method, different preferences can be incorporated into the process of consolidation. In this regard, we study the performance for two preferences, i.e. minimizing the energy consumption or minimizing the number of container migrations. For each time of container consolidation, if we always select the consolidation solutions with the minimal energy consumption, we achieve the simulation results indicated as NSGA-II (min-Energy). On the other hand, if the solutions that prefer the

Table 1. Configuration of PMs, VMs, and containers.

Type #	CPU	Memory (GB)	P_{idle} (Watt)	P_{max} (Watt)	Quantity
PM #1	4 cores * 37274 MIPS	64	86	117	100
PM #2	8 cores * 37274 MIPS	128	93	135	100
PM #3	16 cores * 37274 MIPS	256	66	247	100
VM #1	2 cores * 18636 MIPS	1	N.A.	N.A.	125
VM #2	4 cores * 18636 MIPS	2	N.A.	N.A.	125
VM #3	1 cores * 18636 MIPS	4	N.A.	N.A.	125
VM #4	8 cores * 18636 MIPS	8	N.A.	N.A.	125
Container #1	1 cores * 4658 MIPS	0.125	N.A.	N.A.	834
Container #2	1 cores * 9320 MIPS	0.25	N.A.	N.A.	833
Container #3	1 cores * 18636 MIPS	0.5	N.A.	N.A.	833

minimal container migrations are deployed all the time, the simulation results are demonstrated as NSGA-II (min-Migration). Our proposed NSGA-II based approach outperforms the other two algorithms over time. Specifically, the one-day simulation results demonstrate our approach consumes about 10% less energy, while the container migrations are also about 15% less on average. The minimal energy strategy has the compelling advantage in energy saving. Meanwhile the minimal container migrations strategy is far superior to avoid service degradation caused by container startup delay.

Table 2. Energy Consumption

Hours	LFHS [14]	CorHS [14]	NSGA-II (min-Energy)	NSGA-II (min-Migration)
3	17.47 ± 0	17.72 ± 0	**15.82 ± 0.19**	16.9 ± 0.09
6	30.02 ± 0	29.72 ± 0	**25.33 ± 0.35**	25.67 ± 0.26
9	41.46 ± 0	40.93 ± 0	**35.21 ± 0.45**	35.71 ± 0.42
12	52.11 ± 0	51.85 ± 0.16	**45.08 ± 0.6**	45.88 ± 0.56
15	62.91 ± 0	62.83 ± 0.21	**55.2 ± 0.71**	55.97 ± 0.63
18	73.88 ± 0.02	73.27 ± 0.4	**65.28 ± 0.83**	66.03 ± 0.74
21	84 ± 0.07	83.12 ± 0.68	**74.71 ± 0.99**	75.97 ± 0.87
24	93.27 ± 0.2	91.62 ± 1.24	**82.9 ± 1.36**	83.62 ± 1.18

5.3 Analysis

To further analyze the performance of our proposed algorithm, we plot fitness results of the solutions generated from the CorHS algorithm and our approach at some simulation steps. In some steps such as at the simulation time 1200.2 s (Fig. 3), there is only one solution left in the end of the evolution, which dominates the solution from CorHS. In this case, we can minimize both objective

Table 3. Container Migrations

Hours	LFHS [14]	CorHS [14]	NSGA-II(min-Energy)	NSGA-II(min-Migration)
3	3399 ± 0	3601 ± 0	3343 ± 115	$\mathbf{3315 \pm 56}$
6	5165 ± 0	5017 ± 0	4603 ± 168	$\mathbf{4561 \pm 76}$
9	6682 ± 0	6267 ± 0	5604 ± 265	$\mathbf{5552 \pm 125}$
12	7854 ± 0	7411 ± 37	6734 ± 296	$\mathbf{6679 \pm 149}$
15	9453 ± 0	8656 ± 38	7837 ± 314	$\mathbf{7758 \pm 148}$
18	10945 ± 53	9802 ± 113	8968 ± 406	$\mathbf{8866 \pm 198}$
21	12459 ± 133	11221 ± 163	10418 ± 429	$\mathbf{10334 \pm 210}$
24	14138 ± 202	12131 ± 287	11256 ± 492	$\mathbf{11178 \pm 253}$

values by implementing this solution. Figure 4 depicts the Pareto front identified by NSGA-II at the simulation time 10200.2 s. In this case, the solution from CorHS is dominated by all the final generated solutions, which means our approach has the flexibility to generate a set of non-dominated solutions instead of one single solution. Therefore, energy-saving-oriented cloud data centers could select the solution in the bottom right corner of the evolved Pareto front, while performance-oriented cloud data centers tend to choose the solution in the top left corner of the Pareto front.

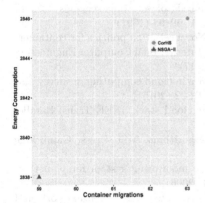

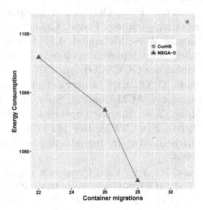

Fig. 3. Simulation time: 1200.2 s   **Fig. 4.** Simulation time: 10200.2 s

6   Conclusion

In this paper, we propose an NSGA-II based approach to the container consolidation problem under the VM-Container configuration. The approach aims to minimize the energy consumption and the amount of container migrations simultaneously. A thorough experimental evaluation using the well-known benchmark dataset and simulator shows that our proposed method can find container consolidation solutions with less energy consumption and fewer container migrations comparing with recent proposed approaches.

References

1. Docker website (2018). https://www.docker.com/
2. Al-Dhuraibi, Y., Paraiso, F., Djarallah, N., Merle, P.: Elasticity in cloud computing: state of the art and research challenges. IEEE Trans. Serv. Comput. **11**(2), 430–447 (2018)
3. Blackburn, M., Grid, G.: Five ways to reduce data center server power consumption. Green Grid **42**, 12 (2008)
4. Calheiros, R.N., Ranjan, R., Beloglazov, A., De Rose, C.A., Buyya, R.: Cloudsim: a toolkit for modeling and simulation of cloud computing environments and evaluation of resource provisioning algorithms. Softw.: Pract. Exp. **41**(1), 23–50 (2011)
5. Deb, K.: Multi-objective Optimization using Evolutionary Algorithms, vol. 16. Wiley, Hoboken (2001)
6. Deb, K., Pratap, A., Agarwal, S., Meyarivan, T.: A fast and elitist multiobjective genetic algorithm: NSGA-II. IEEE Trans. Evol. Comput. **6**(2), 182–197 (2002)
7. Durillo, J.J., Nebro, A.J.: jMetal: a java framework for multi-objective optimization. Adv. Eng. Softw. **42**(10), 760–771 (2011)
8. Goldberg, D.E., Deb, K.: A comparative analysis of selection schemes used in genetic algorithms. Found. Genet. Algorithms **1**, 69–93 (1991)
9. Hanafy, W.A., Mohamed, A.E., Salem, S.A.: Novel selection policies for container-based cloud deployment models. In: 2017 13th International Computer Engineering Conference (ICENCO), pp. 237–242. IEEE (2017)
10. Kaur, T., Chana, I.: Energy efficiency techniques in cloud computing: a survey and taxonomy. ACM Comput. Surv. (CSUR) **48**(2), 22 (2015)
11. Mann, Z.A.: Resource optimization across the cloud stack. IEEE Trans. Parallel Distrib. Syst. **29**(1), 169–182 (2018)
12. Mitchell, M.: An Introduction to Genetic Algorithms. MIT Press, Cambridge (1998)
13. Park, K., Pai, V.S.: Comon: a mostly-scalable monitoring system for planetlab. ACM SIGOPS Oper. Syst. Rev. **40**(1), 65–74 (2006)
14. Piraghaj, S.F., Dastjerdi, A.V., Calheiros, R.N., Buyya, R.: A framework and algorithm for energy efficient container consolidation in cloud data centers. In: 2015 IEEE International Conference on Data Science and Data Intensive Systems (DSDIS), pp. 368–375. IEEE (2015)
15. Piraghaj, S.F., Dastjerdi, A.V., Calheiros, R.N., Buyya, R.: ContainerCloudSim: an environment for modeling and simulation of containers in cloud data centers. Softw.: Pract. Exp. **47**(4), 505–521 (2017)
16. Quan, D.M., Mezza, F., Sannenli, D., Giafreda, R.: T-alloc: a practical energy efficient resource allocation algorithm for traditional data centers. Futur. Gener. Comput. Syst. **28**(5), 791–800 (2012)
17. Sharma, N., Guddeti, R.M.: Multi-objective energy efficient virtual machines allocation at the cloud data center. IEEE Trans. Serv. Comput. (2016)

18. Tan, B., Ma, H., Zhang, M.: Optimization of location allocation of web services using a modified non-dominated sorting genetic algorithm. In: Ray, T., Sarker, R., Li, X. (eds.) ACALCI 2016. LNCS (LNAI), vol. 9592, pp. 246–257. Springer, Cham (2016). https://doi.org/10.1007/978-3-319-28270-1_21
19. Zhang, D., Yan, B.H., Feng, Z., Zhang, C., Wang, Y.X.: Container oriented job scheduling using linear programming model. In: 2017 3rd International Conference on Information Management (ICIM), pp. 174–180. IEEE (2017)

Text Mining and NLP

Enhancing Decision Boundary Setting for Binary Text Classification

Aisha Rashed Albqmi[1,2]($\boxtimes$) (iD), Yuefeng Li[1] (iD), and Yue Xu[1] (iD)

[1] School of EECS, Queensland University of Technology,
Brisbane, QLD, Australia
a.albqmi@hdr.qut.edu.au, {y2.li,yue.xu}@qut.edu.au
[2] Department of CS, Taif University, Taif, Saudi Arabia

Abstract. Text classification is a task of assigning a set of text documents into predefined classes based on the classifier that learns from training samples; labelled or unlabeled. Binary text classifiers provide a way to separate related documents from a large dataset. However, the existing binary text classifiers are not grounded in reality due to the issue of overfitting. They try to find a clear boundary between relevant and irrelevant objects rather than understand the decision boundary. Normally, the decision boundary cannot be described as a clear boundary because of the numerous uncertainties in text documents. This paper attempts to address this issue by proposing an effective model based on sliding window technique (SW) and Support Vector Machine (SVM) to deal with the uncertain boundary and to improve the effectiveness of binary text classification. This model aims to set the decision boundary by dividing the training documents into three distinct regions (positive, boundary, and negative regions) to ensure the certainty of extracted knowledge to describe relevant information. The model then organizes training samples for the learning task to build a multiple SVMs based classifier. The experimental results using the standard dataset Reuters Corpus Volume 1 (RCV1) and TREC topics for text classification, show that the proposed model significantly outperforms six state-of-the-art baseline models in binary text classification.

Keywords: Text classification · Uncertainty · Decision boundary
Sliding window technique · Support vector machine

1 Introduction

With the explosive growth of data, the massive amounts of unstructured data that is available in an electronic form continue to increase. This requires the existence of efficient and successful methods to manage and extract useful information from this data for later retrieval and use [1]. Different methods and algorithms have been developed for text classification including Support Vector Machine (SVM) [2], Naive Bayes probabilistic Classifier (NB) [3], Rocchio Similarity [4], K-Nearest Neighbour (KNN) [5], and C4.5 integration Decision Trees [1].

© Springer Nature Switzerland AG 2018
T. Mitrovic et al. (Eds.): AI 2018, LNAI 11320, pp. 799–811, 2018.
https://doi.org/10.1007/978-3-030-03991-2_72

There are two different approaches to text classification. One approach assigns each document to a single category and the dataset has two or more classes (multi-class) [6]. The other approach is to allow documents to be categorized into all categories that it matches well (multi-label) [7]. Binary classification is a special multi-class with two predefined categories, namely, relevant or irrelevant classes [8], on which our research focuses. A binary text classifier determines a decision boundary to classify documents into two groups: positive and negative classes [6]. However, drawing a clear boundary between the positive and negative classes of text documents is not easy for a classic binary text classifier [8, 9].

Among the binary text classification techniques in recent years, SVM has gained increasing recognition and popularity among researchers due to its ability to handle high-dimensional data such as textual documents [10]. SVM performs classification by finding a decision boundary (separating hyperplane) that partitions the feature space into two distinct classes of data, positive and negative, with the maximum margin and represents the decision boundary using a set of support vectors (SV) generated from the training dataset [11, 12]. However, it is difficult for an SVM-based classifier to deal with non-linearly separable data because the margin between positive and negative objectives is still unclear. In such situations, due to the uncertainty, an SVM classifier might not be completely effective in providing the optimal classification.

An important issue related to text classification is that many datasets have some noise documents which make more difficult the finding of the optimal line to classify related objects, and a full separation of relevant and irrelevant documents would require a curve. However, it is not easy to achieve the curve in a direct way with high precision because it requires too much computation [8]. Even if this were possible, there is no guarantee that it can be applied to completely classify all unknown testing samples because of the differences between training and testing document sets [9]. Thus, a nonlinear classifier is inefficient for a prediction task where uncertain boundary exists in the training set. It is, therefore, desirable to design a classifier model able to linearly cope with non-separable data. Therefore, the hard question this research tries to answer is: how to cope with data having uncertainties in the learning phase to improve the performance of the classifier?

The aim of this research is to present an effective boundary setting model, that we call an SW-based model, in order to overcome the limitations of the existing classifiers and to achieve the best performance in linear SVM for data having uncertainties. Different from traditional binary classifiers, the SW-based model aims to understand uncertainty by partitioning training samples (with two labels) into three regions (namely, positive, boundary, and negative regions) in order to understand the decision boundary. Allowing this partitioning of the training set can help to describe relevant and non-relevant information. This partitioning, at the decision boundary stage, can be conducted by applying an efficient SW technique over positive and negative ranking documents. At the second stage, based on three regions which are identified by SW, new training sets will be created to support the construction of multiple SVMs based classifier. We build up three different SVM classifiers (SVM_P, SVM_N, and SVM_B), each of which is trained using its own training set. The training set for each classifier is different in order to obtain a greater improvement of the prediction result, to increase the certainty of all objects in positive and negative regions and to resolve the uncertainty in boundary region. The basic motivation for using multiple SVMs to classify new incoming documents is that a problem which requires expert knowledge will be better solved by a committee of experts rather than by a single expert [6].

This research made *three innovative contributions* to the fields of text classification: (a) A new and effective model that deal with the uncertain decision boundary for text classification. Our proposed model uses only training set with minimal experimental parameters to identify the uncertain boundary, which makes it efficient; (b) An alternative solution for the hard uncertain boundary problem that was traditionally solved by non-linear SVMs; (c) A structure to guide the design of multiple classifiers fusion. To test the effectiveness of the proposed model, substantial experiments were conducted, based on the RCV1 data collection and TREC filtering track. The results show a significant improvement on F_1 and *Accuracy* in the performance of binary text classification.

2 Related Work

Binary text classification is a significant research problem in information filtering and information organization fields [14]. It provides a way to determine a decision boundary that classifies textual documents into two distinct classes: relevant or irrelevant class. Several approaches to binary text categorization, such as NB, KNN, decision tree, Rocchio, and SVM, have been developed to identify an efficient way to separate all related documents from a large dataset to determine a clear boundary between the classes in the text dataset [1]. However, in practice, the decision boundary includes much uncertainty because of the limitation of traditional machine learning algorithms, presence of noisy in text documents and feature scalability [15, 16].

SVM represents the training dataset as vectors, where each vector comprised of its words with their frequencies, and then try to locate the linear hyperplane which separates two classes [12]. SVM can solve linear and nonlinear classifications and works well when applied to many practical problems [17, 18]. Although nonlinear SVM is effective when classifying nonlinear data, it has much higher computational complexity than linear SVM when making predictions for sparse data [18]. In addition, linear SVM performs better than nonlinear SVM when the number of features is very high, for example, in document classification [19, 20]. Therefore, if the number of features is extremely large, it is better to select linear SVM, due to the difficulty in finding the optimal parameters of a classifier when using nonlinear SVM [21]. However, linear SVM still has no effective way to deal with the uncertain factors, therefore, it is desirable to have a classifier model with the efficiency of a linear classifier to deal with data having uncertainty. The linear SVM is chosen in this study due to its computational and algorithmic simplicity.

The above limitations can be alleviated by setting the decision boundary using the SW technique and then designing a multiple SVMs based classifier. Through calculating the relevancy of the training samples to the topic, the SW- based model can divide the ranked documents list into three regions based on scores that present their degree of relevance. Recent advances in our proposed model mean that the SW technique can be optimized by using Entropy. The entropy measurement is chosen in this research because it is a commonly understood measure in information theory and it is a fundamental measure for describing randomness and uncertainty of data [13, 22].

3   Decision Boundary Setting

To achieve the best performance in binary classification, the objective is to determine a decision boundary between classes. Decision boundary setting is the first stage in an SW-based model. Our proposed model uses the training set only to set the decision boundary and to explore the uncertainty situation, as shown in Fig. 1.

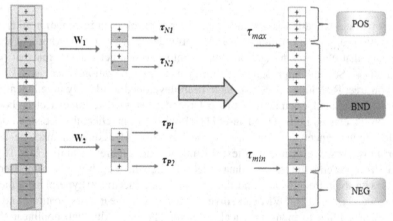

Step 1: A sliding window technique over ranked documents

Step 2: Indicates the boundary values and three regions.

Fig. 1.   Decision boundary setting.

3.1   Document Scoring

Scoring documents to indicate their importance is an effective way for ranking relevant information. For a collection of documents in the datasets consisting of two sets (positive document sets, D^+; and negative document sets, D^-), the SW-based model calculates the weight of terms extracted from D^+ and ranks them to use the *top-k* features based on their values. However, identifying the value of k is experimental. In our proposed model, we use the Okapi BM25 as a term weighting function. BM25 is a probabilistic state-of-the-art retrieval model [23], which can be calculated as follows:

$$w(t) = \frac{tf.(k_1 + 1)}{k_1.\left((1 - b) + b\frac{DL}{AVDL}\right) + tf} \cdot \log \frac{\frac{(r+0.5)}{(n-r+0.5)}}{\frac{(R-r+0.5)}{(N-n-R+r+0.5)}} \tag{1}$$

where N is the total number of training documents; R is the number of relevant documents; n is the number of documents which contain the term t; r is the number of relevant documents which contain the term t; tf is the term frequency; DL and $AVDL$ are the document length and average document length, respectively; and k_1 and b are the tuning parameters.

The reason for using the BM25 to calculate term weight is that the BM25 is a probabilistic model and in binary text classification we deal with uncertain information [23]. Probability is the measure used to understand the uncertainty in the information. Therefore, probability theory is the best way to quantify uncertainties. Next, the weighted terms are used to calculate the scores for all training documents $d \in D$ as follows:

$$score(d) = \sum_{t \in T} w(t).\tau(t, d) \tag{2}$$

where $w(t) = BM25(t, D^+)$; and $\tau (t, d) = 1$ if $t \in d$; otherwise $\tau (t, d) = 0$.

Once the scores of the documents are calculated, the documents are ranked in descending order based on their scores.

3.2 Sliding Window Technique

After ranking the training documents in the previous step, the most related document will be located at the top of the list, while irrelevant ones will be located at the bottom of the ranked list, as shown in Fig. 1 (step1). However, in most cases there are regions in which positive and negative document are mixed due to uncertain boundary. To find this area with many noisy documents, a sliding window technique and entropy are used to effectively determine the boundary region. Ko and Seo [24] used entropy and a sliding window to remove noisy data and solve the problem of the One-Against-All method. Our proposed model extends this idea to use a sliding window and entropy measurement to construct the decision boundary.

In this research, the sliding window was used to identify the boundary values which denote the region with the highest rate of noisy documents [24, 25]. The window size in this paper was set to 5 documents. The model starts to slide the window from the top documents in the ranked list, and then calculates the entropy value for the window. The window then slides over one document and yields a new entropy value. It continues to slide and stop when the entropy is greater than the threshold. We choose a high entropy threshold (95%). The same process applies from the bottom of the ranked list as shown in Fig. 1 (step1).

3.3 Entropy Algorithm

Entropy is commonly used to define the uncertainty of variable [22, 25]. For example, for data containing only two objectives, A and B, the entropy (E) can be denoted using the following formula:

$$E = -p_A \, log_2(p_A) - p_B \, log_2(p_B) \tag{3}$$

where p_A and p_B are the proportion of A and B separately.

In this paper, for each sliding window, the entropy value can be calculated using the following function based on the number of positive and negative documents as follows:

$$E = -\left[\frac{P}{P+N} \, log_2\left(\frac{p}{p+N}\right) + \frac{N}{P+N} \, log_2\left(\frac{N}{P+N}\right) \right] \tag{4}$$

where P and N are the numbers of positive and negative documents in SW, respectively.

Next, we select two windows with the greatest degree of entropy value. The first window (W_1) is from the top of the list and the second window (W_2) is from the bottom of the list. For W_1, the irrelevant documents are denoted as τ_N. For W_2, the relevant documents are denoted as τ_P. In this study, the values of the boundary are calculated based on the scores of the relevant documents (τ_P) and the irrelevant documents (τ_N); we selected the highest score of irrelevant documents in W_1 as a maximum threshold (τ_{max}), and the lowest score of relevant documents in W_2 as a minimum threshold (τ_{min}) as shown in Fig. 1 (step2). Hence, the upper and lower decision boundary values τ_{max} and τ_{min} are calculated as follows:

$$\tau_{max} = \max_{d_i \in D^- \cap W_1}\{Score(d_i)\} \tag{5}$$

$$\tau_{min} = \min_{d_i \in D^+ \cap W_2}\{Score(d_i)\} \tag{6}$$

3.4 Three Region for Partition the Training Set

Our proposed model aims to group training sets into three regions rather than two classes. The training set D can be split into three regions based on the document scores and threshold settings in the previous step: the positive region (POS, possible relevant); the boundary region (BND, uncertain); and the negative region (NEG, possible irrelevant). The ranges of these regions are defined as follows:

$$POS = \{d{\in}D|score(d) > \tau_{max}\}$$

$$BND = \{d{\in}D|\tau_{min} \leq score(d) \leq \tau_{max}\}$$

$$NEG = \{d{\in}D|score(d) < \tau_{min}\}$$

The boundary region BND contains many positive and negative documents under uncertain decisions, therefore, two other subsets of the BND region are produced: $B^+ = BND \cap D^+$ and $B^- = BND \cap D^-$.

4   Design Multiple SVMs Based Classifier Using Three Regions

The SW-based model attempts to use the training dataset effectively to improve the accuracy of the classifier. Our model uses SVM as a high performance model and generates new training data based on the three regions, as indicated in the previous section. However, a single SVM may not be sufficient to classify all unknown testing samples. Therefore, we propose to use multiple SVMs based classifier. This stage contains two phases including a training phase and a testing phase, as shown in Fig. 2.

4.1   Training Phase

In the training phase, building a classifier is achieved by training the SVM using chosen training documents via three regions. As shown on the left side of Fig. 2, we constructed three different SVMs classifiers; SVM_P, SVM_N, and SVM_B. To explain this process, the Algorithm 1 describes the training phase to learn the classifiers. The First classifier, SVM_P (step 8), takes strong positive documents POS and all negative documents ($B^- \cup NEG$) as input, and uses the SVM classifier to build a predication model. The SVM_P generates the hyperplane between POS and ($B^- \cup NEG$) to maintain the maximum margin between them. However, a potential problem with this approach can arise when the number of training samples in the POS part is very low and, in this case, the boundary of class would not be accurate due to insufficient positive training samples provided for text classification. To overcome this issue, we use a *pseudo feedback* technique. We select *top-k* scoring documents from the unlabelled testing set U and add them to the POS part as shown in step 1 to step 6. Different numbers of *top-k* have been tested and we found that using 5 documents improved the performance compared with using $k > 5$, which reduced the performance. The second classifier, SVM_N, is constructed from the all positive documents ($POS \cup B^+$) and strong negative documents NEG as in step 9. For SVM_B, it is difficult to construct a classifier from the documents in the boundary region because SVM is very sensitive to noise, especially when noise is large, and in this case, the classifier will be very poor. Therefore, we used the complete training set (D^+, D^-) to build SVM_B in our model, as in step 10.

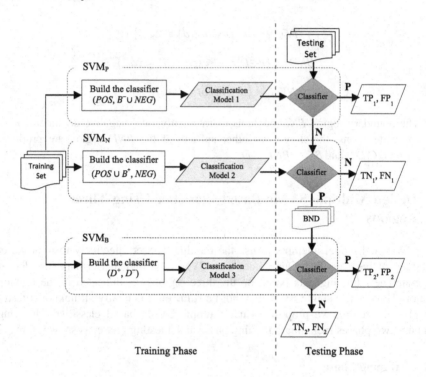

Fig. 2. Architecture of a multiple SVMs classifier.

Algorithm1: Multiple SVMs classifier Learning

Input: POS, NEG, BND, D^+, D^-; and parameter k;
    Unlabelled document in testing set, U;
    SVM classification model;

Output: SVM classification models, SVM_P, SVM_N, SVM_B;

    // Add *top-k* unlabelled documents to build first classifier

1 let $n = |U|$

2 **forall the** $d \in U$ **do**

3 $\quad$ $score(d) = \sum_{t \in T} weigh\ (t).\ \tau(t, d)$

4 **end**

5 let $P = \{\ d_1, d_2,..., d_n\}$ in descending ranking order,

6 $D_P = \{d_i\ |\ d_i \in U,\ 0 < i \leq k\};$

    // Learn training dataset using SVM classifier, get SVM models.

7 $B^+ = BND \cap D^+,\ B^- = BND \cap D^-;$

8 $SVM_P = Classifier_{SVM}\ (POS \cup D_P,\ B^- \cup NEG);$

9 $SVM_N = Classifier_{SVM}\ (POS \cup B^+,\ NEG);$

10 $SVM_B = Classifier_{SVM}(D^+,\ D^-);$

4.2   Testing Phase

In the testing phase, each stage has a different classification model, as shown on the right side of Fig. 2. The SVM_P classification model concentrates on identifying positive documents. In this stage, the documents that are classified as positive are denoted by TP_1 (true positive one) if they are true positive or grouped as FP_1 (false positive one) if they are actually negative. The objective of this stage is to achieve a high precision rate for positive documents and to minimize the FP rate, with an acceptable False Negative rate FN. The SVM_N classifier, which is generated in stage two, is applied to classify the documents that were predicted as negative in stage one. This stage focuses on increasing the precision rate for negative documents. In this stage, the documents that are classified as negative are denoted by TN_1 (true negative one) if they are negative or grouped into the FN_1 if they actually are positive. However, as the documents that were predicted as positive in this stage are still uncertain, the classifier will collect them into the boundary set BND. To classify these documents, we used the final classifier, SVM_B. This classifier can then assign those documents as positive or negative and produce four outputs, namely, TP_2, FP_2, TN_2, and FN_2. In our proposed classifier model, true positive $TP = TP_1 + TP_2$, false positive $FP = FP_1 + FP_2$, true negative $TN = TN_1 + TN_2$, and false negative $FN = FN_1 + FN_2$. The testing phase of our proposed model is outlined in Algorithm 2.

Algorithm 2: Multiple SVMs Classifier Testing

Input:	Incoming document without label for testing, U;
	SVM classification models, SVM_P, SVM_N, SVM_B;
Output:	Positive documents POS, and negative documents NEG;

```
1    POS := NEG := BND := ∅;
2    forall the d ∈ U do
         // Predict label the new documents d_unlabeled using SVM_P.
3        d_labeled = SVM_P (d_unlabeled, Model_1);
         // If SVM_P label document as positive, the label of the
            document is positive
4        if d_labeled is positive then
5        |   POS = POS ∪ {d};
6        else
7            d_labeled = SVM_N (d_unlabeled, Model_2);
             // If SVM_N label it as negative, the label of the
                document is negative
8            if d_labeled is negative then
9            |   NEG = NEG ∪ {d};
10           else
11               BND = BND ∪ {d};
         end
     end
         // Predict label the rest documents in BND using SVM_B.
12   forall the d ∈ BND do
13       d_labeled = SVM_B (d_unlabeled, Model_3)
14       if d_labeled is positive then
15       |   BND = BND - {d}; POS = POS ∪ {d};
16       else
17           BND = BND - {d}; NEG = NEG ∪ {d};
     end
```

5   Evaluation

The main objective of this research is to set an effective decision boundary to increase the performance of binary text classification using the SW technique and multiple SVMs. To support this idea, we conducted an experimental to evaluate the performance of our proposed model.

5.1   Dataset and Evaluation Metrics

We evaluated the performance of our proposed model on the RCV1 dataset, which is most frequently used in text classification and information retrieval. It consists of 100 topics. Each topic has been divided into training and testing sets with relevance judgements. The RCV1 corps has more than 804,000 documents which are news stories in English published by Reuters journalists [26]. The first 50 topics were developed by the National Institute of Standard and Technology (NIST). The last 50 topics were constructed artificially rather than by humans. Therefore, in our experiments in this study, we used the first 50 topics where the experiments are more reliable.

Two evaluation metrics were used to measure the effectiveness of our proposed model and the baselines. The measures are the F_1 score and *Accuracy*. These evaluation metrics are widely used in text classification research. For more details of these measures refer to [6].

5.2   Baseline Models and Settings

We compared our proposed model with six different baseline models. These models are the state-of- the-art influential models including statistical method libSVM, SVMperf [27], J48 [28], NB [3], IBk (Instance-Based Learning), and Rocchio. All six models were trained and tested with the same training dataset to conduct the experiments. The baseline models were run with their best settings obtained through experimental practice and a *top-k* terms are selected for final classification in the baselines and the final proposed system. For *libSVM*, some default settings were utilized because the F_1-scores of the classifier are low when using the default setting. Different types of kernel functions and values of C were conducted, and we found that if we set $k = 0$ (linear kernel) and $C = 1$, we could get better results. In addition, we set the value of C in SVMperf based on the recommended value of 10. Our proposed model is based on SVM and we used the linear kernel because it is quick and efficient with very large numbers of features as in document classification. We used the same parameter, C, for all our experiments. For BM25, k_1 and b values were set at 1.2 and 0.75, respectively.

5.3   Experimental Results

The evaluation results of our model and the baselines are presented in Table 1. These results are the average of the 50 collections of the RCV1 dataset. The comparison between the proposed model, SW-based model, and other six baseline models was completed using two measures, F_1 and *Accuracy*. The results in Table 1 have been categorised into two groups. The first group includes two SVM models (*libSVM and* SVMperf); the second group includes a popular influential classifier.

Table 1. Evaluation results of our model compared with the baselines.

Models	F_1	Accuracy
SW-based model	**0.402831**	**0.86743**
libSVM	0.3271	0.8557
SVMperf	0.2864	0.8001
Improvement%	**32%**	**5%**
J48	0.3449	0.8263
Naïve Bayes	0.1851	0.8131
IBk	0.297	0.8404
Rocchio	0.3681	0.5646
Improvement%	**45%**	**17%**

Table 1 shows that our model outperformed all baseline models for text classification. It was significantly better on average by a minimum improvement of 5% and a maximum improvement of 45%. Compared with the SVM models, F_1 and *Accuracy* of the SW-based model were significantly improved by 32% and 5%, respectively.

In order to test the effectiveness of using multiple SVMs in our proposed model, we performed the same experiments with a single SVM classifier which used the original training set. The aims of using multiple SVMs is to provide a way to make the decision boundary better. Table 2 shows the results of the performance of a single SVM classifier and multiple SVMs on the RCV1 dataset. We used the precision, F-measure and the accuracy as measures for comparison. In Table 2 we found that using multiple SVMs achieved an average increase of 27% for F_1 and 2% for *Accuracy*.

Table 2. Result comparison using single SVM and multiple SVMs on RCV1.

Models	Precision+	Precision⁻	F_1	Accuracy
Single SVM	0.5016	0.8623	0.3187	0.8543
SW-based model (multiple SVMs)	**0.5509**	**0.8778**	**0.4028**	**0.8674**
%improvement	9%	2%	27%	2%

When considering precision value, multiple SVMs showed the best performance, especially for the relevant part (Precision+). It is clear that using multiple SVMs instead of a single one can lead to better classification and improve the overall accuracy with data having uncertainty.

Based on the results presented earlier, the SW-based model improved the binary classification with the highest score in both F_1 and Accuracy (and particularly in F_1) that best expresses the real situation in text classification.

6 Conclusion

An SW-based model was proposed to address the uncertain decision boundary and to improve the performance of binary text classification. This model uses the training set effectively to achieve super machine learning with high classification accuracy. It tries to establish an uncertain decision boundary by dividing the training set into three regions, namely, positive, negative, and boundary in order to improve the certainty of both relevant and irrelevant parts and reduces the impact of uncertainty in the boundary part. The decision boundary was established by applying an effective SW technique and threshold setting, and then organizing training samples to generate new training sets. After the boundary region is identified, we used multiple SVMs instead of a single one to learn the classifiers and to classify new incoming documents. The proposed model was tested for binary classification on the standard RCV1 dataset and TREC assessors' relevance judgements. The experimental results show that our model achieved significant improvements in F_1 and Accuracy, especially F_1 and outperforms existing classifiers, including state of the art classifiers.

References

1. Jindal, R., Malhotra, R., Jain, A.: Techniques for text classification: literature review and current trends. Webology **12**(2), 1–28 (2015)
2. Joachims, T.: Transductive inference for text classification using support vector machines. In: ICML 1999, San Francisco, pp. 200–209. ACM (1999)
3. John, G.H., Langley, P.: Estimating continuous distributions in Bayesian classifiers. In: UAI 1995, Canada, pp. 338–345. ACM (1995)
4. Aggarwal, C.C., Zhai, C.: A survey of text classification algorithms. In: Aggarwal, C., Zhai, C. (eds.) Mining Text Data, pp. 163–222. Springer, Boston (2012). https://doi.org/10.1007/978-1-4614-3223-4_6
5. Cover, T., Hart, P.: Nearest neighbor pattern classification. IEEE Trans. Inf. Theory **13**(1), 21–27 (1967)
6. Sebastiani, F.: Machine learning in automated text categorization. ACM Comput. Surv. **34**(1), 1–47 (2002)
7. Forman, G.: An extensive empirical study of feature selection metrics for text classification. J. Mach. Learn. Res. **3**, 1289–1305 (2003)
8. Zhang, L., Li, Y., Bijaksana, M. A.: Decreasing uncertainty for improvement of relevancy prediction. In: Proceeding of the Twelfth Australasian Data Mining Conference, AusDM 2014, Brisbane, pp. 157–162 (2014)
9. Li, Y., Zhang, L., Yue, X., Yiyu, Y., Raymond, L., Yutong, W.: Enhancing binary classification by modeling uncertain boundary in three-way decisions. IEEE Trans. Knowl. Data Eng. **29**(7), 1438–1451 (2017)
10. Wardaya, P.D.: Support vector machine as a binary classifier for automated object detection in remotely sensed data. In: IOP Conference Series: Earth and Environmental Science, vol. 18, no. 1. IOP Publishing (2014)
11. Joachims, T.: Text categorization with support vector machines: learning with many relevant features. In: Nédellec, C., Rouveirol, C. (eds.) ECML 1998. LNCS, vol. 1398, pp. 137–142. Springer, Heidelberg (1998). https://doi.org/10.1007/BFb0026683

12. Burges, C.J.: A tutorial on support vector machines for pattern recognition. Data Min. Knowl. Disc. **2**(2), 121–167 (1998)
13. Shannon, M.: Forensic relative strength scoring: ASCII and entropy scoring. Int. J. Digit. Evid. **2**(4), 1–19 (2004)
14. Lau, R.Y., Bruza, P.D., Song, D.: Towards a belief-revision-based adaptive and context-sensitive information retrieval system. ACM Trans. Inf. Syst. (TOIS) **26**(2), 1–38 (2008)
15. Bekkerman, R., Gavish, M.: High-precision phrase-based document classification on a modern scale. In: KDD 2011, San Diego, pp. 231–239. ACM (2011)
16. Li, Y., Algarni, A., Zhong, N.: Mining positive and negative patterns for relevance feature discovery. In: KDD 2010, pp. 753–762. ACM, New York (2010)
17. Fu, Z., Robles-Kelly, A., Zhou, J.: Mixing linear SVMs for nonlinear classification. IEEE Trans. Neural Netw. **21**(12), 1963–1975 (2010)
18. Rodriguez-Lujan, I., Cruz, C.S., Huerta, R.: Hierarchical linear support vector machine. Pattern Recogn. **45**(12), 4414–4427 (2012)
19. Gao, Y., Sun, S.: An empirical evaluation of linear and nonlinear kernels for text classification using support vector machines. In: FSKD 2010, Yantai, pp. 1502–1505. IEEE (2010)
20. Lan, M., Tan, C.L., Low, H.B.: Proposing a new term weighting scheme for text categorization. In: AAAI 2006, Boston, pp. 763–768. ACM (2006)
21. Hsu, C.W., Chang, C.C., Lin, C.J.: A practical guide to support vector classification. Technical report, Department of Computer Science, National Taiwan University, Taipei (2003)
22. Du, L., Song, Q., Jia, X.: Detecting concept drift: an information entropy based method using an adaptive sliding window. Intell. Data Anal. **18**(3), 337–364 (2014)
23. Robertson, S., Zaragoza, H.: The Probabilistic Relevance Framework: BM25 and Beyond. Now Publishers Inc., Breda (2009)
24. Ko, Y.J., Seo, J.Y.: Issues and empirical results for improving text classification. J. Comput. Sci. Eng. **5**(2), 150–160 (2011)
25. Hall, G.A.: Sliding window measurement for file type identification. Technical report, ManTech Security and Mission Assurance (2006)
26. Lewis, D.D., Yang, Y., Rose, T.G., Li, F.: Rcv1: a new benchmark collection for text categorization research. J. Mach. Learn. Res. **5**, 361–397 (2004)
27. Joachims, T.: A support vector method for multivariate performance measures. In: ICML 2005, Germany, pp. 377–384. ACM (2005)
28. Quinlan, J.R.: C4.5: Programs for Machine Learning. Morgan Kaufmann Publishers, San Francisco (1993)

Stability of Word Embeddings Using Word2Vec

Mansi Chugh$^{(\boxtimes)}$, Peter A. Whigham , and Grant Dick

Department of Information Science, University of Otago, Dunedin, New Zealand
chuma964@student.otago.ac.nz, {peter.whigham,grant.dick}@otago.ac.nz

Abstract. The word2vec model has been previously shown to be successful in creating numerical representations of words (word embeddings) that capture the semantic and syntactic meanings of words. This study examines the issue of model stability in terms of how consistent these representations are given a specific corpus and set of model parameters. Specifically, the study considers the impact of word embedding dimension size and frequency of words on stability. Stability is measured by comparing the neighborhood of words in the word vector space model. Our results demonstrate that the dimension size of word embeddings has a significant effect on the consistency of the model. In addition, the effect of the frequency of the target words on stability is identified. An approach to mitigate the effects of word frequency on stability is proposed.

Keywords: Word2vec · Embedding dimension · Similarity · Stability

1 Introduction

An analysis of the distributional structure of language, first formally described by Harris [6], suggests that both the syntax and semantics of utterances can be inferred. This assumes that words in a similar context should have similar properties, such as roles in the structure of the language (e.g. nouns), concepts (e.g. country names) or relationships between words giving high-level meaning (e.g. analogy). The concept of word co-occurrence is formally defined by the concept of an n-gram model, where models use the 'n' neighbors of a word in a corpus to build a representation for each unique word, and words with similar context are clustered together. Early work by Schütze [12] proposed the creation of word vectors that represent the semantic and syntactic meaning of a word. This was achieved by performing unsupervised learning on a corpus for identifying the "word vector space". Proximity of words in the vector space implied semantic similarity and was measured using Cosine distance. The technological limitations restricted Schütze from putting his ideas into a computational model. The concept was revived and gained popularity with the word2vec algorithm [8,9]. The vectors were subjected to analogy and similarity tests and the results were comparable to human performance. The most famous example to show the success of the model was its ability to answer the question: if man is to woman then

© Springer Nature Switzerland AG 2018
T. Mitrovic et al. (Eds.): AI 2018, LNAI 11320, pp. 812–818, 2018.
https://doi.org/10.1007/978-3-030-03991-2_73

king is to what? These word vectors (more popularly known as word embeddings) were hence argued to contain both semantic and syntactic information. Following word2vec's success, two other models gained moderate attention for creating word embeddings. The first model was GloVe (Global Vectors for Vector Representation), which in addition to utilizing the local context of words for creating word embeddings (similar to word2vec) also used the co-occurrence of words present in the corpus globally [10]. The second methodology, known as SVD PPMI (Singular Value Decomposition on Positive Pointwise Mutual Information Matrix) applied the singular value decomposition to a high dimensional sparse matrix in which each row represents a word in the vocabulary and each column a possible context [2,3].

After words have been embedded in a vector space, words with similar contexts should ideally be placed close to each other in terms of cosine distance measured between their embedding vectors. Additionally, after training is complete, the vector space should ideally be identical over multiple re-buildings of the model with the same corpus and same hyper parameters. A recent study [7] examined the embeddings generated from these three models from the perspective of "stability" and found that the word2vec model does not produce consistent embeddings. The term stability in these studies refers to the consistency of the neighborhood of words around a given target.

This paper will consider the stability of the word2vec model with regards to the size of the word embeddings and the frequency of words in a given corpus. We will explore the somewhat contradictory results from the literature and propose some solutions for using Skip-Gram Negative Sampling (SGNS) version of word2vec in a stable manner.

2   Stability of Word2vec Model

There are two elements that make the word2vec model non-deterministic. First, the weights of the hidden layer (which represent the word embeddings) are randomly initialized. Hence, every run of the model (keeping all other factors constant) will proceed from a different point in the vector space. Second, the training example generation process brings another element of randomness. The selection of words and their contexts through a sampling process results in variation in the examples that are presented to the model. Even if similar examples might be presented to the model in different runs, their order will vary. The non-deterministic nature of the model as seen above raises an issue about the stability of the model and its corresponding word embeddings. For example running a stable model with identical corpus and hyper parameter settings should result in the same neighbors of a given word determined by a similarity measure. Although there is an ordering to the similarity of words, this work will consider similarity by treating a list of neighbors as a set (and therefore ignore ranking). For example the nine nearest neighbors for the word "Nine" are identical.

$Nine : eight, four, one, zero, seven, six, two, five, three$
$Nine : one, eight, two, seven, six, zero, five, four, three$

To measure the stability of a given word, the Jaccard similarity index is calculated between the pairs of sets of neighbors generated during different runs of the word2vec model. Jaccard similarity returns values in the range zero (no matching) to one (both sets identical) with values closer to one indicating greater consistency in the neighborhood of a given word. The model will be examined for stability of word embeddings for words selected across the entire word frequency range to allow the question of frequency and stability to be considered. The frequency spectrum has been split into high, medium and low frequency words to allow more general statements to be made regarding stability.

3   Background Literature

The stability of word embeddings came into prominence due to work by Hamilton et al. [5], where the authors utilized word embeddings to study the change of word neighborhoods over time and have cited the example of the change of meaning of the word *gay* over time. This method seemed appropriate because, as per the distributional hypothesis, the words belonging to a cluster help to identify the category of each word. In order to achieve conclusive results for the above study it was necessary to obtain consistent neighborhood of word embeddings as the entire premise of understanding the meaning of a word relies on the neighborhood. Hellrich and Hahn utilized English and German text for a similar human diachronic language study and applied SGNS, GloVe [10] and the SVD PPMI models [7]. Their results showed that only SVD PPMI produced consistent results whereas the other two models produce inconsistent clusters. The authors attribute the inconsistent behavior of SGNS to the non-deterministic nature of the model. The SVD PPMI model performance matched the conclusions of Levy et al. [4].

Following this previous work, other researchers began examining the consistency issue of word embeddings. Pierrejean et al. [11] have listed some factors behind the variability of word embeddings which they consider to be "intrinsic to the word, corpus or model". One of these features is the frequency of words in the corpus. Their experiments concluded that the words in the lower and higher frequency ranges are more prone to variability compared to words in the middle range. Antoniak and Mimno [1] considered the variability of word embeddings in regards to three factors related to any corpus: order and presence of documents, size of corpus, and the length of the documents in a corpus. They segregated their data into "fixed", "shuffled" and "bootstrap" categories based on the sampling method applied to each corpus and applied this sampled data on LSA, SGNS, GloVe and PPMI models. A common theme amongst all of these recent papers is the inconsistent conclusions generated by the skip gram models through word embeddings. None of the word embedding models has been a clear winner and neither has there been a coherent identification of any features which can reliably explain the variability of word embeddings.

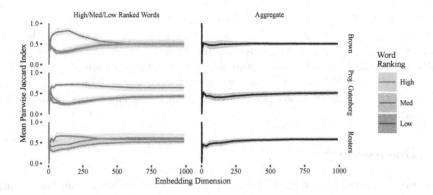

Fig. 1. Jaccard index for nearest neighbors of target words with different frequencies selected from 3 different corpora for specific frequency range (left side) and over aggregated frequency range (right side).

4   Experimental Setup

The experiment was performed on three corpora: Brown, Project Gutenberg and Reuters. The Python gensim[1] package has been used for creating the word2vec models. Below are the steps for generating the results.

1. Split the corpus into sentences, remove all punctuations and zero length strings and convert to lowercase.
2. Tokenize all the sentences and save the top 10,000 most common tokens and their frequency. This step is executed to define a fixed vocabulary size over multiple corpora. Replace the remaining words with "UNK".
3. Select 10 words from the top (0–10), middle (4995–5005) and bottom (9990–10000) frequency range.
4. For 100 runs of the model for a specific corpus and hyper parameters:
   For each dimension size ranging from 1 to 377 following the Fibonacci series:
   (a) Create a word2vec model with 100 iterations and window size of 2.
   (b) Save the 10 nearest neighbors of top, middle and bottom frequency words using the word embedding created in the previous step.
5. In every frequency range, calculate the average and standard deviation of Jaccard index between pairs of sets of neighbors of all the words.

5   Results

Figure 1 shows the Jaccard index for the three corpora. There are two plots for each corpus, one broken down into high-mid-low frequency groups, and one aggregated over the entire frequency range of the vocabulary. The left hand side graphs from all three corpora depict a consistent pattern: the similarity (hence

---

[1] https://radimrehurek.com/gensim/.

the stability) of high frequency words gradually increases and then eventually decreases to a stable value. In contrast, the similarity values of both the mid and low frequency terms initially decline and then gradually increase to a steady value of around 50%. The right hand side graph depicts an almost static value of stability of around 50% over the aggregate target words. The dimension size at which the similarity index peaks for the high frequency words varies across the corpora.

6   Discussion

Some of the results presented here align with our assumptions and the results of previous work, with high frequency words showing greater stability. However, there are also several observations which do not match the results seen in previous work. Much work using word2vec mentions use of an embedding size of 100 or 300 without providing justification for this choice. As can be seen from the results presented here, optimal embedding dimension for maximum stability is corpora-dependent. Given that word2vec is a standard single hidden layer feed forward neural network model, the number of nodes in the hidden layer is an important factor for the model to perform well both on training and test data as it is a bias-variance trade-off. The vocabulary size and frequency distribution of words will determine how many features (dimension size) are needed to capture the semantic and syntactic relationships in a consistent manner. Hence care should be taken to identify the optimal size of the hidden layer (word embedding dimension size) for a specific corpus and a specific natural language processing problem. The other factor presented in this work is the influence on stability for words based on their frequency. Words with high frequency are presented more frequently as examples to the model. Hence the model is likely to have greater accuracy when recognizing these high frequency words compared to both low and mid frequency words. However our results show that both low and mid frequency words perform equally worse. Additionally, the direction of the Jaccard index is opposite for high frequency words (increasing) compared to both low and mid ones (decreasing) when the embedding size is small. This effect cancels out the positive impact of high frequency words on the stability and the aggregate stability is around 50% over any embedding size. Hence the structure of the model is preventing it from receiving a balanced set of training examples across all the frequencies and therefore producing a consistent embedding relationship.

7   Conclusion

The word2vec algorithm has been a major milestone in developing representations of word structure, as evidenced by its popular application in natural language processing. However, word2vec has recently come under scrutiny when the word embeddings generated by this model were utilized in varied fields of studies. The stability of word embeddings is one such factor that has been identified as being of concern. While some studies aimed to find models that performed better than word2vec in creating stable embeddings, others have tried to understand the factors which cause this phenomenon. This work examined two factors that might affect model stability, and contributes to this debate by examining embedding dimension size as one causal factor. Even though the process of tuning hyper-parameters to achieve good performance is now a standard practice in machine learning, selecting an appropriate embedding size for a given corpus should also be part of this process. Choosing an arbitrarily large value might work well for some scenarios, but overall is not likely to be optimal over all instances and hence care is required when choosing this parameter. The second factor considered is the influence of embedding stability due to the frequency of the target words. Even though high frequency words exhibit higher stability, every English corpus will always have low and mid frequency words following Zipf's law, which will reduce the overall stability of the model. Further work is required to determine how models might be able to overcome the issue of improving model embeddings on low and mid frequency words. One simple approach would be to use the inverse of word frequency as a probability for repeated re-sampling when training the skip-gram model, however this will lead to an increased training time for stable results.

References

1. Antoniak, M., Mimno, D.: Evaluating the stability of embedding-based word similarities. Trans. Assoc. Comput. Linguist. **6**, 107–119 (2018)
2. Bullinaria, J.A., Levy, J.P.: Extracting semantic representations from word co-occurrence statistics: a computational study. Behav. Res. Methods **39**(3), 510–526 (2007)
3. Church, K.W., Hanks, P.: Word association norms, mutual information, and lexicography. Comput. Linguist. **16**(1), 22–29 (1990)
4. Goldberg, Y., Dagan, I., Levy, O.: Improving distributional similarity with lessons learned from word embeddings. Trans. Assoc. Comput. Linguist. **3**, 211–225 (2015)
5. Hamilton, W.L., Leskovec, J., Jurafsky, D.: Diachronic word embeddings reveal statistical laws of semantic change. In: Proceedings of the 54th Annual Meeting of the Association for Computational Linguistics, Berlin, Germany, 7–12 August 2016, pp. 1489–1501 (2016). Association for Computational Linguistics
6. Harris, Z.S.: Distributional structure. Word **10**(2), 146–162 (1954)
7. Hellrich, J., Hahn, U.: Exploring diachronic lexical semantics with JESEME. In: Proceedings of the 55th Annual Meeting of the Association for Computational Linguistics-System Demonstrations, Vancouver, Canada, 30 July–4 August 2017, pp. 31–36 (2017). Association for Computational Linguistics
8. Mikolov, T., Chen, K., Corrado, G., Dean, J.: Efficient estimation of word representation in vector space. https://arxiv.org/pdf/1301.3781.pdf
9. Mikolov, T., Sutskever, I., Chen, K., Corrado, G., Dean, J.: Distributed representations of words and phrases and their compositionality, p. 9. https://arxiv.org/pdf/1310.4546.pdf
10. Pennington, J., Socher, R., Manning, C.: GloVe: global vectors for word representation. In: Proceedings of the 2014 Conference on Empirical Methods in Natural Language Processing (EMNLP), Doha, Qatar, 25–29 October 2014, pp. 1532–1543 (2014). Association for Computational Linguistics

11. Pierrejean, B., Tanguy, L.: Towards qualitative word embeddings evaluation: measuring neighbors variation. In: Conference of the North American Chapter of the Association for Computational Linguistics: Student Research Workshop, New-Orleans, United States. Proceedings of NAACL-HLT 2018, pp. 32–39 (2018)
12. Schütze, H.: Dimensions of meaning. In: Proceedings of the 1992 ACM/IEEE Conference on Supercomputing, pp. 787–796. IEEE Computer Society Press (1992)

Using Word Embeddings with Linear Models for Short Text Classification

Alfred Krzywicki[1]([⊠]), Bradford Heap[1], Michael Bain[1], Wayne Wobcke[1], and Susanne Schmeidl[2]

[1] School of Computer Science and Engineering, University of New South Wales, Sydney, NSW 2052, Australia
{alfredk,b.heap,m.bain,w.wobcke}@unsw.edu.au
[2] School of Social Sciences, University of New South Wales, Sydney, NSW 2052, Australia
s.schmeidl@unsw.edu.au

Abstract. Text documents often contain information relevant for a particular domain in short "snippets". The social science field of peace and conflict studies is such a domain, where identifying, classifying and tracking drivers of conflict from text sources is important, and snippets are typically classified by human analysts using an ontology. One issue in automating this process is that snippets tend to contain infrequent "rare" terms which lack class-conditional evidence. In this work we develop a method to enrich a bag-of-words model by complementing rare terms in the text to be classified with related terms from a Word Vector model. This method is then combined with standard linear text classification algorithms. By reducing sparseness in the bag-of-words, these enriched models perform better than the baseline classifiers. A second issue is to improve performance on "small" classes having only a few examples, and here we show that Paragraph Vectors outperform the enriched models.

1 Introduction

In many domains the relevant information from documents is contained in short "snippets" of the text. One such domain is the social science field of peace and conflict studies, where documents are "coded" by human analysts who identify important snippets in the text and classify them according to a domain-specific ontology. This is a difficult task for human coders due to the limited amount of text in a snippet, the large number of classes, the imbalanced class distribution (with frequent overlap between smaller classes), the requirement for all classes to be well-classified, and the amount of disagreement between human coders. Towards the goal of automating such coding, the task addressed in this paper is multiclass classification of short texts or *snippets*. Our task is further characterized by having a large number of classes (in this paper a minimum of 64) and a highly imbalanced distribution of instances over the classes. Accurate classification of instances in less-populated classes is important in this domain.

© Springer Nature Switzerland AG 2018
T. Mitrovic et al. (Eds.): AI 2018, LNAI 11320, pp. 819–827, 2018.
https://doi.org/10.1007/978-3-030-03991-2_74

Two specific aspects of this task are addressed. These can both be seen as problems of data "sparsity", but in different senses. First is the problem of rare terms in short text snippets. We investigate two methods to solve this problem: (i) a method using learned word embeddings [7] to augment short text snippets before classification by a linear model; and (ii) a version of Paragraph Vectors [5] to learn classified word embeddings. Our empirical evaluation compares these classification methods on two corpora exemplifying different writing styles. Second is the problem of classifying documents into "small" or sparsely populated classes. The problem here is that because there is limited data in smaller classes, supervised text classification methods are often less accurate for these classes [3]. We use the same methods for this problem as for the problem of rare terms, but compare classification performance on small and large classes.

2   Methods

2.1   The Bag-of-Words Model and Its Limitations

A text snippet T is defined to be a sequence of individual word tokens $T = [t_1, t_2, \ldots]$. The bag-of-words model maps each text snippet T to a vector M_T of dimension $|V|$, where the vocabulary V is the set of all tokens in the training data. The bag-of-words vector M_T contains the term frequency of each token from V that occurs in T, where the value of the vector is 0 for every token in V that does not occur in T.

The key limitations of the bag-of-words model addressed in this paper are: **Vocabulary Size** – this can affect calculation of class-conditional term probabilities, in classes with a small class-conditional vocabulary, or a small number of training examples; and **Rare and Out of Vocabulary Words** – due to the extremely skewed distribution of word usage in typical text (following Zipf's law) words that occur only very infrequently do not give a learning algorithm sufficient information to determine their correct influence on classification and words that do not occur in training data are discarded by the bag-of-words model.

2.2   Bag-of-Words Enrichment with Word Vectors

Word Vector (WV) models are constructed using neural networks [7] by projecting all the words from a corpus into a dense vector space. Word vectors are widely used as input to neural networks, but since in this domain interpretable models are valuable for analysts, we combine word vectors with linear classifiers.

The process of enriching the bag-of-words model involves a number of steps:

1. Obtain a Word Vector model W that models the vocabulary and language of the training set. In this paper we always use the Google News model.
2. Given a text snippet T to be classified:
   - For each token $t_i \in T$ with a frequency in the labelled training data less than n (i.e., t_i is a *rare word*), if t_i is represented in W, find its m (here 10) nearest neighbours in W, then take up to k of these words that also

occur in the training set (*enriching words*), chosen in order of closeness to t_i.

- For each such rare word t_i, construct a new bag-of-words vector M_{t_i} with the enriching words for t_i that occur in the training set assigned a term frequency of 1, and all other words in the vector assigned the value 0.

3. From the original bag-of-words vector M_T, create an enriched bag-of-words vector M_T^+ by adding M_T and each individual rare token's nearest neighbour bag-of-words vector M_{t_i}:

$$M_T^+ = M_T + \sum_i M_{t_i} \tag{1}$$

As a result of this process, T is now classified using the enriched bag-of-words vector M_T^+ instead of the original bag-of-words vector M_T.

The following example text snippet from the ICG dataset (see Sect. 3.1) illustrates the enrichment process: "Army integration is a particularly delicate subject, as many Banyamulenge soldiers in Kabila's army were killed in camps at the beginning of the RCD rebellion in 1998." In this snippet there are 26 words ("1998" is not counted and "army" is counted twice). Rare words are "delicate" and "subject". Both rare words have neighbours in the WV model. For the word "delicate", enriching words are "fragile", "sensitive" and "complicated", and for "subject", enriching words are "concerning", "relating" and "subjects". The enriched vector has non-zero entries for these six additional words, so the final vector for this text snippet has 32 non-zero values.

When evaluating word enrichment options, enriching rare words in *both* the training and test sets was considered. However, the results of this method on the ICG dataset were slightly worse than enriching only the test set.

Once a bag-of-words is extended with words from the Word Vector model, it can be used by any machine learning method capable of using the bag-of-words model. In this work, three classifiers are used to make predictions about the classification of text: our implementation of Multinomial Naive Bayes (MNB), Weka's[1] implementation of SVM using the SMO algorithm, plus the DeepLearning4J[2] version of Paragraph Vectors (see Sect. 2.3). The classification performance of these models is evaluated with and without enrichment of test instances with word vectors.

2.3   Paragraph Vectors

Paragraph Vectors [5] (PV, also called *doc2vec*) extend the *word2vec* word embedding algorithm [7] by introducing extra embeddings for "paragraph IDs" which are then combined with word vectors when classifying text.

Paragraph IDs serve as proxies for the contexts in which words appear. In the DeepLearning4J implementation, paragraph vectors and word vectors are defined in the *same* vector space. Furthermore, in our setting the paragraph IDs

---

[1] http://www.cs.waikato.ac.nz/ml/weka/.

[2] https://deeplearning4j.org/.

are just the class labels so, in effect, the training phase produces an embedding for each class label in the same space as the word vectors.

We also use a simpler method than [5] to classify new text. Our paragraph vectors (which are vectors for class labels) are in the same space as the word embeddings, so the following "nearest neighbour" approach is adopted. Given an unseen new text, we simply calculate the centroid of all the word vectors for those words in the text that are also in the original training vocabulary (weighting word vectors by the number of times they occur in the text). The label corresponding to the paragraph vector with the highest cosine similarity to this centroid vector is then assigned as the label of the new text.

Since both the WV and PV models are constructed in similar way, no improvement is expected by combining the two models, which was confirmed by empirical evaluation.

3   Empirical Evaluation

3.1   Datasets

ICG DRC Dataset. This dataset contains text snippets from 15 International Crisis Group (ICG) reports on the Democratic Republic of Congo (DRC) during the period 2002–2006. To construct the dataset, a domain expert read 8,836 sentences across the 15 reports and extracted 2,159 text snippets which were then each given one or more of 64 class labels. The dataset contains 3,366 unique words, with a mean snippet length of 25 words. Previous work has shown that classification of this dataset is very difficult for state-of-the-art algorithms [2].

Reuters-21578 Short Text Dataset. This corpus contains news reports from 1987 and is a benchmark dataset widely used in many previous text categorization evaluations. For our evaluation on short text, we extract a subset of the reports where the length of the article body is 100 words or fewer (approximately two sentences). Any article belonging to the 'earn' class is excluded, as these documents have share ticker information and do not form full sentences. This dataset, which we call Reuters-ST, contains 7,213 unique words in 3,003 articles labelled by 91 categories. The mean length of each document is 70 words.

3.2   Approach

Around 10–20% of the instances in both ICG and Reuters-ST datasets are classified into more than one class. To simplify this problem, our classifiers are configured to only produce a single classification label and an article is considered to be correctly classified if the model correctly predicts one of its ground truth labels. In this setting, micro precision is equal to micro recall. We also measure class macro precision, recall and F1, as these metrics equally weight all classes. Effectively, comparing micro and macro metrics gives an indication of performance for less frequent (smaller) classes. Separately, the methods are evaluated for small (less frequent) and large classes.

The evaluation setup is a 10 × 10-fold cross validation. The Paragraph Vectors model is trained using 60 epochs for each fold. Other parameters are default in DeepLearning4J (learning rate = 0.025, vector dimensions = 100). For each dataset we use Mikolov's Word Vector model pre-trained on Google News. This model is used for enrichment of the test set without any pre-processing of the text.

For each dataset and classification model, hyperparameters are tuned for word frequency n and the number of additional words from the Word Vector model k using a grid search over the first fold of the dataset. Optimal values of these parameters were $n = 3$ and $k = 3$ for both datasets and all methods. These values are then used in all 10 × 10-fold cross validation runs. A publicly available paired t-test calculator[3] with $p < 0.05$ is used to determine statistical significance.

3.3   Results

In Table 1, it is evident that on both datasets the word vector enrichment improves the micro-averaged performance for the linear classifiers, with SVM being better. Macro-averaged performance shows that enriched SVM obtains the best F1 on both datasets, although MNB has the best precision on ICG and unenriched SVM on Reuters-ST. PV has the best recall on both datasets and, as expected, WV enrichment does not improve the PV model. On ICG, all comparisons of the enriched models to baseline models are statistically significant.

Table 1. Classification results for ICG and Reuters-ST datasets

	ICG				Reuters-ST			
	Micro	Macro			Micro	Macro		
	Prec./Rec.	Prec.	Rec.	F1	Prec./Rec.	Prec.	Rec.	F1
MNB	0.2999	**0.4515**	0.1154	0.1833	0.7647	0.8087	0.1778	0.2909
MNB enriched	0.3247	0.4337	0.1307	0.2003	0.7729	0.8019	0.1863	0.3018
SVM	0.3745	0.4043	0.2151	0.2801	0.8417	**0.8473**	0.4434	0.5810
SVM enriched	**0.3933**	0.4078	0.2330	**0.2961**	**0.8430**	0.8340	0.4489	**0.5825**
PV	0.3697	0.2885	**0.2576**	0.2716	0.8254	0.6349	**0.4792**	0.5449
PV enriched	0.3600	0.2776	0.2445	0.2595	0.8217	0.6337	0.4761	0.5426

Overall, comparing the results in Table 1, it can be seen that word vector enrichment improves macro recall and F1 for linear MNB and SVM, although the baseline SVM for the ICG dataset is improved more than for the Reuters-ST dataset. This is possibly because ICG categories are much more difficult to predict, which is reflected by the lower values in the above table.

---

[3] http://www.socscistatistics.com/tests/ttestdependent/Default2.aspx.

The micro-averaged metrics reflect more the performance on larger classes (i.e., those containing more examples), whereas macro-averaged metrics give a better indication of prediction performance over all classes.

3.4 Small and Large Classes

Of special interest is how enrichment affects classification accuracy for classes with fewer instances. To investigate this, the set of classes was ordered by the number of instances in each class and divided into two approximately equal-sized subsets, the "large" classes and the "small" classes. This gave 32 ICG small classes with 15% of all instances and 46 Reuters-ST small classes with only 4.4% of all instances. The Reuters-ST dataset is much more skewed towards larger classes, with the largest category containing 37% of all instances, whereas for the ICG dataset, this value is only 6%. Results were obtained for each class separately and aggregated for the small and large classes.

Table 2. Classification results for small and large ICG classes

	Small classes						Large classes					
	Micro			Macro			Micro			Macro		
	Prec.	Rec.	F1	Prec.	Rec.	F1	Prec.	Rec.	F1	Prec.	Rec.	F1
MNB	1.000	0.004	0.008	0.063	0.002	0.004	0.299	0.293	0.296	0.329	0.175	0.161
MNB Enr.	0.905	0.006	0.011	0.078	0.003	0.006	0.324	0.317	0.320	0.318	0.197	0.186
SVM	**0.376**	0.081	0.134	0.147	0.051	0.072	0.374	0.354	0.364	0.396	0.296	0.319
SVM Enr.	0.367	0.095	0.151	**0.157**	0.061	0.083	0.394	**0.370**	**0.382**	**0.412**	**0.319**	**0.344**
PV	0.150	**0.181**	**0.164**	0.112	**0.156**	**0.120**	**0.419**	0.335	0.372	0.364	0.307	0.322
PV Enr.	0.144	0.165	0.154	0.112	0.137	0.114	0.406	0.327	0.362	0.347	0.295	0.307

Table 3. Classification results for small and large Reuters-ST classes

	Small classes						Large classes					
	Micro			Macro			Micro			Macro		
	Prec.	Rec.	F1	Prec.	Rec.	F1	Prec.	Rec.	F1	Prec.	Rec.	F1
MNB	0.000	0.000	0.000	0.000	0.000	0.000	0.765	0.642	0.698	0.445	0.209	0.233
MNB Enr.	0.000	0.000	0.000	0.000	0.000	0.000	0.773	0.649	0.705	0.442	0.220	0.241
SVM	**0.754**	0.188	0.301	**0.203**	0.094	0.123	0.843	0.698	0.764	**0.815**	0.508	0.589
SVM Enr.	0.749	0.193	**0.307**	0.203	0.097	**0.126**	**0.844**	**0.699**	**0.765**	0.797	0.513	**0.591**
PV	0.348	0.228	0.275	0.147	**0.118**	0.121	0.843	0.683	0.754	0.662	**0.548**	0.563
PV Enr.	0.355	**0.232**	0.281	0.148	0.118	0.120	0.839	0.679	0.751	0.664	0.544	0.560

By decomposing the results for Table 1, we can see from Tables 2 and 3 that the greater contribution to the classification performance for all three methods is on the large classes (on both datasets), although PV performance on the small classes is best (for ICG), or at least more balanced between precision and recall (macro-averaged, Reuters-ST). This is evident on the large classes (for both datasets) in the macro results, which are more representative of all the classes in the large class subset. Furthermore, the small class performance is *reducing* overall performance (F1, both datasets), although not for MNB.

We can see that for SVM there is improvement due to enrichment on both small and large classes on both datasets. However, while performance for the small classes on both datasets as measured by micro-averaged F1 is approximately double that of macro-averaged F1, for the large classes it is approximately equal. This can be interpreted as showing that, for the small classes, the smaller the class, the harder it is to learn to predict. Although predictive performance of PV is weaker, it is more balanced in terms of micro and macro-averaged results, at least on ICG, which is the more difficult dataset.

Importantly it is evident that enrichment usually increases (and never reduces) recall for both linear classifiers, on both datasets, for small and large classes, measured by both micro- and macro-averaged metrics. This is a significant advantage given the intended application of our approach, where it is often more time-consuming for human analysts to search in a document for potential indicators of conflict that have been missed by an automated method (i.e., false negatives) than to correct for false positives [2].

This could be due to the fact that the Word Vector model is trained using an *unsupervised* approach and thus lack class-conditional information. In contrast, in our approach PV is trained in a supervised manner, consistent with a better balance between precision and recall, although overall performance is less than the linear classifiers, possibly since PV is a much simpler learning algorithm.

4   Related Work

Many approaches for transforming the bag-of-words model or modifying linear models to increase classification accuracy have been proposed in previous work. Some of the most relevant to our approach involve using dictionaries [6] or encyclopaedias [10] to find synonyms for rare terms. Use of word embeddings in text processing includes query expansion [4] and named entity recognition (NER) [1]. The research described in this paper differs from the above work in that we use word vectors to classify short text snippets by enriching only rare words or words unseen in the training set. Word vectors were used to augment short text for similarity measures [8]. Using a unified architecture for word embeddings and classification (for example, a Convolutional Neural Network [9]) is something worth further investigation, although it does not result in the kind of interpretable model required for our domain.

5   Conclusion

In this paper we were motivated by the social science goal of automatically predicting conflict-related categories for short text segments or "snippets". Such domains typically have a large number of classes, many of which are sparsely populated in datasets and are closely related semantically. Additionally, class distributions tend to be imbalanced, and snippets often contain words or terms appearing infrequently in the corpus. Since classification methods are eventually intended as a tool to aid human analysts, it is desirable to have interpretable models and to reduce the risk of missing information relating to potential conflict. Our hypothesis was that enrichment of the standard bag-of-words representation by a Word Vector model (here the Google News model) would improve the performance of standard linear classifiers on this multiclass problem. This hypothesis was supported by empirical evaluation on two datasets, one on conflict data from ICG reports and the other a subset of short texts from the benchmark Reuters datasets. A key benefit of the enrichment approach is that it does not require any change to the training of linear classification models. However, improvements due to enrichment for the linear classifiers were mainly due to better performance on the larger classes. We also tested a classification-based Word Vector model and found that it gave better recall on smaller classes. For future work, a promising avenue is to investigate hybrids of these models.

Acknowledgment. This work was supported by Data to Decisions Cooperative Research Centre. We thank Josie Gardner for coding the ICG DRC dataset.

References

1. Guo, J., Che, W., Wang, H., Liu, T.: Revisiting embedding features for simple semi-supervised learning. In: Proceedings of the 2014 Conference on Empirical Methods in Natural Language Processing, pp. 110–120 (2014)
2. Heap, B., Krzywicki, A., Schmeidl, S., Wobcke, W., Bain, M.: A joint human/machine process for coding events and conflict drivers. In: Cong, G., Peng, W.-C., Zhang, W.E., Li, C., Sun, A. (eds.) ADMA 2017. LNCS (LNAI), vol. 10604, pp. 639–654. Springer, Cham (2017). https://doi.org/10.1007/978-3-319-69179-4_45
3. Joachims, T.: A probabilistic analysis of the Rocchio algorithm with TFIDF for text categorization. In: Proceedings of the Fourteenth International Conference on Machine Learning, pp. 143–151 (1997)
4. Kuzi, S., Shtok, A., Kurland, O.: Query expansion using word embeddings. In: Proceedings of the 25th ACM International Conference on Information and Knowledge Management, pp. 1929–1932 (2016)
5. Le, Q.V., Mikolov, T.: Distributed representations of sentences and documents. In: Proceedings of the 31st International Conference on Machine Learning, pp. 1188–1196 (2014)
6. Mansuy, T.N., Hilderman, R.J.: A characterization of WordNet features in Boolean models for text classification. In: Proceedings of the Fifth Australasian Data Mining Conference, pp. 103–109 (2006)
7. Mikolov, T., Chen, K., Corrado, G., Dean, J.: Efficient estimation of word representations in vector space. CoRR abs/1301.3781 (2013)
8. Song, Y., Roth, D.: Unsupervised sparse vector densification for short text similarity. In: Proceedings of the NAACL:HLT Conference, pp. 1275–1280 (2015)

9. Wang, P., Xu, B., Xu, J., Tian, G., Liu, C.L., Hao, H.: Semantic expansion using word embedding clustering and convolutional neural network for improving short text classification. Neurocomputing **174**, 806–814 (2016)
10. Wang, P., Domeniconi, C.: Building semantic kernels for text classification using Wikipedia. In: Proceedings of the Fourteenth ACM SIGKDD International Conference on Knowledge Discovery and Data Mining, pp. 713–721 (2008)

Towards Compiling Textbooks
from Wikipedia

Ditty Mathew[✉] and Sutanu Chakraborti

Artificial Intelligence and Databases Lab,
Department of Computer Sciene and Engineering,
Indian Institute of Technology Madras, Chennai 600036, India
{ditty,sutanuc}@cse.iitm.ac.in

Abstract. In this paper, we explore challenges in compiling a pedagogic resource like a textbook on a given topic from relevant Wikipedia articles, and present an approach towards assisting humans in this task. We present an algorithm that attempts to suggest the textbook structure from Wikipedia based on a set of seed concepts (chapters) provided by the user. We also conceptualize a decision support system where users can interact with the proposed structure and the corresponding Wikipedia content to improve its pedagogic value. The proposed algorithm is implemented and evaluated against the outline of online textbooks on five different subjects. We also propose a measure to quantify the pedagogic value of the suggested textbook structure.

1 Introduction

Nowadays, most self-learners depend heavily on online resources for learning. Among online resources, Wikipedia has rich content in almost all areas. Hence, online readers often tend to have a stopgap recourse to Wikipedia to satisfy their learning goal. Though Wikipedia has good reference value and broad coverage, its pedagogic value is typically less compared to carefully crafted learning resources like textbooks. This is because Wikipedia content is not necessarily structured with the goal of assisting graded learning of topics [13]. In contrast, a textbook author organizes content to satisfy the intended tutoring goal. However, crafting authoritative textbooks is an exercise that is highly demanding in terms of time, effort and human expertise. Moreover, textbook content is relatively static and may be inherently restricted in its coverage. It is thus intriguing to envisage design of tools that, given a subject, can aid in composition of textbooks from relevant pages in online resources like Wikipedia.

Agrawal et al. [11] studied the characteristics of well-written textbooks. An ideal textbook presents concepts[1] in a sequential manner, i.e. a concept is defined or explained before it is being referred anywhere in the textbook in order to explain other concepts (an exception being the set of concepts the textbook

---

[1] The term "concept" is loosely used to refer to a topic or idea. Here, we use this term interchangeably to correspond to either Wikipedia article titles or textbook topics.

© Springer Nature Switzerland AG 2018
T. Mitrovic et al. (Eds.): AI 2018, LNAI 11320, pp. 828–842, 2018.
https://doi.org/10.1007/978-3-030-03991-2_75

assumes the learner to be familiar with). In contrast, Wikipedia supports flexible hyperlinking between related articles, with the goal of enhancing its value as a ready reference. Mathew et al. [13] observed that Wikipedia tends to have circular dependencies between articles, i.e. article A hyperlinks to article B and vice versa. More generally, concepts in Wikipedia are not sequentially structured in a way that ensures that all prerequisites of a given concept are presented before they are used to explain the concept. This adversely affects the usefulness of Wikipedia for a learner who wishes to be guided through a set of neatly structured topics, graded in terms of learning difficulty.

It is hard for even humans to organize the content of a book. Hence, it would be overtly ambitious to target a fully automated solution for this problem. A more pragmatic goal would be to examine the extent to which tools can be devised that can effectively aid humans in this task. A Wikipedia tool named *Book Creator*[2] provides an option to compile books from Wikipedia by manually adding relevant Wikipedia articles in an order given by the end user. However, this tool does not estimate the pedagogic value of the book, or guide the user in enhancing the content with the goal of making it pedagogically richer. Another project named *Wikibooks*[3] allows editors to collaboratively organize and write the content of book, and currently, Wikibooks contains only 66 featured books (books with high quality). Hence, designing a tool that guides human in compiling books from Wikipedia can help editors in contributing more featured books. We propose an algorithm to suggest the book structure from Wikipedia on a given subject. We also conceptualize a decision support system that allows the user to interact with the proposed structure and the corresponding Wikipedia content to improve its pedagogic value. The system flags regions which are largely affected by circular dependencies. The process of resolving such circularities in order to enhance the pedagogic content is referred to as *grounding* [13]. The system can guide users in identifying concepts that need to be grounded. The user then grounds a concept by rewriting part of the content, or adding images or videos, so that prerequisites are satisfied. The tool intimates the user of the impact of the change on the pedagogic value of the learning resource, and also of any fresh circularities that may have formed as a result of the grounding.

To the best of our knowledge, this is the first attempt towards compiling textbooks from Wikipedia on a given theme. The contributions of this paper are: (i) an algorithm to suggest the book structure from Wikipedia based on a set of seed concepts which act as chapters of the book, (ii) an approach to identify regions that need to be grounded in the proposed structure, (iii) a score to estimate the pedagogic value of the predicted textbook structure. We evaluate the proposed book structure quantitatively, and also report findings based on user studies.

---

[2] https://en.wikipedia.org/w/index.php?title=Special:Book&bookcmd=book_creator.

[3] https://en.wikibooks.org/wiki/Wikibooks.

2   Identification of Book Structure from Wikipedia

We first identify the book structure from Wikipedia based on a given set of ordered seed concepts. This book structure can be used as reference for compiling a textbook from Wikipedia. Figure 1 depicts an example of book outline for a book on *Automata Theory* from the seed concepts *Finite state automaton, Regular grammar, Context free grammar* and *Turing machine*.The expected structure of a book from Wikipedia is a hierarchy of concepts recursively organized in terms of chapters, sections, subsections and so on. We consider each chapter as a parent of its sections and each section as a parent of its subsections. In this hierarchy, we make simplifying assumptions that there is a relation between each parent-child pair, i.e. the *introduction to the parent concept* is a prerequisite of its *child*. For example, *introduction to sorting* is a prerequisite of *bubble sort*.

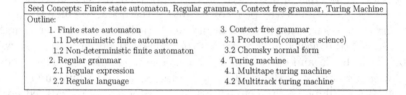

Fig. 1. An example of book outline from Wikipedia for a given set of seed concepts

In our work, seed concepts act as chapters of the book. We propose an augmentation algorithm to identify section concepts for augmentation under seed concepts which can be recursively used to add subsection concepts and so on. We then order concepts under each chapter, section, subsection, etc. We first discuss the augmentation process and then the concept ordering process.

2.1   Concept Augmentation

At this step, an augmented graph $AG = (\mathbb{V}, \mathbb{E})$ is constructed where each vertex represents a concept and each edge $(u, v) \in \mathbb{E}$ is a directed edge which signifies that v is augmented to u. The construction of AG begins with seed concepts as vertices. For each seed concept, a set of candidate concepts are selected for augmentation from their corresponding Wikipedia articles; the mapping is currently done manually (see Sect. 4). These candidate concepts form candidate edges (*CandidateEdges*) where for each $(m, n) \in CandidateEdges$, n is a candidate concept that is proposed to be augmented to concept m. Concepts from these candidates are selected for augmentation by analyzing the extent of subordination of candidate concept under the concept to which it is proposed to be augmented and any circular dependency that may result due to augmentation. We characterize the extent to which a candidate concept is subordinated by its parent concept based on (i) the prerequisite relation between them, (ii) semantic relatedness, (iii) non-violation of prerequisite relationships down the hierarchy. In the rest of this section, we present measures to capture these factors.

Prerequisition Score. Liang et al. [14] proposed a simple link-based measure called *reference distance* (*RefD*) to estimate the strength of prerequisite relations among Wikipedia concepts. This method is based on the intuition that if a concept c_1 and its related concepts refer to another concept c_2 a lot in their description but not vice versa, c_2 is more likely to be a prerequisite of c_1. Liang et al. [14] propose to use links in the Wikipedia article c_i as related concepts of c_i. Thus *RefD* measure is based on the hyperlink structure of Wikipedia and accounts for articles that are referred directly by a page. However, if a concept A is referred to by B and B is referred to by C, then A is being indirectly referred to by C. This kind of transitive or higher order reference is not captured by *RefD* score. In order to address this gap, we propose a revised measure called *PReqScore* for estimating the strength of prerequisite relation. The *PReqScore* is defined based on the hyperlink network in Wikipedia, where an edge from article A to article B indicates that article A is hyperlinked in article B (which means concept A is used to explain concept B). The intuition of *PReqScore* is: *a concept c_i is likely to be a prerequisite of c_j, if there are more paths from c_i to c_j compared to the paths from c_j to c_i in the hyperlink network.*

To compare the paths between c_i and c_j, we propose a measure called *PathScore*(c_i, c_j) for all directed paths from c_i to c_j. The presence of noisy edges can lead to meaningless paths. Hence, we use *RefD* score to ensure that each edge in a path results in a meaningful prerequisite relation. As the path length increases, the prerequisite connections get digressed from the source concept. Hence, we weigh paths based on their path lengths. *PathScore*(c_i, c_j) is defined as,

$$PathScore\,(c_i, c_j) = \sum_{path \in Paths(c_i, c_j)} \frac{1}{length(path)} \prod_{(u,v) \in Edges(path)} \frac{1 + RefD(u, v)}{2} \quad (1)$$

where $Paths(c_i, c_j)$ contains all paths from c_i to c_j. Since the range of *RefD* varies between -1 and 1, we scale its value between 0 and 1 using the term $(1 + RefD(u, v))/2$. The product of scaled *RefD* scores of edges in each path are taken to consider the noise in the path. Using these scores, we define *PReqScore*(c_i, c_j) which estimates the extent to which c_i is a prerequisite of c_j as,

$$PReqScore(c_i, c_j) = PathScore(c_i, c_j) - PathScore(c_j, c_i) \quad (2)$$

PathScore(c_i, c_j) takes non-negative value. Hence, a concept c_i is considered as a prerequisite of c_j if *PReqScore*$(c_i, c_j) > 0$. While computing *PathScore*, we further limit the paths based on path length up to 4. This value is fixed based on cross validation in CrowdComp dataset [12].

Augmentation Score. To characterize the extent to which a candidate is subordinated under its parent, we consider *PReqScore*, semantic relatedness, and the prerequisite violation cases in the book structure when the candidate concept is augmented to its parent. Let $seed(c_i)$ be the seed concept that is the ancestor of c_i. A case of prerequisite relation violation occurs when a seed concept that is ordered after $seed(c_i)$ is a prerequisite of the candidate c_i, or any descendant of a seed concept that is ordered after $seed(c_i)$ is a prerequisite of candidate c_i. The former case is shown in Fig. 2 and the latter one in Fig. 3. In Fig. 2, *Finite State Automaton(FSA)* and *Regular Expression(RE)* are seed concepts; *Regular Language(RL)* is a candidate concept for *FSA* and *RE*; *RE* follows *FSA* in ordering and is a prerequisite of *RL*. Hence, while finding the extent to which *RL* is subordinated under *FSA*, prerequisite violation with *RE* has to be considered. Figure 3 illustrates a case of higher (second) order prerequisite violation. Here the concepts *Deterministic Finite Automata(DFA)* and *Regular Language(RL)* are augmented in the first iteration; *Pumping lemma for Regular Languages* is a candidate for *DFA* and *RL*; the $seed(RL)$ (i.e. *RE*) follows $seed(DFA)$ (i.e. *FSA*) in seed concepts ordering. Hence, the prerequisite violation of *Pumping lemma for RL* with *RL* has to be considered while estimating the extent to which *Pumping lemma for RL* is subordinated under *DFA*.

Fig. 2. An example for prerequisite violation case during first iteration

Fig. 3. An example for prerequisite violation case during second iteration

We propose a measure called $AugScore(c_i, c_j)$ which estimates the extent to which c_j is subordinated under c_i based on *PReqScore*, semantic relatedness, and the prerequisite violation case. It is defined as

$$AugScore(c_i, c_j) = \frac{SemRel(c_i, c_j) \times PReqScore(c_i, c_j)}{1 + \sum_{\substack{c_k \in parents(c_j) \\ Index(seed(c_k)) > Index(seed(c_i))}} PReqScore(c_k, c_j)} \tag{3}$$

where $Index(seed(c_j))$ is the position of $seed(c_j)$ in the seed concepts order. The denominator accounts for the case where the ancestor of c_j is a seed concept which is positioned after $seed(c_j)$ in seed concepts ordering. In such cases the $AugScore(c_i, c_j)$ is penalized by the $PReqScore(c_k, c_j)$. The addition of 1 in the denominator is to handle the case when there are no prerequisite violations. The $SemRel(c_i, c_j)$ captures the semantic relatedness between c_i and c_j, for which we use a measure called Normalized Wikipedia Distance (NWD) [9] which is based on Wikipedia link structure. This measure is based on the occurrences of Wikipedia concept links in Wikipedia articles. Wikipedia concepts with common links indicate relatedness, while concepts without any common links suggest the opposite. The normalized Wikipedia distance measure is defined as,

$$NWD(c_i, c_j) = \frac{\log(\max(|L(c_i)|, |L(c_j)|)) - \log(|L(c_i) \cap L(c_j)|)}{\log(|W|) - \log(\min(|L(c_i)|, |L(c_j)|))} \tag{4}$$

where $L(c_i)$ is the set of Wikipedia concepts that link to c_i and W is the set of all Wikipedia concepts. $SemRel(c_i, c_j)$ is measured as $1 - NWD(c_i, c_j)$.

Augmentation Algorithm. Algorithm 1 recursively augments concepts to the augmented graph while ensuring that circular dependencies are minimized. This algorithm inputs a set of seed concepts, and the number of levels in the hierarchy to which the concepts are augmented (lvl). First, the seed concepts are added to the augmented graph (AG). The candidate concepts of each seed concept are generated from hyperlinks that are referred to by the corresponding Wikipedia article. Candidate edges are drawn from each seed concept to its candidate concepts. The candidate concepts and candidate edges are tentatively added to the augmented graph. The algorithm selects some candidate concepts and corresponding candidate edges for final augmentation by retaining them in the augmented graph. The final selection of concepts from candidates is based on the extent to which a candidate concept is augmented by its parent.

Algorithm 1. Augmentation Algorithm

Input: Seed Concepts, No of levels (lvl)
Output: Augmented Graph AG
Initialize $AG = (V, E)$ with V =Seed Concepts
$AugmentedConcepts \leftarrow$ Seed Concepts
$CurLevel = 0$
while $CurLevel < lvl$ **do**
    $CandidateEdges \leftarrow$ Empty
    for each cpt in $AugmentedConcepts$ **do**
        $\mathbb{C} \leftarrow CandidateConcepts(cpt)$
        $\mathbb{C} \leftarrow \mathbb{C} - AugmentedConcepts$
        $CandidateEdges \leftarrow CandidateEdges \cup \{(cpt, c_j) \mid \forall c_j \in \mathbb{C}\}$
        $V \leftarrow V \cup \mathbb{C};\ E \leftarrow E \cup \{(cpt, c_j) \mid \forall c_j \in \mathbb{C}\}$
        Estimate $PReqScore(cpt, c_j)$
    Normalize $PReqScore$ of all $CandidateEdges$
    for each (c_i, c_j) in $CandidateEdges$ **do**
        Estimate $AugScore(c_i, c_j)$
    Cluster $CandidateEdges$ based on $AugScore$
    $AugmentedEdges \leftarrow CandidateEdges$ in the cluster with candidates having highest $AugScore$
    $E \leftarrow E - \{(c_i, c_j) \mid (c_i, c_j) \in CandidateEdges$ and $(c_i, c_j) \notin AugmentedEdges\}$
    $AugmentedConcepts \leftarrow \{c_j \mid (c_i, c_j) \in AugmentedEdges\}$
    $CurLevel = CurLevel + 1$

The algorithm uses $AugScore$ to measure the extent to which a candidate concept is fit to be augmented to a graph. $PReqScores$ are normalized at each level to compute $AugScore$. We cluster candidate edges using jenks natural breaks algorithm [21] based on $AugScore$ and use elbow method [5] to find the best number of clusters. The candidate edges in the cluster, which have the highest $AugScore$ are chosen as the edges for augmentation. Similarly, in subsequent iterations, concepts are augmented to those suggested concepts in the previous iteration. This process is repeated for lvl times. Although we restrict our scope to augmenting concepts in the cluster with the highest score, the interface can provide an option to the user to choose the candidates based on a threshold.

2.2 Concept Ordering

We order concepts that are suggested for augmentation under a parent concept based on the idea that *if two concepts A and B are in the same level, and A comes before B, then B may not need A as a prerequisite, but definitely A does not need B as a prerequisite.* Using this idea, we identify inequalities between pairs of concepts that are taken for ordering. Let $\{c_1, \ldots, c_m\}$ be a set of concepts taken for ordering. For a pair (c_i, c_j), if $PReqScore\ (c_i, c_j) \leq 0$, c_j does not require c_i as a prerequisite. Hence, c_i can come after c_j in the ordering. This forms an inequality $c_j < c_i$. Thus, we find all such inequalities between concept pairs in the given concept set. We construct a directed graph based on these inequalities where vertices represent concepts and each edge (u, v) denotes $u < v$. The PageRank [7] score of concepts in this graph is computed for aggregating the pairwise comparisons to a global ranking of concepts [20]. A concept with high PageRank should be ideally ordered after all other concepts. Hence, we order concepts based on PageRank in the ascending order.

3 Identification of Regions for Grounding

The Wikipedia article contents are mostly affected by circular dependencies [13] and due to these circular dependencies the user has to flip back and forth between Wikipedia articles while reading the content. Hence, the pedagogic value of the content of Wikipedia concepts in the proposed structure is expected to be less compared to a well-written textbook. To guide the user in improving the pedagogic value of the content, we propose a method to identify regions which need attention. These regions are addressed by (i) *perceptual grounding* by providing links to videos, images etc. (ii) *linguistic grounding* by redefining the concept [13]. In Fig. 4, we illustrate an example of suggestions of regions for grounding in *Deterministic finite automaton* article in Wikipedia with respect to a book outline. The suggested regions are highlighted in red.

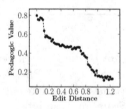

Fig. 4. An example of regions for grounding in *deterministic finite automaton* article (Color figure online)

We construct an extended augmented graph (AG_{ext}) to check for circular dependencies in the article content of concepts in the augmented graph. AG_{ext} contains all vertices and edges of augmented graph AG, and apart from that the interlinks between concepts in the augmented graph based on Wikipedia hyperlink structure is added to AG_{ext}. More precisely, if u is a hyperlink in article v, and u and v are vertices in the augmented graph AG, we add an edge from u to v in AG_{ext}. We propose a measure called $CycleScore$ to estimate the extent to which the addition of a concept in the extended augmented graph introduces circular dependencies. This measure is inspired by the work of Levary et al. [18] who studied the loops in dictionary network and observed that meaningful loops (those that do not digress from the source) are quite short. The lesser the number of concepts involved in cycles, the stronger the dependency between concepts. Hence, for a concept that is involved in many short length circular dependencies, we incur overheads in terms of learning difficulty. Based on these aspects, we define $CycleScore$ for each edge (c_i, c_j) in AG_{ext} as,

$$CycleScore(c_i, c_j) = \frac{GraphScore(AG_{ext}) - GraphScore(AG'_{ext})}{GraphScore(AG_{ext})} \tag{5}$$

where AG'_{ext} is a graph same as AG_{ext} except that the edge (c_i, c_j) is removed in AG'_{ext} and the $GraphScore(AG)$ is

$$GraphScore(AG) = \sum_{cyc \in Cycles(AG)} \prod_{(u,v) \in Edges(cyc)} PReqScore(u, v) \tag{6}$$

where $Cycles(AG)$ consists of all cycles in AG and $Edges(cyc)$ is the set of edges in a cycle cyc. The product term gives less weight to a cycle when there is a noisy edge and its length is large. After computing $CycleScore$ for all edges in AG_{ext}, we suggest the edge with maximum $CycleScore$ for grounding. Let (c_i, c_j) be the edge with maximum $CycleScore$. So it will be suggested for grounding, which means the hyperlink c_j in article c_i needs to be grounded with the help of human by either perceptual or linguistic grounding.

4   Estimation of Pedagogic Value

In this section, we attempt to estimate the pedagogic value of the proposed book structure. The proposed pedagogic value depends on three factors: (i) prerequisite and subordination conditions between every parent and child concepts in the book structure(AG), (ii) ordering of concepts under each section in the book structure(AG), (iii) percentage of concepts suggested for grounding in the extended augmented graph(AG_{ext}); the lower the percentage, the higher the pedagogic value. For each parent-child pair in AG, the first factor is captured by $AugScore$. The ordering of child concepts under each parent concept is checked based on the condition that there should not be any concept which acts as a prerequisite for a concept that is positioned before it in the given order of concepts. Using this idea, we propose a measure called $OrderScore$ as,

$$OrderScore(G) = \frac{\sum\limits_{(u,v) \in \mathbb{O}} 1 - P(v, u)}{|\mathbb{O}|} \tag{7}$$

where $\mathbb{O}$ is a set of all ordered pairs of concepts within each parent section in the book structure. $P(v, u) = 1$, if v is a prerequisite of u; 0 otherwise. The higher the $OrderScore$, the lower the prerequisite violations of concepts at the same level. Based on all these aspects, we define the pedagogic value for the augmented graph $AG = (V, E)$ as,

$$PedagogicValue(AG) = OrderScore(AG) * \frac{\sum\limits_{(c_i, c_j) \in E} AugScore(c_i, c_j)}{|E|} * (1 - \frac{|E_{ground}|}{|E_{ext}|})$$

(8)

where E_{ground} is the set of edges suggested for grounding and E_{ext} is the set of edges in AG_{ext}. The $PedagogicValue$ of an augmented graph (AG) is high when the $OrderScore$ is high, the edges in AG have high $AugScore$, and the percentage of concepts suggested for grounding is less.

5   Experiments

We quantitatively evaluate the proposed method for predicting book structure from Wikipedia by using the structure of actual books. We used five online books, namely *Automata, Data Structures and Algorithms (DSA), Compiler Design(CD), Basic Electronics (BE)* and *PreCalculus (PC)*. The first four books are from tutorialspoint[4] which contains online content on various subjects, and the last one is from openstax[5] which is a collection of open-access books. From the book outline, we manually mapped chapter/section/subsection titles to the corresponding Wikipedia concepts. The number of Wikipedia concepts mapped to chapters, sections, and subsections for each book are given in Table 1. The Wikipedia concepts that are mapped to chapter titles of the book are used as seed concepts. The order of seed concepts presented in the book is retained in the predicted outline. We extracted candidates for each seed concept from the corresponding Wikipedia articles. In our experiments, hyperlinks present in the first three paragraphs of a Wikipedia article are used as candidates for augmentation. This is based on the F1-score analysis on all five books with different candidate sets taken from first k paragraphs where $1 \leq k \leq 5$.

Evaluation of Book Structures Before Grounding: Using Algorithm 1, we obtain the predicted structure for all five online textbooks. The chapter names in the actual book structure are treated as seed concepts to predict till two levels i.e., sections and subsections. We compare the predicted structure with the actual structure by analyzing the tree edit distance [6] between them. The intuition is to estimate the cost incurred in revising the predicted structure to make it equivalent to the actual structure. We consider insertion, deletion and relabel operations while computing edit distance with costs 0.5, 0.5 and 1

---

[4] http://www.tutorialspoint.com.
[5] https://openstax.org/details/books/precalculus.

Table 1. Textbook concepts to wikipedia concepts mapping statistics

Textbook	No of mapped concepts		
	Chapters	Sections	Subsections
DSA	9	24	3
Automata	6	19	0
CD	7	19	7
BE	13	17	9
PC	5	16	0

Table 2. Evaluation of suggested book structure based on online textbook structure and the structure revised by human

Textbook	Using online textbook structures			Using human revised structures			Pedagogic value
	Edit dist.	Precision	Recall	Edit dist.	Precision	Recall	
DSA	0.428	0.296	0.94	0.295	0.634	0.972	0.266
Automata	0.449	0.358	0.96	0.229	0.719	0.977	0.358
CD	0.479	0.253	0.815	0.372	0.373	0.921	0.405
BE	0.484	0.158	0.75	0.424	0.271	0.846	0.265
PC	0.478	0.138	0.904	0.287	0.549	0.997	0.342

respectively. The edit distance is computed for all five textbooks and normalized with respect to the size of the actual and predicted structure [2]. We also analyze the precision and the recall of concepts augmented in the proposed structure based on the actual book structure. The results are shown in Table 2 and we can see that *Basic Electronics* has the highest edit distance and least pedagogic value. We can also observe that the recall over all five books are high whereas the precision is less. This is because while the system is able to correctly recommend most sections and subsections mentioned in the actual textbook, many concepts that are augmented are not present in the actual book structure.

We perform human evaluation of predicted structures by asking humans to revise the structure by removing undesirable sections or subsections, reordering and inserting concepts if required. Each predicted structure is revised by 5 experts in the given field. We use the structures revised by humans to evaluate the predicted structure by computing tree edit distance between the predicted and the revised structure. We also estimate the precision and the recall of augmented concepts in the predicted structure with respect to the revised structure. The average of the edit distance, precision and recall based on the revised structures by humans are given in Table 2. Based on the edit distances, it is observed that the predicted structures are closer to the revised structures than to the actual book structures across all five books. We can also notice that the precisions are increased for all books when evaluated based on revised structures. This shows that many desirable concepts are recommended by our system which are not present in the actual book structures. The recall based on revised structures depends on the number of concepts inserted in the revised one.

Evaluation of Book Structures After Grounding: To evaluate the effect of grounding, we make a simplistic assumption that links contributing to cycles are removed. Hence, for grounding, we remove the edge with maximum *CycleScore*. Once a concept is grounded, the book structure is again generated based on the updated link structure. This process of grounding is continued until contents of the proposed structure are cycle-free, or the user chooses to ignore any further suggestions made by the tool. The final book structure is evaluated both quantitatively and qualitatively as was done on the predicted structure before grounding. For these evaluations, we use tree edit distance, precision and recall of the predicted final structures with respect to the actual book structures and the revised structures provided by humans respectively. It can be seen in Table 3 that for both qualitative and quantitative evaluations, the edit distances are less after grounding compared to the corresponding edit distances before grounding which is given in Table 2; precision values also improve after grounding for all textbooks. We can also observe that the *Pedagogic Value* of all predicted structures increase while their edit distances decrease after grounding. This signifies that this score can be used to guide the user as she interacts with the system to edit concepts by iteratively resolving prerequisite violations and circular dependencies. The result shows that in both evaluations, *Basic Electronics* has the highest edit distance, least precision and least *Pedagogic Value*. This points out that certain books are difficult to compile from Wikipedia. It may be noted that while the actual process of grounding may involve editing content in addition to links, the scope of the paper with respect to evaluating effects of grounding is restricted to evidences that can be gathered from links.

Table 3. Evaluation of book structure obtained after grounding based on online textbook structure and the structure revised by human

Textbook	Using online textbook structures			Using human revised structures			Pedagogic
	Edit dist.	Precision	Recall	Edit dist.	Precision	Recall	value
DSA	0.352	0.398	0.972	0.224	0.694	0.976	0.393
Automata	0.375	0.538	0.96	0.076	0.768	0.977	0.449
CD	0.438	0.318	0.815	0.225	0.585	0.995	0.453
BE	0.473	0.188	0.813	0.423	0.49	0.994	0.329
PC	0.4442	0.221	0.904	0.272	0.627	0.994	0.449

| Outline:
1. Finite state automaton
  1.1 Deterministic finite automaton
  1.2 Non-deterministic finite automaton
2. Regular grammar
  2.1 Regular expression
  2.2 Regular language | In the theory of computation, a branch of theoretical computer science, a deterministic finite automaton (DFA) is a finite-state machine that accepts and rejects strings of symbols and only produces a unique computation (or run) of the automaton for each input string. DFAs recognize exactly the set of regular languages, which are, among other things, useful for doing lexical analysis and pattern matching. DFAs can be built from nondeterministic finite automata using the powerset construction method. |

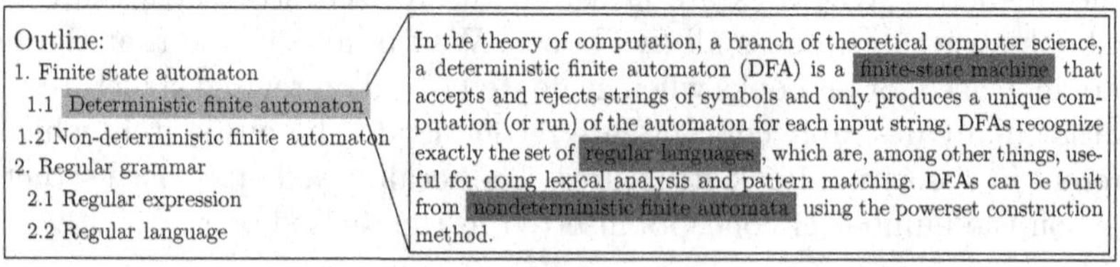

Fig. 5. *Pedagogic Value* analysis: using an online textbook

Sanity of *Pedagogic Value*: The sanity of the proposed measure to estimate the pedagogic value of a book structure is evaluated using Stanford online textbook on Information Retrieval[6]. This book contains hyperlinks to navigate

---

[6] https://nlp.stanford.edu/IR-book/html/htmledition.

between pages. We extracted the hyperlink network in this online book and it is used to compute its *Pedagogic Value*. Then, the sections and subsections in the book are randomly shuffled to observe the variation in *Pedagogic Value*. The extent of shuffling is measured using tree edit distance. The *Pedagogic Value* of each shuffled book structure and its tree edit distance with the actual book structure is illustrated in Fig. 5 and it shows that the *Pedagogic Value* is high when edit distance is 0 and it decreases with increase in edit distance.

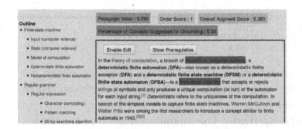

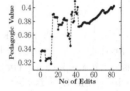

Fig. 6. A screenshot of the interface

Fig. 7. *Pedagogic Value*
Analysis: using interface

We designed an interface to assist user in compiling the book from Wikipedia[7]. A screenshot of the interface is shown in Fig. 6 where the book outline generated by the proposed algorithm is given along with the content of a section with regions flagged for grounding. The pedagogic value of the book structure and scores for computing pedagogic value are also shown in the screenshot. We compiled a book on "Automata Theory" using the interface. The pedagogic value of the book structure is analyzed while editing the content during the compilation process and the pedagogic value after each edit is show in Fig. 7. We can observe fluctuations during the initial edits. This is because some revisions create new circular dependencies and some eliminate quite a few existing circularities.

Comparison of *PReqScore* and *RefD*: We evaluate the effectiveness of the *PReqScore* by comparing it with *RefD* score using CrowdComp dataset [12]. This dataset includes binary labelled concept pairs from five different domains - *Global Warming, Parallel Postulate, Public Key Cryptography, Meiosis* and *Newton's Laws*. The classes are balanced by oversampling the minority class and we analyzed the accuracy of test data based on 5-fold train-test splits. The accuracies obtained when trained using *PReqScore* are 74.2% (*Global Warming*), 74.8% (*Parallel Postulate*), 72.2% (*Public Key Cryptography*), 72.6% (*Meosis*), and 80.1% (*Newton's Laws*) which are conspicuously better compared to the accuracy figures obtained when trained using *RefD*, which are 60.1%, 69.9%, 65.3%, 65.1% and 56.9% respectively. The improvements are statistically significant ($p<0.05$, paired t-test).

---

[7] A demonstration of the interface and a book compiled using the interface can be found at https://sites.google.com/site/compiletextbooks/.

Comparison of *AugScore* with Baselines: We compare the *AugScore* used in augmentation algorithm with baseline measures such as semantic relatedness and Wikipedia category tree based score. The semantic relatedness between concepts ($SemRel(c_i, c_j)$) is measured as discussed in Sect. 2.1 The intuition of Wikipedia category tree based score is that a concept c_i is a prerequisite of c_j if there is a category of c_i that is an ancestor of any category of c_j in the category tree. The extent to which c_i is a prerequisite of c_j is measured by the path length between those categories. Thus the Wikipedia category based score is,

$$CatScore(c_i, c_j) = \min_{\substack{u \in Cat(c_i), v \in Cat(c_j) \\ u \text{ is ancestor of } v}} \frac{1}{pathlength(u, v)} \tag{9}$$

where $Cat(c_i)$ implies Wikipedia categories of concept c_i. These baselines are compared based on the F1-score of book structure generated by using these scores with respect to the actual book structure and the F1-score values are given in Table 4. It is clear that empirically, the augmentation algorithm based on *AugScore* performs significantly better than the baselines.

Table 4. Comparison of *AugScore* with baselines

Dataset	SemRel	CatScore	AugScore
Automata	0.38	0.22	**0.52**
DSA	0.37	0.29	**0.45**
Compiler	0.33	0.32	**0.39**
BE	0.13	0.18	**0.26**
Precalculus	0.13	0.12	**0.24**

6   Discussion and Related Work

Authoring a textbook is hard even for experts. This paper aims at a relatively modest goal of helping humans in compiling books from Wikipedia by utilizing its hyperlink structure. Although there are different aspects to be considered in pedagogically organizing the content, experimental results provide support for using *PedagogicValue* to guide humans in adapting Wikipedia content to meet pedagogic goals. Even though we made a simplifying assumption that in a book structure, introduction to a parent concept is a prerequisite of its child, it may be noted that links in Wikipedia do not necessarily carry the semantics of referring to the introduction to the target article. To address this issue, we need to classify each Wikipedia link based on its context to decide if it refers to the introduction of the target or the whole content. While we have assumed that the user provides as input a set of ordered concepts, it should be straightforward to adapt the tool to take advantage of the proposed ordering method in situations where the user is unsure of the ordering between seed concepts. Also, while we have demonstrated the effectiveness of grounding in an automated way, the grounding of a concept by redefining content can lead to creation of fresh circular dependencies. In such cases, changes in *Pedagogic Value* scores can be exploited by the interface to guide the user to choose a grounding operation that can reduce such side effects.

A method to increase the coverage of textbooks by linking textbook content to web resources is proposed in [1]. Mathew et al. [13] distinguished between pedagogic and encyclopedic resources and observed that circular dependencies tend to occur more often in encyclopedic resources like Wikipedia; the authors do not, however, prescribe a concrete approach to semi-automate the task of converting encyclopedic resources to pedagogic ones. A study towards measuring the extent to which prerequisite relation between knowledge concepts in MOOCs is performed in [3]. A computer facilitated interactive system to create books using open access textbooks is proposed in [10]. Wang et al. [16] proposed an approach for extracting concept map from textbooks which use prerequisite relations that are estimated based on topical relatedness and complexity level differences between concepts. Our work differs from most of these approaches in terms of its overall goal, and is motivated by the goal of aiding humans to construct a textbook out of relevant Wikipedia articles. It aims at an end to end interface that uses human feedback to structure the content of the textbook and help users in grounding concepts that are involved in circular dependencies.

7 Conclusion

We presented an approach to help users in compiling books from Wikipedia. This involves two steps (i) identify book structure on a given subject (ii) flag regions for grounding in Wikipedia content corresponding to topics in book structure. We evaluate the effectiveness of proposed algorithm for identifying book structure both quantitatively and qualitatively and also propose a measure to estimate pedagogic value of a book. We could also characterize the books empirically based on how hard it is to compile them from Wikipedia resources. While the results presented are encouraging, practical deployment of the tool may need significant work to go into building of better interfaces and empirically evaluating the end-to-end effectiveness of the tool using ablation studies over different configurations of the proposed modules.

Acknowledgements. We thank Prof. Marti A. Hearst for the fruitful discussion and feedback, and the members of AIDB lab for their insightful comments. This work is partially funded by TCS Research Scholar Program, India.

References

1. Agrawal, R., Gollapudi, S., Kenthapadi, K., Srivastava, N., Velu, R.: Enriching textbooks through data mining. In: ACM DEV, p. 19 (2010)
2. Li, Y., Chenguang, Z.: A metric normalization of tree edit distance. Front. Comput. Sci. China **5**(1), 119–125 (2011)

3. Pan, L., Li, C., Li, J., Tang, J.: Prerequisite relation learning for concepts in MOOCs. In: Proceedings of the 55th Annual Meeting of the Association for Computational Linguistics, vol. 1, pp. 1447–1456 (2017)
4. Jain, P., Hitzler, P., Verma, K., Yeh, P. Z., Sheth, A.P.: Moving beyond sameAs with PLATO: partonomy detection for linked data. In: Proceedings of the 23rd ACM Conference on Hypertext and Social Media, pp. 33–42 (2012)
5. Milligan, G.W., Cooper, M.C.: An examination of procedures for determining the number of clusters in a data set. Psychometrika 50(2), 159–179 (1985)
6. Mateusz, P., Nikolaus, A.: Tree edit distance: robust and memory-efficient. Inf. Syst. 56, 157–173 (2016)
7. Page, L., Brin, S., Motwani, R., Winograd, T.: The PageRank citation ranking: bringing order to the web. Stanford InfoLab (1999)
8. Cilibrasi, R.L., Vitanyi, P.M.: The google similarity distance. IEEE Trans. Knowl. Data Eng. 19(3), 370–383 (2007)
9. Witten, I.H., Milne, D.N.: An effective, low-cost measure of semantic relatedness obtained from wikipedia links. In: Wikipedia and AI: An Evolving Synergy, pp. 25–30 (2008)
10. Liang, C., et al.: Bbookx: an automatic book creation framework. In: Proceedings of the 2015 ACM Symposium on Document Engineering, pp. 121–124 (2015)
11. Agrawal, R., Chakraborty, S., Gollapudi, S., Kannan, A., Kenthapadi, K.: Quality of textbooks: an empirical study. In: ACM Symposium on Computing for Development (2012)
12. Talukdar, P.P., Cohen, W.: Crowdsourced Comprehension: predicting prerequisite structure in wikipedia. In: 7th Workshop on Building Educational Applications Using NLP, pp. 307–315 (2012)
13. Mathew D., Eswaran, D., Chakraborti, S.: Towards creating pedagogic views from encyclopedic resources. In: 10th Workshop on Innovative Use of NLP for Building Educational Applications, pp. 190–195 (2015)
14. Liang, C., Wu, Z., Huang, W., Lee Giles, C.: Measuring prerequisite relations among concepts. In: Proceedings of the Conference on Empirical Methods in Natural Language Processing, EMNLP, pp. 1668–1674 (2015)
15. Agrawal, R., Golshan, B., Papalexakis, E.E.: Toward data-driven design of educational courses: a feasibility study. In: Proceedings of the 9th International Conference on Educational Data Mining, EDM, p. 6 (2016)
16. Wang, S., et al.: Using prerequisites to extract concept maps from textbooks. In: Proceedings of the 25th ACM International Conference on Information and Knowledge Management, CIKM, pp. 317–326 (2016)
17. Liang, C., Ye, J., Wu, W., Pursel, B., Giles, C.L.: Recovering concept prerequisite relations from university course dependencies. In: (2017) Proceedings of the Thirty-First AAAI Conference on Artificial Intelligence, pp. 4786–4791 (2016)
18. Levary, D., Eckmann, J., Moses, E., Tlusty, T.: Loops and self-reference in the construction of dictionaries. Phys. Rev. 2(3), 031018 (2012)
19. Agrawal, R., Golshan, B., Papalexakis, E.: Data-driven synthesis of study plans. Data Insights Laboratories (2015)
20. Negahban, S., Oh, S., Shah, D.: Rank centrality: ranking from pairwise comparisons. Oper. Res. 65(1), 266–287 (2016)
21. Jenks, G.F.: The data model concept in statistical mapping. Int. Yearb. Cartography 7, 186–190 (1967)

Measuring Language Complexity Using Word Embeddings

Peter A. Whigham$^{(\boxtimes)}$ ⓘ, Mansi Chugh ⓘ, and Grant Dick ⓘ

Information Science, University of Otago, Dunedin, New Zealand
{peter.whigham,grant.dick}@otago.ac.nz, chuma964@student.otago.ac.nz
https://www.otago.ac.nz/info-science/people/peter-whigham.html

Abstract. The analysis of word patterns from a corpus has previously been examined using a number of different word embedding models. These models create a numeric representation of word co-occurrence and are able to capture some of the syntactic and semantic relationships of words in a document. Assessing language complexity has been considered for many years through the use of simple indexes and basic statistical properties (word frequency, etc.), however little work has been done on using word embeddings to develop language complexity measures. This paper describes preliminary work on measuring language complexity using clustered word embeddings to produce network transition models. The structural measures of these transition networks are shown to represent basic properties of language complexity and may be used to infer some aspects of the underlying generative grammar.

Keywords: Word embedding · Language complexity · Word2vec
Grammar · Network

1 Introduction

This paper considers the use of word embeddings to estimate the structural complexity of English sentences. The concept of word embeddings involve the mapping of a vocabulary to a low dimensional vector that represents the positional context between words within a sentence or stream of words. Several models for word embedding have been proposed, including Skip-Gram with Negative Sampling (SGNS) [13,14], Latent Semantic Analysis (LSA), Global Vectors for Word Representation (GloVe) [16] and PPMI [7]. The reader is referred to the review paper by Li and Yang [12] for further details regarding these and other methods. These models vary in the way in which they construct the embedding vectors, however they all have the same goal of creating a mapping from a high dimensional n-gram space to a lower dimensional representation. Although word embeddings have been previously used as structural information to enhance parsing methods [1], they have not been used for evaluating structural language complexity in terms of clustering and graph representations. This work is motivated by an early discussion paper by Harris [10], where he described the distributional

© Springer Nature Switzerland AG 2018
T. Mitrovic et al. (Eds.): AI 2018, LNAI 11320, pp. 843–854, 2018.
https://doi.org/10.1007/978-3-030-03991-2_76

structure of language and the implications of their meaning. Harris considered grouping the words of a corpus language as classes (sets) with certain properties and argued that co-occurring words with different meanings would have different distributions. Further, he suggested that having produced a method for grouping elements of a language that these could be combined if a measure of similarity was constructed, thereby identifying roles such as nouns, adjectives, etc. The implication was that the underlying structural properties (i.e. complexity) of a grammatical generator for a language could be inferred by suitable operations on the distributional properties of sentences. The model presented here is one approach to capture these underlying distributional properties and resulting structural features by creating generalised hierarchical representations of word dependencies.

This paper is structured as follows: Sect. 2 presents related work in the field of language complexity and the use of word embeddings; Sect. 3 presents the proposed model for measuring language structure; Sect. 3.1 shows a toy example to motivate the work; Sect. 4 describes the corpus data and model parameters used for the experiments; Sect. 5 presents the results and discusses the implications of the model; and Sect. 6 concludes the work.

2   Related Work

Language complexity has a long history in natural language processing (NLP) [2], often framed around the issue of readability [11,18]. Simple statistical methods, such as the Gunning Fog Index [9] (a measure of the proportion of the number of words versus number of sentences, and complex words versus simple) are often used to measure readability, and this in turn is used as a surrogate for complexity. The work of Yasseri et al. [18] considered complexity in terms of the Gunning Fog index and n-grams of speech and part of speech tags. Although these traditional methods do capture complexity, they are simple statistical measures. More relevant to the work described here is the use of word embedding vectors as inputs to complexity measures.

Early work on the use of n-grams and statistical co-occurrence [4] discussed the concept of partitioning a vocabulary of words into classes using a greedy mutual information measure. There concepts were framed around information theory and the statistical properties of word occurrence. Although word embedding models such as word2vec were not available at the time of this research, they showed that both syntactic relationships and their semantic similarity could be constructed. The mathematical basis of this work was limited to bi-grams, however the implications of the work clearly support the methods presented here. The work by Bullinaria and Levy [5] examined how models of co-occurrence could be used for semantic analysis of words. Although they do not address language complexity directly, the work showed that a range of statistical measures could be created and used as a basis for psychological models to evaluate meaning in documents. Andreas and Klein [1] posed the question: "How much do word embeddings encode about syntax?". They used word embeddings to support statistical parsing by using neighbourhood relationships in the embedding vector to enforce common behaviours between words. In addition they used the vectors to create features (based on the first two principle components of a PCA projection of the embeddings) that could be used as input to a lexical parser. Although they did demonstrate that the embeddings captured syntactic information they could only demonstrate marginal improvements in terms of state-of-the-art parsers. Of relevance here is that they showed the syntactic concepts of a language were represented in the word embeddings.

Recent work has examined the use of clustering for word embeddings [6] for readability prediction. Here a K-means clustering method was used with the word embedding vectors (K was tuned between 10–200 using validation data), and the text then pooled into the clusters. A histogram of the distribution of words in each cluster was then used as input to a support vector machine to produce a regression model for readability. Here the clustering model was used to just produce one set of clusters (with a fixed K for any corpus). Our model extends the use of clustering by creating a set of different models defined by a range of dissimilarity measures. These clusters and the text corpus can then be used to construct transition networks represented as a Markov chain model of transitions between words and groups of words. We propose that this type of model captures a generalised representation of the underlying grammar used to create the corpus, and can therefore be used as a measure of complexity.

3 Methods

The approach taken here is to assume that word embeddings represent underlying syntactic structures that can be used to estimate the complexity of sentences. Although previous work has shown that syntactic information from word embeddings is redundant [1] for constituency parsing, we do not aim to construct a formal parser, but to assess the structural complexity of the language represented by the embedding. To demonstrate this concept we use the Python gensim[1] package to create the word embeddings (word2vec), clustering using a dendrogram, and a transitional network (graph) to measure complexity. The finite-state machine (network) model and dendrogram were implemented in the basic R [17] implementation, and used the *igraph* package [8] for measuring the network properties and display purposes. The model steps are defined as follows:

1. Create an embedding E for the corpus C using an embedding size S and vocabulary size $|V|$;
2. Cluster the embedding E using a dendrogram using a Euclidean distance metric for similarity and inter-cluster agglomeration method "average";
3. For a range of dissimilarity cut-points d_i in the dendrogram:
   (a) Create a finite state machine F where each state represents cluster of words at d_i. Include two additional states: S (the start symbol that links to the first word in a sentence) and END (the end state linked from the last word in a sentence);

---

[1] https://radimrehurek.com/gensim/.

(b) Sample sentences from C, updating the transition matrix for F based on the order of words from a sentence and their associated states (clusters);

(c) Construct a directed graph D_i that represents F; and

(d) Measure the structure of D_i using the graph properties of clustering coefficient (transitivity) and mean path length.

4. The structural measurements of D_i can be used as features to infer the complexity of the language that generated C.

We note that there are many possible graph measures of D_i. Our choice of transitivity and mean path length was that they are relatively fast to calculate for large networks, and they capture basic structural information for graphs. Transitivity measures the probability that adjacent vertices of a vertex are connected, and therefore represents the clustering of words or concepts in a language. The mean path length calculates the average directed path length between all pairs of vertices. A language with no structure would therefore likely have a large mean path length.

3.1   Motivational Example

The following example shows how the structure of D_i varies by creating a simple language defined by a context-free grammar (CFG). The purpose here is to demonstrate that structural information regarding the grammar used to produce a text can be inferred by using the dendrogram and associated transition networks for a range of similarity cuts.

A context-free grammar is a tuple $(N, \sum, S, P)$, where N is the set of nonterminals, $\sum$ is the set of terminals, $S \in N$ is the designated start symbol and P is the set of rules or productions. A rule is a pair (l, G), where $l \in N$ is the left-hand side, and $G = g_0 g_1 \ldots g_n$ is the right-hand side, with $g_i \in N \cup T$.

The grammar G_{simple} generates a simple language with a small amount of structure based on the position in a sentence of nouns, verbs, adjectives, conjunctions, pronouns and determinants.

$G_{simple} =$
  $S = S$
  $N = \{NP, VP, \ldots, Conjunction\},$
  $\sum = \{nouns, verbs, \ldots, and, or, but\},$
  $P =$
    $\{S \rightarrow NP \quad VP \quad | \quad NP \quad VP \quad Conjunction \quad S$
    $NP \rightarrow Pronoun \quad | \quad Det \quad Nominal$
    $Nominal \rightarrow Noun \quad | \quad Adjective \quad Nominal$
    $VP \rightarrow Verb$
    $Conjunction \rightarrow and \quad | \quad or \quad | \quad but$
    $Pronoun \rightarrow we \quad | \quad me \quad | \quad you \quad | \quad it \quad | \quad \ldots | \quad most$
    $Det \rightarrow the \quad | \quad a \quad | \quad an \quad | \quad this \quad | \quad these \quad | \quad that$
    $Noun \rightarrow n0 \quad | \quad n1 \quad | \quad \ldots | \quad n19$
    $Verb \rightarrow v0 \quad | \quad v1 \quad | \quad \ldots | \quad v19$
    $Adjective \rightarrow a0 \quad | \quad a1 \quad | \quad \ldots | \quad a19$
    $\}$

Twenty unique nouns (n0-n19), verbs (v0-v19) and adjectives (a0-a19) were used in the language so that the dendrogram could be easily visualised. One example sentence generated by G_{simple} is *"these n1 v0 but this a2 n8 v6"*. A small number of terminals were used for each of the non-terminals Conjunction, Pronoun and Det. A corpus of 5000 sentences was generated using G_{simple} and embedded using the method previously described. Figure 1 shows the dendrogram and two transition networks (D_i) produced using one embedding of the corpus generated from G_{simple}. The dendrogram shows that the nouns, verbs, adjectives, conjunctions, pronouns and determinants all form initial clusters, indicating that the structural roles these words play in the language have been represented by the word embeddings. The network shown in panel B was produced by cutting the dendrogram at a dissimilarity height of six. Of interest here is that this transition network in panel B represents the underlying structural relationships defined by G_{simple}. The network in panel C is more complex since some nouns and adjectives are still treated as separate groups.

4   Corpora

A simple set of different styles of text from the Brown Corpus have been selected to examine the properties of the proposed model. The Brown Corpus is a commonly used collection of text for NLP problems with a set of corpora divided into 15 theme categories. Figure 2 shows a summary of the structure for each category. Panel A shows word frequency (note outliers to the box plots not shown), panel B shows the distribution of sentence length, and panel C plots the number of sentences versus number of unique words in each corpus. The corpora were accessed using the Python interface to the nltk package [3]. The following preprocessing steps were carried out for each category of text:

1. remove all punctuation from the text;
2. convert all text to lower-case;
3. construct a unique word table and calculate word frequency; and
4. keep only the first 10, 000 most frequent words, replacing the remaining words in the text with the symbol UNK.

Figure 2 shows that the different categories vary in their basic structure. In particular, panel C shows that the science fiction, humor and religion categories have fewer unique words and number of sentences. Panel A also shows that word frequency is low for science fiction, reviews and humor. The sentence length (Panel B) shows some differences, with adventure, fiction, mystery, romance and science fiction having somewhat shorter sentences than other categories.

Early experiments with the model described in Sect. 3 indicated that direct comparison between corpora may not be appropriate due to behavioral differences caused by word frequency, sentence length and the size of the documents. Hence a set of baseline text documents were created for each corpus that directly reflected the structure of each document. Three baseline texts were created as follows:

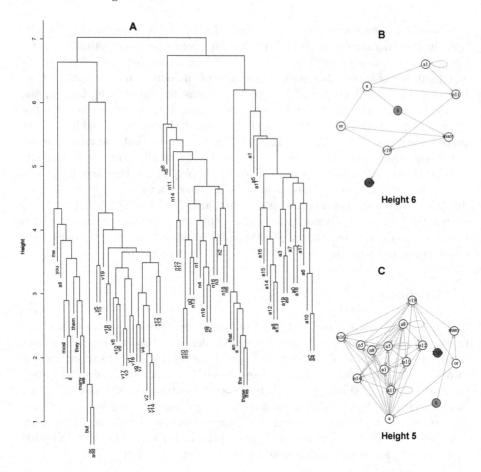

Fig. 1. The dendrogram (A) of an embedding for text generated by G_{simple}. The resulting graph structure when cut at a dissimilarity height of 5 (C) and 6 (B). Note that the graph nodes are labeled with an example from the cluster (class) represented by that node.

1. Random: For each sentence in the document, create sentences of the same length with words randomly selected from the corpus.
2. Random Frequency: For each sentence in the document, create sentences of the same length with words selected proportional to their frequency.
3. Random Sentence: For each sentence in the document, create sentences by randomly reordering the words in the sentence.

Each category corpus will be compared against these three random texts based on structural measures of the transition networks for a range of dissimilarity cuts in the dendrogram. The similarity ordering for the random models compared to their original text should be that the Random Sentence text is more similar than the Random Frequency which is more similar than Random. Comparisons

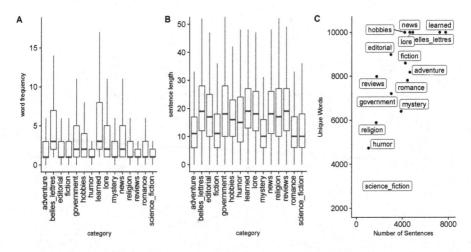

Fig. 2. Word frequency (A), sentence length (B) and total sentences vs unique words (C) for each category. Note that outliers are not shown in A and B, and the axes in C are drawn with different scales.

between corpora can then be made be considering how they behave against these baseline random texts. The word embedding dimensionality has been set to 20, based on [15], and each category corpus is iterated through *word2vec* 100 times. The context (skip-gram) window was set to 2. The model was run 10 times per category corpus and random data, with the network measures presented with a 95% confidence interval about the mean for transitivity and mean path length. Although these parameters may not be optimal for each corpus (this is a general issue when using any neural model) they are suitable for our initial investigations given the small corpus size - in addition, since we are using aggregated clusters the issues with inconsistent word distances in the vector space should be reduced.

5   Results

The results for both network measures as the dissimilarity measure for the dendrogram is increased from 1 to 8 are shown in Figs. 3 and 4. The mean distance between vertices (Fig. 3) has a similar pattern for all corpora in that the random text model has the greatest distance for large networks (small values of the dissimilarity cut) and gradually decreases to be similar to all other text models as the agglomeration process increases. In particular, the ordering of distance is consistent for all corpora, with the original text having a slightly larger mean distance than the random sentence text, with the random frequency text having the lowest distance. The random frequency is likely to have the lowest distance measure since words that are more commonly selected will also be more likely to be in the same sentence. Therefore, although in the original text a word may appear commonly, it might be that is only occurs once in each sentence - by sampling the words using a probability these common words are more likely to

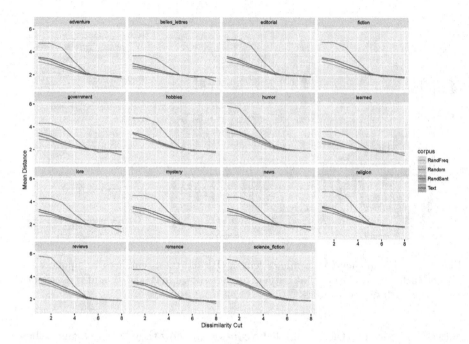

Fig. 3. Graph mean distance between vertex pairs for each category cut at dendrogram dissimilarity measures 1–8.

be co-occurring and therefore the network structure will cluster more rapidly. Therefore this would result in shorter mean paths in the network. Of more interest is the two categories where random text distance is close to the original text: "belles lettres" and "learned". These texts have the largest number of sentences and unique words (see Fig. 2) and large sentence length distributions and word frequency counts. Clearly this measure is representing the overall complexity of the corpus in a similar manner to the concept of readability.

The transitivity coefficient (Fig. 4) captures a different measure of complexity. Of interest here is that the three corpora ("humor", "reviews" and "science fiction") show very different patterns compared to their corresponding random models. Examining Fig. 2 would suggest that this is a result of word frequency, given these three corpora have very low word frequency distributions (panel A). These texts also have the smallest number of sentences and unique words (panel C). Since transitivity measures the clustering of nodes in the network this implies that these text documents have a more rigid structure and do not use different words for the same semantic role. There is also some support for this from Fig. 3 where these texts have a slightly larger mean path length compared with other corpora. All other texts in Fig. 4 show a consistent ordering of transitivity with random frequency > text > random sentences. In addition, the spike in transitivity for the random text around a dissimilarity cut of approx. Six is consistent across all of these corpora. Why this spike occurs, and what it

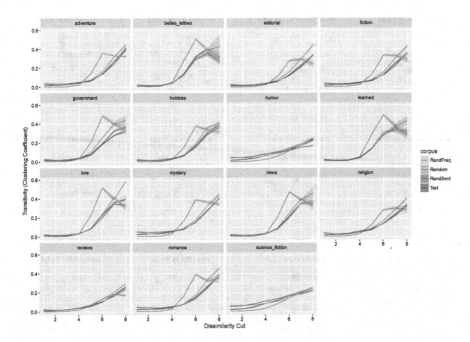

Fig. 4. Graph transitivity (clustering coefficient) for each category cut at dendgrogram dissimilarity measures 1–8.

represents in terms of the underlying sentence structure, is currently not known, but certainly identifies future work. Given the three corpora mentioned above do not show this spike with the random model suggests that it is a consequence of word frequency, but currently we do not have a good explanation as to why this should occur at these particular levels of clustering.

These preliminary results demonstrate that the model has captured some structural measures of complexity and therefore achieves our original goal. However, this preliminary work does not demonstrate that new insights regarding the underlying grammatical structure of the language used to generate these texts can be inferred. Our choice of graph measures was made largely based on simplicity and computational efficiency, rather than from a theoretical argument regarding finite-state machines and language structure. There is clearly an opportunity here to investigate different graph properties and develop a range of measures that can be interpreted for complexity. In addition, we have used a comparison against a set of random models rather than a direct comparison between corpora (although this has been done to some extent). It is an open question whether network measurements from this model can be used to directly compare against different documents and what inferences can be made with this model. Finally, the model uses Euclidean distance for the dendrogram clustering, whereas cosine distance is often used for measuring word embedding similarity. Since a distance measure is fundamental for determining clustering future work

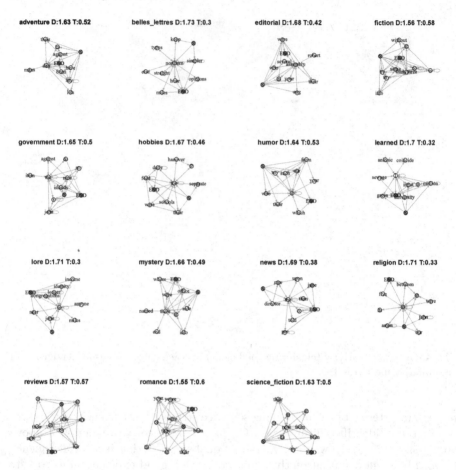

Fig. 5. Network structures for each text category where the number of clusters is fixed at 9. In the caption for each network D shows the mean path length, and T the transitivity.

is needed to determine the most appropriate metric to use when measuring similarity. In addition, the assessments of structure have cut the dendrogram using a dissimilarity measure, whereas the networks could also be constructed by fixing the number of clusters. An example is shown in Fig. 5, where a network for each corpus has been constructed with exactly 9 clusters. Variation in the complexity of these networks could be used as a tool for direct comparison, and is left for future work.

6   Conclusion

This work has introduced a new method for measuring the complexity of a text document using word embeddings, clustering and finite-state machines (networks). The use of graph measures to represent the underlying structure of the networks appears to capture several properties of the corpora that have been examined, however there are several issues that require future work. In particular, for a method to be useful it must provide information regarding the complexity of a language that cannot be derived from a simple set of statistical measures. This work shows some promise in extending the ability to understand language complexity from the perspective of grammatical structure, however at this stage there are many open questions that still need to be addressed.

References

1. Andreas, J., Klein, D.: How much do word embeddings encode about syntax? In: Proceedings of the 52nd Annual Meeting of the Association for Computational Linguistics (vol. 2: Short Papers), pp. 822–827. Association for Computational Linguistics, Baltimore (2014)
2. Baumann, J.F.: Vocabulary and reading comprehension: the nexus of meaning. In: Israel, S., Duffy, G. (eds.) Handbook of Research on Reading Comprehension, chap. 15, p. 24 (2014). https://doi.org/10.4324/9781315759609-28
3. Bird, S., Klein, E., Loper, E.: Natural Language Processing with Python (2009)
4. Brown, P.F., deSouza, P.V., Mercer, R.L., Pietra, V.J.D., Lai, J.C.: Class-based N-gram models of natural language. Comput. Linguist. 18(4), 467–479 (1992)
5. Bullinaria, J.A., Levy, J.P.: Extracting semantic representations from word co-occurrence statistics: a computational study. Behav. Res. Methods 39(3), 510–526 (2007). https://doi.org/10.3758/BF03193020
6. Cha, M., Gwon, Y., Kung, H.T.: Language modeling by clustering with word embeddings for text readability assessment. In: Proceedings of the 2017 ACM on Conference on Information and Knowledge Management, CIKM 2017, pp. 2003–2006. ACM, New York (2017). https://doi.org/10.1145/3132847.3133104
7. Church, K.W., Hanks, P.: Word association norms mutual information, and lexicography. Comput. Linguist. 1(1), 22–29 (1990)
8. Csardi, G., Nepusz, T.: The igraph software package for complex network research. Int. J. Complex Syst. 1695(5), 1–9 (2006)
9. Gunning, R.: The fog index after twenty years. J. Bus. Commun. 6(2), 3–13 (1969). https://doi.org/10.1177/002194366900600202
10. Harris, Z.S.: Distributional structure. WORD 10(2–3), 146–162 (1954). https://doi.org/10.1080/00437956.1954.11659520
11. Huang, Y.T., Chang, H.P., Sun, Y., Chen, M.C.: A robust estimation scheme of reading difficulty for second language learners. In: 2011 IEEE 11th International Conference on Advanced Learning Technologies, pp. 58–62 (2011). https://doi.org/10.1109/ICALT.2011.25
12. Li, Y., Yang, T.: Word embedding for understanding natural language: a survey. In: Srinivasan, S. (ed.) Guide to Big Data Applications. SBD, vol. 26, pp. 83–104. Springer, Cham (2018). https://doi.org/10.1007/978-3-319-53817-4_4
13. Mikolov, T., Chen, K., Corrado, G., Dean, J.: Efficient Estimation of Word Representations in Vector Space. arXiv:1301.3781 [cs] (2013)
14. Mikolov, T., Yih, S.W.T., Zweig, G.: Linguistic Regularities in Continuous Space Word Representations. Microsoft Research (2013)
15. Patel, K., Bhattacharyya, P.: Towards lower bounds on number of dimensions for word embeddings. In: Proceedings of the Eighth International Joint Conference on Natural Language Processing (vol. 2: Short Papers), pp. 31–36. Asian Federation of Natural Language Processing, Taipei (2017)

16. Pennington, J., Socher, R., Manning, C.: Glove: global vectors for word representation. In: Proceedings of the 2014 Conference on Empirical Methods in Natural Language Processing (EMNLP), pp. 1532–1543. Association for Computational Linguistics, Doha (2014)
17. Team, R.C.: R: A Language and Environment for Statistical Computing (2017)
18. Yasseri, T., Kornai, A., Kertész, J.: A practical approach to language complexity: a wikipedia case study. PLoS ONE 7(11), e48386 (2012). https://doi.org/10.1371/journal.pone.0048386

Author Index

Printed in the United States
By Bookmasters